NELSON

The Sword of Albion

ALSO BY JOHN SUGDEN

Nelson: A Dream of Glory

Sir Francis Drake

Tecumseh

NELSON

The Sword of Albion

JOHN SUGDEN

THE BODLEY HEAD
LONDON

Published by The Bodley Head 2014

2 4 6 8 10 9 7 5 3 1

First published in Great Britain in 2012 by
The Bodley Head
Random House, 20 Vauxhall Bridge Road,
London SW1V 2SA

www.bodleyhead.co.uk
www.vintage-books.co.uk

Addresses for companies within The Random House Group Limited can be found at:
www.randomhouse.co.uk/offices.htm

The Random House Group Limited Reg. No. 954009

A CIP catalogue record for this book
is available from the British Library

ISBN 9781847922762

The Random House Group Limited supports the Forest Stewardship Council® (FSC®), the leading international forest-certification organisation. Our books carrying the FSC label are printed on FSC®-certified paper. FSC is the only forest-certification scheme supported by the leading environmental organisations, including Greenpeace. Our paper procurement policy can be found at www.randomhouse.co.uk/environment

Typeset by Palimpsest Book Production Ltd, Falkirk, Stirlingshire
Printed and bound in Great Britain by
Clays Ltd, St Ives plc

This book is dedicated to
Will Sulkin, an editor among editors,
and to Terri and Philip,
the three who were there at the beginning

Contents

Book Three: The Glorious Race

List of Illustrations

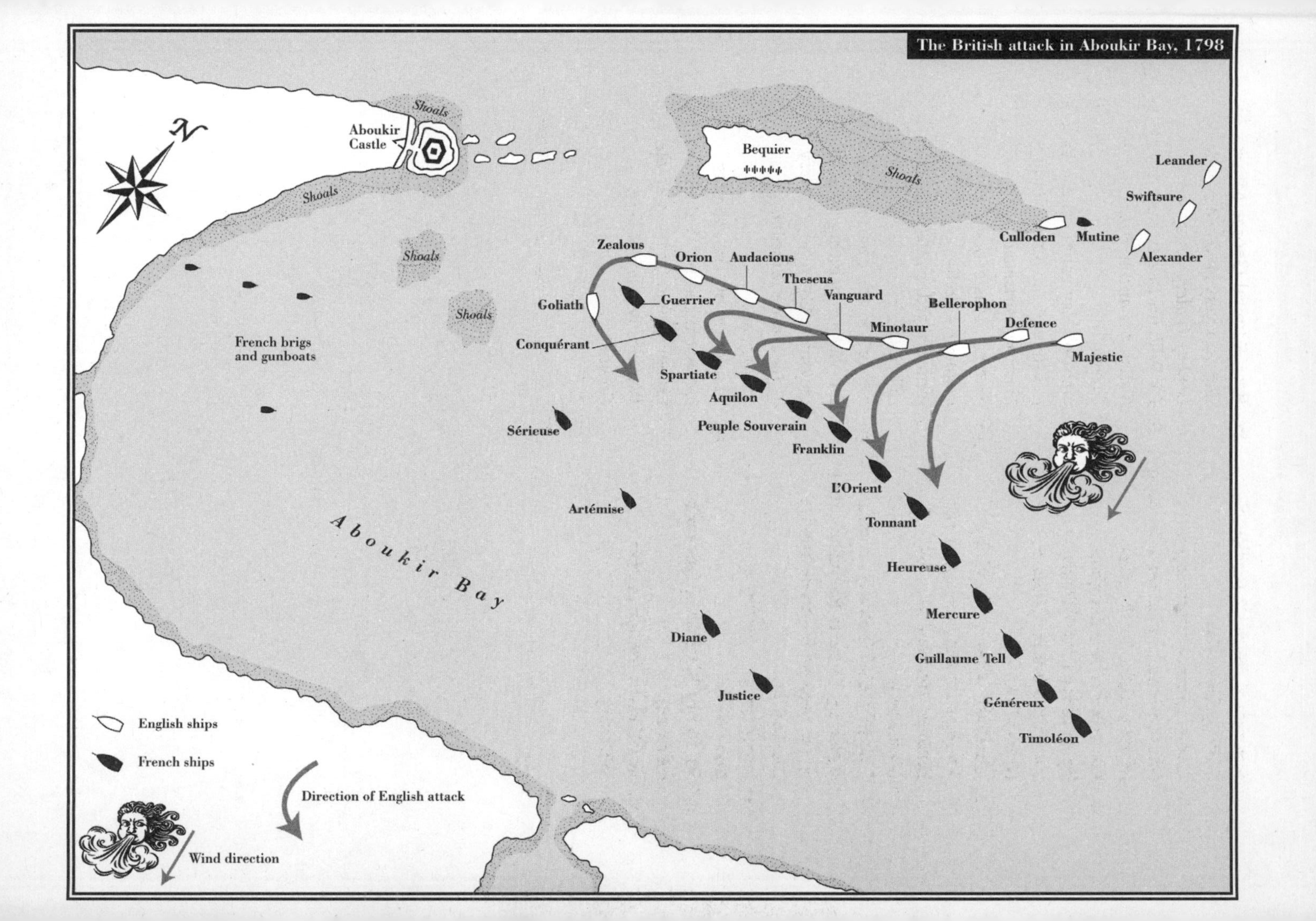
The British attack in Aboukir Bay, 1798
N
Aboukir Castle
Shoals
Shoals
Shoals
Shoals
Shoals
Bequier
Leander
Swiftsure
Culloden
Mutine
Alexander
Zealous
Orion
Audacious
Theseus
Vanguard
Bellerophon
Defence
Minotaur
Majestic
Goliath
Guerrier
Conquérant
Spartiate
Aquilon
Peuple Souverain
Franklin
L'Orient
Tonnant
Heureuse
Mercure
Guillaume Tell
Généreux
Timoléon
French brigs and gunboats
Sérieuse
Artémise
Diane
Justice
Aboukir Bay
English ships
French ships
Direction of English attack
Wind direction

Italy on the eve of the war of 1798-99
AUSTRIA
CISALPINE REPUBLIC
PIEDMONT
Turin
Milan
Verona
Mantua
Parma
PARMA
Modena
Bologna
LIGURIAN REPUBLIC
Genoa
LUCCA
Florence
TUSCANY
Leghorn
Siena
ROMAN REPUBLIC
Tiber
Trieste
Fiume
Venice
Cherso
Ancona
Ligurian Sea
C. Corse
Elba
CORSICA
STATO DEGLI PRESIDII
Civita Vecchia
Civita Castellana
Rome
Ajaccio
Strait of Bonifacio
Maddalenas
Asinara
SARDINIA
Cagliari
Gulf of Palmas
Pula Bay
Adriatic Sea
Ragusa
NAPLES
Apulia
Gaeta
Capua
Naples
Ischia
Castellamare
Bari
Brindisi
Taranto
Otranto
Tyrrhenian Sea
Calabria
Lipari Islands
Palermo
Marettimo
Messina
SICILY
C. Spartivento
Ionian Sea
Syracuse
C. Passero
Pantelleria
Mediterranean Sea
MALTA
Valletta
N
0
50
100
150 miles

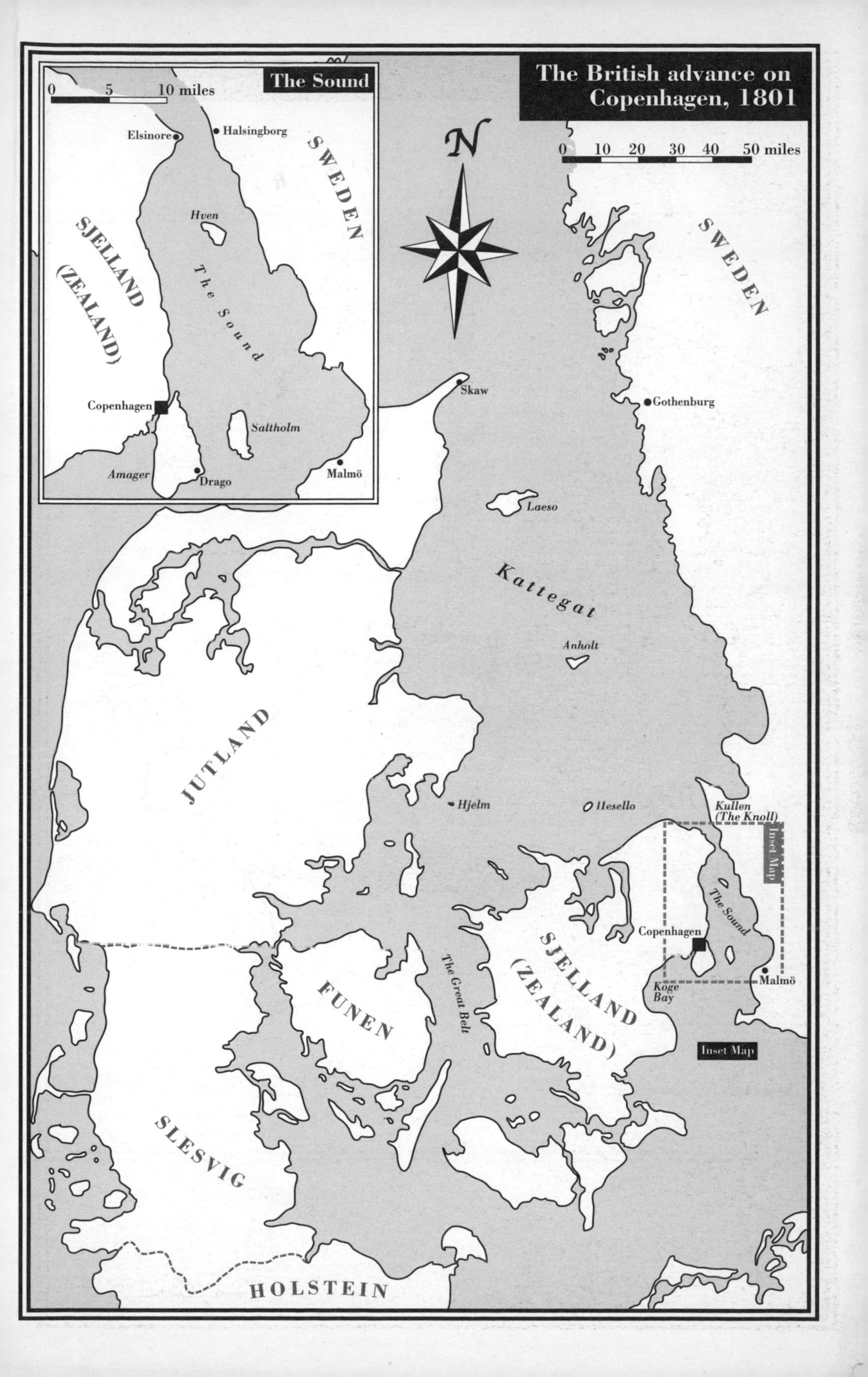
The British advance on Copenhagen, 1801
0 10 20 30 40 50 miles
N
The Sound
0 5 10 miles
Elsinore
Halsingborg
SWEDEN
Hven
SJELLAND (ZEALAND)
The Sound
Copenhagen
Saltholm
Amager
Drago
Malmö
Skaw
Gothenburg
SWEDEN
Laeso
Kattegat
Anholt
JUTLAND
Hjelm
Hesello
Kullen (The Knoll)
Inset Map
The Sound
Copenhagen
Malmö
Koge Bay
SJELLAND (ZEALAND)
The Great Belt
FUNEN
Inset Map
SLESVIG
HOLSTEIN

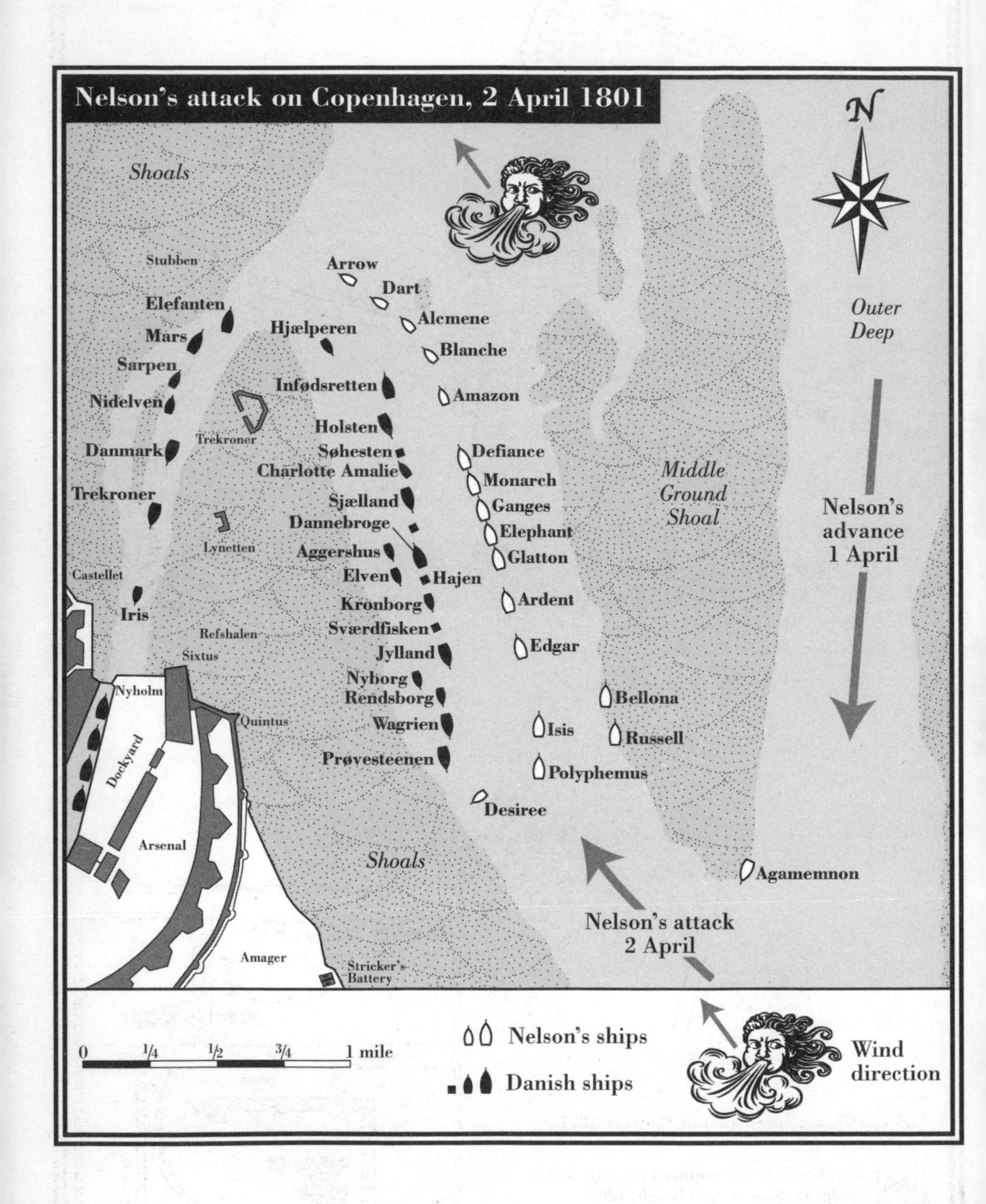

Nelson's attack on Copenhagen, 2 April 1801
N
Shoals
Stubben
Arrow
Dart
Alcmene
Blanche
Amazon
Elefanten
Mars
Hjælperen
Sarpen
Infødsretten
Nidelven
Holsten
Trekroner
Danmark
Søhesten
Defiance
Charlotte Amalie
Monarch
Trekroner
Sjælland
Ganges
Dannebroge
Elephant
Lynetten
Aggershus
Glatton
Castellet
Elven
Hajen
Kronborg
Ardent
Iris
Refshalen
Sværdfisken
Sixtus
Jylland
Edgar
Nyborg
Nyholm
Rendsborg
Bellona
Quintus
Wagrien
Isis
Russell
Dockyard
Prøvesteenen
Polyphemus
Desiree
Arsenal
Shoals
Agamemnon
Outer Deep
Middle Ground Shoal
Nelson's advance 1 April
Nelson's attack 2 April
Amager
Stricker's Battery
0 1/4 1/2 3/4 1 mile
Nelson's ships
Danish ships
Wind direction

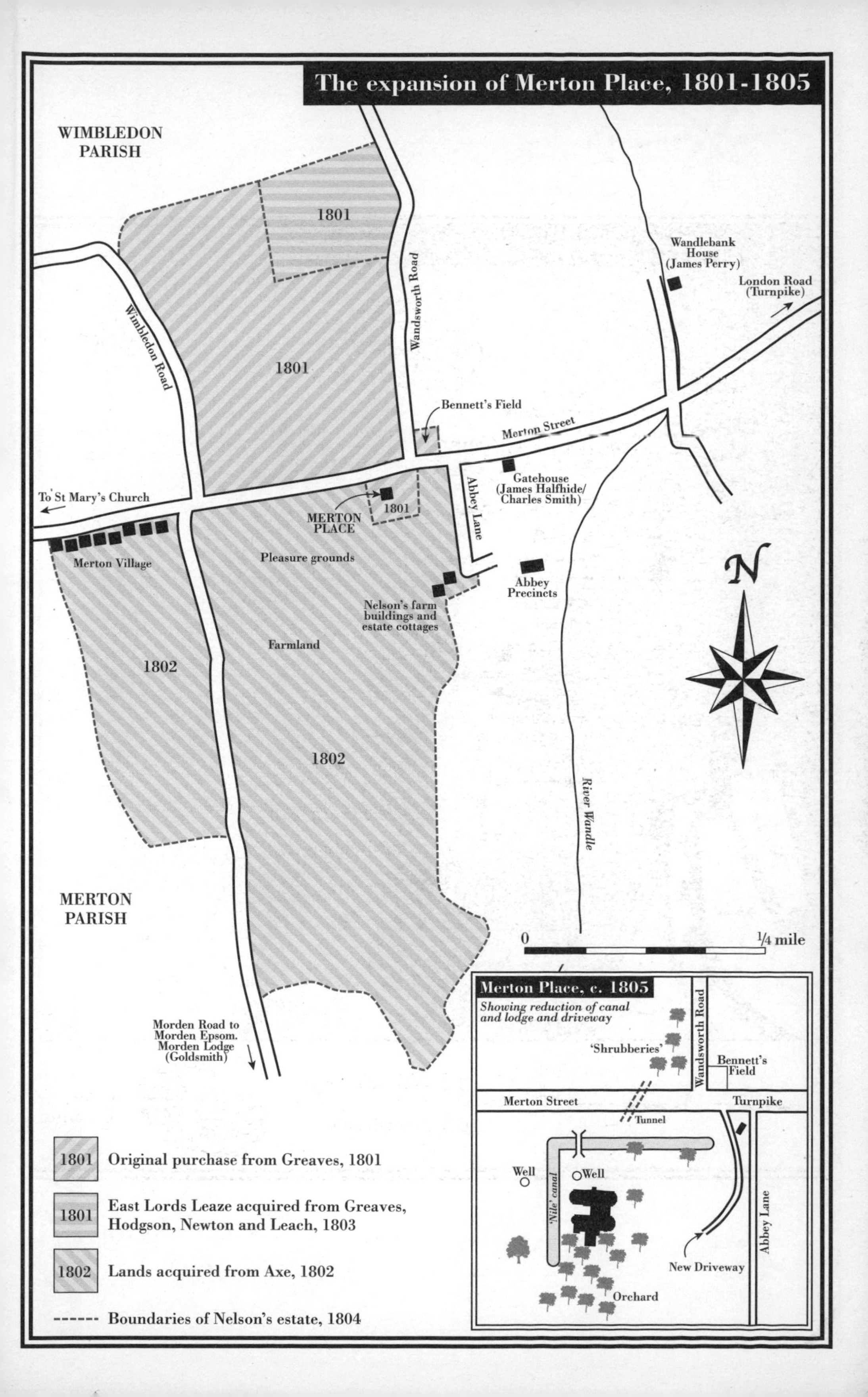

The expansion of Merton Place, 1801-1805
WIMBLEDON PARISH
1801
Wandlebank House (James Perry)
London Road (Turnpike)
Wandsworth Road
Wimbledon Road
1801
Bennett's Field
Merton Street
Abbey Lane
Gatehouse (James Halfhide/ Charles Smith)
To St Mary's Church
MERTON PLACE
1801
Merton Village
Pleasure grounds
Abbey Precincts
Nelson's farm buildings and estate cottages
N
Farmland
1802
1802
River Wandle
MERTON PARISH
0
¼ mile
Morden Road to Morden Epsom. Morden Lodge (Goldsmith)
Merton Place, c. 1805
Showing reduction of canal and lodge and driveway
'Shrubberies'
Wandsworth Road
Bennett's Field
Merton Street
Turnpike
Tunnel
Well
Well
'Nile' canal
Abbey Lane
New Driveway
Orchard
1801 Original purchase from Greaves, 1801
1801 East Lords Leaze acquired from Greaves, Hodgson, Newton and Leach, 1803
1802 Lands acquired from Axe, 1802
Boundaries of Nelson's estate, 1804

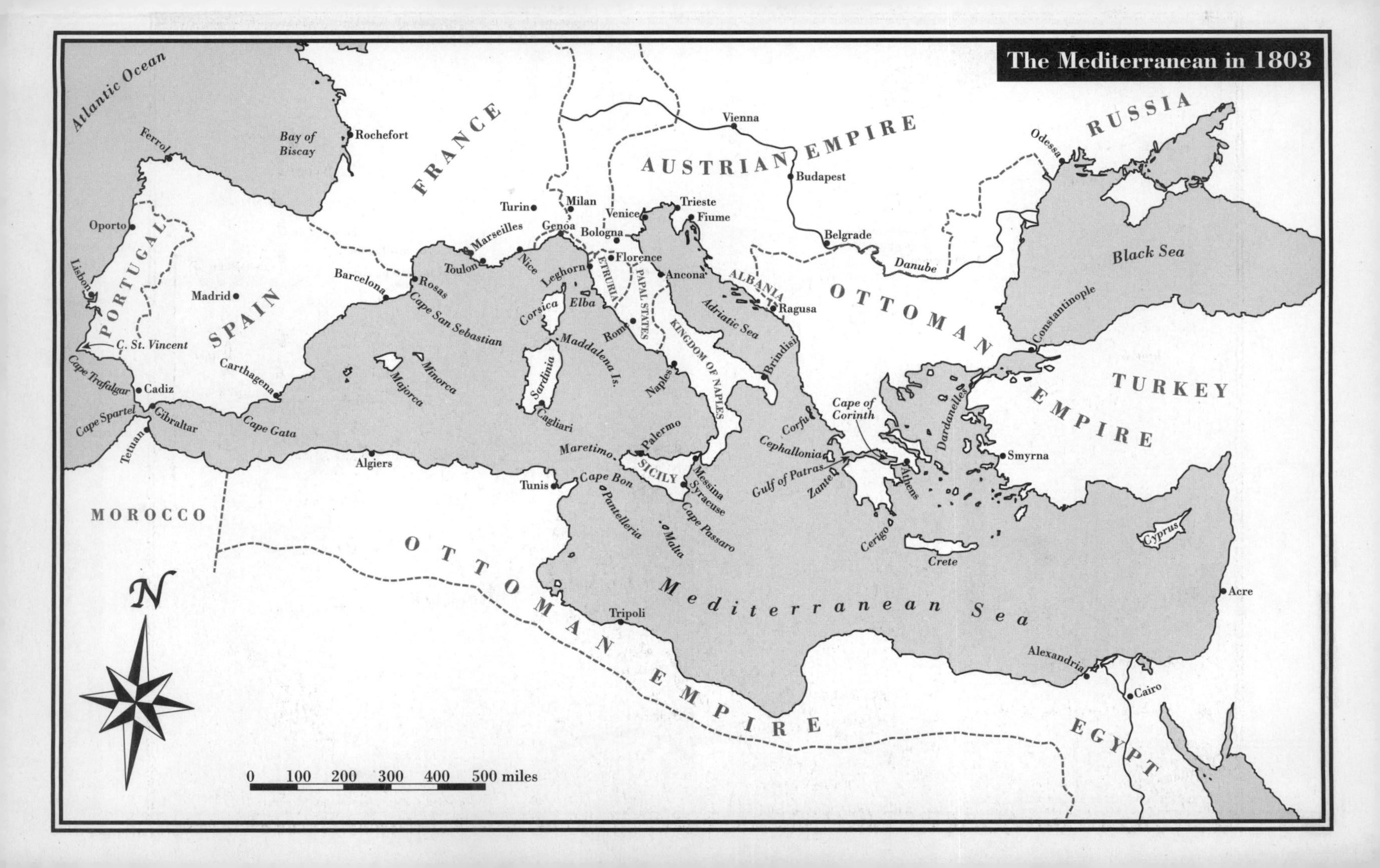
The Mediterranean in 1803
Atlantic Ocean
Bay of Biscay
Rochefort
Ferrol
Oporto
Lisbon
PORTUGAL
Madrid
SPAIN
C. St. Vincent
Cape Trafalgar
Cadiz
Cape Spartel
Gibraltar
Tetuan
Carthagena
Cape Gata
Barcelona
Rosas
Cape San Sebastian
Majorca
Minorca
Algiers
MOROCCO
FRANCE
Toulon
Marseilles
Nice
Turin
Milan
Genoa
Bologna
Venice
Trieste
Fiume
Florence
Leghorn
ETRURIA
PAPAL STATES
Elba
Corsica
Maddalena Is.
Sardinia
Cagliari
Rome
Naples
KINGDOM OF NAPLES
Ancona
Adriatic Sea
ALBANIA
Ragusa
Brindisi
Palermo
Maretimo
SICILY
Messina
Syracuse
Cape Passaro
Cape Bon
Tunis
Pantelleria
Malta
Tripoli
Vienna
AUSTRIAN EMPIRE
Budapest
Belgrade
Danube
OTTOMAN EMPIRE
Corfu
Cephallonia
Gulf of Patras
Zante
Cape of Corinth
Athens
Cerigo
Crete
Dardanelles
Smyrna
Constantinople
Black Sea
Odessa
RUSSIA
TURKEY
Cyprus
Acre
Alexandria
Cairo
EGYPT
Mediterranean Sea
N
0 100 200 300 400 500 miles

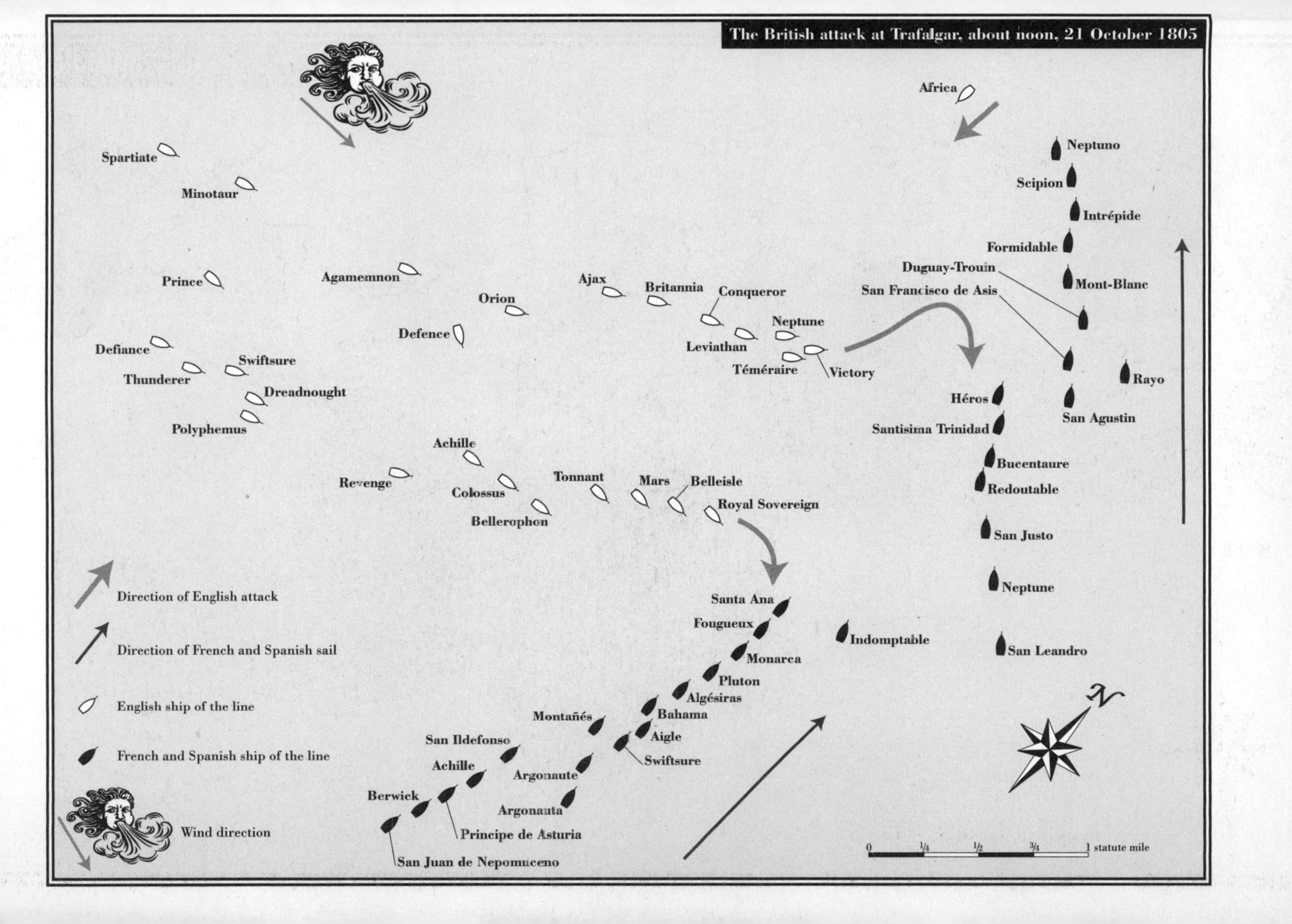
The British attack at Trafalgar, about noon, 21 October 1805
Africa
Neptuno
Scipion
Intrépide
Formidable
Duguay-Trouin
Mont-Blanc
San Francisco de Asis
Rayo
Héros
San Agustin
Santisima Trinidad
Bucentaure
Redoutable
San Justo
Neptune
Indomptable
San Leandro
Spartiate
Minotaur
Prince
Agamemnon
Ajax
Britannia
Conqueror
Orion
Neptune
Defence
Leviathan
Victory
Téméraire
Defiance
Swiftsure
Thunderer
Dreadnought
Polyphemus
Achille
Revenge
Colossus
Tonnant
Mars
Belleisle
Royal Sovereign
Bellerophon
Santa Ana
Fougueux
Monarca
Pluton
Algésiras
Bahama
Montañés
Aigle
San Ildefonso
Swiftsure
Achille
Argonaute
Berwick
Argonauta
Principe de Asturia
San Juan de Nepomuceno
Direction of English attack
Direction of French and Spanish sail
English ship of the line
French and Spanish ship of the line
Wind direction
0
1/4
1/2
3/4
1 statute mile

INTRODUCTION

In eight short years Horatio Nelson, already a rear admiral and a national hero, turned himself into a major international figure and a deathless icon. Rich in the admiration of his countrymen and women, he was almost universally acknowledged to be the nation's champion during a period of grave danger. At his peak his opinion on naval affairs carried more weight with ministers and prime ministers than that of any other officer, and his ability to inspire a fleet was unmatched. Appointed commander-in-chief of the Mediterranean in 1803 he bore one of the most awesome burdens of any public servant, commanding an area three times the size of Napoleon's European empire with a handful of ships and influencing the destinies of half a dozen great powers and as many other significant nations. A perfectionist, constantly reaching for heights greater than he or anyone else had scaled, he delivered one sensational success after another in circumstances that would have repelled most contemporaries. In the parlance of today he was simply Britain's one and only superstar. As the Earl of Malmesbury remarked, Nelson possessed 'the singular power of electrifying all within his atmosphere, and making them only minor constellations to this most luminous planet . . . Every victory was greater than the last. Every additional difficulty seemed only to bring some new proof of the combination and powers of his mind, as well as the invincible force of his arms.' His life was a mission with the essence of a tour de force, hurrying towards a bloody climax in the greatest clash of armour of the war, and one that would shape the fate of empires.[1]

Nelson may have seemed an Achilles, but he was not without the proverbial heel. His was no steady upward trajectory, but a career of ups and downs in which victories were sometimes snatched from crippling reverses, not all of his making. And throughout, those closest to the revered warrior saw another man, emotional, disappointed, irritable, lonely, embittered and above all acutely vulnerable. He searched for glory and what he called happiness, for him no less than the utilitarian philosophers a condition to which man naturally aspired, but while the former gathered in full measure, the latter eluded him to the end. As his achievements thrust him before an ever larger public, the fault lines in his character were exposed, and his marital relations became the meat of public ridicule.

The Nelson record has been much distorted, most grossly by those who have deified or denigrated the admiral, but mystification had its roots in the man himself, for no man wanted more to be a hero. He exhibited his trophies, stage managed public appearances and manipulated the press to shape the desired image. When soliciting a vote of thanks from the London Corporation after his victory at Copenhagen, for example, he personally suggested an appropriate wording. Not wishing to appear immodest, he claimed to have taken it from the letter of 'a dear friend'. The tribute pronounced him 'the Victor of the Nile, the conqueror of Copenhagen, St Vincent's prop, the hero of the 14th February [battle of Cape St Vincent], the terror and stop of the Northern Confederacy, the restorer of the King of Naples, the preserver of Rome, the Avenger of Kings, and the Guardian Angel of England. The only man who in this war has been 127 days in battle and ever came off covered with glory, honor, virtue and modesty, The pride of his country and friends.'

But of course no one but Nelson himself so assiduously counted his actions, or the enemy ships destroyed or taken in his train, and when the original eulogy is traced the 'friend' reveals herself as none other than Emma Hamilton, the admiral's mistress and most extravagant partisan. Yet even her embellishments were not enough for Nelson, who added to the litany of accomplishments. It was he who inserted the claim to have been 'the terror and stop of the northern confederacy', and whereas Emma had described him as 'the man of men' who had triumphed in 127 engagements, the admiral made it 'the *only* man' who had emerged from 127 days of battle. In this, as on many other occasions, Nelson sought to place every strut to his fame on public record.[2]

The early biographers reflected Nelson's interest in his posterity. Theirs were 'monuments' erected to praise a famous man, written under the gaze of influential patrons and participants they could not afford to offend. They dodged controversies to dwell upon the more splendid of their hero's public services. Shortly after Nelson's death Lady Hamilton hired James Harrison, the editor of a series of British classics, to write a biography and he spent much of 1806 and 1807 at her home in Merton, accessing confidential papers and interviewing witnesses. With a large family to support, Harrison's affairs were 'desperate', and he depended entirely upon a frugal stipend from his publisher and Emma's legendary largesse. The *Life* was published in 1806. It is by no means as worthless as most subsequent writers would have us believe, but betrayed its origins, traducing the wronged Lady Nelson, who thought it a vile publication, and offering a spotty coverage of an illustrious career. A planned revision never appeared. On his part, William Nelson, the admiral's brother, who received an earldom from a grateful nation, engaged a cleric named Nott to produce a rival publication using papers in his possession, but on learning that the Prince of Wales was patronising a third project he deferred to its authors, John McArthur and James Stanier Clarke, the editors of a ponderous but popular serial entitled *The Naval Chronicle*.

Although Clarke claimed to have studied 'naval literature' since 'early life' it was McArthur (1755–1840), doctor in law, who was the key figure in what came to be recognised as the official life of Nelson, launched in two spacious volumes in 1809. He had been a prize agent and long standing promoter of the admiral. In 1799 he ferried Nelson's only fragment of autobiography into print, and – if his own story is to be believed – persuaded the admiral to accept him as the authorised biographer. In all walks he had been a thorough partisan. When Sir Hyde Parker approached him with a vindication of his shaky performance as commander-in-chief of the Baltic, McArthur advised against its publication, since it contained 'so many improper and ill founded strictures' upon Nelson's 'conduct' during the campaign. Clarke and McArthur's book reflected the support of many naval friends and acquaintances as well as the Nelson family, but it too confined itself largely to the creditable. McArthur's reputation has see-sawed. Once uncritically plagiarised by legions of successors, he is now as lazily dismissed as an irrelevance. His work is certainly a difficult one, partisan and stuffed with inadequately rendered documents, but much quarried from the admiral's papers found its only home in the book's pages and some of the eye-witness testimony has lasting value. However, from inception it was a commemoration, not a balanced portrait.[3]

In the 1840s the worthy Nicholas Harris Nicolas, who abandoned the navy for a career as a lawyer and historian, published what is still the most scholarly and comprehensive collection of Nelson's letters and dispatches, but even he felt constrained in treating the more delicate aspects of his hero's life. On their way to high Victorianism, with its emphasis on sobriety and strict morality, the educated classes did not relish dwelling upon the shortcomings of their national hero, especially at a time when the naval power he had bequeathed was transparently a pillar of the nation's security, world-wide empire and prosperity. Works exposing a shabbier side to the coin were usually unsuccessful. *The Letters of Lord Nelson to Lady Hamilton*, published by Thomas Lovewell of London in 1814, was condemned as fraudulent and fell into lasting disrepute. Its 'editors' have never been identified, although Emma Hamilton, who was injured by the publication, insinuated that Harrison was to blame. The hostile reception received by the book aborted a promised sequel. However, originals of some of the published letters have since come to light, and show that the transcriptions were generally accurate, even if one of the deletions preserved the secret of the parentage of Nelson's daughter, Horatia.

A similar fate befell Thomas J. Pettigrew's documentary biography of Nelson, published in 1849. Among the hundreds of additional documents it published, often in an abridged form, were proofs that the admiral had sired a daughter by another man's wife. Like the *Letters*, the book was fiercely resisted, its author denounced as a fraud and a blackguard who had published calumnies that should never have seen the light of day. It was only with the issue of Alfred Morrison's collection of Nelson–Hamilton papers in 1893 and 1894 that the actual relationship between Nelson, his mistress and daughter was finally conceded. Over a far longer period a different but equally heated tit-for-tat exchange was occurring over the events of June 1799, with accusers marshalling every specie of evidence, tainted or no, to condemn Nelson's handling of Neapolitan Jacobins in Naples, and apologists as vigorously defending the admiral's own version of his conduct.

For long we have expected more of biography than this, and today it might be said that no corner of the lives of past public men and women escapes modern scrutiny. During the twentieth century Nelson continued to attract attention, but most of the important works were studies of specific aspects rather than biographies. Julian Corbett and Edouard Desbriere on Trafalgar, William Hardman on the blockade of Malta, Ludovic Kennedy on Nelson's professional relations, Dudley Pope and Ole Feldbaek on the Baltic campaign, and Brian Lavery and Michelle Battesti on the Nile, among a few others, count as major contributions to our understanding of Nelson's service career. Several important collections of documents also appeared, but the biographies reflected a popular rather than a scholarly tradition, and while some were pleasing and worthwhile introductions, few made much of an impression on the mass of imperfectly known primary sources. This tradition also contaminated the evaluation of the literature, and many unadventurous titles were hailed as standard works, while serious efforts sometimes went unsung. There was little appreciation of what needed to be done. In truth, the century produced one major Nelson biography, Carola Oman's magnificent *Nelson* of 1946. In 1905 Walter Sichel's *Emma, Lady Hamilton* surpassed all existing Nelson biographies in terms of scholarship. Of later biographical studies, Jack Russell's *Nelson and the Hamiltons* (1969), though undocumented and cloaked in a folksy language, and Winifred Gerin's *Horatia Nelson* (1970), a study of Nelson's daughter, were the only ones to be based upon an extensive study of the relevant manuscript and published primary evidence.

A lacuna in interest in Nelson lasted from the late 1960s to the 1990s, when military topics fell into disfavour, and academic historians shunned narrative history in favour of socio-economic analysis. In a post-war and post-imperial world it was also easy to forget what Britain had owed to her navy. I can vividly remember an Oxford Don flatly advising me to abandon naval history on the grounds that it 'didn't contribute much to knowledge'. And if Nelson remained widely respected he possessed, as a reviewer of one of the more successful biographies grudgingly acknowledged, 'the wrong magic'. Nevertheless, from that hiatus there emerged a number of enthusiasts who appreciated the weaknesses of the existing studies and the need for a renewed assault upon the forbidding collections of underused or unexplored manuscript materials. My own awakening occurred in the seventies, when working on a doctorate relating to Nelson's time, and the immensity of that stock of material came into view. I knew how Lewis and Clark must have felt gazing upon what seemed to be a primeval wilderness west of the Mississippi, beckoning to be explored for all its difficulties and hidden pitfalls. It was clear to me that it was time for another major reappraisal, one that would initially eschew the secondary books and build the portrait anew from its true foundations. For long the project simmered, but after six years of concentrated work my earlier volume, *Nelson: A Dream of Glory* (2004), was published. It was the first biographical study to trawl the full range of primary sources and to tackle the admiral's earlier life in depth, and judging by a considerable correspondence it has been useful, although I am still finding new material I wish I had used.

I did not realise when I embarked upon the book that others would be pursuing similar ideas, but the first years of the new century, coinciding with the bicentenary of Trafalgar, produced an explosion of refreshing close-grained scholarship. A number of valuable monographs appeared, and a few multi-sourced and penetrating biographies. Professor Roger Knight's *The Pursuit of Victory* (2005) is magisterial, an extensive well-researched and eminently judicious work with a particular emphasis on the naval aspects. Indeed, in that respect it is to be doubted if it will ever be superseded, for no previous biographer had brought to the subject such a command of the nuts and bolts of the eighteenth-century navy, gained in a lifetime of study. Meanwhile, a fine German scholar, Marianne Czisnik, completed an unusually conscientious doctorate on Nelson for the University of Edinburgh, and turned it into *Nelson: A Controversial Hero* (2005), a book that also deserves a place on the top Nelson shelf, as well as a more robust edition. Her forthcoming collection of the correspondence of Nelson and Emma Hamilton will lay foundations for the major life that this mercurial woman so obviously needs. Like Czisnik, Professor Andrew Lambert, our most visible naval historian, was particularly interested in the use posterity made of the admiral's memory. An admirer of Nelson and a Norfolk man to boot, he sympathetically reviewed the admiral's life in *Nelson: Britannia's God of War* (2004) and demonstrated his continuing contribution to the naval tradition, drawing upon a formidable expertise in the navy of the nineteenth century. The appearance of these studies coincided with *The Command of the Ocean* (2004) in which N. A. M. Rodger, arguably the greatest British naval historian since Julian Corbett, surveyed his country's rise to naval superiority in a richly faceted history. Never had so much erudition been focused upon Nelson and his age.[4]

The naval aspects were particularly well served by these studies, but none came close to exhausting the enormous amount of material available. The British Library alone holds 129 volumes of relevant Nelson and Hamilton papers. Some areas of Nelson's life remained relatively unexplored, and myths continued to abound; as fast as some were knocked down, others pressed forward. Partisans of Nelson have searched for reasons to exalt. Their hero has been described as a great seaman, although few who knew him gave him that reputation. His ships occasionally performed surprising navigational feats, but this was largely because he drove his captains, masters and pilots to do what they might not otherwise have attempted. More surprising are the repeated claims that Nelson possessed literary talent. Undoubtedly his letters yield occasional vivid phrases, but Nelson, who knew eighteenth-century literature and letters too well, frankly admitted that his was the unlettered pen of a seaman. His friend, Collingwood, may have brought a certain Richardsonesque quality to his communications, but not Nelson.

On the other hand, in other quarters there has been an accentuation of the negative. Nelson is sometimes portrayed as a war-monger and political reactionary. He certainly revelled in naval glory, which he equated with personal honour and patriotic endeavour, but the long contest with Revolutionary and Napoleonic France, and the catalogue of human disasters that he was forced to witness, developed in him a clear view that war was to be seen primarily as a road to peace. His later correspondence is peppered with allusions to the importance of pacifying Europe. 'God send a finish to it for the benefit of mankind', he wrote in 1804. 'I have only to wish for a battle with the French . . . That over . . . I most sincerely hope that by the destruction of Buonaparte that wars with all nations will cease.'[5]

It is even more misleading to damn him as a reactionary, although he defended largely unreconstructed monarchies, and the war – a struggle for national survival on an unprecedented scale – drove Nelson, as many others, into more extreme positions than they would have ordinarily taken. As I explained in my earlier volume, at their roots Nelson's views were unremarkable among eighteenth-century Englishmen of his class. Rather he was distinguished by his earnestness. From his father, the rector of Burnham Thorpe in Norfolk, he took a more prominent piety than most. 'I own myself a believer in God,' he wrote in 1801, 'and if I have any merit in not fearing death, it is because I feel that his power can shelter me when he pleases, and that I must fall whenever it is his good pleasure.' He shared with his countrymen a common patriotism, with its suspicion of foreigners, but adopted the deeper commitment to public duty espoused by his uncle, Captain Maurice Suckling, who mentored him during those first years in the navy. Likewise, Nelson subscribed to the standard conservatism, and believed that the English constitution, with its creaking balance between Crown, Lords and Commons, theoretically protected the property and liberties of all. But within those parameters he was, as that freethinker Sir William Hamilton said, of a liberal tendency. He saw nothing unnatural in a social order full of distinctions, except that he strongly advocated the reward of merit, and espoused an increasingly old-fashioned paternalism, which emphasised the duties of those above to those who served them below. The central role of government was to protect and reward loyal subjects, and to address their just grievances. This took him far from reactionary politics.[6]

Failures of paternalism, at home or abroad, tended to arouse Nelson's sympathies. He spoke up for impoverished agricultural labourers and abused seamen in England, for the peasants of Sardinia and the Two Sicilies, and the client underlings of the Ottoman Porte. He disliked the French Revolution not only because it threatened his country and the stability of Europe, but also because regimes that wilfully oppressed, massacred and robbed sections of their peoples were the very antithesis of paternal government. Nowhere did he express his view of government more vividly than in relation to Bronte, the Sicilian duchy awarded him by a grateful king of Naples. 'My object at Bronte', he said, 'is to make the people happy by not suffering them to be oppressed [and] to enrich the country by the improvement in agriculture.' The theme occurs and reoccurs in his correspondence. A combination of benevolent rule and loyal service would create Bronte the Happy, or so he hoped.[7]

Many of the misconceptions have arisen from partial views of the evidence. But the quantity of letters to, from and about Nelson, and the supply of relevant public documents now available are so vast as to be almost inexhaustible, and furnish the materials for a comprehensive and intimate portrait. The present work is not a history of the Royal Navy or the war at sea, although both figure prominently. It is a biography, and must address the many different facets of its subject with equal care. Like most people, Nelson was driven by public and private aspirations and anxieties that competed for his time and attention, and they intermingle here as they did in life. The fighting admiral, fleet manager, diplomat and self-publicist; the patron, friend, lover and father; the disillusioned patriot, the patient plagued by bodily infirmities, and the commoner looking for security in a society dominated by lineage, land and property; the estate improver; the strong man and the weak are among the many Nelsons with their attendant tragedies and triumphs with whom we must contend to recreate the whole man. As Sir Winston Churchill said of his biography of Marlborough, his illustrious ancestor, 'It is my hope to recall this great shade from the past, and not only to invest him with his panoply, but make him living and intimate to modern eyes.'[8]

Following my usual practice, I built this book from primary sources gathered in more than fourteen years of research. The bulk of them are unpublished, but the original manuscripts of those that have been printed were used wherever possible or practical. I attempted to approach the subject as objectively as possible, without axes to grind, and to allow my conclusions to develop naturally from the accumulation and evaluation of evidence. My constant concern has been whether my account fairly reflected the evidence seen, irrespective of whether it supported, contradicted or modified received opinions where they existed. I believe that readers are best served by forthright independent scholarship, unconditioned by preconceptions, and the advantage of going to the secondary sources at the end of a project, when a mastery of the evidence has been acquired, is that the historian quickly learns which authors stand on firm ground. In my notes I have alluded to those I have found most useful, although I am sure there are others in such well-tilled fields. Their conclusions are not necessarily the same as mine, for scholars look through different eyes, but they will give the deeper enquirer a range of qualified opinion.

I hope this book will be enjoyed by intelligent lay men and women, as well as those with more permanent or professional commitments in the area. In the interests of clarity I decided to modernise most of the spelling and punctuation when quoting original material, but the wordings and meanings have been scrupulously preserved. Footnotes are a serious problem. Had I acknowledged every source, they would have filled a large volume of their own. I opted to identify quotations and the lesser known pieces of evidence, but have skimped the great published collections, most of which are conveniently organised on a chronological basis.

Nelson: A Dream of Glory told of a young man driven by a need to achieve, using the navy to make his way through Georgian society. We followed his search for a command of his chosen profession, promotion, the patronage of influential persons and a good marriage. He endured much routine service, chequered levels of support and a prolonged spell of unemployment, but from the beginning showed flashes of an unusual spirit and physical and political courage, and after the outbreak of the French wars in 1793 established a solid reputation in the Mediterranean. Nevertheless, it was not until 1797 that he became a national hero by an astonishing display of initiative and bravery in the battle of Cape St Vincent and became a rear admiral. Within months of these achievements, however, a disastrous attack on Tenerife and the loss of his right arm threatened to end Nelson's active naval career. The possibility of a peace contributed to his despondency, and we left the disabled Nelson at the age of thirty-nine, returning home to an uncertain future.

Fortunately for him, the country had need of her admirals.

When Nelson was invalided home in 1797 Britain had been fighting France for more than four years. She had no powerful allies, and because the war had been financed by expensive loans her national debt had spiralled. The cream of her relatively small army had been lost in poor-paying disease-ridden campaigns in the West Indies, and at a time when military strength still depended upon the foot soldier, she was further disadvantaged by her modest population of eleven million. France's armies had been depleted, and she would introduce conscription in September 1798, but her population of twenty-five million gave her a large reserve of muscle. In these circumstances, the navy was Britain's essential safeguard, protecting her trade, colonies and wealth, and of course the realm itself. An island, Albion had long since invested in her wooden walls, outstripping her rivals in dockyard facilities (she had three times as many dry-docks as France and Spain combined) and her reservoir of experienced seamen. Her growing industrial power, itself stimulated by naval and military demand, was also delivering some technical advantages, including – in the earlier years of the war – superior numbers of carronades, the heavy guns that gave British ships such powerful hitting power at shorter ranges. Yet even at sea the British could not be complacent. Using conscript labour, her naval rivals could often build ships faster than Britain, and they were able to annex the dockyard facilities of numerous satellite powers. Had it not been for Britain's battle superiority and ability to destroy, capture and purloin enemy ships, the naval arms race would have been in doubt.

Britain never needed her wooden walls more, for the wars in Europe were embarking upon a new and more dangerous phase. In 1799 Napoleon Bonaparte overthrew the French Directory and used a new constitution to consolidate power, originally as the first of three ruling consuls. In 1804 he had himself crowned hereditary emperor. Some of Napoleon's internal reforms, in the realms of finance, law and order, administration and jurisprudence, were far from contemptible, but he also became a dictator far distant from popular sovereignty, dominating the government, turning the press into an organ of state propaganda, censoring or controlling education and the arts and creating the elements of a police state. Of wider import, he was consumed by dreams of empire, and turned Europe into a battlefield. As one German diplomat, charged with accepting Napoleon's claim to hereditary kingship too readily, tartly replied, he would build Bonaparte a statue of gold if he would only leave Prussia alone. Of those willing to resist, Britain was Napoleon's most stubborn foe, and unsheathed her navy as the principal weapon of her survival.

Returning home in 1797, almost broken by the fatigues and afflictions of years of war, Horatio Nelson could not have predicted that eventful future. If there was peace, it was not clear what use Britain might make of the disabled veteran of a bloody defeat, and a retirement on 'half pay' seemed as likely a prospect as any. Yet within months he would go forth as his country's champion in a new round of hostilities, and attempt, as he often said, what Man can do.

BOOK ONE

THE BAND OF BROTHERS

'I had the happiness to command a Band of Brothers . . . Each knew his duty, and I was sure would feel for a French ship.'

Nelson to Lord Howe, 8 January 1799

'His activity and zeal are eminently conspicuous even amongst the Band of Brothers. Each, as I may have occasion to mention them, must call forth my gratitude and admiration.'

Nelson to Earl Spencer, 25 September 1798

I

RECOVERING

From Gallici Bonaparte sailed,
Nelson from Albion's sea;
Chains were our lot had one prevail'd,
The other sets us free.

'Imitation of a Greek Epigram', *c.*1798

I

As soon as he arrived at Spithead in the *Seahorse* frigate on 1 September 1797, Rear Admiral Sir Horatio Nelson wrote to the Admiralty for permission to haul down his flag and go ashore to restore his health. Between five and six in the afternoon he disembarked at the new sally port in Portsmouth to a novel welcome. A waiting crowd raised 'three cheers' and the admiral 'very politely thanked' his admirers. It was the first time that Nelson had returned to such a greeting, a measure of his growing celebrity and a good omen. Another quickly followed. A day later a private note from George, Earl Spencer, the first lord of the Admiralty, complimented Nelson upon his 'very glorious though unsuccessful attack on Santa Cruz' and wished him a speedy recovery in Bath. The gesture revived the wounded admiral's spirits, for it suggested that, although he had lost his right arm, the esteem of this powerful patron had not been diminished by Nelson's bloody repulse at Tenerife, and that there were prospects of receiving another command.[1]

Nelson immediately took a coach for Bath, and sped towards the two people who loved him the most but from whom he had been separated these past four and a half years, Fanny, his adoring wife, and his father, Edmund, still the rector of Burnham Thorpe in Norfolk, where Nelson had been born, but now visibly showing his seventy-five years. For ten years they had been a triumvirate – Nelson a rising star of the British fleet but so often at sea, and Fanny and Edmund, the keepers of the home fires, as often waiting and praying for his safe return. The last letter Fanny had received from her husband, written in the tortured, unfamiliar scrawl of his remaining hand, had told its own dreadful story, and now she longed to nurse him back to health. On the evening of Sunday, 3 September (the day before the official dispatches about Tenerife were published in London) the admiral's coach arrived at her rented house at 17 New King Street, a plain, terraced three-storey dwelling with dormer windows above and servants' quarters below, and interiors cheered by the pictures Fanny had hung on the walls and the notes from her pianoforte. Her father-in-law, who had recently returned to Bath from one of his peregrinations, used the house whenever he could, especially in the colder months.[2]

The Reverend Edmund Nelson was frail and narrow shouldered but his long grey locks and soft, gentle face added distinction to the dark clerical clothes, while at thirty-six Lady Nelson remained petite and brown-haired with fine features that were interesting rather than beautiful, and a habit of demonstrating with dainty hands. The admiral himself was another matter. A local newspaper thought he looked 'in good health and spirits', but Fanny would have seen further. Thirty-nine years had not erased the distinct boyishness in Nelson's appearance, and his thin voice still reflected the unmistakable country drawl of his native county, but the shock of long sandy-brown hair, as uncontrollable as ever and pulled into a pigtail that greased the collars of his uniform coats in long hauls, was streaking with grey, and his sensitive face was looser and more lined. The scars of four years of war were painfully plain. The left eye looked bright because the pupil of the right, effectively sightless, was unnaturally dilated and part of the eyebrow above was missing. The admiral still suffered occasional pain from an abdominal hernia caused by a blow received off Cape St Vincent, but most obviously of all, his right sleeve was empty, where the arm had been cut off below the shoulder after being shattered by grape shot. He had the look of a man who was still sick.[3]

Nelson was occasionally feverish, but the unhealed stump of his arm was the constant irritant, and only opium suppressed extreme pain and allowed fitful sleep. One of the silk ligatures sealing his arteries still protruded from the wound at the end of the stump, refusing to come away, and preventing it from closing as well as inviting infection. The patient suffered excruciating pain each day when a surgeon tested the ligature in the course of redressing the wound. In Bath a surgeon named Nicholls reported for daily duty, while the services of a local physician, Dr Falconer of 29 The Circus, and Joseph Spry, an apothecary, attended more intermittently. Fanny also rallied to her broken husband with courage and care. She was shocked to see the arm cut 'so high towards the shoulder', but eventually mastered the grisly dressings, and assumed innumerable burdens, from writing Sir Horatio's letters to cutting his meat at the table. Thus accommodated, Nelson waited impatiently for his wound to close, stirring at every sign of improvement. After one fairly quiet night he informed his brother that his 'personal health' was 'never . . . better' and his arm 'in the fairest way of soon healing'.[4]

Physical dependency pushed Nelson closer to his wife, and their relationship remained strong, despite the admiral's guilty secret. Like many officers exiled for long periods on far-off stations, he had not been strictly faithful to the woman fretting back home. He had taken a little Italian mistress in Leghorn, Tuscany, in 1794, maintaining her in a house, and on one occasion carrying her aboard his ship to Vado Bay, where he had been temporarily stationed. The French occupation of Leghorn in 1796 had driven a wedge between Nelson and Adelaide Correglia, but they continued to communicate through Genoa until resuming their physical relationship at Porto Ferraio on Elba at the turn of the year. It was there that Nelson had last seen Adelaide in January 1797, only eight months before the reunion with Fanny. A newly discovered account shows that Nelson's passion for Adelaide had been strong towards the end, and that he would brook no male competition. Our witness is James Noble, one of Nelson's lieutenants, who was recuperating from wounds at the time, and found himself escorting Signora Correglia when his commander was otherwise detained. His unpublished autobiography records:

> The following occurrence was near costing me the commodore's [Nelson's] friendship, from a false feeling and unjust suspicion, viz. – while at Porto Ferraio the officers of the *Blanche* gave a ball [January 1797], and thinking it would amuse me . . . although my wounds were unhealed, I asked permission to go, which was granted, and I was asked to take Adelaide, which I readily consented to, being sure that I would be the more welcome. The commodore . . . [requested] that when I came away I should put her on shore, and let [Israel] Co[u]lson, the coxswain, see her to her lodgings. I was induced to stay much longer [at the ball] to gratify her than I should have done otherwise. When I put ashore, [it] being very cold, and having some distance to row afterwards, I was induced [by Adelaide] to walk up with her and take a cup of chocolate, making Colson accompany me. This gave rise to unworthy ideas [in Nelson], which the emaciated state of my frame ought to have protected me from, if no other. A great coolness ensued for some days . . . I refused to dine in the [commodore's] cabin. He sent for me the third day. An explanation having taken place, I dined there that day, and the commodore showed me afterwards more kindness than ever.[5]

Naval officers were used to such liaisons, which were generally regarded as temporary affairs of convenience, and in the Mediterranean most fellow officers knew about Nelson's relationship with Adelaide, but none of them spoke of it in England, not even Fanny's son, Josiah Nisbet, a petty officer on his stepfather's ships, who surely had some inkling of what was going on. Such was the confidentiality shrouding the episode that half a century later Noble deleted the incident from a printed version of his autobiography.

Nelson did not regard his two years of trysting in Italy as a threat to his marriage, but kept it from Fanny, who seems never to have known about it. But that autumn of 1797 Sir Horatio was able to bring his wife good news – of her son. Josiah was a mere seventeen-year-old. He lacked the years and experience to qualify for a commission in His Majesty's navy, but had nevertheless shot precipitately through the lower ranks. On 26 May that year, when still apparently sixteen, he had been appointed a lieutenant in Nelson's flagship, *Theseus*, in flat contravention of the rule that six years of 'sea time' and a minimum age of twenty were indispensable for such an appointment. To get Josiah commissioned while under age, Nelson had done 'a little cheating', falsifying Josiah's record and finding three loyal captains to sign the 'passing certificate' that testified that the applicant had passed the necessary examination. Not only that, but Nelson had even gerrymandered his stepson over the next slippery step up the ladder, and persuaded his commander-in-chief, Earl St Vincent, to appoint the boy acting commander of the *Dolphin* hospital ship, a post confirmed by the Admiralty on 18 September. Josiah Nisbet was absurdly young and immature for the honour, but there he was, master and commander of one of His Majesty's ships of war. It was one of the most spectacular examples of nepotism on record, but sitting by her fireside in New King Street Fanny was delighted. If her boy could make post-captain, his next step, he would probably become one of the youngest admirals in the service.[6]

Bath, that town of restorative waters, apothecaries, doctors and enfeebled but fashionable gentry in search of health, was a favourite resort of the Nelsons, and Sir Horatio had first come here as a junior captain recuperating from the pestilential climes of the Caribbean. Now old haunts brought many chance encounters with friends and acquaintances, one 'Honest Bob' Man, the admiral who had blotted his record the previous year by abandoning the Mediterranean fleet and sailing to England without orders. Man was worried that his flight had cost him a share in the prize money taken on the station after his departure, and wanted Nelson's support. Sir Horatio's convalescent state deterred Man from pressing the subject immediately, but he reserved it for long letters.[7]

Nelson had his own anxieties about status and prize money. He had certainly risen in rank and reputation, achieving national fame as the hero of the battle of Cape St Vincent, but his subsequent defeat at Tenerife and his disabling wound raised questions, especially if the war ended, as some thought likely, and the size of the naval establishment withered. What future could a half-blind, one-armed admiral expect? The press was speculating that he might be offered a place on one of the 'public boards' but that was neither certain nor appealing for a man of Nelson's age and energy. And yet he had little money to fall back upon. He had made little prize money, and when arrears of pay had been made up, he would be left with quarterly payments of 'half pay' (the stipend awarded unemployed officers), amounting to no more than £77 9s. 9d. for a man of his rank, and about £2000 of savings in government stocks. On 6 October his main account with his bankers, Marsh, Page and Creed of Norfolk Street in London, stood at a mere £2248. Another £4000 lay in an account under the name of his brother, Maurice Nelson, and his friend Alexander Davison, but every penny of that had been left to Fanny by her uncle. It was all a very small fortune with which to confront the expenses and expectations held of an admiral and Knight of the Order of the Bath. The most embarrassing deficiency was his complete lack of property, that indispensable symbol of eighteenth-century English gentrification. There was no ancestral home for any of the Reverend Edmund's extensive brood to inherit. Their father had been one of the relatively indigent middling classes, a respected, educated, but property-less clergyman who had been content to spend his days serving his fellow man while remaining a life tenant of the rectory of Burnham Thorpe, a patrimony of a relative, Lord Walpole. Returning from the wars, Sir Horatio was immediately challenged by the need to find a modest, affordable property that would support his status and house his family.[8]

Nelson had always regarded glory and honour, rather than money, as his motor, but that too depended upon further employment. Fanny and Edmund would probably have been content to see Sir Horatio retired, a respected war hero, even if they had to struggle on stinted means, but Nelson's ardent need to achieve would never have allowed him to settle for it, and as his wound healed he yearned for a summons from the Admiralty. His hopes of active service rose in the late summer. It was clear that he retained the confidence of Spencer, as well as St Vincent, his old commander-in-chief, and far from damning him, the news of Tenerife seemed only to increase the admiration of the public. Knowing nothing of Nelson's role in conceiving and planning the attack, the press saw him as the gallant executor of a misconceived adventure, the hero of a hopeless mission. *The Times*, for example, aired many doubts about the wisdom of the attempt to capture Tenerife, which did 'not appear to have been judiciously planned', but the gallantry of those charged with the attack was beyond all praise. Nelson's role was even exaggerated, for *The Times* depicted the desperately wounded admiral 'exert[ing] himself in snatching from a watery grave a number of gallant fellows that were paddling about him' as his boat carried him back to his ship, and told how he had scaled her side without the aid of a 'boatswain's chair', assistants or his shredded right arm. The sympathy for him was almost universal. 'This gallant and valuable officer is already able to write with his left hand,' one paper consoled its readers in September. 'It is indeed a curious fact that he had for some time practised with his left hand, in case any accident should happen to his right.' Several weeks later another confidently predicted that Nelson was soon to be re-employed in 'command of a secret expedition', and there was 'no officer in His Majesty's fleet more capable of executing any service of difficulty or danger'.[9]

To Nelson such praise was a tonic. He derived enormous pleasure opening the stream of admiring letters. Hood, the old commander-in-chief who had been his greatest role model, sent congratulations. So did the Corporation of London, and Sir Horatio's old friend the Duke of Clarence, who welcomed his return 'covered with honour and glory' and declared that he wanted to be among the first to shake his remaining hand. The London Guildhall and that famous venue for public meetings, the London Tavern, rang with toasts to his name, and the freedoms of Bristol and Norwich were on their way. Old neighbours sent gifts of game, including the mighty Coke, who dominated the politics of northern Norfolk. Coke talked about getting the county magistrates to send a public letter of thanks and sent sixteen partridges, five pheasants and four hares. In January the town hall of Norwich proudly exhibited the sword Nelson had taken from the dying Spanish admiral off Cape St Vincent, suspending it from the flukes of an anchor with the hero's new coat of arms below. It was sharply energising. 'The moment I am cured I shall offer myself for service,' Nelson wrote to St Vincent, 'and, if you continue to hold your opinion of me, shall press to return with all the zeal, although not with all the personal [physical] ability I had formerly.' Be damned to the blind eye and missing arm![10]

After a brief interlude in Bath, Nelson and Fanny were back in London by about 18 September with business in mind. Nelson's uncle, William Suckling, had offered them lodgings at his house in Kentish Town, but Maurice Nelson, the admiral's brother, had found a more convenient address, apartments at 141 Bond Street, an area of interesting shops and circulating libraries only a short walk through Piccadilly to St James's and the Admiralty. It was a flat-roofed house on the south-west side of the street, consisting of three storeys over a shop, lit by a trio of regular windows to the front. The landlord, a young fellow named Jones, was connected to Admiral Man. 'I am persuaded he will do everything in his power to render his apartments agreeable,' wrote Man, 'and any service you are pleased to tender him will I am sure be gratefully acknowledged.'[11]

The move put Nelson close to the heart of public affairs, and on better days he ventured about town. He reached Greenwich Hospital, where he took his old Mediterranean friend, Sir Gilbert Elliot, to dine with the governor, their mutual comrade, Lord Hood, and where he renewed his friendship with the lieutenant governor, his beloved 'sea-daddy', Captain William Locker, who was invited to Bond Street. Other naval friends and acquaintances exchanged news here and there, or grumbled about prospective unemployment in these leaner times. In November Betsy Fremantle called at Nelson's apartments with the news that her wounded husband, Nelson's colleague Captain Thomas Fremantle, who had shared the miserable voyage home in the *Seahorse*, was still in pain but at least would keep his arm. Also arriving at the convalescent's door was Captain Richard Bulkeley, an army friend from West Indian days, who brought two sons to see the hero of Cape St Vincent. Sir Horatio showed the boys his sword, and the youngest, an eleven-year-old, was so spellbound that he resolved at once to go to sea.[12]

The constant visitors must have tired one in such pain, but he was forever hospitable. A Norfolk man learned how 'happy' the admiral was to meet a 'countryman', and relatives he had not seen for many years crowded into his quarters. Maurice, the loyal brother with the 'open frank manner', lived only a short walk away in Rathbone Place, and must often have called with Sukey, his common-law wife. More wearing was the Reverend William Nelson, Horatio's other older brother, who arrived at the end of September grubbing for favours as always, 'the roughest mortal . . . who ever lived', according to Fanny. He wanted to attend Nelson's investiture into the Order of the Bath at St James's, and was even more interested in securing a prebendary stall, the 'nearer home and the *larger* the income the better'. Armed with a list of those within the gift of government, his heart was set upon the stall said to have become vacant in Norwich Cathedral. The report proved to be ill founded, but before scuttling back to Hilborough, where his parish church sat in an attractive Norfolk lane near the Wissey, William had impressed upon his brother the need to grovel before the great while 'the iron is hot' to wheedle some comparable appointment. The admiral's brother-in-law, Thomas Bolton, was far more agreeable, and became a constant companion during his brief stay in the capital. No doubt Nelson managed the journey to Kentish Town to see Uncle William Suckling, now at the summit of his career as comptroller of customs, though far from well. The last of his children were off his hands – the daughter married and the youngest son, Horace, about to receive the living of Barsham in Suffolk, a family home – but the old patriarch who had done so much for the young Nelson had only another year to live.[13]

If those who met Nelson at this time expected a self-pitying invalid they would have been surprised. Rarely was the paradox of physical weakness and mental determination so evident as in those months after his return to London, when he adjusted to mutilation and disability. As Sir Gilbert Elliot remarked, Nelson was obviously in 'a great deal of violent pain' but 'better and fresher than I ever remember him'. As on so many occasions, his strength of mind and purpose overcame pain and disability.[14]

2

The iron surely grew hotter as the war with revolutionary France neared the end of its fifth year and peace negotiations stalled. Britain was confronted with impossible terms. France demanded compensation for the destruction of her ships in Toulon in 1793, and wanted the Cape of Good Hope returned to Holland, which she controlled, a concession that would have threatened Britain's communications with India, a hub of her trade empire. The elected five-man Directory that now governed France may have been less doctrinaire than its predecessors, but belligerence remained a stock tool, partly, perhaps, because its restless army was better employed abroad than destabilising the regime at home. To fuel Britain's pessimism, her one effective ally, Austria, made a separate peace with France at Campo Formio in October, leaving the island power the sole significant adversary of the military colossus of Europe.

Britain would fight on, but no one was quite sure how. William Wyndham, Baron Grenville, the foreign secretary, was a gritty warrior, determined to contain France within her pre-war geographical boundaries, and to keep the Low Countries, from which Britain could be threatened with invasion, out of hostile hands. Britain's best course, he said, was to bring Austria, Prussia and Russia into an anti-French coalition, a formidable diplomatic task given the exhaustion, diverse interests and mutual distrust of the great powers, even if oiled with British money. But Pitt's hard-working secretary of war, Henry Dundas, was reluctant to mire the country in the continental entanglements that were unfortunately necessary for complete victory, and favoured a defensive campaign in which the navy – still superior if not supreme at sea – would secure Britain and its interests and inflict maximum damage on enemy commerce and colonies. His policy presaged a long-drawn-out economic struggle. Whichever road was pursued, the country had need of her fleets and admirals.

On 18 September, upon returning to London, a frail one-armed officer arrived at the Admiralty in Whitehall. He may have spoken to Spencer in the oak-panelled first-floor boardroom, but was also entertained in the adjacent Admiralty House, where the first lord resided. At least Countess Spencer, if we can believe a second-hand account, thought the visitor 'so sickly it was painful to see him'. It took a little conversation to reveal a man who knew his business.[15]

In the Spencers Sir Horatio had unquestionably secured his most important patrons to date. George John, Earl Spencer, was the same age as Nelson, and the brother of the influential Georgiana, Duchess of Devonshire. Tall and well-put together, he was nevertheless reserved, polished and gentle rather than flamboyant. A well-connected top-drawer Whig, Spencer had split from the radical Foxite wing on the outbreak of the war and aligned himself with Pitt, whose assessment of the nature of the threat to Britain was much the surer. On that Nelson entirely agreed. Spencer had headed the Admiralty since 1794, and long corresponded with Nelson, recognising in him an officer not to be wasted. His wife, Lavinia, the daughter of the Earl of Lucan, was herself a pillar of London society, famed for beauty, conversation and charm. The historian Edward Gibbon admiringly said that she brought 'the simplicity and playfulness of a child' to 'sense and spirit'. Nelson, with his ready eye for handsome females, would also have been impressed by the thirty-five-year-old petite, big-eyed and interesting face peering from beneath huge hair, and appreciated the liveliness and wit. The Spencers, he found, also had a personal connection. The earl's uncle, Dr Charles Poyntz, of North Creake, Norfolk, was a personal friend of the Nelsons, and in fact had stood godfather to Sir Horatio's youngest sister,

Kate. The Spencers knew the county well, and could interlace their table talk with East Anglian gossip about such ghosts from Nelson's past as Sir Mordaunt Martin.[16]

Armed with the good opinions of the Spencers and Admirals Hood and St Vincent, Nelson had never felt securer, and for the first time the king's favour also seemed within his grasp. Nelson had been ushered into the august presence of George III as early as 1783, when he had been a young protégé of Admiral Hood, but four years later struck up a close but unfortunate friendship with the king's wayward sailor son, Prince William Henry, later destined to become the Duke of Clarence and King William IV. Grossly inexperienced, Nelson hoped to strengthen his influence, or 'interest' as eighteenth century folk called it, by the relationship, but the king thought him an inadequate mentor who failed to improve his son's behaviour. The prejudice lingered, and George was one of the few who criticised Nelson for the failure at Tenerife, which he viewed as an empty display of valour. Nevertheless, a rapprochement with the king was necessary, as Nelson had to be formally inducted into the prestigious Order of the Bath, the knighthood he had won off Cape St Vincent, and Spencer repaired the necessary bridges so well that Nelson became a familiar figure on the royal fringe during the months that followed.

Attendance at the royal levees, when courtiers, foreign envoys, ministers, major office holders, Church leaders, diplomats, peers, knights and leading officers of the armed services were admitted to the king's presence at St James's Palace for one or two hours on stipulated weekday afternoons, not only conferred a degree of royal favour but afforded opportunities to meet the movers and shakers in contemporary Britain. At 12.30 on Wednesday, 27 September, Nelson duly appeared, probably chaperoned by Spencer, but bringing in his train his brother William and two naval protégês, John Waller and Jonathan Culverhouse. It was customary for officers returning from service abroad to be presented to His Majesty, where they bowed to kiss the royal hand, and when the levee closed the king retired to his closet to prepare to formally invest a new public hero with the Order of the Bath.

The vacancy among the 'knights companions' had been much coveted, among others by Charles O'Hara, the governor of Gibraltar, and Robert Calder, Lord St Vincent's captain of the fleet, but there was no dissent that day. The Privy Chamber, which hosted the ceremony, was crowded with the knights and officers of the order in ceremonial garb, as well as some of the great men of state. They shuffled serenely into the king's closet, 'making the usual reverences' to His Majesty: the deputy 'king of arms'; the 'Windsor herald', Francis Townshend, in his mantle, chain and badge of office, with the sceptre of the Bath in his hands; George Naylor, the genealogist of the order; the bearer of a cushion of crimson velvet, upon which Nelson's red ribbon and star were reverently borne; and behind, the knights in a solemn body. At a command from 'Farmer George'

Nelson was admitted, and led forward by Naylor, Sir William Fawcett, an army officer, and the diplomat James Harris, Lord Malmesbury, who delivered the sword of state to the sovereign. Admiral Nelson bowed to receive first the accolade of knighthood, and then the ribbon and star, handed up by His Royal Highness Frederick, Duke of York, the 'grand master' of the order, and placed over the admiral's right shoulder by the king. Nelson kissed the royal hand, the procession returned to the Privy Chamber in the order in which they had come, and the deed was done. It was cemented the following day, when Nelson's party returned to St James's Palace to appear at the Queen's 'drawing room', a subordinate levee open to women as well as men. Apart from the usual parade of ministers and public servants, including Lord Loughborough, the Lord Chancellor, whom William Nelson thought a useful means of advancement, Nelson found many familiar faces in the throng, including Clarence, the Spencers, Hoods and Howes, and the Hon. John Trevor, his diplomatic colleague, who had arrived from Turin with his wife.

The two days of pomp may have taken their toll, for one witness remarked that 'Sir Horatio Nelson's health does not appear to be much mended, if we are to judge from his appearance at the levee on Wednesday. He looked very sickly.' But they thawed the frost between Nelson and his sovereign. Sir Horatio wrote to St Vincent that His Majesty had asked after the earl's health, and we may conclude from Nelson's tone that the interview had gone satisfactorily. According to one of several questionable versions of the meeting, George jocularly remarked that though Nelson had lost a limb his 'country has a claim for a bit more of you'. If true, it implied an anticipation of his return to active service.[17]

The warm glow of royal favour must have been infinitely pleasing to a Church, king and country man like Nelson, and that it seemed genuine rather than a mere matter of duty was suggested by the admiral's regular attendance at the levees that followed. In this surreal, glittering world the parson's boy from Norfolk rubbed shoulders with the elite of the nation, nearly all of them far wealthier than he, if poorer in honour. In a world dominated by the social network, patronage and the giving and receiving of favours, they were a crucial cast of characters. Nelson attended the levees six times between 4 October and 20 December, mixing regularly with Spencer, Sir Andrew Hamond (comptroller of the Navy Board) and fellow admirals, some of them friends from way back, such as Sir Robert Kingsmill and Charles Pole. The great political luminaries shared their views, including the Earl of Chatham, a former first lord of the Admiralty, Malmesbury the diplomat, Charles Grey, father of the Whig reformer, Grenville the foreign secretary, and his cousin, Pitt himself, the first lord of the Treasury and chancellor of the exchequer, who in modern terms was the prime minister. Among these august figures there were voices that spoke highly of Nelson's abilities, and not simply as a naval officer. All three of the senior diplomats who had worked with Nelson in the Mediterranean – Trevor, Francis Drake and Sir Gilbert Elliot – had come home to add to the chorus of approval. Trevor we have seen, and Drake attended the levee of 4 October.[18]

These encounters familiarised Nelson with the manners and mores of the ruling class, created connections and increased his 'interest'. Further access came through invitations from these new acquaintances. On 15 November he duly appeared at a 'grand entertainment' mounted by the Speaker of the House of Commons at his home in Palace Yard, where Chatham, Spencer, Hood, Duncan, Vice Admiral Sir Richard Onslow, Pitt, Dundas, the Lord Mayor of London, and the Master of the Rolls jostled for prominent places. A particular admirer willing to open doors was William Windham, the secretary at war, whose pride in Nelson stemmed from his Norfolk heritage and position as the member of parliament for Norwich. On 25 November Nelson joined Windham for breakfast with Lord William Bentinck, a 'Portland' Whig destined to become a liberal governor general of India, and three days later for dinner with the Lord Chancellor, Grenville, Sir Gilbert Elliot, now Earl of Minto, and two politicos, Richard, Lord Lavington, and George, Earl of Cholmondeley. The next day, 29 November, Nelson endured his most fulsome public tribute yet, when he was the guest of the Corporation of London at a Guildhall dinner and received the freedom of the city in a golden box. The occasion was crowned by an admiring speech from the city chamberlain – none other than the once notorious radical John Wilkes, now a solid member of the Establishment and within weeks of his death. It was tiring but entirely satisfying to a man as hungry for attention as Nelson, and the conversations about public affairs that accompanied these ceremonies and repasts must have considerably enlarged the sea views that Sir Horatio brought to the table.[19]

Never before had Nelson been so admired and visible. It was the beginning of an acclamation that would reach extraordinary unprecedented proportions in the years to come. Though a defeat, Tenerife had enhanced the image of the daring admiral created by the battle of Cape St Vincent. These first steps in deification were taken by a man who was, however, still in great pain, and unsure of where his health might take him. Much as he longed to return to duty, and as his political masters were disposed to oblige him, that physical barrier had yet to be overcome.

3

The ligatures binding the arteries in the stump of his arm should have come away about ten days after amputation, but one remained, week after week and month after month, protruding from the bottom of the stump and preventing the wound from closing. In Bond Street, William Cruikshank, an eminent

London surgeon who dressed the arm daily, gently tested the stubborn ligature, but it shot excruciating pain through the patient and refused to come away. John Rush, an army surgeon and inspector general of hospitals, James Earle of the Surgeons' Company and St Bartholomew's Hospital, Thomas Keate of St George's Hospital, and Dr Benjamin Moseley, who had once brought Nelson through malaria, were all enlisted in the battle for his health, to no obvious avail.

The misery was compounded by additional nerve pain, including phantom sensations that Nelson thought he felt in his missing hand, and the medics believed that a nerve had been accidentally bound with the artery during the amputation. Unfortunately, the problem was situated some two inches into the wound, and a further amputation to rectify the damage was pronounced impracticable and dangerous, particularly as Nelson had so short a stump to work upon. Nelson grimly resolved to endure the pain until the ligature slipped away of its own accord. He dispensed with the expensive services of Cruikshank, turned the daily dressings over to his old ship surgeon, Michael Jefferson, and waited.[20]

For several months Nelson led a see-saw existence between discomfort and almost unbearable pain, suppressed only by laudanum. His attempts to resume business were sometimes stifled, and we find him dictating a letter to the widow of a Royal Marines officer, slain at Tenerife, dutifully promising to aid her petition for relief as best he could, but pointing out that 'it cannot be expected I can exert myself much at present as I feel great pain at times from my wound'. One story of Nelson's sufferings, although preserved in an unreliable source, seems to have come from the dependable Lady Nelson and was probably true. On 11 October Britain won another great naval victory, when a fleet under Admiral Adam Duncan decisively thrashed the Dutch fleet off Camperdown on the coast of Holland, taking nine small enemy ships of the line and two frigates. Coming as it did after the famous naval mutinies of 1797, it was a welcome reassurance of Britain's naval power. An air of expectancy had lingered in London for days. On 9 October Duncan had led his force from Yarmouth upon learning that the Dutch had left the Texel. Long afterwards John Drinkwater, who had advertised Nelson's heroics at Cape St Vincent in a pamphlet, recalled visiting Nelson about that time. When the subject of a probable battle with the Dutch was aired the admiral 'started up in his peculiar energetic manner, notwithstanding Lady Nelson's attempt to quiet him', and extending his remaining arm, declared, 'Drinkwater, I would give this other arm to be with Duncan at this moment!'[21]

Then, on 13 October, an extraordinary number of the *London Gazette* announced the victory of Camperdown. Bells rang throughout London, flags were hoisted and guns fired at the Tower in the customary salute, while the theatres and many principal streets of the capital were illuminated in celebration after dark. The rejoicings climaxed three nights later, when the 'illuminations were general' and those in the Admiralty building 'most brilliant' in appearance. 'The streets were everywhere as light as in the daytime,' remarked one journalist. 'We hardly witnessed a single house in darkness, nor had the "sovereign people" any occasion . . . to exercise its . . . right of breaking windows.' Most householders, it was true, hastily placed lamps and candles at their windows to spare them from the patriotic mobs roaming the streets, but there were exceptions. In Fleet Street the famous radical Thomas Hardy declined to illuminate, and fighting broke out between the mob and his supporters. 'Several persons were taken up and many got broken heads,' it was reported, and the windows of the house were smashed before soldiers dispersed the crowds.[22]

Another of a very different stamp also braved the jubilant populace. As Fanny remembered it:

> During the month of October, whilst he continued in this state of suffering at the lodgings of a Mr Jones in [141] Bond Street, Nelson had one night retired to his bed-room after a day of constant pain, hoping with the assistance of laudanum to enjoy a little rest, when the exhilarating news of Admiral Duncan's victory threw the whole metropolis into an uproar. The first idea that presented itself to the family was an alarm of some dreadful fire. The mob knocked repeatedly and violently at the door, as the house had not been illuminated. It was at length opened by a servant, who informed them that Sir Horatio Nelson, who had been so badly wounded, lodged there and could not be disturbed . . . 'You will hear no more from us tonight,' exclaimed the foremost of the party, and that universal sympathy for the health of Nelson which pervaded even the minds of the lowest of his countrymen was clearly shown, no subsequent visit being paid by the mob, notwithstanding the tumult that prevailed.[23]

Sir Horatio was nevertheless as exhilarated by Camperdown as anybody, and recognised it as a victory of unprecedented completeness, one he would have loved to have won himself. Following the examples of Howe and St Vincent, Duncan had used two divisions to cut the enemy line of battle, attacking from windward and fighting their way to leeward in order to prevent a Dutch retreat before the wind. Though Duncan's tactics were dictated less by careful planning than an urgent need to prevent the enemy from escaping, they rewarded him with nine sail of the line as prizes, setting a new standard for victory. Nelson cheered with the rest. On Thursday, 19 October, he helped organise a commemoration dinner at the Shakespeare Tavern, its clientele almost entirely naval officers. 'Sir Horatio Nelson', it was reported, 'has taken some pains to procure a full meeting', and 'almost every flag officer and captain in London' attended the event. It was followed by a celebration the East India Company laid on at the London Tavern on 6 November, in which Nelson joined a hundred or so guests, including the Lord Chancellor, Spencer, Pitt, Dundas, George Canning (under-secretary of foreign affairs) and Admirals Hood, William Young and Onslow, the latter a hero of the battle. In the course of the evening the strains of a new ballad, 'The Fight off Camperdown', were heard.[24]

Throughout Nelson continued his own daily battle to accomplish the most commonplace tasks, familiar since childhood, but now frustrating, time-consuming and sometimes humiliating. He rarely alluded to it in letters, except in apologies for his shortcomings as a correspondent, and dwelt directly upon his disability only whimsically, when he signed an amusing petition compiled by his brother and sister, William and Kate. In the document Nelson's 'Left Hand' complains that while right hands were 'favoured', educated and trained to perform all manner of skills, from greeting friends with a handshake or wielding a sword against the Dons, the left was suffered to hang 'awkwardly, dangling by the side, except now and then when called in to assist in some drudgery which the right hand does not choose to do by himself'.

Such levity as the 'Left Hand's' petition may have helped Sir Horatio come to terms with his predicament, but life now required the almost constant attendance of assistants. Among innumerable inconveniences a particularly public embarrassment was the cutting of food at the table. Fanny bore the burden when she could sit beside him, but Lavinia Spencer sent him one of his few specially manufactured aids, a combined knife and fork that could be used one-handed, one of the four prongs having been given a cutting edge. Other contrivances eventually included linen shirts made with short right sleeves, their cuffs capable of being drawn over the stump of the arm by a tape, and armchairs with pads upon which the stump might be rested. We hear so little of these difficulties that biographers virtually eliminate them from their accounts, yet that silence itself speaks volumes about the spirit of their subject, and his determination to conquer substantial and endless obstacles.[25]

The disability would last for ever, but on Monday, 4 December, Nelson awoke to find that the pain in his arm had gone. When Jefferson arrived, he effortlessly pulled the remaining ligature away. An elated Sir Horatio described himself as 'perfectly recovered and on the eve of being employed', and on the 13th was discharged by his surgeon, who assigned to Fanny the task of further dressings. Thus, the year that had raised him to national celebrity only to plunge him into despair had ended in jubilation and hope. Spencer had promised him a brand new ship of the line, the *Foudroyant*, and he could visit her at Chatham dockyard with a new anticipation. On 10 December, at a Sunday service in the church of St George's, Hanover Square, the Reverend Greville read out a note that had been sent to him. 'An officer,' he read gravely, 'desires to return thanks to Almighty God for his perfect recovery from a severe wound, and also for the many mercies bestowed upon him.'[26]

Sensible of the debt owed to the navy, the state planned its own impressive thanksgiving in St Paul's Cathedral for the victories of the war. Seats were reserved for available admirals who had been present at the capture of one or more enemy ships of the line. The morning of 19 December was bright and crisp, and the crowds thronging the winter streets seemed greater than anyone remembered. Three major processions converged upon the cathedral, and redcoats lined the streets to keep milling townsfolk off the carriageways, while windows overlooking the scheduled routes were full of faces. The naval procession left Palace Yard in Westminster about seven, a cavalcade of horse artillery carriages bearing captured enemy flags, escorted by divisions of seamen, marines from the barracks at Chatham and Portsmouth, and bands of musicians, and followed by the private coaches of several admirals, including Samuel Cranstoun Goodall, Charles Thompson and Adam Duncan. Soberly rumbling towards the cathedral, it received 'the loudest acclamations that perhaps were ever uttered by the greatest concourse of people ever assembled'. Pitt and the members of parliament had a more subdued reception as they passed through the streets, but the royal party, which included Nelson's friend Clarence, in a coach and six, made heavier going of it, and the king did not reach Temple Bar, west of St Paul's, before eleven. The naval wagons reached the south-west gate of the churchyard, discharging the flags into the hands of naval lieutenants for delivery into the cathedral, and the seamen and marines entered the holy precincts after wiping their feet. As for Nelson, one of the stars of the celebration, he appears to have waited inside, accompanied by two other *Agamemnons*, Edward Berry and James Noble. The navy was honoured with a general upstanding and a service of thanksgiving with two anthems set to music, and it was about 2.30 in the afternoon before the king left as he had come, flanked by the bishops of London and Lincoln.[27]

In the past Horatio Nelson had sometimes complained of official neglect and indifference. His thirst for glory, his personal insecurity and need for affection and attention had so often been thwarted, leaving him dissatisfied and unfulfilled. But no year had ended in greater promise and acclamation.

4

Justly proud of his achievements, Nelson was as interested in commemoration and consolidation as thanksgiving. In terms of the upper gentry, his was a new family, raised on the back of naval endeavour, but to establish itself it needed to acquire the trademarks of its new status. With the knighthood, for example, came the privilege of creating a family coat of arms, which he designed with the help of his brothers and the guidance of the College of Arms, which ensured that new heraldry did not encroach upon existing patents. Nelson's pattern boldly drew attention to his humbling of the Spaniards at Cape St Vincent. Its crest showed the stern of the *San Josef*, one of his prizes, and the shield was flanked by a British tar, carrying the pendant of a commodore, the rank Nelson held in the action, and a lion, both despoiling the Spanish colours. This last was inspired by Ralph Miller, Nelson's flag captain at Cape St Vincent, who had replaced the crumbling figurehead of their ship, the *Captain*, with an effigy of a rampant British lion shredding the Spanish flag only days before the battle. Officials of the College of Arms, principally Sir Isaac Heard, the Garter King-of-Arms, and George Naylor, had some difficulties with the design, but after negotiations in person and in writing the parties came to a satisfactory accommodation. The use of a sailor as a 'supporter' was unprecedented but admitted, and in fact set a new trend in naval heraldry, but the use of the royal ensign of Spain was ruled out, and the lion had to content itself with chewing a flag bearing the Spanish colours of red and gold.[28]

A coat of arms was an important symbolic step in the rise of any new family, but no less essential indications of status, especially if martial victories had to be commemorated, were portraits. Portraits were done to commission, but artists were keen to paint popular heroes because they could provide likenesses to engravers and profit from the public hunger for prints. Since Cape St Vincent the few earlier portraits of Nelson had been engraved, but now there was a demand for an up-to-date likeness, and during the eight months Sir Horatio remained in England he sat to no less than five artists.

Henry Edridge appears to have been the first in the field. Edridge was no big canvas painter, but his pencil and ink full-length, probably sketched in his house in Dufour Place, near Bond Street, would have been worth turning into a new commemorative portrait. Nelson posed in the undress uniform of a rear admiral, with the gold medal awarded him for Cape St Vincent and the ribbon but not the star of the Order of the Bath on his breast. The famous action itself was depicted raging in the background. Apparently the work was commissioned by Sir Henry Englefield, a notable collector and antiquary, perhaps at the behest of his brother-in-law, Nelson's friend Richard Bulkeley. Daniel Orme and Henry Singleton also made sketches from which half-length oil paintings and engravings were produced, and an Irish sculptor, Lawrence Gahagan, created an attractive marble bust after securing seven sittings in Bond Street. Alone of all the images, the bust captured Nelson's smile, although when it was exhibited at the Royal Academy the admiral's cousin, Elizabeth Wigley, thought it made him look 'too old'. Nevertheless, Gahagan turned it to profit with additional sculptures in bronze, marble and plaster.[29]

However, no one made more of an industry of Nelson than Lemuel Abbott, hitherto a competent but jobbing portrait painter. A handsome, eager-faced man in his thirties, he was reputedly tight-fisted, perhaps no surprise in one whose living depended upon so frugal a profession as art, but at this time he showed no obvious signs of the mental illness that would soon lead him to the madhouse and death. His respectable canvases included portraits of several of

Nelson's friends, including Captain William Locker, who was shown with his trademark eye-glass cane. Locker, one of Nelson's early captains, was immensely proud of the important part he had played in Sir Horatio's career, and already owned the most famous of the earlier portraits made of him, by Francis Rigaud. Now he commissioned Abbott, and Nelson is said to have given a couple of sittings in Locker's quarters at Greenwich Hospital, where the little Eliza Locker, the captain's daughter, remembered helping the admiral off and on with his coat. The resultant half-length oil painting of Nelson in his informal dress uniform with the St Vincent medal and ribbon and the Bath star, was probably done about October 1797, and shows the unsmiling, austere face of a man still ravaged by pain.

Almost immediately, Abbott was being approached for variations and copies, and produced canvases for Fanny and Nelson's prize agents, John McArthur and Alexander Davison, among many others. Increasingly he varied the portraits, painting Nelson with and without hats, but there is room for disagreement about which of the earlier likenesses was the most accurate representation of the admiral's features. Scholars have praised the Locker portrait, and a sketch upon which it might have been based, as the more authentic works, adding, as they do, a strained quality to Nelson's countenance. But it might equally be argued that they gave him an uncharacteristic severity at a time of physical stress.

Fanny may have thought so, since Nelson did an additional sitting for the portrait she commissioned from Abbott, and the face in her half-length has the softer lines of a recovering patient. Fanny and Edmund thought it a fine likeness. Once completed, and engraved for a mezzotint, it found a home opposite the east window of a sitting room in the Nelsons' new house, Roundwood. 'I am now writing opposite your portrait,' Fanny wrote to her husband. 'The likeness is great. I am well satisfied with Abbott . . . It is my companion, my sincere friend in your absence. Our good father was delighted with the likeness.' Opinions differed, but one thing is certain. Several dozen different Abbott portraits of Nelson found their way into the print shops, supplying thousands of illustrations in the years that followed. But it is the portrait that he did for Lady Nelson, now in the National Portrait Gallery in London, that has above all others become, if not the definitive representation of Nelson, certainly the most iconic.[30]

More important than coats of arms or portraits was serious property, for this was a society that saw houses and lands as the essential qualifications for becoming a member of the governing classes. Indeed, the most powerful argument used against the idea of universal suffrage was that the vote had to be restricted to property owners, because only they had a stake in society, only they had something to lose, and could be trusted to act responsibly. The trouble was that Nelson had little money. When damages were allowed against him on account of the *Jane and Elizabeth*, a prize he had seized in 1786, he had to appeal to the Treasury to protect him for doing what had been an act of public duty. Nevertheless, something had to be done, and the admiral began a house hunt. He considered Norfolk, close to the family homes of Burnham Thorpe and Hilborough, but it was too far from London for a man of public affairs, and when the Reverend William Bolton, Thomas's brother, spotted a property a mile or so out of Ipswich in Suffolk on the Rushmere road, a suitable halfway location seemed to have been found.[31]

Advertised in the local newspaper, Roundwood (named for a circular area of timber in the grounds) was lot 3 of the estate of the late John Kirby, due to be sold at auction at the sign of the White Horse in Ipswich on 26 September. The 'particulars' issued by Messrs Roper and Doughty, the auctioneers, described

> a modern built messuage, consisting of a small hall, 2 genteel parlours, a dressing room, kitchen, back kitchen, dairy, cellar, 3 wine vaults, 4 good bed chambers, 2 dressing rooms, and 2 servants' chambers; also a large barn, stables, cow-house, and other offices; a well-planted garden, together with 50 a[cres], 1 r[od] and 35 p[erches] by survey of exceeding rich arable land in high cultivation, situate[d] in the parishes of St Margaret, in Ipswich, and Rushmere, and in the hamlet of Wix Ufford in Ipswich.

This was not the small cottage Nelson had dreamed of in simpler times, but a modest country villa and farm. It could be seen until the mid-twentieth century, standing among 'fine old trees of elm and sweet chestnut' and a yew hedge, a 'plain and pleasant house with white stucco walls and grey slate roof' and 'several long windows opening to the lawn, two of them having curious round fanlights heading them'.[32]

The auction failed to unearth a suitable purchaser, and at the end of October Sir Horatio and Fanny inspected the property and within days agreed to buy it. The deal was sealed on 13 November, and witnessed by Captain Berry. Nelson agreed to pay John Kirby of Lincoln's Inn £2000 by 5 January, plus an amount for 'fixtures' yet to be decided. Nelson was also liable for annual charges of £8 on account of land tax and an ancient quit-rent due to Withepole House in Ipswich. A sitting tenant, Captain William Edge, from whom rents were now due, was put on six months' notice.[33]

This, then, was Nelson's first property, yet ironically he would never spend a night beneath its roof, because he returned to sea before gaining access. It was not until May 1798 that Fanny and Edmund took possession. They were delighted, and while the old parson saw the need for fresh paintwork, he conceded that it was withal 'a neat, strong, well built and convenient house, consisting of 2 parlors, a small han[d]some vestibule and staircase, 6 bedrooms and 2 dressing rooms, with offices of every denomination and good cellars. The little pleasure ground and small garden are laid out in good taste and all looks like a gentleman's House . . . The farm is 50 acres of good land adjoining, divided into several small enclosures.' At the time neither saw the flaws in the property, but Fanny would find it too cold to inhabit in deep winters and remote from the sort of society she had grown accustomed to in Bath. And yet it fulfilled one of her dreams, and when her husband returned to active service enthusiastically took up the task of possession and improvement, assisted by Edmund, William Bolton and their local solicitor, John Foster Nott.[34]

Sir Horatio Nelson, Knight of the Bath, of Roundwood, Suffolk, had at last dug himself a niche in the tiered society of eighteenth-century England, but he had expended almost the whole of his fortune to do it. He had no money to improve his property, despite his imminent re-employment with the chance of additional prize money. The probability was that he would have to borrow from his banker and prize agent, William Marsh, to equip himself for his next command, setting it against future pay and prize money. Not surprisingly he was alert to possibilities of additional income. Prize money, compensation for disabilities incurred in the king's service, and indemnification for professional expenses looked the likeliest prospects.

With regard to the former, it was necessary to tread carefully. He had already been reckless enough to invest some of the payments he had received in government stocks while appeals against the legitimacy of the prizes were still going through the courts. Had the stocks fallen, and those payments been reclaimed, he could have been hard put to repay the money. Sir Horatio also got embroiled in litigation with brother officers over the distribution of freight and prize money, a common misfortune that ruined many a naval friendship. In this case Nelson acceded to a plan concocted by the cantankerous Admiral William Parker, with whom he had had his own differences in the past. Parker wanted all the Mediterranean flag officers to share the freight money the fleet had earned shipping goods, a perk currently being cornered by the commander-in-chief. 'I am sure Lord St Vincent will never pay one half penny,' complained Parker. 'Indeed, he has told me he will not.' Parker and Admiral Charles Thompson proposed to go to law, and tried to persuade Nelson and Sir William Waldegrave to join them in a suit against St Vincent. As encouragement, Parker insisted that the action would not 'make any alteration in the respect or friendship that may be subsisting between any of the parties and the commander-in-chief.'[35]

Nelson was not so sure. St Vincent had been a friend and patron, and he preferred to settle the matter privately as 'brother officers'. However, the four admirals eventually initiated a suit for the recovery of their shares of freight money between October and 13 December 1797, and contributed £100 apiece to a fighting fund. Nelson wanted their submission toned down, suggesting that a statement that St Vincent *abrogated* the whole of the freight money 'to himself' be softened to one that said he had merely *claimed* it, and he recommended that three lawyers and other admirals be consulted before going further. Legally, it was a grey area, and the opinions proved indecisive. Five commanders-in-chief owned that they, too, had received all the freight money earned by their fleets, but two of them, Hood and Duncan, were unsure of their right to do so.[36]

While this hare was still running, Nelson applied for a disability pension, allowable according to rank and severity of injury. Leaving the issue of his arm for the moment, Nelson harked back to 1794, when his right eye had been damaged besieging Calvi. On the day of his investiture into the Order of the Bath, Nelson gave to Spencer a résumé of his services and certificates describing his injury, including an up-to-date reappraisal made by William Cruikshank and H. Leigh Thomas on 20 September 1797. It 'found the sight entirely lost, without the smallest hope of his ever recovering it again'. It all sounded conclusive, and to strengthen his claim Nelson slipped in the stomach injury he had sustained off Cape St Vincent.[37]

Sir Horatio did not enjoy testifying to his disabilities. It was humiliating enough to go cap in hand, but the bureaucracy made him feel that his claims were doubted. He felt the discomfort many proud independent souls experience in asking for what some might have deemed charity. 'I have, my dear sir,' he thundered at the Navy Board, 'positively asserted . . . that I have lost my right eye, and . . . sent them such proofs as none can doubt.' He was instructed to attend the Surgeons' Company at 6.00 in the afternoon of the first and third Thursday of each month to have his eye monitored, but protested that his 'present weak state' prevented him doing any such thing so late in the day. Disgruntled by the entire process, he observed to Thomas Bolton that no doubt he would also be required to bring documentary proof of the loss of an arm, since the one injury was as plain as the other. Nonetheless, on 12 October, at 'a private court . . . holden in . . . Lincoln's Inn Fields', seven medics gave Sir Horatio their written opinion that his wound was 'fully equal to the loss of an eye'. When presenting the report to a hapless clerk in order to receive his money, the admiral explained that it was 'only for an eye; in a few days I shall come for an arm, and in a little time longer, God knows, most probably a leg!' But the ordeal was worthwhile, for Nelson received an annual pension of £763 16s. 0d.[38]

He also received compensation of £135 for medical expenses incurred since his return from the Mediterranean, a claim that passed through the Surgeons' Company and the Sick and Hurt, Admiralty and Navy Boards before it was judged 'reasonable and allowed' in the spring. It followed a successful petition for an additional ten shillings a day in pay covering responsibilities Nelson had undertaken as an acting commodore between 4 April 1796 and the following 11 August, when the post was finally confirmed by the Admiralty. That Nelson pressed these suits, entirely justifiable in themselves, indicates the shaky financial situation in which he was placed.[39]

A coat of arms, commemorative portraits, property and a measure of financial security were essential to the world that Nelson now entered, but nothing mattered more than 'interest' – the social influence that one could command. While proud to have won his place through courage, duty and enterprise rather than mere connection, heredity or institutionalised wealth, he had nevertheless sprung from a socially insignificant family that relied heavily upon one vital connection, a link through Nelson's mother to the once mighty Walpole clan. That connection had given Edmund his parish, his son Horatio his early success in the Royal Navy, and brought the Nelsons invitations to Wolterton Hall, the ancestral Walpole pile in Norfolk. As Nelson advanced in the service, he repaid some of the early favours he had received, finding places on his ships for the relations and protégés of those patrons who had furthered his own career. That was how the eighteenth century worked. Though merit sometimes played its part, especially in the navy, this was still an age of patronage, when appointments and opportunities generally came through access to powerful and well-disposed persons, when the amount of 'interest' an individual wielded was of paramount importance, when favours carried an obligation to reciprocate, and when a 'good' marriage was one that connected two strong families and made them stronger. It was a world of competing 'interest' groups, and the fortunes of a family rested on the success of its members in creating opportunities.

Now that Nelson had achieved prominence, he considered it a fundamental duty to repay obligations and elevate his family and friends, and to that end it was time to hobnob with the powerful, create some bonds and test his new found 'interest'. 'Such a son falls to the lot of few fathers,' Edmund wrote thankfully, but in truth Nelson's early attempts to manipulate the privileged were only partially successful. His youngest brother, the feckless Suckling, then a struggling curate at Burnham Thorpe, was one beneficiary. In October 1798 Edmund proposed resigning the rectory of Burnham Sutton, with its dependent responsibilities for Burnhams Norton and Ulph, if Sir Horatio could persuade the Lord Chancellor to pass it to Suckling. Nelson duly addressed Lord Loughborough with complete satisfaction. 'Your great services,' wrote the Lord Chancellor, deserved 'every mark of attention.' Accordingly Edmund resigned the living of Burnham Sutton, retaining for himself that of Burnham Thorpe, and Suckling gratefully succeeded, the last of the siblings to leave the nest.[40]

On the other hand Nelson could do little for his brother William, who epitomised the shabbier end of patronage by milking Sir Horatio for everything he could get. When Nelson asked what preferment would satisfy his brother, the pastor of Hilborough fairly salivated at the mouth. No living in the gift of the crown would content him. 'Any living is out of the question. A prebend in any cathedral and of almost any value is my wish. When I say a prebend I mean a residentiary, for there are many prebends which are not residentiaries, and have only a small stipend of ten or twenty pounds a year and no stall. They are not what I mean. It must be a stall, no matter where, only the nearer home, and the larger the income the better.' The naval brother balked at admitting such greed, and miserably wrote to the Lord Chancellor that 'any residentiary stall will be acceptable, the nearer Norfolk the better'. Though he plugged away for William, Nelson's greater sympathies were for his oldest brother, Maurice, trapped in his clerkship at the Navy Office. He tried to have him made a commissioner of the navy, but entirely without success.[41]

A tyro in this business of lobbying government, Nelson supposed that his claims upon the country merited a satisfactory return, but he underestimated the sheer number and power of his competitors, and the positions within the gift of the administration. The king's governments had nothing like the unfathomable pot of sinecures, posts and pensions that Whig propagandists claimed. It was a lesson that Nelson never really learned, and he was doomed to suffer continual disappointments.

5

Patronage was less objectionable when it served the deserving, and while Nelson sought and rewarded favours like any other naval officer, he also believed in sponsoring merit. The promotion ladder of the Royal Navy was more accessible than many of the alternatives, such as the army, where commissions were purchased, and officers from relatively humble backgrounds, among them St Vincent and Troubridge, reached exalted positions. However, historians have sometimes expressed too strongly the idea that the navy was a career 'open to talent'. Letters from the junior ranks were peppered with complaints about the inequities of the struggle.

Nelson was susceptible to unhappiness in others and hard luck stories, and derived great pleasure from relieving problems and anticipating needed favours. One of his first acts upon reaching England was to write to Ann, the wife of Ralph Miller, his flag captain, giving her early notice that her husband had survived the debacle at Tenerife unhurt. He and Fanny also visited the family in Old Burlington Street, and sent the captain word of his 'very fine' daughter, 'little Charlotte', adding that her guardians were 'good people' who would care for her. 'It will be the pride of my life to preserve the early notice you were so good as to send her [Ann] on your arrival,' Miller wrote from the Mediterranean. Of such gestures was Nelson's leadership fashioned. By them he endeared men to him, and fulfilled the contract that he believed governed all good relations between commanders and their men, the one supplying protection and assistance when it was needed, and the other loyal service in return. Every success Nelson scored for a follower justified that bond; it made his side of the bargain good and legitimised his leadership.[42]

Nelson's commitment to supporting followers, even long after their paths had divided, was a major facet of his managerial style. His correspondence contains hundreds of such appeals, and many found him during his period of convalescent leave. Here Mary Lucas, the widowed mother of Lieutenant William Lucas of the *Agamemnon*, wrote to tell him that her son, invalided home after an injury, had died in February. There a seaman, John Coulson, spoke of the bad times that had visited him and his sick wife, and beseeched help. Lieutenant Thomas Withers wanted a testimonial, and boatswain Joseph King gratefully acknowledged Nelson's assistance in getting a warrant from the Navy Office, and wished the admiral to be godfather to his new child, Mary Nelson King. A former purser, Thomas Fellows, who had most recently obliged Nelson by getting a bust of Cleopatra he had imported from Italy shifted from Portsmouth to London, was thankful for his transfer to the *Superb*. 'To you only, sir, am I indebted for this ship . . . I accept her with pleasure, and return you every thanks that can flow from a great full heart.' Some of these correspondents wrote to him time and again, using his helping hand to surmount the obstacles they met throughout their careers.[43]

It grieved Nelson to see officers distinguish themselves under his command, only to falter through indifference and neglect, but he recognised that his best efforts were not always enough. Upon returning to England he had learned the fates of two of his finest *Agamemnons*, Peter Spicer and James Noble, whom he had successfully pressed the Admiralty to promote to the rank of commander for their meritorious conduct in the battle of Cape St Vincent. Unfortunately, this well-intentioned support placed them at a level exceptionally vulnerable to unemployment. By 1797 the shortage of experienced officers that had existed at the beginning of the war, four years earlier, had been more than cleared, and there was such an excess of commanders and captains that unemployment became a common fate of newly promoted officers. In 1800 only 40 per cent of commanders had ships, and the following year St Vincent, then first lord of the Admiralty, attempted to freeze further promotions.[44]

Both of Nelson's protégés fell foul of the situation. Spicer's father, Lieutenant William Spicer, had never made commander, but he impressed St Vincent (then Captain John Jervis), who rescued him from 'a mean captain' and brought him into his own ship, the *Foudroyant*. When the elder Spicer died of disease he left his son to the protection of Jervis and the ship's purser, Evan Nepean, and it was with their help that Peter had reached the rank of lieutenant, and served efficiently in the Mediterranean under Nelson. After being promoted commander, partly as a result of Nelson's persistent advocacy, he returned to England, but was unable to secure anything more than temporary or stopgap commands. Even elevated to post-captain as part of the general promotion that followed the Peace of Amiens in 1802, he had to content himself with unsatisfying appointments in the Sea Fencibles, a marine home guard, and the impress service, and died in 1830 after fourteen years on a humiliating 'out pension' from

Greenwich Hospital. James Noble, a handsome, open-faced young man with blue eyes and brown hair, would endure an even more instructive career profile that ultimately squandered his gallantry and enthusiasm. Like Spicer, Noble distinguished himself at Cape St Vincent and became a commander at Nelson's behest, and like Spicer he returned to England and unemployment. Nelson invited Noble to join him at the naval thanksgiving at St Paul's at the end of 1797, no doubt hoping to remind Spencer and other senior naval figures of his existence, but Noble shared much of Spicer's fortune, including the promotion to post-captain in 1802 and a spell in the Sea Fencibles. A mere twenty-three years old when he was made a commander in 1797, Noble fancied himself on the brink of a distinguished career. In fact, he was already at the summit, for he never did get a ship, and the empty, demoralising decades ahead were filled with hopeless applications to one first lord or another. Both of Nelson's Cape St Vincent heroes were effectively thrown into a waste basket. This, often, was the fate of the officer without a heavy battery of 'interest'.[45]

Nelson felt deeply for such men. He remembered his own vulnerability as a junior officer. He had benefited from considerable nepotism, but never really felt secure because he had been overdependent upon one source of patronage, his uncle, Captain Maurice Suckling, a significant if self-effacing officer in his day. Suckling's early death had left his twenty-year-old protégé somewhat bereft. Nelson had tried to cultivate new patrons, such as Hood and Prince William Henry, but the process was often chastening and the results indifferent. Sir Horatio could still remember the five bleak years he spent at home in Norfolk, brooding over the failure of his 'interest' until the outbreak of war in 1793 rescued him.

If commanders such as Noble and Spicer were beyond his immediate assistance, Spencer's promise that Nelson would receive the *Foudroyant*, a new and unmanned ship, gave him the privilege of naming his flag captain and lieutenants, and therefore the pleasure of sending good news. As it happened, work on the *Foudroyant* had not yet been completed, and Nelson was offered the seventy-four-gun *Vanguard*, a twelve-year-old 'third-rate' being fitted out at Chatham, instead. He chose two relatively uninfluential officers to be his seniors. The Admiralty agreed that Edward Berry, another *Agamemnon*, might be his flag captain. Berry was engaged to marry Louisa Forster of Norwich, and the admiral wrote that he should seal the bargain quickly because he expected to summon him to Chatham 'every hour'. All else seemed to Nelson's satisfaction, for his new ship was reputed to be 'choicely manned'.[46]

Lieutenant Edward Galwey, an officer seriously weakened by his lack of 'interest', also received excellent news. He had gone to sea as a purser's servant in the *Swallow* in 1786, and the following year as a midshipman to Captain Robert Fancourt of the *Bulldog*. Since 1792 he had been out in the Mediterranean, becoming lieutenant in the *Princess Royal*, the flagship of Admiral Goodall, in time for the battle off Genoa in 1795. Later Galwey passed to the *Nemesis* and *Seahorse*, and it was in the last ship that he had helped bring the wounded Nelson home in 1797. Nelson liked Galwey, and after returning to London found the willing young lieutenant useful in winding up his affairs at Portsmouth, ready to steer the bronze figures, drawings, china, oil, soap and wine the admiral had brought home through the customs house with as little expense as possible. Unfortunately, Galwey could get nothing for himself but a routine appointment to the *Arethusa*, sitting in Portsmouth, and must have seen Nelson's invitation to visit him as a timely rescue. On the morning of 22 November the expectant young lieutenant found the apartments in Bond Street heaving with visitors, but Nelson took him aside and offered him the post of first lieutenant of his new ship. Galwey returned to Portsmouth in a whirl. 'I greedily accept it,' he wrote the next day, 'and trust my conduct when under your command will ever be such as to meet your approbation.' Nelson wrote to the Admiralty about Galwey on 14 December and on 20 January 1798 he was commissioned first lieutenant of the *Vanguard*.[47]

Before the end of December Berry was at Chatham, getting the *Vanguard* ready for sea, and Galwey joined on 2 January. 'Upon the whole we are well-officered,' Berry wrote to Nelson in February. 'The quarter-deck looks respectable. Mr [John Henry] Kremer, the Hanoverian [midshipman], towers above everybody.' By then – in fact by Christmas Day – Nelson had returned to Bath, where he and his lady joined a surprisingly vigorous old parson for a few final months of leave. By now, however, his mind was firmly upon the sea.[48]

6

With the routine responsibilities for his ship in hand, Nelson had time to linger in Bath worrying about the larger question of destination. The press thought he would be given a light squadron briefed to counter any French attempt to invade England from Holland, but the Channel fleet was another possibility. Watching the enemy's principal fleet in Brest was a crucial task, but Sir Horatio did not have a high opinion of Vice Admiral Sir Charles Thompson, who conducted the blockade by popping in and out of Portsmouth. He preferred the Mediterranean fleet, still under St Vincent and currently wintering in the Tagus. Despite the impending dispute over freight money, as far as Nelson was concerned the formidable earl was not only an important patron but a commander of the first water. Though separated, the two men continued to correspond. On the spot in England, Nelson performed small acts of friendship for St Vincent, while on station the earl watched over Josiah, William Hoste and other followers of his one-armed subordinate.[49]

In Bath Nelson spent several weeks with his father and wife. His sister Kate (Catherine) and her adventurous husband, George Matcham, were also lodging in the city, while selling their main home, Shepherd's Spring, near Ringwood, Hampshire. Nelson brought a new servant to Bath, a Thomas Spencer, hired upon a written reference, but Fanny shouldered most of the burden of caring for her disabled husband. Despite their childlessness, their relationship was strengthened by her sense of duty, and there is no evidence that they were unhappy at this time. Fanny's infertility has been the subject of some speculation, and Nelson's greatest twentieth-century biographer, Carola Oman, referred to Lady Nelson as 'a one-child sterility case', a diagnosis supported by 'her record of joint-pains and hysteria'. More recently Edgar Vincent suggested that she suffered from minor puerperal sepsis, an infection that can occur after childbirth. In truth the records are silent about Fanny's latent childlessness, but in the long run it was certainly costly, denying the couple a bond that might have kept them together.[50]

But that winter in Bath there seemed few long shadows. The Nelsons were entertained by Martha Saumarez, whose husband was still in the Mediterranean. About town Nelson met William, Lord Lansdowne, who offered him his place in one of the boxes in the Theatre Royal. After sampling the privilege, Nelson wrote that Lansdowne had neglected to tell him of 'all its charms', for the box was also used by 'some of the handsomest ladies in Bath'. If he had been single, he confessed, he would have been tempted, 'but as I am possessed of everything which is valuable in a wife, I have no occasion to think beyond a pretty face'.[51]

The most striking testimony to their bond at this time came from the Countess Spencer, who was accustomed to having Nelson to dinner when he was in London. Some time in late March 1798, just before he joined the *Vanguard*, Nelson called upon her to give 'a most solemn farewell', and asked her to protect Fanny if he was killed. He seemed fully conscious of all his wife had done for him, describing her as 'an angel, whose care had saved his life'. It was not the custom of the Spencers to invite officers' wives to dinner, and Lavinia had never met Fanny, but Nelson explained that 'if I [Lavinia] would take notice of her, it would make him the happiest man alive. He said he felt convinced I must like her. That she was beautiful, accomplished, but above all, that her angelic tenderness to him was beyond imagination. He told me that his wife had dressed his wounds, and that her care alone had saved his life.' Lady Spencer thought it wise to meet Fanny, and invited her to accompany her husband to a farewell dinner the day before the admiral left for Portsmouth. Nelson's 'attentions to her were those of a lover', Lavinia told a friend. 'He handed her to dinner and sat by her, apologising to me by saying that he was so little with her, that he would not voluntarily lose an instant of her society.'[52]

There was no hint of the betrayal and sadness that lay ahead.

7

On 19 February Nelson and his wife left Bath for London, where they were met by William and his son Horace on the morning of the 25th and took new lodgings several doors from Jones's house, at 96 Bond Street. The property was similar to those previous Bond Street lodgings, with a shop surmounted by three floors and a flat roof, and it survives to this day, dilapidated but recognisable. Behind, in Bath, the Reverend Edmund Nelson wondered if he would ever see his son again. The old man's health was fair, though his eyesight was poor and his hours too often empty, with more time to reflect than was perhaps desirable. Nelson had spoken breezily of a short war and a speedy return, but the parson had heard such stories too often to believe them.[53]

The few weeks in London were dominated by Nelson's impending departure and leave-takings. He took his wife to Kentish Town, as it happened for the last time, because old Uncle William Suckling was closer to death than anyone suspected. Brother William called, still in pursuit of an ecclesiastical sinecure, and was sent back to Norfolk with a letter telling their old aunt, Mary Nelson, that Fanny would be sending her two pounds of tea, but that she should 'call upon' Nelson 'for anything in particular'. Fanny was entrusted with £100 for Edmund. He would protest that it was too much, Nelson said, but it might enable him to visit Suckling in Norfolk. On 21 March Sir Horatio also signed a will, leaving £200 to Maurice, £500 to Josiah, £50 to an old manservant, Frank Lepée, and the rest to Fanny, who was the sole executor.[54]

Other farewells, personal and official, were made, to the Spencers, Locker and Waldegrave, who bestowed advice and entrusted Nelson with managing his prize affairs on station. Sir Horatio took his leave of the royal family at a 'drawing-room' function at St James's on 1 March and a levee thirteen days later, in which he also saw Hood, the Lord Chancellor, Earl Chatham and Admiral Lord Keith. Returning to London also plunged Nelson back into the prestigious dinner gatherings, and two for March appear in William Windham's diary. They were primarily naval occasions, one hosted by the Admiralty secretary, Evan Nepean, and the other by the Spencers at Uxbridge. The guests included Keith and Hamond, and significant political figures such as Lavington, Earl Bathurst, Grenville and Trevor. At Nepean's a 'Governor Philips' who had just returned from the Mediterranean briefed Nelson about St Vincent's blockade of the Spanish fleet in Cadiz. Fanny, who knew more than most about the agonies of being left behind, also troubled to visit the newly wed Mrs Berry, so quickly to be parted from her husband. 'It was excessively kind calling on her so soon,' Captain Berry wrote from Chatham. 'She requires consolation after parting from me, but this is only teaching her discipline of what necessarily must happen to sailors' wives.'[55]

It was not until 16 March that Nelson was ordered to Spithead to raise his flag in the *Vanguard* and await further orders. A stream of signal books and instructions followed until 27 March. Taken together, they answered Nelson's wishes, for he was to take a hired cutter as a tender and sail on 1 April, collecting transports and merchantmen from Spithead and Falmouth and conducting them to Oporto and Lisbon in Portugal. From there he was to regain his old Mediterranean station and join St Vincent off Cadiz, where the fleet was trying to contain Britain's most powerful naval adversaries, France and Spain. He could not have been happier had he written the orders himself.[56]

Early that March the *Vanguard* was still at Chatham. Berry's reports made interesting reading in Bond Street. There were over 150 supernumeraries on board, some destined for the Mediterranean on business of their own, and a few hoping to slot into naval vacancies that might occur on station, but 'on the whole' the ship's company was 'very tolerable', and included a thirty-one-year-old seaman from the *St George*, Thomas Johnson, who had specifically lobbied for the post of boatswain's mate on the *Vanguard* to be reunited with his old commander, Admiral Nelson. The men received their advance pay on the 10th, six months' provisions were stowed away, and, after disembarking the three hundred wives and prostitutes who had come aboard to fraternise with the men, Berry sailed for Portsmouth. He turned an eye to the comforts of his admiral, and advised Sir Horatio to secure a floor cloth to place beneath his large dining table, a carpet for the side of his cot, a two-foot mirror in a deep frame and curtains for the quarter galleries of his cabin. Additional curtains might be needed to supplement the shutters on the stern windows.[57]

At Portsmouth the port admiral was one of Nelson's favourite benefactors, Sir Peter Parker. Lady Parker had mothered several young naval officers, Nelson and Fremantle included, and Mrs Fremantle thought her 'the most civil kind woman I ever saw' and Sir Peter 'very kind likewise, but the oddest figure in the world . . . a most excellent caricature'. Parker had decisively intervened in Nelson's early career, putting him on the all-important list of post-captains, and he, his wife and daughter were as ready to oblige now, receiving Nelson's luggage and personal stores as they poured into Portsmouth, four locked boxes, a boat cloak and a wagonload of provisions from Bristol. Wine and spirits were always high on Nelson's list, for an admiral was expected to offer a good table. Nevis rum arrived, a present from John Pinney the Bristol merchant, and a cutter from Guernsey with Nelson's considerable regular order. From afar the admiral monitored the deliveries with his obsessive attention to detail, sending meticulous instructions to his secretary, John Campbell. He was to ensure the score of 'dry fed' sheep were 'of the best but not largest kind' and that all chickens, ducks and geese, as well as sugar, water, 'tripe', oysters and 'essence spruce' were in order.[58]

Like most admirals bound for the sea, Nelson was besieged with requests for places and favours. In sifting through the applications he was drawn to the relatives of naval officers, whom he regarded as his brothers in arms. A few streets north of Nelson's lodgings in Bond Street lay Queen Anne Street, where there lived Lady Elizabeth Collier, the widow of Vice Admiral Sir George Collier. Four of her six children were sons, and she desperately needed a protector for young Francis Augustus, who was then about fifteen years old. Francis had served a couple of spells in ships in the Irish Sea and English Channel, but his last two years had been spent studying for a naval career at Greenwich, where his tutor found him 'an excellent character'. Lady Collier's letter reached Nelson as he prepared to attend a royal levee, but he agreed to see her the same day, happy to have 'so very fine a lad under my wing' and satisfied that it was his 'duty to be useful to the children of our brethren'. Lady Collier fussed dreadfully, and bombarded Nelson with notes about her son, but he understood and rated the boy a 'first class' volunteer in the *Vanguard* on 21 March, thus making him one of the 'young gentlemen of the quarter-deck' in training for posts as commissioned officers. Nelson undertook to supervise the youngster, and promised his mother that his pocket money would not be squandered ('he will be a very lucky fellow if he gets on shore twice a year'). Lady Collier was deeply grateful for Nelson's 'great kindness' towards her 'dear boy', and young Francis himself was manifestly 'delighted with his situation'. He would die a rear admiral of the white in 1849.[59]

Nelson parted with his wife on Thursday, 29 March, he to take a coach for Portsmouth, she to return to Edmund in Bath to begin again the long home watch. The *Vanguard* had been at Portsmouth since the 15th, and the admiral's flag rose above her on the 28th. Some thirty men were either hospitalised or absent without leave, so Nelson appealed to the Admiralty for replacements and Sir Peter extricated nineteen Maltese seamen from the *Diadem*. Beyond that only wind and tide stood in the way of sailing.[60]

He went on board the last day of March, but visited naval friends and officials about the town, among them the Parkers and Captain Thomas Lloyd, a long-standing friend. Falling sick soon after parting from Nelson, Lloyd 'bolstered' himself 'up' in bed to wish his old comrade well. 'Among all your friends you have not one more anxious for your success and safety,' he wrote. 'God bless you, my good fellow.'[61]

The last few days in London had been hurried and confused, with a turnover of servants feeding the chaos. As Nelson pored over his baggage in Portsmouth, he fired complaint after complaint about missing items, linen stockings, a black stock and buckle he had purchased eighteen years before, three Portuguese pieces and the keys to his dressing stand. He had only eleven of an intended thirteen silk handkerchiefs, sixteen cambric handkerchiefs instead of thirteen, eleven of twelve cravats, three of six Genoa velvet stocks, and twenty of thirty huckaback towels. A watch was missing. On the other hand he unearthed items that belonged to Fanny, including some weights from her scales and a blue pillow. In Bath Fanny found the subject 'mortifying', and urged her husband to check his boxes and trunks more carefully, including the one belonging to his servant, Tom Allen. Her assistants, including Kate, were as sure as she that some of the items reported as missing had been packed. 'I think we can't all be mistaken,' she said. On the other hand, Fanny admitted that preparations had been rushed, and promised 'more care' in the future, when she hoped they had 'proper servants'. Look as he would, Nelson could not find everything he wanted, and grumpily remarked that he had had to buy a new stock and buckle at double the price of his old one.[62]

Fanny may have been careless, but she had much on her hands. She was emptying the house in Bond Street of their possessions, placing some in storage and transporting others to Bath; discharging errands for her husband, from safeguarding papers relating to his investments to distributing prints of Abbott's portrait to their friends; and preparing for the move to Roundwood, imminent now that Edge was due to quit the premises in the first week of April. In addition, she had Edmund to render comfortable, and found herself ill served by her staff, a sixty-year-old Catholic cook, a fourteen-year-old girl named Ryson, and 'Will', a worthless ne'er-do-well, who Suckling, Nelson's brother, would only agree to have back at Burnham Thorpe provided he had nothing to do with the garden.[63]

In Portsmouth it was the ship and its mission that most concerned Nelson, and he saw little of which he could complain. As an admiral, he was released from the routine management of his ship, which properly belonged to his flag captain, but bore the ultimate responsibility for the wellbeing of the ship's company of near six hundred. The team of officers inevitably reflected his patronage. Up until sailing he continued to slot people into positions according to grace and favour. He took an acquaintance of the Reverend Thomas Weatherhead, a Norfolk friend; the son of a clerk with William Marsh's banking house; Midshipman Clement Ives from Hull, recommended by Uncle William Suckling; Edward Naylor, a twenty-year-old landsman from London, to oblige Thomas Rumsey of the Excise Office, the aforesaid Uncle William's father-in-law; Thomas Meek, master's mate, to please his brother, Suckling, as well as Coke of Holkham; and Captain William Faddy of the Royal Marines, and his teenage son, a midshipman, associates of William Locker. Unavoidably, Nelson also had to disappoint. He could not wait for Thomas Morris, the chaplain of his last ship, the *Theseus*, who wanted to join him, and had to appoint the Reverend Stephen George Comyn in his stead, to assist which spiritual mentor, the admiral also made his customary appeal to the Society for Promoting Christian Knowledge for a supply of prayer books and Bibles.[64]

At least five of the six lieutenants were personally known to Nelson. Galwey had been with him in the *Seahorse*, and William Standway Parkinson in the *Boreas*. Henry Compton was a stalwart follower. Born in Limerick in 1774, he had trained for the sea at an academy in Deptford, joined the navy in 1789 and made his first voyage in the *Actaeon*, sent to the Caribbean. Since then he had served in five ships belonging to the Channel or Mediterranean fleets, including the flagships of Hotham and St Vincent, and it was the latter who had passed him to Nelson in 1796. Compton followed Nelson through four ships, during the course of which he executed a particularly tricky mission to Genoa in 1796. Of the other lieutenants, John Miller Adye was related to the attorney who had assisted Nelson in the Leeward Islands, and the Honourable Thomas Bladen Capel, aged twenty-one, was a son of the Earl of Essex and a protégé of the Spencers. The only lieutenant without an obvious connection to Nelson was Second Lieutenant Nathaniel Vassal, eight years a commissioned officer, and possibly a recommendation of his old patron, Lord Hood. Among the senior warrant officers in the *Vanguard* was another old *Agamemnon*, Michael Jefferson the surgeon, who was less than satisfactory but had earned some return for his recent treatment of Nelson's arm.[65]

The other contingent that greatly reflected the patronage of the admiral was its quota of junior quarter-deck officers aspiring to a lieutenant's commission. They were rated either midshipmen, master's mates or volunteer 'boys, 1st class', and there were about twenty of them in all. Some were, in fact, mature men, perhaps late climbers recruited from the more able of the 'lower deck' ratings, although more often men of limited ability, stuck in their neophyte status because of their inability to master the lieutenants' examination. In the *Vanguard*, John Weatherstone of Berwickshire, variously a master's mate and midshipman, was twenty-seven years old; James Quick of Plymouth, originally rated a coxswain, was thirty-five; and Daniel Legg, a master's mate from Aberdeen, older still at thirty-seven. The majority of the contingent, however, were 'young gentlemen' of whom Midshipman William Faddy might have been the youngest at about thirteen years.[66]

When vulnerable youngsters went into a hard world of men, it was inevitable that anxious parents pleaded for the oversight of captains and admirals. Nelson's interest in young people made him particularly susceptible to such appeals, and he often opened his purse to alleviate the difficulties of boys far from home. Granville Leveson Proby, later third earl of Carysfort, was seventeen or so when he joined the *Vanguard* as a 'first class' boy. His father, the first earl, an Irish peer and Whig of some influence, notified Nelson that he would provide his son with £40 a year, 'but if any circumstances should call for a further expense, you would . . . judge . . . the necessity of it, and draw upon me for whatever you should think proper'. Simon Antram of the *Enterprise* also applied to Nelson to take his son, George, who was accordingly rated midshipman. 'I am happy in your promise of attending to him,' wrote the father, 'and as I observed to you he has not learned navigation, [I] flatter myself you will (should you not have a school master) get him instructed therein by some person on board, and, as he has never been at sea, I could wish him in some mess the least expensive, having seven more [children] to attend to. I fitted him as well as my finances could do, but should he be in want during the voyage shall rely on your goodness to advise . . . and supply him at your discretion, which I shall at all times cheerfully pay to your agent.' Sir Horatio may have been an admiral charged with matters important to the realm, but he was also expected to act *in loco parentis* and to defray the extraordinary expenses of the boys on the promise of reimbursement.[67]

Nelson trusted people and was sometimes abused. The Reverends Dixon Hoste and William Bolton had allowed him to bear the financial burden of supporting their sons in the *Agamemnon*, and now history repeated itself. The recruit in question was fifteen-year-old Henry Cooper, a striking, spare, dark-eyed, round-faced lad with black curls, rated a 'first class' boy on 28 March. Sir Horatio paid out £45 on his account, and looked certain to incur further charges. However, the boy's father, Charles Cooper, a Norwich lawyer of Oby Hall, near Yarmouth, was suspiciously silent, and on the eve of sailing Nelson had to write to him. He considered the elder Cooper's behaviour to be 'shameful'. When Nelson sailed the matter had to be left to Fanny, who discovered that 'nine tenths of the year' Cooper was with the bailiffs; in fact, although no one knew, he was on his way to the debtors' prison. Nelson probably lost his money, but he did not send the boy home, as Fanny recommended. Fortunately, he was not out of pocket long, because Henry left the navy soon after the battle of the Nile, 'disliking the service'.[68]

By the time Nelson reached the *Vanguard*, the relentless process of enforcing discipline was being implemented. Soon after his arrival, on 3 April, four men received twenty-four lashes each for disobedience, and the day after the ship put to sea three more were punished. The offences were theft, drunkenness, uttering mutinous expressions and neglect of duty. Punishment, like the day-to-day running of the ship, was in Berry's hands. Nelson believed it 'a virtue to lean on the side of mercy', but punished firmly when the efficiency of the ship and the wellbeing of its company required it. As an admiral he rarely interfered in disciplinary matters, even when his most famous flag captain, Thomas Hardy, ran a rigorous regime.[69]

Nelson tried to get to sea with a convoy of eleven ships on 1 April, but the wind swung to westward and forced him back into St Helen's, where strong gales and rains imprisoned him for more than a week. As he waited for his luck to change he received a surprising farewell from a friend who wished him

> the most prosperous voyage and the most robust health. The only thing I do not wish you is more honours and glory. Your stock is sufficiently large already, and wants no increase, and I want exceedingly to see you once more and for very many years to come. I am afraid, however, that there will be times when you will

not think as I do on this subject, but I will not alter my opinion for all that. Be sure your dear son [Josiah] shall not be forgot [in the event of Nelson's death]. Ever yours, my dear Sir Horatio, with all regards and true esteem, Lavinia Spencer.[70]

Understandably, Lavinia echoed the feelings of Fanny and Edmund, who cared more for their hero than for any battles he might win. Nelson saw matters differently. While consoling his loved ones with the thoughts that the campaign might be a short one and his wife was 'uppermost in my thoughts', he thrilled at the sea chase. Fanny's farewells expressed, in her subdued way, the deepest feelings of her heart. 'God grant you his protection,' she said, and 'a continuance of the great successes which has attended you, and a happy meeting to us in Old England, and that soon.' She looked forward to the years they might spend together, certain as anyone could be that no clouds stood between them but those of the enemy and the sea. 'I hope, as some years are past,' she wrote, they had had 'time enough to know our dispositions' and that 'we may flatter ourselves it will last.'[71]

II

THE BAND OF BROTHERS

Ye saw with sails all swelling white,
Britain's proud fleet to many a joyful cry,
Ride o'er the rolling surge in awful sovereignty.

W. L. Bowles, *Song of the Battle of the Nile*, 1799

I

ON 9 April Nelson sailed from St Helen's, and gathered some twenty sail in Falmouth, most bound for Lisbon. Despite being short-handed, the *Vanguard* sailed exceptionally well, and could make eleven knots before the wind. She arrived off Portugal in good time, and there was only one alarm. Soon after seeing some of his charges into Oporto, Nelson was alerted to the approach of eighteen strange sails early in the morning of the 22nd, and the *Vanguard* cleared for action. But it was only a neutral Portuguese convoy, and Nelson ushered the rest of his convoy into the Tagus the next day. At Lisbon he restocked with fresh water, bread and beef, and large supplies of lemons and onions to fend off scurvy.[1]

Sir Horatio was at this point able to tell Fanny of his reunion with her son, Josiah Nisbet, now commander of the *Dolphin* hospital ship. Since receiving this first command, 'Captain' Nisbet had spent most of his time moving back and forth between Gibraltar and the Tagus, delivering stores, shepherding convoys and chasing small enemy privateers as well as providing a hospital facility for the fleet. In two days in September his boats even brought in six small prizes. Surprised, the exacting commander-in-chief of the Mediterranean, St Vincent, wrote that Nisbet had 'acquitted himself marvellously well', and that despite his natural ungraciousness appeared to have 'a great deal' of good 'stuff' in him. Nelson, who saw his stepson during the four days *Vanguard* was in the Tagus, remained sceptical and merely told Fanny that the youth was 'very well', but had failed to cultivate the acquaintance of His Majesty's local consul. Such officials were vital sources of goodwill, local knowledge and intelligence. Still, he had hopes that Josiah would 'make a good man, when we shall be happy'.[2]

At ten in the morning of 30 April the *Vanguard* joined St Vincent off Cadiz, where his fleet of eighteen ships of the line was blockading the Spanish fleet and keeping an eye towards the Strait of Gibraltar in case any French or Spanish ships from Toulon or Cartagena attempted to escape from the Mediterranean. Aboard the flagship, *Ville de Paris*, Nelson found that differences over prize money had not seriously damaged his relationship with the craggy commander-in-chief. In fact, St Vincent confessed to Spencer that Sir Horatio's arrival had put 'new life' into him. While some old jealousies stirred at the return of the star of the Mediterranean fleet, Nelson's friends rallied enthusiastically, receiving the news and letters that he had brought from home. 'He is really grown fat,' Captain Cuthbert Collingwood wrote with evident satisfaction.[3]

Eager to resume an active role, Nelson fancied that the Spaniards were shuddering at his return, but it was a surprise that awaited him off Cadiz. For as the *Vanguard* had blithely cut her way towards the fleet, great events that would change Nelson's life for ever were unfolding, and he stood on the brink of a great adventure. The Mediterranean station had suddenly been thrown into the vortex of the international struggle, and it would fall to him, a diminutive one-armed admiral, to go forth as his country's champion. The prize was the effective mastery of the entire Mediterranean, and his antagonist the most explosive military talent of modern times, Napoleon Bonaparte.

There were two crucial developments, the first a major diplomatic initiative which Nelson had probably heard something about before he left England, perhaps from conversations with Lord Grenville, the foreign secretary.

Grenville was a little like Nelson, a man who detested the principles and atheism of the French republicans, but whose concern was less the internal affairs of France than her threat to the peace and stability of Europe, and Britain in particular. With that quintessentially English notion of balance, Nelson and Grenville both saw the expansive energy of France as destabilising. To contain it within acceptable geographical boundaries, it was necessary to unite the other European powers in an anti-Gallic coalition. Nelson probably sailed knowing that Grenville was already bending himself to the enormous task of rebuilding an allied coalition, but he had few illusions about the difficulties involved. He had personally experienced the frustrations of working with the Austrians on the Riviera coast two years before.

Austria had been a powerful but unreliable coalition partner. She distrusted Prussia, her German rival, and had made a separate peace with France at Campo Formio in 1797, defaulting upon the repayment of British loans in the process. However, Austria was also afraid of France, and her suspicions grew as it became clear that the peace had not quenched French imperialism. In 1797 France occupied Switzerland and north-western Italy, establishing the Helvetian, Ligurian and Cisalpine satellite republics on the western and southern flanks of Austrian territory, and early in 1798 the papacy was sequestrated, and the Roman Republic added to the bag. The motives for these incursions were complicated, but they sent shock waves through southern Europe. Especially fearful was the kingdom of the Two Sicilies (Naples and Sicily), which controlled the peninsula of Italy south of Rome but was militarily weak and an undisguised foe of the French, for Naples was not only a monarchy, but also had a queen, Maria Carolina, who had lost her beloved sister, Marie Antoinette, the late queen of France, to the guillotine.

Naples had been Britain's most constant ally in the Mediterranean since the outbreak of war in 1793, and now appealed for help. 'We are threatened again with invasion,' Sir John Acton, her first minister, wrote to Sir William Hamilton, His Britannic Majesty's Envoy Extraordinary and Minister Plenipotentiary to the court of the Two Sicilies. 'The troops which the French are bringing into Genoa . . . those even from the Roman State . . . have the Two Sicilies for their destination . . . Will England see all Italy and even the Two Sicilies in the French hands with indifference?' Similar appeals went to Russia and Austria, which Naples also regarded as protectors. Maria Carolina, queen of Naples and wife of Ferdinand IV, was a daughter of the late empress of Austria, Maria Theresa; a sister of two Austrian emperors; and mother-in-law of the current Holy Roman and Austrian emperor, Francis II, as well as of Ferdinand III, the Grand Duke of Tuscany. To dynastic loyalties were added strategic imperatives, for Austria and Naples needed each other. Although the city of Naples was the third largest in Europe, the kingdom was a weak international player, but she also guarded Austria's vulnerable southern flank.[4]

Austria's influential foreign minister, Baron Franz Maria von Thugut, was unfortunately unfathomable. By the spring of 1798 he knew that the peace of Europe depended upon checking France, and that a united front was necessary, but he shrank from grasping the nettle and attempted to appease. To some extent his vacillation was understandable. Britain's military power was naval, and if Prussia or Russia could not be involved she alone would have to confront France's prodigious armies. On the other hand, in April the massing of French military power in northern Italy seemed a direct threat to Naples, and anti-Gallic sentiment in Austria rose. When the French ambassador in Vienna raised a tricolour above his hotel there were riots, and he quit the country. As relations with France deteriorated, Thugut notified Grenville that Austria believed a new war was unavoidable, and he was willing to talk about a Quadruple Alliance with Britain, Russia and Prussia. Austria's provisos were that Britain would finance the campaign and send a naval squadron into the Mediterranean.[5]

In Whitehall there were doubts. Grenville, noting the historic slipperiness of Austria, was determined that she must commit herself to repaying outstanding loans before new subsidies would be provided, and to supporting Britain's war aim of clearing the French out of the Low Countries. Moreover, if Britain sent ships into the Mediterranean, where she had no base, Naples would have to provision them and it would be necessary for Austria to back the Neapolitans in the event of French reprisals. Spencer doubted that the Royal Navy had the capacity to re-enter the Mediterranean a year after it had been abandoned to the French. With France in the Low Countries, Britain had to focus her sea power in protecting the English Channel. St Vincent's Mediterranean fleet was already at full stretch blockading Cadiz, where it was also strategically placed to protect Portugal and watch the Strait. Despite such reservations, on 28 April the British cabinet made an historic decision. As a positive step towards a new allied coalition, St Vincent would be ordered to send a task force into the Mediterranean, using reinforcements from the Channel fleet to replace the ships he detached. It was a bold move, one that brought Austria and Britain closer to an alliance. Austria seemed to respond. Naples received 'news of the most assured assistance of the [Austrian] emperor if we are attacked', and in May Austria and the Two Sicilies drew up a defensive alliance. Though not ratified until July, it committed Austria to covering Naples if the latter was attacked for provisioning the British naval squadron.[6]

Britain's decision to re-enter the Mediterranean, which had been a French lake for almost two years, was driven not only by plans to create a new coalition, but also by alarming intelligence from Toulon, the great enemy naval base inside the Strait. Using funds stolen from a subservient Switzerland and Genoa, the French were creating a huge overseas expeditionary force, led by their greatest general, Bonaparte. That was where Britain's fragmentary intelligence ended. Although her representatives abroad used 'secret service' money, provided through the Civil List, to buy information and employ spies, they could not penetrate the great design. Only ugly rumours were trawled up. Reports in the Parisian *Moniteur* and from John Udny, the British consul in Leghorn, and Captain William Day in Genoa, all suggested that the expedition was bound for Naples and Sicily, but it was entirely conceivable that the French were deliberately spreading that story to disguise Bonaparte's true destination. Day considered Portugal or Spain as credible alternatives, while Thomas Jackson, Britain's minister plenipotentiary in Turin, thought the amount of biscuit the French were baking and the number of ships and men being gathered betokened 'a hostile and distant object'.[7]

France had been assembling troop transports in her northern ports, but the tides and harbours did not favour an attempt to invade England over the Channel, and Bonaparte and the French foreign minister, Charles Maurice de Talleyrand, had begun to look to the Mediterranean as a surer way to strike a blow against their most stubborn adversary. Under the Directory the French navy had improved, but it remained chronically undermanned, inexperienced, ill-officered and defensive in nature. Nevertheless, when the British withdrew from the Mediterranean in 1796 to concentrate their defences nearer home, they had left France the strongest naval power within the Strait. Assembling men and materials in Toulon, Marseilles, Corsica and Genoa and Civita Vecchia in Italy, the French mustered 30,000 troops, nearly 300 transports and 20 warships for Bonaparte's expedition.[8]

On 24 April, as alarm spread throughout Europe, a cultivated, upright man in his forties, his greying hair adding distinction to already strongly etched and handsome features, called at the British Admiralty with a suggestion for Earl Spencer. Sir Gilbert Elliot, Lord Minto, was a resolute Whig, a liberal man tutored by David Hume and schooled in the Pension Militaire, Mirabeau, as well as Oxford and Lincoln's Inn. A governor of Corsica in 1794 to 1796, he had been a close associate and admirer of Captain Horatio Nelson, and in 1797 was staggered to witness Nelson's heroism in the battle of Cape St Vincent. Minto was impressed not only by the admiral's naval skill, but something perhaps rarer – his willingness to learn about the grimy politics of the Mediterranean from diplomats such as Drake, Trevor and himself. Nelson, in fact, struck Minto as the ideal inter-service man, capable of working with naval, diplomatic and military colleagues. Minto told Spencer that Nelson was 'the fittest man in the world' for a command inside the Strait because he had 'proved' himself 'quick and sharp with the enemy' and 'possessed [of] the spirit of conciliation with all friendly neutral powers' to a 'remarkable degree'. In conclusion, Minto told Nelson, 'I added . . . that your disposition to consult confidentially, and to act in concert and harmony with those on shore had been conspicuous on every occasion.' His message to Spencer was clear. If Britain wanted to return to the Mediterranean, Nelson was the man to lead her.[9]

Spencer had already thought about the matter, knowing full well that the Toulon armament as well as the need to respond to Austrian and Neapolitan pleas for help would probably send a British squadron back into the Strait. He, too, had considered Nelson the ideal commander, despite his junior standing on the list of flag officers, and the doubts about him in some quarters. The king himself, mooting the events at Cape St Vincent and Tenerife, admitted a terrible 'fear' that Nelson would 'do something *too* desperate'. The final decision, he told Minto, rested with St Vincent, the commander-in-chief, but the Admiralty would make their own preference for Nelson clear. Minto was so encouraged that, remembering Nelson's love of amphibious operations, he wrote to the Admiralty the same evening, suggesting that a couple of bomb-ketches and additional marines and troops be allocated to the detached squadron.[10]

The day after the cabinet's decision to re-enter the Mediterranean, the first lord dated a letter to St Vincent. He thought the French armament 'very probably in the first instance intended for Naples', but hinted that it was not the sole reason for the [detached] squadron, for 'the fate of Europe' might rest upon it. It was 'time to run some risk in order, if possible, to bring about a new system of affairs in Europe, which shall save us all from being overrun by the exorbitant power of France'. In other words a viable coalition, indeed the course of the war, as well as Bonaparte's sortie, depended upon those ships.[11]

Accordingly, Spencer sent a detachment under Sir Roger Curtis to reinforce St Vincent and enable him to construct a task force of twelve capital ships and some frigates. Nelson, Spencer suggested, would make a good commander. The squadron had a specific task: to find and destroy the French expedition. Venturing into an area where there were no British bases, it would be empowered to seize what supplies it needed from any port that refused provisions and water, barring those in Sardinia, which was peculiarly circumstanced. But at this stage the service was not regarded as permanent. There was no commitment to an indefinite British return to the Mediterranean. The squadron would simply complete its allotted duty and return.[12]

2

In May, after Nelson joined the fleet, the British were still ignorant of the purpose of the Toulon armament. Even in the Mediterranean an almost impenetrable mist shrouded the venture, and in June Bonaparte was reportedly stopping neutral vessels leaving his ports to prevent intelligence leaking out. Jackson, at Turin, received regular reports from Genoa and sent spies to Toulon, but although the massing of men, money, munitions and ships was notorious, there were few clues as to intent. Indications that the French were shifting strength from Toulon to Genoa or Corsica encouraged a belief that the expedition was bound eastwards, for Italy or perhaps southern Greece, part of the vulnerable dominions of the creaking Ottoman empire. Intelligence from Paris, however, curiously revealed that 'documents and characters of the Eastern Language' were being sent with the 'men of letters' accompanying the French army, and in Vienna Britain's ambassador, Sir Morton Eden, picked up a rumour that Bonaparte intended to invade Egypt and use it as a bridge to British India. Thugut discounted the idea, while Eden admitted that his 'great apprehensions' were for Naples. Then again, intelligence from Jackson and Day that the Toulon ships had only three months' provisions and those being fitted out at Genoa looked unable to withstand deep Atlantic rollers implied a voyage within the Mediterranean. No one really knew. St Vincent continued to regard Ireland as a possibility, while Spencer's money was on the Two Sicilies, the Levant or perhaps Spain, where he feared an army might be landed to march against Portugal. In Lisbon the Portuguese took the threat seriously.[13]

Unravelling the French plan was to be the major theme of the campaign. Even before receiving Spencer's orders to detach a squadron to seek and destroy Bonaparte's expedition, St Vincent had acted to clarify the matter, sending Nelson to Toulon to reconnoitre with a light force. He gave Nelson two capital ships, the *Orion*, Captain James Saumarez, and the *Alexander*, Captain Alexander John

Ball, and five cruisers, the *Emerald*, *Terpsichore*, *Flora* and *Caroline* frigates and *Bonne Citoyenne* sloop. Sir Horatio realised the sacrifice his commander-in-chief was making, because this represented a substantial part of his cruising strength. Nelson was to discover what he could, but if the enemy seemed set upon coming westwards towards the Strait, he was to fall back immediately so that St Vincent could prepare a reception. At this stage Nelson's job was primarily one of gathering intelligence.[14]

On the scent, Sir Horatio wasted no time waiting for his forces to gather. He took the *Emerald*, which was immediately available, and escorted a convoy to Gibraltar, where he picked up the remainder of his force, barring the *Flora* and *Caroline*, on 4 May. Rear Admiral Sir John Orde was there, partying aboard the *Princess Royal*. Forty-six years old, an admiral since 1795, and formerly a governor of Dominica, Orde was furious to learn that Nelson had been chosen for the detached service, when senior flag officers such as Sir William Parker and himself remained in the fleet. Nelson was the fourth most junior admiral on an Admiralty active list of ninety-four. In a difficult meeting, Nelson tried to mollify Orde but a couple of months later St Vincent told Nelson that Parker and Orde were part of 'a faction fraught with . . . ill will to you'. General O'Hara, the military governor of Gibraltar, had coveted the vacant Order of the Bath that was given to Nelson, but showed no hard feelings when he visited the *Vanguard*. Success, Nelson was discovering, was inseparable from envy, and that increased his burden. Knowing the trust placed in him, and the sacrifices superiors were making to send him forward, made it all the more imperative for him to deliver.[15]

Completing watering on the 7th, and storing 210 tons in the *Vanguard*, Nelson ordered his small squadron to weigh anchor at dusk the following day, slipping away in the descending darkness to escape hostile eyes in the Spanish fort at nearby Cape Carnero. Daylight found the ships still painfully warping from their anchorages, and the Spaniards fired as they passed. A shot lodged under the main chains of the *Alexander*, but the squadron was soon clear and bowling into the blue Mediterranean. In his first major order that day Nelson established the spirit that would govern his mission. 'In order that every ship . . . may be ready at day break to make a sudden attack on the enemy, or to retreat should it be deemed expedient, the decks and sides are to be washed in the middle watch, the reefs let out of the topsails whenever the weather is moderate, topgallant yards got up and everything clear for making all possible sail before dawn of day.' His force was tightly focused on its quarry, primed like a coiled spring.[16]

For all his decisiveness, Nelson was flesh and blood, and like all admirals charged with grave matters felt the loneliness of command. In that respect, he was fortunate in having a sympathetic and kindred spirit at his elbow. Not Berry, who was a sword rather than a head, nor even James Saumarez, his senior captain, who was a year older than the admiral. Sir James, a gallant Guernsey man, had been knighted for his spectacular capture of a French frigate in 1793, and won not a few accolades since. He had served under Nelson off Cadiz in 1797, and his wife, Martha, Lady Saumarez, had been a convivial comparer of naval news and gossip with Fanny back home, but Saumarez was rather an aloof, superior being, and – like Nelson – apt to petulance and grievance-mongering. The two men were not close. As the campaign progressed, however, Nelson developed a warmer relationship with Ball of the *Alexander*. Yet he began knowing relatively little of this forty-two-year-old son of a Gloucestershire squire. Indeed, Sir Horatio had once thought him 'a great coxcomb' for wearing epaulettes in the French style in 1783, two years before they made their appearance in the Royal Navy, and had not yet outworn that prejudice. But Ball was not only an accomplished seaman, but also loyal, sympathetic and a fund of advice and common sense. Educated in his native Stroud, the captain was a long-faced, grave-looking, bookish man, given to enlarging his views by wading through tomes of non-fiction, although he used to say the pages of *Robinson Crusoe* had inspired him to go to sea. His greatest qualities were his studied and controlled conduct and ability to find compromises, and his weakness optimism. But he emerged from the campaign a close confidant of Nelson, and a perfect complement to his more emotional and volatile personality.[17]

Within the Strait, Nelson was in hostile waters, but his line of battle ships were under orders to keep together, while the frigates and a sloop fanned out as scouts. Nelson had left orders for the missing *Flora* and *Caroline* to meet him at an appointed rendezvous along latitude forty-two degrees twenty minutes north, between Cape San Sebastian in Spain and Toulon, but neither ship showed up. The small squadron had gained the initiative, however, for its presence in these seas was unknown, and it surprised several enemy vessels, one the *Pierre*, a French privateer of eight guns and 'swivels' and sixty-five men, taken on the 17th. Nelson interrogated his prisoners individually, but got little information. Bonaparte's ships were still at Toulon, but the men did not know when they were due to sail or to where. Nelson sent the prize back to Gibraltar, placing one of his 'young gentlemen', Charles Harford, in command with a dispatch hinting that he might be made lieutenant. As he put his followers through their paces, he happily pushed the most promising forward. In Gibraltar he had already written to St Vincent about Galwey, whom he rated 'by far the very best [officer] in the ship'. There was a suggestion that he would make a likely commander if a suitable ship became available.[18]

Nelson got the squadron to his stated rendezvous off Toulon, but before he could reconnoitre the port his expedition was suddenly overtaken by disaster some twenty-five leagues south of Hyères. The storm that came was one of unusual ferocity, and Nelson's steward told his parents, 'while I breathe the recollection of that night will ever be before me. We expected every minute to go to the bottom.'[19]

In the afternoon of Sunday, 20 May, shortly after a small prize laden with cotton was taken, the wind quickened but some of the captains continued to set their yards, sails and rigging for fine weather. Berry had the flagship's topgallants and royals raised to catch additional wind, and Saumarez also set his topgallants. About ten in the evening the north-westerly breeze sharpened, whipping into an angry squall. After midnight the ships were engulfed in a terrifying tempest, tossed almost helplessly in tremendous seas while vivid flashes of lightning stabbed through the darkness above. Even reefed, the topsails of the *Orion* and *Alexander* burst, and the latter lost her foresail. Berry reduced his canvas to a storm staysail, but the flagship's main topmast snapped and swung crazily down, lunging at the mainmast rigging with every roll and pitch. Its topsail yard had been lined with struggling seamen, clinging to the yards and slippery footropes, but all but two were rescued from the wreckage. Of the others, one plunged to his death on the booms and his companion was swept into the sea. Half an hour later the ship, rolling wildly as the seas slammed into it broadside, also lost its mizzen topmast and after three the foremast itself, which cracked like a twig above the deck and fell in two pieces across the forecastle, smashing the bowsprit in several places. Until cut away by a frantic work party, part of it hung by its rigging about the bows, the debris, including a huge three and a half ton anchor, beating violently against the hull.

For two nights and an intervening day the battle continued. With its foremast and topmasts down, the flagship was in a miserable condition, frantically floundering in violent wind, rain and spray. Unable to sail close to the wind, she took the gale on her port side and was carried east-south-east towards the perilous rocky coasts of Corsica. Berry and Nelson tried to turn the ship around by wearing so that they could steer southwards, but without masts or sail she was virtually unmanageable. Only when the weather abated after daybreak could the helm be used and a spritsail hung under the damaged bowsprit to wear the ship and put her head south-south-west instead of north-east. Thus, almost miraculously, *Vanguard* fought her way clear of Corsica, but she was still taking a dreadful beating, and storm-savaged seamen worked feverishly to clear wreckage, cutting away a main anchor, relieving what pressure they could upon the mainmast, and cutting holes in the lower gun deck to allow water to escape into the hold, from which pumps worked ceaselessly to remove it. Thomas Meek, one of the 'young gentlemen', was washed overboard, and a cutter was lost.

The gales slackened in the early hours of the 22nd. The smaller ships were scattering in the darkness and spray, but, obeying their orders to remain in company at all times, the ships of the line remained close by. Nelson signalled the *Alexander* to take the shattered flagship in tow, and in the afternoon a cable was got across with great difficulty, and Ball set his topsails and courses and began to tow the crippled *Vanguard* towards the neutral islands of Sardinia, looking for shelter. The wind now dropped completely, but there was little relief, for it left a strong swell carrying the crippled flagship towards the craggy margins of San Pietro. By midnight they were close enough to see the surf breaking ominously over foam-streaming rocks, but no anchorage could be seen, and daylight found the ships in a perilous position five or so miles offshore. Fearing both ships might be lost, Nelson nobly ordered Ball to cast off the tow and save his ship. But Ball – Ball the man Sir Horatio had disliked for fifteen years – refused, even when, by his own account, his admiral grew 'impetuous' and 'passionate' in his threats. At six a saving north-westerly enabled the *Alexander* to pull the crippled flagship around the fearful rocks to windward of San Pietro. Another six hours and they were anchored in the sheltered harbour of the island's principal town.[20]

The bad weather lasted until the morning of the 23rd, and Nelson marvelled at his escape, concluding that

> the accidents which have happened to the *Vanguard* were a just punishment for my consummate vanity, I most humbly acknowledge, and kiss the rod which chastised me. I hope it has made me a better officer, as I believe it has made me a better man. On the Sunday evening I thought myself in every respect one of the most fortunate men, to command such a squadron in such a place, and my pride was too great for Man. But I trust my friends will think that I bore my chastisement like a man, and it has pleased God to assist us with His favour in our exertions to refit the *Vanguard*, and here I am again off Toulon.

He commended the exertions of Ball and Saumarez, and realised that he had seriously misjudged the former. Officially, Nelson wrote of Ball's 'unremitting attention to our distress'; privately, he enrolled the captain into his own pantheon, and as long as he lived could never do enough to serve him.[21]

Nelson made no criticism of Berry's handling of the ship. In fact, although the admiral had not been on deck when the storm approached, he would almost certainly have been aware of what was happening. He had displaced Berry from the captain's cabin at the stern of the ship, and slept in its forward part, reserving the roomier sections lit by the stern windows for the business of the day. Nelson's custom was to retire early in the evening, and rise early, long before the boatswain's mates turned the men from their hammocks at about seven each morning. But the partition between him and the people at the steering wheel above was a thin one, and at no time was he completely divorced from the comings and goings of the handling of the ship. It is impossible to believe he remained an idle spectator during the storm, and much of the handling of the ship was almost certainly his own. But throughout he remained in his 'usual spirits,' relatively unmoved by the disaster.[22]

The storm blighted Nelson's mission, scattering his ships, and sending the sail of the line limping towards a neutral haven for repairs. On the morning of 23 May they arrived at Carloforte, a small port off south-west Sardinia, in the island of San Pietro, where they encountered a very different problem. The following morning Giovanni Segni, the port captain, arrived in a boat to establish the identity of the stranger. Nelson and his officers leaned expectantly over the side of the crippled *Vanguard* to hold a brief but disturbing conversation. The kingdom of Piedmont-Sardinia did not permit ships of the Royal Navy to enter their ports, Segni explained. 'Since when?' asked one of the disgruntled British officers, perhaps Berry. Segni alluded to a treaty concluded with France the previous year, but Nelson knew it was pointless negotiating with an officer of that rank, and asking the name of the local governor said that he would send someone ashore to speak with him.[23]

Nelson was encountering the reality of a Mediterranean left to the mercy of the French for more than a year, and none had lingered under that uncertain shadow more fearfully than the Italian states. Some had fallen under effective French control and been bled of resources. A British officer in Genoa, one such place, wrote that the

> people here are heartily tired . . . of the French. Their Council of Sixty has voted all the plate &c. of the convents and churches to be sold in order to raise the sum of 800,000 livres demanded by the French for this [Bonaparte's] expedition, and a proclamation has been issued by the [French] Directory forbidding all persons giving their opinions on the propriety or impropriety of this measure, and so great is their fear [that] the vote of the council will be resisted by the country people that a body of troops has been sent to the different parts of the coast . . . to act in case of opposition. The French have also informed the government that the sum of 9,000,000 livres will be wanted for this and the ensuing year.

Moreover, in addition to a France eager to control and despoil them, the Italian states had deep-rooted problems of their own. Rising costs of corrupt and inefficient administrations, cash-strapped governments and the reluctance of nobles and clerics to shoulder fair shares of economic burdens were creating widespread distress and discontent. Radicals, whether mere modernisers seeking to limit the powers of hereditary rulers, moderate democrats, or outright republicans, were to be found among the educated and middling urban classes, and the French were not insensible of their use in destabilising regimes and opening them to foreign intervention. Gallic interference was predominantly cynical and self-interested, despite the rhetoric of liberation. Venice, for example, was occupied by the French in 1797, used as a prize to tempt Austria into the peace of Campo Formio, and then gutted of valuables and abandoned. As one contemporary remarked, the French 'left behind an infamous memory of robbery . . . no more rapacious army has descended on Italy since the Landsknechts'. Thus, the Italian states were threatened by an aggressive and imperialist power that knew their Achilles heels – the internal discontent that they could promise to redress, and from which they could fashion a useful if not entirely controllable fifth column.[24]

Piedmont-Sardinia, with her mainland territories sandwiched between France and her satellite, the Genoese (Ligurian) Republic, was particularly vulnerable, and there were considerable divisions within, between royalists loyal to King Carlo Emanuele IV of the ruling house of Savoy, radicals influenced by France and discontented peasants. In 1797 the country had bought a measure of peace by signing a treaty with France, consenting to allow French troops to garrison her principal cities, Turin and Alessandria, to close her ports to British warships, to supply France with troops on demand and to reserve for her the use of San Pietro and San Antioco. Despite this the kingdom was in perpetual fear of being invaded and revolutionised, and with good reason. As far as Bonaparte was concerned, France was 'a giant embracing a pygmy' which it would sooner or later 'crush . . . in its arms'. In April the new French ambassador to Piedmont-Sardinia was equally blunt. The survival of the Italian state depended entirely upon her slavish adherence to French interests. Even as Nelson's ships began their mission, Piedmont-Sardinia was in an acute state of uncertainty and unrest. To add to her perplexities, an internal rebellion near her Genoese frontier had involved her in difficulties with Genoa, whose troops seized Loano in June.[25]

The British government appreciated some of Sardinia's problems, and had specifically excluded her from a general instruction that the task force could coerce any port that refused him entry. But at this stage, Nelson was ignorant of those instructions. He naively assumed Sardinia to be a neutral power willing to extend the common hospitality of the sea to warships of His Britannic Majesty. In Turin Jackson knew better, and predicted that while a British squadron would be welcomed by the Sardinian people, it would be an unwelcome embarrassment to the government. And so it had proved.[26]

The same day that the port captain at Carloforte visited the *Vanguard*, a Sardinian fort fired a salute, which Nelson, pleased at least to be acknowledged, returned with an equal number of guns. As promised, he also sent an officer ashore to meet the governor, Francesco María de Nobili, and after making little progress, asked Saumarez to take over the following day. Armed with scrupulous courtesy and a profusion of compliments, Saumarez referred to the friendship between Britain and Sardinia, and requested livestock, vegetables and onions. De Nobili protested the scarcities of his region, but over that day and the next furnished a few slaughtered oxen, two bullocks and a quantity of onions for cash. The *Vanguard* took aboard 310 lbs of beef.

De Nobili had contacted the viceroy, Marquis Don Filippo Vivaldi, in Cagliari, and was told to stand firm, refuse to admit the British to the port and to give Nelson notice to depart. Accordingly, on the evening of 27 May the governor boarded a sloop and gingerly approached the British ships offshore. Seeing him coming, Nelson put his head out of a window and invited him aboard the flagship, hurrying out to meet him 'with great courtesy' as he came over the side. A seven-gun salute was fired, and Nelson conducted De Nobili to a 'well appointed cabin' and heard the hapless official out. The admiral, 'a youthful 38 year old' according to the governor, was not taken aback by the viceroy's orders, but, rather, laughed, and said, smiling, that he understood how uncomfortably De Nobili was circumstanced. But showing sudden if fleeting force and gravity, he added that his ships had nevertheless to be repaired, he needed a friendly port and would even go to Cagliari, the Sardinian capital, if necessary. However, Nelson promised to try to have his ships ready to leave the next day. After being escorted back to the ladder, and receiving another salute, De Nobili reported that he could not 'express . . . how many compliments, kindnesses and graces' he had received. He carried letters Nelson had given him to forward to the British officials at Turin and Leghorn.

The governor could not prevent Nelson from seizing the port, but there was no need for such extremities, which in the end created few friends. The seamen, therefore, worked with an astonishing will to prepare the ships for sea. At stake was the *Vanguard*, which might otherwise have had to return to Gibraltar, forcing Nelson to raise his flag on one of the consorts. The hero of the hour was James Morrison, carpenter of the *Alexander*, who worked wonders, digging into the resources of all three sail of the line to replace or repair masts, yards, shrouds, rigging and stays. By 28 May the ships were ready to sail, and Nelson was able to save the Sardinians further embarrassment. They appeared to appreciate it, and fired a nine-gun salute as the British ships left their anchorage.[27]

The Sardinian incident told Nelson that in the Mediterranean, where His Britannic Majesty had no bases and the French free rein, potential allies only jeopardised themselves by encouraging British ships. Only the maverick state of Algiers offered help gratuitously, but it was too distant, inadequate and unreliable. And no sooner had Nelson got his ships to sea again than he met another reverse. Off San Pietro the *Orion* seized a Spanish snow of six guns and 'spoke' a neutral ship that had vital intelligence. She had just left Marseilles, and revealed that the very day the gales had attacked Nelson's ships the French expedition had sailed from Toulon!

3

While Nelson was in south-western Sardinia, Bonaparte's fleet had been at La Maddalena, on the north-eastern side of the island. Pushing forward as fast as he could, Nelson reached his station off Toulon on 3 June, without finding any of his missing cruisers. These small, fast ships were the handmaidens of every fleet, the scouts, couriers, chasers and errand-runners, facilitating the necessary flow of provisions and information. Without his 'eyes' Nelson's effective horizon was the view from his mastheads, twelve miles or so in good weather, but usually less in the customary haze.

Two days later a solitary cruiser appeared, but not one of the missing ships. It was the brig-sloop *Mutine*, under Thomas Masterman Hardy. Hardy, a large, broad-shouldered twenty-nine-year-old, was one of Nelson's favourites, a thorough professional in all that appertained to the management of a ship, and a loyal, self-sacrificing if uncomplicated man. Hardy brought bad and good news. Some days back he had encountered Captain George Hope in the *Alcmene* frigate, sent to reinforce the admiral. Unfortunately, Hope had failed to find Nelson, but had come across his missing cruisers. Deciding that Nelson must have returned to Gibraltar to repair storm damage, he had taken it upon himself, as the senior captain present, to withdraw the entire detachment from the rendezvous and redeploy them in the southern and eastern Mediterranean. Nelson was rightly enraged, and grumbled that Hope should have known him better. Without making any appreciable efforts to find the admiral or divine his probable intentions, Hope had dispersed an essential part of the admiral's force, and even his encounter with Hardy, who thankfully held his course, had not prompted a revision of his faulty judgement. In the next few days Nelson had to risk using his capital ships as cruisers, sending them to chase sails and gather information.[28]

But Hardy also brought compensatory news. Hope had intelligence that a mighty French armada of some 230 transports and escorts had been seen off Nice, apparently bound south-east, as if to pass north of Corsica towards Elba. What was more, Hardy delivered new instructions from St Vincent that completely transformed Nelson's mission. An additional eleven ships of the line were on their way to give him a fully-fledged task force, and his job was no longer to reconnoitre, but to find Bonaparte's expedition and destroy it. The news was met with 'universal joy' in Nelson's little squadron, and when the reinforcements arrived in the afternoon of 7 June the admiral was inspired to discover that St Vincent had sent him 'the elite of the navy of England'. Ten of the ships were third-rates of seventy-four guns, the fighting ships most prized for combining power and speed, and they were captained by some of the ablest officers of the fleet.[29]

After Nelson had left the fleet, St Vincent had received Spencer's orders to detach a squadron to destroy the French expedition, and acted as soon as Curtis's reinforcement arrived. The new mission, to return to the Mediterranean in force, was momentous, and it aroused great competition in a fleet of ambitious officers, not simply among the flag officers who had coveted Nelson's command, but in the captains. However, to head the reinforcements St Vincent chose the legendary Thomas Troubridge of the *Culloden*, a hero of Cape St Vincent and Tenerife, whose skill the commander-in-chief rated above all others, Nelson included. It was a good choice, for Nelson and Troubridge had not only been the twin warheads of the Mediterranean fleet, but soulmates, sharing dreams, deeds and a hatred of the French. Troubridge was a fine sea officer, amazingly energetic and tigerish in disposition, but he was too quick-tempered, artless and emotionally unstable to command a complicated theatre. Yet the two men worked well in tandem – almost too well. Their friendship had attained a rare intensity, not so surprising in Nelson, whose feminine sensitivity fuelled deep attachments and innumerable kindnesses, but more remarkable in a figure as masculine, bluff and brutally blunt and down-to-earth as Troubridge. Any stresses that beset their friendship frequently reduced both men to tears.[30]

Appropriate as it was, Troubridge's appointment created some difficulties. Behind, in the fleet, a senior captain, Cuthbert Collingwood, one of Nelson's oldest naval friends, simmered at what he regarded as outright favouritism. Already disliking his commander-in-chief, he resolved to quit the fleet 'from that day'. Off Toulon, Sir James Saumarez also felt inconvenienced by Troubridge. In the official pecking order Sir James would remain Nelson's second in command, but it was to Troubridge and increasingly also Ball that the admiral effortlessly related. 'Who shall dare tell me that I want an arm,' Sir Horatio once declared, 'when I have three right arms?' And so saying, he indicated his own and the adjacent figures of Troubridge and Ball. Aware that Saumarez had recently considered returning to England, St Vincent gave him permission to leave the task force as soon as the reinforcements arrived, but scenting a battle Sir James swallowed his pride and insisted upon remaining.[31]

Of the other captains who joined Nelson, Henry d'Esterre Darby of the *Bellerophon* was next in seniority to Troubridge, 'a good-humoured, blundering Irishman, who will make you laugh', according to St Vincent. Looking more like an amiable shopkeeper than a sea fighter, he never became one of Nelson's closest confidants, but did his duty well enough. Among the remainder, though, were faces that Nelson knew and respected – Samuel Hood, the tall, gawky, handsome captain of the *Zealous*, a cousin of Admiral Hood and veteran of Tenerife, who added to the skills of seaman a bent for military fortification and a useful smattering of languages; Benjamin Hallowell of the *Swiftsure*, a bulky North American whom Nelson had known in Corsica, capable if somewhat unpredictable, with a 'spirit . . . certainly more independent than almost any man's I ever knew'; and the entirely likeable and righteous New Englander, Ralph Willett Miller of the *Theseus*, who had been Nelson's flag captain in three desperate encounters at Cape St Vincent, Cadiz and Tenerife. The other newcomers were Thomas Louis of the *Minotaur*, John Peyton of the *Defence*, who had come to the Mediterranean as a passenger in the *Vanguard*, Davidge Gould of the *Audacious*, Thomas Foley of the *Goliath*, George Westcott of the *Majestic* and Thomas Thompson of the fifty-gun *Leander*.[32]

This, then, was the elite corps who would chase Bonaparte's fleet, and who Nelson would famously dub his 'band of brothers'. The quotation was from what was apparently the admiral's favourite Shakespearean play, *Henry V*. On the eve of Agincourt, Henry described, in words Nelson could never match nor forget, the bond that often developed between colleagues in combat, the sacred fraternity solemnised in the face of deadly danger, that Nelson believed should never be betrayed:

> We few, we happy few, we band of brothers;
> For he today that sheds his blood with me
> Shall be my brother; be he ne'er so vile
> This day shall gentle his condition.[33]

Raised to fourteen line of battle ships and a brig, Nelson's force made an impressive sight. The two-decked capital ships, some 170 feet in length and carrying a principal armament of powerful thirty-two pounders, were strikingly painted, most in yellow with black adornments, but a few blood-red with a yellow or black line running horizontally between the fearsome gun ports. They were in excellent order, the men regularly drilled in the use of great and small arms, and the ships making eleven knots in good weather. Each 'seventy-four' was manned by six hundred or so men and boys, and a handful of women were in the fleet, most of them wives following their men. In all necessities but bread and wine, of which they had as much as room afforded, the ships were victualled for six months.

The stubborn weakness was an almost total lack of cruisers. St Vincent had done his best, assigning no less than nine cruisers to the task force and thinking it 'well off', but his best efforts had been overthrown by misadventure. Two of the five assigned to Nelson's original detachment had never joined, for no fault of their own. The other three were separated in the storm, and then lost in the southern and eastern Mediterranean by the sixth recruit, Hope's *Alcmene*. This stripped Nelson of four cruisers in the crucial phase of his campaign, and two later reinforcements, the *Seahorse* and *Thalia* frigates, did not find the fleet until it was far too late to play a significant part. Only one of the nine cruisers the commander-in-chief had tried to supply, the tiny *Mutine*, was there to do their work. In what became a complex game of 'hide and seek' the lack of cruisers severely disabled Nelson's fleet. Nor did the admiral feel comfortable spreading out his ships of the line to extend the area of sea they covered. In this his thinking was dominated by memories of Admiral William Hotham's operations in 1795, when the contrary winds common to these waters divided a large British fleet, leaving one part of it isolated and becalmed and at the mercy of a superior French force. To prevent such fragmentation, Nelson regularly insisted that his capital ships maintained fairly close order. As he instructed his captains on 18 June, 'on no account whatever' were they to 'risk the separation of one of their ships'.[34]

The lack of cruisers also rebounded upon the battle plans that Sir Horatio was now beginning to devise. He was in pursuit of a huge force, actually consisting of some 22 warships, 130 transports and 11,000 men. Ideally, Nelson would have attacked the enemy battle fleet with his ships of the line and left his cruisers to fall upon the convoy, which would be carrying the bulk of the artillery and army. But he had no cruisers, and his capital ships would have to deal with both. The admiral therefore divided his fleet into three squadrons, one of six line of battle ships under his immediate supervision, another consisting of the *Orion*, *Goliath*, *Majestic* and *Bellerophon* under Saumarez, and the last, the *Culloden*, *Theseus*, *Alexander* and *Swiftsure*, with Troubridge. If the French were encountered in the open sea, he planned to engage their escorts with two divisions, leaving his remaining division to do its best with the transports. Given the reported size of the French expedition, Nelson's force was thinly stretched indeed, and more capable of scattering than destroying the enemy.[35]

Bonaparte had quit Toulon on the 19th, but Nelson had no reliable evidence of his intentions. St Vincent's latest instructions of 21 May, brought by Troubridge, had nothing new to say about the subject. He cautioned Nelson to take 'special care' to keep the French in the Mediterranean, but his greatest worries within the Strait were for Naples and Sicily. Indeed, the commander-in-chief promised Sir William Hamilton that he would aid the threatened kingdoms, and notified Emma, Sir William's demonstrative wife, that 'a knight of superior prowess' was 'charged with this enterprise, and will soon make his appearance at the head of as gallant a band as ever drew sword or trailed pike'. Nothing Nelson had learned detracted from this idea that Bonaparte was on his way to settle old scores with the Two Sicilies. Clearly, the French were not sailing westwards. None of the British ships coming from the Strait had encountered any such force, even though Hardy had come north of the Balearic Islands and Troubridge south of them, and Nelson had passed from southern Sardinia to Toulon. Furthermore, all the intelligence picked up from prizes or passing neutral ships pointed to an eastern destination. One of a pair of Spanish prizes taken on 7 June informed the British that seventy transports and a frigate were waiting for Bonaparte in Genoa, suggesting that the main French force would sail eastwards along the Riviera to collect them. And a ship the *Leander* 'spoke' the following day reported Bonaparte even more advanced, somewhere in the vicinity of Naples. Everyone had different views of the ultimate French target, and mentioned Naples, Crete [Candia] and Malta, but every scrap of intelligence currently pointed eastwards.[36]

With no remit but to find and destroy the French, a frantic chase was now afoot. Bonaparte was closer to home, and at least knew where he was going. But Nelson's squadron seemed almost lost in a vast blue sea of more than a million square miles, scratching for every clue, without a single British base to inform or sustain them. Provisions were likely to run dangerously low. So far the squadron had kept reasonably healthy, but some fevers and ulcerated legs were being treated in the sickbays. Nelson's people ate beef, pork or poultry on some days, and oatmeal, bread, butter and cheese, but they needed fresh provisions, as well as palliatives such as onions and lemons, to maintain bodily vigour and counter scurvy. The stored provisions would only last three to six months, and then the squadron would need friends. In Italy, Tuscany and the Two Sicilies were possible sources of aid, but they lived in terror of French invasion. Malta affected strict neutrality, and would be unlikely to risk a partial course, while further east the far-flung dominions of the Ottoman Porte had been inclined to lean politically towards France.

Nelson's was a charge of unusual diplomatic and logistical, as well as military, difficulty.

4

Far away many minds lingered anxiously upon Nelson's quest.

In England Earl Spencer, who had recommended a junior admiral to lead Britain back into the Mediterranean, was sure that Nelson would acquit himself gloriously, given the chance of battle. The news that Bonaparte had sailed from Toulon, and that Nelson was after him, raised feverish expectations in Britain, where an exciting if frightening encounter was expected. Most had no doubt that the Royal Navy would add another naval victory to its matchless record; as Pitt remarked, the French embarkation was 'agreeable' because it augured 'some good event'. But there were underlying doubts. At sea, no one had invested more in Nelson than St Vincent, who watched his task force swallowed up by the Mediterranean, and spent agonising weeks waiting for news. In the meantime his relations with Orde spiralled down in fierce recriminations. When Orde tried to bring his commander-in-chief before a court martial, Spencer rightly quashed it, and St Vincent shipped the simmering rear admiral home. More than a year later St Vincent also reached England and Orde was taken into custody after challenging him to a duel. Though Orde's career survived, his mind was poisoned for life.[37]

Fanny and her father-in-law were again before the home fires, and Edmund returned to monitoring his growing infirmities and wondering whether he would live to see his son again. 'I am decreasing, bearing away,' he wrote in his big bold hand, 'bad eyes, bad pen, glad only that I am able to add your affect[ionate] father.' As usual also, Fanny started at every report of a battle in the Mediterranean. Nelson's letters had been neither extensive nor satisfying. 'You must tell me the truth,' she said in search of more about her son, but what information there was shrivelled once the chase had begun. On 15 June Nelson warned his wife that she would have to be content with short letters. He never seems to have understood how much she loved him, and how even the briefest accounts of his fortunes allayed her troubled mind. 'No one period of the war have I felt more than I do at this moment,' she wrote in July. 'I really am so affected that it has enervated me beyond description.' Getting few letters from her husband and none from her son, she continued to fall victim to every rumour.[38]

Initially, Fanny had much to divert her, using captains departing for the Mediterranean to carry long and disjointed letters to her husband, along with jars of cherries, currant jelly and apricot; answering irritating requests for patronage; paying bills, including the duties on wine imported from abroad, and attempting to reclaim occasional sums Nelson had advanced on behalf of 'shabby people'. At the beginning of May she left Bath for Kentish Town, from where she visited the Royal Academy to see if her husband's portrait was being exhibited. Proud of Sir Horatio, she rejoiced at the brisk sale of the engravings, and purchased two second-hand silver plates, which she had engraved with the Nelson arms.

On 20 May Edmund and Fanny took possession of Roundwood after a journey with their footman from Bath. The house occupied a rather exposed spot, the highest for ten miles around, and Fanny planted trees to add beauty and shelter. Edmund thought it had 'everything needful to a family of moderate income', and wanted only some papering and painting here and there to make it fully acceptable. He was happy to tell his son that he could explore the neighbourhood, for he was fit enough to walk to the Ipswich market. On her part, Fanny admired the crops, the larks and blackbirds, and set about repairing the water pump and shutters, restoring the garden wall, tackling damp spots, fixing leaks and buying furniture, though she thought everything expensive, including her three female servants. Sir Horatio urged her not to stint on necessities, for glory, rather than money, was his object, but Fanny was careful by nature. 'The expense of housekeeping is very great,' she complained, 'altho' we dine off cold beef, not being able to procure fish or fowl.' Her real complaint was the lack of the good company she had known in Bath. The Boltons lived nearby, but they were 'cunning people', happy to shift their expenses to Nelson, with William in particular, ensconced uncomfortably close by in Akenham Hall, so 'officious' that even the mild-mannered Edmund could barely suppress his distaste.[39]

It took time to fit into a new community, and Fanny was never comfortable pushing herself forward, especially as she often suffered colds, felt stressed and worried about her eyesight and hearing. Once the bustle of moving was over, life settled into a slow, quiet and lonely routine. 'We see few people,' she owned, as 'there was no neighbourhood.' Some of the 'country families' had four-horse carriages, and lived in 'great style' but remained aloof, save the affable Middletons. Sir William Middleton of Shrubland Hall was a veteran parliamentarian and high sheriff, who had once built a seventy-four-gun ship for the nation, and his wife, Lady Harriet, had family in Norfolk. Less amenable neighbours included a gambler and flirt ('no gentlewoman ever went to his house'), who lived among 'indecent ornaments' of nude figures, and 'as arrant a courtier as ever lived' who opened her home 'to all card players'. The service families were more acceptable, and Vice Admiral Samuel Reeve, Captain John Bourchier and a 'Major Heron' were occasional escorts. In particular Fanny formed a friendship with Louisa Berry, with whom she went to races, balls and social events, or tackled sofa covers and cushions. There were moments of excitement, in one of which Fanny caused some comment by declining to flee her house when strange ships off the coast stirred a local invasion scare. But generally time hung heavily, and Fanny and Edmund spent too much time talking and thinking about their missing hero, and searching for news in the papers. Visitors of the fleet were especially welcome. One day John Thompson, an old *Agamemnon*, called, now disabled, emaciated, and unable to stoop or go aloft after a spell in a French prison. 'He wished himself often enough with you,' Fanny wrote to her husband.[40]

Of the other Nelsons, none waited more anxiously for news from abroad than his brother, William, whose thoughts were constantly about the personal benefits to be reaped from another victory. 'If any fortunate circumstance should occur to put it in your power,' he wrote to Sir Horatio, 'I hope you will not forget your promise to me that you would remind the Lord Chancellor of what passed between you and him about a church dignitary for me.' William was short of money, and had to pull Charlotte from school and tutor her at home, but his avarice went far beyond mere subsistence. Rubbing his hands together and 'building castles in imagination', he was already dreaming of a peerage that might ultimately pass from his childless brother to his own posterity.[41]

Nelson's mind was no less concentrated. On 8 June he decided to sail around Cape Corse and south towards Naples to cover the most urgent danger points. Three days later he wrote to his commander-in-chief that 'the French have a long start, but . . . you may be assured I will fight them the moment I can reach, be they at anchor or under sail'.[42]

5

With fair winds Nelson made Telamon Bay on the Italian coast on 12 June, but when Hardy took the *Mutine* inshore he got no news. Two days later, however, a Tunisian warship reported that the French had been seen off Sicily ten days before, and it looked as if Bonaparte was menacing the Two Sicilies as so many had speculated. The British therefore steered south. Nelson's head was crowded with the politics of the moment, but there were natural wonders to entertain less occupied minds. Off Elba on the 13th the squadron observed a large water spout, which 'frequently varied its form, and was often of a bended shape, like an S' but at length 'burst' leaving 'the space where it fell . . . whitened with foam'.[43]

While approaching the Bay of Naples on 15 June, Nelson wrote to Lord Spencer, broaching what many would have considered a novel idea. Though none of his orders had mentioned it, might not Egypt be Bonaparte's destination? The idea had not been plucked out of the air. It originated with John Udny, the British consul at Leghorn, who had written to Nelson of the possibility as early as 20 April. Nominally a part of the Ottoman empire, but governed by the Mamelukes, Egypt was a land of discontented Arabs and Egyptians who might welcome the French as liberators, and Alexandria, the gateway to the interior, was poorly defended. The darker scenario opened by this thought was the possibility that, once in control of the region of the Red Sea, Bonaparte could find a way to India and team up with the anti-British forces of Tippoo Sahib, the Sultan of Mysore, who dominated much of the southern part of the subcontinent. Britain's eastern trade empire, a significant prop of the nation's commercial strength, would be at risk. The idea sounded visionary, but Udny pointed out that the late empress of Russia had spoken of it some years before, and that Bonaparte, if anyone, was capable of turning it into a reality.[44]

More, Nelson hoped, would be clearer at Naples, the capital of the Two Sicilies, where the debauched and boorish King Ferdinand IV and his powerful wife, the astute Maria Carolina, headed a regime as stubbornly opposed to the French as Britain. Nelson himself had been rapturously received in Naples in 1793, and in the three years that followed the twin kingdoms had proved the staunchest of Britain's allies, sending troops, ammunition and ships on demand. But much had changed since the British withdrew from the region in 1796, leaving their friends to deal with a resurgent France as best they could. A treaty had been concluded between Naples and France in October 1796, creating an uneasy peace that both parties judged a mere expediency. The Neapolitan government was forced to pay eight million francs to avoid invasion, but since France showed little respect for her treaties the next two years had brought little relief. In every direction the French closed in. They occupied the Greek Ionian Islands on the south-eastern flank of the kingdom of Naples, and in February 1798 invaded the papal state on her northern border, proclaiming it a republic and deposing the eighty-year-old pope, who was bundled into exile. Switzerland – a road between France and Italy – almost immediately followed, and in June 1798 20,000 French soldiers were struggling through the mountain passes, eastwards into northern Italy. With the enemy massing on their frontiers, and the mighty French armada afloat, their Sicilian Majesties shuddered. It seemed that their end had come.

The French Directory made no secret of its dissatisfaction with Naples, which they systematically bullied, peremptorily demanding the removal of Ferdinand's pro-British foreign minister, John Acton, and the withdrawal of the Neapolitan troops that had for some time been occupying two papal principalities, Benevento and Pontecorvo. The king gamely resisted, but eventually agreed to replace Acton with the more pliable Marzio Mastrilli, Marquis di Gallo, and to pay an additional twenty million francs to hold the disputed principalities. Joseph Garrat, the French ambassador in Naples, explained that Bonaparte's expedition had no business with the Two Sicilies; he planned to occupy Egypt and cut a canal across the Suez isthmus, but his word carried no credence in Naples. For one thing, it was this same Garrat who had announced the death sentence to the French king, Louis XVI, Maria Carolina's brother-in-law. For another, whatever was said in Naples, in Paris the Neapolitan minister was flatly told that if Naples failed to deliver the new levy for the principalities, Bonaparte might invade and revolutionise the kingdom. It amounted to saying, 'Deliver your money or I will blow your brains out!' fumed Sir William Hamilton, Britain's ambassador in Naples.[45]

While willing to stand up to France if she had to, Naples naturally looked to her safety and appealed to Austria and Britain. A secret defensive treaty with Austria, which would give Naples 60,000 imperial troops if she was attacked, was awaiting ratification when Nelson's fleet arrived on the coast. Nelson saw himself as the deliverer of Naples, but the situation of the kingdom was altogether more complicated. Even if the British fleet defeated Bonaparte's armada, it could do little to prevent an armed invasion overland through northern Italy. And given Britain's two-year absence from the Mediterranean, there was no guarantee that she would stay for long. If Naples confronted France too hastily, she could easily find herself left in the lurch. Much as their Sicilian Majesties thrilled to the news of Nelson's appearance, they had to play their few and pitiful cards with the utmost caution.

In Naples there was little doubt that France intended to overthrow the kingdom, but much disagreement about how, or when, to resist. Acton was inclined to put his faith in the Austrian army, which had some 80,000 men in Italy, and the Royal Navy. In April Hamilton had also urged strong measures, complaining of 'the miserable station' to which the country was being 'reduced' by its '*mezzitermini*, or half measures'. But Gallo counselled appeasement. The Austrian treaty had not been completed, and it was in any case a defensive treaty, that did not cover a war begun by any act of Neapolitan aggression. It was not even clear where the country stood in relation to provisioning the British fleet. The existing Franco-Neapolitan treaty of 1796 had stipulated that no more than four foreign warships could be allowed in a Neapolitan or Sicilian port at any one time. Naples could hardly victual and water a British fleet without violating that treaty. If conflict broke out over the issue, would Austria regard France or Naples as the aggressor? And, for that matter, would the British remain in the Mediterranean to protect Naples from the fallout, or withdraw as they had in 1796? The dilemma of the kingdom was that, while she needed the support of Britain, and regarded the fleet's arrival as a godsend, she dared not antagonise the French until more guarantees were in place.[46]

The dilemma was no less thorny for Britain. She had responded to the appeals for help from Naples and Austria, and to what Grenville termed the 'plain and undisguised declarations of the French government of their intention to overwhelm the dominions of His Sicilian Majesty'. But Britain had no bases in the Mediterranean, and could not maintain a presence without dockyard facilities and supplies. Grenville assumed that Austria and Naples would provide his task force with the necessary logistical support. At first he demanded the fleet receive 'free and immediate admission' to Neapolitan and Sicilian ports, 'unrestricted' supplies, three thousand seamen to meet a manpower shortage and a commitment to closing those ports to the French. These 'essential' requirements were scaled down, but the demands for provisioning and dockyard facilities could not be waived, as they underpinned the basic survival of the task force. The diplomatic impasse had not entirely been bridged when Nelson arrived, although the Neapolitans had assured Hamilton that the fleet would not be denied supplies. Gallo's letter, promising that 'the English fleet will be welcomed and treated with all the facilities and advantages *which will be suitable to circumstances*', stopped short of promising to break with France outright, but Hamilton considered it as 'fair and satisfactory' as could then be expected. Writing to Emma Hamilton on 11 June, the queen also explained that giving Britain free access to Neapolitan ports would risk 'open war' and that Naples had to 'act circumspectly', but whether by 'admitting vessels into neighbouring ports, or . . . in terms of refreshment, provisions, assistance, news, all will be provided . . . with pleasure and promptness.'[47]

On 12 June, as the admiral steered towards the fabled city of Naples, nestled between the dazzling blue of the sea below and the lush green mountains behind, he wrote a letter to Hamilton, desiring to know what assistance he could expect. He talked about supplies, intelligence and pilots, and his need of frigates or fast vessels to compensate for his lack of cruisers. The requests were understandable, but despite his experience in Sardinia the admiral had still not quite grasped the vulnerability of Mediterranean states living under the French shadow. A few days later, with Mount Vesuvius towering in the distance, Troubridge went ahead with the letter in the *Mutine*, and sped into the luxurious bay.

The French were nowhere to be seen, but Nelson spent Tuesday, 17 June offshore, just over the horizon, tacking back and forth and waiting for Troubridge to return. Ashore, Sir William Hamilton was expecting him, for letters from St Vincent had already been delivered by the *Transfer* brig. Now he wasted no time in escorting Troubridge to Acton, who continued to work behind the scenes after being driven from office by the French. Troubridge learned that two divisions of Bonaparte's fleet had united off Sicily, making a total force of 16 ships of the line, over 20 smaller warships, 280 transports and 40,000 men. It had bypassed the Two Sicilies to fall upon Malta further south. No one could quite see why. The island was ruled by the Knights of St John of Jerusalem and had a fine and formidably fortified harbour in Valletta, but it was unlikely to have been an objective in itself. Strategically located between the western and eastern basins of the Mediterranean, it was probably being seized to provide a base for an attack somewhere else. In Naples it was known that a French officer had landed on an island in Sicily, and said that Bonaparte had no hostile intentions towards the dual kingdom, but no one put much faith in the claim. With regard to Troubridge's other request, the amount of support Nelson could expect, Hamilton explained that he had been badgering Acton about that very question for weeks. Now Troubridge pocketed an order, signed by Acton in the king's name, requiring the governors of his ports to supply the British with provisions on demand, and declared himself 'satisfied'. The captain also arranged for pilots to be made available for a voyage to Sicily, and within two hours of landing was back on the *Mutine*, making his way back to the fleet.

Nelson was not so impressed. He wanted more, including new masts, ammunition and the use of Neapolitan frigates. Even the written assurance that Troubridge had brought about supplies was not as clear as it might have been. That said, Nelson was led to believe that while Naples was afraid of 'an open breach' with France, 'private orders' would be sent to the port governors to ensure that the British would be granted 'free admission'. In fact, this was not quite what was said. As Hamilton explained to St Vincent, 'every assistance . . . *that would not absolutely be a direct violation of their treaty with the French republic*' would be made available. Acton also wrote that while 'every *proper* order' would be sent to Sicily, some 'restriction' would have to be imposed. Later he explained that 'orders in Sicily for admitting any English squadrons of whatever number could not be openly given', but implied that the 'governors' would make 'demands' of the British before supplying them to provide 'an excuse . . . in case of a rupture, to show that we are . . . forced to admit them above the fixed number'. If the French threatened reprisals, or Austria blamed Naples for being unduly provocative, she would answer that she had bowed to superior force.[48]

Writing to Hamilton on 18 June, Nelson reassured the Neapolitans that he would not withdraw his squadron from the Mediterranean without 'positive orders' from his government, unless – he added innocently – it could not be provisioned. If they depended upon him, they would not be disappointed. But they had left him short of the wherewithal. 'My distress for frigates is extreme, but I cannot help myself and no one will help me.' But he begged his regards to Lady Hamilton. 'Tell her I hope to be presented to her crowned with laurel or cypress . . . God is good, and to Him do I commit myself and our cause.'[49]

With concrete news of the French whereabouts, the speed of the campaign increased, and Nelson pressed rapidly forward in the hope of reaching Malta before it fell. His ships passed the smoking cones of Stromboli and Etna, where columns of black fumes rose through the haze, and used local pilots to navigate between the famous Scylla rock, crowned with its ancient castle, and the Charybdis whirlpool, the legendary home of a mythical sea monster, to enter the narrow strait between Sicily and the mainland. Here the squadron glided along a ruggedly picturesque passage with the wild Calabrian mountains falling away to port and contrasting cultivated fields to starboard. Everywhere the Sicilians hailed the British as liberators. Vast crowds cheered from the shore, boats full of visitors pulled vigorously to the ships, and at Messina the admiral was welcomed ashore with a 'demonstration of joy'.[50]

The *Leander* 'spoke' a fishing boat and heard that the French were anchored off the island of Gozo, which they had seized as a base for their attack on Malta. Sir Horatio contemplated flushing them out with gunboats, fireships and bomb vessels, and went so far as to order Ball to convert a prize into an incendiary. But he simply lacked enough vessels, and appealed again to Naples, explaining that if Bonaparte had taken and entrenched himself in Malta a protracted blockade would have to be imposed, and that would need long-term and extensive supplies. Quoting words the Neapolitans had once sent to him, he asked if 'the Ministry of their Sicilian Majesties' would 'permit these fine countries to fall into the hands of the French?' Surely Naples would help Malta, for a Malta in enemy hands opened a 'direct road to Sicily'.[51]

At Messina the British consul, James Tough, came aboard the *Vanguard* with important news. Malta had fallen. Nelson skirted the east coast of Sicily hoping to catch the French before they left, and on 22 June reached a position south of Cape Passero and east of Malta. At this point Hardy came to Nelson with crucial intelligence he had acquired from a neutral Ragusan trader that had been in Malta the previous day. Bonaparte had installed a garrison in Valletta, begun the usual process of plunder and political reform, and then left with his fleet and transports on the 16th. The informant had nothing to say about whither they were bound, but some had said Sicily. Nelson's plan had to be revised again. There was no immediate need for bomb vessels, fireships and assault boats, but, with the French loose on the sea again, the want of cruisers remained as bedevilling as ever.

Before we follow Nelson in a dramatic new twist to his campaign, we must briefly trace his developing correspondence with Hamilton, letters that sent important ripples swirling about the Italian shores left behind. Although flattered by Sir William as 'a guardian angel' wielding a sword to 'protect . . . poor Italy', the admiral had now been disappointed twice, in Sardinia and Naples. Four letters sent by Hamilton supplied important intelligence, including the bizarre but significant titbit that Bonaparte had astronomers and mathematicians in his expedition, strange passengers for a campaign in territory as well known as Italy.

But of physical aid there had been almost none. Nelson's opinion was that Britain alone could not save these kingdoms, and that Italians must contribute more to their deliverance.[52]

Nelson was speaking of the aid he needed to wage his naval war, but Hamilton, the conduit for these notions, had ideas of his own. As we have seen, he had been complaining of the 'half measures' being adopted by Naples for her defence as early as April. Now, inspired by the appearance of the British squadron, he produced a remarkably bold plan to expel the French from central Italy and draw both Naples and Austria into an alliance with the British. If he had learned anything in the last few years, it was 'as clear as daylight' that the primary purpose of French foreign policy was to 'take all they can, in this and every other port of the world'. Sir William believed that attack was the best form of defence, especially at the present moment, when the French military build-up in Italy was as yet incomplete. Hamilton argued that as the Crown of the Two Sicilies had a claim upon the sovereignty of Malta, and the capture of that island threatened Sicily, the Neapolitans could attack the French on grounds of self-defence and invoke their new treaty with Austria. On 20 June Hamilton wrote to Grenville that it was time for Naples to act 'offensively' against the French, and six days later he put the bones of a full-blown plan to Nelson. The French ambassador should be dismissed, and Ferdinand's forces sent north to expel the Gallic army from the Roman Republic, supporting a popular rebellion already underway in that quarter, and calling upon Austria and Britain for their assistance. Britain had a squadron to hand, and, when completed, the defence treaty between Naples and Austria would oblige the latter to act. To delay was to throw away a rare chance. Ferdinand was 'giving time for the French to pour fresh troops into Italy. Ten thousand are already arrived and twenty-five thousand more are coming from Marseilles.'[53]

It was Hamilton, not Nelson, as stated or implied in innumerable histories, who authored the British war plan of 1798. Grenville found himself reading:

> How can this government [Naples] be so blind as not to see that the Kingdom of the Two Sicilies must necessary be one of their [France's] immediate objects, and when alone money can be found in Italy? And yet no active measures are taken . . . They say here that they wait to be sure of the support of the Emperor of Germany [Austria], and as I understand [it] the Emperor is waiting to be sure of that of the King of Prussia, and in the meantime the French are pouring a fresh and formidable army into Italy, and in my humble opinion, unless some unforeseen and fortunate event should prevent it, the French will pass their Christmas merrily at Naples.[54]

His fire also went directly to the Neapolitans through Acton. Though the emperor was needed 'to complete the business' Naples must stand up, the ambassador told him. 'It is impossible that this government can keep the mask on much longer, and in my humble opinion the sooner it takes it off the better. Now is the moment for a religious war. The Pope will be of no use in Spain. Bring him here. Put him into a litter and let him be marched at the head of the army with his cardinals, many of which are at Naples, and with all the pomp of the head of the church. You would see what multitudes would join!'[55]

Historians have said little of Hamilton's role in the Neapolitan war, and almost nothing of the contribution of Sir Morton Eden, Britain's Envoy Extraordinary in Vienna. Eden influenced Sir William's thinking as much as Nelson. The two diplomats were close confidants, regularly exchanging ideas, information and copies of their dispatches. In pursuit of Grenville's coalition, Eden was urging the Austrians to pre-empt French hostility by joining Britain in open warfare, opining that the republican forces in Italy should be struck before they had time to reach full strength. He was instrumental in pressing Austria to modify her treaty with Naples to allow the Neapolitans to supply British ships without forfeiting the emperor's support, and enthusiastically endorsed Hamilton's attempts to stir the Two Sicilies to action. 'Your reprobation of the Two [Sicilies's] half measures . . . is perfectly just,' he carolled. 'They must inevitably lead to destruction.'[56]

Eden had many meetings with Thugut. He took a more sympathetic view of the Austrian minister than many, but still found him a shifting shoal. Thugut looked upon a war with France as 'inevitable' and regularly assured Eden of 'the determination of the emperor to protect Naples against hostile attack'. In May and June the promise was also twice given to the Neapolitan chargé d'affaires in Vienna. Since these were verbal statements, their extent is difficult to gauge. Some of Austria's remarks implied merely that Naples would not be abandoned if attacked – a reiteration of the principle of the defence treaty – but others were more bullish. In May, for example, the emperor explained that he 'could not march an army in support of Naples till the [British] fleet arrived, but that then he would decidedly carry into execution the assurances which he had given if it became necessary, and . . . would . . . peremptorily . . . insist on the French withdrawing their troops from the Roman State, and on their ceasing to molest the court of Naples'. Whatever was said, it created in Eden, and thereby in Hamilton, a belief that Austria would intervene if Naples, her sister state, came to blows with France, however it arose. Eden and Hamilton no doubt believed they were furthering Grenville's plan for an anti-French coalition, and looked for the promised positive response to Britain's re-entry into the Mediterranean. The ball, in modern parlance, was in Austria's court. The two ambassadors genuinely believed that it was in the interests of Naples to clear the French from her northern border while she could, but they also saw a Neapolitan war as a means of drawing a prevaricating Austria into the war.[57]

Reading Hamilton's letters, Nelson knew that Hamilton was trying to provide the tangible aid the fleet needed and, by his own lights, furthering Grenville's ambition for coalition warfare. Lady Hamilton's letters were also chasing the admiral, supporting her husband in the singular impetuous, warm and personal style that could be so endearing. 'God bless you, and send you victorious,' she wrote, 'and that I may see you bring back Buonaparte with you. Pray send Captain Hardy out to us, for I shall have a fever with anxiety. The Queen desires me to say everything that's kind, and bids me say with her whole heart and soul she wishes you victory. God bless you, my dear sir. I will not say how glad I shall be to see you. Indeed, I cannot describe to you my feelings on your being so near us. Ever, ever, dear Sir, your aff[ectiona]te and gratefull Emma Hamilton.' She forwarded a letter she had 'received *this moment* from the Queen. Kiss it, and send it back by Bowen, as I am bound not to give any of her letters.' The queen's letter was undated, but probably written about the 17th. In a neat hand it wished Nelson well, and expressed regret that her circumstances did 'not allow us to open our ports and our arms entirely to our brave defenders', though 'our gratitude is none the less'. Nelson replied the same day. 'My dear Lady Hamilton, I have kissed the Queen's letter. Pray say I hope for the honor of kissing her hand when no fears will intervene.'[58]

Emma reiterated her husband's views, barely containing her contempt for Gallo, whom she regarded as a fop and appeaser:

> We have still the regicide minister here, *Garrat* [the French ambassador], the most impudent, insolent dog, making the most infamous demands every day, and I see plainly the court of Naples must declare war if they mean to save their country. *Her Majesty* sees and feels all you said in your letter to Sir William dated off di Faro Messina in its true light. So does General Acton. But alas! Their First Minister Gallo is a frivolous, ignorant, self-conceited coxcomb, that thinks of nothing but his fine embroidered coat, ring and snuff-box; and half Naples thinks him half a Frenchman; and God knows, if one may judge of what he did in making the peace for the Emperor, he must either be very ignorant, or not attached to his masters or the *Cause Commune*. The Queen and Acton cannot bear him, and consequently [he] cannot have *much* power, but still a First Minister, although he may be a minister of smoke, yet he has always something enough, at least enough, to do mischief . . . In short, I am afraid, all is lost here, and I am grieved to the heart for our dear charming Queen, who deserves a better fate.[59]

6

On 22 June Nelson was less worried about the extent of Neapolitan aid than he had been. His problems had moved on. Hardy's intelligence had told him that Bonaparte's expedition had left Malta on the 16th and was out there at sea, and his job was to find it.

Unfortunately, all the conventional wisdom about Bonaparte's intentions had been proven wrong, and credible alternatives were close to exhaustion. The French had not sailed for the Strait, nor molested the Two Sicilies. They had taken Malta, but surely that must have been a means to a greater end rather than an aim in itself. If Bonaparte had turned back towards Sicily after leaving Malta, Nelson must have heard of it. Furthermore, the winds were west-north-west, difficult for a cumbersome convoy trying to regain Sicily, but fair for sailing east. Where, then, had the French gone? Turkey was one possibility, but Nelson's mind reverted to a thought he had come up with before, but which he might have then judged fanciful – Egypt.

It was an odd idea, and easy to dismiss. Back in London, Henry Dundas, a member of the East India Board of Control as well as a government minister, had started to worry about Egypt on 9 June, but after warning Spencer he confessed to having been the victim of 'whimsical' fears. Only later, as reports of the scientists and Egyptian and Indian books with Bonaparte came in, did Dundas's concern for India deepen.[60]

Nelson now conceived a bold voyage to Alexandria, in waters relatively little known to the Royal Navy, if familiar to Levant traders. It was a serious gamble, risking the Two Sicilies, and he needed reassurance, signalling his senior captains, Saumarez, Troubridge, Darby and Ball, to come aboard. In his cabin Nelson sifted through the facts and inferences. Nelson threw in his own preference, Egypt. 'Should the armament be gone for Alexandria and get safe there, our possessions in India are probably lost,' he said. 'Do you think we had better push for that place?' He was so insecure that he asked the captains to put their opinions in writing. He got a unanimous mandate, and the fleet was signalled to bear up and sail eastwards within two hours. Not everyone was convinced. 'We are crowding sail,' Saumarez wrote, 'but . . . at present it is doubtful whether we shall fall in with them at all, as we are proceeding upon the merest conjecture only, and not on any positive information. Some days must now elapse before we can be relieved from our cruel suspense; and if, at the end of our journey, we find we are upon a wrong scent, our embarrassment will be great indeed.'[61]

By an unhappy coincidence, this new phase of the search got off to a poor start. The morning that Nelson heard from Hardy that the French had quit Malta six days before and held his council-of-war, the *Leander* went in chase of four sails seen at east-south-east. At 6.45 Thompson signalled that the ships were frigates, and by implication enemy frigates, but Nelson called him off. He was still afraid that his fleet might become separated, and also guessed that if Bonaparte had left Malta six days before, as Hardy's intelligence indicated, these frigates must have become separated from the main French fleet and to pursue them might lead him on an expensive wild goose chase. On balance, the need was to get to Alexandria as soon as possible. But in reality those frigates were the tail end of Bonaparte's fleet. It had not left Malta on the 16th, as the Ragusan had reported, but three days later, on the 19th. As Nelson was making his decision to run to Egypt, Bonaparte was actually only a few miles eastwards, steering in the same direction but a little south. The two forces had narrowly missed each other, and if Nelson had had frigates to reconnoitre ahead and on his flanks, there would probably have been a naval battle involving the two greatest commanders of the age.

There was a good breeze, and the eight hundred miles between Cape Passero and Alexandria were covered in six days. Information was as thin as ever, and the few vessels 'spoken' had no news to relieve the tension. No one had seen the French fleet, not even a ship from Alexandria bound for France, which was stripped of supplies and burned. On 28 June Nelson stood off the port, looking at a long low line of buildings with three hills behind them and Pompey's Pillar stretching skywards from the seafront. His ships had prepared for action, but by sunset all hope had faded. The only ship of the line in Alexandria was Turkish, and Hardy returned from a visit ashore bereft of tidings. The Egyptian authorities had not seen the French, nor did they believe they were in danger.[62]

This fresh reverse sunk all previous disappointments into insignificance. Hitherto, Nelson had acted conventionally, abiding by his instructions to protect Naples, and pursuing such clues as became available, but now, on an inspired hunch of his own, he had been drawn into a visionary chase, wasting six days travelling nearly a thousand miles to learn little more than he had known before. Worse, while he was being diverted to Egypt, Bonaparte was free to operate elsewhere, and there was no telling what damage might have been done. Nelson took it personally, feeling that he had betrayed those who had put their faith in him. After Alexandria, said Berry, Nelson was lost in a 'deep and anxious disappointment', groping for an answer amidst stress, mental exhaustion, suspicion and self-doubt.[63]

Sure that his reputation was at stake, he wrote St Vincent a painful vindication on 29 June. 'The only objection I can fancy to be started is, "You should not have gone such a long voyage without more certain information of the enemy's destination." My answer is ready – who was I to get it from? The governments of Naples and Sicily either knew not, or chose to keep me in ignorance. Was I to wait patiently till I heard certain accounts? If Egypt was their object, before I could hear of them they would have been in India. To do nothing, I felt disgraceful. Therefore I made use of my understanding, and by it I ought to stand or fall.' The faithful Ball thought the letter premature, as it started the idea 'that your judgement was impeachable' before it had been criticised. 'You, sir,' he added, 'are in search of a French fleet without any intelligence or guidance, but that of your own judgement', and that judgement had been reasoned. Why would Bonaparte have taken Malta, at the entrance to the eastern Mediterranean, if he did not intend venturing into those regions? How could Nelson have delayed even twelve hours seeking intelligence while he still had the chance of overtaking Bonaparte and thrashing him before he could disembark his army? And, anyway, Nelson might still have protected Egypt, for it was entirely possible that Bonaparte had changed his plans after learning that Nelson was in the Mediterranean, and been deflected towards Corfu. No, as far as Ball was concerned, far from being a fool's errand the voyage to Alexandria had been 'a wise measure'.[64]

But what was to be done? The huge French fleet had simply disappeared in the vastness of the Mediterranean. Hastily reforming his plans, Nelson left Alexandria and steered north towards the Turkish possessions. It was just possible that the French were after a piece of the crumbling Ottoman empire, and Nelson needed water as well as information. They took a few miserable prizes on their way, including a French merchantman, which was burned, but got little enlightenment. In fact, during the period 9 May to 1 August few of the thirty-eight ships stopped, 'spoke' or captured had yielded much information. Finding nothing to the north, Nelson finally turned west again on 2 July, near Cyprus, almost dreading what he might find. What might Bonaparte have done in all that time? The voyage back was a hard one against the winds, and when Nelson put into Syracuse Bay, Sicily, in the afternoon of 19 July, after a voyage of over 1900 nautical miles, he was cursing that 'the Devil's children' had 'the Devil's luck!'[65]

He was immensely relieved to find that the French had not doubled back to Sicily behind him. Mysteriously, no one had heard a reliable word about the French. They seemed to be phantoms, capable of materialising and dematerialising at their pleasure. But there was a fresh aggravation. After the ships and the castle at Syracuse had raised their flags, the governor, Don Guiseppe della Torre, sent a launch with three officers to inform the newcomers that his standing 'orders and instructions' from the king forbade him from allowing more than four warships at a time to enter the port. Put differently, he was supposed to abide by the Franco-Neapolitan treaty. The launch was met part-way by a British boat, in which a senior officer brandished the 'credential' that Troubridge had got from Acton on 17 June, promising that Nelson's ships would be fully supplied at Sicilian ports. The British officer landed and made 'the most pressing royal entreaties' to have the port thrown open, and the fleet supplied 'well beyond the usual impediments'. Sir Horatio, who had understood that private instructions would be sent to port governors, almost exploded, and angry letters flew to the Hamiltons. 'Our treatment is scandalous for a great nation to put up with,' he told Sir William, and 'the king's flag is insulted at every friendly port we look in.' To Emma he raged that 'if we are to be kicked at every port of the Sicilian dominions, the sooner we are gone the better. Good God! How sensibly I feel our treatment. I have only to pray that I may find the French and throw all my vengeance on them.'[66]

This new inconvenience could not have come at a worse time. After such a long and exhausting voyage, stores had to be replenished, and the health and energy of the squadron restored. The flagship had not watered since 6 May, and several ships had only enough for another ten days. The enduring heat had also taken its toll, despite clean air and refreshing breezes in July, and Peyton of the *Defence* was so drained that he was asking to be relieved of his command. Sir Horatio had inherited basically healthy ships, and supported them with sensible precautions. The lower deck of the *Vanguard* was washed twice a week, and such unhealthy places as the cable tiers, the cockpit and the well fumigated three times a week. Every ship fought similar battles, some better than others. The *Swiftsure* was blessed with an excellent surgeon, James Dalziel, who considered that his captain's 'attention to and support of the sick' exceeded 'anything I have ever met with'. But the *Defence* and *Audacious* had the longest sick lists in the squadron.[67]

Intermittent tertian fevers, sometimes accompanied by sore throats and inflammatory complaints, had been difficult to eradicate, despite doses of opium and 'large quantities' of Peruvian bark (cinchona), which contained quinine, a treatment for reducing temperature, deadening pain and arresting recurrent attacks. Dalziel suspected that dampness contributed to the fevers. The *Swiftsure* often sailed with her lower gun ports open to air the decks, but the practice increased the amount of water that sloshed in. More alarming were symptoms of scurvy and the persistence of sea ulcers. In some cases ulcers, like swollen gums, denoted scurvy, but by no means all ulcers were scorbutic. The skins of some sailors were so fragile that any abrasions, boils or contusions exposed to sea water could develop into unpleasant and stubborn ulcers, and legs were particularly vulnerable. The sick lists of most ships had examples. In June and July ulcers accounted for half the thirty-odd men put on the sick list of the *Vanguard*. Adequate clothing and hygiene, dry and warm environments and diet were important, but medicines such as 'yellow' and Peruvian bark were used, and citrus fruits, which contributed crucial vitamin C, were invaluable. Men with symptoms of scurvy were given five or six lemons a day in the *Swiftsure*. While the exact causes of these ailments were still being explored, access to fresh water and food were universally relevant, and Nelson needed those supplies at Syracuse.[68]

In the end, Nelson was supplied. On the 19th all the boats went in for water, and for several days sweating sailors bullied empty butts a quarter of a mile upstream to avoid the pollution in the lower reaches. On the second day the admiral went ashore to speak to the governor himself. Torre had wanted the British to split their force, sending four ships into Syracuse, four into Augusta and holding the rest offshore, awaiting their turn, but Nelson would have none of it. Nevertheless, he was not unduly provocative, and ensured that only officers and boats' crews landed, and that all were withdrawn each day when the gates of the piazza were closed after sunset. The governor had no alternative but to give way. Nelson's ships put in regardless, and Torre was unable to resist. Acton's note, written in the king's name, carried obvious authority, and the local people were so eager to sell the British provisions that 'in overflowing exhilaration [they] had rushed to the port, and would have taken the ships home one by one if possible'.

As a result fresh beef and vegetables and wood were produced daily. The *Alexander* received 2814 lbs over five days, and the *Vanguard* a total of 664 lbs of fresh beef and twenty-one live bullocks. Wine, and the lemons and onions necessary in the fight against scurvy, were also made available, with the *Zealous* alone stowing away 400 lemons and 536 lbs of onions. The only deficiency was bread, for which item Sir Horatio had to put his men on two-thirds of their allowance within four days of leaving Syracuse. A final boon was the ability to get linen laundered. It was clear that some Sicilian worthies were unsure about where they stood, and declined to fraternise with the British. Only one noble, it was said, invited officers to his house, but the common traders were delighted. 'They [the British] spend a lot of money,' reported Torre, 'even the lowest sailors, paying double for what they buy, despite the publication of a ban to prevent locals from raising the prices of food.' When all was said and done, Nelson contentedly told Hamilton that, despite the failure of the 'private orders', Syracuse had withal been a 'delightful harbour, where our present wants have been most amply supplied, and where every attention has been had to us'.[69]

Acton did not deny the problems, but was able to counter with good news. The Austro-Neapolitan defence treaty arrived from Vienna on 30 July, and through British pressure it provided for any fallout from the Royal Navy's use of Neapolitan and Sicilian ports. On 4 August Hamilton was joyously gloating that the king's 'half measures' might now come to an end, a new liberal provision of Nelson's fleet would provoke a French reaction and Austria would be bound to support her weaker sister. Indeed, it might be advisable for Ferdinand to 'take advantage of the present discontent and rising of the Roman peasantry . . . and march on to Rome'. The effect of the Austro-Neapolitan treaty and return of the British had made Hamilton dangerously bellicose.[70]

The recess in Syracuse was important. 'Our entering the harbour of Syracuse was attended with great benefit,' reported Dalziel. 'Before that many had symptoms of scurvy and even accidents where the skin was removed [and] terminated in a foul . . . ulcer', but 'the large supply of fresh beef, vegetables, &c.' soon created 'a change for the better'. The social diversions were also important. The sailors saw the local people crowding the seafront to behold them, some comely sisters of the convent of Monte Virginis, and others in gaudy liveries and elegant dresses with their carriages waiting in a queue. On shore some of Nelson's officers enjoyed the ruins of the amphitheatre, the caverns and temples, and the mummies in the monastery, and even the fabled 'fountain of Arethusa', which proved to be no more than 'a dirty pool issuing from a hollow rock' near the harbour, in which washerwomen stood waist deep beating linen upon broken boulders. Nelson's men were recharged in body and mind.[71]

7

The interlude also enabled the admiral to attend to some aspects of management. The fourth lieutenant of the *Orion*, expelled from the mess table by his fellows, was court-martialled on a charge of sodomy, 'infamous and scandalous actions unbecoming the character of an officer and a gentleman'. The captains were spared the investigation when the defendant fled before the court could be convened.[72]

It may have been at Syracuse that Nelson inducted his captains into the principles that would govern a battle with the French. Nelson's management style has been much praised for its informality, efficiency in the transmission of orders, plans and ideas, and the encouragement it gave officers to use their own initiative. The issue of communications was certainly important. This was an age when warfare was increasing in scale, and ever more a matter of large forces occupying wide fronts. Ideally, better methods of getting messages between commanders and subordinates were needed to avoid a breakdown of control. At sea the problem of communication was particularly acute. Naval warfare still relied on ships' order books, in which the admiral's pre-planned instructions were copied for everyday reference, and upon visual signals such as flags, the position of sails and the distribution of lights. St Vincent's signal book contained almost two hundred messages. But any system of visual signals remained inflexible and slow, and ultimately depended upon whether it could be seen. Powder smoke, bad weather, darkness and the position of the ships could all destroy visibility.[73]

As classically described by Berry, Nelson's preferred leadership style was of a much more personal nature:

> The admiral . . . placed the firmest reliance on the valour and conduct of every captain in his squadron. It had been his practice during the whole of the cruise, whenever the weather and circumstances would permit, to have his captains on board the *Vanguard*, where he would fully develop to them his own ideas of the different and best modes of attack, and such plans as he proposed to execute upon falling in with the enemy, whatever their position or situation might be, by day or by night. There was no possible position in which they could be found that he did not take into his calculation, and for the most advantageous attack of which, he had not digested and arranged the best possible disposition of the force which he commanded. With the masterly ideas of their admiral, therefore, on the subject of naval tactics, every one of the captains of his squadron was most thoroughly

> acquainted; and upon surveying the situation of the enemy, they could ascertain with precision what were the ideas and intentions of their commander, without the aid of any further instructions; by which means signals became almost unnecessary, much time was saved . . .[74]

Berry's account is an attractive picture of the 'band of brothers' imbibing their leader's principles in friendly but detailed face-to-face discussions. On his previous expedition to Tenerife, Nelson had certainly discussed his plans with his captains, and perhaps even suffered by it, for it was they who persuaded him to attempt a final disastrous assault. But the popular concept of the admiral educating his captains in free-flowing conversations over dinner tables stems as much from Berry as anyone else. It has been said that, more than any other great commander of his time, he had solved the problem of command and control. Bonaparte, for example, tended to keep his tactical ideas to himself, and often left officers bereft of direction at critical moments. Nelson disseminated his tactical objectives so that his officers could interpret them according to their individual circumstances, reducing an excessive reliance upon signals.[75]

Berry's description of the 1798 campaign is, nevertheless, misleading, a caricature that exaggerates the novel at the expense of the traditional. Nelson did not dispense with centralised control through order and signal books, nor was his consultation process as complete or as systematic as Berry implied, and possibly only involved the senior captains.

Nelson began issuing written orders the day Troubridge joined him off Toulon, and his demand that 'every [standing] order and instruction of the commander-in-chief [St Vincent]' was 'to be most strictly complied with by this squadron under my command' was no doubt intended to include any supplementary directions that he might make. There was little room for manoeuvre or initiative here. His first ideas governing battle entered the order book the following day, 8 June. He explained that if he came across the enemy in the open sea, he would attack their line of battle from the rear, pitting ship against ship. As there were probably more French than British, some of the ships at the head of the enemy line would not be engaged, but they would have to execute a laborious turn to support their rear and centre, and thus hopefully give Nelson time to gain an advantage. A separate, equally terse, directive stated that if the British found the enemy anchored on a lee shore, each ship should take a suitable position by anchoring by the stern and putting a spring on the cable. These were practical instructions that helped ships to hold their battle positions in a potentially dangerous wind, while allowing minor adjustments to extend their arcs of fire. Since Nelson's tactics usually embraced the principle of concentration, that is massing superior firepower against a part of an enemy line, it is worth mentioning that neither of these brief orders explicitly referred to the idea.

Nelson's most elaborate written order was dated 18 June, and confronted two omissions in the previous instructions: the enemy transports, and the possibility that the French might be caught in the open sea with their capital ships deployed irregularly, rather than in a formal line of battle. To meet such circumstances, Nelson had already reorganised his squadron into three divisions under Saumarez, Troubridge and himself. Now he declared that the transports, which contained the bulk of the French army, were to be the principal, indeed the 'sole', object of an attack. He would direct part of his force against them, while the rest entertained the escorting warships. His greatest worry was that his squadron might become dangerously fragmented during such a comprehensive attack, and emphasised that captains were to 'strictly' obey the signals of their divisional commanders, avoid being diverted and maintain 'close order' so that 'the whole squadron may act as a single ship'. The attack on the transports was to be continuous. The British ships should quickly disable any prizes by removing masts and bowsprits, and install skeleton prize crews, so that they could move on to continue the assault. Notwithstanding Berry's evidence, Nelson's order was prescriptive, rather than permissive. Such leeway as was offered was confined to the divisional commanders, who were empowered to make such signals as they thought 'proper'. And it was probably on these key officers that Nelson focused his face-to-face discussions.[76]

These orders covered several possible battle scenarios, but they were neither detailed nor unambiguous, and did not preclude some of the verbal communications that interested Berry. The flag captain's evidence cannot be thrown out, because he was privy to most of Nelson's discussions with visiting officers, but it was exaggerated. Historian Brian Lavery has used Nelson's signal book to investigate whether all the captains were briefed in this way, as Berry claimed. Saumarez, the second in command, was summoned aboard the flagship at least four times between 10 June and 20 July. Troubridge and Hardy, who were sometimes detached on missions and needed regular briefings and debriefings, received more invitations than anyone else, respectively nine and five. Ball was summoned four times, Darby and Hallowell twice, and Hood, Foley and Thompson once, but none of the remaining five captains received an invitation. Only one occasion on which Nelson met a substantial number of captains is recorded, that of 22 June, when the admiral discussed the possible destination of the French fleet with Saumarez, Troubridge, Darby, Ball and Berry. This analysis supports the conclusion that, while Nelson did confer with captains, he concentrated upon the senior officers. But this is perhaps too pessimistic a view. The signal book does not give the whole story. Saumarez's diary, for example, provides evidence that in breakfasts, dinners, councils of war and visits he was on the flagship at least six times from 29 May. On 29 June he spent most of the day on the *Vanguard*. At Syracuse there were probably opportunities for Nelson, the most socially accessible of commanders, to meet all of his captains. And as late as the eve of battle Nelson had 'several captains' on his flagship. Berry's account is best regarded as an exaggeration of a truth.[77]

Nelson left Sicily on 24 July, refreshed in all but news. He continued to believe that French ambitions lay eastwards. Unknown to him, those same thoughts were running at home, where evidence that the French had equipment to help their ships through shallows had encouraged Spencer to consider whether Bonaparte intended passing the Dardanelles to attack Russia or Turkey. At the end of July, as the smoke of an eastern venture thickened, Constantinople still seemed a potential target. Nelson decided to grope his way eastwards again, towards the Greek archipelago and Cyprus, looking for information. He could think of no alternative.

Then, suddenly, the long silence was broken. A Ragusan brig from Malta was 'spoken' and reported hearing that the French had attacked Crete three weeks before. On the 28th a good wind brought the British to the Gulf of Coron (Koroni) in the Greek archipelago, and Troubridge went in with the *Culloden*. Soon he was hurrying back with a prize French merchant brig in his train. Within hailing distance of the *Vanguard*, Troubridge called that he had interviewed the Turkish governor ashore, and that Bonaparte had been off Crete a month before. However, he was now believed to have gone to Egypt. Moreover, the prize brig had been told by the master of a German ship that Bonaparte was already at Alexandria. At last, Egypt! Nelson's instincts had been right all along.

8

Thus far, the campaign had been an astonishing story of mistakes and missed opportunities, with Nelson blundering like a blind man after an egocentric Corsican who wanted to rival Alexander the Great.

Disappointed at the dismal prospects of invading England, Bonaparte and Talleyrand had looked eastward. Egypt, internally troubled and militarily backward, was easy game but a conquest that could generate trade to compensate France for losses in the West Indies. Better still, Egypt could be used to inflict a grievous wound upon the British. She was a dominion of the ramshackle Ottoman empire. France had a reasonable relationship with Turkey, but Bonaparte cared little for that; if her empire was folding, France might as well profit from it as anyone else. On 12 April the Directory had ordered Bonaparte to control and occupy Egypt. India was not mentioned, but the drift of Gallic policy was obvious. Still, the complacency of the French was remarkable. The expedition would obviously alarm Britain and alienate the Ottoman Porte, and the use of Malta as a springboard would likewise annoy Tsar Paul I of Russia, who regarded himself as the protector of the island. Bonaparte was almost building a coalition against himself.

After leaving Malta, he had taken a more north-easterly course to Egypt than Nelson. Afraid of open water, where the British might find them, the French hugged the coast of Crete, and were actually overtaken by Nelson's ships, which struck a more direct course further south-west. At times the two fleets were less than a hundred miles apart. On two occasions Nelson was within a hair's breadth of intercepting Bonaparte at sea.

The first was on the morning of 22 June, when a Ragusan neutral had misled Nelson with her report that the French had left Malta on the 16th. As we have seen, Bonaparte was much nearer to Nelson than he imagined, and his fleet had crossed the path of the British force the night before. On the fateful 22nd the adversaries were only twenty miles distant, and Thompson of the *Leander* spotted the French frigates. If Nelson had chased them instead of pressing on with all sail to Egypt he would probably have overtaken the French armada. The second near-miss had occurred at Alexandria. A mere twenty-five hours after the British departure, Bonaparte's fleet arrived off the port! On both occasions Nelson was within a whisker of intervening in the Corsican's meteoric career. It was on those occasions, when Nelson had Bonaparte's career in his open hand, that the absence of the missing British frigates was most cruelly felt.

But history could not be undone, and Nelson now made for Egypt again under a full press of sail. The winds blessed him, blowing from the north and west, but the admiral's nerves were wire-taut at the expectation of what might be found. Probably Bonaparte would have disembarked his army. Perhaps he had dispersed his fleet, or perhaps it would be sitting in Alexandria, and compel Nelson to resort to a wearisome and expensive blockade. Nelson slept and ate little, but paced long hours, and on 31 July was close enough to send *Alexander* and *Swiftsure* ahead to make their report. He expected a battle and invited 'several captains' to his flagship that day, no doubt discussing possible tactics for what lay ahead.[78]

The first of August 1798. Early that afternoon Ball's *Alexander* approached Alexandria for the second time and signalled the squadron coming up behind. The news was crushing. Bonaparte's transports were in the harbour, sure enough, secure from naval attack, and the troops had landed and raised French colours over the castle. As for the battleships, they were missing, apart from a couple of sail of the line and six frigates.

The escape of the French army was devastating, but Nelson's priority then became their fleet, for without that Bonaparte would be marooned in Egypt, and whatever he achieved would ultimately serve little purpose. Thinking quickly, Nelson reasoned that, having discharged its duty to the transports, the French fleet might seek a safe harbour from which to await further orders. Corfu, which was in French hands, was one possible sanctuary. Saumarez spoke for many of the brotherly band that night when he wrote, 'I do not recollect ever to have felt so utterly hopeless or out of spirits as when we set down to dinner.'[79]

Before continuing his weary search, Nelson sent the *Zealous* and the *Goliath* a score of miles to the north-east to check the anchorage at Aboukir Bay, where the water was deep enough for a fleet to lay. Sixteen-year-old George Elliot, a son of Lord Minto, was signal midshipman of the *Goliath* that day, and he was on the fore royal yard as she approached the bay, swaying spectacularly above ship and sea with his telescope to his eye. Suddenly he saw something, but, rather than hail the deck and alert their rival, the nearby *Zealous*, he slid down a backstay to report to his superiors. A signal was soon being prepared for the *Vanguard*, but a rope broke or snagged. Thus it was at 2.45 in the afternoon that the flags of the *Zealous* ran up their historic message, 'Sixteen sail of the line at anchor bearing East by South.'[80]

They had found Bonaparte's fleet, thirteen ships of the line, four frigates and five brigs and bomb vessels, apart from gunboats. Throughout the British ships there were instant signs of great joy, as the long suspense of the chase gave way to the hot blood of coming battle. On the *Orion* Saumarez drank a toast to success with his officers in his cabin and then went on deck, where his appearance was greeted with three cheers from the crew. Similar scenes occurred on other ships. In the *Vanguard*, Rear Admiral Sir Horatio Nelson felt the tension draining away. Ahead lay a bloody battle against a foe superior in numbers, but for the result he had no fears, and he immediately recalled the *Swiftsure* and *Alexander*. The light was beginning to fade, but he did not even wait for them to come up. Like a tiger transfixed upon its prey, he immediately attacked.[81]

III

'VICTORY IS . . . NOT A NAME STRONG ENOUGH FOR SUCH A SCENE'

Of all the places that I have passed thro'
None pleases me so much as you.
For here I learnt that Nelson beat,
Took or destroyed the whole French fleet,
Excepting two that ran away
To tell that they had lost the day.

Inscribed on a window of the
Angel Inn, Doncaster, 1798

I

NELSON'S fleet was scattered when the *Zealous* signalled. *Alexander* and *Swiftsure* were in pursuit of an enemy vessel several miles to the south, while the *Culloden* was seven miles astern of the main body, towing a prize with a valuable cargo of wine. The rest of the ships were spread over three miles, sailing smoothly under their topsails in no particular order. Sir Horatio signalled his ships in, but would not wait for them. It was about three in the afternoon, and it would take him several hours or more to reach the enemy fleet, about nine miles away. That would leave him little enough daylight to take his squadron into a strange shoal-ridden anchorage and engage an enemy moored in a strong defensive position. But the band of brothers responded well, and only Troubridge of the *Culloden*, whom St Vincent rated the finest fighting seaman in the service, would miss the fight. Though he cast off his prize to surge impetuously forward, he ran his ship aground and experienced the most frustrating night of his life.

Nelson might have waited until first light, boxing the French in during the hours of darkness to make a safer attack, but it was not in the admiral's nature to dither with an enemy in sight. The north-north-westerly wind was ideal for entering Aboukir Bay, where François-Paul de Brueys d'Aigelliers, the French admiral, had anchored his fleet, and, having come so far, Nelson had no intention of giving the French any opportunities to slip away. He was ready for a night action, and had ordered his ships to raise four horizontal lights at the mizzen peak to distinguish them from the enemy. Besides, he was sure of the superiority of the British fighting machine and the men who led it. 'I had the happiness to command a band of brothers,' he said. 'Therefore, night was to my advantage. Each knew his duty, and I was sure each would feel for a French ship.'[1]

Nelson flew signals 53 and 54 at 3.00 and 4.25, ordering his ships to prepare for battle. Aboard each warship men answered the stirring drum tattoo with silent and speedy intent. All obstacles to the guns on the decks were stowed away or thrown overboard, bulkheads, furniture, partitions, hammocks and impedimenta of every kind. Ten live bullocks were cast kicking over the side of the *Zealous*. Decks were sluiced with water to reduce the risk of fire and gritted to prevent running feet from slipping, and fire buckets were placed in convenient places. Gun crews assembled, ports creaked open and the huge rumbling pieces, three tons of wood and iron, were loosed from their lashings and prepared for action. While heavy iron shot was lifted from racks and powder and cartridges hurried from the magazines, carpenters readied themselves to plug holes, repair damage and clear wreckage, and surgeons prepared the cock-pits below decks for their even bloodier work.

With signal 54 Nelson gave his ships an important advantage over his opponents. Seeing that the battle would be fought at anchor, he ordered each ship to secure a cable to the forward bitts or the mizzen (rear) mast and pass it out of a stern port, where it could be attached to a large sheet anchor. As a ship approached its intended firing position, the anchor would be dropped at the bow so that the vessel would shortly be brought up with a shudder at the stern. Had the ships been anchored by the bow, with the wind behind them, they would have been swung round and exposed to dangerous raking fire. More predictably, Nelson also required his ships to attach 'springs' or ropes to the anchor cable, by which the positions of the anchored ships could be adjusted and the guns given wider arcs of fire. These arrangements advantaged the British squadron over its more immobile opponent.[2]

Admiral Brueys had not wanted to anchor in Aboukir Bay. His preference had been for Corfu, but Bonaparte, in another of a catalogue of errors that marked his progress across the Mediterranean, wanted the ships close by, where they could support the army he had landed at Alexandria, and so there Nelson found them, tucked into the south-western margins of the wide bay. The enemy fleet was supported by a couple of indifferent shore batteries, which Brueys had commandeered, one a castle situated on Aboukir Point at the western terminus of the bay, and the other, consisting of half a dozen mortars and twelve-pounders, thrown up on Bequier Island about two miles off the point. Between the point and the island, and therefore between the two batteries, there was a channel, but the broken, discoloured water betrayed dangerous shoals impassable to large vessels, so the whole formed a sandy hook sweeping north-eastwards across part of the entrance to the bay and sheltering the French fleet within. The shore batteries were within range of the head of the French line, which lay less than a mile from the island, but were neither powerful nor efficient enough to provide protection.

Far more formidable to any attackers than the shore batteries were the extensive shoals in the bay itself, many invisible to the naked eye. Some of them extended the hook at the entrance of the bay a mile north-east of the island, forcing ships to stand well out to round the point. Others lined the south-western shore of the bay, leaving only a mile of clear water between them and the larboard side of the French line of battle. Brueys relied upon these last to protect his larboard, or left, flank, but had also dispersed his small ships – four frigates, a couple of brigs, three bomb vessels and a flotilla of gunboats – in the intervening shallows to give additional support. From the beginning the shoals were a problem to the British, who knew little about the bay that was not distilled from an obsolete seventeenth-century English 'pilot' or navigational guide. Foley of the *Goliath* had something better, apparently Jacques Bellen's *Petite Atlas Maritime*, published in 1764, and Nelson possessed a chart he had taken from a recent prize. Captain Hood thought Nelson's chart 'very good', although the chaplain of the *Swiftsure* dismissed it as 'an ill drawn plan'. The shoals along the south-western edge of the bay could not be ignored, however, because the wind was blowing towards them. If a ship was disabled, it could be driven aground and wrecked.[3]

As the British got closer, what had seemed to be a formidable French line betrayed weaknesses. It ran NNW to SSE, the ships with their heads forward exhibiting, from above, the shape of a slightly flexed longbow, with the extremities closer to the dangerous south-western shoals. It was apparent, however, that the French expected any attack to begin against their rear. Perhaps they supposed that the shore batteries and shoals at the head of the line would deter an attack upon their van, or they expected the British to sail wide into the centre of the bay before sweeping south west and west to engage the rear. Whichever, Brueys's flagship, the massive 120-gun *L'Orient* (larger than any ship in the Royal Navy) commanded the centre of the French line, flanked by two big eighty-gunners, *Le Franklin* ahead, bearing the flag of Rear Admiral Armand-Simon-Marie, Chevalier de Blanquet du Chayla, and *Le Tonnant* astern. The other eighty-gunner, *Le Guillaume Tell*, the flagship of Rear Admiral Pierre-Charles de Villeneuve, was the eleventh ship in the French line and commanded the rear. Nelson probably picked out the preponderance of the big French units in the centre and rear, for at about five o'clock he signalled his intention to attack the enemy van and centre. However, the wind was also an important consideration, because it blew more or less down the French line from its van. This more than facilitated a British attack on the head; it made it difficult for the French rear to work forward to assist their consorts. Nelson's signal advertised his intention to concentrate his smaller force against part of the enemy line, eradicating his numerical inferiority, and in a way least expected by his opponents.[4]

On paper the adversaries looked well matched. The French line consisted of nine seventy-fours, three eighties and one 120-gunner, a total of thirteen sail of the line, but it was supported by four frigates, three of forty guns, which possessed a considerable nuisance value. According to an analysis by the historian Michele Battesti, the seventeen ships carried a nominal total of 1182 guns firing 26,740 pounds of metal, a firepower exceeding that of the 'grand army' of half a million men that Napoleon took into Russia in 1812. Against it Nelson ranged thirteen seventy-fours and a fifty with a nominal firepower of 1012 guns and 21,134 pounds of metal. However, in addition to their standard long guns both sides used unknown numbers of carronades, heavy auxiliary armaments that were extremely destructive at short range. Battesti believed the French fleet fielded seventy-four heavy carronades firing 2664 pounds of metal, and the British 116 of varying sizes firing 2452 pounds. The picture is certainly muddier than this, but the French do seem to have possessed a marginal superiority in firepower, especially as the French pound was slightly larger than the British pound. Their ships carried more and often larger guns, including thirty-six-pounders, rather than the thirty-two-pounders that formed the principal British main deck armament.

That said, this overall superiority was of little ultimate importance. Much of the French armament would not be deployed, because Nelson focused his attack on only a part of the enemy line, and in any case it was the skills, speed and tactics of the gunners that were the keys to the fight. British gunners were apt to double- or triple-shot their cannons during firing, upsetting simple calculations based on nominal weights of metal, and they were far more experienced. As engagement after engagement showed, whether between fleets or single ships, the British consistently outgunned French and Spanish opponents. Their ships were better manned, some of their guns equipped with fast-firing flintlock mechanisms, their superior powder gave greater range and velocity and their gunners had not spent most of their time in ports under blockade. They had been at sea, sharpening their seamanship, discipline and teamwork, drilling with their guns and not infrequently firing them in anger. As French theorists were admitting, British gunners had also developed more destructive gun tactics. Whereas the continental navies tended to fire defensively at longer range, firing high at masts, sails and rigging to cripple the mobility of an enemy, and wasting much shot in the process, the British preference was for close-range fire that punched destructive holes through hulls and maximised damage, injury and death to enemy gun decks. Nelson's ships were tried battle units. The *Vanguard* recorded eleven gun drills between 3 May and 31 July, and the *Goliath* only two between 7 June and 31 July. But the cumulative effect of their experience produced awesome results. In a few hours the *Minotaur*, for example, would inflict most of the three hundred casualties suffered by the French *L'Aquilon* at a cost of only eighty-seven in return.[5]

The French navy had improved since the days Nelson had tested and found it wanting in 1795, when revolutionary chaos had torn deep inroads into its officer class and discipline. The new French Directory had retrieved some of those lost officers, and Brueys himself was a rare survivor of the upheaval. Now forty-five, he had been at sea since the age of thirteen, and his rear admirals had also considerable service. But far too many unproven or inexperienced officers manned the French service, many plucked from the merchant trade or prematurely promoted from the lower ranks, and the Gallic navy as a whole remained elementally weak in gunnery, seamanship and confidence. Its crews were badly understrength, drawing upon a merchant marine only half the size of Britain's. For the most part recruited for spasmodic service or confined to ports, they lacked opportunities to develop expertise. Army infantry, rather than professional sea gunners, often manned their artillery. The French had courage, but it was not enough.

Brueys knew this. 'Our crews are weak, both in number and quality,' he wrote. 'Our rigging in general out of repair, and . . . it requires no little courage to . . . undertake the management of a fleet furnished with such tools.' At Aboukir his fleet had eight to nine thousand men, and was about 16 per cent short of its ideal complement. According to Admiral Blanquet 'at least 200 good seamen' were needed for each capital ship. The suddenness of Nelson's attack aggravated these problems. Brueys had hundreds of men onshore, digging wells, manning batteries or standing guard against prowling Arabs, and could not regain them all in time. In desperation, he had his frigates send several hundred of their men to his capital ships, and rushed an appeal for reinforcements to Alexandria. It brought a few thousand men tumbling towards Aboukir, but only a few were in time to make a contribution.[6]

Brueys had added to his disadvantages with tactical errors. Some in the fleet confidently thought themselves 'moored in such a manner as to bid defiance to a force more than double our own', but others had reservations, including Villeneuve, who complained that Brueys awaited 'the enemy at anchor against all prescribed laws of tactics'. Despite the twenty-five days the French had had to prepare a credible defence, Brueys laboured under the delusion that his larboard flank could not be turned. Yet there were two ways to do so. Despite the shoals and cruisers to larboard of the French line, there was still sea room for an enemy to squeeze into that space by attacking from either the head or the rear. Moreover, the French line of battle ships were too widely spaced, with some 175 yards between them, sufficient to allow the British with a good wind to attack from starboard and cut their way through to larboard. Brueys belatedly saw the danger and ordered his ships to run a cable to the next astern and put a spring on the anchor hawse to increase manoeuvrability, but not all of the captains complied.[7]

Nelson issued no further instructions about the mode of attack, except for one calling for close action shortly after firing began. At about 5.30 he signalled the squadron to form line of battle ahead and astern of the flagship as convenient. In light breezes and moderately clear weather, the fleet gradually wore to clear the shoals off Bequier Island and loop around them to the south-west to make their attack on the head of the French line. A French brig approached, trying to lure the British into the shallows, but the attack was a disciplined one and refused to be diverted.[8]

The problems of bearing up around the island were considerable, and an overeager captain might easily turn too tightly and run upon the shoal. Nelson found the water shelving below his flagship, and hailed Hood of the *Zealous*, who was to starboard, asking whether they were far enough eastward to bear up around the shoal. Hood had no chart, but his lead line was telling him that he was in eleven fathoms, and he offered to go ahead of the *Vanguard*, sounding a safe way forward. The admiral raised his hat in acknowledgement, and the *Zealous* groped onward with lead and line at work. But it was not Hood who was to have the honour of leading the British ships into action. Nelson saw *Orion*, *Audacious* and *Theseus* pass him, while the *Goliath*, abreast of the *Zealous*, used her position on the inside of the turn to forge ahead under stay and studding sails.[9]

Boldly, Nelson's ships snaked around the shoals, their sails gilded red by a huge setting sun that seemed in strange accord with the scarlet cross emblazoned bravely on the English colours. The greatest naval battle of the eighteenth century was about to begin.

2

From the start it looked like a stiff fight. The French did not fire prematurely, in the hope of dismasting the enemy ships at long range, as they so often did. Instead, they 'received us with great firmness and deliberation,' said Berry, waiting silently at their guns as the British ships rounded the shoal and advanced, exposing their vulnerable bows in the process. Only when the leading British ships got within 'half gunshot' range did the French raise their colours and loose the first thundering salvoes. Neither these nor the shore batteries, which were flinging futile discharges across the water, muted the vigour of the British attack.[10]

Thomas Foley, captain of the lead ship, the *Goliath*, quickly saw the tactical blunder committed by the French. Instead of tucking their line snugly against the shoals along the south-western shore of the bay to larboard, they were anchored too far out. As Foley approached the head of the enemy line he saw that there was room to cross the bows of the leading French ship, *Le Guerrier*, and turn to larboard to pass along the inside of the enemy line, between it and the shoals to leeward. The French could then be engaged from both sides, trapped in a crossfire; indeed, it was possible that they had not even troubled to prepare their larboard batteries. Foley was the only British captain to possess a reasonably up-to-date chart of the bay, and his suspicion that there was sufficient water on the inside of the French line for him to use might conceivably have come from it, because it showed twenty-four or more feet about the head of the enemy line. But, equally, Foley may simply have relied upon his experience of nearly thirty years at sea. The French ships were anchored by their bows, so that they would swing to point into the wind from whichever direction it blew. An easterly would have taken their sterns further inshore towards the shallows. Foley probably realised that, anchored as they were, the French must have had sufficient deep water along both sides to swing on their cables, especially as the huge *L'Orient* and the three eighty-gunners displaced more water than any British opponent. Without visible hesitation, at about 6.15 in the evening Foley put up *Goliath*'s helm to take her across *Le Guerrier*'s bows. Behind *Goliath* Hood of the *Zealous* was surprised at Foley's manoeuvre, but followed in the more experienced captain's wake.[11]

Nelson's ships were frightening fighting machines. Their main lower-deck guns were thirty-two pounders, fourteen on each side, measuring ten feet in length and weighing some three tons apiece. They detonated with an almost deafening roar and clouds of black smoke, recoiling viciously upon their breech ropes like berserk beasts, and hurled one, two or even three iron balls, almost six and a quarter inches in diameter, with terrific force. Accurate to about two hundred yards, these smooth-bored guns could wreak chilling destruction, smashing star-shaped holes through four foot of solid oak wall, dismounting guns and scattering lethal splinters in all directions. Seven men served each gun, bandanas bound around their heads to suppress the relentless roar, and stripped to their trousers in cramped, crowded, dark decks. In an action like this those decks became incarnations of Hell, filled with stifling, choking air starved of oxygen by the explosions and filled with powder smoke, and reeking with the sweat of desperate human energy and the blood of broken bodies. A gun captain adjusted elevation and aim, while others sponged burning refuse out of the bore, rammed cartridges, shot and wads home, pierced the cartridges through the breech touch-hole and hauled the heavy pieces into position, ready for ignition. Standing back from the teams, uniformed midshipmen or lieutenants supervised sections of the gun decks, coordinating firing and handling emergencies, while men and boys scuttled back and forth with ammunition and cartridges. Nelson's men could fire far faster than their relatively unpractised opponents, creating a great superiority of firepower.

A few women shared that miserable torment in the British fleet. 'The women behaved as well as the men,' one sailor recalled, 'and got a present for their bravery from the Grand Signier [of Turkey].' In the *Goliath* Ann Taylor, Elizabeth Moore, Sarah Bates and Mary French, were subsequently 'victualled at two thirds allowance in consideration of their assistance in dressing and attending on the wounded, being widows of men slain in the fight'. All four would be discharged on 30 November, 'their assistance not being required'. The gunner's wife carried ammunition and plied her husband and his assistant with needed refreshments. Two other women in *Goliath* fared less well. Samuel Grant, the purser, recorded that at 7.36 'Mrs Holcom's skull [was] fractured in ye larboard wing by a shot 'tween wind and water'. She survived till 4 August when she 'tumbled to pieces tonight'. Later a 'Mrs Brierly' also died. John Nicol, a second gunner in the *Goliath*, subsequently recalled that a Scottish woman had given birth to a son during the battle, but he probably confused his memories of two births which actually occurred on 17 July and 16 September. In another ship, the *Majestic*, Christian White, according to her own testimony, was also widowed that day, but during the fighting 'attended the surgeon in dressing the wounded men, and likewise atten[d]ed the sick and woun[d]ed durring theare passage to Gibberalter, witch was 11 weeks on bord . . .' Nor were the women, boys and inexperienced the only ones who may have felt they had to prove themselves that day, as one by one the British ships entered the smoke and fury of battle. In Nelson's forces were the ex-members of a detachment of Austrian soldiers, captured by Bonaparte's armies in 1796, and afterwards rescued by the admiral, who had invited them to join the fleet as volunteers. Some were men who bore grudges, and now stood grimly waiting to take their revenge.[12]

The French van, consisting of five seventy-fours, *Le Guerrier*, *Conquérant*, *Spartiate*, *Aquilon* and *Peuple Souverain*, was the weakest part of the defence. As Foley may have anticipated, Captain Jean-François Trullet of *Le Guerrier* had only readied his starboard guns. 'Her [inside] lower deck guns were not run out,' recalled an officer in *Goliath*, and the upper deck ports were obstructed by lumber of all kinds. Once engaged, Trullet frantically redistributed his crew to work both broadsides. At fifty-two years, the second French ship in the line, *Conquérant*, was the oldest and flimsiest of the fleet, as well as the most undermanned and underarmed. Uniquely, she mounted only twelve- and eighteen-pounders, and carried less than four hundred men.[13]

Goliath reserved her fire as she led the British line in a serpentine course that curled around the head of the French line. Taking in most of her sails, she slowly crossed the inviting bow of *Le Guerrier* and delivered a devastating raking broadside at point-blank range. Passing to the inside of the French line, Foley intended anchoring opposite *Le Guerrier*, but failed to control his anchor cable as it raced from the stern gunroom, and ran as far as the second enemy ship, *Le Conquérant*. The British ship dealt out far more punishment than she received, but once the French got over their initial surprise they began a desperate fightback. Within ten minutes of firing, the surgeon of the *Goliath* was receiving the first casualties, and another forty minutes saw them coming 'down fast'. Behind Foley, Hood's *Zealous* shortened sail as she approached and rounded the head of the enemy line, when she likewise raked the miserable *Le Guerrier* within range of a pistol shot. In a mere seven minutes the Frenchman's foremast was down, the first concrete sign of success that raised cheers from the British ships coming behind. Nelson had signalled his ships to engage more closely, and Hood anchored his ship opposite *Le Guerrier*, taking the place Foley had wanted. He left enough room for following consorts to squeeze between the *Zealous* and her opponent, sparing them the trials of the shallower waters beyond, but the third of Nelson's band, Saumarez of the *Orion*, swung wide after raking *Le Guerrier*, and passed around the offside of the *Zealous* before closing upon the quarter of the fifth French ship, *Le Peuple Souverain*, and the big bow of *Le Franklin* astern. As *Orion* completed her manoeuvre, she fired a devastating double-shotted broadside into *La Serieuse*, a thirty-six-gun frigate attempting to intervene. The frigate had already been hit, but was now hulled below the waterline and driven into the shallows, where she sank on to the sandy bed with wavelets lapping her upper works and her head beneath the surface. Her masts soon fell, and, although most of the crew struggled ashore, the captain and thirty unhappy survivors had to surrender to a boat's crew from Miller's *Theseus*. The other small warships made little attempt to stay the tide of battle. The forty-gun *Artémise* frigate and *Hercule* bomb ran aground while trying to save themselves, and the other bombs and brigs huddled under the Aboukir seeking the sanctuary of the batteries.[14]

Gould's *Audacious* and Miller's *Theseus* also rounded the French line. The first scourged *Le Guerrier* and then joined *Goliath* in savaging the hapless *Conquérant*, which was already outmatched. Miller did better. As he approached the French line from starboard, he noticed that the enemy were firing high, as usual, and ran in closer to get under their arch of fire. He had ordered the guns of the *Theseus* to be loaded with two or three round shot each, but waited until he was crossing the 'T' and lining up the remaining masts of *Le Guerrier* before letting fly. The broadside was fired only feet away from the French jib boom, and hurled missiles the entire length of the unfortunate Frenchman, bringing down her main- and mizzen masts and leaving her a ruined hulk. Yet her men fought for three more hours, their upper desks wasted and cleared by canister and musketry from the *Zealous*, their hull pummelled so mercilessly that several gun ports were smashed into one and their fire reduced to the occasional report of a single gun. Even Hood was moved to pity, and several times called upon *Le Guerrier* to surrender. She did so after dark, and, as she had no masts, she had to signify her submission by raising and hauling down lights.

Theseus was the last British ship to flank the French line by its head, and she threaded between the *Zealous* and *Guerrier* and around the *Goliath* to anchor adjacent to the third enemy ship, *Le Spartiate*. Five of Nelson's seventy-fours had thus turned the French line to punish it with exemplary gunnery. *Le Guerrier* was finished, and the weak *Conquérant* made a 'very inefficient resistance'. Her main- and mizzen quickly went down, her men were driven from her upper gun deck, and over two hundred, half her complement, were scythed down in a 'dreadful' slaughter. For a while she struggled on, 'every now and then' firing 'a gun or two' in defence of her flag, but it was useless.[15]

The British had flattened the head of the French line, but Nelson's men were not unscathed. On the *Goliath* a boy was found dead, sitting upright on a cartridge chest with his eyes open and not a mark on him. Another lad, perhaps a playmate, performed a remarkable feat of heroism. He raised his arm to apply a slow match to his gun only to see it almost ripped off by enemy fire. Calmly, he stooped to retrieve the fallen match with his remaining hand and fired his gun before going down to the surgeon.[16]

The flanking movement led by Foley came to an end with the sixth British ship, Nelson's own *Vanguard*, which wore to descend the outside of the French line until she reached and engaged the third enemy ship, *Le Spartiate*. Once the flagship had anchored, men scrambled from aloft or their positions at the braces to strengthen the starboard gun crews, and for two hours poured a murderous fire into the Frenchman at a range of less than half-pistol shot. It was needed, because *Le Spartiate* was a new and strong vessel, and captained by Maurice-Julian Emeriau, a surprisingly pugnacious adversary.[17]

In performing his manoeuvre, Nelson exploited Foley's doubling of the French line and began the desired concentration. *Le Spartiate* was the first of the French ships to be caught in a crossfire, since she was already engaging Miller's *Theseus* to leeward when Nelson attacked from windward. The effect was immediate, because she was undermanned, and had barely enough crew to work both larboard and starboard batteries. But, although a gallant captain, Miller seems not to have understood Nelson's desire to concentrate force, because as soon as Nelson joined the fray he abandoned *Le Spartiate*, 'giving up my proper bird to the admiral', and moved down the enemy line to confront *L'Aquilon*. The upshot was that Captain Emeriau was able to redeploy what gunners he had, re-man his full starboard broadside, and intensify his fire upon the British flagship. The issue was not in doubt, but Nelson's battle with *Le Spartiate* became considerably grimmer. According to one account the *Vanguard* lost fifty to sixty men in ten minutes.[18]

Receiving the full fire of *Le Spartiate* and some forward raking fire from the French number four, *L'Aquilon*, the *Vanguard* suffered serious damage. Wreckage fell from above, obstructing the upper deck and trapping men and guns, and wooden splinters, round shot, fragments of chain and iron and musket balls flew devilishly about the decks, cutting men down. The pressure only eased when Captain Louis followed Nelson's example and anchored the *Minotaur* to the windward of the enemy line, firing upon *Le Spartiate* from her aftermost guns and more fully upon *L'Aquilon*. Even so, *Le Spartiate* made a plucky defence. Between them Miller, Nelson, Louis and Gould knocked seventy-six holes about or below her waterline, flooding her hold with nine feet of water, and forcing many of the men to abandon the guns to throw themselves upon the ship's pumps. Her main- and mizzen masts went over the side, and she suffered 214 casualties before surrendering at about nine o'clock.

Le Spartiate was a bloody conquest. The British flagship alone lost 105 killed and wounded subduing her, and one of the casualties was Admiral Nelson.

3

He had always been where action was thickest, and rarely emerged unscathed. In Corsica he had been lucky when splinters had only bruised his back, but less fortunate a few months later when the sight of his right eye was lost besieging Calvi. In the battle off Cape St Vincent in 1797 a blow to the stomach inflicted lifelong health problems, and five months afterwards his right arm was lost at Tenerife. Now a piece of iron fired by *Le Spartiate* struck Nelson on the right side of the forehead, laying bare the cranium for more than an inch and slicing the skin for thrice that length. Berry was beside him on the quarterdeck when he fell. 'I am killed,' he said, 'Remember me to my wife.' Possibly blinded by the frightening rush of blood running into his remaining eye, he was carried below to the surgeon's cockpit.[19]

In the cockpit below decks, Michael Jefferson the surgeon, and his assistant, twenty-two- or twenty-three-year-old Samuel Cotton, were working under swinging lanterns to alleviate pain and save life. Twenty-seven casualties had come down before Nelson arrived, the first of them a twenty-one-year-old landsman or inexperienced sailor, Richard Craden of Buckinghamshire, who had volunteered for service. He had a compound fracture of the left leg, but was luckier than Philip Murphy, a fellow landsman from Cork. Murphy, only a year older than Craden, was brought down the ladders with his skull laid bare and his right eye gone. Twenty-five-year-old John Tripp arrived with a wound in the abdomen and his right forearm almost torn away. All three were destined for the hospital at Gibraltar and 'smart' or injury pensions. A number of the ship's officers had also preceded Nelson to the cockpit, including two 'young gentlemen', John Weatherstone, a master's mate nursing an arm injury, and twenty-year-old Midshipman George Antram, whose damaged thigh would lay him up for one and a half months. The arm of Michael Austin, the ship's boatswain, had been mangled by a musket ball and had to be amputated. He would survive the hideous operation and die at Gillingham in Kent in 1844 at the respectable age of seventy-two.[20]

Wiping away the blood, Jefferson found that Nelson had a jagged, irregular cut running a full three inches, beginning at the left-hand side of his right eyebrow and coursing upwards and to the right. As best he could in the appalling conditions of the cockpit, the surgeon brought the edges of the wound together and applied strips of 'Emp. Adhesive' to hold them in place. No stitches were used, but the patient was given opium. The admiral was judged to be out of danger pretty quickly, though he was sick during the night, and the gruelling headaches he reported for many weeks suggest post-concussive trauma. Three days after the injury Jefferson removed the dressing and applied more sticking plaster with lint, and on 1 September he was able to pronounce the wound 'perfectly healed', though 'the integuments' were 'much enlarged' so he applied a wet compress and 'embrocation' nightly. The treatment lasted a month and proved 'of great service', but it left an ugly scar that Nelson took to hiding by brushing his hair forward.[21]

For some time Nelson was uncertain about his fate. Among several stories told about those first black moments in the cockpit, one appears to have been true in its broader elements. After nine in the evening, with the battle still raging, Nelson asked Lieutenant Capel to take a boat to the *Minotaur* to fetch Captain Louis to the flagship. Perhaps still unsure whether he would survive, the admiral could not rest until he had thanked Louis for relieving the *Vanguard* by attacking *L'Aquilon*. According to Lieutenant Hill of the *Minotaur*, who probably had it from Louis, the meeting was 'affecting in the extreme'. As Louis leaned over, the wounded admiral reportedly said, 'Farewell, dear Louis, I shall never forget the obligation I am under to you for your brave and generous conduct, and now, whatever may become of me, my mind is at peace.' Both the drama and the desire to reward were typical of Nelson.[22]

Above, the sun had gone and the battle continued in a smoke-thickened darkness illuminated only by the moon, the distinguishing lights hoisted to the mizzens of the British ships and the sudden and repeated stabs of vivid horizontal red, orange and yellow flame from the guns. By now, however, the attack on the van was complete. All five leading French seventy-fours were in the process of defeat, and by about 8.30 *Le Peuple Souverain* and *L'Aquilon* had struck, the latter with her main- and mizzen masts cut, half her guns dismounted and three hundred men and boys down, one of them her captain, who expired almost immediately after both of his legs were blown off. About the same time Lieutenant Galwey of the *Vanguard* led a party of marines to *Le Spartiate* and returned with the enemy captain's sword. Two swords were surrendered to the *Vanguard*, one that Nelson eventually sent to Prince Leopold of Naples, and another which Berry took down to the cockpit to cheer his injured admiral, and which he consequently received as a gift.[23]

With the van defeated the French centre became the crux of the battle. There sat the biggest fighting units in the bay, two eighty-gun two-deckers, *Le Franklin*, under Rear Admiral Blanquet and Captain Maurice Gillet, and *Le Tonnant*, sandwiching between them one of the largest warships afloat, the mighty three-decked, 120-gun *L'Orient*, the French flagship, with her formidable pieces double-shotted for action. One of the most spectacular scenes in modern warfare was about to be enacted.

4

The first British ships venturing against the heavily defended French centre had been severely handled.

Darby's *Bellerophon* had come upon the starboard side of *L'Orient*. Perhaps he had mistaken her in the smoke and darkness for *Le Franklin*, or perhaps like Foley he had had difficulties with his anchor. Whatever, *Bellerophon* found herself broadside to broadside with a French giant almost twice her strength, and fought her for half an hour single-handed, while also suffering a galling fire from the forward starboard batteries of *Le Franklin* for good measure. Though the British guns smashed into the huge warship, inflicting serious damage, the sheer weight of the French flagship's broadside was overpowering. Two of *Bellerophon*'s masts fell, most of her sails were cut to ribbons and sixteen of her guns disabled. She suffered nearly two hundred casualties, more than any other British ship, and they included Captain Darby, severely wounded in the head, and several lieutenants killed. Eventually, with his third mast about to fall, Darby had his cable cut, exactly when is unclear, and used a spritsail to limp painfully eastwards, past the French rear and out of the fight. Illuminated by the fires that shortly broke out in *L'Orient*, the wounded *Bellerophon* was fired upon by *Le Généreux*, near the end of the French line, but ended up several miles away totally dismasted.

The *Majestic* also took a savage beating. She ran upon *Le Tonnant*, one of the eighties, enmeshing her jib boom in the Frenchman's fore shrouds, and was hammered by that ship and the seventy-four-gun *L'Heureuse*, astern, while unable to bring her main guns to bear effectively. Captain George Westcott was fatally wounded early in the fight, hit in the neck by a musket ball, but the first lieutenant, Robert Cuthbert, took command with such ability that Nelson made him an acting commander after the battle. Disentangling the *Majestic*, Cuthbert judiciously tried to place her athwart the stern of *L'Heureuse* and the bow of the next Frenchman, *Le Mercure*, to rake them both, but ran upon a cable thrown between the two French ships and was unable to complete his manoeuvre. *Majestic* received another mauling, losing her main- and mizzen masts and sustaining almost as many casualties as the *Bellerophon*, but she gave a sound account of herself. When the commandant of *L'Heureuse* ordered his men to board the British ship in the teeth of her fire the men flatly refused the order.

Peyton's *Defence* joined the battle by pounding *Le Peuple Souverain*, an old ship that had already been heavily punished on her larboard side by the *Orion*. After three hours the dismasted Frenchman was silenced at about ten o'clock. Then both British ships turned their full attention to Blanquet's *Le Franklin*, a ship that had already come under their secondary fire.

Later Admiral Blanquet excused the French defeat by claiming inferiority of numbers, but during this early stage of the battle his contention was not justified. Although Nelson's ships came into action quickly, with no more than forty minutes elapsing between the beginning of the fight and the anchoring of the *Majestic*, the concentration the British had wanted did not fully take place. Only *Le Guerrier*, *Conquérant*, *Aquilon* and *Peuple Souverain* had truly engaged more than one antagonist simultaneously. On the other hand some of Nelson's ships had also fought at a disadvantage. The *Vanguard*, *Bellerophon* and *Majestic* were all at one time or another outgunned. Indeed, in the first two hours of the battle ten British ships had principally engaged nine French, some of the latter considerably larger. Their success had not primarily been due to numbers, but to fighting efficiency. It was only after eight o'clock, when the last British ships came up, that the complexion of the battle changed and Nelson began to concentrate superior force.

Ball's *Alexander*, Hallowell's *Swiftsure* and Thompson's fifty-gun *Leander* clinched the battle in the centre and hastened the end. Notable for its absence was the *Culloden*, under the fiery Troubridge. He had been so eager to put his stamp on the battle that he had got ahead of Ball and Hallowell, only to run aground on the edge of the shoal east of Bequier Island. Probably, the captain had been trying to clip minutes off his time by bearing up too quickly around the shoal, an action almost reckless as the light faded over such unfamiliar waters. It was a tragedy, for it deprived Nelson of a seventy-four, and of all seventy-fours the *Culloden*, captained by the most tigerish officer in the fleet. It was even worse for Troubridge. He, more than any, had been Nelson's confidant; he above all others but Nelson, had a reputation to defend; and he, more than most, hungered for those rare opportunities to participate in full scale naval actions. But now, as the band of brothers took their ships into mortal danger, when they needed him the most he could only act the distant spectator. His feelings are almost unimaginable. Troubridge jettisoned provisions, shot and empty wine pipes to lighten his ship, but, even assisted by the *Mutine* and *Leander*, his boats could not haul the *Culloden* free. Their efforts only increased the damage, as the stricken ship's rudder came away, her timbers buckled and water poured into the hold at a rate of three feet an hour. What could be done, Troubridge did. He flew signal number 43 to advertise his plight and warn the *Alexander* and *Swiftsure*, which he saw 'hauling considerably within me', away from the shoal, and he ordered the *Leander* to leave him and help Nelson in the fight.[24]

It was thus left to the *Alexander*, *Swiftsure* and *Leander* to penetrate the smoky, flame-seared blackness that shrouded the battle and break the enemy centre. But as Gamble of the *Swiftsure* remarked, 'Two fresh ships coming in made a wonderful difference.' It was fortunate that their arrival was not offset by any corresponding action on the part of the French rear, which remained supine. Two enemy sail of the line and two forty-gun frigates were barely to enter the battle at all. Their failure allowed Nelson's numbers to accumulate, and wipe out the narrow advantage in guns that the French fleet as a whole had possessed.[25]

Ball's attack went straight to the heart of the resistance. The *Alexander* cut the French line behind the huge *L'Orient*, unleashing ferocious broadsides into the stern of the flagship to the right and the bow of the eighty-gun *Tonnant* to the left as she did so. Then she positioned herself on the vulnerable larboard quarter of *L'Orient* and the bow of *Le Tonnant*, avoiding their full broadsides while lashing them with her own devastating volleys. The *Swiftsure*, under Hallowell, was hit on the waterline early on, but as her men strove to pump four feet of water from the hold, she stationed herself on the outside of the French line, training her after guns on *Le Franklin* and her forward ones upon *L'Orient*, neither target more than half a cable's length away. The *Leander*, though a little 'fifty', had to make up for the loss of the *Culloden*, and squeezed between the stern of the defeated *Le Peuple Souverain*, now drifting helplessly out of her line, and the bow of *Le Franklin* to fire into the latter. Some of her shot passed over or through *Le Franklin* to multiply the misery of *L'Orient*. These three new arrivals gained the upper hand in the centre, where *Le Franklin* of eighty guns was being engaged by *Leander*, *Defence*, *Orion* and *Swiftsure*; the flagship *L'Orient*, after fighting off the *Bellerophon*, was exchanging blows with *Alexander* and *Swiftsure*; and *Le Tonnant*, another eighty, having survived an onslaught from the *Majestic*, was now scourged by both the *Swiftsure* and the *Alexander*.[26]

Though her tricolour flew defiantly from the mainmast, *L'Orient*'s fate was inevitable, without the men to man any but her heavier guns and beset by new and implacable assailants. 'We tried to spin our starboard cable and turn on the stern,' wrote a French officer, 'but as we were too bound by our mooring this operation became impossible.' Her opponents had no such inhibitors. 'In regard to the *Swiftsure*, it was impossible for men to behave more cool or collected,' wrote one on board. 'Had it been only general exercise there could not have been less confusion; every man seemed to be perfectly acquainted with the duty allotted to him, and this was one good attending general exercises, which we had once or twice a week before the action. Captain Hallowell had given positive directions that not a gun should be fired until the order was received from him. This was strictly attended to . . .' As his ship hurled wrathful broadsides into the enemy flagship, Hallowell could not have been cooler traversing a ballroom floor.[27]

Aboard the tortured flagship, its formidable fire wilting at last under the assault, Brueys was wounded in the head and arm, and, soon after, as he came down from the French poop, was 'almost cut . . . in two' by a shot in the belly. He lived for another fifteen minutes or so, but insisted on keeping the deck to the end. Commodore Aristide Aubert Dupetit-Thouars of *Le Tonnant* was similarly served, losing both arms and a leg, but he doggedly refused to surrender his ship, attempting to encourage his men as blood and life spilled from his desecrated body.[28]

The end for *L'Orient* began in one of the after cabins, perhaps the result of a raking broadside from the *Alexander*. About nine o'clock a fire was observed near the mizzen chains, and soon it had spread to the shrouds and poop. The origin of the flames has never been satisfactorily explained. Ball later told Coleridge, his secretary and biographer, that one of his lieutenants tossed an incendiary into the enemy flagship. It had been prepared for use as a last resort, and was thrown without the sanction of the captain. Others claimed that containers of oil or paint left on the deck of *L'Orient* after repainting fed the blaze. However that may be, there was chaos. The fire pump was shattered, battleaxes needed to clear wreckage to get at the flames were buried under debris and fire buckets had been scattered far and wide. Seeing the conflagration, Hallowell also turned some of his guns upon it to drive away the fire fighters. The blaze raced hungrily up the rigging and along the yards, and quickly enveloped the ship from head to stern in a terrifying apocalypse, the lurid red and yellow bursting through the billowing black smoke to illuminate the night sky. So intense was the heat that pitch began to run from the seams in the sides of the nearby *Swiftsure*. After a forlorn attempt to drown the powder, all order on the French flagship broke down and it was every man for himself.[29]

Berry reported the fire to Nelson, who insisted upon being assisted to the quarterdeck to see it. It was obvious to him that the great ship was finished, and some of her men were jumping overboard even as others stuck to their guns below. When the fire devoured its way to the middle-deck, there was a wild scramble to evacuate the ship. 'Such a scene of misery I never beheld before,' wrote a seaman of the *Minotaur*, 'to see the men alongside of her like a swarm of bees a few minutes before she [*L'Orient*] blew up.' Among the lucky ones was Rear Admiral Honoré-Joseph-Antoine, Comte Ganteaume, who got in a boat which took him to one of the smaller French vessels and ultimately to safety in Alexandria. Commodore Luce-Luzio-Quilicio Casabianca, then about thirty-six, and his ten-year-old son, Giocante, were not so fortunate. The boy had given 'proofs of bravery and intelligence far above his age', but neither his father nor anyone else could protect him from destruction. Legend asserts that the youngster lost his leg, and his father refused to leave him, but Blanquet's report tells us only that the Casabiancas jumped into the black litter-strewn sea together, sought each other out in the water and clung to the remains of a mast. Then, when the flagship violently exploded, both were killed in a tragedy that inspired one of the most moving, if sentimental, poems in the English language, Felicia Hemans's 'The Boy Stood on the Burning Deck'. On seeing the horrifying scenes aboard the enemy ship, hostility was suspended in many

British hearts. Nelson ordered Galwey to prepare *Vanguard*'s remaining boat to pick up survivors, an 'example' which the admiring Berry claimed was 'immediately followed' by his captains, as if they were not capable of being moved by the same emotions of common humanity.[30]

As *L'Orient* turned into a ball of fire, the ships around her looked to their own safety. Everyone knew that there was going to be an explosion when the flames reached the magazine, and friend and foe alike began cutting cables to escape the blast. They included *Alexander*, *Majestic*, *Le Tonnant*, *L'Heureuse* and *Le Mercure*; even the rearmost ships in the French line, *Le Guillaume Tell*, *Le Généreux* and *Le Timoléon*, let out more cable so that current and wind would bear them further eastward. Others were not so well placed. The durable *Franklin*, ahead of the flagship, was boxed in by the *Leander*, *Defence* and *Orion*, and could put no more water between herself and the blazing *L'Orient*. Though the ship had been firing well, both her captain and Admiral Blanquet had been seriously wounded and carried below, and she had already been damaged by fire. About 9.45 a chest of musket cartridges had blown up and kindled several fires on the poop and quarterdeck, but they had all been extinguished. Captain Hallowell of the British *Swiftsure* was not dissimilarly circumstanced. His vessel, like *Le Franklin*, was upwind of the blazing flagship, and therefore less vulnerable to flying wreckage than the ships to the east, but with astonishing presence of mind Hallowell decided that his very proximity to *L'Orient* would save him and send the imminent explosion over his head. He continued to pummel *L'Orient* and *Le Tonnant* until the last moment, hauling on the spring on his cable to sweep his fire this way and that. But preparations had to be made, and a guard was placed beside the principal cable to prevent any panic-stricken sailors or officers from cutting it. As he judged the time of the dying enemy flagship was fast approaching, Hallowell shut his gun ports, covered magazines and hatchways, tightly furled and wetted sails and placed buckets of water and wet swabs in convenient spots. His final orders were for the men to take cover, and Gamble, just coming up from the lower deck, hid under the booms. Similar scenes were being enacted on almost every ship able to respond.[31]

L'Orient went up after ten in what was perhaps the most shattering moment of eighteenth-century warfare. The ship died in a man-made volcano that 'made the whole element shake'. In one searing red blast one of the largest ships afloat simply disappeared as an entity, its stern and bows, where the powder had been kept, blown off, and the hundreds of tons of wood and iron, miles of rope and two acres of canvas propelled upwards and outwards into the night in thousands of fragments or sent to the bottom. The vivid flare, eventually occluded by sinister black smoke pierced by flashes of luminescence, and the thundering roar travelled over miles of sea and sand, creating alarm in Alexandria and among Bonaparte's bivouacked troops. At Aboukir it lit up the entire bay, revealing crowds of Mameluke and Arab spectators lining the shore in rapt amazement. Debris, including masts, yards, blazing stubs of wood and chunks of iron, traced fiery trails through the darkness, some climbing to a vast height before curling down to scatter their remains across a huge area. Big guns were twisted and tossed a couple of hundred yards or more, and a fifteen-ton rudder was flung nearly eleven hundred yards. Many of the British observers shared similar thoughts. It was 'a most grand and awful spectacle,' said an aghast Captain Miller. A purser thought it 'the most melancholy but at the same time most beautiful sight I ever beheld'.[32]

As if shaken into disbelief by what mere mortals had done, or suddenly moved by the terrible plight of fellow creatures consumed in such appalling carnage, the men of both fleets fell silent and the guns stopped. There was an almost eerie silence, 'most profound', 'awful' and 'death-like', broken by the falling wreckage hissing into the sea and the occasional cries of survivors thrashing in the black water. Some of the descending debris bombarded the ships and forced men out of their stupor. A port-fire fell into the main royal of the *Alexander*, and the blazing sail had to be cut down and dropped over the side. The ship's jib boom, spritsail and topsail yards were also cut away, but fires still broke out in the ship, and flames ran up the stays to the masthead before being brought under control. It took two hours to beat out the flames completely, and the men were so fagged that Ball allowed them to sleep at their guns for several minutes. Aboard the *Franklin* French sailors also fought fires caused by the remains of the dead flagship. But the *Swiftsure*, as Hallowell anticipated, remained largely unhurt, suffering nothing more serious than damage to her main and fore tops, caused by the falling timber.[33]

Apart from a few small fires, the obliteration of *L'Orient* returned the bay to relative darkness, in which the fight remained in solemn suspension. 'The sea around us was covered with the wreck,' said one, 'and . . . it was shocking to hear the cries of the wounded, and people who had escaped who were floating upon pieces . . . they had been able to catch hold of, without our being able to give them any assistance.' Nearly eight hundred souls had lived in the French flagship. What boats the British still had were soon out, combing the wreckage-strewn water for blackened, traumatised and bleeding survivors. Some were hauled naked from the sea, and gallant tars stripped off items of their own clothing to cover them, while captains ordered pursers to issue slops from the stores. But most died: the *Vanguard*, *Orion*, *Alexander*, *Goliath* and *Swiftsure* saved only about seventy from the sea.[34]

People almost lost track of time, and disagreed about how long the ceasefire lasted. Perhaps it was ten to fifteen minutes. Then, groggily reconnecting with their business, exhausted men struggled back to their guns, which slowly, almost apologetically, barked into life, one, two and then more. Ironically, it was Blanquet's battered *Le Franklin*, sitting closest to the empty space where the great flagship had once been, that led the renewal, spitting hopelessly at a ring of enemies. 'She was surrounded by enemy ships,' reported Blanquet, 'some of which were within pistol shot, and who mowed down the men with every broadside.' Her main deck guns were dismounted, her main- and mizzen masts jagged stumps and wreckage, and two-thirds of her men were down, but still her lower-deck guns replied through the thick smoke. The outstanding performance of the entire battle, it was worthy of a far better cause than Bonaparte's megalomaniac campaign, but about 11.30, with only three guns left, *Le Franklin* struck. An officer sent from the *Defence* to take possession found her decks scenes of almost indescribable destruction.[35]

With the destruction of *L'Orient*, the capture of *Le Franklin* and the flight of *Le Tonnant*, *L'Heureuse* and *Le Mercure* to the rear, the French centre was broken before midnight, and the seven headmost enemy ships of the line captured or destroyed. South and east, however, lay the fractured rear of the enemy fleet, six capital ships and three frigates. After six hours of fighting, Nelson's ambition to annihilate the French force was still unfulfilled.

5

In the first hours of 2 August the French rear was more than a mile from its original position, and scattered in the peripheries of the bay. *Le Tonnant*, *Guillaume Tell*, *Généreux* and *Timoléon*, the last three largely undamaged, and the frigates *Diane* and *Justice* were afloat to the south-east, capable of stiff resistance. Further inshore and more directly south *L'Heureuse* and *Mercure* and the frigate *Artémise* had all run aground in trying to escape and were open to attack. Unfortunately, only two British ships were in action in the small hours. Cuthbert's *Majestic* had opened fire upon the two stranded ships of the line, and Ball's *Alexander* was focusing upon the eighty-gun *Le Tonnant*, neither receiving much fire in return. At about three in the morning *Le Tonnant* was dismasted, and for the second time cut her cable; she had no alternative but to run ashore.

Initial efforts to support *Alexander* and *Majestic* failed. Only Miller's *Theseus* got back into the fight, using stay sails to struggle past the *Majestic* and to anchor in a line with the *Alexander* to throw some shot at the grounded ships. Nelson sent Capel in a boat to rally other ships, urging them to get underway as soon as possible to attack the disorganised French rear, but most of the British were working flat out to repair serious damage and control prizes. Saumarez's *Orion* could not move before emergency repairs to her fore- and mizzen masts had been completed. The *Goliath* was similarly placed, but Foley scribbled Nelson a note promising to rejoin the fight as soon as he could secure his mainmast. True to his word, he eventually cut his cable and dropped southwards using a fore topsail hung on either side of a stay, but by then both fleets were exhausted, and firing was subsiding. Miller took advantage of the cessation by allowing his men to rest at their guns, and saw them fall 'asleep in a moment in every sort of posture'.[36]

If the French pondered the growing scale of their misfortunes in what was left of the night, they might have wondered what they could have done, given the weakness of their defensive position and the vigour of the British attack. The inaction of the rear under Villeneuve of *Le Guillaume Tell* had not helped. It had done nothing until driven from its anchorage by the destruction of *L'Orient*. Yet those capital ships could have made a difference had they worked their way up to support the centre. Many of the British ships had been partially disabled. The *Theseus*, one of the more serviceable vessels, had been hit by eight shot, some of which had passed through both sides, while *Swiftsure* was injured aloft in masts, sails and rigging, and eight inches of water an hour were entering her perforated hull. The French rear could not have turned the battle around, but they could have made Nelson's victory much more expensive. Also culpable were the two unengaged forty-gun frigates, *Diane* and *Justice*, which scarcely fired a shot in defence of the tricolour. One wonders, for instance, why an attack was not made upon the dismasted *Bellerophon* which lay to the eastwards, in danger of going ashore. Blame for French inaction fell most heavily upon Villeneuve, who commanded the rear. In after years he tried to blot the event from his mind, but he made an unconvincing attempt to explain himself to Blanquet. His view of the battle was certainly clouded by the dense powder smoke being blown downwind towards him, but he must have seen the British throw their last ships against the French centre without leaving themselves any reserves. At thirty-four years old, he seems to have been overawed by his responsibility and unwilling to revise unsatisfactory orders, which afforded him no specific instruction to leave his station and assist the van and centre. Even when the British attack massed around the French centre, he continued to hold his position, passively awaiting his own destruction. Intervention, it was true, would not have been easy. The wind was blowing down the French line, against Villeneuve, so he could only have attacked indirectly, first sailing north-easterly into the bay on the larboard tack and then coming about to re-enter the battle. Nevertheless, the failure of the rear to act, instead of grimly watching the van and centre being annihilated, is difficult to excuse.[37]

It was now too late to remedy past mistakes, and action resumed at about five as 2 August dawned moderate and clear. After less than two hours at rest, the *Theseus*, *Alexander* and *Majestic* reopened fire upon the French rear, and they were soon reinforced by the *Leander* and *Goliath*. The *Artémise* frigate was pounded into defeat, but, after hauling down his colours, Captain Pierre-Jean Standelet evacuated the ship, his men jumping into the water and swimming for the shore, and set her afire before the British boats could take possession. Miller thought it a dishonourable act, but the sound of the frigate's magazine going up was music to other ears. 'The explosion was the most beautiful I ever witnessed, as she had a very large quantity of shells on board, which all burst [into a] column of smoke,' it was reported from the *Swiftsure*. *Le Tonnant*,

L'Heureuse and *Mercure* were all aground and close to defeat, and the last two had endured heavy losses without being able to make adequate replies.[38]

Villeneuve wisely decided to save what was left. His three surviving ships of the line had been reinforced by three hundred men from Alexandria, rowed out in small boats early in the morning, and with their assistance he got underway. There was one more tragedy to witness, however. *Le Timoléon*'s masts, rigging, sails and rudder had been so crippled that she ran aground trying to wear, and a mast went over the side. Flight was now impossible, but Captain Louis-Léonce Trullet was worth his uniform. When Villeneuve hailed him, he said he would fight his ship as long as he could and then set her on fire rather than surrender. 'Bravo!' the admiral shouted back.[39]

Before noon the four chastened survivors, the capital ships *Guillaume Tell* and *Généreux*, and the frigates *Diane* and *Justice*, formed a tiny line of battle and made for the open sea. Hood's *Zealous*, the nearest British ship, exchanged broadsides with them as they passed, but the French fired too high as usual, and Hood suffered only one casualty and additional damage to his upper masts and rigging. At first Nelson signalled *Audacious*, *Goliath* and *Leander* to support Hood, but then he realised that his ships were in poor shape for a chase and called them off.[40]

Inside the bay the remaining resistance crumbled. The captain of the stranded *Tonnant* tried to negotiate a safe passage to Toulon for the 1600 men on her decks, but eventually accepted the inevitable and surrendered to a party from the *Leander*. The last of the Nile ships to fall was *Le Timoléon*. As her captain had promised, she was evacuated during the following night and morning, and set on fire before noon of 3 August. In a final display of fire and thunder the battle of the Nile ended.

What was left in that corner of the bay of Aboukir was utter desolation, with even the victorious ships scored with shot and in different degrees of mutilation. The stained water was strewn with debris, the bones of smoking ships and scorched, swelling, semi-naked corpses, already being tormented by scavenging fishes and birds. Nelson had not lost a ship; even the *Culloden* got afloat, albeit with her pumps constantly at work. The British had captured or destroyed eleven sail of the line, two frigates and a brig. The human casualties were equally disproportionate. Nelson had lost 895 killed and wounded, with the severest casualties suffered by the *Bellerophon* (197), *Majestic* (193), *Vanguard* (105) and *Minotaur* (87), and the lowest the *Zealous* (8). But in his possession were some 3305 prisoners, including about 800 wounded, while Saumarez later conferred with French officers and estimated that another 2949 men had been killed on the ships taken or destroyed. This gave about 6254 killed, wounded or captured, apart from additional casualties suffered on the ships that escaped and ashore, where desert Arabs slaughtered some of the fugitives. Nelson's own estimate of 5000 killed or missing alone, while possibly originating in conversations with the senior French prisoners, who he had to dinner one afternoon, appears to have been an exaggeration. Whatever the true figure, Bonaparte's fleet had been destroyed. In its scale and completeness Nelson's victory was the most spectacular naval triumph in living memory, more total and overwhelming than either Quiberon Bay or Camperdown. As the admiral wrote to Fanny a few days later, 'Victory is certainly not a name strong enough for such a scene as I have passed.' [41]

On 2 August, before the last French ship had struck, Nelson sent his congratulations to the squadron and announced a general divine thanksgiving in all ships. The service in the *Vanguard* began at two the same day. A religious man, Nelson was sure that the Almighty had delivered him his enemies. 'The hand of God was visibly pressed on the French,' he told his father. 'It was not in the power of man to gain such a victory.' He also understood that if the victory belonged to the Royal Navy, he had made an important personal contribution. In the circumstances, other good officers might have annihilated the French fleet as effectively as Nelson. Troubridge would have fallen upon it as fiercely, and Saumarez as efficiently. But judged as a whole, Nelson's campaign had been as strategically and tactically flawless as resources and intelligence allowed. He had driven it forward with immense energy and courage, taking the necessary calculated risks without hesitation. The decisions to make the first voyage to Egypt and the immediate attack upon the fleet in Aboukir Bay would probably not have been taken by many admirals, but events had vindicated his judgement. Minto, Spencer and St Vincent had stuck their necks out for Nelson, but they had not mistaken their man.[42]

More important than any personal considerations, however, were the political aftershocks. The battle had transformed the balance of power in the Mediterranean, and changed the course of the war. For if Bonaparte's fleet was gone, so ultimately was his army, because without naval support it was marooned on an inhospitable shore of the general's own choosing. That army would survive longer than Nelson, or many others, bargained for, and would have to be defeated in the field by a British expeditionary force three years later. But with neither an effective supply line nor a means of retreat or reinforcement its defeat, and with it the overthrow of the whole Egyptian adventure, was almost written. At a stroke Britain had regained the command of the Mediterranean she had abandoned almost two years before, and the shadow that France had thrown over the region had withered. Indeed, the victory crushed the morale of the French navy for years. Like the battle of El Alamein a century and a half later, the conflict in Aboukir Bay heartened a cowed Europe, and told it that republican France, for all its ambition, aggression and success, was not invincible.

Even in so isolated and remote a place as Aboukir, Nelson saw the ripples of what the brothers had done. For three nights beginning on 2 August the whole coast thereabouts was illuminated in a ghostly light. Some French prisoners wondered whether the local tribesmen were celebrating a victory over Bonaparte's army, but they were mistaken. They were celebrating the destruction of his fleet in Aboukir Bay.

6

Nelson had passed the last few weeks in a state of nervous tension. The diverting scenes of the Mediterranean held no fascination for him, for he was no dilettante able to turn his mind to the rich landscapes, natural wonders and antiquities with which the region was so famously endowed. He remained utterly, obsessively focused on finding and destroying the French, seeking them out with the unerring single-mindedness of a modern guided missile, twisting here and there, but inexorably hounding the quarry to its death. Now his principal task was done, and the irritability lifted. Miller, who visited the admiral as the battle was closing, found him in his cot, 'weak, but in good spirits' and eager to capture the last enemy ships. A day later Berry was able to report that 'the rage' was 'over'.[43]

New, if less frenetic, problems now confronted the admiral. He was two thousand miles from Gibraltar, the nearest British base, and his ships, men and prisoners needed urgent attention. The sounds of battle had scarcely faded before orders began to flow about finding provisions for the sick, identifying those who would have to be hospitalised in Gibraltar and salvaging stores from the prizes. Troubridge and Hallowell attended to the French. The captain of the *Swiftsure* led a quick assault upon Bequier Island off Aboukir Point on 8 August, and seized it without encountering much resistance. Troubridge conducted a hard-nosed discussion with the commandant of the castle at Aboukir, securing an agreement that enabled him to land 3100 paroled prisoners. A few who refused to be paroled had to be kept in captivity in the prizes, while some Maltese, Genoese and Spaniards found among the French crews seized the opportunity to enlist with their captors. Nelson needed every man he could find if he was to get his ships and prizes back to Naples and Gibraltar. Troubridge also secured fresh provisions ashore, including onions and other commodities needed in the sickbays, but this was not a coast that promised ample supplies.[44]

Other, sad, duties intruded upon the ritual of repair and rejuvenation. Dead comrades were sewn into hammocks, placed beneath their country's colours, and after doleful readings before assembled companies slipped into the sea or buried on the island. In most ships the few pathetic possessions of the dead were auctioned before the mast. Every ship enacted her own sorrowful scenes. Captain Westcott of the *Majestic* was buried at sea, while in *Orion* Saumarez, nursing an inflamed thigh and side grazed by a flying splinter, particularly mourned the loss of Midshipman Charles Miell, who died resigned to his fate in 'a good cause'. Saumarez told his wife that 'a better young man . . . never existed'. In the flagship, too, the men bade farewell to fallen comrades. The departing included Midshipman Thomas Seymour, and two 'young gentlemen of the quarter-deck', John Taylor and Richard Martin, the last only seventeen years old. No less moving to Nelson than the destruction of such young life was the plight of William Faddy, a fourteen-year old midshipman, who survived the battle. The boy had dreamed of going to sea, and had accompanied his father, Captain William Faddy of the marines, into the *Vanguard*. But Captain Faddy was slain in the battle, and his boy and a large family at home orphaned. On 19 September, Nelson wrote to Spencer, urging that the youngster be promised a commission in the marines as soon as he had completed his schooling and reached an appropriate age. 'May I request that his name may stand as an *eleve* of the Admiralty,' he remarked, 'and Mrs Faddy acquainted of it, which must give her some relief under her great misfortune.'[45]

The ships also needed attention, especially the prizes. Rigging had to be repaired, masts and spars reinforced or replaced, guns remounted, damaged hulls sealed, sails replaced or patched and small boats repaired. The *Majestic* had been left with one mast, and the *Bellerophon* with none at all. Nelson's *Vanguard*, already scarred by the storm off Sardinia, needed extensive provisional repairs, despite shortages of materials. Her mizzen was 'fished' or reinforced, a fore topmast was fashioned from a spare main topgallant mast, and a mizzen topsail yard and mizzen topgallant had to serve the mainmast. On the *Alexander* 'the masts [were] shot through in several places. Fore [and] main topgallant masts and mizzen topmast shot away, the yards all shot through, the greatest part of the standing and running rigging shot away. All the sails shot through, and a number of shot in the sides.' With her masts in danger of falling, she desperately needed a regular dockyard. Most worrying of all, perhaps, was the *Culloden*, which spent nine gruelling hours on the shoal. Her rigging and upper works were respectable, but the heavy swell had driven her hard aground, ripping off her false keel and rudder, and she was shipping so much water that two canvases had to be passed beneath her hull to keep her afloat. Troubridge reckoned that the 'poor' ship was 'almost finished . . . for this war'. And while his capital ships were in such disarray, Nelson was doubly embarrassed by his lack of cruisers. 'Was I to die this moment, "Want of Frigates" would be found stamped on my heart,' he wrote to Spencer. 'No words of mine can express what I have, and am suffering.'[46]

Nelson bore his problems while still suffering from an uncertain injury. As it turned out, the wound to his temple was more unsightly than dangerous, but the admiral suffered for a month or more. His head was 'splitting' and he had difficulty concentrating. 'My head is so upset,' he told St Vincent, 'that really I know not what to do.' Briefly he considered turning the command over to Troubridge as soon as he could get back to Naples, and sailing for England.[47]

An early chore was the victory dispatch, addressed to his commander-in-chief. It gave Nelson pleasure to report to one who had agonised over what was happening to him for several weeks. St Vincent, in fact, had heard nothing of Nelson beyond his arrival at Naples, but supposing that he might be blockading Malta, was sending the *Colossus* and four store ships to support him. On 3 August Nelson opened his dispatch from 'the Mouth of the Nile' with an exultant 'My Lord, Almighty God has blessed his Majesty's Arms in the late Battle by a great Victory', but he felt neither the vigour nor the necessity for a full narrative. He was giving Berry the honour of taking the dispatch home. The captain was not known to stint on details, and Nelson felt obliged to him for the patience he had shown during a period when the admiral had been at his most emotional. 'I shall never forget your support for my mind on the 1st of August', he told him.[48]

Unfortunately, Nelson also confronted the dilemma of every victorious admiral. Who was and who was not to be singled out in a public dispatch destined for mass consumption, in this case for the edification of all Europe? It was a task that most admirals bungled. Howe, Hood and St Vincent had all created resentment in first-rate officers who felt themselves undervalued in dispatches, and Nelson's dissatisfaction with the public record had led him to prepare his own accounts for publication, in effect appointing himself his own press agent. Now the shoe was on the other foot; for he was the victorious admiral with careers to make or maltreat. He could leave the bald facts to seal his own reputation as the victor of 'the Nile', but although he wanted his captains to take centre stage, there were two thorns to avoid. One was Troubridge, a master-spirit of the enterprise who had failed to get into the battle, and the other the hypersensitive Saumarez, who as second in command would expect special notice.[49]

The day Nelson wrote his dispatch Saumarez felt well enough to visit his chief on the quarterdeck of the flagship, where the admiral was conversing with other officers. In good humour, Saumarez tactlessly began to express his regret that the British had not all anchored on the starboard of the enemy line. It insinuated that Foley's flanking movement had been dangerous, and perhaps counter-productive, since had the British fought ship to ship they might have prevented the escape of the French rear. Nelson did not wait for the full import. 'Thank God there was no order!' he snapped petulantly, and went down to his cabin, from which an invitation was soon issued for Captain Ball to join him. Shortly Ball was back. 'Nelson says there is to be no second in command,' he said. 'We are all to be alike in his dispatches.'

And so it was. The 'high state of discipline [of the squadron] is well known to you,' Nelson wrote, 'and with the judgement of the captains, together with their valour, and that of the officers and men of every description, it was absolutely irresistible. Could anything from my pen add to the character of the captains, I would write it with pleasure, but that is impossible.' The only officers to be mentioned by name were Berry, who had commanded the *Vanguard* after Nelson was wounded; the slain Westcott, and Lieutenant Cuthbert, who had stepped in his place; and Hood for his lone attempt to stay the flight of Villeneuve. Neither Saumarez, who sought distinction, nor Troubridge, who feared elimination, were mentioned. He had treated them equally as the band of brothers he believed them to be.

Reflecting, Saumarez remembered that the day before the dispatch was written he had spoken to Ball, who had suggested that Saumarez would reap particular rewards as second in command. In his enthusiasm Saumarez had replied, 'we all did our duty – there was no second-in-command'. Later he wondered whether Ball had fed that remark to Nelson, and encouraged its sentiment. Anyway, he was privately disappointed, but at least had the sense to realise that he would forever be deified as one of the Nile captains. The day of the dispatch Saumarez wrote Nelson a letter on behalf of all the captains, saying that they intended to commission a commemorative sword for their chief and to establish an 'Egyptian Club' in honour of the battle, a cadre of elite naval officers that had shared the glorious day. Saumarez asked Nelson if he would have his portrait painted so that it might hang in rooms the club would hire back home. Of course Sir Horatio was flattered, and agreed whole-heartedly. In a smooth recognition of his own as well as his captains' credit, he replied, 'My prompt decision [to attack] was the natural consequence of having such captains under my command; and I thank God I can say that in the battle the conduct of every officer was *equal*.' Both men recognised the underlying tension between them.[50]

The plight of Troubridge particularly troubled Nelson, for he foresaw that the *Culloden*'s absence from the battle could not be hidden, and might be used to deprive the captain of a share in the glory. Indeed, he appended a note to his dispatch to St Vincent, authorising the commander-in-chief to add a paragraph to his dispatch if he thought it to Troubridge's advantage. Troubridge, he later emphasised, deserved his place with the other brothers. He it was who had equipped the squadron so quickly at Syracuse; who had shouldered the essential tasks of command during the admiral's convalescence after the battle; and saved the *Culloden*. 'He is, as a friend and an officer, a *nonpareil*.' But this was a fight for his friend that was only just beginning.[51]

The dashing Berry, whose inadequacies as an independent commander were not yet apparent, could look forward to the customary rewards granted the bearers of victory dispatches. On 5 August he sailed in Thompson's fifty-gun *Leander*, complete with the captured flag of Admiral Blanquet, but his journey would not be straightforward. Thompson was ordered not to deviate on any pretext whatsoever, but thirteen days out the *Leander* had the misfortune to encounter *Le Généreux*, a superior seventy-four-gun warship as well as one of the survivors of the Nile, and he was forced to surrender after heroically trading broadsides for six and a half hours and repelling boarders on several occasions. Thompson's claim to have inflicted 288 casualties for the 92 he sustained may have been close, when the superiority of British gunnery is considered. The captain himself suffered four wounds, and limped ever after to prove it. After receiving some abominable treatment from their captors, Berry and Thompson got to Trieste, but they did not reach England until 25 November. Despite his failure to deliver dispatches, Berry was knighted within a month.[52]

Anticipating such risks, Nelson had sent a duplicate dispatch to the Admiralty by Thomas Bladen Capel, the junior lieutenant of the *Vanguard*, who had proven himself 'a very good young man' despite the favouritism he had received as a protégé of the Spencers. To do this Nelson brought Hardy into the *Vanguard* as Berry's replacement, and made Capel acting commander of Hardy's *Mutine* with orders to take her to Naples, where he would hand the command to a companion, Lieutenant William Hoste, and continue his journey to England overland. Hoste, one of Nelson's favourites, was then ordered to cruise off Sicily until the admiral could get there with his squadron. By these arrangements, therefore, Nelson had been able to reward five followers, for Berry, Thompson and Capel would gain by their roles as couriers, Hardy became an acting flag captain and Hoste an acting commander, a promotion St Vincent obligingly confirmed. Both Hardy and Hoste had earned their places. The log of the *Mutine* reveals how often Nelson had consulted Hardy during the chase of Bonaparte's fleet, and although his talents lay in seamanship and ship management rather than intellectual power, he made an ideal flag captain, releasing the admiral from the daily routines of the ship. As for Hoste, now eighteen years, he was a special case. The son of an indigent Norfolk parson, Hoste had come to Nelson more than five years before, recommended by two of the admiral's associates, Lady Anne Townshend, to whom Nelson was related, and the Whig magnate Coke of Holkham. The boy had followed Nelson from ship to ship, becoming in all but blood a son. As Nelson now wrote to Lady Hamilton, William combined 'the gentlest of manners' with 'the most undaunted courage. He was brought up by me, and I love him dearly.' In their voyage to Naples Capel also fell under the youth's spell, thinking him 'as fine a fellow as ever was'.[53]

The official reports done, Nelson turned to other matters. There was more writing than a one-armed man could accomplish, and his secretary, John Campbell, wielded so leaden a pen that the admiral sent him to the *Franklin* prize as a purser. On 11 August Nelson dispatched Blanquet's sword to the Corporation of the City of London. The most important missives went to Britain's representatives in Austria, Naples and Turkey, potential allies who were vitally touched by the battle, while Lieutenant Thomas Duval of the *Zealous*, a relative of Francis Drake the diplomat, sped overland to Bombay to reassure British India. Nelson believed that the French had planned to take Suez, but had no evidence that they intended to menace India; however, if such an aspiration had existed, Bonaparte's teeth had now been drawn. Nelson claimed that his command of the Mediterranean was preventing 12,000 men from sailing from Genoa to reinforce Bonaparte.[54]

Among such furious quill-driving Nelson did not neglect the financial benefits to be gained from his victory, for prize money of one kind or another still remained a crucial inducement to those enduring the hardships of service. In Drake's day plunder had been an almost inescapable feature of large-scale naval expeditions, because Elizabeth I's impoverished government needed private enterprise and treasure to share the burdens of the state. Nelson lived in a more prosperous Britain, committed to maintaining a powerful navy, but the lure of prize money was still essential to recruitment. Indeed, naval prize lasted until the Second World War. Nelson's interest, therefore, reflected his time, and the natural aspirations of both commanders and their men. He suggested that his captains appoint his old acquaintance Alexander Davison as their London agent. Conducting his affairs from an impressive pile at 9 St James's Square (now number 11), Davison was new to the prize business, but had been encouraged to bid by Nelson's brother Maurice, who still worked in the Navy Office. Now he landed a dream contract, securing the business of Nelson's squadron on explicit assurances that all would be conducted with rigour, speed and probity. Fearing accusations of self-interest, Nelson's only reservation was about his brother, whose personal finances had once been chaotic, and he warned Davison not to admit Maurice to any part of the agency. Maurice was peeved at being squeezed out, but Nelson never regretted the confidence he placed in Davison.

Strict 'prize money' was due on the usable prizes, which could either be taken into the navy or sold as the Admiralty saw fit, but there were problems about three of the captured ships, *L'Heureuse*, *Mercure* and *Guerrier*, which were beyond practical repair. Between 17 and 19 August Nelson burned them. 'I never saw so awful and magnificent a spectacle,' marvelled a young British officer as one of the ships disappeared before his eyes. 'You could count her ports through the flames, and her masts seemed to be illuminated.' Nelson wrote to Spencer that the ships now destroyed to expedite the service would have yielded the captors £60,000, and called for compensation. Their lordships at the Admiralty thought the measure irregular, but saw the logic of the argument, and eventually allowed £20,000, rightly pointing out that the three ships had been among the least valuable of the enemy line. The government would also be indulgent over the matter of 'head money', the sum awarded for the destruction of enemy warships in battle, assessed according to the size of their complements. Technical flaws were found in Nelson's submission for £45,000, but through the good offices of Hamond, the comptroller of the Navy Board, and George Rose, secretary to the Treasury, Davison got it passed. Nelson's remaining claim, an unprecedented suggestion that the Admiralty compensate the captors for cargoes lost in the ships that had been destroyed in the battle, was, however, dismissed. It had been a long shot, prompted by a false report that *L'Orient* had carried £600,000 of treasure looted from Malta.[55]

It was while the squadron was putting itself together that some of the cruisers Nelson had craved at last came in, after tracking him painfully across the Mediterranean. On 13 August *Alcmene*, *Emerald* and *La Bonne Citoyenne* arrived in the bay, and four days later the *Seahorse* with welcome letters, desperately needed naval stores and a Mr Littledale, who had been appointed agent victualler to the squadron with the authority and money to purchase essential provisions. Between these valuable reinforcements a small brig arrived from Tunis in the afternoon of the 15th bringing Nelson a personal problem. It was his stepson, Josiah Nisbet. Though Fanny's pride and joy, Josiah troubled Nelson, who admitted that he had probably spoiled the boy. Josiah's continuing immaturity, deplorable manners and lurking ineptitude were disappointing. How different, Nelson must often have thought, were Josiah and young William Hoste. Both boys had learned their trade under Nelson, sharing quarters in the *Agamemnon*, *Captain* and *Theseus*, and in his letters to Fanny Nelson had bracketed them as if they had been brothers. But the boys had matured so differently, and did not even seem good friends. At least, William's letters home, which spoke affectionately of his associates, never mentioned Josiah; and, on his part, Josiah never wrote to anybody. Regardless, Nelson saw the duty a man owed a stepson, and more besides, because Josiah had truly shone that night in Tenerife, when Nelson's arm had been shattered in the attack on Santa Cruz. The boy had saved his life, tying a tourniquet around the wounded limb and piloting his stepfather to safety through the darkness in an open boat. But how best to repay? That was a question that caused Nelson constant anguish.

He had used what influence he had with formidable results, sweeping aside regulations and propriety alike. In theory, an aspirant needed to be at least twenty to pocket his first royal commission as a lieutenant. Josiah had done it at sixteen, and had made commander at seventeen. We can forgive Nelson his urgency, perhaps. In such a dangerous business as war, no admiral could say how long their lives or their influence might last, and if young officers did not get a foothold on the list of post-captains at an early age they had few chances of reaching flag rank. If Sir Horatio could get his stepson on that list he could relax, because thereafter Josiah would rise steadily by seniority, always supposing, of course, that he did not seriously blot his record and get himself struck off. So, like any good father, Nelson had done his best while he could, but inside he feared that Josiah had been promoted prematurely and was simply not up to the responsibilities of command. He clung to a hope that the boy would suddenly mature.

Josiah's arrival surprised Nelson. It was obvious that St Vincent was trying to please him by rescuing Nisbet from the relative drudgery of the *Dolphin* hospital ship and appointing him to head the twenty-gun sloop, *La Bonne Citoyenne*, a cruiser that offered greater scope for excitement and more prospects of prize money. The new command had already been sent after Nelson, so Josiah followed it, taking passage from Gibraltar in *L'Aigle* frigate, which was bound to join Sir Horatio wherever he might be found. Sadly, on 19 July *L'Aigle* was shipwrecked on a rocky island near the Gulf of Tunis, and Josiah and the rest of her company were lucky to get ashore without losses. Reaching Tunis, Josiah was put on a brig by the British consul, and caught up with his stepfather in Aboukir Bay. Nelson had just sent *La Bonne Citoyenne* on an errand, so he placed Nisbet on the books of the *Vanguard* while he considered the next move. It was gratifying to see the boy favoured with a better ship, of course, but with the news Josiah also brought a disturbing letter from St Vincent. The commander-in-chief had been optimistic in his last assessment of Josiah's progress, but this new reappraisal was blunt. It was St Vincent at his brutal best. Nelson read that while Josiah had been entrusted with a cruiser 'it would be a breach of friendship to conceal from you that he [Josiah] loves drink and low company, is thoroughly ignorant of all forms of service, inattentive, obstinate and wrong-headed beyond measure, and had he not been your son-in-law [sic] must have been annihilated months ago. With all this he is honest and truth-telling, and I dare say will, if you ask him, subscribe to every word I have written.' It was a devastating broadside, dispelling all hope. The boy had become one of a class the commander-in-chief despised, a privileged but unworthy officer robbing better men of vital appointments.[56]

In reply, Nelson could only make a brave face. He hoped that St Vincent was 'a little mistaken' because the boy was 'young' and had 'a great knowledge of the service'. 'Depend upon it,' he wrote even more bravely in another letter, 'he is very active, knows his business, but is certainly ungracious in the extreme.' Yet while Sir Horatio continued to press for Josiah's promotion to post-captain, he doubted that St Vincent would swallow it, and warned Fanny that there was no immediate prospect of that desirable end. Time quickly proved that the pessimism rang a true note. After some clash with the teenager, Troubridge suppressed an impulse to make a formal complaint, and informed Nelson of Nisbet's 'ingratitude to you, and strange insulting behaviour to me'. Worse, the youngster declined to show remorse, and told Troubridge 'that he knew it would happen, that you [Nelson] had no business to bring him to sea, that he had told you so often, and it was all your fault'. When Troubridge upbraided him for his 'black ingratitude' he refused to 'alter his language', leaving the captain in no doubt that 'he has a bad cut about him'. The outburst sheds crucial light on Josiah's problem. Despite initial excitement, he had no real vocation for a naval career, little talent for it and had been put to the profession largely on account of a lack of satisfactory alternatives. Nelson would have preferred the law, but his purse was not deep enough, and, rather than leave the boy stagnating at home with an overindulgent mother, he had hoped that Josiah would eventually take to the navy as many youngsters did. But he did not, and as early as 1794 Nelson had admitted that 'Josiah would give up the sea for anything we can wish him to do'. There, perhaps, we have the core of it. Trapped in disagreeable work, outshone by the likes of Hoste and numerous other highly motivated 'young gentlemen' with whom he was unable to compete, Josiah faced a peculiarly hard road. If he succeeded, there were sneers that he owed it all to his stepfather; if he failed, ship gossip sighed that he would never fill the admiral's shoes. As himself, he was privileged but not respected, exhorted to follow in the footsteps of a man he could not possibly begin to emulate, and promoted beyond his experience or abilities. He may have been a commander, but he was also an adolescent, four years short of his legal majority, and in that difficult period of adjustment when boys became men, and often muddled, unhappy, insecure, frustrated and rebellious. It tore at Nelson's heart strings, but he hoped on, believing that Josiah might 'yet make a good man'.[57]

7

With the enemy fleet destroyed and his own regenerating, Nelson had to redefine his objectives and redistribute his ships. He had no one to guide him, and when St Vincent eventually acknowledged the glorious news, he admitted that he could make no 'sense' of 'prospective events' and must therefore leave Nelson to his 'own impulse'. The eclipse of French naval power in the Mediterranean allowed Nelson to return as many ships of the line to St Vincent as possible, along with the prizes. After all, the great task of the commander-in-chief, to keep the Spanish fleets in Cadiz and Cartagena apart, and both from sailing north to threaten England, was still the priority. On 12 August Nelson therefore ordered Saumarez to take *Orion*, *Minotaur*, *Defence*, *Audacious*, *Theseus* and the badly damaged *Bellerophon* and *Majestic* to Gibraltar, towing with them six of the French prizes. The contingent sailed three days later. Nelson, still recovering from his wound, was thinking too hurriedly, and soon sent revised orders after Saumarez, redeploying the *Minotaur* and *Audacious* to Naples, and asking his second-in-command to send back all his surplus provisions. It added up to a gruelling voyage for Saumarez. At the beginning of September he was reduced to a month's supply of two-thirds rations of salted provisions, with the balance to be made up from flour, but the sluggishness of the damaged prizes and bad weather prevented him reaching Gibraltar until 18 October.[58]

Despite his success, Nelson could not quit the Mediterranean altogether, for Bonaparte's army had to be prevented from escaping or flourishing. The French controlled Alexandria and some coastal settlements eastwards towards Damietta, and advancing up the Nile they seized Cairo. Nelson expected the French to march into Syria, but after intercepting enemy dispatches, he suspected that they would be sorely tried by the heat, disease, famine and shadowing Mamelukes. An active naval blockade could contribute by shutting out reinforcements and shrivelling supplies, and on 15 August Nelson ordered Hood to cruise along the coasts with *Zealous*, *Swiftsure* and *Goliath* and four cruisers. A few prizes were quickly picked up, including a vessel of three guns and seventy men. But Bonaparte was not entirely dependent upon the sea, for he could shift some supplies by camel train, or, in one month of the year when the Nile rose, by small canal boats. The harbour at Alexandria, thronging with French transports and store ships, was a tempting target, but Nelson lacked the bomb vessels to shell the enemy positions or the manpower to storm the town.[59]

The blockade could only be maintained from a base, and the obvious place was Naples, where there were dockyard and provisioning facilities, and where the squadron could poise itself within striking distance of both the western and eastern basins of the Mediterranean. Furthermore, a station at Naples was in keeping with an important object of the mission, the protection of Britain's staunchest ally, the kingdom of the Two Sicilies. Nelson had no specific instructions on this head, but he had divined the thinking of the British foreign secretary, Lord Grenville, who suggested to Spencer before hearing of the Nile that a squadron might be based in Naples with a view to cooperating with the Turks and Russians in a blockade of Alexandria.[60]

Nelson's plan to take *Vanguard*, *Culloden* and *Alexander* to Naples for repairs, stores and provisions depended, of course, upon the willingness of that kingdom to commit itself more fully to Britain. One of the letters the admiral gave Capel on 14 August was addressed to Sir William Hamilton, warning that, while the battle had been a 'blessing' that should encourage Austria to join a coalition, the naval squadron now needed tangible help and there must be no blanching. 'I hope there will be no difficulty in our getting refitted at Naples,' he said sternly. '*Culloden* must be instantly hove down, and *Vanguard* all new masts and bowsprit.' On this score he needed to have no fears, though. The ratification of the defence treaty with Austria and Nelson's victory had cleared the gloom in Naples, and created an entirely new and brighter climate. Suddenly France cut a more modest figure. Acton, regaining his influence, assured Hamilton that the needs of the British squadron would be fully satisfied, and even ordered Neapolitan ships to put their masts and spars at the disposal of their allies. Supplies of biscuit were to be baked. A month later Nelson asked for more, explaining that liberal supplies would be needed for the ships blockading Alexandria, and hinting that he might call for bomb and fire vessels to destroy the enemy shipping.[61]

Nelson knew the importance of capitalising on a success, and that his battle had changed things, stirring potential allies and breathing credibility into Grenville's embryonic coalition. Most immediately he needed concrete help to achieve his new naval objectives, and it was on account of all these considerations that he began to intervene in the wider political affairs of the region.

The blockade of Alexandria necessarily drove Nelson's thoughts in that direction, because it was difficult to mount 1200 miles from Naples. Without bomb vessels or troops to attack Alexandria, Hood could only cruise along the coast as long as his provisions lasted, exchanging blows with the fortifications and falling upon vessels trying to pass in and out of the enemy ports. The campaign had its successes. *La Fortuna*, an eighteen-gun French privateer, was taken by the *Swiftsure* on 10 August, and fifteen days later the boats of the *Goliath* cut out the *Torride*, a seven-gun French war ketch hiding under the guns of Aboukir Castle. Among other prizes were small victuallers and perhaps more importantly packet boats with mail from the French army. Three weeks into August, Hood's men intercepted the *Legare*, a gunboat trying to sneak out of Alexandria. The French threw their dispatches overboard, but two British seamen from the *Alcmene* instantly dived into the sea to retrieve them. On 2 September it was the turn of the four-gun *Anemone* cutter, also trying to slip letters through the blockade. The vessel was driven onshore, and her men, including a general and one of Bonaparte's aids, struggled to the beach only to be despoiled and butchered by Arabs, and their dispatches purloined. A few fled in terror, floundering back to the surf to surrender to the British. But to do more Nelson needed help, and he looked to the power that claimed Egypt and Syria as its dominions, the Ottoman Porte.[62]

The Porte claimed suzerainty over a vast area, from Algeria to Eritrea and Bosnia to the Caucasus, an area of thirty million people, but it had long been in decline. Its weak leadership had allowed many far-flung provinces to drift under the control of autonomous heads (*ayan*, or 'local notables') and brigand chiefs (*derebeys*, 'lords of the valley'), their economies stagnating and their inefficient administrations festering in disorder and corruption. Egypt was a case in point. A Turkish governor, or *vali*, collected taxes for Constantinople, but control was largely in the hands of the Mamelukes, and the governor only survived by playing off rival indigenous factions. Selim III, the Sultan or 'Grand Signior' of Turkey, had enough problems of his own to worry about wars in Christendom, but self-interest had hitherto pushed him towards the French, mainly because France shared the Porte's fear of Russia. For much of the century Turkey had been hard pressed by an expansionist Russia, and in 1795 recognised the French Republic. There was even an informal agreement by which the Porte pledged to stay out of anti-French coalitions in return for aid in the event of a Russian attack upon Turkey. However, much had changed of late. A new tsar of Russia, Paul I, had adopted a policy of rapprochement with Turkey, and conversely it had been France that had cast the greediest eyes upon the Porte's unstable dominions. By the treaty of Campo Formio (1797) the French had occupied the seven Ionian Islands, based on Corfu, in the Turkish Adriatic, alarming both Russia and the Porte. Selim rightly suspected the French of using their new bases to tamper with disaffected elements in such remote parts of his empire as Bulgaria and Albania, and began shifting his loyalties. A proposal for an Anglo-Turkish alliance was received by the British, and, more surprisingly, the sultan began cooperating with his old enemy Russia. The sudden fall of Malta reinforced Turkish fears for their possessions in the Morea and Albania, but even the sultan was shocked by the flagrant French invasion of Egypt that followed. News of the French landings reached Constantinople on 17 July and created anger in the streets.

For a while Selim wavered, unsure about whether to stand against the Gallic colossus, but when word of the 'battle of the Nile' reached Constantinople on 14 August and a Russian squadron from Sebastopol arrived he went into action, arresting French diplomats and merchants in the city and confiscating their property. A new 'Grand Vezir', or chief executive officer, was appointed and on 2 September the Porte declared war on France. The war message emphasised religion, an aspect in which Nelson also saw political capital. 'This is a war of religion,' he wrote to the tsar. 'Justice and humanity against atheism, oppression and assassination.' As far as Egypt was concerned, Selim's local *vali* was incompetent, so the sultan turned to the nearest powerful overlord, 'the butcher' Ahmed Jezzar Pasha, governor of Acre and Sidon, and ordered him to coordinate resistance to Bonaparte. The Barbary states of Algiers, Tripoli and Tunis, semi-autonomous principalities that thrived on plunder, were urged to join the British in harassing French seaborne communications.[63]

Nelson's victory, and his new diplomatic initiative, therefore arrived at an opportune time, when opposition to France was growing but hesitant and in need of a stimulus. Writing through Britain's minister in Constantinople on 27 August, Nelson urged the sultan to send ships of the line, bomb vessels and an army of 10,000 men to destroy the French shipping in Alexandria and to snatch the port from a reduced and diseased enemy garrison. Turkey was, as Nelson knew, technologically backward and politically weak, but she had done much to increase her navy in recent years, launching a series of new ships modelled on French designs. In 1796 the Porte had seventeen ships of the line and twenty cruisers. The sultan's response was consequently immediate. Two tenders and three corvettes under Halil Bey were sent to cooperate with Nelson's squadron, and a generous purse was bestowed upon the British seamen wounded at the Nile. Nelson himself, lauded as a defender of the empire, was awarded a sable fur or pelisse, a box set with diamonds (the special gift of the sultan's mother) and, most spectacularly of all, a diamond-encrusted aigrette taken from the imperial turban. Known as the 'chelengk', the aigrette was a remarkable piece of jewellery shaped in the form of a flower spray bound by a love knot. The nucleus, surrounded by petals, rotated by clockwork to catch the light, and the thirteen arms of the plume, one to represent each French warship taken or destroyed, vibrated. Nelson would grow to love it, and never tired of pinning it to his hats when sitting for important portraits or turning out for gala occasions.[64]

The French campaign, Britain's re-entry into the Mediterranean and Nelson's stunning victory breathed life into Grenville's nascent coalition. If Turkey responded immediately, Russia, too, flexed her muscles. Like the Porte, Tsar Paul I was deeply suspicious of the eastward spread of French influence, but the unprovoked attack upon Malta, of which the tsar was a patron, was the last straw. It is not surprising, therefore, that the news of the Nile created 'the greatest sensation' in St Petersburg, and that the tsar, no less than the sultan, made a personal overture to the British admiral, sending his portrait worked in diamonds on a snuff box. And Russia was a significant player in the power game, lifted into the front rank by its enormous reserves of manpower. Given the indifference of Prussia, she was the one power capable of fielding major land forces in support of Austria, and her naval power was far from contemptible. Vice Admiral Feodor Ushakov, commanding a Russian squadron sent into the Mediterranean to collaborate with a Turkish fleet under Abdul Cadir Bey, wrote to Nelson from the Dardanelles in September. It was not entirely good news. The priority for the Russo-Turkish fleet was to expel the French from the Ionian Islands, and it would station itself at the mouth of the Venetian Gulf, about Zante, Corfu or Cephalonia. However, apparently believing that Britain was strong enough to handle matters elsewhere, Ushakov and Abdul Cadir Bey sent only four Russian and Turkish frigates and ten gunboats to Alexandria.[65]

After a summer barren of allies Nelson felt a tide growing beneath his cause, and he was already looking forward to the involvement of the Two Sicilies and Austria. He told Minto that he intended 'to put matters in a fair train for the advantage of Italy and ourselves', and expected that Austria would have acted of her own volition before he reached Naples. 'As this [Egyptian] army never will return, I hope to hear the [Imperial] Emperor [of Austria] has regained the whole of Italy', Hamilton learned. Wyndham, the British minister in Florence, was told that Nelson anticipated that 'the Emperor and many other powers' would be 'at war with the French, for until they are reduced there can be no peace in this world'. The united effort he envisaged included Naples, from which he hoped to acquire bomb vessels for an attack on Alexandria. 'As for Naples,' the admiral confided to St Vincent on 1 September, 'she is saved in spite of herself. They have evidently broken their treaty with France, and yet are afraid to assist in finishing the vast armament of the French. Four hours, with four bomb vessels, would set all [in Alexandria] in a blaze, and we know what is an army without stores.' In fact, he planned to spend no more than five days at Naples, and then to take those ships to Hood himself.[66]

Letters brought to Nelson by his frigates encouraged the admiral's essay into diplomacy. St Vincent transmitted secret tidings that Britain was about to seize

Minorca from Spain and use it as a permanent base in the Mediterranean, something essential to a revival of the anti-French coalition. If nothing else, it signalled Britain's new commitment to the region, and it became Nelson's duty to curry the support that his country was inviting. In addition the admiral learned an existing ally, Portugal, had sent four sail of the line under Rear Admiral Don Domingo Xavier de Lima, Marquis de Niza, to Naples to reinforce Nelson. Portugal had remained within the British orbit when bigger guns had been silent or had made common cause with France. Her navy was a small one and when Nelson saw the Portuguese ships he doubted their ability to cruise or fight, even captained as most were by British officers who had learned their trade in the Royal Navy. The Portuguese squadron also brought new tensions to the growing coalition, because Portugal and the Porte were actually in a state of war. Nevertheless, on 8 September, after hearing that Niza was on his way, Nelson hurried a letter to the Portuguese admiral, urging him to spell Hood off Alexandria, allowing the British contingent to return to Naples for supplies.[67]

It had been an eventful summer. In a few short weeks, indeed perhaps in less than twenty-four hours of appalling destruction, Nelson had destroyed the French fleet, restored British naval supremacy throughout the Mediterranean, isolated Bonaparte's army, and secured the active support of Naples, Turkey, Russia and Portugal. The possibility of a weighty triple alliance of Britain, Russia and Austria looked a distinct possibility. Sea power had created a new phase of the war.

8

The shock wave started near the mouth of the Nile swept across and beyond Europe, creating jubilation and fury, relief and anguish, energy and despair. The news reached Naples on 4 September, Smyrna in the Levant two days later, Vienna on the 8th and Berlin on the 23rd. States threatened by the French felt the grip of their oppressors loosening. The tidings 'caused a great ferment throughout Italy' and the British minister to the Sardinian court was hastily informed that, while the governors of their ports would continue to object to British ships entering their harbours, no resistance would be offered, and supplies would now be furnished. After dropping Capel at Naples, Hoste of the *Mutine* took the tidings westwards, reaching Gibraltar on 26 September, where twenty-one guns roared in triumph at midnight, and St Vincent off Cadiz the next day, where the commander-in-chief lapsed into paroxysms about the greatest achievement of all time. Under pressure for his use of a junior admiral, St Vincent had replied from the mouths of Nelson's cannons.[68]

In Britain despondency had grown over the summer, breeding in the silence about Nelson's progress, the news of the fall of Malta and the first whisperings that the French had successfully landed in Egypt. Unconfirmed rumours of a battle, reaching the country from different directions, created a nail-biting expectancy. Politicians and admirals paced, and the literate public scanned daily gazettes as the clocks tolled the hours and days.

In Roundwood the other members of the family triumvirate waited. Little had come from Nelson ('a letter of one line will rejoice my heart,' Fanny prompted her husband) while Josiah, her 'dear child', had obviously 'quarrelled with his pen'. Lady Nelson read the London papers to Edmund, whose eyesight was deteriorating, but decided that the quill-pushers were 'despicable creature[s]' for circulating such alarming tittle-tattle. Edmund toasted his old legs before the fire, took snuff and started at every caller. Among others, none waited with more anticipation than the Spencers. Lavinia remained in a 'state of agitation' that was 'impossible to describe', speculating on how these 'grand and splendid events' would reflect upon her husband. Though 'entirely overcome' and in a 'whirl', she had an instinctive belief that 'our dear Nelson' would, after all, deliver. A verse kept running through her head:

> Fair laughs the morn and soft the Zephyr blows,
> While proudly riding o'er the azure realm,
> In gallant trim the gilded vessel goes,
> Youth on the prow and valour at the helm.[69]

Early that autumn, as the trees turned in England, a travel-worn naval lieutenant crossed the Channel from the German coast after a long and exhausting journey from Egypt, through Naples, Trieste and Vienna. About 11.15 on the morning of 2 October, Thomas Bladen Capel hurried through the Adam screen before the Admiralty building in Whitehall and delivered Nelson's sensational dispatches to the first lord. A messenger was soon speeding to the king. Crossing Hounslow Heath he was stopped by a highwayman, but upon being told what the packet contained, the robber returned it unopened and waved the courier on. The guns of the Tower of London were fired, compositors threw themselves into a special edition of the *London Gazette*, and the capital erupted in rejoicing, illuminations and pealing bells. Theatres slipping impromptu allusions to the victory into their productions received roars of approval. Admiral Duncan, who was at the Admiralty when Capel arrived, instantly rushed a private note to Roundwood, bubbling with satisfaction, and explaining that while Nelson had been wounded he was now 'perfectly recovered'. The next day flags were on steeples and houses in Ipswich, people spilled into the streets, troops paraded, guns and rockets roared, bands played and bells rang lustily. Fanny, always respected, became a local heroine overnight.[70]

As word of his doings crackled furiously, Nelson finally got to sea on 19 September with the *Vanguard*, *Culloden*, *Alexander*, *Seahorse*, *Emerald* and *Bonne Citoyenne*, cruising briefly off Alexandria before beginning the long journey to

Naples. Five days out he ran into Saumarez's division off Cape Caledonia, and was able to deliver letters brought by the *Seahorse*. He also conferred with his second in command before they parted off Crete on the 28th. Saumarez found the admiral in 'perfect health'; and Nelson, knowing how modesty sometimes begat complications, insisted that the other, still recovering from his injured thigh, include the injury on the official casualty list.[71]

Nelson's voyage was a slow one, delayed by the struggling *Culloden*, which had a canvas pulled tight under her hull to keep the water at bay. On 12 September the *Flora* frigate joined, and was packed off to support Hood, and the next day the admiral reached Messina, where fruit, lemons and other supplies were secured. Here another frigate, the *Thalia* under John Newhouse, arrived, having been to Alexandria in search of Nelson and been redirected by Hood, who took the opportunity to forward his report with captured enemy dispatches. And here, too, the admiral finally put Josiah into *La Bonne Citoyenne* and gave him his first order, to press ahead to Naples and prepare berths for the crippled ships that were following.[72]

Sir Horatio's head was a little better, but a cough gripped him so powerfully that every hour he thought his lungs would be thrust through his mouth. He needed rest, but one more dramatic event had to be dealt with before he reached Naples. The *Thalia* brought news that Niza's squadron had reached Alexandria, as Nelson had ordered, but instead of releasing Hood to return to Naples, the Portuguese had turned back towards Italy without performing any service whatsoever. Niza had not even thought to reprovision Hood from his own supplies, and left Alexandria the morning after arriving. Nelson's plan to relieve Hood was overthrown, but paradoxically Niza's return enabled the admiral to meet a sudden dilemma.[73]

Off Sicily Nelson was hailed by a Maltese vessel. It carried two delegates of the island's national congress, Luigi Briffa and Francesco Ferrugia, and they came aboard the British flagship with a stirring story. The Maltese had risen against their French conquerors, and the delegates were on their way to Naples for help. The indigenous islanders had not particularly enjoyed the rule of the Knights of St John. The Knights, of whom two-thirds were French, had excluded the native Maltese from prominent positions and refused to subject themselves to Maltese law, and they were widely disliked for their exploitation of the local women. But the brief French occupation introduced by Bonaparte suited the islanders even less, particularly when the victorious soldiery plundered the churches, confiscated property and provisions, and suppressed the religious houses much beloved by a deeply Catholic society. Inspired by Nelson's victory, the Maltese rose in revolt on 2 September – men and women of all classes – murdering some of the French and driving the rest into the strong fortifications at Valletta and elsewhere. Angry islanders ridiculed the corpses of dead bluecoats, stuffing their mouths with parsnips, decapitating them and bearing their heads in triumph through the streets.

The Maltese elected leaders, formed themselves into combat units and hauled whatever guns they had into position. Lead was melted down for ammunition, and bedding turned into gun wads. Yet theirs was a situation of extreme difficulty. Under General Claude Henri Belgrand, Comte de Vaubois, four thousand French remained posted behind fortifications of astonishing power with some 640 cannons and mortars, while the Maltese were short of every species of arms and ammunition. To add to the rebels' vexations, three of the four French ships that had escaped the Nile, Villeneuve's *Guillaume Tell* and two frigates, had arrived at the island to succour Vaubois.

Nelson had no orders covering Malta, but he knew that it occupied a strategic position in the Mediterranean, and could not be left in French hands. Nor could he help but empathise with the islanders attempting to liberate their country from invaders. A cogent reason for immediate action was the presence of the Nile ships in Valletta. Apart from assisting the French garrison, those ships threatened British supply ships coming to Naples, and Nelson knew that the *Colossus* under Captain George Murray was bringing just such a convoy from Gibraltar. To keep supplies out and the French ships in, Valletta had to be blockaded, and as Niza was now on hand, Nelson sent him to immediately seal off the French positions.

And this time Niza's squadron did rather better. It ran into Saumarez's division and joined him in sending a flag into Valletta on 25 September, demanding the surrender of the island and the three French warships. Nelson tended to be cavalier about fortified positions, and gullibly thought the French positions might be taken 'with little exertion'. Even the more cautious Saumarez got the impression that 'their situation is such that they cannot hold out many weeks without supplies, which they are entirely cut off from'. Vaubois did not agree, and rejected the summons. The British and Portuguese had to content themselves with giving the rebels 1062 muskets with ammunition, and imposing a blockade.[74]

The Maltese rebellion encouraged Nelson to revise his priorities yet again. He had intended to refit and return to Alexandria, but now Hood, hopefully aided by Turkish ships, must do his best while the admiral attended to Malta. As Nelson told Spencer, 'The moment I can get ships all aid shall be given to the Maltese.'[75]

Nelson's ships would do nothing if they could not be repaired, however, and their need was emphasised on 14 September, when the admiral's small force was engulfed in wind and rain off the volcanic island of Stromboli and tossed to and fro between angry seas and skies. At 7.30 in the morning terrific gusts wrenched away the *Vanguard*'s foremast, jib boom and part of her main topmast, sweeping four clinging seamen to their deaths. In the elemental struggle further casualties were incurred. William Warne, a twenty-three-year-old able seaman, fell from the foretop yard and suffered a compound fracture of the left leg, and James Dawson was stunned by a falling block. A party of axe men attacked the wreckage, losing the foreyard and sail as they fought, but for the second time that summer the flagship had to be taken in tow, this time by the frigate *Thalia*. A jury foremast with an improvised foresail was eventually raised, and the tow was cast off three times in five days, but on each occasion *Thalia* had to return to the rescue. Thus the flagship of the victorious fleet had the indignity of being towed into the Bay of Naples on Saturday, 22 September.[76]

Nelson had not entirely looked forward to his return to Naples. 'I detest this voyage to Naples,' he told St Vincent. 'Nothing but absolute necessity could force me to the measure. Syracuse, in future, whilst my operations lie on the eastern side of Sicily [i.e. off Malta and Egypt], is my port, where every refreshment may be had for a fleet.' But he also needed rest. In the middle of August the weather had changed, with the cooler weather retreating before warm, squally conditions and rain. An occasionally violent 'catarrhal fever' spread among the seamen, associated with delirium, pulmonic inflammation and 'an obstinate and troublesome cough which remained for several weeks'. Sometimes dysentery or intermittent fevers developed. This, at least, from the estimable surgeon of the *Swiftsure*, who blamed the change in atmosphere and dampness, which he relieved by using fires between the decks. The condition had probably infected most of the ships and claimed Nelson as one of its victims. He told St Vincent that his severe cough had attacked him after the battle and deepened into a fever, which had 'very near done my business. For eighteen hours my life was thought to be past hope. I am now up, but very weak both in body and mind from my cough and this fever.' Then, with what would become a familiar appeal for sympathy, he added, 'I never expect, my dear Lord, to see your face again.' Despite his own predicament, not for the first time he exaggerated the general state of health in his squadron, telling St Vincent that he had 'not a sick man in the three ships with me'. Even the ship musters, which we have already found so inadequate a reflection of the squadron's health, were then showing nineteen sick on the vessels to which Nelson alluded, eleven of them on the *Vanguard*. Men as well as ships needed putting in order in Naples, and the admiral had been promised that soft pillows awaited him in the Palazzo Sessa, where the Hamiltons lived.[77]

The *Mutine*, *Bonne Citoyenne* and *Alexander*, even the labouring *Culloden*, had been sent ahead to precede the *Vanguard* into Naples, but it was the flagship and her hero that the city was waiting for. The king and numerous small boats had gone out to meet Ball and Troubridge, believing that Nelson had arrived, smothering the sailors with adulation, but disappointed to find that the admiral was not among them. Just over a year before at the new sally port in Portsmouth Nelson had returned to his first cheering crowd, but nothing in life or imagination prepared him for what awaited the broken *Vanguard* as the *Thalia* towed her into the Bay of Naples that sunlit Saturday morning of 22 September 1798.[78]

IV

'NOSTRO LIBERATORE!'

See our gallant Nelson comes;
Sound the Trumpet, beat the Drums;
Sports prepare, the Laurel bring,
Songs of triumph, Emma, sing;
Myrtle wreaths and roses twine;
To deck the Hero's brow divine.

Emma Hamilton's modified
'See, the Conquering Hero', 1798

I

NAPLES, in its resident population of 350,000 the third city in Europe, compensated for its relative political impotence by an unmatched reputation for art, science and decadence that had made it the indispensable stop on the European grand tour. The stunning blend of blue sea, green hills and white buildings that feasted the eye in the bay often paled before the frightening but compelling pyrotechnics of Vesuvius, looming dark and ubiquitous, sometimes smouldering menacingly and at others ablaze with fumes and flames that bathed the landscape in red and black shadows. It was the volcano that attracted the natural scientists; the ruins of Pompeii, Herculaneum and the Phlegrean Fields that drew archaeologists, connoisseurs and collectors, and inspired neo-classical styles throughout Europe; and the city itself, where magnificent palaces, churches, theatres, striking villas and baroque-bound squares contrasted with a proliferation of coffee shops, taverns, ice-cream parlours, squalid narrow alleys and sunlit courts that housed a cosmopolitan society that throbbed with life. Here ran nobility, living upon the proceeds of their feudal estates, an omnipresent clergy tripping in and out of numerous religious houses, doctors and lawyers, merchants who had made the city a conduit for goods moving east or west, artists, writers, scholars, dancers and harpists, and the famously colourful *lazzaroni*, who idled about the streets, regarded by some as indolent and others as liberated, but contributing to the sultry pleasure-seeking live-for-today atmosphere of that remarkable place.

Almost anything seemed possible in Naples. 'Naples is a paradise,' Goethe declared. 'Everyone lives after his manner, intoxicated with self-forgetfulness.' The streets were full of monks, musicians and prostitutes. Some of the latter did well, attended by liveried servants, and 'painted like Jezebel, dressed with such fine muslins that you might see their shapes to the greatest nicety, their breasts exposed in the most wanton manner, heads decorated and wreathed with pearls and artificial flowers, hair hanging down their bosoms in beautiful ringlets, lascivious attitudes, their breath as fragrant as the spices of Arabia'. Not surprisingly, this was not the place for everyone. 'Everything gives way to their cursed pleasures,' growled Troubridge.[1]

Though the city was governed by the great families, the *nobiltà di piazza*, the Bourbons still ruled here from their four palaces, hating the French and looking upon Austria and Britain as natural allies. During the eighteenth century Neapolitan life owed much to royal example, in its ornate buildings and gardens and its industries, but the 'golden age' was melting before the flinty realities brought by the French Revolution, stalling what tentative steps were being taken to reform a creaking administration and focusing the monarchy upon the grimmer game of survival. Ferdinand IV of Naples and Sicily was a boisterous, big-featured buffoon, a disagreeable looking man, more physical than cerebral, who knew nothing of books or public affairs, but readily pursued processions of courtiers about his palaces, shrieking in a shrill falsetto; serially indulged in childish if benign rib-tickling oafishness; and butchered thousands of animals in vile royal hunts. He could be generous, and mixed with the common people, many of whom loved him, but it was fortunate that he took little interest in politics. His queen, Maria Carolina – 'Charlotte' to friends – was the thinking half of the partnership. Though she had striking chestnut hair, dark blue eyes, and a dimpled smile that relieved an oblong face, the queen was not a handsome woman, and when excited accompanied a hoarse masculine vocal delivery with wild movements of the arms and a trembling of the entire face. By the time she was forty-five, she had given birth to seventeen children, nine of whom survived, and seemed forever surrounded by princes and princesses, whose welfare was a perpetual preoccupation. Maria Carolina has been damned more than sainted, a political football between academics and writers of one persuasion or another, but none could deny her strong qualities, astonishing strength of purpose, great courage and energy. It was she who had gradually taken over the management of the realm, securing a seat in the council of state in 1776, and using her principal minister, John Acton, the son of an Englishman, to strengthen the twin kingdoms of Naples and Sicily in an increasingly dangerous world. In 1798 Acton was fifty-two, slim, intelligent and pleasantly mannered. Born in France, he had served in the navies of that country and Tuscany, whence he passed to Naples in 1778, charged with putting the Neapolitan navy in order. He made enemies, but prospered in the queen's favour, and as a field marshal and minister of war considerably improved the armed services. Acton, everyone knew, remained English at heart, and he also understood that weak Naples, confronted with an unfriendly power as great as France, had to cultivate the dominant sea power for its own survival.

That September of 1798 the gloom had suddenly lifted. The defence treaty with Austria had helped, but the news that the *Mutine* brought to the city on 4 September created a sensation. Capel and Hoste had been accommodated and feted by the Hamiltons, who paraded them about the town in an open carriage, her ladyship wearing a bandeau around her forehead inscribed 'Nelson and Victory', relishing the ecstasy of the crowds as if the glory was her own. Before Capel left for Vienna he scribbled a note to Nelson telling him that both she and the queen had fainted on receiving news of the Nile. Hoste, who stayed longer, received a diamond ring from Her Majesty and a purse of two hundred guineas for the ship's company. 'You can have no idea of the rejoicings that were made throughout Naples,' he wrote home.[2]

Sir William strutted like a peacock, suddenly looking a decade younger than his sixty-seven years. His father had been the third Duke of Hamilton, his mother the daughter of the sixth Earl of Abercorn, and he had been reared in the court of the Prince of Wales with the future George III as his foster brother. But a youngest son, he had shifted much for himself in the world, and after an education at Westminster School and a spell in the army, he married an heiress to lands in Pembrokeshire and was appointed to Naples, a billet that lacked the importance of Paris, Vienna, Madrid or St Petersburg but fitted his studious fascination for music, art and natural sciences like a glove. Hamilton had been in the city since 1764, five years longer than the queen, a lean, tall, dark-complexioned, hook-nosed man, who interposed diplomatic business with the more congenial activities of fishing, hunting, playing cards with the king, entertaining visiting worthies in the Palazzo Sessa, his three-storey house overlooking the bay, and patronising arts and sciences. He was known far beyond Naples for his taste, extensive collections of paintings, sculptures and classical antiquities, and his research into vulcanology – and, it has to be said, for the charms and talents of his second wife, Emma, Lady Hamilton.

Thirty four years his junior, she was an arresting presence in the prime of life, tall, strong-limbed, voluptuous, her stunningly beautiful countenance as expressive and commanding as it was classical, cast within an enormous angry auburn mane, and all held in the service of an energetic, vibrant and often tempestuous personality. She was constitutionally histrionic, besotted with attention, noise and company, in which she thrived and shone, and never more in her element than in those heady days after the battle of the Nile. 'Delirious with joy' and bursting with patriotic pride, she attired herself 'à la Nelson', throwing a navy blue shawl over a costume festooned with gold anchors. 'In short, we are be-Nelsoned all over,' she declared, and walked 'in air'. The French chargé d'affaires complained that the Hamiltons had publicly insulted the arms of the republic displayed on its consulate in the Piazza Santa Lucia, but few were listening. The queen, whose close confidante Emma had become, was more intelligent though no less emotional, and after recovering from the initial shock of the Nile, paraded here and there, crying, kissing and embracing all and sundry, and repeating in ecstasy, 'Oh brave Nelson! Oh, God bless and protect you, our brave deliverer!' The country, too, seemed 'wild with joy'. Naples was illuminated for three nights, and the Hamiltons alone raised three thousand lights, some creating a blazing Maltese cross adorned with Nelson's initials. 'Not a French dog dare show his face,' said her ladyship.[3]

Into this hothouse came the crippled *Vanguard*, which found herself beset by hundreds of small boats while still miles from her anchorage. The waterfront was lined with spectators, many with their carriages. First to reach the British flagship was the Hamiltons' barge, with a band behind striking up patriotic songs. Sir William and Emma were soon on board, with their friends, Miss Ellis Cornelia Knight, a vivacious and intelligent forty-one-year-old, and her mother, the widow of Admiral Joseph Knight. Sir William brimmed with emotion, but Emma flew forward, collapsing upon the frail little admiral with a tearful, 'Oh God! Is it possible?' More calmly Miss Knight observed that the hero was 'little and not remarkable in his person', though distinguished with 'great animation of countenance and activity' and 'unaffectedly simple and modest' manners. The royal barge shortly came alongside. The queen was ill, but Ferdinand and his heavily pregnant hereditary princess, Clementina, disembarked on the *Vanguard* to a thundering salute of British guns. The king grasped the admiral's remaining hand with great warmth and rattled through a heartfelt eulogy about Nelson, King George and Britain. They had met before, in 1793, and now, with obvious sincerity, Ferdinand swore that he regretted only that he had not been with Nelson in the battle. The royal and Hamilton parties joined Sir Horatio for breakfast in his cabin, where the guests were amused by a small bird that hopped freely about the admiral's quarters. Nelson explained that the creature had taken refuge in the *Vanguard* the evening before the battle and remained ever since, fed by the sailors who regarded it as an harbinger of good fortune. Evidently, its task was done because it seems to have flown away soon after Nelson reached Naples. But in that cabin Nelson renewed his acquaintance with a very different portent, Francesco Caracciolo, a forty-six-year-old court favourite and senior officer in the Neapolitan navy, who had been entrusted with supervising the naval apprenticeship of Prince Leopold, the king's second son. Caracciolo had been attached to the British fleet in 1795, when he had some differences with Nelson, but whether any ill feeling survived is unclear. Nothing marred this occasion, and Ferdinand remained in the *Vanguard* for three hours, during which time he inspected the ship, spoke to members of the crew and personally thanked those in the sickbay. Thus honoured, the British flagship was towed through the armada of craft towards the mole, where the welcome sight of the *Alexander* and *Bonne Citoyenne* greeted her, and where she anchored close to the Health Office.[4]

Ashore guns crashed in salute, banners were hoisted and a flock of birds released, and excited crowds were joyful 'beyond description'. 'Viva Nelson!' rose from hundreds of throats, and the admiral struggled to control his emotions at the roar that greeted his landing. The Russian ambassador and his legation welcomed the British admiral, joining hands in a new political symbiosis. Nelson was then shown to a carriage and whisked between cheering crowds and crowded balconies to the Palazzo Sessa, close to the royal Palazzo Reale. That evening Sir William hosted a dinner for the hero, his captains and the principal British residents in Naples, for the city was again illuminated not just in honour of a fleet but a nation. It was 'the most distinguished reception that ever, I believe, fell to the lot of a human being', Nelson reported. He felt 'the most humble of . . . creation, full of thankfulness and gratitude'. There was no need for him to exaggerate his achievements any more. 'All Naples called him "Nostro Liberatore" [Our Liberator], and printed eulogies were appearing on the streets.'[5]

For days the attentions flowed. The 'liberator' was passed from ball to banquet, acclaimed out- and indoors, saluted by the Neapolitan fleet, paraded at court and daily deified in addresses and verses 'from all parts'. On the evening of Monday, 24 September, Nelson and the brothers were formally received at court, and the following day the admiral rashly assured Ferdinand that he would restore Malta to the kingdoms of the Sicilies. Maria Carolina, who was still indisposed, had to wait another seven days to be officially reintroduced to the admiral, who, being Nelson, used the occasion to lobby Acton about his need of masts and a spar. Acton had Nelson to dinner on 27 September, and two days later it was the turn of the Hamiltons, who celebrated Nelson's fortieth birthday with an extravaganza that cost them a thousand pounds. At one end of the ballroom a rostral column was inscribed with the names of Nelson and his captains, and commemoration plates had been produced for the occasion in the royal porcelain factory at Capodimonte Palace. Everywhere ribbons and buttons bore Sir Horatio's monogram. 'There was nothing to be seen or heard of but "Viva Nelson!"' declared Ball. Eighty sat to dinner in the afternoon, over seventeen hundred attended the evening ball, and supper was served to eight hundred. Among the songs, sonnets and speeches that drowned the feted hero was a verse Miss Knight had added to the British national anthem, and which Sir William had already rushed to the king's printers:

Join we great Nelson's name
First in the roll of fame,
  Him let us sing;
Spread we his praise around,
Honour of British ground,
Who made Nile's shores resound,
  God save the King.

There were few blemishes, but the refined Miss Knight spat on Admiral Blanquet's sword, and Josiah was said to have become so ungracious in his cups that Troubridge and another officer had to hustle him away. It took only seven days for another eruption of congratulations to occur, this time on the poop of the Neapolitan frigate *Sannita*, where Nelson, the Hamiltons and the British captains were guests of the king, Francis the hereditary prince, Prince Leopold and Caracciolo. Gallo, the first minister, was there with three of the king's lords in waiting. Emma had taught Nelson to despise the cautious Gallo, and after the admiral agreed that 'we are different men'. After dinner the king toasted His Britannic Majesty and 'Sir Horatio Nelson and the brave English nation', which the British returned with three cheers and the frigate complemented with her own gun salute. These were no mere formalities, but the heartfelt congratulations of an alliance in the making, and all within full view of the harbour-side window of the new French ambassador.[6]

It was an electric time for Nelson, something beyond anything he had seen or could realistically have expected. He had wanted to be a hero, and now he was, acclaimed by people and rulers alike. The commoner from Norfolk stood on the international stage, bathed in light and bowing before the rapturous applause of his audience. It was a dangerously intoxicating draught. Flattering remarks from the king, he admitted on 25 September, were 'enough to make me vain. My head is quite healed, and if it were *necessary*, I could not at present leave Italy, who looks up to me as, under God, its protector.' The implication was that this heady cocktail was capable of drawing him from duty, but he had not quite succumbed. Two days later he was writing that 'nothing shall again induce me to send the squadron to Naples whilst our operations lie on the eastern side of Sicily. We should be ruined with affection and kindness.' He viewed Syracuse, rather than Naples, as his best station. Nevertheless, an earlier prediction that he would leave Naples within five days was not to be fulfilled.[7]

Recovering his health with the help of a course of asses' milk, Nelson fell inexorably under the spell of his obliging hosts. For reasons no one now can safely diagnose, the admiral had always needed sympathy and praise. Perhaps it had something to do with his largely motherless childhood, or an adolescence spent at sea. No one really knows. But he desperately needed love and praise, becoming sullen and resentful under neglect or criticism, but flying to the heavens when acknowledged and admired. There was no shortage of attention at the Palazzo Sessa, especially from Emma, who daily fussed over him, tending to ailments, cutting food and pouring wine at the table, all the while trumpeting his achievements with an extravagance that would have been repellent had it not been entirely sincere. He soon felt that he belonged to this household, which treated him as one of its own, sharing his triumphs and disappointments, standing by him in all matters, caring for him when present and missing him when apart.

Infusing all, Emma also brought a magnetic, bewitching personality and a powerful sexual attractiveness.

The speed at which this new triumvirate bonded has not always been appreciated. The weeks only added to the Hamiltons' admiration. 'So fine a character I really never met with in the course of my life,' Sir William wrote to Eden. As for Nelson, within three days of arriving in Naples, he was telling Fanny that he hoped 'one day to have the pleasure of introducing' her to one of the finest of women. 'She is one of the very best women in this world. How few could have made the turn she has. She is an honour to her sex and a proof that even reputation may be regained, but I own it requires a great soul. Her kindness with Sir William to me is more than I can express. I am in their house, and I may now tell you it required all the kindness of my friends to set me up. Her ladyship, if Josiah was to stay, would make something of him, and with all his bluntness I am sure he likes Lady Hamilton more than any female. She would fashion him in 6 months in spite of himself. I believe Lady Hamilton intends writing you.' It was not a tactful letter, raising as it did the spectre of a husband incarcerated in the house of an attractive and designing woman, and one, moreover, whose ability to chisel the 'rough' edges off Josiah exceeded that of Fanny herself, but the very artlessness of it suggests that Nelson was then totally innocent of any threat to his marriage.[8]

More flowed in letter after letter. The Hamiltons' 'goodness' was 'beyond everything I could have expected or desired', and the improvement made in Josiah was 'wonderful'; indeed, Emma seemed 'the only person he minds'. It took a mere ten days for the couple to supplant all of Nelson's friends, barring only those two dearest of all, who maintained the home watch. 'The continued kind attention of Sir William and Lady Hamilton must ever make you and I love them,' he wrote to Fanny, 'and they are deserving of the love and admiration of all the world . . . My pride is being your husband, the son of my dear father, and in having Sir William and Lady Hamilton for my friends. While those [four] approve of my conduct I shall not feel or regard the envy of thousands.'[9]

Fanny did not see the implications at this time, but Nelson was saying something that was nevertheless significant. He was telling Fanny that the old trio of father, son and wife was gone. It had become a quintet.

2

Emma Hamilton was one of the essential sights of Naples. 'The environs of Naples are truly Classic Ground,' wrote the painter William Artaud in 1796. 'I have visited Lake Avernus, have been in the Elysian fields, in the baths of Nero, and in the tomb of Virgil. I have . . . descended . . . 100 [feet] into the crater of Vesuvius . . . I have been at Herculaneum and Pompeii, and the museum at

Portici, and saw Lady Hamilton's Attitudes.' In Naples Emma had been bewitching audiences with her 'attitudes' for years. 'Dressed in this [Greek costume], letting her hair loose and taking a couple of shawls, she exhibits every position, variety of posture, expression and look so that at last the spectator almost fancies it is a dream,' gushed Goethe. Emma was born to perform, and as fully impelled towards applause and affection as Nelson himself. In her case it reflected the long, remarkable journey she had made, from the miserable cottage of the illiterate Cheshire blacksmith who had fathered her, to fame as an artist's muse, singer and actress, and political influence at the Court of the Two Sicilies.[10]

In 1798 she was thirty-three, and, although increasingly overweight, still endowed with beauty. Baptised Amy Lyon and raised at Hawarden by her widowed mother, Mary (née Kidd), she had entered domestic service as many working-class girls did, but eventually found herself in London, relying upon her blooming looks to wring a livelihood out of more disreputable trades. Contemporary rumour made her a common prostitute, and as early as 1791 Thomas Rowlandson satirised a belief that she had posed naked for the artists of the Royal Academy. Neither story may be true, but there is credible evidence that she was being groomed for 'gentlemen' when she passed into the hands of the first of a series of wealthy protectors, each of whom left her legacies of one kind or another. By the first, Sir Harry Featherstonhaugh, she had an illegitimate child at the age of sixteen, fostered out to indulgent relatives. The second, Charles Greville, a son of the Earl of Warwick, polished her social accomplishments to ease her entry into 'gentle' society as 'Emma Hart', and arranged for her to sit to some of the ablest portrait painters of the day. Finally, deciding he would marry an heiress, he dumped Emma on his uncle Sir William Hamilton. It was under Sir William's management that she put her status as an unmarried paramour behind her, and became a toast of Naples. She did not convince everyone, however. The Countess de Boigne was not alone in dismissing her as vulgar and lacking in intelligence.

Emma benefited from protectors because of her looks and talents, for she had no independent name or fortune, but she rose to each challenge with enthusiasm. Fine painters fought to capture her beauty, and one, George Romney, documented his infatuation with her in some fifty likenesses. In Naples Sir William set another hare running. Noting his lover's similarity to the faces of antiquity, as well as her ability to pose, he invented the famous 'attitudes'. Their nature and content were the brainchild of Hamilton, who harnessed the fashionable scenes of the Classics (refreshed by such recently discovered images as the wall paintings of the 'Herculaneum dancers') to the ancient art of pantomime, in which performers presented a sequence of silent tableaux, rather like a constantly metamorphosing gallery of statues. But although the old knight handled the lighting effects, it was Emma herself who raised the act to the sublime. With almost uncanny instinct she effortlessly portrayed the subtle shades of human character. 'The face of Lady Hamilton remained always beautiful, as it was,' said the painter Wilhelm Tischbein, 'yet with the slightest movement, say of her upper lip, she was able to express contempt which made her beauty fade away.' 'Her features,' thought William Hayley the poet, were 'like the language of Shakespeare' in their depiction of 'all the feelings of nature and all the gradations of every passion, with a most fascinating truth and felicity of expression'. The mimes spoke without words, but many were instantly recognisable to a classically educated audience. No less alluring, as art they legitimised titillation, exhibiting as they frequently did a handsome female in flimsy garments performing what one observer described as 'most voluptuous and indecent poses'. The fame of the 'attitudes' travelled, and Hamilton had Frederick Rehberg's drawings of them published in Rome in 1794. Nor did Emma's talents stop there. She discovered a credible singing voice, danced in the style of the Neapolitan street performers, and could host the most elaborate gatherings with a seemingly tireless appetite for banter. Sir William had found a veritable powerhouse of entertainment, and the Palazzo Sessa became a *dernier ressort* of artists, notables and curiosity seekers.[11]

Emma's strengths lay in social interaction and the visual and musical arts, not analysis or abstract reasoning, for which her passionate theatrics were wholly unsuited. Nonetheless, they unlocked doors in the Neapolitan court and enabled her to exercise a definite if ultimately indefinable influence upon the public affairs of Naples. Maria Carolina was far more intelligent and astute than Emma Hamilton, and unquestionably used the willing ambassadress to further her own cause, but she was also charmed by her obvious loyalty and verve, and wrote to or entertained her on a regular, sometimes daily, basis. Between queen and *cortigiana* there developed a close bond, in which Emma acted the sympathetic intermediary and broker, filtering ideas and information back and forth between the monarch and first the British ambassador and then Nelson. The extent of this influence can never be effectively gauged, since so much that passed between the two women was private and unrecorded, and the truth has been obfuscated by Emma's exaggerated, even dishonest, claims about her diplomatic achievements. But that she had loyalties to the Queen of Naples and Britain, and that she tried to serve both and to bind them in a bipartisan cause, is undeniable.

Emma was much admired. She worked hard for love and friendship, and her loyalty, basic kindness and generosity were outspoken. But she wore virtues and faults loudly, and aroused prejudice and hostility, especially among her own countrymen and women. Her humble origins, readily revealed in provincial speech and discordant manners, led many to describe her as 'coarse'; her relentless socialising and tiresome histrionics, sometimes manifested in emotional outbursts, hyperbolic assertions and swooning, suggested shallow attention-seeking; her disposition to be ruled by her heart rather than her head did little to inspire confidence in her judgement; her glaring interest in and attentions to men stirred fear and resentment among vulnerable females recognising hard-to-beat competition; and her tendency to drink, eat and gamble to excess repelled the upright and decorous. Even her successes as a public performer, and her association with artists, persons of all reputations and 'the promiscuous herd' all aroused charges of impropriety. She was, withal, a spendthrift, incapable of living within her means and ruthless and unscrupulous in her own cause. It was a powerful indictment.[12]

Gossip about her 'former life' and her bonds with powerful people laid her open to repeated charges of being an undesirable influence. Apologists for Sir William, Maria Carolina and Nelson all found her a convenient scapegoat for misfortune or wayward behaviour. Some even spoke of her as an 'evil genius'. But possibly more than anything else Emma was driven by passion and insecurity. She bore the scars of past deprivation and her passage through a critical class-conscious society. The extravagant gifts and ridiculous praise she bestowed upon people, the extreme professions of love and steadfastness, her eagerness to please, hunger for applause and admiration, interest in improving her manners, language and temper and her smothering attentiveness all betokened a simple basic need – to prove herself worthy and to be accepted. Even more than Nelson, Emma reflected the difficult journey she had made in the company of more privileged beings.[13]

For Emma, Nelson provided a heaven-sent opportunity to take centre stage, for she suddenly found herself not only confidante to the Queen of Naples but also personal assistant to a new international hero who had transformed the politics of Europe. Never had she been happier.

3

Back home in England there were many others who basked in their relationship with the victor of the Nile. Sir Horatio proudly read their letters of congratulation – from Sir Mordaunt Martin of Burnham Westgate, a figure from his childhood, who now spoke of raising a public subscription for the families of the killed and wounded; from his old 'sea-daddy', Captain Locker, now failing in health but vindicated in his admiration for his most apt pupil; from old comrades in arms, such as Bulkeley, Collingwood and the Duke of Clarence who had toiled with him in the West Indies, James McNamara, with whom he had journeyed through France, and Admirals Hood and Goodall.

Lady Parker and Lady Spencer were among the most obviously delighted. Lavinia had spent weeks fretting, partly for her husband, whose reputation and reign at the Admiralty rested on what was happening in the Mediterranean. The news of the Nile, brought by Capel with a personal note for her, hit like a thunderclap.

> What with joy, gratitude and exultation I have really been very near killed [she wrote to the Dowager Countess]. I am still far from sober, and when I shall get to rights I know not . . . Dear little creature [Nelson], I forgive him all he has made me suffer. What a letter was his! How sublimely excellent! So truly humble, so magnanimous by [being] forgetful of himself, so laudably vehement in the praises of his valiant band. How perfectly he fulfilled my notion of a Christian hero! But then how he has been rewarded. What a victory!

To the admiral himself she was no less herself:

> Joy, joy, joy to you, brave, gallant, immortalized Nelson! May that great God, whose cause you so violently support, protect and bless you to the end of your brilliant career! Such a race surely never was run. My heart is absolutely bursting with different sensations of joy, of gratitude, of pride, of every emotion that ever warmed the bosom of a British woman on hearing of her country's glory, and all produced by you, my dear, my good friend! And what shall I say to you for your attention to me in your behaviour to Captain Capel? All, all I *can* say must fall short of my wishes, of my sentiments about you.

Like Lady Parker, she was soon worrying about Nelson's health. His frailty, she said, 'goes to my heart', for 'every letter' from him 'increases my respect for his character'.[14]

Fanny, now fully expecting to become at least a baroness, followed much of the excitement through the pages of the *Ipswich Journal*, which predicted that Nelson would 'set the mode' for the current fashion season and attire 'our ladies . . . *à l'Egyptienne*'. On Tuesday, 16 October, she and Edmund experienced a prouder day than they had ever known when a ball and supper was held in their honour in the illuminated Assembly Rooms.

> At 7 o'clock the company began to assemble [said the *Journal*]. About 8 Lady Nelson's arrival was announced by the ringing of bells and repeated huzzas of a vast concourse of people in the street. Her ladyship was introduced into the ball room by Admiral Sir Richard Hughes [Nelson's old commander-in-chief, then living at nearby East Bergholt Lodge, Suffolk], who conducted her to the top of the room, attended by the Rev. Mr Nelson, the venerable father of the admiral. Then followed Captain [John] Bourchier, leading up Miss Berry, sister to Captain Berry of the *Vanguard*. On their entrance they were welcomed by the grateful respects of the company, the regimental bands playing 'Rule Britannia'. It is not easy to conceive the sensations that at this time prevailed; all seemed to feel in their hearts an event so glorious to the king and country that had been the means of concentrating the principal families in the town and neighbourhood. Dancing soon after commenced and continued till near 12, when the company, consisting

> of 300, were regaled with an elegant supper. Many appropriate toasts were drunk, and much social harmony exhibited during a festive period of 2 hours. Dancing was then resumed and continued till the morning. The ballroom was ornamented with wreaths of flowers. At the top was a whole length transparency of the gallant admiral, surrounded by naval trophies, with a drawn sword in his left hand, and his right foot upon a cannon. On the side of the room were two other transparencies, one representing the battle of Bequiers, and the other Neptune, ploughing the ocean, with the Hero of the Nile in his car.[15]

Until now Fanny had felt herself isolated in an indifferent community, and she was not convinced by the sudden stream of callers. 'They ought to have found their way to the cottage before,' she wrote. But she had much bigger fish to fry now. The Nile had turned one national hero among several into a superman, the country's foremost warrior. Nelson had become a subject of political cartoons in January, but no less than eleven additional works grimaced from the print shops during the last three months of the year. A torrent of memorabilia spilled out of workshops, factories and presses, pamphlets, songs, poems, sonatas, plays, prints, jugs, mugs, snuff boxes, watches, fans, linen, a commercial medal designed by Thomas Wyon, even, as the Ipswich rag had predicted, clothes. In London it was soon fashionable to dress 'à la Nile' and while the two oldest royal princesses began sporting turbans and diamonds in imitation of the chelengk, in Vienna 'Nelson overcoats', anchor shaped earrings and 'crocodile' bonnets became the latest fads.[16]

Everyone, it seemed, wanted a piece of the hero. John Pitt, Earl of Chatham, Lord President of the Council, wanted an introduction, and suggested his countess present Fanny to the queen. When Lady Nelson and Edmund arrived in London in November, taking her old lodgings at 141 Bond Street, both seemed 'well' enough to confront 'the amazing bustle of congratulation'. The adoration reflected on all close to the admiral. When Berry reached Norwich, after being paroled by the French, he was 'received . . . with mad joy. In short, I'm so great a man that I am sung in and out everywhere to the great annoyance of my pocket and the distress of my feelings.' Fanny weathered all such tribulations, including the queen's 'drawing room' events in November and July, with both prim feet firmly on the ground, although she had to borrow suitable apparel from Lady Walpole of Wolterton. Even though Nelson had briefed her for the attentions of high society ('Don't mind the expense. Money is trash!') Fanny resolved to 'go on in the same careful way' and used her time in London to serve the family. Brother-in-law William had always seen Nelson as a means of his own advancement. He now 'thinks the mitre is very near falling upon his head', his sister Kate remarked. William happily lumbered Fanny with his daughter, Charlotte, who was to be educated in the capital, whenever she was 'in town'. Maurice and Sukey were still close by, and Nelson's ailing uncle, William Suckling of Kentish Town, the deputy collector of customs, required a visit. He was, in fact, near the end, but died only after Fanny had taken Edmund to Bath for the winter.[17]

Fanny did not know it, but this was, in fact, her personal summit. There were no obvious clouds. Nelson was still declaring that 'the happiest [day of his life] was that on which I married Lady Nelson', and the only fly in the ointment seemed to be Josiah. Charles Peirson, an old *Agamemnon*, assured her that Nisbet was well thought of in the fleet, and even Nelson shielded his wife from St Vincent's bleak opinions. Apart from Josiah's questionable future, Fanny's horizon had never glowed more.[18]

Despite the public celebrations the official British rewards for the victory were niggardly. Initially the plan was to make Nelson a viscount, and on 4 October the secretary of war so informed Spencer. Pitt also told Admiral Hood, who dutifully relayed the happy news to Fanny, but then the king intervened. Judging from comments His Majesty made to Davison, the king had abandoned his earlier prejudices against Nelson, but did remember that after the battle of Cape St Vincent the admiral had objected to a barony on the grounds that he lacked the financial means to support a peerage. So now George recommended that Nelson be given a handsome pension instead. Spencer was in a quandary, for, while it was the sovereign's prerogative to confer peerages, to deny one to Nelson would not only be manifestly unfair but court public outrage. He persuaded the king to compromise. Nelson would become a lord, but only a baron, the lowest rank of the peerage, and Pitt and Spencer covered their embarrassment by referring to the relative youth of the recipient, and remarking that, unlike Howe, St Vincent and Duncan, Nelson had not been an actual commander-in-chief when he won his victory. Most people saw it as a downright paltry response to the greatest British victory since Quebec, but it set a pattern for the future. In one sense Nelson had himself to blame, for, had he not shunned a barony in 1797, he would certainly have become a viscount in 1798. But many were justifiably angry. 'Never was a more flimsy reason given,' wrote Hood after hearing Pitt's unconvincing defence of the decision in the Commons. 'Viscount at least!' Goodall raged to Nelson. 'I shall clamour for more, but shall not rest till I have you viscount!' When the secretary of the Admiralty told Maurice Nelson about the barony he was too stunned to reply, and merely bowed and left the room, while out in the Mediterranean the Hamiltons were livid, and Nelson grumpily wove another grievance into what would become a rich tapestry of neglect. Nevertheless, it was done, and on 6 October Sir Horatio Nelson became Baron Nelson of the Nile and of Burnham Thorpe in the County of Norfolk. The patent was not entirely satisfactory. It confined the succession to two heirs of Nelson, who was likely to remain childless, but the disgruntled admiral was proud enough to start signing himself 'Nelson' rather than 'Horatio

Nelson' and using seals that showed his provisional coat of arms and an Egyptian palm tree.[19]

The family made the best of it. Edmund consoled himself with the knowledge that the name 'Nelson' had been incorporated into the official title, and William began looking for ways in which the title might ultimately revert to his children, since both his older brothers lacked issue. Eagerly, William also began designing a livery for the new Lord Nelson's servants, who, he decided, should adorn their yellow and black uniforms with buttons stamped either with the crest of the admiral's coat of arms or an engraving of the Turkish chelengk. Unfortunately, a second blow soon fell. As expected, the British parliament voted Nelson an annual pension of £2000 to go with his peerage, backdated to the day of the battle and transferable to the next two heirs. It was a considerable sum, but the Irish parliament was too embroiled in the Act of Union to find time to provide a customary increment of £1000. Thus, once again, Nelson was disadvantaged compared to St Vincent and Duncan, whose victories had been far less important.[20]

Barring the unequal treatment of Nelson, the government acted according to expectations, organising votes of thanks from both houses of parliament, striking gold medals for the Nile captains and promoting their first lieutenants. Galwey, who arrived in England with further dispatches, found himself a commander in December, and if his career was later blighted by rheumatism he died a rear admiral in 1844. Not to be outdone by officialdom, Davison, the squadron's prize agent, determined to show his gratitude by bestowing a medal on every Briton surviving the battle. They were struck at Matthew Boulton's famous Soho works in Birmingham, gold medals for captains, silver for lieutenants and copper medals for the ordinary seamen and marines. For Nelson himself there were also personal gifts of a pair of Derby mugs, bearing the same designs used for the medals, two wine coolers and other pieces of china. The marine insurers Lloyd's raised its usual subscription for the relief of the families of the British casualties, and received donations from as far away as the West Indies and Calcutta. The public served its new hero extremely well. New honours included the freedoms of Thetford, Liverpool, King's Lynn and the prestigious Drapers' Company of London, gifts from the Turkish Company, the Corporation of London and Lloyd's Patriotic Fund, and, of more practical importance than any, no less than £10,000 voted by the directors of the East India Company, a reward for ridding them of the menace of Bonaparte. Ever the family man, Nelson immediately arranged for £2500 of the East India award to be shared equally between his father, brothers and sisters, and the balance to be invested in government stocks.[21]

At home Fanny handled these attentions, including the financial repercussions, with what Marsh called 'admirably sensible, judicious and proper' care, but in the Mediterranean another flow of presents and tributes reached the admiral direct. There were diamond boxes, commemorative plates and swords from Ferdinand of Naples, Paul of Russia, the King of Sardinia, and the islands of Zante and Sicily, none quite replacing in Nelson's favour the enchanting chelengk. They were testimony to the debut of a significant new international player, and one who had shifted the balance of power in the Mediterranean world. It was that world that Nelson had now to address.[22]

4

In Naples plain old Sir Horatio Nelson, KB, as yet unaware of his elevation to the British peerage, was experiencing something else new: what it was to command an entire theatre of war. St Vincent may have been commander-in-chief, but he was watching Cadiz, shielding Nelson from threats from outside the Strait. In the Mediterranean itself Nelson was the ranking officer, and Naples and Sicily were his logical bases. With the French battle fleet gone, and only a few weak Venetian ships of the line in Toulon, Nelson's principal tasks lay eastwards, where Italy needed support and the blockades of Malta and Alexandria had to be maintained. There the naval forces opposing him were few. One capital ship, a survivor of the Nile, was bottled up in Valletta, while at Alexandria two underpowered Venetian ships of the line and a dozen cruisers had taken refuge. The French army in northern Italy was the most worrying enemy, for Nelson realised that sea power alone could not prevent it sweeping south-eastwards throughout the peninsula. To contain or expel the French a coalition of land and sea powers was necessary. Bonaparte had helped, alienating Russia and Turkey by his attacks on Malta and Egypt, but Austria, which had solicited Britain's re-entry into the Mediterranean in the first place, was the other important participant.[23]

The first task was to refit and provision his squadron at Naples, and put the operations at Malta and Alexandria upon an efficient footing. The aid of Naples was crucial at this point, providing dockyard facilities, artisans and supplies. The *Culloden* was berthed in Castellammare, across the bay to the south-east, and her keel and stern-post replaced. Eight thousand pounds' worth of repairs were done up to the middle of October. Troubridge, her captain, also needed attention. His disappointment at the Nile was followed by news of his wife's death in Plymouth in June, and Nelson worried unduly about his friend until 26 September, when he heard his familiar voice scolding the men at work and knew that the captain was mending. The admiral fiercely resisted attempts to exclude Troubridge from the honours the brothers had earned. 'I well know he is my superior, and I so often want his advice and assistance,' he told St Vincent. Meanwhile, at Naples itself, where the heavy swell hindered work, the *Vanguard*'s masts had to be fished again because the spares sent by St Vincent had now to replace the main- and mizzen masts of the *Alexander*. Hardy, who had succeeded

Berry in command of the flagship, now proved to be invaluable, pitching into every kind of work that was needed, while Ball drove the repairs to his ship forward with an energy 'conspicuous even amongst the band of brothers'. Taking advantage of the overhaul, the captains replaced vermin-ridden provisions and replaced depleted or worn medical and naval stores. After three weeks, the ships were ready and victualled for six months.[24]

The human resources had also been reappraised. Lengthy periods in port always provided opportunities for desertion, and Nelson imposed St Vincent's dictums prohibiting the men to go ashore or from one ship to another unsupervised. However, he maintained that his ships were 'in the highest health and discipline', with some justification. Between 1 September and 10 December only four new cases of intermittent fevers and five with sea ulcers were reported in the flagship. The situation deteriorated a little thereafter. The reports for 24 December to 8 June show the ship free of scurvy, but mentioned 20 patients with continuous or intermittent fevers, 4 of whom died in the ship, 29 cases of sea ulcers and 30 of venereal complaints, and 22 men were recovering from wounds or injuries. Again, the Italians helped. Seriously ill patients were invalided to Gibraltar or Minorca but more regular use was made of the hospital at Palermo. By 9 October Nelson's small detachment of ships was ready to sail. It had, by then, also been reinforced. The *Colossus* and *Alliance* store ship had arrived with a convoy of victuallers from Gibraltar, and the *Goliath* and *Terpsichore* frigate returned from Alexandria. Two ships of the line, *Audacious* and *Minotaur*, originally detailed to accompany Saumarez to Gibraltar, had also been recalled. Nelson now had seven British capital ships with which to prosecute his campaign.[25]

If Nelson looked in vain for advice from the Admiralty or his commander-in-chief, his own assessment of the tasks before him very much mirrored that of government. 'The protection of the coasts of Naples and Sicily, and an active cooperation with the Austrian and Neapolitan armies are the objects to which a principal part of the squadron should be most particularly directed,' Spencer told St Vincent on 3 October. And Malta and the eastern Mediterranean, where Britain had commercial as well as strategic interests, were also important. Grenville contended that a British presence in the Levant was 'absolutely necessary' to encourage Turkey and Russia, and that Nelson was best located 'in the neighbourhood of the Two Sicilies', where he could provide 'courage and support' to Naples and excite 'a powerful resistance . . . in that part of the world'. St Vincent passed Spencer's orders to Nelson, but there was nothing in them that he had not already in train.[26]

Nelson's task was one of unusual complexity, however, particularly for one whose resources remained frugal. He had to conduct distant blockades while withholding sufficient strength to support Italy, and there was a major diplomatic impasse. Russia, Turkey and even the Two Sicilies seemed disposed to join a united front, but Austria dragged her feet. Whitehall saw real prospects of purging Italy of the French by squeezing their armies between Britain and Naples in the south, Austria in the north and Russia and Turkey in the west. Grenville had supposed that Austria would commit to the coalition if British subsidies could be arranged and tangible support provided. Nelson's task force was followed by an amphibious expedition under Commodore John Duckworth and General Charles Stuart, and on 19 November Minorca was seized from Spain and a garrison of redcoats installed at Port Mahon. There could be no clearer declaration of Britain's determination to remain in the Mediterranean, for a squadron based at Port Mahon was ideally situated to watch Cartagena, Toulon and northern Italy, releasing Nelson to focus upon the Two Sicilies, Malta and the Levant. But nothing half so positive came from Vienna, and Spencer feared that Austria might make some 'shabby bargain' with France. Grenville doubted her willingness to cooperate so deeply that he began transferring his attention to subsidising Russian forces.[27]

Austria's procrastination was all the more frustrating because of the massing of French forces in northern and central Italy. Returning from Egypt, Nelson found an Italy close to panic but as divided as ever about how to react. The Ligurian, Cisalpine and Roman republics, which the French had carved out of the peninsula, were effectively satellites, although rural disaffection in the Roman Republic was causing France some concern. Orders from Paris forbade them from admitting British ships of any description to their ports, and Grenville had replied by declaring that any haven so acting would be deemed hostile and liable to a damaging blockade. By contrast, Sardinia-Piedmont and Tuscany affected to be neutral, but both had been cowed into silence by France, which had told them that their liberties depended entirely upon them keeping their heads down. Displaying the iron fist, French troops had occupied parts of Sardinia-Piedmont and turned the king into a supplicant in his own land. They would soon banish him to the island of Sardinia. But the population at large hated the French, and Thomas Jackson, Britain's minister to the Sardinian court, secured secret permission for Nelson's ships to enter Sardinian ports, providing the governors could pen a protest to the British to provide themselves with a pretext.[28]

Tuscany and Naples were sister states of Austria. Ferdinand III, the Grand Duke of Tuscany, was the brother of Francis II, Emperor of Austria, and both were sons-in-law to Maria Carolina of Naples. Yet Tuscany dared not even go as far as Sardinia's furtive invitation to British warships. She had been warned that any part of her realm being compromised by the British would be occupied, and lived in fear of triggering a French attack. Both Sardinia-Piedmont and Tuscany were nervous about the outbreak of major conflict in Italy. In Sardinia-Piedmont fear of France was increased by a belief that Austria would bargain rather than stand up to her. But by mid-September Tuscany believed that a war between France and Austria was inevitable, and in that event the Grand Duke would throw in with his brother. Two months later Tuscany was refusing to loan the French two million livres for their war chest.[29]

Further south, Naples, with her 60,000 troops, would have liked to have driven the French from Italy, sandwiching them between Austrian, Neapolitan and British forces, but dithered uneasily. Nelson's ships had defanged Bonaparte's expedition, but could not protect Naples from a land invasion from the north, and Austria's treaty with Naples was limited by its essentially *defensive* character. Their Sicilian Majesties were in an extremely parlous situation. They were sure that the French were massing to invade Naples, and that a pre-emptive strike to throw them off balance before they could reach full strength made military sense, especially as the stroke could be supported by British naval power and insurgent forces in the Roman Republic. But would Austria deem such an action defensive, and come to Ferdinand's support, or would she argue that it was *offensive*, and beyond the scope of the Austro-Neapolitan treaty? On the other hand, the other option of waiting for a clearer signal from Austria seemed doom-laden, since it merely gave the French time to build a vastly superior force. Urgent appeals went from Naples to Vienna, seeking a solid promise of support, but Vienna demurred and the Neapolitans dithered. The king, influenced by Gallo, was more cautious than his queen, who appeared willing to take stronger action.[30]

But one day Austria was a hawk and the next a dove, and Britain's return to the Mediterranean failed to clarify her position. There were issues about the financial subsidies to be had from Britain, and a mistrust of Prussia, which Austria feared might attempt to profit from any conflict with France. Austria would have liked to liberate Switzerland, regain territories she had lost in Italy and support her sister states, but until July no potent land power would stand beside her. That month Russia promised to send 60,000 men to Austria's aid, in addition to some already guaranteed under a treaty, and these battalions began to enter imperial territory in the third week of October. Yet even this failed to stir the emperor to action.[31]

Hamilton had urged Naples to reel Austria in by means of their defence treaty. One idea was to cite Bonaparte's seizure of Malta, to which Ferdinand had some political claims, as an act of French aggression against Naples, and another, probably inspired by Grenville's suggestion that the displaced Pope Pius VI be used as a figurehead, was to call for a holy war to drive the French out of the papal dominions. Both appeals would have been difficult for Austria to resist, given that the emperor was not only the protector of Naples but also Holy Roman Emperor, sworn to defend Christendom. Nelson, a more impatient man than Hamilton, added his huge authority to the strategy. 'What precious moments the two courts [Naples and Vienna] are losing,' he said. 'Three months would liberate Italy; this court is so enervated that the happy moment will be lost.'[32]

In the light of later misfortunes, many historians have criticised Nelson's intervention. Indeed, the latter part of 1798 is one of the least understood periods of his career, partly because it concerned Nelson the diplomat rather than Nelson the admiral. At the onset it is important to distinguish between the 'truths' contemporaries believed, and the hindsight available to later generations. The actions of Hamilton, Nelson and Ferdinand need to be judged in the light of their knowledge and circumstances, as well as ours. Unlike most of his critics, Nelson had no access to the certainties of past events, only the possible outcomes of different untried options, none of which was risk-free.

It has sometimes been said, for example, that the French had no intention of invading Naples at this time and had resisted the invitations of Italian Jacobins to do so, repeatedly expressing their pacific intent to Ferdinand's court. Possibly so, but this was not the view of vulnerable Italian states whose prevailing dispositions were inimical to the republican cause. Few in Piedmont-Sardinia, Tuscany, the papal dominion or the Two Sicilies would have believed the assurances of such an aggressive, opportunist, untrustworthy and volatile regime as France, nor were her messages unambiguous. It was the actions, not the words, which carried the most weight. Naples had seen the French create puppet regimes in northern Italy, and seize Switzerland, the papacy, the Ionian Islands, Malta and Egypt, and she had suffered constant intimidation, with threats that the kingdom risked conquest if she failed to satisfy Gallic demands. Most of all there were those thousands of republican troops marching into Italy towards the Neapolitan frontier. Even after snow filled the higher Swiss passes and retarded the menacing flow, some troops got through by way of the Riviera coast and Mount Cenis. Fifty thousand republican soldiers were now thought to be in Italy. However studiously inoffensive were the words of the new French minister to Naples, Lacombe St Michel, they were drowned by the noise of those marching feet. If France needed a pretext to invade Naples, she already had it in Ferdinand's support of Nelson's fleet.

Given such facts, whatever France's intentions, the conclusion that Naples, the remaining Italian thorn in the French foot, was to be reduced to obedience was natural, compelling and widespread, even among men whose function was to sift scanty intelligence. 'We are acquainted from every tide, Paris, Madrid, Milan, Genoa, Florence and Rome,' wrote Acton, 'that [the] French are making and hurrying their preparations against us, and Vienna still thinks of delays and nonsensical reasons for keeping their forces still in garrisons. They shall certainly sustain us, but we may be too late for depending on their help.' British diplomats throughout the region sang the same song. From Turin Jackson reported that 'all the accounts from Italy and Paris mention the invasion of the kingdom of Naples as resolved upon and approaching'. Intelligence from the Roman Republic declared it 'certain'. In Florence, Wyndham fired increasingly hysterical warnings to Hamilton. Early in November he had intelligence of 'undoubted authority' that Modena was being used as a rendezvous for troops destined for Naples. 'The King of Naples must make haste,' he urged on the 7th, 'and I think I may prophecy that if he is not at Rome in the course of this month, he will never be there.' A week later he was giving Ferdinand ten days to save his kingdom; if he allowed himself to be 'humbugged' he would be 'lost'. Under such imperatives, Hamilton and Eden agreed with their Sicilian Majesties that an attack on Naples was imminent, and Nelson merely echoed the common refrain when he wrote to Emma that '*all know* [the French] are preparing an army of robbers to plunder these kingdoms and destroy the monarchy'. Roger de Damas, the most talented soldier in Neapolitan service, later scoffed at those claiming wisdom after the event. 'Certain circumstances that afterwards occurred may have given rise to the belief that, if the Neapolitans had not made the attack, the French would not have taken the initiative, but at the time appearances did not favour this view. To make the attack was the only prudent course, and it was more the manner of it and the time chosen that were in fault.'[33]

Equally, some historians, seeking to portray Hamilton and Nelson as aberrant amateurs, have pictured Britain's foreign secretary, Lord Grenville, as a critic of their policy. It is certainly true that on 3 October Grenville wrote to Hamilton that he had cautioned the Neapolitan ambassador in London of the dangers of attacking France 'without the fullest assurances of support from the Court of Vienna', but his full letter did not end there. Grenville went on to say that 'it could not be denied' that the 'alternative' to an immediate offensive 'was also full of danger' and risked insult and aggression. That being the case, he left the decision to the Neapolitan court, which would, he presumed, have access to the freshest intelligence. The following month he was firming up his opinion. 'The intelligence received here respecting the intentions of the Directory coincides with that of the Court of Naples,' he wrote to his man in St Petersburg, 'and it seems even doubtful whether the plan of the Neapolitan government [to attack] may not even yet be anticipated by the operations of the French army.' War, he had concluded, was imminent, and, what was more, it could rebound to the good of the coalition. He could not see Austria standing idly by, despite her prevarication, and Britain should support Neapolitan appeals to Russia. In a subsequent letter to Hamilton, Grenville owned that the battle of the Nile had given Ferdinand an 'opportunity . . . to rescue himself and his kingdom by a vigorous exertion from the state of terror and subjection in which they had been held by the French, and the ruin which has long been meditated against them'. Hamilton was, therefore, to 'omit no occasion of expressing His [Britannic] Majesty's fervent hope that the opportunity thus afforded will not be suffered to be lost'. When the war began, Grenville rejoiced, believing that Ferdinand 'could not avoid it in the end' and that it made Austria's intervention almost inevitable. In other words, Grenville did not demur from the policy that Hamilton and Nelson were developing on the ground, as several historians have claimed. On the contrary, both he and Spencer were led to the same conclusions and the same recommendations.[34]

Nelson's strategy for surprising the French and engaging Austria in the allied coalition was not quite the headstrong action of a naive admiral, pursued in the face of common sense. It was one of several risky alternatives, the outcomes of which could not then be known. Nor, as some have said, was the result 'Nelson's War'. The evidence reveals a more complicated birth. The plan originated not with Nelson, but with Hamilton, Eden and probably Acton. Although the Neapolitan government would probably not have embarked upon the adventure had the French fleet not been destroyed, it was worked out in some detail before Nelson's counsel was solicited. The admiral seems to have first been consulted at Acton's dinner of 27 September. 'We all dined with General Acton yesterday,' he wrote, 'and he told me that this country was determined to declare [war], and not wait for the emperor; that they well knew the plan of the French against them.' Reporting the same discussion to Grenville, Hamilton wrote that the battle of the Nile had 'induced this government to . . . march . . . immediately . . . without waiting for the decision of the Court of Vienna and [to] take possession of Rome'. Shortly afterwards, on the occasion of a visit to the queen on 1 October, Nelson was briefed by Acton about a proposed two-pronged campaign. Ferdinand would lead the army to Rome and liberate the papal possessions, while another force – possibly carried by sea – would seize Leghorn, in Tuscany, in the rear of the French, securing a retreat for the Grand Duke of Tuscany if it was needed, and a beachhead from which the enemy rear could be threatened. Acton asked Nelson if the British could be relied upon for help. Nelson approved in principle, assuming that Austria would not fail the Neapolitans. There was logic in taking the initiative while numbers, momentum and surprise were in the king's favour, and to put the French between two fires. Once signed up, Nelson urged their Sicilian Majesties to suppress self-doubts. As Hamilton acknowledged on 16 October, 'the conferences we [he and Nelson] have had with General Acton have certainly decided this government to the salutary determination of attacking rather than waiting to be attacked'.[35]

Acton believed Naples had little choice. 'God, I hope, will bless our endeavours, directed only to avoid plunder and destruction,' he explained. 'The arms are the only measure at present. It may appear a desperate one, but no other afford[s] any prospect of success with a traitorous set of people as those towards who we march in our defence.' But deep down no one expected that Austria would fail them. Strategical security, dynastic loyalty and national honour and pride would surely urge her forward. Optimism was increased at the beginning of October by the arrival in Naples of Karl Mack von Leiberich, an experienced forty-six-year-old general of some reputation, who was employed to command Ferdinand's army. Mack had been in Austrian service, and came with the emperor's blessing. As Nelson heard it, he carried a message that Ferdinand could depend upon Austria's support, but it seems fairly certain that he had been cautioned to act defensively, in keeping with the Austro-Neapolitan treaty. Nelson knew that Austrian military aid was essential. 'Without the assistance of the emperor, which is not yet given, this country cannot resist the power of France,' he wrote. But he expected the Neapolitans to put their army into shape, and quickly sized Mack up. They met at dinner in the opulent royal palace at Caserta, north of Naples. The queen urged Mack to be another Nelson, but the admiral saw that he could not move without five carriages in his retinue. 'I heartily pray I may be mistaken,' he confided to Spencer.[36]

A war of terrific savagery was now coming fast.

Neither Nelson nor Hamilton was privy to the inner deliberations of Neapolitan government, but they learned much through Acton and the queen. Acton, who headed the departments of war and marine, two of the three for which there was a secretary of state, and the queen, who mainly liaised through Emma, were both anti-French, Maria Carolina especially so. The daughter of Marie Theresa of Austria and sister of Marie Antoinette, she was of a line of strong women. 'I am not and never shall be on good terms with the French,' she wrote. 'I shall always regard them as the murderers of my sister and the royal family [of France], as the oppressors of all monarchies, as the villains who have seduced and put poniard and poison into the hands of all classes and peoples against legitimate authority, and who have consequently blighted my existence.' What little of the enlightened monarch there was about Maria Carolina disappeared after the French Revolution, but Nelson saw her in the context of the continental struggle, and was inspired by her stubborn, often lone, stand in an intimidated Europe. 'She is . . . a *great king*,' he told Fanny.[37]

After agreeing to participate in the campaign at the beginning of October, Nelson was surprised at the slow pace of the preparations. That month the Austrians blew hot and cold. At the beginning a Neapolitan appeal for help drew a lukewarm response from Vienna, agreeing to consider fielding a force once 20,000 promised Russian auxiliaries had arrived. This was reminiscent of a stronger but as yet unfulfilled undertaking made in May that the emperor's forces would march after the appearance of the British fleet. It was one of several 'vague and unsatisfactory' communications that characterised the Austrian government over the following weeks. In this cooler climate Ferdinand shuffled between Gallo and his appeasers and a war party stirred by Acton, Hamilton and Nelson. The admiral 'scolded' the government with 'plain truths' about the folly of delay with the intention of smoking Austria into the open. 'Inducing the emperor, &c. to go to war,' he said, 'is my very greatest reward, and I desire no other.' The Neapolitan war would thus be a mere hors d'oeuvre leading to a powerful tripartite coalition of Britain, Austria and Russia, one capable of winning the war in Europe.[38]

Further progress had to await meetings at the royal palace at Caserta on 12 and 13 October, when Nelson and Hamilton got the impression that Austria had actually given Naples the go-ahead. 'The emperor has desired the King of Naples to begin, and he will support him,' the admiral wrote to St Vincent on the first day of the deliberation. Hamilton later told Nelson that he had seen Acton that morning, and been shown 'a letter from Monsr. Baptiste, the Neapolitan Charge d'Affairs at Vienna, with a message to him from the Baron Thugut, in the emperor's name, advising the King of Naples to act openly against the French at Malta as His Imperial Majesty would certainly support him. This takes off all the difficulties.' Sir William reported to Grenville that the emperor had 'assented, and even promised his powerful support'. The reality was less definitive. Apparently the king had written on the specific issue of the Maltese rebels. If Naples supplied the Maltese, as they had the British, would Austria support them if the French retaliated? According to Eden, the emperor replied that if their Sicilian Majesties were 'determined for war' he 'would not examine too closely if the *casus faederis* existed with this court, but would faithfully support him'. Put simply, if Naples felt she had no alternative but to fight, Austria would not use a strict interpretation of their treaty to deny her aid. This was hardly an endorsement for outright war against the French. It is not clear that Nelson understood this, but Acton admitted to Hamilton that the letter amounted only to 'a kind of promise to support'. It was in view of this less than unqualified support that Acton moderated his plan of campaign, emphasising its defensive character. The 'hostile views' of the French compelled Naples to take 'proper positions of defence for this kingdom', but the Neapolitan army would 'act as protectors and certainly not invaders of that country [the Roman Republic]', and there would be no declaration of war. To underscore the defensive nature of the campaign, Mack resolved to advance slowly, advertising his approach as he went, so that his adversaries had the opportunity to withdraw without fighting.[39]

The plan was finalised on 13 November. So complete was the temporary ascendancy of the 'war party' that the cautious Gallo found himself manoeuvred out of essential meetings, which were convened as informal rather than formal council proceedings. Thirty thousand men were to advance to the northern frontier to secure the strategic areas, occupying a line starting at Rome and proceeding north and east via Terni and Foligno to Macerato near the Adriatic coast. Thus posted, the army would remain in camp until it was learned that the Austrian troops were also in motion. Then the Neapolitans would advance into Umbria, possibly supported by a simultaneous amphibious thrust towards the French rear through Leghorn. Events were now very much as Nelson wished, and his success in war and diplomacy was being much applauded by his superiors. St Vincent thought him as 'great in the cabinet as on the ocean' and told him that his 'whole conduct fills me with admiration and confidence'. So, too, said Spencer. On 30 September he wrote to Nelson that 'as the French will lose no time in falling upon Naples for having treated you with ever common civility, it must be a principal object to give that country all the protection which naval operations can give it, and if the Neapolitans will heartily and actively assist us with what force they have, I think it will be no very hard matter to regain Malta'. Upon learning of the Neapolitan offensive to the north he expressed equal pleasure. In Whitehall, then, policy followed the trail blazed by Hamilton and Nelson, and deviated in only one significant respect. Whereas Hamilton did not discourage the Neapolitans from believing that Britain might provide some financial as well as naval support, and Nelson emphasised Ferdinand's shortage of money, Grenville saw no available resources.[40]

The Neapolitan war impacted upon Nelson's existing operations. It aborted a plan to use Syracuse as a base to complete the work in Egypt. Despite shortages of provisions, Hood was still blockading Alexandria and Aboukir, taking a score of provision vessels in one fortnight, but seeing no end to his troubles. He had neither the strength to storm or bombard Alexandria nor the supplies to sustain an indefinite blockade. A Russo-Turkish fleet of twelve ships of the line and half a dozen large frigates was in the eastern Mediterranean, under Ushakov and Abdul Cadir Bey, but it disappointed. Russia and Turkey were deeply concerned about French interference in the Adriatic and Ionian seas, where they might use their bases in eastern Italy and the Ionian Islands to tamper with volatile and disaffected regions of the Ottoman empire. Ushakov therefore concentrated on clearing the French out of the Ionian Islands, a task that took him until the following March. It was important work, but with some justice Nelson blamed the Russian admiral for leaving the British to handle Egypt alone.[41]

The Turks, who had denounced the French as enemies of God in their declaration of war, rather attracted Nelson. He was a deeply religious man, as befitting a son of the Church of England. 'I own myself a believer in God, and if I have any merit in not fearing death it is because I feel that his power can shelter me when he pleases, and that I must fall whenever it is his good pleasure,' he said. Although religious, Nelson was never a bigot. A Protestant, he felt a unity with people of faith, whether Italian Catholics or Turkish Moslems, since all stood apart from the atheist undercurrent of French republicanism. The effectiveness of Turkish support was another matter, however. Between 19 and 21 October, seven cruisers and a dozen gunboats from the Turkish fleet arrived off Egypt, but four of the former ran out of provisions and left straightaway, and none of the latter were the bomb and fire vessels Nelson had requested. In action they hindered rather than helped. Hood thought the Turks 'deceitful' and 'impossible' to motivate, and all but one of their officers 'very bad'. Hallowell, who mounted several attacks upon Aboukir on successive days, was reduced to fury by the indiscipline of such allies. 'The cowardice of the Turks is not to be described,' he thundered. 'I made use of every argument in my power to get them forward. I kept in my boat ahead of them to lead them on, sometimes coaxing, sometimes damning and swearing at them for poltroons, but to very little effect.' Nelson hoped to mount a rescue, bringing Neapolitan warships and bomb vessels to attack Alexandria, but although Acton ordered the preparation of six mortar vessels 'for the service of Sicily, we shall say', the impending Neapolitan war soon swallowed every energy and resource. It was on such occasions that a disgruntled Nelson wished himself at sea. 'I am very unwell, and the miserable conduct of this court is not likely to cool my irritable temper,' he wrote at the end of September. 'It is a country of fiddlers and poets, whores and scoundrels.'[42]

If progress in Egypt was out of the question for the moment, Malta – Nelson's other ongoing operation – was not. At the beginning of November, Ball was due to supersede Niza in command of the blockade of Valletta, and Nelson saw an opportunity to make his first reconnaissance of the operation. He had overcome the greatest obstacle to the blockade by arranging for Sicily to supply the rebels and support the British and Portuguese ships. Sicily, in fact, claimed Malta as an historic possession, lost in the sixteenth century when the Knights of St John had assumed control. Now that Bonaparte had expelled the Knights, it was natural for Ferdinand to reassert his sovereign right, and Nelson saw no objection to it. At least it gave their Sicilian Majesties a stake in liberating the island, and provided a source of supplies. The admiral agreed that if he freed Malta he would restore it to Sicily, providing that Ferdinand undertook never to cede it to another power without British consent, and relinquished all captured French property to the captors. When Nelson sailed to Malta, therefore, he offered a basis for the blockade: the islanders accepted Sicilian sovereignty and raised Neapolitan colours, and in return could rely upon Ferdinand as well as the British for support.

Nelson had again anticipated his political masters, for on 3 October Grenville had written to Hamilton that if a war between Naples and France broke out the effective blockade of Malta would become a 'first' object. Although the island's political future had not been considered, he had added that while Britain had no ambitions to possess the island, Naples and Russia might have claims upon it. When Grenville was penning his letter, Ball was already preparing to leave with the advance guard of Nelson's force, the *Alexander*, two cruisers, *Terpsichore* and Josiah's *Bonne Citoyenne*, and a fireship, and on 15 October the admiral followed with the *Vanguard*, *Goliath*, *Minotaur* and *Audacious* ships of the line, the *Alliance* store ship and the *Earl St Vincent* cutter. Before leaving, Nelson entertained the Hamiltons, Ferdinand with other assorted royals, and his captains on his ship. He kissed the royal hand, and the king gave him 'a most cordial embrace'. Nelson swore he would 'serve him with the same zeal as he served his own royal master', and gave young Prince Leopold a 'long message' to take to his absent mother. Behind Nelson left Troubridge with the

Culloden, a cruiser and three transports, to stand on guard at Naples. Ahead, on the rocky, limestone, sun-baked island of Malta, the destiny of 90,000 souls was in his hand.[43]

5

Malta could not be ignored. Set in a ninety-mile narrows between Sicily and North Africa it controlled the traffic between the western and eastern basins of the Mediterranean. In the hands of the French, it would have been the perfect station for incursions into southern Italy, the Adriatic, the Levant and Egypt. Apart from his sympathy with the struggle of a small population seeking freedom, Nelson knew that Malta was a position that had to be secured. The question was how to do it.

It took Nelson nine days to reach Malta, where Niza, Ball and a Maltese deputation came to the *Vanguard* to brief him about the situation. Ball reckoned the French had 3000 men, of whom 700 were hospitalised, and 1500 Maltese levies of dubious loyalty. As the enemy fortifications needed 10,000 defenders, Nelson got the rosy notion that had he enough troops he could have gained control of one side of the Grand Harbour at Valletta and destroyed the enemy shipping. With no such force at his disposal, he unsuccessfully summoned the enemy to surrender, and then consigned himself to the one remaining option, a blockade that threatened to tie down ships, men and resources for many months.[44]

From the beginning Ball was far too optimistic. As early as 11 October he had predicted that the French would run out of powder and surrender 'in a few days'. A month later he was writing that the enemy had 'very few shells left, and only a small number of shot for their eighteen and twenty-four pounders. Great discontent prevails in the garrison. The soldiers want to capitulate and get home, and say they must cut off the heads of three of their principal men who are thieves . . .' Yet it is difficult to imagine that Nelson, who had cracked such hard nuts as Bastia in Corsica and Porto Ferraio in Elba, could have looked at the fortifications at Valletta other than with dismay. This was arguably the world's most impregnable fortress. Valletta was situated at the end of a peninsula that jutted out of Malta's eastern coast, dividing a bay into two harbours, one on either side. The town itself, a maze of streets in a grid formation, was encircled by huge fortifications. In three directions they overlooked water, and on the landward side the massive walls rose a hundred feet above deep, dry ditches. Across the harbours on either side of Valletta were further lines of fortifications, enabling the French to control all traffic in and out. In all, these fortifications extended for eight miles or more. They contained four powerful forts, St Elmo on the point of the peninsula, Ricasoli and St Angelo across the Grand Harbour to the south-east, and Manuel across Marsamxett Harbour to the north-west. Elsewhere the defences bristled with huge stone walls and multiple walls, star-shaped bastions, thirty-foot-thick parapets, commanding cavaliers, bomb proofs and tiers of guns. The Cotonera lines, which protected the rear of the Grand Harbour, alone contained ten bastions and demi-bastions and a curtain wall five thousand yards long. In the Grand Harbour sat three survivors from the Nile, *Le Guillaume Tell*, *Diane* and *Justice*; a Maltese sixty-four and a frigate that had been pressed into service; and a cutter and six galleys and gunboats, most beyond the range of any British guns. The French had more regulars than Nelson suspected, about four thousand, but if their numbers were too few for the ground they held, their real strength was their leader. Vaubois was one of the most experienced artillery officers in the French service, a veteran of the historic siege of Mantua, and perhaps the most obdurate opponent that Nelson ever faced. In Vaubois the Maltese and British had encountered a man who would hold his ground to the last extremity, a human stone wall.[45]

On the other side several thousand motivated but untrained Maltese held few strongpoints or arms. A dozen futile battering guns barked at the French positions, and what musket ammunition had been landed by Saumarez and Niza had been expended in violent exchanges. In November two fierce French sorties were bloodily repulsed, according to Ball with a loss to the enemy of 618 killed and wounded. None of the arms and supplies the Neapolitans had told Nelson they had sent had arrived. Barely able to hold their own, the Maltese could do nothing except shut the French out of the interior and cut some water pipes that were supplying the enemy garrison. Both Nelson and Vaubois recognised that this struggle would depend upon supplies. The British admiral landed twenty barrels of powder for Emmanuel Vitale, the principal Maltese leader, and sent the *Emerald* frigate to Naples to collect what had been promised. He told the rebels that if they drew up a petition covering their wants he would carry it to Ferdinand. The Maltese were being treated with 'total neglect and indifference' by the Two Sicilies, he stormed to Hamilton. Why, even a military officer they had sent was old, tired and palsied. He wanted 2000 muskets with ammunition, 4 or 5 mortars and howitzers, and 2500 shells. This was a tirade he would have to repeat time and again.[46]

Ball, and to some extent Nelson, underestimated the difficulty of winkling the French from their positions. Ultimately, the blockade would be the principal weapon, slow but inexorable. Nelson's prompt action in stifling French communications the previous month had made a fair start, but victuals and fresh water had to be kept flowing to the Maltese as well as the blockading squadron, and the ships themselves needed regular maintenance to withstand the wintry gales. The seas around the craggy Maltese shores were dangerous, and in November the *Emerald* was damaged when she ran ashore at a speed of nine knots. Nelson asked the Maltese to raise night lights at dangerous points to guide his captains in dark or dirty conditions. With Valletta in French hands, the British and

Portuguese used St Paul's Bay to the west and Marsa Scirocco (Marsaxlokk) Bay in the south of the island to shelter or land supplies, but neither were entirely suitable. Another complication was Niza's Portuguese squadron, which until now had borne the brunt of the blockade. Their ships were ill manned and in poor shape, and Nelson sent them to Naples to refit and reprovision, half suspecting they might use the opportunity to hightail it for Lisbon. Happily, he did his allies a great injustice. As Miss Knight remarked, Niza was 'a well-bred, good-natured man, much liked by all', including the British, and Nelson learned that he possessed the virtues of loyalty and commitment. Ball, who knew him better than most, spoke of his 'good abilities and very great merit'. Gathering experience, the Portuguese turned into major assets, and only one difficulty between the two allies developed. The English captains of Niza's ships affected to hold Portuguese ranks as 'commodores' and bucked at receiving orders from Ball and other senior British captains, all of whom had been schooled to an efficiency no other European service approached. After taking advice, Nelson was able to apprise them that the rank they held, *chef d'division*, did not equal the British commodore, which was effectively on a par with the Portuguese *chef d'escadre*. He ordered the 'commodores' to place themselves under Ball's orders.[47]

For a while ample supplies of bread and the wells inside Valletta saved the French from famine, but they also had to feed a substantial civilian population living within the fortifications, and imports were a necessity. The British and Portuguese shut down most of this traffic, except when northerly and north-westerly winds swept ships from their stations. Four of five dispatch boats from Toulon were intercepted, and between November and January perhaps a dozen provision boats were caught, trying to slip in from Sardinia, Spain and France, some coming by way of Tripoli using passes wangled from the British consul general of that port. Ball also intercepted vessels leaving Valletta, and burned one of several Greek vessels as a warning to the others not to return. Nonetheless, it was difficult to close Valletta completely. Vaubois was said to have got one set of dispatches out by means of a courier who represented himself to Nelson as a deserter from the French army.[48]

Having satisfied himself that the blockade was in as good order as could be expected, Nelson sent Ball to summon the surrender of a small French garrison that had been holding out in the neighbouring island of Gozo. This isolated outpost, held by 217 men, had refused Niza's summons ten days before, but yielded immediately to Nelson on 28 October, turning in twenty-four pieces of artillery, some powder and small arms, and a supply of corn. While the prisoners were taken aboard the *Vanguard* and *Minotaur*, no doubt relieved that their trial was over, Nelson retrieved the French colours, which he eventually delivered to Ferdinand with the claim that he had gained the king 16,000 new subjects.[49]

Leaving the *Alexander*, *Audacious* and *Goliath* ships of the line with Ball, Nelson eventually sailed for Naples with the *Vanguard* and *Minotaur*, sending Josiah ahead with the squadron's prizes. The British admiral reached the Neapolitan capital on 5 November, emerging from a storm that had carried away the flagship's main topsail yard and split some sails. He went straight to the Hamiltons at Caserta, but the next day forcibly tendered a list of the supplies needed at Malta to the king, sugaring the pill with the captured French colours. He was successful, and three Neapolitan warships were shortly on their way to Malta with guns, mortars and two thousand muskets for the rebels, while in December Nelson was able to spare a detachment of gunners, sent to Ball in the *Strombolo* bomb vessel.[50]

Nelson had promised to return for the first week in November, and his appearance was no doubt a relief. Mack had returned from reconnoitring the northern frontiers of the realm, and had a plan of campaign. Naples stood ready to challenge the most powerful military power in Europe. No one doubted the gravity of what was being attempted, and amidst continuing rumours of the build up of French forces in the Roman Republic, Maria Carolina begged Nelson to leave a ship in the bay lest their venture went badly. 'Our position is really deplorable and disastrous,' she wrote to Gallo. 'It is hoped that Heaven will produce a miracle in our favour.'[51]

V

NELSON'S GREAT GAMBLE

Thou great preserver, no 'twas thine
To snatch from faithless subjects and from
barbarous foes
A kingly race, from anguish and despair,
To save a royal heroine and prop
The tottering ruins of a falling state.

Cornelia Knight, 'Lines written after a walk
at Villa Luichesi, near Palermo, with
Lady Hamilton and Lord Nelson,
March 31, 1799'

I

THE brief voyage to Malta provides us with a fresh clutch of letters between Nelson and the Hamiltons that indicate how the bonds between them were tightening. This new triumvirate was more intense than the old, for whereas Fanny and Edmund had managed Nelson's domestic affairs, they were not intrinsic partners in his professional career. Theirs were quiet retired existences, away from the babble of public affairs, of which they knew relatively little. The Hamiltons were different. They talked politics, policies and princes, and could counsel as well as listen. When Nelson was away they opened his mail and often acted on his behalf. They were invaluable intermediaries between an admiral who knew no Italian and a government that had little English, and were steeped in the etiquette, customs and nuances needed in Neapolitan society. All three regarded the interests of Britain and Naples as one and saw few contradictions in serving both. Theirs was a partnership of both the private and the public, and therefore the more inextricable.

Nelson had raised the Hamiltons to the summit of their influence in Italy, and Emma in particular, starved of status in times past, was particularly electrified by her role as a highway between Naples and Britain. Maria Carolina was often unwell and regularly communicated with her friend by letters which betray the tenor of their face-to-face meetings. 'How I envy you the sight of the hero!' ran one royal missive. 'Tell him all I feel of pride, admiration and gratitude for him and his brave companions . . . Send me word . . . what news he brings of our enemies. In a word, let your kindness inform me of everything.' In so singular a position, as confidante of a lonely monarch, an ageing ambassador and a disabled and ailing admiral, Emma imbibed a great deal of political information that, with her bilingual skills, enabled her to function in their company.[1]

The letters she sent after Nelson, gloriously misspelled and unpunctuated, tumbled excitedly from one subject to another, vibrant, enthusiastic, loving and flattering, and a man so constitutionally in need of care found himself being pleasurably sucked into the world they were making together. We can imagine Nelson, alone in his cabin and desperate to feel important to somebody, opening these endearingly familiar outpourings from a beautiful woman. On 20 October she was infusing the queen with 'our spirit and energy' but confessed 'how miserable we were for some days' after he left for Malta. But 'now hopes of your return revives us'. He must write and 'come soon, for you are wanted at Caserta. All their noddles are not worth yours.' A few days later she was telling him about the arrival of a Kelim Effendi, sent by the sultan with the chelengk and scarlet pelisse lined with sable that Nelson had been awarded. She was beside herself with joy, but 'if I was King of England I would make you the most noble puissant *Duke Nelson*, *Marquis Nile*, *Earl Alexander*, Viscount Pyramid, Baron Crocodile and Prince Victory that posterity might have you in all forms'. I give the next letter exactly as she wrote it:

> How you are beloved, for not onely with her Majesty, but of [at] the Generals [Acton's] house you was our theme, and my full heart is fit to Burst with pleasure when I hear your honored name but enugh now for the day . . . I must see the [Turkish] present[.] how I shall look at it smel[l] it taste it & tuch it put the pelice over my own shoulders look in the glas & say vivo il Turk . . . god bless or Mahomet bless the old Turk [Effendi] but how every body loves & esteems you Tis universal from the high to the low oh do you know I sing now nothing but the conquering hero I send it you alter'd by myself & and sang it comes very fine & affecting I sang it to Trowbridge & [John] Waller [of the *Emerald*] yesterday . . . your statue ought to be made of pure gold & placed in the middle of London never never was there such a Battle . . . & the Queen yesterday said to me the more I think on it the greater I find it & I feel such gratitude to the warrior the glorious Nelson that my respect is such I could fall at his honer'd feet & kiss then you that know us boath & how alike we are in many things that is I as Emma Hamilton & she as Queen of Naples imagine us *boath* speaking of you we talk ourselves into Tears of rapture wonder respect & admiration & conclude Thir is not such another in the world I told her Majesty we onely wanted Ldy

> Nelson to be the female tria juncta in uno for we all love you and yet all three differently & yet all equaly . . .[2]

As the reference to Fanny implies, at this time Emma had no idea of supplanting her, and remained contented with her own husband, whatever his shortcomings. 'He is the best husband, friend, I wish I could say father also, but I should be too happy if I had the blessing of having children, so must be content,' she said. Nonetheless, her growing dependence upon Nelson was showing. 'Thank God the first week in November is near . . . for we love you dearly,' she added. It was music to Nelson's ears, and, struggling with a bad cough brought by the sea air, he looked forward to the hospitality the Hamiltons provided. By the middle of October he was writing to them almost compulsively, even when he had nothing to say. 'My dear Madam,' he wrote on 16 October, using a form of address fast disappearing, 'I honor and respect you and my dear friend Sir William Hamilton, and believe me ever, your faithful and affectionate Nelson.' It was the first letter Emma received in which Nelson used his new title, as word of his peerage reached him at Malta. On the face of it, Nelson also maintained the status quo, but the personal attractiveness of his female host, and its potentially destructive nature, was not being missed. 'I am writing opposite Lady Hamilton,' he wrote to his commander-in-chief as early as 4 October. 'Therefore, you will not be surprised at the glorious jumble of this letter. Was your Lordship in my place, I much doubt if [you] could write so well. Our hearts and hands must be all in a flutter. Naples is a dangerous place, and we must keep clear of it.'[3]

The intimacy that was developing within the walls of the Palazzo Sessa was important, not least because of the role it played in Nelson's professional career. The admiral had orders from his government to support the kingdom of the Two Sicilies, and knew the loyalty they had shown Britain between 1793 and 1798. Apart from these obligations, Nelson had come to recognise the political instrumentality of Naples, which he now saw as a lever to reach Austria and Russia. These were solid reasons for the close attention Nelson paid the Two Sicilies, but they were being reinforced by powerful personal emotions. No country, not even his own, had valued Nelson as much as Naples, a recognition he found deeply satisfying. And Emma's tremendous affection for the Queen of Naples was another kind of cement. Extraordinarily close to both the admiral and the queen, Lady Hamilton enthused about both, and strengthened the view each held of the other. Nelson felt a growing emotional commitment to the Italian kingdom and the possibility of a conflict of interests. As he wrote to Emma in October, 'all my views are to serve and save the Two Sicilies, and to do that which their [Sicilian] Majesties may wish me, even against my own opinion'. His 'whole study' was to meet the queen's approval. To Sir William he admitted, 'Now I feel employed in the service of their Sicilian Majesties.'[4]

As Nelson was solidly in tune with his responsibilities and orders, few saw anything untoward about the admiral's relationships with the Hamiltons or their Sicilian Majesties during these months. Among the brothers the most sceptical was Troubridge. During Nelson's excursion to Malta, he was at Naples, directing a storm of intemperate letters to Hamilton, peopled with 'an Irish rascal who calls himself the American vice-consul', a British vice-consul at Sicily who had authored 'a dirty trick', a 'crimp', deserters and 'shabby' Neapolitan office holders, all of whom, in one way or another, had obstructed his duties. Speedily descending into furious rants ('Dear Sir, The plot begins to thicken'), Troubridge showed little inclination to compromise ('To get rid of the fellow send him a copy of the deposition if you think it necessary') and was developing a hatred of the Neapolitan administration. 'I will *serve them, and serve them well*, but by God, I will *ever despise them*,' he raged. Recognising the potential for trouble, Hamilton tried to calm him down. Sir Thomas was under terrific strain, suffering professional frustration and personal bereavement, and he was the avowed foe of inefficiency and corruption, but as yet he had no criticisms of either the royal family or Nelson. That disillusionment lay in the future.[5]

Fanny's letters were also free of overt suspicions in those last months of 1798. The letters that Nelson addressed to his wife were full of the Hamiltons, and extolled Emma's success in reforming Josiah. Hoping to please, Emma herself sent Fanny an 'ode' Miss Knight had written in honour of the hero and a fan mount, and said that the company at Naples only wanted her with them to be 'completely happy'. She heaped praise on Josiah, but perhaps unwittingly trod on a dainty foot when admitting that 'although we quarrel sometimes, he loves me, and does as I would have him'. A more suspicious woman than Fanny might have wondered if she was being replaced as a wife and a mother. But it does not seem to have been so. Davison twice wrote to Nelson of Fanny's anxieties and indifferent health. The admiral had 'done enough' and his 'object now ought to be that of contributing to that tranquillity and comfort of your inestimable wife, whose anxiety may be conceived but never expressed by words'. The prize agent wanted Nelson home, but not as far as is known because of any dark suspicions of his fidelity. Fanny's worries probably related to her husband's head wound. If we may believe Miss Knight, Nelson was speaking of his wife 'with the greatest affection and respect' and referring to his wedding day as the 'happiest' of his life.[6]

Yet for all this the Hamilton–Nelson relationship moved forward with considerable speed. St Vincent, at least, saw the danger, remembering Nelson's liaison with his Italian mistress, Adelaide Correglia, and wrote to Emma on 28 October. 'Pray do not let your fascinating Neapolitan dames approach too near him,' he warned, 'for he is made of flesh and blood, and cannot resist their temptations.'[7]

2

Nelson had left Naples in October in 'perfect' health but returned considerably the worse for wear, and full of insinuations of impending death. Such ominous predictions often appeared in his letters, usually when he felt both ill and ill used, and sometimes they denoted nothing more than an appeal for sympathy. News from England had dried up, and only a thin trickle of private letters from Spencer reached his desk. Even St Vincent was unusually silent. Nelson, now used to constant acclamation, felt ignored and isolated. The truth was that his superiors had nothing to add to Nelson's knowledge of affairs off Italy, and were in entire agreement with his activities. Their relative silence was a tribute to their belief in him. But the little admiral did not see it that way. Spencer was neglecting him, and St Vincent jealous of his newfound fame.[8]

Nelson's dissatisfaction is, nevertheless, understandable. He was effectively handling the affairs of the Mediterranean with one hand and no formal secretariat. John Tyson, a purser, was a scribe, but Nelson drafted much of his correspondence himself, tied for long hours to his desk at the Palazzo Sessa, Villina (a country house the Hamiltons owned some sixteen miles from Naples) or in his cabin. Emma helped, and also forced him out for an hour's constitutional every day. Indeed, both Hamiltons treated him with 'inexpressible goodness', Sir William thinking his friend 'the most humane and active man I ever met', and Emma idolising the deck beneath his feet. Still, these long laborious hours and a hacking cough convinced the admiral that his health was failing and that he would not be able to maintain his command for long.[9]

Two developments accentuated his unease. His relationship with Emma was deepening, something that was as troubling as it was intoxicating. This is the import of letters Emma sent after Nelson when he sailed to Leghorn in November. They hint at the jealousy that would be such a striking feature of their mature romance in 1801, when mutual distrust led the couple to ban each other from meeting dangerous members of the opposite sex whenever they were apart. This singular custom first appears during the Leghorn expedition, and we can suggest why. The Hamiltons almost certainly knew about Adelaide, the mistress Nelson had maintained in Leghorn a few years before. Our last record puts her in Porto Ferraio in 1797, but the arrangement was temporary, and it is entirely possible that she had re-established herself in her old home. Whatever, for the first time Emma tried to prevent Nelson going ashore. 'Pray keep yourself well for our sakes,' she wrote on 24 November, '*and do not go on shore of Leghorn*. There is no comfort there for you.' And the next day she wrote again, 'Everybody here prays for you . . . but Sir William and I are so anxious that we neither eat, drink, or sleep, and tell [till] you are safely landed and come back, we shall feel much . . . Lady K[night], Miss K[night], Campbell and Josiah dined today with us, but alas, your place at [the] table was occupied by Lady

K. For God's sake, turn back soon. Pray do you have no occasion *to go on shore at Leghorn*. I could have cried and felt so low spirited.' Though missed by most writers, these underlined allusions – which replicate one of the most astonishing and destructive features of the fully-fledged passion – tell us that Emma's feelings for Nelson had already gone beyond that of the dutiful hostess and admiring friend. The most reasonable inference is that she feared Adelaide, or someone like Adelaide.[10]

Nelson and Emma both had histories to live down. Emma's was the most notorious, but Nelson had a number of relationships behind him, including a mild flirtation with a married woman, who, like Emma, had been more than thirty years younger than her husband. He would not have missed the significance of Lady Hamilton's remarks, although it would be some months yet before he put his true feelings on paper. 'You and good Sir William', he would write in May, 'have spoiled me for any place but with you.' The words were vividly prophetic.[11]

The other reason for Nelson's unease during the autumn of 1798 was far more momentous than any private affair. The whole of Italy was suddenly convulsed by war. To the east great powers were joining the struggle earlier than Nelson anticipated. He planned to send Troubridge to Corfu, hoping to stimulate the Ionian islanders to rise against their French masters, and was preparing inflammatory proclamations to that effect. Suspicious of the spread of Russia, his idea was to gain an early foothold in those islands, but Ushakov anticipated the ploy and by mid-November the Russo-Turkish fleet had expelled the French from all the Ionian Islands save Corfu, where an enemy garrison held out until the following March.

But if Russia moved, Italy's recognised defender, Austria, remained paralysed. In fact, her evasive messages grew more disillusioning as the extent of the Neapolitan preparations for war became apparent. Towards the middle of October, France delivered one thunderbolt by threatening to retaliate against Tuscany and the papacy if Austria went to war. The Grand Duke (the emperor's brother) and the pope would be taken to Paris. There seemed little doubt that conflict would embroil all three sister states, Austria, Naples and Tuscany, and probably others, too. Austria warned the Grand Duke to prepare a line of retreat, and remove his most valuable effects to safety, and poured cold water on the Neapolitan war plan. The liberal interpretation of her defence treaty with Naples, which had recently encouraged Ferdinand, was now withdrawn. In November, Thugut emphasised that Austria would not support a hostile move on the part of Ferdinand, and that the emperor was prepared to 'leave him to his own means'. This was not illogical. Despite her part in bringing Britain to the Mediterranean, and suggestions that she would support the expulsion of the French from Italy, Austria had done little to prepare her army and saw the winter approaching. Her policy was one of procrastination, perhaps hoping for a more propitious time to fight a war that even she regarded as inevitable. However, the future remained an unknown place. Britain, Russia and Turkey were already engaged, French naval power had been annihilated, and Naples – weighing the grim tidings to the north, and listening to intelligence that largely pointed one way – did not feel she had time to wait.[12]

The thought that Austria might actually abandon Naples sent an icy shiver through coalition diplomats. In Vienna Eden was so baffled that he wondered whether some personal enmity between Thugut and Acton might be behind it, while in Whitehall a despairing Grenville could only suppose that Austria was secretly negotiating a separate peace with France. Emma's letters had warned Nelson that negotiations with Austria were not going well. Though the queen had written to her daughter, the empress, and sent Gallo to Vienna to argue Ferdinand's cause, the emperor had sent a 'cold, unfriendly, mistrustful frenchified' letter 'saying plainly – help yourselves', and then appeared to relent. 'The Emperor [h]as thought better,' Emma said, 'and will assist them. The war is to be declared religious.' Emma urged Maria Carolina to act anyway rather than forgo the advantages to be gained by a pre-emptive strike, for 'sure, their poor fool of a son [in-law, the emperor] will not – cannot – but come out.' According to her own account, Emma told the queen that posterity would castigate her if she allowed her country to be ruined, the royal family destroyed and her friends sacrificed rather than fight the enemies of her religion and murderers of her sister.[13]

Something also had to be done about Tuscany. She, no less than Naples, was sure that the French forces marching into Italy were to be wielded against her. Intelligence from Italy and the Tuscan minister in Paris convinced the Grand Duke that his kingdom was on the brink of an invasion. He, too, appealed to the emperor (his brother) 'to save this country' and likewise received unconvincing 'promises of protection'. Another appeal went to Ferdinand, whom the Grand Duke begged to 'make overtures to Admiral Nelson, requesting their [Britain's] powerful assistance in these perilous times'. Wyndham, the British minister in Tuscany, added his voice. The Grand Duke's benevolent and tolerant rule had endeared him to Tuscans, but he lived in daily 'dread . . . that the next day may finish his reign'. Through Hamilton, Wyndham called upon Ferdinand 'to save this country from French invasion' by marching a force into Tuscany to secure Orbetello, a port in the southern part of the realm. The objectives, he said, were to 'protect Tuscany from any insult, give a safe retreat to this court in case of surprise, and place His Sicilian Majesty in a situation not only to preserve this country, but also to cut off the enemy's retreat from Rome by this way, and place the French and Romans between two fires'. Although Wyndham hoped that Austria and Naples could act in concert, he solicited unilateral action from Naples.[14]

These, then, were the circumstances that met Nelson upon his return from

Malta. Their Sicilian Majesties called a council of war on 12 November, and Nelson and Hamilton were invited to the camp at San Germano, below Monte Cassino, where the army was mobilising. The review of the troops on the appointed day was spectacular. Thirty-two thousand horse and foot were drawn up for inspection, and the queen moved along their front line on horseback, attired in an imposing blue riding habit with a gold fleur-de-lis collar and a white plumed hat. Mack told Nelson 'that he had never in all his experience seen so fine a body of men'. Nelson agreed about the soldiers, but not about Mack, who managed to get himself surrounded in manoeuvres. Damas saw more. The Neapolitan army had been increased from fifteen to fifty thousand troops in six weeks, but neither the veterans nor the recruits had been in a battle. Most were 'peasants in uniform, who had never been drilled before and were afraid to fire their muskets'.[15]

That evening the basics of the campaign were agreed. Mack's army, with Ferdinand as its figurehead, would march from San Germano on about the 23rd, leaving a second force of 30,000 to maintain a defensive position in Naples. Nelson proposed an answer to some of the concerns of Tuscany. Pursuing an earlier suggestion, he would take a small squadron of ships and five thousand Neapolitan troops to Leghorn and seize the port, providing Ferdinand gave him a letter to the Grand Duke facilitating entry. Moreover, he was ready to begin the following morning. Such a move could threaten the French rear and would prevent them from using Leghorn to import supplies or reinforcements, but the principal objective was to secure a retreat for the Grand Duke and his retinue and government. True to his word, Nelson had a squadron ready to embark the necessary troops and equipage at six the following morning, but when he called at Caserta to take leave of the royal family he found them 'in great distress'. A courier had brought another discouraging response from Vienna, emphasising that for Austria to join Ferdinand the French, not the Neapolitans, must be the aggressors. Nelson had no patience with such timorous talk, and flatly urged the campaign forward, if necessary without the prior agreement of the emperor. As he reported it, 'I ventured to tell their Majesties directly that one of the following things must happen to the king, and he had his choice: either to advance, trusting to God for his blessing on a just cause; to die with *l'épée à la main*; or remain quiet and be kicked out of your kingdoms. The king replied he would go on and trust in God.'[16]

At the time Nelson's involvement satisfied his superiors, although there was some criticism after the event. But something had changed. Nelson had ventured upon an enormous gamble. He now knew that the campaign was going ahead without the approval of Austria, although the emperor's military support was essential. 'The event God only knows,' he wrote, 'but without the assistance of the emperor . . . this country cannot resist the power of the French.' He was bargaining that whatever the emperor or Thugut had said beforehand, they would not stand by and watch Naples, and by implication Tuscany, fall. He was using Naples to bounce Austria into the coalition by presenting the Austrians with a situation they could not ignore. Probably most British diplomats, had they put their hands on their hearts, would have predicted that the emperor would intervene rather than see his sister states cut to pieces. Nelson gambled that it was so. If it went well, he stood to bring a mighty coalition into being, capable perhaps of ending the European war. But if it failed kingdoms were at stake. No one expressed the grim mixture of apprehension and resolution that ensued better than the queen. 'Each step of the troops is a stab in my heart,' she said. 'The die is cast.'[17]

The decision was based on several unsafe premises. Apart from anything else, the Neapolitan treasury was not up to a protracted struggle, and Ferdinand hoped Britain might contribute to his war chest. Yet Hamilton, who was drafting a treaty of alliance between Britain and Naples, had been forbidden from agreeing to any such subsidy. Ferdinand urged Hamilton to appeal, and Nelson threw his weight behind it, but how far either Briton thought the subsidy a reasonable aspiration is open to question. Hamilton must have known the prospects were poor. As for Nelson, he expected the Austrians to rally, but underestimated the elemental weaknesses in the Neapolitan army which would have to bear the brunt of the initial fighting. Most fundamentally of all, no one in the Neapolitan high command, lest it was Gallo, gauged the true extent of Austrian intransigence.[18]

Nonetheless, on 22 November the Neapolitan army marched north in seven columns, trudging over difficult, rain-sluiced, rutted roads beneath leaden skies, and fording a river, the baggage labouring behind in wagons that constantly sank axle-deep in mud. Despite Mack's reconnaissance, no bridge had been thrown across the River Melfa, and the men forded it, slipping and stumbling with the water surging rapidly under their armpits, their muskets, cartouche boxes and packs held over their heads. Most of the baggage had to be abandoned. Ferdinand and Acton, the former representing himself as the defender of the faith and champion of liberty, accompanied the advance in their carriages, tossed from rut to rut. As they struggled towards the French positions they found that even this had surprised their opponents, who had never quite believed that the Neapolitans would try it. Jean-Etienne Championnet, the Gallic commander in the Roman Republic, had 26,000 men, but he bleated specious protests about breaches of a treaty with Naples that his own government had effectively torn up by their illegal occupation of the papal dominion, and withdrew without fighting to play for time. The campaign had started, painfully but to plan, though none could say where it was going.[19]

Nelson immediately did his part. He had no reservations about committing British ships to the enterprise, for the sake of Tuscany if no other. If Leghorn was not secured, he said, it would be lost to the French within 'one week' of the opening of the campaign. His worry was that the Tuscans might object to any part of their territory being occupied, even by a friendly power. It was agreed that Ferdinand would smooth the way with letters to the Grand Duke and his minister in Tuscany, the Duke of Sangro, officially notifying them that Nelson was coming to occupy Leghorn in response to the requests for protection and that his only object was the support of the Grand Duke and his 'family, country, laws and neutrality'. These letters, supported by one Hamilton addressed to Wyndham, left Naples in the *Terpsichore* frigate on 18 November. Acton expressed gratitude for Nelson's cooperation. 'This is another service of importance which Lord Nelson renders to Italy in saving Leghorn with this expedition,' he wrote.[20]

For a few days troops, baggage and artillery were embarked on the British ships, but they got away on 22 November, encountering the same miserable weather that battered the Neapolitan army. Two Neapolitan ships under Caracciolo sailed for Palermo to collect two regiments of cavalry for Leghorn, but Nelson led the main force direct from Naples in the *Vanguard*. With him sailed the *Culloden* and *Minotaur* ships of the line; two small cruisers, *La Bonne Citoyenne* and the *Balloon*; the *Alliance* store ship and a cutter; the Portuguese capital ships *Principe Real*, *Alfonso d'Albuquerque* and *St Sebastian*, and a brig, *Benjamin*. They carried 5123 infantry, including a detachment of artillerymen, battering guns and army stores and provisions under the command of an elderly lieutenant general named Diego Naselli, who sailed on the flagship. Most of Ferdinand's own warships, and the *Rheine de Portugal* remained at Naples to provide security for the royal family, and Nelson promised to return as soon as possible. Before marching upon Rome, the king had begged Nelson to station himself at Naples, both to 'advise' the queen in his absence and 'in case of accident to take care of her and her family'. Whatever Ferdinand's deficiencies, this was a man going to war and entrusting Nelson with the safety of the family he left behind, and the admiral saw the duty as 'sacred'.[21]

Heavy and persistent rain and wind dogged Nelson's voyage north, and during the first night Josiah's *La Bonne Citoyenne* and all three Portuguese seventy-fours were scattered. The *Alliance* disappeared later in the day. When Nelson got into the northern road of Leghorn at about three in the afternoon of 28 November, he had lost some half of his troops at a critical moment. Nor was the reception quite what Nelson expected. He had come, he thought, to aid Tuscany at the behest of her government, but quickly discovered that the Grand Duke's administration was deeply divided about how to handle the crisis. On the one side the appeasers under the Marquis Manfredini shrank from offending France and wanted to negotiate for whatever shred of independence they could salvage. To them Nelson was an unwelcome provocation. Those seeking his intervention were led by the nation's first minister, Chevalier Francesco Seratti, and, although they had the ear of the Grand Duke, they by no means commanded impregnable ground. Indeed, the emergency appeal to Naples and Nelson had apparently been sent secretly by the Grand Duke, Seratti and the British minister, Wyndham, without being laid before the national council. The admiral had not come to a country ready to receive him as a deliverer, but to one unsure of what steps to take.[22]

On arrival Naselli summoned the fortifications to yield in the name of the King of Naples without thinking it necessary to ask Nelson to add his signature. 'I am certain that I was never more hurt in my life,' chafed the admiral, 'being clearly considered by the general as nothing, as a master of a transport.' Before Naselli's boat could reach the mole it was intercepted. The *Terpsichore* had brought the explanatory letters from the King of Naples and Hamilton to Leghorn on 23 November, and the Grand Duke had decided to receive Ferdinand's force but he had to manage the matter delicately. As soon as Nelson appeared, Wyndham and Sangro, the Neapolitan minister, put out in a boat, turned Naselli's back, and made for the British flagship to discuss protocol with Lord Nelson. In a long interview the ministers said that the summons would carry more weight countersigned by Nelson, and satisfied themselves that the newcomers had come to rescue the port from the French and not to destroy its neutral status. Thus armed, they personally took the revised summons ashore, and conferred with Seratti and the governor of the town, De La Villette. Nelson demanded possession of the port, and stated his readiness to use force if refused. This was not in itself undesirable. If the Tuscans needed to deny their complicity in the occupation of Leghorn, they could present the document as proof that they had merely submitted to a greater power. The formal document of capitulation, which included the signatures of Sangro and Wyndham, went back to the *Vanguard* at about 8.30 in the evening. Despite the darkness and a gathering gale, Nelson landed the troops under Naselli and Troubridge and occupied the forts before midnight. The next day, 29 November, he took possession of the batteries at the mole head and the task was almost complete. Leghorn was secured.[23]

Perhaps the Grand Duke hoped the Neapolitan soldiers could keep Leghorn out of enemy hands until his own forces were brought up to strength. A voluntary loan was being collected, arms stockpiled in Leghorn and an army of 40,000 men recruited. Momentarily, even the Tuscan council seemed to be in accord, but revealing difficulties with the occupying force soon arose. The catalyst was the shipping Nelson found in Leghorn, which included a score of French privateers and seventy to eighty Genoese merchant vessels, almost all of which had been shipping provisions to the French. The admiral knew that the French had been abusing the neutrality of the port, which should have been open and safe to ships of all flags. Gallic privateers had been using it as a base from which to pounce upon British ships, with the result that none dared approach except in convoy and under armed escort. The French had also been using the port to send grain to their troops in Italy, hiding the shipments under neutral flags and false papers that described them as the legitimate imports of Leghorn merchants. In fact, early on 29 November a Genoese merchantman arrived in the roads laden with corn for the French, and two Genoese warships, the *Equality* of twenty-two guns and the *Tigre* of eighteen guns. Nelson took all three, and claimed that he had seized 'the *whole* Ligurian navy'.[24]

Unabashed by seizures that might have been interpreted as a breach of the neutrality of the port, Nelson then went further. In the negotiations that led to the surrender of the fortifications, he had undertaken to honour the neutrality of Leghorn. But now he effectively tore up the agreement, and decided to seize all the French and Genoese ships in the port. Wyndham was horrified, and hurried a letter to the admiral. Surely Nelson had come as a protector, not a conqueror; he had come to rescue the Grand Duke, not force him out of his neutrality and lay his weak kingdom open to reprisals from the French. He pointed out that even if Leghorn itself was temporarily protected by Nelson's force, the other Tuscan ports were almost defenceless. The admiral himself had written from Caserta, promising that the Grand Duke would suffer no injury. If he had had reservations about the capitulation, he should have returned it at the time, stating his disapproval. Wyndham trod gingerly, avoiding provocative words, but explained to Hamilton that while 'neutrality is not violated' the port might become compromised through a 'misunderstanding'. He obviously felt that the British were not playing fair, and it even crossed his mind that a spirit of revenge might be abroad, a form of payback for 1796 when the French had occupied Leghorn and confiscated considerable property owned by the resident British merchants. Not only had London always instructed him to respect the neutrality of Leghorn, the minister said, but the Grand Duke had agreed to submit the British claims for the losses of 1796 to the judgement of any European sovereign Britain named.[25]

There is little doubt that Nelson wilfully broke the terms upon which he had secured the surrender of Leghorn. He admitted as much in a private memorandum written for the Hamiltons on 2 December. When he saw the capitulation, he said, he disapproved of the reference to Leghorn's neutrality being respected, but declined to raise the issue: 'although I considered this part of the paper signed by the ministers as impossible, and although the governor's acquiescence to the admission of the troops was founded in appearance on the good faith of the paper signed by the ministers of the two courts, I thought my object was to get possession [of the port] on any terms, and that I should be ready to take all or any part of the odium of breaking them for the advantage of His Royal Highness the Great Duke and the King of Naples'. Put bluntly, once the fortifications were in British–Neapolitan hands, the terms could be dishonoured in the wider interests of the countries concerned. The ends justified the means.

After receiving Wyndham's mildly worded protest, Nelson replied that, although he could not regard Leghorn as neutral, he had not come to plunder, and would go ashore to ensure order. Despite wind and rain he did so, and claimed that 'all Leghorn turned out to show due respect'. At some time the Russian minister in Tuscany tipped him off that the French privateers at the mole were planning to break out that night. Nelson accordingly had the *Flora* cutter and several ships' boats patrolling off the mole head throughout the hours of darkness with orders to board any privateer that attempted to leave.[26]

It is not difficult to see Nelson's logic. As the presence of nearly an hundred privateers and victuallers showed, Leghorn's neutrality was being ritually abused by the French. Unprotected British ships dared not approach, and if they had by some marvel got in, they could not have left without being chased by corsairs. Tuscany had simply been too weak to preserve effective neutral status. Now that Nelson had scooped all this shipping up, he had no intention of loosing those corsairs on British commerce, or allowing the supplies from French-controlled Genoa to succour the army that was confronting Ferdinand on his march north. It was true that Nelson was meeting one abuse with another, but, in a war this desperate, fire had sometimes to be met with fire. That, at least, was presumably how the admiral looked at it. His answer to Wyndham, who worried about reprisals, was that the Grand Duke should disavow what had occurred, for Nelson was quite happy for the 'odium' to descend upon 'the Neapolitan general and myself'. This, justifying what some would have seen as a dishonourable deception, was nothing if not the voice of a hugely self-confident man sure in his service to the greater good.[27]

Naselli, though, felt uncomfortable under such a glare, and protested with an argument that had nothing to do with Tuscany. Naples had studiously avoided declaring war on France so as not to appear an aggressor. Her army had advanced providing opportunities for their enemies to fall back peacefully, but what was going on in Leghorn was an act of war. As the commander of a British squadron, Nelson might have replied that *his* country most certainly was at war, a muddy contention tantamount to taking the 'odium' upon himself rather than let it fall upon his Neapolitan partners. But in this case he insisted Naples itself flexed its muscles. Referring to the blockade of Malta and the march north, he remarked that a conflict existed of a sufficient scale to justify the seizure of the privateers. Naselli was persuaded to leave matters be until he had received further orders from the king, On 3 December the admiral sent his own letter to Hamilton, demanding that authority be sent to seize the privateers. Naselli, he said, lacked backbone. 'The general prudently, and certainly safely, awaits the orders of this court, taking no responsibility on himself. I act from the circumstances of the moment, as I feel it may be the most advantageous for the honour of the cause which I serve, taking all responsibility upon myself,' he said.[28]

Nelson needed to return to Naples to redeem his promise to the king, and declining an invitation of the Grand Duke to dine at Pisa, he sailed on 30

November. Troubridge remained with the *Culloden*, *Minotaur*, *Terpsichore* and *Bonne Citoyenne*, armed with orders to cruise to and from the Riviera, destroying as much of the Genoese trade as possible, and to look regularly into Leghorn to support Naselli and collect any fresh instructions. No shrinking violet, Troubridge was contemptuous of 'the old fool' who commanded the Neapolitan troops, and decisively pushed matters forward. On Nelson's recommendation, he packed 250 French agitators, mostly privateers, into a couple of boats and shipped them to Genoa, and disarmed and disbanded all their vessels. The cargoes of the Genoese merchantmen were confiscated before the ships were released with single ballasts. No claim appears to have been made on the part of the British for prize money. As Nelson remarked, 'The world, I know, think[s] that money is our God, and now they will be undeceived as far as [it] relates to us.'[29]

Nelson was back in Naples on 5 December feeling ill and low. He saw a city racked by uncertainty. The French minister, Jean-Pierre Lacombe St Michel, finally got away with his legation on 10 December, only to be captured at sea by a Tunisian cruiser and reduced to beseeching a British consul for his release and safe passage. The Neapolitan government issued a proclamation rallying their people behind the king's crusade to restore the supremacy of the Catholic Church in the Roman Republic, but no one knew what would happen if the French reached their gates.

The smell of political instability unleashed many underlying tensions. All monarchies, even 'enlightened' ones such as Tuscany, were threatened in such circumstances, and the Kingdom of the Two Sicilies had many springs of internal discontent. To strengthen her government and raise additional revenues to reform the armed services and meet the rising costs of administration, Maria Carolina had confronted the fiscal exemptions and privileges of the Church, the feudal nobility and such city oligarchies as those in Naples and Palermo. The reforms had faltered after the outbreak of the French Revolutionary wars, easing the pressure upon the *ancien régime* and frustrating advocates of change, calling for a widening of the access to wealth and power and greater rewards for talent and enterprise. In 1792 some strands of this radical critique, gaining among the educated, professional and middle classes, had even extended to Jacobinism, espousing the benefits of republicanism. A relatively bloodless purge had tempered but not extinguished the movement, which simmered in an urban minority, but there was no telling what opportunities it might make of a French invasion. The Bourbons had grounds to question the loyalties of several elements within, from disgruntled aristocrats to re-emergent Jacobins. They felt relatively sure of the support of the clergy, in whose cause they had ostensibly marched to Rome, but vested their greatest faith in the common people and poor. The monarchy's attempts to reform land tenure and create a class of peasant farmers may not have made much headway, and army conscription was unpopular, but

Ferdinand still commanded the overwhelming fidelity of the humbler classes. In this complicated mix, Nelson had no doubt that his role was to stand ready to protect the regime if events took a dangerous turn. He was not blind to the need for reforms in the Two Sicilies, and often ventured to say so, but he believed he was serving the majority of the Neapolitan and Sicilian peoples, who supported their king, as well as his country's most faithful ally.

His spirits were also depressed by a letter Spencer had written to St Vincent about the expected promotion of the first lieutenants who had been at the Nile. 'I sincerely hope this is not intended to exclude the first [lieutenant] of the *Culloden*,' Nelson wrote to his commander-in-chief angrily. 'For Heaven's sake, for my sake, if it is so, get it altered. Our dear friend Troubridge has suffered enough . . . His sufferings were in every respect more than any of us [at the Nile]. He deserves every reward which a grateful country can bestow on the most meritorious sea-officer of his standing in the service. I have felt his worth every hour of my command. I have before wrote you, my dear Lord, on this subject. Therefore I place Troubridge in your hands.' To Spencer he repeated that the *Culloden*'s 'misfortune was great in getting aground, while her most fortunate companions were in the full tide of happiness'. But 'Captain Troubridge on shore is superior to captains afloat'.[30]

Nelson felt for Troubridge, but also saw the Admiralty's neglect as a slight upon himself, in keeping with the long silences and parsimonious rewards. As usual on such occasion, he dwelt upon his bad health and talked about going home. His short, drifting letter to Spencer on 18 December suggests that he was writing almost for the sake of it, referring despondently to his mortality as he often did. Without doubt he was feeling the weight of his awesome responsibilities, and a lack of interest and reassurance.[31]

With minimal resources Nelson was fighting his war on four weighty fronts, and, despite the consumption of lemons and onions, scurvy was appearing in the ranks of his forces. Ball was blockading Malta with a skeleton force, devoid of such basic supplies as slops and bedding, and trying to inspire a native population without bread in its mouth. In Egypt Bonaparte's army had been thrown back from Cairo, and was rumoured to be dropping with disease and disaffection, but Hood would have run out of provisions himself had he not found sources of supply at Rhodes, Cyprus and Acre. His ships were taking turns to fall out of the blockade to replenish supplies, and when they reached suitable ports they were hampered by the difficulty of cashing British Treasury bills at reasonable rates. Nelson's attempts to persuade the Russo-Turkish fleet that Egypt was 'the first object, Corfu the second', and to support Hood continued to be futile. Meanwhile, in the Gulf of Genoa Troubridge was simultaneously trying to shield Tuscany and blockade Genoa, in which activities the artless young Captain Nisbet of *La Bonne Citoyenne* was as much a hindrance as a help. All of these considerable duties paled before the cloud thickening over northern

Italy, and monitored by Nelson at Naples. There the outlook, at first promising, had blackened. Dreadful and dire stories of disaster were coming from the front. Ferdinand's army was in deep trouble.[32]

As Acton wrote to Hamilton from Rome on 28 November, 'If the emperor moves we shall be saved. Otherwise . . .'[33]

3

The Neapolitan army had advanced, sodden, disorganised and dishevelled, but the French fell back before them, abandoning Rome except for four hundred men left to garrison the fort of St Angelo. While Championnet, the enemy general, gathered about 12,000 men further north at Civita Castellana, Ferdinand entered Rome unopposed on 29 November, and Civita Vecchia and Viterbo to the north-west fell as easily soon afterwards. There was considerable praise for the king's action in Europe. *The* (London) *Times* informed its readers that 'The king . . . cannot be too much admired for his prompt and decisive conduct, as he had certain information of its being the intention of the French to attack him.' And some allies were stirred to support, including the Tsar of Russia. In September he had dispatched auxiliary troops to Austria, and now he ordered another 10,000 to cross the Adriatic and disembark at Ancona to march directly to Ferdinand's assistance. 'The manly and vigorous measures of the King of Naples have been duly appreciated here,' wrote Charles Whitworth, Britain's minister in St Petersburg, 'and the emperor [tsar] has not hesitated a moment in sending this body of troops to his assistance.' This ran as Nelson had bargained – thus far. Yet Austria, on whom Naples had placed its greatest reliance, remained frozen to the spot. Arguably, the Neapolitans ought to have consolidated their hold on Rome and awaited help, but Mack recklessly advanced 20,000 men towards Civita Castellana to uproot the enemy's main force. Even so unsure a judge of army matters as Nelson sensed danger. He knew that however impressive Mack's recruits had looked in their new uniforms, they were 'wretchedly officered' and unlikely to survive a prolonged contest. 'If Mack is defeated,' he fizzed on 6 December, 'this country, in fourteen days, is lost, for the [Austrian] emperor has not yet moved his army.'[34]

The day Nelson wrote those words the French Directory declared war on Naples, and within another twenty-four hours Ferdinand's carriage was rattling out of Rome the way it had come, fleeing home as fast as its wheels could grip the wet and muddy roads. His offensive crumbled as the well-drilled French troops chewed into the raw Neapolitan recruits. The king's rank and file, in desperate need of effective leadership, were burdened by appalling officers, many appointed by Mack, most ignorant and uncommitted, and some downright cowards. One general defected and another fled with his men wild-eyed, discarding cannons, arms, tents, baggage and a war chest in the process. Shaking their heads at such behaviour, common soldiers muttered about betrayal and sabotage. Mack and Prince Cette attempted to rally reeling detachments, but the king was advised to flee. In the fevered city of Naples the news created panic, dismay and disbelief. Surely so many soldiers could not have collapsed so quickly? Hamilton railed about 'treachery and stinking cowardice', while Nelson curtly remarked that 'the Neapolitan officers have not lost much honour, for God knows they had but little to lose, but they lost all they had!'[35]

Blame also belonged, of course, in other places. To some the hawks in Naples, including Nelson, Hamilton, Acton and perhaps the queen, were culpable for gambling that Austria would support a war she had not sanctioned, a credible argument still favoured today. But Nelson, and many another victim of the change of fortune, blamed Thugut's timid foreign policy, and Austria's failure to back repeated assurances that she would protect Naples from destruction. Nelson saw the emperor's conduct as dishonourable, pusillanimous and blinkered, squandering the opportunity to crush the French between Austrian and Neapolitan offensives. The events of the following year suggested that the French might well have crumbled in such a vice, but little but blood is certain in war. However, Nelson was sure that only solidarity would defeat France, and without it the allies would fall one by one. As he argued through Eden, even if he was able to rescue the Neapolitan royal family and the Grand Duke of Tuscany, his ships alone could not save Italy. 'All must be[come] a republic if the Emperor does not act with expedition and vigour. "*Down, down* with the French!" ought to be placed in the council-room of every country in the world.'[36]

The admiral was not alone in his disgust. In Tuscany Seratti and Wyndham voiced their anger at Austria, which, they said, had 'promised protection' to the Grand Duke and encouraged Naples, only to abandon both. From Sardinia Jackson wrote of the 'most surprising and unaccountable' behaviour of Austria, and in Vienna Eden lamented that 'all the promises and assurances, so often given upon which his Sicilian Majesty had built his measures, were now forgotten or set aside by observing that circumstances had changed'. This, he continued, after Thugut had 'systematically encouraged' Naples in a line of conduct that could only have led to war. Most usefully, the turn of events caused dismay in St Petersburg, where Whitworth found the 'mysterious and wavering conduct' of the Austrians unfathomable, and the tsar branded it a flat betrayal. Indeed, as far as Britain was concerned, the most positive fallout from the Neapolitan campaign was the change it brought in Russia and new opportunities it created for clearing the French out of the Low Countries, an important strategic area. Russia renewed an application for British subsidies, and undertook to contribute 45,000 men to a British campaign to help Belgian rebels throw out the French. Moreover, the tsar promised an army for Italy and in January declared his intention to make any further aid to Austria conditional upon her supporting Ferdinand. Austria, of course, fidgeted under such widespread condemnation, and her explanations differed according to the audience. Her army was unprepared because of difficulties over British subsidies; Ferdinand had not consulted her in advance of his campaign, and – more credibly – failed to inform her of Nelson's expedition to Leghorn; and, again with some justification, Britain had pushed Naples into war and tried to lever Austria into the coalition. Nevertheless, despite these protestations, Austria's reputation for duplicity, mixed signals and shifting policies must share the blame for the disaster of 1798, and her credibility was further tarnished by the affair.[37]

Within a single month the war turned around. Championnet reoccupied Rome and marched south towards the city of Naples, while Mack attempted to bar his path near Capua. Ferdinand slipped into his city and joined Maria Carolina on a royal balcony to receive frenzied huzzahs from the crowd, but a sense of imminent disaster overhung the capital. Charges of treachery and cowardice flew left and right, and the minister for war found himself under arrest. Royalist mobs hunted Jacobins in the streets, while monarchists shivered at the thought of falling into the hands of the French and their collaborators. Their Sicilian Majesties did not know whether to stay and rally the city, risking being taken, or to save their children and flee to Sicily, where the British fleet might protect them and where they could form a government-in-waiting and try to rally the southern provinces. Nelson's great gamble had substantially failed, and the debris was falling about his ears. However, he was determined to pick up the pieces, and became the one certain rock upon which the monarchy depended. Mindful of his evacuation of Bastia in 1796, he prepared for the worst. Leaving the *Terpsichore* at Leghorn to provide for the Grand Duke, he recalled the *Culloden*, *Minotaur* and the *Goliath* from their respective stations and organised three transports to accommodate the substantial numbers of British who might wish to leave Naples.

By the third week in December, with the French army closing in, their Majesties committed themselves to flight, even at the risk of forfeiting public support. Gallo would speed to Vienna and St Petersburg with full powers to conclude a treaty with anyone who would save the kingdom, and in the meantime the court would transfer to Sicily, leaving a regent, Francesco Pignatelli, in Naples. Secrecy had to be the watchword, to avoid anger, interference or sabotage, and for several days the principals in the plot lived double lives, presenting a business-as-usual face to the world, while covertly preparing an ambitious midnight flight. Tensions rose. Volatile mobs commanded the streets, and every furious rider from the front portended the imminence of a relentless enemy. The queen could not rid her mind of the chilling memory of her sister's desperate, ill-fated flight to Varennes seven years before, when her coach was intercepted and the family hauled back to Paris and the shadow of the guillotine. Trusted couriers daily slipped between Acton, Nelson, the royal family and their senior officers as the complicated arrangements needed to move a government and its national treasury to the ships without public knowledge were put in place. Many of these notes still survive, expressing the fear and anguish. 'The agreement with our liberator [Nelson] stands,' 'Charlotte' wrote to 'Miledy'. 'I rely upon it, and abandon myself to him with ten innocent members of my family. My heart is dying with grief.' Emma wrung her hands in sisterly angst. 'My adorable, unfortunate Queen!' she endorsed one royal letter. 'God bless and protect her and her august family! Dear, dear, dear Queen!'[38]

After dark on 17 December one of the queen's most trusted retainers, Saverio, called furtively at the Palazzo Sessa, the Hamiltons' residence, with 60,000 gold ducats and a collection of diamonds. It was 'our all', according to the queen. The following two nights coffers of linen, clothing and heirlooms also arrived, and Emma carefully stowed them away until they could be surreptitiously removed to the *Vanguard*. By the 20th they were safely on board, according to Hamilton and Nelson, amounting to two and a half million pounds' worth of valuables. The same day Acton arranged for the transfer of the state treasury, brought from castle strongrooms to the *Alcmene* frigate. Captain George Hope's log records that 271 kegs were received, 'said to contain money'. The ships had also to be prepared for their exalted passengers, and additional cots were built, the wardroom and offices under the *Vanguard*'s poop given a fresh coat of paint, and extra linen and bedding brought from the Palazzo Sessa. It was a huge operation, not the least because other vulnerable worthies, including the Hamiltons and many of the British merchants and their families, would also expect to be evacuated. Sir William had four properties, the Palazzo Sessa with its 'secret treasure vault . . . crammed with works of art and junk', the Villa Emma beach house near Posillipo, the Villa Angelica on the foothills of Vesuvius and a villa near the royal palace at Caserta, and days were spent stripping their rich galleries and rooms of the most treasured items and preparing them for shipment or storage. A priceless collection of vases, paintings and sculptures was eventually stored in the *Colossus*, bound for England, but went to the bottom of the sea when the ship foundered off the Scilly Isles. When the court and government had been secured, last-minute whispered warnings had other British residents gathering their effects for a flight to any British or Portuguese warship that Nelson could supply. Among the most fearful inhabitants in Naples were French émigrés, who had fled the revolution in France to seek exile with their queen's sister in Naples. They had the least claim to republican mercy, and Nelson hired a couple of Greek polacres to carry them to safety.[39]

On 18 December a letter from Mack arrived, informing their Majesties that he could no longer hold the French army and that they should flee. Nelson agreed, and the next day his plans for the royal evacuation were approved. The admiral had drawn them up conscientiously, conferring with Acton and Prince Belmonte, the king's major-domo, and if they had a flaw it was in their treatment of the Neapolitan navy. The speed of the army's defeat and unrest in the city had convinced the royal family that their armed forces were riddled with traitors. Frightened of putting themselves in uncertain hands, their Majesties insisted on using Nelson's force for the evacuation. Caracciolo had a Neapolitan ship of the line and a frigate ready for sea, but there were doubts about her crews, of whom 1500 deserted in a single night. Nelson filled the gaps with Portuguese and British seaman, and ordered the two ships to accompany him to Sicily, but only as auxiliaries, and Caracciolo was cut to the quick. Cornelia Knight, who saw him at a dinner at about that time, recalled, 'I never saw any man look so utterly miserable. He scarcely uttered a word, ate nothing, and did not even unfold his napkin.' Five other Neapolitan ships of the line and cruisers were in the bay, but they were unmanned. The king had invested a great deal of money in his 'beautiful' ships and refused to destroy them, so Nelson duly had them anchored out in the bay, beyond the reach of shore batteries, and outside Hope's *Alcmene* and Niza's squadron, safe from harm or mischief. Ultimately, Nelson intended bringing them to Sicily, but in the meantime they were left under the care of Captain Campbell of the Portuguese service, who had orders to destroy them if the French or their Jacobin adherents gained control of the city. These arrangements ultimately failed, because, left to his own devices, Campbell burned thirty-one ships and ninety gunboats prematurely when they could have been saved.[40]

An icy north wind blew through Naples on Friday, 21 December, and the queen found herself shaking, wasted by worry and uncertainty. The city seemed to be slipping into anarchy, and wild stories had an inflamed mob seizing the castles, arsenal and town gates and distributing arms. That morning Count Marchese Carlo Vanni, a judge noted for his severity to liberals, convinced himself that the French would take Naples and shot himself with a pistol. Later a royalist crowd mistook one of the king's messengers for a French spy and dragged him half dead beneath the king's balcony before pitching him dying into a sewer. Afraid of being arrested in their own capital, the royals no longer hesitated. After an avalanche of notes from Acton, including lists of the royal retinue to be led to safety, Nelson had completed his arrangements and put his plan into action when darkness fell.[41]

The wind was fuelling a powerful and choppy sea, but the admiral went ashore, blithely attending a social function with Sir William, Emma and Mrs Cadogan as if nothing unduly amiss was about to take place. Outside, where the lights and laughter from the chandeliers and wine faded into the icy darkness, two rescue parties were being coordinated by Hardy. At about seven in the evening three barges and a cutter, filled with men armed with cutlasses and grapnels, assembled silently about the *Alcmene*, moored in the bay. Under the command of Hope, they were to help Nelson take off the first and royal party. Over at the *Vanguard* a second flotilla gathered, some of its launches mounting carronades. Hardy would lead them forward if the first party got into difficulties, and stand by for the remainder of the royal retinue. In the palace, where the anxious fugitives assembled, in the ships and boats, and ashore amidst the clink of wine glasses there was growing apprehension. That day Acton wrote, 'Trust we in God.' Emma endorsed the latest note from the queen, 'God protect us this night.' Maria Carolina wrote of her 'terrible and cruel resolution', adding, 'If I do not die in pain now, I shall never die!'[42]

At the appointed time Nelson and the Hamiltons casually dismissed their servants, explaining they were going for a walk, and asking to be collected in two hours' time for supper at the Palazzo Sessa. They strode briskly to the waterfront, where a boat from the *Vanguard* waited to take them to the flagship. Once the Hamiltons had been delivered, Nelson joined Hope's flotilla to rescue the royal family. The boats pulled silently towards the embarkation point, a *molesiglio*, or 'little quay', near a corner of the arsenal, north of the lighthouse. Leaving all boats bar the flagship's barge secreted behind some rocks, Nelson and Hope continued to a wharf known as 'La Victoire', where they met a muffled figure, Count de Thurn, a trusted Austrian in Neapolitan service. 'All goes right and well,' said Thurn – the passwords for the go-ahead – and Nelson followed him into some 'little rooms' that accessed a long secret passage that led from the waterfront to the queen's bedroom in the royal palace behind the arsenal. He emerged to find forty worried persons waiting for him, including Ferdinand and Maria Carolina; Francis, the twenty-one-year-old hereditary prince, with Clementina, his princess, and their baby daughter; Princes Leopold and Carlo Albert, both beyond their usual bedtime; and three young princesses, Christina, Amelie and Antoinette, destined to become the Queens of Sardinia, France and Spain respectively. With them were leading members of the government, including Acton, Prince Belmonte Pignatelli, Prince Castelcicala (Fabrizio Ruffo) and the Duke of Gravina, as well as a number of attendants. A singular scene ensued, as one of the first families of Europe, among the last of the endangered Bourbons, in fear of their lives and their throne, followed a parson's son from Norfolk as he led the way down a black stone stairway beneath the feeble light of a 'dark lantern', carrying a cutlass and pistol. 'I was trembling like a leaf,' recalled the queen, 'and without my virtuous and attached Mimi [Princess Christina] I would have fallen a thousand times.' Outside in the cold night a signal brought Hope's boats gliding in, and within an hour the royal family and principal officials had been snatched from the capital and lifted into the *Vanguard*. When Nelson's boats left the landing place, Hardy, whose men had been laying on their oars off the arsenal waiting for signal fires, swept in for the remaining twenty-two or so persons, most of them attendants such as nurses, tutors, doctors, servants and a confessor. The king was so relieved that he gave Hope a diamond ring and rewarded the barge crews with silver.[43]

Once the royals had been evacuated, with some other high-profile notables such as the Russian and Turkish ministers, word went to others who might wish to leave, and several converged on the waterfront to await boats. They were difficult hours, but the fortunes of the Knights and their two Italian maids must stand for the many. Cornelia and her mother were alerted by a note Nelson sent to their hotel, and found a place in a boat making the long pull out to the *Vanguard*. The flagship was full when they reached it, and they were directed to a Portuguese ship, *Rheine de Portugal*, where they found fifty-five fellow refugees, including the Russian consul, nobles, generals, émigrés, the queen's secretary, Head the painter with his wife and child, and an English physician. Captain Stone was an ungracious host and his crew 'a strange medly of Negroes, mulattoes, and people of different nations without order, discipline or cleanliness'. Hearing of their plight, Nelson sent a written apology the next morning, and suggested they waited for the *Culloden*, which was coming from Leghorn. The lady, her daughter and servants eventually reached Palermo on the *Alliance* store ship, which arrived at Naples on 4 January.[44]

On 22 December, Naples thus awoke to see the royal standard flying on the *Vanguard*, rocking at single anchor in the blustery weather. On board the queen and her children commandeered the admiral's ill-lit cabin, most of them afraid and tearful, while the king, hereditary prince, the Hamiltons and other dignitaries displaced Hardy and his officers from the repainted wardroom and elsewhere. Ferdinand at least was calm, content to pace the deck and discuss the fine hunting to be had in Sicily, but business could not entirely be forgone and when the weather improved boats began pulling out to the flagship. Cardinal Zurlo, Archbishop of Naples, alone gained royal access that day, imploring Ferdinand to remain in the city, but on the Sunday morning the miserable Mack appeared, bringing 'news to freeze one's blood'. The remains of the army were still at Capua, but Naples could not be saved, and the French were even rolling into Tuscany. The general was worn to a shadow and close to emotional and physical collapse.[45]

On 23 December Nelson sailed for Palermo at seven in the morning, in the company of the two Neapolitan warships, the *Archimedes* ship of the line and *Sannita* frigate, a corvette and some twenty merchantmen and transports. Behind he left the *Alcmene* to bring out some hired transports, as well as four Portuguese ships. The passage was a difficult one. The next day a powerful westerly brought driving hail, and at 1.30 in the afternoon a 'sudden heavy squall' tore all three of the flagship's topsails to pieces and destroyed the fore topmast staysail and the driver. For a few hours it 'blew much harder than I ever experienced since I have been at sea,' said Nelson. Hardy organised parties of axe men to cut away damaged rigging or fell masts if the ship was in danger of capsizing. To the civilians, unused to such pitiless elemental furies, it was terrifying. Sir William retired to his sleeping quarters with a loaded pistol by his side, determined to blow his brains out rather than drown, and Count Esterhazy, the Austrian ambassador, was so afraid that he threw a snuff box adorned with a nude portrait of his mistress into the sea lest it compromised him with his maker. The royals in the admiral's cabin clung and cried, some prone and one on her knees vomiting into a basin, and Princess Amelie and Prince Leopold asked for a priest to conduct a confessional. Emma rose to the occasion magnificently, keeping her head and tending to every need while the domestics floundered, and her mother busied herself sorting out the men below. In the afternoon the storm eased a little, and replacement sails were raised, but the wind remained strong into the early hours of Christmas Day. Tragedy struck at nine that morning, when the youngest of the princes, the delicate six-year-old Carlo Albert, began convulsing and after several hours died in Emma's arms. The wind changed direction and the ship clawed its way from dangerous, dark shores to reach Palermo at about three in the afternoon. All their consorts save the *Sannita* had separated, most finding shelter in Messina, but at two the following morning, with Ferdinand's standard on the main topgallant mast, the flagship was towed to the mole. The queen, too upset to face her public, landed discreetly with her family, but Ferdinand made an official entry in Nelson's barge, to a considerable if muted welcome from the people. His treasure was whisked away in a carriage.[46]

The monarchy had been saved, but the future had never looked less certain, and the kingdom of Naples, if not Sicily, looked to be lost. Acton admitted 'a broken heart'. As he wrote to Sir William, 'I did love that country, my dear sir, as you did likewise, and by gratitude to the sovereigns did what I could to save it.'[47]

4

For days the weather was stormy. On 26 December all the gunboats at Naples foundered in their anchorage, and the *Alliance*, which had sailed for Palermo with additional royal property and refugees, was driven back into the bay. Palermo was cloaked in snow and ice. It symbolised the gloom that had settled upon Nelson's affairs. A year that had begun in hope and risen on an unprecedented triumph had ended in frustration and defeat.

Palermo was a city of lofty imposing houses, fountains, marble statues, nunneries and ornamented churches. The central square was the nucleus of two intersecting main streets leading to gates on each of four sides, and residents could thread through carriages and loafers to patronise the shops on Cassano, or exercise along the impressive marine promenade outside the walls. Two thousand refugees fled Naples, and accommodation was scarce, so many of the arrivals thought themselves poorly housed. Their Sicilian Majesties occupied a cheerless semi-furnished pile in the Chinese style, situated in the Conca d'Oro, above the walls on the north side and surrounded by religious establishments. Almost oblivious to the loss of most of his kingdom and revenue, the king buried himself in hunting at their country house in the Colli, a mountainous timberland west of Palermo, or retired to another residence at Bagaira, on the other side of the city. But wherever located, the queen entombed herself in grief and confusion, complaining of pains in her head and chest. The future was unpredictable and unsafe, for she feared more treachery, and suspicion was an insidious and poisonous enemy, difficult to root out. A revolt could happen in Naples, and in Sicily, for while Nelson's ships could keep the French out of the island, they were not proof against disaffection and revolution within. Maria Carolina spoke of accepting exile and surrendering her wealth to 'vultures', committing herself to an impoverished and dishonoured existence in Sorrento, 'withdrawn in a corner'.[48]

The British community fared variously. The Knights found an inhabitable room in the only inn in Palermo, across a narrow street from the common jail, while Nelson and the Hamiltons were directed by their Majesties to the 'very pretty villa' of Montalto, situated near the beautiful Flora Reale gardens at the end of the promenade. It had been designed for summer use, and lacked fire-places and chimneys, and a few weeks of cold and damp played havoc with Sir William's health. The party moved to the Palazzo Palagonia, a commodious building formed from what had been separate houses by the Palagonia family earlier in the century, and situated closer to the mole. Hamilton was 'worn out' but Emma grieved for the queen more than her husband thought healthy, and Nelson had royal access 'night and day', enjoying the status of a deliverer and principal counsellor.[49]

The outlook at the end of the year was disturbing. Nelson's gamble had drawn Russia to the fore, but it had not stirred Austria, and brought Naples down about their ears. The French were only thirty miles from the city, and Tuscany was in confusion. As late as 23 December, Wyndham, ignorant of events further south, was still soliciting a Neapolitan army to rescue Tuscany ('Unless the King of Naples comes with great force . . . all is lost'), while Seratti was trying to resign, and the Grand Duke was swinging towards appeasement, begging Ferdinand and Nelson to withdraw their provocative force from Leghorn. Also fleeing chaos, the King of Sardinia-Piedmont appeared in Leghorn in search of a passage to the island of Sardinia, where he might be safe. The whole of Italy was on fire. Not only that, but while an anti-French coalition of a kind had formed, embracing Britain, Russia, Turkey and the Two Sicilies, it was uncoordinated; the allies had come together one by one, with their separate agendas, rather than in accordance with a grand strategic plan. The differences between Nelson and Ushakov, the Russian admiral, reflected that clash of priorities.[50]

With the help of the Neapolitans, Nelson had made his squadron serviceable, but it was widely scattered, with eight ships of the line, four cruisers, a store ship and a few bomb and fire vessels divided between Egypt, Malta, Palermo and northern Italy. *La Bonne Citoyenne* would be soon on her way to Constantinople to return the Turkish ambassador, Kelim Effendi, and carry letters. For the most part the ships remained active throughout the squally winter seas, and Manley Dixon's *Lion* took a French national corvette, the ten-gun *Chasseur*, just after Christmas as it tried to run between Alexandria and Toulon. All of their missions required more ships than were available.[51]

Nelson was also growing embittered. A man who invested time, effort and money into friendship, he was hurt by anything resembling ingratitude. Even in these troubled times, we find him generous with now forgotten benefices. William Compton, a Norfolk man then in Italy, received 'a great many favours and kindnesses' from Nelson, and most especially 'the kind interest' taken in sealing his union with a wife who made him 'the happiest of mortals'. Anne, the aforesaid spouse, said that the admiral's 'good heart' had made her 'as happy as I can possibly be on this earth'. The Admiralty, on the other hand, was constantly reminded of the other side of this trait in Nelson's personality, his constant complaints of neglect. His morale, subject to imaginary as well as real disappointments, was forever rising and falling, and at times he lapsed into sulky attention-seeking. The admiral's allegations that Spencer was ungrateful and St Vincent envious were not shared by the accused. Though conscious of the inadequacy of the barony, Spencer believed that he was serving Nelson as a friend and a patron. He had secured ministerial agreement to compensate the squadron for the burned Nile prizes, sent several bomb vessels and the *Foudroyant* ship of the line to reinforce Nelson, given Troubridge his Nile medal and slated the first lieutenant of the *Culloden* for an early promotion. If he had been able to do little for Maurice Nelson, an employee of the civil branch of the service, he had done a reasonable job of attending to other Nelson protégés, such as Faddy. The promotion of Josiah to positions utterly beyond his experience or ability was an undoubted boon. Followers, as well as patrons, took fire from the prickly little admiral. He was soon grumbling that Capel had not written to him.[52]

And the year had one more cruel twist for Nelson. It came in the form of Sir William Sidney Smith, an ambitious naval firebrand with fifteen years' standing as a post-captain, a Swedish knighthood, astonishing dash and enterprise and a talent for upsetting people. Even the unflappable Collingwood would find his head so 'full of strange vapours' more aggravating than an enemy fleet, and suspected that the Admiralty had taken to posting him to far-off stations merely to rid themselves of a 'tormentor'. Nelson knew him and thought his mouth outran his achievements, but he was a cousin of Grenville and had powerful friends, including Spencer. Now this stormy maverick came out to the Mediterranean in the eighty-gun *Tigre* with some very special orders. He was not only a captain in His Britannic Majesty's navy but also a minister plenipotentiary to the Ottoman Porte, a position he was to share with his brother, John Spencer Smith, who was already in post at Constantinople. The credentials in his pockets came from both the Admiralty and the Foreign Office.[53]

Smith explained his bizarre appointment by alluding to his previous experience with the Turks. As Britain was committed to cooperating with the Turks in the Levant, he was an obvious choice for a command in the eastern Mediterranean. As for his ministerial hat, it had been necessary to ensure that he would not be outranked by any Turkish admiral, and that Britain's professional point of view carried weight. In October, when Smith was sent out, his appointment made some sense, even if it originated with Spencer and smacked of nepotism, but it was tactless, since it invited a clash of volatile spirits. Smith came to the Mediterranean with clear instructions to place himself under the command of St Vincent and Nelson, but he would almost inevitably use his unusual diplomatic powers to interfere with their commands. It was not long before abrasions appeared. 'It is vexatious to see the manner in which this Hero of Romance imposes upon all our ministers,' St Vincent snarled to Nelson. 'The bombast he has written to Lord Spencer . . . has made me sick, and I have reams to wade through . . . He has no authority whatever to wear a distinguishing pendant unless you authorize him, for I certainly shall not.'[54]

Smith was a stranger to circumspection. Getting to Malta, he wrote two letters on 11 December, advertising his arrival in the most inappropriate fashion. Sir William Hamilton was told that the captain of the *Tigre* was on his way to Alexandria, where 'the zealous Hood', being an inferior officer, would 'naturally' fall under his orders. In unsaid words, he would take take command of Nelson's brothers as a matter of course. Worse, when Smith also wrote to Nelson to assure him that he would be subject to the orders of senior officers, he dropped the remark that he was not at liberty to reveal the instructions he had received from Lord Grenville. This must have struck Nelson as a slap in the face, because it implied that he, charged with the management of that quarter and in a good measure the architect of state policy that governed it, could not be made privy to information affecting the command. More, Smith – a mere post-captain – effectively treated his admiral as the inferior officer. The same day Smith tried to bypass Nelson by seeking direct permission from St Vincent 'to dispose of the force I find in the Levant' as he wished, 'the captains . . . there being junior to me'.[55]

Coming as it did on top of so many other tribulations, Smith's appointment hit Nelson with unusual force. On the last two days of the year he wrote searing letters to his commander-in-chief asking to withdraw and turn his force over to Troubridge. His 'weak constitution' needed convalescence and the arrival of a 'much abler' officer in 'the district which I had thought under my command' made his further presence unnecessary. 'My dear Lord,' he added, 'I *do feel, for I am a man*, that it is impossible for me to serve in those seas with the squadron under a junior officer. Could I have thought it? And from Earl Spencer! Never, never was I so astonished as your letter made me.' His other immediate thought was to send Troubridge to Egypt. Unlike Hood, Troubridge was senior to Smith, and he would not only do everything possible to destroy the shipping in Alexandria, but also bring 'the Swedish knight' under control. 'The knight forgets the respect due to his superior officer [Nelson],' the admiral complained to St Vincent. 'He has no orders from you to take my ships away from my command, but it is all of a piece. Is it to be borne? Pray grant me your permission to retire, and I hope the *Vanguard* will be allowed to convey me and my friends, Sir William and Lady Hamilton, to England.' To Spencer he was more restrained, but simply craved 'ease and quiet' and permission to return to England for a few months.[56]

Nelson managed a civil reply to Smith, directing him to Alexandria to take command as his orders required, but his mortified protests served their purpose. St Vincent replied on 17 January, reprobating Smith's 'bold attempt' to wrest part of the squadron from Nelson, and speaking of his surprise at the 'interest' he had commanded at home. He urged Nelson not to abandon their Sicilian Majesties at such a critical hour, and suggested employing Smith in situations suitable to his talents, arbitrating between him and other senior captains when necessary. St Vincent could sympathise, because he too foamed at the mouth about Smith, and had already fired a characteristic blast at the secretary to the Admiralty denouncing the captain for living in 'a continual maze of errors and imposture'.[57]

The Smith affair seems a minor irritant at a time when Italy blazed, but of such are human relations often made, and it deeply disturbed Nelson. 'Believe me, my dear friend,' he wrote Cornwallis, 'I see but little real happiness for me on this side [of] the grave.' Home suddenly looked more attractive. Roundwood, the house in Ipswich, was adequate as a country seat, but a peer of the realm who walked on the world's stage really needed a property in or near London. Something like a house his late Uncle Maurice had owned. Fanny was sent looking for a home with 'a good dining room and bed chambers', servants' quarters, stables and a coach house suitable for a 'neat carriage'. Nelson detested 'the other side of Portman Square' and Baker Street, but Hyde Park, near the Admiralty, would be an excellent location. 'You will take care I am not let down,' he warned Fanny. 'The king has elevated me and I must support my station . . . Sooner or later a house in London must be had, furnished and ready for us.'[58]

But he would not be going home just yet.

VI

'THE MAINSPRING'

Though Vice and Guilt their numerous
conquests boast,
Yet Virtue has her sails unfurl'd
To save a sinking, a deluded world;
Her sons assert her empire o'er the main,
Spread terror round each hostile coast,
And teach mankind to bless her generous reign
Britannia's palms shall break the guilty charm,
Rouse latent valour, and bid Europe arm.

Cornelia Knight, *The Battle of the Nile, A Pindarick Ode*, 1798

I

THAT New Year Nelson festered at Palermo, a 'detestable' place, living with the Hamiltons, 'all unwell and full of sorrow'. 'My dear lord,' he told St Vincent, 'there is no true happiness in this life, and in my present state I could quit it with a smile.' Nelson's health fluctuated, with bowel complaints being reinforced by the return of fever in the spring, and the queen felt enough to send him a 'douche' or shower appliance. Grimly, during this nadir in his fortunes, he stuck to his task. His government was on the other side of Europe, and his commander-in-chief in Gibraltar writing letters that revealed how little he knew of Nelson's situation. John Duckworth, promoted a rear admiral in February, was nearer at Minorca, but his eyes were fixed on the enemy naval bases of Cartagena and Toulon. Further east Nelson was effectively a 'Secretary of State' and commander-in-chief, revising his country's foreign policy as he thought best. He was more still, for their Sicilian Majesties, rocking on their throne, saw him as their lifebelt. Jealous officers in Ferdinand's service complained that 'everything' was 'subject' to 'Nelson's ruling', which went too far, but the admiral was certainly the chief 'councillor' in all that concerned defence. He had a point when he boasted, 'I am here the mainspring which keeps all things in proper train.' [1]

Nelson was nevertheless surrounded by the debris of his recent intervention in the politics of Europe. Never again would he hazard such a move. His bold ploy to create an alliance, drive the French from Italy, and change the course of the war had misfired; it had stirred Russia, but at the cost of bringing Britain's staunchest ally, the Two Sicilies, to the brink of oblivion. And yet his means to rescue Naples and slow the French advance were few.

In March Nelson had sixteen ships of the line, four of them Portuguese, and some twenty smaller cruisers, carrying mail, passengers and freight, escorting convoys, gathering intelligence and supplies and hitting the enemy where they could. They covered thousands of miles of sea, snaking through the Aegean and up and down the Adriatic. Supported by dockyards in Naples, Castellammare and Sicily and the hospital at Palermo, as well as by what Britain could supply through Gibraltar and Minorca, Nelson kept his force in a relatively good condition. The losses he suffered came mainly from accidents and disease. Problems of supply led to sporadic outbreaks of scurvy, and a day on which Nelson reported his squadron 'very healthy' the *Lion* landed twenty scurvy-ridden patients she had brought from Egypt in Sicily. A month later the surgeon of the *Goliath* was dead and several of the ship's officers 'in a dreadful state', while 'virulent ulcers' were shortly reported in the *Minotaur*. At Malta fevers contracted by shore parties were a complication, and at the end of March the sick on the *Alexander* had quintupled to twenty-seven, and Ball was commandeering a house to isolate cases. Nelson's *Vanguard* spent more time in port than many, enjoying the support of the local hospital and the regularity created by Hardy's firm discipline. Fully-fledged scurvy was kept at bay but the number of men suffering from ulcers of the limbs and loins and intermittent and continuous fevers increased during the winter. The state of the hospital, the acquisition of oranges and lemons for the sick, and the needs of those being invalided to Mahon were important features of the admiral's letters and orders.[2]

An enormous body of paperwork descended upon a disabled admiral without a proper secretariat. Letters, dispatches, commissions, contracts, safe passports, surveys, sick reports, tallies of stores, duplicates and all manner of miscellaneous documents involved not only Nelson and John Tyson, his secretary, but also willing helpers such as the Hamiltons and their banker, Edmund Noble, in the 'very serious operation' of mastering paper. Occasionally Nelson wrote or dictated 'from morn till night and sometimes all night', producing a fast-flowing stream of dispatches, letters and orders. Amid such desktop fury the admiral's private correspondence retreated, although he did manage some lengthy letters to Clarence.[3]

The labour and anxiety that followed the flight to Palermo were partly relieved by the agreeable company that assembled in the Palazzo Palagonia, where Nelson and the Hamiltons made their home. It was a four-storey building enclosing ample gardens, its plain front punctuated by shuttered, full-length, windowed doors that opened on to private balconies, all suggestive of the many apartments into which the upper floors were divided. Here there came exiles of greatest use to the admiral and his friends, some to lodge and others to visit. Emma's mother, weathered Mrs Cadogan, 'a little old woman', answered the door of the Hamilton apartments in a white bed gown and black petticoat, as if she was a housekeeper, but shared an apartment of her own with a female attendant. She normally joined the ménage for dinner, enjoying chattering to Tyson, but retreated to her room on the grand occasions that made her feel out of place. Others often within doors were the bankers Abraham Gibbs and Edmund Noble, and John Andrew Graefer, a naturalised German who had distinguished himself as a gardener in Whitechapel before arriving in Naples with a letter of introduction from the botanist Sir Joseph Banks, President of the Royal Society. Encouraged by Sir William and Maria Carolina, he had created a fifty-acre English garden in Caserta. Now he frequently appeared in, and perhaps inhabited, the Palazzo Palagonia with his wife, Eliza, and their children, struggling to master dancing and French. Occasional weddings were held in the house, and Miss Knight enlivened social occasions, as 'good' and 'charming' as ever, and, poised to inherit a substantial legacy, ever more eligible. One Harryman, an army officer, pursued her, but the Lady Knight's opposition left 'the poor man almost mad with anger', and Cornelia herself had eyes for Captain Davidge Gould, one of the brothers. Lady Knight was failing, and Nelson and Sir William chivalrously promised to watch her daughter. When the old woman died in the summer, Cornelia also moved into the Palazzo Palagonia. In moments of absence Lord Nelson spoke longingly of the community that graced the house in Palermo, speaking briefly in his letters of such mysterious beings as Dr Nudi, the Hamiltons' physician, 'little Mary' to whom he sent kisses (perhaps young Mary Gibbs), and Mira, Emma's dog.[4]

In these weeks Nelson's involvement with the Hamiltons passed the point of no return, and his infatuation with the wife of the English ambassador was leaking out – sometimes almost innocently, as in the admiral's request that Smith, the minister in Constantinople, shop for two or three Indian shawls, for which 'the price' was 'no object'. Perhaps he intended them for Fanny, but more likely they were tools for Emma's noted 'attitudes'. In letters that might fall into the wrong hands Nelson masked his love for Emma in polite effusions about Sir William and his lady, but the drift was clear. 'To tell you how dreary and uncomfortable the *Vanguard* appears,' he wrote to Emma during a rare spell at sea in May, 'is only telling you what it is to go from the pleasantest society to a solitary cell; or from the dearest friends to no friends. I am now perfectly the *great man* – not a creature near me. From my heart I wish myself the little man again! You and good Sir William have spoiled me for any place but with you. I love Mrs Cadogan. You cannot conceive what I feel, when I call you all to my remembrance. Even to Mira, do not forget your faithful and affectionate

Nelson.' Emma, too, may have been confiding in her closest female friend. 'I *also* suffer through the departure of our dear virtuous admiral,' the queen wrote to her. 'How I feel for you.' By the middle of January the subject was hot gossip. Among those taking it westwards was Captain George Hope of the *Alcmene*, who left Palermo on 16 January and reached Gibraltar on 7 March. On 10 April Admiral Lord Keith, newly arrived there, wrote to his sister that Hope and other officers had said that Nelson was 'making himself ridiculous with Lady Hamilton, and idling . . . in Palermo when he should have been *elsewhere*'. That word 'ridiculous' was exactly the one Captain Fremantle had chosen to describe Nelson's behaviour with his previous mistress, Adelaide Correglia, three years before. Soon afterwards Keith remarked that Nelson was 'cutting the most absurd figure possible for folly and vanity'. In view of his remarks, Charles Lock does not seem to have completely exaggerated when he described Nelson's 'extravagant love' as 'the laughing stock of the whole fleet' the following June. Lock disliked Nelson, but others told the same story. Damas, the talented French military officer in Neapolitan service, claimed that Nelson's own officers were 'mortified and disgusted' by his conduct.[5]

In England Fanny knew nothing of this chatter, but there was one person in the Mediterranean for whom it was a peculiar burden. No one had the effrontery to confront Nelson, but Josiah Nisbet, the troubled teenager, probably suffered considerable ridicule during the spiteful and almost childish banter that usually enveloped him, even if only in behind-the-back whispering and furtive asides. He was already visibly failing as a commander. Without the personality or experience to impress, he resorted to an abuse of power to maintain discipline. In seven months he flogged nineteen men in the *Bonne Citoyenne*, inflicting an average of twenty-six lashes per punishment. At that time officially a sentence of more than a token twelve lashes could not be imposed without a court martial, but almost all captains waived the regulation as impractical. Nevertheless, Nisbet went far beyond moderation. A man who attempted to desert received forty-eight lashes, a thief seventy-two and a forty-five-year-old able seaman a savage eighty-four, none with the benefit of a court martial. Ultimately such leadership was sterile. It won Nisbet no loyalties, followers or respect. It merely advertised a young man losing control of his ship.[6]

Almost everywhere Josiah went he made trouble. Cruising off Italy under Troubridge, he seized what he took to be a French privateer in Longone Bay, Elba, in December. Unfortunately, the island belonged to Tuscany, and the prize was a Tuscan merchantman sailing under French flags of convenience in waters infested by Gallic privateers. To make matters worse, the boy quibbled when Troubridge ordered him to return it, and Wyndham had to mollify the angry Tuscan authorities. Disappointed, Nelson packed *La Bonne Citoyenne* off to Constantinople, where Josiah was to land Kelim Effendi, the Turkish ambassador, and his staff, and deliver dispatches to the British minister. Josiah left

Palermo on 10 January, and performed his task reasonably, though he used 'an officer' to conduct the diplomatic business in Constantinople, rather than attending to it himself, another indication of his lack of confidence. Back in Palermo on 7 February, the boy was soon heading for Malta with a convoy freighting ammunition to the insurgents.[7]

None of this convinced a despairing Nelson. On 17 January he went so far as to tell Fanny that there was 'nothing good' about her son, who 'must sooner or later be broke'. Soon after he added that Josiah had 'had more done for him than any young man in the service, and made, I fear, the worst use of his advantages'. These were hard words for his wife to swallow, however honest. Nelson was disappointed not only that Josiah was proving incapable and ungrateful, but that he was also something infinitely more depressing – ineducable. Instead of repairing his behaviour, he denied faults, rejected advice and sulked. George Cockburn, an efficient if dour frigate captain, kindly offered to supervise the boy, but when Nelson put it to Josiah, he flatly refused. It augured very badly indeed.[8]

Nisbet's main problem was his youth. He had been pushed forward too quickly, and was not up to the difficult challenges of command, work for which in any case he had neither interest nor aptitude. Added to this, the stigma of being an unworthy product of nepotism, destined to disappoint, was corrosive, and the whisperings about his mother and stepfather, about which he could do nothing, cruel. How could he answer them? Perhaps he felt obliged to defend Nelson, but, if so, it was a defence in which he had no faith, for if Josiah was young, he was assuredly not blind and could see that his mother was being betrayed. One obscure piece of evidence to this effect is found in a letter one of Fanny's maids wrote to her brother in 1806. 'Captn. Nesbitt,' she wrote, 'was in the ship with Lord Nelson, and he said Lady Hamilton [was] a bad woman and [she] and Lord Nelson lay together and his blood boiled to see them, so he took it up and offered to fight a duel with him, and said he would never sail in the same ship with him again, and Lord Nelson drank Lady Hamilton's health, and Captain [Nisbet] said it was through [such] wh[ores] that his mother was used ill . . .'[9]

This is second-hand, a memory of what Josiah had said, and his actual words may have been less than the truth themselves. For example, Nelson and Josiah were never rated on the books of the same ship during the period of the admiral's relationship with Emma, nor is any more heard of the duel, though Nelson once complained that Josiah 'may again, as he has often done before, wish me to break my neck, and be abetted in it by his friends, who are likewise my enemies'. One observation seems justified, however. Josiah's relationship with Nelson deteriorated most sharply at the time the affair between the admiral and Emma developed, and the two were unlikely to have been unconnected.[10]

In April Nelson's relationship with his stepson took its last hopeful turn. The boy had been off Malta with Ball, a more amiable officer than Cockburn and more stable and sympathetic than Troubridge. Ball was positive, noting that Nisbet had successfully convoyed corn vessels from Girgenti to Malta. 'I have sincere satisfaction in observing that his conduct on two occasions . . . evinced good judgement,' he wrote to Nelson. Soon after something untoward happened. Despite Josiah's indifferent showing as a commander, Nelson had continued to press for his promotion to post-captain, though with an increasing sense of futility. But Spencer and St Vincent felt they owed their star admiral favours and in the spring news reached the fleet that Josiah had been made 'post' on Christmas Eve 1798 and placed in command of a fine thirty-six-gun frigate, the *Thalia*. He shifted to his new ship on 2 April, so hurriedly that he failed to submit satisfactory musters and accounts for his previous command and delayed his pay for at least five years. Nevertheless, his promotion had been a truly spectacular feat of naval jobbery. Josiah was eighteen years of age, and as many months short of the minimum age needed to hold *any* commission, let alone a post-captaincy. His elevation rivalled the well-known instance of nepotism practised by Rear Admiral Sir Alexander Cochrane, who got his son Thomas John 'posted' in 1806, shortly after his seventeenth birthday, but with this difference: Cochrane proved to be a respectable officer, and Josiah did not. In fact, particular care was taken to support the youngster. The ship was well-manned, the first lieutenant, Samuel Colquit, 'highly spoken of', and Ball also transferred John Yule, an experienced and capable lieutenant of the *Alexander*, to the *Thalia* to keep the boy out of trouble.[11]

The sudden promotion raised Josiah's morale, and made him reappraise his relationship with his stepfather. Reaching post rank at eighteen gave him an almost unparalleled chance of becoming an admiral, for once on the captains' list an officer plodded towards flag rank by seniority, relatively invulnerable to the influence of merit and the machinations of more favoured candidates. Ball continued to brandish the carrot. 'I have lately had a great deal of conversation with Captain Nisbet, who is very much attached to his ship [the *Thalia*], and expresses himself extremely satisfied with the service and his station off here,' he informed Nelson. 'I have endeavoured to impress him with an idea of his being the most fortunate young man in the navy, to have such a friend, a father and protector. I believe he is more sensible of it than ever. That alone will stimulate him to prove himself worthy of it. I have told him that your Lordship's friendship to me has made me the happiest fellow in the world, and that it will enable me to smile at the common ruffles of this life.' Thus enthused, young Nisbet actually wrote to his patron, acknowledging him to be 'the only person on earth who has my interest truly at heart', and promising to redouble his efforts to please. 'He is now on his own bottom,' Nelson said dryly, 'and by his conduct must stand or fall'.[12]

It was sad because it might have been so different. Nelson loved children, and had always wanted a child of his own, a child Fanny had failed to provide. He must have wondered whether that was his fault or hers. Had Josiah been a different person – had he been, say, the dutiful, grateful, admiring, achieving fellow that William Hoste had shown himself – he would certainly have captured the admiral's love. And that parental love could have been the cement that Nelson's marriage needed. Josiah, in short, might have been the one person capable of keeping Nelson and Fanny together, and of sparing the family the tragedy that lay ahead; instead, his churlish resentment only pushed Nelson further away. Josiah was no saviour. He was one more temptation to abandon his old life, and create another.

2

The collapse of Naples and the threat to Sicily remained the inescapable landmarks in a bleak picture embellished by the stream of couriers and refugees that reached Palermo from the mainland. Occasional news from home, including fulsome parliamentary tributes and, on 14 February, a promotion to the rank of rear admiral of the red squadron, failed to lighten the prospect, for Nelson was sure that Sicily, no less than Naples, would succumb to the French. The dismal conclusion seemed eminently logical as resistance on the mainland crumbled and the Strait of Messina was only a couple of miles wide.

In the city of Naples Nelson's timely evacuation of the royal family was soon vindicated. Francesco Pignatelli, whom the king had left as 'Vicar-General', lost control as anarchy and murder spiralled in a vicious struggle between nobles, Jacobins and royalists. He destroyed his popular credit by negotiating an armistice with Championnet, agreeing to surrender Capua, Gaeta and Naples to the French, and to pay reparations of two and half a million ducats. He followed other fugitives to Sicily, leaving organised military resistance to the invaders collapsing. Poor Mack gave himself up to the French and pleaded for a passport that would allow him to slink home. On 22 January the French seized Naples and began to suppress the fanatically royalist mob and turn the kingdom of Naples into the 'Parthenopean Republic', whipped on by Jacobin reformers, a small minority of the population gleaned from the propertied and wealthier classes. The Directory in Paris had not wanted to go so far, viewing a new republic as a liability. They replaced Championnet with Marshal Jacques-Etienne Macdonald, and sent the slavish Guillaume Faipoult to strictly enforce orders from the centre. Given the French triumph in the city, as well as residual resentments against the toppled monarchy, several Neapolitan towns also declared for the republicans, but resistance was stronger in the countryside, and rebel bands under such leaders as Michele Pezza of Itri, known as 'Fra Diavolo' (the Great Devil), harried French communications. The French replied savagely, and when their soldiers took the town of Andria in February they slaughtered four thousand inhabitants. The crusade to liberate Rome had turned into a bloody civil war, in which the French and Jacobin collaborators were pitted against royalists in a pitiless struggle for survival.[13]

These misfortunes contained innumerable cuts, and one that bit particularly deep into the stricken monarchy was the destruction of the Neapolitan navy. Numerous gunboats had been destroyed to keep them out of enemy hands, and on 8 January, before the capital fell, one of the Portuguese captains, Donald Campbell, set fire to four Neapolitan ship of the line and several cruisers, bathing the Bay of Naples in a lurid flickering firelight that lasted throughout the night. Five days earlier Nelson had ordered the destruction of the ships upon the approach of the French, but Campbell's act was premature, and their Sicilian Majesties greatly upset by the loss of such a huge investment. Nelson suggested that Niza discipline his subordinate, but with too few men to work the Neapolitan ships and most of them unserviceable, their sacrifice was merely a matter of time. On no account could they be left behind to endanger Sicily, and the queen sensibly allowed the whole unfortunate matter to be dropped, however dispiriting to the royalist cause.[14]

The British government was uncertain how to respond to the new Italian crisis. It felt obliged to support the unseated Bourbons, but although Grenville advanced a £100,000 in specie to aid Ferdinand's cause, he would not tie Britain to the possibly unrealisable goal of restoring the king to his throne. But for Lord Nelson it was a matter of personal honour. He had been shaken by the scale of the king's defeat, and the ease with which 12,000 French had routed an army more than four times their number. It seemed so 'extraordinary' as to be 'a dream'. But he who had helped bring their Sicilian Majesties to this pass, whose great gamble was paying dividends far too late to save the kingdom, could not forsake such faithful and grateful allies. 'I would, indeed, lay down my life for such good and gracious monarchs,' he told St Vincent.[15]

The king was embittered, but cushioned from the worst by his ability to concentrate on simpler pleasures, sometimes seeming, said his wife, to regard Naples as remote as the land of the Hottentots. The prince royal grew irritable, erupting in sudden fits of anger and violence. Maria Carolina's lamentations were highly visible, for she was an emotional woman, and brooded deeply over the pell-mell loss of her kingdom, a son, her family's prospects and her reputation. The *Monitore Napoletano*, the organ of the new Parthenopean Republic, scourged her with virulent abuse. She felt betrayed by her son-in-law and nephew, the emperor, and by fifth columnists, the 'vile animals and cowards', who alone, she concluded, could have caused her so sudden a fall. She feared it would happen again in Sicily. 'The dangers we run here are immense and real,' she wrote. 'You may imagine what I suffer. Before forty days revolution will have broken out here. It will be appalling and terribly violent.' Nor did she like how these misfortunes were changing her as a person. 'This infamous revolution has made me cruel,' she admitted.[16]

The queen's anger, grief and anxiety gushed unchecked in Italian to Emma, and through her in English to Nelson. The admiral sometimes accompanied Emma to visit Her Majesty, so that she could confer with 'le brave amiral' about her situation, but more often Emma served as the courier, carrying words and letters from one to the other. By both means the queen begged him not to desert her and throw her and her children to her enemies. Nelson felt obliged to comfort and agreed. After all, only British ships could ultimately protect Sicily – and the monarchy, with its government in waiting – from invasion. 'Without the British this monarchy is undone . . . no attack can be made [on us] but by sea,' said Acton bluntly. Technically, Nelson had no authority to allow foreign sovereigns to dictate where His Britannic Majesty's ships should go and what they should do, but he had no alternative but to base his squadron in Sicily, both to protect that island, the monarchy and the blockade of Malta, which depended on both. No one doubted this decision, and when Nelson threatened to resign over the Smith affair St Vincent begged him 'not [to] think of abandoning the royal family'. If Nelson courted controversy, it was in his commitment to maintain his station for an indefinite period. But the admiral had been part of the Neapolitan strategy, and could not in honour leave them in danger, and as a man he felt for those who had trusted him. After several days trying to reassure the terrified queen, he put his promise in writing in a letter to Emma. 'My dear Lady Hamilton,' he wrote on 25 January, 'I grieve on reading the Queen's letter to you. Only say for me, Nelson never *changes*. Nelson never *abandons* his friends in distress. On the contrary those are the moments that knit him closer to *them*. Nelson, you know his heart. Vouch for the uprightness of your old friend, Nelson.' In a postscript he affirmed, 'Nelson never quits Palermo but by the desire of the Queen.' He meant it, and reported his action to St Vincent and Spencer. Abandon their allies? *'No. That I will not, while God spares my life, and she* [the queen] *requires my feeble assistance.'*[17]

Nelson's undertaking steadied some nerves, and at the beginning of March the city of Palermo presented him with its freedom, 'an honour,' boasted Hamilton, 'never conferred before to any foreigner, except to Louis XI, King of France'. Syracuse followed suit. Then and since, however, it fuelled much spiteful criticism of the type Hope carried to Gibraltar. The charge that Nelson idled in Palermo because of his obsession with Lady Hamilton was unfair at this time, as we have seen. As a matter of fact, Nelson's promise to support the Sicilian monarchy threatened to part the admiral from his beloved, rather than keep them together. Sir William's health was so bad that spring that he talked seriously about an imminent return home, especially after Charles Lock, the newly appointed consul, arrived to handle part of the diplomatic business. And although Syracuse might have been a better operational base than Palermo, the latter port was by no means unsuited to the admiral's responsibilities. With St Vincent at Cadiz or Gibraltar and Duckworth at Minorca, Nelson's brief was eastwards, in Italy and beyond. And a station there would alone, perhaps, have reassured the stricken regime.[18]

There is more truth in the charge that Nelson was losing his ability to act independently of the Sicilian monarchy. To some extent this was a matter of its parlous circumstances, which pleaded for protection, but Nelson was also flattered by royal attentions and grateful for them. Moreover, he unquestionably admired his allies – particularly the queen – and found her hard to refuse, backed as she also was by a passionately partisan Emma Hamilton. At times he spoke of Maria Carolina as if she was the fourth member of their cabal. Thus, addressing St Vincent, he spoke of 'our great queen, who truly admires you, our dear invaluable Lady Hamilton, our good Sir William, and give me leave to add myself to this excellent group, have but one opinion of you, viz., that you are everything which is great and good. Let me say so.'[19]

Notwithstanding, Nelson was not entirely uncritical of the Sicilian monarchy. He understood their desire to root out subversive elements, but made the occasional protest. Their Majesties lived in a world of real and imaginary fears, which was not surprising at a time when treason was rearing its head left and right, and some of the regime's most trusted friends and servants turned their coats in an effort to square themselves with the new political reality. The most wounding desertion was that of Caracciolo. The commander of the Neapolitan navy applied for permission to return to Naples to protect his property from being confiscated by the republicans, and left Sicily with their Majesties' blessing. But in Naples Macdonald, the French commander, saw uses in this able and significant officer, 'overcame' Caracciolo's 'reluctance' to switch allegiances, 'and attached him to our side', installing him first as a common soldier and then as the commander of the small republican flotilla being prepared to defend the city. When she learned the shocking news, Maria Carolina's paranoia knew no bounds, and she denounced her late admiral as 'that great scoundrel'.[20]

Obvious targets for royal suspicions were the French émigrés, those pitiful refugees who had fled revolutionary France to find asylum in Naples, but who now found themselves condemned and distrusted on both sides of the political schism. Although they had given everything to escape the republicans, they could not venture on to Sicilian streets without risking verbal or physical abuse. When the émigrés from Naples arrived in Sicily, Ferdinand refused them permission to land, and ordered them to be shipped to Trieste. The ménage at the Palazzo Palagonia had qualms about the treatment of these wretched exiles, whom Nelson had first seen being expelled from Toulon in boatloads in 1793. He offered an alternative voyage to Tangier for any who wanted it, while Hamilton used Treasury bills to provide financial support, drawing to the tune of £20,000 by the end of the year. One petition in particular made the hearts of the triumvirate 'bleed with sorrow'. It came from a blind seventy-five-year-old Frenchman who had lived in Palermo for fifty years, but now faced expulsion as part of the policy of ridding the island of Gallic influences. 'For God's sake, for the sake of a virtuous king and queen, stop this cruel process!' Nelson beseeched Acton. 'If you have proofs of his infamy, send him to the devil. If not clear proofs of his guilt, pray let him remain.' Acton apologetically explained that the Frenchman in question had 'continually' criticised the monarchy, but he agreed to lay Nelson's protest before the king.[21]

A more fundamental reservation about Sicilian royal policy was its failure to adequately address the need for internal reform. General Charles Stuart, who we will meet shortly, believed that the inhabitants of Sicily were 'enjoying a mild, free representative government, as established under the old laws of Aragon, whereby the people regulated the price of their own produce, taxed themselves, and even appropriated the produce of their taxes'. This, he said, accounted in some way for their 'independent spirit'. This was not Nelson's view. He believed that any government, whether a monarchy or a republic, survived inasmuch as it served its people, rewarding their loyalty and service with protection. He had always been an advocate and exponent of paternalism, in government as in ships. By his lights the government manifestly failed in Sicily. Nelson and Hamilton complained of the 'want of justice and good government' on the island, and the dire poverty of so many of its people. As far as Nelson was concerned, the 'proud' Sicilians were 'an oppressed people' who 'in fairness . . . ought to be consulted on the defence of their own country'. He urged their Majesties to temporise, and vowed to set an example and act so 'as to meet the approbation of all classes in this country'.[22]

Tactfully, Nelson pointed out that good government was not only a virtue in itself, but a necessary weapon against the French juggernaut. He had no time for the French Revolution, which not only destabilised Europe and terrified its neighbours with its aggressive imperialism, but also failed to protect the liberties, property and lives of its citizens. There had been worthwhile reforms, but Nelson knew little of them. The Parisian 'Terror' and the genocide in the Vendée, of which he had read, and the treatment of the royalists of Toulon and Marseilles, which he had seen, had exposed to him the vicious underbelly of the revolution. In the years that followed he had seen the unscrupulous imperialism of restless Gallic armies, as they spread eastwards along the Riviera and into Italy, the Ionian Islands, Malta, Egypt and Syria, looting under arms. He determined to spare his country such oppression, and others if he could, but he also understood that the rhetoric of the revolution, at least, was persuasive, seducing the desperate, the discontented and the idealistic, and introducing enemies within. The answer, he believed, was to remove the springs of that discontent by a wise, benign and just rule.

However, if Nelson was not always in agreement with the Sicilian monarchy, he no less than they had been scarred by the treachery and brutality of the Neapolitan war that he had helped unleash. Generally benign by nature, he lived in an unsafe world, and had learned that values and liberties could only be protected by a firm, and if needs be, a ruthless defence. That ruthlessness was readily invoked by treachery. To him there was nothing worse than a traitor. Men had the right to demand the redress of legitimate grievances, as had the Spithead mutineers of 1797, who had remained solidly patriotic and whom he applauded. However, those who subverted the safety of the realm or tried to betray it into the hands of foreign enemies, like the mutineers at the Nore, deserved severe punishment.

The collapse of the kingdom of Naples merely underscored the dangers without and within, and we can detect a hardening of the admiral's attitude towards those he held responsible. On 20 January a French vessel with 140 soldiers, most of them sick, arrived in Augusta (Sicily) from Egypt. They were quarantined in a house by the seashore, but twenty days later a frenzied mob attacked the building, tearing the roof tiles away to get at the inmates. More than eighty of the French were killed, some on their knees, and their officer was 'torn to a thousand pieces' after trying to feign death. The survivors took refuge in a Neapolitan ship, but Nelson was unsympathetic. 'What a fool!' he remarked of the vessel's master.[23]

It was probably an instinctive remark, and one that would have moderated in reflection, for Nelson stoutly defended French prisoners of war. One of his principal charges against Bonaparte would be his 'murder' of four thousand Turkish prisoners at Jaffa in March 1799. But the underlying flintiness it betokens was noticed by newcomers less inured to the increasing ferocity of the war. A couple of tourists, Archibald, Lord Montgomerie, and Major Pryse Lockhart Gordon, and Charles Lock, the newly appointed consul to Naples, and his wife Cecilia, were in Palermo about the end of January. Hamilton had requested a consul to ease his burden, but the Locks were in their twenties and wholly inexperienced. They came well recommended though, not the least by St Vincent, who described Cecilia as 'an excellent young woman'. Darby of the *Bellerophon* was likewise charmed by the 'nice Mrs Lock'. Unfortunately, though her handsome husband had secured his post through relationships to Lord Robert Fitzgerald and such Whig notables as Fox and Lord Holland, he was very much a man on the make.[24]

When Montgomerie and Gordon called upon the Hamiltons they found Emma, her luxurious hair encompassing an 'expansive form and full bosom', bewailing the fate of Naples in a subdued 'melange of Lancashire and Italian'. Nelson emerged from a corner in which he had been writing, and cross-examined the travellers about the situation in Naples, which they had just left. Though Sir William was also present it was with Emma that Nelson exchanged 'some very significant glances' as Montgomerie expounded on the collapse of support for the king in the city. Then, apparently dissatisfied with the visitors' attention, Nelson pointedly asked Gordon if he had heard of the battle of the

Nile. The major owned that he had, upon which Nelson explained that the action had been 'the most extraordinary . . . ever fought' for it occurred at night, and at anchor, and had been won by an admiral with one arm! 'To each [point] . . . I made a profound bow,' Gordon remembered, 'but had the speech been made *after* dinner, I should have imagined the hero had imbibed an extra dose of champagne.'[25]

The tourists gained a darker insight early in March, when the Hamiltons hosted a dinner to welcome a Turkish captain who had arrived from the Russo-Turkish fleet with a message for Nelson from the tsar, sent with a snuff box set in diamonds. The receipt of the gifts had been stage-managed by Emma, who insisted that Nelson accoutred himself in the sultan's gifts, his sable pelisse and famous chelengk. The Turkish captain had thrown himself at Nelson's feet, but after dinner the next day Gordon decided that he was 'a coarse savage monster'. Emma seated herself next to the Turk with a Greek interpreter at hand, and listened to an inebriated account of the captain's exploits. Boasting of capturing a ship carrying French invalids from Egypt, the fierce fellow drew a sword and claimed that he had used the very weapon to behead twenty of the prisoners. Moreover, the blood was still there to prove it. According to Gordon, Lady Hamilton 'beamed with delight'. Crying, 'Oh, let me see the sword that did the glorious deed', she caressed it with ring-regaled fingers before kissing it and passing it to Nelson. 'Had I not been an eye witness to this disgraceful act I would not have ventured to relate it,' recalled Gordon, a scruple that did not prevent him from purchasing the weapon and giving it to Montgomerie as a keepsake. By Gordon's account the evening was a disagreeable one. Mrs Lock fainted and had to be removed before an indifferent hostess. Emma, said Gordon, was 'jealous' of the younger woman, and alluding to her relationship to an Irish nationalist (her brother, the late Lord Edward Fitzgerald, had participated in the 1798 rebellion) and the green ribbons she wore at the table, insinuated that she might be a Jacobin. 'The toad-eaters applauded, but many groaned and cried "shame" loud enough to reach the ears of the admiral, who turned pale, hung his head and seemed ashamed.' Written long afterwards, these memoirs might have been coloured for publication, but the Locks certainly grew to detest Emma, blaming her for keeping Hamilton at his post and frustrating their own ambitions. There was 'nothing so black and detestable as that woman', wrote Lock, and 'there are not five dissenting voices among our many countrymen here with regard to her'. Cecilia told her mother, the Duchess of Leinster, that Lady Hamilton was 'artful, malicious, envious and detracting'.[26]

With the kingdom of Naples imploding, and the French hammering at the door, it is not surprising that a black mood prevailed among those who manned the final bastion that Sicily had become. No one had emerged from the catastrophe of 1798 unscathed, and nothing looked good ahead. Nelson predicted the monarchy would fall. But it did not. There were yet twists to the tale.

3

In January Ferdinand and his advisers came up with a plan, based on frail shards of light that glimmered dimly on the political horizon. Nelson's ships had saved him from the French and protected him in Sicily but his was to be a government in waiting, hoping for the defeat of his enemies and the restoration of his kingdom. There was a possibility of encouraging a popular counter-revolution using Britain's control of the sea to shield incipient royalist forces from any seaborne reinforcements from France or northern Italy.

Despite posing as liberators, democrats and even defenders of the Catholic Church, French incursions into Italy ran a predictable course involving extortion and plunder, a refusal to accept any political system that did not conform to their own ideas, order that rested on the power of occupying armies, and, whether wilfully or no, the unleashing of an anti-clericalism contrary to the sentiments of most of the indigenous populations. In the city of Naples a succession of unsatisfactory provisional governments were supported by disaffected nobles, well-intentioned reformers in search of a better society, radicals and opportunists, but relied upon French troops and a conscript militia to guard a disarmed population. Discontent, fanned by the confiscation of public and private property, a crippling financial levy, food shortages and a curfew, grew. Beyond the simmering city open revolts flared in the provinces before the end of January. Modern historians have shown that these 'church and king' movements rose from different roots, blending nationalism, anger at the levy and attacks on the Church, and complicated personal and municipal rivalries. Whatever, something remarkable was happening. Austria had left Naples to her fate, but now, against all predictions, Naples, with the aid of the British, began to save herself. An Italian legend, the legend of the *sanfedisti*, the popular counter-revolution, was being born.

Popular counter-revolutions had recently occurred elsewhere, in Liguria, southern Piedmont and the papal territories, but this one, at first sporadic, scattered and uncoordinated, and consisting of armies of undisciplined and untrained peasants led by members of local elites, surged forward with a singular momentum. Ferdinand judged it right to encourage and control these incipient protests. Perhaps, shielded from enemy reinforcements from France and northern Italy by Britain's control of the sea, they could succeed where the regular Neapolitan army had failed.[27]

To manage this rebellion Ferdinand turned to a fifty-four-year-old, white-haired cleric named Fabrizio Dionigi, Cardinal Ruffo. A cardinal who had never taken holy orders, a treasurer to the pope and governor general of the Neapolitan royal palace at Caserta, Ruffo was an unlikely general, but he was brave, loyal and circumspect, and had written military treatises. Now he proposed to raise his native Calabria, in the south of Italy, for the king, and on 25 January Ferdinand commissioned him Vicar-General, authorising him to act as the monarch's alter ego and use all means to conjure resistance. Ruffo landed at Punta del Pezzo on 7 February with a banner proclaiming his daring mission for Church and king, but little money or arms. Yet by the end of the month he had raised 15,000 men. Soon the ragged *sanfedisti* were gaining victories and advancing north beneath the white cross and red cockade of the Bourbons. Ruffo was a humane man, but had limited command of his motley forces, and French garrisons who resisted were slaughtered with their Jacobin collaborators. The 'Army of Holy Faith' took few prisoners, established its own inquisition, and dealt brutally with traitors as it went.

At the beginning little faith could be pinned upon this strategy, and until the spring the best hope for the reclamation of the kingdom of Naples lay in Russian and Austrian intervention. Russia had already rallied, salvaging some success for the great Hamilton–Nelson gamble. In London she had concluded a formal alliance with Britain on 29 December. The tsar received British subsidies, and agreed to field an army in Holland and put nine thousand men into northern Italy. Another three thousand were to be sent directly to Naples. Russia also sent urgent invitations to Austria, calling upon her to join the common cause; there must be an end to her obfuscation, and she should make an open and fair declaration of her views. Austria fumbled and mumbled, blaming Britain for what had happened, but finally agreed to renew hostilities. But in the meantime the security of Sicily itself rested squarely on Nelson, who stationed the *Vanguard* at Palermo and Portuguese ships in the narrows between Sicily and the mainland. Supervising the land defences, the admiral discovered that the king's regular force consisted of no more than four thousand men. He advised raising ten times that number of regulars and militia, but Mack's experience had taught him the unreliability of levies, and he recognised the need for regular troops. Batteries also needed to be improved. Messina was the danger point, but although its castle could be made defensible, it had few troops to man it. Nelson ordered gunboats to be fitted, and cast around for professional help. Through Wyndham and Eden he appealed to Vienna, and in January and February hurried a plea to the Russo-Turkish fleet blockading Corfu. As Nelson perhaps suspected, Russia moved clumsily. When Ferdinand, with the admiral's approval, sent Chevalier Antonio Micheroux to Corfu to hasten the troops Russia had promised, he arrived on 9 April to find Admiral Ushakov signally ignorant of the wider war. He knew nothing of Ruffo's mission to Calabria, the Anglo-Russian treaty or Austria's belated entry into the fighting. The Russian admiral also protested that it would be too expensive and time-consuming to ship Russian troops direct to Naples and Sicily, but he would link with Ruffo by way of the Italian west coast. In May several hundred Russian troops, accompanied by Micheroux, were landed in the Gulf of Manfredonia, and five of Ushakov's cruisers patrolled the coast in support, but it fell far short of what the tsar had promised.[28]

None of this solved Nelson's problem, which was the immediate defence of a woefully weak Sicily, but then another miracle occurred. In the middle of February, Nelson's plea for a thousand British troops fell upon the desk of the commander of the garrison at Minorca, and he was none other than Lieutenant General Charles Stuart, one of the few senior army officers whose energy, talent and volatility were comparable with the admiral's own. Nelson had been with Stuart at Calvi in 1794, and knew him to be a difficult but brilliant commander. 'What a state we are in here without troops, and the enemy at the door,' Stuart read. Even a thousand redcoats could save Sicily. Stuart did not hesitate. In itself Sicily was important, and it might be used as the base for a diversionary strike against the French on the mainland when Austro-Russian forces attacked from the north. On 10 March the general appeared off Palermo like a caped deliverer. With him were the *Aurora* frigate and seven transports containing a thousand men of the 30th and 89th regiments. Despite gout in both feet, Stuart immediately went ashore, and, taking no more time than it took to confer with Nelson and the Hamiltons and secure full powers from their Majesties, he continued to Messina. Fifty thousand cheering people welcomed him, and something of 'an electrical shock' swept through the town as the redcoats marched into the castle, restoring hope where it had faltered or died.[29]

With his usual decisiveness Stuart withdrew the unreliable Neapolitan troops from the castle, in which the British were now supported by Sicilian militia; charged Acton with ensuring a flow of supplies and additional artillery; and improved the fortifications. He then sailed for Malta, where he commended Ball's 'very judicious dispositions' but pronounced his hopes of an easy conquest 'sanguine'. Back at Palermo the general produced a comprehensive plan for the defence of Sicily. Nelson's coastal batteries would not do. They merely created an extended line of weak defences that could be bowled over in succession. Power had to be concentrated in key fortifications, each capable of raising substantial bodies of supporting militia, and serviced by a string of coastal signal stations. Plans had to be made to close what lines led into the interior of the island at short notice.[30]

Stuart left Sicily on 30 March, and it took almost another month for a permanent successor, Colonel Thomas Graham, to take up his quarters in Messina. But Stuart had provided the professionalism that Nelson had wanted, raising morale all round. The queen declared that he had saved Sicily.

4

Between them Nelson and Stuart had given Sicily credible defences. Even if a powerful enemy managed to cross the Strait of Messina and mounted an attack, the entrenched redcoats were probably capable of resisting until British naval forces arrived to tip the balance irrevocably in their favour. His lordship's responsibilities ran much further, however, and for the only time in its history the elegant portals of the Palazzo Palagonia became the nucleus of strategic planning that affected the whole eastern Mediterranean.

In Italy Nelson could offer little more than vigilance. The papal territories had again sunk under foreign dominion, and Tuscany, which Nelson had tried to protect by his expedition to Leghorn, was set to follow. On 28 December Wyndham predicted that she would not last a month. 'We must either have great force or none, for the present Neapolitan troops in Tuscany [at Leghorn] are not equal to save it, and many of the officers are Jacobins.' Nelson's advice was singularly stupid. Despite the collapse of the Neapolitan army and the torpor of Austria he said that unless the Tuscans acted 'like men' and took 'the chance of war' they would be conquered and republicanised. 'I cannot agree with your lordship that this country could save itself by a vigorous effort,' replied the horrified minister. 'Surrounded as it is by republicans with large armies, well disciplined, on their confines, without an officer, without artillery or artillery men, with few troops, with a people that can never be made courageous and warlike, without a penny in the treasury, without a chance of assistance, this country would only by opposition draw upon itself more cruel terms in the moment of ruin. Under these circumstances the Grand Duke must negotiate . . . That horrid monster [Antoine Christophe] Saliceti, member of the Council of 500, is here declaring openly [that] Tuscany will be revolutionised this Lent . . . I am confident . . . that we are on the eve of a revolution.'[31]

The Tuscans did lie low, and the Grand Duke reaffirmed the neutrality of his country. As Naselli's Neapolitans were now both useless and provocative, he formally begged them to withdraw. Ferdinand's troops left on 5 January, marking the complete futility of Nelson's expedition. When Naselli reached Naples he blindly sailed into French hands. His dejected army was disarmed, and the Neapolitan corvette and convoy which had brought his force home confiscated. These gestures on the part of the Grand Duke worked temporarily, because French columns that marched into Tuscany in January quickly withdrew after extracting a levy of two million livres. Nelson's ships could do little, but a succession of officers maintained a presence off the coast to protect British merchantmen plying those waters, and to provide a retreat for political refugees. Gage's *Terpsichore*, Louis's *Minotaur*, Darby's *Bellerophon* and Niza's *Principe Real* all stood their turns. And they proved their value. With Piedmont, part of his kingdom, under French martial law, Carlo Emanuele IV of Sardinia, fled his lonely exile in Florence. His escape was carefully managed by Louis, who spirited the sick king and his suite into a Danish neutral at Leghorn, and had her escorted to the island of Sardinia, the safest part of the troubled realm. After a few weeks of shaky neutrality, the French invaded Tuscany again in March, seizing Pisa, Leghorn and Florence. The Grand Duke ran for Austrian territory, but Wyndham, the Russian, Portuguese and Neapolitan ministers, and such members of the Tuscan government as Seratti and Manfredini also had to escape by sea, to Palermo. Nelson declared Tuscan ships legitimate prize to prevent them carrying supplies to the enemy and sent the *Lion* to attempt the relief of a Neapolitan garrison at Longone in Elba, but felt barely able to protect British trade. Nevertheless, he had to keep some ships on that station. 'It is essential at least to show we have not forgot them,' the admiral wrote.[32]

Of other issues, the two biggest were Egypt and Malta. Wrestle as he might with them, Nelson found them intractable. Off the sun-drenched, sandy shores of Egypt his ships were pinning the remaining French vessels in Alexandria, while Bonaparte's disease-ridden and dwindling army lashed out with an increasing lack of purpose. Leaving Cairo in January, Bonaparte headed north for the Turkish territory of Syria, cutting a ruthless and bloody swathe and massacring thousands of prisoners at Jaffa.

One reason why Egypt raised Nelson's temperature can be summed up in five letters – Smith. Aggravating as if born to the business, Sir Sidney wrote to Nelson in what the admiral considered a 'dictatorial' style to get more ships. He soon found that he had met a rock in the hero of the Nile. 'I shall, my Lord,' Nelson told St Vincent, 'keep a sufficient force in the Levant for the service required of us, but not a ship for Captain Smith's parade and nonsense – Commodore Smith – I beg his pardon, for he wears a broad pendant. Has he any orders for this presumption over the heads of so many good and gallant officers with me?' Nelson tried several ways to rein Smith in. As we have seen, the government had unwisely joined Smith to his brother's post as minister plenipotentiary to the Ottoman Porte, creating a dual naval and political appointment intended to strengthen Sir Sidney's standing in any joint British–Turkish operations that might arise. The trouble was that it also encouraged Smith to lord it over his British naval colleagues and mess with Nelson's command. Spencer might assure Nelson that Smith had no authority 'to take a single gun boat . . . from your command' and that he was bound to obey the orders of naval superiors, but Smith needed none. The Admiralty had created a thoroughly ambiguous situation. On 5 January, for example, the Smiths signed a defensive alliance with Turkey, undertaking to blockade Alexandria and to cooperate with Jezzar Pasha's attempts to defeat the French army. Without any appreciable knowledge of Nelson's other obligations, Sir Sidney then proceeded to use the political commitments that he had made to pressure the admiral to increase the naval force in the Levant, claiming that it was all consistent with his instructions from Grenville. On 31 May he pointed out that 'no latitude could be left for the judgement of any of His Majesty's servants' since 'a positive stipulation had been entered into that the British naval force in these seas should always be proportionate to the enemy'. Smith put the British contribution at two capital ships and three cruisers. Nelson's complaint that his command had been compromised was, therefore, justified, and, being

Nelson, he took it personally and decided that the Admiralty simply wanted 'to lower my importance'.[33]

Nelson countered Smith's pretensions by insisting that both Smiths sign any diplomatic letters, thus stripping the upstart captain of any political authority independent of his brother. On 8 March he also warned the captain of the *Tigre* neither to redeploy any of his ships nor interfere with communications passing between Palermo and the Russo-Turkish fleet at Corfu or Constantinople. To make it absolutely clear that he, rather than Smith, controlled naval affairs, Nelson wrote directly to the British consul at Corfu and the Turkish commander-in-chief.[34]

Nelson's preferred solution was to send Troubridge, who outranked Smith, to clear up the principal business at Alexandria by destroying the enemy shipping in the harbour once and for all. A success for Troubridge might also help him bear the latest cut from the Admiralty, which had refused to include his first lieutenant in the list of Nile promotions. Nelson, who had begged Spencer not to do it, was frank about the latest 'stab'. 'We know of no distinction of merit,' he wrote to the first lord, 'and yet, unfortunately, it has been found out so many hundred leagues distant, not found out from public dispatches, but from private information.' On 6 January the admiral ordered Troubridge to gather as many ships and bomb vessels as he could raise and proceed to Alexandria, calling at Malta on his way to see if Ball could use timely help. If the enemy ships in Egypt could not be destroyed, Troubridge was to bring Hood's squadron back to Syracuse, leaving Miller's *Theseus* to support Smith in continuing the blockade. The expedition left Syracuse on 7 January, but before the end of February dispatches were telling Nelson of its failure. Alexandria was well defended, and sported places where the French ships could huddle beyond range of British shells. Troubridge's bomb vessel had burst her mortar, and seven fireships, converted from prizes taken off the coast, were lost in bad weather. 'I believe we did but little damage,' admitted the captain grimly. A Genoese polacre was sunk, that was all. Demoralised, he had no alternative but to return to Palermo. 'My ill fate still sticks to me in these seas,' he told Nelson. 'I was in hopes I should have wiped the stain off at the Admiralty.'[35]

It disappointed Nelson, too, prolonging the strain upon his wavering resources, and further aggravations materialised when Troubridge reached Palermo on 17 March. It was Smith again, clamouring for the additional ships to which he thought himself entitled. Troubridge had forbidden him to detain any capital ships except the *Theseus*, which Nelson had already assigned to the Levant, but had been inveigled into temporarily loaning him the *Lion*. More worrying, to get Bonaparte's army out of Egypt Sir Sydney was talking about allowing it free passage to Europe. Nelson exploded, and with good reason. He had destroyed the French fleet, and, if Britain remained resolute, guaranteed ultimate victory over their army. French papers intercepted by the *Seahorse* suggested that Bonaparte's men were not in as bad a way as the British had been led to believe, but they were still trapped in a desolate, disease-ridden region with few resources. Nelson wanted the total victory that this war of national survival demanded. Yet now, for the sake of expediency, Smith was throwing away that prize. The admiral fired a furious letter at Smith, declaring that his proposal was 'in *direct opposition* to my *opinion*, which is *never to suffer any one individual Frenchman to quit Egypt*', and that he was '*strictly*' to desist. So upset was Nelson that similar barrages went elsewhere. 'I consider it nothing short of madness to permit that band of thieves to return to Europe,' he stormed to Wyndham. On 29 April Nelson ordered his ships to pay 'no attention' to Smith's passports, but to send any ships intercepted with French soldiers to Palermo.[36]

Nelson was not mistaken about Smith. Without consulting Nelson or St Vincent, he informed Grenville on 6 March that his new course had followed 'conferences at the Porte'. The French would be allowed to evacuate the territories they had invaded provided they surrendered their arms. They do not even seem to have been required to remain on parole until formally exchanged for allied prisoners of war. From the beginning Nelson had suspected that Smith would exceed his powers, and that he lacked judgement. He was right on both counts. Soon the blockade Hood and Hallowell had maintained so well began to creak. Troubridge intercepted one ship that Smith had allowed out, full of sick French soldiers, and matters deteriorated further when enemy cruisers got out of Alexandria between 5 and 18 April, after Sir Sidney had sailed north to Acre to aid the Turks against Bonaparte's army. Nelson heard of the escape in May, when he suspected the enemy ships might have fled to Tripoli, and sent Campbell of the *Alfonso d'Albuquerque* to investigate. But Smith always packed surprises, and while Nelson was frowning at the damage done by one, he was busily unveiling another. It was the most sensational naval success the admiral's forces had won since the Nile. Throwing himself into Acre and animating its Turkish defenders, he met Bonaparte and his army head-on and stopped them in their tracks. It was a performance worthy of Nelson himself.[37]

For Nelson, nailed to Palermo by his promise to a queen, Egypt was a profound worry in the hands of such an unpredictable subordinate, however spasmodically brilliant, but Malta, perhaps the most difficult task the admiral had to entrust, was at least in steadier hands. Ball, grave but kind, was professionally and socially the most supportive of all his lordship's colleagues. St Vincent read that Nelson's 'obligations' to him exceeded the admiral's command of words, while Spencer learned that he possessed 'judgment, gallantry and the most conciliatory manner that ever man was blessed with'. On his part Ball thought Nelson's friendship 'an inestimable treasure', and particularly valued the unexpected small gifts, from portions of fresh cheese to positions for the captain's protégés, all bestowed 'at a time when you are so fully occupied with national concerns'. The huge task given Ball, the reduction of one of the most powerful bastions in the world, got harder in unusually punishing winter gales. Winds that blew Ball's ships off their station, tearing away their clawing anchors, and keeping sailmakers and carpenters working at full stretch, also brought French victuallers from Toulon, Marseilles, Genoa or Trieste, and a few got through. The frigate *Boudeuse* and five or so small vessels sneaked into Valletta in January and February, replenishing the garrison's diminishing supplies. Nevertheless, Ball's blockade largely held up. His ships took occasional prizes, several in April that included a privateer and a provision ship carrying four hundred much needed barrels of pork and beef and fifty-three pipes of wine, and deterred most of the others, leaving the dogged French soldiers precariously clinging to Malta malnourished and scurvy-ridden.[38]

As Ball was master of the local situation, Nelson's job was largely one of logistical and political support. The island's mixed economy of farming, fishing and light cotton industry, which had once created the impressive blend of baroque and classical architecture that marked Maltese city skylines, had long since failed to support its growing population. Even in good times it fed only half the inhabitants, and necessitated extensive imports. Now, it was blighted by war and most of Malta's existing banks and granaries were situated within the French lines and inaccessible to most of the islanders. As the fractured livelihoods of these sturdy people disintegrated, Nelson's role in keeping corn, clothing, powder and shot coming from Sicily, Minorca and Gibraltar became a crucial key to success.

The idea of a dire, drawn-out contest, haunted by the shadowy faces of the starving, was difficult to accept, and for a while hopes were entertained that direct military action might produce a speedier result. After the French lost thirty or more men during a futile sortie against the allied lines in November, Vaubois put his faith in a dogged defence and hopes of eventual relief or rescue. Provisions, including medical supplies, were unsatisfactory, but he had plenty of fresh water and some corn. Nelson and Ball were tantalised by the idea of a sudden victory rather longer. The admiral's complaints to Ferdinand in November had brought three Neapolitan cruisers and some mortars and ammunition to the fight, and the British spared bomb vessels and a detachment of Royal Artillery gunners under Lieutenant John Vivion. So fortified, Ball landed three mortars and a carronade and threw shot and shells from ashore and afloat with improved effect. The three survivors of the enemy Nile fleet in the Grand Harbour all took direct hits. The French had reinforced them with 'armour plating' but they struck their topmasts, removed their powder and squirmed into more inaccessible refuges under waterfront storehouses. Overall, however, the results were disappointing. In one six-day bombardment in December two mortars cracked and their beds disintegrated, but only one small enemy vessel was sunk. Ball, like Troubridge at Alexandria, found his enemies beyond reach.[39]

Ball was patient and optimistic by nature. He saw the best in people and situations, but although these qualities made him an effective arbiter, able to unite such fractious beings as the Maltese chiefs, they led him into serious military misjudgements. He believed wild exaggerations of French losses, including reports that placed their casualties as high as two thousand in October and November, and encouraged Nelson to believe that the capitulation of Malta was imminent. Ball's most ambitious attempt to break the stalemate occurred on the night of 11 January. The French themselves admitted that there were 'scarcely . . . seven or eight families' who were 'truly loyal to the republic' in Valletta, and Ball attempted to synchronise an attempt to storm the lines with an internal uprising. A red flag was raised over the Maltese batteries to initiate furtive meetings between those inside and outside the garrison at recognised trysting places. The rebels inside Valletta, led by a 'Captain Guilermi, an old religious privateer and a colonel in the service of Russia', planned to gather inconspicuously at strategic places, such as the sea gate at the Floriane, the National Gate, Cavaliers and National Palace, and attempt to seize them at the pealing of bells on the night of 11 January. On his part, Ball's Maltese would storm the town through the opened gates. The 'bold stroke' was an abject failure. Inside, the plot was leaked by a prostitute, as well as by the number of suspicious assemblies, while outside the attackers were wasted by superior fire. 'They were over the first ditch and retired, *damn* them!' stormed Nelson, without the slightest knowledge of what they had been up against. As for Guilermi, he and forty-four of his followers died before firing squads in the public square. Although Emmanuele Vitale, the leading Maltese commander, tried to create a cadre of disciplined native troops, a *coup de main* now looked out of the question, and the realisation that the tedious blockade had to continue, sank in. The cumulative investment in Malta was enormous. In a sampled five months of 1799 the blockade employed, fully or occasionally, eight British and Portuguese ships of the line, ten smaller warships and three bomb vessels, as well as transports and victuallers. Even the blustery winter months did not stop them more or less closing Valletta, but at considerable cost. The *Audacious* had fifty men on the sick list in January. Ashore Ball fought another battle to sustain morale and unity in a courageous but starving people. It was no mean feat managing such diverse materials as Vitale the notary, Francesco Caruano the priest and Vincenzo Borg the landowner, but he organised regular meetings and spasmodically 'united all the chiefs in the most perfect harmony'. Lord Nelson lobbied the Sicilian government for food, fuel, money and military stores, and then lobbied again.[40]

It was towards the end of January that the spectre of famine first threw its ubiquitous shadow over the operation, and the Maltese petitioned Ferdinand for relief. When no one responded, Nelson personally appealed on 2 February and within twenty-four hours obtained a promise of six thousand 'salms' of corn. But maintaining a fluid flow was impossible. Ships were delayed by bad weather and stringent quarantine restrictions, bureaucracy moved slowly, food supplies and prices fluctuated, and merchants were reluctant to deal with an island that manifestly lacked credit. On 12 February three Maltese deputies, Ludovico Savoye, Baron Fournier and Luigi Aguis, arrived in Palermo with a fresh memorial to Ferdinand. Among the usual requests for provisions, the deputies wanted permission to raise British as well as Sicilian colours over the island in an attempt to gain additional security under the protection of His Britannic Majesty. They had Nelson's full support. His flagship had brought them from Malta, and they lodged at the Palazzo Palagonia. A month later they left for home with promises of additional aid, including a personal donation from the queen. Their Majesties supplied £7000 and 10,000 'salms' of wheat, and they also supported the attempt to court the British, keen to share the burden of liberation.

Part of the new arrangement placed Ball ashore as civil governor, while Niza conducted the naval blockade. The idea originated with Nelson, who saw his subordinate's skill in dealing with the Maltese. Providing the work counted towards his naval service, Ball liked the idea, and even consulted Hamilton about the possibility of securing some decoration from the British crown to support the dignity of the proposed office. With uncanny prescience, Ball foresaw that Malta might become a British protectorate under his stewardship, but at this stage Nelson considered its ultimate future as a possession of the Two Sicilies. Nevertheless, Ball used his residence at the Villa San Anton as the venue for a new national congress, its members elected in the *casals*, or parishes. The first meeting on 18 February chose Aguis as the presiding judge. The same month Ball was suggesting that the Maltese regiments be incorporated into British service, from which improvements in pay and provisions could be expected.[41]

Malta's agony featured prominently in Nelson's workload for two years. Barely mentioned by biographers obsessed with the big battles, it was nevertheless the most gruelling of his operations against a specific enemy force, and involved the greatest loss of life. Nelson prosecuted it with totally inadequate means, too few ships, soldiers, guns, food, stores and finances, but as he gradually wore down Vaubois's miserable defenders, crouching behind ramparts laced with lethal glass and metal fragments and loaded shells – presaging the barbed wire and minefields of later wars – his own Maltese lived daily with malnutrition, disease, disruption and death. Their volunteers braved the severest weathers, 'almost naked, without pay and their only nourishment bread and a small allowance of pork'. At times the people survived on locusts, and at other times they starved. As the blockade bit into the besieged garrison, Vaubois conserved supplies by driving Maltese civilians trapped in Valletta outside his lines. Twenty thousand men, women and children had been dispossessed and thrown out by June 1799, and others were still following a year later. The job of feeding these refugees thus effectively passed from the besieged to the besiegers, multiplying

Nelson's difficulties. Fortunately, Ball's forces suffered but light casualties, although occasional tragedies can be found in his voluminous correspondence. One April night a guard boat blew up, killing and maiming nine of the occupants, including 'one of the finest lads, without exception, I ever knew'. But in general it is the daily fatigue and endurance that stands out. 'We have had a continuation of the worst weather I ever experienced,' wrote Ball in May. 'The ships have parted their cables twice and were driven to the eastward. Capt. Foley says his ship is leaky. She makes thirteen inches [of] water an hour and requires refitting. Some of his people have the Maltese fever . . .'[42]

Few of the problems found a lasting solution, and crisis after crisis ran seamlessly together. In April Nelson was again telling Acton that without further provisions the islanders might be forced to make their peace with the French, and the exasperated recipient explaining that the Sicilian government, now stripped of its mainland revenues, had much less money than the admiral supposed. Nevertheless, some £2000 in goods or money was stumped up. 'Your Lordship's humanity and ardour in procuring . . . these supplies has been the means of saving the lives of thousands,' wrote Ball.[43]

In the longer term the patience of the Two Sicilies was strained by a deal that Russia and Britain, the senior allies in the coalition, tidily stitched up between themselves. Nelson regarded Ferdinand as the legitimate sovereign of a liberated Malta, if under British protection, and in that belief had called upon the Sicilians to support the blockade. But in Whitehall wilier politicians saw Malta as a tool that could be used to bind Russia more tightly into the coalition. The tsar, it was known, had turned the expelled Order of St John into a private obsession, even assuming the mantle of its new Grand Master in November 1798. In April Britain and Russia agreed that once the French had been ousted from the island, it would be jointly occupied by British, Russian and Neapolitan troops until there was a permanent peace, and then restored to the Order of St John. Whitworth, Britain's minister in St Petersburg, explained that Russia had no ulterior designs on Malta, but many, including Nelson, suspected that territorial ambitions lurked beneath.[44]

On a more positive note, Russia's increased interest in Malta suggested another potential source of aid. For many months Nelson expected that Ushakov, whom he now suspected to be no more than a blackguard, would send reinforcements from the Russian fleet at Corfu. He was not sure he liked the idea of the Russians making a belated appearance to share in the glory of liberation, and went so far as to write to Whitworth to ask the tsar to recognise the achievements of the captain of the *Alexander* by creating him a Knight of the Order of St John. Acton, too, had mixed feelings, and began to wonder why the Two Sicilies should spend such pain and treasure upon an island that seemed to be drifting towards Russia, and that without Ferdinand having even been consulted. Ball promised Nelson that he would collaborate with the Russians if they appeared, but secretly hoped that Britain would assume ultimate sovereignty, a view widely favoured among the Maltese but as yet far from the hearts and minds in London.

In the meantime the blockade went on. The fight to get supplies in and out continued. The French clung like limpets to their positions, starved and harassed by the British, Portuguese and Maltese warriors no less determined. Ball still stared fixedly towards a brighter horizon . . . The enemy in Valletta were dropping with disease . . . their hopes of reinforcement and supply were crushed . . . a new battery was throwing shot the length of the Grand Harbour and scoring solid hits on the defences . . . And while they fought the people of Malta continued to die.[45]

5

Trying to bring these operations to a fruitful end, Nelson found himself thrown into strange company, and relations with them were not always straightforward. Across the Mediterranean from Malta, but uncomfortably close both to the south and west, situated on the burning shores of North Africa lay three dusty city-states that had become bywords for piracy, slave trading and murder. For centuries the dreaded 'Barbary corsairs' had poured from the ports of Algiers, Tunis and Tripoli to scourge Christendom.

Ostensibly they were client states of the Ottoman Porte, but in truth they had become largely independent Islamic entities, pursuing their own foreign relations through war or diplomacy as they saw fit, and thriving on the proceeds of commerce, plunder and blackmail. Willing to turn almost anything into money, Algiers even levied a charge for the gun salutes with which ports normally heralded the arrival of the warships of foreign nations. Britain, France and Spain, the superior sea powers, got discounted rates of sixty Spanish dollars; those of other nations paid seventy-six dollars. But the Barbary powers were not strictly pirates, if we define the latter as unlicensed sea raiders who were generally outlaws rather than instruments of any national policy, so much as state-sponsored corsairs or privateers who preyed upon nations with whom they were at war, but who accepted the diplomatic representatives of agreeable powers and affected to observe treaties. Countries reacted to them differently. Some bought immunity from attack with money and others exchanged like for like. Sweden, for example, would purchase the freedom of 132 of her nationals and peace for 300,000 Spanish dollars in December 1800. Britain's formidable naval power made her relatively impregnable to the predations of these corsairs, and relations were cordial; in fact, some of the North African states furnished provisions for the Royal Navy and the British troops in Gibraltar. But inevitably, with their system of protection or plunder, and wholesale enslavement of thousands of white Christians, whom they sold, forced to labour or held for ransom, they were hated throughout Europe and America, as if they were living fossils from an ancient and more barbaric world. Ironically, the Barbary powers would eventually be humbled by the United States and Britain, states heavily involved in human traffic of their own, the African slave trade.

Nelson disliked the Barbary states, but with bigger fish to fry he supposed that the best he could do at the moment was to bring them into the anti-French coalition, especially as the Porte itself was an enthusiastic member. Tunis and Tripoli, the nearest of the Barbary states, were both intriguing with the French, and helping to smuggle supplies to the beleaguered garrison in Valletta. One ship, sailing from Tunis under Neapolitan colours, was intercepted by the British and discovered to hail from Marseilles. But there was more than this at stake, because the desperate Maltese depended upon seaborne imports and exports, and in their present condition were in no position to sustain attacks from Barbary corsairs. Tunis and Tripoli were at war with Portugal and the Two Sicilies, and if Nelson could broker a general peace, he would not only have harnessed allies but also temporarily rid Malta and the Two Sicilies of inveterate enemies.

Not that seducing the North African states was going to be easy. They were notoriously capricious, temperamental and quarrelsome, even with each other. The Bey of Tunis and the Bashaw of Tripoli were consumed with mutual long-standing grievances and fears, and both were jealous of the more powerful Algiers. Perkins Magra, the British consul at Tunis, stigmatised Hamooda Pasha, the bey, as haughty and intemperate, incapable of 'uniformity of conduct', and described dealing with him and his advisers as akin to 'reasoning with mules'. Furthermore, the bey was complaining about a Gibraltar privateer that had seized one of his vessels in 1797. O'Hara, commanding at Gibraltar, had ordered its release, but it still remained in the possession of the captors.[46]

Tunis and Tripoli also had long-term self-interests to protect, and were economically inseparable from plunder. They stood with their backs to barren desert hinterlands inhospitable to agriculture, husbandry or industry, and therefore spent huge sums on the armed forces that gave them a livelihood. Additionally, before Britain regained command of the Mediterranean at the Nile the French had ruled this sea. Britain had abandoned it to their enemies in 1797, and as far as the Barbary states knew might do so again. If so, anyone who had prematurely thrown in with His Britannic Majesty stood to suffer retaliation. It behove these relatively small, if troublesome, powers to choose their friends carefully. Despite all this, the early signs were good. Using Magra, the British consul, the Bey of Tunis had already begun sending Nelson intelligence about the French garrison in Valletta, gleaned from vessels that had come from that port and fallen into the hands of his cruisers. He seemed amenable, and on 4 January even declared war on France, enslaving French citizens in his city and setting his corsairs upon their commerce on the high seas.[47]

A discerning diplomat, Magra saw an opportunity for Nelson to establish a rapport with the bey, and suggested the admiral write to him in a spirit of reciprocality. Consequently, on 17 March Lord Nelson praised the bey, pointing out that the French were 'the enemies of God and His Holy Prophet' and merited 'the vengeance of all true Mussulmen'. He knew that while Tunis had cordial relations with Britain, she was at war with her allies, Portugal and Naples. A thousand Neapolitans and Sicilians were said to be enslaved in Tunis at that very moment, and on his part the bey was angry at the capture of two of his cruisers by the Portuguese, and the alleged enslavement of their crews. So Nelson now told the bey that he had dissuaded his Portuguese ships from attacking Tunisian vessels, and had secured the release of twenty-five Moors and Turks and sent them to Constantinople. He offered to be the honest broker of a peace: 'at this moment all wars [between us] should cease, and all the world should join . . . to extirpate from off the face of the earth this race of murderers, oppressors and unbelievers.' It was heady stuff.[48]

It was a rugged road. The case of the Tunisian ship held at Gibraltar was investigated, but remained in dispute at the end of the year. On the other side, in March a corn brig, the *Nostra Signora Della Grazie*, which had been taking provisions to Malta under Neapolitan colours, was brought into Tunis as a prize, even though she had a safe pass from Nelson. Confronted by Magra, the bey drew himself to his full height and declared that the ship's bill of lading had proved her to be a Neapolitan, and as he was at war with Naples the British had no business interfering. However, should Lord Nelson wish him to issue Tunisian passes to a few victuallers he would oblige. To add fuel to the fire, at the end of the month, while the corn brig festered in the bay, her cargo spoiling and her crew in captivity, the corsairs brought in two feluccas which had been carrying wine to the British squadron off Malta, both with passes signed by Ball.[49]

Nelson sent *L'Entreprenant* cutter to strengthen Magra's arm, but she was refused permission to enter Tunis and had to drop off the admiral's packet of letters. Both sides then jockeyed for position. By detaining the corn brig, the bey hoped to draw a senior British officer to Tunis so that he could parade his grievances about ships being held by the British and Portuguese, but in the meantime he pressed it into his service and included it in a commercial convoy bound for Minorca and Spain. Magra responded by refusing the convoy British passports, and urging Duckworth to seize the disputed vessel if it appeared in Minorca. Yet in this case patience and forbearance were rewarded. By May Nelson had paved the way for Ferdinand to send a representative to Tunis to negotiate a truce on behalf of Sicily, albeit one oiled with sufficient money to liberate existing prisoners. Acton acknowledged that the treaty, signed on 26 June, was 'entirely obtained by your Lordship's support and powerful mediation'. And the following month the *Strombolo*, sent to Tunis to collect the Sicilian envoy, was also ordered to land a Portuguese officer with powers to negotiate a similar deal for his country. Magra, a firm but practical politician, was fundamental to the success of both negotiations, especially as the Sicilian envoy, a lawyer, made enough unreasonable demands to ruin the business. In June the truces were concluded for the duration of the present war, and Nelson was encouraged to go further. In August he asked the bey to moderate his financial demands in order to secure an agreement with yet another Italian state suffering from Tunisian depredations, Sardinia. The King of Sardinia, he explained, had been 'cruelly treated' by the French, and had little money. A reputation for even-handedness was essential to the role of an intermediary, and in September Nelson took up the case of a Tunisian vessel seized by the Sicilians.[50]

These diplomatic successes, almost unknown to Nelson biographers, made a significant difference to Malta and Italy during a particularly stressful period. Relations between Britain and Tunis remained unsteady. Nelson, tiring of wrangling, privately resolved to seize the Neapolitan corn brig by force at the first opportunity, while Magra felt so unsafe that he dissuaded his family from coming out to join him in Tunis. However, after the truces the bey manifested a 'most gracious disposition'. In the last months of 1799 the indefatigable Magra was even able to shuttle between Tunis, Palermo and Malta to organise Tunisian supplies for the stricken island. Some of these provisions were furnished at prices lower than those the produce commanded in Spain, and made the voyage to Malta in Tunisian ships carrying the British passports the bey had so recently condemned.[51]

Tripoli and Algiers were harder nuts to crack. Yusef Pasha, the governing bashaw of Tripoli, was particularly afraid of France, and had failed to support the Porte's war against the invaders. He had become disillusioned about Britain's ability to protect him from the French after she refused to send a ship to Tripoli's aid in 1797. Nelson's information, which came express from Simon Lucas, the British consul in Tripoli, was that Yusef had actually concluded a secret pact with Bonaparte on 24 February, offering a refuge to the French army should it retreat that way. Worried about the consequences, Lucas appealed to Nelson to protect the British residents. In March the admiral sent Hardy in the *Vanguard* to Tripoli with messages for the bashaw and Lucas. Hardy reached his destination on the 26th, and received 'a submissive answer' to his complaints about Gallic influence. The bashaw immediately ordered the French in Tripoli to be imprisoned, and their property confiscated. Another report from Lucas soon reawakened Nelson's concerns, however; according to him, the bashaw had rescinded all his actions after the *Vanguard*'s departure.[52]

The Barbary powers were volatile entities, and Britain needed a sound and steady diplomatic presence to inform and negotiate. Lucas, our man in Tripoli, was no Magra. His adopted son, the surgeon and secretary Bryan McDonough, complained of his 'frolicks' with 'a dame of easy virtue', and Ball came to regard him as 'a sad fellow' prone to scare stories. None was severer than St Vincent, who thought 'a greater rascal' did 'not exist in public or private life'. When

Lucas appeared in Palermo and began auctioning his valuables it was not clear whether the bashaw had driven him from Tripoli because of his attempts to combat the French influence or as a result of a personal tiff. Nevertheless, Nelson played safe and penned a second letter to the bashaw thanking him for his hospitality to Hardy but complaining again of the 'evil counsellors' about him. To carry the letter – and Lucas – back to Tripoli, the admiral now turned to Campbell of the Portuguese *Alfonso d'Albuquerque*, the same who had blotted his record by the premature destruction of the Neapolitan ships at Naples. But now Campbell entirely redeemed himself in a difficult mission. He was ordered to land Lucas with an uncompromising message. Portugal and Tripoli were officially at war, but Nelson had hitherto prevented his Portuguese allies from menacing Tripoli. He was prepared to withdraw his injunction, however, if the bashaw failed to signal compliance with several tough demands within two hours and to supply hostages to guarantee that any promises would be fulfilled. The French consuls and their retinues were to be surrendered to the British, and any French vessels in the harbour were to be destroyed. 'These folks must be talked to with honesty and firmness,' Nelson told St Vincent.[53]

Campbell made no bones about the matter upon his arrival on 6 May. He opened negotiations with the bashaw through Lucas and McDonough. At first the bashaw resisted, denouncing Lucas as a pernicious rumour-monger, and explaining that the French could not be surrendered as the sultan had demanded their shipment to Constantinople. Campbell wisely declined embroiling himself in any controversies about Lucas, but threatened to blockade Tripoli if his demands were not met. More, he proceeded to do so, making obvious preparations to cut out or destroy the Tripolitan cruisers with his boats while engaging the batteries with his ship. Poor weather prevented this strong action, but the Portuguese attacked one of the bashaw's vessels, of eighteen guns and 150 men, drove it ashore and set it on fire. They also cut off the bashaw's largest frigate, and were lowering boats to seize it when a Tripolitan flag of truce intervened. The bashaw backed down, handed over forty-two French prisoners, and made a candid statement about the French vessels in the port. Two, it appeared, had been sold to Greek merchants, and another lay stranded and unserviceable. A fourth Campbell allowed the bashaw to retain as a reward for his cooperation. The business was concluded with a peace agreement between Portugal and Tripoli that promised a degree of future stability. Back in Palermo, Nelson was impressed by what Campbell had achieved, and no doubt owned that he had misjudged the commodore.[54]

Nelson attempted to broker a peace between Tripoli and Naples, as he had done for Tunis, but the bashaw's regime survived upon plunder and he complained that if he made peace with Naples he must either declare war on another or lay up his cruisers. Of course, if Naples paid him adequate compensation . . . While the bargaining continued, Nelson contented himself with his more moderate success, nursing the consoling thought that he had at least eliminated one safe haven for any of Bonaparte's ships attempting to escape from Egypt.[55]

Algiers, he knew, was the most powerful Barbary state, but it was also more removed from Nelson's operations than Tunis and Tripoli, and for long less of an irritant. With so many pressing problems, the admiral felt neither the leisure nor the inclination to deal with Algiers until the close of 1799, when her nuisance rating significantly increased. Her ships still skimmed across the blue Mediterranean, seizing defenceless vessels or striking suddenly at isolated coastal communities. In November Tuscany appealed to Nelson for help after an unusually destructive raid on the port of Giglio, and Hoste was sent to patrol the coast. The Algerian privateers were not noted for chivalry. When a brig laden with bullocks for Minorca was captured by a notorious corsair named Rais Alvaz, her master was bastinaded for refusing to help with a boat. 'Never let us talk of the cruelty of the African slave trade, while we permit such a horrible war,' the admiral grumbled. More, the Algerians stepped up their attacks upon merchantmen plying about southern Italy, and that same month the American consul at Algiers, Richard O'Brien, estimated that twenty-two vessels with British passes from Nelson or Ball had been seized, and 245 Neapolitans, Sicilians and Maltese were enduring a miserable imprisonment with scanty rations and hard labour. If true, this was a significant toll of the provisions that were being procured for Malta with such labour.[56]

The new Dey of Algiers, Mustapha Pasha, had few reservations. 'He would capture his enemies wherever his corsairs met with them . . . and those in his possession he would keep' was his regular refrain. And like his counterpart in Tunis, Mustapha also saw prizes as hostages, and constantly met British protests with demands for the restitution of two or three cargoes taken by Gibraltar privateers. Moreover, he refused to allow provisions to be exported to the British unless traders paid for a licence in Algiers. Informed agents attributed much of this anti-British hostility to an influential group of Jewish merchants headed by Joseph Bacri and Naphtali Busnach, who shipped cargoes to the French under neutral flags, cargoes Britain defined as contraband. 'On this hinge,' said O'Brien, 'turns all your difficulties.' Another problem was the new consul general Britain had appointed to Algiers at the end of 1799. According to the dey, John Falcon, though a competent thirty-two-year-old, was 'too young and giddy' and it was with some difficulty that the Algerians could be persuaded to accept him.[57]

At the end of the year Nelson sent the *Phaeton* to Algiers with protests about the seizure of vessels with British passes. A supporting message from Constantinople was sent ashore in the same packet. The dey's predictable reply was that he was happy to issue as many of his passes as Nelson needed, provided attention was paid to Algerian grievances about the activities of the British privateers based at Gibraltar. Falcon, who did not get to Algiers and his new post until May 1800, made little more progress. The dey demanded British safe passage for an Algerian convoy bound for Constantinople and a huge sum in compensation for prizes held at Gibraltar as the price of his cooperation. 'He plainly told me he never intended to give up any of the Sicilians, Maltese or Neapolitans captured under English colours,' said Falcon. Rebuffed, the consul general withdrew to Malta without taking up his post.[58]

An agreement of any kind with the dey had to wait until December, after Nelson had left the Mediterranean, but difficulties continued more or less unabated. Another fifteen years would have to pass before there was a fierce and bloody reckoning.[59]

VII

COMING BACK

What powerful call shall bid arise
The buried warlike and the wise;
The mind that thought for Britain's weal,
The hand that grasped the victor steel?

Sir Walter Scott on Pitt and Nelson, 1808

I

As the winter of 1799 paled and the spring oleanders flowered red on the walls in Palermo, it seemed to Nelson that a dark corner had been turned. If Egypt and Malta remained running sores, the situation of Sicily had improved, and the wider political context was brightening with the blue skies. The allied coalition had formed raggedly, one power committing after another, in a piecemeal fashion. There was little overall strategy or a consensus about war aims, but the odds against France were distinctly lengthening.

On 12 March Austria finally added her weight, as an ally of Russia rather than Britain. The Austrians had the effrontery to write to Ferdinand, asking him to reopen a war that the emperor would now support. The Austrian plan involved holding the French in Germany and Switzerland, while collaborating with Russia in expelling them from Italy. The commander of the combined Austro-Russian army in Italy was Field Marshal Alexander Suvorov, one of the greatest warriors of the age. A ribald and elemental Russian of seventy years, his slender frame, sagging, lugubrious face, large, sad eyes and innumerable eccentricities (one a vampiric hatred of mirrors) belied a tigerish energy. Suvorov reached Vienna in March and was in the field the following month. About the same time the fall of Corfu finally released the Russo-Turkish fleet under Ushakov to play its part in the Italian war.[1]

Like the famous Spanish revolt of 1808, immortalised in the paintings of Goya, the war for the kingdom of Naples was unusually brutal, with atrocities flooding fiercely from both sides, some passing through massacre and mutilation to cannibalism. Ruffo was inherently humane, ready to forgive so that he could reconcile, but he led forces impelled by revenge and plunder as well as piety and patriotism. On their part, the French high command had its own way of dealing with rebels, and torched towns and slaughtered routinely. In Trania, Ceglie, Carbonara and other places the accumulating human cost of resisting invasion rose into thousands. Even some hardened French veterans complained of such a 'cruel and barbarous' conflict, while a sixteen-year-old Jacobin would carry into old age his vivid memories of the 'terrible slaughter of the vanquished'. None of it stopped the counter-revolution, however. With Suvorov in the north and the insurgents gaining control all around, in the Cilento, Basilicata, Apulia and Molise, Macdonald, the French commander-in-chief, warned Paris on 17 April that he could not hold Naples. The military assumption that had underpinned Nelson's great gamble – that the French could be successfully squeezed between Neapolitan and Austrian forces – had been intrinsically sound.[2]

It was time for Nelson to resume the offensive. 'The moment the Emperor moves,' he told St Vincent, 'I shall go with all the ships I can collect into the Bay of Naples to create a diversion.' Naples, he believed, was short on supplies and held down by only two thousand French soldiers, aided by a militia of 20,000 'weathercocks' who would shift with the balance of power. He admitted to Spencer that their Sicilian Majesties would be unlikely to 'consent to my leaving them for a moment', but his determination to mount an attack was unshaken.[3]

The question of who was to command the new naval offensive was answered when three of the brothers, Troubridge, Hood and Hallowell, returned to Sicily after the abortive attempt to attack Alexandria. Nelson did not rule himself out from leading the expedition, but when Acton put the plan before the king on 18 March he approved it with one serious cavil. 'Their Majesties, however,' Acton wrote, 'in confiding an operation so important to their service to your Lordship have another and dear interest at heart, the safety of their numerous family. They cannot bear [the] thought of remaining alone in Palermo without the possibility of leaving it with security under your protection, till . . . the venomous seed of disaffection and of rebellion is . . . extinguished . . . Their Majesties require me to desire your Lordship to remain with them for your useful counsel and for the motive explained above.' They wished Nelson to stay in Palermo 'while their Majesties and family keep their residence in this capital', and recommended his place in the squadron be filled by Troubridge.[4]

The return of such trusted comrades provided sounding boards for his ideas and enlivening social occasions. There was time to chew over their triumph at the Nile, newly recounted in an effusive image-building pamphlet written by Berry, which Nelson pronounced 'well drawn up'. We have a few glimpses of their leisure moments. On Easter Sunday the four friends joined the Hamiltons, Mrs Lock and the minister of the *Swiftsure* in a visit to an ancient Capuchin monastery, about a mile from the southern gate of the city. It was a macabre occasion. They descended into its subterranean cemetery, where thousands of the city's mummified ancestors occupied 'niches' in the walls on either side of the pathway, hanging from hooks in simple cowls or their crumbling finery, men, women and children with heads bent as if in prayer, staring through black holes, with hanging jaws and bony claw-like hands. In a chapel where the nobility and gentry rested, their guide lifted the body of a small prince, clothed after the fashion of an earlier time, but the ladies recoiled in disgust as the head of the corpse fell off. Nevertheless, the party steeled themselves for an account of how fresh bodies were placed in coffins and dried in an oven so that their skins could be hardened like tanned leather. Indeed, a portly military officer who had died the previous day was receiving those very attentions at the moment. Not surprisingly, the women quit the tour, but on 26 March all found suitable entertainment in a ball and supper hosted by Hallowell on the poop and quarterdeck of the *Swiftsure*. Neapolitan and Sicilian notables and nobility enhanced the occasion, on which the cabins were given over to card parties.[5]

The serious business had still to be faced. In Naples the French were already stretched for food, forage for their horses, and silver, and Macdonald had resorted to sequestrating supplies by force. Relatively little was to be had in the city itself, and imports from the countryside had been stifled by the growing insurgency. Now Nelson planned to seize the islands of Procida and Ischia off the northern point of the Bay of Naples and Capri to the south, using them to shut the port down.

On 31 March a powerful flotilla sailed bravely from Palermo, Troubridge's *Culloden*, Louis's *Minotaur*, Hood's *Zealous*, Hallowell's *Swiftsure*, the Portuguese *St Sebastian*, *El Corso* brig and *Perseus* bomb. The next day the *Seahorse* frigate joined. With orders from Nelson and the king in his pocket, Troubridge had full military and civil authority, as well as a detachment of Neapolitan troops. He was to base his operations at Procida, where there was a decent harbour, and to restore the islands to their king, raising royal colours and establishing temporary governments. Nelson emphasised that Troubridge was to use 'every means in your power to conciliate the affections of the loyal part of the inhabitants', but traitors would obviously answer for their actions. Nelson opined that a 'speedy reward and quick punishment' were the 'foundation of good government', but the former governor of Procida, Michele de Curtis, and several other trusted officials accompanied the expedition to advise and assume local authority.[6]

After Naples fell to the French, Nelson had got the Sicilian government to acknowledge that her ships were liable to seizure as legitimate prize, and the principle had been extended to Tuscany in April. Prize money was anticipated, and Hoste's *Mutine* had opened the season in February by cutting a fourteen-gun polacre from the Bay of Sorrento. While Troubridge was charged with protecting areas under royal colours and stimulating and assisting the counter-revolution far and wide, he concentrated his activities in the Bay of Naples, extending his patrols occasionally to include Gaeta and Civita Vecchia on the Roman coast. He was not, however, to fire upon the city of Naples itself without licence from the admiral. In all, Nelson hoped that the campaign would demonstrate Britain's continuing commitment and encourage resistance to the 'modern Goth'.[7]

Procida and Ischia surrendered immediately on 2 April, throwing the gates of their castles open to landing parties without resistance, and the few enemy gunboats that sallied from Naples to investigate quickly retreated without firing a shot. The republican 'liberty trees' and tricolours were destroyed, and Troubridge garrisoned and strengthened the fortifications. 'Such loyalty you never saw,' he reported. 'The people are perfectly mad with joy, asking for their beloved king.' The islands of Capri, Ventotene, Ponza and Palmarola also submitted within two days, and a blockade of Naples and the coast was imposed. The *Culloden* seized a privateer, and the *Seahorse* burned five vessels trying to run provisions to Valletta on the 6th. The matter of justice was much more complicated, and Troubridge did not act consistently. He understood that legal affairs were best left to the Sicilians, and thought attempts to burden the British with them as efforts to 'throw the odium on us'. But he was not reluctant to express ferocious opinions on how the process should develop. He disliked trials of absent defendants, but was typically brusque about the guilty. A captured priest 'must have his head [taken] off', and the overturned republican commander of Ischia, once a Neapolitan officer, was 'double' ironed in the *Culloden* after being rescued from an angry mob who had torn off his uniform. Some thirty-five other miscreants were shackled in the ship, and others incarcerated in the castle of Ischia, awaiting examination and potential execution. More significantly, though Troubridge admired Curtis as 'a truly honest and valuable subject', he railed against the judges. When one explained that a bishop was needed to deconsecrate disloyal priests before they could be executed, the captain 'told him to hang them first, and if he did not think the degradation of hanging sufficient, I would piss on the[ir] damned Jacobin carcass[es]'. As far as Troubridge was concerned, convicted traitors needed no masses or confessionals, for 'Hell was the proper place for them'. Considering the available judge 'frightened out of his senses', he wrote to Palermo for another so that 'eight or ten' of his prisoners could be strung up as examples.[8]

As in the case of Malta, Nelson was both adviser and a conduit for necessary support. Troubridge's needs extended from gunboats to elm for repairing boats, but here, as in Malta, the big item was food. The islands in the Bay of Naples had no mills to grind corn, and once restored to the king they were barred from obtaining flour from the occupied mainland. Fifty thousand people were thrown upon the ability of Sicily to export, and such shipments as Nelson badgered out of the government were consumed within days of their arrival.

Troubridge dug into the supplies of his squadron and his own pockets to supply or buy what he could. He opened a public subscription, and cannonaded Palermo with frantic letters, lashing the Sicilians for breaking their promises and releasing so little of their plentiful supplies. 'No king or ministers could ever exert themselves more to save a nation that these do to lose it,' he foamed. In fact, if all the king's orders had been carried out there would have been a sufficiency of provisions, but his administration let him down. The combustible Troubridge identified the most culpable minister as Count Trabia, 'a complete monopolizer' and 'vagabond', who had turned the British into tools of his deception. When supplies that Trabia was supposed to have sent failed to arrive from Palermo, Troubridge approached Messina for alternative provisions in May, but his boats were turned away. Even amidst this distraction, Troubridge knew that Nelson was doing all he could. The admiral issued numerous passes to ships carrying provisions, eleven on 6 May alone, and forcefully took up Troubridge's complaints. He had the queen summoning Trabia to the court to account for the failure in supplies, and the king foraging in his private coffers to buy cargoes of corn. 'For my own part I feel so much indebted to your lordship for your constant attention to me,' said Troubridge, 'that I feel I can never do enough.' Troubridge's daily avalanche of emotional, sometimes almost hysterical, letters probably alarmed Nelson, but he trusted the inherent strength of the man, and fought the battle for him that he was fighting for Ball, using the same arguments. Adverting again to his belief in paternal government that protected the people, he told Acton that 'If His Majesty loses them [the islands] again, it will be very difficult to recover them. Therefore, it is my opinion that the very greatest care should be taken that the islanders are supplied with the greatest abundance of provisions, and at the very cheapest rate. Those who cannot afford to buy it should be given. In short, the greatest care should be taken that these people who retain their allegiance should have plenty to eat, and that the rebels should be forced to confess the difference of situation.' The 'terrible' boat incident in Messina infuriated him, no less than Troubridge, and he demanded a general order be sent to all ports to admit vessels from the islands.[9]

While wrestling with such systemic difficulties, Troubridge applied himself to the task of discomforting the enemy. The captain estimated that the French had over two thousand men in their five fortresses, three of which were located in Naples and two to the west as far as Baia. There were, of course, also substantial numbers of Jacobin adherents, but Troubridge believed that the vast majority of the people were loyal to the king and would rise en masse in a showdown. So weak did the Parthenopean Republic appear that Troubridge reckoned that no more than a few thousand regulars were needed to make 'a glorious massacre' and itched for the fight. The admiral warned Troubridge against precipitate landings on the mainland, when foreign troops were still expected, and had directed his attention to the blockade. But Troubridge lived for action ('Oh, how I long to have a dash at these thieves!'), and in anticipation of reinforcements began mounting naval artillery on field carriages and carts to turn them into siege guns. In April and May several hundred additional troops, the requested judge and some provisions came by three frigates under George Cockburn and Count Thurn. But the first attacks were disappointing. In April the British began skirmishing with the enemy gunboats in Baia, rounding up any Neapolitan vessels they saw and firing upon enemy positions ashore. Troubridge's pinprick assaults were annoying, and one of his boats inflicted fifty to sixty casualties on an enemy force assembling on a beach to oppose them, but his bigger thrusts failed. On 28 April the *Minotaur* and *Swiftsure* landed sixty soldiers at Castellammare, a little south of Naples and captured the port. Unfortunately, even reinforced they had to be withdrawn before a vigorous French counterattack, leaving several prisoners and guns to fall into enemy hands. The sole British spoil was a mortar boat. Much the same happened at Salerno, an unfortified town south of Naples that stood in the path of Ruffo's army as it marched north. On 25 April a detachment of marines from Hood's *Zealous* gained control of the town and distributed arms to local insurgents, but enemy reinforcements drove the British back two days later. Hood lost sixteen men extricating his soldiers. For several days the struggle see-sawed as the French and Jacobins fled, regrouped and attacked again, while the *Zealous* tried to savage them with terrifying broadsides. When the dust settled, the French abandoned the position on 3 May, and the British had secured a small foothold. Macdonald fantasised about Troubridge's casualties at Castellammare and Salerno in his official dispatch, exaggerating in true Napoleonic style, but admitted a loss of thirty to forty of his own men.[10]

More effectively, Troubridge communicated with Ruffo and the other insurgent forces converging upon the French positions. Important leaders were cultivated. Brigadier Tschudy, a Swiss soldier, slipped from Naples to visit Troubridge, and returned with orders to prepare other loyal officers, while on 26 April Fra Diavolo, the brigand turned revolutionary who claimed the power of raising 20,000 men at a day's notice, was on board the *Culloden* discussing an attack on Gaeta. Most of the insurgents and would-be insurgents were short on arms, and Troubridge was hamstrung by his own shortages of cartridges, powder and shot. Hood had to advise royalists to fire stones, and was daily cutting up boat spikes to make artillery rounds 'of some sort'. Similarly the great numbers of defectors escaping from the mainland to join Troubridge exacerbated the squadron's victualling problems, a difficulty he partly solved by persuading many to return to Naples to prepare for the return of the king's government. His presence alone raised expectations among the people, who, as Macdonald told the French Directory on 17 April, grew ever more impudent. He confessed that a general insurrection seemed imminent, and doubted that he could contain it, even before learning that Suvorov had defeated the French at Cassano and opened the way to Milan. In these last days of the Parthenopean Republic, Macdonald hit hard at the encircling adversaries, sacking the towns of Castellammare, Gragnano, Lettere, Cava and Victri, but everything was against him: the insurgency, the British naval presence and the ominous success of Suvorov. On 7 May it happened. Breaking into and looting shops and houses as they went, Macdonald's forces withdrew from Naples, leaving a thousand well-provisioned diehards holed up in the strong hilltop fortress of St Elmo, and retreated north towards Capua. If necessary the French in St Elmo could negotiate a surrender according to the accepted usages of war, but the Neapolitan Jacobins who had betrayed the Bourbon regime were effectively abandoned to their enemies, forting up in the remaining castles, where they listened to the stories brought from fleeing refugees from the south, spine-chilling yarns of the vengeful *sanfedisti* advancing purposefully towards the city with blood on their hands. The Jacobins had dreamed of a new order, but the world beyond their walls had suddenly become a lonely and dangerous place. No sooner had the blue-coated Gallic horde gone than Troubridge sent Hallowell to reclaim Castellammare. The British commanders looked upon the defeated Jacobins with stony faces. After taking Salerno, Hood, who shared Troubridge's hatred of the 'infernal set of vagabonds and rascals', used the absence of a judge to encourage the jubilant local royalists to dispose of the captured Jacobins as they wished. It augured ill for those who had collaborated with the invaders.[11]

The tide had turned. Suvorov was getting the better of the French in the north, while Ruffo, rather more than the 'swelled up priest' of Nelson's imagination, was regaining the south, and screening them all from unwelcome intrusions were the British ships. The admiral sent a 'handsome compliment' to Troubridge's squadron, and was able to inform Spencer that a mere ten days might see their Sicilian Majesties back in their kingdom. Acton also felt new blood in his veins as he prepared fourteen hundred foot and horse and provisions to support Troubridge's beachhead.[12]

2

As the restoration approached, the tangled issue of the treatment of the treasonable Jacobins naturally pushed itself to the fore. Two theories about how they might be handled were developing. The one favoured by Ruffo emphasised forgiveness, reconciliation and conciliation, and the return of the wayward to the fold. On 17 April the cardinal published a general pardon to those who would recant and return. The other approach, adopted by their Sicilian Majesties and Nelson, was firmer. It also emphasised reconciliation. As Ferdinand stated in his instructions to Ruffo, dated 1 May, 'It is my intention . . . in accordance with my duty as a good Christian, and the loving father of my people, to forget the past entirely, and to grant all a full and general pardon, which will protect them all from any consequences of any past transgression. I shall also forbid any investigation, believing as I do that their acts are due not to natural perversity, but to fear and cowardice.' But there would be exceptions, for, unlike Ruffo, the king and queen had to return to a place of potential danger, placing their lives and those of their family among those who had ousted and betrayed them. They had been lucky, for the British had been on hand to save them, but such a fortunate circumstance would not continue indefinitely. The queen, in particular, was so damaged by the treachery she had experienced, so fearful of the murderous consequences of French republicanism, and so nervous for the future, that she doubted she could ever live in Naples again. Like all people, the monarchy craved security. For them, if it was necessary to forgive and repatriate the many who had been seduced or intimidated into joining the Jacobins, it was equally necessary to expunge the few severely disaffected, subversive and unreconstructed elements that were deemed a threat to the stability of a restored regime.[13]

This was an issue that deeply embroiled Nelson, and it is worth developing in a few paragraphs. The template for the king's view was outlined in Acton's letter to Ruffo of 4 April and Ferdinand's instructions of 11 April and 1 May. A keystone was the principle that the right to grant clemency rested with the crown alone. Pardoning, Acton told Ruffo, was 'a peculiar and natural prerogative of the crown, as is well known'. However, for the cardinal's guidance, their Majesties outlined the principal exemptions to the general pardon, those who would be subject to arrest and judicial review, and who – in the most extreme cases – would warrant exile or execution. Particularly culpable, said Ferdinand, were those who had held office under the republican regime, in the government, police or forces, especially those who had formerly enjoyed positions with the king; who had sat on commissions inquiring into the alleged misdeeds of monarchical rule; who had written or distributed seditious literature; and nobles who abrogated their oaths of loyalty and obligation to the king to assist the enemy. Such individuals actually taken in arms were to be shot 'without any legal formalities, and according to the usages of war'. After sifting, the graver cases would face a specially appointed commission, and convictions could lead to the forfeiture of property, exile and execution. As the queen emphasised to Ruffo, the rebels could make 'no terms' with the king, but simply throw themselves upon the judicial process and his mercy.[14]

The royal search for security, in effect a *sine qua non* for a restoration of their regime, saw the purging of the most dangerous Jacobins as essential. Its extent depended on the nature of the offences and the mood of the victors. The queen was willing to reward 'the faithful' and punish 'the wicked' with equal enthusiasm, and though she hoped she was not vengeful, she found herself relishing the prospect of a general massacre of the Jacobins. The king advocated 'no pity' for the purveyors of gross treachery.[15]

The language of the royals and their ministers was echoed by Nelson. He regarded the king's statement of the 'few exceptions' to be made to a general pardon as 'very handsome'. Sharing the queen's view that 'rewards and punishments' were a key to 'all good government', he accepted that the punishment of the grossest offenders was just and necessary to remove corrosive and destructive elements and act as a deterrent. These principles were unexceptional in an eighteenth-century man. Moreover, over and above such beliefs, and his duty to support the most faithful British ally, Nelson was identifying with their Majesties emotionally. He saluted their stand against France, felt the queen's fear and misery, and saw their plight, and he stood much as a loyal friend might do, ready to assist an injured comrade in distress. 'Lay me at the feet of their Majesties,' he told Acton. 'Tell me how I can best serve them.'[16]

No one who has studied Nelson's justice at sea can fairly characterise him as a severe man. In normal circumstances, he believed in reclamation and second chances, but he had always stood absolutely firm against those who would jeopardise the welfare of their fellows. As far as governments were concerned, nothing alarmed him more than foes within, who would destabilise a realm – even one in need of reform – by gnawing at its foundations and delivering it into the hands of malignant enemies. He met such threats firmly, even ruthlessly. Among the Jacobins, for example, he particularly condemned the nobles and former office holders who betrayed the privilege and trust that had been reposed in them, and iced their treachery with ingratitude.

Thus did Caracciolo and Marshal Charles Edward Yauch fall from grace. Yauch had been sent with a detachment to relieve Neapolitan garrisons holding out in Orbetello (Tuscany) and Longone (Elba). Troubridge ordered James Oswald of the *Perseus* to transport the force from Procida, but did not enjoy reading his report. At Longone, which the *Perseus* reached on 2 May, they found the French delivering a smart fire, and Yauch declined to land. He repeated his disinclination immediately afterwards at Orbetello, which had been under attack for five days. When *Perseus* returned, the irascible commander of the *Culloden* summarily ordered Yauch out of the ship, and sent him to Procida. Orbetello was lost, but Longone struggled on. Troubridge called upon Nelson to urge the king to 'hang' the 'coward', whose 'dirty villainy distresses me beyond description'. No less Nelson, whose thoughts were with the abandoned defenders of Longone. 'The king must instantly order his trial, and if guilty of cowardice or treachery, he must be shot in the most infamous manner,' he stormed. 'What a villain! Good God! To see shot flying and not taking the post of honour entrusted to him by his gracious master! If an example is not made of this wretch, for he has not one inch of a man about him, the king will never be well served . . . Excuse my feelings, but I cannot bear such gracious monarchs should be so ill-served. More than ever hasten the troops. *Think* of Longone!'[17]

That said, the correspondence of 1799 runs with an unusually callous undercurrent that reflected the scars of a brutal civil conflict. The war had reached a bloody, pitiless phase in which republicans and royalists threw themselves at each other like pit dogs, giving and expecting no quarter. Sheer survival, and the knowledge that failure could result in the extinction of self and loved ones, was turning humanity into a disposable luxury. In every direction there were bereaved people with wrongs to right. Even relative outsiders, such as the British, seem to have been tainted with its corrosive influence. Troubridge was unusually forthright, but hardly unique, and the tone was set by Nelson himself, who stonily urged the captain of the *Culloden* to 'send me word some proper heads are taken off' for that 'alone will comfort me'. Troubridge was literally willing to oblige, but the decapitated head of an alleged Jacobin was not forwarded because of the hot weather.[18]

It is difficult to escape the conclusion that the stresses of these past months were affecting Nelson and compounding his poor physical state. 'In short, my dear lord,' he admitted to Spencer on 17 April, 'I am almost blind, and so fagged by all things not doing as I wish that I often think that no consideration ought to keep me here. God bless you. I am out of spirits and with great reason.' The possibility of returning home seemed real. The Hamiltons had long had ministerial permission to take leave, and had remained in Naples largely on account of the difficult political situation. Now England beckoned more imperiously, especially as her winter was over, and Sir William's rheumatic hip might give him less trouble. At Naples he was also running low on money, trying his purse by oiling the wheels of diplomacy and keeping a lavish table. If the French could be expelled from Italy and Ferdinand restored to his throne, as now seemed possible, the Nelson–Hamilton entourage might return to London on a high note. Professionally, Nelson's superiors were still fully supportive. Most recently, on 12 March, Spencer had written that his conduct in protecting Naples was 'honourable and glorious'.[19]

But then, in its unpredictable way, the world suddenly changed. For during the evening of 12 May a small brig, the *Espoir*, under Captain James Sanders, reached Palermo with alarming news. A large French fleet of over thirty sail had escaped from Brest, and been spotted off Oporto in Portugal, steering for the Mediterranean. Britain's naval supremacy within the Strait was about to be overthrown.

3

The night of 25 April had been foggy and dark in the approaches to the English Channel and Vice Admiral Eustache Bruix, commanding the French fleet bottled up in Brest, seized his opportunity. He squeezed through Lord Bridport's loose blockade, released five Spanish capital ships from Ferrol, which joined him, and headed for the Mediterranean. His orders, unknown to the British, were relatively flexible, but directed the admiral to succour the army in northern Italy and then rescue Bonaparte in Egypt. Corfu and Malta were also mentioned as desirable objectives. Whatever, the French fleet was a full-blooded challenge to British control of the Mediterranean.

Bruix first encountered the British Mediterranean fleet off Cadiz, where Vice Admiral George Elphinstone, Lord Keith, was shutting seventeen of the Spanish line in the port with fifteen of his own. Keith was therefore greatly outnumbered when Bruix made his appearance, but boldly stood between the French and Spanish, effectively daring the enemy to attack him. Bruix's business was elsewhere, and he passed by, reaching the Strait of Gibraltar on 5 May. St Vincent was at Gibraltar that day with a single capital ship, and had no alternative but to watch thirty-five enemy ships, nineteen or so of them of the line, materialise through the rain and stream past into the Mediterranean under dark clouds. The old commander-in-chief had never been in a more serious pickle, for he had only fourteen capital ships within the Strait, and they were widely scattered: four with Duckworth at Minorca; a like force with Troubridge off Naples; one ship at Palermo carrying Nelson's flag; three under Ball at Malta; and two off Egypt with Smith. Even with the support of three available Portuguese men-of-war, those detached units were capable of being wiped out piecemeal.

The old tiger stirred. He dispatched the *Espoir* and *Cameleon* up the Mediterranean with warnings, and, bringing Keith to Gibraltar by 10 May, assumed command of his force and sailed after the French. In doing so he had to leave Cadiz open, and risk the escape of the Spanish fleet. Soon Don Frederico Carlos Gravina was leading his ships through the Strait and the Mediterranean was awash with big battle fleets. Joining Duckworth at Minorca, St Vincent fielded twenty of the line, but hardly knew which way to turn. Above – somewhere – was Bruix, bound whither no one really knew, while below were the Spaniards, who posed a distinct threat to Minorca at any time the island was left uncovered. The British commander-in-chief shifted inconclusively between the two dangers, first towards one and then the other, and then he fell ill.[20]

After nine months in command of the Mediterranean, the British admirals were fighting to regain control. When the news reached Nelson, his instinct was to reinforce St Vincent and Duckworth with as many ships of the line as he could muster, though St Vincent had not required it. *L'Espoir* was soon flying to Troubridge at Procida, the *Mutine* to Dixon off Leghorn and the little *Penelope* cutter to Ball, calling in their capital ships. 'No time must be lost,' Ball was informed. A wave of energy swept through the brothers. *L'Espoir* reached Troubridge on 14 May, and he instantly recalled Hood from Salerno, left the blockade of Naples to Foote of the *Seahorse* and pointed his capital ships towards Palermo.[21]

Taking the news to the royal palace at Colli, Nelson saw the queen close to panic. The arrival of a French fleet at such a time, when the counter-revolution was at a critical moment, was potentially disastrous. An enemy fleet of that size appearing off Naples would completely overturn the odds, or, worse, side-step Nelson and overwhelm Sicily. There were only two British regiments at Messina, supported by weak Neapolitan battalions, and while Graham and the local governor, Danero, had improved defences at the citadel, clearing adjacent ground, it was without a counterscarp and vulnerable to attack from both the harbour and beach. So great was the alarm that by 15 May Ferdinand was issuing a proclamation calling upon all Sicilians to prepare to repel invasion. Writing to St Vincent three days earlier, Nelson relayed a change of plan. 'I am only sorry that I cannot move to your help, but this island appears to hang in my stay. Nothing could console the Queen this night but my promise not to leave them unless the battle was to be fought off Sardinia [Sicily?].' Tortured by visions of falling into the hands of the French with her children, Maria Carolina's hysteria was understandable, but her attempts to cling to Nelson were short-sighted, for her ultimate security rested upon the ability of the British to eliminate the enemy fleet. The queen reluctantly accepted this, but she was sore afraid, since Bruix reportedly had so many ships and Nelson transparently had so few. He told her he could defeat the French with half their number, but she shook her head as the little admiral left to fight her battle. 'Though inferior in strength, he wants to attack them with the seven [ships] he already has,' she wrote to Gallo. 'I watch him go with regrets, for himself, being a brave man, and for us, because the chances in the sea are doubtful.'[22]

Nelson was indeed in a quandary. Free, he would have joined St Vincent, improving his chances of winning a decisive victory, but he was not free, for he guarded a theatre at a critical pass. 'Should you come upwards without a battle,' he wrote to the earl, 'I hope in that case you will afford me an opportunity of joining you, for my heart would break to be near my commander-in-chief, and not assisting him in such a time. What a state I am in! If I go I risk, and more than risk, Sicily, and what is now safe on the continent [mainland] . . . As I stay, my heart is breaking, and to mend the matter I am seriously unwell. God bless you. Depend on my utmost zeal to do as I think my dear friend would wish.'[23]

To cover both obligations as well as he could, Nelson made a courageous decision. He would concentrate as many ships as possible to the north of the island of Marettimo, just west of Sicily, a position from which he might block hostile threats to Sicily, Malta and the east, and at the same time be ready to respond to a summons from his commander-in-chief. Never had the little man stood taller. With barely a dozen capital ships he planned to stand truculently in the way of an enemy fleet of twenty – perhaps nearer forty if the Spanish and French had combined – ready to tear the heart out of their force, destroying it for anything else, even if it caused his entire destruction. As he wrote to St Vincent, 'Your lordship may depend that the squadron under my command shall never fall into the hands of the enemy, and before we are destroyed I have little doubt but that the enemy will have their wings so completely clipped that they may be easily overtaken.'[24]

He sent an express to St Vincent and Duckworth, alerting them to his intention, and inviting the latter to fall back upon him so that they could at least 'look the enemy in the face'. Lieutenant Philip Lamb, his agent for transports, was left at Palermo to redirect calling ships to the new rendezvous and the *Petterel* – commanded by the brother of Jane Austen – tried to find Ball, while the admiral sailed with the advance of his force on 20 May, *Vanguard*, *Culloden* and the *Principe Real*, as well as the frigate *Minerve*. Slowly the brothers gathered around. Hallowell's *Swiftsure*, Louis's *Minotaur* and another Portuguese, the *St Sebastian*, soon fell in, and Hood of the *Zealous* caught up on the 21st. Two days later Nelson reached his rendezvous, but there was no sign of Ball or Dixon. Nevertheless, the admiral reckoned that their arrival would eventually give him eleven ships of the line.[25]

The day Hood joined, dispatches arrived by a Portuguese ship, notifying Nelson that Duckworth was awaiting St Vincent and that for the time being he was on his own. However well-fought, he would be greatly outnumbered, but Nelson put a 'new plan of attack' to Troubridge, Louis, Hood and Niza, and won their approval. 'They all agree it must succeed,' the admiral claimed. What he meant by success is not clear. Against such odds the possibility of a defeat was strong. Nelson's plan has never been found, but both the nature of the proposed encounter and the clarity of the tactical vision behind it emerge from terse remarks. Thus he wrote to Emma, who nervously awaited every mail, that whatever happened, 'I will cut them up [so] that they will not be fit for even a summer's cruise, and one of them shall have the [*Incendiary*] fire-ship laid on board.' The import is that Nelson intended a point-blank and almost nightmarish combat, using every means at hand to defeat the French or, failing that, to destroy their operational capability. If he was defeated, so be it, but it would be a defeat that would transform itself into victory.[26]

Whether any of it sufficiently answered the overall strategic situation is another matter. St Vincent and Nelson had independently opted to confront the Franco-Spanish threat with two undersized fleets, one based on Minorca and the other Sicily. St Vincent dithered about whether to pursue the French or guard Minorca, and whether to reinforce Nelson or not. It was not until 31 May that news of approaching reinforcements from England persuaded him to send Nelson four additional ships. Nelson's grasp of the big picture was also blurred. He complained that Duckworth had not come instantly to his support. 'If he shelters himself under nice punctilios of orders, I do not approve of an officer's care of himself,' he grumbled to Emma. But this was hardly charitable. Duckworth's small force had been charged with the protection of Minorca. Confronted with the threat of two large enemy fleets, his duty was to stay at his post if practicable or rally to St Vincent's advancing force, rather than to dissipate its strength. The Bruix cruise had exposed not only the fragility of Britain's command of the quarter, but also the differing priorities of her admirals.[27]

Despite bad weather Nelson cruised off Marettimo for several days, expecting to fight the battle of his life and flinging small vessels out north and south to ensure that Bruix did not steal past along the coasts of Italy or Barbary. In an acute state of prolonged nervous tension, he suffered seasickness, migraine, sleeplessness and loss of appetite, and longed for the reassuring presence of Ball. The latest intelligence put the French fleet at twenty-four sail of the line. Dixon joined, bringing the admiral's force to only eight or nine of the line, but in black moments Nelson feared that Ball had run foul of the French at sea. As if to rub in apprehensions, Captain Hallowell, whose sense of humour tended towards the macabre, chose this time to give Nelson a present made from the main mast of *L'Orient*. It was a coffin! 'When you are tired of life you may be buried in one of your own trophies!' said Hallowell. Nelson scarcely needed reminding of the prospect, and two days later added a codicil to his will in favour of the Hamiltons, but he enjoyed the gift nevertheless. Ultimately, it would serve the very purpose that Hallowell had suggested.[28]

By 28 May matters had eased with intelligence from St Vincent that put the French fleet in Toulon. Nelson decided to return to Palermo, where he planned to hold his force in readiness and complete water and provisions. Back in Sicily on the 30th, he had concocted a 'plan for the defence of Palermo' that 'should prevent the whole French fleet destroying us'. Though physically exhausted, he was soon advising the government on suitable places for the establishment of new shore batteries.[29]

The day after Nelson's return Ball reached Palermo, and on 1 June the *Alfonso d'Albuquerque* gave him thirteen capital ships. The naval part of Nelson's 'plan' for the defence of the city emerges in an order he had provisionally issued to the fleet on 28 May. Twelve ships of the line were anchored across the shoreline of Palermo bay, covering the whole of the waterfront. *Vanguard* was a cable's length from the lighthouse in the north-west, and the other ships extended roughly south-east with intervals of two cables between them, standing in oblique line abreast rather than line ahead, and held in place by two anchors. The line's weakness was the open right flank three miles from the *Vanguard*, and guarded by the *Audacious* and *Minotaur*.[30]

The crisis had emphasised the potential incompatibility of Nelson's position. He could not always effectively protect Naples and serve his commander-in-chief simultaneously, and a solution to the Neapolitan problem was urgently needed. Back in the Bay of Naples the Jacobins had taken advantage of the absence of the British ships of the line by mounting a counterattack upon the king's flotilla at Procida. Only the Neapolitan frigate *Minerve*, under Count Thurn, the *Perseus* bomb and seven gun and mortar vessels were at Procida on 17 May, when Caracciolo made a determined assault using twenty-three small vessels. He was beaten off in a stiff fight which cost both sides casualties. A few days later the arrival of *Seahorse, Mutine, San Leone* (a Neapolitan corvette) and a bombard taken from the enemy at Castellammare prevented a renewal of the attack.[31]

In Malta, too, the French took advantage of the fleet's absence, and here the consequences were more serious because Vaubois used a flotilla of half-galleys, launches and *speronaras* to become 'complete masters of the seas' around the island. They shut down the two principal British ports, St Paul's and Marsa Scirocco, carried boats into Valletta, and disrupted the supplies that were now 'almost daily' coming to the Maltese from the mainland. Rarely had the importance of Nelson's paper-thin blockade been more immediately demonstrated.[32]

The interlude may have set the blockade back months. Vivion of the marines, who had been left in charge, painted hideous pictures of the destitution, disease and desperation that gripped the besiegers, and without Ball's conciliating influence the 'lower classes' rebelled against their chiefs and Maltese society was 'torn to pieces' and reduced to 'the greatest despair'. Conversely, the French, who had been wringing money from the islanders still in their power, filling impromptu hospitals with sick and dying, and suppressing a spirit of mutiny among their troops were lifted by the possibility of being relieved by Bruix. Vivion fitted out some privateers to contest the enemy's control of local waters, but the issue remained in doubt until the beginning of July when Dixon returned to the station with the *Lion* and three cruisers. However, those few weeks may have enabled Vaubois to replace enough supplies to push the blockade into its second year.[33]

Nelson had much to ponder in Palermo, as he waded through the packets of mail the Hamiltons had saved for him. Of several dangers, two had priority. The French fleet was still out there, capable of appearing on the doorstep at any time; and the counter-revolution in Naples screamed for decisive support. Others could advise, but only Nelson could make the crucial but lonely choice as to where he would go next.

4

For several weeks the crisis continued as Bruix roamed unchecked. At Toulon he took aboard supplies and shipped them to the Gulf of Genoa, where he also landed a thousand men to support the French army in northern Italy. His orders entreated him to join Gravina's Spanish fleet from Cadiz and relieve Bonaparte in Egypt, but his offensive fizzled out. The Spanish fleet was so knocked about by its voyage from Cadiz that it could go no further than Cartagena, and Bruix did not relish going it alone with British fleets both ahead and behind. Withdrawing to Cartagena he pondered his next move.

Not once did the British intercept him, though they came close on 7 June, when he was anchored in Vado Bay. Four days earlier Keith, who had taken up the pursuit while St Vincent recuperated in Minorca, wrote to Nelson that he would follow the French to Leghorn if needs be, 'although it is contrary to my orders'. But when knowingly within striking distance of his prey on the 7th, he called off the chase to answer expresses from St Vincent redirecting him to Majorca, where the Spaniards were threatening Minorca. It was an almost unforgivable failure, and when Keith withdrew to Majorca there was nothing to prevent Bruix from sailing south to challenge Nelson's inadequate force, especially as the wind favoured such a voyage.[34]

While confusion reigned below, Nelson remained anxiously at Palermo. He was sucked into such inconsequentialities as the king's birthday fete at the palace, but was impatient for action, especially as St Vincent sent him four additional ships of the line on 1 June. His reinforcements included the *Leviathan*, flying the flag of Rear Admiral Duckworth, and perhaps the most formidable ship he now had, the newly built *Foudroyant*, with eighty guns and eight carronades and a complement of about 650 men. By spreading her principal armament on two rather than three decks, she had the speed of a seventy-four and the hitting power of a second-rate. St Vincent had thought the *Foudroyant* in 'a vile state', but a temporary captain put the crew in order and they arrived in Palermo disciplined if a tad inexperienced. Nelson decided to turn her into his flagship. His flag and principal followers, including Hardy, their surgeon, chaplain and most of the lieutenants, midshipmen and masters' mates, made the transfer on 7 June. Although Nelson found his cabin more cramped and uncomfortable than the one he had left in the *Vanguard*, many considered *Foudroyant*'s French design superior, and Nelson grew to love the ship as he had once loved the little *Agamemnon*, in which he had made his reputation.[35]

Among Duckworth's tidings was the unwelcome news of the commander-in-chief's deteriorating health. It shocked Nelson to think that St Vincent might quit a critical campaign, and equally that, if he left, the dour Keith, a less familiar and possibly unsympathetic entity, would take his place. 'For the sake of our country, do not quit us at this serious moment,' he pleaded on 10 June. Keith was not a St Vincent. 'We look up to you as we have always found you, as to our Father, under whose fostering care we have been led to fame. If, my dear lord, I have any weight in your friendship, let me entreat you to rouse the sleeping lion. Give not up a particle of your authority to anyone.' Two days later he was urging him to join the hunt for the French. 'If you are sick, I will fag for you, and our dear Lady Hamilton will nurse you with the most affectionate attention. Good Sir William will make you laugh with his wit and inexhaustible pleasantry. We all love you. Come, then, to your sincere friends.'[36]

St Vincent did not come. He was tired and sick, and besides had his heart upon commanding the Channel fleet, the most important naval duty of all.

Resigning his active command to Keith on 16 June, he was soon on his way to England, closing one of the most glorious tours of duty of any Mediterranean commander-in-chief but, paradoxically, leaving his forces in disarray.

In Palermo the king's expedition to Naples was almost ready, with an advance guard of 1700 soldiers, 660 horses, and artillery about to leave in twenty-five transports. Acton was imploring Nelson to lead it, and on 10 June Ferdinand wrote personally, asking the admiral to escort his force to Naples and secure the surrender of the enemy garrisons. He worried that Ruffo's advance might stimulate 'premature ardour' in his supporters in the city, provoke an untimely insurrection and unleash 'the fury of the rebels . . . upon . . . many faithful subjects'. In that case, Ruffo's irregulars might not be able to restore order when they reached the city, and a cadre of trained foreign troops was essential. The situation demanded Nelson's 'valuable assistance and direction'. The hereditary prince (Francis) and Acton, supported by such top-level dignitaries as the dukes of Gravina and Ascoli, were at the head of the expedition, but the admiral would have supreme command. In passages of general instructions issued to guide the soldiers, the king introduced an unfortunate ambiguity about the treatment of rebels, however. While reserving the right of clemency to the crown, and demanding a general adherence to his declaration of 1 May, Ferdinand opened a significant loophole by stating that 'the power of stipulating for their departure may be extended to several rebels, even to the leaders, according to circumstances, if the general good, the promptitude of the operations, and reasons of weight make it advisable'. In other words, if circumstances demanded it, the Jacobins might be allowed to quit the kingdom. But this and all other decisions were only valid if sanctioned by Nelson and the Prince Royal.[37]

Nelson was unsure about the wisdom of entangling his fleet in the recovery of Naples with Bruix still loose. Fortunately, the last from St Vincent, dated 31 May, suggested that the French were in Toulon and the Spaniards in Cartagena, the latter in a wretched condition. This gave him space. Nelson consulted his senior officers, but it was the queen who finally persuaded him to go. In a heartfelt letter she begged to entrust him with 'ungrateful Naples . . . which I still love in spite of all', and asked as a mother if he would care for her son, 'who feels honoured and contented at being on board your ship and under your orders'. Emma Hamilton also spoke up. Coming hotfoot from an interview with the queen on 12 June she reported Her Majesty 'very miserable', convinced that the 'quietness and subordination' of Naples depended upon the appearance of Nelson's fleet. 'She therefore begs, entreats and conjures you, my dear lord, if it is possible . . . to go to Naples . . . For God's sake consider it, and do. We will go with you if you will come and fetch us. Sir William is ill. I am ill. It will do us good.' Nelson agreed.[38]

For Nelson this was a period of indecision, in which the loneliness of command rested upon him heavily. After days of doubt, he opted to take fourteen ships of the line and a bomb and a fire vessel to Naples, hoping to restore Ferdinand's authority before Bruix presented himself. 'You may be assured that I will not risk a mast,' he promised St Vincent. On the morning of 13 June Nelson picked up the Prince Royal and Acton with their staffs at the 'waterhole' outside the Palazzo Palagonia, and took them, with the Hamiltons, out to his flagship. Their Sicilian Majesties came aboard to wish all farewell, and then in almost indescribable pride and expectation watched the *Foudroyant* use a fair wind to get under way, her topgallants and royals set and the royal standard billowing. Nelson, they believed, was going to save their kingdom, and Acton had a printing press and several chests of money to ease the return of monarchical government. But Nelson had barely got out of Palermo than two sail of the line appeared. They were the *Bellerophon* and *Powerful*, sent by Keith, and they carried a letter from the stony Scot, reporting that, far from being in Toulon, the French had got to Vado Bay in the Gulf of Genoa, much nearer to Nelson than he had bargained. Worse, Keith had given up his pursuit within thirty leagues of the enemy fleet and returned to Minorca, leaving Bruix with an open passage to the south and a fair wind. Nelson glanced at the date of the letter. It was 6 June, a whole week before. Why, the French might already be here, in the vicinity of Naples, Sicily and Nelson's fleet![39]

Keith had not only failed to engage an enemy at arm's length; he had also put Nelson in great peril, sending in the process a derisory reinforcement of two ships of the line. Nelson instantly put back to Palermo. On 14 June the ships speedily disgorged the prince and his soldiers while the admiral rehashed his plans. To allay panic in Sicily, where the disappointment was crushing, he promised Acton 'never to lose sight of the defence of His Sicilian Majesty's dominions', and vowed that the French would only reach them 'through his heart's blood'. That night his fleet was at sea again, heading not for Naples but for the station off Marettimo, which he had chosen as the best position to intercept the enemy.[40]

After Ball and Foley had joined on 18 June, Nelson had eighteen ships of the line and a fireship, the *Incendiary*, a far healthier force than the one at his disposal in May. But he was still outnumbered. According to the latest intelligence, the French were fielding twenty-five ships of the line, including four first-rates against which Nelson had nothing to show, and although the British were well provisioned they had no frigates. Apart from their value as scouts, cruisers were essential in a battle, for they could tow crippled ships out of danger or secure prizes. From his rendezvous Nelson had to write to Foote, who commanded in the Bay of Naples, asking if he could spare a brig and bomb vessel.

Nelson's new quandary was whether to remain on the defensive off Marettimo, barring the road to southern Italy, Malta and the east, or whether to go on to the offensive, pre-empting the French by seeking them out. The temptation to spring upon the enemy, gaining the advantages of surprise, was great, but he doubted whether his inferior force was up to it. If another reinforcement arrived, he wrote to Keith on 16 June, he would 'go in search of the enemy's fleet, when not one moment shall be lost in bringing them to battle, for I consider the best defence of His Sicilian Majesty's dominions is to place myself alongside the French'. However, what if there were no reinforcements? Nelson was on the rack. His old zest for combat was still there, urging him forward with whatever he had, but now it was tainted by a fear of failure, and what that might entail both for his own coveted reputation and the trust those he defended had placed in him. 'I long to be at the French fleet as much as ever a Miss longed for a husband,' he told Emma in one of his daily missives, 'but prudence stops me. Ought I to risk giving the cursed French a chance of being mistress of the Mediterranean for one hour?'[41]

Nelson had never made the lack of force a sufficient reason for not fighting the enemy before, and a letter he received from Sir William on 20 June revived his warrior spirit. Hamilton had heard the French were at Leghorn, embarking some of their forces with the treasures they had looted from Tuscany. Sir William opined that 'I still think your lordship will not be many days without a proper reinforcement, but I fear the precious moment will have been lost, and that the French fleet with the plunder of Tuscany and remains of their army will have got to Toulon before you could get alongside them.' Differently put, a golden opportunity to do the enemy serious harm was slipping away.[42]

The Hamiltons were now Nelson's closest confidants, even professionally. He still enjoyed the company of his officers, and we catch glimpses of him dining with his captains and listening in amazement to their tales of the 'Palermo ladies' and the prostitute on the Portuguese flagship who protested her respectability while offering herself for 'a great deal more, I am sure, than she is worth'. But it was Emma and Sir William who had become his missing right arm, handling matters as personal as sending him his 'new plain hat' and attending to laundry, and as crucial to the affairs of state as sifting his incoming correspondence and forwarding the latest news and opinions. Their views of what could and should be done had become important. The admiral's response to Sir William's vision of a glorious victory open to a hero ready to seize it was terse. 'I am agitated, but my resolution is fixed,' he wrote on 20 June. 'For Heaven's sake suffer not anyone to oppose it. I shall not be gone eight days. No harm can come to Sicily . . . I am full of grief and anxiety. I must go. It will finish the war. It will give a sprig of laurel to your affectionate friend.'[43]

Events were racing now, and the dash to Leghorn was not to be. The very day that Nelson decided to risk it the Portuguese *Swallow* arrived with a letter Keith had written three days before. It reported that St Vincent had relinquished his active command, and more importantly that Minorca was now secure, partly because of the imminent arrival of sixteen sail of the line from the Channel fleet. As acting commander-in-chief, Keith felt free to resume his pursuit of the French fleet. The ball had returned to his court.[44]

While the exact location of Bruix still caused apprehensions, Nelson felt the pressure ease. Keith had enough ships to deal with the situation in the north, and, reshaping his priorities, Nelson sailed for Palermo on the 21st. His decision was influenced by news Hamilton had sent him the previous night. Ruffo's forces had reached Naples, where the French occupied the powerful Fort St Elmo and the Jacobins the powerful seaside fortresses of Uovo and Nuovo, but the enemy had been greatly encouraged by the proximity of Bruix. St Elmo still seemed willing to hear terms, but the Jacobins were making 'continual' sorties and Ruffo was in 'a disagreeable position'. In these circumstances the king was desperate to see Nelson's fleet end the stalemate and bring the affair to a satisfactory conclusion. On 20 June the capital appeared to be sliding into chaos, and with his invariable respect and courtesy Acton tried to call in the admiral's promise to assist Naples as soon as the threat of the French fleet subsided.[45]

Racing to Palermo, Nelson arrived within hours, and did not trouble to anchor. He went ashore on the 21st, found a delighted king, and had time to dine on board the *Serapsis* with a party that included the captain and Cornelia Knight. Then, with the Hamiltons in tow as interpreters and secretaries, he returned to his fleet off Ustica Island. Emma vowed to serve the queen with 'heart and soul' if it cost her her life, and appointed herself Her Majesty's personal foreign correspondent. Nelson suspected that Keith might criticise him for sailing for Naples while the wider picture remained so murky, but was satisfied that he had to discharge his promises and respond to the appeal the king had sent through Acton.[46]

And thus, without a day's release from the tensions of the Bruix crisis, Nelson sailed into the most controversial episode of his career.

5

The tension in the sultry air of Naples had never been heavier as the forces of the Parthenopean Republic made their last stand against the counter-revolutionary forces enveloping them. Cardinal Ruffo's motley army of several thousand, assisted by 530 Russians and Turks chaperoned by Micheroux, Ferdinand's minister plenipotentiary, scurried through the streets to seal in the remaining bastions of republican power, while Captain Edward James Foote of the *Seahorse*, commanding Nelson's small squadron, closed off any retreat by sea. Inside the tightening net few Jacobins knew who they could trust, and they arrested and executed each other. Those who had hitherto served the republic through fear of injury or disadvantage now began to rebel as the balance of power changed. The civil guard the Jacobins had established refused to fight, while the cowed royalist *lazzaroni* rose once more to their feet to hunt down the enemies of the crown or drive in their remaining fortifications. As soon as Ruffo's *sanfedisti* began spilling into the city on 13 June they murdered and ransacked, and the Carmine castle had no sooner fallen than its garrison were butchered. Ruffo used edicts, sermons and patrols to curb the rising violence to no great avail. Hordes of dirty and ragged brigands roamed the streets, smoking suspects out of their homes, and killing and looting. The cardinal set up his headquarters at Maddelena Bridge on the southern fringe of the city and tried to gather prisoners in a nearby granary where they should have been protected, but dozens were slaughtered before his eyes.

The remnants of the French army were penned in St Elmo, sitting on the hill of San Martino behind the city, and in Capua and Gaeta outside, while their Jacobin allies held both Uovo and Nuovo. Foote's skeleton force, which then consisted of his frigate and eight smaller British and Neapolitan consorts, had vigorously contributed to the enemy's discomfort, blockading their positions and landing powder, ball and shot for Ruffo's irregulars. On 13 June, Foote used a couple of intimidating broadsides to force Fort Granatelli to surrender, although the royalists who rushed in happily butchered the garrison of two hundred. Two days later the British captain induced Castellammare and Revigliano, a fortified rock, to surrender their ordnance, stores and fourteen gunboats. Perhaps a thousand prisoners fell into British hands. The leaders were held in a xebec riding off Procida, but the rank and file seem to have been shipped to Toulon, except for some of the Jacobins who appear to have returned to the city and joined their companions in the Castel dell'Uovo. Foote had then turned his attention to the remaining strongpoints, especially Uovo, a large featureless fortification almost surrounded by sea. For several days gun and mortar boats pounded the castle until 19 June, when an armistice came into force.[47]

This armistice was a centrepiece of the ensuing controversy. The allies allowed themselves to be stampeded into it, and a capitulation that followed on its heels. Although the position of the French and Jacobins was dire, it was not yet quite hopeless. Some of the defenders spoke of an illusory French relief force from Capua, and rather more pinned their hopes upon Bruix's missing fleet, which – larger than any force the British had in these seas – was capable of transforming the situation. It was the French fleet that worried some of the allies, and drove Foote forward with undue haste. Admitting himself 'too much interested' in concluding negotiations while he could, he pressed Ruffo to strike a bargain with the Jacobins, even though he expected that it would lead to excessively 'favourable' terms being offered them. Ruffo was not blind to Foote's concern, but added others of his own. If the siege was prolonged, the French fire from St Elmo might damage the city, and if he was forced to storm the enemy positions his violent irregulars might lose control and murder indiscriminately.

Consequently the cardinal allowed Micheroux to open negotiations. By 19 June a three-week armistice was established. This leeway would enable General Oronzio Massa, the Jacobin commanding from Nuovo, to discuss a general capitulation of all the garrisons with his colleagues, the commandant at Uovo and Colonel Joseph Méjean of the 27th Brigade of French Light Infantry, who held St Elmo. Micheroux was a principal architect of a draft agreement. He leaned towards clemency, and wrote to Ruffo asking whether it was acceptable to offer a general pardon to those 'who had not committed any positive crimes, and a safe conduct to France for those who see fit to depart, with liberty to sell their property or to remove it within a given space of time'. Although this breached the crown's prerogative to grant clemency, in itself it was not greatly inconsistent with Ferdinand's idea of a general pardon for the Jacobin rank and file.[48]

Ruffo was conciliatory. He believed in returning the disaffected to the fold, draining their opposition by renewing their access to place and favour. Laudable in some respects, this policy soon ran into difficulties. It aroused suspicions in the court, and opened as well as healed wounds, creating anger among royalists who believed that disloyalty was being rewarded and their own fidelity undervalued. But in any case, if Micheroux is to be believed, Ruffo scarcely troubled himself with the details of the capitulation. Ruffo, Baillie (the Russian commander) and Foote were, in Micheroux's words, too 'eager . . . to get rid of this business', and the cardinal signed a capitulation 'without examining it, and indeed without even allowing me to point out the inadmissible articles to him'. Ruffo, in fairness, was fraught with all manner of difficulties, but the king probably had a point when he later accused the one man authorised to negotiate on his behalf, and to protect his interests, of inattentiveness. Afterwards all the allied principals had misgivings about the capitulation. Micheroux, who guiltily understated his responsibility, denounced the agreement as 'reprehensible'; Foote thought it 'very favourable' to the enemy, although he forwarded it to Nelson on 23 June; and Ruffo declined to report any detail to their Majesties during negotiations, but vaguely warned Acton on 21 June that the terms offered the Jacobin 'rascals' would be 'very merciful for a thousand reasons'. This letter did not reach Acton until after Nelson finally left Naples.[49]

The completed capitulation of 23 June bore the signatures of Massa, Méjean, Ruffo, Foote and the Russian and Turkish commanders. It was a thoroughly unsatisfactory document. It did not provide for the surrender of the French garrison, the key adversary, and covered only the Jacobin castles, which were to be yielded, and their inmates suffered to march out with the honours of war to ground their arms. Those who wished could board transports for Toulon, with all their baggage and property, but any who chose to remain in Naples would be allowed to do so 'without being molested either in their persons or families'. These conditions applied to all the republican prisoners, irrespective of degrees of complicity. Moreover, the allies were bound to send four hostages into St Elmo, to be released by Méjean when he had received confirmation that the transports had reached Toulon.[50]

Predictably, all this infuriated their Majesties as soon as they saw it. Point after point insulted them. Ruffo was authorised to conclude a treaty, but not to flout clear-cut instructions. Those orders stipulated that clemency rested solely with the crown, which would attempt to weigh degrees of guilt, but by this capitulation every Jacobin would escape punishment and remain free to offend, in Naples as elsewhere. It did not even remove the disaffected from the capital. In their Majesties' opinion this was not the way to stabilise the realm and give it permanence. As the queen had explained to the cardinal on 19 June, her aim was 'to reorganise the kingdom in such a way as to ensure lasting peace, and to prove to the faithful inhabitants how truly we are grateful'. Moreover, the allies had given hostages 'as though we were the conquered'. And, just as bad, the treaty had not been made subject to the king, whose forces commanded the situation, but to the commander of a French fort that should have been taken. Traitors, the queen raged, had been exalted and allowed the honours of war, something 'so infamous and absurd', she cried, 'that it revolts me even to speak of it'. All in all, said she, 'this is such an infamous treaty that . . . I look upon myself as lost and dishonoured . . . This infamous capitulation . . . grieves me a great deal more than the loss of the kingdom and will have a far worse effect.' The royal principles had been clearly outlined, as recently as 14 June, when the queen had written to Ruffo that 'there must be no treaty with our rebel vassals. The king in his clemency will pardon [some of] them, will out of kindness reduce their punishments, but he will never negotiate or enter into capitulations with guilty rebels who . . . being caught in a trap like mice are unable to harm us as they would wish to do.'[51]

The details of the negotiations had not reached Palermo when Nelson sailed, but rumours had begun to fly. Prophetically, Hamilton had sent a report to Nelson when the latter had been cruising off Marettimo, noting that 'what we suspected of the Cardinal Ruffo has proved true, and I dare say when the capitulation of Naples comes to this court, their Sicilian Majesties' dignity will be mortified'. He believed that Ruffo would try to conclude the entire business himself, and lumber the king with an unsatisfactory treaty. Three days later the king himself was writing to Ruffo about a rumour that the Jacobins were to be allowed to leave their castles 'safe and sound', declaring that he could 'never believe it, for (may God preserve us from it!) to spare these savage vipers and especially Caracciolo, who knows every inlet of our coastline, might inflict the greatest damage on us'. The queen's hatred of the hapless Neapolitan naval commander stood on somewhat different ground. He had been in Palermo and seen her pain and tears, she said, only to drive the dagger deeper.[52]

Nelson's task, therefore, was to pre-empt such unsatisfactory proceedings, secure the surrender of all the enemy castles, and establish public order. Hamilton said that he possessed 'full instructions' about these matters, but in fact no fresh written orders from the king have been found. Nonetheless, there can be no doubt that the admiral was given full powers to take control of the situation. Thus the queen wrote to Ruffo on 21 June that 'Nelson will demand a voluntary surrender, or failing this, he will procure it by force', for 'to continue negotiating would be a useless and degrading task'. She was incensed at the faithlessness of some of the Jacobins, who had broken an earlier ceasefire by launching sorties from their castles. Four days later the king told the cardinal that Nelson had 'an understanding to fulfil my instructions, according to which junior [rebel] officers, or minor offenders shall be deported . . . while ill-famed offenders and leaders . . . shall be put to death'. There could be 'no capitulation' with the rebels, 'and even if it had been agreed on, it shall be void and null without my ratification'. Acton said the same. 'We hope in him [Nelson] for a relief of what is against His Majesty's dignity and interests,' he said. 'The cardinal . . . ought to send the treaty . . . for His Majesty's approbation.' The admiral sailed with a clear mandate. In accordance with the king's former pronouncements, he alone had the power to pardon; and he intended to use it by exiling the less culpable, and reserving punishment for what he deemed to be a rotten core.[53]

It was a grim mission and none on board the *Foudroyant* was in a good mood. The Hamiltons were ill, Emma 'low-spirited with phantoms in her fertile brain', and her husband devoid of appetite and finding solace in sea-bathing and doses of Peruvian bark. Nelson, physically and emotionally drained by the prolonged double crisis, was in his darkest mood. As he had written to Foote on 6 June, 'Your news of the hanging of the thirteen Jacobins gave us great pleasure, and the three priests, I hope, return [from Palermo, where they had been defrocked] in the *Aurora* to dangle on the tree best adapted to their weight of sins.' But whatever his personal feelings, he went as an officer, charged by his government with supporting their Sicilian Majesties, on a clearly defined mission to – in Ferdinand's words – 'end all matters with proper honour and decorum' in a way that would 'guarantee the future tranquillity for my dominions'.[54]

In hindsight it is regrettable that the expedition did not include senior members of the Sicilian government capable of handling the political dimensions. For, despite his fidelity to Ferdinand, Nelson was a foreign officer in the service of another monarch. Military or naval aid was one thing, but internal administration and justice were properly matters for the Sicilians alone. Nevertheless, a purpose ran through the whole fleet. As Hamilton graphically wrote from the flagship, 'Our admirals and captains are impatient to serve His Sicilian Majesty and save his capital from destruction.'[55]

VIII

THE BOURBON RESTORATION

Vile Outcast France, at last thy fate's decreed,
And Europe now from Tyranny's freed,
No more shalt thought the Rights of Man
invade,
Or make of human gore a constant lake.
Italia's sav'd, swift liberty restor'd,
All Europe will unite with one accord.

Sir Edward Newenham,
'Admiral Nelson's Victory, 1798'

I

On the afternoon of 24 June, a cloudy day, Nelson's ships entered the Bay of Naples using full sail and a moderate breeze. They grandly passed the outlying forts of Baia and Puteoli, firing rumbling salutes in recognition of the royal colours flying over the garrisons, and stood towards the harbour, eighteen ships of the line, a frigate and two or three smaller vessels. It was a magnificent mix of beauty, grace and power, and affected everyone in Naples. To some, desperately wishing the arrival of the French fleet, the sight brought despair; but to others those British and royal colours signalled an imminent liberation.[1]

The details of Ruffo's 'treaty' were on their way to Sicily, but Nelson was still largely ignorant of them when he reached Naples. He knew that a three-week armistice had been established, and that the rebels had been offered terms allowing them to evacuate their castles and take passage for France. From his experience of such ceasefires, he assumed that there was an understanding that the enemy would surrender on those terms if they had not been relieved within the three-week period. Agreements of that kind were always subject to change according to shifts in the military circumstances. Terms could be withdrawn, revised or refused. In this case the British, not the French, fleet had arrived, and Nelson planned to dissolve the armistice and demand an outright capitulation within two hours. If successful, Nelson was prepared to ship the French home 'without the stipulation of their being prisoners of war', a minor inducement that absolved them from the necessity of being exchanged before returning to service. But he deemed the Jacobins to be dishonourable participants, and they would have to yield unconditionally and throw themselves upon the king's mercy.[2]

Studying the city through spyglasses, Nelson and his officers saw that it was still in the grip of war. The French tricolour flew over St Elmo, which stood on a hill, its guns dominating the city below. But the armistice seemed to be in place, because white flags could be seen above the Jacobin castles – on the left the egg-shaped Uovo, situated at the end of a causeway protruding into the bay, and surrounded by water once its drawbridge had been raised, and to the right Nuovo on the foreshore near the royal palace, which it partly controlled. Ruffo's batteries also held their stations, menacing Uovo from the Chiaja Quay, the royal park and the Pizzofalcone at the foot of the causeway, and Nuovo from the seafront and the Castello del Carmine to the south. But the area around the royal palace looked to be in enemy hands. A Liberty Tree stood there defiantly, and the red cap of liberty was perched cheekily upon the stone head of a giant statue nearby. Sweeping their glasses towards the west of the bay, the British could see Foote's *Seahorse*, riding off Posillipo, also showing a flag of truce.

Nelson's first concern was to shield the city from any possible intervention by the French fleet. He ordered the *Bulldog* sloop to cruise west of Ischia to provide an early warning of the approach of any large force, and spent much of that day and the next putting his fleet in a strong defensive position. Anchored in soft, black mud, it was drawn up in a close 'line of battle', about one and a half miles from the waterfront, each ship two-thirds of a cable apart and sitting in forty or more fathoms of water. Running from the naval arsenal on the seaside, where the line was flanked by the Castel dell'Uovo, it stretched NNW to SSE towards Portici, and commanded the principal waterfront, including the mole, lighthouse and Ruffo's headquarters at the Maddelena Bridge. Nelson placed *Foudroyant* in the van, though he planned to switch to the centre if the French fleet appeared, and he positioned twenty-two gun and mortar boats he had brought from Procida on his flanks. Guard boats were appointed to row back and forth at night. Nelson's other immediate need was for supplies, and boats quickly began plying to and fro to gather water, beef, wood and lemons.[3]

About three o'clock in the afternoon of the 24th, Nelson signalled that the truce was at an end. Foote, still reasonably confident that matters were proceeding satisfactorily, was disabused of his complacency as soon as he came on board the flagship and made his report. Nelson was now learning about the capitulation that had been signed the day before. A copy sent by the governor of Procida had reached him as he entered the bay, and now it was confirmed by the chagrined Foote. It took two days for the captain of the *Seahorse* to place a written justification of his part in the 'treaty' before a stony commander-in-chief. He had signed the capitulation because he had assumed that Ruffo had the authority to conclude it, and the cardinal had wanted a speedy possession of the forts. The captain had not been without his reservations, but the only clear-cut objection that he voiced was his disapproval of the order of signing, which placed Britain below Russia and Turkey. However, he had protested at 'everything that could be in the least contrary to the honour and rights of my sovereign and the British nation'. In truth, given his state of ignorance about Ruffo's authority and instructions, and the danger from Bruix, Foote had probably done his best, and Nelson did not ultimately hold him to blame.[4]

Nelson now realised that the situation before him was rather more complicated than he had supposed. The armistice of the 19th had been superseded by the capitulation or 'treaty' of the 23rd, which put the matter on a different footing. Nevertheless, he got Sir William to write to Ruffo, expressing his entire disapproval of the capitulation and his refusal to stand neutral. The letter went to Ruffo with the admiral's previously written 'observations' on the nature of an armistice and draft summonses to the castles. One, to the French in St Elmo, demanded surrender within two hours. Those to the Jacobin castles made it clear that their inmates would not be allowed to depart and must surrender unconditionally. Troubridge and Ball apparently made two trips to Ruffo's headquarters, on 24 June and the following day, soliciting his cooperation. Ruffo probably realised that Nelson's action was appropriate to a mere armistice, but it took no cognisance of the formal capitulation, solemnly signed in good faith by the Jacobins, French and available representatives of Naples, Russia, Turkey and Great Britain. That, he insisted, must stand. The talk grew so bitter that Micheroux found himself smoothing feathers. Ruffo refused to countenance any abrogation of the treaty, and indicated that he was 'tired of his situation' and would withdraw from it. When Troubridge asked him if he would cooperate in an attack on the castles if Nelson broke the armistice, he declined to contribute either men or materials. Moreover, he refused to send in Nelson's summonses.[5]

However, Ruffo did visit Nelson on the *Foudroyant* to thrash the matter out on 25 June. Nelson and Hamilton were congratulating themselves on frustrating a dishonourable capitulation that would have demeaned their Majesties and destabilised the city, and were heartened by the enthusiasm of the people. The night the fleet arrived the town was illuminated in celebration, and the next day a flotilla of small boats packed with people came flocking to the flagship, eager to pay their respects. There was music and shouts of '*Viva il Re!*' But an efficient reduction of the enemy positions by force also required the cooperation of Ruffo's forces. On 25 June Nelson had dispatched his summons to the French garrison in St Elmo, envisaging that it would resume firing that very day. But the admiral's suspicions of the cardinal were deepening. Visitors were bringing complaints, grumbling about the rapacity and indiscipline of Ruffo's

Calabrese, and the favours he was bestowing on Jacobins. Their story was that loyal royalists were being excluded from power, while the cardinal was surrounding himself with venal and evil-minded counsellors. Hamilton and Nelson thought they saw deep divisions between what was going on and royal policy. While the king wished to punish erring nobles and abolish feudalism to 'caress and reward the people', Ruffo seemed to operate on a reverse principle. None of it boded well for the meeting between the two would-be liberators of Naples.[6]

That afternoon a salute of thirteen guns welcomed the cardinal to the flagship, and talks occupied the cabin, with the Hamiltons interpreting. 'I used every argument in my power to convince him that the treaty and armistice was at an end by the arrival of the fleet, but an admiral is no match in talking with a cardinal,' Nelson told Keith. The two were coming from opposite directions. Ruffo kept referring to the Jacobins as 'patriots', which Nelson considered a prostitution of the word. If he had breached his orders, he said, it had been done to prevent Naples being reduced to 'a heap of stones'. In word and writing Nelson – following his instructions from the king – contended that the treaty could not be executed 'without the approbation of His Sicilian Majesty', and Ruffo apparently made it clear that if the treaty was annulled he would feel obliged to inform the castles of the fact, and withdraw his troops to the positions they had occupied before the agreement. The viewpoints were irreconcilable, and threatened to destroy cooperation between the allied forces, although later in the day Ruffo requested that Nelson send him 1200 marines to strengthen his military positions before St Elmo, which were now vulnerable to counter-attack.[7]

During the day Nelson's demand to the French at St Elmo was delivered and rejected by Méjean, who intimated that the city would be damaged if hostilities were renewed. A few shots seem to have been fired from the castle in the evening, effectively marking the end of the armistice. On his part, Ruffo warned Massa of Nuovo that, while he stuck by the treaty, the admiral did not, and he suggested the Jacobins try to escape by land. He even sent a trumpeter through the city warning the citizens against molesting any republicans who sought to do so. By daybreak of 26 June Nelson's demand for the unconditional surrender of the Jacobin castles was delivered, apparently with a note signed by Ruffo and Baillie, the Russian commander, that they were withdrawing their troops to their former positions. Certainly, the Russians retreated from the space surrounding the castle and palace to the Spirito Santo, and considerable alarm spread through the city at such tangible indications of imminent bombardment. Several thousand people began evacuating the town, shops closed and streets emptied. In St Elmo threats were made against the four hostages the French were still holding. Ruffo may have still hoped to deter Nelson from breaking the treaty, for after his meeting with the admiral he is said to have conferred with Baillie, Achmet and Micheroux, parties to the agreement, and encouraged them to make a formal protest declaring the abrogation an abomination.[8]

Despite this, Nelson's action was arguably defensible. Ruffo had clearly exceeded his orders, and produced a capitulation that was unacceptable to his masters. Nor had Foote any authority to sign for Britain. As yet neither party had materially executed its provisions. A few Jacobins may have opportunely slipped away, and their prisoners had been released, but four hostages were still held at St Elmo. That being so, Nelson's contention that the treaty, having neither been ratified by the king nor concluded according to his dictates, was illegal had some force. The right to overturn treaties between states, if the signatories had lacked 'sufficient powers', had been admitted by Emir de Vattel, the leading authority on emerging international jurisprudence, although more specifically he had also acknowledged that treaties of capitulation signed by generals without sufficient powers should nevertheless be binding, 'especially when they cannot wait for the sovereign's orders'. Vattel's view seems to have been that unless capitulations were rigorously upheld, there would be uncertainty about whether anyone might surrender safely. These were issues that were arguable in law. Some have seen the admiral's behaviour as unreasonable, and largely the product of a vengeful queen, through her manipulation of Emma Hamilton. Gordon, for example, who we encountered in Palermo, thought Nelson's 'natural disposition' to be 'mild and conciliating' was twisted by Lady Hamilton, 'a female fiend'. But while Nelson was undoubtedly moved by the predicament of their Majesties, whether mediated through the Hamiltons and Acton or not, and was influenced by his views of what had to be done to resist the march of French republicanism, his annulment of the treaty was entirely consistent with the instructions he had received from the king.[9]

But then something surprising happened. Nelson suddenly performed something of a turnaround. Early on 26 June, Sir William wrote a brief letter to Ruffo, informing him that Nelson had now 'resolved to do nothing which might break the armistice'. Seeking reassurance, Ruffo wrote to Nelson, and received a similar pronouncement, namely, 'I will not *on any consideration* [my italics] break the armistice entered into by you . . . I hope Your Eminency will be satisfied that I am supporting your ideas.' The following day Hamilton wrote to Ruffo again, 'I can assure your Eminence that Lord Nelson congratulates himself on *the decision he has arrived at*, not to interrupt your Eminence's operations, but to assist you with all his power to put an end to the affair which your Eminence has so well conducted up to the present in the very critical circumstances in which your Eminence found yourself.'[10]

Given the views of the king and the trust placed in Nelson this extraordinary step back – rather than the earlier annulment of the unauthorised and unsatisfactory treaty – is the more inexplicable act. It was nowhere described or explained, and only thin clues and insinuations point to a solution. Not even the voluble Hamilton, who had written to Palermo of Nelson's repudiation of the treaty, ventured much to account for the change in his next letter to Acton, dated two days later. He merely mentioned that some 'cool reflection' had helped calm the situation. That unspecified reappraisal may have been primarily the work of Hamilton, who had said that 'a little of my phlegm was necessary between the cardinal and Lord Nelson' to avoid a rupture at their first meeting, and that he later helped 'stem the torrent' of Nelson's 'impetuosity'. Another witness, an English resident of Naples, would also remember finding Nelson 'in a great passion' when he visited the flagship soon after she arrived, and an embarrassed Hamilton quietly reassuring others that the admiral would be 'calmer next morning', as indeed he appeared to be.[11]

Nothing Nelson ever did was more controversial than his 'cool reflection' of 26 June, or ultimately proved so damaging to his memory. The paper war continues to the present, setting admirers and detractors of the admiral at each other's throats, trashing each other's sources, conclusions and integrities, and producing a mosaic of obfuscation, confusion and outright myth as well as reasoned advocacy. To clear some of this away, certain facts have to be recognised. First, we are not dealing with story-book saints or knights here, but flesh and blood people in complex, dangerous and challenging circumstances that rarely lent themselves to straightforward solutions. There was no satisfactory road ahead of Nelson. All his options involved difficulties and invited criticism. Second, a change *did* take place that morning, and it is not good enough to contend that Nelson merely restated his previous position in different words.[12]

Nelson's intentions cannot be separated from the actions that flowed from them. Briefly, as a result of assurances from the admiral, Ruffo implemented his capitulation the same day, 26 June; the Jacobin rebels left the castles, not in a manner compliant to Nelson's military summonses, but generally in accordance with the treaty of 23 June; and British detachments from the ships were parties to the operation.

Neither Nelson nor Hamilton reported their actions with complete candour, and they spoke so loosely that historians have argued about their meanings. That a distinct change in their position took place emerges, however. Thus Nelson writing Acton on 28 June, said, '*Had I followed my inclination*, the capital would have been in a worse state, for the cardinal would have done worse than nothing.' And the same day, Hamilton, who was at the core of events, wrote, 'Lord Nelson, *having at first entirely differed in opinion with the cardinal*, continues the same, but does not refuse any assistance that he thinks can be of service to His Majesty. In short, all will be confusion if some regular government is not soon established.' Though wary, both statements acknowledge a change, and imply that its motive lay in the state of the city. More bluntly still, Hamilton informed Acton the day after the evacuation of the castles, that '*If we cannot do exactly as one could wish, one must make the best of a bad bargain*, and that Lord

Nelson is doing.' That last phrase, which has hitherto escaped published versions of the letter, speaks loudly. It meant that Nelson accepted that he was stuck with the 'bad bargain' already struck by Ruffo.[13]

Historians have long noted that on 26 June both Nelson and Hamilton used the word 'armistice' rather than 'treaty' in realigning themselves closer to Ruffo, and some of the admiral's apologists have argued that on 26 June Nelson's assurances only extended to a renewal of the armistice, and never endorsed the capitulation. But this, in my view, is unsustainable. The armistice had ended. The French in St Elmo had already reopened a weak fire, and the ceasefire with the rebels, created to facilitate negotiations, had been superseded by the treaty of 23 June, granting them a conditional surrender. Having disallowed that treaty and submitted his demand for the unconditional capitulation of these castles, Nelson might certainly have now wanted to restore a temporary ceasefire to enable the Jacobins to reflect upon their new position. Following that scenario, had the rebels opted to resist, Nelson would have crushed them by force at the expiration of the new armistice. The trouble with this interpretation is that Nelson neither acted nor spoke as if this was his intention.

As we have seen, Hamilton assured Ruffo that Nelson had now decided to 'assist' rather than 'interrupt' the cardinal's 'operations' to bring affairs to a conclusion. The issue between Nelson and Ruffo was not the defunct armistice, but the current capitulation or treaty, and it was this that the endorsement therefore implied was now supported. Sir William actually said so when writing to Grenville on 14 July. 'Lord Nelson,' he explained, 'assured the cardinal at the same time that he did not mean to do any act contrary to his Eminency's treaty, but as that treaty could not be valid until it had been ratified by His Sicilian Majesty, his Lordship's meaning was only to secure His Majesty's rebellious subjects until His Majesty's further pleasure should be known.' This tactlessly – and perhaps unfairly – admits the key charge later made against Nelson: that he had misled Ruffo and affected to accept the treaty solely to induce the rebels to put themselves into his power pending the king's judgement. In other words, if we take Hamilton literally, the admiral had played a dishonourable trick.[14]

That Nelson's reappraisal of the 26th and tacit endorsement referred to the capitulation, rather than any prolongation of the ceasefire, is further indicated by what he expected to follow from his assurances. The same day Nelson sent Troubridge and Ball to confer with Ruffo about the evacuation of the castles. A note the captains supplied Ruffo said they were 'authorised to declare to his Eminence on behalf of Lord Nelson that his lordship will not oppose the embarkation of the rebels'. In other words, Nelson was now willing to allow the evacuation of the castles as agreed in the capitulation. Had the Jacobins surrendered according to Nelson's military summons, the manner of their leaving would have been different. In that summons Nelson had declared that he would 'not permit them to embark or quit those places'. They would all have been held pending the king's mercy.[15]

Ruffo and the other key players certainly took Nelson to be referring to the treaty, not a restoration of the armistice, and acted on that understanding without any contradiction from the British. The cardinal wrote to Micheroux at ten the same morning informing him that Nelson had consented to carry the capitulation into effect, and that in consequence the Russian troops should return to their previous positions, and the Jacobin garrisons be reassured. Later in the day the rebels marched out to ground their weapons. Nelson told Spencer that they were not accorded the honours of war, but the evidence divides on the point. However, they were not incarcerated, as Nelson's summons would have required, but separated in accordance with the capitulation, some electing to return freely to their homes and others embarking with their baggage and side arms on the fourteen polacres assembled for a voyage to Toulon. One hundred and thirty-five of the 265 rebels in Castel dell'Uovo dispersed in the city rather than board the polacres. The process was facilitated by five hundred British marines and some sailors, who then manned the evacuated forts in about two hours to the satisfaction of civilian bystanders. Royal colours were raised above the castles at about sunset, and the republican flags delivered to the *Foudroyant*, while Captain Hood remained on shore to restore a relative tranquillity to the disturbed city. That the British went ashore to assist in an embarkation in the manner agreed between the cardinal and the rebels is a further indication that they endorsed the capitulation, and not a mere extension of the ceasefire. The *Culloden* log records, 'Captain and a lieutenant on shore. Disembarked sixty privates and two officers of marines to take possession of the two lower forts and embark Jacobins on board of transports.' Troubridge himself reported to Nelson that 'agreeable with your lordship's orders, I landed with the . . . marines . . . and after embarking the garrisons of the castles . . . I put a garrison in each.'[16]

Momentarily there were huge sighs of relief. Ruffo tendered his thanks to Nelson, British and Neapolitan flags were brandished vigorously in house windows, and the night was brilliantly illuminated in celebrations that spilled into the next day. Bells rang, the 'Te Deum' was sung gustily and the people rejoiced to regain their city. Troubridge sent a work party to hack down the Liberty Tree in front of the palace, where it was ignominiously burned to public applause. The statue lost its liberty cap. There was a general belief that Nelson had reflected, decided to honour the treaty, gained possession of the Jacobin castles and sealed the fate of the French in St Elmo. This was probably substantially the case. But if so, why had Nelson changed his mind about the treaty? And was his action a mere pretence, designed to gull the Jacobins into his hands as Hamilton had clumsily insinuated, or did he, in fact, act more candidly, fulfilling a treaty that he personally disliked, but in good faith?

Grounds for believing that Nelson was trying to behave honourably, and had retraced his steps after a practical reassessment of his circumstances, are cogent. The statement Hamilton made to Acton on 27 June ('We *now shall* act *perfectly* in concert with the cardinal, though we *think* the same we did at first as to the treaty [my italics] . . . If we cannot do exactly as one could wish, one must make the best of a bad bargain and that Lord Nelson is doing') indicates that the admiral had compelling reasons to adopt his second-best alternative, but that he intended to proceed sincerely rather than cynically. We can guess what those reasons were: chaos and disorder in the city.

Nelson had probably been shaken by Ruffo's threat to refuse cooperation in further operations, for although the British could take over his batteries and reinforce the Russians, who were threatening St Elmo from the foot of the hill, they were little equipped to both mount the sieges and police the city. The immediate results of Nelson's annulment of the treaty were a renewal of fire from St Elmo and transparent preparations to recommence hostilities. This, said Micheroux, caused 'incredible consternation' in the city. Fearing shelling, thousands of inhabitants quit their homes within hours. Disorder spread, and, stimulated by the establishment of a council to try offenders, both Ruffo's rapacious Calabrese and the urban *lazzaroni* rooted out Jacobins, or anyone sporting the short hairstyle associated with the breed, to rob, abuse or murder. Bodies were reportedly burned or brandished aloft on swords or poles, and almost anyone was at risk. Robert Smith, a contractor who was supplying the British ships, was twice almost murdered by the *lazzaroni* while going about his business in the town, and once delivered to the *Foudroyant* as a Jacobin. While the initial panic may have begun to subside, Nelson's efforts to address the problem appear to have been counter-productive. As early as 25 June the Hamiltons were conferring with 'the loyal party' in Naples, hoping that the *lazzaroni* might supply the place of Ruffo's Calabrese in maintaining order. A local chief named Egidio Pallio promised 90,000 loyal subjects if arms were forthcoming. Through Nelson, Emma supplied Pallio with his weapons, telling him in confidence that he should keep the city quiet for the ten or so days it would take the king to return. But it soon became apparent that raising another party was only a recipe for further disorder. According to Ruffo's not unprejudiced secretary, Domenico Sacchinelli, these 'English' *lazzaroni* began seizing people and sending them to Procida for judgement, rather than to the cardinal. They tore down Ruffo's edict of 15 June, by which he had tried to protect non-combatants, and accused Ruffo of shielding republicans. The machinations of the Hamiltons increased, rather than curbed, disorder.[17]

Nelson's new course provided a few days of relative stability. Matters were put in train to reduce St Elmo, Ruffo reneging on the strict terms of the capitulation in response to a plea from Nelson that the fort needed to be taken quickly. As recently as 26 April news had reached Naples that enemy forces from

Capua had routed a royalist force and advanced as far as Caserta. The British and Russians, who were professionals, took the lead, but Ruffo sent up to three hundred men to man the captured castles of Nuovo and Uovo and release marines for a thirteen-hundred strong assault force of British and Portuguese being formed under Troubridge and Ball. A printed edict also shut further supplies from the garrison. Troubridge and Ball conferred somewhat unsatisfactorily with the Russian leaders, but both sides threw themselves into establishing batteries and secondary fortifications.[18]

With cooperation of a kind prevailing in the allied camp, Nelson felt secure enough to write to Keith and the Admiralty, and to request Ruffo to send Caracciolo and a dozen other noted Jacobin leaders the royalists had rounded up to the flagship. Plainly, the idea was to secure them for trial, and to prevent them claiming the protection promised in the treaty. This action was significant because it represented a compromise on the part of Ruffo, and perhaps the beginning of a bridge between himself and Ferdinand. By meeting Nelson's specific objections that his capitulation had left the major offenders unpunished, Ruffo thus addressed one of the king's gravest concerns. But, of course, the senior Jacobins themselves suffered dearly. The miserable Caracciolo had been tracked to Calvizzano, where his mother's family had property, and hauled from a well where he had been hiding, disguised as a peasant. Still in his mean attire, he was returned to Naples and incarcerated in the granary. Hamilton supposed that Nelson would send the unlucky thirteen to Procida for trial, and that Caracciolo would perish as a mutineer, hanging from the yardarm of one of his sovereign's ships.

Nelson's position at this time is by no means clear. Hamilton had written to Acton on the 24th and 25th, reporting Nelson's disapproval of the treaty, and the king's response to Ruffo's conduct was expected within a short time. But after the rapprochement with Ruffo the British tone moderated. On the 27th Hamilton spoke of the benefits of cooperating with Ruffo, the ensuing 'calm' and 'joy' of the people, and 'the good of His Sicilian Majesty's service'. If nothing was said for the Jacobins who had evacuated the castles, there was no further disapprobation of the treaty. 'I hope the result will be approved by their Sicilian Majesties,' Hamilton suggested. He did state that the 'rebels on board of the polaccas cannot stir without a passport from Lord Nelson', thus opening the prospect of a reversal of the existing process, but those vessels were not then under confinement, and it was Caracciolo and the dozen other 'most infamous' rebels demanded of Ruffo that Hamilton believed ought to be tried at Procida.

Nelson began a report to Keith on the same day, which as submitted continued to speak of the 'infamous' treaty, but that dispatch was not finished until three days later, when circumstances had changed again. We do not know exactly what course of action he might have recommended had he finished the dispatch on the 27th, and not on the 30th. It is entirely conceivable that Nelson and Hamilton were not cynically executing Ruffo's treaty, determined to overthrow it when an opportunity presented, but genuinely resigned to its implementation. The seizure of the notorious Jacobins may have been a significant means of reconciling their Majesties to the capitulation. But the next day, the 28th, was another day, and the pendulum swung again, heralding another sensational chapter in what had become a tragicomic farce.

2

That morning a vessel arrived from Palermo with a packet of letters for Nelson and the Hamiltons. A letter from the king was addressed to Nelson, two for Emma came from the queen, and there were three Acton had written to Sir William. There was also a letter Ferdinand had sent to Ruffo. All but one dated three days previously, they were written in ignorance of the exact nature of Ruffo's treaty and the latest letters adopting a moderate line, but replied to reports sent earlier from the *Foudroyant* and Procida.

Taken jointly, these letters carried a clear message. The dignity and stability of the monarchy were at stake, and a dishonourable peace that allowed rebels to escape unpunished and disaffection to reseed was unacceptable, 'for,' said the queen, 'without it the king could not for six months peacefully govern his people, who hope for some recompense from his justice after having done everything for him'. Nor was Ruffo now trusted. Their Majesties were suspicious of the people he was employing, suspected him of favouring Jacobins and nobles at the expense of loyal subjects and were sure that he was disobeying his instructions in the matter of offenders. Acton wondered whether the cardinal was raising an anti-monarchical party of his own, and noted that he had resurrected the office of *regente di vicaria*, or minister of police, already proscribed by the king. To make themselves clear, the court re-emphasised the essentials. The French should be compelled to surrender and leave, the exact terms of their capitulation to be ratified by the king, but there could be no negotiations with Jacobins, who must throw themselves upon the mercy of the king's tribunal and await acquittal, pardon, exile or execution as the process determined. Nelson not only had full powers, including the right to overrule Ruffo, but the moral burden of defending their Majesties' security and honour. Both king and queen entreated the admiral's support. 'I count on your arrival with the squadron, and on the firmness of the admiral,' the queen wrote to Emma. 'I have made up my mind never to set foot again in Naples if things are done in a way which brings us little honour, and which is such as to make one fear a relapse in the future. My trust is altogether in you all.' Ferdinand was just as categorical with Ruffo, who had been 'deceived' into employing dubious, possibly potentially hostile, persons. As for the treaty, if it did not comply with his instructions, 'it shall be void and null without my ratification'. Again, the king's reliance upon Nelson to 'fulfil my instructions' resonated.[19]

The action demanded by the court was consistent with Nelson's original annulment of the treaty, but not his subsequent retreat. Nelson and Hamilton had tried to bridge the gap between Ruffo and their Majesties by proceeding with a modified version of the treaty that yielded the thirteen rebels deemed most culpable to the king. But these new letters gave no room for such compromise. There can be little doubt that Nelson wrestled with his conscience, but he had been sucked into a hole from which there was no honourable escape. Either he dishonoured the treaty with the Jacobins or he dishonoured the court and government who had put their trust in him. It was a dismal impasse, but given such a choice his obligations lay principally to the monarchs who had stood with Britain against revolutionary France since 1793, and whose uncommon spirit had brought about their misfortunes, and not with the republicans. As for consequences, he had to weigh the abrogation of a treaty with Jacobins and perhaps some residual disorder in Naples (now being controlled to a degree by British marines), distasteful as they must have been, against the stability, security and restoration of an important ally. In the Leghorn affair of November, Nelson had already shown a readiness to break an agreement in the interests of what he deemed to be a greater good, and now he apparently went down a similar path.

His conduct at Naples seems to have largely been one of damage limitation. With difficult choices, he searched for the lesser of evils. On the 26th he had judged it right to support a treaty he hated to spare the city, and now he felt compelled to renege on his word to secure an unappeased monarchy. In both cases he opted for what he considered the least damaging course of action. Accordingly, Hamilton wrote afresh to Ruffo, explaining that the king had rejected the treaty and ordered the seizure of the prisoners, and that the polacres and their inmates would be impounded. As for those rebels who had returned to their homes, a proclamation would be published demanding their surrender within twenty-four hours upon pain of death.[20]

It was unquestionably a breach of faith with the Jacobins now sitting in their polacres waiting for the promised voyage to Toulon. It dishonoured the signatories of the treaty, as well as Nelson, and some British officers also felt that it dishonoured them. According to the gossipy Gordon, even Hallowell, George Martin, Hood and Troubridge objected to breaking faith with the rebels and suggested that they be given their arms and put back into the fortresses. Lock, who arrived in Naples about 3 July, also told in private letters of the 'abhorrence expressed by the whole fleet' at the betrayal of the Jacobins. Lock was no admirer of Nelson when he wrote the fullest of his three accounts of the business to Graham, the military commander at Messina, in August. According to that version, Hood and Hallowell were summoned to the *Foudroyant* on the morning of 28 June and told to station each of the Jacobin polacres under the stern of a line of battle ship. Fifteen Jacobin officers among the prisoners were to be transferred to the British ships and ironed. Neither officer was happy, and appealed to Rear Admiral Duckworth, the second in command, to visit the flagship and intervene. In the meantime Hood suggested to Nelson that the act would be deemed treacherous. Their beloved admiral would be accused of decoying the prisoners out of the castles under false pretences. Nelson replied that he acted under the king's orders, and 'that it was not his doing', which was not entirely devoid of truth. Hallowell supported Hood with 'great earnestness' and suggested the Jacobins be returned to the castles, and both captains 'engaged with their lives to reduce them by force in twenty-four hours'. Duckworth arrived to embolden the argument, but Nelson shut down further discussion. 'I see you are all against me. I am determined to obey my orders. Right or wrong, it shall be done. I will be obeyed.' The revolt was thus silenced, and the captains went sadly to work.[21]

Almost certainly Nelson and Hamilton were concerned about the deed, and dissimulated in their official reports. On 14 July Sir William told Grenville that the polacres, laden with rebel prisoners, were already there when the British fleet arrived in Naples. Nelson immediately ordered his boats to bring them under the sterns of the British ships to prevent them sailing. Thus the salient facts about the evacuation of the castles on 26 June were omitted. The day before Nelson had been no less close-lipped in writing to Spencer. In his account the rebels had been called upon to surrender unconditionally and 'came out . . . with this knowledge, without any honours, and the principal rebels were seized and conducted on board the ships of the squadron'. The rest had been loaded on to the polacres. This version linked the summonses Nelson had sent into the castles with the evacuation, but entirely missed out the prevarication between. The dispatch also misled when it stated that the rebels had been seized on the 26th, whereas many had then departed to their homes, and the rest had only been made prisoners on the 28th, when the treaty was abrogated. Nelson continued to mislead when Charles James Fox later publicly criticised his conduct in the British parliament, protesting to Davison that 'nothing [was] promised by a British officer that His Sicilian Majesty had not complied with', as if Foote for one had never existed. These adjustments are instructive, for they tell us that Nelson and Hamilton were ashamed of their conduct, and probably would have preferred it otherwise.[22]

For shame is one thing, blame another, and lazy judgements do violence to what were complex, frustrating and quickly evolving events. The admiral's apologists have underestimated his occasional unscrupulousness, and invested his conduct at Naples with an unconvincing uprightness. Critics have underestimated his general honour and described a thoroughly cynical trickster, wilfully gulling the Jacobins into a faithless surrender. Neither seems to be true.

Here, I have suggested that Nelson acted with open intentions, but found himself in the grip of impossible circumstances. Perhaps, with hindsight, he should have stuck to his first plan, disavowing the unauthorised treaty, returning the combatants to the positions they had occupied before it was signed, and squarely facing the consequences. But confronted by increasing chaos and alarm, he had tried to spare the city, and endorsed Ruffo's treaty. It seems that he was acting honestly, and had tried to shear the treaty of its most objectionable elements to make it more palatable. But the royal response aborted the compromise, and Nelson reneged upon the treaty in aid of the smooth restoration of the monarchy that was for him the ultimate as well as by far the most important objective.

By the end of the day the deed was done, and letters to the effect were speeding to Palermo by the *Earl St Vincent* cutter. The British fleet adjusted its position, and three guard ships advanced to cover the fourteen polacres with their guns. Armed boats from the fleet hurried to the mole to usher them out of their berths. Quickly the polacres were transformed into prison boats, secure under the sterns of the British ships, and the Jacobin leaders were unearthed, deprived of their side arms and removed for incarceration in the fleet. The rest of the prisoners remained aboard the polacres in squalid conditions. If their complaints are to be believed, their diet consisted of bread, water and wine mixed with seawater, and the boards below them served as beds. Exercise was limited, and some of the prisoners fell sick.[23]

The newly expressed authority of the king hamstrung Ruffo's ability to resist, and he slipped thenceforth into the background, distrusted by his superiors. Nelson continued to interpret his actions darkly, suspecting him of attempting to shield former Jacobins, but amid the confusion Nelson and Hamilton got some things right. They now insisted that the royal family and ministers return to Palermo to restore civil authority. This was essential. It was no part of the duty of a British admiral to meddle in the internal affairs of a foreign nation. 'I approve of no one thing which has been and is going on here,' Nelson told Acton. 'I see nothing but little cabals and complaints, which in my humble opinion, nothing can remove but the presence of the King, Queen and the Neapolitan minister, that the regular government may go on.' A ruling junta under the Sicilian Duke of Salandra had been established but an authoritative unifying figure was needed. Foote's frigate and a cutter were soon on their way to Sicily to collect. The response was immediate. On behalf of the king, Acton thanked Nelson for the 'proper measures' he had taken for 'saving His Majesty's honor from . . . the capitulation', and promised that Ferdinand would return to Naples. On the evening of 3 July the king sailed, accompanied by Acton, trusted adherents such as Prince Castelcicala and the Duke of Ascoli, and about 1700 soldiers. Despite Nelson's entreaties, the queen herself declined to go, fearing that she was so hated in Naples that her presence could only be counterproductive.[24]

To his credit, Nelson did not entirely turn his back upon the discredited Ruffo, to whose heroic efforts the monarchy still owed a great deal. On 29 and 30 June more letters from Palermo, all dated the 27th, strengthened Nelson's hand. Their Majesties had now read the actual capitulation and listened to a trickle of aggrieved suitors from Naples, complaining of Ruffo's patronage of ex-Jacobins. 'I cannot express the desolation of both their Majesties for the shameful operations of that man,' Acton wrote to Hamilton. The packet arriving on board the *Foudroyant* on the 30th was the crucial one. It enclosed a letter the king had written to Ruffo, firmly coaxing him into line. Ferdinand presumed that Ruffo had supported Nelson's demand for the unconditional surrender of the Jacobins, since to do otherwise 'would be equivalent to declaring yourself a rebel, which is impossible after the many proofs of fidelity and attachment given me in the past'. In another letter to Ruffo, Acton demanded his immediate return to account for his conduct. Nelson was armed with letters to the Duke of Salandra, 'General' Jean-Daniel de Gambs and Baron Tschudy, appointing them to the military and civil commands in Naples, and in case Ruffo resisted a warrant for his arrest. No one wanted it to come to that. To his credit Nelson did not abuse his power in the matter of Ruffo, and kept the entire royal packet locked firmly in his writing box, preferring to ease the cardinal along with as little disruption to the king's service as possible. Indeed, on 30 June Nelson and Hamilton were informing Palermo that the cardinal had been badly informed, and though misguided was not disloyal. The court was much relieved, and shelved plans to depose Ruffo, and on 2 July the queen even wrote to the wayward cardinal, saying that while she disapproved of the capitulation and the employment he had given scoundrels, she still hoped he would remain at his post and complete his great task.[25]

As far as he felt able, Ruffo did so. He appears to have refused to print any proclamations on behalf of Nelson, but supported the British, Russian and Portuguese artillerymen who opened a formal siege of St Elmo on 29 June. He also took responsibility for maintaining order in the city, although such 'anarchy and confusion' returned to the streets that the cardinal asked Troubridge to contribute to patrols. There was no appreciable interference with Nelson's new policy towards the Jacobin prisoners, though petitions began to reach the *Foudroyant* from the mystified and miserable inmates of the polacres, terrified that their vessels sat under guard when the weather was suitable for sailing, and that no victuals for a voyage appeared to be coming aboard. Similarly, Nelson's demand that those Jacobins who had left the castles for their homes should return to receive a parole pending the king's pleasure, backed as it was by threats of the ultimate sanction, was bringing in worried persons and petitions. Nelson resisted adding them to the bag, and gave them leave to remain in their homes, providing they promised not to 'stir out of them until His Sicilian Majesty's pleasure is known'. A few others were rounded up in the town, and some simply absconded rather than trust themselves to a royal tribunal.[26]

Nelson's earlier demand for key Jacobins from the granary, where Ruffo held his prisoners, was met on the morning of 29 June, when thirteen named 'wanted' were brought on board the *Foudroyant*. They included the former Neapolitan admiral Caracciolo, along with Domenico Cirillo (former president of the legislative commission), Gennaro Serra, Giuliana Colonna (a noble) and Nicola Pacifico, an obese, white-haired priest. A search of the polacres was uprooting other significant Jacobin leaders, including 'General' Gabriele Manthone and Massa. Many of these were also brought aboard the *Foudroyant* for a preliminary assessment before being imprisoned in other British ships.[27]

The captives were a distressing sight. On the quarterdeck of the flagship the Hamiltons, who knew Cirillo, formerly the king's physician, entreated him to petition for royal clemency, but found the old man unshakeable. He was born, he said stubbornly, in the reign of a tyrant, and had acted the part of a patriot in the fallen republic. His case was deferred for judicial review with all the others bar one, the pitiable figure of Caracciolo, who stood handcuffed in his dirty peasant disguise, his pale face obscured by a long, dishevelled beard and his eyes downcast. A thick-set, short, strong man of forty-seven, he appeared fatigued and 'half dead'. Hamilton had anticipated that the rebel admiral would have been shipped to Procida for trial before Sicilian authorities, and so he should have been, but Nelson did not wait. The man was shabbily treated, and denied the means of preparing a defence or the right of what would have been a futile appeal to the king's clemency. Nelson had internalised the king and queen's anger at Caracciolo, and decided to make an example of him. Without seeing the wretched prisoner, he sent an order to Count de Thurn, over whom he had full authority as commander-in-chief, ordering him to fetch five senior Neapolitan officers to the *Foudroyant*. When they arrived the admiral supplied them with an order. They were to form a court martial on board immediately, try the prisoner for the attack on the king's ships on 17 May – an attack that had cost the lives of several loyal seamen – and if they judged him guilty to recommend his punishment. Informed of the proceedings, Caracciolo asked to be tried by British officers. Perhaps he sensed vengeance in the Neapolitans, for Thurn himself had commanded the royalist flotilla attacked by Caracciolo on 17 May, but it was clearly not a job for the Royal Navy. Nelson would have seen nothing unusual in mutineers being judged by the fleets they had betrayed, and the trial went ahead as ordered.[28]

Midshipman George Parsons, who later claimed to have been present, remembered the accused defending himself 'in a deep, manly tone' that only faltered when describing the damage he believed would have befallen his family had he not 'succumbed to the ruling power'. The only surviving contemporary report, by Thurn, says little. Caracciolo could not deny the role he had played, which was notorious enough, nor had he fled the enemy service and returned to duty when opportunities presented themselves. Rather he excused himself by claiming that all he had done had been performed under the threat of being shot. In a few hours a majority verdict was returned, and the death sentence recommended. Nelson received it stonily. Thurn stated that it was usual to grant a condemned man twenty-four hours 'for the care of the soul,' and Hamilton agreed, but Nelson confirmed the sentence and ordered it to be carried out at five the same afternoon.[29]

We will never fully understand Caracciolo. That he had been an able and gallant naval officer is undeniable, but he seems to have been downcast by the king's distrust of the Neapolitan navy, and may have felt more valued elsewhere. It is also impossible to discount fears of retaliation against his loved ones. Whatever, he met his end bravely. Returned to his former ship, the Neapolitan frigate *La Minerve*, upon which he had made his fateful attack, he is said to have told Lieutenant Parkinson, who formed part of a guard, that he would rather have been shot than hanged. But he was swung from the foremast yardarm at the appointed hour. The body hung until sunset, beheld by numerous small boats that put out to view the corpse, and was then cut down, weighted with round shot and thrown into the sea.[30]

Caracciolo's guilt was undeniable, and Nelson executed him as a deterrent to traitors, but the manner in which he was pushed towards his end and the refusal to allow him a Christian burial, excommunicating the departing spirit, was precipitate and vindictive. Moreover, Nelson showed poor judgement involving himself in judicial matters that rightly belonged entirely to the Neapolitans. Compared with the other enormities committed during this bitter conflict it may have seemed insignificant, but even though he acted within the authority granted him by the king and queen, it does not rebound to Nelson's credit.[31]

3

Nelson could not allow even such events as these to obliterate the wider war. On 26 June the *Lion* and three sloops left to restore the blockade of Malta, which had again become a casualty of the crisis. Ball had been serving ashore at St Elmo, but on 3 July he too left for Malta, with the *Alexander*, *Alfonso d'Albuquerque*, *Success* and *Bulldog*.

One more fortification in Naples, the formidable castle of St Elmo, garrisoned by a thousand French troops and twenty-eight artillery pieces, had yet to be subdued. With walls sixty to eighty feet high, too tall for scaling ladders, it stood on a hill in the rear of the city, presenting three fire-proof gateways, each reached by drawbridges that spanned the surrounding ditch. The only ground commanding the castle was a hill in its rear, occupied by the convent of Calmandolese, but that was beyond point-blank range of artillery. The garrison of St Elmo was low in powder and had been firing sparingly, using a single charge each time, but there were few quick ways to subdue it. The ground was soft enough to mine, but that would have been a time-consuming business, and Troubridge, the effective leader of the attack, opted to breach and storm, though he typically dispensed with the conventional parallel approaches, and dug more direct and exposed trenches for his batteries. Seven thirty-sixes and eight mortars were initially deployed, some within seven hundred yards, trying to knock breaches into opposite angles of the castle. Other guns made use of the available cover, including the convent and the grounds of the Capo di Monte palace, which offered accommodation for troops.[32]

Cut off from succour, Méjean had no hope of making a successful resistance, but needed to satisfy his masters that he had offered a creditable defence. On the 29th Nelson landed the remaining marines from his fleet, bringing Troubridge's contingent of British up to thirteen hundred. With five hundred Russians, a Swiss regiment, some Portuguese gunners and an untold number of Calabrian irregulars, they formally invested the fortress the following day. To satisfy protocol, the Duke of Salandra was named titular head of the operation. Troubridge soon experienced problems with his irregular sappers, who, he said, refused to work at night and were scared to put their heads up by day, but he drove the trenches forward, promoting and praising the meritorious and placing halters around the necks of persistent shirkers. His equipment also inspired complaints of poor ammunition, powder too weak to throw projectiles far or hard enough, dilapidated mortar beds and unserviceable guns. Nevertheless, the allied fire told. Though the French officers scurried for a bomb-proof shelter, the commandant's house and some storehouses were set on fire or destroyed, and a reported twenty-six casualties inflicted in the first two days. By 4 July Nelson was allowing Méjean to send a courier to the French garrison at Capua. If they could not assist him he agreed to surrender.

The next day one of the British batteries was destroyed by enemy fire, and another two thirty-sixes had to be rolled up as replacements. Four mortars were added on the 6th. But to deliver a decisive stroke Troubridge began constructing a third battery of six thirty-sixes, masked by a bank of trees about 180 yards from the citadel walls. When the guns were ready the hazardous job of removing the screening trees was undertaken. Some of the labourers blanched at exposing themselves to enemy grape and the way had to be shown by Troubridge, Hallowell, Tschudy and, most remarkably, one Monsieur Montfrere, a French schoolmaster in the *Seahorse*, who revealed unsuspected talents as an engineer. Showered by dirt and branches hurled left and right by the French fire, they hacked away the trees, adjusted the guns, and at daylight on 11 July opened a new and more deadly bombardment. It took only two hours to dismount most of the enemy guns, destroy their works and bring a French officer to the walls with a white flag. Firing stopped, terms were concluded and the weary and dusty French bluecoats marched out in the morning of the 12th, drums beating, and stacked their muskets outside the gates. Then, as the Neapolitan colours rose above the castle to enthusiastic salutes from the guns of the fleet, they began their journey home. They had lost 135 killed and wounded.

The siege had cost the allies 125 casualties, seven of them British, and in an appreciative dispatch Nelson urged his superiors to recognise the value of Troubridge, who had suffered so many disappointments. The captain of the *Culloden* also had the privilege of bringing the keys of the castle and captured enemy colours to the *Foudroyant*, where he was able to deliver them not to Nelson but to Ferdinand himself, for the king had coincidentally arrived the day before with Acton, two frigates and fresh troops. His standard, now flying with Nelson's own on the big eighty-gun *Foudroyant*, jubilantly proclaimed the return of the Bourbons.[33]

The news of the king's appearance, noisily advertised by the guns of ships and forts, flashed through the city like an electric current, and flotillas of tiny boats soon surrounded the British flagship, filled with smiling people clamouring to see their leader. At every appearance, Ferdinand inspired tremendous cheers, provoking sights, Sir William said, 'as never can be forgotten'. Troubridge had brought His Majesty one gift with his news of the collapse of the last pocket of resistance in the city, but there were other reasons to be satisfied. Thanks in part to Hood's day and night patrols, performed by British marines quartered in the Castel Nuovo, public order had improved, and the streets had been cleared of royalist mobs. The discipline of the British force was scrupulously monitored by its officers to ensure that it remained an example of purpose and regularity. Nelson probably exaggerated when he claimed that 'no capital is more quiet than Naples', for much remained to be done. Troubridge warned that Ruffo's favouritism to former Jacobins had fuelled 'great discontents . . . among the people', and that if the king did not 'establish a government I fear the place will not continue tranquil long'. Ferdinand was already planning to reward those to whom he believed he owed his restoration. The nobles, professionals and intelligentsia had been at the core of the disaffection, he believed, and the common people his bedrock of support. He talked about abolishing the *sedile* (the annual assembly of Neapolitan nobles) and the feudal system, by which he said the aristocracy oppressed the poor.[34]

For some time the everyday needs of the king added to Nelson's frustrations. Ferdinand took over the cabin of the *Foudroyant*, except for a small ante-room that Emma and her English secretary used as an office and reception room for endless visiting ladies, and from which the regular correspondence between the royal 'Charlotte' and her 'Miledy' passed in and out. The king conducted daily levees on the quarterdeck, flanked by Acton, Castelcicala and an attendant. For four long weeks he held court with innumerable visitors, whilst Nelson, the Hamiltons and secretary Tyson withdrew to rooms in the lieutenants' wardroom. Ferdinand assisted with the Sunday religious services, but for most of his spare time was content to fish, bag seabirds with his musket and leave affairs to his principals. Emma he called 'his Grande Maîtresse', but she continued to fawn upon the admiral. He was, she said, 'here and there and everywhere. I never saw such zeal and activity in anyone as in this wonderful man.' But the bustle of business was not the whole story. On 9 July the *Foudroyant* hosted the wedding of two of the British residents of Naples, Dr William Compton, the Chancellor of Ely and a relative of the Earl of Northampton, and the eldest daughter of the late Knipe Gobbet of the West Norfolk Militia. Nelson gave away the bride. Midshipman Parsons remembered those days nostalgically, noting the great improvement the king made to the ship's mess, Emma's 'graceful form' bending over her harp to bestow 'heavenly music' upon the diners on the quarterdeck and the large-decked galley, flush with opera singers, that glided alongside to serenade the sunset of each day.[35]

One tense moment impressed itself on several witnesses, however. The details they give vary, but it seems that Nelson occasionally took the flagship out into the bay to please the king, perhaps to facilitate his appetite for fishing. But one day they beheld an eerie sight, the bloated corpse of Caracciolo bobbing upright in the water, its feet still held down by the remains of the shot that was supposed to anchor it to the seabed. Ferdinand was startled by the apparition, supposing at one time that it had been a prank, contrived by means of 'corks, planks, weights, etc.' But once he had regained his composure, he agreed that the body should be taken ashore for burial. A boat retrieved the remains, which were sewn into a hammock and laid to rest beneath a modest stone in the church of Santa Maria della Catena.[36]

Despite such distractions, Nelson prepared to bring the campaign to an end. The city of Naples was free, a measure of order established and Ferdinand restored to his kingdom, but to the north two French garrisons remained, at Capua and Gaeta. Both were being harassed by insurgents under Fra Diavolo, but Capua alone was believed to shelter fifteen hundred French regulars, and a regular investment was necessary. On 19 July Troubridge and Hallowell left for Capua, a town twenty miles inland, with about 1000 British marines and 4000 Portuguese, Russian, Swiss and Neapolitan troops. They arrived at their destination three days later, with orders Nelson had refined in collaboration with Ferdinand. If they surrendered immediately the French would be allowed free passage home and excused the status of prisoners of war; otherwise they risked 'as degrading terms as it is in your power to give'.[37]

It was on 13 July, while preparations for this operation were underway, that Nelson received a discomforting letter. It was from Lord Keith, his acting commander-in-chief.

4

Keith had been vainly searching for Bruix in the northern Mediterranean. Fortunately, the French fleet had not been adventurous, and after transporting several thousand soldiers from Vado Bay to Savona, it recoiled towards Toulon. Keith also continued to fret about Minorca, with its modest British garrison, now exposed to attack from three directions – from the French fleet, the Spanish fleet in Cartagena and an assemblage of forces in Majorca. On 27 June he wrote to Nelson asking him to send any spare ships to cover the island.[38]

Nelson had expected the summons, and warned Spencer that if it came he would have to judge whether Minorca or Naples was the greater priority. Engaged in delicate operations of his own in Naples, Sicily and Malta and with a superior French fleet at large, he had a point, and Keith's reference to *surplus* ships provided a temporary loophole. Nelson immediately replied that he would send what he could as soon as Naples and Sicily were 'secure' and 'a thorough cleansing' had restored 'tranquillity'. But Keith's next orders, dated from Minorca on 9 July, were more peremptory. They informed Nelson that the Spanish and French fleets had combined in Cartagena on 22 June, creating a huge force of forty-three capital ships, and sailed apparently for the Strait. It looked as if they were leaving the Mediterranean, but Keith intended to pursue, leaving Minorca to Nelson's protection. As a couple of Spanish ships of the line with a few frigates and gunboats could attack the island the moment Keith left, the acting commander-in-chief thought it imperative that 'all or the greatest part' of Nelson's force now be deployed to defend it. He allowed no leeway. 'If this island is left without ships, it will fall,' he wrote. 'You must, therefore, either come or send Duckworth . . . until I can determine to a certainty the intention of the enemy.' Enclosed was intelligence that Spain had been assembling a flotilla with several thousand men, hundreds of pieces of artillery, powder, munitions, floating bridges, scaling ladders and provisions for an assault.[39]

More sensitive than Keith knew, Nelson was already feeling aggrieved by almost everything that came from his new superior. On 28 June Keith had ordered him to send Smith whatever 'ships or ammunition or other articles he . . . may want with all possible despatch', apparently oblivious of the bone of contention that Sir Sidney's demands had become. Now Nelson flatly refused the order to reinforce Minorca. 'Your lordship,' he replied, 'at the time of sending me the order was not informed of the change of affairs in the kingdom of Naples, and that all our marines and a body of seamen are landed.' There followed a lecture about priorities. 'I am perfectly aware of the consequences of disobeying the orders of my commander-in-chief, but . . . I have no scruple in declaring that it is better to save the kingdom of Naples and risk Minorca than to risk the kingdom of Naples to save Minorca.' Spencer also got it straight from the shoulder. 'At this moment I will not part with a single ship, as I cannot do that without drawing 120 men from each ship now at the siege of Capua, where our army is gone this day.' He would send eight or nine ships to Minorca as soon as the French 'scoundrels' had been ousted. 'I have done what I thought right,' he added. 'Others may think differently, but it will be my consolation that I have gained a kingdom, seated a faithful ally of His Majesty firmly on his throne, and restored happiness to millions. Do not think, my dear lord, that my opinion is formed from the arguments of any one. *No*; be it good, or be it bad, it is all my own.'[40]

Nelson had a history of disobedience, of course, some of it ultimately productive. He had ascended the San Juan River in 1780 against orders; flouted the orders of his commanders-in-chief, Sir Richard Hughes in 1784–5, Hotham in 1795 and Jervis in 1796, and famously taken an independent line in the battle of Cape St Vincent the following year. Perhaps more radically, he believed that political courage, the willingness to act independently, and to modify, even to reject orders, as changing circumstances dictated, was an essential quality for a naval officer, an eminently logical if dangerous tenet most recently expressed in his condemnation of General Naselli the previous November. Here, however, the hero of the Nile demonstrated his distinctive independence of mind with increased effrontery. His letters carried more than a hint of insubordination; they flaunted it, almost inviting 'a trial for my conduct'. This was brazen indeed.[41]

The ranking officers in the Mediterranean were coming from different directions. Nelson did not believe that Minorca would be attacked, but he had seen and suffered with the Two Sicilies, and at this stage was desperate to fulfil his commitments to them. His latest decision was probably influenced by a heartfelt plea from Ferdinand not to desert him at this critical moment. Through Acton, the king alluded to a work in progress, one of his forces having marched into the Roman state to secure his frontiers on 18 July and another for Capua the day after. Nelson's 'fleet and excellent advices have procured every success', and without them 'His Majesty cannot exert, as intended, his endeavours for the common cause, nor be easy in the reacquired possession of his kingdom'. These were not responsibilities that Keith fully understood. In contrast to Nelson, he talked about Minorca as if it was by far Nelson's most significant responsibility. In eight letters shot at Nelson between 13 and 17 July, Keith told him to reposition his force at Minorca, stationing a few ships at Gibraltar to preserve communications with England and protect convoys proceeding up and down the Mediterranean. When Italy was mentioned, it was to remind Nelson to support the allies on the Riviera coast. Naples and Malta, he believed, could be left to the Portuguese and their own devices.[42]

On 22 July Nelson went so far as to detach Duckworth with three ships of the line to Minorca, minus their marines, who were serving ashore with Troubridge, and another two followed at the beginning of August. It was probably sufficient for the purpose, although far smaller than Keith had wanted, and the embryo commander-in-chief left the Mediterranean highly dissatisfied with his more glamorous subordinate. He stressed to his superiors that he had written 'in the strongest terms' to Nelson, but failed to bring him to heel. His negativism probably damaged Nelson at the Admiralty, where the board realised that the flight of Bruix had restored Britain's supremacy in the Mediterranean, and that Nelson had the force to protect Minorca and Italy, a view that gained strength with the advantageous turn that affairs had taken in Naples.[43]

With St Vincent and Keith elsewhere, Nelson was free to pursue his country's interests in the Mediterranean as he saw them, and as Duckworth had a token force at Minorca, he focused upon completing the liberation of Naples. He remained in the bay, continuing to police the city and supporting the forces he had sent against Capua and Gaeta, the two remaining Neapolitan fortresses in enemy hands.[44]

Before Capua, which nestled inside a loop of the River Volturno, his little army dug in on both banks, the infantry under Generals Emmanuel de Bourcard and de Gambs fording the river on the left to threaten the enemy rear, the British holding the centre before the front of the city, and a six-hundred strong Swiss regiment under Colonel Tschudy securing their right. Acton, reliving his martial career, took charge of the cavalry, while the Turks and wild Calabrese who had attached themselves to the expedition skirmished on the flanks, peppering the fortress with a distracting small arms fire and driving in a French advanced post. To facilitate communications between the different detachments a pontoon bridge was thrown across the Volturno on 22 July, and at 3.30 on the morning of the 25th two batteries of howitzers, mortars and heavy long guns opened fire from ranges of five to seven hundred yards.

The enemy castle stood on a gentle hill. It was stronger than the allies expected, containing 2817 regulars, perhaps 800 Jacobin supporters, 108 pieces of artillery, 12,000 muskets, 68,000 lbs of powder and 414,000 cartridges, but few of their guns were in a condition or position to bear, and the men had little stomach for a fight. Nevertheless, the defenders refused the first offer of terms, which Hallowell brought under a white flag, and on the first night made a disruptive sortie against the encircling army. By daylight of the 28th, however, Troubridge had driven his siege trenches to within a few yards of the glacis, where he erected two new four-gun batteries, and in a few hours the French capitulated. They marched out to stack their arms on the glacis the following day, the French no doubt relieved that they were going home, and their Jacobin adherents, who had been excluded from the protection of the capitulation, fearfully throwing themselves upon whatever justice waited in Ferdinand's hands. It had, in all, been another creditable achievement for Troubridge, who had met his old enemy – the inadequacy of men, supplies and tools – with great determination. A lack of suitable siege guns was met by fitting 'land beds' to sea mortars in the Naples arsenal, and the carpenter of the *Culloden* had scoured the fleet for good quality gunpowder. One day in the siege was lost through the failure of the bread supply. Moreover, although the sappers performed essential work, labouring through darkness to build batteries and redoubts, there were too few of them, and they were apt to scatter under fire. Nerves remained on a knife edge. 'An unfortunate shot took a horse's head off and killed one of the workmen,' grumbled Troubridge. 'The rest set off' and 'hid in the corn'. Even worse, the siege had to continue without Baillie's Russians, who took umbrage at some unstated difficulty and refused further cooperation. Whether this was due to some inadequacy in Troubridge's management of a multi-national force is unclear, but at least he successfully prevented it from looting the captured town or gratuitously bullying prisoners.[45]

Only the nearby port of Gaeta remained to be cleared. On 25 June Nelson had sent Hoste with the *Mutine* and *San Leon* sloops to blockade and bombard the place, and to collaborate with the local insurgents. Brigadier General Antoine Girardon, the French commander at Capua, also agreed to treat for the subordinate post, and included it in the surrender of his own garrison on the 29th. When Louis of the *Minotaur* duly appeared at Gaeta to receive its capitulation, he was astonished to find the commander of the garrison jibbing at complying, though he was low on food and ammunition. Nelson seems to have concluded that Louis lacked the necessary steel. 'I was sorry that you had entered into any altercation with the scoundrel,' Nelson wrote to Louis unhelpfully. 'There is no way of dealing with a Frenchman but to knock him down.' The rebuke from an idolised chief deeply hurt the sensitive and utterly loyal captain, and he redoubled his efforts to regain Nelson's confidence. In the meantime Gaeta knuckled under, and eighty-five guns of different types, 1498 French and a hundred or so Jacobins surrendered. A delay in the arrival of Neapolitan troops needed to form a new garrison postponed the embarkation of the prisoners until 3 August, when Louis's men struggled to keep Fra Diavolo's angry insurgents from plundering the dejected soldiers marching to the boats.[46]

The kingdom of Naples was free – for most – but the further consequences for those who had dared to challenge the groaning regime had yet to be endured. Among them were occasional unfortunates swept up through no fault of their own, perhaps guilty only by association. An Englishwoman, caught up with the republican forces just before the restoration, was among those rotting in a Neapolitan ship, though the French had taken all she had. At Naples the rebel prisoners were eventually transferred from the dark, stifling and fetid transports to penitentiaries ashore, and brought before a couple of juntas. The *Giunta di Stato*, which tried civilians, was reputedly severe; the other, the *Giunta di Generale*, which examined the cases against military officers, was reckoned to be a fairer instrument. Regrettably, few records of these proceedings have survived, and rumours have been left to rage unchecked, but there can be little doubt that injustices were done. Public executions of those convicted of the grosser offences began at the Porta Capuana on 7 July 1799 and lasted until September 1800. The beheadings and hangings before baying crowds in the Mercato square attached to the Castello del Carmine made for grim entertainment indeed. Some of the victims earned sympathy through their bravery and transparent patriotism, while others perished amidst derision and joy. A cleric, it is said, died at the end of a rope, with a grotesque hangman swinging obscenely on his shoulders, boasting that he had never before ridden a bishop. The scale of this purge may have been negligible measured against the thousands slaughtered in the Italian war, but among the hundred or so executed were some idealistic if gullible men and women, who in other circumstances might have benefited their country. However just some of the penalties seemed to British officers, the spectacle as a whole depressed the most hardened. Troubridge, who remained in command off Naples when Nelson returned to Palermo, was disturbed by the thin evidence used to convict some of the prisoners, and argued for a general amnesty. 'Today,' he wrote on 20 August, 'departed this life princes, dukes, commoners and ladies to the amount of eleven, some by the axe and others by the halter. I sincerely hope they will soon finish on a grand scale, and then pass an act of oblivion. Death is a trifle to the prisons.' But the trials continued. Eight thousand were indicted, of whom some nine hundred suffered further imprisonment or exile and a little over a hundred were executed.[47]

For her part Emma Hamilton seemed generally sensible of the brutality of it, and received many petitions for clemency from those who believed that her voice carried weight with the queen or Nelson. Her Majesty was certainly embittered, and in letters to 'Miledi' (as she called Emma) freely dispensed strong opinions about people and events, fuelled by the latest from Naples. But her mood varied. Despite the reconquest of her kingdom, she remained tortured by a fear that dangerous traitors might survive to destroy her once the supporting military and naval forces had gone. 'As soon as the king's back is turned, they will be worse than ever before, as they will manage matters more skilfully through their previous experience,' she complained. She was therefore assiduous in singling out perilous opponents. Yet at other times she recognised and rued her intemperate pronouncements, and it testifies to her loss of influence with her husband that she sometimes used Emma to entreat Nelson to intervene. 'I solicit . . . a good word for them from you, if the tutelary hero Nelson approves it,' Maria wrote on behalf of three defendants on 28 July.[48]

In passing observations through Emma, the queen understood her friend's distaste for the business. On 7 July we find 'Charlotte' chiding 'Miledi' for her generous heart. 'I beg you to restrain your benevolence, and think only of those on whom real misfortunes have, or are promptly about, to fall,' said she. Sir William was no less aware, remarking that his wife 'had no other fault than that of too much sensitivity'. Yet Emma features ambiguously in the sources, according to the disposition of the scribe. An emotional person, she was as capable of strident denunciations of supposed enemies as she was of empathy, and people who saw the one attribute did not always see the other. Where the likes of Gordon saw a fiend, others beheld an angel. Midshipman Parsons took that last memory to his grave fifty-five years later. For him Emma remained an 'unjustly treated and wonderful woman' whose 'generosity and good nature were unbounded', and whose 'heart was of softer materials than to rejoice in the sufferings of the enemies of the court.'[49]

On the whole Nelson and Hamilton avoided entangling themselves in the judicial process. With a few exceptions, Nelson was not sympathetic to the rebels, but he regarded their fates as matters for the king's government. Emma, he complained, 'has time so much taken up with excuses from rebels, Jacobins and fools that she is every day more heartily tired'. Perhaps wisely, he referred the complaints and petitions he received to the king.[50]

Among those who did appeal to Nelson were the officers of the *Leviathan*, who spoke up for a family then being held on board, allegedly repentant of their republican service, as well as for Domenico Cirillo. A noted philanthropist and botanist, correspondent of Linnaeus and fellow of the Royal Society of London, Cirillo was nearly sixty. Hitherto he had adamantly refused to appeal to the king, whose physician he had once been, even when entreated to do so by the Hamiltons, but incarcerated in the *St Sebastian* he eventually recanted, writing separately to both Emma and Nelson, explaining that his house was a ruined heap, his mother missing and his prospects ruined. He had been appointed to Championnet's provisional government, but quickly resigned, and only served on the Legislative Commission of the Parthenopean Republic under duress, avoiding, he said, taking any oath against the king or defaming his name. 'What could I do, how could I and what could I oppose?' he pleaded with unassailable logic. It is difficult to see how Cirillo could have endangered the restoration, except in inciting a royalist crowd that had decided that his treason was too notorious to overlook. 'Now, Madam,' he addressed Emma, 'in the name of God, do not abandon your miserable friend.' She must have felt guilty, since she it was who had copied his name on to a list of Jacobin prisoners and sent it to the queen. For whatever reason, Nelson seems to have secured him a relaxation of the conditions of his captivity aboard ship, but later said that his suit had come 'too late . . . or the queen would have begged his forfeited life of the king for the sake of his age and good mother'. Cirillo died on the gallows with three comrades on 29 October. 'So much wisdom, so much learning, and so much honour were thus lost to Italy in one day,' mourned one who had seen the good in him.[51]

5

The Bourbon restoration closed a whirlwind period in which redemption and reclamation were snatched from disaster. British ships had played an important part in the counter-revolution, saving and preserving the royal family in Sicily, shielding the insurgency from Bruix, helping expel Macdonald from the city, and in the recent campaign spearheading the expulsion of seven to eight thousand French and Jacobin forces from Granatelli, Revigliano, Castellammare, Naples, Capua and Gaeta. Nelson was not naive enough to believe that Ferdinand's apparent enthusiasm for beneficial reforms, especially to reward the majority who had stood by him, would greatly benefit the people. He had long convinced himself that the state was inherently inefficient and corrupt, and believed that Acton and Belmonte were the king's only honest servants. But at least an important ally, essential for Britain's control of the eastern basin of the Mediterranean, had been put back upon his feet.

He milked the success on behalf of his officers, packing favourites off to England with dispatches announcing the liberation of Naples and testifying to their services. James Oswald of the *Perseus*, who had repulsed Caracciolo's flotilla in May, was promoted post-captain, and two flag lieutenants, William Standway Parkinson and Henry Compton, became commanders, the latter slipping into the post just vacated by Oswald. Compton's departure to the *Perseus* allowed Lieutenant Andrew Thompson to enter the flagship, always a coveted base for advancement. When Nelson was able to appoint John Lackey, another *Foudroyant* lieutenant, to command a cutter, he replaced him with one of St Vincent's protégés, Frederick Langford, who had been marking time in the *Principe Real*. Most of all Nelson's recent success was rooted in three sterling members of the brothers. Troubridge's 'merits speak for themselves', Nelson told Nepean. 'His own modesty makes it my duty to state that to him alone is the chief merit due,' although 'the brave and excellent Captain Hallowell' had been his support throughout, and Hood had restored order to the streets of Naples. In another reflection of the value he placed upon naval personnel serving ashore, he supported a petition for their officers to be awarded the 'bat and forage' money available to their counterparts in the army.[52]

After astonishing highs and lows the first anniversary of the battle of the Nile was reached with satisfaction, and Ferdinand honoured Nelson with a dinner, a royal salute fired by his remaining Sicilian warships and a celebratory evening in which a boat mocked up as a Roman galley rocked gently alongside the *Foudroyant*, awash with two thousand lights and the admiral's portrait, furnishing a musical tribute to the hero. Nelson issued an order to the fleet 'that no heart may have cause to be sad on such a day', urging his captains to 'forgive faults committed' and entreating that a half pint of wine be issued to every man so that the health of His Britannic Majesty could be drunk at six in the evening. Six, of course, was the hour at which the feted engagement had begun.[53]

There was more to be done, as Nelson realised. The counter-revolution in the south and the triumphant opening of the Austro-Russian campaign in the north had closed upon the French like the jaws of a tiger, splintering and pulverising the opposition, but Troubridge would remain off the coast to quieten Naples and secure her northern borders. Nelson advised Wyndham to return to Tuscany, where the minister found 50,000 Tuscan insurgents in arms against the evaporating French forces, many equipped only with fowling pieces. He set about organising a chain of communication between Nelson and the allied armies in the Gulf of Genoa. By the end of July Tuscan territory had been liberated relatively bloodlessly to 'joy and exhilaration beyond description'. The former Roman state still harboured French holdouts, and on 18 July Ferdinand's troops had again crossed the border, this time as part of a general allied offensive. Nelson had three capital ships and more than half a dozen cruisers on the coast of northern Italy in July and early August, collecting information, protecting trade, harassing enemy communications and cooperating with allied armies ashore. The most active of these ships were quite effective. Cockburn's *Minerve* took or destroyed about eighteen vessels between April and 2 August, including a French privateer, *Caroline*, on 2 June, and with help from the boats of the *Petterel*, a felucca and a half-galley found in Diano Bay two months later. But this was a theatre that would need further attention.[54]

The Hamilton–Nelson trio could also contemplate home. Age, health and revolution had drained Sir William's spirits, though he had mixed feelings about leaving Italy. He felt and looked worn to the bone and his personal losses had accumulated. Eight cases of treasures had gone down in the *Colossus*, wrecked off the Scilly Isles, and he was urging Greville to salvage at any expense, but his own attempts to rescue what was left of his fortune in Naples had not been successful. In April the Hamiltons had made enquiries about possessions they had left in the Palazzo Sessa, only to learn that everything was gone, while Emma herself had visited the remains of that house and the Villa Emma after the restoration and been distressed at the sights that greeted her. To these losses could be added the expenses incurred in conducting King George's business in Palermo. The king's permission to retire had been in Sir William's pocket for more than two years, but he had stayed to see out the crisis. Now, dreading an English winter, he talked about living quietly in Palermo until the spring, and then going home.

When Nelson and his friends prepared to sail for Palermo early in August, they were satisfied that they had performed an important service. Emma optimistically hailed the achievement as 'a glory to our good king, to our country, to ourselves that *we* – our brave fleet, our great Nelson' had had 'the happiness' of restoring a 'much loved king' to his people 'and been the instrument of giving a future good and just government to the Neapolitans'. Sir William was more sceptical about the future of Naples, but equally self-satisfied. 'Lord Nelson and I, with Emma, are the *Tria Juncta in Uno* that have carried on affairs to this happy crisis,' he said. In England Matthew Boulton, the Birmingham ironmaster who had struck Davison's Nile medal, celebrated Nelson's part in Ferdinand's restoration with a new medal.[55]

But there were others who took a different view, and in due course criticisms filtered back to Nelson. In Whitehall Lord Spencer, hitherto almost slavishly in agreement with Nelson, first parted company over the Bruix affair. When the admiral reported that a thousand of his men had marched inland to attack Capua, the board penned a mild rebuke, pointing out the impropriety of embroiling so many men in a land operation with a French fleet on the loose. Spencer knew that a measure of independence was necessary in a ranking officer in the Mediterranean, which was so far from government advice or control and generally a diplomatic maelstrom. No less was he aware that Nelson was the best fighting admiral he had. He therefore handled him carefully, tempering criticisms, trying to reward his followers and paying plenty of tributes. On 19 August Spencer gingerly approached the admiral's blatant disobedience to Keith. 'You have already, my dear Lord, done wonders', and while Keith had been within his rights to issue the disputed orders, Spencer understood the importance of Nelson's operations and the difficulty of extricating forces involved in activities ashore. However, he nudged, the admiral must also recognise the importance of ensuring that his force was ready to respond to urgent demands, and would no doubt assist Minorca as soon as he could. Even such moderate censures as this stung Nelson, who admitted 'great pain' in reading them when they arrived in Sicily in September. He was entirely unrepentant, and declared that he would never 'shelter myself under the letter of the law' if it was 'in competition with the public service'. More mollification was needed from Admiral Young, one of the other members of the board, and afterwards Spencer reiterated his full commendation of the operations in support of Naples.[56]

The Admiralty's worries were serious ones, for all that. The departure of Keith left Nelson de facto acting commander-in-chief of the Mediterranean, with much wider responsibilities than he had ever known. It was essential that he was weaned from the Two Sicilies and repositioned, probably in Minorca, so that he could respond adequately to events in the western as well as the eastern reaches of the theatre. Spencer hinted at this on 8 August when he expressed a hope that the restoration of the Bourbons would leave Nelson little to do there from the naval point of view. But in addition to apprehensions for current operations, the Admiralty was beginning to hear disquieting whispers about Nelson's recent activities. None of them came from Nelson's own officers, although some had not approved of all that the British had done at Naples. George Magrath, a surgeon with the fleet and one of the admiral's great admirers, still refused to talk about it after long decades had passed. 'Let us not speak of that,' he would say. 'He was not the first man infatuated by a petticoat, and will not be the last.'[57]

The key whistle-blower, in fact, was the peeved young consul, Charles Lock, who wanted to be chargé d'affaires at Naples, but who had not been included among those who had accompanied Nelson and the Hamiltons to Palermo. He turned up later, and soon marshalled other grievances. Lock saw a profitable sideline in brokering local contracts to supply British ships with fresh beef, wine and other provisions, a way of turning his office as consul to greater account. No sooner was he in Naples than he began badgering Nelson to grant him a monopoly of such supplies. At that time the power to procure fresh provisions lay with the individual captains and pursers of the squadron, who had been ordered to attend closely to both price and quality. The system seemed to have been working well, and Nelson saw no reason to risk it in hands as inexperienced and opportunist as those of Lock. And from such mundane beginnings there grew an altercation that would rebound against Nelson's public reputation.[58]

Lock was 'much agitated' at his rebuff, and instantly declared that he would force Nelson to act, if only to curb 'flagrant abuses' and 'great impositions practised against government that it was his duty to correct'. At dusk on 23 July there was an ugly public conversation on the quarterdeck of the *Foudroyant*, when Lock insinuated that the pursers were abusing the current system. 'How d'ye mean?' snapped the admiral promptly. Lock replied that he had evidence that suggested pursers were charging the government more than the cost of the victuals they were receiving. 'Aye, aye,' said Nelson, 'how do you know this?' Lock sensed that he was getting into deep water and declined to name either the cheats or his source. 'By God, I will sift this matter to the bottom!' Nelson pronounced in his most decisive manner, and summoning Hardy he immediately set in motion an order to the captains of the fleet, telling them to check their pursers' receipts before signing the vouchers they sent to government.

Nelson's sharp mind had discerned the drift. There was probably no substance to Lock's allegations, which had been carelessly cobbled up to discredit a system he wanted to replace for personal advantage. But Nelson also realised that Lock had a malignant spirit, and that it was necessary to cover himself from any charge of shielding abuses. After such a public accusation, broadcast openly on the flagship's quarterdeck, there had to be an investigation. The conversation crackled fiercely, and Nelson brought it to an end. 'Here!' he told Hardy, 'Take him from me. I am afraid, by God, he'll strike me.' The burly flag captain bulked beside his admiral, transfixing Lock with a resolute and intimidating eye, and the consul rapidly trod water. Ten more minutes found Lock outside Hardy's cabin beneath the poop, attempting a faltering apology and pleading that an investigation would 'ruin' him. But Nelson told him that the matter was out, and could not be dodged. He walked away leaving Lock hovering helplessly in obvious distress.[59]

While the captains trawled through the accounts of their pursers, only to discover nothing amiss, Lock's name turned to mud and the pursers of the fleet angrily refused to have any dealings with the purveyor of such 'malicious insinuations'.

The consul was soon performing a double act, denying in Naples that he had intended any offence and simultaneously trying to justify himself at home through confidential innuendos. He had already been writing of the Hamilton–Nelson ménage behind their backs, depicting Emma as 'a superficial, grasping and vulgar-minded woman' who wished to sustain an 'unfit' husband in his station, a station Lock would have liked for himself. More, on 13 July Lock told his father that the fleet was shocked at Nelson's breach of faith over the surrender of the Neapolitan castles. The danger for Nelson lay in Lock's powerful Whig connections, for he was a cousin by marriage to the voluble Fox; a protégé of Fox's nephew, the grandee Henry, Baron Holland; and a son-in-law of the Duchess of Leinster. His family walked in elevated circles, and his views, right or wrong, had legs. As early as 30 July Lock was urging his father to bypass Nelson in his campaign for an appointment as agent victualler, and to raise the matter with the king through the offices of Lord Grenville. In the summer he was telling his father that he had a full account of the violation of Ruffo's treaty in preparation.[60]

Nelson sent his investigation into his pursers to the Victualling Board in London, but remarks about the allegations against them had also reached members of the board through letters Lock had written to his family. Moreover, although the consul got cold feet about submitting a detailed attack upon Nelson's handling of the Jacobins, his remarks went around in private circles and probably occasioned the hostile comments that began to appear in the British press. On 12 August the Whig *Morning Chronicle* accused Nelson of seizing some of the rebels 'contrary to an express engagement, on the faith of which they had acted'. A year later, on 3 February 1800, Fox attacked Nelson in the House of Commons. Fox's view of the events was clearly muddled, but he had heard that the rebels had left their castles believing they could sail to Toulon, only to be subsequently imprisoned.[61]

It all touched upon the Achilles heel in Nelson's operations, and one he and Hamilton had written out of their dispatches. Nelson valued his reputation as a man of honour, and tried to be one. Some shortcomings were so unpleasant that he found them difficult to live with, and coped by denying that they had ever happened, perhaps trying to convince himself as much as anyone else. Nelson responded hotly to Fox's aspersion with a letter he authorised Davison to publish or circulate. It repeated the abridged account that he had offered before ('I sent in my note [summons] . . . on which the rebels came out of the castles *as they ought . . . to be hanged* or otherwise disposed of, as their sovereign thought proper') and ingenuously claimed that 'there has been nothing promised by a British officer that His Sicilian Majesty has not complied with'. The following year he was equally annoyed with Helen Maria Williams's *Sketches . . . of the French Republic*, a manifestly prejudiced and inaccurate book which also mentioned British bad faith. But he was fortunate that the story did not gain a wide circulation until after his death.[62]

Thereafter the attacks became more barbed. Incensed by a remark in Harrison's *Life* of Nelson, published in 1806, Captain Foote finally broke his silence about the treatment of the rebels, and in his *Vindication* of 1807 charged the admiral with having become so 'infatuated' with Emma that 'the balance of his mind was lost at a critical moment' and created 'unjustifiable' measures. He alerted James Stanier Clarke, another 'official' biographer of Nelson, to the change of mind that had brought the rebels from the castles under false expectations, but found him an unwilling listener. Clarke had already been 'put on my guard respecting the castles Uovo and Nuovo' by Hardy, and declined to use the story. It was left to the less reverent but equally admiring Robert Southey to give Foote's not entirely accurate version widespread circulation in his popular *Life of Nelson*, published in 1813.[63]

The critics had a searing point but Nelson might still have justly complained, for few understood the complicated circumstances in which the admiral had been placed. As the nineteenth century progressed a new united Italy arose upon the ashes of the old, and the minority of 1799 became the majority. Generations of Italian scholars, such as Benedetto Croce, imbued with a spirit most of their forebears would not have recognised, subsequently lionised the martyred 'patriots' of 1799 as the ancestors of political unification and democracy, and demonised their conquerors as vengeful tyrants, ignorant peasants, superstitious clerics and, of course, a manipulated British admiral with a backstairs dragon in tow. Nelson might not have been surprised, because he had lived long enough to learn the ways of the world. As he remarked to Clarence, 'the generality of mankind judge from what *is now*, and not *what was then*'.[64]

Those he had served saw it in an entirely different light, from the common people who cheered the restoration and clamoured around him, to the queen. 'Without' the British, she said, 'we would already be pensioners or beheaded or imprisoned, for none of our ships would have sailed to Sicily [in 1798] . . . Within a fortnight Sicily would have followed the example of Naples, and everything would have been lost . . . They have saved us personally, preserved Sicily, and will recover Naples. Whatever the motive, the service is real, and we cannot fail to be everlastingly obliged to them.'[65]

IX

DUKE OF BRONTE

An heart susceptible, sincere and true,
An heart by Fate and Nature torn in two –
One half to duty and his country due,
The other better half to Love and you.

Nelson's verses to Emma Hamilton,
Autumn 1800

I

On 6 August three ships, the *Foudroyant*, *Principe Real* and a Neapolitan frigate, left Naples for Palermo, a smooth passage that lasted two days. Nelson's flagship carried the king, with his baggage, hunting dogs and guns. The Sicilian capital was languishing in a disagreeable cocktail of heavy rain, bright sun and a hot sirocco wind when the ships arrived, but stirred to greet the triumphant monarch. The queen and Prince Royal dined on board, and then at Ferdinand's insistence, Nelson and the Hamiltons accompanied them to the landing place to the roar of guns. A 'Te Deum' in the cathedral and a surfeit of celebrations and illuminations followed.[1]

And in Palermo, despite everything anyone could say, the king remained. He visited country houses and bagged game, but bristled at representations about Naples, as if the whole subject was too painful. Suspicious of his own forces, and with enough foreign troops to instil confidence in the security of Naples, he refused to return and a provisional government had to act for him. The queen offered to go to Naples if it would help, but she who could once have excited her husband by merely drawing long, white, tight gloves over her arms, was finding herself increasingly estranged. She still attended council meetings at the Colli, but spent too much time writing to Emma or Gallo of her poor health, endless sadness and prospective retirement and death.

The kingdom of Naples remained hamstrung by sporadic lawlessness, corruption and appalling administrative inefficiency. Nelson, who, as Hamilton said, generally manifested a 'liberal way of thinking', naively hoped that a spirit of benevolent reform might mark Ferdinand's renewal. Troubridge, now flying the broad red pendant of a commodore authorised by Nelson, supported public order in Naples with several ships of the line, but called for public investment and an amnesty for political prisoners. 'If some act of oblivion is not passed,' he wrote, 'there will be no end of persecution, for the people of this country have no idea of anything but revenge.' Hamilton, deeply disturbed by the execution of Cirillo, joined Nelson in urging the king to establish himself in his capital, grant a 'general pardon' to offenders and 'seriously' apply him 'to the formation of a better government'. A veil had to be drawn over the past. Acton and the Prince of Cassaro, who had replaced Ruffo, agreed, but wheels still moved slowly. Even after fifteen hundred Russians reached Naples in November the king would not return, and it was not until May 1800 that an amnesty was proclaimed and the gallows could be removed from the market square.[2]

Neither Nelson, the Hamiltons nor Mrs Cadogan felt well when they were reunited in the Palazzo Palagonia, where the temperature sometimes topped ninety. But in the weeks that followed the ménage was showered with gifts from a grateful court. Nelson's captains were given gold jewelled snuff boxes, watches and rings. Tyson received a diamond ring, and the men of the *Foudroyant* £1150 to share between them. Emma's haul included a gown, earrings, an aigrette, a diamond necklace and portraits of the king and queen set in jewels, and Sir William's a 'thumping' diamond ring. On 13 August the king gave Nelson a sword once owned by Louis XIV of France and presented to Ferdinand by his father, Charles III of Spain, upon his accession to the throne of the Two Sicilies. It was a small weapon with a gold hilt, chased and spirally fluted, and studded thickly with diamonds, but to the king it was 'a symbol' of the 'preservation' of his kingdoms, bequeathed by his father. 'To you, my lord, I consign it, in remembrance of the obligation I then contracted, an obligation you have put it in my power to satisfy.'[3]

Prince Luzzi, the secretary of state for foreign affairs, notified Nelson of the greatest reward. The king made him a Sicilian Duke, thus conferring the grandest of the three peerages that he would receive in life, and one that vividly contrasted with the paltry barony forked out at home. With it came a 35,000-acre estate in the north-western foothills of Mount Etna, newly constituted a feudal tenure and duchy for the purpose. It took its name from the nearby town of Bronte, an impoverished community of nine thousand souls, where pleasing orchards mixed with fossilised streams of volcanic lava, sprouting cacti and foraging black swine. At a stroke Nelson had become a landowner, but knew nothing of his acquisition. It contained a ruined castle, a twelfth-century abbey on the River Saracena, enough woodland to support creatures as large as boar and deer, and water to irrigate crops and power mills. About three-quarters of the land had been given over to arable and pasture farming, which maintained some sixty tenant farmers and several thousand serfs. However, in former times the monks had run the estate down before donating it to the Great Hospital of Palermo in the fifteenth century. Although recovered and transferred to Nelson, it remained deeply burdened with debts, and the only property capable of being turned into a gentleman's residence was a farmhouse named La Fragilia with views of Mount Etna to the south.[4]

The king's gift entitled Nelson to sit in the Sicilian House of Peers, though he never did so, and it gave him the jurisdiction over all civil, criminal and religious affairs within his duchy, including the right to appoint public officers. Ferdinand waived a sum normally payable upon such an investiture, but not his right to demand a quota of men for royal service. Nelson was, however, eligible to receive an annual tariff previously paid to the Great Hospital, and rents from the estate estimated to be worth about £3000 a year. The admiral was certainly flattered, and busied himself with the repercussions for his family and posterity. He planned to assign his father £500 as an annual pension, and to preserve the gift in the event of his death, originally settled the succession of the estate upon his father, brothers and the male heirs of his brothers or sisters. In 1800 he obtained the right to name any successor to the dukedom, whether related or not. More immediately, Nelson wrote to the English College of Arms to discover how to incorporate his fresh acquisitions into his existing arms, signature and attire, and enjoyed experimenting with his signature. Should he be 'Bronte Nelson' or 'Bronte Nelson of the Nile'?[5]

The new Duke of Bronte was a strong believer in that much admired if indifferently encountered commodity known as English paternalism. He accepted inequalities in society as natural and God-given, but genuinely supposed that a first duty of those above, and especially government, was the protection of those below who provided loyalty and service. Typically, some of his first thoughts about Bronte – thoughts that illustrate his inherent kindness of heart – ran in this direction. 'I am determined . . . that the inhabitants [of Bronte] shall be the happiest in all His Sicilian Majesty's dominions,' he wrote to Davison, and to kick-start his regime he declared that he would forgo rents for two years to enable the people to improve their holdings. The estate, he proudly told Fanny, would become 'Bronte the Happy'.[6]

But of course nothing was that simple. Unable to go to Bronte himself, Nelson employed his friend John Graefer, the landscape gardener, to oversee the estate. Graefer had considerable experience under his belt, having created the fifty-acre English garden at Caserta and managed a workforce of several hundred, and left for Bronte with his wife, Eliza, in the autumn. The last leg of their journey took them over a ragged road from Adrano by mule and jolting litter, but when the Graefers arrived at their destination they were enthusiastically greeted by a troop of horse, volunteers with drawn swords and trumpets, the estate militia standing stiffly to attention and 12,000 vassals. Notwithstanding the 'universal joy' Graefer was somewhat dismayed by the scale of his task.

Reconnoitring the property, he allocated eight hundred acres as Nelson's personal holding (the *boschetto*), and began rehabilitating La Fragilia as its country house, but hopes that it could be turned into a model farm that would inspire the neighbouring tenants to reach a blissful state was beset with difficulties. Almost everything was wanting: tools, equipment, wagons, seeds, knowledge and skilled workers. The estate had no roads and few amenable paths, and its impoverished inhabitants scratched a subsistence livelihood from gleaning and cultivation, but suffered from excessive royal taxation. As in Ireland, tenants divided their farms between their children, condemning each new generation to survive on less ground than the last. So sure was Graefer that the peasants could not both pay their taxes and survive throughout the winter without selling possessions and cutting food supplies to the bone, that he begged Nelson to ask the government to postpone gathering its due until after the harvest. Lastly, the new estate manager discovered that the means of collecting rents were haphazard and that the duchy was sinking under debt. Graefer could only clear the existing debts and raise funds for improvement by taking new loans from the Archbishop of Bronte and Chevalier Antonio Forcella, a lawyer.[7]

Graeffer also encountered social protest. The majority of Nelson's subjects welcomed the admiral as a 'saviour', but there were very different views about what needed to be done. Some expected him to parcel out the land in equal lots and supply subsidies and livestock. Nelson's own plan was very eighteenth-century English. He wanted the land leased to likely farmers, stipulating that they must be *Brontesi* rather than 'strangers', who could improve the land and provide employment to the landless labourers. By December Graefer had leased every farm bar one, but some disappointed aspirants threatened violence. A priest came forward with frightening details of a plot to murder those who collaborated with Graefer, and to begin their bloody work at the pealing of the bells on Sunday, 8 December. The malcontents were swiftly arrested, but as Nelson declined to taint his rule with executions, they were expelled from the duchy. On the whole, the admiral remained in high esteem in Bronte. One of the better-off tenants, a brother of a Sicilian baron, returned from a visit to the new duke 'quite entranced'. Several hundred signed a card wishing him a happy new year.

For Nelson, Bronte would always be an unfulfilled dream. For years it conjured an image of an idyllic retreat, in which he and Emma could escape from the world, but he was destined never to see a paradise that he had heard was beautiful. He was spared total disillusionment. However, amidst the early enthusiasm for his new duchy Nelson also enjoyed other smaller but tangible awards. Deal boxes had begun to arrive from England containing consignments of seven thousand medals that Davison had minted in Birmingham to reward the British crews at the battle of the Nile. Nelson received two of the gold medals given to captains and flag officers, and surrendered one to Hardy, who had accidentally been omitted from the distribution, and the other to Hamilton. He was pleased to learn that Davison had shown the medals to George III and received royal approval.[8]

That year rewards and awards flowed fast. In October the island of Zante, attributing the liberation of the Ionian Islands to British sea power, sent Nelson a gold-hilted sword and a gold-topped cane adorned with twenty-three diamonds. Ali Pasha of Albania added a sword, gun and silver pitcher. From the Sultan of Turkey, whose 'daily . . . veneration' of Nelson had already produced important gifts, came a drawing of the battle of the Nile and the admiral's second order of knighthood. Selim had previously sent the chelengk, of course, but that was a purely military decoration. Nelson now became the first knight of a new civilian order named the Order of the Crescent. The magnificent diamond star reached him in November, its heart a brilliant blue enamel that contained a star and crescent. Nelson, who saw himself as a sword of God, approved of this 'flattering' symbol of the 'approbation from all religions', and started styling himself 'First Knight of the Imperial Order of the Crescent' at the head of his orders. He brandished such honours because they testified to courage, exertion and duty rather than birth, money or patronage, and advertised him as self-made in a world of wealthier men.[9]

Nelson dwelt longingly on every appreciative remark. A copy of a tribute Minto had paid him in the British parliament was kept close by, and he and Emma often read it together. 'Oh, how he loves you!' Emma wrote to its author. And here in the Two Sicilies, more than any other place, his worth was taken at his own estimate. In port his ship was often surrounded by small boats, shouts of acclamation greeted his public appearances, and sooner or later someone would strike up 'See, the Conquering Hero Comes'. The public enthusiasm exceeded anything Nelson had yet seen in England. Although the demonstrations nauseated some, George Parsons, the young midshipman of the *Foudroyant*, remembered the 'refined Italian flattery, incessant balls and feedings, the smiles of beauty and the witchery of music' that marked the period. Private gatherings were equally sumptuous. On Emma's birthday in April 1799 the admiral brought his ship into the mole, and threw a ball to all who had been with her ladyship at the queen's drawing room that morning. Nelson's fortieth birthday the following 29 September also prompted an elaborate celebration, hosted by the Hamiltons, who employed four mounted troopers and a couple of infantrymen to control the numerous carriages.[10]

Earlier, on 3 September, a royal fete at Colli, celebrating the day Naples first heard of the battle of the Nile, graphically illustrated the surreal nature of these events. Nine-year-old Prince Leopold, whose idolisation of Nelson was returned by sincere fatherly affection, hosted in his midshipman's uniform, though their Majesties received the company. The three princesses and the consort of the Prince Royal decorated the occasion, dressed in white with garlands of laurel over their shoulders and around their heads. Around their necks were ornaments honouring Nelson's victory. The fireworks in one of the gardens represented the same engagement, and concluded with a dramatic representation of the destruction of *L'Orient* as well as a burning of the tricolour. Nelson and Emma, who wore laurel wreaths for much of the evening, watched from a balcony with the queen and the newly arrived Turkish and Russian admirals, Cadir Bey and Ushakov, whose captains also attended. Nelson wore the diamond-encrusted sword given him by Ferdinand, and Emma a medal and a portrait of the queen. 'On this day last year,' the queen observed to Cadir Bey, 'we received from dear Lady Hamilton intelligence of this great man's victory, which not only saved your country and ours, but all Europe.' Ever gracious, the Turkish admiral beamed. After a eulogistic cantata, ices and sweetmeats, the queen led the way into a brilliantly illuminated garden, where pavilions had been swathed in honour of each of her allies, Portugal, Britain, Russia and Turkey. The imperial ambassador, who was present, dolefully noticed the absence of Austria. 'No one but my master is forgotten here,' he complained. But opposite the entrance a magnificently lit Greek temple proclaimed the supreme hero. In the vestibule, propped up by columns and accessed by steps, were life-sized wax effigies of Nelson and the Hamiltons. Like a religious idol, the mock 'Nelson' occupied the centre of the display in his uniform, while Emma's effigy was garbed in a white dress and a blue shawl embroidered with the names of every one of the Nile captains. Inside the temple an altar depicted 'the figure of glory characteristically habited' with a representation of Ferdinand in a triumphal car. None of this slush abashed the British admiral. The four princesses stood as priestesses, while Leopold ascended with a crown of laurel and placed it on the head of the Nelson effigy as the band struck up 'Rule, Britannia'. The queen admitted her son's tribute to be an inadequate one, but the admiral was deeply moved, and in the silence that followed advanced to the child and knelt and kissed his hand. The boy threw his arms around the admiral's neck in a loving embrace. Afterwards the queen showed her guests around the gardens, drawing attention to inscriptions commemorating the Hamiltons, Niza, Troubridge, Hallowell, Foote and other heroes. Gordon the tourist watched uncomfortably, and noted that after the royals had withdrawn Nelson and his 'satellites' continued to parade for hours, followed by an admiring entourage. 'How lamentable to see the greatest sea captain submit to and glory in being made such a puppet,' he remarked. Roger de Damas agreed. 'Nelson came out of the temple more vainglorious . . . than he entered it,' he remarked, shaking his head that such 'natural watchfulness and activity' could be reduced to lethargy. As he remembered it, some officers of the fleet declined to attend. Nelson, however, was entirely happy. He sent Cornelia Knight's account of the event to his brother Maurice, who duly inserted it into the *Sun* and the *New Briton*.[11]

Back home there was indeed a sustained demand for Nelsoniana. James

Gillray supplied ugly caricatures for the print shops, one depicting the hero bashing crocodiles into defeat with a club of British oak, and another standing pompously garbed in his scarlet, fur-lined pelisse and oversized chelengk. Josiah Wedgwood did a busy trade in basalt busts and profiles on jugs, vases and urns. In Italy, however, artists had the real man to capture. A Cumbrian artist, Guy Head, got a single sitting for a portrait that may have been commissioned by Nelson himself, and in Palermo someone produced several states of an unflattering stiff-necked profile that Nelson and Emma nevertheless circulated to friends.

Two of the new portraits got closer, however. One was a full-length by a Palermo artist named Leonardo Guzzardi. In many respects, the Nelson it showed is not one his admirers would like. There is the bombast expected in a formal commemorative portrait, with the battle of the Nile raging in the background and the hero in the full-dress uniform of a rear admiral standing with the trophies of war around him. On his rakishly poised hat gleams the dazzling chelengk, while draped over an adjacent chair lies the accompanying pelisse. The Cape St Vincent medal and the Bath star and ribbon are clearly visible, and updated versions added the official Nile medal, Davison's medal and the star of the Order of the Crescent. But this martial drumbeating contrasts with the insipid figure of Nelson himself, who looks the very antithesis of an energetic hero. The face is tired, flushed and ravaged by war, with a formidable red scar over the right eye and half an eyebrow missing. The fragile frame stands almost languidly, as if barely able to raise the surviving arm. This is the Nelson some certainly saw, vain but vulnerable, pompous but pitiable, sick and weak.

By far the finest Italian portrait of Nelson, and perhaps the best likeness ever made, was an unfinished pencil sketch by Charles Grignion. Grignion, who had already made a strikingly lifelike portrait of Sir William in 1794, had arrived in Naples with two Altieri Claude masterpieces that Nelson helped him to send to England. On 7 February 1799 the admiral sat for his portrait in Palermo. A sharp contrast to the posed formality of most of the other portraits, Grignion's sketch shows a relaxed admiral, his arm propped over the back of a chair in which he palpably lounges, as if off duty in his cabin or house. The informality is enhanced by the relative lack of ornamentation. Nelson's uniform is undress, and there are no bragging medals. The Bath ribbon and star are there, but the former is obscured by Nelson's empty sleeve and the latter hides behind his left hand. Nevertheless, the figure as a whole is strong and confident, a believable man of business, and the failure to turn this portrait into oils is one of the greatest losses to Nelson portraiture.[12]

Somehow the two portraits, the one good and the other bad, reflect the two sides of Nelson's Italian journey.

2

On 19 August Nelson learned that Keith had left the Mediterranean in pursuit of Bruix and that he was de facto commander-in-chief, a position acknowledged in an Admiralty letter written the following day. He already had a collection of letters from Keith, including instructions of 16 July and most recently two communications of the 24th, in which the departing admiral ordered Nelson to entrust Neapolitan affairs to the Russians and Portuguese and to deploy his own ships between Minorca and Gibraltar. His attention was also directed to Cadiz, where a few unseaworthy Spanish ships of the line were moored, and to the Gulf of Genoa, where the allied armies were mopping up the remaining French resistance. These were the last of a series of letters in which Keith had attempted to reposition Nelson's ships further west, especially at Minorca, all of which had been resisted to a greater or lesser extent.[13]

The two admirals did not think highly of each other. Influenced by reports that Nelson was dawdling in Palermo, infatuated with Lady Hamilton, Keith saw Nelson as an unsafe commander-in-chief, nailed to the Kingdom of the Two Sicilies to the neglect of wider obligations. On his part Nelson condemned Keith for throwing away the one good opportunity to bring Bruix to battle, and thought him obsessed with Minorca and under-appreciative of the critical state of southern Italy.

The Franco-Spanish fleet had gone, leaving the Mediterranean to the British. Naples had also been reclaimed. On these grounds the Admiralty agreed with Keith that Nelson needed to shift the focus of his operations westward. Only by placing strong forces between Cadiz and Minorca could Nelson maintain adequate communications with England; protect the flow of commerce to, through and from the Mediterranean; keep a close eye on the nine enemy ships of the line scattered in the naval bases of Cadiz, Cartagena and Toulon; and remain within striking distance of the Riviera coast, where the Austrians were still embattled. If Bruix or any other French admiral made another sortie inside the Strait, Nelson needed to intercept or monitor him early in order to minimise potential damage. All of these needs were best met by a force in the western Mediterranean.[14]

Despite his earlier complacency about Minorca, Nelson gradually accepted the more comprehensive picture of his responsibilities. In some compliance with Keith's orders, he directed Duckworth to blockade Cadiz and secure the safety of the Strait with six ships of the line, suggesting he base himself at Gibraltar, and fall back to protect Minorca if threatened by a superior fleet from Brest. 'No one, my dear admiral [Duckworth], be assured, estimates your worth as an officer and a friend more than *we* of this house,' Nelson encouraged on 20 August. Later he also assigned *Goliath* and *Swiftsure* to the area between Cadiz and Minorca. The remaining distribution of his capital ships – one in the Gulf of Genoa, three with Troubridge at Naples, two off Malta with the four Portuguese consorts, and his own ship, the *Foudroyant*, then returning the King of Sardinia to his court on the mainland – was not entirely injudicious. But he differed from some of his superiors in the weight he gave to the needs of Naples and Malta, which absorbed nine or ten British and Portuguese capital ships.[15]

For most of that time he was ashore, though that in itself did not prevent him from managing affairs in the Mediterranean. Indeed, St Vincent would shortly be controlling the Channel fleet from Tor Abbey. Nor did Nelson tie his flagship to Palermo. Under Hardy the *Vanguard* and *Foudroyant* were constantly in motion, carrying out missions to Tripoli and Sardinia or supporting the blockade of Malta. Nelson's practice was to fly his flag from any convenient vessel, including transports such as the *Samuel and Jane* and the *Alty*, and even from a balcony of the Palazzo Palagonia. But in hindsight it is still difficult to excuse Nelson's limpet-like attachment to Sicily from the summer of 1799, when a base at Minorca would have increased his flexibility, and still enabled him to leave three or four capital ships at Malta, Palermo and Naples, in addition to the Portuguese contingent. Keith's notion that Lady Hamilton had something to do with it cannot be dismissed. Nelson had now become heavily dependent upon Emma's feminine company, and indeed upon Sir William's grasp of Mediterranean affairs. In fact, though the Hamiltons had leave to go home, and the Bourbon restoration might have signalled an appropriate moment to do so, it was Nelson who pleaded with them not to desert him. The king would be upset if he left, said the admiral; moreover, how could he himself continue, knowing no Italian, if deprived of his right arm? As rheumatic Sir William did not fancy going home to an English winter, he decided to remain until the spring.[16]

One reason why Nelson maintained a substantial presence off southern Italy was his lack of confidence in his Russian and Turkish allies. Two Russian ships arrived in the Gulf of Genoa, enabling Nelson to reassign Martin's *Northumberland*, commanding off that coast, to Duckworth's squadron. Unfortunately, the Russians proved to be poor substitutes, for half of their crews were sick and the ships uncoppered, sluggish and unfit for anything but summer cruising. Ten more Russo-Turkish ships of the line arrived at Messina in August. Nelson formed a quick attachment to the Turkish admiral, Cadir Bey, whose eighty-gun flagship ('*Il Leone Marinho*') always appeared in clean and good order. 'A man of more conciliating manners does not exist,' said Nelson, 'and he has gained all our hearts in this house, in which he is considered as a brother.' Unfortunately, while the Turks were 'good people' they struck Nelson as inexperienced and undisciplined. In any case relations between the Moslem Turks and Catholic Sicilians were far from amicable, and early in September a dreadful fracas developed between the parties in Palermo. More than a hundred Turks as well as fifteen Sicilians were killed, wounded or scattered. Enraged, the Turkish sailors threatened the town with the guns of their four ships and might have fired had not Cadir Bey intervened. Even so, the Turks were so angry that they mutinied and insisted their admiral take them back to Corfu.[17]

But if the Turks were undisciplined, the Russian ships were transparently in a poor physical state and their admiral, Ushakov, difficult. Unlike Cadir Bey, he did not fraternise with the British, and when the two admirals exchanged visits to their respective flagships in Palermo on 2 and 3 September they did not see eye to eye. The Russian admiral found Nelson dismissive; the Briton saw narrow thinking and an eminently dislikeable disposition. Ushakov upset Nelson by striking a Turkish captain with his cane, and refusing to release the British *Leander* (the Nile ship captured by the French but retaken by the Russians at Corfu), even though it had been promised by the tsar. Within days of their meetings Nelson rated the Russian force 'a dead weight'.[18]

The Portuguese squadron had grown in experience and stature, but these new arrivals did not look up to strenuous duties, and Nelson decided that a leavening of British ships was still necessary. But there were more fundamental reasons for Nelson's refusal to release all of his ships from their duties in southern Italy, as Keith had ordered. The blockade of Malta depended upon the flow of supplies from Sicily, and a strong presence to ensure that it was not disrupted. And Naples was still struggling to secure her northern border. The Roman Republic was still in the hands of the French and 'dangerous mobs' of Jacobin supporters. True, Russo-Austrian forces were clearing northern Italy, but in such dangerous times even that was not without its implications. In particular, Ferdinand and Maria Carolina distrusted Austria. The imperial chancellor, Thugut, was already alienating his Russian allies with a 'grand policy . . . to spare his army', leaving Suvorov to do the lion's share of the fighting. In addition, it was widely recognised that Austria coveted some of the Italian territories, including the papal ones, to make good disappointments in central Europe. One prevalent view in diplomatic circles was that Austria wanted to strip Sardinia of Piedmont, compensating the king with a dissolved Roman Republic. True or not, in the Two Sicilies Ferdinand thought the pope a better neighbour than Austria, and saw only one way to pre-empt the imperial land grab. He would liberate the Roman Republic first, and, in an uncanny replay of the previous autumn, his troops marched across the border on 18 July. He needed Nelson's help.[19]

On the quarterdeck of the *Foudroyant* the king had formally pleaded with Nelson not to desert him. Face to face it was almost impossible for Nelson to refuse, and Acton pressed the suit in writing the day after the army crossed the frontier. The king, said Acton, was doing his utmost to secure his northern borders, but no hope of success could be entertained 'if your lordship does not protect His Majesty's operations'. Moreover, with 'secret enemies' skulking 'in every department', Naples itself could not be left 'to its own force' and needed dependable foreign assistance. In short, the kingdom was not ready to stand alone on its shaky legs, and needed Nelson. There is some evidence of the British admiral's unease. Tired of 'fetes and rejoicings' he laid some proposals before the king, who came back with his reservations. He asked Nelson not to entrust the blockade of Malta to the Portuguese, emphasised his difficulties in maintaining order in Naples and conducting the Roman campaign, and said one more thing. 'My formal demand,' said Acton, 'is, however, to beg of your lordship to protect the Two Sicilies with your *name and presence* till at least all Italy is perfectly secured . . . and the quiet and order are entirely recovered in the kingdom of Naples.'[20]

The truth was that the revolution had badly frightened the royal family, as well it might, since it threatened their lives as well as their kingdoms. Hamilton, who knew it, wrote, 'Their Majesties are not easy if His Lordship is absent from them one moment.' These fears, as well as the admiral's importance to ongoing operations, continued to tie Nelson to Sicily. The royal importunings suggest that Nelson had broached the idea of transferring his base to Minorca before resigning himself to remaining in Palermo. Critics saw him as a limpet, enslaved by his obsession with Lady Hamilton, and that portrait was gaining credibility, but at this time it may still have been an injustice.[21]

So they remained in the Palazzo Palagonia. Nelson was neither the first nor the last commander-in-chief to base himself ashore, but it sat badly with the man who had been considered the most energetic flag officer in the fleet.

3

The Roman expedition rolled forward quickly. In August Nelson sent Hallowell of the *Swiftsure* to Civita Vecchia, the port of Rome, to prepare the ground. Apart from blockading the place, Hallowell corresponded with the French commandant, and ascertained that the garrisons of both cities would surrender to a regular force. Nelson tried to borrow a couple of regiments of redcoats from Major General James St Clair Erskine in Minorca, but the general declined to weaken his garrison for what he regarded as a dubious cause. He had a point. Though Bourcard was marching towards Rome with 9000 men, 7000 of them were mere 'vagabonds' if Troubridge was to be believed, and there were doubts about whether the people would welcome Neapolitans a second time. As it plodded on in bad weather, Ferdinand's army suffered defections. Some men had to be shot to encourage the others.[22]

Ferdinand was preparing an additional force of eight hundred Swiss regulars under Tschudy, and Nelson had authorised Troubridge to carry them to Civita Vecchia to demand the surrender of the remaining French garrisons in the Roman Republic. Their departure was delayed because the marines attached to the British ships were still maintaining order in the capital by regular twenty-four-hour patrols. Naples was so quiet that Troubridge 'walked all the town over' one night without encountering the slightest danger or untoward noise. Ushakov proved to be the solution. Supported by Nelson and Acton, Ferdinand pressed the Russian to transfer his ships from Messina to Naples to relieve Troubridge's force. On 5 September Ushakov finally agreed. As the king was suspicious of Austrian and Russian attempts to liberate Rome, he was less than candid about Troubridge's intentions. Nelson's instructions to Troubridge were marked 'most secret' and the Russian admiral knew so little about the Roman campaign that when he arrived at Naples on 18 September he began conferring with Ruffo about mounting a joint campaign under his own leadership.[23]

With an Austrian army of 10,000 men under Lieutenant General Franz Frehlich on its way to Rome, there was no time to lose. Troubridge sent Louis ahead with the *Minotaur*, two small cruisers and a bomb vessel, and they arrived off Civita Vecchia on 16 September to send in a summons and mount a blockade. Leaving Tschudy's troops to follow, Troubridge hurried to support in the *Culloden* and threw some shells into the defences on the 21st. The next day he offered the terms that had been accepted at Gaeta. The French could keep their small arms and colours, and obtain a passage home without the inconveniences attached to formal prisoners of war providing they surrendered the forts, artillery and public property. A few days of envoys shuttling back and forth followed. *Général de division* Pierre Dominique Garnier, commanding at Rome, had just thrown back the advancing Neapolitan army at Monte Redondo, but he knew that if the Austrians or Russians arrived he would be lucky to get anything like the terms offered by Troubridge, and on the 26th accepted them on behalf of all the French troops still occupying the former Roman Republic. Troubridge put 108 marines and seamen into Civita Vecchia three days later, and sent parties to take possession of Tolfa, Corneto and Rome on the 30th. Louis was rowed up the Tiber in his barge at the head of a token force to receive the surrender of the castle of St Angelo at the fabled heart of an ancient empire, just as Bourcard's regrouped Neapolitan troops began to arrive. 'Thus,' marvelled Hoste, whose *Mutine* had been with Louis, 'was the whole Roman state, with its capital, once mistress of the world, taken by about three hundred Englishmen!' According to Nelson, the event had been foretold by a seemingly preposterous prophecy made just a year before in the Palazzo Sessa. A visiting Irish Franciscan, Father Michael McCormick, had told him that he would 'take Rome with your ships!' And so it had come to pass.[24]

Troubridge was soon driven to distraction finding transports and provisions for six thousand prisoners, and ensuring that they were not making off with any plunder. As in the Bay of Naples, he dug into his own purse to meet expenses. Protecting the hated invaders from the angry crowds that gathered to insult them was another difficulty. Hoste and three fellow officers once had to march the French general arm-in-arm through a hostile mob. To add to the chaos, Frehlich's Austrians now appeared on the scene, furious about being beaten to Rome, and angrily disputing Troubridge's authority to make the conquest. When Garnier's troops were marched from St Angelo to the transports at Civita Vecchia on 30 September they were attacked by Austrian soldiers and suffered eleven casualties. For an ugly moment it looked as if Troubridge's redcoats would have to confront Frehlich's soldiery in defence of their prisoners. The storm rumbled afield. Not only was Frehlich 'in a great passion for not being master of Rome' but at Naples Ushakov was 'highly enraged' at the furtive and independent actions of the British. 'Nevertheless,' said Acton, 'we rejoice much at this event.' The aggrieved retired muttering. When an outraged Thugut condemned the generous terms offered the French, Minto (who had succeeded Eden as Britain's Envoy Extraordinary and Minister Plenipotentiary in Vienna) flatly defended Troubridge and threw back Frehlich's attempt to interfere with the evacuation of the prisoners. Thugut returned to the defensive, his common position, protesting that the general would not have attempted to carry out his threat. Whatever the ructions, Nelson had opened the path to a papal restoration. Troubridge raised colours bearing the papal cross keys without the tiara, and Ferdinand sent Naselli to Rome as an interim governor who would in effect act as a regent until a newly elected pope, Pius VII, willing to resist Austria's impositions, could reclaim his historic prerogative.[25]

The Roman campaign purged the leg of Italy of French troops, except for a single garrison at Ancona on the east coast, and completed Troubridge's principal work. For Nelson there was the satisfaction of completing the task of 1798, especially one that so pointedly stood up for faith. One Robert Sagar created a rostral column commemorating Britain's part in the liberation, and proposed to erect it in the Piazza di Spagna in Rome. It chose to emphasise the preservation of Italian art treasures, but the British were not entirely disinterested parties in that respect. Troubridge reckoned that under British law the squadron would have been entitled to some three million pounds of prize, most of it 'salvage' for treasures rescued from the French. In the end he settled for £60,000, but even that was hard to find. An enfeebled Rome protested its inability to contribute anything to the pot, and Ferdinand had to stump up the money by selling some of his foreign property. Troubridge, hugely embittered by his personal expenses, got an additional £500 as indemnification.[26]

The Roman campaign was the most important of several services Nelson performed in Italy that autumn. He lent a hand whenever he could. Further north, Suvorov, worrying about the supplies his army had to bring by sea, appealed to him for protection. In August Nelson therefore loosed Martin's *Northumberland* in the Gulf of Genoa, and seven or eight prizes were taken within a month. Martin kept the seas until relieved by two Russian ships of the line, although the latter, their ships unseaworthy and their men sick, soon disappointed. On a very different errand, in September the *Foudroyant* and *Mutine* assisted the court of Sardinia, carrying the king from Cagliari to Leghorn to enable his court to be re-established on the mainland, and the king's brother in the opposite direction, landing him in Sardinia to rule as regent.[27]

The other outstanding item that benefited from Nelson basing himself in Sicily was Malta, where Ball, back from Naples, resumed his struggle to isolate the French by land and sea. As the blockade entered its second season of autumnal and winter storms, Ball had some new problems to add to the old. The summer disruption had damaged relations between the Maltese factions, and from exile the old Grand Master of the Knights of St John had deployed *agents provocateurs* to strike down the new plan to restore the island to the knights under the aegis of the Russian tsar. But Ball's cruellest enemy remained famine. On Sicily the harvest of 1799 was so poor that the king thoughtlessly prohibited the export of corn, and Malta had to import food from the mainland, often at tip-top prices. No one brought more weight to Malta's cause than Nelson. Between July and December five separate appeals produced shipments of corn and £10,000 in cash, some of it painfully extricated from the king's personal coffers. Yet Ferdinand's resources were not infinite, and by November Acton was advising his monarch against depositing more money into the bottomless pit that Malta had become. Ferdinand had then expended £27,000 on food, war materiel, clothing and wages for those under arms; 372,104 bushels of wheat and barley were shipped from Sicily in the eleven months since 1 October 1798. Still the crisis deepened. Early in December Nelson had urgent discussions with Hamilton, Acton and the Chevalier Italinsky, a newly arrived Russian minister who was also an acquaintance of Sir William, about how the burden of supporting the island might be shared. It was doubtless through Hamilton and Nelson, as well as the Neapolitan minister in London, that British support was increased, and Hamilton was able to use Treasury bills to provide needed cash. Certainly Ball claimed that if it had not been for Nelson and Hamilton 'thousands of Maltese would have perished'.[28]

But if Malta undoubtedly benefited from the admiral's close oversight and advocacy, clinging to it to keep ships at sea and supplies moving, the other enduring business of Egypt had slipped from his grasp, with Smith doing much as he wanted for good or ill. Nelson was alternately elated and depressed by the mercurial 'commodore'. The astonishing victory at Acre, when Sir Sidney's *Tigre* and Miller's *Theseus* helped a few thousand poorly equipped Turks defeat Bonaparte's army in a sixty-day siege and halted its tide of conquest in the Middle East, was an heroic enterprise by any lights. It was saddened by the loss of eighty men in an explosion that rocked the quarterdeck of the *Theseus* on 14 May, one being Nelson's old flag captain Ralph Miller, a Nile brother, whose chest was ripped open by a splinter, but Nelson instantly embraced the wayward Smith with a letter that virtually welcomed him as a substitute. 'Be assured, my dear Sir Sidney, of my perfect esteem and regard, and do not let anyone persuade you to the contrary,' he wrote, 'but my character is that I will not suffer the smallest tittle of my command to be taken from me, but with pleasure I give way to my friends, amongst whom I beg you will allow me to consider you.' He allowed Smith to fill the vacancies in his detachment, including Miller's acting successor, thus endowing him with the means of rewarding his followers. Some he also promoted directly himself.[29]

Smith was almost impossible to encourage, however. For every step forward there was a step back, and Nelson continued to oppose Sir Sidney's attempts to allow the French to evacuate Egypt peacefully. Some boats of invalids from Bonaparte's army had been intercepted, trying to steal home. One, containing a general, 104 men and dispatches, got almost as far as Toulon before being captured by the *Vincejo* on 4 December. The intelligence from such coups all indicated the abysmal shape the Army of Egypt was in. As Nelson pointed out, only British mishandling of the situation could save it.[30]

While Nelson continued to perform important services, a question about his efficiency as a theatre commander remained. He did not think so. Stung by the Admiralty's criticism of his disobedience and involvement in the terrestrial campaigns in Italy, he stood unbowed. Fame and success had increased Nelson's confidence and probably his spirit of independence, and he vigorously defended his conduct. On 21 September, for example, he shot a bolt straight into Keith. 'Common sense told me that Minorca could be in no danger by my breach of orders,' he wrote to Spencer, and 'I only wish that I had been placed in Lord Keith's situation, off Cape dell Mell [in June]. I would have broke the orders [from St Vincent] like a piece of glass. In that case the whole marine of the French would have been annihilated, and all the fagging anxiety attending the watching of Brest would have been at an end.' As for Capua and Gaeta, had he obeyed Keith's orders, those 'two keys of the kingdom' would have still been in the hands of the French. Brashly he asserted, 'I do not believe any sea officers know the sea and land business of the Mediterranean better than myself.' This was straight talking. Keith had got his priorities wrong, and his slavish regard for orders, however inapplicable, had cost an opportunity to destroy the French fleet. 'I restored a faithful ally by breach of orders,' he grumbled to Davison. 'Lord Keith lost a fleet by obedience, against his own sense. Yet as one is censured, the other must be approved.'[31]

This was a robust defence. It could be argued that Minorca, despite its vulnerable British garrison, was not as important as Italy in the new coalition warfare, and that some amphibious warfare was indispensable to its security. The key issue, though, was neither Minorca nor Italy, but the supremacy of the British fleet upon which everything hinged, and the Admiralty was surely right to be concerned about the effectiveness of vital ships at a time when the naval control of the Mediterranean was still in the balance.

After Keith left, Nelson had transferred some strength westwards in acknowledgement of the wider responsibilities that had fallen upon him, but his continuing residence in Palermo understandably raised eyebrows. The successful completion of the Roman campaign at the end of September could have allowed Nelson to redefine and refocus his command, shifting its strategic centre westwards, where the biggest threats to his command of the theatre were likely to materialise, and playing the more energetic role for which he had been famous.

Two sudden scares in October put his options in starker relief.

4

First there was a serious double-headed threat to the blockade of Malta. Back in February Lisbon had recalled their Portuguese detachment from the Mediterranean. Niza's squadron had visibly grown in stature under Nelson's direction, and their presence off Malta had given the blockade its bite. The blow threatened to fall just as intelligence reached Nelson that France was launching a major attempt – her first – to relieve Valletta, and fitting out a convoy of provisions in Toulon using five polacres and two Venetian ships of the line. One thread of this intelligence came through Nice, Turin and Florence to British ministers in Sardinia and Tuscany. Nelson kept a cruiser looking out for the convoy between Toulon and the Riviera, but studying his charts he fixed upon the areas from Toulon to Ajaccio in Corsica and between Tunis and Malta as the best places to intercept such reinforcements. The Portuguese were now even more essential. Their marines were ashore, manning Maltese batteries, and their ships standing offshore, closing the sea lanes to enemy vessels. On 3 October Nelson took the unusual step of asking Niza to postpone his departure for Lisbon. Week by week he cajoled the Portuguese commander to remain, protecting the precious blockade. 'Again, and ten times again,' he wrote, 'I direct you, I entreat you, not to abandon Malta.' The words did not fall on stony ground, for, relatively young as he was, Niza was worthy gold dust. He was still at his post on 10 December. Ball remarked that 'his zeal and persevering conduct will reflect great honour on him. There are very few foreign officers who would not have availed themselves of the orders he had to have withdrawn from a tedious and difficult blockade at such a season of the year.'[32]

But the blockade had never looked frailer. It had already been deeply troubling to Ball and Nelson, who saw its drudgery and pain intensifying as it approached another bracing winter. Looking for a way out, the two officers were again being tantalised by chimerical visions of quick solutions, against their better judgement. Inside the French lines, it was said, cats, dogs, horses and mules were being ravenously consumed, and that, although Vaubois had a year's supply of corn, his other provisions were running out. Despite this black situation, the French commander contemptuously disregarded all summonses to surrender, and pinned his hopes on relief from France. Just how could this stubborn general be moved? French deserters encouraged Ball to believe that Vaubois might surrender to a more imposing military force. It made some sense, because Vaubois would have had difficulty justifying himself at home if he yielded his command to a transparently diminutive opposition. Apart from 500 marines, Ball had only 1500 Maltese under arms, of whom perhaps a mere 600 were fit for service, and they were already occupying more ground than they could have defended against a determined counterattack. Ball decided that if he could strengthen the investing force, bolstering it with regular troops to make it more credible, he could get a capitulation. He asked Colonel Graham, commanding the British garrison at Messina, whether any of his troops might be transferred to Malta, making play with the greater security of Sicily now that the threat from the mainland had been lifted. And Graham, anxious to turn his acting rank as brigadier general into a permanent one, was interested. He said that if the enemy fort, Ricasoli, on the eastern point of the Grand Harbour of Valletta, was taken it might be possible to dominate the entrance to the port and shut it down. But he would need permission from Erskine, his superior at Minorca.[33]

Ball convinced Nelson that the plan was plausible. Indeed, almost anything was worth trying if it could terminate such a torturous contest. Consequently, his lordship began devoting much time trying to collect a polyglot force capable of doing the job. He asked Acton to pump Ushakov, who was still at Naples, for seven hundred Russian soldiers, and backed Ball's bid for the British regulars, securing with 'great difficulty' Ferdinand's consent to a transfer of strength from Messina to Malta. The British high command proved the impossible rock, however, even though Erskine had been reinforced as recently as August. Asking the major general for twelve hundred men with entrenching tools and ammunition, Nelson appealed to his dormant sense of military glory. 'Pardon what I am going to repeat,' he wheedled, 'that either in Malta or on the continent [Italian mainland] a field of glory is open.' He was not surprised by the result. 'Sir James enters upon the difficulty of the undertaking in a true soldier way,' he sighed. Both men were conditioned by their previous meetings in Corsica, when Erskine had allowed himself to be overawed by the French opposition, and Nelson had tigerishly but unsuccessfully urged him forward with little knowledge of the strength of the enemy positions. Distrusting Nelson's military judgement, Erskine now decided that 'no officer would have been justified . . . in forming a project for besieging 5000 men [in Valletta] . . . with a corps of 500 men only', as if that was what Nelson had actually proposed. He escaped from the prospect by pointing out that he was in any event due to be superseded by Lieutenant General the Hon. Henry Fox, who alone would control Britain's Mediterranean army. For the time being, therefore, the naval blockade would have to continue.[34]

While the threat of the French relief force in Toulon remained in the air, an even more forbidding spectre suddenly returned, the haunting presence of another Bruix! The *Phaeton* frigate brought Nelson a report that thirteen enemy sail of the line had been seen off Cape Ortegal on the north coast of Spain, raising the disquieting possibility that it might be coming into the Mediterranean. Even if the hostile ships did not pass the Strait, placed as they were they could sever communications between England and the Mediterranean, and wreak havoc among convoys trafficking back and forth. Hundreds of merchantmen and transports were at risk. Here was a pretty kettle of fish. Nelson now had two enemy forces to worry about, one in Toulon threatening to relieve Malta, and the other even more formidable bearing down outside the Strait. Although Niza stood in the goalmouth before Malta, Nelson acted decisively. He would personally meet the threat from beyond the Strait with ten or more sail, putting Minorca into 'a proper naval defence' into the bargain. In short, he would shift strength westwards, towards Toulon and the Strait, as the situation clearly demanded. Nelson's position at Palermo was no longer tenable.[35]

On 4 October he hoisted his flag on *Foudroyant*, and ordered Troubridge to meet him with the *Culloden*, *Northumberland* and *Minotaur* at Minorca. He even called upon Smith to review whether one or both of his ships of the line might rally to Nelson's aid at this time. Cold reality cut through the frivolity at Palermo like a hot knife in butter. That day the flagship was festooned with colours in celebration of the Prince Royal's birthday, and in the afternoon the admiral, the Hamiltons and the queen attended a rowing gala. Young Mary Nisbet Elgin, who was accompanying her husband, Lord Elgin, to Constantinople, where he was to assume ministerial duties, declined to use Nelson's boat on the occasion. She was thoroughly disenchanted with Emma, who had advised her to dress modestly for a royal dinner the previous evening, only to pitch up herself in 'a fine gold and coloured silk worked gown and diamonds'. Mary had found herself apologising to gracious royals, and hurrying home to change. The event coloured what she had to say about the admiral and his lady. 'You never saw anything equal to the fuss the Queen made with Lady Hamilton,' she wrote, 'and Lord Nelson, whenever she moved, was always by her side . . . Lady Hamilton has made him do many very foolish things.' Indeed, said she, so completely was the admiral tied to his mistress that 'people' were 'laying bets' that even now – in this new crisis – Nelson would not leave Palermo.[36]

But Nelson confounded the doubters. He sailed the next day in the teeth of impending squalls, only to intercept the *Salamine* brig from Port Mahon with news from Darby of the *Bellerophon*, which was stationed there. Darby had heard that the enemy relief force for Malta had actually left Toulon, and was heading south-east with an escort of two sail of the line and several frigates. Sending the *Salamine* on to alert Niza, who had seven capital ships and ten cruisers, Nelson pressed forward with all haste towards Minorca and Gibraltar. He was at Port Mahon six days later. All seemed in order, and *Bellerophon* was at her post with several smaller ships of war. The admiral had no time to land, but signalled Darby for the latest intelligence and an up-to-date report on Minorca's defences, and hurried a letter to Erskine, the military commander, notifying him that as soon as he had satisfied himself that there was no danger from an enemy fleet, he would return to talk some more about the troops needed at Malta. This was the old Nelson, bursting with purpose and energy.

Troubridge's division had not arrived, so Nelson left instructions for him to follow and resumed his voyage to Gibraltar to support Duckworth. Fortunately, he did not need to go that far, for on 13 October he fell in with the *Bulldog*, ten days out from Gibraltar. In her was Sir Edward Berry, returning to serve his old chief after recuperating from his tribulations in the *Leander* in England. Nelson had expected Berry to reclaim his old position as Nelson's flag captain, but was secretly disappointed, for if Sir Edward was a good fighting subordinate, he lacked decisiveness in command and ran a sloppy ship. With Hardy as his captain, Nelson had always been free to concentrate on matters germane to a commander-in-chief, but Berry's shortcomings had the admiral frequently intervening in the running of the ship as if he was a common captain. Troubridge had been kept at his habitual boiling point by Berry. 'I really was ashamed and astonished to see Berry sitting still and your lordship going out to carry on the duty,' he wrote. He marvelled that Nelson 'did not set him to order'. Moreover, with Berry in the *Foudroyant*, inefficient but devoted as a dog, Nelson had to find another post for the displaced Hardy. His lordship gave Hardy the temporary command of a captured French frigate, the *Princess Charlotte*, assuring Spencer that the big captain from Dorset would 'make a man-of-war of her very soon', and then sent him home with dispatches and powerful recommendations to the Admiralty and Clarence, among others.[37]

Berry's good news was that during his voyage he had seen nothing of the enemy detachment rumoured to be on the loose off Spain, and the report was being discounted at Lisbon. Moreover, he brought letters from Duckworth that revealed that the outward-bound convoy from England had safely reached Gibraltar. In truth, the enemy squadron had been Spanish, not French, and it had gone harmlessly into Ferrol on 29 September. The spirit of Bruix immediately dematerialised, and Nelson rearranged his priorities. He turned back for Port Mahon, which he reached the following day. As there were no threats from ships of the line, Nelson decided that Minorca could be protected by ten cruisers, and sent *Bellerophon* to reinforce Duckworth. The only flag officers on the station, Nelson and Duckworth, agreed to share such emoluments of command as freight and prize money. There would be no bickering over any spoils. 'My only wish is to do as I would be done by,' Nelson wrote.[38]

There was more to do in Minorca. Nelson confirmed a capital sentence passed on a boatswain's mate who had threatened a superior with mutinous expressions, and the wretched fellow was hanged one morning on board a prison ship.

He ordered ships to be refitted at the arsenal, arranged convoys, packets and patrols, and had provisions and naval stores purchased at Leghorn, using government bills cashed in the town. The important issue to address was Malta. 'I am in a fever about these ships seen steering towards Malta,' Nelson admitted. He sent the *Vincejo* towards Toulon to investigate the French relief force, and directed Troubridge and Martin to reinforce Niza, putting, as he said, nine British and Portuguese capital ships and four cruisers 'in the track' the French would have to use to reach Malta. However, the threat evaporated almost as quickly as the scare in the Atlantic. Five warships had left Toulon, but they got no further than Ville Franche on the Riviera coast, where they deposited stores and provisions for their forces ashore before scampering home. The naval threats to Nelson's command of the sea had both risen and fallen as one.[39]

The disappointment was the conference with Erskine. Aggressive, eager to probe the weaknesses of the enemy, and willing to take risks to attain great objects, Nelson ran into a man who was cautious, safe and prone to be paralysed by doubts and dangers. 'He sees all the difficulty of taking Malta in the clearest point of view, and therefore it became an arduous task to make him think . . . the thing was possible,' Nelson grumbled. Actually, on this occasion, there was more to be said for Erskine's opinion than Nelson's. Valletta was, as the general wrote, 'one of the strongest places in Europe', and its defenders were determined to hold out as long as their stores. Nelson and Ball saw that with only some five thousand men Vaubois could not adequately defend works that needed three times that number. The French must therefore have been deployed thinly, and not always in places where they could support each other. It was true that their four main forts were located on three peninsulas and an island, but even had the British been capable of taking some of the outlying defences, it would not have compromised the awesome defensive power of Valletta itself. Despite their differences, Erkine and Nelson agreed that a force of at least five or six thousand men would be needed to provide even the chance of a military solution, but there unity divided. Nelson spoke optimistically of cobbling up a collection of marines, Russians, Maltese and British regulars, while Erskine was suspicious of such motley outfits and did not believe 'that any inconsiderable addition of numbers will afford the least prospect of ending the business'. And he apprised a frustrated Nelson with the news that the British garrison at Minorca was not only weaker than the admiral supposed, but had been warned that it might be withdrawn. Finally, Erskine passed the buck. He agreed to prepare fifteen hundred men with appropriate supplies for shipment to Malta if Fox, who was due to succeed to the command of Minorca, gave the go-ahead. 'It has cost me four hours' hard labour,' Nelson scoffed, 'and [the result] may be upset by a fool.'[40]

Nelson might have remained at Minorca, where he was more centrally positioned and well placed to tackle Fox; tried to track down and destroy the Toulon convoy; or reinforced Troubridge and Niza off Malta, but he left Port Mahon on 18 October to do none of these things. He was back in Palermo four days later. Nelson told Berry that he planned to visit Malta, as Ball had been urging him to do, but remained on shore for another three months.[41]

In lieu, it was left to his captains and commanders to carry the war to the enemy, in large ships and small. George Cockburn of the *Minerve* took a large twenty-gun privateer manned by 140 men in December and another almost as formidable the following spring. Henry Blackwood's *Penelope* took a Spanish ship from the Canaries and destroyed two French privateers in the Strait in October, and the following month assisted the boats of the *Vincejo* to cut six vessels from the harbour of Monaco, while in December Jahleel Brenton's small *Speedy*, shuttling a convoy through the Strait, beat off a dozen Spanish gunboats. Duckworth's division alone took or destroyed nine enemy vessels, five of them privateers, and recaptured two British ships between 19 September and 4 December.[42]

However, there was one very important vessel that they failed to intercept. On 9 October a twenty-eight-gun ship named *La Muiron* slid quietly into Fréjus on the French coast, towing a weathered felucca. That felucca had made a long and dangerous journey from Egypt, sneaking unseen past the *Theseus* and several Turkish vessels that had thrown a screen west of Alexandria, and making its way to France by way of Corsica. It dodged British men-of-war all along the way. When Nelson heard about her escape from one of the prizes Blackwood took from Monaco on 17 November he was extremely angry, and blamed the Admiralty for starving him of enough ships to cover all contingencies, especially when Malta absorbed so many of his resources. Some of the French fugitives from Egypt had been intercepted, but that obscure little felucca inflicted a terrible blow upon Nelson and Europe. It was almost the admiral's costliest failure, for it snatched a remarkable passenger from the clutches of British sea power. His name was Napoleon Bonaparte.

The complexion of the war was already beginning to change. By the end of November a British incursion into Holland had been abandoned and the troops withdrawn, while in Switzerland Suvorov was retiring before superior forces. The return of Bonaparte added huge momentum to this swing of the pendulum. Forsaking his disease-ridden Army of Egypt and his tattered dreams of eastern empire, the little Corsican rapidly refocused upon the crisis in Europe. He abolished the Directory by a coup in November, making himself the First Consul of France with a new constitution, and then threw himself into the war against Austria and Russia with manic energy. He would scourge the continent for another fifteen years.

5

Anyone who bet that Nelson would not leave Palermo had been wrong, but not far wrong. Within three weeks he was back, as if drawn by a magnet. The excursion to Minorca demonstrated that Palermo was the wrong place from which to confront the larger business of his acting command. He knew this, and tried to justify himself. When Hardy left for England he was instructed to explain his 'extraordinary' position to the Admiralty. His Sicilian Majesties insisted he remained at Palermo, 'for if I move they think the country is in danger and that they are abandoned. If my flag is in a transport they seem contented.' No doubt their Majesties were clinging to Nelson, as he said, but the time had come to explain that his overall responsibilities did not necessarily jeopardise their security; indeed, they enhanced it. Sir William gave the rest of the story. 'Without Emma and me,' he said, Nelson would no longer have been at Palermo. Since the previous year Nelson and the Hamiltons had been purloining the motto of the Order of the Bath, to which the men belonged, and referring to themselves as the *tria juncta in uno*, the three joined in one. A day after returning to Palermo Nelson repeated it to Minto. 'We are the real *Tria juncta in uno*,' he proudly asserted. That relationship had become crucial to Nelson, and could only thrive in Palermo.[43]

To some it was a repugnant cell of self-congratulation, flattery and manipulation under royal patronage. For Emma, sniped the hateful Gordon, 'flattery was as necessary . . . as the air she breathed'. The queen, the trio's beloved 'Charlotte', was no more restrained, and 'flattered . . . beyond all credibility' according to Countess Elgin. 'I never saw three people made such thorough dupes of as Lady Hamilton, Sir William and Lord Nelson.' The young countess assumed the compliments were cynical, but this hardly seems to have been the case. The personal letters of these individuals, the queen as well as the triumvirate, glitter with affection and unbounded admiration. To the more reserved their unrestrained professions oozed sycophancy, but they expressed actual emotions. Hamilton ever remained ecstatic about Nelson. 'Take him all in all,' he wrote in a typical line, 'I never met with his equal.' Their friendship would 'be the pride of the rest of my days'. The day Nelson had left Palermo on 5 October Emma had wept at a toast to the absent hero.[44]

Of the trio it is Hamilton who has surprised the most. The flirtatious relationship between Nelson and Emma was notorious, even in England, where a November issue of *The Times* likened the pair to Antony and Cleopatra, and spoke of Emma's famous performances as 'Admiral attitudes'. At home people assumed that the usurped husband would disapprove, and one wild tale credited Sir William with killing Nelson in a duel. Out in Palermo British visitors such as the Elgins also recoiled at the bizarre spectacle: Emma, an overweight, blousy seductress of thirty-four or thirty-five, full of animal magnetism and an armoury of attention-seeking skills; Sir William the scraggy, rake-thin seventy-year-old aesthete grumbling about his disordered stomach, rheumatism and missing art treasures; and the 'mean' figured, badly disabled admiral disappearing beneath an unseemly display of medals, ribands and orders. Nelson did not look well. Lord Elgin thought him 'very old' and noted that he had 'lost his upper teeth', developed a film over 'both' eyes, and suffered 'pretty' constant pain on account of the head wound sustained at the Nile. Yet for all their incongruities the three clung together like limpets, with Hamilton seemingly indifferent to the goings-on between the other partners. Elgin thought Nelson 'completely managed' by Emma, and his countess thought it 'a pity' that such a hero 'should fling himself away' in such a 'shameful manner'. At one dinner she admitted that Emma was 'very handsome' though 'quite in an undress' and 'very vulgar'. 'It is really humiliating to see Lord Nelson. He seems quite dying, and yet as if he had no other thought than her.'[45]

Sir William must have known that Nelson was involved with his wife, but he had long accepted that he would eventually become incapable of satisfying a partner thirty-four years his junior. As long as his own needs were fulfilled, he was philosophical enough to ignore inconvenient facts. However astonishing many Britons found the ménage, Sir William and his wife, long immersed in a libertine Neapolitan society, regarded it as common practice. Emma was merely doing what upper-class women with ageing husbands, or indeed husbands of any age, did in Naples. They found a lover, a *cicisbeo*. As Madame de Saussure wrote of the city, 'All the women, old and young, ugly or pretty, have lovers. The Princess of Belmonte usually has three . . . Since the court has been in Naples we have seen Princess Ferolito's husband at her parties every evening, [and] he appears to be on excellent terms with her lovers. The customs of this country are very strange.' A French diplomat found Neapolitan husbands 'far more tolerant than those of other nations. Marchese Santo Marco . . . decided to claim exclusive rights to his wife when he married, but he soon became aware that this was unreasonable.' And a surgeon in Nelson's fleet marvelled at how forward, vivacious and lascivious the Sicilian ladies seemed, compared with his own countrywomen. It was 'very customary for every married man to have some favourite, either single or wedded, and his wife, her gallant'. The Hamiltons, like other English who spent years abroad, imbibed aspects of different milieus, and became supra-national in ways that surprised their narrower countrymen and women at home.[46]

Emma and Nelson were more transparent. The admiral sucked in the attention she loved, and struck her as a possible protector after her ailing husband had gone. Nelson was so enchanted by her that he had stopped thinking of his wife back home. His letters to Fanny had become brief, uncommunicative and matter-of-fact, without any significant traces of emotion or longing. Occasionally he offered her self-congratulatory tidbits of information, but nothing that allowed her to glimpse pictures of the fleet, Naples or Palermo. He had simply stopped sharing information with her. But he did unjustly upbraid her for not writing to Emma, and for failing to send prints of the battle of Cape St Vincent, which he wanted to give to his mistress and to Prince Leopold.

Nelson's health accentuated his dependency. His eyes particularly worried him. To add to his standing problem, long exposure to wind and sun had given him bilateral pterygiae, in which an overgrowth of the conjunctival tissue over the whites of the eye was effecting the cornea, spreading like a 'film' across the pupil and iris and reducing vision. Both his eyes, the good as well as the bad, were attacked, and in the process became badly inflamed, probably the result of bacterial conjunctivitis, which turns the eye red, sticky and irritable. 'I really have not the power of writing,' Nelson told Duckworth. 'I am really blind.' Dangerous surgery was a possibility, but by the end of the year Nelson had embarked upon a quite different treatment, and was using 'electricity', to attempt to restore the sight of his dead right eye. During the eighteenth century pioneering physicians had begun to investigate 'electrotherapy', employing friction machines capable of delivering a single charge of electricity at a time. In England John Neale had published *Directions For Gentlemen Who Have Electrical Machines* as early as 1747, and John Wesley was a famous devotee, advocating the practice to treat cramp, lameness, inflammation and even deafness. In Italy Luigi Galvani did demonstrate that electric shocks could activate muscles, even dead ones, and documented a notion that would inspire Mary Shelley to write her gothic shocker, *Frankenstein*. Nelson stoically underwent 'a course of electricity' and by 4 July 1800 Sir William was able to announce that though his friend was still troubled by 'pains in the head, a swelling of the heart and inflammation of the eyes', he was no longer blind in his right eye![47]

'The eye that was totally blind has been . . . by electricity recovered sufficient to distinguish objects, and hopes may be entertained of his lordship recovering that eye,' said Hamilton. How far this improvement continued, or held its ground, is difficult to say, but it may explain a hitherto baffling and much derided statement made in *The* (London) *Times* of 4 October 1804. 'We beg to state, for the satisfaction of those . . . who are not personally acquainted with him,' ran the item, 'that Lord Nelson is not blind of either eye. It is true that he, for a short period, lost the sight of one eye, but it has happily been restored. He has also a speck on the other eye, but that he could see with both . . .' This, said to have come from 'his lordship's own information', was exaggerated. Nelson is supposed to have said that 'he could *see best* with what people called his *worst* eye'. It is doubtful that the damaged right eye was ever effective, but the traditional picture of the one-eyed admiral might have to be adjusted. The state of both Nelson's eyes continued to trouble him until the end, and the opinion of his last surgeon was that had he lived long enough he would have gone blind.[48]

The *tria juncta in uno* were interdependent financially as well as professionally and emotionally. Hamilton had always been in debt, but it grew as the years passed. At the moment he owed merchants and bankers £13,000, and his rakish nephew, Greville, reckoned the total figure stood at £19,000, far beyond the reach of the annual yield of his mortgaged estate in Pembroke, Wales, which had been withered to £850 by taxes and interest payments. Though the Bourbon restoration had enabled him to recover his houses in Naples and Caserta, the possessions that had been left in them had gone, including all his furniture, three carriages, paintings, glassware, antiquities and marble tables. Nelson bore at least three-quarters of the expenses at the Palazzo Palagonia, but in January still had to loan Hamilton £927 which remained unsettled.[49]

Their finances deteriorated at the Palazzo Palagonia, because both Hamiltons lived forever beyond their means, entertaining constantly and lavishly, sometimes as a function of their official duties but often out of a sheer generosity of spirit. Nelson told Fanny that he wrote for much of the day, except for occasional evening walks with the Hamiltons. In fact, the house was much livelier. It, and occasionally Nelson's flagship, hosted a spate of parties and fetes, and regular short-term guests boarded at the Palazzo Palagonia, including Maltese deputies, Turkish officers on their way to Algiers with dispatches, and numerous naval officers, including, in 1800, the returning Lord Keith. Hamilton chaffed to Greville that 'to keep an inn as I have done for 35 years' should have been 'impossible' on his income, 'but then a comely landlady calls more company than I could wish to my house'. But Nelson was almost as willing to throw his door open. 'No person in this world is more sensible of your worth and goodness in every way than myself,' he exhorted Berry. 'Let all pass over, and come and dine here. As you are ready to execute my orders, take this . . . as a positive and lawful one . . . When I see a ship better ordered than *Foudroyant*, I will allow you to confine yourself on board.'[50]

Emma was the star of those evenings, hosting the dinners and for most of the time providing the entertainment, singing movingly or amusingly, according to the piece, dancing a tarantella, tambourine in hand, or unleashing a full-blown performance of her 'attitudes'. 'Others have tried to imitate Lady Hamilton's talent,' said the Countess de Boigne, 'but I doubt if any one has succeeded . . . To equal her success, the actor must first be of faultless beauty from head to foot, and such perfection is rare.'[51]

But complicating the situation, Emma had taken an ill-advised leaf from the queen's book, and began rounding off evenings with late-night sessions gambling for money. The ferocious hours staggered naval colleagues, who knew the long days Nelson kept, and it was not surprising that he declined to play himself and was regularly to be seen dozing at the table while Emma sat beside him, studying her cards and gratuitously dipping into the £500 or so in stake money that lay before her. Nelson did not wholly approve of gambling, though he enjoyed the occasional wager, and had a fifty guinea bet with Duckworth about how long the war would last. Nevertheless, he may have lost considerable sums at Emma's hands. Sir Arthur Paget, who arrived in the spring, spoke of the 'great losses . . . both His Lordship and Lady Hamilton have sustained at faro and other games of hazard'. By then absurd rumours had reached Berlin that the admiral's losses had reached a preposterous £12,000![52]

Henry Aston Barker first visited the house on Saturday, 7 December. 'In the evening dressed and went to Sir William's conversazione,' he wrote. 'There was a large assemblage of the nobility of Naples and many very beautiful women. Gambling went on to a great extent, in which Lady Hamilton and Lord Nelson were principal actors. I pitied Lord Nelson. He seemed quite tired of the noise and bustle which was very great. The hero of the Nile sitting by Lady Hamilton was every moment dropping asleep and reminded me not a little of Hercules and Omphale. Before the bustle began Lady Hamilton introduced me to Sir William, who I found very affable and kind, assuring me that I should have every assistance in his power. I was introduced also to Miss Knight, a lady who draws extremely well and . . . [was] intimately acquainted with A[ngelica] Kauf[f]man[n] [the painter].' Barker found it tolerable enough to return the following day, when heavy rain reduced the number of guests, but on his third successive attendance 'I found Lady Hamilton sitting at a small wheel spinning and an Italian princess busy with a spindle and distaff. Lord Nelson then came into the room with whom I had a little conversation. We soon went to dinner. Lord Nelson sat on Lady Hamilton's right and she cuts his meat. He was very lively. He amused himself after dinner teaching the princess to say "Damn your eyes!" for an English blessing. A quarter of an hour after dinner we all rose from [the] table and Sir William showed me some curiosities and beautiful remains of the antique gems, also a head [likeness] of Lady Hamilton cut on a pebble in a very masterly style.' However, these daily ordeals may have tried anyone less obsessed with noise and company than Emma. Barker, unlike many, emerged with favourable memories. Apart from being 'so kindly treated' he took away a vision of Emma, her robe trimmed with roses from neck to foot, and her face lit up with 'lovely dark eyes'.[53]

Of the brothers none loved Nelson more than Thomas Troubridge, once the admiral's soulmate. None had shared his highs and lows, from the exhilaration of the battle of Cape St Vincent to the stormy, shot-slashed hell of Tenerife. They had dreamed dreams together. But now it was increasingly the Hamiltons who provided Nelson with that close, confidential and emotional support, and Troubridge's increasing bellicosity may have had its roots in jealousy. He was certainly not a man to dissemble. In December 1799 he wrote to Nelson about the gambling, which he feared was exhausting the admiral and damaging his eyes as well as his reputation and purse. Lady Hamilton, he said tactfully, was used to such 'horrid hours'; he was not, but 'the other day' even she had barely kept her eyes open and stifled yawns. The game, he said, gave Nelson no pleasure, so what was the point of it? Nelson avoided the central issue in his reply, but Sir Thomas returned to the attack. 'Pray keep good hours,' said he. 'If you knew what your friends feel for you, I am sure you would cut all the nocturnal parties. The gambling of the people at Palermo is publicly talked of everywhere. I beseech your lordship, leave off . . . Lady H[amilton's] character will suffer. Nothing can prevent people from talking. A gambling woman in the eye of an Englishman is lost.' He was so concerned that he got Ball to rally to his aid, and Emma finally and good-naturedly responded. On 8 January she promised that she would 'play no more'. 'You may not know that you have many enemies,' Troubridge cautioned her six days later. 'I therefore risk your displeasure by telling you. I am much gratified you have taken it as I meant it – purely good.' The embattled sea dog spoke too soon, however, for if Paget and Keith are to be believed the nocturnal sessions were still in progress several months later.[54]

Palermo, despite the seasonal winds and humidity, was not without its other attractions. At times the air hung with the scent of orange blossom, oleander, pomegranate and syringa. The yellow rocks were colonised by climbing plants and the gardens were ablaze with flowers in the spring. But there was an intoxicating sultriness about the Palazzo Palagonia, fatally attractive like a delicious sin that compels as it disturbs, sowing feelings of guilt, extravagance and waste. It has been said that Emma was popular with the officers and men of the British fleet, and that she stood as their patroness, advocating their cause. To some extent that was true, but by no means all took such a generous view. There were those who lamented the powerful influence that she exerted upon their chief, and saw a beautiful spider ensnaring an admiral, drawing him from his rightful business and sullying his reputation. From the autumn of 1799 it was a charge that was difficult to refute.

6

As the winter set in Nelson could reflect upon a year of mixed fortunes. The road back from the disaster of 1798 had been expensive, bloody and barbarous, but there had been real achievements. Despite meagre support, Nelson had maintained an effective naval squadron, preserved Sicily and significantly contributed towards ridding Italy of the French. He had contained Bonaparte's activities in the east and kept a blockade of Malta in place, one that at times had looked almost impossible to sustain. In the course of these operations, he had influenced the political complexion of the Mediterranean, easing Turkey and Russia into the allied coalition, and forging pacts between the Two Sicilies, Portugal and the Barbary states. He had consistently pre-empted the thoughts of his political masters in England, and until recently they had satisfied themselves that he had been a steady hand in difficult circumstances.

But now the accusations were mounting, painting a colourful canvas of decadence and neglect. Adultery, gambling and idling in Palermo all blotted a falling reputation. In some respects the indictments were unjust, but although Nelson superintended his fleet from ashore, he was acting against type. If nothing else, Nelson had been synonymous with enterprise, restless energy and impatience with delay or inaction. He added one more minor success to his collection before the year ran out, however. Nelson was still banking on raising troops for Malta, and Russia was believed to have sent a detachment, but it never appeared. Even after three thousand soldiers reinforced Ushakov at Naples, his promises to prioritise Malta remained empty. Nelson got no further writing to the tsar. Russia wanted Malta to be restored to the Knights of St John, and Paul was Grand Master, but the country left Naples and Britain to bear the financial burden of liberating the island. Nelson estimated that the blockade alone had cost His Britannic Majesty a staggering £180,000.[55]

Nelson's success was with the British, and an adroit manipulation of Lieutenant General Fox. Erskine had undertaken to discuss the needs of Malta with Fox, but there was a danger that the incoming military commander would imbibe the negativity of the old. On 15 October Nelson wrote to Governor O'Hara at Gibraltar, briefing him about Malta in readiness for his meeting with the new military commander-in-chief. He also ensured that when Fox reached Minorca, he would be met by letters from Ball and Hamilton, as well as himself, all stating the case for an expeditionary force to be sent to Malta. Fox would encounter a wall of positive professional opinion. At the same time Nelson strove to convert Erskine. Back from Minorca in October, the admiral told Sir James that whether Fox arrived or not, Graham's garrison at Messina should be ordered to Malta to protect the most advanced siege works from French counterattack, especially as the Portuguese would have to withdraw their marines when they returned to Lisbon. Failure to supply these reinforcements could cost the island. 'This is a great and important moment,' said Nelson, and if Erskine had his doubts, 'I wish to take all the responsibility.' But, of course, Erskine had not been given his responsibility to pass it to another. 'Sir,' Nelson sighed to Clarence, 'I find few think as I do, that to obey orders is all perfection. To serve my king and to destroy the French, I consider as the great[est] order of all, from which little ones spring, and if one of these little ones militate[s] against it . . . I go back and obey the great order and object – to *down*, *down* with the damned French villains. Excuse my warmth, but my blood boils at the name of a Frenchman. I hate them *all*, royalist[s] and republicans.' He told Spencer that 'much as I approve of strict obedience to orders, even to a court-martial to inquire whether the object justified the measure, yet to say that an officer is never, for any object, to alter his orders is what I cannot comprehend.' Spencer had rarely, if ever, read such letters. Here was an admiral who doffed his hat at orders, but made a virtue of disobeying them.[56]

Nelson's machinations were effective. When Fox reached Gibraltar, O'Hara handed him the admiral's letter, and he was so anxious to help that he immediately wrote to the secretary of state for war reiterating the need for greater military resources in the Mediterranean. At Port Mahon he found not only the collection of letters Nelson had arranged, but Duckworth and Troubridge to help him weigh pro and con. Fox kept his head, though. Apart from the 28th Regiment, which had been recalled, he had only 6638 soldiers in Minorca, 348 of them sick. With Duckworth based at Gibraltar, too far away to give immediate assistance, the general judged that at present he could not weaken his force in Minorca, but at least authorised Nelson to transfer Graham's two regiments from Messina to Malta. An excited Troubridge arrived at Sicily with Fox's orders on 26 November, and two weeks later the *Culloden* and *Foudroyant* landed Graham and eight hundred soldiers in St Paul's Bay in Malta. They then sailed south-east to deposit guns and stores at Marsa Scirocco.[57]

This fillip painted the Maltese service in fresh colours, introducing new faces and minds. Ball retained control of civil affairs, but Troubridge succeeded Niza at the head of the naval blockade with four British ships of the line and orders to protect the troops ashore and to collaborate with any Russians who condescended to arrive. Ushakov was difficult, but Nelson recommended Sir Thomas to use Italinsky, 'one of the best foreigners you ever dealt with'. But in the meantime the force ashore now stood at 400 British marines, shortly to be put under Acting Major James Weir; Graham's 800 line infantry; about 1500 Maltese; and a reserve of about another 1000 Maltese.[58]

Yet there was a sting in the tail. The additional men exacerbated the dire shortages of provisions, and Nelson was disturbed by an odd statement in Fox's orders to Graham. Graham was to take necessary military stores and equipment with him, but there was a question about whose responsibility it was to feed them. If the army would not supply Graham's force with victuals, then who could, Nelson wondered? 'If nobody will pay it, I shall sell Bronte and the Emperor of Russia's [diamond snuff] box,' he said, 'for I feel myself above every consideration but that of serving faithfully.'[59]

Then, too, the military introduced some overdue realism. Despite his initial enthusiasm, Graham patently lacked confidence, and his uncertainty was underpinned by Fox's orders, which cautioned him against placing his troops in unjustifiable danger, and authorised him to withdraw completely if necessary. Graham did valuable work, improving Ball's existing dispositions, devising and protecting lines of retreat and creating defensive redoubts, but he was defensively minded. Indeed, he was so afraid of provoking a French counterattack that he was loath to make any offensive move of his own. This mood was influenced by Lieutenant Colonel Lewis Lindenthal, who arrived with Fox's orders to make a full military report. The result was a thoughtful and sobering document. The enemy positions were too strong to warrant a regular siege with less than 13,000 men equipped with an artillery detachment, entrenching tools and trained engineers and sappers, and even that would offer no more than a 'hope' of success. But there was no such army, and no such equipage. Lindenthal saw a great deal to admire, including the Maltese, who were 'very much attached to us' and had 'performed wonders', and Vivion, who offered a hand in 'almost every department', but the stubborn fact remained that with the resources to hand the only viable strategy was that of blockade. 'All . . . said of a speedy surrender of the place, in case we could make a show of regular troops, has no foundation whatsoever.' The Ball–Nelson bubble had well and truly been pricked.[60]

The army did not dispel all the bolder visions. Ball continued to support an attack upon Fort Ricasoli, while Nelson clung to a fading hope that the Russians might yet supply the wanted strength. Troubridge, whose military experience exceeded Ball's if not Nelson's, took a more jaundiced view, and predicted that three times their force would be needed to conquer. Martin of the *Northumberland* agreed, and concluded that Ball's 'sanguine' temperament had 'deceived many other people as much as himself'.[61]

The job would remain with the navy, and more besides. As Nelson had predicted, the Russian navy performed badly, and the Austrian generals were soon clamouring for British ships to support their army in the Gulf of Genoa. 'The Russians do not approach the coast,' Wyndham wrote to Nelson, and the siege of Genoa, which otherwise proceeded satisfactorily, was faltering through the attrition on allied lines of communication and supply at sea. Nelson wanted assurances that Britain would be a full partner in any negotiations for the surrender of Genoa, but agreed to send Martin with a small naval force back to the gulf to restore allied superiority at sea.[62]

Genoa, where Austria and France were poised to fight a final battle for the control of northern Italy, and Malta were outstanding areas of conflict, but elsewhere the French imperialist broil had retreated, in Egypt, the Ionian Islands and central and southern Italy. On the face of it, it was not an unsatisfactory legacy to leave to the next commander-in-chief of the Mediterranean. The job had taxed Nelson to his limits. He had lost weight, and those who had not seen him before thought him almost skeletal. Though he confronted the enormous paperwork associated with theatre command, he had no proper secretarial assistance, and was often barely able to see. Yet he did not doubt that he had earned the right to be named a full commander-in-chief. He had told Spencer so, advertising his mastery of many Mediterranean affairs and the deficiencies of Lord Keith. Although Keith had three years' seniority as a flag officer, the import of Nelson's language was plain.

Yet when St Vincent went to the Channel fleet, the Admiralty named Keith the new commander-in-chief of the Mediterranean on 15 November. There must have been misgivings, for the board was entrusting an important theatre to two flag officers who shared a strained past. That Nelson would take Keith's promotion badly, and see it as another reflection upon his services, was a certainty. The political situation in the Mediterranean was not unfavourable, but it was notoriously volatile, and needed a strong British presence. There were troubles enough ahead. Out on station, in sultry Palermo, Nelson faced a new year sick at heart.

BOOK TWO

HOPING FOR HAPPINESS

'I have naturally been thinking and hoping for future happiness.'

Nelson to Emma, 11 March 1801

'I am fixed as to the plan of life I mean to pursue. It is to take a small neat house, six to ten miles from London, and there to remain till I can fix for ever or get to Bronte. I have never known happiness beyond moments, and I am fixed as Fate to try if I cannot obtain it after so many years of labour and anxiety.'

Nelson to Emma, 12 May 1801

X

'COME BACK TO YOUR FAMILY HERE'

Come, cheer up, fair Delia, forget all thy grief,
For thy shipmates are brave, and a hero's their
chief.
Look round on these trophies, the pride of the
Main,
They were snatched by their valour from Gallia
and Spain.

Cornelia Knight, Verses for
Emma's Birthday, 1800

I

SIR Thomas Troubridge, Baronet, was about forty-one years old, a time of life when many reflect and take stock, accepting the departure of youth, with its sense of invulnerability and endless tomorrows, and weighing how the remaining years might best be spent. Turning forty had been a stressing period for Troubridge, professionally and privately, and he had emerged scorched. The loss of his wife, Francis Richardson, a widow, in June 1798 had left him with six or seven children to support, two his own, and he had not sprung from a well-to-do line. His rise in the service owed much to merit, and its recognition by a vulnerable succession of chiefs, half of whom were now dead. At present St Vincent and Nelson were his principal props, and under them he had seen his great years as a fighting captain, distinguishing himself at Cape St Vincent and Tenerife and in the Italian campaigns of 1799. Yet Troubridge thought himself unlucky, even damned. He deeply resented the Admiralty's attempts to deny him a Nile medal and debar his first lieutenant from a customary promotion. Grief and frustration propelled him into a frenzy of work, but it left him on the brink of financial and physical collapse, venting at the incompetence and corruption that encircled him, and every new misfortune. Throughout, he remained devoted to Nelson. 'I long much to see Lord Nelson,' he wrote to Hamilton. 'I love him, and have much to say which I cannot trust to paper.'

But even he furrowed Troubridge's brow, as the admiral sank into the febrile lacuna that was Palermo.[1]

Troubridge's latest assignment, the blockade of Malta, for which he assumed responsibility in December, got off to a difficult start when *Culloden* ran upon a rock while trying to land shot and artillery at Marsa Scirocco. She got to her anchorage without a rudder, pintles and false keel, the captain cursing the 'vagabonds' who had supplied him with false charts, and feeling 'so low and dejected . . . that I am quite unhinged'. On 23 December Nelson wrote to Spencer that if Troubridge was not given another ship his irreplaceable services would be lost to the Mediterranean, but the Admiralty decided that the captain was needed in the Channel fleet and took the opportunity to order Troubridge to bring his damaged ship home. A longer-term consequence of the mishap at Marsa Scirocco may have been Troubridge's deep interest in the accurate charting of the Mediterranean, something that made him a key figure in the development of the Admiralty's hydrographic department.[2]

This was a mere beginning, and before the end of the year Nelson was receiving a torrent of letters from Sir Thomas, some written daily or even twice daily. His lordship tried to reassure. 'Your resources never fail,' he encouraged, 'and you would contrive something, I dare say, if the ship's bottom were knocked out.' Nelson knew that Troubridge was ailing. He had problems with his chest and one hand, but it was his friend's mental state that most worried, with its seamless processions of thought – through outrage, instability and irrationality. Others could not help but notice. Ball thought Troubridge had brooded too long about his misfortune in Aboukir Bay, while Hamilton confessed his inability to persuade him all men were not rogues. Nelson shook his head at Sir Thomas's violent denunciations of all and sundry. Dixon, whom Ball thought 'one of the best fellows in the world', was in Troubridge's view 'deranged', while Berry had been so 'destroyed with pride' that he was best back to his wife. Both deserved to face courts-martial. Occasionally the captain owned, however, that he was 'soured with the world'.[3]

Perpetually pivoting on despair and fury, Troubridge's letters poured white hot from a burning soul, and they were not always easy to follow. Forced to oil his service with his own money, he scourged the Sicilian administrative, supply and financial systems. In October he had even threatened to return a ring and jewelled box that Ferdinand had given him that nothing of 'such unprincipled people' would be left 'about' him. His anger at Admiralty neglect was also finding new fuel in Nelson's failure to get his rank as an acting commodore confirmed, and he may have resented Ball landing the position of governor of Malta. Another irritant was Nelson's involvement with the Hamiltons. But the origins of some of his attacks are mysterious. 'The German [Austrian] interest prevails,' he ranted obscurely at the turn of the year. 'I wish I was at your lordship's elbow for one hour. *All*, *all* will be thrown on you, rely on it. I will parry the blow as much as is in my powers . . . *Trust not the court of Palermo, particularly the female part*. God bless your Lordship. I am miserable. I cannot assist your operations more.' A week later he 'really' thought 'it dangerous . . . to trust the Queen. Women never could keep a secret, or ever should be trusted with one.' Nelson would not have missed the veiled shaft at Lady Hamilton.[4]

The food shortages in Malta were the root of Troubridge's latest outbursts, reminding him of his troubles in the Bay of Naples the previous spring. Once again he flagellated members of the government for inflating the price of corn for their own benefit. His favourite target was Trabia, and there was an explosive scene when the two men met at a dinner at the Palazzo Palagonia sometime in December. One witness said that Troubridge foamed with rage and flew at the minister, and that he had to be restrained while Emma and Nelson restored a degree of equanimity. Probably more accurately, Troubridge admitted telling 'that gambler . . . of his tricks . . . in good English', and branding him a 'villain' as well as 'a disgrace to his country'. But he also confessed to Nelson, 'I long to have a [pistol] shot at the villain. I never told your Lordship of half the ill treatment I received from that fellow . . . I have really fretted until I am seriously ill, and I believe a little deranged.'[5]

Troubridge took up the festering issue of Malta's sustenance with a vengeance. It had been enhanced by the arrival of the newly installed British forces. Although a responsibility of His Britannic Majesty, Graham's soldiers depended upon a laborious system of cashing government bills and the regularity of victuallers and store ships dispatched from Minorca. At the end of 1799 they were flat out of some commodities, including oatmeal, while others were being distributed at two-thirds the normal ration. It was not until February that the redcoats and Troubridge's ships felt their provisions were up to par. The Maltese remained as vulnerable as ever, and were hit in the spring by shortages caused by the poor harvests in Sicily in 1799. With Malta's main source restricted, Ball looked for alternatives as distant as the Levant and Barbary, and appealed again to Nelson, who had worked his magic with the king on some six or seven different occasions over the past year. Troubridge was less diplomatic. From 23 December he fired angry demands that the export ban in Sicily be lifted. 'I have this day saved 30,000 people from dying,' he stormed on 5 January, 'but with this day my ability ceases. As the King of Naples, or rather the Queen and her party, are bent on starving us, I see no alternative but to leave these poor unhappy people to starve, without our being witnesses to their distress. I curse the day I ever served the King of Naples . . . I assure you on my heart, if the Palermo traitors were here, I would shoot them first and then myself.'[6]

No one had fought harder for Malta than Nelson, but he knew that the king's resources had been seriously depleted by the war and that he had already borne a disproportionate share of the burden of the blockade. Whatever his faults, he had always responded to Nelson's appeals, and sometimes made substantial personal donations. The admiral also realised that Sicily was herself short of food, and what was available was hamstrung by inefficient distribution systems and unreliable sailing weather. Not so Troubridge, who denied the scarcity in Sicily, and railed about 'worthless' monarchs and corrupt civil servants. Nelson, with his 'honest, open manner', was too naive to understand 'their infamous tricks', he warned, and would be turned into their tool. 'We have characters, my lord, to lose. These people have none. Do not suffer their infamous conduct to fall on us.' In the present situation, Girgenti was 'full of corn', and Troubridge had the money to buy it were it not for the machinations of saboteurs and profiteers. The situation was so serious that he felt like withdrawing the troops and leaving the island to the French. But Sir Thomas had a more practical solution. He sent ships to Girgenti and Messina to purchase corn; if they were refused, they were ordered to seize the supplies by force.[7]

Nelson tried to avert Troubridge's action, which he tactfully suggested should only be used as a last resort. 'I know all your wants, and it is always my sorrow when I cannot relieve the wants of my friends,' he soothed, but it was quite 'useless' to 'fret yourself to death, because you believe that all the world are not so honest as yourself'. There were victuallers in Palermo destined for Malta, but they were trapped by bad weather. However, Sir William and Acton had arranged for the corn in them to be unloaded for the use of Palermo. An express was being sent to Girgenti directing that their corn, earmarked for Palermo, now be shipped direct to Malta instead. But Troubridge outran Nelson, and his ships seized two corn vessels at Girgenti and carried them to Malta. The admiral found himself explaining to Acton that no disloyalty or disrespect had been intended; given the desperate situation in the island, Troubridge had merely anticipated his Sicilian Majesty's orders to release those cargoes. It was a nice interpretation. Nevertheless, Troubridge's no-nonsense approach, softened by Nelson's advocacy, paid off because other food and supply vessels began to arrive in Malta, and the king promised that in the future nothing essential to the blockade would be refused at Sicilian ports.[8]

In every Italian service Troubridge had bordered on the paranoid and the hysterical, but he always delivered. His campaign against the French garrisons had been flawless, and one way or another he kept the Maltese blockade in place throughout that second winter and spring. Though Hamilton attributed the latest success to 'Lord Nelson's and my strong remonstrances to this government', as well as to a few British Treasury bills, others had a clearer picture of what Troubridge was achieving. Hearing that Keith was on his way to replace Nelson as commander-in-chief, Graham urged the incoming chief to visit Malta 'that you may judge of all our innumerable wants and the total impossibility of abridging the blockade' without more soldiers. He was very clear about his greatest asset. 'For God's sake,' he implored Keith, 'don't take Troubridge away.

He is invaluable to us or to any service' and it was 'impossible to unite more zeal and activity or any service than he does'.[9]

Troubridge, a mighty warrior and diplomatic embarrassment within a single frame, was impossible to reform. When Emma innocently offered her services as a broker, his resentment at the court boiled over. 'I feel their ill-treatment and deep intrigues too much ever to forget or forgive them,' he replied tartly. 'I feel so conscious I did not deserve it from them or their ministers, nor can I even thank them for the corn [finally sent].' He could not look for compromises, and would not be drawn from his world of enemies. 'Does the worthless traitor [Trabia] think he can deceive me by his hackneyed villainy? No, be assured not, I keep a watchful eye on them all – they do not carry on their intrigues, even with the assistance of Mr [James] Tough [British consul in Sicily], unnoticed.' But Emma might do something about the ruin of his finances. His campaign in Naples had cost him £500 in expenses, and he had turned over to the king 'all I got at the islands, which certainly was the property of the captors' for no reward. Even the British government had been spiteful, actually docking his pay for the period in which he had served ashore instead of on the *Culloden*. Though some agreement had been reached over the prize money for the Roman campaign, he estimated that he had recently spent another 7000 dollars on corn for the Maltese. 'I should have been a very rich man if I had served George III, instead of the King of Naples,' he said bitterly.[10]

By comparison Ball, who had also thrown private resources into public service, took a more temperate position, viewing matters more dispassionately than either Nelson or Troubridge, and providing a steadying influence. As far as he was concerned, Sir William was 'the most amiable and accomplished man I know, and his heart is certainly one of the best in the world. I wish he and her Ladyship would pay me a visit. They are an irreparable loss to me, for I am convinced that but for their influence with their Sicilian Majesties and his ministers the poor Maltese would have been starved, and my head would have been sacrificed in their moment of despair.'[11]

Yet Malta remained an intractable conundrum, and no one wanted to help. For long Nelson hoped the Russians might add their weight to the British regulars and force a capitulation. For a moment Ushakov gave wing to these hopes by returning from Naples to Messina with half a dozen capital ships and 2500 men, but he only lingered purposelessly for a short while before discovering urgent orders to return to Corfu. Flabbergasted, a 'greatly' distressed Nelson spent a morning with Acton, considering what could be done to repair the damage. Acton undertook to put 2600 Sicilian soldiers with their provisions under Graham's command, but when the plan was put to the latter he would have none of it. With some justification, Graham pointed out that the inexperienced and undisciplined Sicilians would merely be 'an encumbrance'. More, the whole sorry business of scratching here and there for a credible military force was futile. 'The quantity of stores, ammunition and artillery we have is trifling,' he said, 'and would only expose us to the ridicule of the enemy were we to fire on the place, as I am frequently pressed to do by Ball.' He told Keith that the defection of the Russians made 'it a hopeless case, for any number of Neapolitans will not hasten the surrender [of Valletta] one hour.'[12]

It was driving Nelson, as well as Troubridge, into the ground, even as he tried to dispel the disillusionment of others. 'You may depend that Graham shall share the fate of our ships,' he wrote to Fox on 7 January. 'I shall never suffer him to want, if I can beg, borrow or steal to supply him.' But inside he was close to despair. Nothing seemed to work. In June his old military comrade William Anne Villettes was sent from England to recruit two Albanian regiments for Malta. With the assistance of the British consul in Corfu, Spiridion Foresti, Villettes got permission from the Porte to recruit within the Ottoman dominions, but he made hard work of it. The Albanians found the ten-year terms of enlistment offered by the British unacceptable, they refused to wear anything but their own national dress as a uniform, and looked wild beyond belief. Ball did not believe that the Albanians and Maltese would work together anyway, and recommended that two regiments of Maltese be raised instead, encouraging them with a guarantee that they would not be deployed outside the island.[13]

It was all highly dispiriting. Nelson was angry that Erskine and Fox had denied him the use of two thousand troops from Minorca, which, he believed, might have forced Valletta to surrender and 'released' his ships 'from the hardest service I have ever seen'. On 7 January he admitted to Keith that Malta had 'almost' broken his spirits 'forever'.[14]

2

Nelson's new year brought another unwelcome letter. It was on the night of the Epiphany that he opened a dispatch from Keith, confirming that he was on his way to take command of the Mediterranean. The letter was dated off Vigo, Spain, on 30 November, and its writer could not, therefore, be far away. In fact Keith had arrived at Gibraltar in his flagship, the *Queen Charlotte*, on 6 December. Nelson's period as acting commander-in-chief was over.

Nelson was hurt. A current string of petty complaints from the Admiralty had suggested that his authority was ebbing, but, despite Keith's seniority (he was a vice admiral rather than a rear admiral), Nelson had hoped that his superior achievements and experience in the Mediterranean would have given him the formal command of the theatre. It was with chagrin that he sent the *Vincejo* to Malta to direct Troubridge to place his detachment under Keith's command. Writing to Spencer, he simply said that Keith's appointment was 'entirely contrary to my expectations'.[15]

Always sensitive to rebuke and criticism, Nelson saw Keith's appointment as an ominous censure. He enjoyed his status as the country's hero, and since 1793 had been manipulating the national press to create it. Most recently he had passed glowing tributes from Ferdinand and Acton to the Admiralty and Davison, instructing the last to give them to the press if the board failed to do so. On 15 October 1799 he had gone further, addressing a brief autobiography to his old prize agent, John McArthur, for publication in a new British serial, the *Naval Chronicle*. This famous 'sketch' of his life, like the narratives of Cape St Vincent and the Nile that his supporters had put into print, bolstered his reputation with material from the fountainhead. It was a self-congratulatory, if not entirely honest, story of how a gallant and industrious public servant raised himself to the pinnacle of his profession by his own exertions. Unfortunately, Keith's appointment suggested that this opinion was not shared by the Admiralty, and that they had reservations about his fitness for theatre command.[16]

There was much at stake for Nelson – self-respect, the opportunity to become an extremely young but fully-fledged commander-in-chief, and financial returns. Everyone knew that a commander-in-chief could earn a fortune from his share of prize, head and freight money. Even an unlucky admiral who missed the big prizes might pocket a handsome increment to his salary. According to one accounting Nelson, though a junior flag officer, earned £3373 on freight and prize money from 30 November 1799 until the date he struck his flag the following summer. The prizes topped 750, including three or four warships and twenty-six privateers.[17]

Spencer's board had no doubt about Nelson's ability as a fighting admiral, but the events of the summer and autumn of 1799 had raised worrying doubts about his judgement, energy and controllability. Judgement because of his apparent overemphasis upon southern Italy, as well as the deployment of his marines ashore with a French fleet at large; energy because of the subsequent sojourn at Palermo; and controllability because of his tendency to overrule orders. There was a suspicion that he was being inveigled from duty by Emma Hamilton, and had become the dupe of their Sicilian Majesties. Keith probably contributed to these impressions during debriefings at the Admiralty after his return to England, but they were in any case becoming notorious. In northern Italy the Russian general Suvorov acidly wrote to Nelson, 'I thought you were going from Malta to Egypt to destroy . . . the remaining . . . atheists of our time. Palermo is *not* Cythere.' More kindly, Admiral Goodall, who loved Nelson and included him in his will, chafed from England that gossip was portraying him as 'Rinaldo in the arms of Armida, and that it requires the firmness of an Ubaldo and his brother Knight to draw you from the Enchantress. To be sure, 'tis a very pleasant attraction to which I am very sensible myself, but my maxim has always been, *Cupidus voluptatum, cupidior Gloria*.' Glory, rather than love, should prevail. No one was more injured by the stories than Fanny, waiting for her husband to come home. The sparse letters, the cool reception that met her plans to sail out to join him and the inability of Davison to answer her enquiries all told their own story. As early as April 1799 she had seen unpleasant writing on the wall. 'Lord Hood always expressed his fear that Sir William and Lady Hamilton would use their influence to keep Lord Nelson with them,' she wrote. 'They have succeeded.'[18]

The debacle between Nelson and Lock was also still doing its work, this time through the Victualling Board in London. Relations between the two remained icebound after Lock's failure to wring a victualling agency from Nelson, and the young consul could scarce bow to the admiral as he entered the room or reply to anything he said in words of more than one syllable. Lock, as we have seen, was also in trouble with the captains and pursers of the squadron for alleging that they had been overspending on provisions. Nelson's enquiries, which vindicated his officers, had been duly reported to the Victualling Board, but in November Lock blabbed to Hardy and Hamilton that the board had nevertheless actually thanked him for his information, which had saved them 40 per cent of their disbursements. Nelson saw red. If true, this indicated that Lock had fed his unsubstantiated allegations about the officers of the squadron to the board, and that they had been believed. Angry at any suggestion that he and his officers were being traduced behind their backs, Nelson wrote sternly to the Victualling Board, stating that his investigations had shown Lock's allegations to be malicious, and that he therefore expected to be supported. Resorting to his worst third-person style of address, he added, 'Nelson is as far from doing a scandalous or mean action as the heavens are above the earth.' The day after writing his letter, which Hardy undertook to deliver personally to the board, Nelson formally demanded that Lock send him copies of all his correspondence on the subject. If any furtive allegations were going about, he intended to root them out.[19]

Lock had an unfortunate predilection for putting both feet in his mouth. He had artlessly attended a royal fancy-dress ball in the whiskers and clothes of a Jacobin, and the king had the consul thrown out of the place. The bad impression stuck, and the court never did like Lock. Now the helplessly inexperienced gallant responded to Nelson's demand by drawing himself up to his full inconsiderable height and declaring that as an employee of the Foreign Office he was not subject to naval discipline, and did not have to produce his public letters. However, he tried to appease, he had not in fact had any correspondence with the Victualling Board, but he would surrender portions of some personal letters that bore on the question.[20]

Angrily Nelson fished through Lock's submissions to discover that the consul's stories originated in letters his relatives had sent from England. His sister, for example, had written on 8 September that she had met the chairman of the Victualling Board at a dinner, and he had expressed gratitude for Lock's intervention and expected to make savings of 40 per cent on reforms. It was clear that Lock had had nothing from the board, and was simply repeating hearsay. On 20 December the board itself confirmed this in its reply to Nelson. Indeed, it stiffly resented that Nelson had attacked them on the basis of mere 'rumour'.[21]

By then Nelson had already fired a crushing broadside into Lock after receiving from him an 'incomprehensible' and 'improper' letter of 3 December. In the new document, Lock had flattered himself that the private stories would be confirmed. Nelson fiercely replied that in that case he would put the whole matter before the Admiralty, and demand that they either supported or removed him. The admiral enlarged this announcement by accusing Lock of fabricating allegations against the pursers and captains for no higher purpose than to secure a contract to supply the navy with beef: 'Your never mentioning the [alleged] extraordinary price paid for fresh beef for the several days you were soliciting to have the exclusive privilege of supplying the fleet, and your refusal afterwards to bring forward any proof of fraud, warrants every expression in my letter to the Victualling Board. If you could bring proof of what you asserted, you are in the highest degree, as a public officer, criminal; and if you could not, your conduct is highly reprehensible.'[22]

The appalling prospect of the Board of Admiralty choosing between the hero of the Nile and an insignificant consul defeated the miserable Lock, who shrank from any further encounters. It was Hamilton who offered him a way out. He invited Lock to the Palazzo Palagonia to tender a written apology. Lock nervously appeared with his submission at the appointed hour, and Sir William effected a reconciliation. Nelson even shook the poor fellow's hand, dined with him a couple of times and offered to serve him. Seldom spiteful in the face of contrition, Nelson dispatched a more conciliatory letter to the Victualling Board. The youth, he explained, had been misled by 'false' and 'nonsensical' friends, and, as any enquiry could only end in his public ruin, Nelson wished to withdraw his request for one. 'It was justice to the public and a vindication of my own honour that I sought, and not ruin to a young man setting off in life with a family of children', a young man who had learned a 'lesson.'[23]

There the matter rested, but not without damage done. It seemed to inspire James Tough, the consul at Palermo, to make a bid for a victualling agency of his own, although the board made sure to leave the whole business to Nelson's management. From the point of view of the admiral's reputation, the letters of Lock's family suggest that allegations against Nelson's squadron had passed around private but influential gatherings. Keith certainly heard about them. Officially, they carried no weight, but informal whisperings can be corrosive, partly because they require neither limits nor verification, and they may have contributed to the undercurrent of dissatisfaction with Nelson's command.[24]

News of the return of Keith was not met in the Mediterranean with universal approbation. The brothers took it badly, for, although Keith was reliable and physically disarming with his thin face softened by sleepy eyes and a good-humoured mouth, he had a reputation for distance, a man who insisted his officers wore old-fashioned pigtails and who moved amidst an entourage of Scottish protégés. Ball, Troubridge, Hood, Blackwood and Louis all expressed their sorrow. 'I really offer myself to follow your fortunes during the war,' the latter wrote to Nelson. 'This comes from my heart.' He was, he said, not fond of new faces.[25]

3

One of Keith's priorities took him to the Gulf of Genoa, where he planned to cooperate with an Austrian army besieging Genoa, held tenaciously by the French. He declared a blockade of the coast and ordered Nelson to meet him in Leghorn, perhaps with a pointed intention of prising the admiral out of Palermo. Keith was careful and gracious. He explained that he had been promised additional military resources, and wanted to talk to Nelson about how they could assist Malta. The new commander-in-chief's views leaned towards Nelson's, for he too hoped to raise enough soldiers to save Britain the 'frightful' expense of the blockade. And Keith would like to serve Josiah Nisbet by sending the *Thalia* into profitable cruising grounds. By taking aboard pet projects of his fiery subordinate, Keith bade for peace and harmony. Nelson did not take the bait. On the evening of 16 January he grudgingly sailed north in the *Foudroyant*, having sent the *Thalia* ahead. He reached Leghorn in a few days, but kept much to his cabin, pestered largely by his servant, Tom Allen, whose broad Norfolk accent and rolling gait exemplified graphic autobiography.[26]

Close to the war in the north, Leghorn was a busy entrepôt for warships as well as merchantmen, and huge battleships like the *Foudroyant* and Keith's three-decked *Queen Charlotte* sat with Nisbet's *Thalia* and Hoste's brig, the *Mutine*. Nelson was unimpressed by Keith, and after an amicable but strained meeting must have found relief in inviting Hoste to dinner in the *Foudroyant*. William Hoste had just returned from Bronte, where he had delivered agricultural implements Nelson had purchased for his farm, and there was much to talk about. His lordship told the captain of the *Mutine* that he had recommended Keith to promote him. 'I leave you, my dear mother, to guess how greatly I was affected by his kindness,' William wrote home, 'for indeed, words will fall infinitely short of what I wish to express. It is exactly seven years since I left Godwick, and believe me, during the whole time he [Nelson] never altered his conduct with respect to me. I think every time I see him, he behaves with more kindness than ever.' Nelson was a 'second father', a touchstone to whom he could always return for advice and support, a veritable 'sheet anchor'. But the admiral himself was disconsolate. Keith was soon taking his force to Palermo, weighing on 25 January. Nelson recaptured a Ragusan prize from a French privateer along the way, but his only real solace was in writing longing loving letters to his mistress.[27]

'Separated from all I hold dear in this world, what is the use of living, if indeed such an existence can be called so?' he wrote on 29 January. Time and distance could not 'alter my love and affection for you. It is founded on the truest principles of honour, and it only remains for us to regret, which I do with the bitterest anguish, that there are any obstacles to our being united in the closest ties of this world's rigid rules, as we are in those of real love. Continue only to love your faithful Nelson as he loves his Emma. You are my guide. I submit to you.' The 'obstacles', of course, were Fanny and Sir William. In the meantime, as he sailed north, he had given Emma 'my word never to partake of any amusement or to sleep on shore'. Perhaps Lady Hamilton still feared that Adelaide Correglia lived in Leghorn, and might kindle some old flame into life. There was little likelihood of that, however, for the next day Nelson was deeming a life apart from Emma 'worse than death', and losing appetite and sleep 'thinking of you, my dearest love', and worrying whether she was being faithful to him and had 'equally kept' her 'promises to me'.[28]

Their love was going to be like this, intense and jealous, each aware of the other's chequered past, each afraid that they might be doomed to become another chapter in it. On 31 January Nelson was being driven 'mad' by the thought that he was twenty leagues further away from her than the day before. The previous night he had been tormented by an erotic dream. 'Last night I did nothing but dream of you, altho' I woke twenty times in the night. In one of my dreams I thought I was at a large table. You was not present. Sitting between a princess who I detest and another, they both tried to seduce me and the first wanted to take those liberties with me which no woman in this world but yourself ever did. The consequence was I knocked her down, and in the moment of bustle you came in and taking me in your embrace whispered, "I love nothing but you, my Nelson." I kissed you fervently, and we enjoyed the height of love. Ah, Emma, I pour out my soul to you.' The following day found him ruefully reckoning that 138 miles divided them. 'No love is like mine towards you,' he wrote to her.

This one letter exposes his inadequacy as an admiral at this time, shackled as he was to an inappropriate station by Love, and it tells us that his relationship with Emma had become one of sexual intimacy. Upon reaching his destination on 3 February he had only dismal news for Emma. 'Having a commander-in-chief, I cannot come on shore till I have made my manners to him. Times are changed . . . In the meantime, I send Allen to inquire how you are. Send me word, for I am anxious to hear of you. It has been no fault of mine that I have been so long absent. I cannot command, and now only obey.'[29]

The Hamiltons, in fact, were still discussing their own latest news. Sir William, who had merely asked permission to return to England for a period of leave, had been told he was to be replaced as Envoy Extraordinary and Plenipotentiary. Hamilton, too, had been undermined by the rumours, and Elgin for one had recommended his removal. In a letter that also reflected upon Nelson, Grenville wrote to Spencer that 'the account' he had received of 'the state of affairs' in Naples and Sicily 'made me judge that there was not an instant to be lost in sending there a man of activity and talent to replace Sir W. Hamilton, whom it was absolutely necessary to supersede'. Accordingly, the Hon. Arthur Paget, the twenty-nine-year-old son of Lord Uxbridge with experience as secretary of Legation in St Petersburg and Berlin, and, what was perhaps more important, the friendship of the Prince of Wales, had been sent to Sicily. When he realised that Paget's appointment was to be permanent, Sir William fretfully thought that he could stand it if the government would give him a pension of £2000 per annum. As he packed to go home, he owned that he was still very much in the dark about the whole thing, and knew not whether he had been 'kicked up or down out of my post'.[30]

Suddenly the community in the Palazzo Palagonia was on the brink of dissolution. The Hamiltons were going home, and with them the queen would lose an important lever on Nelson. Nelson, forced to bend to the will of a rival he disliked and doomed to be deprived of his muse, had little to keep him in Palermo. Sir William saw it and on 7 February urged, 'Advise get yourself well and come to your sincerely hearted friends, and let us go home together.' Even their great patron, General Acton, was sensing that change was in the air. Sixty-four years old, he was talking about retiring to England with his new wife – his thirteen-year-old niece!

Paget did not arrive in Palermo until 9 April, but Keith had already established a rapport with their Sicilian Majesties. On the day he arrived, Keith accompanied Nelson and the Hamiltons to the palace, where the new commander-in-chief was told that the survival of the kingdom was owed to 'Great Britain and the indefatigable zeal of Lord Nelson'. On 9 February the king and his senior ministers paid an official visit to Keith on the *Queen Charlotte*, reserving the *Foudroyant* for a breakfast appointment the following day. Keith was not impressed by what he saw in Palermo, not least the 'fulsome vanity and absurdity' of the Nelson–Hamilton household, in which he and his flag lieutenant and secretary were briefly accommodated. The hours the ménage kept, he noted, were 'beyond belief'. He knew he had a prima donna on his hands, but Keith was determined to put Nelson to work.[31]

Keith was not long in Palermo, but during those days Nelson met one of the commander-in-chief's lieutenants, a tall, gangling, red-haired Scot named Thomas, Lord Cochrane, the eldest son of a brilliant but impoverished peer. This was the sole occasion on which the two most spectacular naval commanders of the age met. Cochrane, then on the brink of his first command, recalled that Nelson was 'surrounded by the elite of Neapolitan society, amongst whom he was justly regarded as a deliverer'. But the admiral found time to give the lieutenant some advice, including the maxim 'Never mind manoeuvres, always go at them'. It was an exhortation to rely on Britain's battle superiority at sea, and to fight at close quarters, where it could tell to the greatest effect. Nelson never had an apter pupil, for Cochrane – the original of the fictional heroes of Captain Marryat, C. S. Forester and Patrick O'Brian – subsequently achieved an unparalleled record for combat against apparent odds.[32]

Determined to inject new power into the blockade of Malta, Keith revisited much ground that Nelson had already found barren. He unsuccessfully appealed to Ushakov and Portugal to stay the departure of their forces, and called in Ferdinand's promise to supply the additional troops Graham had once refused, as well as some small warships and gunboats. Almost immediately he ordered Nelson to accompany him with the first seven hundred of the Sicilian troops the king had supplied. On 12 February the *Foudroyant*, having embarked her quota of 154 soldiers, sailed with the *Queen Charlotte* and a frigate.[33]

Nelson's parting with Emma was difficult. Indeed, he commenced a period of full sexual relations with her the very day he left, if a letter he wrote in 1801 can be believed. 'Ah! My dear friend, I did remember well the 12th February, and also the two months afterwards. I shall never forget them, and never be sorry for the consequences.' Those consequences were, in fact, Emma's pregnancy, for their daughter, Horatia, was conceived about the end of April. Once afloat, he certainly detested every humiliating moment he was with Keith, and every league that took him further from Palermo, writing constantly about them, or to them:

Diary, 12 February: 'Sent my letters on board: two for Sir William, two for my lady.

Diary, 13 February: 'Wrote a line to Lady Hamilton, but no news or opinions, as they might be opened out of curiosity . . . Sent on board the *Queen Charlotte*. Had the pleasure of receiving letters from Sir William and Lady Hamilton.'

Letter to Emma, 13 February: 'To say how I miss your house and company would be saying little, but in truth you and Sir William have so spoiled me that I am not happy anywhere else but with you, nor have I an idea that I ever can be.'[34]

4

Nelson's opinion of Keith had not improved. Breakfasting with the commander-in-chief in the *Queen Charlotte* on 14 February, he could only note in a fragment of diary that 'everything was dirty and the table cloth not changed since he sailed. Got no indication of Lord Keith's intentions about me.' It was the anniversary of Cape St Vincent, and, back in his own flagship, Nelson summoned all the officers and midshipmen who had participated in the victory to his dinner table. But he felt unwell, lonely and dispirited. The next day they made Malta in a hard wind, and just in time.[35]

As long ago as December, Captain Blackwood of the *Penelope* had got intelligence from a ship that another significant relief force was fitting out in Toulon. It was not clear whether it was bound for the Genoese coast, Malta or both. In fact, the return of Bonaparte had raised the profile of Malta in France, for the island represented the vestige of his ambitions in the east. If it could be held, it could still be used to threaten southern Italy or invade the Levant or Egypt. A serious effort was soon underway to relieve Malta. Rear Admiral Jean Baptise Perrée flew his flag on *Le Généreux* of seventy-four guns, one of the two capital ships to escape at the battle of the Nile. The other, *Le Guillaume Tell*, was already trapped in Valletta. With Perrée was a large armed store ship, *Ville de Marseille*, the *Badine* frigate of twenty-four guns, and a couple of eighteen-gun corvettes, *Sans Pareil* and *Favorite*. Carrying extensive provisions and stores and nearly four thousand regulars to strengthen the dwindling garrison in Valletta, they left Toulon on 7 February. The importance of such a detachment was difficult to overestimate. If Perrée got into Valletta, he would greatly alleviate Vaubois's supply problems, and, more crucially, more than double the French military and naval forces, greatly imperilling the already inferior British, Maltese and Neapolitan besiegers. In short, Graham's force stood to be destroyed and the siege broken.[36]

It was truly remarkable that this, the most ambitious French attempt to break the stalemate at Malta, should approach its destination just as Keith and Nelson arrived on the station. Even now an engagement was by no means inevitable, given the stormy and foggy weather that prevailed. But the day the British admirals arrived at Marsa Scirocco Bay, south-east of Valletta, where they planned to land troops and stores, Keith learned that the frigate *Success* had seen five enemy sail off the west end of Sicily steering south-east. That this was a relief force seemed obvious. Postponing the landings, Keith signalled enemy ships to windward at SSE, and placed his huge three-decked flagship, the hundred-gun *Queen Charlotte*, with a few smaller ships in front of Valletta, blocking the goalmouth if we may borrow a sporting phrase once more. He directed the *Lion* to protect the passage between Gozo and Malta, the *Alexander*, commanded in Ball's absence by Lieutenant William Harrington, to guard the south-east side of the island, and Nelson to chase to windward with the rest of the squadron in search of the French. The wind, a powerful south-easterly, was foul for hunters and hunted, and visibility was reduced by savage rain, but Nelson carried what sail he could as his old fighting spirit reclaimed him.[37]

By dark Nelson was east of the island, and impatient for a new piece of glory. Scattered about were Gould's *Audacious*, Martin's *Northumberland* and Harrington's *Alexander*, as well as the *Success* frigate under Shouldham Peard and the tiny *El Corso*. For more than two days the search continued in poor conditions, while the wind veered to the north-west. On the afternoon of the 17th the *Lion* signalled an enemy to the NW, and the ships chased that way as best they could. Then, at about five or six in the morning, as dawn spread its shadows over the sea, the men on the flagship heard signal guns barking to the north-west, and Nelson bore up under full sail. The *Alexander*, standing to the westward since the previous afternoon, had encountered four of the French ships, and firing upon the *Ville de Marseille* store ship forced her to strike in about seven minutes, at about a quarter past eight. Apart from stores, she carried three hundred soldiers and a crew of two hundred. Coming up, Nelson signalled *Audacious* and *El Corso* to secure the prize, while he pursued the others with three sail of the line and a frigate. At 1.30 in the afternoon the French ships tacked to the west, but their flagship was unable to do so without engaging the oncoming *Alexander* and bore up eastward. She was soon being overhauled by the nimbler *Foudroyant* and *Northumberland*.[38]

One can sense Nelson's revived spirit in the accounts of the chase, especially after he realised that the enemy flagship might be *Le Généreux*. He told Berry to 'make the *Foudroyant* fly', something that would have pleased the captain, since *Le Généreux* was the same that had taken the *Leander* in 1798, and in which Berry and Thompson had spent an undignified captivity. When *Northumberland* appeared to gain the better of *Foudroyant* during the chase, Nelson became excited, 'working' the stump of his amputated arm as he was wont to do on such occasions, and driving his men with a good-natured but firm urgency. 'This will not do, Sir Ed'ard,' he said. 'It is certainly *Le Généreux*, and to my flagship she can alone surrender.' After rounding on the quartermaster at the conn ('I'll knock you off your perch, you rascal, if you are so inattentive') he observed a British sail to leeward. 'Youngster,' said he, addressing the signal-midshipman, 'to the masthead. What! Going without your glass, and be damned to you? Let me know what she is immediately.' When the boy shouted that the stranger was the *Success*, Nelson signalled the undersized cruiser to attempt to cut off the French seventy-four. 'Great odds though,' he reflected. However, when firing began, and Nelson noted the alarm in the face of one of his 'young gentlemen', he patted the boy on the head and 'asked him jocularly how he relished the music', consoling him 'with the information that Charles XII [of Sweden] ran away from the first shot he heard, though afterwards he was called "The Great" . . . from his bravery. "I, therefore," said Lord Nelson, "hope much from you in future."'[39]

Parsons cannot have remembered the details as comprehensively as he would have us believe, and he is manifestly in error in places, but his impression of Nelson's energy finds confirmation in notes that the admiral wrote as the event actually unfolded. It was as if he needed to record his own exhilaration and triumph. 'Pray God we may get alongside of them,' he scribbled. 'The event [result] I leave to Providence. I think if I can take one 74 by myself, I would retire and give the staff to more able hands.'[40]

About four o'clock the *Success* boldly lay across the Frenchman's hawse 'with great judgement and gallantry', raking him with one broadside and then wearing to deliver the other. In return she took a broadside from *Le Généreux*, suffering ten casualties, including her master, but at 4.30 *Foudroyant* and *Northumberland* came up and the battle ended quickly. The French had courage, and cheered the British ships as they arrived, almost as if they willed an end to their adventure. Unperturbed, the *Foudroyant* fired two ranging shots at the French flagship, and she returned a token broadside and then surrendered to escape a serious mauling. Berry's first lieutenant, Andrew Thompson, took a prize crew aboard and found twenty-four dead and wounded on the Frenchman, including Admiral Perrée, who lay dying on the quarterdeck after both his legs had been taken off by a shot from the *Success*. But the ship contained numerous provisions and stores and 1300 men, 500 of them soldiers. The incident took place ten leagues off Cape Passero, in Sicily, and Nelson detailed the *Northumberland* and *Alexander* to escort the prize to Syracuse, the nearest port, while the flagship herself attempted to find the remains of the enemy convoy. Nelson characteristically closed the account in his diary with the words, 'Thank God'.[41]

It had not been the most dramatic victory, but it was certainly an important one – the decisive engagement of the entire two-year blockade. Two ships, one of them of the line, had been taken, and their convoy scattered, and Graham was released from the 'damned funk' he had got himself into. None of Perrée's vessels got to their destination, and the blockade of Malta was rescued from disaster. As usual, Nelson's dispatch of the same day praised effusively. 'I attribute our success . . . principally . . . to the extreme good management of Lieutenant William Harrington, who commanded the *Alexander* . . . and I am much pleased with the gallant behaviour of Captain Peard . . . as also with the alacrity and good conduct of Captain Martin and Sir Edward Berry,' he wrote to Keith. He was excited about his own role, too, and enthusiastically wrote to Minto that he had now been instrumental in taking nineteen ships of the line and four admirals during the war.[42]

The sequel was less satisfying. The French prisoners were riddled with typhus fever, a potentially fatal malady associated with insanitary and overcrowded conditions, and the *Northumberland* soon had forty men down and 'more [were] falling down every day'. By the middle of March Captain Martin had isolated 106 men in a camp ashore, and Nelson had authorised additional provisions and medicines. Only less irritating, when Nelson rejoined Lord Keith off Valletta the day after the engagement he found him 'too great to appear pleased at the captures'. More disconcerting as far as Nelson was concerned, when he slipped in his notion of returning to Palermo or hauling down his flag completely, the commander-in-chief showed little alarm. Keith refused to grant permission for the admiral to return to Palermo, which was 'too far out of the way of everything', particularly when the commander-in-chief would soon have to leave Malta for Genoa. However, if Nelson's health forced him to withdraw to Sicily, he might do so as long as he did not take a capital ship from Malta. Keith was doing his best in a difficult situation, but a better manager could have closed the rift between the two admirals at that point by praising Nelson's achievement and enthusiastically insisting that his presence was indispensable to Malta. That was the type of language Nelson understood. He freely used it to others, and craved it in return. All Keith offered was indifference. The commander-in-chief rubbed it in by using *Le Généreux* to reward his followers. Dixon was eventually appointed to command the prize, Lord William Stuart and Jahleel Brenton moved up to the *Lion* and *Guerrier* respectively, and Lord Cochrane, who piloted the crippled *Le Généreux* through terrible storms to Minorca, got his first command in the *Speedy* sloop.[43]

Nelson was happier in the exaggerations of friends. He sent the French admiral's flag to a delighted Prince Leopold and his sword to the tsar. Ball gushed to Emma about 'a heaven-born admiral, upon whom Fortune smiles wherever he goes', and emphasised the extraordinary fact that Nelson had appeared off Malta just as the first serious attempt to break the blockade in sixteen months occurred. But his success was due to more than luck, Ball added: 'We shall not meet such another. Such rare qualities seldom combine in one person.'[44]

Nelson agreed, and used the late engagement to make further distinctions between the commander-in-chief and himself. To be fair, he was provoked by Keith's dispatch of 20 February. Keith emphasised his own contribution to the success, claiming that Nelson's squadron had only acted in accordance with his signal to chase on the 15th. 'His Lordship,' said Keith, 'has on this occasion, as on all others, conducted himself with skill and great address in comprehending my signals, which the state of the weather led me greatly to suspect.' This ignored Nelson's independent initiative over the following three days, and sounded suspiciously like self-promotion. Nelson boiled, and sent Spencer extracts of his journal to prove that *Le Généreux* was taken according to 'my plan' and not Keith's. In fact, said Nelson, Keith had directed a chase to the south-east, which Nelson subsequently altered to the north-west at his 'own risk', using his knowledge of the area to predict a different course for the French convoy. The success, therefore, depended upon Nelson's established disobedience to the instructions of incompetent superiors.[45]

It was unseemly of both parties, and Nelson's jealousy of Keith was never clearer than in this untypically mean attempt to besmirch his commander-in-chief. The spoils in prize and head money might have been a minor factor. Half of the agency concerning the prizes was surrendered to Keith's brother and secretary to keep the commander-in-chief happy, but when Cochrane took *Le Généreux* to Minorca Nelson made sure that his secretary and local prize agent, John Tyson, was aboard to handle such formalities. However, the issues between the two men were largely personal. In insisting that Keith had had no part in the victory, he did not stop to realise the importance, for example, of Keith's timely reinforcement of the blockade, and – even more telling – that, had Nelson not been ordered to Malta, entirely against his inclinations, he could never have captured *Le Généreux* in the Palazzo Palagonia.

For the first time Keith saw for himself the strength of the enemy defences at Malta, but, like Ball and Nelson, he refused to be defeated, and detected three places where he suspected the French might be vulnerable. His answer was theirs, and he wrote to Fox and Whitehall for reinforcements, eventually helping to bring two additional regiments to Malta. In the short term, however, he seemed to be baying at the moon. When he urged Fox to spare two thousand men to strengthen Graham's force against enemy counterattacks, the general replied that not only had he no authority to release such a force, but also that if Graham was in 'any danger' his force should immediately be withdrawn. Graham's morale was in steady decline. Even the arrival of the Sicilians only gave him 2092 regulars fit for duty. A new Maltese Light Battalion was being formed, partly at Graham's expense, and two companies, clad in blue-grey sashes and nankeen trousers, and armed with French muskets, were being drilled by April, but Graham voiced little faith in them. As he complained to Hamilton, 'from the first I have strongly felt the disadvantage of being employed where such sanguine hopes had been so unaccountably raised with a force not only totally inadequate to any exertion that could contribute to realise them, but which in strictness, according to my instructions, scarcely justified my remaining here'. Exaggerating the strength of his enemy, he even declined to harass the French for fear of provoking a counterattack he could not handle. In fact both forces seemed sapped of confidence or aggression, and sat stubbornly watching each other over the fortifications, hoping some external intervention would put an end to their misery.[46]

Nelson and Keith shared the view that something might be done to end the blockade, but beyond that their relationship remained dysfunctional. On 26 February Keith turned the blockade of Malta over to Nelson, and returned to his duties further north. There was an unfortunate pedagogical element in the instructions he left behind, as if he was admonishing an unreliable schoolboy. Nelson was pointedly told that Palermo was too far away to be a satisfactory base, and that he should use Syracuse instead. Moreover, he should keep his ships ready to 'proceed upon distant service' at all times – an echo of the Admiralty's charge that Nelson had locked ships into campaigns from which they could not be retrieved – and 'at this critical time I cannot consent to any of them quitting your station' except in the unlikely event that Nelson received substantial reinforcements. Nelson resented being disciplined, and replied the same day. His health was so bad, he said, that he had to return 'to my friends at Palermo for a few weeks, and leave the command here to Commodore Troubridge. Nothing but absolute necessity obliges me to write this letter.' Without rest, he was 'gone'. Wearily, Keith offered no more resistance, but went north to cooperate with the Austrians, who were besieging Genoa, now without their Russian allies who had withdrawn from the war. His reply, when it came, almost accused Nelson of a dereliction of duty. He regretted that Nelson should feel unable to remain at Malta, for the blockade was reaching a 'momentous' phase; Troubridge was ill; and Keith's flagship, *Queen Charlotte*, had been accidentally destroyed by fire with a huge loss of life, preventing him from returning to Malta. The rebuke administered, Keith demanded that if Nelson did retire to Sicily he should at least ensure that the *Foudroyant* was restored to its station off Malta.[47]

Ball and Troubridge also urged Nelson to stay. *Le Guillaume Tell*, *Diane* and *Justice*, the last of the Nile ships, were still in Valletta but ready for sea, perhaps preparing to run for it with the French high command, papers and treasury, leaving the fortifications to the allies. The blockaders sensed that their travail was coming to an end, and it was fitting that Nelson, whose campaign it had largely been, should be there to receive the surrender. 'I dined with his Lordship yesterday, who is apparently in good health,' Ball wrote to Emma, 'but he complains of indisposition and the necessity of repose. I do not think a short stay here will hurt his health, particularly as his ship is at anchor, and his mind not harassed.' Guessing that Nelson was really missing the Hamiltons, Ball suggested that they come to Malta. 'What a gratification it would be to us if you and Sir William could pay us a short visit. We could make up a snug whist party every evening for Sir William.' Nor was it a contemptible ploy. As a result of Nelson's overtures to the tsar, both Ball and Emma had been awarded the Order of St John of Jerusalem on account of their service to the island, and Ball had taken to addressing Lady Hamilton, the first Dame of the order, as his 'dear lady and sister'. Flattered to bits with her honour, Emma was telling Sir William that she would at least like to see Malta before she returned to England.[48]

To all entreaties to remain Nelson protested his health. Morbid references to decline and death in his letters betokened general unhappiness as much as physical ailment, but the months at Palermo had improved his material condition. The occlusions in his eyes persisted, and he was 'always in a fever'. On 26 February he 'dropped with a pain in my heart', and started worrying that 'the vessels of the heart' were becoming inflamed with stress, especially as he recalled having endured a similar affliction during that worry-ridden voyage from Egypt to Syracuse in the summer of 1798. A modern authority has related the attacks to a severe hiatus hernia, although his last surgeon, William Beatty, was sure it was indigestion. Nelson also believed that he had gout, a common ailment of eighteenth-century gentlemen, and wrote to the British consul at Corfu seeking the 'infallible remedy' for that complaint said to exist in those parts.[49]

During their brief reunification at Malta, Nelson and Troubridge continued to relate to each other with an exceptional intensity, each ready to protest tearfully at any fancied lapses of attention from the other. Nelson complained that Troubridge had not called upon him, and the other replied that the accusation had 'really so unhinged me that I am quite unmanned and crying. I would sooner forfeit my life, my everything, than be deemed ungrateful to an officer and friend I feel I owe so much to. Pray, pray acquit me, for I really do not merit it. There is not a man on earth I love, honour and esteem more than your Lordship.' Troubridge knew about illness. He was jaundiced, feverish and spitting blood, but perhaps because he loved Nelson so much he begged him to stay at Malta. Why, Sir Thomas was ready to raise Nelson's flag in the *Culloden* to get him away from the negligent Berry. 'Everything shall be done to make it comfortable and pleasing to you. A month will do all. If you comply with my request, I shall be happy, as I shall then be convinced I have not forefeited your friendship.'[50]

But Nelson would not stay. For several weeks of dirty weather, he persevered, using ten or so warships, including five of the line, *Alexander*, *Foudroyant*, *Audacious*, *Lion* and *Culloden*. One night at the beginning of March a squall drove Nelson's ship towards the French batteries and one of their shots bit a chunk from his fore topmast, but this necessary if dreary service could not compete with the attractions of Palermo. Fresh beef and repairs claimed much of Nelson's attention, as well as the disagreeable court martial of one of his captains, George Miller of the *Minorca*, on charges of abusing his crew, but little happened afloat or ashore. Graham showed no offensive capability, so convinced of his military inferiority that he dared not hit out lest the enemy struck back. Both sides looked across miles of fortifications they could not possibly man, overwhelmed by their weaknesses, and exerting themselves only with a spasmodic and useless fire, waiting for starvation or a relief force to change their situation.[51]

Unfortunately, during Nelson's watch a French corvette slipped into Valletta with provisions on the night of 4 March, giving the faltering French garrison another few months of food. The admiral may have been at fault. His ships were apparently stationed to the north-east of Valletta, and Ball said that he should have had a cruiser north-west of Gozo to intercept vessels stealing along Malta's northern shore. Nelson did post the *Success* in that area before he left, but too late to shut out the provision ship.[52]

On 10 March he finally handed the command back to Troubridge, pleading 'illness' and promising that the *Foudroyant* would be sent back to Malta as soon as possible, although it must be kept ready to collect him 'at a moment's notice'. Once at Palermo, Nelson switched his flag to a transport, sent the *Foudroyant* back, and ordered four Neapolitan gunboats for Malta, but it scarcely exonerated him. Troubridge, racked with fever, was no fitter than Nelson, but stoutly resisted Hamilton's invitation to join the Palermo set. 'I must stick to my post as long as I can, as Death does not give me much concern,' he answered grimly. The temporary absence of the *Foudroyant* deprived him of the most powerful and nimble ship of the line at a time when the French eighty-gun *Guillaume Tell* looked about to run the blockade and only nine British ships of all sizes were fit to keep the sea. Troubridge had to send the decrepit *Culloden* out cruising. Of his other ships, the *Northumberland* was scourged with sickness, the *Lion* short of water, and the only ship he had capable of catching the *Guillaume Tell* was the *Penelope*, an outgunned frigate. During the eighteen days the *Foudroyant* was missing the British were fortunate that only one small settee with dispatches got into Valletta. While Troubridge did what he could Nelson brooded in Palermo. Unable to gain perspective, to confront his own shortcomings or envisage the world through Keith's or Spencer's eyes, he was sick at heart, and hated serving under Keith. As he confessed to Emma, 'to say the truth' it was his 'uneasy mind at being taught my lesson like a school boy' that aggravated. 'We of the Nile,' he wrote to Troubridge, 'are not equal to Lord Keith in his estimation, and ought to think it an honour to serve under such a clever man.'[53]

In Palermo a Roman Catholic priest named Henry Campbell, formerly attached to the Neapolitan embassy in London, had arrived with papers for the Sicilian court. He also brought a rumour – a false one as it happened – that Keith's spell in the Mediterranean would be short-lived. Nelson wondered whether he would become commander-in-chief after all, but there was no longer any question of his remaining on station when the Hamiltons were being recalled. In letters written to Nelson at Malta, Sir William said all that needed to be said. 'If possible, let us go home together,' he wrote. And more forcefully, the next day, 'Come back to *your family* here, who love you and honour you to the bottom of their souls.' The hero of Aboukir was going home.[54]

5

During the first week in June Genoa surrendered to the Austrian and British allies, and the French were pushed westwards. It was the high-water mark of the coalition's success, because suddenly, with terrifying speed, its situation deteriorated. Just as Nelson consigned himself to quitting the Mediterranean, the pendulum of war swung fiercely in the opposite direction.

Until then the theatre had been deceptively quiet. If we review his situation, Nelson's tasks were largely in the way of unfinished business. Finding more space, he had the idea of settling with the Barbary powers, for despite his progress with Tunis and Tripoli, Neapolitan and Maltese ships were still being taken, some possessing Nelson's passports. Nelson considered making a punitive strike against Algiers, where sixty-five Maltese and Neapolitan prisoners remained captive in November 1799. 'Demand nothing that is not just, and never recede, and settle the whole [issue] in half-an-hour' was his lordship's advice to Spencer.[55]

In Egypt Nelson's demand for total surrender had almost been destroyed by a new round of negotiations between the French army and the Ottoman Porte. After Bruix's failure to reach Egypt, the luckless Jean-Baptiste Kléber, who had succeeded to the command of the isolated force, was as eager to escape his imprisonment as the Turks were to oust him, and a 'treaty' of El Arish was concluded in January 1800. It allowed the enemy passage to France, with all stores, artillery and baggage, and guaranteed the safety of their shipping in Alexandria. Despite Nelson's positive orders to Sidney Smith that the French must not leave except as prisoners of war, Britain's representatives in the east made no appreciable attempts to halt the process. The Smiths condoned it, and Elgin, who took over the diplomatic mission in Constantinople, helplessly accepted it as a *fait accompli*. When Nelson heard of the 'treaty' in March, he instructed his captains to seize any vessels coming from Egypt, whatever passports they carried, and so wrote to all allies concerned. The *Santa Dorotea* did intercept two vessels loaded with French in April. But the El Arish affair imploded in chaos. The British government disapproved of the agreement, but felt they were honour bound to abide by it, and sent new orders to the Mediterranean through gritted teeth. It was too late. Acting on his previous orders from the Admiralty, and without any knowledge of El Arish, Keith had already reinforced Nelson's policy. Furthermore, mistakenly assuming that Britain had rejected the treaty, Kléber renewed hostilities and effectively buried it himself. Another year would pass before a British army finally landed in Egypt, defeated the French and brought the whole sorry saga to an end.

The other open wound, Malta, also lurched towards closure during Nelson's remaining days in the Mediterranean. Perrée's failure, like Bruix's, had greatly discouraged the Gallic holdouts. The corvette that had run the blockade in March had given Vaubois another few months, but the end was plainly in sight. In the first hours of 30 March the largest of the French ships, *Le Guillaume Tell*, tried to break out, perhaps hoping to relieve the pressure on the garrison's dwindling supplies, perhaps in a last desperate attempt to bring relief from outside. Alerted by lookouts they had posted ashore, the British were ready, and a three and a half hour fight ensued in which three British ships, two of them inferior in firepower, overpowered the last of the Nile line of battle ships. Flying the flag of Rear Admiral Denis Decrès, *Le Guillaume Tell* was exceptionally well armed, her total armament of eighty-six guns consisting of lower-deck thirty-six-pounders, main deck twenty-four-pounders, quarterdeck twelve-pounders and poop deck thirty-two-pound carronades. She carried 1220 men, including a few Maltese Jacobins, and statues and artworks stolen from the island. Much of the credit for her defeat belonged to Captain Henry Blackwood, whose frigate, the *Penelope*, intercepted and engaged the big eighty-gunner, firing ruthless raking broadsides into the stern of the giant Frenchman within musket range, and bringing down his topmasts and yards. Dixon's sixty-four-gun *Lion* joined the fight at daylight, and belatedly also the *Foudroyant* under a sluggish Berry. *Le Guillaume Tell* surrendered after losing all masts and two hundred casualties. The frigates *Diane* and *Justice*, remained in Valletta Harbour with six other warships, but now the battle fleet that had resisted Nelson's attack in Aboukir Bay had been effectively annihilated.

Troubridge would have given a thousand guineas to have seen Nelson there, and Berry too, it seems. 'I had but one wish,' he told Hamilton. 'Need I tell you it was the presence of him who first led me to glory, one who has impressed me with sentiments far above myself, which I am ever reflecting on with gratitude.' Having said that, the engagement also demonstrated how Nelson had endangered the blockade when he removed the *Foudroyant*, 'If the *Foudroyant* had not arrived here, nothing we have could have looked at her,' said Troubridge. But the admiral was jubilant for the men who had performed well in a stiff fight that had cost 127 British casualties, seventy-five of them in the *Foudroyant*, including several wounded midshipmen, Granville Proby, Thomas Cole, and Edward West whose upper right thigh was slashed to the bone by a splinter. The ship herself had sustained significant damage to her masts and bowsprit, and Nelson's cabin had been swept by shot that damaged Emma's chair, the admiral's wardrobe and bookcase and a portrait of King Ferdinand. The role of his favourite flagship thrilled Nelson immeasurably. 'I love her as a fond father, a darling child, and glory in her deeds,' he told Spencer. And to her captain he assured, 'I have no cause for sorrow [at not being there]. The thing could not be better done, and I would not, for all the world, rob you of one particle of your well-earned laurels . . . Thanks, ten thousand thanks, to my brave friends!' Keith learned, 'I Thank God I was not present, for it would finish me could I have taken a sprig off these brave men's laurels. They are, and I glory in them, my darling children, served in my school, and all of us caught our professional zeal and fire from the great and good Earl of St Vincent.' He got in words for Ball, Captain George Ormsby, a volunteer aboard the *Penelope*, among others.[56]

To Blackwood he was particularly grateful, recognising in him a genuine kindred spirit. Before being consigned to the daily battle with the spring gales off Malta, he had distinguished himself cruising, and cut out six vessels from Monaco. Now the skill and courage he had shown in his unequal battle with *Le Guillaume Tell* had given him a permanent place among the great frigate captains. 'My dear Blackwood,' Nelson wrote to him, 'is there a sympathy which ties men together in the bonds of friendship without having a personal knowledge of each other? If so, which I believe, it was so to you. I was your friend and acquaintance before I saw you. Your conduct and character in the late glorious occasion stamps your fame beyond the reach of envy. It was like yourself – it was like the *Penelope*! Thanks, and say everything kind for me to your brave officers and men.' No words were more deserved or would ever be treasured more.[57]

When the battered *Foudroyant* brought the prize into Palermo, and reclaimed Nelson's flag, she was beset by visitors, among them the queen and three princesses, who insisted on seeing the wounded, including poor West, a 'fine apple-cheeked bold boy' who 'had shrunken into a withered . . . old man . . . a ghastly spectacle'. If Parsons is to be believed, the youth died in their presence. He had come out to the Mediterranean in the *Vanguard* in 1798. Knowing that the wounds were gangrenous, Nelson took the dying midshipman by the hand, praising his courage, and whispering whatever beautiful lies he hoped might keep him alive. West closed his eyes for the last time believing that he had been promoted a lieutenant on account of his gallantry.[58]

Nelson took the event as the final release from his toil. 'Thus,' he wrote to Nepean on 4 April, 'owing to my brave friends is the entire capture and destruction of the French Mediterranean fleet to be attributed, and my orders from the great Earl of St Vincent fulfilled . . . My task is done, my health is finished, & probably my retreat [retirement] for ever fixed.'[59]

6

For all Nelson's self-righteousness, he must have known that he was disappointing members of his profession, the brothers who had begged him to stay off Malta as well as his superiors in London and on station. He who had once been the fleet's greatest asset was now underperforming and becoming a hindrance to his commander-in-chief, a prima donna turning into a passenger. Minto wrote that Nelson did 'not seem at all conscious of the sort of discredit he has fallen into' or that he was 'being foolish about a woman who has art enough to make fools of many wiser than an admiral'. Nelson was certainly capable of denying unpalatable truths, but the references to sadness and broken spirits that appear in his correspondence at this time suggest that inside he knew that his reputation was being tarnished and that it was in a good measure his own fault. Because he wanted so much to be his country's hero, and because he had consciously striven to achieve more than any other, he felt his failure. But, paradoxically, it was at this time that he was finding a rare solace, in the domestic sphere. His passion for Lady Hamilton was now more intense than ever before, and she and Palermo had become the centre of his world. He was happy in that world, behind closed doors, but when the doors opened and he strode on to the public stage, he no longer felt he commanded it, and the audiences sounded muted. A strange combination, this private ecstasy and public sorrow.[60]

Of many troubled by Nelson's behaviour that spring, few had more at stake than Earl Spencer, first lord of the Admiralty. The first lord was used to the admiral's anguished letters and usually tried to oblige and humour him, although he had not always satisfied. Most recently he had been unable to make Maurice Nelson a commissioner of the Navy Board or promote Lieutenant William Bolton on account of the engagement with *Le Généreux*, and he had not felt justified in appointing Nelson commander-in-chief of the Mediterranean when a steady hand like Keith's stood expectantly by. On 25 April, Spencer reminded

Nelson of the favours he had done his 'eleves and followers', and complained that the admiral's veiled charge of ingratitude was unjust.[61]

Spencer also approved of Keith's attempt to energise Nelson, and tried to support it. He was convinced that Palermo suited neither Nelson's pocket nor his health. It would be a pity if Nelson quitted the station, he wrote to the wayward hero, because Malta and *Le Guillaume Tell* were his particular 'due'. But for the admiral's sake as well as the good of the service, Spencer ventured some home truths. If the enemy fleet reappeared in the Mediterranean, he said, 'I should be much concerned to hear that you learnt of their arrival . . . either on shore or in a transport at Palermo.'

Keith's problem was that he had an admiral pleading incapacity and waiving, contradicting and interfering with most of the commander-in-chief's orders. The misuse of the *Foudroyant*, the best ship the British had in those parts, was one example, and the *Speedy* sloop another, which Nelson redeployed to Malta, any contrary orders notwithstanding. On 3 April, Nelson wrote to Keith from Palermo. He wanted 'a temporary release' and permission to return to England with the Hamiltons, springing further demands on the commander-in-chief's ships. As Keith had lost his flagship, the *Queen Charlotte*, in a fire, Nelson no longer felt justified in asking for permission to use the *Foudroyant* for his passage home. But he hoped she might carry his retinue to Gibraltar, and supposed Keith 'would not think it right to send me home in a store ship or in anything less than one of the large frigates', as 'our family' consisted of not less than six persons with their 'innumerable' servants. In addition, he indicated that Maria Carolina was thinking of travelling to the mainland with her family and before he left the station he might need the *Foudroyant* to give them passage.[62]

On 9 May the first lord authorised Keith to use the first ship he sent to England to bring Nelson home, if he wished to leave the Mediterranean. The same day he also wrote to Nelson, repeating his belief that Malta still needed his attention; but if he was truly 'exhausted' the first lord was 'quite clear, and I believe I am joined in opinion by all your friends here, that you will be more likely to recover your health and strength in England than in an inactive situation at a foreign court, however pleasing the respect and gratitude shown to you for your services [there] . . . I trust that you will take in good part what I have taken the liberty to write to you as a friend.' Spencer was saying that it had to be Malta or nothing, and Nelson did not like what he read. In June he complained that the letter, and that word 'inactive' had caused him 'much pain'.[63]

Spencer's well-meant attempt to bring Nelson into line was wounding because it confirmed the admiral's deep-seated fear that his reputation, honour and sense of duty had been compromised. He owned that he was 'a broken-hearted man', and the Palazzo Palagonia was scarcely a restful place, especially after 9 April, when Sir William's successor, Paget, finally arrived in Palermo. The situation replayed the meeting of Nelson and Keith, with stony exchanges, in which

Hamilton stubbornly insisted that he was only returning to England temporarily on health grounds, and was in no sense making way for the newcomer. He delayed presenting Paget's credentials to the court, the indispensable act by which one diplomat turned over his affairs to another. Paget replied in kind. He declined to disclose his instructions to Hamilton, sought no advice as if the older man had none of value to give, and bristled when he discovered that Emma was stigmatising him to their Majesties as 'a Jacobin and coxcomb, a person sent to bully and to carry them . . . back to Naples'. Paget reported to Grenville that 'Lord Nelson has given more or less into all this nonsense', and according to Keith the admiral had 'been violent with Mr Paget'. Nelson was present when Paget was finally introduced to the queen. The new ambassador waited for the best part of an hour before Maria Carolina, followed by Nelson and the Hamiltons, entered the room and spared him a mere sentence or two in welcome. Acton was kinder, but upon hearing of it the usually tranquil Sir William exploded, complaining that Acton had 'trod upon' and 'betrayed' his old comrade. The winners and losers of the palace revolution slipped into opposite camps. Paget, in fact, lodged with the Locks and went riding with them, and he corresponded with Lord Keith, who even revived the consul's ambition to become an agent for provisions. They lacked the glamour of the famous ménage and were all hated by their Majesties (the queen thought Paget 'one of those young folks devoted to the chase and coursing the hare'), but they were the new powers with whom the monarchy would have to deal. Paget's letters said little of Nelson, which speaks as to how how irrelevant the admiral had become.[64]

To escape, the ménage retreated to the *Foudroyant*, where friends abounded and it was possible to believe that the world was other than it was. The *Foudroyant* reappeared in Palermo on 21 April, in accordance with the admiral's wishes, and Nelson restored his flag to her. The voyage was not devoid of business, since Nelson intended visiting Malta, but bore more the character of a relaxing cruise. The Hamiltons abandoned the court and their squabbles to Paget and shipped aboard, along with such cronies as Cornelia Knight, a Maltese nobleman named Mushkin Pushkin, Lieutenant Thomas Staines, formerly of the *Petterel*, and an unidentified elderly English couple. Nelson offered a 'good but unostentatious' table in a cabin furnished with such novelties as the latest publications Fanny had sent from home, four muskets captured on the *San Josef* three years before, the flagstaff of the *L'Orient*, and part of William Tell's plumed cap from the figurehead of *Le Guillaume Tell*. They sailed on 24 April, but contrary winds made the opening leg of the voyage to Syracuse overlong and disagreeable, and Nelson 'suffered' throughout, probably of seasickness. Spirits were so low that when Emma celebrated her thirty-fifth birthday on board the ship, Miss Knight composed verses to the tune of 'Hearts of Oak', and all joined in song:

Come, cheer up, fair Delia, forget all thy grief,
For thy shipmates are brave and a hero's their chief.[65]

There was, nevertheless, a bittersweet element to this cruise, which took an eighty-gun ship beyond the ken of a needy commander-in-chief, and secured moments of peace with a select company. Cornelia recorded it in twenty-six recently discovered watercolours, portraying sketches of the memorable sights they saw, just as a modern tourist might accumulate holiday photographs. Beginning with a view of Torre d'Orlando on the southern coast of Sicily, she sketched the wonders of Sicily, Syracuse, Malta and Palermo, and in one portrayed Nelson and his mistress proceeding by boat into the Anapo River to examine the ruined Temple of Zeus. They breathe the tranquillity that Nelson remembered. Almost a year later he wrote to Emma wistfully, 'When I consider that this day nine months was your birthday, and that although we had a gale of wind, yet I was happy, and sung "Come Cheer up Fair Emma." Even the thought, compared with this day, makes me melancholy.' He spoke of the cruise as a lost treasure, but he had also gained one, for on it, or perhaps in Malta, the lovers conceived the child that was to be Horatia.[66]

They arrived in St Paul's Bay on the north-east coast of Malta on 3 May. The motive for the visit to Malta is uncertain. Emma had wanted to see the island since being made a Dame of the Order of St John, and both Troubridge and Ball had urged Nelson to return, Ball preparing a furnished house for the ménage a few miles from his own. They stayed on the island until the 20th, dining occasionally with Ball at San Anton palace, a seventeenth-century mansion that served as his seat, some four miles west of the Grand Harbour of Valletta. Troubridge received them at Marsa Scirocco Bay, where the crippled *Culloden* was moored and a depot for stores and provisions had been established, and the admiral found time to confer with Graham. The situation of the island naturally figured prominently throughout these discussions, but Ball gave up trying to persuade Nelson to stay when he saw how 'harassed and fatigued with anxiety' he was.[67]

Keith, wrapped up in the operations off Genoa, could barely discover what his second in command was doing. Nelson had written from Palermo to say that he was bound for Malta, but almost all his other news was disturbing. As he had the Hamiltons aboard, the purposes of the voyage were somewhat mystifying, and references to the *Foudroyant*'s need for repairs to her masts and bowsprit and his own health indicated that Nelson was flagging up an ominous desire to have the ship for his voyage home, where both could be put in order. Even more alarming to Keith, Nelson's last from Malta stated that he intended to withdraw both the *Foudroyant* and *Alexander* from Malta to carry the queen's suite to the Italian mainland. To deprive the blockade of its two best ships of the line, leaving the undersized *Lion* the only seaworthy capital ship on the station, was close to negligence. And it may have prolonged the blockade for up to another three months, because nineteen days after Nelson left another French corvette, *La Marguerite*, brought provisions into Valletta. Keith regarded Nelson's action as irresponsible, and so did the Tsar of Russia, who darkly suspected that the British were deliberately allowing ships through their blockade to stop the island being restored to the Knights of St John and falling under Russian influence.[68]

Nelson's biographers have not concerned themselves with Keith's dilemma. The French were 'straining every nerve' to reinforce Malta, and Keith's ships intercepted another corvette bound for the island soon after it left Toulon. With Vaubois approaching his last gasp, a real chance of closing the Maltese affair was being damaged by Nelson's interference. Perhaps Nelson's complacency was based on a belief that British troops might be on their way to reinforce Graham, as he wrote Acton, but his conduct was still negligent. Equally infuriating to Keith, Nelson was almost routinely denying the commander-in-chief control of his ships, sequestrating them for comparatively frivolous purposes of his own. Despite this, Keith remained composed. Writing to Nelson on 6 May he was 'in wonder what Hamilton is to do in Malta', but emphasised what should have been obvious, his distress for ships. When Keith heard that Nelson had returned to Palermo with *Foudroyant* and *Culloden*, his letter of 5 June was stronger. 'I can by no means admit of the king's ships being, at this moment, directed to another service from which I have appointed them to perform, except in some public or most pressing demand indeed.' He ordered both the ships of the line to be immediately returned to Malta. The next day Keith reiterated his orders, adding that he would make provision for the queen as soon as circumstances allowed. He must now have realised that the only crumb of comfort in this miserable exchange was the intention of this persistently obstructive subordinate to go home. Reporting the latest events to Spencer, the commander-in-chief admitted himself 'as much grieved as surprised'.[69]

A difficult voyage from Malta had returned Nelson to Palermo on 1 June. He did not see matters through the same eyes as Keith. His commitment to Naples ran deeper than any of his countrymen suspected, and even now he was considering making his permanent home in Sicily. The Hamiltons had not abandoned the notion either, and Sir William still hankered after reclaiming his diplomatic post in Naples. Nelson saw Bronte as a potential retreat for them all, although Graefer was reporting all manner of difficulties in the duchy, including a class of selfish 'middle men' who managed some of the farms for absent landlords and oppressed the peasants, and the accidental omission of the farmhouse, La Fragilia, now being turned into a residence befitting an English gentleman, from the patent of Ferdinand's gift. Notwithstanding, Nelson told Acton, 'My object is to make the people happy by not suffering them to be oppressed' and 'to enrich the country by the improvement of agriculture'. Once personally in command, he would improve life for his subjects and 'never . . . consent to do an unjust act'.[70]

Over and above the importance of Sicily as a future sanctuary, however, Nelson was determined to discharge what he saw as his final duty to the Queen of Naples. In fact, before receiving either of Keith's orders about returning the ships of the line to Malta, he had already embarked the royal party. The Hamiltons, Maria Carolina, three princesses (Christina, Amelia and Antoinette), Prince Leopold and a score of staff, with a few ministers, such as Prince Castelcicala and his wife, who were to take over the Neapolitan embassy in London, Prince Belmonte and the Prince of Luzzi, were accommodated in the *Foudroyant* with so many coffers of family plate, jewellery and baggage that Nelson could hardly 'stir'. Another two dozen passengers boarded the *Alexander*. Apart from the obvious inconvenience of unravelling the arrangements, it would have been, in Nelson's view, an intolerable breach of trust. Nothing now would sway him from what he considered to be a sacred personal obligation, not even Keith's explicit orders to return his two ships of the line to Malta. 'Until I have safely got rid of my charge nothing shall separate me from her,' he told Spencer. 'I should feel myself a beast could I have a thought for anything but her comfort.'[71]

Nelson's heart was ruling his head, but for the first time in his life he had become an impediment rather than an asset to the service he had loved.

7

The queen had been drifting from Ferdinand for more than a year. She wanted him to return to Naples, where the city itself was fairly quiet, but he seemed afraid of leaving Palermo. Maria Carolina finally decided to go to Vienna to see her daughter, the empress, and to take her family with her in search of suitable future marriages. It was to provide her with a passage to Leghorn that Nelson had offered the *Foudroyant* and *Alexander*. The admiral and the Hamiltons would accompany the royal party, using the voyage as the first leg of their own journey home.

Amidst preparations there was genuine sorrow. The Hamiltons were reluctant to leave Italy, and their Majesties paid munificent tributes. 'Believe that nothing shall ever change our principles,' the queen wrote to Emma, 'and that if the country is base, we shall be ever honest and true. Say so to our friend, liberator and saviour.' There were parting gifts. The king's existing orders of chivalry could not be conferred on Protestants, so he created a new knighthood, installing Nelson, Suvorov and the tsar as the first three Knights Grand Cross of the Order of St Ferdinand and Merit. It was the admiral's third knighthood, and its privileges included the right to wear a hat in the royal presence. Troubridge, Ball, Hood, Louis, Hallowell and Blackwood were all made Knights Commander of the same order. This time money, as well as honour, was on offer. Ball pocketed

£500 for personal expenses. Emma, encouraged by Nelson, had lobbied for rewards for the aggrieved Troubridge, who received £500 in expenses and the same amount as a perpetual annuity. Sir Thomas was surprised. He had asked for 'a very moderate sum' but expected nothing extra from 'that—set!' It did not assuage the formidable captain, who doubted his pension would be paid, but it increased his sense of obligation to Nelson. In any case he was very ill, and also on his way home.[72]

Unlike Troubridge, Nelson had always believed Ferdinand a good if timid man, whose benevolent intentions had been thwarted by venal and inept servants. He gave the king one of Davison's Nile medals as a keepsake, and applied himself to preparing the ships for the queen and her suite. The king was grateful for this final benefice and thanked Nelson 'for not abandoning in this critical situation Her Majesty and family'.[73]

And Ferdinand was only the most elevated of many who viewed the departure of Lord Nelson with sadness. Naval officers and politicians such as Blackwood and Spiridion Foresti, the consul in Corfu, expressed their 'heartfelt' gratitude for what he had done for them. His generosity and sympathy had rarely failed to enchant. 'The more I hear of you,' he had written to Foresti, 'the more I am impressed with your extraordinary attention to the business of your office. Never have I seen anything to equal it, and I shall feel an honour to be called upon to bear my testimony of your worth.' Surely, Keith could never have written such a letter to an obscure consul beavering manfully in remote climes? Protégés, high and low, lamented the loss of a powerful patron, none more sincerely than Hoste. 'To you I owe everything, and it will always be my greatest pride to avow it,' he wrote from the Gulf of Genoa. Troubridge wondered 'how I am to thank and acknowledge your Lordship' for his 'attention to my affairs'. 'Every letter' young Collier wrote home gushed with 'the deepest regret of the loss he has sustained' by Nelson's departure. Civilians were among the well-wishers, some now almost lost to history, and the favours Nelson had done them forgotten. Anne Compton spoke of the 'great many favours and kindnesses' she had received from his lordship, especially 'the kind interest you showed in the affair of my marriage' to her husband, William. It had made her 'as happy as I can possibly be on this earth'. James Tough, the consul in Palermo, told the admiral that 'Old Gamelin and his grand children are full of gratitude for your having averted the storm that was going to overwhelm this unhappy family in an inevitable ruin. The ardent prayers of afflicted old age, of the innocent, of the widow and fatherless are sent up to smiling Heaven for your welfare and preservation.' We will never know what he did for them, but their gratitude is undeniable.[74]

Typically, the departing admiral attempted to find places for individuals he no longer felt able to serve. There was an unsuccessful plea for Ormsby's position as acting captain of the *Alexander* to be extended, and requests on behalf of Louis Remonier, a surgeon's mate of long acquaintance, the son of a merchant who had lost an arm in an explosion on a sloop, a clerk, a carpenter's mate, a boatswain and sundry midshipmen. On the other hand relatively few of the fleet had angered him, among the last a lieutenant who resigned his command of the *Earl St Vincent* rather than answer charges of 'bestiality' brought against him by his crew. Nelson was particularly fond of the men of the *Foudroyant*, many of whom had come out with him two years before. He begged Berry to 'assure all the *Foudroyants* of my sincere regard and affection for them. *They may depend upon me.*' He had a history of standing up for old shipmates, and almost always told departing companies of his readiness to serve them. A note in an unpractised hand, but containing only two misspelt words, was written by the admiral's barge crew:

> It is with extreme grief that we find you are about to leave us. We have been along with you (although not in the same ship) in every engagement your Lordship has been in both by sea and land and most humbly beg of your Lordship to permit us to go to England as your boats crew in any ship or vessel or in any way that may seem most pleasing to your Lordship. My Lord pardon the rude stile [sic] of seamen who are but little acquainted with writing and believe us to be, my Lord, your ever humble and obedient servant, barges crew of the *Foudroyant*.[75]

One by one the brothers had left the scene of their glory. Miller was dead, Saumarez, Hood, Foley, Hallowell and Hardy had gone home, and while Ball remained at his post, Troubridge was also bound for England with every expectation of receiving a key appointment in the Channel fleet, which St Vincent was to command. When Nelson sailed for Leghorn on 10 June, the *Princess Charlotte* and *Santa Dorotea* accompanied his two ships of the line. All of these ships could have been serving Malta. The admiral had a Neapolitan brig and four gunboats sent to the island, but they made a poor exchange.[76]

He left at an inauspicious time. The Russians had already withdrawn from the war. Left by the Austrians to face overwhelming odds in Switzerland, Suvorov had barely been able to extricate his forces, and the tsar, at any time an unstable element, had had enough. The reluctant Austria was left the only potent land power confronting France, but Bonaparte was massing to counterattack. Nelson was leaving the Mediterranean as he had found it, in crisis.

XI

'A WEAK MAN IN BAD HANDS'

Nelson, the flag haul down,
Hang up thy laurel crown,
While her we sing.
No more in triumph swell,
Since that with her you dwell,
But don't let her William tell
Nor George, your King.

Anonymous verse, London, 1800

I

FOUR storm-battered ships arrived at Leghorn at seven in the morning of 14 June 1800. Two were British ships of the line, *Foudroyant* and *Alexander*, and their consorts were a frigate, the *Princess Charlotte*, and the *Santa Dorotea*.[1]

The passage from Palermo had started so fair that those on board one ship could speak to passengers on another, but a savage storm had overtaken them north of Elba. Nelson, who spent four days of the seven ill in his cot, had to rise and face the very real and frightening prospect of the *Foudroyant* going down with all hands. Princess Amelie, then about eighteen years old, left the most graphic account of the voyage in her diary:

> June 14, awake at 4.30 and delighted at once to learn that we had passed Monte Cristo and were between the islands of Elba and Capraia, that during the night we had covered 80 miles and should be at Leghorn by evening. Towards 11 o'clock Lord Nelson came up. After a little conversation we descended to be shown around the vessel, which is smart and as clean as a mirror. At dinner Lord Nelson and the captain [Berry] both rose more than twenty times to check that we were still outside cannon range from the island of Capraia, which belongs to the French, and whether the wind was rising. When they returned they said laughing, 'The wind will be here in ten minutes, which will bring us to Leghorn.' Around 3

o'clock the motion increased considerably and the wind blew with unbelievable violence. We found Milady [Emma] kneeling on a mattress in the middle of the cabin. Toto [Princess Antoinette, Amelie's younger sister] cried, 'It's all over, we're dead, we're swamped!' Mama [the Queen] ordered us all to sit on the floor, pressed against the beds [to avoid being thrown down], and this we did, Mama, Toto and Ruffo on one side and Milady, Castelcicala and myself on the other. We were more dead than alive. Nelson came in from time to time to comfort us, saying that there was no danger and that by 7 o'clock we were sure to reach Leghorn. Milady took me in her arms. There was a gust of wind so strong that the vessel dipped under[water] three times. Nelson went as pale as a sheet and rushed out. Milady began to scream and to roll about on the floor. Mama said to us solemnly, 'Commend your souls to God,' and began to recite aloud a prayer in German. Then we recited the litanies of the saints and the thirteen Credos, doing nothing but praying and weeping.

At five minutes to seven we dropped anchor in the harbour at Leghorn, as Nelson had foretold. We learnt the pleasant news concerning Genoa's surrender. Mama wrote two letters in English, one to my good Lord Nelson, which was signed by all four of us, and the other to Captain Berry to thank them for all the kindnesses they had shown us throughout the voyage. She appended to the first a medallion containing a portrait of papa [Ferdinand] with his own initials, surrounded with large brilliants [diamonds and emeralds] and anchors wreathed in laurel; to the second a snuff box with his monogram and a ring. Nelson and Berry came to thank Mama heartily by word and gesture and, kneeling down, wished to kiss her hand as well as ours. We had all been terribly frightened, for the wind had been very violent and the motion dreadful, that [we were afraid] the two anchors would be lost and the vessel run upon the rocks.[2]

Even after their arrival the weather prevented landing for two days, during which essential repairs were made to the flagship's foretop. The following day was a Sunday, and after a private mass the guests joined Nelson in worship above decks. 'At 11 o'clock' on the 15th, wrote the princess, 'everybody gathered on the poop deck, which was furnished like a room with flags and seats. Then divine service was held. Between the wheel of the tiller and the captain's cabin cushions were laid out, on which Nelson knelt, along with Emma Hamilton, wearing a white blouse with her hair practically down over her shoulders. Each had a book, reading and praying with admirable attentiveness and devotion. Following dinner we went out on the poop deck to take coffee. Later we went below to listen to Milady, who, despite the swell, which was increasing at the time, sang several musical items.' When the queen and her party left the *Foudroyant* they were honoured with a gun salute and the cheers of the company. As usual, Her Majesty responded generously, presenting 2500 Sicilian crowns to the ship's company, and then her people made for the cathedral for a thanksgiving amid cries of 'long life' to the queen, the Austrian house and 'Milord Nelson' from a jostling crowd. The royals retired to the palace, where the duration of their stay was spent at the expense of the Grand Duke of Tuscany, the queen's nephew and son-in-law, while Nelson and the Hamiltons paid their respects to the British consul.[3]

Though he essayed into the town occasionally (once to stand as godfather to a boy of naval parents who was being christened in the chapel of the British Trade Factory) Nelson remained much occupied with business, including attending the royal family and monitoring their situation. After one such dinner on 19 June, records Amelie, the admiral showed the princesses the 'superb sword' presented to him by the Nile captains, its gold hilt tooled to represent a crocodile. At this stage Nelson believed that the promise he had given Ferdinand to see his family safe had been discharged, and that his immediate concern was to wind up his naval affairs and take the Hamiltons home, but no sooner had the storm at sea been overcome than an equally threatening political maelstrom brewed with astonishing speed.[4]

Upon landing Nelson received Keith's orders of 15 June, superseding his previous and ignored instructions with a new directive to send all ships to join the commander-in-chief at Genoa. Nelson still hoped to commandeer the *Foudroyant* for his voyage home, and grumpily replied she would proceed to Genoa but that the *Alexander* was wanted at Malta. Sir William made his own application for the *Foudroyant*, citing the needs of his antiquities and Nelson's health in extenuation. Keith, however, had to respond to the military exigencies of the situation, and they were changing by the day. Around them, the second coalition suddenly fell apart. On 6 June Genoa had fallen to the allies, but a mere matter of days later Bonaparte's army inflicted a crushing defeat on the Austrians at Marengo on 14 June, transforming the aspect of the entire theatre. Many of the allied conquests of the past year were instantly rolled up as the Austrian general, Michael Melas, agreed a hasty and unfavourable armistice to extricate his army, yielding a dozen fortresses to the French, including those at Milan, Turin, Savona and Genoa. The Cisalpine (Milanese) and Ligurian (Genoese) republics had no sooner been liberated than restored to vassalage. For the time being Tuscany remained neutral, and the new pope, Pius VIII, retained his seat, but Bonaparte plainly had the papal territories and Naples in his sights, and, had it not been for the opposition of Russia, his armies might have marched instantly. As it was, panic spread through Italy. In Tuscany thousands of people took to arms to defend their country, and art and national treasures were hidden in inviolable places.[5]

Keith, so recently master of Genoa, saw it reoccupied by French armies on 22 June, and rapidly reappraised his predicament. New orders flew to Leghorn. On the 17th he ordered Nelson to repair with all ships to the Gulf of Spezia,

1. Rear Admiral Sir Horatio Nelson, K.B., painted in London by Lemuel Francis Abbott in 1797. Abbott produced numerous versions of what became the most famous of all Nelson portraits, but this one appears to be that made for Lady Nelson, based on an additional sitting. 'The likeness is great,' she concluded. Nelson wears his Star of the Order of the Bath and the medal commemorating the battle of Cape St Vincent.

2. Perhaps the most accurate likeness of Nelson, showing him in Palermo in 1799. A pencil sketch by Charles Grignion, it was never turned into a formal portrait in oils. However, in its depiction of the face as well as its overall informality the sketch offers a unique glimpse of the admiral as many must have encountered him. Even the display of decorations, so obligatory in commemorative portraits, is moderated, the Star of the Order of the Bath on Nelson's undress coat being hidden by his remaining hand.

3. Frances, Lady Nelson (1761–1831), about 1800, after a portrait attributed to Henry Edridge. This portrait seems to capture the strain of her anxious wait for the return of her husband, and her care of his ailing father.

4. William, Earl Nelson (1757–1835), the admiral's last surviving brother, who benefited from the nation's gratitude for Trafalgar. An indulgent self-seeker of limited principles, his 'amiable qualities' were also marred by 'a rough exterior and abrupt manners' and relatively few remembered him with real affection.

5. Once 96 Bond Street, London, this property was leased to Nelson and his wife in 1798, and became his base when preparing to return to the Mediterranean after recovering from the loss of his arm. The house, which was renumbered in the nineteenth century, is one of a very few of the admiral's temporary homes to survive.

6. During his lifetime Nelson had three principal homes in England: his birthplace at Burnham Thorpe and two houses he purchased after achieving prominence as an admiral. Only one survived into the age of photographs, Roundwood, near Ipswich, which appears in this grainy early-twentieth-century picture. Nelson bought the house in 1797 but never spent a night under its roof, although his wife and father made it their home for more than two years while he was in the Mediterranean. The family sold the house in 1801, and it was demolished in 1961.

7. Sir William Hamilton (1730–1803), Envoy Extraordinary and Plenipotentiary at Naples, portrayed in this engraving of a fine miniature of 1794, painted by Grignion. A collector of antiquities, patron of the arts, pioneer of vulcanology, hedonist and diplomat, he tarnished his reputation by his association with the Neapolitan counter-revolution of 1799 and the Nelson–Hamilton ménage.

8. The Palazzo Sessa, Naples, in the early twentieth century, once the luxurious home of the Hamiltons, where Nelson recuperated after the battle of the Nile.

9. Emma, Lady Hamilton (1765–1815), as she appears in *The Ambassadress* painted by George Romney in London in 1791, shortly after her marriage to Sir William Hamilton. The last of Romney's portraits of his famous muse, the work captures Emma's beauty at its ethereal best.

10. Maria Carolina, Queen of Naples (1752–1814) in a typical likeness by Vigée Le Brun. The daughter of the famous Maria Theresa of Austria, she was married to Ferdinand IV of Naples and Sicily in 1768. She encouraged the arts and moderate political reform until alarmed by the excesses of the French Revolution. Haunted by the fate of her older sister, Marie Antoinette of France, she feared for her crown and family and became a bitter opponent of the French and firm ally of Britain. She looked upon Nelson as an indispensable prop to her threatened kingdom.

11. Sir John Acton (1736–1811), of mixed English and French descent, inherited an English baronetcy in 1791. After distinguished service in the Tuscan navy, he became an efficient instrument of Maria Carolina, reforming the Neapolitan armed services and rising to the position of principal minister. Under Acton the Two Sicilies strengthened their leanings towards Austria and Britain. He was the main intermediary between Nelson, Sir William Hamilton and the Sicilian monarchy.

12. The Palazzo Palagonia, Palermo, as it survives today after considerable reconstruction. Traditionally the home of the Palagonia family, it is believed to have been the headquarters of Nelson and the Hamiltons during most of their stay in Sicily in 1799 and 1800.

13. One of the residents of the Palazzo Palagonia was Ellis Cornelia Knight (1757–1837), the daughter of an English admiral. His widow died in Sicily in July 1799, leaving Cornelia to the protection of Nelson and the Hamiltons, with whom she freely associated, celebrating them in songs, poems and watercolour sketches. She parted with the ménage after its return to England, and deftly aligned with the disapproving establishment, becoming an official companion to Princess Charlotte. Her appearance is here preserved in this painting by Angelica Kauffman.

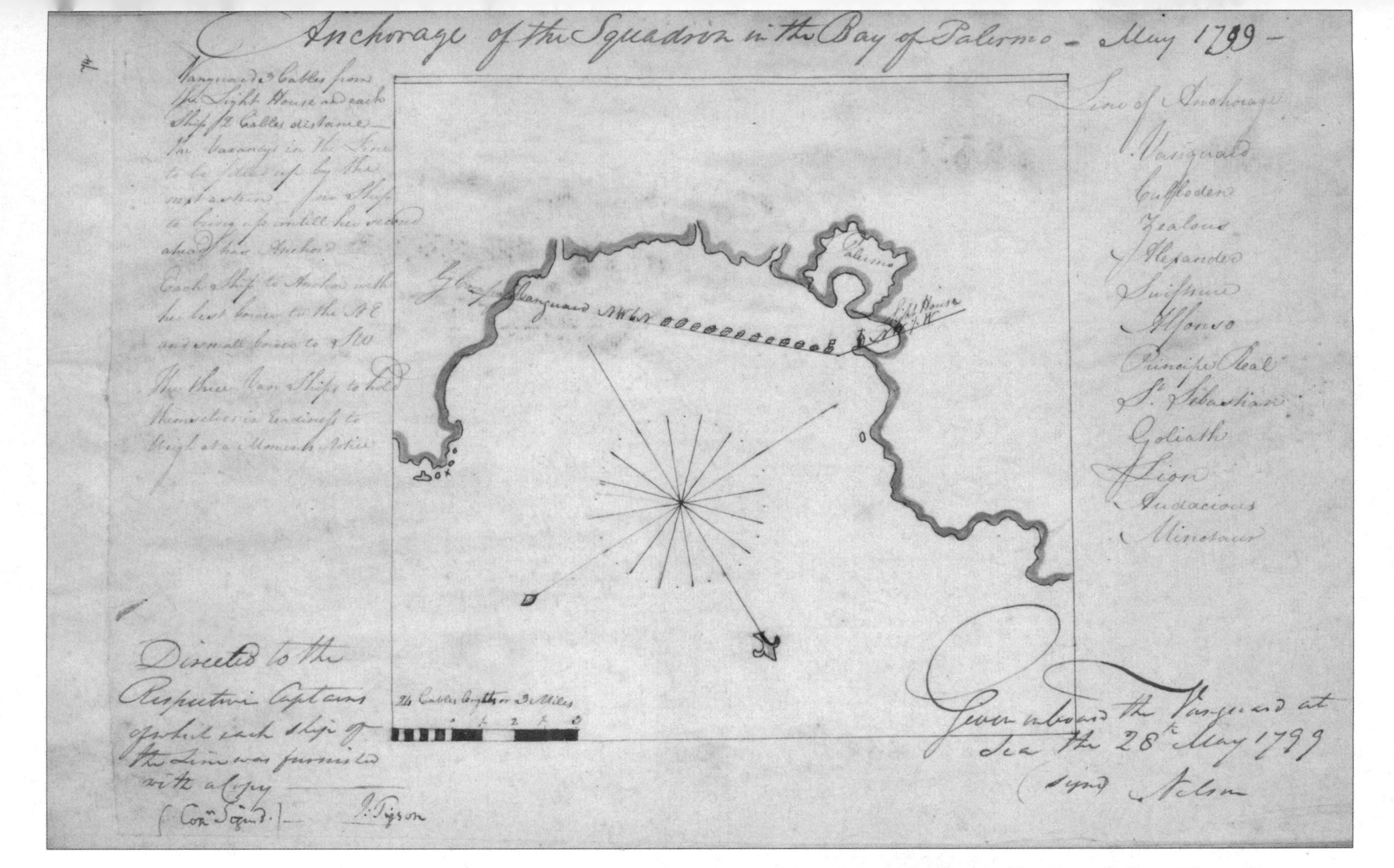

14. Nelson's plan for the defence of Palermo, threatened by the possible appearance of a superior French fleet. The order was issued at sea on 28 May 1799, as Nelson was returning to Palermo after cruising in search of the enemy.

north of Tuscany, to seize garrisons in the bay that were being evacuated by the Austrians, and destroy or carry off their artillery, arms and munitions before the French arrived. Without any time for more nonsense from Nelson, Keith insisted his orders were 'final'. His concern was understandable, since he needed all the ships of the line he could get. The orders reached Nelson at night, and he and Emma went to the palace with the news, waking the queen to alert her to the astonishing misfortune. There is no direct evidence, but as the royal family was now in serious danger of being cut off by their enemies, Nelson almost certainly consoled them with a promise to keep a ship at hand to secure their retreat, even though it led to a further defiance of orders. Instead of sending all ships, he ordered the *Santa Dorotea* and *Alexander* on the errand to Spezia, but withheld the *Foudroyant* to ensure the safety of the royal party.[6]

Keith was not pleased, and virtually admitted to Spencer that he had lost control of his force, and hardly knew what to make of Nelson's thinking. On 19 June he bombarded his resistant subordinate with no less than four firm but respectful communications that outlined his own construction. Every ship of the line had to be returned to service, and the *Foudroyant* was now ordered to Minorca, where she could be remasted before resuming her duties. But recognising the danger facing the queen at Leghorn, he reluctantly offered the *Princess Charlotte*, with the pointed remark that even his temporary loss of that frigate might cost the allies Sardinia. It was indeed a difficult conundrum. Possibly Keith felt that the queen could have used the three Neapolitan frigates at Leghorn, but if so he underestimated the deep scars left by the collapse of the Neapolitan army and Jacobin revolution of 1798 and 1799, which ingrained in Maria Carolina a deep fear of relying upon her own forces. As for the ménage, Keith continued, if Nelson struck his flag and got to Minorca by the *Foudroyant*, he could there pick up the *Seahorse* frigate, or a troop or store ship bound for England. Protesting at his inability to do more at a time when 'the late unfortunate events make me tremble for all Italy', he included a plea remarkable in a commander-in-chief's address to a subordinate. His orders 'must . . . be final . . . so, my dear friend, let me insist that my ships instantly follow my further orders'. It was almost a plea to allow him to command.[7]

Keith also decided to go to Leghorn himself, though dreading being 'bored by Lord Nelson to take the Queen . . . to all parts of the globe'. Nelson, however, had an eye to those vengeful French armies sweeping back into northern Italy towards his royal charges. The new crisis had first shocked Maria Carolina, giving her two apoplectic fits and depriving her of memory and senses for several days, and then thrown her into panic and indecision, fed by the sight of miserable fugitives from the Austrian army dribbling into Leghorn and lying about the streets. Should she proceed to Vienna, perhaps to plead with the emperor to include Naples in any peace with the French, return to Sicily to stand with her people behind the British shield or continue by sea to the Austrian port of Trieste? In her letters she vacillated, here believing a peace to be essential, and there wishing the Austrian army had the pluck to make a stand. Exiled with her vulnerable family in a fear-ridden town, she expected 'every moment to see the enemy', and dreaded falling into their hands. 'I am a woman, after all,' she admitted, but she was in truth much more. She was a rank foe of the French, who had coveted her kingdoms, scourged them with civil war and murdered her sister. A flight was inevitable, but although her experiences at sea had made the prospect of another voyage terrifying, the land journey across Italy to Ancona, from which she could ship to safety in Austrian Trieste, looked no less perilous. French soldiers were already closing in, penetrating Massa, some forty miles north of Leghorn; to within eighty miles of Ancona on the east coast; and to points north of a line connecting Modena, Bologna, Imola and Faenza. Studying all the roads, the queen could see none that did not require a French pass. She waited on tenterhooks for advice from Vienna, and Nelson could not find it in himself to desert her. When a rumour went around that the Brest fleet had escaped again, and might threaten the Two Sicilies, Malta or Egypt, even Keith began to panic, and frenzied notes were fired at Nelson. 'My dear Lord,' he wrote on 21 June, 'Get the Queen to Naples . . . or to Palermo.' Then, in a second, reflecting on the dangers to Sicily and the Mediterranean seaways, 'Let the Queen go to Vienna as fast as she can. If this fleet gets the start of ours [for] a day, Sicily cannot hold out . . .'[8]

Keith's arrival in Leghorn in the *Minotaur* three days later was followed on 1 July by the appearance of two thousand redcoats, part of a modest British expeditionary force from England, commanded by Generals Ralph Abercromby and John Moore, then on their way to Malta. Unfortunately, these transients did not ease the situation. In a tearful interview, the queen asked for the use of a line of battle ship to facilitate her escape and troops to defend her kingdoms, and Nelson separately protested that the *Princess Charlotte* was no fit place for the royal suite. But Keith was in no position to comply, with every ship of the line needed to meet the French, and the military force far too small to assume major commitments on the continent and barely adequate to securing Minorca, Sicily and Malta. Keith ordered Berry to take the *Foudroyant* to Minorca, and Nelson to transfer his flag to the *Alexander*, which could temporarily remain in Leghorn to give the queen a retreat in an emergency. No one was satisfied. Maria Carolina thought it a poor return for the sacrifices her kingdoms had made to support Britain, regarded Keith as 'detestable', and vowed she would never enter a coalition again, while Nelson was thoroughly dissatisfied with the *Alexander*, where he 'had not the least thing for comfort of any kind'. His hurried evacuation of the *Foudroyant* left him worrying about mislaid possessions, including some of Cornelia's letters left in a book 'in one of my drawers', and he missed his old shipmates. 'God bless you and all the *Foudroyants*,' he wrote to Berry. Nelson had been reduced on this occasion to little more than an onlooker, and perhaps a curiosity. Moore, who had known him in Corsica, felt 'melancholy' to see a hero 'cutting so pitiful a figure' beneath his stars, ribbons and medals that he looked 'more like the prince of an opera', and Wyndham, the British representative in Tuscany, and Keith were almost as blunt.[9]

On the night of 3 July Her Majesty at last received a courier from her daughter, the Austrian empress, pointing out that the armistice with France had been extended until 12 July and the queen should get to Vienna while a measure of stability prevailed. Keith agreed, and relented to the point of agreeing to release the *Alexander* for a voyage around the foot of Italy to Trieste. Nelson had resigned himself to using the *Seahorse* to begin his journey home, but minding his promise to place the royal family in 'perfect security' now abandoned the idea, and promised that he would accompany the queen to safety by sea or land.[10]

As the royal fugitives dithered about which route they feared the least, and gathered intelligence, events moved suddenly to a head on 8 July, when alarming news reached Leghorn that four hundred French soldiers had occupied Lucca, barely a day's march away. The next day the streets were in turmoil, as a patriotic but unruly mob paraded up and down throughout the day declaring their determination to confront the invaders, and demanded the local arsenal be thrown open. They descended upon the Grand Duke's palace, baying for action, reminding the terrified queen of the disorder that had driven her from Naples in 1798. Some of the crowd demanded that Nelson lead them against the French. According to an account Emma gave nearly six years later, the admiral was summoned to the scene, and pushed his way through the rabble-rousers to gain admission to the palace, where he found Maria Carolina on an overlooking balcony with her frightened children. From this vantage point the admiral addressed the crowd, explaining that he would put himself at their head, but only after they had returned their arms to the arsenal and restored order. Some noisily dispersed, and Nelson used the lull to rush the royals and their principal possessions to the *Alexander*, where they were secured aboard the same night. The bare bones of the story are supported by contemporary accounts, and Cornelia Knight credited Nelson with pacifying the crowd. Emma probably enhanced her own part in the drama, but Nelson may have used her as an interpreter.[11]

Tension hung in the air like a raised axe, and several unsatisfactory days passed. Despite the efforts of Acting Captain George Ormsby, Princess Amelie thought the *Alexander* a 'villainous vessel', stinking, cramped and running with cockroaches, but she tried to read on the poop, while Emma indulged in her 'usual extravagances' during the stifling heat. By the morning of the 11th the royal party had landed again, having finally convinced themselves that the land journey was the surer escape route, although Cornelia, Berry and the officers of the *Alexander* were astonished that anyone would even consider it. No wonder. The queen's destination, Ancona, remained in Austrian hands, but inland her route passed within fifty miles of places already known to have been reached by the French, and uncomfortably close to the Bolognese people, who were believed to have been seriously influenced by Jacobinism. The French army was thought to be intending a march through Romagna to threaten the Roman and Neapolitan states, and no one could be certain that the roads would be clear of their cavalry, or what treatment the queen and her daughters might receive if they were captured. Nevertheless, without further procrastination, Maria Carolina and her retinue slipped out of Leghorn on the evening of 11 July and took the road for Florence.[12]

Nelson and the Hamiltons would also have made capital prizes, although Emma was also afraid of the sea and Sir William felt so ill that he doubted that he would survive whichever route he went. The admiral realised that he could do little if their worst fears materialised, but felt obliged to remain with the queen during the dangerous leg of her journey. On 12 July he hauled down his flag, and shortly afterwards embarked with his party upon the hot, dusty and dangerous road inland. Among them was Cornelia Knight who suspected she might be heading for a French prison.

2

In Vienna Lord Minto represented his country as the Envoy Extraordinary and Minister Plenipotentiary to the court of the imperial emperor. He admired, even loved, Admiral Nelson, and had been a principal mover of his appointment to the Mediterranean in 1798. But Minto and his wife were disturbed by what they heard from Italy, and struggled to see the Nelson they had known. It was said, for example, that the admiral was 'a weak man in bad hands', whose public 'zeal' had been 'entirely lost' in 'love and vanity'. The Nelson–Hamilton circle merely 'sit and flatter each other all day long', Lady Minto wrote, oblivious of the opinions of outsiders. The hero of 1797 and 1798 had begun to look like a weak and unsafe commander.[13]

The charges have appeared and reappeared ever since, and some of Nelson's best friends, such as Minto, subscribed to them. Troubridge plainly regarded the admiral as the dupe of a venal court, and particularly of those designing females, the queen and the English ambassadress. Modern historians have agreed, lamenting like Keith that Nelson had so readily placed His Britannic Majesty's ships at the service of the Two Sicilies when they were needed elsewhere, and there is some truth in the charge. As we have seen, Nelson had stepped beyond the duty to his own sovereign in the summer of 1799, and during the ensuing year he had both frustrated Keith's plans to redeploy his forces and loosened control of the blockade of Malta. It is impossible to exonerate Emma's influence, especially in the failings of August 1799 to June 1800, but the ultimate responsibility was his rather than hers.

In acknowledging these indictments, we should nevertheless remind ourselves of the admiral's own sense of mission. Britain's diplomats, admirals and generals were, of course, the country's servants, but it is impossible to cultivate goodwill in foreign courts, particularly those of allies and potential allies, without showing empathy for the associated power and an appreciation of its individual circumstances. Indeed, the trust between allies depends upon such intercourse. It was necessary for public servants to alert their government to the concerns of allies, and to explain them, but also occasionally to negotiate between two points of view. Many, and among them the most respected, even gained credibility if, within reasonable bounds, they were prepared to support allies in cases of principle against the inclinations of their own political masters. It is a difficult brief, as Nelson discovered during his Italian interlude.

Many Britons, then and since, saw Nelson as a weak man, allowing the Neapolitans to manipulate him, not always to his country's advantage. But looked at another way, he was a strong man. The government of the Two Sicilies, and indeed a few other Italian states, saw him as almost their one dependable support. In every crisis – the disastrous war of 1798, the defence of Sicily, the reclamation of Naples and the papal territory, and the threat from Bruix – he had stood staunch and strong. Even those final distressing squabbles with Keith arose from an iron adherence to the safety of the royal family. This 'Sicilification' as he called it not only reflected simple gratitude for the honours these kingdoms had lavished on him, and the influence of Emma, but also Nelson's genuine sense of obligation to one of the few allies to stand solidly against the French. For Naples had succoured his fleet at Syracuse in 1798 when no other would, enabling him to win the battle of the Nile. British warships had drawn upon the dockyards and arsenals at Naples, Castellammare and Palermo, as well as the hospitals for untold amounts of supplies and materiel, and had it not been for Ferdinand's support, focused by Nelson and Ball, the blockade of Malta would have been impossible.[14]

Prince Belmonte, whom Emma hated, organised the march, but the royal party with a total entourage of some eighty persons maintained its station ahead of Nelson's, partly to alleviate the strain upon roadside accommodation. Nelson's more modest cavalcade headed east in two coaches, transporting the admiral, Emma, Sir William, Mrs Cadogan, Miss Knight and eight retainers (five of them Italians and three of them women), all encumbered with a considerable amount of baggage, including many of the more impressive gifts Nelson had received during the last two years. Twenty-six hours of bumping, during which the travellers heard that they had passed within two miles of the French advanced posts, brought Nelson to Florence and a brief rest. The enemy were in Bologna, their cavalry biting ever deeper into the heart of Italy, so when Nelson's coaches continued they detoured south-east to Arezzo and Perugia before striking north-east again towards Ancona, on the Adriatic. When

Nelson showed his face in the towns along the way he was cheered, but at Castel del Giovanni a wheel on his coach collapsed and the carriage overturned, injuring Cornelia and both Hamiltons. A quick repair, effected amidst many worried glances up and down the road, got them to Arezzo, where the wheel gave in again and precipitated a hasty and worried conference. If the French caught Nelson or the Hamiltons the allies would suffer a severe blow, but Cornelia and Mrs Cadogan, who might pass as a lady and companion, were unlikely to be recognised. Their danger, indeed, lay in being caught in Nelson's company. Therefore the women waited in the hospitable town of Arezzo for three days while Nelson and the Hamiltons went on in the remaining carriage. The road between Arezzo and Ancona was infested with Neapolitan deserters and starving peasants, but though the coach shook its occupants night and day it arrived in Ancona without significant mishap. On 15 July Nelson wrote to Acton that the queen had not yet arrived, but was believed to be close. Much heralded upon their more leisurely journey, the royal entourage reached Ancona two days later.[15]

Attention was now turned towards getting a voyage to Trieste, where feet could be finally set upon safe Austrian territory. The dangerous part of their journey seemed to be over, but Nelson had attracted attention on the road, and French soldiers were already on his trail. The admiral, with the Hamiltons and Miss Knight, found accommodation in the house of Alexander Comelate, a young Englishman with a large family and an appropriately commodious property. Shortly after Comelate left with his guests, having agreed to accompany them to Trieste, a French detachment arrived at his house and ransacked and trashed his place, particularly venting their anger on the room that Nelson had occupied. By then the fugitives had flown. An Austrian frigate, *Bellona*, had been available, but she was poorly armed, and Nelson recommended using the alternative, a Russian force of three frigates and a brig. A short, unpleasant but safe voyage to Trieste was the result. Nelson, the Hamiltons and the queen both sailed on the forty-four-gun flagship *Monarchia*, where the eleven beds crammed into a single cabin for the use of the royal party created the appearance of a hospital ward. Moreover, the captain, Count Voinovitsch, was ill, and the trip was managed by Lieutenant Capaci, whom Nelson rated an upstart. But Nelson did enjoy the occasional company of Thomas Messer, the English captain of one of the consort frigates, *Casanski Bogorodeto*, in which Cornelia and some of the other travellers were housed. Nelson was missing the *Foudroyant* dreadfully, and referred to her again and again in brief conversations, but sometimes he allowed his professional interests to intervene and was heard discussing ships, harbours and battle plans with Messer and other naval officers. Fortunately there was only one scare, during the night of 28 July, when a high wind suddenly engulfed the ships and threw them this way and that. Nelson and Emma immediately tumbled out to attend to their charges, she entering their cabin partly dressed to reassure, and he outside in a 'dressing gown and beret' concerning himself with the handling of the ship. The admiral later said the ship could have sunk. But the crisis over, the ships reached Trieste on 1 August. The royal children found Nelson below decks to congratulate him upon the anniversary of the Nile, and then everyone disembarked, the queen leading her people to the 'Grand Hotel', while Nelson furnished Messer with a recommendation to his emperor, and joined the Hamiltons in more modest rooms in the Emperor's Eagle inn.[16]

For almost a fortnight the royal progress, with its attendant celebrity circus, was stymied in Trieste. Sir William was shaken to the core and took to his bed for days, while a mild fever went through the queen and some of her retinue. But the town was safe and far from disagreeable, and there was no damper upon the public enthusiasm for the visitors. Nelson sent notes back and forward, including one to Fanny, joined the royals to hear a 'wonderful' symphony in honour of the Nile, and showed himself on the streets. 'He is followed by thousands when he goes out,' Miss Knight informed Berry, 'and for the illumination . . . this evening there are many "Viva Nelsons" prepared.' The news was eagerly consumed here and afield, because Nelson's hazardous overland journey had fed wild rumours. It was being said that Sir William was dying, Emma had lost her teeth in the accident upon the road, Nelson was going blind and Prince Luzzi was on his deathbed after dislocating his neck.[17]

When the cavalcade got underway it resembled the baggage train of a large army. Three divisions set out a day apart, with more than a hundred horses and seventeen coaches and wagons. The queen went with the first party, and Nelson travelled in the last with the Hamiltons and their servants. Cornelia had some German, but the British vice-consul at Trieste, a Mr Anderson, consented to accompany Nelson to Vienna as his interpreter. Journeying roughly easterly and northwards, the procession groaned and creaked over an erratic zigzag course. Nelson visited the limestone cave at Adelsberg (Postojna) and on 14 August broke the journey at Laibach (Ljubljana, Slovenia), sixty miles from Trieste, where the local philharmonic society welcomed him with a musical celebration of the battle of the Nile. The next day mercilessly taxed the ailing Hamilton as the route traversed the Loibl Pass through the Karawanken mountains, the coaches jolting violently in oppressive heat, and struggling up and down such fierce gradients that the passengers were frequently obliged to alight to spare the horses. But at the crest, at 3500 feet, they were rewarded with a remarkable view of the Drau Valley.[18]

The descent took them to Graz in Styria, on the River Mur, where they stayed at Schmelzer's Gasthof by a bridge. Nelson admitted inquisitive citizens to his room and appeared on the streets with Emma on his arm, inciting much interest and applause. Locals were astonished to gaze at a famous warrior who was small, lean, pale and hollow-cheeked, in the company of two striking women, his decidedly overweight but beautiful big-boned lady with newly trimmed chestnut locks, and the attractive figure of Fatima, Emma's black maid. Little is known about this particular favourite of Emma's, who now makes her debut in recorded history. She was about eighteen years old, 'a Copt, perfectly black', who had been in the seraglio of Murad Bey, a Mameluke leader defeated by Bonaparte at the Pyramids in 1798 and driven into upper Egypt. Fatima's husband was killed in the fighting, but she fell into French hands and was incarcerated in what has variously been described as a warship and a slave ship. When the vessel was taken by the British, Nelson presented Fatima to Emma, who became her protector. Though some observers disliked her Negroid features, she attracted considerable attention on the streets of Graz, looking 'a counterpart in black beauty of Lady Hamilton's noble charms'.[19]

Another rugged stretch of the journey was accomplished on 16 August, when the tourists passed along the Mur to Bruck and struck east into the picturesque valley of the Murz before climbing the Semmering Pass on the border of Styria and Niederösterreich. It had been arranged that the Queen would wait for them at Gloggnitz, so that all could enter Vienna together, but to Emma's chagrin the emperor had already met his aunt and mother-in-law and personally conducted her people to the capital before the ménage arrived. Nelson's own roadshow reached Weiner Neustadt, where it lodged at the Zum Hirschen on 17 August, and set off at four the following morning to avoid the fearsome midday heat. Later that day they passed the Schönbrunn Palace, the home of the emperor, and two miles beyond entered the fabled capital of European culture.

After the tension of the first days on the road, Nelson's journey turned into a triumphant *tour de force*, for here in Austria the little admiral was seen as a hero of the struggle against the French. And his progress was documented by some of the most revealing descriptions of the ménage that we have. His coach sped into the centre of the city to Graben Square, an elegant area between the Kohlmarkt and Habsburgergasse ennobled with fountains, shops, imposing houses and a marble column. The travellers disembarked at the Inn For All Honest Men, a five-storey building with a store at ground level, and an ornate façade, behind which the Villar family were noted for serving choice steaks. Only 150 yards away the greatest church bell in Europe reposed in St Stephen's Cathedral. Three hundred miles of road from Trieste had exhausted Hamilton, and he had no desire to stir in a temperature that sometimes reached the higher nineties. Twelve days later he still looked as if he would never see England. But during that time crowds gathered about the hotel, straining to see the hero. Women dusted off their 'Nelson' bonnets, dresses, earrings, topcoats and robes, the trappings of the last two fashion seasons, to visit him, or held out babies for him to touch. Nelson and Emma lapped it up, venturing into the streets, the admiral sometimes seeming a mere 'shadow . . . as motionless and silent as a monument', while Emma 'never stopped talking, singing, laughing, gesticulating and mimicking'. Despite her voluminous figure, enhanced by a secret pregnancy, she was now credited with popularising 'the light diaphanous draperies which leave nothing to be guessed at by lovers of the fair sex'.[20]

They attended such theatres as the Hofburg or the Leopoldstadter in the Praterstrasse, sitting through productions of Niccolò Piccinni's *Griselda*, Joachim Perinet's three-act operatta *Raoul, Herr Von Crequi*, three works by Carl Friedrich Henslar, and a comedy entitled *Kaspars Schelmereien*, the adventures of a sharp-witted but unworldly peasant boy which afforded Nelson considerable amusement. 'He is . . . said to be a great lover of gay comedies,' reported one. Nelson responded graciously to the thronging crowds, and was exceptionally gratified to witness a fireworks display in his honour on the Danube. Sometimes it seemed that Vienna was catching Nelson fever, as shops and inns were renamed for him, and storekeepers displayed the admiral's portrait above their premises. The hero patronised some of these establishments, sending a consignment of wine to Graefer.[21]

Nelson had, in fact, been admired here since news of the Nile had 'filled' the 'whole city' with 'joy'. In addition to the fashions in women's clothing, poems, pictures, plans of the battle, commemoration snuff boxes, a play and a couple of musical pieces had been devoted to Nelson. Among the visitors paying court was Heinrich Füger, a tall, fine-looking and prestigious portrait painter in search of a subject. He had possibly been pointed towards Nelson by the Queen of Naples, for whom he had done some work, and the admiral eventually commissioned portraits of the queen, Emma and himself, arranging for payment through a Viennese banker, Leopold von Herz. The artist was suffering from eye problems but produced two arresting likenesses of Nelson, marred only by a thinning of the lips that conveyed an excessive air of cold ruthlessness about the man. The version in uniform rings true, with its display of all three orders of chivalry and the usual three medals, two struck by the crown to commemorate St Vincent and the Nile, and the third the private contribution by Davison. Another version has the distinction of being the only formal portrait to show the admiral in civilian dress, and if the outfit was genuinely one of the admiral's own rather than a studio prop, his early penchant for dark, sober clothes appears still to have been flourishing. The portraits Nelson commissioned from Füger were not finished until the following summer, but even more important as far as his iconography is concerned was the life mask made by the Viennese sculptor Franz Thaller. Thaller made some money selling copies of his mask, and it probably deserves to be remembered as the best representation of Nelson's features, although the artist Sir William Beechey later remarked that Nelson 'pursed up his chin and screwed up his features when the plaster was poured in', thus unfortunately reducing the breadth of his face and pointing the chin. The sitter himself was much pleased with the result, and immediately commissioned Thaller and Matthias Ranson to produce busts based upon it.[22]

Old acquaintances were encountered in Vienna, including Francis Oliver, an elderly but active friend of the Hamiltons, who furnished the necessary local lore and as a German speaker took the place of the British official from Trieste for the rest of their Austrian tour. But Nelson was most thrilled to meet Lord and Lady Minto, his old Mediterranean friends. Lord Minto had been saddened by the gossip about Nelson, but was inclined to leniency nevertheless, having a great affection for the man and a sound sense of Lady Hamilton's attractions, even compared with 'the other ladies of Naples'. Years before he had commented upon her 'barmaid' manners and readiness to flirt. 'With men her language and conversation are exaggerations of anything I ever heard anywhere,' he had said.[23]

Minto had a fine house on the side of a hill, overlooking the Wien, at St Veit, and the day after Nelson and the Hamiltons arrived in Vienna they received a dinner invitation. Lady Minto was forgiving. 'He has the same shock head, and the same honest simple manners,' she wrote. 'But he is devoted to Emma . . . and she leads him about like a keeper with a bear.' She sat beside him at dinner to cut his meat, and he carried her pocket handkerchief. Nelson was 'a-gig' with decorations but behaved 'just the same with us as ever'. There were several other visits, in which Nelson was brought up to date with the progress of the negotiations between France and Austria. On the Saturday before their departure Nelson remarked upon the sadness of the Queen of Naples, and urged Minto to visit the 'neglected' monarch, who was usually to be found in her apartment at the Schönbrunn Palace between five and six of an evening.[24]

As Nelson's comments indicate, the ménage regularly dined with the weary queen. Conscious that the emperor really wanted her here, at a time when delicate negotiations were underway, Maria Carolina was pleased to see her eldest daughter for the first time in ten years, together with numerous grandchildren. Royal obeisance was also extended to Nelson by the crowned heads of the Austrian empire, though the noise of five children led Nelson to leave the empress after less than an hour on 21 August. However, while many Austrians thought Britain had dragooned them into the war with France, they almost all admired Nelson. Two days after his retreat from the royal children, Nelson had an audience with Francis II himself, probably in the Hofburg townhouse less than two hundred yards from the admiral's hotel. The following morning there was an official reception in the imperial palace, during which Minto presented the admiral and the Hamiltons to the court. The emperor and empress were there, and the Queen of Naples and Elector of Cologne, and the place was awash with diamonds. 'Admiral Nelson alone had a whole treasury on his person,' said one eyewitness. Here Nelson was feted by powerful rulers who did not balk at his chosen lady, something that would never occur in Britain. After the reception Nelson joined a lunch for fifty at the Augarten Palace, presided over by the emperor's uncle, Duke Albrecht of

Sachsen-Teschen, and was then driven in a six-coach parade to a park in the Danube Meadows, where the admiral received the cheers of thousands of people. At the end of August the emperor's court moved out to Baden, and it was the duke who performed duties in the capital. On 4 September Nelson and the Hamiltons joined nearly thirty others at one of his dinners. The admiral drank too much and returned to Vienna ill, but he was with the queen for breakfast on the 6th and found her unusually upbeat. The emperor, she said, was reviewing his troops, which gave her some hope of a strong stance against the French.[25]

After Nelson's official reception set a precedent, invitations from members of the elite poured in. The Arnsteins, Jewish bankers, received the admiral and his lady, the latter carrying Nelson's hat under her arm, and Prince Stanislaus Poniatowski, a nephew of the King of Poland, showed them around his jewel collection at the Chateau of Lichtenstein. Sir William was too ill to accompany many of these excursions, and Mrs Cadogan kept out of the way lest she embarrass her daughter, but Miss Knight more than made up for any lack of conversation. She talked a lot, and corresponded with Berry, who shared her penchant for sycophantic verses in Nelson's honour. Cornelia had several on offer, three celebrating the Nile and the captures of *Le Généreux* and *Guillaume Tell*, and additional verses for the national anthem much to the same effect. Armed with these, she accompanied Nelson and the Hamiltons when, on 6 September, they embarked upon their most memorable expedition, to the magnificent palace of Kismarton (Eisenstadt) in Hungary, situated forty miles south-east of Vienna in a countryside of lush farms and vineyards.

Their host was Prince Nikolaus Esterházy II, one of the greatest of the Hungarian nobles, who had known the Hamiltons in Naples and now laid on a four-day fest in honour of the Britons. As usual the admiral presented himself in full uniform with his medals and orders, but talked 'very little', managing the occasional stilted conversation in uncertain French or Italian. 'He praised the charming landscape of our homeland,' said a fellow guest. 'Then I mentioned that a number of learned inhabitants of this . . . country [had] made fine Latin verses in his praise . . . two years ago' and he 'showed his joy and gratitude in looks and words'. Referring to some of the sumptuous gifts Nelson had brought with him from the Mediterranean, the witness added, 'He carries with him fabulous treasures.' The next day, a Sunday, there was an evening fireworks display in the prince's park, and on 8 September a ball. On Tuesday, 9 September, the last day, the guests joined one of the prince's infamous hunting parties. Eighteen hunters and over a thousand bearers and beaters were used to destroy 713 birds and animals in three hours, and a reinvigorated Sir William claimed the revolting distinction of the prize bag, no less than 122 birds. At a supper for seventy, held in a fine hall ceremoniously guarded by one hundred six-foot grenadiers, a toast to Nelson's health was followed by a flourish of trumpets and the thunder of guns in the grounds.[26]

Hamilton loved music, playing the violin and viola, and sometimes kept violinists and cellists as another might servants. The first Lady Hamilton had been an excellent pianist, and composed to boot; the second trended in the same direction, singing, some said beautifully, and often using a guitar or tambourine to accompany her words in the Neapolitan way. Among the many musicians the Hamiltons had entertained in Naples were the Mozarts. The highlight of Nelson's visit, at least for them, was probably the concerts arranged and conducted by the prince's resident musician, the great Joseph Haydn. In a session organised by the princess on 6 September, Haydn accompanied Emma on the pianoforte as she sang his 'Spirit's Song'. Her performance made the audience 'ecstatic' and Haydn gave her a copy of the work.[27]

One who was present painted a discordant picture. James Harris, a nephew of the Mintos and son of Lord Malmesbury, found Nelson a modest man, eager to praise his men, but Emma 'the most coarse, ill-mannered, disagreeable woman I ever met', whose behaviour with Nelson was 'really disgusting'. By his account, at one of the concerts Emma impolitely ignored the musicians and 'sat down to the Faro tables and played Nelson's cards for him, and won between £300 and £400'. If true, Troubridge's homilies about gambling had fallen upon stony ground, and Nelson was risking scarce resources. He was now unemployed, and since Sir William was in debt, funding the expenses of both the Hamiltons and himself. Between 13 July and 18 November Nelson paid out £3432, of which Hamilton owed him £1349. But other evidence implies that in some respects Harris may have exaggerated. According to another source, Lady Hamilton 'never left Haydn's side', and relations between the great composer and the ménage remained good. While in Vienna, Nelson had vainly published Miss Knight's eulogy of September 1798 as a fourteen-page pamphlet entitled *The Battle of the Nile, A Pindarick Ode*. With supreme effrontery he handed copies round, and one reached Haydn, who, at Emma's request, set it to music. Thus was produced *Nelson's Aria* for soprano and piano, using nine of Cornelia's seventeen verses. Haydn may have met the English party again, in Vienna, and presented them with the score before they left. Certainly it would be published in London as *The Battle of the Nile* in 1802.[28]

Nelson was not devoid of an appreciation of good culture, and enjoyed reading. Haydn's friend and biographer recalled that Nelson asked the musician for a pen he used for his compositions, and in return presented Haydn with his watch. Naturally, though, the admiral was predominantly interested in his profession, and probably found more to his liking in an aquatic demonstration organised on the Danube by the Hungarian count Theodor Batthyany, who put an experimental vessel of his own invention through its paces. It had machinery that enabled it to work against the current. Nelson pronounced the device 'prodigiously ingenious' but doubted that it could be a practical success. The exact nature of the vessel is unclear. As early as 1784 the count had produced a vessel capable of working upstream by means of an Archimedian screw attached to the bow. His invention was still protected by a patent, but it was probably an improvement upon it that Nelson saw, for in 1797 the resourceful count had produced 'a new hydraulic engine . . . which . . . could sail upstream without the aid of human hands'. The day seems to have been a satisfying one. Before going to the display the party had fished at Brigittena near the Augarten, and landed their dinner.[29]

Nelson and his friends left Vienna in pouring rain on the morning of 26 September, after five and a half exceptional weeks. Nelson had seen the queen at Schonbrunn on 18 September, but probably took a tearful farewell on the 23rd. The queen assured Emma in a letter that she would always be her friend and sister, and hoped to see her again in Naples, but begged one more service, and gave her letters to deliver in London. Two of the letters, addressed to the Queen of England and Lady Spencer, may have recommended Emma to their protection.[30]

The news for the queen grew blacker during the following months. A letter from Edmund Noble told Nelson that the *Success* had captured the *Diana* frigate as it tried to escape from Valletta, which left the *Justice* the only Nile frigate to escape. Better, soon after, on 5 September, Vaubois surrendered Malta to the British, and the islands were finally liberated. Fifteen hundred British troops under Major General Henry Pigot had belatedly turned up in July, but the French had been starved into defeat, conquered not by soldiers but the British and Portuguese ships that had mounted a two-year blockade. Barely remembered by Nelson biographers, Vaubois had nevertheless been one of the admiral's most obdurate foes, and the Maltese blockade his most costly operation. In addition to the men slain, wounded and captured on ships taken trying to enter or leave Valletta, the losses on the island itself had been appalling. In 1803 Ball, whose services were rewarded by a well-deserved baronetcy, estimated that the Maltese had lost only 300 casualties in the actual fighting, but mourned 12,000 deaths through consequent sickness. Some have put those losses as high as 20,000. Vaubois surrendered 3272 men, all that was left of his regular force. Of the rest, some had been taken in the *Généreux*, *Guillaume Tell*, *Diana* and other vessels, and the others were dead, claimed by disease. Scurvy and fever alone killed 825 of his garrison.[31]

But for the queen and Nelson there was a sting in the tail. Despite the expense and trouble to which Naples had been put during the blockade, her claims upon the island were discarded and her representatives shut out of the capitulation. Captain George Martin of the *Northumberland* and Pigot took the surrender, and Ball's attempt to sign on behalf of Naples, in whose name he had reigned as civil governor, and to have Neapolitan colours raised with the British, were brushed aside. It is easy to see why. When Malta fell the allied coalition was crumbling, and the French were regaining ground. Russia was showing signs of instability, and the Two Sicilies palpably lacked the power to defend Malta. In these circumstances, Britain preferred to retain control of such a highly strategic position, and today it is an independent nation within the British Commonwealth as well as one of Nelson's most enduring legacies. Yet at the time Nelson was angry at the insult to Naples, which had enabled him to take Malta. Certainly the matter could have been handled better, but as it was the queen was left a dupe, drained of resources to help the British during the blockade but discarded as soon as she became inconvenient.

A bitterer pill still awaited Ferdinand and Maria Carolina, after the treaty of Lunéville ended the war between France and Austria in February 1801. France acquired Belgium, Luxembourg and some German areas west of the Rhine, and she turned Piedmont, the Cisalpine and Ligurian republics, Tuscany, Parma, Modena and Lucca into Gallic satellites. Northern Italy had again become a French sphere of influence, and a threat to such neighbours as the papal state. Naples was not even mentioned in the treaty, and had to conclude her own humiliating peace with France at Florence on 18 March, bereft of potent support. The king had to yield a few areas in the north, such as Porto Longone in Elba, and was compelled to pay an indemnity of 120,000 ducats, supply three frigates and submit to the military occupation of portions of his realm, a process he was also expected to fund and provision. In effect, Naples had survived as a chastened vassal, her only consolation the rapidly changing fortunes of these wars. Their Sicilian Majesties could only hope the wretched agreement would stave off a full-blown French invasion until another turn of the wheel of fortune might play to their advantage.

3

A party of eighteen crossed the Danube and rumbled north in their carriages towards Prague. Nelson made a brief stop at Hollabrunn, and it was seven in the evening of 27 September before the travellers finally reached the famous capital of Bohemia. Their billet was the Black Lion hotel, but they had received an invitation from the Archduke Charles, Austria's greatest general as well as a nephew of the Queen of Naples, who resided at the Hradschin Palace. The following day the tourists duly presented themselves at the palace for a convivial meeting, and then did some sightseeing before closing the day with a visit to the King's Theatre. On Nelson's birthday the party returned to the palace for a celebration, and Prague was illuminated in his honour, although the Black Lion shrewdly charged the cost of its additional lighting to its illustrious guests. A second round of birthday festivities got underway at the hotel, where a collection of counts and viscounts and their ladies dined off meat with goose and apple sauce and listened to Emma's rendition of 'God Save The King'. More interesting, she sang 'some charming stanzas written by the amiable and witty

Miss Knight in honour of the hero'. It is quite likely that there, in the Black Lion in Prague, Emma gave the first public performance of Haydn's *Nelson Aria*.[32]

Nelson's expenses at Prague, including £76 for thirty-eight baths and £13 for the use of a pianoforte, which were covered by bills drawn on von Herz in Vienna. Then on 30 September the travellers moved on, towards Dresden, the capital of Saxony. After forty-five miles, half the distance, they halted at Lobositz on the Elbe and transferred to a couple of gondolas, which the archduke had suggested would make a more comfortable mode of conveyance. Sailing leisurely downstream, Nelson enjoyed marvellous vistas of the Elbsandstein mountains before disembarking in Dresden and installing himself in the Hotel Pologne in the Schloss Strasse.[33]

Hugh Elliot, the British ambassador, a brother of Lord Minto, was spending the summer in 'a very pretty villa' in Dresden, and had the admiral and the Hamiltons to dinner on the evening of 3 October. Present was Mrs Melesina St George, who entered a spiteful but amusing description in her diary:

> Dined at Mr Elliot's with only the Nelson party. It is plain that Lord Nelson thinks of nothing but Lady Hamilton, who is totally occupied by the same object. She is bold, forward, coarse, assuming and vain. Her figure is colossal, but excepting her feet, which are hideous, well shaped. Her bones are large, and she is exceedingly embonpoint . . . The shape of all her features is fine, as is the form of her head, and particularly her ears . . . Her expression is strongly marked, variable and interesting, her movements in common life ungraceful, her voice loud, yet not disagreeable. Lord Nelson is a little man without any dignity . . . Lady Hamilton takes possession of him, and he is a willing captive, the most submissive and devoted I have seen. Sir William is old, infirm, all admiration of his wife, and never spoke today but to applaud her. Miss Cornelia Knight seems the decided flatterer of the two, and never opens her mouth but to show forth their praise; and Mrs Cadogan, Lady Hamilton's mother, is – what one might expect. After dinner we had several songs in honour of Lord Nelson, written by Miss Knight, and sung by Lady Hamilton. She puffs the incense full in his face, but he receives it with pleasure, and snuffs it up very cordially. The songs all ended in the sailors' way, with 'Hip, hip, hip, hurra' and a bumper with the last drop on the nail, a ceremony I had never heard of or seen before.[34]

On the morrow the pair seemed 'wrapped up in each other's conversation' in Elliot's box at the opera, but when the ambassador attempted to present the ménage to the court of the Elector Friedrich August III he experienced a hitch, for the latter's wife, Marie Amalie, flatly declined to receive Lady Hamilton. It was the first harbinger of what lay ahead in England, an official refusal to associate with a woman of notoriety. Consequently, on 5 October Nelson, 'a perfect constellation of stars and orders', with the chelengk pinned to his hat, and Ferdinand's jewel-encrusted portrait supporting his medals and orders, and Sir William appeared alone. The private audience was later supplemented by an official dinner. It has been said that Saxony was not as liberal as Austria or Italy. Whatever, Emma met only one royal, the elector's brother, Prince Xavier, who had known them in Naples, but she did join her comrades for a dinner with the wife of the foreign minister of Saxony. Moreover, Emma was in evidence when the party visited the porcelain factories and toured the Dresden Gallery, for which the elector had supplied a guide. While Sir William fussed over the exhibits, others were as eagerly inspecting the famous trio. 'Nelson is one of the most insignificant looking figures I ever saw,' recalled one. 'His weight cannot be more than seventy pounds. A more miserable collection of bones and wizened frame I have never yet come across. His bold nose, the steady eye and the solid worth revealed in his whole face betray in some measure the great conqueror. He speaks little, and then only in English, and he hardly ever smiles . . . He was almost covered with orders and stars . . . As a rule Lady Hamilton wore [carried?] his hat . . . She behaved like a loving sister towards Nelson, led him, often took hold of his hand, whispered something into his ear, and he twisted his mouth into the faint resemblance of a smile . . . She did not seek to win hearts, for everyone's lay at her feet.'[35]

Elliot arranged for the party to sail for England from Cuxhaven, but they decided to proceed towards that port by water, and Nelson ordered their gondolas to be modified to provide toilet and cooking facilities and a screened area. During the additional time spent in Dresden he and Emma sat for a beautiful pair of pastels, which Elliot commissioned from the court painter, Johann Heinrich Schmidt. Her ladyship boasted her Maltese Cross in a likeness that was altogether too innocent and placid to believe, but which became one of two 'guardian angels' in Nelson's cabin in HMS *Victory*. Nelson sported his St Vincent and Nile medals as well as the Bath sash and three orders of knighthood, but his portrait captured a boyishness that reasserted itself after years of physical pain and mental anguish in white-hot love and war.[36]

There was time to treat Dresden to at least two performances of Emma's 'attitudes'. The first, on 7 October, began to melt even Mrs St George, if only a little. 'It is a beautiful performance,' she admitted, 'amusing to the most ignorant, and highly interesting to lovers of art.' But afterwards Emma sang in a strong, good voice that was nevertheless 'frequently out of tune' and neither sweet nor flexible. 'She does not gain on me,' concluded the witness. 'I think her bold, daring, vain even to folly, and stamped with the manners of her first situation . . . Her ruling passion seemed to me vanity, avarice and love for the pleasures of the table . . . Mr Elliot says, "She will capturc the Prince of Wales, whose mind is as vulgar as her own."' A second performance of the 'attitudes', accompanied this time by the tarantella, took place at a breakfast at Elliot's on

9 October, interspersed with repeated acclamations from Nelson. But Melesina was chiefly entranced with the amount of alcohol consumed in the ensuing evening. Emma declared herself 'passionately fond of champagne' and proved it, and Nelson, far from a big drinker, imbibed furiously, calling 'more vociferously than usual for songs in his own praise, and after many bumpers proposed "the Queen of Naples", adding, "She is *my* Queen, she is Queen to the backbone!"' Sir William would not be outdone and 'performed feats of activity, hopping round the room on his backbone, his arms, legs, star and ribbon all flying about in the air'. Melesina sighed, 'Poor Mr Elliot.' When the guests had finally gone the host begged his wife, 'Don't let us laugh tonight. Let us all speak in our turn and be very, very quiet.'

The next day the bizarre outfit collected at the gondolas, ready to descend the Elbe to Hamburg, and Mrs St George noticed how the 'attitudes' and flourishes vanished as soon as they were on board. Emma's maid, Fatima, 'began to scold in French about some provisions which had been forgotten, in language quite impossible to repeat, using certain French words which were never spoken but by men of the lowest class, and roaring them out from one boat to another'. Emma contributed by 'bawling for an Irish stew, and her old mother set about washing the potatoes . . . They were exactly like Hogarth's *Actresses Dressing in the Barn*.'[37]

Eventually the vessels got underway. Equipped with a large main sail, each was about eighty feet long and designed for shifting goods in bulk. Sometimes they sailed side by side in tandem, steered by a single tiller, and were punt-poled around shallows and obstacles. As the vessels slipped downstream they passed bridges, banks and overhead windows jammed with excited spectators, and Nelson politely acknowledged their acclamations. Once the city had been left behind, the boats meandered blissfully through hills cloaked in vineyards and vivid autumnal colours until the landscape flattened out. Every bridge had the crews scurrying to lower or raise the tall masts, which perhaps reached a height of eighty feet. And thus, gently, did they descend towards the North Sea.

Often riding ahead, or using coaches, Francis Oliver announced the imminent arrival of the celebrities, preparing the numerous customs and staging posts, and finding food and rooms. Though nicknamed 'The Jackal', Oliver was not always able to scavenge to satisfaction, as the waterside inns offered little more than sanded floors, beds that brutalised backs, chairs that bit into bottoms, and barely edible provisions. Nor could his efforts always produce the reception the celebrity travellers had come to expect. These, it seemed, were cooler, more sceptical climes.

On 14 October they went ashore at Vockerode, south of Dessau, to be greeted by Prince Leopold Friedrich Franz von Anhalt-Desau, who had once scaled Vesuvius with Sir William. The ensuing day brought them to Magdeburg in Prussia, where they lunched near the cathedral at the King of Prussia in the

Praelaten Strasse. But there was no official reception. Lady Hamilton, acting as interpreter, got them through 'the Bridge Gate' by negotiating with a young officer. With all the appearance of 'a woman full of fire' she adverted to the hero's many wounds and his alleged 120 engagements at sea, and soon Nelson's party was ensconced at a nearby inn as sightseers gathered excitedly. 'He dined with open doors and had wine and refreshments handed out to the crowd of onlookers of every standing,' the same Prussian officer wrote. 'Lady Hamilton helped him to his food.' With an eye to quick profit, the landlord of the inn hired out a stepladder to those who could not get to the doors but were willing to gaze at the admiral through a high window! Nelson was in no way inconvenienced. He discovered several Britons from a 'commercial school' and began 'assuring them that he was nothing less than a great man, [but] they must be loyal and industrious, [and] then they would do equally well; but he above all urged upon them an eternal hatred of the French'. Not only that, but he summoned the officer in immediate command and 'confirmed him heartily in his hatred of the French'. By the time Nelson got back on his boat the banks of the Elbe were filled with people, and skiffs plied busily around. The admiral doffed his hat to the cheering crowd, but there was almost a tragedy. One of the skiffs caught the bow of a gondola and capsized, and Nelson encouraged his people to pull the floundering unfortunates from the water.[38]

Passing downstream, Nelson visited the attractive peninsula of Hitzacker, formed between the meeting of the Jeetzel and the Elbe, and on the afternoon of Tuesday, 21 October arrived at the largest port in Germany, Hamburg, perched on a saltwater estuary. Here, at last, were the smells of home. Again, no official welcome had been prepared, but Oliver had reserved eight rooms in the King of England in the city centre's Neuenwall, and prompted the authorities to provide a guide, Lorenz Meyer. The informal interest in Nelson was considerable. 'All ranks of people, the magistrates as individuals, as well as the inferior classes were eager to receive him with shouts of applause,' observed a resident. In quiet moments during their stay the admiral and a recuperating Sir William enjoyed games of cribbage, a pursuit said to have been brought to England by the admiral's ancestor Sir John Suckling, the cavalier poet. By day Nelson inspected fortifications, dockyards and the harbour, and two evenings were spent at the German Schauspielhaus theatre. Unfortunately, the performance of Kotzebue's *Gustav Wasa* jarred with the admiral's politics, and a play about Richard the Lionheart was marred by a Jacobin gang, which attended for the sole purpose of barracking Nelson before being forcibly ejected from the building. The magistrates blamed the theatre for announcing in their published programme that Nelson would be the guest of honour.[39]

There were interesting people to visit, however. At the home of Baron Breteuil, a former French ambassador to Naples, in Hamm the tourists met the Duke de Guignes, an ageing diplomat, and the exiled French general Charles

François Duperior Dumouriez, the hero of the battles of Valmy and Jemappes, which had saved revolutionary France from being snuffed out at birth. A short, plain man in his sixties, the general had since repented, and fallen on hard times, unemployed and trusted by no one. Nelson found an articulate and intelligent warrior who was fiercely eager to return to the field, though this time in the cause of the allies, and was moved by the man's poverty, giving him £100 with the words that 'he had used his sword too well to live only by his pen'. No doubt he also saw a reclaimed sinner. Nelson suggested Dumouriez offer his services to the British, and for a while the two warhorses, foes turned into friends, enjoyed fantasising about a campaign they might lead together. Why, said Dumouriez excitedly, with Nelson at sea and himself on the land they could save Italy. The meal at Breteuil's may have inspired the report in *The Times* of London, which said that Emma struck up a song, omitting some of the customary verses that Nelson thought might offend a Frenchman. Dumouriez noticed and wept, Emma wiped the hero's tears from his furrowed cheeks, and Nelson cried in solidarity. Certainly the strange friendship flowered, and Nelson visited the general again at his lodgings in the Ottensen. When he got home he sent Dumouriez a complete set of Shakespeare's works, and for a few years the general was refining their plan of campaign against Bonaparte. Nelson encouraged him and recommended him to the British government, but worried that his partner's ebullient self-confidence might irritate ministers, and warned him not to 'make enemies by showing he knows more than some of us'.[40]

The sketchy accounts of Nelson's time in Hamburg refer to other pleasing encounters, at Nienstedten with John Parish and his wife, the parents-in-law of his great friend Hercules Ross; at Altona with the British consul, who proved to be the brother of another friend, Captain George Cockburn; with Sir Brooke Boothby, who claimed to be a poet; and with the aged Friedrich Gottlieb Klopstock, who most assuredly was a poet, but whose formidable appearance, incoherent ramblings and foul tobacco almost drove the Britons from the room. Emma kissed him nevertheless, and promised a performance of her 'attitudes', and he was impressed, writing to a friend that the British admiral was 'a man of heart' who 'sometimes' smiled 'in a particular way'. Of many who visited the ménage, perhaps the most moving was an elderly Lutheran pastor, who appeared at Nelson's apartment one morning, having walked thirty-five miles to have 'the saviour of the Christian world' sign his altar Bible.[41]

The most mysterious, however, made an alarming appearance at Nelson's apartment early one morning. Summoned to see a caller, Sir William met a well-spoken but strange Englishman, who declined to reveal his identity or business but said that he had something to communicate to Lord Nelson in private. Hamilton did not like his manner, and noticed that the visitor kept one hand hidden under a coat, and when he found Nelson he advised him to have the caller sent away. Nelson replied that he had done no man ill, and therefore feared none, and conducted the visitor into a separate room. Some anxious moments passed before Nelson re-emerged to tell the Hamiltons that the man had acknowledged himself to be Major Semple, the notorious 'king of swindlers'. While warning Nelson of a plot to kidnap him when he tried to embark at Cuxhaven, he had not neglected to recount his own sad life as an outcast and his desperate need of money. Instinctively kind-hearted, Nelson supposed the fellow had made a mess of his early life, when he had lacked proper guidance, and descended helplessly into ignominy. 'What shall we do for the poor devil?' he asked. The triumvirate cobbled up a purse of twenty guineas. This is the last known reference to Semple, and may have been his last recorded confidence trick, but Nelson took his intelligence seriously enough to change his planned port of departure from Cuxhaven to Oevelgoenne.[42]

The English community in general were much enamoured of Nelson's appearance in Hamburg. Poems were printed in his honour, and a number of celebrations organised, perhaps by Power and Thornton, two leading merchants. Nelson and the Hamiltons were invited to inspect the local British Trade Factory, and on 27 October a reception was held that drew some thousand people to a house called The English Bowling Green in the vicinity of St Michael's Church. The dinner, concert, ball and supper were graced by a play depicting the battle of the Nile, and a finale of fireworks. Nelson had a speech prepared. Recalling how he had been accidentally shut out of the gates of Hamburg after returning late from nearby Altona the other day, he observed that he trusted the town would defend itself as assiduously against the French. They laughed. Unfortunately, it was apparently that evening that Nelson lost a large diamond from the pommel of the King of Naples' sword, which he had worn for the occasion, and it could not be recovered even with a reward of 1000 reichstaler. Nevertheless, the day after the 'English' event, Emma was performing 'bewitching apparitions of sublime figures' to another audience.[43]

These were his final days on the continent, and amidst the comings and goings, the giving and receiving of presents, and the many public and the few private moments work had to be done. In a shopping expedition Nelson bought a court dress for his wife, and Cornelia helped him choose fine lace to trim it. On 30 October Meyer and Cockburn were bade farewell. The next day Nelson and the Hamiltons graced a waxworks on the Neuen Markt, where an effigy of the admiral was being installed, and then embarked from Oevelgoenne on a hired packet, *King George*, under a Captain Deane. On board they found Lord Whitworth, Britain's former representative in St Petersburg, returning from the funeral of Suvorov.[44]

Sailing was delayed by winds a few days, but a stormy voyage over a grey, cold sea eventually brought the travellers to Yarmouth in the county of Nelson's birth, on Thursday, 6 November. He had been away for two and a half years.

4

As Nelson moved closer to home the temperature had cooled in more ways than one. The attentions of the common folk were diluted by a growing scepticism in government circles. Surrounded by flatterers, Nelson showed a disturbing sense of unreality, capable of any degree of frivolity and innocent of impropriety. He tended to deny his grosser errors, or to explain them by putting others in the wrong, but it is difficult to believe that he was privately untroubled. He had only one good eye, but was far from blind to criticism and gossip, and as he journeyed home knew that uncertainty, unhappiness and trouble lay ahead. He was, after all, a married man returning with his adulterous love, threatened with being unmasked by the secret child growing inside her, and her cuckolded husband. Nelson's professional reputation had also taken a beating in quarters that mattered. Even Lord Spencer had reluctantly come to the opinion that Nelson's further employment in the Mediterranean 'cannot . . . contribute either to the public advantage or his own'. In a sense Nelson had jealously abused his heroic status, disobeying his commander-in-chief in ways that no commonly circumstanced flag officer would have dared, and the price to be paid was still unknown.[45]

The disappointments cut both ways, however. Spencer had befriended Nelson's protégés, as far as the recognised practices of the service allowed, but he had been unable to promote Maurice Nelson to one of the public boards. If Nelson had taken a more realistic view of Spencer's influence, his other brother, William, would not have permitted matters to stand, for he was determined to stir grievances. 'I feel you have cause for complaint that not one relation of the victor of the Nile has been noticed,' Nelson replied. 'I wrote to both Mr Pitt, Mr Windham and Lord Spencer. The two first never answered my letter. The latter has told me he does not know how he can be useful to my brother Maurice. So much for my interest!' Apart from the family disappointments, Nelson had not forgiven Spencer for passing him over in favour of Keith, and complained that he had incurred the expenses, but not the benefits, of being a commander-in-chief.[46]

Nelson was now solicitous of re-employment, but Spencer was not the only relevant actor in that respect. The other crucial figure was St Vincent, the admiral who had nurtured Nelson's earlier career and recently taken over the Channel fleet. In 1796 St Vincent had inherited an efficient fleet trained by Hood, but Lord Bridport, his predecessor in the Channel fleet, had been an altogether inferior admiral and left, as the new commander-in-chief sneered, 'old women' in command of the ships. Immediately St Vincent had set about raising the efficiency of the Channel fleet, tackling procedures, health, discipline, the command structure and the efficiency of the officers. He particularly wanted to mount a rigorous blockade that would confine the enemy to Brest in all weathers, although an admiral who expected his captains to ride out the winter at sea while pleading ill health to enjoy the comforts of Tor Abbey, near Dartmouth, ashore, could expect criticism. A part of St Vincent's plan was to import his Mediterranean men to spearhead reform. He had Troubridge, Collingwood, Saumarez, Foley, Thompson and Fremantle, and he was not ignorant of the value of Nelson.

And yet his opinion of Nelson had also shifted. He disapproved of the involvement with Lady Hamilton, and must have listened grimly to all the returning Troubridge had had to say. Certainly he now doubted Nelson's suitability to theatre command. He was just not a team player. He had always been happiest on detached service, in command of a squadron away from the main fleet, and would probably 'tire' of the mundane but arduous work in the Channel fleet, seeking instead 'a predatory war (which is his metier) on a coast that he is entirely ignorant of, having never served in those seas'. In other words, St Vincent scented trouble, and there was even a hint of jealousy of the man who had displaced him as the nation's most admired sailor. 'He is a partisan,' Nepean, the secretary of the Admiralty, was told. 'His ship always in the most dreadful disorder, and never can become an officer fit to be placed where I am.' At this time Britain was contemplating taking strong action against the Baltic powers, but on 7 December St Vincent recommended that Sir Hyde Parker be given the command of the expeditionary force, on account of his supposed experience of work in that region.[47]

St Vincent's relations with Nelson were also being damaged by disputes over prize money. The two men had skirmished over prize before, but the new dispute endured and festered at a time when Nelson was still to some degree dependent upon the other for his advancement. In October 1799, shortly after St Vincent left the Mediterranean, one of his cruisers, the *Alcmene*, had participated in the capture of two Spanish treasure ships from Vera Cruz, the *Santa Brigida* and *Thetis*, off Cape Finisterre. They contained valuable cargoes of sugar, cochineal and indigo, and bullion worth a staggering £661,200! The captors scrambled for pickings, including those interested in the eighth of the proceeds assigned to flag officers. Although St Vincent had come home to recuperate his health, he had not resigned his command until a month after the prizes were made, and further claimed that the *Alcmene* had still been cruising according to his unrevised orders. Therefore, he was entitled to the lion's share of the flag eighth, and his secretary and prize agent, Benjamin Tucker, accordingly received £14,000 on his account. But Nelson had been the acting commander-in-chief of the Mediterranean that October, ultimately accountable for its doings, and contended that St Vincent had seized his just entitlement. Both officers were surprised at the claims of the other, and in November 1800 St Vincent wrote to Nelson to urge him not to resort to law. 'God forbid I should deprive you of a farthing!' he said. Nevertheless, he sensed the weakness in his position, and engaged the most eminent legal counsel, including Sir William Scott and Sir John Nichol. Davison managed Nelson's campaign, hiring Frederick Booth and William Haslewood as solicitors, and sounding opinions from prize agents and sea officers as well as legal men, and in December Nelson authorised him to proceed against Tucker for the rights of the commander-in-chief.[48]

Nelson's attitude to prize money was far from consistent, but he was genuinely surprised by the earl's resistance to his suit, and was not an officer who readily laid claim to the just emoluments of others. He conceded, for example, that he had no rights in a vessel taken by the *Dover* store ship, and accepted the prize regulations of the time, even when big money was involved. These conventions had enabled St Vincent to do very well out of Nelson, netting him the lion's share of the prize money for the Nile, even though he had neither been in the action nor near enough to direct it. In fact, Nelson had received less for his victory than any participating captain, and only as much as five other junior flag officers who had not been in the battle. The St Vincent suit aside, the extras Nelson had earned as acting commander-in-chief had been comparatively modest. Freight money and his dues from 780 prizes yielded him only £3374 on one account.[49]

Nelson's relationships with the most powerful figures in the navy were not, therefore, what they had once been, and he expected that a measure of rehabilitation might be necessary. He needed to put the unhappiness and guilt of the past year behind him if he could. In his favour there remained his unparalleled reputation as a fighting admiral, the hero of Cape St Vincent and the Nile. Nelson returned to England when relations with the northern powers were deteriorating, and a major expedition was in the making. St Vincent recommended Sir Hyde Parker for the overall command, but there was a serious risk of combat, and Nelson's name would soon be in the hat. As Henry Addington, the Speaker of the House of Commons, remarked, if it came to a fight, Nelson 'was the most likely [officer] to strike a great blow'.[50]

5

But his profession was the least of his problems, for Nelson knew that a family awaited him in England, and one that had the power to sink what happiness he had found with his mistress. It was a family that would place him under diverse pressures. Some members wanted to know what he might do for them, and expected him to break ice for them in hitherto cold, inaccessible regions of social influence. Nelson's social status had changed since he last stood on English soil. He was now of the peerage, and must cut a figure appropriate to a member of that powerful class. He must live to some extent as they did, entertaining in a degree of style, patronising local charities and exercising leadership in the community. Unfortunately, the annuity of £2000 granted by parliament, his modest property near Ipswich, uncertain earnings as a naval officer and slender reserves put him at the poor end of the titled heads. Some of his humbler relatives had little understanding of the expenses that accompanied an exalted social position, and those who did knew that if Nelson's purse was relatively small, his name and reputation rang throughout the land. The eighteenth century thought much of family standing and honour, and constantly weighed the interest and fortune of one house against another. It was natural that Nelson wanted to share his success with relatives, and his nature was in any case a generous one that derived pleasure from giving. There were some, however, who thought him a milch cow to furnish the money, appointments and prestige beyond their own reach, a veritable highway to advantage.

Nelson's family had suffered losses to three generations in the years he had been away. The oldest of his surviving paternal aunts and uncles, Mary, had died at the age of eighty-one on 16 March 1800, after a long decline that Nelson had tried to ease with financial contributions. Only two aunts remained, Alice and Thomasine. The admiral's last maternal uncle, his old patron William Suckling, had also gone. He had lobbied for his nephew, supplied allowances and even borne part of the cost of outfitting him for sea in 1793. Nelson was named an executor to the will of the deceased, but also felt a great obligation to Mary, his widow, and four offspring. Mary, who lived in Hampstead, had sold a family estate in Suffolk and was holding a small legacy for Nelson. The admiral had also lost his last younger brother, Suckling, who had perished in a sudden fit on 30 April 1799, and been laid to rest in the Norfolk village of his birth. His ecclesiastical living at Burnham Sutton reverted to his father, Edmund. Edmund's extensive brood had not been a healthy one. Only five of eleven children survived, Maurice, Susannah, William, Horatio and Kate, and between them they had a current tally of eight nieces and four nephews, some of whom were already beginning to write letters to their famous uncle. Susannah had recently been struck by tragedy, when her second son, George Bolton, died on his way to join his uncle in the Mediterranean in 1799.[51]

Nelson's patronage was expected to extend far, and although he had distributed part of the East India Company grant to his father and siblings, the admiral remained conscious of disappointing. Of the siblings and in-laws the ablest and most independent was George Matcham, husband of Nelson's youngest sister, Kate. His family were comfortable, but George was thinking of selling his home, Shepherd Spring near Christchurch, and moving to the continent when a peace had been signed. At the moment the Matchams were living in Kensington Place, Bath, where Kate was carrying another child, Horatio. Nelson's older sister, Susannah, was happily married to Thomas Bolton at their farm at Cranwich, five miles from Hilborough. Brother William was jealous of the property, but Bolton had actually over-reached himself to acquire it, and dunned Fanny for loans or used Nelson's name to obtain credit. Susannah's grubby and ill-natured twins, Catherine and Susannah, were often boarded on the long-suffering Fanny, and Bolton wanted Nelson to get him a position on a public board.

Nelson's brothers pressed him the most, and since he was childless they had an additional importance as potential suppliers of heirs for the admiral's titles. The older brother, Maurice, had been clerking in the bills and accounts department of the Navy Office for most of the last quarter of a century. He had no children, and waived his place in the succession to William, his younger brother, but he did hope that Nelson could save him from his lowly status and find him a more remunerative public position. Maurice had a couple of modest homes to maintain, as well as his 'wife' Sukey, whose physical condition was deteriorating. Her eyesight was failing, and she suffered 'contractions' in her hands. Nelson loved Maurice, and felt the more committed to helping him after disappointing his brother in the matter of the Nile prize agency. The Admiralty had so far resisted the admiral's solicitations, however, but in April 1801 Maurice would get a minor promotion and a salary of £400 per annum.[52]

The most insistent beneficiary of Nelson's patronage was his other brother, William, the insufferable rector of Hilborough whom the admiral characterised as a natural 'big wig' too fond of food and drink, the truth of which was evident to all who saw his growing corpulency. His wife Sarah, his 'jewel', had given him Charlotte, now a beautiful teenager, and Horace, both being educated under the supervision of relatives. Charlotte was at Whitelands School for young ladies on the King's Road, Chelsea, and within commuting distance of Fanny, whenever she was in London. Horace had been placed at Eton, a few miles from Laleham, where Maurice had his small country retreat, and he was willing to show the boy the sights of London during vacations. The two had been there when the *Lord Nelson*, a merchantman, was launched at Deptford.[53]

William was not well liked. He had not felt it necessary to ride forty miles to see his younger brother, Suckling, dying in a fit in 1799, nor were the words he had said at the funeral deemed charitable. His manipulation of Nelson's interest for his own advantage was notorious in the family. 'I dare say the mitre is very near falling on his head now,' Kate wrote after the battle of the Nile. While Nelson was away William had continually traded on his triumphs, sometimes with a belligerence that frightened timorous souls. Fanny thought him 'the roughest mortal, surely, that ever lived', and a man driven by 'ambition, pride and a selfish disposition'. It mortified her to see him pestering his aged and sick father to lobby William Windham, member of parliament for Norwich and a secretary of state, or the Lord Chancellor, in his campaign for a bishopric. 'I must write . . . and beg him not to be so tiresome,' Fanny complained, 'for truly I am nursing and doing everything I can to make your father comfortable, and . . . he is quite upset by . . . these epistles.' Deflected, William turned on Nelson, telling him that in 1799 the Lord Chancellor had only given him a small living that would clear no more than £120 per annum, though deaneries and prebendal stalls had been allocated to others. No sooner had he met Emma than he began plumbing her 'interest' for what he could get.[54]

Returning to Yarmouth, Nelson knew that his brothers would be gathering, eager to push him to exercise an influence he doubted he had, but he loved them anyway, and his key anxieties lay elsewhere. They were with the most constant of all his supporters, the two people who thought more of him than anyone in England, and who had waited for his return through the years. With him, they had once been the nucleus of his life, the other members of the old triumvirate, his wife Fanny and Edmund, his old father. But his life, and theirs, had changed forever.

6

The paths of Fanny and her father-in-law had thoroughly intertwined, as Edmund once reminded his son in acknowledging that he had arrived at the 'last stage of human life'. 'I well remember that on my receiving a wound [the death of his daughter, Ann, in 1783], you promised to heal it by giving me another daughter. Indeed, you have. Lady Nelson's kindness as a friend, a nurse, a daughter, I want words to express.' Fanny had become the beloved substitute of that lost favourite, and in increasing decrepitude was a rare comfort. She was, he said, 'the very counterpart of her great and good husband'.[55]

Edmund relied upon Fanny for company, care and the shared longing for Nelson's return. Approaching seventy-nine years, he had nearly died in the hard winter of 1799–1800, when he and Fanny had temporarily exchanged Roundwood for a few rooms in St James's Street, London, for a weekly rent of seven guineas. His appearance had much altered, as he ate little and coughed and wheezed inside a paper-thin frame, on the verge of mental agitation. He seemed, said Maurice, about to slip away 'like the snuff of a candle'. Aware of his frailty, Edmund stayed in London, where medical men were close by, but spent much time slumbering in his chair before a fire in his back drawing room, the long white locks falling forward about the drooping head and lined cheeks. Even the children sensed they were losing something valuable. Young Charlotte sadly noticed how 'very much broken' the old man had become, and how he sat for whole evenings without a word when she remembered a man once so cheerful. Fanny bore the brunt of caring for the old man. She planned to use sedan chairs to get him out, and despite her own coughs, indispositions and rheumatism stayed constantly at his side. 'I have never left him since this severe illness but once,' she wrote on 23 February. 'That was at his own desire [that I was] to dine at Mr Davison's, who had a cheerful dinner company.' Edmund was so ill that the portrait painter William Beechey had to come to his lodgings to give him a sitting. One problem seems to have been an acute hernia, for which surgical procedures were occasionally necessary. 'His body comes down too frequently, even turning in his bed quickly,' Fanny explained. The manservant had to be taught how 'to put it up', while an ailing prostate led to the patient's urine also having to be 'drawn off'. That Nelson's father survived that terrible year to gaze upon his son again was largely down to Fanny. The old man knew it. 'The hope of seeing his son, I verily believe, keeps his good father alive,' she told Davison. 'It is impossible to describe how very feeble he gets.' But 'he told me yesterday, if he lived to see him [Nelson], the first thing he should say to him was to take care of me'.[56]

It was not the first time that Fanny had sustained an ailing Nelson. She it was who had eased the final days of the admiral's younger brother, Edmund junior, during his 'deep decline' in Burnham Thorpe. 'I was his friend and nurse to the last,' she said. And then she had been beside her husband as he made his painful recovery from the loss of his arm. Fanny and the Reverend Edmund were indeed the heart of Nelson's waiting family. While her husband was away, Fanny improved Roundwood, managed servants and finances, dealt with the numerous appeals for patronage, kept up with friends, and, moving between Burnham Thorpe, Ipswich, London, Bath and Clifton near Bristol, represented Nelson in society without incurring a known word of reproach. She had Charlotte and Horace to stay when she was in London and they on vacation, enjoying their respective charming childhood chatter about pearl earrings and pet rabbits. Although a daughter of the 'gentle' classes, Fanny had never been a natural society belle, but she visited the palatial properties of the Cokes and Walpoles in Norfolk, and was received at court in London several times after Nelson's elevation to the peerage, appearing four times in the queen's 'drawing room' functions between November 1798 and March 1800. She made friends, and people liked her, even after the whispering started. Fanny's was not a complicated mind, and her letters were disjointed and parochial, but she had solid qualities, including the vastly misnamed attribute of common sense. She was seldom bowled over by flattery, saw through silly shibboleths ('every man who refuses a challenge [to a duel] exalts himself,' she said), and realised that in her circumstances living 'in the style of a gentleman's family' meant keeping within means. There must be 'nothing fine' about a carriage, and when William chided her for the economies she practised in London, she had to remind him that she was keeping two homes whenever she stayed there. On fiscal affairs, she took advice from Davison and William Marsh. Fanny was throughout a compassionate woman (we find her typically looking for a hospital place for a sick housemaid), sweet-natured and forgiving, loyal, dutiful and self-sacrificing, and she hardly deserved the fate that was engulfing her.[57]

The trouble was that Nelson no longer loved her, and found her very presence an irritation. He had moved on in two and a half years, into a different world of monarchs and international diplomacy, a world understood and shared by the Hamiltons, in whom he now confided. He returned hopelessly in love with Emma, the father of her child, and was incapable of living apart from her. She and her husband, not the homely Fanny and Edmund, were the other members of the triumvirate that now mattered to him. Away, Nelson had lived two lives, but now he had to reconcile the old world with the new. He fancied that he could avoid separating from Fanny, but maintain a close relationship with the Hamiltons, and probably his illicit affair with Emma. From Vienna a letter went to London in search of 'a house or good lodgings' where he might handle town business, and, of course, live in close proximity to the Hamiltons.[58]

A battle between the rival women was looming, one in which Fanny was decidedly disadvantaged, for she was ill at ease in the grand theatre that was Emma's forte, and could not compete with the other's energy, talent and flair. Fanny was understated and domestic, not flamboyant and worldly; quiet, unobtrusive and discreet, rather than loud, theatrical and attention-seeking; mild-mannered and decorous instead of wilfully beguiling; and plain and measured, not a tempestuous beauty, extravagant in word and deed. She was also handicapped by her greater honesty and decency. 'Some women can say or do anything; I cannot,' she admitted. She was proud of her husband, but, like Edmund, wished for a safer life for him, which she could share in honour and peace, and deep down she was frightened of Nelson's fighting spirit. Emma, at least at the moment, stoked it up to drink hungrily from the reflected glory. Perhaps most of all, Fanny had never been able to excite her husband as Emma did, nor give him a child.[59]

Fanny had resisted criticising or confronting her husband, but conversations with Hood and St Vincent in 1799 had aroused her suspicions, and before the end of the year Nelson's relationship with Lady Hamilton had reached the British press. Fanny was sure that the Hamiltons were brewing 'mischief' and shared her concerns with Davison, who tried to befriend both parties. Nelson's letters also told their own story. While Fanny wrote about once a fortnight, the replies were few, short and emotionless, containing little more than brief allusions to business and self-congratulation. Despite the 'most affectionate' finales to these dutiful documents, there was little love in them. At one time Fanny supposed someone was intercepting and stealing her husband's letters, so few had made their appearance, and she probably paused to wonder at her husband's reaction to her suggestion that she join him in the Mediterranean to improve her health. He abruptly dismissed the idea. Whatever constructions she might have put on some or all of these things, she had a brave face for visitors. St Vincent found her 'in good health and spirits' at the end of 1799, and 'most kind and attentive' as always. In her letters to her husband she made no reference to the rumours, and pretended nothing had changed. 'Make my best regards to her,' she wrote of Lady Hamilton, and she sent her a cap and kerchief. Truly, she said, 'it has been my study to please and make you happy.'[60]

Starved of news, Fanny and Edmund waited long months, thrilling at the occasional visits of officers with the fleet. When Lieutenant Edward Parker arrived at Roundwood late one night, paying his respects while his chaise waited at the door, Fanny was charmed by 'the young man's extreme gratitude and modesty', and felt 'so glad to see anyone who could give me such late accounts of my dear husband and my son that . . . I could not hear or see, and was obliged to call in our good father, who made many enquiries'. Hardy, Berry, Foley, St Vincent and Oswald were among the others who brought first-hand tidings of the Mediterranean, while in London and Bath she was delighted to meet naval friends and acquaintances, such as Waldegrave, Locker, Boyles, Hood and the Parkers, Nepeans and Spencers, who had had private letters from the fleet, or plain old service gossip. Most suppressed anything amiss that they had heard, or prevaricated, and some gave the impression that Nelson was actually eager to come home. But to such a woman as Fanny any rumours were unsettling, and must have made her wait an eternity.[61]

There were apprehensions aplenty as the ménage travelled home, and not merely in Nelson. Sir William's health and finances were broken, and he craved rest and a respectable pension, which he intended to supplement by selling some of his art treasures and antiquities. Free thinking, he cared relatively little for the way the world viewed him so long as he was free to indulge in a little fishing and intellectual stimulation in his twilight years. At thirty-five Emma was more vulnerable. The days when she could bedazzle a great city had gone, and she worried about how a less permissive and more sceptical society, which hardly recognised her undoubted patriotism, would receive her. The London set were far from salubrious. The Duke and Duchess of Devonshire both had children by other partners, one of whom, Lady Elizabeth Foster, lived in the same house. But it could not compete with Naples. Unfortunately, Emma needed attention, and could no more have sunk into a quiet provincial life than Fanny could have walked upon a stage. But despite her artistic abilities and the remains of beauty, her social background, dubious past and scandalised present were all against her. Her last visit to London in 1791 had spawned a Rowlandson cartoon showing her posing naked for lecherous artists in the Royal Academy. Displayed in West End print shops and coffee houses, such artefacts were important arbiters of popular taste and discussion. Nelson had been the subject of no fewer than a dozen of them in 1798, but they were heroic in character, the most famous James Gillray's energetic depiction of the admiral furiously clubbing 'revolutionary' Nile crocodiles into submission and harnessing them to his train. But Emma only entered the grotesque if effective world of caricature to lower the tone, and just twelve days after the ménage arrived in Yarmouth George Cruikshank's *A Mansion House Treat, or Smoking Attitudes* had her comparing the sexual potency of her lovers with the words, 'Pho, the old man's pipe is always out, but yours [Nelson's] burns with full vigour!' As Mrs St George testified,

Emma feigned indifference, but returning to such ridicule, she was deeply worried about what the future held. Prestige and respectability, she knew, would be hard to regain, not the least because the proof of her infidelity was growing in her belly, but she was also financially insecure. Sir William had never looked frailer, and if he died beset by debts, as seemed probable, how would she maintain herself? She needed another protector, and her eyes were upon Nelson, whom she certainly loved, and whose standing as a hero could open doors that might otherwise be closed. Emma was not naturally cruel, but in her own interest she could be ruthless and must have realised that ultimately she might have to destroy Nelson's marriage, and usurp Fanny from both the admiral's home and family.

The complications that Nelson and Emma's fervent romance had avoided far away in sultry Palermo had now to be faced. There had to be serious casualties.

7

In the struggle that Fanny and Emma would wage for their man, two other actors would play crucial roles, Josiah Nisbet, Fanny's son and Nelson's stepson, and Emma's unborn child.

Nelson had always loved children. He spoke of them as symbols of love that would stand as legacies long after the original partners had been gathered to their fathers. Had Fanny provided Nelson with a child, vulnerable to any disputes between the parents, he might have fought for his marriage. Her failure to do so must have raised fears in Nelson that he was sterile, given that she had borne her first husband a son. But even as a stepson, Josiah might have been the glue that kept the couple together. His story has not interested biographers, yet for several years the relationship between stepfather and son had been a source of continuing pain and sadness. Had Josiah been a William Hoste or Edward Parker, he could have been a powerful bond. Instead he became a liability, another aspect of Nelson's old life that he wanted to leave behind.

Nelson had done everything he could to bring Josiah forward, but he had constantly disappointed. With considerable adjustments to the truth, he had got him posted captain of the *Thalia* frigate in 1799, for any ambitious young officer an enviable billet. The boy was still legally a minor, eighteen years old, and almost as many months short of the minimum age theoretically needed to hold a commission as a naval lieutenant. Yet here he stood, two steps further up the ladder on the list of post-captains, won by a singular example of naval nepotism. Thus situated, he had an excellent chance of proceeding by seniority to flag rank, even on the back of barely adequate service. Moreover, against his better judgement, St Vincent, then commander-in-chief, had given him his smartest and best-manned cruiser, hoping it would 'not be thrown away' on such an unpromising officer. Josiah was inexperienced, but furnished with talented officers. First Lieutenant Samuel Colquit was 'highly spoken of', and he was supported by Lieutenant John Yule, who had proved himself on the *Alexander*. The master, Alexander Briarly, had the reputation of a man who knew his business, and counted himself a veteran of the Nile. If Josiah was to redeem his undistinguished record in the *Dolphin* and *La Bonne Citoyenne*, this was the ship and ship's company to help him. Ball, who had shown more patience with Josiah than anyone else, tried to be positive, but Nelson had already despaired of his stepson ever making much of himself. For his part, Josiah kicked against the traces like many a troubled young man, and more. He had no liking for the sea, he protested, and resented being told how lucky he was when he was constantly failing. Furthermore, he did not like Emma, and resented the way she had displaced his mother in Nelson's affections.[62]

Occasionally Josiah looked as if he might confound the doubters. Joining the blockade of Malta, he took a few prizes. When Nelson had placed his puny squadron off Marettimo to intercept Bruix in May 1799, the *Thalia* had done some useful work plying between Sicily and the Barbary coast in case the French came that way. Later, when operating in the Gulf of Genoa under Martin of the *Northumberland*, he had even shown initiative. The governor of Orbetello told him that the French were about to evacuate Civita Vecchia, the port of Rome, and might surrender if their retreat was cut off and reasonable terms offered. Accordingly, Nisbet delayed joining Foote in Leghorn as ordered, and proceeded to Civita Vecchia, where he summoned the garrison on 23 July, emphasising its unenviable position. It could have worked, but did not, and Nelson was unimpressed, though he admitted 'it was done for the best'. The *Thalia* returned to cruising, taking a couple of boats carrying corn to Civita Vecchia and a privateer.[63]

Unfortunately, the complaints piled up with disturbing speed. In September Darby of the *Bellerophon* reported that the physical condition of the *Thalia* was so poor that a refit would be needed to keep her at sea during the winter, and, what was perhaps worse, it became obvious that the teamwork, discipline and spirit of the ship's company were being destroyed under Nisbet's leadership. Repeating former errors, Nisbet wielded an excess of force common to many weak commanders, who used the articles of war to supply what leadership and personality lacked. At least forty-two floggings were administered on the *Thalia* during a twenty-month period. The average sentence amounted to about twenty-three strokes, but a gross seventy-two lashes punished one man for theft, and four other heavy sentences consisting of forty to fifty lashes were handed out.[64]

Stories were soon reaching Nelson of his stepson drinking and keeping low company, and that the *Thalia* was an unhappy ship, in which Josiah's inability to maintain a proper distance between a captain and his subordinates was breeding a dangerous familiarity. Not the familiarity that bound a Nelson to his juniors in mutual respect, but a type that bred contempt for an overpromoted and graceless boy losing control. Instead of keeping a table in his cabin, to which he might invite guests, Nisbet messed with inferiors in the gunroom, and the place contained two women, one an Italian, who may have trifled with and compromised the adolescent captain. Between 14 August and 18 September Josiah took sick leave ashore in Leghorn, and according to Martin his ailment arose 'from the venereal'. Even there he could not avoid trouble, and offended an Austrian general for ordering one of his privateering vessels broken up for firewood. Troubridge wanted Nisbet to apologise and pay compensation to abort a complaint from Vienna. Whatever the result, Nelson considered Nisbet's sojourn on shore a dereliction of duty, and had curtly ordered him back to his ship.[65]

Josiah was soon at odds with his principal officers. Lieutenant Colquit, a protégé of Captain Isaac Coffin, now an irascible dockyard commissioner, was ambitious and resented playing nursemaid to an unworthy upstart. He had, in fact, already captained the frigate on an acting basis, and no doubt hoped to regain command. Colquit's log is remarkable. Although a public document, legally owned by the Admiralty and capable of being called in and examined, it was used by the lieutenant to criticise his captain in an extraordinary way. Possibly Colquit thought the captain's log did him less than justice. It did not, for example, record that Colquit had to resume command of the ship while Nisbet was on sick leave, and it failed to pay satisfactory homage to the lieutenant's role in the ship's few successes, all omissions Colquit conscientiously corrected in his own account. But there was also direct criticism of Nisbet, venomous in its nature because it was secretly entered in a log that would eventually be submitted to the Admiralty. The best example concerned an incident that occurred on 30 March 1800, when Colquit described the chase of a strange sail. 'Found ourselves to gain fast upon the chase, which appeared to be an enemy armed vessel,' he said. 'At 8 (to the astonishment of everyone) Captn. Nisbet ordered the ship to be hauled to the wind, and left off the chase, assigning as his reason that the ship was only 5 leagues from the land, though no reckoning made it nearer than 9 leagues . . . The enemy must have been captured.' The lieutenant's and captain's logs did not even agree on the ship's longitudinal position, which the former placed at 12 degrees 23 minutes, 36 leagues from Allegranza in the Canaries, and Nisbet at 10 degrees 44 minutes, 26 leagues from the Moroccan coast. The next month Colquit returned to the attack, describing the loss of the frigate's main topmast in a strong northwesterly on 8 April. 'This loss was occasioned by too much top weight and want of judgement in carrying sail,' he said. The hostility between Nisbet and Colquit was soon widely known, but in this case Nelson seems to have backed his stepson, and displayed a 'cool' demeanour to the embattled lieutenant.[66]

A more immediate personnel problem had arrived when the admiral was at

Port Mahon, Minorca, in October of 1799. Captain Darby, commanding there, passed him a formal letter from Josiah. Dated 30 September it demanded a court martial on his lieutenant of marines, William Fisher Bulkely. His lordship must have sighed, but had little choice but to comply. He also ordered the *Thalia* to Gibraltar to serve under Duckworth, to whom he opened his heart in a private letter. 'I wish I could say anything in her [*Thalia*'s] praise, inside or out,' he wrote. 'Perhaps you may be able to make something of Captain Nisbet. He has, by his conduct, almost broke my heart.' But, said the despairing admiral, if 'no good can be got out of either ship or captain' Duckworth should send them home with a convoy and be done with them. Duckworth promised to do his best with Josiah and 'bring him round'.[67]

The court martial was convened at Port Mahon three days after Christmas, with Louis of the *Minotaur* presiding and Captain Hoste as one of the judges. Hoste had been with Josiah in the old *Agamemnon*, and had not liked him. On this occasion the testimony revealed a trivial episode that a witness, John Richards, commander of the *Courageuse*, nevertheless described as 'one of the most disagreeable I ever experienced during the whole of my service'. The evening of 29 September had found Josiah in Port Mahon, dining in the gunroom of his ship with some of his officers according to his custom. A few guests were also present, but apparently not for the first time Josiah's table conversation began 'tending to the obscene' until Lieutenant Bulkely rose from his place angrily denouncing 'such blackguard discourses'. In an ugly confrontation, Bulkely threatened to seize Nisbet by the nose unless he left the room, and Josiah called his accuser 'a damned rascal' and said he would run him through with a dirk. Mr Briarly, the master, and other officers intervened, and got the captain up on deck, but the court martial did neither party any good. Bulkely was dismissed from the ship and demoted to the bottom of the list of marine lieutenants, but Nisbet's charges of insubordination were only 'partly proved' and if nothing else demonstrated the captain's poor standing among his officers. In reporting the proceedings to Nelson, Louis recommended that several officers, in addition to Bulkely, be removed from the ship. 'I really think the familiarity too great,' he observed.[68]

Initially, Nelson got happier news from Duckworth, who thought 'much better' of Josiah 'than your Lordship' and gave some 'most favourable' reports. Among other creditable services, Nisbet had saved the crew of a transport which had gone down in heavy December gales. When Nelson encountered his stepson at Leghorn at the beginning of 1800, he was pleased to find him 'much improved'. Even Troubridge, who had had his difficulties with Nisbet, was upbeat, informing Nelson that he had received 'a very pleasant letter from [Captain John] Inglefield, telling me how well Captain Nesbitt [sic] has behaved at Gibraltar. I am sure it will give your Lordship pleasure to hear it. Get him among us that we may wean him from too much familiarity with his officers.' For the first time in a year or more, Nelson saw a glimmer of hope.[69]

But it was only raised to be dashed. Back in Leghorn, Josiah went ashore in flagrant breach of the port's quarantine and health regulations. Keith, then commander-in-chief, feared an enquiry that would ruin the boy, and wrote Nelson an embarrassing letter. 'Now, my good lord,' he said, 'for God's sake let this young man write a letter of apology to the Grand Duke [of Tuscany, and] his Senate, because you know if it comes to me in [official] form what must be done, and it may end ill for him.' Another unseemly incident showed how Nisbet was speedily resorting to violence to settle differences or impose his authority. During an altercation at a Leghorn theatre he beat a man so badly that Briarly 'begged' the captain to 'let him alone' lest it provoked retaliation from a hostile mob. Captain Louis thought Briarly one of the dubious influences on Nisbet, but the records suggest his effect was rather more palliative, and he certainly sent a timely warning about Josiah's waywardness to Nelson's secretary, John Tyson.[70]

Ironically, it was Briarly who next crossed swords with Captain Nisbet, over the issue of stores in the *Thalia*, which the master claimed fell within his prerogative. Attempting to assert his right in February 1800, he was 'accosted' by Nisbet and called 'a damned rascal', evidently one of the captain's favourite phrases. In a prolonged rant, Josiah successively threatened to drive the hapless master overboard, make of him 'a broom stick who I can make do as I think proper', and turn the ship into 'a Hell' for him. 'Damn your eyes,' he was quoted, 'you are no more an officer than the boatswain or carpenter, I will recommend them, if ever you refuse to sign the[ir] expense [for stores] to knock you down.' Briarly appears to have restrained himself in the face of such appalling behaviour, although he later accused Nisbet of turning the other ship's officers against him with 'the most infamous and false' lies 'that ever disgraced the mouth of man'. The captain's bullying extended to the surgeon, who was 'struck . . . a blow on the quarter-deck' and placed under arrest. Unlike Briarly, the surgeon demanded his day in court, and he was not alone. By June 1800 a well-officered ship had been turned into a bed of discontent. Duckworth at last owned that he had failed, and sadly informed Nelson that Colquit had such 'a string of complaints' that would 'quite destroy Captain Nisbet's reputation' if they got to a court martial. For the sake of the boy's stepfather, Duckworth began shuffling officers around to head off a glut of damaging trials. While poor Yule, who also disliked Nisbet, remained in the *Thalia*, the surgeon was discharged in March, Colquit invalided out of the ship in July and Briarly discharged in Minorca in September, even though the frigate was left without a master. No doubt the officers concerned were relieved to transfer to other duties, but Colquit for one had not finished with the captain of the *Thalia*.[71]

Nisbet's career as a frigate captain was not without *any* redeeming features. Between 24 June and 7 August 1800 he took five prizes, including two privateers, and recaptured two enemy prizes, and he earned praise for his cruises west of the Strait. When Keith withdrew him from that area, a Madeira merchant even appealed against the decision, explaining that Josiah 'kept us so free of enemy's cruisers that a variety of arrivals have brought us most seasonable supplies and relieved a threatened scarcity. He now further obliges the trade by seeing clear of the island all the vessels in readiness to sail, and they are forward in expressing their wishes that your Lordship may allow of Capt. Nisbet's return to take care of us.' But Keith, who had done his best to keep the youngster out of trouble to oblige Nelson, was not impressed, and ordered *Thalia* home with dispatches. Thus, while Nelson made his way home overland, Josiah went by sea. He was at Plymouth on 6 October, and took a convoy into Deptford on 17 November, hauling his pendant down on 12 December.[72]

Josiah did not know it, but the navy would never employ him again; before he had even attained his legal majority, his career was finished. In some respects his had been a most singular experience. Formally, an aspirant in the navy needed to be twenty years of age, and show six years of relevant sea time to be eligible for a lieutenant's commission. The steps to commander and post-captain might never be achieved, but few gained them without several years of respectable service and a degree of luck and 'interest'. Consider, then, Josiah's spectacular climb. By gross acts of nepotism on the part of Nelson and St Vincent, a thirteen-year-old boy entering the navy in 1793 had been promoted post-captain at the age of seventeen on 24 December 1798, with less than six years of experience at sea under his belt. More, he held a golden opportunity in his hand, cruising for prizes in wartime with a fast frigate and strong crew. Stationed on the captains' list at such an early age, he had to do almost nothing but live and keep a clean record to rise by seniority to flag rank. Nelson had engineered his promotion, on account of which St Vincent, Keith, Duckworth, Troubridge and Ball, among others, had tried to favour and guide him. It had all been for nothing, and the boy had written himself off at twenty. As Nelson admitted, it broke his heart.

Josiah was responsible for his failures, but not entirely. He had never wanted to go to sea, and growing and working alongside the likes of Hoste or even William Bolton he had quickly recognised his short comings. Promotion had not won respect. If anything, it pointed him out as the worst kind of officer, who owed everything to connection and little to merit. The scandal involving his stepfather and mother was an additional burden, hard on a mere teenager. But when all was said and done, Josiah and Nelson were both victims of a flawed system. The road to flag rank, traversed according to seniority, was long if not always laborious. The captains shuffled sluggishly up their list in a queue system, waiting for appointments, retirements and deaths above to clear a way forward. Most started their journeys too late in the day to get their flags. To succeed it was necessary to begin early. A beneficiary of nepotism himself, Nelson had done extremely well, making flag rank at forty, but he had been fortunate to become a post-captain at twenty. In these circumstances, the urge of well-intentioned naval officers to push young protégés forward as fast as possible was natural. Unfortunately, Josiah's is perhaps the best example of the downside of the process. He was too immature for the responsibilities of command. In short, a boy was being asked to do a man's job, and a difficult one at that. He failed, spectacularly. Given ten more years at sea, he might have turned into a jobbing captain, but at twenty he was lost, and there were no more chances. The verdict would stand.

Inevitably, that failure rebounded upon the relationship between Nelson and his stepson, and they exchanged several hard words. The admiral found his advice ignored, and the opportunities he had won squandered. He tired of unloading an ungrateful and abusive boy on luckless subordinates, and of bailing him out of hot water. Yet Nelson desperately wanted a son, and channelled immense love and attention upon Hoste and later Parker. Had Josiah been like them, he might have saved his mother's marriage. But as he was, Josiah became simply another problem that came with a wife he no longer loved. Rather than a bond holding Nelson and Fanny together, he pushed them further apart.

Fanny was truly unlucky, in her son as in her two husbands, the one fatally sick and the other unfaithful. Through Emma, however, Nelson had another shot at fatherhood. If he had any lingering doubts about the road to future happiness, the little girl who saw light for the first time in January 1801 would have dispelled them. Fanny's fight to save her marriage was doomed to failure.

XII

DOMESTIC STRIFE

A heart *susceptible*, sincere and true;
A heart, by Fate and Nature, torn in two;
One half to duty and his country due;
The other, *better half*, to love and you!

Sooner shall Britain's sons resign
The empire of the sea;
Than Henry shall renounce his faith,
And plighted vows to thee!

'Lines [written] . . . in the late gale',
Nelson to Emma Hamilton, 16/2/1801

I

ONE question was quickly answered. Not since Drake's circumnavigation of the globe in 1580 had a returning English sailor been so welcomed by the public. The town corporation and a gaping crowd greeted Nelson when he landed at Yarmouth, the mob unhitching the horses of the ménage's carriage, imported from Germany, and man-hauling it to the Wrestlers Inn in the centre of the town amid unbridled applause. The freedom of the town was bestowed, foot soldiers paraded before the hostelry and while a regimental band struck up muskets and artillery spat salutes that lasted until midnight. The ships in the harbour raised their colours and the town was illuminated. During the hullabaloo Nelson penned a note to the Admiralty to inform their lordships that his health had been 'perfectly established' and that he was 'immediately' ready to serve. The next day local officials accompanied Nelson's party to the church, where an organ piped 'See, the Conquering Hero Comes' and thanks were given for his safe return. Nelson donated £60 to the poor of the town, and when he left, a detachment of volunteer cavalry escorted his carriage to the county boundary.[1]

He headed to Roundwood. Nelson had found letters from Fanny waiting at

Yarmouth, but only opened one of them, the wrong one. Fanny had not received a letter Nelson had written from Vienna, telling her to meet him in London, and when she had eventually learned about her husband's plans there was no time to prepare accommodation in London. Fanny therefore rushed letters to Yarmouth and Harwich, ports Nelson might use, inviting him to Roundwood first. Nelson's party accordingly divided. Mrs Cadogan and Cornelia made straight for London, while Nelson, the Hamiltons and Fatima reached Roundwood on the morning of Sunday, 9 November. To their surprise no one was at home, and Nelson had to content himself with inspecting his only home for the best part of an hour. Reportedly he was 'much pleased with the improvements Lady Nelson had made'. But then the party sped into Ipswich for lunch at Bamford's Hotel. The town was as excited as Yarmouth had been, and Nelson's visit was marked by roaring crowds and the ritual unhitching and hauling of his carriage.[2]

The confusion at Roundwood had arisen because, after sending her first letters to the ports, Fanny had been persuaded by Davison to meet Nelson in London after all, and she and Edmund had taken rooms at Nerot's Hotel in King Street, not far from the prize agent's own townhouse at 9 St James's Square. She had written revised epistles, but Nelson had not troubled to open the one at Yarmouth. The consequence was that Fanny had been put in the wrong through no fault of her own, and her first meeting with her husband in the new century would have to begin with an explanation. It was not a good sign. The air was pregnant with anticipation. Troubridge, Hardy and Berry were also in London waiting to greet Nelson, the first two with news that the *San Josef*, a massive Spanish first-rate Nelson had taken in 1797, was being earmarked as his new flagship, with an appointment to the Channel fleet under his old chief, St Vincent. Knowing Berry's inadequacies, Troubridge had colluded to ensure that Hardy would be Nelson's captain. As for Hardy himself, he had taken lodgings in Duke Street, a few doors from Nerot's Hotel, and shared the family's apprehensions. The old parson, in whose ancient heart there still burned a fierce pride in his favourite son, was visibly impatient, but Hardy secretly suspected that Nelson was deliberately delaying the family reunion. 'I know too well the cause of his not coming,' he confided to a friend.[3]

That Sunday saw the worst thunderstorm many Londoners could remember, but the news of Nelson's return soon had sightseers converging upon the hotel. When the admiral finally alighted about three in the afternoon, predictably clad in full uniform and regalia, he made 'a low bow' to the cheering multitude before hurrying his party inside to meet Fanny and Edmund in the lobby. Emma, at last face to face with her rival, later maintained that Lady Nelson received her husband coldly, but it is impossible to believe, and one of the London daily newspapers reported otherwise. The old triumvirate showed its years, and Edmund in particular had aged more than Fanny's powers of description had been able to convey. Lady Nelson herself was fortyish, and though still slim, had lost the perky prettiness of earlier years, while Nelson was fit but desperately thin, his countenance careworn, and he covered the ugly scar on his head by combing his hair forwards. The scene, however, was brief, because one of Hamilton's cousins, the Duke of Queensberry, arrived only minutes after them. The dinner that followed a couple of hours later was probably stilted, although Fanny lightened it with the news that Nelson was to receive the *San Josef*, and at 7.30 the admiral and his legitimate lady left for the Admiralty in a 'chariot'. Despite the last eighteen months, the Spencers remained enchanted with Nelson, and while the earl discussed his prospective employment, Lavinia entertained Fanny. It was all calculated to raise Nelson's spirits, but the fate of poor Berry remained a fly in the ointment, and it may be upon this occasion that the admiral secured a promise that his former flag captain would not lack alternative employment.[4]

During the days that followed Nelson remained 'constantly upon the wing', rising early to receive visitors by eight or nine in the morning. Monday opened with a breakfast shared with Hardy and Berry. As Hardy was to join him in the *San Josef*, Nelson insisted he remained close throughout much of the busy day. The new Lord Mayor of London was to lead a parade of livery company barges along the Thames, as part of the ceremony in which he was sworn in at Westminster Hall, but Nelson offered a one-man counter-attraction. After another call at the Admiralty that morning, the admiral strolled through the neo-classical Adelphi district and along the Strand with a 'gentleman' who may have been Davison, and soon attracted a crowd large enough to be described as 'troublesome'. It was briefly thrown off at Somerset House, which the admiral entered to visit his brother Maurice at the Navy Office, but fell in behind as soon as he reappeared, crowing in the admiral's wake as he continued his progress to Lord Grenville's office in Whitehall. Fanny and Princess Castelcicala, who was attached to the Neapolitan minister in London, enjoyed the Lord Mayor's procession from a terrace at Somerset House, but perhaps the greater spectacle was to be seen that afternoon when Nelson, Hardy and Sir William answered an invitation to dine with the Corporation of London. At Ludgate Hill their carriage was uncoupled, and the mob dragged it to its destination, around St Paul's churchyard and along Cheapside and King Street to the Guildhall, between walkways and windows crowded with shouting sightseers and waving handkerchiefs. After toasts Nelson was presented with the sword the corporation had voted him after the Nile, a splendid trophy with a gold hilt incorporating anchors and the figure of a crocodile. Under a triumphal arch created for the purpose, Nelson raised the weapon in his remaining hand and vowed to use it until France had been driven back to her 'proper' limits, a sentiment that generated tremendous approval. By comparison the next day was an anti-climax. Nelson ordered a beaver hat and cockade at James Lock's the hatters, of 6 St James's Street, and accepted a dinner invitation from his old friend the Duke of Clarence.[5]

Court sanction came at a levee at St James's on 12 November. Nelson and Sir William attended, the admiral with his chelengk, orders and medals, not the most tactful regalia, given that the customary royal permission to wear all of these foreign decorations had not yet been granted. That evening Nelson and Fanny again dined with the Spencers, and the following day Lavinia presented Lady Nelson at the Queen's Drawing Room. Nelson was present, attended by Hardy and other Nile veterans, but he was angry that Sir William showed up without his wife, to whom no invitation had been extended. It was the first chill wind, for where the king led, innumerable sycophants followed.[6]

For all the celebrations these were, in fact, difficult days. The ménage had hoped to preserve itself, accommodating the additional presence of Fanny, who could be little more than a spare part. Thus, close physical proximity was maintained. While the Nelsons lodged at Nerot's, the Hamiltons found a nearby hotel in St James's Street. These arrangements were, of course, temporary, and within days the Nelsons took a year's lease of a large furnished house at 17 Dover Street from R. and H. Chipchase. Most of their baggage went into storage with James Dods of Brewer Street, Soho, an agent recommended by Davison, and Nelson patronised glaziers, silversmiths, coachmakers and tailors to add additional comforts. So many servants were hired – to Fanny's maid and Samuel the coachman were added a cook, housemaid, kitchen maid, footman and French butler – that Edmund thought the premises swimming in shoals of staff and visitors. Nevertheless, it was a convenient town base that allowed Nelson to plan what to do about Roundwood and meet important callers. One found the Nelsons at breakfast with Edmund, Josiah and the admiral's brother, William. The Hamiltons, however, were not shaken off. Before November was out their friend William Beckford loaned them a property at 22 Grosvenor Square, where Sir William installed a bust of the admiral and enthusiastically told visitors 'in every other sentence' that Nelson was 'the pride and glory of his life'. Thus, the Nelson residence at Dover Street was roughly equidistant from, and within easy walking distance of, both Grosvenor Square and Davison's house at 9 St James's Square. Much fraternisation was envisaged, and the moves had barely been effected than Fanny found herself reading a long letter from Lady Hamilton, advertising her low spirits, and praying a continuance of a friendship that would, she trusted, be 'forever lasting'. As 'Sir William and self feel the loss of our good friend', the Nelsons were invited to dine at Grosvenor Square the following day. Nelson was equally bereft. 'Sunday I dine with Mr Nepean,' he wrote to his real love. 'From my heart I wish you could have dined here.'[7]

The strains upon such inadequate arrangements must have been tremendous, enveloping the old and new triumvirates in mutual misery. Unable to accept blame himself, Nelson turned it outwards, and became irritable. Lavinia Spencer, who cared for the Nelsons as much as anybody did, saw the underlying tension. According to one of her confidantes, the admiral was morose at the table during a dinner they shared, and thrust aside a walnut Fanny had shelled for him so violently that a glass was broken. When the ladies withdrew a tearful Fanny confessed to Lavinia 'how she was situated'. The story may have been exaggerated, but even Cornelia Knight testified to the 'very unpleasant' turn Nelson's relations with his wife had taken. Now having to make her way in London society, Cornelia continued to socialise with some of her old friends, and remained rather taken with Captain Gould, but felt increasingly uncomfortable associating with the Nelsons and Hamiltons. Her first night in the capital had been spent in an Albemarle Street hotel with Mrs Cadogan, but Troubridge had called that very evening to advise her to detach herself from the ménage, and accept an invitation to lodge at the house of Evan Nepean, the chief secretary of the Admiralty. She took the hint, and wound down her engagements with the troubled couples. One of her last outings with them, at a private dinner with Prince Augustus (the king's sixth son) and Lady Augusta Murray on 17 November, was barely enjoyable. 'What a bitch that Miss Knight is', Nelson eventually concluded.[8]

The social calendar was difficult for everybody. Not only did Nelson's wife and mistress dislike each other, but no one could predict who would or would not find Emma acceptable, whatever their own private peccadilloes might have been. Many old acquaintances such as the Prince of Wales and Prince Augustus, and relatives of Hamilton, including Queensberry, Greville, Lord Abercorn and Lord William Gordon, were happy to associate with Emma, but even in close circles opposition could surface. Members of Greville's family, for example, only fraternised with Lady Hamilton to avoid injuring the ailing diplomat. Greville's sister even told Sir William that she 'could not be in their society, but hoped he was assured of my affection', to which the old man laughed and said kindly that 'everyone must follow their own plans'. Emma showed less equanimity, for she needed attention, applause and society as much as Nelson craved naval glory. She contested her exclusion from court by developing a tale that she had used her influence with the Queen of Naples to get the British fleet watered at Syracuse in 1798, a story Nelson himself endorsed. Her husband tendered a petition for her admittance, enclosing one of the letters of recommendation Maria Carolina had given Emma before their final farewell, but whether an official answer was received or not, the response was plain enough in the continued royal indifference. The only echo of Emma's former glory as a courtesan was the continued friendship of Prince Castelcicala, the ambassador from Naples, who was established with his wife and staff in Wimpole Street.[9]

Appearances were nevertheless preserved for a while. Both the old and new triumvirates were at the Theatre Royal at Covent Garden on 18 November, sitting out a comedy called *Life* and Thomas Dibdin's more topical musical tribute to the hero, *The Mouth of the Nile*. The visit had been well advertised, and the house overflowed with well-wishers, and when the admiral in a fully decorated uniform appeared in his box the band struck up 'Rule, Britannia'. Nelson's party occupied two boxes next to the stage, opposite that reserved for the king, and the admiral sat flanked by Fanny and Emma. Although the latter, 'rather embonpoint' but 'highly graceful' and 'extremely pretty' in a blue satin gown and plumed headdress, was the more voluble, it was Fanny who attracted the greater compliments in the press, dressed in a white gown and a violet satin headdress decorated with a small white feather. 'Her ladyship's person is of a very pleasing description,' said one of the dailies. 'Her features are handsome and exceedingly interesting, and her general appearance is at once prepossessing and elegant.' Yet her position as one of two bookends can hardly have been enviable, especially as Sir William sat behind his wife, and Edmund was accommodated in the adjacent box. When Munden, the actor, introduced a popular Nelson ballad to the performance, and declared that the admiral would thrash the French again if it became necessary, the crowd erupted in delight, the hero rose and bowed from his box, and the old parson's eyes swam with tears. But a second excursion to see *Pizarro* at the Theatre Royal in Drury Lane was less successful. On this occasion the party included Princess Castelcicala. There were more cheers, lustily rendered patriotic airs and a song to trumpet Nelson's triumphs, but the heat was such that Fanny 'fainted away' towards the end of the third act and had to be assisted from her box.[10]

The papers speculated about her ladyship's indisposition, but Fanny was well enough to attend her husband, the Hamiltons and Princess Castelcicala at a dinner hosted by the Marquis and Marchioness of Abercorn at their home, the Priory, at about the beginning of December. The Abercorns were related to Sir William, and Fanny may have found this alien ground, but whether it was the occasion of a famous confrontation between the rival women is unknown. The details are vague, coming as they do through second-hand informants who were not actually present. Fanny's friend Sir Andrew Snape Hamond, sometime comptroller of the Navy Board, gave one version to the diarist Joseph Farington, while another passed into the *Memoirs of Lady Hamilton*, published in 1815, possibly through Francis Oliver, then an estranged former member of the Hamilton entourage. Apparently Emma grew dissatisfied with the attention she was receiving at the table from Fanny, who sat beside her, affected to swoon – something that Hamond plainly regarded as a mere artifice to solicit Nelson's support – and had to be conducted out of the room. Nelson is said to have attacked his wife for not attending to the sick woman, and the following morning arose early from the conjugal bed in great agitation. He seemed intent on leaving, and his wife took him by the hand to ask whether he had ever suspected her of infidelity, to which the admiral confessed, 'Never.' Even if half true, it indicated the total implausibility of Nelson's plan to live with one woman while loving another.[11]

The public displays of unity thinned out towards the close of the year. The last appears to have occurred on 19 December, when the Nelsons, Hamiltons, and other friends joined Colonel Havilland Le Mesurier for a dinner at the Crown and Anchor in support of 'the Friendly Assembly'. Beyond, the cocktail of public adulation and private anguish only grew bitter beyond endurance.

2

Emma aside, the Establishment showed few reservations about Nelson, and the king and his government saw political capital in his popularity. The admiral was invited to a second royal levee on 26 November, where he was reunited with Prince Castelcicala, and swaddled in silly robes, he was inducted into the House of Lords on 20 November, chaperoned by Lords Grenville and Romney, the Duke of Norfolk, Sir Ferres Molyneux and the Garter King-of-Arms, Sir Isaac Heard. The ceremony over, the admiral took his place in the house 'next below' Lord Seaforth. As employees of the government, naval members of either legislature were commonly regarded as placemen, invariable supporters of the sitting administration, and at this stage Nelson saw no reason to rock the boat. On 31 December he joined Hood in conducting the king to his throne in the Lords at the beginning of a new parliament, and listened to him condemn Russia's detention of British ships and the growing alliance of neutral nations that was challenging Britain's presumed rights at sea. Both admirals were implicit reminders of the force the country could bring to its elbow in a crisis. By this time Nelson was also confiding in Pitt, the prime minister, who was as respectful as his distant personality allowed; his successor, Henry Addington, was more welcoming, and rated Nelson's opinion of Mediterranean affairs highly.[12]

Charities also saw uses for the admiral, who could draw large numbers of potential donors to their functions, as well as supply a contribution himself. On Monday, 17 November, Nelson and his uniform were at the Little Theatre, where a performance in aid of John Bannister, a famous comedy actor, was being held, and two weeks later he celebrated St Andrew's Day alongside Hamilton, Spencer and other 'benefactors and friends' of the Scottish Corporation at a dinner in the London Tavern. A popular singer, Dignum, was on hand with a stirring repertoire, of which a new composition, 'Nelson's Return', had the company joining in a rapturous chorus. The purpose of this charity of 1664, to raise money for needy Scots in London, was fulfilled with numerous donations, but Nelson also strengthened bonds with such notables as the Prince of Wales, Earl Chatham, Lord President of the Council, William Pitt, Henry Dundas, secretary of war, and his junior, William Windham, secretary at war, all men capable of pulling strings if favourably disposed. As we have seen, the admiral also turned out for 'the Friendly Assembly', but it was on 30 November that he made his first recorded appearance at a charity that would become a particular favourite, the Asylum for Female Orphans in Lambeth, where he attended the Sunday service.[13]

Many private dinners were held in Nelson's honour, and he found himself a guest of Admiral Robert Man and his relative, George Walpole, a member of parliament, among others. Davison, who had benefited himself as Nelson's prize agent, went further than most, staging a grand dinner in his honour at his house on 29 November, and bringing a collection of influential royals, peers, politicians and naval men to exalt an admiral who still felt in need of patrons. But an even more elaborate tribute was staged by the East India Company, which had already voted £10,000 to a man credited with rescuing the nation's possessions in India from the monster Bonaparte. On Wednesday, 19 November, the directors showed the admiral around their new buildings at East India House, and on the third day of the next month followed up with a gala dinner for up to two hundred at the London Tavern. There were few inhibitions. East India House was illuminated, a troop of cavalry drawn up, an image of Britannia presiding over the burning *L'Orient* was raised in the tavern, and a veritable who's who of the male Establishment sat at the tables, including Frederick, Duke of York, military commander-in-chief, the second and ablest of the king's progeny, and Pitt and Addington. Nelson, the immodest focus of all this homage, sat between Dundas and Lord McCartney, former governor at Madras, but used part of the extraordinary opportunity to introduce relatives to potential patrons. William Nelson could bore Lord Loughborough, the Lord Chancellor, and George Matcham, bubbling with a scheme to send emigrants to Port Jackson in Australia, made a useful contact with Philip King, the governor of New South Wales. It was not until midnight that the diners dispersed to their carriages.[14]

Looking at the almost frenzied programme that Nelson endured in those last months of 1801, a continuous round of dressing for show, travelling, wining and dining, basking in hyperbolic accolades, shaking admiring hands and cultivating friends, one suspects that while incessant sycophancy pumped adrenalin into the admiral and rarely seemed to tire him, it also furnished underlying gratifications. These hectic events gave the admiral much to do in company, and reduced opportunities for private torment, whether longings for Emma, arguments with Fanny or the silent reproof of his father. As if there were not enough sores, Josiah arrived in London in mid-December after bringing the *Thalia* into Deptford. Out and about Nelson could escape; only reflection, solitude and an illness of ease awaited him at home.

At home visitors provided similar relief. Nelson's nephew, Horace, received 'a positive order' to leave school and bring his mother and Charlotte to visit. A mounting correspondence, some of it stirring old memories, also helped. Most of the writers wanted help. Lieutenant Thomas Brown, who had shared 'Gunner'

Whittington's quarters in the old *Triumph* with Midshipman Nelson, had been twenty years a lieutenant, and was now seeking a shore appointment after sustaining an injury. George Barrons, a former captain of the top in Nelson's *Theseus*, had been wounded in the explosion that killed Captain Miller, and wanted a medical discharge. Thomas Atkinson, a thirty-three-year-old Yorkshireman from the same ship, excitedly told his former captain that he had qualified as a master of a third-rate and desperately wanted to serve under him again. A John Barry recalled meeting him at Mr Horsford's near English Harbour in Antigua, while a surgeon on the *Boreas*, which Nelson had commanded in those islands, hoped that he no longer suffered the 'repeated attacks of fever' that had then so often laid him low. But other letters sought to give. There were satisfying missives from the King of Naples and the Marquis of Niza congratulating him upon his safe return, while one letter conferred the freedom of Salisbury and another notified the admiral that he had been elected a member of the Ancient Order of Gregorians, a friendly society similar to the Freemasons, that met for an annual feast of venison at the White Swan at Norwich. The famous Coke of Holkham had long and recently been the society's president.[15]

As usual, Nelson lapped up the tributes. Though he struck some as shockingly 'shrunk and mutilated', he loved his public, to whom he appeared in full uniform, bedecked with marks of distinction. He walked openly in the streets, and there are glimpses of him purchasing a dog for Emma in Holborn, and ordering a commemoration dinner service from Rundell and Bridge at the sign of the Golden Salmon on Ludgate Hill and another hat from Lock's. The service was financed by £500 Lloyd's had awarded him after the Nile, and finally appeared in April in plain but heavy silver, decorated with gadroon borders, a baronial coronet and coat of arms. Soon after Lloyd's granted an additional sum for the battle of Copenhagen, and the admiral was able to expand his set to some 154 pieces. Nelson was accompanied to Lock's by his father on 6 January, when the old triumvirate was in its very last days.[16]

Despite his continued public exposure, Nelson was not particularly fastidious in dress, although he usually opted to appear in uniform with the intention, no doubt, of attracting attention. In themselves there was nothing exceptional about the uniforms, which were made of jobbing blue broadcloth, lined with a silk twill, 'serge' weave or even a simple serviceable linen, and supplemented by woollen kerseymere breeches. It was the orders of knighthood that festooned his left breast that Nelson wished the public to see. Indeed, he arranged for some of these trophies to be displayed in December at Admiralty House. Perhaps even more remarkably, Nelson also hit upon a way to spare the originals from wear, and ordered complete sets of full-sized imitations to be embroidered. Made of coloured silk, spangles and gold and silver purl wire fixed to a linen base, they were then sewn into the admiral's different uniform coats and thus displayed or discarded with the garments. The first surviving example of these singular manufactures appears on a full-dress coat made after Nelson's promotion to the rank of vice admiral of the blue squadron on 1 January 1801, and was probably made for him by King and Company, his London tailors, or perhaps Meredith of Portsmouth.[17]

No reader will be surprised to learn that Nelson's return to England was distinguished by a fresh round of portraits, as the admiral tried to flaunt his appearance and recent decorations for posterity. 'That foolish little fellow Nelson has sat to every painter in London,' scoffed the Earl of St Vincent, probably not a little jealous of the reputation of the younger man. He exaggerated, but when most public figures settled for no more than half a dozen paintings done in their lifetime it must have seemed so. Within a few short weeks Nelson sat to perhaps as many as eight artists, including the rival luminaries Sir William Beechey and John Hoppner, who produced the last great Nelson canvases. Beechey, who had already painted the admiral's father, was commissioned by the City of Norwich. The resultant full-length, possibly done at the artist's house in George Street, Hanover Square, was finished in May 1801. It is resplendent, showing Nelson in his usual finery, but for all its majesty has not always been considered a good likeness. Nelson's eyes were blue, not brown, his hair sandy, and in 1800 he was altogether paler and thinner than the healthy, robust figure portrayed. Hoppner painted Nelson for the Prince of Wales. Although he also gave Nelson brown eyes, one of the admiral's closest associates in his final years, Dr Scott, proclaimed the likeness one of the two best he had seen. The praise was more justified if applied to Hoppner's preliminary sketch, rather than his finished portrait, for it convincingly captured the once notorious boyishness seared by present troubles, with the sheepdog hair carefully arranged to cover the scar on the forehead.[18]

Among the lesser known portraits, the unsophisticated profile produced by Simon De Koster, a Dutch artist, on 8 December was thought by Nelson to be his truest likeness. Beechey, Scott and reputedly Hardy also commended it, and it agrees closely with Grignion's more proficient but unfinished portrait of 1799. About the same time Nelson sat to the sculptor Mrs Anne Seymour Damer, and Robert Bowyer, a miniaturist much patronised by the royal family, who left an attractive watercolour on ivory. In the handling of Nelson's expression about the mouth, Bowyer's picture resembled the classic 1797 portrait by Lemuel Abbott, though it made the eyes look larger and sadder. Bowyer's niece was the wax modeller Catherine Andras, and it was probably through him that she also got a sitting from the admiral. She was the first to portray Nelson in the undress uniform of a vice admiral, and must therefore have finished her work after his lordship's promotion on New Year's Day, the same day the union of Britain and Ireland was accomplished. A few months later, at Yarmouth, a local artist named Matthew Keymer painted Nelson in the full-dress uniform of a vice admiral.[19]

Nelson's return should have been a period of unrelieved triumph and celebration, for Fanny and Edmund as well as Nelson, but they quickly realised that the rumours about Nelson and Lady Hamilton were true, and that whatever goodwill the admiral had had for his wife was rapidly disappearing. With remarkable speed Nelson's plan to remain with one woman while loving another disintegrated. After Nelson's death Emma (and indeed a few others) told stories about those final days that justified the break with Fanny. Lady Nelson, we are told, was by nature cold, a damper on her husband's career, eager to believe the public scandals, and unable to stand the noisy nephews and nieces with whom her husband liked to play, and who, she believed, threatened Josiah. Contemporary letters do not bear out this picture of Fanny, whose forgiving, patient and kind disposition took on a new dignity during the years of spiteful character assassination. Though vastly overpowered, she tried to keep her husband, attempting to live with his obsession with another, and his increasing distance.

Nothing, perhaps, augured the end of their marriage more than the Christmas of 1800. Nelson had not shared a Christmas with his wife in three years, but he chose to leave her at home with his sick father to recapture the life he had led with the Hamiltons, free from the old triumvirate and public criticism in an episode as surreal and obsequious as any that had occurred in Palermo.

3

William Beckford, the seriously rich second cousin and old friend of Sir William Hamilton, was forty-one years old. Despite a degree of artistic eminence, Beckford was *persona non grata* in fashionable society, and something of a law unto himself. His imagination reached such taboos as homosexuality and a predilection for young boys, something he had once confessed to Sir William's first wife, and found rein in astounding literary and architectural fantasies. In his twenties he had written the dark and psychological *Vathek*, and now he was spending an enormous fortune building a gothic extravaganza within his walled estate at Fonthill in Wiltshire, its keystone a huge abbey looming like a cathedral over the trees, its focus when finished an octagonal tower that formed the hub of four arms, and the whole designed by James Wyatt, whose classical buildings included Oxford's Oriel College Library and the Canterbury Gate of Christ Church.

A maverick he may have been, but Beckford craved a degree of respectability and permanence. He coveted a peerage, and saw Sir William as a possible means of getting one. Hamilton had no clear-cut heirs, but lacked money, and had laid his case for a public reward before the crown. Beckford therefore suggested that Hamilton pitch for a peerage, and in return for the reversion offered to make good any shortfall in the public annuity the old diplomat was expecting. In the end all these aspirations foundered. Hamilton's pension was unsatisfactory, providing an annuity of £2000 for the term of his life, and therefore leaving Emma's future clouded. Moreover, his claim for £23,000 as compensation for expenses and debts incurred in service was refused, and no one mentioned a peerage. But it was in November, while the dream was on the wing, that Beckford invited the Hamiltons to spend Christmas with him at Fonthilll. He also saw a way of improving his personal standing by commandeering the 'victorious presence' of Nelson, and urged the admiral to enjoy 'a few comfortable days of repose, uncontaminated by the sight and prattle of drawing-room parasites'. In a cruel twist, he did not invite Fanny, and Nelson did not insist on her presence. Perhaps she was unwell, or disinclined, for in truth she would have hated the extravagant frivolity that Beckford was planning. In every way, therefore, Beckford offered Nelson an opportunity to recapture the gratuitous homage that had constituted the worst excesses of the ménage in Naples and Sicily, an escape into a work of living art and fantasy that could shut out the icier climes outside.[20]

The idea found Nelson sinking into depression, as his separation from Emma and her unborn child, misery, guilt, the ridicule and rejection of his mistress, the innuendo and jealousy that sometimes seeped from beneath the flattery and celebration, and the crippling financial implications of the split from Fanny insinuated the hopelessness of his current situation. When the Hamiltons, including Mrs Cadogan, finally drove towards Fonthill he was with them. On 20 December they passed through Salisbury. Several miles outside the town their coach was intercepted by a detachment of yeoman cavalry, which conveyed the party to the house of Alderman James Goddard in the marketplace. From thence they proceeded to the town hall, where the admiral received the freedom of the city in an oak box and addressed an admiring crowd outside, calling several veterans forward to receive thanks and gifts. When a survivor of the attack of Tenerife brought forth a treasured piece of cloth which he said had come from Nelson's sleeve at the time his right arm had been amputated, Nelson could scarcely hold back tears. Before leaving to fulsome cheers, Nelson gave the mayor £20 for the poor. Then, with the military escort to point their way, the party resumed their journey. Everywhere, the ordinary people wanted to applaud their champion.[21]

Beckford had deployed hundreds of workers to finish enough of his abbey to fulfil his ambitions for the distinguished guests. At the park gates to Fonthill the carriage was met by a mounted detachment of his own uniformed volunteers, who presented arms and then flanked the party as it made for the main house. A band welcomed the visitors with 'Rule, Britannia'. When the party reached Beckford's mansion the volunteers formed into a line upon the lawn and fired a *feu de joye*, while the band played the national anthem, and Beckford excitedly issued forth to greet his guests. From the dearth of powerful men and women inside, Nelson may have deduced that Beckford was not quite accepted in fashionable circles, but among the exotic collection of French émigrés, a Portuguese nobleman and members of the local gentry, the most imposing guests were artists of one kind or another, musicians such as the Italian soprano Brigida Giorgi Banti, who enjoyed a reputation for manners similar to Emma's; the satirist and poet Dr John Wolcot, known as 'Peter Pindar'; and the painters Joseph Clarendon Smith, Henry Tresham and Benjamin West, president of the Royal Academy, whose painting *The Death of Wolfe* Nelson is said to have admired. In this company the Hamiltons, if not Nelson, saw much for conversation.[22]

A fastidious table had been prepared, served by bustling retainers, and during desserts Emma, Madame Bianchi and one Sapio performed for the company, which heartily joined in the choruses of the better known patriotic songs. The Misses Beckham declared that the music 'delighted' everybody, but later the guests divided for cards, music and talk until a midnight supper closed the day. Two days of eating and mingling followed, but Beckford is reported to have found his premier guest somewhat withdrawn and less adventurous than expected. When he took the admiral for a drive in his four-horse phaeton, giving fine views over the grounds, Nelson grew so alarmed at its speed that he demanded to be set down, and Beckford walked the vehicle back.[23]

The major event was reserved for Tuesday, 23 December. As daylight faded the guests, armed with printed programmes, boarded carriages at the front of the mansion and were escorted by the volunteers towards the abbey itself. With pride of place, Nelson's carriage was the first to pass through a turreted archway in a wall that surrounded the abbey grounds and into the 'fairy scene' inside. Observers seemed lost for words to describe it. The pine woods on either side of the path 'glittered' with 'variegated lamps' that formed 'vast vistas of light' and defined 'the distant perspective as clearly as in sunshine'. At various points bearers stood with blazing flambeaux, and hidden from sight along the route groups of musicians greeted the travellers with 'inspiring marches, the whole effect being heightened by the deep roll of numerous drums, so placed in the hollows of the hills as to ensure their reverberations being heard on every side. The profound darkness of the night, the many tinted lamps, some in motion, others stationary, here reflected on the bayonets and helmets of the soldiery, there through coloured glass, and so arranged as to shed rainbow hues on every surrounding object.'

The procession reached the abbey, its battlements, turrets and flying buttresses festooned in lights, and its tower 'shooting up three hundred feet' until lost in the enveloping darkness, and passed through an eastern postern where a double file of troopers and the 'national banner' and 'admiral's flag' were on full parade. The guests ventured into a 'groined Gothic hall' at the southern end of the abbey, its galleries and corridors reverberating to the sound of a booming organ. Across the hall 'the Cardinal's parlour' occupied the south-western side of the ground floor, with its tapestry-cloaked walls, arched windows and long curtains of purple damask flickering in the light of huge wax candles and a cedar log fire. The visitors were seated on ivory-studded chairs before an enormous dining table that ran almost the length of the fifty-two and a half foot room, and served the 'fare of other days' upon singularly designed and opulent silver and agate ware. But this was merely the beginning of the entertainment. The dinner over, the admiral and his friends were conducted up the grand winding staircase nearby, later known as 'Nelson's Turret', climbing to the first and principal floor between cowled 'monks' standing like sentinels with waxen flambeaux in their hands. They found themselves in the 'yellow withdrawing rooms' on the south-western side of the building, the first and outer an apartment 'hung with gold-coloured satin damask, in which were ebony cabinets of inestimable value, inlaid with precious stones and filled with treasures collected from many lands', and east of it a library with 'crimson velvet' hangings 'embroidered with arabesques of gold' and lit in daylight by stained-glass windows. Continuing in the same direction, the company passed above the gothic entrance hall below into a gallery in the monastic style that extended 270 feet northwards. It was filled by music that appeared to have no discernable source. But at its terminus at the northern end of the building was an oratory, where 'a lamp of gold' illuminated a marble and alabaster statue of St Anthony, situated in a mosaic and jewel-studded 'niche' where candlesticks and elaborate silver-gilt candelabra 'in stands of ebony inlaid with gold and multiplied by huge pier-glasses' contributed to 'the surpassing brilliancy of the scene'. Beckford's musicians were hidden from view behind the shrine, in an octagon tower designed to be a focal point of the abbey but as yet unfinished.

The jaw-dropping tour effectively complete, Nelson and the other guests returned to the yellow withdrawing rooms, where spiced wine and fruit were pretentiously presented in gold baskets, and seats were taken for entertainments. It was at this point that Emma Hamilton appeared as Agrippina, carrying the urn containing the ashes of Germanicus to the Romans and inciting them to revenge. With a few changes in headgear, she 'displayed with truth and energy every gesture, attitude and expression of countenance', using 'classically graceful' movements of the head, hands and arms. A finale, in which 'a young lady of the company' joined as her daughter, was said to have moved the audience to tears. This closed the proceedings after midnight. Bands, supported again by the thundering organ, struck up 'most exhilarating airs' and the guests departed down the turreted staircase the way they had come, 'scarce able to believe that they had not been enjoying an Arabian night's entertainment instead of an English one'. Leaving was, said one account, like 'waking from a dream'.

Beckford was desperate to repeat the experience, and in 1805 would beg Emma to persuade Nelson to return to Fonthill. Nelson was a very different man from Beckford, and could never have made him a congenial companion, but there was food for thought at Fonthill. For Beckford had created a world of his own to counterbalance the colder one outside, and Nelson's mind was turning in the same direction. He, too, needed a sanctuary. But he was cruelly awoken from such reveries the day after Christmas, when he left for London. On the 27th he learned the sad news that his old captain and patron, William Locker, lieutenant governor of Greenwich Hospital, had died at the age of seventy the previous day. Locker had been a great influence on the young Nelson, both as a friend and a mentor. His stories of the capture of the *Telemaque* in 1757 had alerted the keen lieutenant to the devastating power of British gunnery, and for many years it had been Locker more than anyone else who had opened doors for him in naval circles. The captain had been failing badly of late, repeating himself in conversation, but he remained cheerful, kind and loyal, offering hospitality in his quarters at the hospital, where he could be found smoking a cigar and resting his injured leg on a cushion, attended by his devoted daughter Elizabeth and his faithful dog, and surrounded by portraits of the country's king and heroes. Nelson had intended to visit, but now it was too late. Ruefully the admiral wrote to Locker's son, John, and on 29 December attended the funeral alone in his carriage, unwilling, it seems, to risk spending much time with naval colleagues whom he feared might disapprove of the life he was leading. 'I dread the fatigue of this day,' he wrote to Emma at six that morning. For though he had 'had my days of glory, yet I find this world so full of jealousies and envy that I see but a very faint gleam of future comfort. I shall come to Grosvenor Square on my return from this melancholy procession, and hope to find in the smiles of my friends some alleviation from the cold looks and cruel words of my enemies.' As the solemn cortege crawled from Greenwich to Addington, Kent, where Locker was laid in a vault beside his beloved wife, Lucy, Nelson may have wondered what his old friend would have said had they met again. Fanny had come to know the Lockers well, and Elizabeth would remain one of her best and lifelong friends. But he continued to befriend the family, and loaned John money for an outfit to take up his appointment as registrar of the vice-admiralty court in Malta in 1804.[24]

On the last day of the year there was a direct snub at a royal levee. Nelson was received 'coldly'. After asking after the admiral's health and observing that he had been appointed to the Channel fleet the king turned to converse with a nonentity. The Drawing Room event on 2 January was less frosty, perhaps because of the presence of Fanny, but it seems as if Nelson's poor publicity had weakened his acceptability at court.

The winter of 1800 was a hard one that smote the poor and provoked public disturbances as it tore the remaining bonds between the old triumvirate apart. The admiral's obsession with Emma, her unborn baby and jealousy of Fanny could brook no compromise, and he pressed forward with a cold-hearted obstinacy, as if his old life had to be expunged forever without a backward glance.

One harbinger was Nelson's decision to sell Roundwood without delay. His legal man, Thomas Ryder, put it on the market on 8 January and the deal was done on 23 March. The purchaser was an existing tenant, Robert Fuller, who paid £3300. Another sign of Nelson's contemplation of a life apart from Fanny was a direction he gave her to send his legal and such important papers as his freedoms to William. Moreover, he asked correspondents to write to him by Lady Hamilton.[25]

Nelson was rescued from living with his wife by the call of duty. Bonaparte's interest in an armistice with Britain was bewitching the country, but the northern powers of the Baltic were forming an alliance, ostensibly to defend the rights of neutral traders from the tyranny of British naval superiority. A clash seemed likely, and Nelson, newly promoted a vice admiral, was in demand. Spencer had posted him to the Channel fleet, but Admiral Hyde Parker was bound for the Baltic with a fleet, and it was intimated that Nelson would be second in command. In the meantime the *San Josef* was ready to receive his flag at Plymouth.

He took his leave of the Admiralty on Monday, 12 January, and with brother William for company travelled to Southampton the following day, leaving Fanny in Dover Street with £400 to cover immediate expenses. There was no sudden walking out, not even a goodbye. Nelson merely left on service, as he had often done before, and wrote briefly to announce his safe arrival later the same day. 'My dear Fanny,' he said. 'We are arrived and heartily tired, and with kindest regards to my father and all the family, believe me your affectionate Nelson.' She had been with him for fifteen years, many of them waiting for his return from the wars, but now it was over. They would never meet again.[26]

4

As usual William was foraging for favours, and early the following day the Nelson brothers went to Cuffnells in Hampshire to see George Rose, a political ally of Pitt. But Rose was not at home, and without more ado they set off for Plymouth. The coach reached Axminster, with attendant crowds and cheers, by the evening, but Nelson was very low. His new commander-in-chief, St Vincent, had invited him to call at Tor Abbey, which he was using as a base, but Nelson did not relish it, and he missed the Hamiltons. On the coach, just before reaching Dorchester, his anxieties had produced one of the 'heart-attacks' he often described. The coach windows had had to be pulled down and a stop made to give the admiral air. He poured with sweat, but felt deathly cold in the evening chill, and thought he was dying on that long and lonely road.[27]

The journey began again on Thursday, 15 January. En route they visited Captain Westcott's mother in Honiton, a depressing experience since that brave man's family was poorly circumstanced. Had they been chimney sweeps, it was still his duty to attend them, Nelson said. The public dragged his carriage out of the town, but it broke down on the road to Exeter. Eventually the Devon mounted volunteers escorted them to their Exeter hotel, now the Royal Clarence, from where the mayor and corporation led them to the Guildhall so that Nelson could receive the freedom. Bells rang and people shouted huzzas.[28]

At Tor Abbey, near Torquay, he found letters from Fanny waiting. 'I have only time to say God bless you and my dear father, and believe me, your affectionate Nelson,' he replied. As for St Vincent, he greeted the traveller 'cordially', and neither then nor in subsequent visits did either mention the lawsuit that divided them. Nelson had a 'broadside' prepared if the subject came up, but confined himself to talking about the possibility of an attack upon Copenhagen. It was as well, since Nelson's emotions brimmed over at the very thought of that purloined prize money. 'How infamous against poor Nelson!' he wrote to Emma in his most disillusioned and self-pitying tone. 'Everybody except you tears him to pieces, nor has he but only you as a disinterested friend.' Gazing upon the man he had not seen in almost three years, St Vincent drew different conclusions. 'He appeared and acted as if he had done me an injury and felt apprehensive that I was acquainted with it,' he told Nepean. 'Poor man, he is devoured with vanity, weakness and folly. [He] was strung with ribbons, medals, etc., yet pretended that he wished to avoid the honour[s] and ceremonies he everywhere met with upon the road.'[29]

Nelson reached Plymouth on the 17th, and his new blue flag was raised on the foremast of the *San Josef* to the acclamations of the fleet. The ship was in the dockyard, completing her refit under Hardy's supervision and not yet fully manned, but she was a magnificent craft, answering most of the admiral's wishes, and the Navy Board had authorised such modifications as he saw fit to make. 'She works like a cutter,' Nelson said admiringly. Moreover, the ship was large, with a principal gun deck that measured more than 194 by 54 feet, and promised more than the usual comforts. Nelson temporarily occupied Hardy's cabin while his own was being prepared, but punctiliously insisted on the prominent display of two portraits of Emma that he called his 'guardian angels'. With Hardy to manage the ship, Nelson found time to make his customary appeal to the Society for Promoting Christian Knowledge for religious books for the crew, and to consider tactical issues. A hope that he might be allowed to pursue a French squadron that had reportedly escaped from Brest died because Spencer had already covered such contingencies, but there was still the Baltic expedition to consider. Neither Spencer nor St Vincent had encouraged his idea of storming fortifications at Copenhagen, but here in the West Country an advocate appeared in the person of John Graves Simcoe, formerly a capable if hawkish lieutenant governor of Canada, who claimed to be 'the only man' to lead such an assault, and not merely because of his familiarity with the Danish defences.[30]

The *San Josef* slipped south to Cawsand Bay on 22 January, ready for sea. Four days later the Admiralty ordered her to Torbay and she arrived on the morning of 1 February. Nelson fancied action against the French, and advised St Vincent to send two vessels to seek intelligence of a reported breakout from Brest, but instead he was ordered to transfer to the three-decked *St George* of ninety-eight guns, which was bound for the Baltic without delay. The Admiralty urged their first fighting admiral to become the 'Champion of England in the North' but when his new flagship arrived in Torbay Nelson was almost heartbroken. She was in 'a truly wretched state', inside and out, with a 'dreary, dirty and leaky cabin' in which not a dry place was to be found, or a window that did 'not let in wind enough to turn a mill'. Looking at her, Nelson felt his rheumatism returning. There were good reasons for Spencer's decision, however. The Baltic promised a surfeit of shallow-water work, and an armada of flat-bottomed boats, sloops, fireships and bomb vessels was being prepared to support the larger warships. It was a difficult billet for a massive first-rate like the deep-drafted *San Josef*. Nelson reluctantly sent Hardy aboard the *St George* with his flag on 12 February, but he exacted an understanding that the *San Josef* would be available for him when the Baltic business had been accomplished. The admiral's furniture, outfit and provisions, including 312 bottles of port and sherry, along with almost fifty officers and men, followed him into the *St George*.[31]

But at this time Nelson's mind was primarily driven by domestic difficulties, and engaged by a life-changing social upheaval his mood darkened. Almost as long as he could remember, Nelson had striven for recognition, using the triple pathways of naval glory, public duty and personal honour. His life had been far from blameless, although his grosser lapses had usually grown from attempts to fulfil obligations to people he valued, whether a loyal seaman running afoul of the law, or a national ally trying to recover his kingdom. He hungered for the acclaim of his fellow men, and by and large received it, as the crowds and an avalanche of Nelson memorabilia testified. Riding on the back of the mass loyalism that characterised the war up to 1806, more than eighty popular songs dealt with Nelson, and all reflected the admiration of the common man. But now Nelson was meeting something else, something largely confined to small but influential sections of society and extremely difficult to live with – derision. Sometimes he seemed to recoil from society, as if afraid of encountering disapproval, and upon other occasions he stubbornly faced it down. But he sensed criticism and isolation. 'I feel as if no friend was near me,' he owned, 'and truly melancholy.'[32]

While his sadness reflected guilt for the damage he had done his wife, father and the cuckolded Sir William, Nelson's key concern was the future, about whether the life past could be turned into the one he wanted to live, and his upcoming child could be shielded from obloquy and harm. Nelson was also an embittered man, sure that he had been sold short by the rulers of his country, and his mistress unjustifiably reviled. Looking for an escape, he talked about retiring from active service and returning to Bronte, where he might fashion a world more to his liking. But at the moment he was trapped in the present, and dangerously emotional and unstable. He saw enemies and ingratitude everywhere. Why, he brooded, had Troubridge and Hood been granted permission to wear their recent foreign orders while his own remained ungazetted? And when he heard an unfounded rumour that the Admiralty was going to remove him to a bad ship, the *Windsor Castle*, he could scarce believe it, but confessed the very thought made him ready to burst into tears.

These musings bore the more heavily because the weather was inhibiting, with deep snow in January and rain and wind that kept ships in harbours, and the admiral's health had again begun to collapse. Soon after he reached Plymouth his pterygium again began colonising 'the outer side over the pupil' of his one serviceable eye, diminishing what remained of his sight and producing 'most acute pain of the forehead'. 'My eye is like blood,' he wrote, 'and the film [over it] so extended that I only see from the corner farthest from my nose.' Thomas Trotter, the physician of the Channel fleet, thought the symptoms 'truly alarming' and recommended a London specialist who might remove the invading membrane surgically. As Nelson was unwilling to contemplate such a procedure, Trotter prohibited wine or porter and prescribed water and plain food. He had the admiral confined to a dark room for three days, and the eye bathed in 'cold syrup water' brought hourly by a servant. The word of his indisposition had apothecaries send eye lotions of all kinds to the admiral's lodgings, but Trotter's process reduced the inflammation unaided, and Nelson gratefully wrote to Emma to have green shades made to protect his eyes from further glare.[33]

Nelson's mood was also depressed by the jealousy that had always gripped his relationship with Emma. Neither trusted the other out of sight, and imposed debilitating curfews, in which their partner promised to shun the company of the opposite sex. Emma's fears were reignited by every minor flirtation that Nelson mentioned. 'Respecting Kingsmill's friend,' he protested, 'I declare solemnly that I . . . could never bear the smallest idea of taking her out to the West Indies. It is now 17 years since I have seen her. I have no secrets.' He continually reassured Emma that he neither met nor wrote to other women, except when compelled by common courtesy, and upon such occasions he hastened to denigrate potential rivals. Thus Troubridge's sister, with whom he lodged ashore when ill, was fifty-five, deaf and pitted with smallpox; the wife of the port admiral, to whom he had to pay his respects, was an aged 'wife dressed old ewe lamb fashion'; and the spouse of the naval commissioner at Spithead not only liked 'a drop' but resembled 'a cook-maid'. But in general, Nelson genuinely tried to keep his promise to remain beyond the reach of company who might otherwise have eased his isolation. On 24 January he met the mayor and aldermen of Plymouth to receive the freedom of the town, but that done 'retired to his carriage amidst the loud acclamations of a very large concourse of people'. And three days later, accompanied by William, Hardy and Commodore Edward Thornbrough Parker, he inspected the citadel. But he usually kept to his ship. It was a dire monasticism, devoid of amusement, and left him imprisoned on board in his own dark world, 'a fish out of water' and 'a miserable fellow shut up in wood'.[34]

He needed counsel, but it was in short supply. Hardy was busy with the ship, and his bluff manliness as well as the mutual dislike between him and Emma did not promise the empathy and wisdom Nelson wanted. Young Parker, an eleve whom Nelson was increasingly loving as a son, fell over himself to be helpful, and even cut the admiral's meat at the table, but simply lacked the years. At Plymouth Nelson managed to dine with the wise and worldly Collingwood, now a rear admiral with his flag in the *Barfleur*. He was the ideal soulmate, but a solid family man to boot, and quickly left when his wife and daughter arrived in town, just before he returned to sea. Later, when the *San Josef* put into Torbay, Troubridge bunked aboard for a short while. He toasted 'All Our Friends', 'The King', 'Success to the Fleet' and 'Lady Hamilton' over dinners, but was too blunt about Nelson's mistress to satisfy a man as sensitive as the admiral.[35]

Nelson's closest male friend was Alexander Davison, his prize agent, banker and man of business. Davison had moved up in the world since their early days together, and now owned an estate at Swarland in his native Northumberland and routinely rubbed shoulders with royals, peers, ministers and leading businessmen. He it was who handled most of Nelson's affairs when the admiral was abroad, and when an income tax was levied to finance the war in 1799, Fanny could find no one who knew her husband's resources better. Davison not only made money out of Nelson; he idolised him. When his wife, Harriet Gosling, a banker's daughter, gave him a son in June 1799, he asked Nelson to sponsor his christening as Alexander Horatio Nelson Davison. By 1801 Davison had also been pressing for permanent monuments to his hero, serving with Pitt on a committee chaired by Clarence to establish a naval obelisk on Portsdown Hill, above Spithead, and planting the trees of his estate to create a panorama of the battle of the Nile. Davison also had the measure of Nelson's emotional nature, having dissuaded him from proposing marriage to a Quebec beauty, Mary Simpson, in 1782. But in the present circumstances he rode a difficult line between the estranged couple, for he had grown close to Fanny during the last few years and to some degree become her adviser.[36]

Nevertheless, Davison twice travelled from London to the outposts to visit Nelson, first arriving in Torbay on 5 February, where he took up a spare bed and spacious cabin aboard the *San Josef*, and the following month at Great Yarmouth. His news brought the latest developments in the St Vincent lawsuit, which was due to begin in the Court of the King's Bench on 4 March, but he also discussed the tangled matrimonial affairs of his hero. Certainly he was aware of the self-denying ordnance, if only because the admiral studiously avoided fraternising with Harriet Davison and a female companion during the period of the visit. When the ladies came aboard to inspect the ship, Nelson pointedly took himself ashore.

Unfortunately, Davison was a rare presence, and Nelson's daily correspondence with 'my dear Lady Hamilton' became his principal lifeline, something to which Sir William willingly contributed when his wife was ill. In order to maintain that stream of correspondence the admiral had boats struggling to and fro despite the most atrocious spring weather. Once, in Torbay, a huge wave almost engulfed a boat with its nine men. 'Oh God!' declared the contrite admiral. 'How my heart jumped to see them safe.' He sent two pounds to cheer 'the poor fellows'. The Hamiltons had taken their own house at 23 Piccadilly, and were selling jewellery, royal gifts and art treasures to furnish it and extinguish other debts. Among items going to auction was one of Romney's portraits, which Nelson secretly ordered Davison to purchase for him for £300 to prevent its loss. In January Sir William was able to repay Nelson £4109. Amidst this bustle they also directed a stream of letters to Nelson. The admiral savoured every delivery though, after reading them several times, he burned Emma's letters in a forlorn attempt to preserve their secrets. On his part, Nelson used his letters to Emma as a commentary on his day, often opening a new one in the morning and adding to it up to four times before retiring to bed. His language was increasingly explicit. His love, he told her was 'as fixed as Mount Etna and as warm in the inside as that mountain'.[37]

It was in this state that Nelson savaged what was left of his relationship with Fanny. He once complained that it was 'very easy to find a stick if you are inclined to beat your dog', and now revealed himself just such a master. Fanny's preparations for his command provided the pretext. She had incurred criticism in that direction before, although on this occasion the work had also involved servants, suppliers and shippers. Some of the items sent to Plymouth by wagon had been ordered by Davison. Whoever was responsible, Nelson opened a sharp salvo upon his wife on 20 January. His containers were all being broken open because only one key had been found, he grumbled. 'My steward says I have no one thing for comfort come, but a load of useless articles from Burgess's and a large chest of green tea . . . I have nothing useful but two chairs . . . [and] know not where I shall be in a week.' Even the 'affectionate' he generally used in signing off his letters to Fanny was dropped in an angry sequel the next day. 'Half my wardrobe is left behind, and that butler . . . ought to be hanged, and I hope you will never lay out a farthing with Mr Burgess. Had the waste of money been laid out in Wedgwood's ware, knives, forks for servants or cooking utensils, it would have been well. But I am forced to buy everything, even a little tea, for who would open a large chest? In short, I find myself without anything comfortable or convenient. In glasses of some kind, the steward tells me he finds a useless quantity of decanters, as yet not one can be found, and if he cannot find them today I must buy. In short, I only regret that I desired *any* person to order things for me. I could have done all in ten minutes, and for a tenth part of the expense, but never mind, I can eat off a yellow ware plate. It is now too late to send my half wardrobe, as I know not what is to become of me, nor do I care. My brother is very well and desires his regards, as I, to Mrs Nelson. Yours *truly*, Nelson.' The barb at the end is evident in a remark he passed to Emma the same day, that he had written 'her a letter of truths about my outfit'. Surprised by such vehemence, Fanny protested and elicited a softer reply on 3 February. It restored 'your affectionate Nelson' to its place but repeated that he had 'nothing and everything. If I want a piece of pickle, it must be put in [a] saucer. If a piece of butter, on an earthern plate. But I shall direct what things I want in future.' He had no decanter stands or keys to open a wardrobe, trunk and case, while some goods sent by Dods had been 'ruined' in the packing. Nails used to secure boxes had damaged a mahogany table and drawers.[38]

Fanny was soon charged with other errors. The sale of Roundwood aside, she had no clear instructions as to how to proceed in respect of properties, and dithered about whether to remain in London or go elsewhere. Edmund retreated to Bath to live near the Matchams, and after consulting Davison, Fanny closed the house in Dover Street and took Elizabeth Locker to help her prepare a new one in Brighton. Perhaps Fanny thought that Brighton suited her health and was close enough to Portsmouth and London for Nelson's purposes, but if so she not only misread his intentions but also played into Emma's hands. 'Let her go to Brighton, or where she pleases, I care not,' he told Emma. 'She is a great fool, and thank God you are not the least like her.' Emma's view was that by leaving London Fanny had effectively abandoned her husband.[39]

While Nelson was at Torbay Fanny made a serious attempt to repair their relationship. After learning from Davison that her husband still spoke of her 'with affection' – a reckless palliative if ever there was one – and from William that Nelson's eye was inflamed, all of Fanny's 'affection', 'anxiety' and 'fondness' for Nelson 'rushed forth', and she wrote from Brighton on 12 February, offering to come and nurse him. The reply shocked her. 'I only wish people would never mention my name to you, for whether I am blind or not it is nothing to any person,' he said acidly. 'I want neither nursing [n]or attention, and had you come here, I should not have gone on shore, nor would you have come afloat. I fixed, as I thought, a proper allowance to enable you to remain quiet, and not to be posting from one end of the kingdom to the other. Whether I live or die, am sick or well, I want from no one . . . I expect no comfort till I am removed from this world.' In other words, he wanted her nowhere near him, and she should reconcile herself to a life apart. 'You may suppose the consternation it threw me into,' she told Davison, no longer knowing what she could do that would not provoke attack. 'My mind has not recovered its natural calmness,

[n]or do I think it ever will. I am now distrustful and fearful of my own shadow.' [40]

Nelson believed that he had provided 'that person' with a satisfactory allowance. He had given her £400 in London, and would grant her £1800 a year in 1801, as well as return to her the legacy of £4000 bequeathed her by an uncle, which Nelson protected in January 1801 by an investment of £6425. But now the couple led separate lives, and their family and friends had to take sides or maintain a difficult neutrality. Fanny at least felt for them. 'A conscious rectitude will carry me through,' she told Davison, 'but . . . I think you had better not mention my name, and leave me to my fate.'[41]

During the three weeks Nelson spent at Torbay the government changed. Henry Addington, Speaker of the Commons, agreed to form a new government on 5 February, after Pitt stepped down over the issue of Catholic Emancipation. Nelson usually approved of Pitt, impressed by his apparent independence of party, and had discussed the Baltic expedition with him. As a new administration formed, it became known that St Vincent would replace Spencer at the Admiralty, and that Troubridge would join him on the board. Pondering how he would be affected, Nelson hoped that Troubridge would not 'forget my kindness', especially as he was finding his son a place on the *St George*. But the admiral was now committed to a lawsuit against the first lord of the Admiralty, and considered his chances sunk. He nevertheless urged Davison not to abandon 'an oppressed friend' and declared that he would sooner remain unemployed than 'give up an inch'. Fortunately, St Vincent knew Nelson's worth, and was likewise sensible of his increased political clout. He asked whether he could rely on Nelson's vote in the Lords, and the younger admiral agreed, because, he said, St Vincent would energise the war.[42]

On 17 and 18 February orders directed Nelson to join Sir Hyde Parker at Portsmouth, and he arrived at Spithead on the 20th. The outgoing government had supplied the Baltic expedition with 895 of 'the most seasoned and experienced troops' available, under a military 'officer of acknowledged ability and enterprise'. Assembled on Southsea Common, ready to embark, the force consisted of the 49th Regiment of Foot under Lieutenant Colonel Isaac Brock, a big, handsome six-footer, later the saviour of Canada and an ally of Tecumseh, and over one hundred sharpshooters commanded by Captain Sidney Beckwith. Their supreme commander was Lieutenant Colonel the Hon. William Stewart of the newly formed Rifle Corps, a son of the seventh Earl of Galloway, in his mid-twenties, who had earned a reputation for bravery during active service in the West Indies and Europe.[43]

In embarking troops and hurrying ships forward, Nelson regained his best form. After his ship had had some repairs at Spithead, he was so eager to position himself for further business that he sailed for St Helens, on the Isle of Wight, with the painters and caulkers still aboard. He paid little more than due respects to Sir Charles Saxton, the naval commissioner, and John Holloway, the assistant port admiral at Portsmouth, though both were old acquaintances. Behind his cabin door, the other, private, deeply troubled Nelson still prevailed. His internal struggle had reached a peak.

5

One dark evening early in February a private hackney coach halted outside 9 Little Titchfield Street in Marylebone, London, and a lady alighted with a very small bundle wrapped in a coat or muff. Inside, Emma Hamilton entrusted Horatia, a week-old baby girl, to Mrs Jane Gibson, who lived in the house with her daughter, Mary, a hunchback child. Mrs Gibson was to care for the child and supply a wet nurse, though occasionally she would be required to bring her to the Hamiltons' residence at 23 Piccadilly. Emma claimed to be acting out of generosity to the child's mother, whom she eventually revealed to be a mysterious 'Mrs Thomson', forever indisposed through either illness or absence. Mrs Gibson received her further instructions by written notes delivered to her house. Thus began the strange life of Horatia Nelson, the only known surviving child of the naval hero, surreptitiously smuggled into the hands of a guardian by a woman who denied her own motherhood, lied about the child's age and hid her from prying eyes.[44]

Though Horatia's father never knew it, this was not the first inconvenient child Emma had passed into other hands. 'Emma Carew', a daughter born to Sir Harry Fetherstonhaugh in 1782, had been deposited with a maternal grandmother and then fostered in Manchester before being put in a convent. Like Horatia she grew to maturity without the security of an acknowledged parentage. Little Horatia's appearance is still obscure. She seems to have been born in the last days of January 1801, yet Emma would delay her christening until 1803 and then supply a false birth date, 29 October 1800, when she herself was travelling home through the continent. From a remark made by Nelson, it is also evident that Horatia was a twin, but nothing reliable has come down about her sibling. Possibly one twin died at or close to birth, or just possibly that was merely what Nelson was told, and the missing twin was fostered elsewhere. No evidence for a death or a fostering has ever been found.[45]

Whatever else might be said, Horatia certainly had the love of her father. He doted upon her from the beginning, and gave constant thought to her future. 'A finer child never was produced by any two persons,' he said. 'It was, in truth, a love-begotten child.' Horatia cemented his bond with Emma. If Fanny had given him a child, or it had been possible for Nelson to love Josiah, his marriage might have held. But after Horatia there was no road back. In order to correspond with Emma more freely, especially about such matters as her pregnancy, Nelson had invented the 'Thomsons' to throw the readers of any intercepted letter off the scent. The fictional 'Thomson' was a hand on Nelson's ship, while his pregnant wife remained in London under the care of Lady Hamilton. In their letters Nelson and his mistress passed messages between the Thomsons, as if merely benevolent ciphers between two lovers, when in truth they were talking about themselves. This unconvincing artifice must have been concocted before Nelson left London, but 'Thomson' made his paper debut in the admiral's letter of 21 January, when he wrote that 'Thomson' the 'poor fellow', desired him to tell 'dear Mrs Thomson' that 'he is more scrupulous than if Mrs Thomson was present'. Decoded, this meant that Nelson was observing his promise to avoid female company. Three days later he asked about Emma's pregnancy. 'Pray tell Mrs Thomson her kind friend [Mr Thomson] is very uneasy about her, and prays most fervently for her safety.' On 25 January Nelson wrote that Thomson was 'very anxious, and begs you [Emma] will, if she [Mrs Thomson] is not able, write a line just to comfort him. He appears to me to feel very much her situation. He is so agitated . . .'[46]

It was 1 February when Nelson heard of the actual birth. 'I believe poor dear Mrs Thomson's friend will go mad with joy,' he wrote immediately. 'He cries, prays, and performs all tricks . . . He swears he will drink your health this day in a bumper . . . I cannot write, I am so agitated by this young man at my elbow. I believe he is foolish. He does nothing but rave about you and her!' Shortly afterwards, slipping carelessly in and out of his disguise as Thomson, he wrote that the young man wished 'the time may not be far distant when he may be united forever to the object of his wishes, his only, *only* love. He swears before Heaven that he will marry you [!] as soon as it is possible . . . He charges me to say how dear you are to him, and that you must, every opportunity, kiss and bless for his dear little girl, which he wishes to be called Emma, out of gratitude to our dear, good Lady Hamilton.'[47]

Horatia, like the separation from Fanny, forced Nelson to reconsider his finances. Of late he had began to approach the expectations of his station, with modest properties at home and abroad, titles and a prospect of a steady if modest income. Now his means were entirely inadequate to the purchase of another English property and making provision for a wife, a mistress and her child, and the heirs of his title. Roundwood would only fetch £3300, and even after realising £6131 through the sale of government consolidated stock, his end-of-year balance with Marsh, Page and Creed only amounted to some £4000, about the same as his annual income. Apart from that he had a number of diamond gifts, many housed in a mahogany box with Davison, and some £8055 invested in consols and India stock. The measure of this thin bread can be gained from his ridiculous, and rightly rejected, claim to receive full pay as an admiral for the period between hauling down his flag in 1800 and raising it again in 1801.[48]

Within a week of hearing of Horatia's birth, Nelson began submitting draft codicils of his will for Emma's consideration, wrestling with one idea after another in an effort to stretch his assets to all deserving applicants. These deliberations eventually resulted in a new and unsatisfactory will and codicils dated 16 March. He did right by Fanny, assigning her an investment sufficient to protect the £4000 her uncle had willed her with an annual interest of £200. In addition he granted her a pension of £1600. Although £1800 was rather a modest income to fund the wife of a peer, it was generous in terms of Nelson's resources. In the event of his death, the pension would be cut by half, but it was thought that £20,000 would still have to be invested to produce it. As far as Nelson's heirs were concerned, he decided that his only property, Bronte, with the sword presented by the King of Naples, the chelengk and all his medals and orders should descend with his titles. Currently that male heir would have to be provided by his brother William, or one of his sisters, and to strengthen the 'dignity' of his successor Nelson assigned his family any residual money or sums due him at his death beyond the £20,000 needed to sustain Fanny's annuity, save for £3000, which he awarded to Emma.

This did little for Emma and Horatia. Apart from the £3000 that Lady Hamilton would obtain if Nelson's liquid estate topped £20,000, she had little more than diamond boxes and gifts from foreign potentates to live upon, items of a considerable commercial value, certainly, but hardly capable of supporting a woman of her extravagance. Horatia did not feature in the final will at all. In one draft codicil Nelson did refer to a female child 'in whom I take a very particular interest'. Her parents, he said, were known only to Lady Hamilton, and he implored her to 'consider the child as mine and be a guardian to it, shielding it from want and disgrace, and bringing it up as the child of her dear friend, Nelson and Bronte'. But to mention Horatia was also to put Emma in the way of embarrassing questions, and both mistress and child were effectively left dependent upon provision Sir William might make for his lady, and future, rather than existing, resources that could accrue to Nelson. As the admiral wrote to Emma, he must 'now begin and save a fortune for the little one'. The most striking feature of Nelson's provisions, therefore, is their inadequacy. He had neither a landed property in England, that indispensable qualification for participating in the political process and maintaining 'gentle' status, nor the means to guarantee the future of those truly closest to him. It puts into context his continual interest in prize money, including the results of the lawsuit against St Vincent.[49]

Horatia's birth also found Nelson wrestling with the first strains in the new triumvirate. Bound in love, friendship and admiration, Sir William, Emma and Nelson all nevertheless had their own agendas. All were differently circumstanced. Nelson wanted a new life with his mistress and child. He felt a husband and father, but was unable to acknowledge or act in either role. He detested the secrecy and deceit, and his desire to claim Horatia as his own was evident in a childish plan to have her christened. He talked about making a flying visit to London for the event, suggesting St George's, Hanover Square, as an appropriate venue. The child's parents could be given as 'Johem and Morata Etnorb'. 'If you read the surname backwards, and take the letters of the other names,' he explained to Emma, 'it will make, very extraordinary, the names of your real and affectionate friends, Lady Hamilton and myself.' To achieve his aims, he was ready to retire from the world of the fleshpots and bigwigs so ready to abuse him, and accept self-imposed seclusion, however it injured him. Feeling as he did ('I might be trusted with fifty virgins naked in a dark room') he had no need of others: 'I long to be alone with you,' he told her. 'I hate company.' And he expected the same of his mistress. 'Only do as I do, and all will be well, and you will be everything I wish.'[50]

The Hamiltons, unfortunately, were not retiring. Sir William would have liked to, and could think of no life more desirable than a quiet, studious existence fishing, visiting galleries and dealers in antiquities, and haunting clubs and learned societies. But he was worried about his debts, and grubbing for a pension, perhaps even a peerage, and until that was settled he needed to cultivate 'interest'. There could be no exile for him. Nor for Emma, the inveterate socialite, grievously wounded by her exclusion from the court, who could no more abstain from what company she could get than Nelson could have turned his back on a battle. She may have loved Horatia in her way, but the child was also a threat to the reputation she was trying to rehabilitate, and had to remain hidden. She was, of course, the one confronting ridicule on a regular basis, not least in the windows of those arbiters of popular taste and innuendo, the West End print shops. Gillray's latest productions were out in February, and they were merciless. 'Dido in Despair' portrayed Emma as the Carthaginian princess lamenting the departure of her lover, Aeneas. It showed a monstrously fat Lady Hamilton rising nightmarishly from her bed sheets in despair, as the admiral sailed away, and bemoaning being left 'with the old antique'. The old antique himself took star billing in a grotesque sequel, in which the withered cognoscenti admired a display of antiquities. Among several salacious facets, the horns of a bust of Apis, the Egyptian god of the Nile, were shown reaching upwards to link two portraits on the wall behind, labelled Cleopatra and Mark Antony, but in fact showing Nelson and a bare-breasted Emma, the latter clutching a bottle of gin. These were the armies Emma had to conquer in her battle.[51]

The Hamiltons' overtures to society produced the first fissure in the triumvirate in February and March. To draw the influential to 23 Piccadilly, they organised artistic evenings, largely to showcase Emma's talents as a hostess, actress and singer, but from the beginning Nelson was suspicious. Was this the same Sir William who 'used to think that a little candlelight and iced water would ruin him?' Far more troubling, in the context of Nelson's own hermitage, was his thought that Emma was being exhibited to 'a set of whores, bawds and unprincipled liars', one of whom was George, Prince of Wales, whom Nelson himself had once invited to a Sunday dinner with vocal entertainments by Lady Hamilton and Madame Banti. At the beginning of February the prince and Sir William resurrected the idea, which assumed a different hue in the admiral's absence. The prince's philandering in and out of brothels was notorious, and Nelson's fears were further stimulated by rumours that Emma had 'hit his fancy' and he wanted her 'as a mistress'. Yet George was obviously a useful tool for the Hamiltons, especially as the king was deep into another bout of insanity and talk of the prince ruling as regent was rife. Nelson entertained the unworthy suspicion that Sir William's campaign for financial rewards might lead him to offer his wife as 'a whore to the rascal'.[52]

The news plunged Nelson into a desperate trough of jealousy, fear, guilt, self-pity and loneliness. Gazing at Emma's portraits, or a lock of hair he kept in a box with one from his mother, mired him in grief. 'Your character will be gone,' he stormed on 17 February, amidst a confused jumble of anger and advice. 'Do not have him *en famille*; the more [people present] the better. Do not sit long at [the] table. Good God! He will be next you, and telling you soft things! If he does, tell it out at [the] table, and turn him out of the house . . . Do not let him sit next you, but at dinner he will hob glasses with you. I cannot write to Sir Wm., but he ought to go to the prince and not suffer your character to be ruined by him. Oh God, that I was dead . . . He will put his foot near you. I pity you from my soul, as I feel you wish him in Hell . . . He wishes, I dare say, to have you alone. Don't let him touch, nor yet sit next you. If he comes, get up. God strike him blind if he looks at you. This is high treason, and you may get me hanged by revealing it. Oh God, that I were . . . why do I live?'[53]

The next day a rambling hysteria was poured on to paper. 'I knew . . . you could not help coming downstairs when the prince was there, notwithstanding all your declarations never to meet him, to receive him . . . but his words are so charming that, I am told, no person can withstand them . . . Hush, hush, my poor heart, keep in my breast. Be calm. Emma is true! But no one, not even Emma, could resist the serpent's flattering tongue . . . What will they all *say* and think? That Emma is like other women, when I would have killed anybody who had said so . . . Forgive me, I know I am almost distracted . . . Do you go to the opera tonight. They tell me he sings well. I have eat[en] nothing but a little rice and drank water. But forgive me. I know my Emma, and don't forget that you had once a Nelson, a friend, a dear friend, but alas, he has his misfortunes. He has lost the best, his only friend, his only love. Don't forget him, poor fellow! He is honest. Oh! I could thunder and strike dead with my lightning. I dreamt it last night, my Emma. I am calmer. Reason, I hope, will resume her place, please God. Tears have relieved me. You never will again receive the villain to rob me . . . May the heavens bless you! I am better . . . Get rid of it as well as you can. Do not let him come downstairs with you, or hand you up.' He returned to his self-flagellation in the *St George* the next day. 'Do not let the liar come. I never saw him but once, the fourth day after I came to London, and he never mentioned you by name. May God blast him . . . Be firm! Go and dine with Mrs Denis on Sunday. Do not, I beseech you, risk being at home.' At times he grew so confused that he spoke about an event scheduled for Sunday, 22 February, as if it had already happened. 'Did you sit alone with the villain for a moment? No, I will not believe it! Oh God! Oh God! Keep my senses. Do not let the rascal in.' And his suspicions were spreading to others. 'Tell the Duke [of Queensberry] that you will never go to his house. Mr G[reville, Emma's former lover] must be a scoundrel. He treated you once ill enough, & cannot love you . . .'[54]

Sir William, whose standing had been damaged by the affair, was also now being seen as an obstacle to marriage. In the Thomson letters, he appeared as Mrs Thomson's uncle. Mr Thomson, said Nelson, 'wishes there was peace, or that if your uncle would die, he would instantly . . . marry you, for he dotes on nothing but you and his child'. But the cuckolded husband, alerted in some way by his wife, joined her in trying to reassure Nelson. The prince had invited himself, he explained, and it had been difficult to refuse. 'I am well aware of the danger that would attend the prince's frequenting our home,' he added, and promised that he would 'keep' the occasion 'strictly to the musical part' with a small select company, and 'get rid of it as well as we can'. Emma went further, and cancelled the engagement completely, promising to take to her bed ill before the dreaded Sunday to provide an excuse. *'Forgive every cross word,'* he wrote. *'I now live!'*[55]

But his self-laceration continued to ebb and flow. Within a day he was condemning 'the shocking conduct' of Mrs Thomson's 'uncle' and saying that he would resign the sea and reject a dukedom with £40,000 a year to preserve her virtue. 'I have been very unwell, and horrid dreams,' he added the next morning. 'If your uncle persists in having such bad company to dinner, your friend [Thomson] begs, and I agree . . . , that you should dine out of the house and take especial care not to go home till you know the wretches are gone . . . After all, if the beast turns you out of his house because you will not submit to be thought a whore, you know then what shall happen.' He now distrusted Hamilton so much that he suggested Emma used another and safe corresponding address. That letter was carried to London personally by Troubridge, who had sailed with Nelson from Torbay to Spithead. As Sir Thomas put it in his coat, Nelson suddenly broke into 'a flood of tears'. Regaining his composure, he explained that the thought of Troubridge seeing Emma in a mere ten hours hence had overwhelmed him, and he would have given his heart to have taken the place of the letter in his pocket.[56]

It had all been sordid and perhaps silly, but Emma pursued her quarry with no less abandon, embarking upon a gift-giving charm offensive to drive Fanny from the Nelson family, using their dependence upon the admiral as a weapon. Few of the Nelson clan were willing to damage their relationships with their hero and benefactor. The first to betray Fanny were brother William and his small and endlessly talking wife, Sarah. William had been flapping around the admiral ever since his return, and eventually used him to forward a petition to Lord Eldon, the new Lord Chancellor, pleading for advancement. Quickly perceiving Fanny to be disposable, William immediately began courting the new power. 'Your image and voice are constantly before my imagination,' Emma learned, 'and I can think of nothing else. I never knew what it was to part with a friend before.' Soon both the reverend and his wife were blithely toasting 'Sir William and Lady Hamilton, and Lord Nelson – God bless them!'[57]

In turn, Emma eagerly cemented her conversion of Sarah, demonising and ridiculing Fanny, whom she nicknamed 'Tom Tit' with schoolyard spite. 'You and I liked each other from the moment we met,' she told Sarah on 20 February. 'Our souls were congenial. Not so with *Tom Tit*, for there was an antipathy not to be described . . . *Tom Tit* might go to the devil for what I care.' There followed a series of letters, a sickening melange that blended venomous references to Tom Tit and her 'Cub', Josiah, with constant adulation of Nelson. 'We can walk and talk, and be happy together,' said she, 'and you will hear all the news of my Hero, great, great, glorious Nelson.' The admiral was no doubt equally interested in reconciling his family to his new situation, and encouraged the fraternisation between Emma and his brother. He would soon arrange for him to stay in London, and paid for the lodgings. His brother was 'a great bore' but Sarah made a 'cheerful' companion.[58]

To see Horatia and 'bury' his woes in Emma's 'dear bosom', Nelson got leave to slip away from Portsmouth on 23 February, travelling all night with Tom Allen and a prediction that 'twins' would 'again be the fruit' of his reunion with his mistress. His eyesight had improved, which he attributed to abstinence from wine, and his depression lifted, and he arrived in London in good humour, taking rooms at Lothian's Hotel. He had warned Fanny not to try to see him, but did invite Josiah to call, and the youngster duly arrived with a letter from his mother, thanking Nelson for anything he might do for the boy. Surprisingly, the admiral welcomed him warmly. He thought Josiah might be reappointed to the *Thalia* with the support of some carefully selected officers, and for a week or so Nisbet hovered. Emma, busy stigmatising Fanny's 'bad heart', disapproved. 'The cub *dined* with us, but I never asked how *Tom Tit* was,' she wrote to Sarah on 2 March.[59]

The few days in London were full, marred only by Emma's poor health. Nelson saw his daughter for the first time at Mrs Gibson's house on 24 February and was thoroughly charmed. Public appointments were reserved for the next day. At the Admiralty he spoke about Josiah's situation, and met Sir Hyde Parker, promising to give him every support in the Baltic. Brother Maurice and

Troubridge were invited to dinner at Piccadilly that evening and the conversation lasted until two the following morning. 'We had a pleasant evening,' Emma reported, but 'the Cub is to have a frigate . . . I only hope he does not come near me. If he does, not at home shall be the answer.' There was a final visit to the Admiralty on the afternoon of the 26th, when Nelson received orders to proceed to Yarmouth, where the Baltic expedition was assembling. He was also to usher some fifteen ships at Portsmouth forward, and collect flatboats and carronades that awaited him in Deal and Dover. The admiral also found time to send 'a poor woman' to Lord Spencer. She was 'a proper object' for the Trinity Charity houses, but the first lord could find no vacancy. The family partings were hard. His niece, Charlotte, who had been brought from school for the occasion, received two guineas. But leaving Emma was like 'tearing one's own flesh' while her heart was 'fit to burst . . . with grief'.[60]

The appointment Josiah had been promised was never made, however. The new board was too familiar with Nisbet's youthful follies, and were probably also influenced by his old rival, Lieutenant Samuel Colquit, who had returned to England in the autumn of 1800, taken lodgings off the Strand, and fired letters in search of half-pay, promotion and another ship. Colquit's mother even attempted to blackmail Nelson into supporting her son. Somehow Colquit's patron, Captain Isaac Coffin, had got hold of a letter in which Nelson had described Josiah in unflattering terms, and Mrs Colquit intimated that she would introduce it into the public arena if she did not get her way. Adding to the blaze, Colquit himself haunted the Admiralty waiting room, ready to twist the knife into Nisbet. Nelson, of course, would not be intimidated and angrily upbraided the board for reneging on its promise to employ Josiah. 'Although I know that Capt. Nisbet does not care if I was dead and damned,' he wrote to Troubridge, 'yet I cannot but be sorry that he is not to have the *Thalia* or some other good ship. His failings I know very well, but as I have the testimony of Duckworth and Inglefield of his improved construct as an officer, I care not what Lieut. Colquitt [sic] may say.'[61]

The board was unmoved. It posted Colquit to the *Hydra* in March and a year later promoted him to the rank of commander. In 1810 another board made him post, and he died a rear admiral. Nelson had done his best for Nisbet, but now washed his hands of his erring stepson. Though still only a minor, Josiah would get no more chances for redemption. 'I have done all for him,' Nelson wrote in March, 'and he may again, as he has often done before, wish me to break my neck and be abetted in it by his friends, who are likewise my enemies, but I have done my duty as an honest generous man.' It was his final verdict, and everybody else's, for Josiah would never command one of His Majesty's ships again. The boy who might have saved Nelson's marriage, but helped to destroy it instead, effectively slipped out of the admiral's life. It is a measure of the distance that quickly developed between the two that when Josiah wanted to contact his stepfather in September, he had to write to Troubridge at the Admiralty for an address.[62]

Likewise, Nelson was also done with Fanny, as he (again slipping in and out of the persona of Thomson) wrote to Emma on the first day of March. 'Now, my own dear wife, for such you are in my eyes and in the face of heaven . . . there is nothing in this world that I would not do for us to live together, and to have our dear little child with us. I firmly believe that this campaign will give us peace, and then we will set off for Bronte. In twelve hours we shall be across the water and freed from all the nonsense of his friends, or rather pretended ones . . . It would bring 100 of tongues and slanderous reports if I separated from her (which I would do with pleasure the moment we can be united; I want to see her no more), therefore, we must manage till we can quit this country or your uncle [William] dies. I love, I never did love anyone else. I never had a dear pledge of love [a child] till you gave me one, and you, thank my God, never gave one to anybody else . . . My longing for you, both person and conversation, you may readily imagine. What must be my sensations at the idea of sleeping with you! It sets me on fire, even the thoughts, much more would the reality . . . My love and desires are all to you, and if any woman naked was to come to me, even as I am this moment from thinking of you, I hope it might rot off if I would touch her even with my hand . . . My love, my darling angel, my heaven-given wife, the dearest only true wife of her own till death.'[63]

That being so, Nelson felt trapped, at least in England. Marriage among the 'gentle' classes was seldom merely a matter of love. It was a tool by which one family increased its prestige, wealth or 'interest' – that marvellous eighteenth-century word meaning political and social leverage – by uniting with another. Though Nelson had been powerfully attracted to Fanny in those early days in the West Indies, he had also conformed to these norms, for his wife had been an heiress of one of the wealthiest men in the islands. Nelson was not so interested in money that the failure of that apparent legacy worried him much, but it had been a factor in the beginning all the same. Now, however, he was surrendering entirely to passion. Emma might give him an heir, something Fanny had failed to supply, but she could endow her lover with neither money nor honour, and little in the way of interest. Nelson's motive was a passionate love, pure and simple. It overruled everything else.

To satisfy that passion, Nelson condemned Fanny to what no woman wanted, a grass widowhood that left her unable to build a new life and an object of pity and innuendo for the remainder of her days. In those times, when marriage was still held to be an indissoluble union, women had no recourse to divorce, and nor, for that matter, did Nelson. To obtain a divorce he would have had to apply for a private act of parliament, a prohibitively expensive and messy process that would have necessitated peers of the realm picking over his private life. Besides, he had no grounds for such a measure, since Fanny had manifestly been neither adulterous nor cruel. Given the expense and inconvenience of divorces, it was not surprising that only 317 cases occurred between 1700 and 1850. The only escape Nelson could see was some kind of exile in a place that cared nothing for irregularities. The admiral prepared for the Baltic campaign in mental torment, but not without a fixed plan. He wanted a quick victory that would bring peace, and then to leave his country to live as he wanted with whom he wanted, in spite of friends and enemies. Effectively, he also wanted to turn the clock back to the better days he had spent in Italy: 'Ah! Those were happy times. Would to God we were at this moment in the Bay of Naples, and all matters for those good monarchs going on as well as it did at that time.'[64]

In this idyllic scene there was no such person as Fanny, Lady Nelson. On 4 March Nelson finally cut the matrimonial cable. 'I neither want [n]or wish for anybody to care what becomes of me, whether I return or am left in the Baltic. Living I have done all in my power for you,' he wrote to her. 'And if dead, you will find I have done the same. Therefore, my only wish is to be left to myself, and wishing you every happiness, believe that I am your affectionate Nelson and Bronte.' There it was at last, a cruel document for all its talk of provision, and one that Fanny would refer to as her 'letter of dismissal'. It told some of what he had done for her, but nothing about what she had done for him, year after year. There was not one word of thanks, regret or real kindness for a woman who had never wronged him.[65]

It even took Fanny by surprise, but, hurt as she was, she continued to protect her husband, understanding that the letters were aberrant reflections of a naturally kind man. 'No one shall know of these harsh and cruel letters,' she wrote, and burned them. But how was she to respond to them? Already friends and relatives were writing and speaking to her without asking after Nelson, as if he had been erased from her life, but she clung to hopes of a reconciliation. No one seemed to be able to advise her. Although Fanny knew William – 'gain, gain is his *motto*' – she owned herself astonished at the speed at which he abandoned her. Kate wrote 'one of the most affectionate letters ever written to a sister in law' but felt unable to even mention her brother, and old Edmund was equally bewildered. He rode out the storm at 3 South Parade, Bath, soaking his disintegrating frame ('broken almost to pieces') in the spa waters under the supervision of the Matchams, but appeared to know little of what was happening. 'Can I contribute anything to the further increase of your comfort, or do[es] your mind feel easy and happy in its present state?' he asked Fanny. Maurice sympathised, but told Fanny to ignore Nelson's letters, as he had forgotten himself. Only Susannah came up with a positive suggestion. 'Will you excuse what I am going to say?' she wrote to Fanny. 'I wish you had continued in town [London] a little longer, as I *have heard* my brother regretted he had not a house he could call his own when he returned [in February]. Do, whenever you hear he is likely to return, have a house to receive him. If you absent yourself entirely from him, there never can be a reconciliation. Such attention must please him, and I am sure will do in the end. Your conduct, as he justly says, is exemplary in regard to him and he has not an unfeeling heart.'[66]

Grasping at the straw, Fanny mounted a search for a new London house, and made another desperate offer to her husband through Davison. 'If at any future time my husband will make my house his home, I will receive him with joy, and whatever happened shall never pass my lips . . . I forgive my cruel enemies . . . I have injured no one intentionally.' But Susannah had entirely misjudged her brother. He wanted Emma, not Fanny. He had warned her not to come to London, and had no desire to see her. Indeed, he excused his own conduct by blaming her for real or imaginary misdeeds. Fanny's overture was utterly futile.[67]

6

Few commanders have prepared for a crucial campaign in such internal turmoil. Nelson continued to obsess about his mistress. 'I shall soon return,' he promised her, 'and then we will take our fill of Love. No, we never can be satiated till death divides us.' The cancellation of the visit of the Prince of Wales and Nelson's whirlwind visit to London had steadied him, but only temporarily, and his letters to Emma were full of dark visions. The villains were Greville ('never meet or stay if any damned whore or pimp bring[s] that fellow to you'), one Hodges ('my senses are almost gone tonight. I feel as I never felt before'), Lord Abercorn and even Sir William, whom he rated a 'pimp' selling his wife for political capital. Emma clearly encouraged these jealousies, and although he insisted she adhere to her 'oath' of fidelity, he never trusted her. 'I dreamt last night that I hurt you with a stick on account of that fellow, and then attempted to throw over [your] head a tub of hot water. I woke in agony,' he rambled. When brother William and a cousin, Robert Rolfe, visited Great Yarmouth to take their leave and ask favours, he almost resented their interruption of his private fantasies.[68]

Yet in the thrall of this anguish Nelson energetically drove the naval preparations forward. The 'instant' he got back to Portsmouth he threatened the fleet with sailing the next day. 'This is impossible,' complained Fremantle of the *Ganges*, one of his closest colleagues. The troops were divided between ten ships, with Stewart and 108 rank and file in the *St George*, and senior field officers in the *Ganges*, *Saturn* and *Defence*, and fourteen ships of all sizes eventually got to sea on 2 March, blundering through a fog to reach the Downs the following day. There, 'a damned stupid dog' of a pilot ran the *Warrior*, Captain Charles Tyler, on to the Goodwin Sands, 'notwithstanding the repeated signals that were made from the *St George* and every vessel that she was standing into danger'.

The ship was eventually hauled off with little damage, but she was unable to continue with her detachment when it proceeded to the rendezvous at Great Yarmouth. During the voyage Nelson's six o'clock in the morning breakfasts fostered another lifelong friendship, this time with Stewart, 'a very good young man', as well as the brother of Lord Garlies, whom the admiral had known in the Mediterranean. For his part, Stewart admired 'the natural liveliness' of Nelson's personality, although he had a tendency to 'interfere in the working of the ship, not always with the best success or judgement'.[69]

When Nelson reached Great Yarmouth on 6 March he found the commander-in-chief's flag flying from the *Ardent*, though Sir Hyde himself lodged ashore in the Wrestlers Inn with his young wife, Frances Onslow, thirty-seven years the admiral's junior. At sixty-two, Parker had seen relatively little action, but his knighthood had been earned in a gutsy if minor operation in the North and Hudson Rivers, New York, in 1778, and he had made a courageous decision to pursue the French to the West Indies in 1796. If nothing suggested that Sir Hyde would be a particularly active leader, he had considerable administrative experience as a flag officer, and in 1791 had been involved in devising an untried plan to force the Baltic. Given the pronounced diplomatic element in his mission, Parker seemed a respectable choice, and a sound complement to his second in command, whose prudence, strategy and judgement had been criticised, but about whose energy and fighting spirit there could be no doubt.

The relationship between the two commanders did not open smoothly. Parker invited Nelson to dinner, but the latter tactlessly declined, perhaps in compliance with his promise to Emma Hamilton. But Parker seemed incapable of rising early, delaying the day's business, and showed little urgency, waiting for straggling detachments to arrive and hoping to prepare more light-draught vessels for operations in the shallows off Copenhagen. In Nelson's view this was sheer negligence. As far as he was concerned, Britain was confronted by a formidable coalition of Denmark, Sweden and Russia, and it was imperative to destroy the hostile navies piecemeal before they could unite. He wanted to dispose of the Danish fleet at Copenhagen, clearing his communication line in the process, before the ice in the Baltic could clear and release the Swedish ships at Karlskrona and the Russian forces at Revel and Kronstadt. Nelson, Hardy and Stewart waited on the admiral in the Wrestlers Inn, but he not only sat tight, but also declined to share any significant information about the campaign.[70]

Accordingly, Nelson set about bypassing Parker, leaking information to those who might apply pressure. He voiced some concerns in a letter to Davison, suggesting he might notify the press. 'Burn this letter,' he counselled. 'Then it can never appear, and you can speak as if your knowledge came from another quarter.' More directly, he complained to his friends in the Admiralty that Parker was uncommunicative, immobile and 'a little nervous about dark nights and fields of ice' when 'these were not times for nervous systems'. And when the fleet should have been on its way to force the Danes to choose peace or war, the commander-in-chief found 'laying abed with a young wife' far preferable 'to a damned raw cold wind'. Nelson was undermining his commander-in-chief, but to some purpose, since Parker had no real grasp of the essential strategy of the campaign, and was threatening its prospects by procrastination.[71]

Nelson's letters upstairs had a salutary effect. When St Vincent learned 'by a side wind' that Parker was delaying sailing to accommodate a ball, he wrote a sharp letter on 11 March, telling Sir Hyde that any delay on account of 'some trifling circumstance' would do the admiral an 'irreparable injury'. Flushed out of his cosy inn, Parker was at sea with forty-six sail the next day. He may have guessed who had moulded the bullet – his wife certainly did – and remained blithely indifferent to his famous second in command. Nelson, for whom such secrecy was incomprehensible, resented being left out, and Admiral William Dickson, who commanded the North Sea squadron, also thought the 'gross neglect' a scandal. By 5 April St Vincent was delivering another boot to Sir Hyde's posterior, with a direct command to consult Nelson and his third man, Admiral Thomas Graves. 'They are straight-forward men without any views except facing the enemy in every direction.' But by then a battle had been fought.[72].

Both senior admirals of the Baltic expedition were in difficult positions. Parker commanded, but Nelson had the prestige, talent and ear of the Board of Admiralty, and had acquired the reputation of a difficult subordinate. Sir Hyde does not seem to have borne many grudges, but Nelson was a different matter. He was jealous of Parker's supreme command, taking it as a reflection upon his previous difficulties with authority, and was eager to accumulate grievances. An order of sailing, issued shortly before the fleet weighed anchor, placed Nelson in charge of a starboard division of eight sail of the line, but it was a comparatively underpowered force compared with the centre and larboard divisions, containing three of the five weakest ships. The captain of the fleet, William Domett, stationed on Parker's *London*, felt badly enough about it to tell Nelson that the order was none of his doing. But scribbling furiously to Troubridge, Nelson said that if his situation did not improve he hoped to be allowed to quit the fleet 'the moment the fighting business is over'.[73]

Fortunately, Nelson's enthusiasm for combat overruled such frustrations. 'Never mind,' he wrote to Emma. 'Nelson will be first if he lives, and you shall partake of all his glory.' He had no doubt about the result of a battle. When Berry mentioned a system for aiming guns more accurately, he agreed to consider it, but added that he hoped 'we shall be able, as usual, to get so close to our enemies that our shot cannot miss their object'. As confident as ever about the destructive power of British naval gunnery, he intended to deliver 'that hailstorm of bullets which is so emphatically described in the *Naval Chronicle* and which gives our dear country the dominion of the seas'. And he was determined that he, not Parker, would be the focus of the action. The campaign, he assured St Vincent, 'will be the best ever performed by your obliged and affectionate friend'.[74]

He had tried to prepare Emma for any bad news with words he thought might resonate with a decided patriot who enjoyed applause as much as he did. 'I know you are so true and loyal an Englishwoman, that you would hate those who would not stand forth in defence of our king, laws, religion and all that is dear to us,' he wrote while in Torbay. 'It is your sex that makes us go forth, and seems to tell us, "None but the brave deserve the fair." And if we fall, we still live in the hearts of those females who are dear to us.'[75]

On 16 February he had sent her the first of several love poems of his own composition, in which he exhorted her to accept an 'unadorn'd' attempt at 'the poetic art' that truly pledged his troth. As the two verses which provide the epigraph for this chapter show, he adopted the persona of 'Henry', identifying himself with the victor of Agincourt. Emma expressed her feelings in seven stanzas of her own, apparently written about this time. Three of the verses ran:

Silent grief and sad forebodings
(Lest I ne'er should see him more),
Fill my heart when gallant Nelson
Hoists Blue Peter at the fore.

For when duty calls my hero
To far seas where cannons roar,
Nelson (love and Emma leaving),
Hoists Blue Peter at the fore.

Oft he kiss'd my lips at parting
And at every kiss he swore
Nought could force him from my bosom,
Save Blue Peter at the fore.[76]

XIII

'CHAMPION OF THE NORTH'

Of Nelson and the North
Sing the glorious day's renown.
When to battle fierce came forth
All the might of Denmark's crown,
And her arms along the deep proudly shone.

Thomas Campbell, *Battle of the Baltic*, 1805

I

THE political storm that swept Parker's fleet into the Baltic had developed quickly, and at a time when Britain found herself increasingly isolated in Europe. The reluctant pacts that Austria and Naples made with France in the spring of 1801 left her devoid of effective allies. Not only had the second coalition collapsed, but Russia, one of its most powerful members, had become Britain's bitter enemy. The unstable tsar, Paul I, was deeply offended by the British retention of Malta. Britain had spent two difficult years securing Malta, and saw no sense in relinquishing such an important prize to a power as unreliable as Russia. True, His Britannic Majesty had recently acknowledged Paul's desire to restore the island to the Order of the Knights of St John, of which he was Grand Master, but his consent had always been conditional upon Russia's membership of the second coalition, and that was an obligation the tsar had begun to shirk.[1]

Russia had immediately reacted by drifting into the opposite camp. On 10 October 1800 Paul made secret overtures to Bonaparte, hinting at an alliance that could dominate Europe. No longer shackled to a doomed adventure in the desert, Bonaparte's star was rising. A military coup had given him the position of First Consul of France, with a constitution that promised control of the republic for ten years. By spring 1801, Bonaparte was on his way towards re-establishing a French monarchy in his own name, and dominated Holland, Belgium, Germany, Spain and most of Italy. Austria had been silenced. In a remarkable turn of the table, it was now Britain that stood alone and defiant.

Paul's dilapidated empire was still a credible force, with enormous reserves of manpower and forty capital ships, and he followed his overtures to France with an embargo on British property, incarcerating three hundred merchant ships in Russian ports and enslaving their crews. To strengthen his position, Paul revived the League of Armed Neutrality, a defunct alliance of the Baltic powers originally formed in 1780 to defend their rights as neutral traders. In the tsar's hand the new League was patently anti-British, and a potential ally of France. On 14 December 1800 a treaty between Russia and Sweden pointed the way. By strictly defining 'contraband' – that is, the goods that it was agreed that neutrals should not ship – as arms and ammunition alone, it allowed other essential war materiel, such as food and shipbuilding stores, to be traded freely to Britain's enemies. More, the treaty denied the Royal Navy's traditional right to stop and search merchant ships, and an attack was made upon the British interpretation of what constituted a legal blockade. These developments put Russia and Sweden on a collision course with Britain, for, had their contentions prevailed, the British would have forfeited the advantages of their naval superiority and watched essential military and naval stores flooding into enemy ports with impunity, some under an unacceptable definition of contraband and others smuggled in under flags of convenience. Locked in a war of national survival, Britain had no alternative but to stand by her own doctrines of contraband and stop and search.

Driven by Russian ambition, the League quickly embraced Prussia (which seized British warehouses in Hamburg and occupied Hanover, an electorate under the sovereignty of George III) and Denmark. Denmark was then ruled by Frederick, the crown prince, who acted for his insane father, King Christian VII, and was greatly influenced by her foreign minister, Count Christian Bernstorff. Men in their thirties, the crown prince and Bernstorff had no desire to clash with Britain, or indeed any one, but they were keen to turn the European conflicts to their own advantage. The Danes had a history of disputing neutral rights with Britain. In recent years they had expanded their trade at the expense of war-torn competitors, and become adept at carrying the cargoes of the belligerent powers under a cloak of neutrality. After a number of incidents at sea, the British ordered their ships to enforce their definition of neutral rights, and a Danish convoy was seized by force. In August the Danes agreed to suspend their convoys in northern waters until the two countries could negotiate a solution, but in January 1801 they signed up to the League of Armed Neutrality.

It was, in fact, the Anglo-Danish dispute that inspired Paul's revival of the League, but Denmark's position was hardly improved by her membership, for she now found herself boxed in between greater powers. On the one hand, she needed Russia, and not just for whatever support Paul might give on the matter of neutral rights. Denmark dreaded Sweden's interest in her Norwegian provinces, and was afraid of any liaison between Russia and Sweden. To prevent Russia and Sweden collaborating in a seizure of Denmark's Norwegian possessions, the Danes felt compelled to cultivate friendly relations with Paul and support his policies. Unfortunately, those policies drove Denmark firmly towards a clash with Britain, the one naval power capable of annihilating Danish overseas trade, and in the first months of 1801 a third big hat went into the ring. Bonaparte threatened to destroy Denmark if she continued her negotiations with Britain. In February the wretched Danish government considered its options, and found only one. They had to defy either Britain or the Franco-Russian-Swedish bloc. Betting on who was likely to emerge from the war victorious, they opted to stand up to the British.

While staving off a Franco-Spanish-Dutch threat with one hand, Britain had now to confront a confederacy of northern powers with the other, but she, too, had no real choice. She had to control the Baltic, because it was essential to the naval balance of power, supplying timber, flax, rope, hemp and other indispensable ingredients of naval might. To preserve the flow of those vital supplies to her dockyards, and to prevent them reaching her enemies, Britain had to define the terms upon which the hitherto non-aligned Baltic powers could trade. By the spring of 1801, with no breakthrough in the diplomacy, both sides were preparing for war. Between them Denmark and Sweden were supposed to contribute fifteen sail of the line to a Russian forty, but the Swedish and Russian fleets would be iced in their harbours until April and May, safe from British attack but equally unable to assist Denmark. The Danish capital, which guarded the entrance to the Baltic, and its fleet were, therefore, both accessible and alone, and Denmark soon had a commission at work, finding ships and men, and strengthening the fortifications at Copenhagen and Elsinore. In Britain Addington replaced Pitt as chief minister early in 1801, appointing Lord Hawkesbury the new foreign minister, but the government remained resolute. A new British secretary of the Treasury, Nicholas Vansittart, was sent to Copenhagen in February in a last effort to persuade Denmark to forsake the League. Among several suggestions, framed by Lord Grenville, the outgoing foreign minister, Britain offered to defend Denmark from Russian retaliation and to conclude a defensive alliance. At the least, Britain demanded access to the Baltic, so that her navy could deal with the Russo-Swedish fleet, and upon the disarmament of the Danish fleet so that the rear and communications of the British task force could be protected. To add muscle to these demands, Britain pushed ahead with her plans to send Parker to the Baltic.

It fell to St Vincent, the new first lord of the Admiralty, to complete the preparation of the British task force. Despite the country's parlous international position, faith in the armed forces remained high, especially after Keith and Abercromby landed a force in Egypt in March, routing the French army and forcing it to surrender, finally closing the book on Bonaparte's ill-starred eastern foray. As shallow water would be encountered, third-rate ships of the line would carry the principal armament, supported by a flotilla of small cruisers, fireships, bomb vessels, gunboats, galleys and barges. Men were harder to find, and St Vincent grumbled that Parker's squadron had 'consumed all the able and ordinary seamen we have'. Nevertheless, the musters were searched to weed out foreigners who might act as fifth columnists, and an effort made to supply charts, up-to-date signal books, pilots and officers with experience of the Baltic, such as Captain George Murray of the *Edgar* and Captain Samuel Sutton of *Alcmene*. Two commanders who accompanied the expedition as volunteers, Frederick Thesiger and Nicholas Tomlinson, had served in the Russian navy, and had ideas about how the fire and explosion ships might best be employed.[2]

Tomlinson, who was hoping to rehabilitate a faltering career in the Royal Navy, certainly grasped the strategic principles that would govern a successful campaign. It would be necessary for the British to force the sound between Denmark and Sweden and deal with the Danish fleet at Copenhagen before the Swedish and Russian ships, iced in Karlskrona, Revel and Kronstadt, could come to its assistance. Once the Danish threat had been eliminated, the British could push up the Gulf of Finland through the crumbling ice to attack the Russian squadron in Revel, which opened about the beginning of May. This would not only prevent it from escaping and combining with the other Russian force at Kronstadt, but still allow time to trap the latter in port, where the ice usually remained a week longer. In this way, argued Tomlinson, Britain could fall upon her enemies piecemeal, and comprehensively overthrow the entire northern coalition. To Nelson, too, that made plain sense, but although Sir Hyde talked to Tomlinson and took him into the *London*, his flagship, he seemed unable to grasp the urgency that underlay his analysis. It all depended upon acting before the break-up of the winter ice.[3]

In some mitigation, Parker's orders of 23 February, the work of Henry Dundas, the former secretary of state, failed to focus on the wider issues of Sweden and Russia, though the latter was the keystone of the enemy alliance. They told the commander-in-chief to round the Skaw at the northern extremity of the Danish peninsula, and try diplomacy before attacking the enemy fleet at Copenhagen. For this purpose he would carry a duplicate of a new dispatch that Hawkesbury had addressed to William Drummond, the British representative in Copenhagen. It gave Denmark forty-eight hours to agree a treaty with Britain along the lines Vansittart had already suggested, requiring the Danes to ditch the League and rely for their protection upon a fleet that Britain would station in the Baltic. Failing that, Parker was also empowered to spare Copenhagen a bombardment if the Danes surrendered their fleet and arsenal. But were Britain's demands to be totally rejected, Parker was to remove Drummond and his people, and destroy the Danish shipping and arsenal. A peaceful settlement was not, in reality, likely. Denmark could not humour Britain without risking disastrous repercussions, and when Vansittart reached Copenhagen on 9 March he achieved nothing. Bernstorff simply denied that the League was hostile to Britain, and declined to disengage from it. Vansittart's diplomatic credentials were not even accepted in the Danish capital, and he was told he would not be received until Britain lifted her embargo on Denmark's ships and refrained from other violent actions against her and her allies.

Parker was a likeable, well-intentioned commander, a full-faced, large-featured, sorrowful looking man, but the expedition would reveal serious military shortcomings. He was slow, indecisive and over-cautious, and neither of his flag officers, Nelson and Rear Admiral Thomas Graves, were made privy to his intentions. It was a managerial style very different from Nelson's, and one that rebounded upon Parker because it increased the burden on his far from confident shoulders, and eventually wasted time in discussions that should have taken place on earlier and more convenient occasions. When the expedition sailed from Yarmouth in a fresh, snow-singed wind and passed its first night in a murk lit only by the flashes of signal guns, both the commander-in-chief and his second in command were very much wrapped in their own thoughts.

2

For Lord Nelson the Baltic campaign was a dual conflict, in which professional and private passions struggled for supremacy. That he was able to throw such clear light upon the naval operation and act so decisively was the more remarkable in the context of his continuing personal instability. His mind constantly shifted between two quite separate worlds. In one he was a servant of the crown with large business in his hands; in the other a jealous lover, desperate to return to the arms of a mistress he didn't fully trust.

Somehow he managed to focus on the big events and produce a performance of outstanding brilliance, but always those dark thoughts lurked inside like a malignant spirit, ready to invade the private moments in his cabin and fill restless nights with disturbing dreams. He spent the night of 15 March tossing in his cot, while the snow, sleet and wind buffeted the windows, dreaming of Emma. 'I saw you all in black and that fellow [the Prince of Wales?] sitting by you. All this must mean something.' In long circumlocutory daily scribbles to his mistress, replete with false starts and erasures, he revealed deep-seated fears. At other times he was calmer, convincing himself that his 'guardian angel' remained faithful, but focused instead upon the loyalties of others. A series of 'no one cares about me, and I need your attention and affection' letters went to Troubridge, who, he suspected, had no further need of him now he had been raised to the Board of Admiralty. At the heart of these pathetic documents was a feeling that he was being used. Parker was twenty-two places above him on the list of flag officers, but Nelson still resented serving as his second. He saw a rerun of his experience in the Mediterranean, where he had won the battles but seen the supreme appointments, with their contingent privileges, going elsewhere. 'They all hate me and treat me ill,' he complained to Emma. 'I cannot . . . recall to my mind any one real act of kindness, but all unkindness.' And as for '*our friend Troubridge*', he 'felt so little for my health that I have wrote him . . . I would never mention it again to him'.[4]

Shot after shot was fired at the erring Troubridge:

7 March: '[As] perhaps I am now unfit to command [a fleet], my only ambition is to obey. I have no wish ungratified in the service, so you may say, but I told you I was *unhappy*.'

8 March: 'You are right, my dear Troubridge, in desiring me not to write such letters to the Earl [St Vincent]. Why should I? As my own unhappiness concerns no one but myself, it shall remain fixed in my own breast.'

11 March: '*Let jealousy, cabal and art conspire to do their worst*, the *St George* is and shall be fit for battle. I will trust to myself alone and Hardy will support me. Far, far, very far from good health, this conduct will and shall rouse me for the moment.'

13 March: 'It never was my desire to serve under this man [Parker] . . . To tell me to serve on in this way is to laugh at me and to think me a greater fool than I am.'

7 May: 'Quiet I must have, to have a chance of restoration to my health, but I dare say I have tormented you so much on this subject that you say, "Damn him, I wish he was dead, and not plaguing me this way." Therefore, I never shall mention to you one [more] word on the subject.'[5]

'For God's sake, do not suffer yourself to be carried away by an sudden impulse,' wrote St Vincent, trying to arrest the malignant tide, but Nelson assumed an effective business air the moment naval matters interrupted his wounded reveries. He remained tetchy, however, looking for further grievances and shortcomings. Most of his complaints were founded in a truth, but their significance varied.[6]

Swollen by reinforcements, Parker's fleet eventually topped fifty sail, led by the powerful three-decked flagships *London* and *St George*. At sea the commander-in-chief divided his ships of the line into three sailing columns, deploying most of the smaller vessels to windward. Parker commanded the centre division from the *London*, aided most by his flag captain and protégé, Robert Waller Otway, and his captain of the fleet, William Domett. Commanding his third-rates were some of Nelson's finest former captains, the Nile veterans Thomas Foley and Sir Thomas Boulden Thompson in the *Elephant* and *Bellona*, and that old Mediterranean man, Thomas Fremantle, in the *Ganges*. The *Ardent*, a torpid sixty-four, was captained by Thomas Bertie, who, as Thomas Hoare, had been Nelson's boyhood shipmate in the old *Seahorse*. The larboard division of Parker's fleet also revived memories for Nelson, for its commander, Rear Admiral Thomas

Graves of the *Defiance*, had sailed as a lieutenant to the Arctic with the fourteen-year-old Horatio Nelson in 1773.

Nelson complained that his starboard division was underpowered, but it was led by his zealous follower George Murray of the seventy-four-gun *Edgar*, who had been almost thirty years in the service, and his own *St George* of ninety-eight guns. However, coming astern were the *Polyphemus*, a sixty-four, and the clumsy *Glatton*, an East Indiaman converted into an experimental 'fifty' with an armament of fifty-six forty-eight and sixty-eight pound carronades, devastating at short range but of limited use over distance. Her captain was notorious, a brilliant seaman and brave in battle, but a poor leader of men, none other than William Bligh, still shrugging off the shadow of the mutiny on the *Bounty*. He never became one of Nelson's intimates.

Several frigates assisted the fleet, the *Amazon*, *Desiree*, *Blanche*, *Alcmene* and *Jamaica*, and it was the captain of the first who proved to be a true kindred spirit. Captain Edward Riou commanded little 'interest' but was possessed of unusual talent and strength of character. In 1789 he had been the commander of the *Guardian* convict ship bound for Botany Bay, which struck a submerged iceberg and began to founder. Some of the crew took to the boats, but Riou remained with those left on board, forged a working alliance with the convicts and brought the holed vessel safely into Cape Town. Now he was to prove himself the outstanding small ship commander of the Baltic expedition. Among the other commanders was William Bolton of the *Arrow* brig-sloop, one of Nelson's in-laws and an old *Agamemnon*.[7]

While Parker kept his own counsel, Nelson fumed aboard the *St George* as it tossed through squalls, ice and snow. He had no great reputation for seamanship, but his journal disapproved of the slow progress of the fleet and its inability to keep together, noting that on 15 March the *St George* was 'the only ship in her station'. The winds were satisfactory, but the stiffened sails and ropes were difficult to work and cracked the skin of wet, cold hands, the visibility was poor, and the hours of daylight short. Navigation was difficult, but with the aid of dead reckoning and the lead line, Parker's vast flotilla groped north-easterly, struggling to keep together. On 13 March, while on course, the commander-in-chief turned northwards towards Scotland for a day before resuming his north-easterly journey, perhaps believing that if he appeared off the west coast of Denmark he might trigger a premature alarm. In fog and rain the fleet approached the opening of the Skagerrak between Denmark and Norway on 17 March, but a frigate mistook it for a position many miles south and Parker tacked needlessly to the north-west. The Skaw at the northerly tip of the Danish peninsula did not blink on the horizon until two days later.[8]

Throughout this grim journey Nelson received no courtesies from Parker, but on the 14th he took the initiative, sending his commander-in-chief a small turbot that Lieutenant Layman had trawled from the depths. But though a boat had to carry the present over a heavy sea, Parker's written acknowledgement revealed only 'a little of his intentions', and that discomforting. The fleet was ordered to anchor at the entrance to the Sound, north of Copenhagen, and to allow the Danes forty-eight hours to respond to a letter submitted through Drummond. To Nelson, this sounded like sheer prevarication on the part of the Admiralty. It was his opinion that, if Britain had to negotiate, it should be done after her fleet had forced the Sound and presented itself in a threatening array before Copenhagen. 'The Danish minister would be a hardy man to put his name to a paper which in a few minutes would . . . involve his master's navy and . . . capital in flames,' he told Troubridge. In other words, a bold front was the best way to avoid war.[9]

On 19 March, off the Skaw, Parker wrote to Drummond to ascertain whether the Danes would treat, and sent the letter by the *Blanche*, which pushed ahead southwards through the Kattegat to reach Elsinore, where the Danish castle of Kronborg guarded the narrow passage that squeezed between Denmark and Sweden and led into the Sound. From there a lieutenant carried the packet overland to Copenhagen. The captain of the *Blanche* had orders to bring Drummond, his suite and any British residents wishing to quit Copenhagen away if the Danes refused to treat. Nelson wanted Parker to advance 'with all expedition', passing the guns of Kronborg, and taking an advanced position inside the Sound, and to that end ordered his ship to clear for action. The day Parker's letter began its journey to Drummond, Nelson invited himself to the *London* and spent an hour with the commander-in-chief, hoping to invest him with a sense of urgency. To him it was as clear as day that time increased the odds against them, giving their opponents greater opportunities to prepare, and risking the unification of their fleets as the ice in the Baltic and the Gulf of Finland receded. Sir Hyde remained relatively tight-lipped, but he was evidently willing to force the Sound if his peace overture failed, and let slip that his present orders said nothing about proceeding against Russia or Sweden.[10]

Left to himself, Nelson would have forced the Sound on the evening of the 19th, but Parker remained in the Kattegat, seaward of the high Koll (Kullen) promontory in Sweden. That night a foul south-westerly wind and heavy sea put the fleet on a hazardous lee shore, and many of the ships scattered for open water. For several days the bad weather continued, scourging the ships with gales, rain, sleet and snow. Yards were struck and got up again, sails reefed and unreefed, and cables hauled in and released. On the morning of the 21st Nelson could count only thirty-eight of Parker's force. The following day the fleet finally beat up around the Koll and proceeded towards the mouth of the Sound, and the same evening the *Blanche* returned. It was not good news. Firmly in the grip of Russia and France, the Danes, Parker learned, had refused to accept the last British diplomat, Vansittart, and peremptorily rejected his ultimatum; in despair, Drummond, Vansittart and several British merchants had fled the city and taken refuge on the *Blanche*. In his baggage Vansittart had a letter he had written to Parker the same day. It declared that negotiations were now at an end, and the fleet must execute its orders. The next words would come from the mouths of cannons.[11]

One advantage was the military intelligence that Drummond and Vansittart were able to bring. Parker was dismayed to hear of the 'great preparations' made to receive him at Kronborg, where the strait into the Sound ran between two hundred Danish guns on the west bank and Swedish batteries of an unknown strength on the eastern side. Meanwhile, the main Danish fleet was drawn into a 'very strong' defensive line at Copenhagen, defended by heavy guns and deadly shoals. Powerful forts, a formidable line of battle, confined waters, the lack of good charts and the pessimism of the pilots the British had brought for their local knowledge now played upon the commander-in-chief. His forte was administration, and perhaps diplomacy, not fighting, and he saw no clear way forward. Miserably, he wrote a short letter to the Admiralty, stating that he would try to carry out their orders, but preparing the board for bad news.[12]

But Nelson had written to Troubridge that he would give his 'firm support and honest opinion' if Parker condescended to ask for it. Finally, he did.[13]

3

The important events of the next few days are so complicated that scholars have given different and sometimes muddled chronologies of what took place.[14]

On the morning of 23 March Nelson and Lieutenant Layman were rowed across to the *London*, which still lay north of the Koll. In the great cabin Parker and Vansittart were gloomy. Vansittart believed the fleet would be beaten if it attacked Copenhagen, and whatever confidence Sir Hyde had brought to the Sound seemed to have evaporated. Now he balked at forcing the Sound, and even talked about sitting outside in the Kattegat, hoping that the combined Baltic fleets might unite and advance to offer battle, a stupid plan that threw away time, place and numbers, and one that Nelson considered 'disgraceful'.[15]

Nelson listened to Vansittart, and according to Layman consulted some of the other people who had just evacuated Copenhagen. There were certainly grounds for caution. Apart from the batteries at Kronborg, which were said to field two hundred guns manned by three thousand men, a truly formidable defence was being readied at Copenhagen. The entrance to the harbour was guarded by the powerful citadel batteries, while nearby two sinister forts, the Trekroner (Three Crowns) and Lynetten, rose on piles from the sea, fielding a hundred guns between them. As if that was not enough, a tight defensive line of ships, hulks and floating batteries, flourishing a wall of guns, occupied a channel known as the King's Deep, situated between the harbour and a large, treacherous shoal named the Middle Ground. Other armed vessels were stationed inside the harbour mouth itself. Vansittart mentioned that the Danes also expected to be joined by thirteen Russian ships of the line from Revel, where a passage was being sawn through the ice, and less immediately by as many as eight Swedish capital ships.[16]

In such moments military insight was needed to distil the relevant information, and in three hours of discussion Nelson established an ascendancy over Parker, squashing the sit-and-wait policy, and returning to the *St George* satisfied that he had 'completely altered' the commander-in-chief's plan. Thus fortified, Sir Hyde penned a revised report to the Admiralty, singing the beneficial consequences of the new proposal, while Nelson, with his usual regard for their public, reinforced the message the following day by urging Parker to consider his posterity. 'On your decision,' he said, 'depends whether our country shall be degraded in the eyes of Europe, or whether she shall rear her head higher than ever. Again do I repeat, never did our country depend so much on the success of any fleet as on this.' Defeatism and doing nothing were not options.[17]

Nelson was not intimidated by the threat posed by Kronborg at the entrance to the Sound, probably because he weighed the width of the strait against the range of the enemy guns. He would have preferred to continue south with the first favourable wind, direct to Copenhagen by the Sound, but he accepted that Vansittart had shaken Parker with his account of the guns at Kronborg, and proposed an alternative route, one that drew Sir Hyde into a consideration of the broader strategy of the campaign. Whatever the Admiralty's orders might have been, the crucial enemy was Russia, not Denmark, and the prime objective the destruction of the tsar's ships at Revel and Kronstadt. If Parker did not want to risk the Sound, he could take the fleet west and south and use a passage called the Great Belt to circuit the island of Sjelland, on which Copenhagen stood, and approach the city from the south rather than the north. From what could be gleaned from intelligence, the Danes had not foreseen such a manoeuvre. They had, for example, weighted their defences to meet an attack from the north, not the south. There the defensive line of ships was at its strongest, and there, too, was situated the formidable Trekroner battery. But as significant as any tactical advantages it might confer at Copenhagen, the plan's strength, as far as Nelson was concerned, lay in its flexibility. For it would not only enable Parker to interpose himself between Copenhagen and any Swedish or Russian reinforcements, but also provide opportunities to strike Russia. In fact, Nelson envisaged possibilities of bypassing Copenhagen altogether, and making straight for Revel and Kronstadt, or of splitting the British fleet, neutralising Copenhagen with one force under Parker while detaching Nelson with another to Revel. The bones of these ideas converted Parker to using the Great Belt on the 23rd, and were developed further in a masterly memorandum submitted by Nelson the following day.[18]

Nelson's alternative contravened the Admiralty's instructions to knock out

Copenhagen and await further orders, but in its readiness to take the war to Russia and Sweden anticipated supplementary instructions which had left London on 15 March but not yet reached the fleet. It was not without its problems, however. The navigation of the Great Belt was tricky and time-consuming, adding a couple of hundred miles and perhaps five days to their journey, and granting the Danes more space to complete their preparations. But while Parker did not relish dividing his fleet, and losing the services of Nelson, the commander-in-chief was momentarily satisfied, and Vansittart was no less enthusiastic. Nelson had not ignored his intelligence, but he refused to be fazed by it, and probed for unseen advantages. When Vansittart reached England, he reported directly to Addington, who commended Nelson's initiative and secured approval for the new plan.[19]

Nelson believed he had given the task force a credible way forward, but the ensuing day of 24 March was one of confusion and lost opportunity. At about ten o'clock in the morning Otway climbed on board the *St George* with an urgent request that Nelson again repair to the commander-in-chief. Sir Hyde had agonised about their plan all night, and was full of reservations. The key figure in this volte-face was Domett. In a letter written some days afterwards, the captain of the fleet listed a series of objections to Nelson's new plan that carry less conviction with the benefit of hindsight. He was reluctant to contravene the Admiralty's orders; worried about the *possible* existence of a battery on Amager Island, which the fleet would have to pass; and incorrectly supposed that an area known as the Drogden shallows would prevent any but ships of sixty-four guns or less making an attack on Copenhagen from the south. Nelson was not impressed, and owned that while Domett was an officer of 'very high character', capable in routine operations, he lacked the 'spur of the moment' thinking necessary in rapidly changing circumstances. His lordship boarded the *London* for another conference of more than two hours, and read a lucid memorandum he had composed to the dithering commander-in-chief. 'Not a moment should be lost in attacking the enemy,' Nelson had written. 'They will every day and hour be stronger.' The Sound could be forced with little damage that could not be put right, but if the Belt was used a westerly wind would give the fleet the option of prioritising Revel rather than Copenhagen. Though ready to implement either plan, Nelson's new preference, developed in overnight contemplation as intense but more focused than Parker's, was for the Belt. 'The measure may be thought bold,' he said, 'but I am of opinion the boldest measures are the safest.'[20]

Parker bowed to Nelson's opinion, and held to their decision to use the Belt. Possibly the commander-in-chief might have been encouraged by the timely arrival of the *Jamaica* frigate with the new instructions from the Admiralty, orders which emphasised for the first time the need to advance upon Revel, Kronstadt and Karlskrona 'without a moment's loss of time'. The Russian ships were to be destroyed, but Sweden was to be offered the same terms as Denmark, and attacked only if they were refused. These orders supplemented, rather than replaced, the earlier instructions to confront Denmark, but the Belt placed the fleet in a position to embrace both, and Parker may have felt reassured. Anyway, Nelson returned to his ship early in the afternoon satisfied that the situation had been stabilised.[21]

Before sunrise on 25 March Parker weighed and steered west-north-west up the Kattegat and towards the Great Belt. No senior officer had been consulted about the course, apart from Nelson and Murray of the *Edgar*, who had navigated the Belt before and been appointed to lead, and the first the fleet knew of it was Parker's signal to tack to the west. It caused amazement, since everyone had assumed that the fleet would force the Sound. But at ten or shortly after, north-east of the small island of Hesselo, Parker hove to, and a boat sped once more to the *St George*. Nelson was no doubt bewildered to read that the commander-in-chief was now uneasy about navigating the Belt 'in case of accidents' and was therefore steeling himself to force the Sound after all. The pilots had been undermining the commander-in-chief's confidence, and, as if to confirm them, a tender ran ashore at eleven o'clock. By this time Nelson must have been tired of the whole business. He called upon Sir Hyde, listened to his explanation, and 'entirely assented' to his decision to force the Sound. At 11.15 the fleet was ordered back.[22]

Three days of dithering thus ran their course. In his official dispatch of 6 April Sir Hyde concealed the confusion, claiming that the delay in forcing the Sound was due solely to the lack of a suitable wind between 22 March, when the diplomatic overture failed, and 25 March. It was less than the truth, for there had, in fact, been a cost. On 24 March, when Nelson had held Parker to the plan to use the Belt, the wind shifted to NNW, ideal for a passage into the Sound. Had the British made the attempt they would have forestalled the final preparations to defend Copenhagen, because at that time only seven of the eighteen units in the Danish line of battle were in place, their manpower was down by a third, and little in the way of gun drill had been attempted. For this misfortune of war the British admirals were to blame. Parker had decided against and then for using the Sound, and Nelson had concocted an alternative that ultimately proved unnecessary, and held his commander-in-chief to it on the very day the wind changed. Not surprisingly, the fleet was baffled. One officer spoke of a 'general surprise' at the failure to use the wind of 24 March. 'Providence,' sighed Stewart, 'seemed to have positively sent the [wind and we] took no advantage of it.'[23]

In some respects this fumbling performance boded ill, but one important step forward had been made. Parker had been unable to present a sound plan of campaign, but he had discovered Nelson's talents, not the supernatural 'genius' beloved by adulators but his ability to apply a self-assured positivism, experience and cold logic to the known circumstances. Before Parker had said nothing to Nelson; now he seemed unable to do anything without him, and had summoned him to the flagship on three successive days. Nor was this educative process one way, for Nelson had responded to the commander-in-chief's obvious good intentions and respect, and something like a team had emerged. Both men supported each other. As Parker told his wife, 'in the very intricate business' of those few days 'no man' could 'have given stronger proof of friendship' than Lord Nelson.[24]

4

The wind blew foul for several days, spending most of its time at SSW, and it was not until the 29th that the fleet got as far as Elsinore. Nelson used the time well, planning how the Sound might be forced and the Danish defences at Copenhagen overcome. Wisely, Parker gave him free rein in both projects, interposing the occasional suggestion that came to him by and by.

On 26 March Parker gave his second-in-command formal orders to take charge of ten sail of the line and fifty-gun ships, eight frigates and sloops, seven bombs, two fireships and twelve gun brigs to attack the Danish capital. Nelson was to make the main attack, while Parker created a diversion with the remaining ten line of battle ships. Given the shallows around Copenhagen, Nelson was authorised to transfer his flag from the three-decked *St George* to Foley's *Elephant*, a third-rate that drew slightly less water. He was no doubt pleased to stand with Foley, who had led the brothers into Aboukir Bay and doubled the French line, but had relatively little time to familiarise himself with First Lieutenant William Wilkinson, Master George Andrews and the complement of 570. With the admiral came a small retinue from the *St George*, consisting of a secretary, Thomas Wallis, Lieutenant Frederick Langford, Midshipman Robert Gill, seven signalmen, and two servants, George White and Tom Allen. Nelson considered taking Midshipman John Finlayson with him, too, but Hardy explained that the boy was only fourteen, and was better remaining with the *St George*, which would only participate in the diversionary attack. Nelson patted the boy on the head and said, 'We must leave you for a future day.' But his portraits of Emma, the 'guardian angels', did make the transfer, and Allen had the foresight to store them safely below when the fighting started.[25]

Nelson had already decided upon the bones of a battle plan. The ships in the harbour and arsenal might be bombarded, but first it would be necessary to destroy the Danish line of battle in the King's Deep. It was strongest in the north, the direction from which the British had now to advance. Nelson's idea was to use a north-westerly wind to force the Sound, but instead of attacking the northern end of the Danish line, he proposed continuing south through a channel known as the Outer Deep, bypassing Copenhagen, and anchoring south of the capital. This would place him roughly where he had wanted to be after navigating the Great Belt. A southerly breeze would then be required to move northwards again, but this time into the King's Deep to make the unforeseen attack upon the enemy line at its weakest point.

Unlike Parker, Nelson believed in communication and a memorandum was soon in the hands of his captains. The attack he contemplated promised work in dangerous waters, and it would be necessary for the ships to hold precise positions. As at the Nile, Nelson instructed each captain to prepare to anchor by the stern, passing cables through a stern port and 'bending' them to an anchor, which could be dropped from the bow to check the ship in the desired position. The kedge anchors and capstans had also to be prepared in case ships needed to be warped off shoals, and the crews of boats, launches, barges and pinnaces instructed in numerous attendant duties. They were to be manned by marines with muskets, as well as seamen, armed with cutlasses, poleaxes, pikes and broadaxes, and each launch furnished by a capital ship or frigate would be commanded by a lieutenant and equipped with a coiled hawser and carronade. Nelson ordered drills in the use of the great guns and small arms, and gave thought to the role of the troops under Stewart and Brock. Both commanders were given key posts. Stewart accompanied Nelson on the *Elephant*, and Brock transferred from Fremantle's *Ganges*, which was originally excluded from the attack force, to the *Agamemnon*. Only when a change of orders allowed *Ganges* to join Nelson's division did Brock return to the ship. For this broad and bluff Guernsey man these were probably among the most inspirational moments of his career, and his future as the defender of Upper Canada would demand just such a combination of daring, judgement and leadership as he witnessed in Nelson that spring. Some thirteen hundred soldiers and seamen were detailed to stand by to storm batteries or positions ashore 'during the smoke . . . if any favourable opportunity occurs', using the numerous prefabricated flats stored in each ship. To reduce confusion on the day, these vessels were assembled, hoisted into the water and exercised beforehand.[26]

Nelson summoned his principal officers to briefings. All the captains were briefed on board the *St George* on 26 March, and later some of the captains and lieutenants were called to the *Elephant*. Gazing at those captains, Nelson saw the reassuring faces of Foley, Fremantle, Murray, Hardy and Thompson, but most were unknown quantities. The attack that Nelson proposed, against powerful forts and a prepared line of battle occupying shoal-ridden water, the whole supported by the resources of a capital city, was one that few admirals would have contemplated. The conference on the *St George* lasted most of the day, and left Nelson unwell. Many doubts were aired, and even Fremantle, the man who had persuaded Nelson to make the hazardous and unsuccessful attack on Tenerife four years before, suspected that the delays had enabled the Danes to mount an almost impregnable defence. 'Lord Nelson,' Fremantle wrote to his wife, 'is quite sanguine, but as you may well imagine, there is a great diversity of opinion.'[27]

At nine on the morning of 27 March, as Nelson entertained the commander-in-chief, a fleet of fifteen merchantmen from Lübeck and Hamburg came northwards from the Sound. Their masters declared that Copenhagen was in a state of confusion and consternation. Nevertheless, Parker felt obliged to put a final piece of diplomacy in place. Captain James Brisbane of the *Cruizer* sloop approached Kronborg under a flag of truce to discover whether the castle would oppose a British fleet entering the Sound. It was 'a weak manoeuvre', complained Stewart, but Sir Hyde may have wanted to strengthen his bargaining position by placing the onus of opening fire upon the Danes, and his fleet was in any case unable as yet to proceed in a weak southerly wind.[28]

More practically, Nelson sent the *Blanche* with two bomb vessels to anchor in a safe position from which they could bombard Kronborg if it opened fire. The 28th brought a useful westerly, and Parker took his fleet closer to Elsinore, where he awaited a reply to his message. At midnight the *Cruizer* returned with the predictable refusal to admit the British, and on 29 March Parker took up an advanced position three or four miles from the mouth of the Sound. Murray's *Edgar* had anchored with seven bomb vessels about a mile north-west of Kronborg, beyond the arc of fire of the Danish guns but where they could provide covering fire for the ships.

It was Nelson's squadron that would force the Sound and challenge the fearsome batteries, said to consist of two hundred Danish guns pointing to sea, equipped with facilities for firing red hot shot, and an untold number of Swedish counterparts on the other side of the strait. That strip of water that divided them was barely five miles wide, just enough in Nelson's view to avoid serious damage. They needed a wind between WNW and ENE to make the attempt, as the current generally ran northwards against them, and on 30 March it was at WNW. Nelson was up early, writing with anticipation to Emma at 5.30, and just before sunrise Parker signalled the fleet to weigh anchor and steer for the Sound.

The forbidding fortress of Kronborg occupied a narrow, low spit of land, its red-brick walls, green copper roofs and three striking, cupola-crowned thin towers conferring a distinctly exotic appearance. A fifteenth-century fortification, it had impressive ramparts and bastions with casemates below. The batteries covered an arc of some 265 degrees, and possessed furnaces for heating shot, but the quality of the guns, powder and ammunition, as well as the experience of the gunners, who had seldom, if ever, fired an angry shot, left much to be desired. Moreover, even the most powerful Danish guns, thirty-six pounders, had an effective range of only one and a half miles, possibly less if their powder was bad. By keeping about two-thirds to the Swedish coast, passing ships could put themselves out of serious harm, especially as a respectable wind would take them through the hazardous stretch in about twenty minutes. One who knew the fortress thought that three British ships of the line could have reduced the castle by passing it by the strait before closing on its more vulnerable southern flank to cannonade it within pistol-shot range. But in the fleet the degree of danger posed by Kronborg was a matter of debate, and even less information was available about the Swedish batteries across the strait. In fact there were only a handful of guns at Halsingborg, and they had no orders to fire upon British ships entering the Sound.[29]

The time had come to make the first test of Denmark's defences.

Parker signalled the fleet to form a line of battle behind the *Monarch*, the first ship in Nelson's division, and placed the smaller vessels in the centre, rather as a herd of elephants might secure its young. On the *Edgar* Murray prepared the bombs to answer any fire from Kronborg. After finishing his letter to Emma, Nelson wrote calmly to Troubridge. 'I now pity both Sir Hyde and Domett,' he said as the fleet stood in boldly. 'They both, I fancy, wish themselves elsewhere. You may depend on every exertion of mine to keep up harmony. For the rest, the spirit of this fleet will make all difficulty from enemies appear as nothing. I do not think I ever saw more zeal and desire to distinguish themselves in my life.'[30]

Captain James Mosse, proud to be chosen to try the batteries first, had the *Monarch* steer about two-thirds towards the Swedish side of the strait, putting the Danish fort at extreme range. He did not have to wait long. As *Monarch*'s colours flew up about six in the morning, Kronborg fired and Murray's bomb vessels were soon spitting in reply. But the British were lucky, because the Swedish guns remained silent, and the ships following *Monarch* were able to haul closer to larboard, even further from Kronborg, and did not even deign to answer the distant puffs of Danish smoke. Neither side did much execution, although the commandant at Kronborg reported that his guns had plied 'with great vigour' and must have inflicted 'great damage' upon the British. In truth, their shot scarcely reached Parker's fleet, and the only casualties suffered by either side were four Danes and some damage to the castle walls inflicted by Murray's bomb vessels. By nine in the morning the British fleet was out of danger and preparing to anchor in Copenhagen Roads. Parker's fears of Kronborg castle, costing six days, had been totally unjustified. 'More powder and shot, I believe, never were thrown away,' observed Nelson.[31]

The entrance to the Sound was now behind them. On either flank stretched a bleak countryside of wintry forests and fields, but ahead was Copenhagen, a small almost circular city, walled and moated, sitting on the islands of Sjelland and Amager. Nothing could now save it from attack.

5

One obstacle removed, Nelson spent the evening sharpening his knowledge of what awaited him at Copenhagen. The Danes had removed all buoys marking the shoals, so the British would have to replace them, and Nelson ordered new markers to be produced. With Parker, Graves and a number of other officers, he boarded Riou's frigate, *Amazon*, to make a reconnaissance two leagues further south. Accompanied by the *Cruizer* and *Lark* lugger, they used a light north-westerly to approach the northern end of the Danish defences at Copenhagen, drawing a feeble enemy fire. Under the obscurity of the night, the *Cruizer* stole forward to sound the shoals along the channel the British would have to use and lay down buoys.

The attack was one of acute difficulty, confronting numerous fortifications of varying power. The harbour was flanked by the ramparts of the citadel (Castellet) to the west and the seventy-seven guns and mortars of the Sixtus and Quintus batteries to the east. Within five hundred yards of the Castellet stood the Amalienborg royal palace, and the heart of an attractive city of elegant spires and green copper roofs, compact and close enough to be vulnerable to bombardment. But north, covering the entrance to the channel leading to that harbour, were the formidable Trekroner and Lynetten batteries. The hexagonal Trekroner fort rose ten feet above the sea and bristled with sixty-six twenty-four-pounders and three mortars, served by furnaces for heating shot. It was respectably manned but the garrison was miserably housed, the men occupying tents on the walls without any protection from a bombardment. One Danish officer confessed that the fort would not have withstood a prolonged attack. As for the Lynetten, the British could only count six or seven guns in it. Prime British targets were the arsenal and dockyard, which were situated inside the ramparts of the southern part of the city, close to a canal between the main island of Sjelland, on which the city rested, and the smaller Amager Island. The opening of this canal, and the southern entrance to the King's Deep, were covered by a battery on Amager Island, known later as Stricker's battery, armed with six thirty-sixes and a couple of mortars.[32]

The naval defence was divided into two. The smaller force, commanded by Lieutenant Captain Steen Bille, consisted of four weak ships of the line, the *Elefanten*, *Trekroner* and *Danmark*, all seventy-fours, and the sixty-gun *Mars*, as well as a forty-gun frigate and two eighteen-gun brigs, and occupied the channel leading to the harbour between the Trekroner fort in the north and the Castellet in the south. This channel was never breached by the British, and the ships inside remained largely unengaged.

But Denmark's main line of battle, under Commodore Olfert Fischer, was securely moored to the east in an irregular but fairly compact line stretching almost south to north for some three thousand yards. Sitting in the King's Deep with perilous shoals on either side, it was a bizarre collection of eighteen units, consisting of four low-lying bulwarked rafts or floating batteries, one unrigged ship of the line, half a dozen capital ships, or 'fifties', converted into blockships, three transports and four frigates or other small warships, half without masts.

Fischer was aware of weaknesses in his line. In an effort to command as much of the limited navigable water in the King's Deep as possible he had anchored his ships some way out in the Channel, and his formation was a close one, with his transports, floating batteries and a frigate filling the gaps between his bigger ships. Furthermore, recognising that the British might double his line, as Nelson had the French at the Nile, he had ensured his units had enough guns, men and ammunition to work to larboard and starboard simultaneously. The southern part of the line, which was slightly the weaker, and derived less cover from shore batteries, was supported by an inside line of eleven gunboats that fielded a total of twenty-two eighteen-pound bow chasers and 759 men. Looking like ancient Mediterranean galleys in rig and hull, they were ordered to rake any ships trying to penetrate gaps in the Danish line. To guard against flames that might spring from one closely situated Danish vessel to another, Fischer also had a squad of small boats ready to throw grappling irons on stricken vessels and tow them to safety.

Each side counted the odds differently, looking for statistics that cast them in the best light, but even if the shore batteries were included the British had the advantage. In a modern analysis Dudley Pope totalled the number of guns in the Danish line of battle, including several gunboats and the two ships of Steen Bille's division near enough to throw long shots, as well as the Trekroner shore battery at 888. Nelson's assault force, excepting a sixty-four that grounded beyond gun range and some redundant brigs and sloops, was put at 954. Additionally, in terms of the quality of the guns and the experience of the gunners the British were greatly superior. Few of the defenders were trained *naval* personnel, and hardly any of those had battle experience. There was a chronic shortage of regular Danish officers, while a naval reserve hurriedly conscripted in Denmark and Norway supplied most of the seamen. About a quarter of the crews were soldiers, some fifteen hundred volunteer civilians, and most of the balance pressed. Nevertheless, the Danes had six thousand or so defenders in the ships and forts protecting the King's Deep, charged with the patriotism that often comes in the defence of a homeland. In the little time available, Fischer and Bille instilled some basic training, but some of the weaponry the men were required to handle only appeared at the last moment, and on 29 March seventeen cumbersome sledge carriages were still being fitted to three units in the defence line. A consolation was that Fischer's line was not expected to manoeuvre, merely to stand its ground and fight. The *Elven* was rigged as a signal frigate, and manned entirely by regulars and seamen, but most of the vessels were held in their place by four anchors and served only as floating batteries. Dogged pluck and gun handling were premiums, but professional seamanship was scarcely required.[33]

Fischer's defence was tighter than the one Nelson encountered at the Nile, running as an almost continuous battery, and although it was comparatively weak in firepower, it had powerful allies. Most of it was within range of the Sixtus, Quintus and Lynetten batteries, and the northern part within six hundred yards of the feared Trekroner fort. From behind, the Danish line could also draw reinforcements and supplies from the dockyard, arsenal and city, while ahead, some thousand yards out into the Sound, lurked a difficult shoal known as the Middle Ground. A mile wide and two miles long, it overlapped the Danish line at both ends, and posed a hazard to the British as serious as any Danish guns. Despite this, Fischer knew that a determined attack would eventually overwhelm his line, and promised at best a hard and intimidating battle. Parker noted in his journal that the defences were 'far more formidable than we had reason to expect'. The word 'formidable' tripped twice off his pen. Nelson did not think so. 'It looks formidable to those who are children at war,' he told Emma, 'but to my judgment, with ten sail of the line I think I can annihilate them.' Again, he looked for the weaknesses as well as the strengths of an enemy, and his experience had given him great confidence in the combat skills of the Royal Navy.[34]

Nelson was sure that a successful attack could be made, despite obvious difficulties. Had Fischer stationed some ships across the narrows in the King's Deep at right angles, with their broadsides poised to rake any intruder, he might have made his position impregnable. But the Danish ships lined the western side of the Deep, leaving enough of a channel to the east open for the British to use. Nelson had long since decided that his attack would come from the south, where the defences were weaker, although this was the most indirect route and arguably the least navigable. Coming from the north, the British would first have to pass southwards by means of the Outer Deep, with the Middle Ground and the city to starboard, and reach the safety of Koge Bay, to the south of Copenhagen. Then Nelson would have to wait for a southerly wind to work his way northwards again, this time standing to larboard to thread into the King's Deep between Fischer's line and the Middle Ground shoal. They would overwhelm the Danish line from the south, while the immobile enemy ships, most unrigged and heavily moored, were incapable of aiding their comrades against the unfavourable wind. Nelson's attack, then, came from an unpredicted quarter and massed firepower and skill against inferior Danish units.

The first object was to pass the city by the Outer Deep. Nelson set Hardy, who had volunteered to serve with the assault force, and the commanders and masters of the *Amazon* and *Cruizer* to work on Monday, 30 March. For three bitter nights, with the temperature below freezing, men slipped through the chilling darkness in small boats with muffled oars, sounding among the floating ice of the Outer Deep and reading their compasses, lines and poles by candle-light. Nelson himself sometimes participated in the operation. A second reconnaissance of the Danish line was also made from the *Amazon* on Tuesday morning to allow the commanders of their bomb vessels to assess the prospects for shelling the dockyard and arsenal. Captain Peter Fyers of the Royal Artillery, attached to the *Sulphur*, who was an expert on bombardment and an associate of William Congreve, the inventor of the celebrated rocket system, contributed to an immediate final evaluation of the attack.

Back from reconnoitring, the admirals held a crucial council of war in the *Elephant*, to which at least some of the principal naval and military officers were invited to examine the artillerists and make the final decision as to whether to attack or no. Fyers explained that the Danish line of battle would have to be removed for the bomb vessels to occupy essential positions, but Nelson met considerable scepticism about his ability to destroy Fischer's force, some of it from Graves, unchastened by his former opposition to what had turned out to be a bloodless passage of the Sound. Nelson would have none of this timorous talk, and grew increasingly impatient, pacing excitedly up and down the cabin, and starting at any 'alarm or irresolution'. When someone suggested that a strong Russian fleet might intervene, he snapped, 'So much the better! I wish they were twice as many. The easier the victory, depend on it.' The vote went in his favour, and Parker handsomely added two additional ships of the line to Nelson's strike force, the *Ganges* and *Edgar*. But not everyone was convinced. The next day Captain James Mosse of the *Monarch* wrote to his wife that 'the enemy are very strong, far beyond expectation, and will I fear make the success of our attack doubtful'.[35]

The morning of 1 April brought a fair wind for the first part of Nelson's task, the navigation of the Outer Deep. By six in the morning he had signalled the masters and pilots of his ships to attend a briefing in the *Elephant*. That done, the admiral was rowed to the *Amazon*, where Riou controlled five small craft charged with opening the way through the Outer Deep. Before eleven Riou had completed buoying the channel, carefully marking the dangerous eastern reaches of the Middle Ground, and satisfied pronounced conditions as favourable as could be expected. Nelson made a final call upon Parker, and then returned to the *Elephant* to signal his division to weigh. As his gig carried him from the *London* he called upon as many of his ships as possible to alert them to the imminent signal. A midshipman of the *Monarch* remembered seeing the admiral's diminutive figure approach amid the creaking of oars, his cocked hat worn square with a 'peculiar slouch', and his 'squeaking little voice' hailing them in a 'true Norfolk drawl'.[36]

About three in the afternoon Nelson's signal raised cheers throughout the squadron, and at about four the ships of the assault force bore up and made sail, falling behind the *Amazon* as it carefully steered southwards through the cold Outer Deep. In Indian file the ships went 'with a correctness and . . . rapidity which could never have been exceeded', enthused Stewart, and Nelson was 'in raptures' about Riou's feat. Despite a few shells from the Danish defences, it took less than three-quarters of an hour for the ships to reach a safe anchorage off Drago's Point, south of the Middle Ground and Copenhagen. The *Ardent* and *Agamemnon*, both sixty-fours, were posted in guard positions for the night, completing the first of Nelson's tasks. His squadron now stood between Denmark and any relief from Russia or Sweden, and although the Danes continued to throw some blind shells towards the British anchorage in the night they had been thoroughly wrong-footed. As far as they could make out, Nelson looked to have forgone the idea of attacking Copenhagen, and intended pushing into the Baltic to deal with Russia. As one of their observers remarked, 'Many affirmed it to be impossible, on account of the shoals, for so large a fleet to act to advantage, and the almost generally predominant opinion was that it was the intention of the English to sail into the Baltic. This was unhappily false.'[37]

From Nelson's new vantage point the Danish line resembled a continuous wall of ships, battle units and guns lining a city skyline distinguished by its impressive spires. The final dinner on the *Elephant* on the eve of battle put doubts aside. In a 'large' gathering of admirals, captains and senior army officers Nelson appeared 'in the highest spirits, and drank to a leading wind, and to the success of the ensuing day'. He shook hands with the departing company, leaving them, said Stewart, 'with feelings of admiration for their great leader' and impatient for the coming conflict.[38]

When the officers had gone, Hardy and the master of the *Amazon* took to small boats to be propelled by muffled oars into the darkness to make furtive soundings towards the enemy line, while Riou and Foley remained with Nelson till past midnight, helping prepare detailed battle instructions for the captains. The admiral was exhausted, and Allen prevailed upon him to recline in his cot, but he continued to dictate. At one in the morning the papers were handed to four scriveners, who set about producing the needed copies before daylight. But Nelson got little sleep. Occasionally he called for news of the state of the wind, or after the progress of his furious clerks.[39]

The wind was the key. Dawn began to reveal a cold sky with some cloud, but the wind had changed direction in the small hours. As Nelson had prayed, it had swung to the south-east and blew fresh, perfect for his attack.

6

Parker's division, standing six miles north-east of the Trekronor fort, was supposed to support Nelson's attack by threatening the northern reaches of the Danish defences with three of his ten line of battle ships, *Defence*, *Ramillies* and *Veteran*. He was already badly placed to fulfil this role. Nelson's squadron was only a mile from the enemy line of battle, within twenty minutes' sailing, and the southerly wind he needed to make his attack northwards was by the same token an ill wind for Parker to come south. It is surprising that Parker did not, as Tomlinson complained, move towards an advanced position at the earliest opportunity, particularly as he had predicted the problem some days before. As positioned, his was a journey of several hours, tacking back and forth, and it condemned Nelson to fight the battle alone.[40]

The second of April 1801. Nelson had dressed and breakfasted before six. His instructions were ready, and, since the enemy line was fixed, unusually precise. To simplify matters Nelson had the orders drawn up on manageable cards that could be held in the hand. Each ship was assigned her space and opponents, and as the British attack would be led by the *Edgar*, *Ardent* and *Glatton*, which had stations towards the enemy centre, the admiral supposed that they would fire into the ships at the front of the Danish line as they passed, weakening them. Later British arrivals would have to pass the disengaged sides of their own ships, and inevitably find fewer opportunities to fire before reaching their station. But Nelson hoped to create superiority in every part of the enemy line. He bargained that the first two enemy ships would be crippled by the fire of British ships passing up the line, and fall easy meat to a British fifty and a sixty-four, which could then move northwards to help their consorts. In any case, he had grouped his ships close enough together to overpower their lighter Danish opponents, and his captains were double-shotting their guns to maximise fire-power.[41]

Riou alone had a roving commission. Placed in command of a reserve of five frigates and two fireships, *Otter* and *Zephyr*, he was given leave to support the attack wherever it seemed necessary. Dancing attendance around the ships of the line were smaller craft, all with important roles to play, including launches and small boats towed behind, primed to take possession of prizes; flats hidden on the starboard side of the battleships, shielded from enemy fire but ready to act as troop carriers and landing craft when their moment came; and bomb vessels, all but two kept close to the flagship, waiting for Fischer's line to be demolished before beginning their deadly work on the dockyard and arsenal.

Shortly before sunrise Nelson began signalling. While breakfasts were hastily consumed throughout the squadron and the final ominous preparations made for action, a stream of small boats arrived at the *Elephant*. Nelson wanted to see the lieutenants of the *Isis* and *Ganges* on small-boat matters; Captain James Brisbane of the *Cruizer*, an eleve of the Duke of Clarence, who was to mark the southern tip of the feared Middle Ground; and the lieutenants, captains, masters and artillery officers, one group after another, who were briefed for their trials. It was among the pilots that Nelson met the last opponents of his plan. Many were used to the merchant service, and wanted as little as possible to do with such dangerous work. They began prevaricating, frightened of running aground under enemy fire in the King's Deep, and Nelson urged resolution, duty and courage. Then Alexander Briarly, master of the *Bellona*, the same who had conspicuously failed to keep Captain Nisbet on the straight and narrow, spoke up, ready to offer the service of his life. He agreed to lead the fleet, and was soon out in a boat, placing a buoy at the end of the Middle Ground, leaving a relieved admiral. The pilots, Nelson wrote, had 'no other thought than to keep the ship clear of danger, and their own silly heads clear of shot'. But even with Briarly's heroism, Nelson would have to fight at twice the range he wanted because the pilots refused to take advantage of the deeper water close to the Danish line.[42]

At eight o'clock signal 14, was hoisted on the *Elephant* – prepare for battle! The ships were to anchor by the stern to keep them in position during a tailwind, and to use springs on their cables to extend their arcs of fire as circumstances required. When the signal to weigh was raised at about 9.30 the outermost ships began slipping away. The Danish line was only three thousand yards away, fifteen minutes if the wind and current were fair, but Nelson hurried them along with signals to make more sail. Under his anxious gaze they fell in behind the *Edgar* like huge swans, and picked their way slowly into the King's Deep, with the Danish line to their left and the Middle Ground to starboard.

Not long after the movement had got underway the dangerous shoals claimed their first victim. The *Agamemnon*, which Nelson had placed fifth in his line, sailed too far to the north-east. Seeing her peril, Nelson swiftly hoisted signal 333 with *Agamemnon*'s pendant, warning her that she was 'standing towards danger', but it was too late. Captain Robert Fancourt released an anchor and desperately reduced sail, but the wind and current drove his ship into the mud. There was a frantic bustle to set her free, sails were furled and a flatboat and launch sent out to release anchors in the deep water so that an attempt could be made to drag the ship from the shallows by means of the capstan. Sadly, she was stuck as surely as the *Culloden* had been on the point of Aboukir Bay. Within minutes Nelson's assault force had lost a ship of the line, and a particularly useful one, because *Agamemnon* was one of the smallest in the British line and suited to confined waters. It was a grim reminder that the Danish guns were not the only dangers ahead.[43]

Agamemnon was supposed to have engaged the first ship in the Danish line, the *Prøvesteenen*, a former three-decker cut down into a double-decked blockship of fifty-eight guns. The Dane's armament was the heaviest in the defence line, consisting of equal numbers of twenty-four- and thirty-six-pounders, and she was the second most generously manned ship, with 529 men on board. Nevertheless, *Prøvesteenen*'s crew was largely unskilled. She had only 182 navy men, three of them officers; of the rest 110 were soldiers, and as many as 225 almost untrained tradesmen who had volunteered the week before.

Now another British ship had to take her on, and Nelson signalled the *Polyphemus*, another sixty-four, to take *Agamemnon*'s place. She had provisionally been ordered to engage a Danish ship of Steen Bille's division, near the north of Fischer's line, and by switching her attack to the *Prøvesteenen* Nelson showed his determination to retain his principle of concentrating force, sacrificing strength at the northern part of the line to maintain superior firepower further south.

But blood pulsed faster through the squadron as Murray's *Edgar* (seventy-four) purposefully entered the King's Deep, with *Ardent*, *Glatton* and *Isis* falling into their allotted places behind. So vigorously did Murray advance that Nelson signalled him to shorten sail so as not to outdistance the more tardy ships in his wake, at the same time urging those behind to increase sail. The sight of the British ships under sail, most of their hulls painted yellow and black, advancing into fire with a silent deadly resolution at a speed of up to five knots was magnificent. 'A more beautiful and solemn spectacle I never witnessed,' remembered a midshipman of the *Monarch*. 'Not a word was spoken throughout the ship but by the pilot and helmsman.' Seldom had a naval battle been witnessed by so many. Ashore the crowds of the capital city had been gathering since first light, thousands of them anxious for fathers, sons, brothers, friends and lovers who grimly waited to defend their country in that Danish line. Spectators jostled for every available piece of waterfront, crowding balconies, clambering on to buildings and scaling cranes.[44]

The first reports and spurts of black smoke came from the battery on Amager Island, as it flung ineffective long-range shots at the oncoming ships. Then, a little after ten, the guns of the most southerly Danish ship, the *Prøvesteenen*, spat smoke, sparks and shot at the *Edgar* some four hundred yards distant. Smoke spread along the Danish line, spurting the length of each vessel as Murray's ship snaked past on her way up the King's Deep, and rising and thickening into a dense pall that blew northwards over the unengaged units. The *Edgar* suffered some damage aloft, but replied 'in a most lively manner' during the five minutes it took her to find her station, opposite the fifth in the Danish line, a mastless two-decked blockship named the *Jylland*, once a seventy-gunner but now fielding fifty-four guns and 425 men. Murray's lethal broadsides tore into the *Jylland* at a range of perhaps five hundred yards, while his after guns found the twenty-gun *Rendsborg* transport, number three in the Danish line, and perhaps also the *Nyborg*, a similar vessel lying slightly behind the Danish line.[45]

By then Thomas Bertie's *Ardent* (sixty-four), was discharging broadsides into the most southerly Danish ships before she deftly passed the *Edgar* to anchor ahead of her upon the larboard bow of a cut-down mastless frigate, the *Kronborg* of twenty-two guns. Bertie's first broadside into the *Kronborg* hurled guns from their carriages and downed two of her four lieutenants. Simultaneously, one of the guns on *Ardent*'s larboard quarter also lashed the *Svaerdfisken*, a box-like floating battery with eighteen guns and 176 men. The third British ship, the clumsy *Glatton* under William Bligh, moved doggedly up the line, savaging the first two Danish ships with a murderous armament that consisted solely of forty-eight- and sixty-eight-pound short-range carronades. Reaching her place ahead of the *Ardent*, she turned her fearsome armament upon Fischer's flagship, the sixty-gun *Dannebroge*, the *Hayen* floating battery of eighteen guns, and the weakly armed *Elven* signal corvette standing behind her line. The *Dannebroge* was now a mastless hulk and, although her crew consisted primarily of experienced sailors and soldiers, her eight-, twelve- and twenty-four-pounders were outmatched by what Bligh brought to the fight and she took a dreadful beating.

The fifth and sixth British ships were small, James Walker's fifty-gun *Isis* and John Lawford's *Polyphemus*, a sixty-four, but they were assigned the tough job of finishing off the three most southerly enemy ships, which Nelson supposed would by now have been severely damaged by the broadsides they had received from the *Edgar*, *Ardent* and *Glatton*. The admiral was so confident that the British would make short work of it that he expected *Isis* and *Polyphemus* to find time to reinforce their consorts to the north. True to his instructions, James Walker brought the fifty-gun *Isis* into action against the second and third Danish ships, the mastless *Wagrien* of fifty-two guns and the twenty-gun *Rendsborg* transport, while *Polyphemus* began pounding the first enemy vessel, the *Prøvesteenen*, with help from the thirty-six-gun *Desiree* frigate, under Captain Henry Inman. The *Desiree* briefly took the ground, where it could be raked by a shore battery, but aided by the *Hasty* brig she silenced the Danish guns and was placed with considerable skill in a position from which she could rake all the first three ships of the enemy line. The battle in the south was not the straightforward one that Nelson had envisaged, however. The *Wagrien*, under Commander Friderich Risbrich, was particularly well fought, throwing accurate and double-shotted broadsides, while the *Prøvesteenen*, Commander Lorentz Lassen, even if firing her heavy shot rather too high, proved to be a most redoubtable slogger, one of the most unyielding opponents in the Danish line.[46]

At this point Nelson's attack had more or less gone to plan. Although the *Agamemnon* was out of action, five British ships of the line (if we may admit the two fifties, *Isis* and *Glatton*, to that distinction) had formed opposite the southern section of the Danish defences, and were pummelling their opposite numbers into defeat, advantaged by their heavier armaments, superior precision and faster rates of fire. James Elsworth, watching from one of the British fireships, thought they were firing two guns to every one of the enemy, and most of those discharges were double-shotted for maximum effect. Brave as most of the Danes quickly proved to be, they were handicapped by inexperience, their use of slow fuses rather than lanyards to fire their pieces and the immobility of their ships and platforms. Unfortunately, as the British shot began to rip holes in the enemy line, inflicting fearful injuries on the busy defenders, Nelson faced his first crisis.

The *Bellona* (seventy-four), on her way to her station ahead of the *Glatton*, ran upon the Middle Ground as she tried to pass along the disengaged side of the embattled *Isis*. Her captain was no unpractised tyro, but one of the original brothers, Sir Thomas Thompson, who had magnificently engaged superior ships of the line in Aboukir Bay and earned a knighthood for his stubborn battle with *Le Généreux*. Furious, Thompson tried to refloat his ship, and in the meantime trained what guns he could upon gaps in the British line, managing to inflict a few hits on the two enemy transports, *Rendsborg* and *Nyborg*, at an extreme range. To cap all, the *Russell* (seventy-four), destined for the northern end of Fischer's line, was blinded by the smoke and also grounded, just astern of the *Bellona*. Like the unfortunate Thompson, Captain William Cuming tried some distant shots at the enemy fleet, concentrating upon his only available target, the *Prøvesteenen*, but the fact remained that three British ships of the line were now on shore, one out of the fight altogether and the others greatly reduced in capability. Nelson had asked for ten sail of the line, and had been given twelve. He was now effectively down to nine.[47]

These were serious setbacks, but despite his heightened nervous state Nelson remained collected and clear, and that 'spur of the moment' thinking he so admired did not desert him. He had seen *Bellona*'s danger, just as he saw *Agamemnon*'s, and signalled accordingly, but probably it was lost in the smoke. Now Nelson made two fast decisions. Passing their consorts on their disengaged sides, his ships were now trending too far to starboard and uncomfortably close to the Middle Ground. By raising signal 16, ordering his ships to engage the enemy more closely, Nelson may have hoped to encourage the ships already engaged to edge to larboard, giving more room for their colleagues to pass to starboard. Second, he immediately reassigned his remaining ships. The next, his own *Elephant*, would take *Bellona*'s place, and as the succeeding ships passed, Nelson hailed them to follow suit, each adopting a station earlier than the one planned. Rather than thinning his line by extending the spaces between his ships, he therefore shortened it, preserving his superiority in the south and centre at the expense of the north.[48]

Nelson's flagship, *Elephant*, coming astern of the unfortunate *Russell*, set an example. She actually passed along the inside or engaged side of the British line, forcing each ship to momentarily suspend her fire to let her pass. This was not necessarily a disadvantage, because it enabled *Elephant* to send close-range broadsides smashing into the Danish units as she progressed towards their van, and gave the British ships a brief respite. Reaching the *Bellona*'s empty station, she anchored in four fathoms of water, where her forward guns could play upon a floating battery, consisting of twenty pieces and breastworks mounted on a square wooden platform moored into position, and further aft concentrate upon the *Aggershus*, a twenty-gun transport, and support Bligh's attack on the *Dannebroge*. To Nelson's indignation, his pilot would not take the *Elephant* close enough to the enemy, and the ship opened fire at a range of about five hundred yards, about two hundred yards further out. It may have protracted the contest a little, but there was one advantage in standing further back. The additional distance enabled Foley's gunners to depress their guns to deal more effectively with the *Aggershus* and the floating battery, both of which lay low in the water.[49]

Nelson's realignment of the British line left the choice duel with the most powerful Danish ship, the *Sjaelland*, a seventy-four with 553 men under an experienced commander, to the entirely safe hands of Fremantle of the *Ganges*. Nelson hailed Fremantle as he passed, pointing out where he might anchor, and the captain got the ship into position himself, after his master was killed and his pilot's arm torn open in the early moments of the battle. Then a ferocious cannonade was opened, with every hand on the *Ganges* put to work. Even the paymaster of the 49th Regiment manned a carronade and received a musket ball through his hat. Captain Mosse's *Monarch* and Rear Admiral Graves's *Defiance*, also seventy-fours, were the last British ships of the line to take up their places. The *Monarch* anchored directly ahead of the *Ganges* and commenced firing upon the *Sjaelland* and the *Charlotte Amalia*, a former merchantman converted into a twenty-six-gun blockship, while *Defiance* hammered the *Charlotte Amalia*, *Søhesten* floating battery and the sixty-gun *Holsten*.[50]

The *Glatton*, *Elephant*, *Ganges*, *Monarch* and *Defiance* made a tightly packed line, outgunning their Danish opponents at every point, but the loss of three ships had shortened Nelson's line and the last two ships of Fischer's line unengaged. It was towards noon that the enterprising Riou, who had been left with a roving commission, made a characteristically bold decision. With the *Amazon* and four other cruisers, *Blanche*, *Alcmene*, *Arrow* and *Dart* – all between thirty and thirty-eight guns – he worked his way up the British line under dense smoke to occupy the empty but dangerous ground at the head of Fischer's line, assisting *Defiance* with the *Holsten* and taking on the remaining two Danish ships, the *Indfødsretten*, a sixty-five-gun blockship, and the *Hjaelperen* frigate with its armament of twenty-two. Scattered in an arc at the extreme northern end of the battle lines, Riou's flotilla also came under fire from the Trekroner fort, a little over a thousand yards away, and the two leading ships of Steen Bille's line, sitting in the mouth of Copenhagen harbour, the *Mars* (sixty-four) and *Elefanten* (seventy). Here, on the extreme northern flank of the battle, the clear superiority that marked Nelson's line further south ceased to exist.

In little more than two hours Nelson's battle line was put in place, their prime casualties falling not to enemy action but the Middle Ground. These losses continued to mount. The *Jamaica* brig-sloop, under Jonas Rose, also failed to clear the large shoal, and her six accompanying gun brigs did not work their way into usable positions until the afternoon. Nor did all of Nelson's bomb vessels take their allotted positions. The *Hecla* and *Sulphur* failed to get up to shell the Trekroner, and the remaining five only dribbled into the action between noon and three o'clock.

But a complicated manoeuvre had been completed with some success. Given that most of the ships fought only one side during the battle, Nelson's attack employed almost 450 guns, including those of the *Bellona* but not the *Russell*. The Danish force is more difficult to assess, because it was sometimes possible to haul unengaged guns to replace engaged weapons that had been dismounted or destroyed. Nevertheless, including the *Elefanten* (but not the *Mars*), Stricker's battery and the proportion of guns at Trekroner that were able to bear, it is difficult to sum the Danish equivalent at any one time at much more than four hundred. If the weight of metal fired is factored into the comparison, the discrepancy increases, because the standard Danish armament was the twenty-four-pounder, and Nelson's seventy-fours carried thirty-two-pounders on their lower decks. The action was fought over a longer range than Nelson had desired, reducing the precision of his fire, especially from carronades. The tendency of these last weapons to fire high beyond point-blank would particularly mar the performance of the *Glatton*. The battle became a series of bruising contests between groups of antagonists, but the admiral must have been relieved that it had gone so well, and observed to Stewart that the British fire was so 'decidedly superior' that the result was certain.[51]

7

It was the Danish centre, defended by Fischer's flagship *Dannebroge* and the *Sjaelland* ship of the line, which crumbled first. Although the Danes fought tenaciously, producing innumerable stories of extreme heroism, the formidable British gunnery was not to be denied.

With help from the *Monarch*, Fremantle's *Ganges* soon battered the *Sjaelland* into defeat. A third of her crew was bloodily scythed down, her masts, yards and rigging shot away, her guns destroyed or smashed from their carriages, and her hull riddled with more than twenty shot below the waterline. In a short time resistance was reduced to a plucky fire from after guns, but two of her officers led a panic-stricken flight into small boats, and after the ship's cables were cut she drifted helplessly out of the line of the battle. During that brutal exchange *Ganges* suffered only eight casualties, but Mosse's *Monarch* took heavier punishment forward from the Trekroner batteries. Having disposed of *Sjaelland*, Fremantle used his 'springs' to haul his ship clockwise so that she could rake the stern of the *Charlotte Amalia*, which had been moored north of the *Sjaelland*, sweeping her low-lying open deck with murderous grape shot, and punching holes into her hull. She surrendered at about 2.45, although some of her men scrambled into boats and pulled for the safety of the Trekroner fort.

Astern of the *Ganges* Nelson's *Elephant* fought a frustrating battle with one of the floating batteries, the *Aggershus* transport and the *Dannebroge*, Fischer's flagship. The floating batteries were awkward, unorthodox opponents, lying so low in the water that shot tended to pass over them, but at close range singularly well placed to drive their own shot horizontally into the hulls of larger assailants. Nelson's antagonist, commanded by young Lieutenant Peter Willemoes, resisted with exceptional courage, and was still fighting at one o'clock, when British grape, cannon and musket shot had downed more than a third of her crew, smashed in her breastworks, destroyed seven of her guns and turned her deck into a butcher's shambles. Even when her moorings were severed by shot, and she drifted from the line, some of her men floundered over to the wilting *Sjaelland* to try to continue the struggle. Nelson was filled with admiration, and later recommended Willemoes to the crown prince. The *Elephant*'s fire was, nevertheless, irresistible. 'I had Nelson's ship constantly under my eye,' wrote one watching Dane. 'It was one of those at anchor, and from the beginning to the end kept up the most dreadful fire.' The poor *Aggershus* became unmanageable after losing her mizzen, sails, sheets, braces, rudder and wheel. One shot sliced the spring on one of the transport's anchors, swinging her vulnerable bow towards British fire, and after further punishment her moorings broke and she drifted away in a sinking condition with a third of her men dead or wounded. Only the arrival of the *Nyborg*, limping north after being driven from the line lower down, saved the *Aggershus*. The *Nyborg* was an unlikely saviour, with only one broken foremast standing, every gun but one dismounted, and her deck littered with dead, wounded and wreckage. But she managed to haul the *Aggershus* beneath the Lynetten battery. One of the two was scuttled, and the other sank to the gunwhale close to the custom house. Throughout it all *Elephant* suffered little damage and only twenty-three casualties.[52]

While the *Elephant* cannonaded the *Dannebroge*, the principal opponent of the two-decked Danish flagship was Bligh's *Glatton*, stationed perhaps a mere cable's length away. Armed with nothing heavier than Danish twenty-four-pounders, Fischer's flagship could not match the lethal onslaught of British shot, especially from Bligh's heavy carronades, and more than a quarter of her men were cut down and most of her guns disabled or dismounted. The *Glatton* also used carcasses, hollow shells filled with combustibles, and the weary defenders of the *Dannebroge* were soon fighting a new battle against fire. Commodore Fischer, his forehead bleeding from a flying splinter, eventually abandoned the doomed ship to flee northwards to the *Holsten*, which was then unengaged. The luckless *Dannebroge* struck at 2.30, but her mooring cables broke and the current carried her towards the Trekroner and out of the battle. Her end came at about half past four when a terrific explosion blew her to smithereens, filling the air with black smoke and fiery red sparks.

Bligh simultaneously engaged the *Elven* and another of the floating batteries, the *Hayen*, of twenty guns. Much of Bligh's shot flew over the *Hayen*, but the rudimentary timber sides and protective bags were eventually smashed away and barbarous discharges of grape hewed down men crouching behind them or exposed on the unprotected deck. Under Sub-Lieutenant Jochum Muller the

Danes maintained the fight as long as humanly possible, heaving guns back on their mounts, and using small boats to bring additional powder from the shore, but the contest was unequal and the battery surrendered towards mid-afternoon. Muller was eventually brought on board the *Elephant*, where Nelson congratulated him on his heroic defence. The *Elven* avoided serious casualties by standing back from the line, but the *Glatton* shot away masts and rigging and put her in a sinking condition. Bligh's victories were not without cost, however. Fifty-five of *Glatton*'s men lay dead or wounded, nine of her carronades were disabled, her sails and rigging shredded, her masts splintered and her fore topmast down. Nelson hailed Bligh and called him to the flagship to receive his personal thanks, and they had been well earned.

The Danish centre, consisting of five ships, two of them of the line, and two floating batteries, was subdued without exceptional difficulty, but resistance from the southern and northern sections of the enemy line persisted longer. Indeed, it was the southern part of Denmark's line, defended by six ships and a floating battery, which engaged first and lasted the longest. This phase was marked by a series of tragedies that rocked the *Bellona*, beginning with her running upon the Middle Ground. Unable to work loose, Thompson prepared to fight a long-range battle as best he could, but his left leg was ripped off by a round shot as he stood on a quarterdeck gun, and he was carried below spurting blood. The command devolved upon First Lieutenant John Delafons, but his men were rocked by separate and unrelated explosions when two thirty-two-pounders on the lower deck burst, one forward and the other amidships. Parts of the main deck were blown away, guns tossed in the air and the lower deck flooded with smoke, debris and dead and maimed men. The fires were put out, but the ship remained wedged on the shoal and suffered a heavy eighty-three casualties in the battle, including the captain, two lieutenants, a captain of the 49th, a master's mate and three midshipmen.

It was the enemy, rather than shoals or accidents, who inflicted substantial losses on the other British ships on the southern flank of the battle. Murray's *Edgar* took a surprising 142 casualties, including one lieutenant killed, another whose arm was shot away and five midshipmen wounded. The crippled lieutenant was back at his post in nine days. 'Such a spirit in the service is never to be overcome', was Nelson's judgement. Despite losses, Murray took only forty-five minutes to smash in the fragile timbers of the *Rendsborg* transport and put her out of action, punching the first hole in the enemy line. He then dismissed the twenty-gun *Nyborg*, which reeled from the line with only one usable gun left and her decks plastered with bodies and severed limbs. He had more trouble subduing the *Jylland*, which sustained serious structural damage and seventy-one casualties but survived into the afternoon. As a longboat of able-bodied survivors pushed off from one side of the sinking vessel, British boarders scaled the other to find only four guns able to fire and dead men strewn about the blood-stained decks.[53]

Bertie's *Ardent*, fighting ahead of the *Edgar*, also endured a hard trial. In a grisly contest with the *Kronborg* frigate and *Svaerdfisken* floating battery almost a hundred of her men were killed or wounded, and her hull and sails punctured by scores of shot. The foresail alone was pierced 138 times. The floating battery fired double shot, bar, grape and incendiaries at the *Ardent*, but surrendered at 2.30 with her best men dead and only one gun operative. On her part the *Kronborg* lost three of four senior officers and all her guns. Some of her men broke and leaped into the surviving boats in panic, but the remaining lieutenant, Søren Helt, refused to abandon his post or strike his colours until British boarders piled over the side. The *Ardent* won her battle, but most of her guns were useless at the close of fire, and her men exhausted. During the battle they had fired 2693 rounds.

The last of all the engaged Danish ships to give up were the first to engage, *Prøvesteenen* and *Wagrien*, on the extreme southern flank of the battle. The commander of the *Wagrien* fought a particularly intelligent battle, and at one stage hurled incendiary grenades into the *Isis*, trying to turn the fight around in his corner of the action. For perilous minutes smoke billowed out of the stricken fifty, but the flames were brought under control, and by 2.30 *Isis* had the victory. All but three of *Wagrien*'s guns had been silenced, sixty-three of her men cut down, and many of the survivors attempted to flee as British boarders climbed over her shot-riddled side. But her surrender had been bought dear. *Isis* sustained 121 losses, almost equal to those of her nearest consorts, the *Polyphemus*, *Bellona*, *Desiree* and *Russell*, combined. Though less skilfully handled than the *Wagrien*, the *Prøvesteenen* survived about another half-hour, helped by her unusually heavy armament. For five hours she traded blows, struggling on as round and grape swept her upper deck and all but two of her lower deck guns were put out of action. Three fires had to be fought. At the end of it some of the men collapsed exhausted beside the monstrous guns they had unremittingly manoeuvred in their enclosed smoke-choked Hades, while seventy-five of their comrades lay dead or wounded in the bloody wreckage of their ship. Some victims of the slaughter suffered horrific injuries, and one lieutenant was almost traumatised at the sight of a round shot smashing a hole through one of his men so large that the deck could be seen through his fallen body.

The conflict at the northern end of the battle had started later, about eleven in the morning, but finished earlier, and it was fought in a drifting black cloud of powder smoke that was constantly being replenished by the furious fighting down the line. Here the most dangerous opponent was the Trekroner fort, for the naval resistance was weak enough. The fully-rigged frigate *Hjaelperen*, sporting specially reinforced sides and a respectable armament of twenty-two guns, sixteen of them big Danish thirty-six-pounders, fired a mere two hundred rounds at Riou's frigates before fleeing her station. She had suffered only six casualties, but her commander defended himself with a cock and bull story that he had been engaged by two British seventy-fours.

This part of the attack was made by the *Monarch*, *Defiance* and the five frigates under Riou, all of which received fire from the Trekroner. The *Monarch* suffered 220 casualties, more than any other British ship, largely from the *Sjaelland* and the Trekroner. Captain Mosse stood on the poop of his ship at the beginning of the battle, his card of instructions in one hand and a speaking trumpet in the other, but he was killed descending to his quarterdeck, and at about the same time the ship's wheel was smashed and three or four helmsmen cut down. Suffering additional damage to sails, sheets and braces, the ship became difficult to manage. Mosse's officers rose to the challenge, serving wherever needed. First Lieutenant John Yelland, who took command, emerged from one potentially lethal shower of splinters 'smiling' as if it was 'his wedding day', and Lieutenant Colonel Hutchinson happily put himself under the command of a seventeen-year-old midshipman and supervised guns or cut wads for their bores. A humbler soldier, Lieutenant James Dennis of the 49th Regiment, lost the fingerends of his left hand. Binding his wounds in a bloody handkerchief, he flung himself into the battle with a courage that raised a 'huzza' from his comrades, and 'flew through every part of the ship, and when he found any of his men wounded, carried him in his arms down to the cockpit'. Yet the mayhem was terrifying. Midshipman John Green had his arm shot off, an eye 'totally lost out of my head', and a severe wound in the side, apart from other injuries. Midshipman William Salter Millard entered the main deck to collect some equipment for the guns and found 'there was not a single man standing the whole way from the main mast forward'. The *Defiance*, anchored ahead of the *Monarch*, also took severe punishment, taking seventy-five casualties and damage to her main- and mizzen masts and bowsprit.[54]

Despite all, the British ships at the northern end of the battle performed as Nelson expected. The *Søhesten* floating battery took severe casualties within minutes of firing, and when she was silenced at 2.30 she had only two serviceable guns left. The *Holsten*'s battle began late, and almost her first sense of the fate overwhelming her consorts further south was gained at about 11.30, when a small boat emerged from the smoke and noise carrying the wounded Fischer. The commodore explained that the *Dannebroge* was finished, and he intended to raise his pendant on the *Holsten*. But then *Defiance* materialised ominously from the gloom after leaving *Søhesten* to the *Monarch*, and began a gruelling hammering match. The British fire was 'like a hailstorm', systematically dismembering the *Holsten* with broadside after broadside. One shot screamed into the lower gun deck of the Danish ship, killing and maiming many of its men and smashing the best bower cable and sheet anchor aft of the bitts. After almost two hours Fischer accepted that his new flagship was also defeated, and fled again, this time to the Trekroner. He had saved his pendant, but not his ship.

Pierced thirteen times below the waterline, its decks scourged by more than 150 shots, it was a wreck with no option but surrender. A boat carried her officers to the *Elephant*, but Nelson allowed her commander, Jacob Arenfelt, to return to tend his wounded.[55]

The last of the Danish ships to relinquish the fight on the northern flank was the sixty-four-gun *Infodstretten*, which withstood a galling fire from the *Defiance*, *Amazon* and *Blanche* for some time. Badly positioned, and with some of her men intoxicated, she twice lost her commanding officer during firing, and ended the action under the charge of a junior lieutenant. Unsurprisingly, her return fire was feeble. There was an unfortunate confusion about the surrender, which occurred at about half past one. Before a British prize crew could get on board, Danish reinforcements from the shore reached the ship, and her flag was raised again. It was a useless waste, however. By three o'clock the colours fell again, this time signalling not only the fall of a ship but of the whole northern section of the line. Further south the much diminished barking of guns marked where the solitary *Provesteenen* was reaching the end of her gallant fight.

By 1.30 an inevitability had settled upon the contest. The Danish line was crumbling from one flank to the other. Although *Prøvesteenen* and *Wagrien* in the south, *Sjaelland* and *Charlotte Amalie* in the centre, and *Søhesten* and *Infødstretten* in the north were trying to maintain an enfeebled fire, the Danish line was crumbling from one flank to the other. Their energy was draining away, and defeat imminent. Nelson had weathered the first crisis of the battle, overcoming the loss of his three capital ships, and was confident of victory.

But then something remarkable happened. A second crisis arose, not from shoals, nor the Danish fire, nor yet from the unconquered Trekroner, which Nelson had a mind to storm. A little after one o'clock it came from Nelson's own commander-in-chief, who was still some four miles distant. About 1.15 or 1.30, depending upon which source is believed, Sir Hyde Parker raised a general signal, which he advertised by the discharge of two guns. It was directed to every British ship engaged in the battle.

The signal was number 39, and meant 'Discontinue the Action!'

8

Three of Sir Hyde's seventy-fours were supposed to be supporting Nelson's attack with a diversion from the north, and, thrown on to the northern flank of the battle, where the assault force was weakest, they would have made an important difference, perhaps threatening the Trekroner and the two ships of Steen Bille's division that lay closest to the open mouth of Copenhagen harbour. Unfortunately, as we have seen, Parker's movement began too late in the day, and when the commander-in-chief did intervene it was with a dangerous signal to disengage.

Parker had probably seen that some of Nelson's ships had taken the ground, as well as the difficult battle the frigates were waging. It is difficult to avoid the conclusion that the commander-in-chief lost his nerve when he raised signal number 39. Throughout the engagement Parker had been in a state of high tension, claiming later that he had not slept properly since 27 March. Afraid of St Vincent, he became indecisive under pressure, frightened of incurring censure. One indication of his erratic behaviour is his dispatch of Captain Otway in a boat to the *Elephant*, a little before he raised his signal. One supposes that Otway was to assess the state of the battle, and ascertain what assistance Nelson wanted, but before the captain could reach the *Elephant*, Sir Hyde decided that he could wait no longer and flew number 39. It was a dangerous, irresponsible act. The signal was a general one, directed not only at Nelson but at every captain under his command, demanding their obedience. Without any clear grasp of the situation, which was partly masked by smoke, he ordered the embattled squadron to disengage while under heavy fire, and withdraw through treacherous waters in which one or more ships were already aground and unable to comply. Parker's intentions were good. Perhaps he wanted to spare Nelson the odium of ordering a retreat, and nobly took the responsibility upon himself, but given that some of Nelson's ships were not in a position to retreat, and others would probably not even see the signal, the order raised the prospect of some ships attempting to withdraw while their consorts fought on. It was a recipe for chaos.[56]

It did its damage at the north flank of the battle, where some of the ships saw and repeated the signal. The *Alcmene* frigate was one, and began to disengage, followed closely by the *Blanche*. On the *Amazon*, which had suffered almost forty casualties, Riou was astonished. He had already been wounded in the head by a splinter, but kept the deck and felt loath to obey the commander-in-chief's order. Only after Graves, his nearest flag officer in the *Defiance* astern, repeated Parker's signal did Riou grudgingly comply, though with a heavy heart and the words – according to what Stewart later heard – 'What will Nelson think of us?' He was spared the ignominy, however, because as his frigate's cable was cut and her topsails released to enable the ship to bear up, she exposed her stern to raking fire from the Trekroner, and a shot almost ripped the captain in two. A clerk and several marines at the main brace were scythed down about the same time. Lieutenant John Quilliam brought the frigate out, but Riou's loss was a severe one. 'A better officer or better man never existed,' Nelson wrote.[57]

Fortunately, only the frigates, the ships nearest to Parker, obeyed his signal, although both the *Desiree* frigate and the grounded *Agamemnon* at the other end of the battle repeated it. The captains saw for themselves that the *Elephant* was neither disengaging nor repeating Parker's signal, and that Nelson's signal 16 for close action remained in place. Graves's flagship, *Defiance*, represented the strange paradox. Though she repeated the commander-in-chief's signal to leave off action, Graves manifestly refused to carry it out, displaying Nelson's contradictory signal at the same time and maintaining his own fire. He later expressed relief that 'our little Hero' had disobeyed an order which courted disaster.[58]

Nelson's response to Parker's signal has, of course, become one of the legendary stories of British history. Like Alfred's cakes, Robert the Bruce's spider and Drake's game of bowls it passed from one generation of children to another. The story of Nelson theatrically putting a telescope to his sightless eye and saying that he could not see the signal, and would therefore ignore it, made 'to turn a blind eye' to an inconvenient truth part of the language. Recently, however, there has been a stampede to disavow the tale, and brand it an invention. But that goes much too far. Let us return to our witnesses, and see what was said.

Eyewitness accounts possess a prima facie authority, but serious historians know they pose innumerable problems, especially if committed to paper many years after an event they describe. Memory is a valuable but treacherous archive. It quickly loses details, confuses chronology, conflates the details of similar incidents and integrates information that only became known after the fact. In other words, it loses, gathers, reinterprets and reconstructs history as it moves along. We have, therefore, to compare and cross-check these accounts carefully, bearing in mind that independent witnesses will rarely remember an event in exactly the same way, and that their statements will vary according to the circumstances, sincerity, precision and recall of the narrator. Gross contradictions should warn us of errors, but accounts that agree too closely also ring alarm bells, because they suggest that one witness may be plagiarising another, or indeed that both may draw from a common and unknown source.

Parker's signal became an embarrassment, and neither Nelson nor Sir Hyde mentioned it in their dispatches, but it was widely spoken of in the fleet. The most voluble witnesses in the *Elephant* came from Stewart's Rifle Corps. First on the stand is Stewart himself, who was beside Nelson at the time. Unfortunately, unable to forecast the fascination of posterity, his earlier accounts were brief, one appearing in his journal, and the other in a letter he wrote to a colleague on 6 April. Both reported Nelson's annoyance at Parker's signal, speaking of the admiral's 'astonishment' or 'hurt', and that he kept his own signal for close action flying. Both also record some of Nelson's words on the occasion, to the effect that he would continue to hammer the Danes 'till they should be sick of it', whether it took three hours or four. According to Stewart's journal, Nelson acknowledged Parker's signal but refused to repeat it. In a letter of 5 April a second witness, Sidney Beckwith, a captain in Stewart's corps, agreed that Nelson talked about continuing the battle for as long as it took. None of these three cursory accounts refer to Nelson using his blind eye, but then none purported to offer a complete account of the episode. However, a fourth reference, albeit of uncertain origin, reached Lady Malmesbury in England on 18 May. She had at least one relative with the fleet, but did not name the informant who told her that when 'an officer' notified Nelson of Parker's signal 'he replied that he could not see them, for he had but one eye and that was directed to the enemy.' The implication was that his blind eye was the only one available for Parker's signal.[59]

By 1806 another account was in circulation, produced by Doctor William Ferguson of the Rifle Corps, who was also in the *Elephant* at the time. Unfortunately, Ferguson's detailed statement has been lost, although it was evidently in the public domain, and may have been published in some newspaper as early as 1801. As it is we have an extract quoted by a biographer, James Harrison, in 1806, according to which Nelson responded to Parker's order with the words, 'Then damn the signal! Take no notice of it, and hoist mine for closer battle. That is the way I answer such signals.' Then he turned to Captain Foley and added, 'Foley, you know I have lost an eye, and have a right to be blind when I like, and damn me if I'll see that signal!'[60]

By far the most famous and fullest account was written by Stewart for Clarke and McArthur's biography, published in 1809. Principally, it added the telescope to Ferguson's previously published account, along with several other details. The signal, said Stewart, caught Nelson marching up and down the starboard side of the quarterdeck, so excited that the stump of his amputated arm twitched. At one time a shot hit the mainmast and showered the admiral and Stewart with splinters. Nelson smiled. 'It is warm work,' he observed, 'and this day may be the last to any of us at a moment, but mark you, I would not be elsewhere for thousands!' A lieutenant duly appeared with word that Parker was flying number 39. Nelson continued his walk, and as he turned the lieutenant asked if the commander-in-chief's signal should be repeated by the *Elephant*. The admiral ordered him both to acknowledge it and ensure that signal 16 was still in place. After striding one or two more lengths in some agitation, Nelson asked Stewart if he knew what Parker had signalled. The soldier confessed he did not. 'Why, to leave off action,' replied Nelson. 'Leave off action!' he shrugged. 'Now, damn me if I do.' He also observed ('I believe to Captain Foley'), 'You know Foley, I have only one eye. I have a right to be blind sometimes', and 'with an archness peculiar to his character' put a spyglass to his blind eye and exclaimed, 'I really do not see the signal.'[61]

Here, then, is the classic story of Nelson's reaction, and while it contains some vivid new details, including the movement of the admiral's truncated stump in moments of excitement, a practice recorded in other reminiscences, it is at once clear that in the matter of the blind eye it closely parallels Ferguson's previously published account. Modern critics have argued that as Stewart omitted any reference to the blind eye in his known (and very brief) accounts of 1801, he must have taken it from Ferguson and elaborated, or fictionalised it, in 1809. The issue is altogether murkier, however. Stewart, Beckwith and Ferguson were fellow officers of the Rifle Corps, shared the same mess, and no doubt influenced each other. Historians have assumed that Stewart took his account from Ferguson, but it could easily have been the other way round. After all, Ferguson was an army surgeon, and the likelihood is that he was below for much of the battle, helping tend the wounded. His knowledge of what occurred on the quarterdeck most likely originated in Stewart, Beckwith or indeed one of the naval officers, such as Foley.[62]

Our final account, offered by Nelson's lieutenant, William Layman, in about 1817, adds little. Layman served in the *Isis* during the battle but would have heard about Nelson's conduct when he rejoined the admiral and his retinue in the *St George* shortly afterwards. He had a good relationship with Stewart, once volunteering to serve as a supernumerary in the Rifle Corps, and mixed much with Lieutenant Langford of the *St George*, who was in the *Elephant* with Nelson. Either could have informed Layman. On the other hand, his account might be no more than a bowdlerised memory of the earlier published accounts. Whichever, in a terse aside to the affair, Layman said that Nelson found it difficult to believe that Parker could have sent such a signal, and when assured that such was the case, replied, 'Well, I cannot see it.'[63]

Much about this iconic incident remains unclear, but the gist or thrust of the evidence – of the account from Malmesbury, and those transmitted through Ferguson, Stewart and Layman – preserve essential components of the legend. They all, in one way or another, allude to Nelson's refusal to *see* the signal. The 'blind eye' has its claim to history. As for the telescope, that only comes from Stewart's last account. Nelson must have been constantly using his telescope during the battle, and one lifting would have attracted no more general attention than another. A witness would have had to have been very close to have understood the nuance of that particular situation. Stewart may have invented it. On the other hand, Stewart seems to have been as good a witness as one could expect, and the telescope story is entirely in Nelson's character. He never forgot his audience. Historians must make up their own minds about whether Stewart is impeachable or not. Frankly, we do not know.

The consequences of Parker's action were far more important. Nelson had never been afraid of ignoring orders, but no matter how sound a relationship an officer might have with his commander-in-chief, it was always risky to disobey a signal in action, because it transferred the responsibility for the consequences from the superior to the inferior officer. If things went badly, it provided an obvious scapegoat.

The pressure on Nelson was therefore intensified by the affair of the signal. Yet he could see the Danish fire slackening and remained confident of victory, despite the reinforcements that the Danes were getting to their ships from the shore. About 171 Danes went out to units that were still resisting. 'Well, Stewart,' the admiral reportedly observed, 'these fellows hold us a better jig than I expected. However, we are keeping up a noble fire, and I'll be answerable that we shall bowl them out in four if we cannot do it in three hours.' Nelson was fortunate that all his ships of the line remained in place, but Parker had stripped them of their frigates while the battle was in progress, and robbed the service of a brilliant officer in Riou. The second crisis of the battle had not been overcome without losses.[64]

9

Towards mid-afternoon Sub-Lieutenant Muller and a few fellow prisoners from the *Hayen* floating battery, newly conquered by the *Glatton*, scaled the sides of the *Elephant* to meet their captor, the legendary commander of the British fleet. Muller discovered a 'small, thin and very straight' man bizarrely attired in a 'green Kalmuk's overcoat and a little three-cornered hat' worn square. With him stood the bulky Foley in full uniform and decorations, and Thomas Wallis, the admiral's purser-cum-secretary, a modest figure of twenty-two years, dressed in a plain blue suit and white waistcoat. During the pleasantries Captain Fremantle of the *Ganges* arrived, and participated in an earnest conversation. Finally, at the rudderhead in the stern gallery of the upper gun deck, Nelson scribbled a note on a sheet of folded paper. It was addressed to 'the Brothers of Englishmen the Danes' and was enticingly vague. 'Lord Nelson,' it read, 'has directions to spare Denmark when no longer resisting, but if the firing is continued on the part of Denmark, Lord Nelson will be obliged to set on fire all the floating batteries [prizes] he has taken without having the power of saving the brave Danes who have defended them.' Thus, Nelson satisfied himself, did he use 'the moment of a complete victory' to create an 'opening' for diplomacy. In his mind he was contemplating a ceasefire.[65]

Some of the Danes saw Nelson's overture as a surprising new move. 'Our right wing was now quite ruined,' said one, yet 'as soon as the fire of our line was silenced, Nelson sent a flag of truce.' This was, however, no simple act of magnanimity, although it was also certainly that. It was a fine calculation by an admiral who was increasingly aware that words, no less than weapons, could be used with effect, and who saw in a diplomatic overture a way to wind up a complicated situation.[66]

As the Danish line collapsed, Nelson's attention had turned towards the problem of securing the prizes. They were worth little in themselves, but obstructed Nelson's bomb vessels, which had filtered in behind the *Ganges* and *Elephant*, waiting to open a bombardment of the forts, harbour and arsenal. The prizes needed to be cleared away to facilitate the next phase of the British attack. Unfortunately, taking possession was unusually difficult. Some ships struck their colours, only to continue or resume firing, either because of genuine misunderstandings or opportunism on the part of Danish officers. The forts were also maintaining their fire, apparently immune to the conventions of naval belligerents. From whatever reason, the confusion about who had or had not surrendered was endangering British boats which set out to board ships that had supposedly struck, and delayed Nelson's ability to clear the enemy ships from the King's Deep. Stewart testified that the admiral 'lost [his] temper' over the abuse of the conventions of war, and vowed to 'stop' it 'or send in our fire ships' to burn the prizes where they lay.[67]

The problem had an obvious humanitarian dimension. Some of the shore batteries fired into their own ships, once they had fallen into British possession, oblivious of the Danish prisoners still aboard, a 'massacre' that Nelson deplored. He could burn the prizes and be done with them, but what would become of the hundreds of prisoners, including wounded, left inside? 'It was a sight which no real man could have enjoyed,' Nelson said later. 'I felt [that] when the Danes became my prisoners, I became their protector.' Humanitarianism was probably not the primary motive for his overture, despite Nelson's later insistence that such was the case, but it was part of it. He took no pleasure from the needless destruction of brave adversaries, and had always had a special regard for the Scandinavians, who, he believed, were unnatural enemies of Britain. His sympathy was genuine. As Stewart noted, the victory left him 'low in spirits at the surrounding scene of destruction, and [he] particularly felt for the blowing up of the *Dannebroge*'. When that ship exploded with a tremendous blast, Nelson sent boats to rescue survivors, but relatively few were saved, among them the Danish captain.[68]

A comparable concern governing the admiral's thoughts was the security of his own capital ships now that their principal work had been done. While none were incapacitated, all still had to be extricated from a narrow and difficult anchorage under the guns of the Trekronor. Nelson considered storming the fort, but it appeared to be strongly garrisoned and an attack might be expensive and bloody, while the alternative, a bombardment, was time-consuming. Nelson realised that a temporary ceasefire would not only allow prizes and prisoners to be secured, but provide an opportunity to withdraw the ships. Both Stewart and Fremantle were candid enough to own that the ceasefire was a 'convenient' means of obtaining a trouble-free redeployment of their assault force.[69]

Wallis, the clerk, was about to seal the envelope with a wafer when Nelson stopped him, insisting on the use of wax and his own seal instead, lest the Danes entertained any suspicions that he was acting in haste or anxiety. Thesiger, who could speak Danish, agreed to take the message ashore, despite the heavy fire, and one of the *Elephant*'s boats, with a flag of truce on an upraised oar in the bow and Nelson's ensign in the stern, was soon pulling northwards under the shelter of the British battleships until they turned to port towards the *Elefanten*, one of Steen Bille's ships. The message reached the crown prince on the Citadel Point at about three in the afternoon.

By then the fighting in the King's Deep was almost over. The Danish line was a smouldering ruin, most of its guns silent, but a few of the British ships had suffered extensive damage. The *Ganges* required no more than a few days' work on her masts and rigging to regain her full powers, but the *Edgar*'s rigging, shrouds, stays and sails had been wasted; a bower anchor and cable ripped away; her bowsprit damaged; mainmast pierced by nine shots, three of them 'through the heart'; bumpkin and mizzen topmast cross-trees shot away; hull seared by 'many shot holes'; and ten guns out of action, two with their muzzles broken or split and another with its breech blown off. However, all of Nelson's ships remained in a fighting condition, and Parker's nearest battleships were approaching within gun range of the Trekroner. The commander-in-chief eventually anchored his force some three miles distant, passive but nonetheless threatening.[70]

Suddenly the remaining Danish guns fell silent, an indication that Nelson's proposal had struck a chord, and soon after the admiral's boat returned, escorted by a Danish vessel and Captain Hans Lindholm, the crown prince's naval aide. Nelson, Foley and Fremantle waited in the great cabin of the *Elephant* with Muller and other Danish prisoners. Without the slightest insincerity Foley had been complimenting the prisoners, remarking that he had fought the French, Spanish and Dutch, but had never been opposed with greater courage than at Copenhagen. Lindholm arrived after three-thirty, impressing Nelson from the beginning. Though Thesiger was again available as an interpreter, Nelson ordered Wallis to pen a reply to avoid any verbal misunderstandings, stating that the 'object' of the flag of truce was 'humanity,' and proposing a ceasefire until he could burn or remove his prizes and evacuate the prisoners, the wounded among whom would be immediately put ashore. The Danes could see no reason to object, for the ceasefire gave them respite and protected their people, and Nelson went further, observing that he would regard this as his 'greatest victory' if his flag of truce became 'the happy forerunner of a lasting and happy union' of the two countries. To cement that, however, the Danes would have to refer to Parker. In the meantime a ceasefire was established until the following day, and Nelson raised a flag of truce on board the *Elephant*. It came in force just in time to nip further hostilities in the bud, as Nelson's bomb vessels had already begun to throw shells. One fell so close to where the crown prince had taken an advanced station that he prudently retired to the citadel, a reminder of the costs of prolonging the action.[71]

After five or more hours of fury and carnage the battle was over, and the King's Deep was left smoking and strewn with debris and shattered and burning ships. Long afterwards Lieutenant Tom Southey of the *Bellona* could vividly remember seeing bodies lying in the shoal water. The jetty at the Danish customs house was filled with the stretchers of dead and dreadfully wounded men brought ashore. Many lacked limbs and heads. Three days later the *Folketidende* newspaper recalled the day as 'a drunken nightmare' and described the mournful carts that were wheeled up to deal with the human wreckage of the fight: 'The column of dead and wounded [brought ashore] were met by columns of reinforcements, led by drummers, going out to the ships. The reinforcements were wearing smocks which the soldiers called "dead shirts" [shrouds].' In all, the British suffered 944 dead and badly wounded, more than in any previous naval battle of the revolutionary and Napoleonic wars, providing a new challenge to Lloyd's Coffee House, which habitually and honourably raised public subscriptions to relieve broken men and broken families. Danish losses were higher, 1035 killed and wounded, 3500 prisoners later released by the British, and 205 missing.[72]

Fourteen of the eighteen Danish battle stations in Fischer's line had been destroyed or taken, including seven ships of the line or fifties. Most of the prizes were unusable, and only one, the *Holsten*, was taken into the Royal Navy, in which she served as a hospital ship and survived to take part in another expedition to Copenhagen in 1807. Four of Fischer's units – a transport, a frigate, a corvette and a floating battery – remained in Danish hands, all of them driven from the line damaged, and one, the *Aggershus*, was salvaged. Fischer's force had been annihilated, but the loss of the three grounded British ships had prevented Nelson from attacking Steen Bille's division and perhaps the Trekroner.

The truce enabled both sides to take stock. While Nelson's bomb vessels, fireships and small boats secured the prizes, removed prisoners, landed the wounded and prepared to resume hostilities, his capital ships effected hasty repairs and disengaged. Boats from Parker brought extra useful hands, but even with their help the assault force found it difficult to extricate itself. Nelson summoned Graves to the *Elephant* and bade him lead the squadron, but some of the damaged vessels handled badly, and Graves's *Defiance* ran aground trying to negotiate the passage. The mutilated *Monarch*, her braces and bowlines cut and her sails flapping limply, ran on to the mud. She was brutally pushed off by the *Ganges*, which accidentally collided, and was drifting helplessly towards the Trekroner before boats got tow lines across and dragged her around into deeper water. The hitherto unscathed *Elephant* also ran on to the Middle Ground after four in the afternoon. Guns were rolled forward to lighten her trapped stern, some of the provisions swung out to a brig, and a signal made for a spare stream anchor to pull her off the shoal. Even so, she was stuck for more than five hours. The sun set at about 6.30, and night found all but *Defiance*, *Agamemnon*, *Bellona* and *Russell* free of the King's Deep. They would need another day. The difficulty of the withdrawal had vindicated the value of the ceasefire, which at least eliminated the complication of Danish fire.

About sunset a boat with a flag of truce left Copenhagen for Parker's flagship to begin the more comprehensive discussions Nelson had recommended. The British commander-in-chief now had a stronger hand, with the Danish line destroyed and the British bomb vessels poised to unleash more fury. He therefore presented the terms he had offered before with greater confidence. Denmark must resign from the League of Armed Neutrality, and conclude a defensive alliance with Britain relying upon the Royal Navy for protection from Russia. But the battle had not changed the broader politics. Denmark had long calculated that she would rather suffer short-term punishment at the hands of Britain than risk the wrath of Russia and France, and the possible loss of Norway to Sweden. Even defeated, she had proven her value to the League because she had delayed the British, and given the Swedes and Russians time to prepare. The Danish emissaries sent to the *London* could only promise that Parker's sentiments would be laid before their superiors.

A battle appeared to have been won, but the peace seemed no closer.

10

Wellington, it is said, once remarked that a battle won was the next saddest thing to a battle lost.

'We have passed some dreadful days,' said a Danish witness. 'The superiority of the English has conquered us, but with honour, for we have defended ourselves in no common manner.' And the victors too, close to exhaustion, seemed unsure about the result. Graves had opposed the attack from the beginning, and saw little to revise his opinion. 'I think we were playing a losing game in attacking stone walls, and I fear we shall not have much to boast of when it is known what our ships suffered, and the little impression we made on their navy,' he wrote, while admitting, at least, that the 'enterprise' of the attackers was 'invincible'. Nelson had a clearer view of what had been achieved, and of what use might be made of it. However, he was not immune to the wounding scenes of destruction. He would write to St Vincent, recommending the British widows and orphans to the protection of government, and prime a compensation fund with £100. The night after the battle, drained by forty or so hours without sleep, hours filled with unremitting exertion and anxiety and the highs and lows of a life-and-death encounter, the losses fell heavily upon him. He said it made his heart run out of his eyes.[73]

Soon after the ceasefire, Nelson left the *Elephant*, still aground, and reported to his commander-in-chief, arriving on board the *London* soon after Lindholm and Parker had started talking. He left to return to his own ship, the *St George*, and the quiet repose he needed in his great cabin. Taking out his journal, he noted the bald details of the battle, claiming that four hours of fighting had given him seventeen of the eighteen Danish units, taken, burned or sunk. 'Our ships suffered a good deal. At night went on board the *St George*, very unwell.'[74]

Then, in a mood of exhilaration, sadness and exhaustion, Nelson did a curious thing, perhaps something no victorious commander had done before. With surprising speed, his mind sank from professional to private problems, and all his insecurities of the spring resurfaced. Writing to Emma, he warned that he 'could not wish to consider you as my friend if you kept such scandalous company as the Prince of Wales'. Then his spirits rallied, and with uncertain starts and erasures he wrote her a poem. In it he imagined holding a conversation with his 'guardian angel', the theme of which was their unity of soul. Said 'Henry' to his angel,

> 'From my best cable tho' I'm forced to part,
> I kept my anchor in my Angel's heart.'

To which the angel replied with the lazy repeat of a rhyme,

> 'East, west, north, south, our minds shall never part,
> Your Angel's loadstone shall be Nelson's heart.'

After eighteen lines he gave up at about nine o'clock and endorsed his verse with a note that he was 'very tired after a hard-fought battle'. It had been a strange, almost surreal day, beginning with a ferocious battle, passing through a ceasefire between two nations, and ending, half sleepily, in a poem.[75]

XIV

CONTROLLING THE BALTIC

With strong floating batteries, in van and rear
we find,
The enemy in centre had six ships of the line;
At ten that glorious morning the fight begun,
it's true,
We Copenhagen set on fire, my boys, before the
clock struck two.

A New Song, 1801

I

AT three in the morning Nelson was up again, writing to Parker about 'a most disgraceful subterfuge'. He had heard that one of the Danish ships that had surrendered, the *Sjaelland*, had refused to allow a prize crew aboard. The cease-fire, it seemed, was being used to redefine what were and were not prizes. 'I think you had better demand her in a peremptory manner,' Nelson suggested, recommending Otway as the man for the job.[1]

Braving a bitterly cold north-westerly wind, Nelson descended early into his gig to return to the King's Deep, where the last British ships of the line were getting off the Middle Ground. 'His delight and praises in finding us afloat were unbounded, and recompensed all our misfortunes,' said Stewart, who had remained on the *Elephant* throughout. After breakfast on board, Nelson rowed to his other ships and prizes, listening to the reports of damage, and learning with some satisfaction that only the *Isis* and *Monarch* needed extensive repairs. He was also told that Otway had gone to Fischer to protest about the *Sjaelland*, as Nelson had recommended, and went forthwith into the harbour to give support. Vindicating Nelson's faith, Otway had already recovered the *Sjaelland*, but the admiral met the Danish commodore in the *Elefanten*, and remembered seeing him back in the eighties in the Danish West Indian islands. Their relationship did not improve in the following days. Fischer would exculpate himself at Nelson's expense, writing a misleading dispatch claiming that the British had used the flag of truce as a ruse to avoid defeat. Nelson would respond passionately, accusing the Dane of setting a cowardly example by abandoning the *Sjaelland*, but both officers were being unfair.[2]

Back in the *St George*, Nelson addressed a characteristic report to Parker, full of enthusiasm for his companions in arms. Adjectival words and phrases dripped off his pen . . . 'unremitting' . . . 'a noble example of intrepidity' . . . 'high and distinguished merit and gallantry' . . . 'brave' . . . A typical feature of his report was the care he took to protect those who had met misfortune, or whose conduct had fortuitously exposed them to criticism. The troops, who had not been able to perform as planned, had 'shared with pleasure the toils and dangers'. The commander-in-chief's signal was not mentioned, and the losses in the frigates attributed purely to the exigencies of the service. Jonas Rose of the *Jamaica*, and the crews of the gun brigs, who had not always been in their appointed places, nevertheless displayed 'merit', while the boats Parker had belatedly sent to assist him deserved 'my warmest approbation'. Though grounded the *Bellona* and *Russell* had rendered 'great service', and Captain Fancourt of the *Agamemnon*, who had never got into the fight, was not in the 'smallest' degree responsible for running upon the shoal. This was the sort of letter that endeared Nelson to followers. He even sent a private note to the distressed Fancourt, who felt that he had let everyone down, and the captain replied with gratitude for 'the exonerations, marked attention and expressions your kind letter was fraught with. Nothing, my lord, could possibly have added more to the peace of my mind.'[3]

Nelson's report certainly contrasted with Parker's dispatch, which was supposed to offer the standard recounting of events. Infuriatingly, the commander-in-chief promoted several of his own followers into the vacancies that had been created by death, injury and indisposition, irrespective of their services in the battle. Four junior commands went to lieutenants of the *London*, and Otway was accorded the privilege of taking the dispatches home. Lieutenant Yelland, who deserved well for taking command of the *Monarch* after Mosse's death, was remembered in a postscript, and would have thereafter been ignored had Nelson not protested, opening the way to an appointment as flag lieutenant. No doubt Nelson recollected that Howe, Hood and St Vincent had all written very unsatisfactory victory dispatches. Now, complaining that 'all my own children are neglected', he sent letters to Troubridge and St Vincent, urging that the omissions be redressed. All the first lieutenants of the ships in his actual assault force deserved to be promoted, along with Thesiger, who had volunteered to serve as aide in the *Elephant*. A bevy of his 'children' were mentioned, including 'our old Mediterranean friends', Lieutenants Bolton, Lyne and Langford ('you must recollect him . . . He has no interest, and is as good an officer and a man as ever lived'), as well as Joshua Johnson of the *Edgar*, who had lost an arm and stood in the place of his first lieutenant after he fell. More gingerly, Nelson also spoke up for the mercurial Lieutenant William Layman, a man whose astonishing ability irritated superiors. He was, said Nelson, 'really an acquisition when kept within bounds'.[4]

Parker's other disservice, in Nelson's view, was the destruction of the prizes, done on the recommendation of carpenters Nelson considered to be rascals. The commander-in-chief described the captures as 'of a class not to be managed', and claimed he had no men to put into them. But when Nelson had destroyed prizes at the Nile, he had at least demanded compensation from the Admiralty to ensure that the men were not deprived of the prize money due on vessels taken into the navy or sold. Parker, already rich on West Indian prize money, had no such sensibilities, and seems not to have given the matter a thought. Nelson regarded the commander-in-chief's action as a 'wanton waste'. The *Sjaelland* and *Indfødsretten* could have been repaired and sold. 'Admirals &c. may be rewarded,' he complained, 'but if you destroy the prizes, what have poor lieutenants, warrant-officers and the inferior officers and men to look to? Nothing!' Angry at what he regarded as a dereliction of responsibility, Nelson appealed to the Admiralty to ask the House of Commons to support 'a gift to this fleet'. His other attempts to intervene in the matter of spoils were not entirely self-serving. He persuaded Parker and Graves to place the flag business with Davison, partly to oblige a friend but also because he trusted his efficient management, and sought better treatment for the soldiers. It had been agreed that the troops would share with the sailors for prizes taken 'at sea' but the special responsibilities of army officers were inadequately recognised. Nelson argued that the field officers should share in the portion of spoil assigned to the naval captains, and Stewart stand with the flag officers, but by no means all naval officers agreed.[5]

After writing his report to Parker on the day after the battle, Nelson took it to the *London* and found that Lindholm and Captain Steen Bille had arrived with Denmark's reply to the demands Parker had made the previous day. Denmark would not leave the League, as Britain demanded, but offered to negotiate between Britain and Russia if Britain agreed to lift her embargo on Danish shipping. This was drawing Parker beyond the simple outline of his instructions, which directed the admiral to demand the surrender of the enemy fleet and arsenal if Britain's terms were rejected. He decided that his vice admiral would be better handling the business, and arranged for Nelson to go ashore to continue negotiations face-to-face with the crown prince. So far Nelson had done the planning and fighting, and now it seemed as if he was expected to do the talking as well.

And thus, in the afternoon of 3 April, Nelson, Thesiger and Hardy were landed at the South Customs House Quay opposite the Sixtus battery to face an uncertain reception from an inflamed crowd. Near the quay the gunwales of the sunken *Nyborg* still peeped above the surface of the water in silent tribute to the destruction wrought by the British fleet. Curious crowds pressed forward to see the famous admiral, but according to Hardy 'extraordinary to be told'

Nelson 'was received with as much admiration as when we went to [the] Lord Mayor's show [in London]'. It was amenable enough for Nelson to decline a carriage and to walk to the palace of Amalienborg, turning left into the wide Amaliegade Street and towards the square on which the palace stood. Soldiers of the royal guard rushed feverishly back and forth to shield the admiral from potential danger, but he passed under a wooden colonnade to be received in the palace without significant jeopardy. A welcoming dinner concluded, Nelson was shown into a sparsely furnished room for a two-hour discussion with the crown prince, whom he had met as long ago as 1781, when he had come to Denmark in the *Albermarle*. Fortunately the other architect of recent Danish policy, the foreign minister, Count Bernstorff, took no part in the talks, though Nelson met him in passing and candidly told him that he had taken 'a very wrong part' in bringing the two countries to blows.[6]

Nelson entered the negotiations singularly handicapped. He had not expected to fill this role, which had aptly belonged to Drummond, Vansittart or Parker, and unlike any resident ambassador or accredited and properly briefed negotiator, knew little of Denmark's concerns. He may not even have been entirely clear about Parker's instructions. Nelson had discussed aspects of the crisis with Spencer, St Vincent and Troubridge in London, and presumably spoke briefly to his commander-in-chief, but had been counselled by no practised mind. Indeed, upon leaving for England after speaking with Nelson on 23 March, Vansittart had realised the admiral's inadequate grasp of the diplomatic dimensions of the dispute, and on 8 April wrote to him from London, suggesting useful 'ideas' respecting 'the measures which it might be proper to adopt' should Denmark seek an armistice. If the admirals had no 'special instructions' they could not conclude a lasting agreement, but might agree 'a cessation of arms' while submitting the enemy's propositions to London. Such an armistice should rest upon 'conditions as may enforce the observance of good faith', such as a Danish agreement to disarm. Vansittart's letter did not reach Nelson in time, and it is a tribute to Nelson's own insight that he had anticipated much that it contained.[7]

Militarily, Nelson had the upper hand. His bomb vessels were ready, anchored just out of range of the shore defences and protected by gun brigs, but their weaponry was unreliable, and damage to the town and civilian casualties could easily increase, rather than weaken, the enemy's intransigence. Nelson's plan was to appease Denmark, and detach her from her allies. As he said a few days later, 'We wish to make them feel that we are their real friends.' But he began his negotiations virtually isolated, without a credible voice to advise him, and was confronted by a phalanx of professional politicians and national advisers. He also lacked key pieces of information, including exactly what was motivating Denmark, and whether any amount of pain he could inflict would achieve Britain's objectives. On their part, the crown prince and his associates had been talking for most of the previous night. Three older ministers urged the prince to agree to the British demands to spare the city, but Bernstorff stood firm. If Denmark went over to the British, then Russia, France, Sweden and Prussia might strip her of Norway, Holstein, Slesvig and Jutland. In the end, the joint wrath of outraged allies and supporters looked a more compelling argument than seven bomb vessels. The crown prince agreed with Bernstorff, and chose to hazard his city and his life; a trenchant attitude, and willingness to take another beating, did not bode well for Nelson's success.[8]

The talks opened badly. Nelson's humanity to the wounded Danes, his praise for the defenders of Copenhagen and his constantly reiterated belief that Britain and Denmark were not natural enemies won respect and sympathy. He presented himself as a well-wisher, ready to rescue the Danes from the malignant foreigners who had misled them. This went part of the way, and Lindholm had already flattered the admiral as 'a friend of the re-establishment of peace and good harmony between this country and Great Britain', but it could not bridge the great chasm between the negotiators. Negotiations opened with a fruitless exchange of irreconcilable views, in which both sides struggled for the moral high ground by stigmatising the other as the aggressor. Nelson said that Britons would grieve to learn that Denmark had fired upon their flag, but the crown prince swiftly interrupted with the observation that it was Parker who had declared war on Denmark. With some justice, Nelson accused the Danes of joining a coalition that was hostile to Britain. Russia's overseas trade was marginal, and she had no genuine intrinsic interest in an alliance of neutral traders. By falling in with the tsar, Denmark had become a serf to his wider military purposes, and was drawn into an inevitable clash with Britain. But the prince demurred, denying that the League was anything but a commercial coalition, with no ill will towards the British. If Russia tried to push Denmark into such a war as Nelson described, the Danes would refuse.[9]

Nor was there any consensus over the prickly issue of neutral rights. The prince explained the indignity imposed upon Denmark every time British ships searched her convoys for contraband. On thin ice, Nelson said that Denmark was advocating complete freedom of the seas. If that condition was admitted, she would suffer as well as Britain. He instanced Denmark's existing prerogatives to control shipping in the Sound and levy duties, and asked how they would be affected if Hamburg or others challenged them on the principle of 'freedom' of navigation. There was little prospect of reaching agreement here.

However, as neither Nelson nor the Danes wanted a bombardment, there remained a frayed thread of hope. The crown prince was willing to open the facilities of Copenhagen to the British fleet, which Nelson stated as one prerequisite for an understanding, and he repeatedly offered to mediate between Britain and Russia. An admiral he might be, but Nelson was smart enough to smell a trap. If he permitted Denmark to stand as an intermediary, her claim to have been an unaligned, honest broker would have been conceded. Nelson rightly replied that Denmark could not be an intermediary, when she was herself an interested party.

The talks were laboured, with pauses for translation, but Nelson made substantial ground. He realised that Denmark's fear of Russia gave her little room for manoeuvre. 'Denmark, situated as she was, could not make a peace with you,' he told Clarence the next month. 'The moment she had done so, Russia, Sweden and perhaps Prussia would have been at war with her, and all her possessions within one week (except Zealand) would have fallen into the hands of her new enemies.' This was a major advance in insight and it helped move the talks beyond unrealistic demands that Denmark repudiate the League. In this context, Nelson told the crown prince that if Britain's terms were unacceptable, there was an alternative. Denmark must disarm, putting herself beyond the power of doing the British harm. This suggests that Nelson had some familiarity with Parker's instructions of 23 March, which implied that if a treaty could not be made the British might find a surrender of the Danish fleet and arsenal satisfactory. This offered a possible escape from the alternatives of compliance or bombardment, and the crown prince asked what Nelson meant by disarmament. Nelson's defined it as dispensing with 'any force beyond the customary establishment'. That 'establishment', he owned, might incorporate the guard ships Denmark kept in the Sound, but probably not the five sail of the line she had in the Kattegat or on the coast of Norway.[10]

Disarmament *per se* was not acceptable to the crown prince, but it might afford grounds for a compromise, and he politely agreed to put the matter to his council. It was therefore agreed that the truce would be extended until 5 April. In the meantime, the prince said agreeably, would Nelson meet the king's son and brother, who both wished to be presented to the famous English hero? Now this was exactly the sort of proposal that Nelson could accept, and he charmingly obliged.

Nelson had got further than Vansittart, who had been refused a hearing. His guns had brought the Danes to the table, and he had successfully projected the image of a state not inherently inimical to Denmark. He had bought two more days, but must have been conscious that time was running out for a successful strike against Russia, the nucleus of the Northern League. After the first day of negotiations no one could truly say whether the battle of Copenhagen had finished.

2

The following day, 4 April, was frustrating. Nelson was desperate to get to Revel before the Russian fleet could unite at Kronstadt, but the ball was in Denmark's court, and the British could only wait. Fremantle, his closest colleague in the fleet, joined Nelson for breakfast in the *St George* that morning, and then the two friends visited poor Thompson on the *Bellona*. He was in a bad way, and

Nelson continued to monitor his progress. 'I charge you not to write a line,' he said in a note of eight days later, 'only send me word how you are.'[11]

The truce was due to expire on 5 April, which was Easter Sunday. Nelson felt a bone-numbing chill that morning, as the temperature dropped with a fierce south-westerly wind and snow, but after an early visit to Fremantle he continued to the *London*, where the Danish negotiators, Lindholm and Major General Ernst Frederick Waltersdorff, formerly a governor of the island of St Croix, duly called upon the commander-in-chief. Nelson was invited to participate, but when the issue of Danish disarmament was revisited, it seemed that the breach had widened overnight. The Danes refused to offer the British fleet full access to their facilities and resources, something that Nelson had thought conceded the previous day, and, on their side, the British would not allow Denmark the number of warships she claimed constituted her 'customary establishment'. However, Lindholm and Waltersdorff proposed an extension of the ceasefire on the basis of a Danish guarantee that her ships would not be rearmed, re-equipped or repositioned during the stipulated time. Parker fished for something more permanent, and finally demanded that Denmark supply a written statement testifying that she would grant Britain the right to provision and repair in her ports, and unequivocally declare that she had no agreements with Russia that were inimical to British interests, nor would she contribute ships to a combined northern fleet. The Danish negotiators left with an extra day to chew it over, but the prospects were gloomy. Above all, Denmark felt unable to repudiate Russia or renege on her commitments to the League.

The impasse only widened on the 6th. Lindholm and Waltersdorff returned with a letter Bernstorff had concocted, but it fell far short of Parker's requirements. British ships would be granted access to Danish ports, but not to naval stores, an offer that granted no more than the general usage accorded ships in distress. As for the relations between Denmark and Russia, the Danes disingenuously declared that they had made no compacts inimical to Britain, but would only make a verbal statement that they would not contribute to a northern fleet, in other words a commitment that could later be denied. It was, as Parker said grumpily, all 'highly unsatisfactory'. Denmark's negotiators returned to their position of the preceding day. If a permanent agreement was impossible, perhaps an armistice covering a limited period of time was the answer, something that trapped neither side in a long-term commitment. At this point Parker took Nelson aside for a private consultation, when he riffled through his papers and instructions for inspiration. The admirals returned to the table stony-faced, and Parker presented the Danes with a written ultimatum. It stated that he had no power to conclude an armistice, only an agreement on the basis of the demands Vansittart had brought the previous month, demands the Danes had then refused to examine. He gave Denmark twenty-four hours to comply. The negotiations had come full circle. Britain wanted Denmark to quit the League and make a defensive alliance with her, and Denmark could do neither. Both parties were now near the end of their patience, and, in an angry exchange, Lindholm declared that he regretted that hostilities had ceased at all, while the British admirals stood by their threat of bombardment.

A deep gloom fell over the protagonists. Parker sent Otway home on the *Cruizer* with dispatches warning that hostilities might have to be renewed, while the next morning found Nelson again in the King's Deep, examining his bomb vessels and sounding the northern reaches of the Middle Ground. The process of stripping the prizes of their usable stores before destroying them urgently continued. Ashore some precautions against a bombardment were being made, including the removal of furniture and artworks from the Palace of Amalienborg. The 7th looked as if it might witness more fighting. The wind was from the south-west, unsuitable for sailing south towards Revel, but not for resuming the attack on Copenhagen.

The issue of war or peace was on a knife edge, and the tension was immense as a boat pulled for the British flagship the following day with the familiar figures of Lindholm and Waltersdorff sitting expectantly inside. They had a surprise for Parker. After studying Sir Hyde's badly written ultimatum, Bernstorff had found a loophole. Parker had demanded the Danes accept a treaty on the basis of Vansittart's proposals, but Vansittart had been refused an audience in Copenhagen, and the Danes claimed to be entirely ignorant of his terms. Probably simply playing for time, they now asked for a copy of Vansittart's submission. It struck home, because Parker had 'taken for granted that it had been communicated' to the Danes. He admitted that he did not have a copy, and lapsed into a deep, humiliating silence. In that case, said the Danes, pressing their advantage, the parties might usefully address themselves to concluding a temporary armistice, as they had argued before, leaving the lasting peace to the politicians.[12]

Parker had outmanoeuvred himself, and was soon exploring the meat of an armistice which he had only recently denied he had the power to make. They discussed a Danish undertaking not to rearm their ships, and a temporary suspension of Denmark's pact with the northern powers pending negotiations between the British and Danish governments. It was disarmament and a suspension of the League of a kind. The Danish negotiators quibbled over the meaning of suspension and the duration of the armistice, which Parker argued should not be less than four months, and departed. It was agreed that Nelson and Stewart would land the next day at noon to attempt a final negotiation.

Nelson claimed that the ensuing armistice was his: 'be it good or bad, it is my own,' he said. In a sense, that was true. The pith of Parker's orders was plain: if Denmark refused to leave the northern alliance and make a new one with Britain, he was to destroy the Danish fleet and its dockyards. Had orders been strictly obeyed, Nelson and Parker would have already been throwing shot and shells into the Danish capital. The notion that Britain would accept something less than a repudiation of the League and defensive alliance had been sown in Nelson's first negotiation of 3 April. The alternative of British access to Copenhagen and voluntary disarmament had become the pivot of the discussions. To this Parker had added the idea of a temporary armistice. Though the two admirals stood together, it was almost certainly Nelson who gave Parker the courage to adjust his instructions.[13]

Nevertheless, Parker and Nelson were acting logically. They needed to advance upon Russia, and further operations at Copenhagen, even successful ones, stood to waste time and resources that could ill be spared. Furthermore, as the British advanced up the Baltic, they needed to cover their rear and communications, and that meant neutralising Denmark in some way. An armistice served both purposes, and it neither prejudiced the outcome of permanent negotiations nor denied Britain leverage in them, especially as it left Danish merchantmen and colonies in her hands, and the Danish fleet severely debilitated. The armistice fell short of what the British had wanted, but in the circumstances it made practical sense.

The deal had first to be made. Early on 8 April, Nelson, Stewart, Foley, Fremantle and Parker's secretary, the multi-lingual Reverend Alexander John Scott, were towed in a barge by a British schooner to the Trekroner, where a Danish barge waited to guide them to the Customs Quay. The wind blew cold from the south-west, the rain descended in torrents and the spray-sodden occupants disembarked to be received by Captain Lindholm. A carriage whisked the Britons to the palace, past bedraggled crowds of spectators, and inside they stood beside a blazing fire to dry their clothes before being conducted into a spartan conference room. Lindholm and Waltersdorff opened for Denmark in a first round of negotiations designed to clear away the less contentious issues. Bernstorff was again conspicuous by his absence, and Nelson was told that he was ill, though, in truth, he was seen as an irritant and kept out of the way. Nelson was probably relieved, for he detested Bernstorff, and later claimed to have sent him a message advising him 'to leave off his ministerial duplicity, and to recollect he had now British admirals to deal with who came with their hearts in their hands'. But with or without the Danish foreign minister, Nelson embarked upon hours of intense concentration, broken only by the delays of translation. The medium was French, at that time the diplomatic language of Europe.[14]

Several articles were agreed fairly easily. A ceasefire would be observed, embracing Denmark and its islands, but not Norway, which was excluded at the request of the Danes. Nelson agreed to land all prisoners, but Denmark would certify the number so that the British would not be disadvantaged in the event of a renewal of hostilities. The Danish warships would remain in their existing state, however damaged, and the Danish ports would be open to British ships seeking non-military supplies; the last a concession Nelson felt compelled to make. Other issues were difficult. Lindholm and Waltersdorff ruled out Denmark relinquishing the League, and were worried about the length of the proposed armistice. Nelson wanted sixteen weeks, to provide plenty of time for him to deal with Russia, but Waltersdorff argued for a shorter period, sufficient only for Danish envoys to go to London and return. The Danes clearly expected Russia to compromise any agreement they made sooner or later, and wanted as short an armistice as possible. At one point one of the Danish negotiators hinted to his partner that a renewal of hostilities might be preferable to yielding to Nelson's demand. Scott grasped the gist, and Nelson said, 'Renew hostilities! Tell him that we are ready at a moment, ready to bombard this very night!' It was enough, and the Danes apologised.[15]

At two Nelson stood up from five hours' talking. Lindholm conducted the British to a nearby stateroom, where a levee was being held, and the crown prince, his brother-in-law and various princes and dignitaries obsequiously attended the British hero. The party then dined, Nelson leaning on a friendly arm as he ascended a staircase after the crown prince. He sat at the prince's right hand, one of fifty guests who ate and drank with conviviality. That done, the second session began. The prince himself represented Denmark, but Nelson, who had now been active for nine unremitting hours, continued for Britain.

The talks jarred and jammed. Nelson defended his demand that the Danes preserve an unqualified neutrality, suspending the operation of the League during an armistice of sixteen weeks, and the prince as steadfastly explained that the extension was far too long. Then something extraordinary happened. Lindholm suddenly entered the room and whispered to the prince. He left, and neither at that time nor afterwards did the Danes hint at what had been said. The prince kept a straight face, but suddenly abandoned his resistance to Nelson's demand for a substantial armistice, and agreed to a period of fourteen weeks. Nelson was satisfied. 'Now, sir,' he tempted. 'This is settled. Suppose we write peace instead of armistice?' But the prince affably declined to go that far. He would be happy to make peace with Britain, he said, but must bring it forward slowly, so as not to sow the seeds of 'new wars'.[16]

The matter was done by 7.30. It was an adequate result, and Nelson was no doubt flattered by the attentions he had received. 'The ladies of the court came to the door during dinner to see Nelson,' Fremantle told his wife, 'and he was received on shore by multitudes.' Tiring, too, for the admiral did not get back to the *London* to make his report until after dark. There were now no obstacles to moving upon Revel, he told Parker, and it was time they were going. Then he returned to the *St George*, where at last he could remove his uniform, sodden once again in the return passage. It was not surprising that after such an exhausting, inclement day he rose the following morning feverish, but after the Danes had brought the armistice to the *London* for signing, Parker still required his vice admiral to carry it ashore for the prince's ratification. He was not back until six in the evening. During the day the two sides disengaged. The truculent bomb vessels withdrew, boatloads of prisoners were rowed ashore and the British hurriedly prepared copies of the armistice for Stewart, who would carry the news to London, and for dispatch to John, Lord Carysfort, who represented His Britannic Majesty in Berlin.[17]

It had been Nelson's armistice, and he knew he would be judged by it. Not surprisingly, he was 'in a fright' about whether the government would approve of what he had done. The Danes were pleased, for they had upheld their honour, escaped further injury and gained space to review their position without committing themselves one way or another. The crucial piece of intelligence that Lindholm had brought the prince during his negotiations with Nelson had thrown a very different complexion upon the politics of the Baltic. The tsar, Paul I, son of Catherine the Great, and fulcrum of the League of Armed Neutrality, was dead! For long he had been alarming the Russian nobility, which he considered degenerate and in need of reform, but in the end it was a party of disaffected officers who had ended the emperor's life. On the night of 23 March they had invaded his rooms in Mikhailovski Castle, pursued him from one piece of furniture to another, and finally, after stunning him with a blow from a marble paperweight, strangled him to death with his own scarf. It now remained to be seen what his successor would do, and whether the anti-British policy would prevail. From being a threat, Nelson's extensive armistice now looked useful to Denmark, providing a period of reflection and re-evaluation while the new Russian policy was assessed.[18]

A by-product of Nelson's diplomacy was a residue of goodwill he had built up in Denmark. When Nelson and Stewart had gone ashore the last time the people were almost enthusiastic. 'Nelson is a warrior,' the admiral wrote to Emma, 'but will not be a butcher. I am sure, could you have seen the adoration and respect, you would have cried for joy. There are no honours can be conferred equal to this.' Despite his usual narcissicism – as in Vienna the admiral distributed self-proclaiming gifts, including a portrait, two copies of the laudatory autobiographical 'sketch' that he had written for the *Naval Chronicle*, two of Davison's Nile medals and a Boulton Neapolitan medal, the recipients being Lindholm, Waltersdorff and the Naval Academy – many of the Danes liked Nelson. Waltersdorff would later visit him in England, while Lindholm became a regular correspondent and kept in touch throughout the Baltic campaign. When Nelson heard of the death of the tsar, he wrote Lindholm a letter of congratulation, hoping that it would smooth the transition to peace. Lindholm agreed, replying that the latest from Hamburg suggested that Russia was now interested in releasing the British ships and goods she had detained. Why, Nelson said optimistically, if Lindholm and he got together he doubted not that they could settle Anglo-Danish affairs 'in half an hour to the mutual honour and advantage of both kingdoms'.[19]

Nelson spent much of 9 April preparing a package for Stewart to carry to London, justifying his armistice to who mattered to him, including Addington, the prime minister, St Vincent, Troubridge, Minto and Clarence. To St Vincent he admitted that he was tired and ready to quit. 'If I have deserved well, let me retire; if ill, for Heaven's sake supersede me, for I cannot exist in this state.' He pointed out that the armistice had been necessary to move Parker forward. Had he commanded, the British would have been in Revel a fortnight ago, and even now he doubted that the commander-in-chief would move before the coming week. Nelson had sought permission to blockade the Swedes in Karlskrona to prevent the Russians joining them, but without success. [20]

Nelson anticipated criticism, but most people appreciated what had been done. Clarence told his '*best* and *oldest friend*' that the victory had been 'the most elusive' and 'brilliant' in naval history, and the armistice an essential step. The prime minister announced the delight of the government, and solicited more private communications from 'the life and soul' of the fleet. Like many sensitive souls, Nelson felt what barbs there were keenly, and reacted sharply to the king's modest assessment that the armistice was acceptable 'upon a consideration of all the circumstances'. 'I am sorry that the armistice is only approved under *all* considerations,' Nelson told Addington. 'Now I own myself of opinion that every part of the *all* was to the advantage of our king and country.' He was right, for on the spot he had seen that the British instructions were unrealistic. 'There was no damage we could do her equal to the loss of everything [she would have suffered offending Russia],' he explained, and Britain had to do the best she could, and confront the crucial opponent. 'I look upon the Northern League to be like a tree, of which Paul was the trunk and Sweden and Denmark the branches,' Addington read. 'If I can get at the trunk, and hew it down, the branches fall of course. But I may lop the branches, and yet not be able to fell the tree, and my power must be weaker when its greatest strength is required. If we could have cut up the Russian fleet, that was my object.'[21]

It was irrefutable logic. The armistice put Denmark out of the way, and opened the seaways to Russia and Sweden.

3

In solitude the admiral at the eye of this northern storm faced the personal demons that crept upon him. Would Emma be alarmed by reports of his visits ashore? The letter he wrote to her on 9 April spoke of the armistice in one breath and his fidelity to her in the next. 'Having done my duty, not all the world should get me out of the ship. No! I owe it to my promise . . .' The wellbeing of his mistress and daughter was never far away. Starting at every threat, he urged Emma to inoculate Horatia against smallpox, and when he thought one of his portraits of Emma was becoming paler, he worried that it portended misadventure, and that she was in danger. Thomson, he said, 'has cried on account of his child. He begs, for Heaven's sake, you will take care that the nurse had no bad disorder, for he has been told that Captain Howard, before he was six weeks' old, had the bad disorder which has ruined his constitution to this day. He [Thomson] desires me to say he has never wrote his aunt [Fanny] since he sailed . . . He does not, nor cannot, care about her; he believes she has a most unfeeling heart. I only recommend the example of dear, good Lady Hamilton. She is a pattern, & do not let your uncle [Sir William] persuade you to receive bad company. When you do, your friend hopes to be killed.' It was a curiously inept document, slipping in and out of the 'Thomson' persona, and totally misconceiving the natures of the people it described. The man with such a clear grasp of the strategy and tactics of the northern campaign completely misjudged his women, entrusting the fascinating little daughter he loved to an irresponsible guardian whom he regarded, despite those recurring fears for the compay she kept, as a suitable 'pattern' for life.[22]

In public he was as brisk for business as usual, and grew irritable at Parker's dilatory progress. Until the 11th the British refurbished, released prisoners and lightened the three-deckers, temporarily transferring stores to transports for the passage over the Drogden shallows between the islands of Amager and Saltholm. Nelson's journal reveals his growing impatience. 'Sir Hyde gave such directions as he thought proper for the watering of the fleet, which I do not expect from my observations to see finished this fortnight to come,' he wrote sarcastically on the 11th. And the next day, 'Fresh breezes at N.W., fine wind to go through the grounds. Why are we here when it is reported that the Swedish fleet is above?' Not all his remarks were so private, for Nelson continued to undermine his commander-in-chief with complaining letters to the Admiralty. 'Nothing can rouse our unaccountable lethargy,' he told Troubridge. He was so frustrated that he planned to serve with the fleet until it reached Revel, after which, if there was no immediate prospect of fighting, he would resign. By the 12th he was asking to be superseded before the end of the month.[23]

The afternoon of the 13th saw the *Ganges* lead a dozen ships of the line, including Parker's *London*, over the shallows, but there were not enough transports to unload both the three-deckers at the same time, and Nelson was ordered to wait with the *St George* and the remainder of the fleet. 'Therefore here we lay perfectly idle,' he wrote in his journal. Once across the shoals, Sir Hyde made for Koge Bay, a few miles to the south-east, and ordered Nelson to join him there as soon as he could. What happened next was almost predictable. Nelson busied himself with getting his ship over the shoals. He hired an American ship, the *Franklin*, to take her guns across the shoals, and loaded sixty tons of water into the *Desiree* frigate. But about six o'clock in the evening of 15 April, before the operation could be completed, the *Amazon* frigate sped in with a message from the commander-in-chief. According to new intelligence the

Swedish fleet was at sea, amounting to fourteen sail, seven or eight of them ships of the line. If the *St George* was still too heavy to pass the shallows, Nelson was to leave it behind and use any means available to reach Koge Bay, where he could transfer his flag to the *Elephant*. Parker now seemed incapable of doing anything significant without Nelson.[24]

Though Nelson was bemoaning his health to every sympathetic ear, with dark intimations of imminent death, he sprang into action upon receipt of Parker's express and provided another of the canonical pictures of his leadership. Calling instantly for a six-oared boat, which he entered without waiting for so much as a cloak to shut out the sharp wind, he began a gruelling twenty-four-mile row through the darkness against wind and current. Briarly, the master who had distinguished himself at Copenhagen, went with him. 'All I had ever seen or heard of him [Nelson] could not half so clearly prove to me the singular and unbounded zeal of this truly great man,' Briarly reported. For five hours they ploughed through the waves, with spray flying about them as day turned into night. Just as in his pursuit of the Nile fleet, Nelson seemed single-mindedly focused on his quarry, unperturbed by the cold that 'struck' Briarly 'to the heart', and he neither ate nor drank, nor accepted an offer of an overcoat. 'Do you not think the fleet has sailed?' he asked. 'I should suppose not, my Lord,' replied Briarly. 'If they are, we shall follow them to Carlscrona [Karlskrona] in the boat, by God!' Nelson remarked. After a remarkable journey Nelson reached Koge Bay, found the fleet, and, boarding the *Elephant* unheralded before midnight, turned into bed in his old cabin without Foley even knowing he was aboard. The *Elephant* was not the happiest ship, and six or seven were flogged in the few days Nelson remained aboard, but the vice admiral was a reassuring presence to many. Among the soldiers, Sergeant James FitzGibbon of the 49th Regiment, saw him daily. 'He appeared the most mild and gentle being, and it was delightful to me to hear the way the sailors spoke of him . . . My greatest wish then was that I had been a sailor rather than a soldier.'[25]

In the meantime, Otway had brought the news of the battle and the opening of negotiations to England. Rumours of Nelson's doings and news of Paul's death had reached Lord Hawkesbury, the British foreign secretary, on 14 April. The next day Otway was in London, and the victory was announced to parliament the following day. Addington boasted 'that Lord Nelson had shown himself as wise as he was brave, and proved that there may be united in the same person, the talents of the warrior and the statesman'. The spreading tidings sealed Nelson's reputation as the country's foremost warrior, and aroused joy in well-wishers. St Vincent, who had expected to lose 'one or more ships' at Copenhagen, enthused that Nelson had outstripped every previous admiral, while Davison swore that the good news had cured his gout. The Hamiltons entertained a distinguished company in Piccadilly, and Emma danced the tarantella with such energy that she wore out three successive partners, her husband, the Duke of

Noia (a Neapolitan nobleman) and a servant, before finishing with Fatima, the whole performance one observer found markedly as indecorous as it was fascinating. William Nelson was there, excited beyond measure at what the victory might bring him. His behaviour 'was more extraordinary than ever', Sir William wrote to Nelson. 'He would get up suddenly to cut a caper, rubbing his hands every time that the thought of your fresh laurels came into his head.'[26]

Spencer had the decency to send Fanny an account of the battle on 16 April, and she wrote to her husband of the 'general joy throughout the kingdom', assuring him at the same time of her undiminished affection for him, and apologising for any neglect or offence she had given. She was always ready to forgive and reach out, but he was in no mood to listen and tried to head off her 'inquiries' by urging Davison to tell her to leave him alone. Though Fanny was still being received at court, her support in the Nelson family thinned when Maurice, the most likeable brother, was suddenly struck down by a serious illness. Nelson's two sisters were still holding firm but most wounded of all was the old rector, Edmund Nelson, torn between his favourite son and his favourite 'daughter'. He had been truly shocked by their separation, and tried desperately to repair the damage. He invited Fanny to Bath, where he and the Matchams were taking the waters, hoping to reunite her with the family, and in a typically pious outpouring to Nelson urged him to 'return to domestic joys' or at least send Fanny 'a line from your own hand'. At home the family crisis rather than the politics of the Baltic predominated.[27]

In Whitehall the British government wrestled with the fallout from Paul's death and the battle of Copenhagen. The defeat of the Danes did not stir as much national enthusiasm as conquests over traditional enemies, and the delicacy of the political temperature led the government to avoid triumphalism. There was no public illumination, and no vote of thanks from the City, though the battle was celebrated in several new songs and poems, and in performances at such places as Sadler's Wells and the Royal Circus. The first task of government was to reassess policy. Early indications suggested that Paul's successor, the young Alexander I, would pursue a pacific course, and on 17 April the Admiralty wrote to Parker, acquainting him with the news and advising a new caution. Hostilities with Russia were now to be temporarily suspended, and Parker was to send a representative to the tsar to ascertain whether the Russian embargo on British ships would be lifted and their crews released. If the answer was in the affirmative, conflict would come to an end. In the event of a refusal to lift the embargo, Sir Hyde was to make the suspension of hostilities conditional upon an agreement to open negotiations to solve outstanding differences. Only if the new tsar rejected conciliation was Parker to declare that either party was free to resume hostilities upon giving twelve hours' notice. Sweden was also to be given an opportunity to restore amicable relations. These instructions left London for the fleet with Otway on Saturday, 19 April.[28]

The day after Otway began his return journey Stewart reached London with new dispatches describing the final armistice. The lieutenant colonel also supplied an authentic verbal account of all that had transpired, revealing the stark dearth of leadership exercised by Parker. Among other events, the affair of signal number 39 now raised its ugly head, despite its absence from the fleet dispatches. St Vincent acted decisively, appointing Nelson commander-in-chief on 21 April and recalling Parker. A letter from Nelson, asking to come home, was already on its way to England, but their lordships at the Admiralty knew nothing of that. Thanks to Stewart, they did know that Nelson's initiative, decisiveness and notorious disobedience had saved the campaign, and that the doubts about his fitness for the role of a commander-in-chief had been dispelled. But there were still uncertainties about how the achievement might be commemorated in such a difficult political climate. The first object was clearly to restore amicable relationships with the Baltic powers, to detach them as far as possible from Napoleon, and to preserve the effectiveness of Britain's naval strength.

When George Rose visited the Admiralty at the end of April, he found St Vincent hesitating. He was determined to issue the medals that normally accompanied a victory on this scale, but worried about whether Parker's division merited inclusion. The other complication, of course, was the effect such a distribution might have upon relations with Denmark at a time when she was being eased out of the enemy camp. In the end medals were not issued to survivors until 1847, and the custom of promoting the first lieutenants of engaged ships equally forgone, a particularly pusillanimous decision given the severity of the fighting. Nelson received rewards, however. Lloyd's added £500 to the sum they had already provided for a commemoration dinner service, sufficient to add soup plates to an order he had placed with Rundell and Bridge. And on 15 May the *London Gazette*, a mouthpiece for the government, intimated that Nelson would be raised in the peerage and become Viscount Nelson of the Nile and of Burnham Thorpe in the County of Norfolk. It superseded the barony, which notwithstanding remained in its own right, but Davison typified a popular reaction when he grumbled that the admiral ought to have been made a viscount long before.[29]

Out in the Baltic and blissfully unaware of his fall from grace, Parker was still hunting the Swedes. Nelson's journal gave his take on the story. 'Received information that on Tuesday the 14th the Swedish fleet of ten sail of the line and two frigates were to the N.E. off Bornholm, six or seven leagues,' he wrote on the 17th. 'Pray God we may get up with them!' After the five hours he had had to endure in an open boat to join the hunt, his anxiety was natural, but two days later the tone had changed: 'The *Shannon* made the signal for a strange fleet in the N.E., going large with the wind on the larboard quarter. Signal for a general chase. At eleven [o'clock] saw they [the Swedish ships] were at anchor in the outer part of the harbour of Carlscroona [Karlskrona]. *Damn them!*' After its foray, the Scandic fleet had scampered back through a narrow harbour entrance to sit securely behind shoals and rocks, leaving Parker and Nelson to fume outside. Nelson advised proceeding against the Russian fleet, leaving a nominal force to blockade Karlskrona, but Sir Hyde had no stomach for such boldness. 'Under all circumstances I do not feel I ought to proceed higher up the Baltic until I hear from England, or that I am joined by Admiral Totty,' he agonised. From this quandary he was rescued by the arrival of a Danish cutter on 22 April, forwarding a letter from the Russian foreign minister, Nikita Petrovich, Count de Pahlen, dated the 20th. It announced the death of Paul. Russia wanted to end the conflict, and trusted that Parker would suspend hostilities in the Baltic. Soon afterwards Sir Hyde also received a letter from James Crauford, Britain's envoy extraordinary in Lower Saxony, urging him to hold fire and await developments. No doubt relieved at such an unexpected deliverance, the commander-in-chief replied to the Russian minister explaining that he was halting hostilities until he heard from London. So saying, he took the fleet back to Koge Bay, and wrote home for new instructions on the 25th.[30]

Whitehall would rightly judge Parker's withdrawal to Koge a strategic error. By stationing himself south of Copenhagen, he had left the Swedes free to leave Karlskrona and join the Russians at Revel, all before he had any assurance that amity would be restored. He should have left a detachment to contain the Swedish fleet. Lord Hobart, the new secretary of war, believed that Parker ought to have informed the Swedes that he would commit no hostilities providing their fleet did not try to leave Karlskrona. This is exactly what Nelson did off his own bat as soon as he became commander-in-chief.[31]

At Koge Bay Nelson was 'struck . . . to the heart' by the after-effects of his reckless voyage in the open boat, although he had regained the relative comfort of the *St George* on the 21st. Sunday, 26 April, was a good day for the fleet. Otway arrived from London in the *Lynx*, handing to Parker a packet that included the reassuring thanks of the king, parliament and Admiralty, and fresh instructions dated eight days before. These were the orders outlining the new policy towards Russia, dispatched before the Admiralty had been briefed by Stewart about the state of the fleet. After reading them Parker sent Fremantle to St Petersburg in the *Lynx* with a letter to Count de Pahlen, asking what Russia intended to do about the embargoed British ships, cargoes and crews. For Nelson it was a day of celebration. Scott performed the Sunday service on the *St George* and Nelson, despite his illness, hosted a function of his own. A flurry of invitations had gone out, each individually worded. 'Sunday the 26th being Santa Emma's birthday, I beg you will do me the favour of dining on board the *St George*, as I know you are one of her rotaries,' read Captain Tyler of the *Warrior*. 'If you don't come here on Sunday to celebrate the birthday of Santa Emma,' Fremantle was admonished, 'damn me if I ever forgive you.' The Reverend Scott, Parker, Graves and twenty-one others were at Nelson's table, and the admiral used the occasion to present Graves with one of Davison's Nile medals, symbolically inducting him into the 'Band of Brothers'.[32]

The rigorous work in wintry weather and prolonged mental strain had taken its toll of Nelson's constitution. On 4 April he had told Clarence that he had 'scarcely' slept over the last eleven days, and the night of the 27th he suffered one of the 'terrible spasms or heart-strokes' that had last laid him low in the Plymouth coach. It was, he recognised, an 'old complaint' but he feared for his life. More regularly, he was coughing badly, bringing up 'what everyone thought was my lungs', endured night fevers, and thought himself gripped by 'consumption'. Devoted officers watched him as if he had been an infant. He awoke each morning between four and five to warm milk prescribed by Foley, but often exercised on the poop until breakfast about six, when his well-kept table attracted sometimes as many as twenty guests, including 'young gentlemen' whose childish jokes he appeared to tolerate with unfailing good humour. He took lozenges contributed by Murray, but for all his hypochondria he was a bad patient and careless of his health and appearance, refusing, for instance, to have anyone but Emma cut the fingernails of his remaining hand until they became inconveniently long and fragile. Depression was his worst enemy, fed by his domestic worries and the sense that he was being used by politicians and admirals alike, some whom he had considered friends. The letters from Emma 'roused' him, encouraging him to believe that he had at least 'one dear friend who would not desert me, although all the world might'. As for the rest, in the fleet 'everybody [was] devoted and kind to me in the extreme', but beyond its confines he felt 'dreadfully pulled down'.[33]

The day after the severe 'heart' attack he asked Parker if he could return home in the *Blanche*, and, as the fighting looked to be over, Parker reluctantly consented, covering himself with a recommendation from the fleet physician. Tom Allen was soon preparing a berth for his master in the frigate, which was ready to sail for England. Nelson's spirits must have lifted at the thought of rejoining Emma, and his plans at this time can be reconstructed. He had no intention of living with Fanny again, but without a home of his own looked towards obtaining 'a good lodging in an airy situation' as a temporary residence. Reflecting, he believed that he had 'never known happiness beyond moments', and longed for peace and contentment. As soon as possible, therefore, he would take Emma back to Italy, where they had both been much loved, and relive those 'days of ease and nights of pleasure'. If there was a general peace, 'nothing shall stop my going to Bronte'. Although Nelson has sometimes been portrayed as a warmonger, which to the extent that he lusted for excitement possesses an element of truth, he entered middle age with a genuine ambition to bring the tiresome conflict to an end, and claim his share of tranquillity and peace. Amidst these reveries, he prepared the ground by writing to King Ferdinand and Prince Castelcicala, the Neapolitan minister in London, and he asked Emma to contact the queen. Ferdinand replied handsomely, promising Nelson 'gratitude, esteem and affection', three words that were music to the admiral's tormented soul. Alas, as yet Nelson knew little about the deteriorating condition of the kingdom of the Two Sicilies, or that it had been compelled to sign a servile treaty with the French. The queen for one doubted that she would ever quit the safety of Austria. But in the Baltic Nelson dreamed on, building into his scenario the approaching death of Sir William Hamilton, and the union of Emma, himself and Horatia – yet another triumvirate – under one roof.[34]

But on 5 May, mere hours before the *Blanche* sailed, the situation was suddenly overturned by the arrival of Stewart with the latest packets from London. Parker was flabbergasted to learn that he had been recalled, and that Nelson was to succeed to his command, after receiving the thanks of parliament and hearing that the armistice had been approved, but he knew that his conduct was less than had been expected, and had written defensively to his wife of his indifference to honours (perhaps anticipating that there might not be any) and his suspicions that 'trouble and anxiety' lay ahead. Friends, such as Fremantle, sensed it, too. Parker 'is afraid of Lord St Vincent, and will never, I am convinced, go to sea again'. In deposing Parker, the Admiralty effectively ended his active career. As Troubridge remarked, 'If Sir Hyde once gets his foot ashore in England, I do not think anything will get him afloat again.' Seldom, indeed, had a commander-in-chief seemed more redundant, and had the old tsar's death not transformed the nature of the campaign, his reputation might have sunk even lower, because his lethargy was seriously threatening the prospects of the expedition. He would, for example, have still been at Karlskrona on 22 April, only eleven days before the Russians made their escape from Revel. Paul's death made their flight academic, but if he had lived a failure by Parker to reach Revel in time would have been unfortunate, if not disastrous. Miserably, Parker sent Otway to the *St George* to inform Nelson that he was now the commander-in-chief, and at noon went over to the new flagship himself, surrendering his 'unexecuted orders' and instructions. At Nelson's request, Domett remained as captain of the fleet, but Scott, for all his flowering friendship with Nelson, was still Parker's chaplain and secretary and chose to accompany him home.[35]

At 4.30 the same afternoon the *Blanche* slid from the fleet with an admiral aboard as scheduled, but it was poor Parker who occupied the berth Allen had prepared for Nelson. Some were sorry to see him go, including, when he heard of it, his good friend Fremantle, who suspected that Sir Hyde would never serve again. But most felt a breath of fresh air had swept him away. There would be no more loitering at Koge Bay, for none knew better 'that idleness is the root of all evil'. When Nelson made his signal to weigh anchor at daylight on 6 May, it was greeted with cheers throughout the fleet.[36]

All knew that a new spirit was abroad. And for Horatio Nelson it was a remarkable day. He had requested leave and got promotion, and was now an official commander-in-chief for the first time. More, with some sixty-eight sail at his back, he was the effective lord of the Baltic.[37]

4

Rarely was so great an honour received so reluctantly. In his private journal Nelson noted, 'At four o'clock the *Blanche* sailed and left me the command to my great sorrow.' He meant it. In a one-sentence acknowledgement of the commission, he wrote to the Admiralty of his 'most wretched state of health'. A second letter of the same date added that if he did not have a change of climate, that is leave to come home, his 'consumption . . . will most assuredly carry me out of this world', but he would attempt to do 'something decisive' in the next fortnight 'if I can hold out so long'. The gloom barely lifted in the following days, and on 17 May he flatly told the Admiralty that he was 'unable to execute the high trust reposed in me' and formally restated his intention of coming home.[38]

To Spencer, the former first lord, he said little more. He had not rested since 23 March, was 'low and miserable' and intended 'to retire from the service and go to Bronte'. Knowing Nelson, Spencer might have thought this another play for sympathy, but the roots of Nelson's discontent had never been deeper. He was sick to death of the navy, and wanted out of it. 'Be that as it may,' he wrote to Emma, 'I will not remain, *no* not if I was *sure* of being made a *duke* with £50,000 a year. I wish for *happiness* to be my *reward*, and not titles or money.' This was serious disaffection.[39]

He was, of course, ill, and told Emma that it was 'downright murder to keep me here', but in his embittered mind the new appointment merely confirmed his belief that he was being used by self-seekers determined to exploit his talents for their own profit. As Stewart was sharp enough to recognise, Nelson was apt to dismiss his considerable physical problems except when suffering from depression. The admiral's 'bad health', he suggested, was due 'more to chagrin than to any other cause'. His 'mind was not at ease' and 'with him mind and health invariably sympathised'. So it was with this latest slough. Nelson could rightly complain that his services had been ill requited in terms of money and decorations, at least in his native country. They had indeed been niggardly. But in his mortification the admiral was apt to pass over many of the favours done him, for despite an outstanding record of insubordination he had been the recipient of opportunities that many flag officers would have craved in vain. He could not see that his conduct in Sicily had created doubts about his fitness for an overall command, and that the combination of Parker and Nelson had seemed a sensible one. Nor did he appreciate the central role Stewart had played in reconstructing the Admiralty's opinion. Loyal to his chief, Otway had been relatively silent about the deficit of leadership in the Baltic command, but not

Stewart, who had visited the Admiralty, War Office and Downing Street. The effect was the immediate replacement of Parker. But Nelson saw it very differently. He was still sore about commanding the Mediterranean in an acting capacity, bearing the burdens of the post without access to its perquisites, and now he thought himself manipulated in a similar way in the Baltic. When there had been fighting to do, and prize money to win, he had been second-in-command; now, when his health was broken, and the service turned into an unrewarding drudge, he was made commander-in-chief. He was debarred, he discovered, from sharing in the prize money taken by Admiral William Dickson's North Sea fleet. And so, behind the affable leader beheld by the officers and men of the fleet, was a deeply aggrieved and brooding man who pictured himself the focus of a mean conspiracy. 'I have now all the expenses of a commander-in-chief, and am stripped even of the little chance of prize money,' he complained to his mistress. '*This* is the honour, *this* is my reward – a prison for debt.' In such circumstances he simply would not serve. 'Why should I die to do what pleases those who care not a damn for me?'[40]

Yet Nelson was still Nelson, the public servant. Although he had to familiarise himself with the instructions given to Parker, and was unclear about what had passed between his predecessor and the Russians, he acted vigorously. Peace was expected, but not confirmed, and it was necessary to keep the constituent parts of the hostile fleet isolated. Rear Admiral Thomas Totty was coming out to join him, and Nelson decided to base him on Bornholm, an island occupying a strategic position in the entrance to the Baltic and some sixty miles SSE of the Swedish naval base at Karlskrona. From there he could use half a dozen capital ships to blockade the Swedish fleet, while Nelson went up the Baltic to Revel and Kronstadt. The Admiralty's last general orders of 17 April, he found, had warned him to treat Russia gently until the disposition of the new tsar was known, but at the same time to keep the northern detachments divided. A nice conundrum! Nelson hoped that by leaving Totty's force and the fleet's bomb vessels, fireships and gun brigs at Bornholm, and proceeding to Revel with a reduced force of eleven capital ships, attended only by a frigate, brig and lugger, he could avoid unnecessary provocation while preserving a necessary amount of force.[41]

At four in the afternoon of 7 May Nelson's force weighed anchor and left Koge Bay, bound upon its difficult mission of restraint and pacification. Stewart, serving in the *St George*, provided rare glimpses of the new commander-in-chief at work. Nelson thought Stewart 'the rising hope of our army', and Stewart saw the admiral as an inspiration, speaking of the 'uniform good health and discipline' that prevailed under his command, and his economic use of resources. Nelson's energy, or, as Stewart put it, his 'command of time', and his attention to individuals appeared to be central to his success. His lordship rose after four in the morning and dressed and breakfasted between five and six, customarily inviting some of the midshipmen on the watch to join him, providing they first bowed to the 'guardian angels' in his cabin. 'I have known him send during the middle watch to invite the little fellows to breakfast with him when relieved,' Stewart recalled. 'At table with them he would enter into their boyish jokes, and be the most youthful of the party.' Routine business was then dispatched by eight. 'The great command of time which Lord Nelson thus gave himself, and the alertness which this example imparted throughout the fleet can only be understood by those who witnessed it,' Stewart remarked. In the afternoons all the ship's officers took their turns at Nelson's dinner table, where the admiral was ever 'a polite and hospitable host'. It was this accessibility that enabled Nelson to impart his ideas and attitudes to his followers. According to Ferguson the military surgeon, Nelson took 'every possible opportunity' to gather his 'different commanders . . . , arranging plans of conduct in the event of finding the Russians friendly or hostile'. This may have been an exaggeration, but it is consistent with other evidence suggesting a commander unusually good at communication.[42]

Nelson's first task was to neutralise Sweden. She was ruled by a twenty-three-year-old king, Gustavus IV, a cousin to the Crown Prince of Denmark, who longed to restore his country's international prestige after decades of steep decline. He hungered to annex the Norwegian provinces of Denmark, and although the League had brought Sweden and Denmark together, they deeply distrusted each other. The Swedes had not fortified Halsingborg, nor tried to prevent Britain from breaching the Sound, but once Parker's fleet actually threatened Copenhagen they grew alarmed, embargoing trade with Britain and ordering their squadron of eight ships of the line at Karlskrona to redouble its efforts to clear the ice and get to sea. The Swedes offered to support the Danish defence line at Copenhagen, mooting plans to place their ships between the shore and the Middle Ground to seal off the King's Deep, or to close the entrance to the Baltic by occupying the Drogden shallows between Amager and Saltholm. Unfortunately, Baltic ice, unfavourable winds and Nelson's timely occupation of the area south of Copenhagen put an end to such schemes.

The Swedish fleet was still in Karlskrona when Nelson found them on 8 May, and to keep them there he sent in a message by the *Speedwell*, explaining that while Britain (at Russia's request) had decreed that Swedish merchantmen might go about their lawful business in the Baltic unmolested, the countries were still in dispute, and he could not permit their battle fleet to leave port. He hoped the Swedish admiral, to whom the letter was addressed, would do nothing to disturb relations at such a critical time. It did the trick. The Swedish fleet remained safe but inactive and isolated in Karlskrona. Totty had not yet arrived, so Nelson gave his detachment to Murray, who had orders to make no hostile moves against the Swedes unless they ventured out, in which case he was authorised to attack. Captain Inman of the *Desiree* was placed in command of the small ships to be left at Bornholm, and Nelson was free to sail up the Baltic.[43]

Nelson's prudent handling of Sweden deftly anticipated the Admiralty orders of 6 May, but was no more than a curtain raiser to the trickier problem of Russia. In that respect, Nelson had relatively little guidance beyond the Admiralty's instructions to Parker to avoid aggravating the new tsar, but to seek a clarification of his intentions towards the British ships, cargoes and crews detained in Russian ports. Parker had sent Fremantle to St Petersburg but nothing had been heard from him since. A Russian lugger, which brought Nelson copies of dispatches from Lord Carysfort, Britain's ambassador in Prussia, did little more than reaffirm Britain's desire to stay hostilities and give negotiation another chance. Preparing to sail to Revel, Nelson opened his campaign with a letter of 9 May, addressed to Count de Pahlen, Tsar Alexander's foreign minister. Referring to his 'pacific and friendly' orders, Nelson stated that he was on his way to Revel and Kronstadt to 'mark the friendship . . . between our two gracious sovereigns'. He thought he might meet Alexander in one of these places, and raised the question of the embargoed British ships, hoping that he might be permitted to bring them home. The force he was bringing to Revel was a token one, he assured Pahlen, without bomb or fireships, and was designed to pay respects rather than threaten. Under a finely balanced veneer of friendship, Nelson hoped to demonstrate Britain's strength in the region, keep the Russian detachments apart and prompt the tsar towards lifting the embargo on the British traders as a practical step towards restoring good relations.[44]

Within a week of taking command, Nelson established the watch on Karlskrona and travelled some six hundred miles or more to Revel (now Tallinn), on the southern shore of the Gulf of Finland, where one of the two principal Russian naval detachments had wintered. He arrived in Revel roads on 13 May to discover that the Russian ships had sailed through the breaking ice for Kronstadt only nine days before. As Nelson had feared, the tardiness of the British fleet had allowed the Russian navy to unite its forty-three capital ships at the western extremity of the Gulf of Finland, near St Petersburg. It was left to him to attempt the other part of his brief, encouraging the restoration of friendly relations. But while Nelson had judged his eleven sail of the line to be necessary to deter a Russian squadron from leaving Revel, it was arguably an excess of force for its more pacific task. The new British chargé d'affaires to St Petersburg hastily wrote to Nelson from Riga that his appearance at Revel was dangerously provocative, and conveyed an aura of unhelpful intimidation.[45]

Nelson, of course, was juggling somewhat contradictory instructions, on the one hand promoting harmony and on the other using armed force to prevent Russia from gaining military advantages during a diplomatic hiatus that might easily be all too short lived. But he played his next card skilfully. He sent the *Kite*, under Captain Stephen Digby, into Revel with a request for fresh meat and vegetables, and advice, which was duly furnished, about a safe anchorage in the outer bay. There was an uneasy exchange of salutes, but beef was supplied and

Nelson invited ashore, a trip that entailed a fourteen-mile round trip in a boat, an excited crowd and meetings with Governor [A.] Balascheff, Baron Dimitri Ortan (Count Sacken) and the local head navy chief. Domett thought that Nelson was 'received with all possible attention and respect', but there was no dinner, and the admiral was glad to leave such a 'horrid nasty place'. To cap the civilities, he had to cough his way around his ship, entertaining thirty sightseeing officers and nobles the governor brought aboard the next day. One of the guests was an army officer who turned out to be Pahlen's son. His father, he said, was in Revel, but there was no explanation for his failure to appear.[46]

Relations remained studiously respectful, but controlled. Nelson stored the defences of Revel in his mind, noting that the roads were open to attack, the wooden mole vulnerable to fire and that a three-decker moored across the mouth of the harbour would be able to rake ships in the entire dock. On 16 May Nelson was about to sit down to dinner when Pahlen's reply to his letter of several days before arrived. It was at once clear that the Russians had been offended. Pahlen expressed surprise that Nelson had brought such a large force to Revel, and the tsar had found it 'entirely opposed to the spirit of the instructions' of the British government. He had ordered Pahlen to request Nelson's immediate departure. Worse, there could be no negotiations about the embargoed British merchantmen with a hostile fleet at the doorstep. The letter contained nothing about Fremantle's mission to St Petersburg.

Considering the matter over a hurried dinner, Nelson rose to compose a credible reply. Russia had misunderstood, he explained. Most of the British ships had been left behind, and his intention had merely been to pay 'a very particular respect' to the new tsar. He pointed out that his letter had invited Alexander to meet him, and that he had only anchored in the outer bay of Revel by the permission of its governor and admiral. However, since his intentions had been so misconstrued, he would leave as they wished. It was a respectably ploy, since Nelson's departure on 17 May effectively placed the burden of restoring good relations on the Russians, who were now shown to have effectively insulted His Britannic Majesty's well-intentioned fleet. So suddenly did Nelson leave in response to the Russian protest that a brig had to be left to collect the last of the ordered provisions.[47]

Nelson now decided to sit tight until Russia made another move, although he sent the *Kite* up the Gulf of Finland towards St Petersburg in a vain search for Fremantle, who almost alone could shed more light on the tsar's intentions towards the detained British ships and crews. In that hope he was to be disappointed. When Fremantle eventually rejoined the fleet off Bornholm, he had no germane information, except that he had been hospitably received. About the future of the League or the release of the embargoed ships there was nothing. Fremantle's only useful gleanings were about the military condition of Kronstadt.[48]

Nelson sailed towards Bornholm, where he intended to unite his fleet, coming across Murray on his way down the Gulf of Finland. Murray's news was that Totty had reached Bornholm, a reinforcement that gave Nelson a total force of twenty-two ships of the line and forty-six smaller vessels, as fine a fleet, he would decide, as ever 'graced the ocean'. Fortunately, the signs that no further shots would need to be fired in anger suddenly began to multiply. On the morning of 20 May, a few days before Nelson made his junction with Totty, he was found by a Russian frigate, the *Venus*, bringing a welcome newsflash. On board was Paul de Tchitchagoff, a Russian rear admiral and special envoy sent in response to the Fremantle mission. He presented a letter seeking clarification. Hawkesbury had written to Alexander, notifying him that the British fleet had been ordered to suspend hostilities, but Parker had implied that offensive operations would resume if Russia did not release the embargoed British merchantmen. It was the same Russian sensitivity to threats that Nelson had met at Revel. Nelson explained that he needed to know Russia's intentions in relation to the detained ships and crews 'in order that he may regulate his conduct', but suggested they move things on with an exchange of notes. A kind of understanding was reached. Tchitchagoff declared Russia's object to be peace; and Nelson reciprocated by stating that, as such was the case, he would commit no act of hostility against Russia, and allow the merchant trade of the Baltic to continue freely, as Parker had indeed already promised. This removed the threat, and Tchitchagoff happily declared that he 'could almost assure me that his emperor would order the immediate restitution of the British shipping'. With that Nelson was satisfied. He wisely declined to discuss Britain's seizure of Swedish and Danish property, knowing that those disputes would appear in a very different light once an agreement had been made between Britain and Russia. At noon both admirals parted with a sense that peace had taken another step.[49]

Most opportunely, a British ship, *Latona*, entered the fleet in the evening of the same day carrying another influential passenger. Alleyne Fitzherbert, Baron St Helens, was His Britannic Majesty's new Ambassador Extraordinary and Plenipotentiary to the court of Russia, with orders to negotiate a treaty of peace between the two nations. Nelson was not well, but immediately went on board the *Latona* with all his relevant papers, including the recent exchanges with Tchitchagoff. The admiral spent three hours briefing St Helens, who owned that 'many important lights' had been shone upon his task. From Nelson's material it seemed, for example, that the Russians had shed the 'exorbitant pretensions' their representative in London, Count Woronzow, had advanced. Greatly encouraged, St Helens continued his journey to St Petersburg that same night, taking with him a cutter, *Lynx*, so that he could keep Nelson informed about his progress.[50]

Amid these international concerns, Nelson confronted more immediate distractions, including a personal tragedy. On 23 May, reading letters brought from England, he was stunned to learn that his oldest and favourite brother, Maurice, had died at the age of forty-eight. His had been a quick decline. About 13 April he complained of violent pains in the head, and his physicians, one the eminent Sir John Hayes, recommended by Davison, spoke of inflammation caused by a 'brain fever'. The patient briefly rallied, but died in a fit on 24 April. Drawing on the admiral's account, Davison and Thomas Bolton, Maurice's brother-in-law, organised a sad funeral at Burnham Thorpe, attended among others by the distressed and sick common-law wife, Sukey, and a representative of Fanny, who had lost one of her last allies in the Nelson family. Out in the cold Baltic, Horatio Nelson's mind wandered back to the sleepy village of his childhood, and the old stone rectory that had once been filled with the noise of children. 'Six sons are gone out of eight,' he reflected.[51]

Maurice's death struck deeply into Nelson, partly because he felt that he had let his brother down. In his mind, it was Maurice who most symbolised the ingratitude of the Establishment. Nelson had beseeched Spencer to contrive his promotion, all to no avail, and Davison had gone so far as to write to Hamond, the comptroller of the Navy Board, offering £3000 to any of his commissioners who would resign from the board in favour of Maurice. Nelson had also approached Hamond, and was finding the current board of Admiralty another obdurate boulder. In the spring his brother was promoted to the position of chief clerk in the Navy Office, but the recipient dolefully complained that it was a tardy return on his services, and that something better was 'a matter of right' rather than 'interest'. Nelson agreed. 'The neglect shown you . . . is what I cannot forget,' he wrote. St Vincent had been working on the supplicant's 'advancement' as a commissioner of customs and excise, but suddenly it was too late.[52]

Nelson loved his brother, but had disappointed him twice, by cutting him out of Davison's prize agency and failing to get him promoted. As a trustee of Maurice's will, which had been signed in 1795, he also felt a responsibility to Sukey. She inherited Maurice's money, with any residue at her death to be shared between Horatio, Susannah and Catherine, but Nelson considered her plight dire and insisted that Davison do 'everything which is right' for the 'poor blind' widow, who deserved 'every farthing which his kindness gave me'. To her he also wrote personally, sending £100 and assuring her that he would attend to her needs. He would ensure she remained at Laleham, and secure her all necessaries, from a horse to a tipple of whisky. And he remembered a black family retainer, James Price, who had passed from Uncle William Suckling to Maurice, and who would never want a home if Nelson had anything to do with it. Sukey and Price apparently retired to Laleham, with a small portrait of Maurice as a remembrance, and when she died 'rather suddenly' in February 1811 the old servant was the sole beneficiary of her will.[53]

Stricken to the core by his tragedy, Nelson may have been grateful for the distraction of a pressing problem: how to supply his huge force with food, water and naval stores. The Admiralty was sending a supply convoy with ten weeks' provisions, but recommended Nelson use local contractors to eke out existing supplies. At Bornholm little other than fish and eggs was to be had, and no one there would cash British government bills or provide credit. Agents at Copenhagen offered a variety of victuals, but the supply was inconvenient and unreliable, and Nelson turned to Alexander Cockburn of Hamburg, the British consul general for Lower Saxony, to furnish provisions through the Prussian ports of Danzig and Rostock. Richard Booth, an able purser of the *London*, sent by Nelson to purchase for the fleet in Danzig, secured 734 head of quality cattle using bills drawn on the Victualling Board. The admiral's practice was to keep part of his fleet off Bornholm with Totty, ready to curb any adventurousness on the part of the Swedes or Russians, while detaching small forces to gather supplies. Three ships went to Koge Bay for water, and Murray, Foley and Tyler went to Danzig. Nelson himself took eight sail of the line and a frigate to Rostock, arriving on 24 May.[54]

Two officers explained the squadron's purpose to the local military commander, and established a basis for trade. Competition to supply the ships was keen, but one contractor undercut all contenders with an offer to supply provisions through Danzig or Rostock. On the 27th a contingent from the town council came out to the ships, its leaders attired in black silk suits and black hats, and Nelson welcomed them in his cabin before arranging for them to transfer to the *London* for a tour of the ship, which at least got them out of his way. In a goodwill gesture of their own the town council sent the admiral four deer from the estate of Friedrich Franz, Duke of Mecklenburg-Strelitz. Here, as elsewhere, the admiral was beset with sightseers, and sometimes more than an hundred private coaches were parked on the beach, some from as far away as Hamburg and Berlin, waiting for their owners to be rowed to and from the ships. Nelson's captains were on orders to create a favourable impression, and for the most part succeeded. One pop-eyed visitor to the *London* reported entering 'a special little world . . . even five females with babies lived on board, and if you see the cleanliness and order from keel to the top deck it is almost a miracle. Friendly officers gave us excellent meat and port wine, and we talked for above half an hour in their cosy cabin. Later we were guided at a leisurely pace through all the decks.' Public relations came to a head when the agreeable old Duke of Mecklenburg-Strelitz himself appeared on 1 June with an enormous entourage of almost a hundred, and Nelson was 'annoyed to death for an hour' conducting them around the *St George*. But he maintained equanimity even after leaving on 2 June. He sent one of the Davison Nile medals to one dignitary, and the following year responded immediately when a local trader wrote to him about an outstanding bill for goods supplied a British officer. He settled the account and apologised 'for the conduct of this officer, so disgraceful to the service and a very improper return for all your attention to the fleet under my command'.[55]

The presence of the fleet and influx of tourists at Rostock drove the prices of local provisions upwards, and Nelson accused a cartel of traders of exploiting the situation. He decided to use Danzig as his main source of supplies, and returned to Koge Bay to water and await the new commander-in-chief he had requested. But Danzig's resources proved 'scanty' and supplies remained a problem. The Admiralty convoy was sent to Nelson at the end of May, but he had to put his force on two-thirds of their normal bread allowance, and was short of wine, which he preferred to issue to his men in lieu of spirits. Some health problems were reported. While influenza troubled several ships, including the *St George*, a product of the inclement weather, the *Ramillies* reported scurvy, a dietary disease.[56]

It was while Nelson was at Rostock that the last pieces of his Baltic diplomacy fell into place. With the Danes out of action, and the Russians ruminating over what course to pursue, Nelson addressed the remaining member of the League, Sweden. On 23 May he sent the *Jamaica* into Karlskrona with a letter, pointing out that Parker had promised not to molest Swedish traders in the Baltic, but regretting that no reciprocal gesture had been made. He asked for an 'explicit declaration' that Sweden would not act against his country. In fact, the Swedish king had already acted. Four days earlier he had replied to Nelson's letter of 8 May by removing all impediments to commercial intercourse between the two countries, and praying that Britain would do likewise. Within days relations between the two countries had been normalised.[57]

About the same time there was more from Russia. On 26 May a Russian lugger, the *Great Duke*, brought Pahlen's reply to the letter Nelson had written in Revel roads. His tact had paid off. The Russians were thoroughly persuaded that they had mistaken Nelson's intentions, and wanted to repair bridges. Pahlen warmly declared his wish for peace, apologised for the misunderstanding and invited Nelson to St Petersburg. What was more, in return for Nelson's magnanimous letter, the tsar had ordered the complete release of the incarcerated British ships and crews. It was excellent news, and had Nelson known that the tsar himself had dictated Pahlen's letter, it would have spelled the end of the Baltic crisis even more plainly.[58]

Nelson had curbed his natural impatience to play the game of diplomacy, and was sharp enough to recognise the implications. After receiving some provisions, the Russian lugger slipped away the next day, firing a salute as it did so. A little later Nelson turned to his secretary and said, 'Did you hear that little fellow salute? Well now, there is peace with Russia, depend on it.'[59]

Nelson's dispatch of 27 May brought the news to London that Russia had lifted her embargo on British ships, arriving just ahead of a confirmation from the British chargé d'affaires in St Petersburg, who reported that Alexander removed the embargo 'immediately after the departure of the English admiral from Revel on Sunday the 17th instant'. Alexander had wanted to end the Baltic crisis, but was afraid of opening his foreign policy with anything that resembled an act of weakness. Nelson's action at Revel, compounded by his reassurances to Tchitchagoff, had addressed and allayed that reservation. Russia not only restored platonic relations with Britain, but also ordered any necessary repairs to the detained British ships to be done, and authorised compensation to be paid to the British subjects involved. She did not even require Britain to return the Swedish and Danish property that had been seized, or raise the question of neutral rights that had been used as a pretext for the Northern League.[60]

Alexander I had inherited a war from his father, and one, moreover, which had brought a powerful enemy into the Baltic. The naval force of one of his fellow members of the League had been destroyed, and the other imprisoned in its port. The Russian fleet had managed to unite in Kronstadt, where an additional tier of guns now adorned the castle and a battery similar to the Trekronor had been erected, but the ships themselves were unfit to cruise and had had to leave the Baltic in the hands of an enemy with the ability to destroy commerce, bombard ports and impose punishing blockades. It is not clear how far the British fleet was reshaping Russian foreign policy, but Alexander had been helped to ditch an unwanted war by Nelson's restraint. When St Helens spoke to the tsar late in May he found him relatively disinterested in such maritime issues as neutral rights, but greatly concerned to retreat with dignity. 'The very handsome manner in which Lord Nelson had withdrawn his squadron had completely removed their unfavourable impressions,' reported the diplomat. The tsar was so pleased with the British admiral that he repeated the invitation to him to visit St Petersburg, and planned an extravagant state welcome.[61]

The northern coalition against Britain had crumbled. Denmark no doubt continued to challenge Britain's interpretation of neutrality, but covertly and without the support of Russia. It was time for Nelson to go home.

5

On 5 June Nelson's fleet returned to Koge Bay, and in its final weeks the campaign ended where it had begun, with Denmark.

At home Nelson's news that the tsar had ordered the embargo on British vessels and subjects to be lifted, together with indications from Denmark that she would acquiesce in any Anglo-Russian agreements, led the British government to revoke their own seizure of Russian, Danish and Swedish ships on 4 June. Peace now moved forward mightily.[62]

There were still some hurdles to jump. Nelson was disturbed by reports that Denmark was abusing the armistice. One problem was Norway. The Danes had refused to include Norway in the armistice, but Parker had generously permitted them to send provisions there. But now came accounts of corn ships bound for England being seized in Norway, an act Nelson hoped would prove to be 'some mistake', and that guns and naval stores were being shipped between Denmark and Norway. On 11 June, Samuel Sutton, the new captain of the *Amazon*, was sent to cruise between Sjelland and the Koll to intercept any such supplies, and to ensure that no Danish warships currently in Norway could return to upset the agreed status quo in Denmark. Nelson went so far as to warn the Danes that British ships were within their rights to capture vessels in flagrant breach of the armistice, and to suggest that Denmark should consult the British government if she wished to modify its terms. Among other issues about the observance of the armistice were concerns about British access to Danish ports and rumours that the Danes were furtively refurbishing their fleet at Copenhagen, rearming and remasting ships and constructing new floating batteries. Trying to avoid a damaging rupture, Nelson sent Stewart to the Danish capital to investigate, and made a vigorous protest to Lindholm in which he nicely supposed the stories to be false. He suspected French agitation might lie at the back of the problem, and reminded Lindholm of a duty 'to turn all French republicans out of our monarchical governments'.[63]

His annoyance grew the more with a nagging conviction that he was being betrayed, and by 14 June he was asking the Admiralty for permission to revisit Copenhagen, and if necessary set it 'in a blaze' if satisfaction was not obtained. This would have been a potentially disastrous move, especially as Russia was on the brink of an agreement that would have inevitably brought Denmark and Sweden into line. Fortunately, temperance remained Nelson's weapon of choice, and the friendship with Lindholm helped. The Danish officer spent 'one of the pleasantest [days] in my life' visiting Nelson's flagship on 9 June. Twenty-five bottles of sixteenth-century wine from the royal cellars, as well as vegetables and strawberries from the king's garden, found their way to the British fleet. Lindholm denied that any ships had been refitted, and Bernstorff reassured Nelson by letter, but the admiral's scepticism was not entirely allayed.[64]

The growth of anti-British feeling in Denmark contributed to Nelson's unease. The news of Britain's capture of the Danish West Indian islands and some notorious examples of the abuse of neutrals at sea by British privateers fanned public anger, and the armistice, now looking decidedly one-sided in practice, was widely condemned. Nelson concluded that the Danes 'hate us' and would retaliate if they could, and Stewart testified that British officers had to be guarded on Copenhagen streets. Fortunately, in the middle of June the news that Britain had lifted her embargo of Danish and Swedish ships eased the situation, and caused 'the most agreeable sensation' in Denmark. The peace held.[65]

Nelson did not remain in the Baltic for the final settlements. On 17 June, Russia, negotiating with Lord St Helens, agreed that neutrals should not be allowed to ship contraband, or cover the movement of cargoes for belligerent nations. Nor would their ships be inviolable to Britain's practice of stop and search. Once Russia had withdrawn her opposition, the Swedes and Danes lamely followed, and the immediate challenge to British control of the sea ended. The death of the old tsar had been the principal agent of change, but Nelson's campaign had played its part in enabling his successor to sculpture a new political horizon.

The expedition had been a testing experience. By and large, it found Parker wanting, and he struck his flag, never to raise it again, submitting instead to a clouded retirement that lasted until his death in 1807. When Nelson finally got home in the summer of 1801 he found the deposed commander-in-chief trying to vindicate himself, hardly knowing whether to risk a court martial in a dangerous attempt to clear his name, or let matters be and wait for malicious tongues to broadcast their own conclusions. Nelson knew that an enquiry would uncover unwelcome home truths, and did not relish being called as a witness, or having his own incriminating complaints to the Admiralty made public. Sir Hyde had been guilty of 'idleness' rather than 'criminality' and it was better buried. He wrote to the disgraced admiral, saying that he would regard Sir Hyde as a valued friend, whether censure, neglect and misfortune fell upon him or not. 'They are not Sir Hyde Parker's real friends who wish for an enquiry,' he told Davison. 'His friends in the fleet wish everything . . . forgot, for we all respect and love Sir Hyde.' If that was true, and Parker had inspired that much affection, he had not failed in every important respect.[66]

Parker's stature had shrunk, but Nelson's scaled formidable heights. By controlling his more impulsive instincts, and measuring pro and con, he had mastered the strategy, tactics, diplomacy and logistics of a difficult campaign and turned in a model performance. Among many minor examples of his forethought, the admiral had taken advantage of his sojourn at Rostock to dispatch Stephen Digby's *Kite*, with the sailing masters of the *St George*, *London* and *Polyphemus*, to survey the Great Belt between 25 and 30 May, providing essential charts and notes for any future British excursion into those waters. Nelson's observations on the defences of Revel, with a plan Stewart had made of the bay, likewise went home to be filed for another day. Stored in the infant hydrographic office at the Admiralty, some of these materials would be dusted off during the Crimean War.[67]

A study of the Admiralty correspondence reveals how completely the Baltic expedition dismissed the earlier reservations about Nelson's broader judgement. Henceforth, the boards of Admiralty almost obsequiously bowed to his pronouncements, sometimes leaving him feeling distinctly underbriefed and short of direction. If Nelson grasped this, it did not remove his ingrained resentment. In June, as the weather improved, so did his health but he would not retreat upon his determination to resign, nor relinquish his grievances. His prize suit against St Vincent went to court on 25 May, and he worried that it might fail through his inability to attend. At the same time he complained that no one paid him enough attention. 'It is . . . thirty-four days since I have had a scrap of a pen from England, so little do the Admiralty think of us,' he grumbled. They were all 'enemies, damn them! I cannot obey the scriptures and bless them.'[68]

Nelson had set his mind on going home, with all the excitement of a schoolboy on the brink of the holidays. Copenhagen china, bottles of hock and prints for Emma's 'Nelson' room were dispatched to London, while the admiral contemplated a tour of Wales, where Sir William had an estate, and such domestic delights as fitting 'little Harris' (a boy Emma had sent to the *St George*) with a full-dress uniform he had been promised. In anticipation of being relieved, he directed that any more letters to him be sent to the Wrestlers Inn in Great Yarmouth, where he expected to make his landfall.

On 12 June, Nelson finally learned that a successor was on his way. Lieutenant Colonel Hutchinson, who had gone home with recent dispatches, had left the Admiralty in no doubt of the admiral's poor state of health, and St Vincent sent Charles Pole to succeed to the command in the Baltic. On the last day of May he informed Nelson, paying him a golden tribute in the process. It would be 'no easy task' to find a successor, wrote the first lord, 'for I never saw the man in our profession, excepting yourself and Troubridge, who possessed the magic art of infusing the same spirit into others which inspired his actions . . . Your lordship's whole conduct . . . is the subject of our constant admiration. It does not become me to make comparisons. All agree there is but one Nelson.'[69]

No doubt St Vincent libelled many able officers, but he had a point. As Ferguson remarked, Nelson worked 'on the affections and reason of man', and was rewarded with a largely trouble-free command. He judged that, apart from 'the glaring misconduct of the officers of the *Tigress* and the *Cracker* gun-brigs, and the charges alleged against the lieutenant on the *Terror* bomb', he had no complaints against his force of 18,000 men, which worked with 'great regularity, exact discipline and cheerful obedience'. As he put it to Clarence, 'We all truly . . . pull altogether'.[70]

Throughout Nelson remained 'the life and soul of the squadron', praising merit, often beyond its deserts, and creating pride, self-respect and a determination to justify his pleasing opinion. Captain James Brisbane expressed his sorrow at learning the admiral was leaving the fleet, and thanked him for 'the many kind attentions and handsome notice . . . experienced at your Lordship's hands', promising to 'endeavour to merit your Lordship's good opinion'. Rear Admiral Totty, who joined the fleet off Bornholm, had never felt more welcomed. 'I cannot find language to express how highly I am flattered by your Lordship's approbation . . . Your lordship's partiality has far over-rated my humble talents.' During the campaign Nelson discovered and used talent that was unfamiliar to him, and men such as Murray and Riou filled crucial positions, but he had also drawn out less obvious potential, and raised performance.[71]

Rear Admiral Graves was a prime example, a competent flag officer who had opposed forcing the Sound and attacking Copenhagen, but done his duty notwithstanding. As a result he found himself a battle hero and a Knight of the Order of the Bath to boot! Delighted, Nelson solemnly invested Graves with the coveted order of knighthood on 14 June. Emma's green chair served as the king's throne, draped in the union flag and placed on the gratings of the quarterdeck skylight of the *St George*, while blue- and red-coated officers and marines stood stiffly beneath the royal standard flapping majestically above. Nelson's sword bestowed the accolade on behalf of the king. Of the three admirals at Copenhagen, Nelson had been made a viscount, and Graves elevated to the Bath; only Parker got nothing.[72]

The effect on Graves was interesting. When Nelson left the fleet the rear admiral wrote of his 'gratitude and attachment' and recorded the great pleasure he took from 'ranking myself among your Lordship's most zealous friends and most enthusiastic admirers . . . It shall ever be my pride to *endeavour* to follow your Lordship's most glorious race in the service of our king and country.' What was more, he meant it. It was a new Graves, not more courageous, but altogether more ambitious and enterprising, who wrote to Nelson shortly afterwards, upon learning that his old commander-in-chief was being employed to counter the French invasion flotilla. 'I think we ought to convince them [the enemy] that these places [invasion ports] are not invulnerable, and I should rejoice in being employed in burning and destroying these mighty preparations of invasion on their own coast, or even in their ports, to impress upon them the futility of their schemes and that the British navy is invincible. As my greatest wish has ever been to be placed wherever the tempest of war blows strongest . . . I trust I shall be pardoned, my dear lord, in most earnestly requesting that your Lordship will permit me to follow in your Lordship's train.' This was the language of a true brother.[73]

Pole arrived in the *Aeolus*, and Nelson sailed from Koge Bay for Great Yarmouth on 19 June. The log of the *St George* recorded, 'at 8.30 [18 June] the Rt. Hon. Lord Viscount Nelson, K.B., left the ship and hoisted his flag on board H.M. brig *Kite*. A.M. [19th] moderate breezes. Sailed hence H.M. brig *Kite* for England.' Stewart supplied the emotions. 'Lord Nelson's resignation was attended with infinite regret to the whole fleet,' he remembered, 'and there was a complete depression of spirits upon the occasion.' And Fremantle remarked upon the consequences: 'The difference of manner and the total change of system', under Pole, he said, 'is by no means pleasant.'[74]

XV

THE GUARDIAN

On the second of August, eighteen hundred and
one,
As we sail'd with Lord Nelson to the port of
Boulogne,
For to cut out their shipping which was all in
vain,
But to our misfortune they were all mann'd and
chain'd.

'On the Second of August', a song of 1801

I

NELSON arrived at Yarmouth on 30 June. The crew of the *Kite* cheered him ashore, and 'large' crowds assembled, summoned by an exalted peal of bells. The admiral, with Commander Edward Parker at his side, walked straight to the hospital, where men wounded at Copenhagen were recovering. He was there for one and a half hours, touring the wards and speaking affably to the patients. 'Well Jack,' he reportedly said to a sailor who had lost an arm, 'then you and I are spoiled for fishermen.' Passing to the Wrestlers Inn amid a concourse of sightseers, the admiral collected his mail and enjoyed refreshments. Parker left for London with dispatches, and Nelson followed, travelling through darkness. He breakfasted at William Ralton's Three Cups Inn in the High Street, Colchester, where he transferred to one of the daily coaches for London, and arrived in the capital on the morning of 1 July. Rooms awaited him at Lothian's Hotel in Albemarle Street, not far from the Hamilton house in Piccadilly, but he was at the Admiralty the same day.[1]

Though hungry for attention, Nelson found some of it difficult. Sir John Orde called at Lothian's on 5 July, when he was out. Orde wanted to explain that there was nothing personal in his anger at Nelson's appointment in 1798, simply a natural disappointment at being passed over by a junior. However,

Orde was also grumbling about Davison's prize agency, and sensing a dog with a bone Nelson discouraged correspondence. On 2 July, after a second visit to the Admiralty, he felt obliged to call upon the crestfallen Sir Hyde Parker, who was demanding his day in court. Nelson knew that the Admiralty had been too well informed of Sir Hyde's shortcomings by Stewart and Tomlinson, and regarded the controversial signal as an act of sheer stupidity. He advised Parker to lie low to avoid embarrassing disclosures, and later assured him 'that whether you are censured or not, with or without titles, in prosperity or adversity . . . I shall always consider myself as your old friend'.[2]

Nelson hoped to avoid an open criticism of his old commander-in-chief, but happily promoted friends, protégés and family members. 'I long to have you home,' he told Stewart, 'and have said so to all parties.' One of the listeners was Addington, who was visited on 3 July. More personable than Pitt, the new prime minister encouraged Nelson, inviting him to a family dinner at his home in Wimbledon. Among other solicitations at this time, Nelson spoke to the Admiralty about his distant relative, Lieutenant George Walpole, the son of the Earl of Orford, and appealed to the secretary at war on behalf of a cousin, Lieutenant Colonel William Suckling, who was chasing a post as barrack master. An Admiralty promise to promote Walpole was soon forgotten, but Suckling succeeded. He was so low on funds that Nelson had advanced him £300, telling him to 'cheer up, and don't be cast down', for no one could think the worse of him for a temporary embarrassment. In helping him to an appointment to the royal barracks at Windsor, Nelson was repaying kindnesses he had received of Suckling's father in years gone by. A more unusual supplicant for the admiral's favour was Madame Brueys, the widow of his adversary at the Nile, who had come to London to crave a British passport to Martinique, where she had family business. Such was Albion's hold upon the sea.[3]

In his own cause Nelson called upon Prince Castelcicala, the Neapolitan minister, to pursue his plan to retire to Sicily. Concerned to remain of use to Ferdinand, Nelson addressed Addington on the king's behalf, emphasising that the protection of Sicily was necessary for British as well as Sicilian interests. The rewards from Copenhagen also occupied the admiral's mind, on his own account as well as that of others. 'I feel myself . . . as anxious to get a medal or a step in the peerage as if I never had got either,' he wrote to St Vincent, misquoting his favourite author, Shakespeare, 'for if it be a sin to covet glory, I am the most offending soul alive'. The trouble was that the government was not interested in striking a Copenhagen medal, and even the commemoration sword Nelson expected to receive from the City of London looked a forlorn hope. No less shocking to Nelson was the Admiralty's refusal to promote the first lieutenants of the victorious ships, the customary reward for achievements of that magnitude.[4]

Once again, foreigners made up for neglect at home, at least as far as Nelson's person was concerned. In October he received his fourth and last knighthood. He had never heard of the Germanic Order of St Joachim, which was only half a century old, but was flattered to become one of their dozen Knights Grand Commander. The king gave his consent in February 1802, and Nelson's new insignia, a thistle shaped 'star' with a green ribbon, duly arrived in June. He then had four stars for his breast, with as many ribbons, the scarlet of the Bath, the blue and gold of the St Ferdinand, the peach of the Crescent and the green of the St Joachim.

When Nelson escaped the public glare, he found refuges at Davison's or in Sir William's house, where Acting Lieutenant William Cathcart, son of the seventh baron and relative of Hamilton, saw him on 7 July. But he decided to take invigorating excursions into the countryside, and turned down an invitation to dine with Lord Hobart, the secretary of war, to do so. On 9 July the ménage was enjoying the Hare and Hounds, 'a very pretty place' at Burford Bridge on the eastern foot of Box Hill, where the River Mole watered its gardens. The middle of the month saw them in the Bush Inn at Staines, where another agreeable garden overlooked the Thames, and Sir William fished, landing a barbel that Nelson thought quite inedible. Emma's letter to Lord William Gordon elicited an original poem from the recipient, painting a vivid and candid picture of the party. Portraying 'Antony, by Cleopatra's side' (that is 'you . . . and Henry') making merry 'cheek by jowl' in a wherry, it reviewed their associates, 'the 'brave little Parker', Tom Allen and 'Norfolk Sally' (Mrs Sarah Nelson), a 'little . . . pretty black-eyed maid', who consoled her daughter Charlotte (she of the 'cheeks of rose . . . teeth of ivory and eyes of sloes') when her sensibilities revolted at the cruelties of angling. No such sentiments deterred Charlotte's gluttonous father:

> Not so the parson! On it let him fall,
> And, like a famished otter, swallowed all!
> Nor, for the gudgeon's sufferings care a groat
> Unless some bone stick in his own damned throat.

That Gordon wrote these words to Emma suggests that she, too, laughed at William Nelson behind his back, despite her niceties. Gordon was much more impressed by Fatima the black servant:

> Let not, poor Quasheebaw, fair lady, think
> Because her skin is blacker than ink,
> That from the muse no sable praise is due
> To one so faithful, so attached and true!
> Though in her cheek there bloom no blushing rose
> Our muse, no colour, no distinction knows
> Save of the heart, and Quasheebaw's I know
> Is pure, and spotless as a one night's snow.

Nelson loved that break. 'I shall never forget our happiness at that place,' he wrote to Emma in September. The party also took the opportunity to visit Maurice's bereaved Sukey, at nearby Laleham. Maurice's estate of £2550 had been modest, and the lease on Laleham was due to expire in October, so the admiral's appearance provided a welcome opportunity to clarify the position. He had already written to the blind widow that 'nothing shall be . . . wanting on my part to make your life as comfortable and cheerful as possible', and now promised that she would not be forced out of her home.[5]

Perhaps the most interesting person in Nelson's new entourage was Edward Thornbrough Parker. The twenty-one-year-old Parker was much in Nelson's company at this time, in and out of the public eye, acting as a companion and general factotum. The two men almost worshipped each other, but the sudden and astonishing closeness of their relationship has not interested Nelson biographers. No one has attempted to identify the charismatic young man, who rose from obscurity to become an effective member of Nelson's family in such a short space of time. Parker was not related to Sir Hyde, but to another admiral, Rear Admiral Edward Thornbrough, his uncle, who was then attached to the Channel fleet. The nephew was born on 14 January 1780, the son of a Gloucester apothecary and surgeon, Thomas Parker, and his wife, Mary, sister of Admiral Thornbrough. Young Parker lost his mother in 1787, but his father still practised, and a sister, Anna Maria, three years Edward's junior, admired her brother so much that she named her son after him.[6]

The navy was an obvious choice for Edward. A great-grandfather had been a sea officer, and Admiral Thornbrough had married a naval daughter and put two sons into the service. Anticipating his nephew's like interest, he had entered the boy's name in the books of his ships, the *Britannia* and *Blonde*, in 1780–81, when the infant was in the nursery, providing him with fictitious sea time. Later a baptismal certificate was produced to add five years to Edward's age by claiming that he had been born in 1775. Both artifices, of course, were designed to short-cut his path to the king's commission as a lieutenant. Young Parker's actual seafaring began in December 1790, when he joined his uncle's latest command, the sixty-four-gun *Scipio*. Under his uncle and associated colleagues, Edward advanced steadily and made influential contacts. Alexander Hood, his captain in the *Hebe*, was first cousin to Lord Bridport, sometime commanding the Channel fleet, who rated Edward a midshipman in his flagship, the *Royal George*. Captain John Trigge, with whom Parker served in the *Mermaid*, was himself a Gloucester man, and brother to a military governor of Gibraltar. And John Orde – the same who was at loggerheads with St Vincent – was Edward's superior in the *Victorious*, *Venerable* and *Prince George*, and became a rear admiral in 1795 with positions to offer aboard his flagship. Not unexpectedly, young Parker did well for a while and, passing for lieutenant on 30 April 1796 at the youthful age of sixteen, he got an early posting to the *Formidable*, flying the flag of Rear Admiral Sir Roger Curtis.

Then something went wrong. In 1801 Nelson said of Parker, 'He is my child, for I found him in distress.' He told St Vincent that the lieutenant was 'abandoned by the world', although 'not a creature living was ever more deserving of our affections. Every action of his life, from Sir John Orde to the moment of his death, showed innocence, joined to a firm mind in keeping the road of honour, however it might appear incompatible with his interest.' Parker himself acknowledged that he had fallen victim to 'calumny' and had to clear his 'professional character', but as yet this crucial episode which drew Nelson and Parker together remains a mystery. Rather unhelpfully, Nelson merely remarked that it was Parker's 'conduct in Orde's business' that 'won my regard'. With nothing more solid to go on, we can only speculate.[7]

In 1797 Parker had been appointed a lieutenant in Orde's flagship, the *Princess Royal*, on the Mediterranean station, but he abruptly vacated his post on 28 April 1798, only days before Nelson joined the fleet in *Vanguard*. It is possible he resigned; leastways, the Admiralty referred later that year to a '*second*' lieutenant as having resigned from the *Royal Princess*. Or, Parker may simply have crossed swords with Orde in some way and been forced to transfer to another ship. Whichever, from being a favoured lieutenant in a flagship, ready to snap up a quick promotion, Parker took backward steps. St Vincent found him a place in the *Virago* gunboat, moored in Gibraltar, from which he exchanged ships with a lieutenant of the little less ineligible *Incendiary* bomb vessel on 2 June. The link between Parker and Nelson may have been Hardy, who once claimed to have introduced 'my little friend' to the admiral. However that may be, Parker was invited to transfer to Nelson's *Vanguard* and left Malta to join the ship at Naples on 12 April 1799. From that moment he grew in Nelson's favour. The admiral treated him as the son he had always wanted, and his rise contrasted strikingly with the habitual waywardness of Josiah Nisbet.[8]

Nelson brought Parker with him to the *Foudroyant* in 1799, and during his period at Palermo had the youngster escort the King and Queen of Sardinia from Cagliari to Leghorn. At their destination, Parker was discharged on 22 September so that he could continue to London overland, carrying dispatches for the Admiralty and the Sardinian minister. En route he collected more mail from Minto and the Grand Duke of Tuscany in Vienna. In London the Sardinian minister was so impressed with Parker that he wrote to Lord Grenville, urging his promotion, and the young man duly found himself a commander. He attributed this reversal of his fortunes to Nelson, and had no sooner set foot in England than he called upon Lady Nelson at Roundwood. Like most people, Fanny was immediately won over. 'The young man's extreme gratitude and modesty will never be obliterated from your good father's and my memory,' she wrote to her husband, even though he 'stayed' but 'a very few minutes, as the express from Vienna was in the chaise at the door'. Parker used every opportunity to acknowledge the 'friendly interest' Nelson had taken in his career, and thanked him for 'the very flattering situations I have been placed in by your goodness while in the *Foudroyant*'. In London he reported to the admiral as if still under his command. He had volunteered to serve with his uncle in the *Formidable* as an interim measure, but his ambition was to return to Nelson. Sure enough, when the admiral reappeared in England, Parker almost immediately joined his train as an unofficial aid and secretary. Spencer could not find a ship for Parker, but his successor temporarily appointed him to the *Trimmer* at Sheerness on 27 February as an early favour to Nelson. Soon after, the young man was accompanying Admiral Totty to the Baltic to rejoin his patron.[9]

Parker impressed Nelson by his loyalty, gratitude and diligence, but the genuine affection between the two exceeded all matters of service. True, Edward does not seem to have been privy to the closest secret that Nelson shared with his mistress. He saw Horatia, but swallowed the story that she was merely Nelson's god-daughter. But apart from that caveat, by the summer of 1801 Parker was as much a member of the Nelson circle as Sir William. Sarah Nelson wrote to her husband that 'Parker is always to live with your good brother, and if he goes to sea he shall take him.' In short, 'dear little Parker' had become the son Nelson had never had, and so, in fact, the admiral called him. Parker was appointed to command the sloop *Amaranthe*, a remarkable privilege given the list of unemployed but senior commanders, but forwent the post purely to remain at Nelson's side. Sadly for both men, that single act of loyalty would have fatal consequences.[10]

The war was petering out, but a bloody footnote had yet to strike England's champion to the heart.

2

The dissipation of the northern crisis removed a serious threat to Britain's maritime superiority, but throughout the land there was a profound weariness of war. The Royal Navy dominated the oceans, and with it much international trade, and Britain's industry was expanding in response to the demands for ships, guns and provisions, but the country was suffering from poor harvests, food shortages, inflation, growing imports of grain, taxation and social discontent. People were tired of war, especially one without allies. Addington, the new chief minister, caught the mood, for he was known as a moderate man, committed to compromise and peace. In March, as the Baltic expedition went forward, the foreign secretary, Lord Hawkesbury, opened negotiations with the French.

However, when Nelson returned home that summer the newspapers were full of a fear of invasion. In ports between Dieppe and Flushing, Napoleon was assembling hundreds of small barges, gunboats and flats, ostensibly to ship his troops across the Channel to England at a favourable opportunity. The focus of this activity was Boulogne, where Rear Admiral Louis-René Madeleine Levassor de Latouche Tréville supervised the operation from a hilltop tower that gave a distant view of the English coast. His problems were many. His harbours were too small, his invasion craft unsuited to the choppy Channel waters, and the weather and tides rarely favourable for a large disembarkation. Above all, while French vessels could slip along their coasts in shallow water, they would soon be spotted in the open sea and destroyed by the superior British squadrons. The whole expensive exercise was so impractical that many historians have dismissed it as a charade, designed largely to weaken Britain's hand in peace negotiations.

Still, the Admiralty did not take the invasion threat entirely lightly. For one thing, Britain's grip of the Channel was rarely total. The Channel fleet attempted to watch Brest, where France's main battle fleet was stationed, but winter gales sometimes drove it from its station. During his tenure as commander-in-chief Lord Bridport had often sheltered in Torbay, relying on his smaller warships to watch the French. He failed to prevent the Brest fleet from striking at Ireland in 1798 or throwing the Mediterranean into chaos in 1799. The new first lord, St Vincent, was a tougher customer. Determined to tighten up the blockade, even at a formidable cost to ships and men, he closed down enemy opportunities, but could never completely eradicate the danger of the French fleet gaining a temporary mastery of the Channel. However wafer-thin the chance of a French invasion appeared, it had to be addressed.[11]

In 1801 Lord Cornwallis organised defences, volunteers paraded in towns and villages and local bigwigs vied with each other to display patriotic zeal. The threatened areas of East Sussex, Kent, Essex and Suffolk fell within three distinct naval commands, Archibald Dickson's North Sea squadron, Alexander Graeme's command at the Nore, in the mouth of the Medway near Sheerness, and Skeffington Lutwidge's, which was based on the Downs further south. Lutwidge had once taken the young Nelson to the Arctic, but to avoid demarcation disputes St Vincent planned a new anti-invasion flotilla to defend the whole coast from Beachy Head in East Sussex to Orfordness in Suffolk, and if practicable to mount pre-emptive strikes against the enemy flotilla. Though this new task force would consist largely of small ships and boats, its commander-in-chief needed to be a man of stature to avoid difficulties with the other admirals, and to reassure the public that the country had nothing to fear. Addington and St Vincent decided there was one name that stood out, and a reluctant Nelson was persuaded to take the job. In this hour of need, the champion of the north would now become the guardian of the coasts.[12]

Some of the groundwork had already been done. Trinity House, the body responsible for lighthouses, lightships and buoys, had placed vessels in strategic channels approaching the Thames and Medway rivers with orders to remove markers and buoys if enemies approached, and out at sea naval squadrons were watching the hostile coasts. A three-year-old defence plan had been unearthed, and a huge heterogeneous collection of vessels was gathering. At the beginning of August, Nelson had 76 to 81 craft at his disposal, many old and expendable; about a month later there were 7 small ships of the line, 7 frigates, 12 sloops, 35 gun vessels, 7 floating batteries, 33 cutters (either hired or courtesy of the revenue and excise services), 13 bomb vessels and fireships, 21 river barges and 8 armed smacks, a total of 143 battle units, mounting 2124 guns and manned by 11,416 men. Lacking big battleships or the prospect of a major action, this was not a command that appealed to Nelson, who saw it as beneath his status, but it was the largest naval force he had yet commanded. He was ordered to go to the Nore and raise his flag in the frigate *Amazon* under Captain Samuel Sutton.[13]

His commission was signed on 24 July, and the following day Nelson gave the Admiralty a full analysis of the task as he saw it. The Baltic command had removed doubts about Nelson's strategic vision, and the Admiralty saw no need for close supervision. 'The whole . . . will be left to your judgement, as [befitting] . . . the unbounded confidence we repose in you,' wrote St Vincent. During the command he was content to say that he had merely 'obeyed' Nelson's 'orders' on many matters. The first lord also knew that Nelson's early years in small boats on these coasts had given him a singular advantage, 'for the manner in which you treat of it conveys greater information to us than any we have received from other quarters'. His only concern was that Nelson would neglect his health, for which purpose he was glad to grant Commander Parker leave from his own command to act as an official aid. Formal instructions from the Admiralty, issued on the 26th, drew upon Nelson's memorandum, as well as their face-to-face discussions.[14]

Bearing in mind the obvious problems facing the French, including their need for substantial bases, short Channel crossings, and landfalls that were away from the major English garrisons or fortifications, Nelson proposed two lines of defence, one inshore and the other at sea. London would be the ultimate target for the French, and the flat expanses near the mouths of the Thames and Medway were vulnerable landing sites. In accordance with existing Admiralty thinking, the accessible channels that ran through these low-lying areas were to be occupied by floating batteries, bulky 'blockships', cutters, and armed barges, smacks and flats, anchored if possible with 'springs' so that they could sweep approaching hostiles. In addition, small offshore squadrons would cover both flanks of the Thames and Medway estuaries. Berry's *Ruby*, from the North Sea squadron, was stationed with other vessels north of the Thames off Hollesley Bay, Suffolk, south-west of Orford Ness, while to the south another squadron would base itself off Margate and the North Foreland. These squadrons were to be supported by flotillas of gun- and flatboats that could be rowed out in emergencies. Nelson hoped these offshore squadrons would intercept and frustrate any enemy attempts to land, or perhaps trap the invaders between themselves and other British ships that would surely be in pursuit further out to sea. But if the French got ashore, his offshore squadrons would surround and isolate them. He also assigned fast rowing boats and luggers to serve the squadrons as couriers, while ashore communications would depend upon a chain of coastal signal stations connected to the Admiralty by shutter telegraph.[15]

So much for the inshore defences, but out at sea was Nelson's offensive arm, the naval detachments watching, blockading and harassing the enemy concentrations on their own coasts. Assisted by reports of enemy movements flashed from the signal tower at Folkestone cliff, this forward defence contained seven bomb vessels capable of shelling enemy positions. Looking at his maps, Nelson identified Boulogne and Flushing as the most dangerous springboards for an enemy attack, and planned to hit them first. On the whole, Nelson's analysis was competent. Time would show that he placed too much reliance upon the Sea Fencibles, a naval militia that was expected to man the inner line of defence, and for some reason he supposed that if the French were foolish enough to attempt an invasion they would make a two-pronged attack rather than a single concentrated thrust, perhaps using a force from Calais, Boulogne or Le Havre to divert attention from a more lethal stroke to be delivered further east from Dunkirk or Flanders. But neither weakness would be tested.

Nelson set out on his new adventure in reasonable health, but the customary cough, seasicknesses, night sweats and bad eyes would soon be reinforced by stomach and bowel complaints, and he would try rhubarb and prescribed magnesia and peppermint. Making his hurried preparations, those worries lay ahead, but on 26 July, before he could take the coach for Sheerness, an old man clad in the dark suit and black, wide-brimmed hat common to his profession struggled with the aid of a cane to his hotel door.

3

The visitor was his father, the Reverend Edmund Nelson. In one sense, Nelson was glad to see him, and had received letters in which the old man intimated that he hoped to call on his way from Bath to Norfolk. But in another respect the visit was embarrassing, for the parson represented a guilt-ridden past the admiral wanted to leave behind. Nelson was determined to rebuild his life around 'a wife more suitable to my genius', and escape with her to some sunlit sanctuary in the Mediterranean. As he wrote to Emma, 'We shall all meet at Naples or Sicily one of these days.' Until that happy day came, Nelson had set his mind upon purchasing an interim house of his own, and separating the possessions he and Fanny had stored at James Dod's warehouse. He had given Emma the task of house-hunting while he was away, and she was already investigating a property at Turnham Green. But now there came to his door this old man stumbling towards death, recalling the life he had chosen to forsake, and a sadness that was difficult to confront. In that Italian future Nelson planned, there was no place for Fanny, or for that matter the father-in-law who had come to depend upon her, and whose days on earth were surely numbered.[16]

Edmund had come from Bath, where he and Fanny had been sharing a house and its expenses, situated close to the Matcham residence. Now a viscountess, Fanny still loved her husband, and, being the woman she was, she took the responsibility for the breakdown of her marriage upon herself. 'I love him,' she wrote to Davison. 'I would do anything in the world to convince him of my affection. I was truly sensible of my good fortune in having such a husband. Surely, I have angered him . . . It was done unconsciously, and without the least intention.' If he would only summon her, she would fly to him instantly and 'obey' his 'every wish or desire . . . with cheerfulness'. Fanny simply could not believe that a man with 'the best of hearts' would wilfully make her 'miserable', and begged Davison to point out any way that she might make amends.[17]

In Bath, Fanny walked out with Kate Matcham, who sympathised to an extent, while Edmund tried to convince himself as much as anyone that Nelson would 'see his error, and be as good as ever'. After all, Horace had always been 'a good boy'. Others also encouraged Fanny to hope for reconciliation, among them Davison. In April, Nelson had asked Davison to tell Fanny not to trouble him again, but the recipient shrank from such severity. Humanely, if unwisely, he propped up the anguished wife with false hopes, telling her in July that he had seen Nelson, who still had 'sincere respect' for her. Not entirely convinced, Fanny made her third overture to her husband in May, when she wrote to congratulate him on his victory in the Baltic, and followed it soon after with her 'warmest' and 'most affectionate and grateful thanks' for the generous allowance Nelson had granted her. At the same time she assured him that her 'every wish' was 'to please the man whose affection constitutes my happiness'. If he ever got this letter, Nelson ignored it.[18]

Fanny also pondered more positive steps to prove her love. While living in Bath, she and Edmund toyed with the idea of jointly taking a house in London that Nelson could use when in town, and in May there came a glimmer of hope. A letter from Nelson arrived. It was a cold document that alerted Fanny to the likelihood that he would be raised in the peerage because of Copenhagen. 'If the king confers any honour on me, I need not point out the propriety of your going to St James's' to acknowledge the royal bounty. She was asked, or perhaps commanded, to 'support my rank and do not let me down'. Edmund, that 'good old man', was afraid that Fanny would run into the Hamiltons in London, but Fanny asked Miss Locker to accompany her, and at the end of May took rooms in the capital at Nerot's Hotel. A royal 'drawing room' event followed, and Fanny modestly reported that she 'did my very best'.[19]

The truth, that Fanny had lost her battle for Nelson, was increasingly difficult to deny, and her links with the family were snapping one by one. In May, William Nelson forbade his daughter Charlotte from spending any more school holidays with Fanny in London. Fanny understood that the Nelson family – her family – were being torn from her, and, worse, that those who cared about her were being pulled in different directions. She could not allow them to destroy their relationships with the hero. Susannah protested. 'Do not say you will not suffer us to take too much notice of you for fear it should injure us with Lord Nelson,' she wrote in May. 'I assure you I have a pride, as well as himself, in doing what is right, and that surely is to be attentive to those who have been *so to us*.'[20]

Edmund loved his daughter-in-law more than any of his daughters. When the news of Maurice's death reached Bath, Kate asked Fanny to break the news to his father, 'as I was so much in the habit of doing everything that was kind and affectionate to him'. The separation hit the old man hard. 'He told me nothing in the world now could give him pleasure,' wrote Fanny. 'I assured him I did not feel half so much on my account as I now did on his.' This was the background to Edmund's visit to his son. The parson had not entirely abandoned his idea of taking a house with Fanny in London, but decided to return to Burnham Thorpe in need of 'a tranquil mind', calling on Nelson as he passed through London. Loath to 'interrupt any of your engagements' and finding his son packing for a new command, he did not tarry, and may not even have mentioned the tragedy blighting the family. He simply reported to Kate that her brother was well and in good spirits.[21]

Whatever Nelson said did not change the old parson's mind about Fanny. In Norfolk he wrote to her that he was 'ready' to join her in a house in London or Bath. 'If you think you shall add any comfort to yourself from my being with you, I will certainly be at your command.' It was Fanny, the self-sacrificing Fanny, who doubted the wisdom of such an arrangement, although she did hire a London house at 16 Somerset Street. In September, Fanny made her customary visit to the Walpoles in Norfolk, visiting Admiral Reeve and the Berrys at Ipswich on her way. Towards the end of the month she dropped in at Burnham, spending her nights in local inns and her days with Edmund at the rectory, updating him about her situation. But soon afterwards we find her writing to her father-in-law, pointing out that although he was welcome in Somerset Street, where Josiah could easily release a chamber by retiring to the back parlour, she saw danger in a prolonged residence. It would drive a wedge between a man at the end of his life and his son. 'The deprivation of [not] seeing your children is so cruel, even in thought,' she said. 'I told Mrs M[atcham] at Bath that Lord Nelson would not like your living with me', but she disagreed. 'I had seen the wonderful change [in Nelson] pass belief,' Fanny concluded sadly. 'She had not.'[22]

Doubtless almost tearfully, Fanny was giving Edmund her blessing to abandon her rather than suffer estrangement, but it was perhaps the worthiest of all the

Nelson tribe who replied on 17 October. 'Be assured I still hold fast my integrity,' said he, 'and am ready to join you whenever you have your servants in the London house . . . In respect of this business, the opinion of others must rest with themselves, and not make any alteration with us. I have not offended any man, and do rely upon my children's affection that notwithstanding all that have been said, they will not in my old age forsake me.' If Fanny thought his plan impracticable, he would winter in Bath, but he needed to know. 'My movements,' he wrote, 'depend now on yourself.'[23]

He had quite sunk into despair. 'I hope the breach will not extend further,' he wrote to Kate. 'My part is very distressing.'[24]

4

Nelson and Parker travelled by coach to Sheerness on 27 April, leaving the servants to bring the baggage by the *Britannia* cutter. The *Amazon* was not in sight, so Nelson raised his flag in *L'Unité* frigate, under Captain Thomas Harvey, and threw himself into his new command with his usual energy. After Vice Admiral Graeme, another one-armed admiral, had briefed him over dinner, he sent a storm of orders to the captains and commanders of the thirty or so ships under his command, directing them to their stations, or to account for any inability to do so. The instructions ranged from adding thirty-seven signals to the signal books to the punctilious presentation of weekly accounts. Parker, who produced the scripts, reported that Nelson's appetite for business 'made every one pleased, filled them with emulation, and set them all on the qui vive'. Two days later the offshore detachments off Hollesley Bay and Margate were directed to hold their positions with a single anchor, so that they could get underway at a moment's notice, and to ensure the men were drilled in great gun and small arms fire. As he could not be everywhere, Nelson required 'the support of every individual' to create a 'cordial unanimity', irrespective of seniority. It was his version of Drake's famous dictum that 'the gentleman' had to 'haul and draw with the mariner, and the mariner with the gentleman', for the sea was a hard taskmaster. However, said the admiral, if the men rose to the occasion he would not fail to represent their actions to the Admiralty 'in the strongest way'.[25]

In this command Nelson would have to rely not only on the Royal Navy, disciplined under the articles of war, but also upon the Sea Fencibles, a muster of local watermen, piermen, oystermen and fishermen, who were expected to serve for short periods on the numerous small vessels that constituted Nelson's inner line of defence. His first meeting with the Fencibles occurred on 29 July, when he broke a journey to the Downs to inspect the detachment at Faversham. Pushing on to the Downs, an anchorage tucked behind the treacherous Goodwin Sands between the North and South Forelands, Nelson dined with Admiral Lutwidge and the following day raised his flag in the sixty-eight-gun *Leyden*

(Captain William Bedford), lying off Deal Castle, and summoned all available lieutenants to a briefing. The admiral quickly gathered that even at this important naval anchorage the Fencibles were proving to be a problem. The musters showed that 247 should have been at hand, but they were tardy at turning out for training, and it was doubted if many would even respond to an emergency. The Fencibles objected to interrupting their normal livelihoods and particularly resisted serving on ships of the Royal Navy, where regular discipline was enforced, despite promises that they would receive the pay of able seamen. Nelson had no powers of coercion over the Fencibles; indeed, men enrolled on the register were immune from naval impressment, so he undertook the 'terrible' work of a 'recruiting sergeant', cajoling and exhorting, and trying to address persistent concerns. He pledged that the Fencibles would be allowed to serve under their own junior officers; that their tours of duty would be as short as possible; and that, whenever convenient, they would be stationed close to their homes. Naval captains were instructed to treat them 'with as much kindness as possible' and give 'all due encouragement'.[26]

Having put the inshore defences and offshore flanking squadrons on their mettle, Nelson turned his attention to his offensive forces on the enemy coasts. Bedford was given the important job of maintaining communications between the nearest of the offshore squadrons, near Margate, and the squadrons blockading the enemy ports, of which two were particularly important. Captain Edward W. C. R. Owen of the *Nemesis* frigate, an energetic thirty-year-old Welshman, commanded a small force watching the area between Flushing and Dunkirk, while to the south-west half a dozen or so vessels patrolled between Dieppe and Calais under Captain William Nowell of the *Ardent* and Commander Philip Somerville of the *Eugenie* sloop. In the irregular triangle drawn between Dieppe, Flushing and Margate, Nelson had some forty-eight ships.[27]

These ships could not completely close down enemy traffic. It could steal along the shore, using shallows, protecting batteries and short legs from haven to haven. The French luggers drew only three and a half feet of water, and were piloted by seamen who knew every mile of the coast. The day after Nelson arrived at Sheerness nine vessels ran from Calais to Boulogne in thick fog, exchanging fire with the British cruisers further out. 'No exertion . . . was left undone to stop them, but it was impossible,' reported Captain Somerville. On 2 August two gun brigs and sixteen flats made St Valéry from nearby Dieppe, and, more telling still, on 17 August a number of luggers 'passed undiscovered during the night', getting into Calais despite two British gunboats 'well in shore', a cutter plying 'off and on' and two or three cruisers watching the port, commanded by an officer equipped with night glasses. That said, the significant fact is that while the British failed to prevent all the light traffic moving along the coasts, and therefore the concentration of vessels in the invasion ports, none of the enemy flotilla successfully ventured into the open sea. The blockade thus held. However, St Vincent thought that Nelson could go further by bombarding the invasion flotilla inside Boulogne, and cited Captain John Gore of the frigate *Medusa* as an authority on the area. As it happened, Gore returned to the Downs from his latest reconnaissance of Boulogne on 31 July, and Nelson immediately transferred his flag to the frigate. Without more ado, the *Medusa* sped back to the French coast, carrying the admiral and Captain Peter Fyers of the Royal Artillery, whose opinions on bombardment had proven so useful in the Baltic. Nine gunboats had orders to follow in the morning.[28]

The signal station at Folkestone had reported that some French ships had come out of Boulogne, but if so they had retreated before Nelson arrived. Nevertheless, here indeed was the focus of the invasion flotilla. Somerville, who commanded the watching cruisers, believed that fifty small boats were hiding in a spacious inner harbour on the west side of Boulogne, beyond the reach of an effective bombardment. An attack would be difficult, for the town was well defended. The entrance to the only channel leading into the harbour was guarded on both sides by a pier, new batteries had been thrown up on both flanks of the town and several thousand horse and foot occupied temporary camps east and west. Over a thousand yards out from the mole, sheltering behind a substantial sandbank, were twenty-six armed brigs, gunboats and flats, moored line abreast, their bows towards the sea, extending across the entire front of the harbour. Some of these vessels had been fitted with mortars to give them extra power, but British telescopes could only make out one that looked a regular ship of war. Still, the news of Nelson's appointment had reached the French, and the whole place was in a state of alert.[29]

On 2 August, Nelson sent a lieutenant to reconnoitre the enemy positions from a small boat, and after receiving a report went forward himself in the *Nile* lugger to double-check. He reached two important conclusions. The first was that the French posed little danger to Britain. The vessels outside Boulogne looked barely capable of crossing the Channel, even in smooth water, and the British cordon was too tight. 'With our present force from Dieppe to Dunkirk . . . nothing can with impunity leave the coast of France one mile,' he told the Admiralty. The French threat was a bluff rather than a reality. Furthermore, he informed St Vincent, there were too few troops in the Boulogne area to support a serious invasion, while at Ostend, which Captain Richard Hawkins of the *Galgo* sloop had reconnoitred, none of the sixty or seventy enemy transports were able to carry more than sixty men. 'Where, my dear lord, is our invasion to come from?' he asked. 'The time is gone. Owing to the precautions of government, it cannot happen at this moment.'[30]

Nelson's other conclusion was that Boulogne was capable of being attacked in favourable conditions. Enthused, he added more signals to the fleet's book relating to the deployment and identification of ships, the exercising of arms, and night work. Numerous small boats and bomb vessels would be needed for a pre-emptive strike at Boulogne, and some had been supplied by the Admiralty. But Nelson ordered a dozen new small attack flatboats to be fitted at Deal, armed with eight-inch brass howitzers or twenty-four-pound carronades. The idea was Vansittart's, not Nelson's. The heavy-duty carronades on some of the existing boats weighed one and a half tons, and were of limited use in shallow and confined waters. The twenty-four-pounders and howitzers were effective but weighed only twelve to thirteen hundredweight each, which gave them greater manageability. Once completed, the flats could be stored in the ships watching Boulogne, ready to be assembled and hoisted out at the decisive moment. Intelligence was also vital, and Nelson asked his local commanders to supply assessments of Dunkirk, Dieppe and St Valéry. To seal off his present objective – Boulogne – he posted half a dozen vessels south and west of the port to intercept enemy reinforcements and gather intelligence.[31]

At dawn on 3 August the first attack was made by five available bomb vessels that Nelson had summoned from the Downs. As they advanced towards Boulogne a courier from the admiral warned them not to anchor until they had found their range, but the wind failed and the menacing little vessels withdrew after throwing only a dozen or so shells. The next day brought a stiffer engagement. With a light but favourable wind at NE and N, the bomb vessels took up their positions at daylight. Nelson had placed them well. The greatest danger to them came from a battery to the east, which the curvature of the bay allowed to cover the harbour mouth and the whole line of French vessels outside. By anchoring his bomb vessels well to the west, Nelson put them in a position to scourge the French line from west to east, while keeping them out of range of the enemy battery on the opposite flank. Covered by the *Leyden* and *Medusa* and several gun brigs, which stood ready to meet any counterattack, the bombs began throwing shells and carcasses at the French ships outside the harbour at about 6.20. Some of the missiles whined overhead, and some shells burst high in the air, but others smashed through the ships' timbers and sank some of them. The French guns replied, but the extreme range was too great for their inferior powder, and their efforts almost futile. By 8.30 several boats full of troops tried to row from the harbour to assist their suffering consorts outside, but at 10.15, when the changing tide caused a temporary suspension of firing, 'most of their gun brigs and vessels being disabled, their row boats with troops run in the harbours again from our fire, they keeping up a constant fire from their batteries'.[32]

Firing resumed in the afternoon, but most of the French guns quickly fell silent, leaving their defences to take an unanswered pummelling. Thousands of spectators were now transfixed on both sides of the Channel, although the fire was so 'very tremendous . . . that the coast' was 'in one continual cloud of smoke', and some observers hired boats to take them out for a better view. Nelson's gig was seen from the shore, shuttling back and forth between his ships. According to Parker, the admiral rowed 'about in his boat . . . in full spirits, some of which he has given to all'. Writing to Emma, Nelson himself exaggerated. The French targeted him, he said, concentrating their fire upon whichever bomb vessel he was seen to board, but in truth the enemy guns had been either ineffective or non-existent, and there were only four British casualties, one of them Fyers, who was injured by the bursting of a shell. At 6.50 in the evening the French resistance was so weak that the British bomb vessels were towed closer to begin bombarding the town and batteries. After an action of sixteen hours, firing was discontinued when the wind swung to the north-west and threatened to push the attackers on to a lee shore. Some 750 shells had been fired at the French, and ten to twelve vessels sunk or driven ashore, a few of which could only be seen by their colours protruding above the surface.

Nelson had enough materiel for another attack, additional supplies having arrived from the Downs by the *Gannet* during the engagement, but judged that little more could be achieved. At first there was a sense of success. 'We now go to Calais, Flushing, &c.,' boasted Parker, 'and before long the whole of their flotilla on this coast will be annihilated.' The enemy vessels would be destroyed 'in their own ports'. But in fact the French managed to salvage and repair most of the damaged craft, and Nelson was more modest when some citizens from Dover rowed out to his ship with a copy of an 'extraordinary' *Gazette* announcing Saumarez's victory over a Spanish squadron at Algeciras. Nelson invited his visitors to an 'excellent dinner' and explained that the late attack was 'but a shabby affair' intended 'to convince the enemy they shall not threaten invasion with impunity, and to do something to quiet the minds of the women and children in London'. This, in fact, was the crucial point. The attack on Boulogne demonstrated the utter futility of any attempt to invade Britain without a command of the sea. As it was, the flotilla had its hands full defending itself in its own havens. The eminently educable Latouche Tréville reinforced his mauled outer line with six merchantmen armed with mortars, restoring it to twenty-five vessels, but covering up in its own corner it was never going to invade England.

Nelson considered striking at Flushing, but an easterly wind retarded progress and pressing business with the Sea Fencibles called him back to Margate. The prospects of a success there were, anyway, poor. Some seven enemy ships were in the roads, while outside rode two small British squadrons, one accountable to Dickson, who had jurisdiction north of the Scheldt, and Nelson's detachment commanded by Owen of the *Nemesis*. Despite some duplication of resources, Owen's force of three cruisers and five gun brigs was unequal to the extent of coastline he was expected to cover, and Nieuport and Dunkirk were occasionally left unwatched.[33]

Owen had made a conscientious study of the situation at Flushing, and warned Nelson that his reputation had gone before him. 'Since your lordship's flag has been hoisted, all [ashore] wears the appearance of bustle and look out.'

Knowing they were dealing with a lethal admiral, the French had improved their defences. Around Flushing a chain of observation points had been created behind sandhills, supported by troops and a signal station. Whenever Owen stood inshore, the news flashed to the harbour and one of the Dutch ships hoisted a flag or fired a signal gun. In a series of considered reports, Owen nevertheless suggested several possible attacks, including a surprise raid by small boats, launched on an incoming flood tide; an assault with fireships; and a more extensive assault with the ships and bomb vessels, targeting a Dutch sixty-four-gun ship of the line. But he also spoke of serious difficulties, including the shoals and narrows in the roads, the problem of getting pilots to take ships in, and the particularly unfortunate fact that any wind suitable for taking the British into the roads would also enable the enemy to retreat into inaccessible or well-defended refuges. Owen was willing to risk an attack, but it would be far from straightforward.[34]

Given the inability of the enemy to put to sea in the face of the British, there was little justification for risky attacks upon their ports, and the matter was not helped by fluctuating intelligence that made it difficult to select priorities. In August, St Vincent remained very much in the dark about whether the French threat to cross the narrow seas was a serious one; a diversion to draw attention from an attack elsewhere; or a complete bluff. He could not say whether Boulogne, Dunkirk, or the Flemish and Dutch ports of Ostend or Flushing would be used. And none of the masters of neutrals going in and out of the enemy havens had firmer ideas. Owen noted the movement of troops from Flushing, and came to the conclusion that Ostend and Dunkirk had the most dangerous concentrations. Nelson, however, had not finished with Boulogne.[35]

5

Back at Margate, Nelson avoided the stream of sightseeing boats that flitted about the *Medusa*. The problems that engaged him did not all lie on the enemy coast. The difficulty of manning and training the widely dispersed units of his in- and offshore defences was proving intractable.

The admiral's letters dealt with everything from extraordinary provisions, the quality of the beer issued at Dover, the state of the sick quarters at Margate and the supply of sufficient pendants and bunting to distinguish the fifty vessels he was bringing into service. Graeme managed matters at Sheerness, fitting out ten small gunboats for use in the local creeks, rivers and bays between 1 and 9 August, but admitting that some of the gun brigs were being delayed by untimely stoppages in the dockyard. The Ordnance Office at Woolwich virtually sprang into action on 7 August after receiving an urgent order from Nelson for eight eight-inch howitzers and seven twenty-four-pound carronades to arm the flat-boats he needed to attack the enemy flotilla. Artificers sweated around the clock to prepare carriages, guns and military stores. By three in the afternoon of 10 August they had shipped off the required ordnance fitted with carriages for flats, two carronades for the *Medusa* and 810 shells, 128 carcasses, 223 case and grape, 1864 filled and 270 unfilled cartridges, 1876 tin and quill tubes, 15 primers, 100 or more round shot for each carronade, and a quantity of fine grain powder. An additional shipment of shells, grape and carcasses followed five days later.[36]

Manning and training were the core problems. In August the *Glatton* could not reach her station because of the lack of hands, and transfers from the *Ruby* were needed. Despite impressments and reinforcements, the *Leyden* and *Medusa* were short of able seamen, and at the Nore and Sheerness the *Ardent* and *Alceste*, and the *Sparkler* gun brig, were immobilised for want of men. The Admiralty tried to bring men from as far away as Scotland, but temporarily filled the vacuum by forwarding rheumatic Greenwich pensioners to get *Serapis* and *L'Unité* underway. Some of the pensioners were ferried direct to their destinations, but 489 passed through the Nore. Of 69 such in *L'Unité*, 12 had wooden legs that disadvantaged them on rolling decks, 8 had ruptures and could not lift or pull on ropes and nearly all were 'very old and infirm men, many of them sickly or scorbutic'. Other vessels were paralysed by a lack of pilots. Some of the older and better pilots refused to abandon their livelihoods on oyster smacks or fishing boats, and sent their less experienced, and therefore less useful, sons to stand in for them, while others refused to serve in inconvenient situations or indeed anywhere, given the government's rate of pay was less than half a guinea a day. Not a few pilots declared that 'scarce any money' could tempt them to face naval discipline. An able and patriotic pilot such as William Yawkins, an old smuggler, was a genuine treasure, for the generality were so self-serving that St Vincent and Troubridge branded them fifth columnists and swore they would drive them to work. To add to such vexations, there were constant fears of real dissidents among the crews, some French and Dutch émigrés who absconded or were considered too unreliable to employ in critical positions, and desertions continued to embarrass. In September seventeen men fled the *Hound* sloop, leaving the authorities sealing off roads and ransacking houses and taverns in search of the fugitives.[37]

The failure of the Sea Fencibles to stir in sufficient numbers was particularly troubling. On 6 August, Nelson ordered the captains of the four divisions into which the local Fencibles had been divided to call their men out. They were to be treated kindly and as volunteers, and if unable to serve because of their occupations would be excused if they could provide a substitute. But this gentle approach reaped miserable results. When Berry sent his boat to collect a detachment at Orford Ness, the men – 'a set of drunken good for nothing fellows' – flatly refused to leave their home district. The Fencibles in the *Alliance* off Harwich would not serve longer than fourteen days, and left on the expiration of their spell whether replacements were available or not, leaving the ship forty men short at her guns. In all four divisions, the captains echoed the same lament. William Shield, writing from Winchelsea, said that only 485 of 816 men enrolled had reported for duty. From his base at Ipswich William Edge wrote that three districts of Suffolk and Norfolk had produced only 68 of an enrolled 538, although some had agreed to come if their service was kept within three weeks. In desperation Edge began striking backsliders off the roll so that they could be impressed into the navy. Different reasons were assigned for the malaise. Isaac Schomberg, who commanded the division based on the Colne and Blackwater, thought his locals 'smugglers and wreckers' with an almost irrational hatred of the revenue cutters that some were now being asked to man. A recruiter in Thomas Hamilton's division at Whitstable and Margate, where the turnout was rather better, saw naval discipline as a deterrent. 'These people look on officers of the navy as monsters and persons of no consideration,' he said.[38]

Weighing the figures from all sections of his command, Nelson was compelled to tell St Vincent on 7 August that only 385 men of 2600 Sea Fencibles supposed to be available between Orfordness and Beachy Head would serve offshore, and most of those were at Margate and declined to do duty for more than two days at a stretch. The failure of men to enrol, of enrolled men to report, or of reporting men to serve where or when they were needed had created chronic shortages of manpower. The coastal defences in the crucial area between Orford Ness and the North Foreland, which included the estuary of the Thames, were short of 1900 men, while at the beginning of September none had come forward in Kent or Sussex, the counties closest to Boulogne. However carefully Nelson had placed his river barges, many lay crippled for the want of hundreds of experienced hands. These were worrying matters. The offshore squadrons had to be manned night and day, and the river craft needed at least some hands with the training to work them under sail. Nelson was experiencing the frustrations familiar to American and British officers leading militia during the colonial wars. But while their lords of the Admiralty fumed and rumbled, threatening to withdraw leave to keep men in service, or discharge malingerers from the Fencibles and impress them in the regular navy, the problem persisted.[39]

It was partly to inspire the Fencibles that Nelson made a visit to Harwich that entered local folklore. Accompanied by a brig and three cutters, the *Medusa* sailed from Margate on 8 August. The ships were struck by a summer squall as they approached their destination, and the frigate's topsail and royal yards were struck as she lurched violently in the swell. A salute finally welcomed the flag of a very seasick admiral, but the Harwich pilots were too afraid of the bad weather to go out to the *Medusa* to guide her to a safe anchorage, and Nelson had to fight his way ashore in the *King George* cutter. By the 10th he had transacted his business, and needed to return to the Downs, but a powerful wind at ENE made the usual route out of Harwich by Cork Sand unsafe, and the pilots again shrugged their shoulders. Seeing the admiral's irritation, one Graeme

Spence, who had been surveying the area for the Admiralty, volunteered to take the frigate out by an alternative but barely used channel through the treacherous 'Naze' shallows that formed the south-eastern flank of Pennyhole Bay. Sailing at about ten in the morning, the ship groped her way across the 'rolling grounds' for several miles, searching for clear water, sometimes with barely five feet of water beneath her keel. Notwithstanding, she made excellent time, and reached the Little Nore the same evening. In fact, the *Medusa*'s only mishap occurred at the end of her journey, when she ran upon shoals as she entered the Swin, between the Nore and Sheerness, and spent three hours getting into deeper water. Spence's passage of the Naze flats, 'never yet navigated by a ship of war of this size', not only won Nelson's immediate commendation, but became a local legend. Spence named his route 'Lord Nelson's Channel' but it has perhaps more fittingly been remembered as 'the *Medusa* channel'.[40]

The errand left Nelson free to prepare a third attack upon the ships outside Boulogne harbour, not a bombardment this time but a daring attempt to cut out or destroy the French vessels forming the line across the harbour mouth. It was dangerous, and given his opinion that the flotilla posed no threat to Britain, perhaps unworthy of a trial. Although Nelson planned a surprise attack, his earlier bombardment had alerted the French, and it was likely that his men would have to advance into heavy fire. If a letter to Emma is to be believed, Nelson expected the enemy to empty their guns and flee, leaving the British to board or destroy their vessels, but he knew nothing about the resilience of the defenders, their short-range firepower or numbers. The latest intelligence, which placed the number of troops in the neighbourhood at two thousand, may have been an underestimate. Nevertheless, when Nelson sailed with the *Medusa* and several small vessels on 14 August he harboured fair hopes of success.[41]

Like almost all of Nelson's attacks, the attempt was planned in detail. The *Leyden* and *Medusa* brought the flatboats from the Downs and distributed them among the ships off Boulogne to stow, arm and tow until needed. The actual assault would be made by five divisions of boats, launched simultaneously at night. Commander John Conn's division of eight flats armed with howitzers would assemble beside the *Discovery* bomb after dark, and push off at the same time as the other divisions left their rendezvous at the *Medusa*, but its distinct job was to cover them, making for the pier head at Boulogne, and pounding the enemy batteries and army positions ashore from fairly close range. The remaining divisions were led by Commanders Philip Somerville, Edward Thornbrough Parker, Isaac Cotgrave and Richard Jones, each consisting of one or two flats mounted with twenty-four-pounders and eleven to thirteen ships' boats. Two boats in each division were equipped to cut cables and tow away prizes, and all carried combustibles 'ready to set the enemy's vessels on fire, should it be found impracticable to bring them off', as well as the usual collection of boarding arms and muskets. The attackers were ordered to don blue and white belts to distinguish them during any hand-to-hand melees in the dark.[42]

Despite the promise of stiff fighting, morale was high. The assault force had been entrusted to officers with the rank of commander, but Captains Gore and Bedford would have gone with Somerville and taken orders from him had Nelson not held them to their posts. Of the four divisions directed against the French line outside Boulogne, Somerville's was to strike first, at the enemy's north-eastern flank, while Parker, Cotgrave and Jones respectively extended the attack westwards, storming each vessel within their allotted sections 'until the whole of the flotilla be either taken or totally annihilated'. Ten speedy revenue cutters had come from the Downs to tow prizes away, freeing the assault force to continue its work unimpeded.[43]

In 1797 Nelson had led a disastrous night attack on the island of Tenerife, where the British forces had separated during a long row through darkness and attacked an alert and prepared defence piecemeal, fatally weakening what was supposed to have been a concentrated thrust at the decisive point. That bloody defeat illustrated the dangers that wind, tide and misadventure posed for expeditions of this kind, and must have been in Nelson's mind now. The admiral tried to ensure that his assault force remained intact. The four attack divisions would leave the *Medusa* together, and Nelson recommended their commanders to advance in sub-divisions, which might be easier to control, and to use ropes to prevent boats from separating during a difficult approach of some twelve miles. The commanders were ordered to take the lead boat in their divisions, and to ensure that their vessels did not 'cut, or separate from one another, until they are close on board the enemy'.

Surprise – or a partial surprise – was important to the plan, particularly as it contained no provision for softening up the enemy targets with heavy preliminary fire. To allay suspicion Nelson sent his revenue cutters eastwards at noon of 15 August, the day appointed for the attack, with orders to return after dark, and the attack force was to be assembled at night, using muffled oars and the watchwords 'Nelson' and 'Bronte'. Standing some distance out to sea, NNW of Boulogne, Nelson hoped these dispositions might mask his intentions, but the French were far too vigilant. After the previous attacks Latouche Tréville had strengthened his defences, especially on the east side of the harbour, increased his force ashore and added extra vessels to his line, equipping some with mortars to extend their ranges. Captain Etienne Pevrieux, who commanded the defence line from a large brig, the *Etna*, was ordered to train the numerous soldiers that filled the complements of his ships. Latouche Tréville also knew that the attack was coming. Troubridge believed that Nelson had an informer in his fleet, because British newspapers had hinted that 'some new expedition' involving the use of 'additional flat bottomed boats' was afoot. However, the French admiral hardly needed such help, because Nelson himself had telegraphed his punch. On the 15th, four British ships, *Medusa*, *Isis*, *York* and *Leyden*, as well as the *Jamaica* frigate, three smaller vessels and a cutter, were stationed off Boulogne with furled sails, close enough for the French to observe them in the cloudy but otherwise clear conditions. Nelson's orders that the attack force be assembled after dark ('as soon after sunset as possible') were ignored or compromised. The *York* received flats from the *Medusa* while in view of Boulogne harbour, and lowered her boats at seven o'clock in the evening, when it was still light, while the *Leyden* was hoisting her flats out and fitting them by noon. The French also saw an unusual number of boats calling upon the British flagship. Whoever was to blame, the French made final preparations to receive the attack. High 'boarding nets' were raised above the bulwarks of the ships in their line to obstruct enemies from trying to get aboard, and some officers were placed on flats and apparently innocent fishing vessels further out with orders to signal any British approach. The night was cloudy and dark, but as Nelson's men pulled towards Boulogne, their adversaries were both ready and heavily armed.[44]

Nelson wanted to accompany them. His place was with his ships, ready to coordinate and redirect as necessary, but throughout his entire life he had put himself at the head of the charge, in Nicaragua and Corsica, and at Cape St Vincent, Cadiz, Tenerife, the Nile and Copenhagen. This time he stayed, and regretted it ever after. That night of 15 August the wind was north-easterly but light, fair enough to make the attempt. The beloved Parker assembled his division astern of the flagship after eight in the evening, splitting it into two groups as Nelson had advised, one to be led by himself and the other by Lieutenant Edward Williams of the *Medusa*. At about eleven the flagship raised the signal – six lanterns – and within twenty minutes the divisions of Somerville, Jones and Cotgrave had joined Parker. Conn had the fifth division ready to leave from the *Discovery*. The last farewells whispered, they set off at about half past eleven, under the colours of St George, and the boats and finally the gentle creak of muffled oars were swallowed by the darkness.[45]

They pulled arduously through several miles of water, battling eddies and tides as they went, but before a shot had been fired the attack had gone awry, eerily echoing the disaster that had overtaken Nelson's boats at Tenerife four years earlier. By and large the precautions the divisional commanders had taken to keep their own boats together worked, but the divisions themselves began to drift apart. Jones's, which was supposed to fall upon the French left at the north-west end of their line, found the tide sweeping it off course, and it would not get into position until daylight, when the fight was over. Somerville's division, destined to attack the opposite flank of the enemy in the south-east, fared almost as badly, being taken too far eastwards. Only three of the five attacking divisions got in position in time to make the planned simultaneous attack.[46]

Closing upon the flotilla after midnight, one of those three divisions ran upon a French flat, thrown out to give Latouche Tréville advance warning of an attack. Although quickly overwhelmed by the British, the flat signalled an alarm, and a furious fusillade from shore and ships met the advancing boats. While roaring batteries lit up the dark with ragged flashes of flame, excited French troops discharged volleys of musketry, and swarmed on to the mole to help repel the attackers. Miles back in the darkness Nelson and his anxious followers heard a sudden burst of firing at 12.30, but knew nothing of the desperate odds that fortune had pitted against their embattled comrades.

Conn's division, which had kept pace with Parker's during the approach, made a valiant attempt to carry out its orders to engage the shore batteries and troops. While his howitzer boats tried to find targets, Conn fought his way towards the pier, behind the flotilla, meeting heavy fire and a strong tide. But he could not hold his position, and fell back, hoping that he might have drained some of the enemy's strength. If the fire of the shore batteries diminished, however, it was largely because they could no longer distinguish friend from foe as the two sides grappled at close quarters. Parker's division found the French vessels strongly moored bow to stern, firing fiercely upon the British boats below. Gaining additional advantages from their height, the French even had huge eighteen-pound cannon balls ready to throw manually over the sides of their ships as the attacking boats came alongside, hoping to smash through their fragile bottom timbers. Somerville's division, which had been charged with engaging the line immediately to Parker's right, was missing, but Parker and Williams threw themselves upon their allotted targets with a fiery energy.

A brief slaughter followed. Parker, now tackling the most southerly part of the enemy line, led his force in a flat towards the *Etna* brig, near the mole head, which he saw was carrying the pendant of a commodore. The brig was full of soldiers, who supplemented the big guns with lethal volleys of musketry, but Parker got alongside and led his men up the side. At the summit they desperately tried to hack their way through the enemy boarding nets in the teeth of scores of flashing flintlocks and thrusting blades on the other side. It was hopeless, and two-thirds of the Britons fell back into the flat, dead or wounded, including Parker, William Kirby, one of the navy's most brilliant masters, and Midshipman William Gore, a first cousin to Nelson's flag captain. The flat was now dismally circumstanced, unable to defend itself or push away, pinned helplessly beneath a relentless musket fire. It was saved by Acting Lieutenant William Cathcart who followed Parker into the storm at the head of a cutter. Cathcart was not yet twenty, but he behaved with a maturity beyond his years. Placing his cutter across the *Etna*'s bows, he cut her cable but could not move her from her moorings. Cathcart then led boarders up towards the enemy bowsprit, but the blast of a carronade above hurled the intrepid attackers backwards into their cutter. One man's eardrums were burst and poured blood, while Cathcart lay momentarily stunned after striking his head and back upon the boat's thwarts and benches. Struggling to his senses, he saw that every man in Parker's flat was down. Disentangling his cutter, which the tide had pushed against the French flagship, Cathcart got a line to the stricken flat despite the fire that was now being turned towards him, and both vessels slunk back into the darkness. After saving the flat, Cathcart grimly set about helping the remnants of its crew. Tying a tourniquet around Parker's upper thigh, he twisted a stick beneath it to staunch the flow of blood that had been pumping from a frightful wound, yet never even reported his own injuries.

Some of Parker's vessels lost their battle with the tide, and barely engaged, but Williams's sub-division mounted a spirited offensive a little further north. It captured a lugger, and attacked another of the brigs before being driven off by a murderous fire. Nearly all of the men in Williams's cutter fell, and the attrition ran throughout every attacking boat of Parker's command. Lieutenant Charles Pelley, who commanded the *Medusa*'s launch, went down, his shoulder blade and collarbone fractured by bullets, and Midshipman Anthony Maitland, his supporting officer, was seriously wounded. The losses suffered in the *Medusa*'s cutter included Master's Mate William Bristow, who was slain, and Lieutenant Langford, another favourite of Hardy and Nelson, who had a bone in a leg shattered by a musket ball.

As Parker's division was bloodied and beaten, Cotgrave's made their attack to the north-west, also focusing upon the largest ship in their part of the enemy line. Leading, Cotgrave's boat came under such a galling fire during its approach that he cut the ropes connecting it to the following vessels and dashed ahead, opening the fight virtually unsupported. His vessel was holed several times and sank so rapidly that the second boat barely had time to come up and haul the floundering commander and his men aboard. The division attempted to close with the enemy, but was cut to pieces by musketry and grape and recoiled in the early hours of the morning.

Back in the squadron anxiety had turned to dread. The firing that had begun about thirty minutes after midnight subsided close to two in the morning, and was followed by an ominous silence. Then, one by one, broken boats and flats began to emerge from the gloom, filled with the pitiful, bleeding remains of the assault force. The tension, as each waited to hear the fate of cherished companions, was intense. At two or three the *Medusa* saw two flats, a launch and a cutter struggling back. In them were Parker, Pelley and Langford, among others severely wounded. And it was not yet over. Before dawn another heavy burst of firing was heard towards Boulogne, lasting for perhaps an hour. It was Somerville's division, alone but defiant, drawing deeply upon a magnificent courage and pride to make a desperate single-handed attempt to turn the course of the battle. This division had been carried eastwards by the rapid tide, and Somerville had ordered his boats to cast off their lines so that they could try to work back unimpeded. Somehow he got his command to the enemy positions in a respectable order just before dawn. The other divisions had retreated, but Somerville vigorously attacked the French right as he had been instructed. In this final fierce spat the British successfully boarded the *Vulcan*, a brig close to the pier head, only to discover it 'secured with a chain' and immovable. By then a storm of grape shot and musket fire was being trained on the attackers from the shore and from four of the other French vessels nearby, and the growing light was stripping them of one of their few advantages. Somerville did the only sensible thing. After an attack of about an hour, he abandoned his prize and retreated. His losses were heavy, and he himself was injured by the discharge of a gun above, but like Cathcart he declined to include himself in the return of casualties.

A lugger was the solitary prize of the expedition. The British claimed that the enemy ships had been moored to the bottom, but this seems not to have been the general case. Given the circumstances, their failure to bring out prizes was not surprising, but they had been defeated so quickly and completely that the alternative plan, to fire the ships with incendiaries, appears not to have been attempted. It had unquestionably been a gallant effort, and Nelson lavished deserved praise. 'More determined persevering courage I never witnessed,' he reported, and a 'greater zeal and ardent desire to distinguish themselves . . . were never shown by all the captains, officers and crews.' 'All' had done well. 'It was their misfortune to be sent on a service which the precautions of the enemy rendered impossible to succeed in.' As for blame, Nelson was no weasel politician, ready to deny or shift complicity in such matters. 'No person can be blamed for sending them to the attack but myself,' he insisted. 'The loss has been heavy,' he tried to console himself, but 'the object was great'.

The British lost 174 killed and wounded, including Cathcart and Somerville, and so many came from the *Medusa* and *Leyden* that reinforcements had to be sought from Sheerness. Sixty-three men of the *Medusa* fell. Latouche Tréville admitted a loss of 40 killed and wounded, and the British took 17 French prisoners, making 57. For what? The ostensible purpose of the French flotilla, to slip out of Boulogne and transport an invasion army to England, had never looked less credible. British eyes were plainly fixed upon the hostile bases, and if the French could not prevent their forces from being mauled at home, they could hardly look for success at sea. But this had already been established, not least by Nelson's former attack of 4 August. Whether the latest attack succeeded or failed, the basic facts remained unchanged. After the repulse Captain Ferrier of the *York* rode off Boulogne with a small squadron, blockading the port as before. At the end of September some twenty French vessels were prepared to push their prows tentatively out of the harbour, but the autumnal weather as well as the British were against them and they posed no effective danger.[47]

The second attack on Boulogne had been unnecessary and expensive. Its most obvious consequence was to hand the enemy the raw material of propaganda. In a manner worthy of Napoleon, Latouche Tréville furnished the French press with a grossly inflated account of a significant victory, a small crumb of comfort in the sorry saga of an invasion flotilla that had been an exercise of almost unrelieved futility. Nelson would not have been Nelson if he had not looked for another victory. He stretched the navy in order to achieve its full potential, and on this occasion had ran his luck too close. At Boulogne, as at Tenerife, Nelson had been unable to surprise his opponents, or weaken their positions before storming them, and he had seriously underestimated their tenacity. Unable to control the elements, his force divided and met a task beyond its capabilities. Nelson, said his old commander-in-chief Lord Hood, had taken 'the bull by the horns, and . . . sacrificed a great number of lives without an adequate object, for the bringing off a few gunboats could not be one, for they could be replaced within a fortnight'. It was a telling judgement.[48]

6

As far as Nelson was concerned the inevitable sequel to any serious action was the care of the wounded and the recognition due survivors. In his book, merit deserved reward, irrespective of success or failure. Most of the wounded from Boulogne were landed at Deal, where they fell under the care of Andrew Baird, a distinguished naval physician Nelson had specifically requested for the duration of his command. A few of the officers went upriver to Guy's Hospital, but Parker and Langford remained on the *Medusa* until Nelson arranged and paid for private lodgings in Middle Street. Both had come to him at Hardy's behest, and served him in the Mediterranean, and Langford, a lieutenant of twenty months' standing, was, like the admiral, a clergyman's son from Norfolk. Nelson spent the evening of 17 August in the hospital at Deal, 'seeing that all was done for the comfort of the poor fellows'. Some were beyond saving, and the morning after his round of the hospital he joined eight captains to follow the bodies of Midshipman Gore and Master's Mate William Bristow to their premature graves. One was seventeen years old, the other nineteen.[49]

For the living Nelson mounted his campaign for recognition. 'A more zealous and deserving officer' than Conn, he told St Vincent, 'never was brought forward', and Somerville had shown exceptional bravery and presence of mind. Despite this testimony neither these nor Cotgrave and Jones were made 'post' until the peace of 1802, when a general promotion of officers occurred. St Vincent had few ships for post-captains and perhaps wanted to spare the officers immediate unemployment, but the situation of lieutenants was easier, and the influential Cathcart was promised a commission as soon as he had passed the necessary examination. Unfortunately, the Boulogne affair created few such promotions and no one could persuade Nelson that the advancement of a few midshipmen adequately reflected the gallantry of the occasion. He, like James Saumarez and

Lord Cochrane, took his failure to assist followers personally, and fired thunderbolts at St Vincent.[50]

The Admiralty commiserated with Nelson over the Boulogne disaster, but there was criticism in the press, and the admiral encountered his first blackmailer. Early in September he received singular 'remarks by a seaman', courtesy of one J. Hill, the relative of a man killed at Boulogne. The paper was highly critical of Nelson's conduct, and, among several accusations, one that he had launched his attack at the wrong state of the tide and compelled the men to row against the flow may not have been entirely irrelevant. Hill threatened to publish his document if Nelson did not leave a £100 banknote for collection at the post office. Nelson penned a short and defiant reply, declaring that he had 'not been brought up in the school of fear', but forwarded the correspondence to the Admiralty with the suggestion that an attempt be made to seize anyone who tried to collect. Accordingly the Admiralty solicitor and a constable made an arrest, but the luckless offender proved to be a mere messenger, hired at the Temple Gate to collect the reply by a man he did not know. A plan to use the fellow to apprehend the real culprit failed.[51]

The frustrated blackmailer responded with a second letter, informing Nelson that he had composed a full critique 'of your conduct since the beginning of the war', and demanding that money be left with Jordan the bookseller of Ludgate Hill. This time the incident did reach the press, not least because the hapless bookseller wanted to exonerate himself, but it simply rebounded upon the blackmailer, who was dubbed a 'vile wretch' by *The Times*. Hill's third epistle on 28 September was somewhat vindicatory, and attempted to justify his extortion on the grounds that he wished to reward the distressed family of a man lost at Boulogne. The headings of his 'critique' of Nelson's career, though not the full diatribe, saw the light in an obscure London weekly, the *County Herald* on 31 October and got little circulation. It seems that Hill had some genuine information, including details of the Boulogne expedition from a member of Somerville's division, but no more was heard of him. He was not, in fact, the only hostile correspondent, because St Vincent referred to another individual who had recently sent anonymous papers to the board.

Nelson refused to be dismayed by the misfortune at Boulogne, and mulled over the intelligence reports that regularly came from the Admiralty, looking for other targets. In a letter of thanks to the fleet, he said that he would personally lead the next attack to 'completely annihilate the whole of them', an announcement designed, no doubt, to raise morale. Although Emma was pressing him not to risk his life in 'this trivial command', Nelson confessed to St Vincent that he had vowed 'never' to allow an attack to go forward without him again. 'My mind suffers much more [waiting] than if I had a leg shot off in this late business.' He remained bullish, however, even at 'great risk', and only begged the Admiralty's support 'in case of failure'.[52]

At Calais additional fortifications, and the retreat of the enemy ships to a position a mile above the pier head, made an attack inadvisable, but on 23 August Nelson wrote to Owen for his latest assessment of the prospects at Flushing. Sailing from the Downs in the *Medusa*, and picking up the Margate offshore squadron, he arrived at the mouth of the West Scheldt two days later with thirty-four sail, including five bomb vessels and a fireship. Nelson envisaged penetrating the meandering waterway towards Flushing, buoying the channel as he went, but extensive consultations with pilots made it clear that 'so many ifs' attended getting in and out of the roads that the expedition was unfeasible. Owen's testimony was particularly authoritative. While game for the attempt, he regarded it as impracticable. Yes, a squadron might just force the Deur Loo channel, which ran between Walcheren, the island on which Flushing was situated, and an offshore shoal, to reach the anchorage before the port, and it might also leave by the Wieling. But any wind favourable for the attempt would also allow the enemy ships to escape up the Scheldt or into 'the Rammekins', a narrow channel beyond Flushing that ran between Fort Rammekins and another shoal. Nelson decided to look for himself, and the intrepid pilot Yawkins agreed to take him into the estuary in the *King George* cutter. The little vessel advanced nervously into the mouth of the river, getting four or five leagues beyond the British ships standing off the estuary. It stole unchallenged past a black Dutch corvette lying lookout in the Deur Loo channel, close to the fortified point of Dishock, her topsail yards up ready to sail. Further in, Nelson saw more enemy warships, the nearest a Dutch brig anchored off Flushing on the left, and about a mile from it the looming *Pluto*, a Dutch sixty-four. Four more Dutch ships were scattered across the channel, and beyond, above the town, a French frigate was at anchor with a couple of luggers. With the corvette and the batteries at Dishock behind and Flushing and the other ships ahead, Nelson had cheekily placed himself between superior forces before withdrawing. Not to be outdone, Owen made another reconnaissance the following day from his frigate, getting almost abreast of the Dutch ship of the line before turning back. Maps show that small British boats outflanked the enemy ships to take accurate bearings. It was a model operation of its kind, involving enterprising and thorough reconnaissance and sound judgement. Reluctantly, Nelson decided that without troops to seize Walcheren, which quartered thousands of French soldiers, an ambitious stroke was impractical, and he returned to Deal on 27 August.[53]

There would be no more major attacks upon the invasion flotilla, but it did suffer further losses. The boats of the *Jamaica*, *Hound*, *Holland*, *Tigress* and *Gannet* captured three gun flats and disabled three others near Etaples on the night of 20 August. Two days later Cotgrave of the *Gannet* reported capturing five or six flats off St Valéry, and compelling the enemy to scuttle a like number themselves. And on 6 September the *Dart* under William Bolton intercepted twenty-three flats and two gun brigs trying to pass between Dieppe and St Valéry and forced them inshore, causing some damage. By September Nelson could justifiably boast that he had so many vessels on the enemy coasts that the invasion flotilla could not stir without him knowing.[54]

Returning to the Downs after the abortive expedition to Flushing, Nelson transferred his flag to Captain Sutton's *Amazon* on 28 August and based himself at Deal. In September the Admiralty broached a plan to use fireboats to attack vessels at Helvoet, north-east of Flushing. Nelson, Bedford and Sutton interviewed its creator, Captain Patrick Campbell of Dickson's North Sea squadron, and judged the project highly vulnerable to wind, tide and mishap, but justifiable. Nonetheless, Nelson declined supervising the attack. As the senior admiral, Dickson would expect to command, and Nelson was tired of fighting battles as a second. The only other interruption to what Gore described as 'a dull, monotonous, uninteresting state of tame defence' was an imaginative proposal to dislodge the French ships outside Boulogne with fire- and explosion ships, sent in on the flood tide, and to finish the job with howitzer boats. Lieutenant W. F. Owen of the *Nancy*, who advocated the plan, predicted good prospects of 'our most complete success'. St Vincent was less sure, but the time had passed. The brisk autumn weather was throwing another obstacle in front of the French invasion flotilla, and peace negotiations added the *coup de grâce*. On 1 October, with the fireship idea still in train, the Admiralty ordered Nelson to prevent any vessels proceeding to France unless carrying dispatches from the French minister in London. Talks between the two countries were reaching a critical stage, and offensive operations suspended. For the time being Nelson would be kept at his post to demonstrate Britain's readiness to fight, but the war was all but over.[55]

By then Nelson was bored and not a little disillusioned. The attitudes of the Sea Fencibles and pilots had disappointed, and Nelson now also detected a 'diabolical spirit' among some of the seamen, a corrosive, morale-sapping insinuation that he needlessly endangered lives. Bedford found it in Margate and Deal, where papers had been put up warning men that they would be butchered if they volunteered for service. Sutton heard similar stories. If true, it was a serious impediment to a command already strapped for hands. Nelson attributed some disaffection to the Admiralty's failure to reward the heroes of Boulogne, but he owned that his reputation had been injured, and cited it as a cause of his disinclination to lead Campbell's Helvoet raid. He went further, for he saw himself being deserted by superiors and subordinates alike. The Admiralty, he hinted, was so jealous of his success that it would happily see him fail: 'If the thing succeeded the hatred against me would be greater than at present. If it failed I should be execrated.'[56]

These are curious sentiments from a man who inspired much adoration, and it is difficult to take them all at face value. The war was losing pace and little worthwhile remained to be done. Nelson's health was failing in the cold weather, his morale plummeting, and his grievances against the Admiralty making him difficult to control. He wanted to go home.

7

We can never feel closer to Nelson than in the six weeks that followed the failure at Boulogne. Though two centuries have passed, it is still possible to feel the depth of the grief of the two principals in the tragedy that had overwhelmed the admiral's new household.

One was Edward Thornbrough Parker, the doomed young commander hovering painfully between life and death, confronting injury, amputation and death with as much courage as he could summon, but sinking into despair as one blow only succeeded another. Parker was a promising officer, but above all likeable, thoughtful and loyal, a favourite of even such matter-of-fact sea dogs as Hardy and St Vincent. Ferrier spoke of his 'temperance, good habit of body, and even disposition', and Troubridge thought his nature 'heavenly'. He was devoted to Nelson. 'His regard and attention to you gained my heart,' Davison wrote to the admiral; now it would be the death of him. He should not have been at Boulogne. The Admiralty had appointed him to command the *Amaranthe*, but he had applied for special leave to accompany Nelson, and even the terrible consequences did not blight his loyalty. 'To call me a Nelsonite is more to me than making me a duke,' he wrote to Emma from his bed two days after the fight. 'Oh God! How is it possible for me ever to be sufficiently thankful for all his attentions! He is now attending me with the most parental kindness, comes to me at six in the morning and ten at night. Both late and early, his kindness is alike. God bless him and preserve him! I would lose a dozen limbs to serve him.'[57]

Parker laid no blame, spoke of no regrets. In the navy death was never far away, and every man went on armed duty in the full knowledge that he might be called upon to make the ultimate sacrifice. Parker had done what all ambitious officers did. He had looked for opportunities, and taken his chances. He had missed Copenhagen, and, Hardy thought, a promotion to post-captain on account of it. Boulogne had been another chance, and Parker embraced it. It had been his decision, and he never shifted the blame to anyone else. To the end Nelson remained 'my dear lord . . . my friend, my nurse, my attendant, my patron my protector'. Nothing had changed that. The other figure in the tragedy was Nelson himself, now facing that most trying of all ordeals, the watching of a cherished life slipping miserably away before his eyes, and finally flickering out. The feeling of helplessness that pervaded such moments, and the knowledge that love is simply not enough, are some of the hardest burdens to bear. Parker had been more than an officer to Nelson. He had attended to his needs at the table, watched over his medication and cheered him when he felt down. He had become a son, and an unusually caring one, and a room had been reserved for him in the property the admiral was purchasing, as if he was an integral part of the family. Now that part of Nelson's dream faded.[58]

Parker and Langford lay sick in a large room in Middle Street, where Andrew Baird, the physician of the fleet, paid regular visits and reported to Nelson. When at Deal, Nelson tended to remain on board, first on the *Medusa* and then the *Amazon*, but unless a heavy sea confined him to the ship he called as often as he could. The fate of Parker increasingly dominated the admiral's thoughts. At times their meetings were brave ones, but often the enormity of the looming tragedy overwhelmed them, striking both to the heart. When Nelson left the bedside to return to his ship on 18 August, Parker 'got hold of my hand, and said he could not bear me to leave him, and cried like a child'. The admiral kept a promise to call the following day, but found his visits increasingly unbearable.[59]

Desperate for support, Nelson tried and failed to get a day's leave to go to London, and then asked Emma to come to Deal 'as a charity to me and Parker and Langford'. The thought raised his spirits, and he paid a stiff tariff for pleasant rooms in the Three Kings, north of the pier on Beach Street, with views over the sea. The guests arrived late on 26 August with Sarah Nelson and a female companion in tow, after a difficult journey in which their carriage broke down near Rochester and they ran out of fresh horses in Canterbury. Nelson and Hardy joined them for breakfast the following morning, arriving so early that Sarah was still abed. The women made the best of the holiday, despite variable weather, taking a bathing machine a mile from Deal and joining Nelson and Sir William in walks along the shore and a visit to Sir Sidney Smith's father at his home near Dover. A Miss Venn and a Mr Turner arrived to enrich the teacup banter, Nelson was free with gifts, including a roll of blue silk which he gave Sarah for a gown, and they dined at the Lutwidges. Catherine Lutwidge, a quarter of a century younger than her husband, was charmed by Emma. 'She adores you,' chided Nelson, 'but who does not? You are so kind, so good to everybody.' As often as twice a day the whole party visited Parker and Langford, supplying a sofa, hamper and get-well letters from Sarah's children, and sharing tea and sympathy. At the beginning of September Parker was 'easy, comfortable and cheerful', but Nelson hardly dared to hope. 'I shall never believe he will get well till I see him walking,' he said. Alas, this pessimism was vindicated. Parker's injured thigh could not be set until the lacerations healed, but nasty discharges from the wounds were followed by gangrene. 'Parker suffers very much today, and I am very low,' wrote Nelson. The patient was soon enduring the horror of a complicated amputation of his mutilated leg.[60]

Encouraged by Emma, Nelson tried to relinquish his command, but others bade him stay. St Vincent held out the promise of the next Mediterranean command, and Nepean said that true 'friends' would tell him that he would do himself 'an irreparable injury' with the public if he stepped down now, sugaring the pill by implying that as operations were being scaled down he could make himself 'comfortable at Deal' rather than suffer at sea.[61]

The friends departed, Sarah on 15 September and the Hamiltons five days later, leaving Nelson chained to his 'miserable' place. Parker had seemed to rally, but at ten that evening of the 20th his great artery burst and the patient became delirious. Baird could get him to take nothing but milk and jellies. Facing his friend's end alone, Nelson's spirits fathomed down into the darkest depths. 'I am prepared for the worst, although I still hope,' he wrote to Baird from the *Amazon*. 'Would I could be useful, I would come on shore and nurse him . . . Say everything which is kind for me to Mr Parker [his father, who was visiting], and if Parker remembers me, say "God bless him" . . . I have been in real misery.' He spilled the news to St Vincent the same day: 'I am full of grief . . . The breath is not yet gone, but I dare say he cannot last the night.' Astonishingly the young man did survive the night, and even regained his senses on the Tuesday. Exiled on his frigate by choppy seas the admiral implored Baird to pass on his wishes. 'You cannot, be assured, say too much of what my feelings are towards him.' For several more days Parker fought for life, and with a stiff upper lip Nelson wrote to Miss Parker in Gloucester to tell her that his 'dear son and friend' would share many more years.[62]

Nelson needed to go to the Downs, but hated to leave. On 24 September he reported that 'if Dr Baird will allow me to see him [Parker] for a few minutes, I intend to go on shore to assure him that I love him, and shall only be gone a few days, or he might think that I neglected him.' Probably he went to Middle Street for that final meeting, for at 4.30 the next morning he sailed. At noon he was overtaken by a courier from Baird, who said that Parker was incoherent and very near the end. The admiral hurried back, reaching the Downs at five in the evening, but was so distressed at the thought of seeing the dying man that he busied himself with the probable sequel, ordering Sutton and Bedford to organise a funeral and asking Lutwidge to stand by to inform the Admiralty. After two tormented nights, Nelson sent Sutton to the hospital on the morning of Sunday, 27 September, with a message that if Parker had regained his senses and wanted to see him, he would fly to the bedside. But Sutton returned grim-faced. Parker had died at nine that morning.[63]

Nelson wrote to Davison, St Vincent, Emma and others in letters sealed with black wax, but seemed almost bereft of words. 'My heart is almost broke,' he told his mistress, 'and I see I have wrote nonsense, for I know not what I am doing.' He could not bear to see Parker's body, but with the permission of the father obtained his hair, which he wished to have buried with him, and 'which I value more than if he had left me a bulse of diamonds'. Striving to be practical, he talked about getting John Flaxman to sculpt a monument, and tried to settle the dead man's affairs. The Admiralty agreed that the money Nelson had paid for Parker's lodgings and nurses would be refunded by the Sick and Hurt Board, but not the funeral expenses, and the admiral forked out additional funds to satisfy some minor creditors. When Parker's father gave a sorry story that his pocketbook and £20 had been stolen in London, Nelson cheerfully provided enough for mourning clothes and his journey home.[64]

The funeral occurred the day after Parker's death. The coffin was conveyed to the shipyard, from which the cortege to St George's Church in the High Street would start, and ceremonies began at 11.30, when the admiral and other officers from the *Amazon* came ashore. The ships wore pendants at half-mast, their yards reversed, and at noon the solemn thud of half-minute guns from the flagship and shore batteries signalled the procession to begin. On they marched in slow and awful majesty, two hundred of the Derbyshire Regiment with their arms reversed; a military band playing the 'dead march' with muffled drums; a chaplain; Captains John Bazely and Samuel Sutton; the two secretaries of the fleet; six officers from the *Amazon*; and Dr Baird. The coffin followed, escorted by six captains and carried by seamen in blue jackets and white trousers, and behind came the mourners, led by Nelson, Lutwidge and Lord George Cavendish, the commander of the Derbyshires, and including sea officers, pilots and servants. The Reverend Mr Brandon took an hour to complete the service in a clear, strong voice, and then Parker was laid to rest behind the church. 'Lord Nelson was visibly affected' as he followed the coffin, reported the Gloucester newspaper, and streamed with tears at the grave. Three volleys of musketry were fired, and the mourners gravely dispersed. Nelson returned to the dockyard 'by a private way' with his secretary, the captains of the fleet and Admiral Lutwidge. 'Half past one,' he wrote to Emma. 'The dreadful scene is past. I scarcely know how I got over it. I could not suffer much more and be alive. God forbid I should ever be called upon to . . . see as much again.'[65]

No more could be done for Parker, but during the remaining days of his command Nelson could still serve the living with the favours that came so easily to him. The mother of young Edward Augustus Enery of the *Acton* could find 'no words' adequate to describe the 'great and unparalleled act of kindness' the admiral had done her son. Gore was surprised to receive a tea kettle from his superior, engraved as a permanent token of the admiral's gratitude and admiration. The tough captain admitted 'sentiments which beggar all description', and probably kept it always. Baird received an engraved silver cup to commemorate the 'humane attention' he had paid the casualties of Boulogne. There was one ungrateful beneficiary, however. Parker's father, Thomas the apothecary, turned out to be a 'swindler' and 'dirty dog'. Nelson learned that the story of the pocketbook was a ruse to secure money; that the surgeon had dunned young Langford for money; and that other deceits had been uncovered by Sutton, Hardy and Bedford. 'Dear Parker's father was here, a very *different* man from his son,' he wrote to Stewart who wanted a keepsake of the dead officer. He had stripped the lodgings of 'everything' but 'I have got a map of England, which you shall have. It was his, dear gallant spirit! But he is gone! I have felt, for I loved him like a child. He died as he lived, a hero and a Christian.'[66]

8

Nelson had lost Parker, but the anti-invasion flotilla employed some outstanding talent, recognised or not, and brought new 'brothers' into Nelson's fold. An example of the former was Captain William Robert Broughton, one of the finest navigators in the service and a hero of Pacific exploration, who here commanded the *Batavier* off Pan Sand. Two of the old 'brothers' were with Nelson, Hardy in the *Isis* and Berry in the *Ruby*. Berry's progress had fumbled and stumbled, but he survived by clinging to his old chief. 'You are the only real friend I ever found in the world,' he said. But a trio of competent officers became part of a new 'select' band which Nelson vowed to employ if he served again. Sutton, Gore and Bedford all had invitations to visit Merton. Samuel Sutton, a forty-one-year-old Scarborough man, had captained the *Alcmene* in the Baltic and succeeded to the *Amazon* after the tragic death of Riou. A steady, reliable officer, he sealed his bond with the admiral by finding places in his ship for Nelson's followers, helping to fit out two 'young gentlemen', Charles Connor and Stanislaw Banti. Connections of Emma, they were both supported by Nelson's purse. At twenty-nine years John Gore of the *Medusa* was younger than Sutton, but he had known Nelson in the Mediterranean, when they had both served under Hood and Hotham. He had influential patrons, including William Cornwallis, but luck played a big part in his career and he had made £40,000 from two Spanish prizes taken in 1799. Another astonishing windfall was to come. William Bedford of the *Leyden* had participated in the first great naval victory of the French Revolutionary wars, 'the Glorious First of June', in 1794. All three officers reached flag rank, and two would be part of the fleet Nelson commanded in the Mediterranean between 1803 and 1805, the one Nelson regarded as his best.[67]

On 2 September the first of the autumnal north-westerlies pinned the enemy craft in their ports and threatened to drive the British blockaders upon lee shores. Nelson allowed his larger ships to retire to the Downs and Margate or to shelter under Dungeness, where fifteen were finding protection at the end of the month. The admiral insisted that his captains remained aboard, ready to put to sea in an emergency, and as soon as the Hamiltons were out of the way set an example by returning each night to the *Amazon*. Whenever they could his smaller ships patrolled the narrow seas to ensure they were clear of enemy sails, and checked the hostile ports. St Vincent broadly approved, although he warned that the French had been known to take advantage of the cessation of gales to slip away before the blockading squadrons could return to their stations. In this instance only one significant ship seized such an opportunity, the Dutch ship of the line in Flushing, which escaped north to the Goree, an island at the mouth of the Maese.[68]

The bad weather increased Nelson's difficulties with pilots, who discovered more reasons to refuse to put to sea. The *York* and the *Alonso* were prevented from performing their duties on account of pilots. Fortunately, after more than eight years of war, peace was imminent. Lord Hawkesbury, the foreign minister, signed preliminary articles with the French minister on 1 October, and an agreement to suspend hostilities was ratified nine days later. A ship from Lutwidge brought Nelson the news, along with gifts of game and fruit from Catherine. On 15 October, Nelson formally substituted a judicious alert for hostile operations, and slowly his great anti-invasion flotilla was dismembered. The hired barges and sailing vessels were decommissioned and their crews paid off at Sheerness, the revenue cutters returned to their normal duties, the bomb vessels retired to the Nore, and ships were laid up or redeployed. By the time Nelson quit the force on 22 October it had shrunk to twenty-three sail, almost all gun brigs except for the *Leyden, Medusa* and *Amazon*. 'All our party will be broke up,' Nelson told Emma, with his usual sadness for departing friends. 'I am sure, to many of them, I feel truly obliged.'[69]

Nelson's health was worrying him. He kept a fire in his cabin, but shivered in cold fogs and winds, especially when icy easterlies swept across the North Sea from Scandinavia. More urgently, he was fed up with the sea and wanted to return to the tranquil life he was building with Emma. He had wanted to quit by 14 September, but more than any other officer, naval or military, his very presence reassured the public and frightened the enemy, and the government would not let him go until the ink on the peace treaty had dried. 'You will then have seen the ship safe into port, and may close with honour a career of unexampled success and glory,' cajoled Addington. Nelson complied resentfully, denigrating the Admiralty as 'a set of beasts' who did not care 'a damn' for him.[70]

After nearly nine years peace seemed an unnatural state, and, as it inevitably portended a shrinking navy, it suggested that Nelson's life as a fighting admiral was over. In a busy, almost frantic, career he had been the hero of three great naval victories and become the greatest man afloat – anywhere. Despite Boulogne, the end had been creditable. During his watch as the 'guardian' no hostile foot had stepped on English soil, nor had a single British vessel been captured within the limits of his station. But in the last two months his thoughts were naturally looking towards a new future, and the little farm he had bought at Merton. He grumbled at every delay in leaving, but finally he was authorised to hand the command over to Sutton. Until the treaty was confirmed his commission would technically remain in force, but he was permitted to take extended leave.

He got away on 22 October. Since his relationship with Emma had blossomed in 1799, he had shuttled uneasily between the sea and shore, an admiral with divided loyalties. In 1800 it had been difficult to prise him out of Palermo, and in 1801 he grew increasingly irritated with extensive spells of service. Domestic bliss and happiness had vied with naval glory for his soul. It remained to be seen whether peace would bring him the craved contentment, or whether the sea would find a way to claim its own.

XVI

LOOKING FOR PARADISE

Retired from tumult and the public care,
While modest Nelson breathes his Merton air,
Why will a nation sigh to give him power
And load with anxious weight this easy hour?
Why force the hero from his rich repose,
Whose happy spirit calmed that nation's woes?

'On Lord Nelson at Merton', *c.*1803

I

The letters Nelson wrote between 1799 and 1802 reveal a discontented, unhappy man. Emma's presence alone soothed him, and in her absence memories of moments with her induced a sharply poignant sense of loss.

There was, for instance, the fine morning of 12 October 1801, when Nelson, Bedford and Sutton landed on a smooth, freshly washed beach at Walmer, where the former prime minister lived in his capacity as Warden of the Cinque Ports. Pitt, who drank deeply and kept odd hours, was still asleep when the visitors called, and Nelson left his card before walking back to Deal by a route he had used the previous month with the Hamiltons and Sarah Nelson. The officers stopped at the army barracks, but Lord Cavendish had gone to London on business, and they finally settled for refreshments with Admiral Lutwidge. But Nelson could not get that earlier perambulation out of his head. 'All rushed into my mind, and brought tears into my eyes,' he confided to Emma. 'Ah, how different to walking with such a friend as you, Sir William and Mrs Nelson.'[1]

Nelson missed Emma immediately. 'I came on board,' he wrote after she left Deal, 'but no Emma . . . My heart will break. I am in a silent distraction. The four pictures of Lady H[amilto]n are hung up, but alas! I have lost the original . . . My dearest wife, how can I bear our separation? Good God, what a change! I am so low that I cannot hold up my head.'[2]

Apart, both lovers became miserable. To satisfy Emma he intensified the loneliness of his service by his appalling resolution to abstain from company. 'You need not fear all the women in this world; for all others, except yourself, are pests to me. I know but one, for who can be like my Emma? I am confident you will do nothing which can hurt my feelings, and I will die by torture sooner than do anything which could offend you.' In this vein he excused trips ashore. His 'business' was purely with the admiral, he explained, and he had been compelled to attend a civic dinner in Sandwich after receiving the freedom of the town. 'I put them off for the moment, but they would not be let off. Therefore this business, dreadful to me, stands over, and I shall be attacked again when I get to the Downs. But I will not dine there, without you say approve, nor perhaps then . . .' Harwich and Margate were disappointed by his unavailability, and he repelled contacts with 'Lady this, that and t'other', who came hopefully alongside his ship. Even his old diplomatic friends the Trevors were accorded the briefest access at Deal.[3]

Like Fanny before her, Emma urged Nelson to avoid endangering his person. 'No more boat work, I promise you,' wrote the admiral. Going further, she encouraged him to resign his command. Despite Emma's protestations that her 'love of his glory' kept Nelson at sea, others saw her as the root of his manifest dissatisfaction with the service. 'That infernal bitch . . . would have made him poison his wife and stab me, his best friend,' St Vincent thundered, certain that Nelson's protestations about his health were mere pretexts. He exaggerated, but others closer to Nelson – indeed, very close – sang a similar song. 'That b[itch] will play the deuce with him. She is now endeavouring to persuade him that the Admiralty are jealous of his proceedings at Boulogne, and it is her alone who is persuading him to go to London to purchase her a villa. His excuse to Lord St Vincent is to plan a little expedition.' The writer of this frank analysis was none other than Commodore Parker, and the recipient Davison, who was obviously expected to sympathise.[4]

Emma, of course, was embittered after her catastrophic collapse of status and influence in England. Excluded from court, ostracised by many 'gentle' folk and lampooned in print, she also faced an impecunious future. Her ailing husband had not returned as the saviour of a valued ally of His Britannic Majesty, but 'a disgraced man', fobbed off with an inadequate pension of £2000, a pension, moreover, that ended with his death and gave no security to his widow. Hamilton – he who had been raised in the household of the king, a scion of Lord Archibald Hamilton, whose wife had been the lover of a Prince of Wales – was now reduced to sitting in ante-chambers awaiting appointments with the private secretaries of ministers in order to plead his case like a distressed pauper. But the government would have nothing to do with his debts and expenses, and he had had to sell art treasures. In a new will of 28 May Hamilton honoured an obligation to bequeath his Pembroke estate to Greville, and left Emma and her mother with a one-off payment of £400 and annuities of £800 and £100 respectively, pittances against the social standing they were expected to maintain and her ladyship's notorious open-handedness. To Emma, who had risen from poverty and striven for respect and admiration, this was a disastrous fall, and she attributed it to the meanness and ingratitude of government.[5]

Emma's fury at 'the vagabonds in power' stoked resentment in others. She told Sarah Nelson that her avaricious husband had been left 'a slave to a little country parsonage' when 'he ought to be in the palace of Lambeth', while Nelson was rightly 'a duke greater than Marlborough'. No one nodded more fiercely than Parson William, whose unfathomable greed shamelessly manipulated his brother's achievements. In the summer of 1801 William was worrying that Nelson's barony, now overtaken by his latest peerage, would either terminate or descend to Josiah as the admiral's stepson. Supported by Emma, he persuaded Nelson to have the official title of the barony extended to include Hilborough, William's seat, and to secure its descent, failing a direct heir, to the parson's line. Through Addington's good offices the change was effected in August, but the dust had not settled before William and Emma were plotting a new campaign. 'Now *we* have secured the peerage, we have only one thing to ask,' William wrote his confidante, 'and that is *my* promotion in the church, handsomely and honourably, such as becomes Lord Nelson's brother and heir apparent to the title. No put off with small beggarly stalls.' Like a vulture, he smelt death on 'two or three very old' prebends of Canterbury, each sitting on £600 a year and a good residence, as well as six 'old' deans close to oblivion. These ambitions and frustrations were relentlessly dumped on Nelson. 'What must we think of [the] gratitude of ministers who pass over your father and brothers almost every day?' William wrote to his brother, twisting the knife. 'Why, four deaneries and prebendal stalls went begging the previous week.' Even his wife, who hated her lonely country life and longed to move closer to Merton, tired of William's ceaseless importuning. 'Your brother does all he can,' she said, 'that *I do know*, so that *I wish* you would never say a word about it.'[6]

It was easy to disenchant Nelson, who marvelled 'that the man . . . pushed forward to defend his country has not from that country a place to lay his head in'. After Maurice's death he was almost constantly out of sorts with the Admiralty, whom he accused of neglecting his followers. He had a point. The failure to reward the veterans of such dogged encounters as Copenhagen and Boulogne had not helped to inspire men to endure serious battle. Nelson had a few successes, such as those on behalf of former shipmates, the Colletts and Joseph Bromwich, and some of his failures were due to his ignorance of the customs of the service rather than Admiralty resistance. Thus Thomas Fellows could not be appointed a dockyard clerk without the necessary seniority, and there was little point in promoting George Tobin commander when there were no ships to put him in. Troubridge, stung by a charge that the board had unworthily pushed Thesiger forward, tried to reassure Nelson. 'I have been turning everything over in my mind and cannot accuse myself or anyone here of not attending to your lordship's recommendations as far as possible.' Nelson refused to believe it.[7]

As soon as Nelson got to Sheerness in July, he also wanted leave to return to London on personal business. If St Vincent saw this as another episode of Lady Hamilton's charms, he did not say. He merely claimed that the admiral's absence from duty at such a time would produce 'the worst possible effects', leaving Nelson to whimper about his 'life of sorrow and sadness'. Tiring of the admiral's applications, Troubridge tactlessly reminded him that Dickson had been at his post for three years and been absent but seven days, but Nelson had firmly decided that the board cared nothing for him and that Troubridge had betrayed his friendship. Sir Thomas lamented, 'I can only say I never meant to give offence . . . you say you never had but one real friend [Emma]. I know many hundreds who certainly are firm friends to your lordship.' For Troubridge keeping Nelson to his task entailed a constant treading on eggshells, rebuttals of insinuations and attempts at reassurance.[8]

On the arguments went, through the summer and into the autumn, when Nelson clamoured to go home before the colder weather bit hard. 'I should have got well long ago in a warm room, with a good fire and sincere friends,' he grumbled. His sense of duty was far from extinguished, but once the obvious need for his services passed, he hated every moment he stayed. 'I am kept here,' he told Emma, 'for what? He [Troubridge] may be able to tell; I cannot.' The villain of the severest tirades was always 'Master Troubridge', who had 'grown fat' in Whitehall while he shivered at Deal or in the Downs. When Troubridge artlessly suggested that Nelson might benefit from wearing flannel shirts, Nelson rejected the advice with contempt. 'Does he care for me? No.' The friendship between these two officers was over. Nelson was jealous of Troubridge and thought him an ungrateful liar. Hardy agreed, and pictured Troubridge as 'a true politician' who stuck by whoever was most 'likely to push him forward'. But Troubridge saw an admiral difficult to control, putting dark constructions upon innocent remarks and brooding over imaginary slights. 'I feel much distressed at the part of your letter, [from] which I construe that this board would envy any success your lordship might have and feast on your failure,' he complained. 'There never was a charge so unmerited . . . Some person has been poisoning your mind against us . . . I am heartily sick of a situation where I see it is impossible to give satisfaction.' The problem of control was the more difficult because in some respects Nelson had actually become bigger than the Admiralty. He often corresponded directly with ministers, and his professional reputation was so high and sensitivities so sharp that it was difficult to contradict him. When Nelson gave up the idea of attacking Flushing in August the board breathed a sigh of relief; their lordships had doubted the wisdom of the attack, but shrank from interfering.[9]

As an incentive St Vincent had promised that when Keith stood down as commander-in-chief of the Mediterranean, Nelson would be named his successor, but the latter was now 'damned sick of the sea', especially when there was 'nothing to be done on the great scale'. With peace around the corner, he doubted that he would be employed again and showed few regrets. 'I hate the noise, bustle and falsity of what is called the great world,' he sighed. He, Emma and Horatia deserved to 'be happy'.[10]

2

Nelson longed to end his homeless 'vagabond' existence, but where would that peace be found? Nelson thought he knew the answer. He would, he said, 'retire and under the shade of a chestnut tree at Bronte, where the din of war will not reach my ears, do I hope to solace myself, make my people happy and prosperous, and by giving advice (if asked) enable His Sicilian Majesty, *my benefactor*, to be more than ever respected in the Mediterranean, and to have peace with the Barbary states'. Italy was his preferred destination, where the climate was kind and he could live with his mistress high in honour and watch his daughter grow. Emma, too, remembered Italy as the 'only . . . country in which . . . I could have been completely happy', while even Sir William, whose infirmity protested at extensive travelling, clung to the idea. It was not until November 1801 that he finally dismissed his staff at the Palazzo Sessa.[11]

Nelson dreamed of Bronte, but had never seen it, and that was the trouble. In July, when he was planning to visit the estate with the Hamiltons, it was already struggling. John Graefer, the manager, had only cleared its old debts by contracting £3700 worth of new ones, most owed the Archbishop of Bronte and Chevalier Forcella. But although the climate was warm and the vast winter snow sent abundant water running in rivulets down Mount Etna in the spring and summer, Graefer was beginning to despair of ever turning the *boschetto* (a copse in the western part of the duchy) into Nelson's model farm. Everything else was in short supply, from furnishings for the farmhouse to necessary roads, craftsmen, tools, flax seeds and plants. Much sent from England rotted before it reached Sicily. Nelson wanted to employ the new equipment he had seen revolutionising agriculture in Norfolk, and shipped out three ploughs, numerous tools, a horse-hoe, a 'skim' and a winnowing machine, but he lacked the resources for a realistic investment. The threshing machine recommended by Captain Alexander Cochrane was probably never purchased. Although the Sicilian government was sympathetic to Nelson's difficulties, and waived some archaic obligations, including a requirement to maintain horsemen for the king's service, the whole project was stymied for want of money.[12]

The tenants of the duchy, who Nelson wanted to turn into a class of prosperous small farmers, also gave Graefer constant headaches. Nelson had ordered him to let properties only to *Brontesi*, but most were ignorant of anything beyond the most basic subsistence farming, and some sublet to 'strangers', including not a few 'bad eggs'. Graefer was considering bringing in tenants from England or Lombardy to set examples. And there were political matters to address, since Nelson was responsible for administering justice, enforcing bylaws in the baronial courts, and mustering enough men to repel the occasional incursion by Barbary corsairs. The tenor of these vexations came to Nelson through Graefer and Noble, but John Tyson, the admiral's secretary, was even then on his way back from the Mediterranean with huge doses of cold water to deliver.[13]

In the autumn of 1801 Nelson had yet to receive these reassessments, and looked upon Merton as a temporary residence that would help him to close his affairs in England. The furniture that Emma was purchasing for Merton, with the goods Nelson had in storage, would 'probably go to Bronte one of these days', for he would 'certainly go there whenever we get peace'. Nelson was even thinking about the staff he might need in Sicily. Scott, Sir Hyde's secretary, who spoke Italian, looked a likely aid, and the admiral offered Hardy a hundred-acre farm on the estate, as well as apartments in the main house. The land appealed, but the captain politely declined the offer of accommodation, which would have brought him into more contact with Lady Hamilton than he desired.[14]

Nelson had left it to Emma to find the temporary home in the London area, but his thin purse was an obstacle, and the latest command had not been much help. 'If I continue this command much longer,' he had written, 'ruin . . . must be the consequence, for I am called upon, being thought very rich, for everything, beyond any possibility of my keeping pace with my rank and station.' Apart from the unavoidable expenses he had incurred as a commander-in-chief, which he reckoned at more than £3000, his 'soul' remained 'too big' for his 'purse', and he assessed his available fortune at £10,000. His pay would be cut as soon as the peace ended his employment, and Bronte was still a black hole. When Tyson arrived and presented his accounts, the admiral had to find £4000 to reimburse him for sums already expended in Sicily. 'I take no shame to be poor,' his bankers, William Marsh and Henry Creed, learned. 'Never for myself have I spent sixpence. It has all gone to the honour to my country.'[15]

He exaggerated, but years of exceptional service had certainly placed him at the poorer end of the peerage, without a house or an acre of home ground, those indispensable qualifications in a society dominated by landed wealth. Once the necessaries were out of the way, he had next to nothing to support his standing. So Emma was given a very lean purse to perform the not uncomplicated task of finding a suitable property, close enough to London for business but sufficiently remote to provide sanctuary. Nelson told her that he had £3000 in hand, but could borrow more at fairly short notice.

Nonetheless, in August she stumbled across Merton Place in the village of Merton, Surrey, which Skinner and Dyke had advertised at £9400, including fittings and garden utensils. Originally known as Moat House Farm on account of its circuitous canal, the brick-built residence had been built half a century before by one Henry Pratt, and subsequently enlarged, improved and renamed by a prosperous hatter and East Indian merchant named Sir Richard Hotham. Now the estate consisted of fifty-two acres in the parishes of Wimbledon and Merton, enclosed by park palings and 'remarkably fine live Quick fences'. It straddled the London to Epsom turnpike – Merton High Street – and was only seven or eight miles out of the city by way of Westminster Bridge and Clapham Common. The house belonged to the heirs of a calico printer named Charles Greaves, his widow (Ann), brother, son and business partner, William Hodgson.[16]

Nelson's solicitor, William Haslewood of Booth and Haslewood of Craven Street, was Emma's principal agent. He was sure the property was being over-valued. If the rental value of the land was £4368, which he believed, the £4632 being asked for the house itself was far too high. He thought £45 would be well spent on a survey, but Nelson impatiently insisted on proposing to purchase without even seeing the property. Haslewood was so sure that the deal was a bad one that he commissioned a survey on his own hock, and J. C. Cockerell of Savile Row, 'a gentleman of great general information as well as professional ability', accordingly took a carriage south-westwards to inspect Merton Place.[17]

His report was damning. Cockerell considered Merton 'altogether the worst place under all circumstances that I ever saw pretending to suit a gentleman's family. It is scarcely possible to find a worse.' From afar Nelson swept all these objections aside. Cockerell, he said, was no judge of his pocket. 'I cannot afford a fine house and grounds,' he said, and it was as simple as that. At £9000 Merton did not seem expensive to him, even if another £3500 would have to be spent furnishing and insuring it, and he ordered Haslewood to purchase without so much as a haggle. 'I never knew much got by hard bargains,' he said. For a man as particular as Nelson, it was a brave decision, and yet it was the right one, for this inauspicious beginning led him to the 'paradise' he had wanted on earth.[18]

The sum was not easy to find. Davison, Tyson and George Matcham offered loans, but prize money and the sale of stock and diamonds created a down payment and a modest reserve. Emma became so irritated by the delays that she dubbed Mrs Greaves a second 'Tom Tit', but she got possession in October. The ménage's fiction of independent living would be maintained, for although the Hamiltons would share Merton, allowing Sir William to fish the canal and the nearby River Wandle, which flowed northwards a little to the east, they would still have their townhouse in Piccadilly, convenient for the Royal and Dilettanti Societies. Nelson was determined that everything in his new home, from the furniture to the servants, would be his own, and restricted Sir William's financial contributions to the living expenses. He sent Emma the keys to his stored chests, imparting instructions about pictures of himself and his exploits, tea urns, furniture, glass and Coalbrookdale breakfast china. With uncomfortable difficulty the possessions of Nelson and his estranged wife were separated at Dods's warehouse in Brewer Street without the parties meeting. With the admiral's consent, Fanny reclaimed her linen, glass and china, possessions 'of no great quantity but of great consequence to me', and took a share of the wine for her new London home in Somerset Street.[19]

Emma's gushing letters about Merton filled Nelson with childlike anticipation. He talked about the 'farm' and enthusiastically bombarded Emma with advice about sheep, cows, pigs, chickens and ducks; the best fish for stocking the stream; and the desirability of acquiring additional properties and a turnip field. She undertook to supervise the whole, setting men to work, and by 26 September Nelson was satisfied that she would turn Merton into 'the prettiest place in the world'. He looked forward to epitomising the paternalism that he had never ceased to believe in. 'None but real friends shall come to Merton,' he said. 'We will eat plain, but will have good wine, good fires, and a hearty welcome for our friends, but none of the great shall enter our peaceful abode. I hate them all!' There must be cots 'for our sea friends', and the local tradesmen would be paid well and promptly. 'To be sure we shall employ the trades people of our village in preference to any others in what we want for common use, and give them every encouragement to be kind and attentive to us.' Oh, and there had to be a 'nice church' in which they would take their places in the congregation and christen Horatia in the spring. Throughout, they would 'set an example of goodness to the under parishioners'.[20]

Nelson could not escape from his ship quick enough, and upon his release travelled through the night towards London. After crossing Westminster Bridge the coach turned south, passing through the urban reaches of Lambeth before coursing south-west across an extensive area of parkland, arable fields and pleasing meadows. About dawn of Friday, 23 October 1801, Nelson's carriage crossed a bridge that spanned the Wandle, passed a small junction where the Wandsworth Road struck north on the right and a lane led southwards to Merton Abbey, and a little beyond found the gates to Merton Place. The admiral must have been at the window to see the coach turn left and mount a stone bridge to cross the moat and reach the north façade of the house. The Hamiltons were there, and Charlotte Nelson, who had been brought from Whitelands school, but Nelson alighted sick and exhausted and flopped into a sofa.[21]

Within hours he was putting signatures to the formalities of his purchase. The agreed price was an immediate payment of £7000, and a rate of 2½ per cent interest on the remaining £2000 until 24 October 1803, when the principal sum became due. Another £1000 got him the furniture and a haystack. With his house Nelson secured a fire insurance policy, and the next day he added a five-hundred-year lease of the East Lords Leaze, a tract of land north of the turnpike road, in Wimbledon parish, which had belonged to Charles Greaves and his business partners, William Hodgson, James Newton and John Leach.

To meet these expenses, Nelson relied upon loans of £4000 from his brother-in-law, George Matcham, and £3000 from Davison.[22]

The village had been illuminated in Nelson's honour, and the Sunday gave Nelson an opportunity to visit the church, where Charlotte dutifully turned the pages of his prayer book, and he met such excited parishioners as the Newtons and Halfhides. James and Mary Halfhide sent Charlotte grapes, but Emma discovered that their generosity was boundless and they would have given 'us half of all they have'. The weekend done, the entourage went into London on Monday, stopping at Whitelands, where Nelson and the Hamiltons persuaded a flattered headmistress, Miss Voller, to allow Charlotte to serve them tea and extend her leave until the following day. At one in the afternoon they were in Sir William's house in Piccadilly, where Mrs Gibson had been summoned with Horatia. Still disguised as a 'Miss Thomson' being sponsored by kind godparents, and now nine months old, the little girl remained for a day. For the time being that would be her life, a residence in Great Titchfield Street punctuated by occasional short visits to Piccadilly or Merton. Her first to Merton occurred on 15 December.[23]

As the possibilities unfolded, Nelson declared himself entirely pleased. He loved Merton Place from the beginning.

3

Owning a home provides the means of hospitality, and no one enjoyed meeting friends and family more than Nelson. Already admirers were appearing. One of the first was Walterstorff, the Danish diplomat, who spent a night at Merton in December. He was grateful for Nelson's testimonial, which he credited with easing negotiations with Addington about Britain's return of the sequestrated Danish colonies. Apart from Horatia, there was one visitor Nelson particularly wanted to include in his new family arrangements – Edmund, his father.[24]

The process proved to be unpleasant, partly because of the machinations of Lady Hamilton. Fighting for her man and her future, she exposed her ruthlessness in a letter she wrote to Sarah Nelson in September. Fanny was defamed as 'a very wicked, bad, artful woman' with a 'cold heart and infamous soul', who had tried to usurp the right of Nelson's 'own flesh and blood' to inherit his titles by pushing Josiah forward, 'a villain'. Nor did Emma exclude the more reasoning of Nelson's relatives from this mischievous bile, accusing the Boltons and Matchams, as well as Fanny, of encouraging Edmund, a 'poor dear old gentleman', to 'act' a 'bad and horrible part' in supporting Lady Nelson and dealing 'a mortal blow' to his famous son. For good measure Emma repeated a completely false charge that Fanny had abandoned her son. A ruse to drive the old man back into the fold was practised about the time this ugly document was penned. The old parson received an anonymous letter, attacking him for his conduct towards his son, and turning his inherent decency into a vice. It is difficult to think of anyone other than Emma who had the motive and mentality to have concocted it.[25]

It was calculated to upset Edmund, and if it was incapable of instilling guilt in someone as sure of his own rectitude, it stoked his fears of being totally separated from his son. Edmund wrote Nelson a couple of letters, inviting him to visit Burnham Thorpe, where he was spending the autumn, and promising 'a joyful and affectionate reception', but also frankly pointing out that he was considering joining Fanny in her new house in London for a while. 'If Lady Nelson is in a hired house and by herself, gratitude requires that I should sometimes be with her, if it is likely to be of any comfort to her.' Nelson was angry, especially at the possibility that he might be expected to visit his father in Fanny's house, and on 26 September he asked Emma's opinion, ranting mysteriously about his wife's supposed 'ill treatment' of Josiah. He also pressed her to accept Edmund into the Merton household. 'Pray let him come to your care at Merton,' he wrote to his mistress. 'Your kindness will keep him alive.' Sadly, Nelson also drafted a strong reply to his father, imbibing some of Emma's venom and indulging in peevish nonsense. Fanny was accused of describing the allowance Nelson had given her as a 'pittance' ('handsome' and 'exceeded my expectation' were words she had actually used in a surviving letter) as well as of abandoning Josiah. He told Edmund that he had given her £2000 a year and £4000 as a lump sum, neglecting to mention that the latter was the legacy that Lady Nelson had inherited from her uncle. And drawing himself up with inflated self-righteousness, he blamed his father for criticising him. 'As you seem by your conduct to put me in the wrong, it is no wonder that they who do not know me and my disposition should [also], but *Nelson soars* above them all, and time will do . . . justice to my private character.' Nevertheless, as far as Edmund's place of abode was concerned, Merton should become his 'home'.[26]

On reflection Nelson tried to withdraw the discreditable document, but it remains an illustration of his refusal to acknowledge himself capable of anything dishonourable. The failure of his marriage was effectively thrown upon his wife, while Edmund found himself aligned with hostile and misguided enemies. Only Nelson, the actual offender, was beyond reproach or regret.

Still, it offered Edmund an opportunity to visit Merton, where bridges might be built, and where the prominent position found for Beechey's portrait of the old parson instilled a notion that this was the family home. Edmund arranged to winter near the Matchams in Bath, and reached London in November, when he stayed a few days with Fanny before pressing on to Merton for a similar interlude. Nelson had failed to destroy his father's friendship with Fanny, but there was a kind of reconciliation. From Merton Edmund wrote to Kitty that his son seemed happier and healthier than he remembered him, surely a reflection of the tranquillity that Emma and Merton had created. Emma, no doubt, applied her charm and while he may not have been the most enthusiastic convert, he appreciated her attention and kindness. Edmund left Merton just as it was blanketed in a heavy fall of snow, but, approaching what was such a special time of the year for fervent Christians, he nursed mixed emotions. He had reconnected with his son, but it was now plain that Nelson and Fanny would never live together again, and the reverend's hope of a reunion was dead. The best he could now do was to shuttle guiltily between the two establishments.

Nelson, who had avoided a distressing family rupture, must have rested easier after his father's visit. He spent the next few days at home, inviting friends to see his new house. Davison was invited to call as often as he liked, and Sutton was told to come as soon as the signing of the definitive peace treaty released him from his vigil at the Downs. The Christmas that followed was far better than the last.

4

As Nelson retired, his dissatisfaction with the Admiralty plumbed new depths, while conversely his involvement with wider politics scaled new but, alas, ultimately no happier heights.

At its heart his problem was grounded in a simple political principle: that government depended upon a written or unwritten contract between subordinates and superiors. The loyalty and service given by a subordinate deserved the reward and protection of the superior. The two were bound in mutual obligation and benefit. When Nelson complained of the inadequacy of his rewards, or his inability to advance dependants and followers, he was essentially accusing his superiors of betraying the trust that his and their service had earned. Duty had been done by one party but not the other.

The larger sore with the Admiralty was Copenhagen, for which Nelson continued to clamour for medals for his captains and the payment of an equitable amount of prize money. Sir Hyde's destruction of the prizes had robbed the victors of the usual compensation, but Nelson had suggested the government grant of £100,000 in lieu. There were precedents, but St Vincent was an economist, and declined to take that route. He promised that a generous payment would be paid for the one prize taken into the navy, the *Holsten*, but otherwise the fleet would have to rely on 'head money', an unsatisfactory alternative based on the manpower of the enemy ships destroyed. St Vincent nervously promised to discourage those of the Baltic fleet who had not been in Nelson's assault force from sharing in the result. The first lord continued to drag his feet in what was a particularly thorny problem, and the only headway Nelson made was in persuading the Ordnance Office to purchase the 214 brass guns taken by the Baltic fleet.[27]

On another front Nelson flagellated the City of London for failing to acknowledge the victors of Copenhagen, even though it had passed a vote of thanks to the British seamen and soldiers who had finally defeated the French in Egypt. On Monday, 9 November, a new Lord Mayor, John Eamer, was sworn in, and, anticipating a more amenable corporation, Nelson and the Hamiltons attended the customary dinner at the Guildhall. Their coach was man-hauled through the streets, and at frequent stops Nelson shook hands with members of the accompanying crowd. Afterwards he wrote to Eamer, demanding an explanation that he could send to the men of Copenhagen; at least they would know that he had not 'failed' them. Another letter went to the prime minister, citing the neglect of the City and St Vincent's unfulfilled promise to strike a Copenhagen medal.[28]

Addington admired Nelson, and saw him as both a fount of naval advice and a potential political ally, but he tried to explain that the issue of medals and triumphalism in the city were provocative at a time when Britain's relations with Denmark were under repair. But in the meantime copies of the admiral's letters had caused an explosion when they reached the desk of the first lord of the Admiralty. St Vincent replied testily that he had never, as Nelson said, promised that medals would be struck; indeed, he had expressed 'the impropriety of such a measure'. St Vincent was aware of the diplomatic aspects that concerned Addington, but also wrestled with difficulties the issue posed for the navy. The failure to reward did little for the morale of the service, but if there was a distribution of medals, and Sir Hyde's division was excluded, it would not only raise questions about what the commander-in-chief had been doing during the battle and spark a court martial, but also set one part of the fleet against the other.[29]

Now it was Nelson's turn to see red. The first lord's denial of his statement that a promise had been made impugned his honour. Angrily, he told Foley that he would never wear his St Vincent or Nile medals until one was also granted for Copenhagen. Furthermore, he declined to receive any further thanks from the City of London or to accept any invitations to dine with the corporation. While the government construed the rewards for Copenhagen in their wider context, Nelson only felt that he had let down men who had fought, bled and died for their country. He returned St Vincent's fire immediately, stating that the earl's letter had left him 'thunderstruck'. Surely his lordship remembered apologising to Nelson for the delay in producing the Copenhagen medals? Whether he did or no, Nelson had informed the captains that they would get their medals on the strength of it, and they would expect the promise to be fulfilled. Nelson told St Vincent that the matter was 'of the very highest concern' to him, but the response was a dry one. St Vincent curtly remarked that Nelson was 'perfectly mistaken' about their conversation.[30]

The two most prestigious admirals alive stood locked in a dispute about honour, the one small and fragile, the other stocky and hunched with a countenance like the Day of Judgement. 'Either Lord St Vincent or myself are liars,' Nelson told Davison. Nelson visited the Admiralty twice in December and once in February, but his correspondence with the board shrank. When Nelson raised another matter six months later, St Vincent frostily replied that there were 'solid objections' to the proposal, as Troubridge had 'very obligingly undertook to explain to your lordship'. What goodwill had existed between them had almost evaporated.[31]

Long before, Nelson had learned that bypassing superiors by appealing to their masters could help as well as hinder a cause. He and Addington had become friends. 'It will give me great pleasure to see you,' encouraged the minister, 'and to converse with you after the very interesting occurrences of the last three months.' The two met on public occasions. In November they were both at the Guildhall dinner, and three days later they were toasted at another, sponsored by the Levant Company at the London Tavern and attended not only by Nile captains but also political powers such as Grenville and the Marquis of Buckingham. At the beginning of December the admiral visited Addington to speak his mind, enjoying a 'very friendly conversation'. It did not produce a medal, but it did make Nelson one of the few sea officers with the ear of government. The relationship between admiral and premier minister was a curious one in some ways, for Addington lacked the strength that characterised Nelson. Nelson had been an early admirer of Pitt. In October the two men had visited each other, Pitt finding Nelson in the *Amazon* and the admiral eventually managing to sample the other's hospitality at Walmer, but their relations remained grounded in respect rather than liking. Nelson found Pitt a cold fish, and complained that his administration 'never did anything for me or my relations'.[32]

Pitt resigned over the issue of Catholic Emancipation and gave his support to Addington, but the two were very different men. More likeable than Pitt, Addington nevertheless lacked political muscle and was considered a lightweight. On the crucial issue of the war, he tended to be defeatist, preferring accommodation to confrontation, but while he was prepared to pay a stiff price for peace he faithfully reflected the country's war weariness. In 1801 Britain had no credible allies and her economy was in trouble. Her balance of trade with Europe had largely been profitable because of the expansion of her overseas trade and re-export of colonial products to the continent, but those surpluses had been eroded by a run of bad harvests that compelled Britain to import grain. The country's gold reserves were falling, and the shortage of bread drove up prices and caused social discontent. In these circumstances Addington's message of peace and economic retrenchment struck a welcome chord.

Nelson was not immune to that message if France could be kept within reasonable bounds. He saw nothing but a long punishing struggle ahead. 'It has somehow . . . been our fate to turn neutrals and allies . . . into enemies,' he said. 'Ours will now be a war of defence, and a very expensive one.' He had seen ambiguous, unreliable, weak and opportunist allies enough, and thought that if Britain could make a lasting peace that protected her interests then she might as well do so. Rather more surprising in one who had argued so passionately for a unified and strenuous resistance to the French, Nelson continued to support Addington even after the unsatisfactory terms of the peace became known.[33]

Addington's aims of peace and retrenchment might have been sound had France not been in the secure grasp of Napoleon, an egocentric for whom peace and war were tools to further imperial dreams. Bonaparte's purpose in negotiating with Britain was merely to gain space in which to prepare for another round of warfare, and if Addington was foolish enough to disarm in the belief that the peace would last so much the better. Nor did Bonaparte need to consider serious concessions when Addington was so eager to please. The result was a peace, finally concluded on 27 March 1802, that divided Britain's leaders. Grenville and Windham, the late ministers handling foreign and military affairs, condemned it as a sell-out, while some Whigs, incapable of seeing the true nature of the French government, applauded it.

Despite his hatred of the French regime, Nelson, like Pitt, thought the peace 'not . . . a bad one, all things considered'. Basically the treaty of Amiens restored the conquests Britain had made in Europe, Africa and the West Indies to their previous owners, except for Trinidad and Ceylon. In return, France's only new concession, over and above what had already been agreed with Austria and Naples in the treaties of Lunéville and Florence in 1801, was an undertaking to evacuate Naples and the papal territories. As for northern Italy, Napoleon had already secured that at Lunéville, when a parcel of petty satellites, including the Cisalpine and Ligurian republics, had been accepted by Austria.

In a revealing letter to Stewart, his Baltic comrade, Nelson wrote, 'I rejoice that we have not kept either Malta or the Cape. The expense would have been too great for us. I wish we could have kept Minorca and Dovego. But Ceylon is a treasure. It secures India to us and its trade for ever . . . Trinidad is worth more than Antigua, Montserrat and the Virgin Islands put together.' This was not a penetrating analysis. The Cape of Good Hope, which was returned to the Dutch, was arguably as important to the security of Britain's position in India as Ceylon or Egypt, guarding as it did the sea route between Europe and the east. And the relinquishment of Minorca meant that Britain was again without a naval base inside the Strait of Gibraltar. Malta, it was agreed, would be restored to the Knights of St John, an arrangement deriving some strength from the guarantee of the great powers, including Britain, Russia and France, to uphold it, but what would that guarantee be worth if France regained control of the Mediterranean? Perhaps Nelson believed that little more could be expected, and that disappointments were counterbalanced by the protection accorded Naples, Sicily and the papal territories. Nelson's greatest reservations were about Sardinia and Tuscany, which he had endeavoured to liberate. In the late round of treaties Sardinia had been stripped of Piedmont, and the Grand Duchy dissolved, although Ferdinand III was compensated with the dukedom and electorate of Salzburg. Tuscany became the kingdom of Etruria, a possession of the Bourbon dukes of Parma, ostensibly independent of France but in reality a client state.[34]

These were not good settlements for Britain, but she could have lived with them if they had been stable. Unfortunately, they were not, and left Napoleon with a stronger grip on the Rhine and bases for expansion in the 'republics' in Holland, Switzerland and Italy. Nelson accepted that there were dangers, and warned that Britain must be prepared to resist any infringements of the Amiens settlement. He doubted that France could voluntarily remain within 'due bounds', and believed that if allowed Napoleon would try to 'degrade' Europe again. As he wrote to a new acquaintance, 'Lord Grenville [and] Windham . . . see the destruction to the country [Britain] from it [the peace], which I cannot. I am the friend of peace, without fearing war, for my politics are to let France know that we will give no insult to her government, nor will we receive the smallest . . . if Buonaparte understands our sentiments he will not wish to plunge France in a new war . . .' Nelson underestimated Bonaparte. He could not believe that anyone could emerge from the dreadful revolutionary conflict of recent years with a hunger for more. But if he was wrong, he told Emma, he would 'with pleasure go forth and risk my life . . . to pull down the overgrown detestable power of France'.[35]

Weak as Addington was, Nelson was ready to support him for the sake of peace, but the needs of his family, friends and shipmates also drove him towards the prime minister. Both men felt a need for the other. Addington's administration was weak inside parliament, and needed important voices and votes to prop it up. He was, jibed George Canning, 'a sheep calling wolves to his assistance'. It was not surprising, therefore, that on 13 October Thomas, Lord Pelham, Addington's home secretary, personally invited Nelson to take his seat in the House of Lords as a viscount. Like other self-servers infesting parliament, Nelson effectively hoped to sell his support for favours. He was blunt about it to Emma. He had 'come on shore good friends with the [Addington] administration', and hoped to 'get something for my brother. For myself it is out of the question. They can give me nothing as a pension at this time, but good things may fall. I shall talk and be much with Mr Addington, if he wishes it.' It is a sad document. The blue-eyed, smooth-faced, idealistic young man of 1784 who had talked about the need for a parliament of independent men, who would judge matters according to the good of the country, had been turned into a government mouthpiece, a grubby placeman willing to do the bidding of the administration in return for favours.[36]

It needs to be emphasised, however, that in this respect Nelson did not stand apart from his parliamentary colleagues. From the borough-mongering provincial elections, in which candidates openly bribed electors, to the scramble of unsalaried members of parliament for positions, sinecures and favours in Westminster, politics was a venal and nepotistic business. Indeed, every administration depended upon its control of favours and perquisites to secure majorities in the divisions, and when parliamentary reform began to bite into the flabby environs of 'Old Corruption' in the nineteenth century there were protests that the crown was in danger of losing its power to govern. In 1800 two decades of minor reforms had made little impact on the system, and even in the Lords, where most members had sufficient independent wealth to stand aside from the blandishments of government, corruption was a norm. Still, some members, whether through wealth, loyalty or tradition, were less amenable than others, and Pitt had to create large numbers of compliant new peers to control the Lords, increasing the peerage by about 50 per cent. Nelson's behaviour was, therefore, par for the course, but in a man who stood so strongly on moral rectitude and the shortcomings of factional politics, it was a depressing compromise.

Emma summoned all her hatred of the Establishment to protest at Nelson's plan, cautioning him against acting the 'time server'. It was an uncomfortable truth that went straight to her lover's heart. Nelson retorted that it was for his brother that he had 'to let them see that my attendance [at the House of Lords] is worth soliciting', though it would be 'a great bore'. As for her charge that he was toadying to ministers, 'What? Leave my dearest friends to dine with a minister? Damn me if I do, beyond what you yourself shall judge to be necessary!' But if he forsook this opportunity 'they will do nothing. Make yourself of consequence to them, and they will do what you wish in reason.'[37]

Overcoming all reservations, Nelson took his seat in the Lords on 29 October, after being introduced to the house by Viscounts Sydney and Hood, the former supplied by the home secretary. He signed the Test Roll of 1801, taking oaths to oppose transubstantiation (Catholicism) and any Jacobite pretenders, and to support the king and his descendants. Shortly he was seconding St Vincent's motion of thanks to Saumarez for a victory over the Spaniards off Algeciras. Nelson flattered both Hood and St Vincent as the founders of the Mediterranean school to which he and Saumarez belonged. Privately Nelson admitted that his maiden performance in parliament had been 'bad enough, but well meant'. In several opportunities to do better, Nelson dutifully spoke up for uncontroversial government initiatives such as the vote of thanks to the triumphant British troops in Egypt or the successful negotiations with Denmark, but a telling episode occurred on 3 November, when he supported the administration in a debate about the terms of the peace. Spencer and Grenville spoke against them, but St Vincent and Nelson replied for the government. Nelson claimed that neither Minorca nor Malta were important to Britain, because they could not be used to blockade the principal French port of Toulon, as if Britain had no other business in the Mediterranean. He admitted, however, that neither should be allowed to fall into French hands. The admiral also affected to see no value in the Cape, which would merely become an unbearable expense, and – wonder of wonders – he even suggested that the French government would likely be a stable one.[38]

This did not deceive everyone. William Huskisson, an intelligent if prickly member of the Commons, marvelled that ministers could 'allow such a fool to speak in their defence', while gazettes carrying the speech abroad brought offence to old friends. Nelson had not suggested that Britain abandon Malta. His true position was that it should be governed by the Two Sicilies under the protection of Russia, and that at all costs it had to be kept out of French hands. He even thought that Britain should step in if Russia failed. But his apparent dismissal of and disinterest in a place important to Britain's eastern trade and vital to the security of southern Italy upset Ball and their Sicilian Majesties. Maria Carolina wrote to Emma that she had been 'greatly distressed' by the speech, which had followed 'the bitter and unjust [Lord] Hawkesbury [the foreign minister], even Pitt and many others, who have decided to leave Italy as a mere French dependent province and the Mediterranean free for them'. It was not only a 'complete abandonment' of her country, but also a 'cruel' return on its fidelity to the British crown. She wrote to Nelson that his idea of abandoning Malta was 'very painful' and he ate humble pie.[39]

Trimming sails to suit the wind worked at sea, but often created unseen problems in the complicated world of politics, and sadly the sacrifices it entailed were often in vain. Nelson certainly had Addington's respect. He dined with the prime minister on 18 December, and a few days later Addington wrote that 'when I have the pleasure of seeing Your Lordship, I hope to have it in my power to tell you that your suggestion respecting Ali Vizier [Pasha] has been carried into effect'. But for all that the rewards the admiral wanted were largely unforthcoming.[40]

These troubles apart, life at Merton was beginning to weave its spell upon the returning hero, and the Christmas of 1801 gave him more happiness than he had known for a long time. The weather was bitter, and Nelson felt ill, venturing little into town, although he and Hamilton attended the levee of 13 November. In Merton the ménage fast became pillars of the local community. Shortly before Christmas they supported a youth theatre, the 'Young Gentlemen of Baron House Academy' at nearby Mitcham, turning out for their productions of *The Siege of Damascus* and *No Song No Supper*, the latter one of the comedies that the admiral seemed to enjoy.[41]

The Hamiltons joined Nelson for his first Merton Christmas, and Charlotte and Horace came from school with a new 'figure dance' to demonstrate. Horace christened a new pair of boots given by his famous uncle. Susannah sent three of the junior Boltons, twelve-year-old Eliza, ten-year-old Ann and their younger brother, Tom. Sarah Nelson made an inevitable appearance, and even little Horatia, though only for a few hours on 15 December. There were friends too, including 'poor Langford', who arrived in January, still recuperating from his wound.[42]

The festive season was altogether more cheerless at 16 Somerset Street, where Fanny spent a relatively lonely Christmas and made her final attempt at reconciliation. On 18 December she wrote to her husband, objecting to 'the silence you have imposed', but offering him 'a comfortable warm house' if he chose to return. With regard to blame, of course she took that upon herself, and spoke of forgiving and forgetting. 'Do, my dear husband, let us live together,' she implored. 'I can never be happy till such an event takes place. I assure you again I have but one wish in the world – to please you. Let everything be buried in oblivion. It will pass away like a dream.'

But Nelson never replied. Her letter was returned with an endorsement in the hand of Davison. It said, 'Opened by mistake by Lord Nelson, but not read.' Truly it was more than the end of a year.[43]

5

The 'gentle' folk of the late eighteenth century were obsessed with their homes. 'Improvement' was a watchword. The expanding population and industrial activity created compelling incentives to develop estates, exploiting mineral resources and enclosing open fields and consolidating holdings to employ new and more efficient methods of husbandry. Seldom had there been a better time to turn land into income as well as social and political influence, and everywhere the *nouveaux riches*, nabobs of trade, captains of industry and luckier public servants legitimised their rising status by purchasing property. However, the availability of country houses was limited by the laws of strict entail, and they were expensive to purchase and maintain. To display their wealth, sophistication and success men and women of mark spent enormous sums landscaping grounds and beautifying houses with ornamental fountains, grottoes and follies, works of art, exquisite handmade furnishings, fine China and glassware, and classical and neo-classical styling. The home and estate was a barometer of status and taste. It was a venue for musicians and painters in a time when the utilitarian Georges had lost the leadership in the arts that had once been a feature of the monarchy. This was the age of 'Capability' Brown, Kent and Repton; of Wyatt, Adam and Nash; of Gainsborough and Reynolds; and of Wedgwood, Chippendale and Sheraton.[44]

Even modestly financed gentry were sucked into the mania for 'improvement', though their houses might be hunting seats or compact country villas rather than the palatial residences of the great families. Indeed, beyond the sprawl of London the country villa was highly desired as a rural retreat for men of business, creating opportunities to recuperate in the tranquil or sublime. To a large extent Nelson's next eighteen months were dominated by the transformation of Merton Place from a condemned residence into a retreat worthy of its beloved inmates. But looking at the property for that first time amidst the golden autumn leaves of 1801, the admiral must have admitted that the surveyor had not been entirely mistaken. The distant noise from the manufactories on the Wandle towards the south-east could be intrusive, while the turnpike road from London, though screened from the house by shrubs and trees, not only ran across its front at no great distance, but sliced right through the estate, creating separate southern and northern portions, each in a different parish. Merton Place itself stood south of the turnpike in Merton parish, but with only one and a half acres of 'pleasure grounds' it was uncomfortably close to neighbours on three sides. Northwards, across the turnpike, were his remaining fifty-one acres, consisting of lawns, paddocks, fields, coppices and walks in Wimbledon parish. To connect the two dismembered parts of the estate without crossing the busy turnpike, a small, dark, leaky subterranean tunnel had been driven beneath the road.

Cockerell had found 'so many insurmountable objections' to the property that he was 'astonished' that any gentleman would consider it. What the Hamiltons saw as a reliable fish stream that circled the house he condemned as a 'dirty black looking canal or . . . broad ditch' that seeped into the flat clay and visited damp upon the building. The canal was, or had been, fed by the Wandle, but Nelson saw the necessity of reducing it and severing its access to the river. As he stood outside his house he also saw the neighbours' arable fields within twenty yards to the east, west and south, and realised that if eye-searing barns or sheds were established on them his view would be ruined. To increase his privacy he needed to extend and strengthen the boundaries of the southern part of his property.[45]

The house itself, said Cockerell, was 'an old paltry small dwelling of low storeys and very slightly built', extended on its flanks by some dubiously constructed rooms and suffering a dilapidated roof. In truth it consisted of two brick-built blocks parallel to the turnpike, one behind the other, attached only on the east side by an entrance hall and ante-room. The northern block, nearer the road, was the principal residence. It faced a small single-span bridge, elegantly adorned with iron railings and two centrally placed lamp-posts, which took the driveway between the house and turnpike over the moat. This block had been recently improved. The original part of it was a seventeenth-century building, about forty-six feet long, with a conventional Palladian-style central pediment and single-gabled roof, three low storeys with five tall windows on each upper floor, and one window on either side of the protruding entrance porch on the ground floor. To this core had been added two-storey flat-topped wings that accommodated a drawing room and a library at ground level. The rear or southern block, which housed the servants, had once been shorter and detached, but it had been extended eastwards so that it was flush with the main block, and the hall and ante-room had been constructed to connect both buildings on that side and create a single eastern façade.

This attempt to make a single residence out of what had been two discrete buildings had struck Cockerell as incoherent. The staff remained in the older section of the rear block, but its eastern extension became part of the 'gentle' accommodation, and provided an elegant dining room. The previous owner seems to have been so pleased with the eastern façade that he considered changing the principal entrance of the house from the north to the east. When Nelson bought it, the entry porch on the north side merely fed into a simple breakfast parlour, whereas the house was entered on the eastern side by means of a centrally placed flight of steps that led into the entrance hall between the double-fronted and bow windows of dining and drawing rooms right and left.

This eastern façade was also the one most enjoyed by the artists and engravers, and it lingered in the memory of all those who knew Merton Place in its heyday. They talked about the light and reflections. The bows appear to have had glass doors that opened into many-sided single-storey verandas overlooking the garden. These, the famous 'miradores', stood upon low trellised balconies, and possessed attractive arches beneath their roof. Perhaps suggesting the influence of the Hamiltons, who had fitted the Palazzo Sessa with a wall of mirrors, Merton Place captured brightness. In 1864 a servant, Thomas Saker, recalled a house 'roomy but not magnificent', distinguished by the 'glass doors in front', 'a long passage with glass doors opening into the lawn behind', and unusual plate glass reflecting doors in some of the principal rooms that created the illusion of light about the interior.[46]

Despite Cockerell's pessimism, Nelson, who had been raised in a cramped, stone-cold rectory, found elegant echoes of a previous owner in the big dining and drawing rooms of the main block, 'fitted up' as they were 'with Sienna, Egyptian and white marble chimney pieces' and 'rich India paper hangings'. Above, the admiral discovered five bedrooms, one or two of them twenty-four-foot square, although some lacked dressing rooms, and the surveyor had thought only one 'fit for a gentleman's accommodation'. According to the sales particulars of 1801, however, there was a modern refinement: a water closet, possibly one of Joseph Bramah's new ball-cock devices. Below the main block Nelson discovered an adequate wine cellar. As for the rear block, which the staff occupied, it sported five small but 'neatly fitted' chambers upstairs and a large servants' hall and kitchen below, together with such necessaries as a secure stone closet behind an iron door, a laundry, and coal and brew houses. Some of the rooms in this block were south-facing, and caught the sun, but Cockerell had deemed it 'even worse than the house'.

Striding out of doors Nelson found more serious difficulties. There was a dairy, pantry and icehouse but little else. 'There is no kitchen garden or a foot of fruit wall,' the surveyor had complained, 'nor any proper situation to make one', and the absence of stables, coach house, sheds or outhouses for stock meant the estate was barely usable as a farm or a gentleman's retreat. Greaves, the last owner, had incomprehensibly sold such conveniences and rented them in less convenient locations elsewhere. Crossing the turnpike to inspect the northern part of his property, however, Nelson saw some fine yews and a beautiful perspective over the open country to the north, but the grounds needed maintenance, and the subterranean tunnel that connected the two parts of his estate pleaded for renovation. All in all, it was a mammoth job, and was ultimately achieved only through the vision of Emma and Mrs Cadogan, who had already revealed new talents. 'It would make you laugh to see Emma and her mother fitting up the pig-sties and hen coops and already the canal is enlivened with ducks, and the cock is strutting with his hens about the walks,' Sir William had written while the admiral was at sea. Emma became such an inseparable partner in Nelson's enterprise that when he left for the Mediterranean in 1803 he insisted on the project remaining in her hands. He would 'admit no display of taste at Merton but hers'.[47]

Nelson speedily tackled the shortage of necessary outbuildings. On 12 November 1801 he leased a plot and its buildings across the turnpike from Thomas Bennett, a calico printer of Wimbledon. The tract was tucked into an angle formed by the turnpike and the Wandsworth road heading north, and was situated immediately east of Nelson's existing holdings in Wimbledon parish. He got the use of the southern part of Bennett's total plot, with barns, stables, a granary, two coach houses, a cowshed and hen houses. Coming from London, Nelson accessed these facilities by a right turn off the turnpike, just before the gates of Merton Place were encountered on the left. At £50 a year the lease was 'a great expense', but it was necessary until the estate south of the road could be enlarged, and alternative buildings erected on it.[48]

Getting the additional space south of the turnpike, around the house, was difficult. The obvious extension was eastwards across a field towards Abbey Lane, 'a narrow lane at the end of the abbey wall', which would then become a natural boundary between Merton Place and Merton Abbey. But that field belonged to William and Ann Axe of Birchin Lane, London, and one Samuel Axe, possibly their son. In fact, Axe owned all the land immediately east, south and west of Nelson's house, and therefore held the key to its future. Two days after arriving at Merton, Nelson wrote to Axe seeking terms for the small field to the east. Axe was not unsympathetic, but explained that his estate and its house had a sitting tenant, Robert Linton. Linton turned out to be a 'churlish farmer' oblivious to Nelson's courtesies and Emma's charm, not unnatural in one who was being uprooted from his home. The admiral was eager to get to work, and as early as April 1802 paid James Bowyer £528 to erect two double coach houses, a six-stall stable, a cow shed and three small slate-roofed staff cottages, but without sufficient land the project had to remain on the shelf.[49]

After a year of indecisive negotiations, Nelson eventually agreed to purchase the whole of Axe's estate in Merton and Mitcham parishes for £8000, payable by Michaelmas of 1804. At a stroke, therefore, he had trebled the size of his property, making it far larger than his biographers have realised. The admiral's land south of the turnpike had expanded from 1½ to 114 acres, dwarfing the hitherto larger 52-acre stretch to the north in Wimbledon parish. George Matcham stumped up half the price by selling government stock invested for his wife's jointure, on condition that Nelson made half-yearly interest payments. But even after transfers had been signed in November 1802, Axe dithered about whether he had full title, and Nelson began to doubt his 'honor' and 'honesty'. Haslewood advised Nelson to put Matcham's money back into the funds until the matter was sorted out, and after consulting eminent counsel in Lincoln's Inn, including the Whig reformer Samuel Romilly, the admiral demanded a bond of indemnity from Axe, covering him against legal repercussions. Linton also pleaded for additional time to find alternative accommodation, and the property did not fully come into Nelson's possession until 29 September 1803, after the admiral had returned to the Mediterranean.[50]

While the extension of the estate remained in abeyance, Nelson concentrated his fire upon making the house habitable. Until the removal to Bronte, it was to be an ancestral home, and his lordship attempted to unify the family portraits, receiving a likeness of Sir Charles Turner, his maternal great-grandfather, from Edmund. There were also gifts to be displayed from all parts, including a Mameluke sabre sent by Captain Hoste, but above all the house must mirror the heroism of its new owner. The walls and grand oak wainscot staircase were festooned with commemorative prints and portraits, some of them reproductions of Captain Fyers's drawings of the Danish line at Copenhagen, while in the entrance lobby in the eastern façade the visitor immediately encountered several other such representations, together with a marble bust of the admiral. The very dining tables were thick with memorabilia. Prominent were the fine 'Nile' and 'Baltic' services that Nelson had been awarded by Lloyd's. The 'Baltic' tea and coffee service, with its decorative greens, browns, white and gold, was inscribed 'Nelson, 2nd April Baltic'. The admiral's silver sauceboats bore a modified coat of arms appropriately inscribed 'Tria Juncta in Uno', ducal and viscount crowns and coronets, and representations of the chelengk and the stern of the *San Nicolas*, a prize taken at Cape St Vincent and included in Nelson's armorial crest. Silver gravy or straining spoons were stamped with the insignia of a duke, viscount and Knight of Bath. Apart from some of the cutlery, which followed Nelson to sea, most of this personalised impedimenta found its permanent home in Merton.[51]

During those first two years a little was also done with the available grounds, and the ménage planned, cut and planted the paths and gardens that surrounded the house, placing laurels, artichokes and apple trees in pleasing places. Emma seems to have particularly treasured the small mulberry tree the trio planted in front of the north façade, not far from the canal, which they almost immediately rechristened 'the Nile'. Thomas Bolton was the professional farmer in the family, but summoning his experience of cultivating his father's glebe, Nelson quickly fancied himself an expert, and happily disseminated advice on such matters as the cropping of hay and the cultivation of turnips. He laid the foundations for a small farm, with varied livestock, some sent by the Boltons. A modest crop was planted in March 1802. When Nelson was ordered to sea again, he gave Linton a one-year lease of Merton Farm, but put part of the businesss in the hands of one Benjamin Patterson of Cowdery Farm, who acted as an agent. Most of the stock was sold off, and a cow and calf, half a dozen piglets and some hens made 114 guineas, although the Merton hay was reckoned to be too 'light and dusty' to fetch a good price.[52]

Like most houses, Merton Place revealed many of its shortcomings gradually, and cost more than had been anticipated, but by the end of 1802 Nelson was the master of 166 acres in Wimbledon, Merton and Mitcham parishes. In the north the estate was relatively unchanged, but in the south its eastern boundary now rested upon Abbey Lane, its western edge extended beyond Morden Road, and to the south the property just fell short of the upper fork of the Wandle. This large expansion created many possibilities, and Nelson's head teemed with plans. He would improve his pleasure gardens, create a new entrance to the estate with a lodge at the junction of Abbey Lane and the turnpike, and fill in the southern and eastern reaches of 'the Nile' to make way for an elegant new driveway that would sweep gracefully towards the east and rear of the house.[53]

'Paradise Merton' was visibly rising before his eyes.

6

Merton was a small parish of few more than eight hundred inhabitants served by three inns, the King's Head, the Six Bells and the Plough, its original heart the grey-chequered flint ruins of a twelfth-century Augustinian priory. The Wandle flowed northwards, passing to the east of Merton Place and powering several calico-printing mills and copper, iron and fullers' works, but the predominant local livelihood was agriculture, and some stretches of the river were quiet enough to allow fishermen to cast for their next meal. Nelson was not as ardent a fly-fisher as Sir William, but villagers remembered seeing him with a rod on the Wandle. The centre of the village lay to the west of Merton Place, beyond where the turnpike angled south and became the Morden Road. It was near enough to London to attract commuters, and embraced more wealth and diversity than most communities of a comparable size.[54]

The villagers were proud to have the national hero as a neighbour, but found him quieter than many expected, 'of a delicate structure' and 'reflective mind, strongly tinged with melancholy, retired and domestic in his habits'. Nevertheless, he joined Messrs Howard, Newton and Leach in appealing to Sir Joseph Banks for information about some local almshouses that he had endowed, and (it was said) he regularly called upon 'the humble tenants' of his estate and took 'the kindest notice of their little ones', relieving their wants when he could. The claim was vindicated by the memories of old residents, who spoke of the admiral's 'genial manners and kind heart', and his readiness to talk to children in the street and to dispense the odd shilling. Locals certainly benefited from his patronage. William Polly got a testimonial from the admiral; Greenfield, Denny, Chapman and Haines supplied meat, Skelton the bread, Woodman the candles and Mason the brown stout, and a Mr Boyes went hither and thither with letters. At Merton Place itself Mrs Perry cooked, Mrs Cummings did the laundry, 'old' John Matthews and William Austin were coachmen, and a housemaid, Phyllis Thorpe, earned £2 13s. 9d. for some three months' work. Francis Cribb, 'an intelligent, plain, fair, correct, well-meaning man', and his wife Hannah supplied groceries, but eventually tenanted one of the cottages erected on the estate, where Francis became head gardener and manager.[55]

The gentrified residents of Merton became good friends. Nelson mixed with Newton and Halfhide, whose calico printing mills were within the walls of Merton Abbey, with Patterson the farmer and Parrott the surgeon of Mitcham, while 'Old Mrs Percy' called for tea. He exchanged visits with James Perry, the Whig editor of the *Morning Chronicle*, who lived in Wandlebank House to the north-east, and with the brothers Abraham and Benjamin Goldsmid, Anglo-Jewish bullion brokers who used Morden Lodge and resided at Roehampton and who commuted to their London offices in Fenchurch Street. When Halfhide went bankrupt in 1804, he surrendered his three-storey gatehouse at Merton Abbey to Charles Smith, whose cousin was the widow of James Cook, the great explorer, and whose brother, Isaac, had shipped aboard the *Endeavour* at the age of sixteen. As close as any to Nelson's heart was the Reverend Thomas Lancaster, whose home at Eagle House, Wimbledon, doubled as a school. An 'old boy' remembered the day when Nelson and Emma listened to the pupils recite in the front parlour, and the admiral requested that the boys be rewarded with a half-day holiday. Lancaster was the curate in the picturesque Norman church of St Mary the Virgin situated among the cornfields of Merton parish, its mature trees shading a collection of higgledy-piggledy gravestones. Nelson and Emma regularly attended the services, according to tradition occupying a square-shaped pew on the north side of the chancel near the pulpit, where the admiral's hatchment is still to be seen, and the reverend heard the children of Merton Place read their catechisms and hymns. Long afterwards Lancaster's daughter spoke of Nelson's charity. 'His frequently expressed desire was that none in that place should want or suffer affliction that he could alleviate, and this I know he did with a most liberal hand, always desiring that it should not be known from whence it came. His residence at Merton was a continued course of charity and goodness.' A book of Easter offerings kept by the church records that Nelson and Emma donated seven guineas. Speaking to the great man, Lancaster quickly grasped his need for a peaceful sanctuary, and produced Latin verses in December 1801 pleading, 'Let Nelson Be'.[56]

At its peak Merton Place was a working community in which a resident staff pursued private relationships that occasionally intruded upon the master and mistress in ways that service generally did. It was the staff that provided the comfort, lighting fires, cooking meals, washing clothes, stocking larders and keeping the dirt at bay. Mrs Cadogan was the housekeeper, and her letters of 1804 show her to have been a capable manager, willing to take all manner of decisions. A workman (one of her relatives, no less) who returned late from a day's drinking at the Plough and attempted to usurp the position of Cribb was dismissed, and valuable plate was packed off to Davison's after a gang of housebreakers committed a couple of robberies in the village. Many of the other staff were long-standing servants of the ménage. John Tyson handled some of the financial business until Nelson found him a post at Woolwich in 1803 and he and his wife Elizabeth looked for a villa of their own. Tom Allen, discharged from the *Amazon* in February 1802, probably offered his services, but Nelson thought him an incompetent manservant and incorrigible liar, and he took his spouse, Jane, to Fakenham in his native Norfolk. The most controversial figure was Francis Oliver, who had joined the entourage in 1800. Emma trusted him with considerable amounts of money, and, what was more telling, the secret of Horatia's birth, and George Matcham talked about employing his linguistic skills on the continent, but Nelson saw a mere 'fool' and regretted that he had ever recommended him to the East India Company, while Sir William positively hated the fellow, branding him a 'most ungrateful and impertinent rascal' – even 'worse' than Sabatello.[57]

Most of these figures, so familiar to Nelson, peep mysteriously at us from the records. Sabatello and most of the domestics had been furnished by the Hamiltons. Of the maids, who generally received half a guinea a month with board and lodging, Fatima the Egyptian 'Copt' was the most vividly remembered, but Nancy nursed Emma 'in many an illness', and Marianne, one of the Italians, doubled as Mrs Cadogan's personal servant and a cook adept at whipping up macaroni, a favourite dish of the admiral's. Julia, another Italian, had the misfortune to acquire an ugly cross-eyed husband and left service after giving birth to a child in 1805. Others, such as Signora Madre, are mentioned only by name, but Sabatini Michele Sabatello, a Neapolitan, was the fly in the ointment that so many extensive households had to endure. Sir William had dismissed him for misconduct at Piccadilly in 1802, but Emma spoke up for the fellow, and Hamilton was soon complaining that he had been smuggled into Merton, where he was hiding. Whatever, Sabatello was soon on his way home to Naples, absconding, Julia protested, with £70 worth of her property. Sabatello's brother-in-law, Gaetano Spedillo, who remained in service at Merton, was a different animal, 'a good man' by Nelson's lights. When Nelson left for the Mediterranean in 1803, Gaetano went with him, apparently homesick for his native city. The admiral assigned him the task of confronting Sabatello about Julia's valuables, and even set Hugh Elliot, Britain's man in Naples, upon the 'rascal', threatening to withdraw Sabatello's 'character' if he did not return what he had stolen.[58]

It would have been strange if Merton had not experienced its ups and downs, but the prevailing atmosphere was cordial. As Elizabeth Tyson wrote, 'I really spent a most happy time at Merton, and a heartfelt joy, being happy with my dear Tyson a whole year . . . I bless you, Lady Hamilton . . . and many, many thanks to good Lord Nelson for all this comfort he has given us.' The master and mistress of Merton were, on the whole, tolerant employers.[59]

Nelson loved wearing uniform in London, but generally reverted to civilian attire at Merton, reprising his lifelong preference for a 'plain suit of black' that contrasted with Emma's love of striking blue. His tastes in dress remained conservative, and when purchasing footwear would suffer 'no square toes or new fashion'. Surprisingly, there are few portraits from the nineteenth months he spent at Merton, and no major ones. John Downham produced a chalk profile in 1802, and at the suggestion of his friend Richard Bulkeley he sat to Henry Edridge for a more ambitious full-length drawing in the summer. It was much inferior to the same artist's sketch of 1797, but was not without curiosities, including a portrayal of the order of St Joachim, which had arrived in June. Perhaps the most interesting likeness is an impromptu pen and ink showing the admiral at Blenheim Palace in 1802. Its artist, James Caulfield, described Nelson as 'very brown' and serious, but not displeasing in countenance and erect of posture. The portrait speaks more powerfully than the prose, however, introducing a rather incongruous, spindly figure in a large uniform coat, sword and cocked hat, and capturing the admiral's habit of leaning on a companion while walking.[60]

Under the Merton regime Nelson regained strength, but he would never be blessed with general wellbeing, and regularly expressed discomfort, so much so that in May 1802 brother William was recommending surgery. This advice may have related to the bowel and stomach complaint that featured in Nelson's correspondence when last at sea. The admiral was diagnosed with worms, probably suffering from enterobiasis, the most common but least harmful of intestinal parasites in Britain that inhabit the lower bowel. Apart from frequent colds, the inseparable consequences of living in indifferently heated places, his other long-term worry was his eyesight. Whatever changes the electrical treatment had brought to his bad eye, it was the other that now frightened him, and he received little reassurance when he consulted his old physician, Benjamin Moseley, now at the Royal Hospital of Chelsea.[61]

In October 1802 Nelson was wondering whether an operation might be necessary, but confessed that he could ill spare another eye. In the end he opted for protection and easement rather than the knife. He began using Oliver as a secretary to reduce the strain of writing, and on 11 February 1803 called at James Lock's, the hatters of 6 St James's Street, to order a beaver hat with a black cockade. He was a valued customer, and since returning from Deal had made four previous visits to order a total of five hats, three for himself, one for Emma and another for a member of his staff. But he wanted his new hat to be fitted with a transparent stiffened shade, covered with green silk, so that it protected his eyes from the glare of the sun. It was worth all of its two guineas, as far as Nelson was concerned, and only days later he was back in the shop in search of a spare shade. These shades were forgotten by posterity, but it was the nearest Nelson got to the mythological black eye patch so beloved in British folklore.[62]

7

In 1815 a biography of Emma Hamilton was published anonymously. Unashamedly hostile to its subject, it was nevertheless well informed, containing enough little-known but accurate information to establish that its author either spent time at Merton or knew someone who had. Among many charges levied against Emma were the social gatherings, collections of 'Italian singers and English performers, newspaper editors and miserable poetasters, adventurers without character', 'ballad makers', 'gamblers', 'rancorous party writers, virulent satirists, and determined republicans', as well as mere 'sycophants whose manners for the most part were as coarse as their principles'. These were 'orgies' in which the 'freedom of the conversation' extended to unpatriotic political comment. One such guest was Dr John Wolcot, an ageing but razor-sharp satirist who used the *nom de plume* of 'Peter Pindar' to lash the likes of James Boswell and Hannah More. He was so inebriated after an evening drinking at Merton that he set the nightcap that Nelson had lent him on fire. When he surfaced the following morning he returned the singed cap with the remark that anything that belonged to Nelson would eventually come under fire.[63]

There are uncomfortable truths in *The Memoirs of Lady Hamilton*, but it was a relentlessly vindictive piece of work written by someone who plainly disliked the woman. The portrait of the soirées at Merton is a case in point. Shunned by many in the regular Establishment, the Hamiltons gravitated towards some eccentric figures such as Beckford, but then Sir William was an academic, an art connoisseur and free-thinker, and Emma a performer, and it was entirely natural that they mixed with like minds, such as Jane Powell the actress. Artists, poets, singers, editors and writers were apt to criticise government and society, but that did not make them unpatriotic revolutionaries. Moreover, there was absolutely nothing unusual in a villa hosting musical, literary or artistic events. It was a retreat from the cares of business, and a recognised venue for performers the land over. To badge Merton as an unseemly den of undesirables with moral and patriotic inadequacies because it offered hospitality to such clientele is to ignore one of the most salient features of late eighteenth-century suburban life.

To speak more accurately, the roll call of guests at Merton was not particularly surprising. It was naturally rich in naval officers, such as Foley, Louis, Plampin, Murray, Sutton and Hardy, though significantly not Troubridge, for whom Nelson's friendship was spent. Old acquaintances such as Hercules Ross and Dr Moseley called to relive bygone days or beg a little patronage. Richard Bulkeley, though an army man, reckoned his son Dick would do better in the navy, where merit counted for more, and arrived to solicit a place. Bulkeley recalled that Nelson had obliged him once before, on behalf of young Francis Beaufort, the future hydrographer, who, Bulkeley had trusted, would not 'discredit . . . either of us'. Sometimes guests collided. Lieutenant Layman, Nelson's protégé, found himself chatting over tea in a drawing room with such old hands as Ball and Sir Samuel Hood. Often guests arrived serially, some leaving as others appeared. The 'Yonges' could arrive for a weekend; Vizunoni, who sang duets with Emma, 'Mr Ottwood' and 'Mr Blake' be resident for the week; and Signora Bianchi, the soprano and wife of the composer Francesco Bianchi, turn up for a fortnight's residence on the Friday.[64]

If visitors disliked anyone at Merton, even unfairly, it was Emma. In March 1803 James Noble, the old *Agamemnon*, found Nelson in Piccadilly and asked the admiral to abide by an old promise to be godfather to his first son, who had just been born in Hythe. 'He said the boy should be called by both his names [Horatio Nelson Noble], and seemed pleased when I told him that his Brother Gossop was Mr Geo. Noble. Lady Hamilton enquired who was to be the godmother. When I mentioned Mrs Wheelock, she appeared greatly disappointed. I am certain, in revenge, [she] did me much harm with Lord Nelson.'[65]

Perhaps the most famous glimpse of Merton was given by Minto, still as attracted as when he had been plain old Sir Gilbert Elliot and Nelson a mere captain. Not a naive, idolatrous or uninformed man, Minto was a humane and liberal Whig, who had dumped the hopelessly idealistic Fox. One day, as governor general of India, he would champion Raffles, Elphinstone and Metcalfe as he had once Nelson, helping them to flower into brilliant colonial administrators. Like Raffles, Minto saw the need for imperial Britain to accommodate the beliefs and customs of indigenous peoples, even to the extent of berating lauded

Christian missionaries. No fool, this pupil of David Hume and graduate of Oxford and Lincoln's Inn was undeceived by the flattery of the *tria juncta in uno*. Like Spencer and St Vincent, the other principal proponents of Nelson's employment in 1798, he had reaped a mixture of pride and disappointment.

Nelson, he knew, had done Fanny a 'shocking injury', but he remained on the best terms he could. He was at dinner at Merton on Saturday, 20 March 1802, an edifying spectacle in which 'Miss Furse' (apparently Charlotte Nelson's tutor) ate too much, vomited and had to be conducted from the room by Charlotte, and Mrs Tyson became so drunk that she talked 'nonsense'. As the weather was too bad for the household to go to church, Minto spent the next morning talking politics with Nelson, while Emma, growing fat on food and wine, wrote another toxic letter to Sarah Nelson. 'The Cub is in town,' she wrote, 'and has called at Tyson's . . . Tom *Tit* is despised and hated and even those that pretend to protect her *fall off*. She is now bursting and *abuses* him, you and us openly, and all our *friends*. I wish she would *burst*, but there is no such good luck.' The epistle had to be concluded to continue preparations for a dinner for nineteen that included Sukey, whom Emma called 'Mother Blindy'. On Monday Minto returned for a second helping, but he was far from enamoured by what he saw. Emma sang with the Jewish tenor, John Braham. 'She is horrid, but he entertained me in spite of her,' said Minto.[66]

'The whole establishment and way of life,' he concluded, 'is such as to make me angry as well as melancholy', largely because he laboured under the misapprehension that the Hamiltons were living at his hero's expense, which they were not. 'She is in high looks, but more immense than ever. She goes on cramming Nelson with trowelfuls of flattery, which he goes on taking as quietly as a child does pap. The love she makes to him is not only ridiculous, but disgusting. Not only the rooms, but the whole house, staircase and all, are covered with nothing but pictures of her and him, of all sizes and sorts, and representations of his naval actions, coats of arms, pieces of plate in his honour, the flagstaff of *L'Orient* &c., an excess of vanity which counteracts its own purpose. If it was Lady Ha.'s house there might be a pretence for it. To make his own a mere looking-glass to view himself all day is bad taste.' Emma wrote an equally frank account of the same occasion, describing how she and Nelson bombarded Minto with the 'ill usage' the admiral felt at the government's neglect of William Nelson. She noted that Minto's brother was Lord Auckland, and Lord Hobart his nephew, and smelt 'interest'. 'I was determined *he* should know all, for he will raise a clamour.' Emma spelled it 'clamer'.

Minto was repulsed by Emma, yet drawn to Nelson, who remained as vulnerable and lovable as ever, even amidst self-pity and excess. The obvious gratitude of the man, his instant sympathy for the tribulations of friends, his readiness to help at cost and trouble to himself, and his consideration could never be denied. So many friends went away sadly shaking their heads, but they kept returning. In a society that still blamed women for infidelities, Emma was the scapegoat for what was obviously the work of both of them, and many who excused the hero loathed her. 'I cannot bring myself to continue to visit L[ady] Hamilton,' wrote a female patrician. 'Her conduct is so censurable.' Another distinction between the master and his mistress lay in their demeanour. While Emma was unfailingly demonstrative, Nelson lapsed into periods of marked introspection. He loved adulation, and not only devoured congratulatory letters but had them copied and sent to friends, but he was quiet by nature and quickly tired of large gatherings and endless small talk. George Matcham junior remembered his uncle's 'quiet conversation', laced with its undercurrent of pleasantry and wit. 'At his table he was the least heard among the company', he drank sparingly, used few coarse expressions and seemed forever 'anxious to give pleasure to everyone about him, distinguishing each in turn by some act of kindness'. Nelson himself owned that 'the smaller the party, the better I shall like it, even was it a tête-à-tête'. At times even the crowds exhausted him. 'I am almost killed with kindness,' he once wrote wearily. This was the downside of genuine celebrity so familiar today. In that respect his inclinations, and those of Sir William, were in conflict with Emma's, whose obsession with hosting and performing created a continuing round of entertainment.[67]

Sir William ducked out of the way of children, but if Nelson wearied of the table talk of mindless adults, he loved young people. 'The greatest of all his joys', said Emma, was 'when he has his sisters or their children with him', perhaps because in some ways he had remained a boy at heart. Probably a man with his sense of posterity also saw childlessness as an unfortunate vacuum. Emma, too, had a way with children, who responded to her warmth and exciting theatrics, and she was bright enough to know that the surest way to the hearts of parents was through their children. Charlotte Nelson, now a dark-haired beauty, spent her time between Whitelands and Merton, where she helped guests with their coats and brushed up her language and musical skills under Emma's tutelage. Her occasional fits of temper were resolved with written apologies. Her brother, Horace, turned up when he could escape from Eton with his tales of battles between the college boys and townspeople. The Boltons had five surviving youngsters, the twins, Susannah and Kitty, now passed twenty; Tom, who made sixteen years in 1802; and two juniors, Elizabeth and Ann. Nelson's youngest sister, according to her sister Susannah, was breeding herself to death, and between 1789 and 1803 gave Nelson three nephews and four nieces.[68]

The result was inevitable, especially during the Christmases, when Merton Place answered the seasonal weather with roaring fires, good food, mirth, music and the squeal of excited children. The festivities of 1802 were special, attracting the three youngest Bolton children as well as Charlotte and Horace. 'Our house is tolerably filled,' said Nelson. 'Tom is still little Tom, but seems a meek, well disposed lad.' Emma taught everyone to dance and sing, played the pianoforte, and laid on an after-dinner theatrical, introduced by flickering candles that were ignited against glittering glass windows. *Favourite Sultana* featured Emma in Turkish slippers, silk trousers and a satin jacket, sparkling in a diamond head-band, strings of pearls and bracelets that shimmered about her arms and ankles. The supporting cast introduced Mrs Cadogan as a Grecian woman, Charlotte Nelson and Catherine and Elizabeth Matcham, Nelson's nieces, heavily disguised as Moorish ladies, and a 'Miss K' exotically garbed and masked as a black sultana. Even the guests could not escape reverting to childhood. Perkins Magra, late consul general for Tunis, joined Tyson as 'Turks of quality', three neighbours, Messrs Blow, Cumming and Jefferson, were 'Moors of Quality' and the artist Thomas Baxter with sundry other unfortunates were cast as slaves carrying 'long pipes and bags'. The festivities spilled into a wintry new year. 'Lady Hamilton gave a little ball last night to the children,' Nelson informed Matcham. 'They danced till three this morning and are not yet up.' It was 'delightful', Emma thought. 'Charlotte outdid herself. Like an angel she was, all night. The little Boltons were charmed. Tom Bolton is a good boy and he is well behaved, and we like him much.' The children themselves evidently agreed. As young Horace wrote to his mother, 'I am as happy as a prince . . . When my cousin [Tom] comes, my uncle [Nelson] says we shall go and see everything worth seeing.' The only irritant was Nilus, Emma's dog, which contrived to lose itself.[69]

William Nelson and his wife were so often at Merton that a room was permanently reserved for their use, he on the lookout for food and advantage, she whose letters spoke of dumplings, afternoon teas and the inconveniences of modern living. The relatives of the Hamiltons were also regular callers. Nelson discovered an affection for the Dukes of Hamilton and Queensberry, but felt less confidence in the Connor tribe, the children of Mrs Cadogan's sister, Sarah. The Connors resided at Ferry, Hawarden, but somehow the youngsters were bundled upon a celebrated 'uncle' renowned for his hospitality and powers of patronage. Nelson had already slotted Charles into the navy, and now housed and fed the sisters, Mary Ann, Sarah and Cecilia. Emma feared that there was a strain of insanity in the Connor family, and later declared that their 'extravagance' almost 'ruined' her, but Sarah and Cecilia shaped up and acted as occasional governesses to the Bolton girls. Among other mysterious 'misses' at Merton Place were 'Miss Reynolds', probably Sarah Reynolds, one of Emma's cousins, and 'Miss Hartly'. Nelson took the latter, a comely girl of twenty in 1802, to be another of Emma's far-flung relatives, but most likely she was Emma's first illegitimate daughter, 'Emma Carew', who was being raised by foster parents in Manchester. For all that she had her attractions, and we find Mrs Tyson, after her removal to Woolwich, begging Lady Hamilton to allow 'Miss Hartly' to accompany her to a parish ball, promising to 'dress . . . and . . . go comfortable'.[70]

The throng of guests at Merton, young and old, caused serious expense.

Both Nelson and Emma were instinctively generous. 'You have no idea of the sum of money it takes to live in the style of a gentleman,' Fanny had once told her husband. William upbraided his brother for his liberality, even as he regularly unloaded his wife and children upon the Merton household. He did, however, draw the line when Nelson paid a debt of thirty shillings owed by Horace. 'You are too good to him,' William complained. 'It is a mistaken kindness. If he gets into debt any more, make him pay it out of his pocket money.' Nelson loaned far greater sums without blanching, and rarely liked badgering his creditors for repayment. As late as the autumn of 1802 Sir William may still have owed him £1000. Merton was also open to any well-wisher who appeared at the door. Matthew Nelson, a member of the younger branch of his father's family, who sent gifts of a turkey and two hares, received an immediate invitation. Yet Emma was much the worst of the two. Nelson knew the ultimate size of his purse, which she did not. 'Your purse, my dear Emma, will always be empty,' he told her. 'Your heart is generous beyond your means.' She was, consequently, regularly in debt. Hamilton paid his wife an allowance, but at the end of 1802 her account with Coutts was down to thirteen shillings, and she had debts totalling £700. A jewellery bill for 1802 and 1803 summed £169, most of it spent on gifts rather than self-adornment. It was a grievous fault, but the admiral loved her for it.[71]

The household expenses at Merton were about £800 a year, and that was but a fraction of the cost of the extension and improvement of the estate. But it was the first time in Nelson's life that he ruled his own castle, and commanded a home from which he could issue invitations and dispense patronage like the paternalist he had always been. Merton was his place in the sun.

The artist Thomas Baxter, whose acquaintance Nelson had made in 1802, captured life at Merton Place in a number of brief drawings, and they stand as testimony to a domesticity that might have come from the pages of Jane Austen. Emma, overweight but still beautiful of face, using the girls in her 'attitudes'; the sprouting Horatia, standing dramatically beside a rocking horse in the garden, dressed in a smock and top hat with a leaf-clad trellis behind her; and Emma, framed by a table candelabrum, seated at cards with five ladies and a gentleman. These seem to have been the sort of pleasurable moments a later generation would capture in sepia snapshots, peaceful moments that explain why Nelson called Merton his paradise. As Emma said, 'Here we are as happy as kings, and much more so.'[72]

XVII

NO COMMON LOVE

Go, say to him, who knows no fear,
Grateful for thy protecting care,
The British Laurel awaits thee here,
Twined by the hands of British Fair!

Lines to Lord Nelson, Rudhall, 20 August 1802

I

HIS accommodation in place, Nelson could attempt to reunify his damaged family. For Emma, the undoubted mistress of Merton Place, the process involved the final exorcism of the omnipresent spirit of Lady Nelson, 'the Creole with her heart black as her fiendlike looking face' who had unworthily ensnared a 'noble' husband. No epithet seemed strong enough to express her hatred for Fanny, whose doings she obsessively monitored:

> She loved her dirty Escalopes [Aesculapius, i.e. Dr Nisbet, Fanny's first husband], if he had love, and the two dirty negatives made that dirty affirmative that is a disgrace to the human species [Josiah]. She then, starving, took in an evil hour our hero. She made him unhappy. She disunited him from his family. She wanted to *raise up* her own vile spew [Josiah again] at the expense and total abolition of the family which should be immortalised for having given birth to the saviour of this country. When he came home *maimed*, *lame* and covered with glory, she put in derision his honourable wounds. She raised a clamour against him because he had seen a more lovely, a more virtuous woman [Emma], who had served with him in a foreign country, and who had her heart and senses open to his glory, to his greatness and his virtues. If he had lived with this demon, the blaster of his fame and reputation, he must have fallen under it, and his country would have lost their greatest ornament.[1]

This travesty was fuelled by intense jealousy, fear and, most of all, passion, for her lover. 'That I adore him above all this world is true,' she admitted, 'and that I would sacrifice my life for his happiness, but I have the vanity and pride to be sure that the happiness of his depends on mine. Ours is not a common dull love. My mind was taken with glory, my heart beats high with his great deeds, and I never can nor ever will try to get the better of my true and virtuous passion that I feel for him.' There is no doubt that in that, at least, she spoke honestly.

Emma had done her best to drive Fanny and Josiah from the family, and Nelson went along with it, but not all the Nelsons believed in the assassination of Lady Nelson's character. Susannah must have remembered the 'good friend' who had stood by her in past 'distresses', and the Matchams did not see the need to sever all relations with the abandoned wife. Both the Boltons and the Matchams were ultimately loyal to Nelson, however, and the former were still financially dependent upon him for the education of three of their children, Tom at Norwich Grammar and the youngest girls boarded out at Edmonton in London. All three youngsters were regular visitors to Merton, and in 1802 Nelson pledged £100 a year towards their education for three years, a donation important enough for Susannah to beg an extension as the expiration date loomed. Bolton's financial straits may also be judged by his dunning Emma for loans. In addition one of the older Bolton girls, Catherine, was engaged to her cousin, Captain William Bolton, whose career was very much in Nelson's hands. In March 1802 Susannah wrote from a snowbound Norfolk to accept Emma's invitation to make a first visit to Merton.[2]

Old Edmund Nelson was another matter, for the powerful spirit that had taken him through life in the company of his god still flickered in the feeble octogenarian. He had resigned himself to the dissolution of the old family triumvirate, but hoped to remain in good standing with both parties. When the snow cleared in the spring of 1802 he intended to make a second visit to Merton. From Bath he wrote to Nelson in February, thanking Emma for her 'polite remembrance' and including only the mild reproof that 'the post of honour is the post of danger, and to be exalted is to be tempted'. In March he wrote again, wishing his son 'an abundance of eternal peace', and trusting that God would bless 'all who dwell under your roof'. The next month one of his letters went to Fanny, telling her about Kate's new baby, and wishing her 'happiness'. He mentioned leaving Bath in May but said nothing about visiting her. Probably, he was tactfully allowing her the opportunity to issue an invitation.[3]

But for Edmund time had now been stolen. He began to fail in February, coughing relentlessly and 'weak in the extreme'. On 24 April, just four days after Edmund's letter to Fanny, George Matcham wrote to Nelson that his father was in 'great danger', a clear hint that the old man was dying. Fanny, who was also informed, went instantly to his bedside, but arrived too late. Edmund Nelson died on 26 April, 'cheerful', it was said, to the end. Nelson remained at Merton, and the day his father died (Emma's birthday) was in the parish church, where he and Lady Hamilton witnessed the baptism of Fatima, their servant, who took the names Fatima Emma Charlotte Nelson Hamilton. The same day he wrote to Matcham, pleading ill health. 'Had my father expressed a wish to see me, unwell as I am, I should have flown to Bath,' he said, 'but I believe it would be too late. However, should it be otherwise, and he wishes to see me, no consideration shall detain me a moment.' He notified William of their father's decline, believing him to be the sole executor, but it was not until the following day that he heard of the actual death. It struck hard. 'My dear Davison,' he managed in a one-sentence statement, 'My poor dear father is no more. God bless you, Nelson and Bronte.' His house went into mourning. The children were kept indoors, and visitors turned away from the gate.[4]

Nelson was an emotional man of tearful partings, as good friends such as Ball attested, and deathbed scenes cut him to the core. Readers will remember his reluctance to see the dying Parker. This, as well as the possibility of meeting Fanny or of being exhorted to reform by a dying parent, may explain his reluctance to stir. For whatever reason, it was also without the presence of his favourite son that the wasted body of Edmund Nelson made its final journey, the mourning coach winding its way from Bath to his beloved Burnham Thorpe, escorted by Abraham Cook, his servant for forty years. Thomas Bolton and William organised the funeral, although Nelson defrayed the expense, and on the morning of Tuesday 11 May a man famed for his charity drew more crowds to his old church than many remembered. Among the six clergymen who carried Edmund's coffin to its resting place, in a brick-lined grave in the chancel, next to his wife, Catherine, were familiar names, including Archdeacon Yonge, William's brother-in-law; Crowe senior and junior, old Burnham friends; and Hoste and Weatherhead, the fathers of two of Nelson's naval protégés. For William, the oldest surviving son, the return to Burnham Thorpe brought 'pleasant' memories of childhood, saddened by the reflection that he was here for 'perhaps the last time'. As for Nelson, he had not seen his birthplace since 1793, nor would he again. The forty-seven year old saga of the Nelsons of Burnham Thorpe had ended.[5]

William wound up his father's affairs, preparing mourning rings, sorting out plate, furniture and other possessions, including a half-length portrait of Lady Turner, Nelson's great-grandmother, which went to Merton, and calling in investments. As William untangled his father's complicated affairs, some £927 came to Nelson through various legacies, but the latter's concern was for the future of Abraham Cook. He asked Davison to find the servant a suitable position in one of the India House warehouses, and to put the man's mind at rest paid a bridging allowance.[6]

With Edmund's death, Fanny lost what goodwill remained in the Nelson family. Susannah wrote her the last letter on 13 May. 'Your going to Bath, my dear Lady Nelson, was of a piece with all your conduct to my beloved father,' she said. However, 'I am going to Merton in about a fortnight, but, my dear Lady N[elson], we cannot meet as I wished, for everybody is known who visits you. Indeed, I do not think I shall be permitted even to go to town.' Thus, with a final salute, did the family bid farewell to Nelson's wife. Susannah made her first visit to Merton in June, meeting her sister, Kate Matcham, there. She joined a 'magnificent' fete at Morden Lodge. All the original family were now united behind Nelson's new domestic arrangements. Fanny still had some access to the social occasions that drove Emma wild, appearing at the queen's 'drawing room' on 17 January 1802, and many other friends. Hardy breakfasted with her that June. 'I am more pleased with her, if possible, than ever,' said the tough salt. 'She is certainly one of the best women in the world.' And although some poisonous material got into print, including a novelette published in the *Lady's Magazine* for 1803 that made her the manifest model of a 'cruel, treacherous and resentful wife', there was also much public sympathy. The niece of Admiral Cornwallis once saw her in Bath, limping from a recent injury. She 'felt ashamed of my red eyes for [my] tiny sorrows in comparison with hers, and longed to support her down the stairs had I not been a stranger to her'.[7]

Having done everything possible to reclaim her husband, Lady Nelson recognised the parting of the ways and accepted her lonely fate. Perhaps her last approach to the family occurred in January 1803, when she called at the Matchams' house in Bath, and left her card without knocking. It was obvious that Fanny feared that they, like Susannah, might not feel free to see her, but Kate, who had been at home, was sorry. 'We should have told her, as we have always declared it is our maxim if possible to be at peace with all the world.' But there was no mercy from the ménage. Emma called Fanny 'a nasty vulgar bad-hearted wretch', the sort of language that came so easily to her. Nelson merely said that the Matchams should have returned the card.[8]

2

The Merton household was a remarkable one, encompassing a generally harmonious union of a man, his mistress and her elderly and disposable husband. To colour the strange picture, the usurped and usurper shared living expenses and professed great friendship for each other. At first Nelson had been troubled with propriety, and suggested that Emma stay at Piccadilly rather than Merton when Sir William was away, but that caution was soon thrown to the wind.

For all its joviality, Merton was a house of secrets. Take Horatia, for instance. She generally remained with Mrs Gibson, and even in the late summer of 1801, when the child was inoculated with cowpox to protect from the far graver dangers of smallpox, she was temporarily isolated in a house in Sloane Street, and superintended by a nurse and Oliver, rather than at roomy Merton. The extent of Sir William's knowledge of her is uncertain. It seems impossible that he had not noticed his wife's pregnancy, even if, as seems likely, the couple had long used different bedrooms. *The Memoirs of Lady Hamilton* has the child being born in his house in Piccadilly. On the other hand, there are indications that Hamilton was not privy to all, and Emma seemed reluctant to have Horatia about her when Sir William was around. Not only was the child kept with Mrs Gibson, when she should have taken her rightful place in Merton, but when the Hamiltons visited Ramsgate in 1802 and Emma wanted to see Horatia, she asked that the child be taken to nearby Margate so that she could inconspicuously slip away to attend her. This is strange behaviour, capable of several interpretations. Certainly, Horatia's identity was a close-kept secret. The girl's christening was delayed, since no satisfactory account of her parentage could be offered, and Nelson warned Mrs Gibson that on 'no consideration' was she 'to answer any questions about Miss Thomson, nor who placed her with Mrs Gibson, as ill-tempered people have talked lies about the child.'[9]

Whatever Hamilton knew about Horatia, his position in the Merton household was unenviable. He was good at looking the other way, and innocently maintaining the fiction of a platonic relationship between Nelson and Emma, even to the parties themselves. 'I love Lord Nelson,' he told her. 'I know the purity of your connection with him.' Often he took himself out of the way, into town or wielding his rod on the Thames, the Wandle or at Merton, where Nelson had stocked a pond with carp, tench and pike. Despite his portrait of Sir William as an undesirable 'uncle' in the Thomson letters of 1801, the admiral preserved the best relationships with Sir William, and the two men evinced a genuine and deep regard.[10]

Sir William might have separated from his wife, but that would have embroiled all of them in fresh controversy. The course he followed involved humiliation. The asides and knowing looks, the sniggering cartoons, and the occasions when Nelson and Emma strode forward in public places, delighting in the crowds, leaving him to totter behind like an elderly retainer, must have taken an awful amount of philosophy to bear. As he confessed to Greville, apart from debt his greatest problem was 'the nonsense I am obliged to submit to here [Merton] to avoid coming to an explosion which would . . . totally destroy the comfort of the best man and the best friend I have in the world [Nelson] . . . However, I am determined that my quiet shall not be disturbed, let the nonsensical world go on as it will.'[11]

Poor Sir William's finances were still a mess. He brought Greville to Merton to discuss his affairs, assuring the man who was Emma's former lover that Nelson's door would be open and that the admiral bore him no ill will. They talked of investments in Milford, Pembrokeshire, where Hamilton had a poor-paying estate and Greville was trying to develop a naval port. Another confidant was Beckford, who was still offering the Hamiltons pensions providing Sir William wheedled a peerage out of the government and granted him the reversion. The problem was how to get the peerage, and the answer seemed to be plain old political bribery. Beckford could put 'two sure seats' in the Lords in the government's pocket, and influence another two in the Commons. At the beginning of July 1802 Beckford sent a Mr Peebles, one of his parliamentary candidates, to talk the matter over with Nelson and Hamilton. Nelson may have been influenced by Beckford's promise to pay Emma £500 a year after her husband's death. Anyway, he was willing to approach Addington with a proposition, but felt that far greater 'interest' than any he and Beckford could wield would be needed, and suggested Sir William lobby his kinsmen, the powerful ninth Duke of Hamilton and his heir, the Marquis of Douglas. The marquis was known to be interested in Beckford's daughter, Euphemia, but after duly writing on 2 July, Hamilton was respectfully declined.[12]

Sir William's plan to live and let live was difficult to endure, as his and Emma's inclinations drew them further apart. She was never happier than in company, and shone at the table, excitedly organising huge gatherings for dinner and entertainments, while Sir William groaned and looked for his rod. Another issue was her extravagance and his straitened circumstances. 'You do not think of shillings and sixpences that in time make up a great sum,' the old diplomat complained. Her years 'with a great Queen in intimacy' had given her 'ideas' that far outstripped his means. The two began to bicker, and soon curious letters and notes were going back and forth between the Hamiltons as they thrashed out their problems on paper rather than in ugly face-to-face confrontations. It was no use speaking to her, Sir William complained, because she was filled with 'passion, humour and nonsense, which it is impossible to combat with reasoning'.[13]

Thus, the triumvirate creaked into its final year, casting a gloom over Nelson's happiest days.

3

London, which Nelson thought hot and fetid in the summers, was nevertheless the hub of public affairs, and the Hamiltons' house at 23 Piccadilly provided a useful town base. Nelson frequently made the journey, sometimes travelling with Sir William and separating for the day's business to reunite later for the ride home. He enjoyed the company of friends. Calling upon Stewart one day in Charles Street, he found the officer away from home, but sent an invitation for him to visit Merton. 'Believe me that I love, honour and respect you, and your friendship is most dear to me,' he wrote. 'Be assured, at no place, not even at your father's house, will you be more welcome.'[14]

Piccadilly was a short walk away from Davison's home in St James's Square, and Nelson liked to call for breakfast to hear 'all that was going on in the great world' or to meet people who had asked to see him. When Davison was absent, at his estate in the north-east or about town, his assistants, John Bowering and the declining Dods, were sometimes available for business. When the latter died in the autumn of 1802, Nelson characteristically offered to help his 'poor widow'. There were other rallying points, including the Navy Club dinners at such places as the Shakespeare Tavern in Covent Garden, for which Nelson paid a four-guinea subscription. Nelson was also spotted shopping, in such places as John Salter's, the silversmith and sword cutler at 35 The Strand, or Rundell and Bridge of Ludgate Hill. He was said to have attended a masquerade in Bond Street, adopting the guise of a Spaniard.[15]

His relations with the Admiralty had atrophied, although St Vincent exchanged formal pleasantries and again promised to raise the matter of the Copenhagen medal with ministers, if not to support it. Nelson had long since decided that the naval hierarchy was jealous of him. '*Three* medals was too much for one admiral to wear,' he grumbled. About most things St Vincent was so close-lipped that Nelson thought him no more informative than a common broadsheet. Addington was more agreeable, and they spoke about a range of subjects from foreign affairs to the state of government stocks. It was through Addington that Nelson sought royal permission to wear his latest foreign orders, the insignia of the Order of St Joachim and a new ribbon sent by the Sultan of Turkey to accompany his Order of the Crescent. Ever fascinated by such baubles, Nelson occasionally burdened his letterheads with the details of all the titles and knighthoods he had harvested, a recitation that could extend to sixty-two words! As he was effectively retired, his visits to London owed much to matters other than the sea, and often he was championing the cause of underdogs. 'If he saw or suspected any difficulty or distress, his mind was that moment occupied in endeavouring to afford some remedy . . . When he beheld anyone unprovided for, of whom he had a good opinion . . . [his] exclamations were generally followed up by naming some situations suitable for the party, and immediately [he began] using all his interest to obtain it.' The statement comes from an admiring contemporary biographer, but no one can work far into Nelson's correspondence without encountering this facet of his personality.[16]

Nelson's charitable work has never been examined, although it reflected his humanity and desire to play the good leader in society. All six of his principal charities concerned the young, for whom he had a particular concern. Brother William knew that way to Nelson's heart, and in pressing the claims of an in-law, Charles Yonge, added, 'When I tell you this young man . . . is an orphan, I am sure, I need say no more to entitle him to your protection.' As long ago as 1793, Nelson had supported the Marine Society, a charity founded by Jonas Hanway to give pauper boys careers at sea, and he had taken seventeen or so such youngsters into the *Agamemnon*. In 1802 he was still sponsoring the society, paying an annual subscription of two guineas, although he got to few of their meetings.

A similar organisation, the British National Endeavour School, later known as the Naval Asylum, was founded by Andrew Thompson in 1798 to educate, house and clothe the orphans of fallen seamen and marines. In 1802 it was situated at Clarence House in Paddington Green, and accommodated forty boys and ten girls between the ages of five and ten, most destined for the sea service. The patron of the asylum was the Prince of Wales, and numerous royals and admirals served as vice presidents, including St Vincent who donated the huge sum of £1000. Nelson and Davison paid £21 each to become life governors with the privilege of commanding three votes apiece at the committee meetings. The annual anniversary of the founding of the asylum was celebrated in the London Tavern in June 1802. A former lord of the Admiralty, Robert, Lord Belgrave, took the chair, but battle-scarred veterans such as Sir Hyde Parker, Sir Sidney Smith and above all Nelson enjoyed most of the attention. Nelson addressed the meeting, children from the asylum sang patriotic songs and a handsome £1317 was raised.

Like other worthy members Nelson had the prerogative of nominating children to the asylum. In 1802 he had no candidates, and gave his nomination to his friend and fellow member Benjamin Goldsmid, who bestowed it upon 'a poor boy named William Hart'. A year later the admiral had his own nominee, Augustus Gravely, the son of a midshipman. But although he was elected a vice president of the asylum, Nelson was by no means a docile member. Early in 1802 Philip Astley of the Amphitheatre on Westminster Bridge offered to stage two benefit nights in aid of the asylum, one at Easter and the other in the summer, suggesting that if Nelson would honour them with his presence 'it would bring a house without the expense and trouble to the governors to issue tickets for the purpose'. The committee happily agreed to approach Nelson, and were no doubt surprised when he turned them down. He gave reasons which are now unknown, but the benefit nights appear to have been abandoned.

Nelson took the view that naval orphans remained a charge on the service, but he also believed in self-help and in about 1798 joined the Amicable Naval Society, a friendly society for naval officers, who paid regular subscriptions so that their widows and orphans might be supported in times of need. On one occasion Nelson intervened in its management, when the committee, which included Captain Locker and six flag officers, voted to receive applications from the families of 'deserving officers whose circumstances would not admit of them being subscribers'. Doubtless Nelson thought that the society's funds would be depleted at the expense of the subscribers, for he angrily withdrew his membership. Afraid of alienating the hero of the Nile, the committee tamely expunged their previous vote and invited Nelson to return to their ranks, which he did. Nelson saw the importance of a network of provision, targeted to different needs. In 1801 we find him recommending the eight-year-old son of a naval lieutenant to the Blue Coat School, a charity institution supported by voluntary subscriptions, and associated with Christ's Hospital in Newgate, London.[17]

Two civilian charities also engaged Nelson, one the Sons of the Clergy, which assisted the orphans of clergymen to obtain suitable employment, and the other the Female Orphan Asylum, founded by Sir John Fielding, the blind magistrate, in 1758 and housed in a stately building and attractive grounds on the Surrey side of Westminster Bridge Road. The latter charity, under the patronage of the queen, had asked Davison to enrol Nelson among its sponsors in May 1799, when he was at sea, and for the sum of £2 7s. 0d. he became one of six vice presidents, among whom another was Earl Spencer. We find Nelson donating £52 10s. 0d. to the asylum in March the following year, and soon after he reached London he attended his first Sunday service in the building on 30 November 1800, watching the girls as they sang in the chapel, frolicked in an excellent playground, or sat at their long benches in the dining hall, neatly clad in black dresses, white caps and aprons, and little shawls, and tucking into their roast beef and potatoes. As a vice president he may have attended some of the committee meetings held on Thursdays, when the president, treasurer and guardians made their reports; in December 1800 he supported the appointment of Philip Dodd as a morning preacher. The charity did some good work, providing girls of five to twelve years with basic education until they could be found apprenticeships or positions in domestic service. While living at Merton, Nelson frequently attended the Sunday worship and complimented the girls on their singing. The son of one of the officials of the charity recalled that his 'father spoke often of encountering the mighty little man walking to the asylum on Sunday mornings, invariably habited in a complete suit of black.'[18]

The stringencies of Nelson's purse prevented him from supporting all he would have liked, and other obligations competed for his time, including those to men who had given faithful service on board his ships. Ever since becoming a captain Nelson had thanked departing crews for their work and promised his continuing benevolence. As one listener remembered it, he promised 'to see the ship's company righted in every point'. Another said, 'You were pleased to tell me at the time of quitting the *Theseus*, that if I ever stood in need of your assistance, to inform you of my distress, and you would relieve me.' This was his acknowledgement of the unwritten contract that he believed bound leaders and followers. Many old shipmates took him up, some remembering incidents forgotten by all but the beneficiaries. In November 1800 Robert Brent of Ludgate Hill recalled a favour done him almost twenty-four years before by Acting Lieutenant Nelson of the *Worcester*. 'I never shall remember but with the most heartfelt gratitude your kindness in being my coxswain in convoying me from your ship to a frigate that I might arrive the more speedily at Lisbon in order to accomplish my marriage.' Those were 'happy days' that left him with a 'most amiable and beloved wife', but the couple had fallen on hard times, and Brent had spent three years living within the rules of the Fleet debtors' prison, with his wife, her widowed sister and her two children to support. In October 1802 Nelson called at the home of the prime minister's brother to speak of Brent, among greater issues. Armed with a letter of introduction from Nelson, Brent took up an appointment in the *Queen Charlotte* the following May. A victim of the vicious system of jailing debtors indefinitely, without affording them any prospect of relief, was Archibald Johnston, formerly a sailmaker on Nelson's *Captain*, who lingered in prison for a debt of seven guineas. The admiral gave him a testimonial that enabled him to apply to a debt relief charity and regain his freedom.[19]

A different call for help came from the depths of the Middle Yard of Newgate prison on 16 November 1802:

> My Lord, From your well known goodness to those who have had the Honour to serve under your Command, [h]as induced me to take this liberty of writing to you. I was under your orders as a seaman at the Battle of the Nile, and likewise at the siege of Bulongue [sic] and every character from your officers will testify my then merritt, but comeing to London and in a state of intoxication became an acquaintance with and found in company of those of bad character. I was taken with them, tried and cast for death in Septr. last, since which I have received his Majisty's gracious respite if your Lordship's humanity should induce you to interceed for me at the fountain of Mercy for such mitigation of punishment as your wisdom shall direct. I hope once moore to to [sic] prove myself not only a loyall seaman but till Death pleases to call your obedient, Humble servant, Samuel Beach.[20]

In presenting himself as a marginal offender, Beach gave a respectably accurate account. About midnight on 19 July a gang had broken into Skillecorn's public house in Little Queen Street, Holborn, making off with property belonging to the owner. Beach was not among the intruders, but when watchmen traced the robbers to a house in Lewkner's Lane, an area notorious for the disposal of stolen goods, the unfortunate tar was inside, dressed in his sailor's jacket, and attempting to hide 720 copper halfpennies that had been part of the haul. Tried at a session of the Old Bailey on 18 September he was convicted of 'taking and carrying' the stolen loot and sentenced to hang. It was probably Nelson's intervention that got his sentence reduced to one of transportation. If so, it may have ultimately done little good. Delivered to the convict hulks at Woolwich in February 1803, Beach absconded, and remained at large for five months before being apprehended in Piccadilly. Hauled once more into the Old Bailey, he was sentenced to death a second time on 14 September. 'I have nothing to say,' said Beach in his defence. 'A man in my situation would do anything to get away. I had not done anything amiss when they took me, but was going to work till I could get a few things, and then I was going on board a man-of-war.' He was only twenty-eight years old.[21]

The day Sam Beach made his appeal to Nelson from his cell at Newgate a posse led by Bow Street officers surrounded the Oakley Arms tavern in Lambeth and arrested thirty-three men. The prisoners were accused of a mad plot to overthrow the government. It was alleged that they were planning to use a cannon to assassinate George III as he returned to St James's Palace after opening the new session of parliament on 23 November, and that armed proletarians would attack the Tower of London, the Bank of England and the Houses of Parliament, while the poor of the industrial towns of the Midlands and the north would be incited to rise in revolt. The supposed plot was penetrated by informers, and the leading conspirators taken into custody, including their instigator, Edward Despard. It came as a shock to Nelson. He had fought alongside Despard in Nicaragua twenty years before, when the Irishman had been a gallant young army lieutenant in the Liverpool Blues. Unfortunately, the fellow had not prospered since. At one time Superintendent of British Affairs in Honduras, he had been recalled after recriminations, and although his name was cleared he remained unemployed and fell into the conspiratorial tavern world of radicals, Irish nationalists and disaffected soldiers that would later breed the Cato Street conspiracy.

Arraigned now for high treason, Despard's case was depressingly hopeless, but he appealed to Nelson for help. The Grand Jury of Surrey witnessed a remarkable sight in the Newington Sessions House in Horsemonger Lane on 7 February 1803, when a brave but crestfallen revolutionary stood in the dock, charged on some very tainted evidence with the gravest offence imaginable, and the first witness took the stand in his defence. Nelson was no friend of revolution, but he told the truth as he saw it, recalling Despard's courageous services on behalf of the country. A courteous interruption from the bench requested him to speak more directly about the character of the accused. 'I formed the highest opinion of him at that time as a man and an officer, seeing him so willing in the service of his sovereign,' Nelson went on. 'Having lost sight of him for the last twenty years, if I had been asked my opinion of him, I should certainly have said, "If he is alive, he is certainly one of the brightest ornaments of the British army."' Unfortunately, Despard's previous character was one thing, and the present charge another, and the evidence was deemed overwhelming. Although the jury recommended clemency, probably on account of Nelson's testimony, Despard was condemned to the traditional and grisly death of a traitor. For the last time in English history the sentence of hanging and drawing and quartering – the same visited two centuries before on the gunpowder plotters – was pronounced.[22]

Nelson's old friend Bulkeley shared the admiral's astonishment but was less sympathetic. 'The king owes to the country that the execution should take place,' he scribbled to Nelson. However, the condemned man wrote the admiral an emotional letter of thanks from Horsemonger Lane, the Surrey county gaol, and enclosed a copy of a petition for mercy to the king and Privy Council; he had a young son and four nephews in the army, he said. It was delivered to Nelson, who passed it to Addington without comment. The admiral was particularly moved by the distress of Despard's wife, Catherine, a spirited woman of African descent and the daughter of a clergyman. She called upon Nelson at Piccadilly on the morning of 20 February. He tried to comfort her, but when Catherine visited the prison later that day she learned that the death warrant for her husband had arrived, and 'the awful sentence' was to be carried out the next morning. 'My Dearest Lord,' she wrote to Nelson immediately afterwards, 'I can say no more, my heart is too full and my mind distracted.' The grim finale for Despard and six companions was enacted upon the roof of the gaol gatehouse before thousands of spectators, but the sentence had been commuted to one of hanging followed by beheading, and Despard met it stoically. The three detachments of troops prepared to suppress any disturbances in favour of the revolutionaries were not needed. There was little Nelson could add to Despard's case, but he believed Catherine to be an innocent victim, and Emma personally commiserated with the widow after the execution. At Mrs Despard's request, Nelson gave her a copy of his trial testimony for her use, and suggested the government consider her for a pension. It was a distant hope, even though Addington admitted that Despard's petition had been a moving document. Nelson told Minto, to whom he read parts of the petition, that the chances of a pension had been damaged by Despard's unrepentant behaviour on the scaffold. The likelihood is that the admiral ended up plumbing his pockets to contribute to a small private purse. At least Bulkeley forwarded a donation, leaving it to the admiral to decide the propriety of its use or not.[23]

A similar but less distressing appeal arrived from a robust naval captain in his mid-thirties, Captain James Macnamara, who had commanded the *Southampton* under Nelson in the nineties. On 6 April 1803 Macnamara had been at Chalk Farm on Primrose Hill, exchanging pistol shots with a Colonel Robert Montgomery over fifteen or sixteen yards. Remarkably, their quarrel had originated in an affray that had occurred in Hyde Park, when the duellists' Newfoundland dogs had attempted to tear lumps out of each other. As neither officer would call his animal off, pistols cracked on Primrose Hill, Macnamara staggered under a grievous wound, and Montgomery fell with a fatal ball in his right breast. However, duelling had slipped dangerously from respectability by this time, and on 22 April Macnamara, now attired in a dark olive surtout and looking 'very much . . . a man of fashion', appeared before a jury at the Old Bailey to answer a charge of manslaughter. He summoned a glittering array of sea officers to attest to his character, including Nelson, Hood, Hotham, Hyde Parker and Troubridge, as well as Lord Minto. Nelson sat through most of the trial 'on the bench', but advanced to be cross-examined by William Garrow, the celebrated criminal lawyer. He swore that 'I never knew or heard that he [Macnamara] ever gave an offence to man, woman or child during the nine years I have had the pleasure of knowing him.' Privately Nelson knew Macnamara to be quarrelsome and intemperate, but he was acquitted and lived to become a rear admiral. But it was the picture of the battling Newfoundlands and his duel with Montgomery that entered literature as the subject of Edmund Blunden's poem, 'Incident in Hyde Park'.[24]

Nelson also had some searing requests from completely unknown people in adversity, but his more relentless burden arose from the innumerable sea officers and men chasing promotion or positions. They came from many hands: an Italian contractor who had supplied the Mediterranean fleet and wanted a permanent post with the British; Captain Louis seeking a cadetship for an eleve at Woolwich; Lady Collier trying to get her boy, Francis, to the West Indies where naval promotion was brisker; Berry wanting evidence for a cause in the prize court; a lieutenant of the *Edgar* needing help to adjust to life without the arm he had lost at Copenhagen; Major Weir, who had distinguished himself at Porto Ferraio and Malta, looking to get his brevet rank confirmed; and old shipmates such as Captain Richard Williams and Langford floundering on the slippery ladder . . . It was a ceaseless flow of supplications. Nelson was usually susceptible. When Stephen Comyn, who had been Nelson's chaplain in four flagships, wrote in October 1801 to remind the admiral that he had promised to help him find a living ashore, he was answered by a plea for patience. 'I never have forgot you,' Nelson reassured. 'That is not my disposition.' And he meant it. Comyn got a preferment in Bridgham, Norfolk, in 1802 through the interest Davison had with his 'friend' Lord Eldon, the Lord Chancellor.[25]

The manipulation of 'interest' was very much a tit-for-tat affair, with favours creating obligations that could be called in. Striving to find places for followers and the protégés friends pressed upon him, Nelson in turn depended much upon the willingness of others to serve him. As everywhere, some took but gave few favours, and Nelson complained that one of the brothers, 'Captain [Samuel] Hood never offered to take even a midshipman for me'. Fortunately, the system often worked. When Windham, the former secretary at war, asked Nelson to fit one of his people into a naval billet, a Captain Page was obliging enough to accept him aboard the *Caroline*. Sutton of the *Amazon* always worked hard for Nelson. He used the admiral to place his own followers, including a steward and a surgeon, but repaid the favours by taking Nelson's protégés, such as young Connor. As Nelson acknowledged, 'few, very few, will take that care of him which you have been good enough to do, and for which we are most truly thankful'.[26]

In all of these causes, personal, professional and philanthropic, Nelson complained that his 'interest' was simply inadequate to answer the expectations held of it. Because he was a national hero, and the most famous man in the realm, it was often assumed that he held extensive sway in and out of the service. Nelson knew the truth, and his attempts to strengthen his hand led him deeper into the mires of 'Old Corruption'.

4

Politics, Nelson thought, was a filthy trade, and he knew he was contaminating himself. It was treacherous ground, too. Nelson believed that Addington was a man of honour, 'but I may be mistaken. I have no confidence in any of the *ins* and *outs*.' Nonetheless, there seemed no other way to achieve the wanted rewards.[27]

In this respect the times were not unpropitious. The general election of July 1802, in which 97 of 658 seats were being contested, was imminent, and Addington's weak administration sensed a battering. William Nelson, hot on the scent of vacant cathedral stalls worth a thousand a year, was enlivened by news of the illness of the Dean of Exeter, who died in July. He urged Nelson to cultivate Addington and 'speak often' in the Lords to get that opening. A vision of his brother as first lord of the Admiralty and member of the cabinet, with all that that might bring, was before him. William put his votes in the county of Norfolk and the University of Cambridge at the disposal of the government, while a reluctant Nelson applied to Addington, referring to his brother's support for government candidates but fearful that his visits to the prime minister would become synonymous with 'soliciting'.[28]

Nevertheless, Nelson dutifully appeared at the hustings in Covent Garden to support Alan, Lord Gardner, a sea officer and ministerial man to boot, who was standing for one of the two seats representing Westminster. On 15 July Sir William Hamilton also went into town to vote for Gardner, but arrived too late, 'luckily' as it happened, since the rival supporters had torn up the hustings and several people had been killed and injured in the fracas that followed. Gardner won his seat, but was a slack parliamentarian, largely because of a flag command in Ireland.[29]

In the Lords Nelson also tried to be useful. On 29 March he voted in favour of the Civil List, whimsically chiding Davison that it would give the agent 'the *enormous* sum' of £153. The Whigs had long argued that the List was being abused by the crown, which employed the money to buy political influence and undermine the independence of members of parliament. In their view, the delicate balance of the constitution, which stressed a sharing of powers between king, lords and commons, was being subverted by a corrupt and overmighty executive. Nelson justified his support by pointing out that not all the Civil List went into the pockets of the king. His record in the House was not a good one, whether weighed by independence or argument, but Emma was in love. 'Don't you think he speaks like an angel in the House of Lords?' she chirped.[30]

Despite all, Nelson's toadying brought little immediate bread. Sycophants and office-seekers often saw the Treasury as a bottomless pot to be milked, and the Whigs and most radicals believed it and backed 'economical reform' to reduce the money available to government and drain its power to bribe. But many in government had a very different interpretation of the king's largesse; indeed, some said that successive reforms had so far eroded the government's ability to control parliament that it could scarce get the country's business done. From this point of view, the problem was the insufficiency of government patronage, corruption if you like, not the surplus of it. Addington told Nelson as much, when he declined to help William Nelson in 1802, despite repeated applications. 'My means are more limited than you imagine,' he said. 'The ecclesiastical atmosphere has been a very healthy place of late, and the succession has proved too slow for even Christian patience.' In other words there were no dead men's shoes for William to wear, and the government could not create more. But when Nelson bemoaned that there was little to be had from ministers, William did not believe it. He assumed that he had priority over everyone else, and when the government nominated another to a stall at Winchester Cathedral, he grumbled about the 'insincerity' of Addington.[31]

At the end of 1802 a further opportunity arose. The home secretary, Thomas, Lord Pelham, invited Nelson to dinner, suggesting over the repast that he second an address that Addington and Pitt intended to present to the House. The peace of Amiens was groaning under clear indications of Napoleon's unreformed ambition, and it was necessary to prepare the nation for a fresh crisis. Expecting to be busy in parliament, Nelson moved the whole ménage to Piccadilly for a month. There was to be a levee, and Lord Mansfield promised to usher Nelson and Sir William 'near the king and queen without [a] crowd'. Hamilton wanted help with his debts, Nelson perks for his brother, and both were after improved pensions.[32]

On 23 November Nelson supported the king's speech to parliament, prevaricating over the faltering peace. Peace was desirable, but not on 'dishonorable terms', and the 'restless and unjust ambition' of Napoleon might call upon the country to 'assert its honour' on behalf of 'the liberties of Europe'. In this he was sincere and, when he spent a day with Minto soon after, he complained about St Vincent's rabid opposition to a renewal of war. Minto said the earl had run the navy down and knew that it was in no shape to fight, and both men agreed that the armed services needed urgent rehabilitation. Nelson also revealed that he was to be sent back to the Mediterranean to signal that Britain meant business. At every smell of gunpowder, the French were threatened with Nelson, as if he had been a nuclear deterrent. For several months the admiral remained available. He attended a levee on 16 February 1803, and was with the king, the Duke of York and several Knights of the Bath who inducted a general into their order.[33]

Unquestionably, the good of the country was paramount for Nelson, but his embarrassing financial position continued to underlie his political activities. Unemployment and the development of Merton Place had taken its toll. On 8 March 1803, Nelson sent a statement of his income to the prime minister. Since hauling down his flag the previous April, he had been on £465 per annum as an unemployed vice admiral. His pension amounted to £2000 a year, and disability payments brought in another £923. Throwing in the £30 that came from a thousand pounds invested in 3 per cent consols brought the whole to £3418. But when Fanny's allowance, Sukey's pension of £200, £150 earmarked for the education of young relatives and interest payments on mortgages were deducted, Nelson was left with less than £1000 to maintain his house, table and staff, pay his taxes and contribute to 'charities necessary for my station in life'. This was fairly close to the truth. A newly discovered account with Marsh and Creed for the last quarter of 1802 shows that despite receiving £375 in prize money and dipping into his savings to the tune of £304 he ended the year with a favourable balance of only £258 6s. 8d. It was a precarious situation for a man of his stature and responsibilities.[34]

True, there were possible windfalls ahead, apart from an understanding that Nelson would be appointed commander-in-chief of the Mediterranean if the political horizon darkened. Two major disputes about prize were in the offing. Plugging away at Addington and the Admiralty, Nelson eventually got an agreement to grant the captors £65,000 for the Copenhagen prizes, including the salvaged *Holsten*, a sum which gave Nelson £700 and Parker, the commander-in-chief, £3000. Authorised by the Privy Council in June 1803, it was less than Nelson had anticipated, but the admiral reckoned that head money and a reward for the captured guns would take the payout close to £100,000. And Nelson's suit against St Vincent over the rich prizes taken in 1799 proceeded unsteadily. Few agreed about it. Canvassing 86 naval officers, prize agents and experts on prize law, Davison found 33 favourable to Nelson's suit, 5 against, 48 either unable to decide or unwilling to venture an opinion. But in November 1802 the judges in the court of common pleas found in favour of St Vincent, contending that the commander-in-chief may have been home when the captures were made but he had not abdicated his command. Nelson was discouraged, but took heart from divisions among the judges and immediately appealed.[35]

When it came to the undesirable alternative of borrowing money, Nelson preferred to keep within close family and friends, and the generosity of George Matcham and Alexander Davison continued to astonish him. In February 1803 Davison offered Nelson up to £5000 worth of credit. Ominously though, the future of both these stalwarts was uncertain. George hankered to live in Vienna or Dresden, a prospect which disturbed Nelson, who tried to persuade him to buy a house near Merton, and Davison was in serious trouble. Examining his accounts as commissary general to Moira's army, the Treasury found irregularities in his charges relating to the supply of barracks bedding. More critically, Davison had indiscreetly bought votes during the late general election to take the borough of Ilchester from its proprietor, Sir William Manners, who cried foul. The result was annulled and Davison faced a prosecution for bribery and corruption.

This was the background to Nelson's new attempt to persuade Addington to augment his public pension, which compared unfavourably to those awarded St Vincent and Duncan. Moreover, he pointed out that, if he died without heirs, as seemed likely, his barony would revert to his brother, who lacked the means to support the rank and dignity of a peer. But all failed, although on 28 December 1802 Nelson pressed Addington so 'strongly' in an emotional interview that he apologised the following day. 'I own I feel when I see other noble lords' brothers gazetted, whose services I can scarcely trace,' he admitted. The outburst induced Addington to promise a sympathetic consideration, but nothing happened.[36]

Nelson disliked being a party man, but his votes were as firmly in Addington's pocket as those of any placeman. He even urged the likes of Hood to back the prime minister, and there is an indication that he offered to help a naval protégé of Sir William Fawcett providing the latter voted satisfactorily. The matter of his proxy demonstrates his sensitivity on the point. When Nelson returned to active service in 1803, he authorised Lord Moira, whom he believed an honourable man, to use his vote in the Lords during his absence. He believed Moira's promises to use the privilege sparingly, and only in ways that Nelson would have supported. 'I hope he will be a firm supporter of Mr Addington,' the admiral wrote, accepting that there was a risk of his trust being abused. Moira was indeed less than reliable, and Emma, whose financial claims were also before government, grew terrified that his behaviour might damage Addington and endanger essential political goodwill. Nelson regretted that he had ever let his vote slip out of his hands.

At sea in 1803, Nelson reflected unhappily about his political entanglements, and at times harked back wistfully to that independence he had once prized, the free mind, unconnected with party, whose votes reflected nothing but the good of the country. 'I will stand upon my own bottom, and be none of their tools when I come home,' he said. That vision of the younger, purer, uncomplicated Nelson he had once been did not last, because he was never secure enough to indulge his inclinations. Instead he justified his compliance by considering himself 'a part of the administration', and therefore bound by some sense of collective responsibility. Later, the next administration met his provisional approval. 'I like both Pitt and Lord Melville [respectively the new prime minister and first lord of the Admiralty], and why should I oppose them? I am free and independent.' But it was conditional. 'If Pitt is attentive to me,' he said, 'he shall have my vote.' Life, he had long since realised, was not always a simple matter of right and wrong and honour and dishonour. If he was to help his family and those who depended upon him, as he must, he had to work within the system that existed and become part of it.[37]

Perhaps it was Nelson's political acquiescence that accounted for his failure to protest St Vincent's destructive management of the navy during the peace of Amiens. Driven by implacable prejudices, including a Whig's zeal for government retrenchment, a seaman's contempt for the efficiency of landlubbers and a conviction that the whole civil branch of the navy was rotten to the core, the first lord initiated a series of damaging 'reforms'. Relations between the Admiralty on the one hand and the Navy Board, dockyards and commercial contractors on the other deadlocked, dockyard resources were depleted and the supply and repair of ships retarded. As the navy was slowly pulled to pieces, Nepean, the Admiralty secretary, resigned and Earl Spencer complained, but from Nelson there was no public expression. Initially, Nelson's complacency might have originated in a belief that the peace would last, but his loyalty to the Addington administration may have been the main reason for his silence.[38]

Nelson did make a small contribution towards the spirit of reform, though. On 21 December 1802 he spoke in the House for St Vincent's bill to establish a Commission of Naval Enquiry to root out irregularities and abuses in naval administration. There was a strong cost-cutting dimension to the investigation, which published its final and fourteenth report in 1806, but Nelson's reservations concerned the intrusive powers of the commissioners. Probably prompted by Davison, Nelson warned that if a merchant's books were impounded for the purposes of the investigation, their confidentiality needed to be protected. That said, his lordship hoped that the commission might improve the system by which the common seamen received their prize money. 'He was sure,' he said, 'the legislature was anxious that the poorest sea-boy should receive its protection. The admiral, the commandant of a fleet, or the captain might find means to obtain their right, but the poor seaman had not a chance of being able to get his money.'[39]

On 1 April 1803 Nelson appeared before the commission, chaired by Admiral Pole, and advocated a reform of the prize laws, an issue that embittered many of those at sea. He did not concern himself with the exorbitant expenses of the prize courts themselves, although he had suffered much under the system. Fifty-five per cent of the proceeds from five prizes taken by the *Agamemnon* and three consorts between November 1795 and May 1796 had been siphoned off by the costs of condemnation. Nor did he question the generous proportions of the proceeds of prize that went to the captains and flag officers. But he did focus upon the distressing delays and dislocations in distribution. Agents sometimes held captors' money for months, even years, for one reason or another, sometimes profiting in the meantime by risking it in loans and investments.

Some seamen died waiting for their money. According to Nelson, unclaimed shares were also ultimately being pocketed by a number of unscrupulous agents, rather than donated to Greenwich Hospital, the naval charity, as the law required.[40]

Nelson's solution was to require prize agents to post bonds of up to £3000 to ensure 'a faithful discharge of their duty', and to stipulate that no prize money due to the captors could be made liable to debts incurred by agents. Moreover, to speed up the payment of prize money, he suggested adjustments to the commissions agents charged. A distribution within three months of the condemnation of a prize would earn a commission of 5 per cent. If an agent had just cause for failing to meet the deadline, he could be allowed an additional three months, but agents in default would surrender their undistributed payments to a special officer, who had the power to reduce the commission payable or put the business into abler hands. These were useful suggestions, but they went largely unheeded. Only the idea of stipulating time limits for the distribution of prize money was adopted, and that without the supporting measures needed to make it successful.[41]

Nelson had touched upon the matter earlier, sending a memorandum about the problems of recruitment, retention and desertion to the Admiralty on 28 February 1803, and claiming that 'fatal consequences' could result from the destruction of such crucial inducements as prize money. Copies went to Addington and Clarence. Again Nelson drew attention to the difficulties men experienced getting their due rewards, in this case pay and pensions for injury or infirmity. To prevent money going to the wrong people, Nelson recommended a system of certification to provide seamen with authoritative documents establishing their identity and testifying to their character. With such credentials seamen could more readily claim their due and find employment.[42]

Another of the admiral's suggestions was designed to promote loyalty and good conduct. A seaman who completed five years of blameless service should become eligible for an annual bonus of two guineas, and the sum should double after eight blame-free years had been completed. Naturally, there would be a cost to government, but Nelson pointed out that the cost of replacing the 42,000 men who deserted in 1793–1801 had totalled £840,000 in bounties, and pragmatically that as most seamen had retired by forty-five the average bonus would not be enjoyed for a great length of time.[43]

St Vincent had little enthusiasm for Nelson's ideas, but Sir William Scott, the great authority on prize law, was attracted to a few of them, including the certification scheme to streamline payments to seamen. These essays into the territory of naval reform suggest that had the admiral the luxury of sitting longer in the House he might have become useful to the service, his opinions coming without the animus of the professional reformers and carrying the weight of his great personal prestige. But nothing had been achieved by 1803, when the collapse of the peace of Amiens sent Nelson upon a very different path.[44]

5

In peacetime the enthusiasm for war heroes fades, and Nelson could have been excused for wondering whether a public with no great need of his services would continue to exalt him. Yet the memorabilia and admiring letters continued to flow, the crowds remained as insistent and societies he did not know clamoured for his membership. In 1800 the attentions of European cities had delighted the admiral, and in 1802 he decided to show himself to his own people, rather as Elizabeth I had done in storied progresses. The streets of London had seen him, and a few other places, but now Nelson would grace widely scattered towns, villages and hamlets in the provinces, and appear before street-sellers, shopkeepers and shepherds, steel workers and small masters. Nelson's seven-hundred-mile odyssey of 1802, with its public dinners, talks and walks, was nothing less than a celebratory road show of a type no commoner had launched before. It took the champion to his people, and added a new dimension to the image of the national hero.[45]

The idea grew out of Sir William's Welsh interests. He had inherited a Pembrokeshire estate, which was managed by his nephew, Charles Greville. Greville was preparing a parliamentary bill to develop the nearby port of Milford as a naval base and ferry port between Britain and Ireland. In the summer of 1801 Sir William had visited Milford and agreed to enlist Nelson's support for the project. With two thousand acres near Milford, as well as investments in the town, Hamilton expected to benefit from the growth of the town; in fact, he rosily predicted it would create 'immense profits to my heirs hereafter'.[46]

The journey owed much to the expansion of turnpike trusts, which repaired sections of roads and recovered the costs through tolls. The motorways of the day, the turnpikes speeded up travel and garnished it with a proliferation of inns, stables and ostlers. Nelson anticipated reaching Milford in time for the anniversary of the Nile, for which Greville would organise appropriate celebrations, while adequate commemoration would be ensured on the way by alerting the towns ahead of the hero's approach. To some extent, therefore, Nelson orchestrated his own *tour de force* for a total cost of £481. It was borne equally with Sir William, and each opened the pot with an initial float of £100. Their accounts covered payments to coachmen, turnpikes, bell ringers, town criers, innkeepers and purveyors of delicacies, such as 'the oyster man'. The party travelled light, using two coaches and eight horses, and consisted of Nelson, the Hamiltons and William, Sarah and young Horace Nelson, but few servants, relying heavily instead upon service staff in the inns along the way.[47]

Leaving Merton on Wednesday, 21 July, the coaches swung and swayed across a soaked heath still haunted by the occasional highwayman to reach Hounslow, west of London. A change of horses got them to Maidenhead and Henley, and striking north-west in the dying afternoon they made Oxford, where thronging crowds and ringing bells chorused the first enthusiastic welcome. George and Kate Matcham, with their son George, were waiting at the Star Inn in the Corn Market, the best lodgings in town, but the party proved to be too large and had to transfer to the Angel in the High Street. The following day Nelson, uniformed to make the most of the crowd, led his party to the town hall by foot, attended by swarms of chattering pedestrians, and accepted the freedom of the town from the mayor, Richard Weston. It was enclosed in an oval gold box and inscribed with the town crest, appropriately depicting an ox. Nelson took the opportunity to demonstrate his belief in the reclamation of sinners by donating a purse to the prisoners in the local gaol. On Friday Nelson and Sir William, both bedecked in the scarlet sashes of the Bath, were at the magnificent Sheldonian Theatre to be honoured by the university. Robert Holmes, a professor of poetry and theology, presided, but the complimentary doctorates in law (LL.D.) were presented by the famous occupant of the chair, William Blackstone, while the parasitic William snapped up another doctorate in divinity. Thus the parson, a man, it was once said, without grace, manners or a shred of academic credibility, found himself double-doctored at the hands of England's premier universities. Thus lauded the party proceeded to Woodstock to lodge overnight.[48]

The Oxford welcome set the pattern that marked the tour. Nelson's 'walkabout' (as it would be called today), in which the admiral passed freely through the people, without bodyguards, distance or cordons, was a distinctive feature that has had few counterparts since. So universal was the love of the people that he was not threatened once during his tour. An unusual note of disapproval was struck on Saturday, however, when the party visited Blenheim Palace, the magnificent ancestral home that Sir John Vanbrugh had created for the great Duke of Marlborough at the behest of Queen Anne. The current holder of the title declined to receive the party, allowing refreshments to be served outside instead, and the visitors retired disgruntled. They sped westwards, through beautiful green Cotswold hills, and entered the ancient town of Gloucester, where they passed beneath the north gate to halt at the King's Head in Westgate Street, close to St Nicholas Church. People quickly fell behind the party as it strolled to the striking grey stone cathedral, where bells pealed a noisy welcome. Nelson seemed relaxed, healthy and good-humoured, and again visited the local gaol.

Sunday, 25 July, saw the party divide. The Matchams left for their home in Bath, while the Hamiltons and Nelsons skirted northwards around the Forest of Dean and penetrated the beautiful Wye valley beneath brightening skies. They breakfasted at the Swan in the High Street of Ross, Herefordshire, and walked it off in pleasant private gardens owned by Walter Hill. With an eye to the welfare of the navy, Nelson had made notes on the Forest of Dean, and later framed them into a proposal he put to Addington. The navy's insatiable demand for timber was denuding Britain's woodlands and putting the future of the realm at risk by increasing a dangerous dependency upon foreign supplies. Nelson reckoned that the 23,000 acres of the Forest of Dean were capable of providing 9200 loads of oak timber for the navy, but their current state was so 'deplorable' that not more than 3500 loads could be expected, and little additional wood was 'coming forward'. The trees had been mismanaged, timber wasted, purloined and sold by impecunious gentlemen trying to satisfy creditors. Calling for strong measures, including the appointment of a qualified 'guardian' and assistant foresters wise in 'the planting, thinning and management' of timber, Nelson predicted that the forest had the potential to furnish important supplies to the navy for forty years.[49]

At Ross the tourists abandoned their carriages for a voyage down the Wye in a pleasure boat gaily decorated with laurels, winding gently through some of the most impressive countryside in the land and beneath the towering walls of Goodrich Castle, Symonds Yat and the Seven Sisters rocks. When they reached Monmouth in the afternoon feverish crowds were waiting, manning the river banks and quay and a flotilla of small boats. The town had voted Nelson their freedom back in February, inviting him to visit their newly erected naval temple, commemorating the victories of the war, and here the warmth of the people completely overcame the admiral's deeply embedded feelings of neglect. He rose to his feet to acknowledge the cheers with a bow and disembarked at the Wye Bridge, where Mayor Thomas Hollings and his corporation waited in eager anticipation. A band of musicians then preceded the party into town thumping out the national anthem, 'Rule, Britannia' and 'See, the Conquering Hero Comes.' At the Beaufort Arms in Agincourt Square Nelson addressed the crowd; inside, over dinner, he explained that the repulse at Boulogne was of no moment. 'I always did beat the French,' he quipped, 'and I always will!' The meal over, Nelson performed another walkabout, chaperoned by a Mr P. M. Hardwick, inspecting public buildings and responding amiably to pressing spectators.[50]

Reclaiming their carriages, the travellers resumed their journey the next day, Monday, 26 July, heading west and north-west into Wales, where they visited Admiral John Gell's large Italianate house at Crickhowell on the River Usk. A journey up the Usk, with the majestic Brecon Beacon hills to the left, then brought them to Brecon, where the Welsh hill-men turned out in force to greet the admiral with such touching adoration that he expressed a wish to return. On Tuesday the trail twisted south through the Beacons to Merthyr Tydfil, which at that time was the largest town in Wales, the home of a hard-working community of seven thousand souls, many of whom earned a physically challenging livelihood in Richard Crawshay's ironworks at Cyfartha. Crawshay, a large, pig-eyed Yorkshireman, had led a fairy-tale existence, fleeing as a shepherd boy to London to seek his fortune, only to find it in these craggy Welsh valleys. He had been hospitable to Sir William in the past, but for some reason the town was surprised by Nelson's arrival and the party had to put up at the Star, an unimpressive two-storey hostelry. Nevertheless, crowds were soon besieging the inn, shops closed for the day and a band and a squad of musketeers hastily turned out to create a noisy welcome. Nelson appeared at an upstairs window, acknowledging every cheer with a bow that instantly raised another roar. Indeed, the excitement was so great that a swivel gun, carelessly fired in salute, injured three people, one a boy whose wounds looked to be fatal.[51]

Putting the tragedy behind them, the visitors were shown around Crawshay's works the next day, and the bulky ironmaster strutted in his best outfit. Nelson appreciated the symbiotic relationship between the iron industry and the navy, one supplying necessary arms and the other the demand essential to industrial expansion. He was impressed by a one-hundred-ton waterwheel that was used to power the four huge furnaces. At Carmarthen, which the ménage reached the same day, records show that Nelson paid three guineas to visit the Playhouse theatre and gave a guinea to a ventriloquist. Two days later, moving west into Pembrokeshire, the party were breakfasting at the Blue Boar at St Clears and inspiring a welcoming peal of bells at Narberth. And finally the same evening they rumbled into Milford, their primary destination, situated on the most westerly reaches of the picturesque Welsh coast, where the Bristol and St George's channels merged. Tolerable accommodation was provided at the New Inn in Front Street, the road which climbed gently from the quay to the new chapel of St Katherine's. Thomas Bolton had come from Norfolk to share the Nile celebration at Milford on 1 August, which included a rowing match, a fair and a cattle show. But it was also expected that Nelson would support the town's aspirations, and at a banquet he expressed his great admiration for Captain Foley, a local hero who lived in Abermarles, near Landovery, and compared the natural advantages of Milford to the port of Trincomalee, which he had seen as a boy. It had high natural tides, ample supplies of wood and iron, and, situated between Britain and Ireland, was well placed to be a haven, naval base and packet terminus. This was music to Milford, which Nelson discovered possessed yet another valuable asset in Jean-Louis Barallier, a French émigré with outstanding talents for designing ships and developing dockyard facilities.

Nelson spoke to oblige Sir William, but whether he believed all he said is another matter. Almost a year later he was recommending Barallier to the Admiralty, suggesting that he could be more 'usefully' employed than at Milford, and St Vincent was not persuaded by Greville's plan for the port when it finally alighted upon his desk. The town's hinterland was undeveloped, and while Milford might serve as a haven for ships in distress, the first lord saw no great benefit in locating a large establishment there. Nevertheless, in the brighter hopes of 1802, Hamilton donated a portrait of Nelson to Milford, a version of the rather sickly interpretation that Guzzardi had made in 1799.[52]

On Monday, 9 August, the tourists used a boat to visit Lord Milford's castle at Picton, and Sir William probably called at neighbouring Slebech, the home of his favourite wife, Catherine, who had lain waiting for him in a waterside chapel for twenty years. The next day they travelled further north to the small fishing settlement of Haverfordwest, where people 'of every class' were enraptured. The crowds unhitched the horses and man-hauled the carriages to the inn, escorted by Milford's mounted yeomanry; and the flags of 'different companies and societies' were everywhere to be seen. The next morning the mayor and corporation caught up with them at the Ridgeway, a two-storey house eight miles out of town owned by John Foley, brother of the captain, where they had breakfasted. The admiral politely received the freedom of the town and borough to the plaudits of a militia band.[53]

It was at Haverfordwest that Greville turned back, but the Nelsons and Hamiltons struck east and south to reach Tenby on Carmarthen Bay on Friday. The king's ships and batteries about the harbour fired salutes, and the people were as jubilant as elsewhere, but a more cynical observer gave the most illuminating portrait of the visitors. Though 'the whole town was at their heels' during another walkabout, the ménage presented a 'ridiculous' and 'pitiable' appearance, with an 'immensely fat and equally coarse' woman arm-in-arm with a 'thin, shrunken' and ill-looking admiral, and 'poor Sir William, wretched but not abashed', struggling after them 'bearing in his arms a cucciolo [lapdog] and other emblems of their combined folly'. Still, the following day the bizarre guests graced a dinner with Lord Kensington and enlivened a ball at the Lion inn.[54]

Nelson returned to St Clears and Carmarthen on the 14th and 15th before detouring south-east to make their return journey by way of Swansea and the south coast of Wales. Swansea was not the important city it afterwards became, but on that Sunday a corps of seamen met the carriages to haul them into the town, and Thomas Morgan, a robed portreeve, led the sprawling procession into Wind Street. During his stay Nelson was entertained by Sir John Morris, a local entrepreneur, at his home, Clasemont, feted in a public banquet, when the inevitable freedom was bestowed, and inspected the harbour and the pottery factory of Coles and Haynes. It was another success, and Nelson's written thanks to the town were later printed for circulation.[55]

After calling at Margam (Port Talbot), where Nelson gave three shillings to a gardener who showed them around a magnificent arboretum and orangery, the tourists took overnight lodgings in Cardiff, then a community of two thousand, before proceeding to Newport to cross the Usk and take the road to Chepstow on the Wye. They spent the night of Tuesday, 17 August, at the Three Cranes in Beaufort Square, and the next day headed again towards Monmouth, which Nelson had forewarned by a letter from St Clears. On the way they called upon Nathaniel Wells, a rich sugar planter from St Kitts, who had just acquired Piercefield Park, where Chepstow racecourse now stands.[56]

Nelson arrived at Monmouth on 18 August, a day earlier than he had predicted. His second visit completed a round tour of Wales that had revealed the admiral to men and women who would never have encountered a great international figure in the normal run of life. It was in many senses an old-fashioned royal progress that united a people with their leader, and it contributed significantly to the admiral's entrenched popular reputation. No distant fox-hunting patrician he, but a man loud in dress but modest in address, who shook grimy, coarse hands, patted the heads of bare-footed children, shed tears at the sight of old shipmates, and talked with all and sundry as equals. By now the national papers were declaring that no one, not even the king, could attract the attention that was greeting Nelson.

On Tuesday the bells of the Church of St Mary in Monmouth announced Nelson's presence, and he emerged from the Beaufort Arms to an immense throng, which cheered his carriage and four as far as the Wye Bridge. From there it climbed several hundred feet along a narrow path to the summit of Kymin Hill, where the naval temple had been erected to honour the service in 1800. Inspired primarily by the victory at the Nile, it was effectively Nelson's first major public monument. Surmounted by the image of Britannia, the temple commanded views as far as the Malvern Hills and the Brecon Beacons, and Nelson reverently inspected the edifice, resting upon the arm of Mr Hardwick as he studied a painting of the battle of the Nile on an inside wall through opera glasses. It was an overdue memorial to the British navy, he said. Nearby there stood a thirty-foot turreted tower, which the mayor and corporation had commandeered to provide the Nelson party with a suitable repast. Once replenished, the hosts and guests descended the hill on foot, passing through 'a beautiful wood' known as the Beaulieu Grove before re-entering the town below.

The civic banquet at the Beaufort Arms late that afternoon gave Nelson another opportunity to deliver his message to the nation. Flanked by the mayor and Emma, who cut the admiral's venison, Nelson made two brief speeches, the uniform coat over his black silk waistcoat bristling with orders and medals. There was little braggadocio in these orations. Showing a modesty that tended to characterise his ordinary conversation, Nelson chose words calculated to seal the bonds between a hero and his nation, bestowing accolades on others rather than himself. The 'distinguished officers' and 'gallant crews' of the navy were the true architects of his successes. 'I had only to show them the enemy, and victory crowned the standard.' And Nelson declared that it was the desire to please the people that spurred the navy on. Certainly speaking for himself, he remarked that in 'whatever quarter of the globe' an officer might serve, he knew that 'the eyes of the country are upon him'. Nor did he omit the army, which had defeated the French in Egypt, from his tribute. 'The fact is,' Nelson explained, 'all the great battles [triumphs] the French obtained were over our allies, and not over the British soldiers, and if those allies had been as faithful to the engagements as ourselves, the French would not have to boast of what they deem their splendid victories.' But it was when he praised the British people that Nelson struck closest to the heart of his popular audience. If the French dodged every redcoat and ship and landed in England, he said, 'the courage of her sons at home' would alone repulse the invaders, 'for they would always find Britons ready to receive them'. Unity was the key. 'So long as the people continue to unite hand and heart . . . we have nothing to fear.' It was strategic nonsense, but instilled pride in the home front at a time when the nation was not entirely out of danger. Music elaborated the theme, with choristers exalting 'The British Grenadiers' and Emma performing Cornelia Knight's supplement to the national anthem, inviting all to join in 'great Nelson's fame', and her reworking of 'Rule, Britannia'. The evening of mutual congratulation closed satisfactorily with coffee in a summer house in the garden of Colonel Lindsay in Monnow Street.[57]

The morning of Friday, 20 August, Nelson and his friends were in Charles Heath's bookshop in Agincourt Square. 'Did not Lord Nelson speak well to you yesterday, Mr Heath,' enquired Emma, forever fishing for compliments. The bookseller gave the visitors copies of one of his own volumes, for which Nelson thanked him 'in the most gracious manner'. Heath was thoroughly charmed, noticing how the great man respectfully removed his hat to address him, and when the bookseller requested permission to print the speeches of the previous day, the other immediately agreed. Struck with Nelson's modesty, Heath remembered it as a favour, but the admiral thought himself the debtor. He later wrote to Heath to thank him for granting *his* wish that the speeches be published in the local newspaper. Leaving the shop, leaning again upon the arm of the dependable Hardwick, Nelson reflected once more upon the British redcoats. Two privates of the 69th Regiment of Foot, he remembered, had helped him board the *San Nicolas* off Cape St Vincent. One fell into the sea in attempting to jump from one ship to the other, but the other got through the Spaniard's quarter gallery after smashing its windows with a musket stock. The admiral's salutes to the army were particularly appropriate in that town, which was the reputed birthplace of Henry V, the military hero whose name Nelson playfully adopted in the Merton household, and whose effigy guarded the square outside Heath's shop.

The same day Nelson's party continued their homeward journey, re-entering the main street of Ross-on-Wye beneath a triumphal arch of oak and laurel, but this time lodging at nearby Rudhall, a gabled manor house with a beamed Tudor façade in which Thomas and Mary Westfaling, friends of Sir William in Italy, had made their home. The evening and early hours of the next morning were surrendered to a grand dinner and dance, in which hundreds of spectators enjoyed fireworks, an arch decorated with a star of variegated lamps and a band, as well as desserts, wine and cider. Here Nelson was astonished to meet a Danish diplomat he had met at Copenhagen, who, he learned, was visiting South Wales to satisfy an interest in industry.

While at Rudhall, Nelson received an invitation from the town of Hereford, and therefore turned north into new ground to arrive at noon on Monday, 23 August. At the bridge over the Wye the townspeople uncoupled the horses and dragged the carriages to Bennett's Inn in Broad Street, where a reception committee waited with a dishevelled oddity, the eleventh Duke of Norfolk, the Lord Chief Steward of the county, at its head. The visitors were promptly conducted to the town hall, serenaded by a band, and the freedom of this focus of the cider industry was appropriately presented in a box of apple wood. Nelson listened to a tribute from the town clerk, and replied in much the same vein as in Monmouth. The day was non-stop. Back at the inn, Nelson held court in a great room thrown open to the public, and before leaving the town visited the cathedral and the bedside of the ailing Bishop of Hereford. But at about two in the afternoon the party continued north through lush fields and apple orchards to the attractive Shropshire market town of Ludlow. The usual hauling of carriages and milling crowds were punctuated by refreshments at the Crown but Nelson found lodgings at nearby Downton Castle, a mock medieval pile set in parklands on the River Teme, owned by Richard Payne Knight and Lucy Knight Ellis, relatives of Cornelia. The apartments and company were agreeable, and the jaded travellers lingered a few days in the area, calling among local friends and acquaintances, including Richard Bulkeley, who lived at nearby Pencombe, near Bromward. On Saturday Nelson collected another freedom in Ludlow and the following day rode eastwards, through Tenbury Wells, where the people pulled the carriages in a triumphant circular tour of the town. The same evening the tourists arrived at the famous porcelain town of Worcester.

No more joyful church bells, earnest booming cannons or excited hordes had welcomed a great new victory or visiting dignitary. People spilled into the streets and crowded windows and roofs to see their hero pass. At the Hop Pole in Foregate Street, a large four-storey building with a plain front, the entourage alighted. Thousands stood outside for hours, even after dark, raising intermittent clamours to see Nelson at a window, and as often as he obliged and bowed reverently his constituents cheered. In the morning a band led the procession to Robert Chamberlain's china factory at Diglis, Nelson walking with Emma on his arm as if she was his wife, and Sir William and the other Nelsons trailing in their wake. An arch at the entrance had been decorated and inscribed in honour of the guests, who toured the works before adjourning to a shop in the High Street where the finished items were to be purchased. Nelson declared the porcelain finer than any he had seen in Naples or Dresden, and the ménage placed orders. Nelson ordered complete breakfast, tea and dinner services decorated with a floral pattern and personalised with ducal and viscount coronets and elements of the family arms. Portraits of the hero and his lady, but significantly not Sir William, found their places.[58]

At lunch in the town hall the Earl of Coventry handed over the freedom of Worcester, this one rolled into an impressive porcelain vase. Nelson spoke as before and examined the cathedral, and before he left in the afternoon the good people had loaded his carriages with gifts, including a pair of carpets and £13 worth of cider and perry. The tour was now winding to a close in the English Midlands, a developing heartland of small industry. Nelson had an invitation from Messrs James Woolley and Timothy Smith, the High and Low Bailiffs of Birmingham, and hoped to see the famous Soho factory in which Matthew Boulton had minted Davison's Nile medals. He passed through Droitwich and Bromsgrove, his coachmen togged out in the short, eye-catching blue jackets of jack tars with gay blue ribbons in their hats. With a population of 70,000, Birmingham was the largest town the tourists had visited so far, and to avoid the inconvenience of potentially dangerous crowds they arrived early at the red-brick Styles Hotel. Once again worthies assembled, bells sounded, throngs gathered, 'every anxious eye' beaming 'with pleasure', and Nelson found himself having to appear 'affably' at a hotel window to meet the lusty huzzas below. Birmingham had not seen anything quite like it before.

That first evening, Monday, 30 August, the guests' carriages were man-hauled to the Theatre Royal in New Street, where a 'pantomime drama,' *Perouse, or Desolate Island*, was pairing *The Merry Wives of Windsor*. Nelson's entrance was the signal for the entire auditorium to rise to its feet while the orchestra thumped out 'Rule, Britannia', and in a special finale to the evening an appropriately named 'Miss Menage' danced the hornpipe. During the performance several asides to the celebrated guest precipitated great cheers, especially a reference to 'the best lord in the land'. The party emerged at midnight, where people were waiting to pull the coaches back to the hotel by the light of blazing torches. William Macready, the theatre manager, knew an opportunity when he saw one. He persuaded Nelson to return the following night, offering to stage whatever the admiral wished to see. Nelson chose *King Henry IV, Part One*, flyers were rushed out, and the box office was 'besieged' with demands for tickets. This time the supporting play was 'a musical farce' entitled *The Review, or the Wags of Windsor*. Not surprisingly, when an instantly recognisable Nelson in uniform and orders again alighted from his coach, he was greeted with a roar of approval, and as he took his place in his box the 'uproar' in the packed house was 'deafening and seemed as if it would know no end'. Once more the play was loaded with opportunist extras, including Miss Menage's 'celebrated' routine and impromptu asides. Nelson, whose voice the son of the theatre manager remembered as 'extremely mild and gentle', sat wistfully at such moments, occasionally rising to bow graciously to the cheers, but Emma laughed aloud, clapped her uplifted hands furiously, and kicked her heels against the footboard of her seat. Macready went to the Styles Hotel to thank Nelson for his patronage the following day, but found the lobby throbbing with other visitors, some of them old sailors waiting to see the admiral. On his way to his carriage Nelson stopped to speak to each as if they had been old shipmates, as some of them may well have been.[59]

On Nelson's second day in Birmingham an official dinner at the hotel gave the High Sheriff and other local notables their opportunities to acquaint themselves with the admiral, but he was probably happier to rekindle his friendship with Captain Stephen Digby, who had brought him from the Baltic. This was a city of small masters and workshops, however, producing everything from buttons and hinges to firearms, and the travellers delighted the 'vast concourse of people' by making several expeditions through the streets. On Tuesday morning Nelson called upon the Japan factory in Newhall Street, owned by the Mr Clay he had met in Deal; W. and R. Smith, buckle manufacturers; Woolley and Deakins, who made swords in Edmund Street; Simcox and Timmins the buckle and ring makers of Livery Street; and Timmins and Jordan, sash makers, of St Paul's Square. At this point muscular citizens man-hauled the admiral's carriage to Francis Egginton's noted stained glass factory in outlying Handsworth, where young girls were on hand to strew his path with flowers. Nelson's last call interested him the most. The Soho factory had not only minted his medals and played its part in supplying the navy with guns, but was also a birthplace of the industrial revolution, the scene of the famous partnership of Boulton and James Watt, which had produced a practical steam engine. Boulton had a serious kidney illness, and his works had been closed to visitors, but Nelson got a viewing and was received at the bedside of the great ironmaster. Boulton felt so honoured that he struck another medal to commemorate the visit.

A second walking tour took place the following day, squeezed between breakfast and leave-taking. The admiral was conducted around Radenhurst's whip workshop, Messrs T. and T. Richardson's toyshop, Phipson's pin factory, James Bisset's 'Cabinet of Curiosities', teeming with fossils, objets d'art and exotica, and the Blue Coat School, where Nelson was delighted by the good appearance of the orphan children. These rambles were appreciated by the craftsmen and women as well as the sightseers, and the steel workers of Birmingham presented the admiral with a steel snuff box lined with gold. Still the same day – Wednesday, 1 September – the ménage left for Warwick, another reception, a fresh peal of bells, and welcome beds at the Warwick Arms. Much of Thursday was spent at the well-preserved Warwick Castle, home of Greville's parents, but as Lord and Lady Warwick were absent the party continued to Coventry and the King's Head Inn on Friday. With hardly any notice of Nelson's sudden approach, the town corporation had minutes to scratch together a reception committee, and apologised profusely for what must have seemed an indifferent display. Nelson was not dismayed, however; the welcome at Coventry, he said, was all the more endearing for not having been stage-managed and he felt doubly indebted. But the road now led irretrievably homewards. There was a final call, when Nelson detoured to pay his respects to Earl and Lady Spencer at Althorp Park in Northampton, and then the coaches rattled single-mindedly on their way, through Towcester, Stony Stratford, Dunstable, St Albans, Watford and Brenton. They reached Merton on Sunday, 5 September.[60]

Nelson's tour of 1802 aroused some cynicism. A few newspapers scoffed, and Sir Joseph Banks sympathised with Greville, who had accompanied the Nelson–Hamilton party on some of its perambulations, for having endured the 'artificial satisfaction of feasts, mayors and aldermen, freedom of rotten boroughs, etc.'. But to Nelson the episode had been a great success. Never before, perhaps, had a commoner presented himself so purposefully to his public to such universal applause, nor would anything vaguely comparable be seen again until, perhaps, the rabble-rousing popular politician 'Orator' Henry Hunt whipped up something of a mass platform for parliamentary reform in the years immediately after the Napoleonic wars. Nelson had captured the mood of the typical Briton, fiercely proud of the freedoms and liberties enshrined in the law and constitution, bullishly resentful of foreign interference, and appreciative of those who stood with rather than above them.[61]

The tour, it must also be remembered, occurred when the admiral was so deeply disillusioned with his country that he had a strong mind to leave it. He felt that he had been used and abused by the government, and his mistress cold-shouldered by society. Now, in the closeted environment of his sanctuary at Merton, those wounds were beginning to heal, and the tour contributed signally to that process, for if the government had sold him short, the people had not. It had demonstrated an important '*comparison*', he told Davison. 'The way in which I have been everywhere received [was] most flattering', and 'although some of the higher powers may wish to keep me down, yet the reward of the general approbation . . . is an ample reward for all I have done'. Amid talk of another tour, this time of the north, Emma was no less ecstatic. Nelson's success, she thrilled, would 'burst' their 'enemies'. The admiral had gone to the people, and received reassurance. He began to believe in his country once again.[62]

6

After their return Emma and her husband went to Margate. Her ladyship enjoyed bathing in the sea, and dragged her husband from his favourite fishing haunts along the Thames. Their relationship was weakening. Apart from the humiliation of Sir William's circumstances, Emma loved spending money and entertaining, and had no talent for silence, while he enjoyed long moments of reflection, craving peace in a world that was closing down. An exchange of notes between the pair attempted to clear the air. She complained that he had wanted tranquillity, but had no sooner got to Margate than he wanted to return to London. 'I neither love bustle nor great company,' Sir William replied defensively, 'but I like some employment and diversion. I have but a very short time to live, and every moment is precious to me. I am in no hurry, and am exceedingly glad to give every satisfaction to our best friend, our dear Lord Nelson. The question, then, is what can we best do that all may be perfectly satisfied?' As Emma needed to bathe for her health, they would stay awhile, but the fishing season was coming to an end.[63]

Back at Merton another large dinner party was needed to celebrate Nelson's birthday on the 29th. The William Nelsons, Abraham Goldsmid and his girls, who performed a concerto, Signora Bianchi and four other Italian singers, and James Perry were there to hear Emma sing of 'Nelson and Glory'. The following month Sir William made a serious attempt to put his life in order, and wrote another frank letter to his wife:

> I have passed the last forty years of my life in the hurry and bustle that must necessarily be attendant on a public character. I am arrived at the age when some repose is really necessary, and I promised myself a quiet home, and although I was sensible, and said so when I married [you], that I should be superannuated when my wife would be in her full beauty and vigour of youth. That time is arrived, and we must make the best of it for the comfort of both parties. Unfortunately, our tastes as to the manner of living are very different. I by no means wish to live in solitary retreat, but to have seldom less than 12 or 14 at table, and those varying continually, is coming back to what was become so irksome to me in Italy during the latter years of my residence in that country. I have no connections out of my own family. I have no complaint to make, but I feel that the whole attention of my wife is given to Lord Nelson and his interest at Merton.
>
> I well know the purity of Lord Nelson's friendship for Emma and me, and I know how very uncomfortable it would make his Lordship, our best friend, if a separation should take place, and am therefore determined to do all in my power to prevent such an extremity, which would be essentially detrimental to all parties, but would be more sensibly felt by our dear friend than by us. Provided that our expenses in housekeeping do not increase beyond measure (of which I must own I see some danger), I am willing to go on upon our present footing, but as I cannot expect to live many years, every moment to me is precious, and I hope I may be allowed sometimes to be my own master, and pass my time according to my own inclination, either by going [to] my fishing parties on the Thames, or by going to London to attend the Museum, R[oyal] Society, the Tuesday Club and auctions of pictures. I mean to have a light chariot or post chaise by the month, that I may make use of it in London and run backwards and forwards to

> Merton or to Shepperton, &c. This is my plan, and we might go on very well, but I am fully determined not to have more of the very silly altercations that happen but too often between us and embitter the present moment exceedingly. If really one cannot live comfortably together, a wise and well concerted separation is preferable, but I think, considering the probability of my not troubling any party long in this world, the best for us all would be to bear those ills we have rather than fly to those we know not of. I have fairly stated what I have on my mind. There is no time for nonsense or trifling. I know and admire your talents and many excellent qualities, but I am not blind to your defects, and confess having many myself. Therefore, let us bear and forbear, for God's sake.

The anguish that prompted that wise outburst can only be guessed, but Hamilton's 'chariot' was on the road in October. He had once defined living as the 'art of going through life tolerably', and had looked for the short cuts to equanimity, irrespective of the popular clamour. On the whole, it was not a bad way, but it had never been harder to sustain.[64]

In the spring of 1803, when snowdrops bloomed, Sir William fell ill. He became delirious, but recovered sufficiently to visit London, where he attended a levee and hosted a huge evening concert in Piccadilly. But he had to absent himself from a meeting of the Dilettanti Society on 27 March, when the publication of some of his manuscripts relating to Vesuvius and the Herculaneum discoveries was discussed, and on the last day of the month made amendments to his will. Supposing Emma to have found another protector, he did less for her than he might. The annual allowance paid her from the Pembrokeshire estate rose to an immediate £800, of which £100 was assigned to Mrs Cadogan. 'My dearest friend, Lord Nelson' received Henry Bone's copy of Le Brun's portrait of Emma, as well as two guns, 'a very small token of the great regard I have for his Lordship, the most virtuous, loyal and truly brave character I ever met with. God bless him.' Emma's debts of £450 were to be settled out of money owed by the Treasury, money that was never likely to be paid. What property Hamilton owned went to Greville. Hamilton once mentioned that some attempts had been made to turn him against Greville, and it is possible that Emma had tried to weaken his commitment to his nephew, but if so she failed.[65]

Slowly Sir William loosened his grip on life. Knowing the end was coming, he transferred to Piccadilly to die upstairs in the bedroom of his own house. Relations came to pay their respects, including Greville, who found the old man embittered at his treatment but resigned to his fate. Moseley attended him, and Emma and Mrs Cadogan kept a twenty-four-hour vigil at his bedside, 'dreadfully afflicted'. Nelson sometimes joined them. 'He is going off as an inch of a candle,' Francis Oliver wrote on 2 April. 'The sorrow and affliction that reigns in this house is distressing in the extreme. I lose a friend who has spoke well of me for thirty-seven years. We have all paid ample tribute of tears. I think the occasion for a flood is very near at hand. God rest his soul.'[66]

It came on the morning of 6 April. Sir William died without 'a sigh or a struggle' in Emma's arms, with Nelson grief-stricken at the bedside. Later that day Emma wrote, 'April 6th. Unhappy day for the forlorn Emma. Ten minutes past ten dear blessed Sir William left me.' Nelson wrote few letters. In one he asked Perry to come to Piccadilly to discuss what the *Chronicle* should say about the departed spirit. In another he told Clarence that 'the world never lost a more upright and accomplished gentleman.'[67]

The obituaries in *The Times* and the *Sun* alluded to his service in Naples, but spoke chiefly of the dead man's contributions to art. *The Times* claimed that he had found domestic happiness, but respectfully said nothing about Nelson. While Emma sank into days of desolation, supported by Sarah Nelson, the admiral left the house and moved into nearby lodgings at 19 Piccadilly until the final act had taken place. Sir William's coffin made its long journey back to Slebech, in Wales, where he was buried beside his beloved Catherine. Mourning apparel for the household amounted to forty-seven items and cost £185. Emma's loss was tempered by an awareness of her own difficult position. Greville, who returned the day after Hamilton's death and stayed eleven days, sharing some expenses with Nelson, was close-lipped about the future, but when the will was read one grim May morning, Nelson saw the nephew's influence in it. As he suspected, Greville was not generous, and declared that Emma's inadequate annuity would be paid after income tax. Moreover, if the furniture in Piccadilly belonged to her ladyship, the house did not and Greville quickly repossessed it, forcing Emma to find an alternative property at 11 Clarges Street.[68]

Nonetheless, when Greville returned Sir William's ribbon of the Bath he did seize the opportunity to ask the foreign secretary whether a portion of the deceased's pension might be allowed his widow. Emma herself petitioned to the same end, making the misleading claim that she had contributed to the Nile campaign in 1798 by securing the Queen of Naples' orders to victual the British fleet. Nelson presented her supplication to Addington on 16 April and found him disposed to turn a kind eye towards the matter, and Minto promised his support. In the meantime Nelson ordered Davison to pay Emma £100 a month until further notice.[69]

Sad as the old diplomat's death had been, it simplified life for Nelson and his mistress. They were a step nearer to achieving the marital union that both wanted. 'I should like to say Emma Nelson,' Lady Hamilton once wrote to Catherine Lutwidge. 'How pretty it sounds.' Fanny, of course, remained the sole but durable obstacle, but after Sir William's death the lovers could live as man and wife in all but name. In Merton they could be whatever they wanted to be, for it was now their kingdom to share.[70]

7

That spring of 1803 Nelson's future might have gone one of two ways. His life at Merton had been relatively idyllic, but on the other side of Europe he had another estate at Bronte, where he was creating a villa and model farm and administrating the duchy. The idea of retiring to Bronte still beguiled like a mirage, and as late as 1805 one who knew Nelson thought he would eventually leave England and make his home in Sicily. For some time the two estates, Merton and Bronte, fought for Nelson's soul, and it was unclear which would win. When he finally laid down his arms, would he bid to become an elder statesman of England or of the Two Sicilies?[71]

The disappointing state of Bronte became a gnawing reservation, although a necessary condition, the continuation of Sicilian royal patronage, remained solid. Acton and Nelson remained on the best of terms. The admiral obliged Acton by sending him information about his family estates in Shropshire, and offering to stand his guide if the Sicilian minister ever made a long contemplated visit to England. More significantly, Acton and their Sicilian majesties understood that Nelson was their best friend near the heart of British government and that the unsettled state of Europe was still threatening. 'If . . . a rupture takes room again, poor Italy is lost,' Acton told Nelson. 'No remedy can save it as the circumstances stand in the continent at this moment.' Thus situated, Naples and Sicily appreciated Nelson's 'loyal and cordial' support. Nelson had made amends for his gaffe over Malta by regularly speaking up for the Two Sicilies, telling Addington that the queen deserved 'all our regards and services'.[72]

The blackest clouds that were drifting over Nelson's dream of a life in the Mediterranean came not from any failure of royal favour, but from within Bronte itself. In August 1802 John Graefer, Nelson's estate manager, died and a period of uncertainty followed. With an eye to survival, Mrs Graefer offered to take the helm with the help of the banker Abraham Gibbs; Acton recommended the lawyer Antonio Forcella, who had invested money in Bronte; but in the end the duty fell primarily upon Gibbs and his banking partner, Edmund Noble, both trusted friends of Nelson. The bad news about the duchy did not reach Nelson until August 1803, after he had resumed his naval career. The *boschetto* and the only satisfactory residence, La Fragilia at Maniace, had soaked up three years of the duchy's rental income, as well as the admiral's initial investments, to little purpose. Indeed, the project had become something of a 'folly'. Everything was underdeveloped, rents were in arrears, and the wages of what reliable workmen had been found had not been paid. Worse, the loan Nelson had originally raised to oil the work had only been repaid by contracting a second debt to the Archbishop of Bronte and that now stood at £4200. His lordship might have been partly at fault. In his hurry to assist his tenants, Nelson had even suggested forgoing rents for a period to enable them to improve their holdings. Graefer may not have taken that route, but he had been a landscaper and gardener, not a manager, and left a bleak financial situation.

At their bluntest, Gibbs and Noble suggested Nelson consider disposing of the place, either by selling it outright to the likes of John Broadbent, a Messina merchant, or surrendering it to the crown for its market value. Nelson was dismayed. Not only was his paradise in the sun disappearing in smoke, but he was inordinately proud of his status as the Duke of Bronte, and was incorporating the town's arms into his own. 'I shall never again write an order about the estate,' he wrote emotionally. A day later he had recovered his composure, and probed the reports for glimmers of hope. Gibbs was already taking matters in hand, calling in outstanding ducal rents, tithes and ducal fees, and leasing out the *boschetto* to promising farmers rather than trying to cultivate it himself, and so far the year was promising a good harvest. Therefore, while all options needed to be explored, Nelson decided to allow Gibbs to run with his leasing plan for a few years to see how matters fared. He empowered Gibbs to receive rents and tackle debts and pensioned Mrs Graefer off with a modest allowance. Gibbs was not entirely despondent about carving a respectable future for Bronte under a new and stringent regime, and predicted that he could extinguish the estate's debts and return Nelson £2000 or £3000 a year within a few years.[73]

Like many Englishmen with property in foreign countries, Nelson found unseen reefs and shoals in abundance. The friars of two religious houses bothered him for an ancient annual payment that in fact was supposed to be paid them by the former owners of the estate, the hospital at Palermo. In these matters Acton approached the king, who invariably supported the Duke of Bronte. After some legal wrangling the hospital was reminded of its obligations, and an impudent claim it had made to the farm of St Filippo di Fragala, which yelded not immaterial rents, was dismissed. A revised 'royal diploma' placed them firmly within Nelson's jurisdiction. As late as 27 March 1803 Ferdinand exempted the estate from the payment of all taxes. And while the goodwill of an impoverished monarchy could not extend to purchasing Bronte, as Gibbs had suggested, in the short term Ferdinand readily consented to grant Nelson the unique right to lease out the estate for a period of ten to fifteen years.[74]

Ultimately, the picture proved to be far rosier than Gibbs had thought, and Bronte rose like a limp-winged phoenix from the confusion, largely on account of his judicious management. He leased out the *boschetto* to produce a regular income, extinguished the debts, and in December 1803 was able to pay Nelson £1000. Even better, as no acceptable candidate would take the lease of the entire estate for the period the king had granted, Gibbs and Forcella jointly stepped in themselves, and engaged to pay Nelson £2800 net per annum for ten years beginning 1 September 1804. At last the admiral could see a way to bolster the inadequate pension Emma had inherited from Sir William. An air of modest but unprecedented prosperity settled upon Nelson's Sicilian estate. Two watermills were built, the foundations of a settlement (named for the duke, of course) laid down, and a stream capable of irrigating one hundred acres of grassland discovered. Nelson's morale began to recover.[75]

The distinctly doubtful prospects in 1803 had nevertheless damaged the admiral's faith in Bronte as a long-term home, while Merton stormed forward as a tangible paradise within his own knowledge and control. Strangely, however, by one of the odd quirks of history it was this unpromising Sicilian estate that, alone of all Nelson's homes, would survive into the twenty-first century. Burnham, Roundwood and even beloved Merton Place would all pass from the earth with indecent haste, but readers of this book can still walk the corridors of La Fragilia, now named the Castello Nelson di Bronte, and capture a fleeting and poignant glimpse of the life of which Nelson had dreamed.

8

Whether they took the English or the Italian road, Nelson and Emma would walk it together. In their sanctuary near the Wandle, they found the happiness that had been eluding them, living more or less according to their own lights and with whom they pleased. Nelson's letters during the final years of his life show much less of the anguish that had marked his correspondence for the previous two years. Between the middle of 1799 and the end of 1801 he had served his country with distinction, but his heart seems to have always been with Emma, and he was no sooner at sea than yearning to return. He had often been on shore when he should have been afloat. The long leave at Merton steadied him, conveying a sense of permanent security, so that when he returned to service in 1803 he left knowing that a beloved place and its occupants would be waiting when the trip was over. That domestic felicity went beyond anything he had enjoyed with Fanny, who, for all her worthiness, had lost the power to hold him and been unable to provide the child he wanted. In 1803 Nelson's unhappiest years were over, and a renewed and more complete man emerged from what had been a dark and turbulent place. That old love of glory, of achieving more than he or anyone else had done, still lured him on, but it was a more self-assured and calmer being that went forward towards the light.

The Mediterranean had long been his preferred station. As a new war threatened, Nelson expected the Admiralty to fulfil its promise to appoint him commander-in-chief, and his mind was set upon winning such a triumph as would raise him among the immortals, deliver his country and hasten the peace the tired continent desired. As Britain and France slid steadily towards a new and decisive round of conflict, Nelson visited St Vincent, urging him to make the manning and resuscitation of the fleet the top priority in the event of a war. And he told Addington, 'Whenever it is necessary, I am *your* admiral!'[76]

He had supported the peace, but evidence of French ambitions mounted. In the treaty of Lunéville, the French had undertaken to respect the Batavian (Dutch), Swiss and Italian republics but Napoleon accepted the presidency of the Cisalpine Republic, annexed Piedmont, intervened in Switzerland, and attempted to shut British exports from Italy and Holland. Unlike Britain, where the armed services had withered, France ominously strengthened her army and navy during the period of peace. Nelson, like many Britons, believed in a balance of power in Europe that deterred overmighty states from aggression. But balances are difficult to achieve, and the growth of France's influence was tipping power towards it. Britain's short-sighted economy-minded government had played into Napoleon's hands, and even Nelson had given the peace a life of some seven years. By the spring of 1803, however, the drift was clear. The British evacuation of Malta required by the treaty of Amiens was postponed, and plans were drawn up to reoccupy the Cape of Good Hope. Then on 17 May the government pre-empted the inevitable by declaring war on France, reintroducing income tax at 5 per cent to fund the massive emergency preparations that were now necessary. It would be a defensive war in which the first object had to be the regeneration of Britain's command of the sea.

When St Vincent told Nelson that he would return to the Mediterranean as commander-in-chief it was a tremendous fillip, for the station suited his health and experience, and gave him another chance to make some prize money and achieve a decisive victory over the enemy. The appointment told Nelson something else, too. The Mediterranean was Britain's most important distant station, but it was miles beyond the immediate supervision of Whitehall, and required a safe and experienced commander willing to use his own judgement and initiative. By appointing Nelson the government was demonstrating that whatever doubts had existed about his strategic or political abilities had been jettisoned with the past. The Baltic had raised Nelson's professional standing to an almost impregnable level. Now he would go forth as the warrior and diplomat the country needed in such an important post. He was truly redeemed.

Rumours of the appointment, and reports of visits he made to the Admiralty, brought Nelson the usual flood of applications from the known and unknown, all eager for a place in the fleet. As far as captains were concerned, Nelson needed men about him who were tried and sure. Sutton was ordered to fit out the *Victory* as Nelson's flagship, and then transfer to the *Amphion* frigate, also destined for the Mediterranean, and Murray was enrolled as the captain of the fleet when Foley pleaded ill health. Murray demurred a little, fearing that the prickly post might damage their close relationship, but Nelson assured him that he would never address him as an admiral would a captain of the fleet, but merely as one man to his 'friend Murray'. No, Murray must face up to it, for Nelson was as 'fixed as fate' at having such an officer and comrade by his side in this big adventure. The captain, a prematurely balding, long-faced but intelligent looking man, must have beamed with pleasure when he read the words.

After all, the only brother to find an immediate place was Hardy, who became Nelson's flag captain.[77]

Lieutenants were a problem, because Nelson was allowed nine on the *Victory* when his list of hopefuls had swollen to twenty. He eventually sent the Admiralty the names of six lieutenants he wanted. In addition, he had numerous 'young gentlemen' to satisfy, including Charles Connor, Emma's cousin, William Benjamin Suckling, Nelson's cousin, and Dick Bulkeley, who were squeezed into the *Amphion*. Among other personnel the admiral judged necessary to his command was Alexander John Scott, the chaplain and secretary he had appreciated in the Baltic. Scott, the son of a naval lieutenant, suffered from the after-effects of having once been struck by lightning, and became insensible once or twice a month, but he knew Danish, French, Italian and Turkish and was devoted to Nelson. His 'constant wish', he had written, was to serve under the admiral. When the call arrived he left his peaceful living in Essex and came at once. Among major and minor warrant officers Nelson switched to the *Victory* were Atkinson, his regular sailing master, and William Bunce, who had been carpenter in the *San Josef*. Inevitably, some felt disappointed, among them John McArthur, who felt unjustly displaced from a long-standing role as purser in the *Victory*.[78]

For the first time Merton was filled with the bustle of an imminent command. Although much that the commander-in-chief would need could be purchased and sent direct to Portsmouth by the suppliers, and John Salter dispatched three cases of tableware and cutlery, including a tea pot and a coffee pot, chests had to be packed at home with sea furniture, clothes, books, instruments and all manner of professional and domestic necessities. Most of the baggage arrived safely in Portsmouth, where Hardy took charge of it, but as usual some went astray, and his 'safe', linen and a favourite chair had to be left behind and sent after him. The financial outlay was considerable, and a simple bill for six sheep, eight turkeys, two stacks of hay, eggs, nuts, wine and tomatoes for the admiral's table cost £132. It was usual for agents to advance sums against future payments of prize money.[79]

On 6 May Nelson was told to prepare to leave, and four days later he was in Craven Street putting his signature to a new will prepared by Booth and Haslewood. If he died in England, his wish was to be buried with his parents in Burnham Thorpe, unless the king deemed a state funeral demanded a grander resting place. And in a further recognition of his birthplace, he left £100 to the poor of the three parishes over which his father had presided.

Nelson had little ready money, and was relying upon prize to rescue him from the £2100 due to Greaves in the coming October. Emma was willed such heirlooms as the 'diamond star' and a silver cup she had once given him, and more substantially received Merton Place, with its furniture, wine and accoutrements. The chelengk, Ferdinand's diamond-hilted sword and various medals and orders would descend with Bronte to the admiral's male heirs, while other heirlooms – the City of London's gold box and sword, the Egyptian Club sword and a cup presented by the Turkey Company – were to be distributed between William, Susannah and Kate. There were a few personal bequests to Davison and Hardy, but the bulk of Nelson's liquid estate was to be converted into money and invested in government stock to support an annuity of £1000 for Fanny. This document remained Nelson's master will, but it would ultimately be amended by no less than eight codicils. The first was added as early as 13 May 1803. It revoked the absolute transfer of Merton to Emma, consigning it to his heirs instead, but granted Lady Hamilton the right to reside there for the remainder of her life.[80]

The day the codicil was added Horatia was baptised 'Horatia Nelson Thompson' in a quiet ceremony at Marylebone Church, where Emma had married Sir William. Her birth date was falsified to read 29 October 1800, and no parentage was given, although both Nelson and Emma appeared as godparents. Mrs Gibson, who lived nearby, administered to the child. There had been no specific provision for Horatia in Nelson's new will, and her welfare must have been a matter of private arrangements with Emma. He had an idea that she might eventually marry Horace, William's son, and thus gain a place in the Nelson succession. Although unsure about how to proceed at the moment, he never lost sight of her security. 'She shall be independent of any smiles or frowns,' he promised. As an interim he instructed Davison to see that £100 a month was paid to cover her maintenance.[81]

On 16 May Nelson received his official appointment at the Admiralty. His orders, dated the 16th and 17th, directed him to proceed to Malta to supersede Rear Admiral Richard Bickerton in command of the Mediterranean, and to confer with the commissioner of the island, his old friend Ball, about its security. Having so done, Nelson's principal business was to blockade the French fleet in Toulon, along with the usual charges of guarding the Strait of Gibraltar, protecting trade and succouring allies. France and the Dutch Batavian Republic were the recognised enemies, but an eye had also to be kept on Spain, which had naval squadrons in Cadiz and Cartagena.

Nelson left for Portsmouth at five in the morning of 18 May, apparently accompanied by a 'secretary' who had spent the night at Merton. Breakfasting at Liphook, they reached their destination at one in the afternoon, covered in dust from the road. Compared with Merton, Portsmouth appeared 'the picture of desolation and misery', and Nelson had his flag raised on the *Victory* the same day, although he slung a cot in the *Amphion* until the larger ship could be readied. In his haste to be gone he missed an important ceremony at Westminster Abbey on 19 May, when he was formally invested in the Order of the Bath, a final technicality that for some reason had hitherto been overlooked. The admiral had been asked to name someone to accept the honour on his behalf and Captain William Bolton had stepped forward. 'Billy' was triple-blessed, because he not only stood in the august company of the Abbey, but also had to be knighted to qualify as Nelson's proxy. Moreover, the day before he had married the admiral's niece, Catherine Bolton, at a private ceremony in Emma's house in Clarges Street.[82]

Admiral Lord Gardner, one of the new members of parliament for Westminster, joined Nelson for dinner the day he reached Portsmouth, and other friends gathered fast, including Sutton, Murray, Hardy and Davison, who arrived from London by separate carriage. The Elliots were also in town. Nelson had promised to take Minto's son, Lieutenant George Elliot, as early as February, but it was not until the eleventh hour that an Admiralty courier had summoned him from a midnight ball and told him that if he could get to Portsmouth in time to sail on the *Victory* he would be given the *Termagant* sloop on station. Assisted by his father and uncle, George tumbled from the ballroom into a coach and rode through the night without a bag to his name. Hugh Elliot, Minto's brother, whom Nelson knew from Germany, had been appointed the new Envoy Extraordinary and Minister Plenipotentiary at Naples, and also had a passage in the *Victory*.

The flagship, fledging from a £71,000 refit, received the admiral on 20 May, and Davison and Minto said their farewells and left just as the *Victory* got under sail. Nelson had stayed with a friend at Shooter's Hill the previous night, but had been troubled at leaving Merton and was persuading himself that he might be home for Christmas. 'I feel from my soul that God is good, and in his due wisdom will unite us,' he wrote to Emma. 'Only, when you look upon our dear child, call to your remembrance all you think that I would say, was I present, and be assured that I am thinking of you every moment. My heart is full to bursting! May God Almighty bless and protect you.' He could not know that he would not see her for more than two years, and that in this world they would only be together for another twenty-five days.[83]

But now he had at least one more great service to perform for his country. As a Portsmouth chronicler wrote on 20 May, 'Such was the anxiety of Lord Nelson to embark that yesterday, to everyone who spoke to him of sailing, he said, "I cannot before tomorrow, and that's an age." This morning, about ten o'clock, his lordship went off in a heavy shower of rain, and sailed with a northerly wind.'[84]

BOOK THREE

THE GLORIOUS RACE

'May that great God, whose cause you so violently support, protect and bless you to the end of your brilliant career! Such a race surely never was run.'

Lavinia, Countess Spencer, to Nelson,
1 October 1798

'The medical gentlemen are wanting to survey me, and to send me to Bristol for the re-establishment of my health, but whatever happens, I have run a glorious race.'

Nelson to Minto,
11 January 1804

'I have had a good race of glory, but are [am] never satisfied.'

Nelson to General Villettes,
6 September 1804

XVIII

‘BY PATIENCE AND PERSEVERANCE’

Adieu, my dear landsmen, dear Emma adieu,
New glories I’ll bring to the islands and you,
That bosom, where honour and truth hold their
seat,
That chides my short stay will approve when we
meet.

‘Nelson and His Nilers’, *c.*1801

I

NELSON had the command he regarded as his own, but the Mediterranean station was not the principal theatre of the new war. Napoleon, soon to style himself emperor of the French and a hereditary monarch, responded to Britain’s declaration by seizing Hanover, her only continental possession, and resurrecting his invasion project. The Royal Navy’s squadrons in the North Sea and Channel were thus firmly in the front line.

The French strategy was in essence as before. Britain’s first battle fleet would be entangled in an exacting blockade of Brest or diverted further afield to provide an opening for landing craft to carry an elite force across the English Channel. Britain had not emerged from the previous invasion scare with any great belief in the practicability of this hoary scheme, but Bonaparte was capable of trying it, and the navy’s protective shield remained indispensable. Though scourged by St Vincent’s economies, now revealed as a monstrous complacency, the wooden walls were being painfully restored. From the Texel in Holland (now annexed by the French and relabelled the Batavian Republic) to Ferrol in Spain, the famous ‘storm tossed ships’ watched the hostile concentrations. They were the great fixtures of the war, battered but defiant and inviolate, shielding the British people from a military machine of overwhelming power. But Britain’s naval superiority had been seriously damaged during the peace and as late as 1804 she could field no more than eighty-eight ships of the line. Moreover, Albion began the new war alone. As yet Spain stood neutral, although in truth she was already an abused vassal feeding France crucial resources. Prussia and Austria sat bowed, distrustful but exhausted, while Russia, if suspicious of Napoleon's eastern ambitions, was as likely as not to negotiate mutually beneficial terms with the world's most formidable land power.[1]

Despite the grave aspect, once again, Britain's bruised naval power covered her vital colonies and trade routes, and took the war to enemy merchantmen and colonies. The Mediterranean, which had been reserved for her great champion, was a redoubtable brief. Few naval commanders-in-chief were mere marionettes, manipulated by the puppet masters of Whitehall, but those closer to home had easy access to the intelligence, directions and support of government. Nelson's principal communication line, however, was a thousand-mile sea road between Plymouth and Gibraltar, and it was expected that he would have to exploit local resources and formulate and execute policy without the benefit of timely orders from on high. Against him was the enhanced might of France, driven by the same dream of European domination, and stronger in central and southern Europe than ever before. Driven from Malta, the Ionian Islands and Egypt in the last war, France had nevertheless stripped Sardinia of Piedmont, turning it into the Subalpine Republic; retained her control of the Ligurian and Italian (formerly the Cisalpine) republics of northern Italy; wrenched Leghorn and Elba from an emasculated Tuscany; and cowed the papal states and Naples. Again Nelson entered the Mediterranean without an ally or disposable troops, and his only British bases, Gibraltar and Malta, were six or seven hundred miles from the focus of his operations at Toulon. He had to master the politics of a notoriously turbulent region, in which half a dozen major imperial powers and as many other significant players pursued their own nationalist interests on frontiers that separated diverse races, cultures and creeds. And with a handful of ships – a force emaciated by injudicious reforms at home – he had to control a vast theatre that extended three thousand miles from Cape St Vincent off the coast of Portugal to the Levant, and contained more than a million square miles of water, an area three times the size of Napoleon's European empire. With the exception of the prime minister, no public servant of His Britannic Majesty bore a more awesome burden.[2]

Such a task called for varied and mature skills and peculiarly fine judgements. To slay or stay the voracious French juggernaut it was necessary to win minds as well as battles, for the Mediterranean was stuffed with unhappy populations ready to rally to anyone who promised deliverance, however disingenuously. In the past Nelson had advised Ferdinand and Maria Carolina to improve the conditions of their peoples in order to drain discontent and counter-revolutionary propaganda, and on his outward voyage in 1803 he was reminded of the problem by an interview with an Egyptian bey at Malta. The Mamelukes, he decided, would welcome the French merely to rid themselves of the Turks. 'It is a nice point to manage,' the admiral told his diary, 'but by a happy medium, by making the Turks do what is just, and making the Mamelukes be content with what is just, I think we may settle the matter to the satisfaction of all parties.' In Sardinia, the Two Sicilies and the dominions of the Porte Nelson saw that defence and internal reform were two sides of a coin.[3]

Another form of balance – creating credible defences at weak spots without provoking the enemy into undesirable, and possibly overpowering, reactions – called for a dangerous political 'brinkmanship' that became a distinctive feature of the campaign. France as well as Britain often held ground with thin forces that were insecure and nervous. In three areas – the Two Sicilies, the Greek Morea and Sardinia – both sides watched each other guardedly, primed to stampede into a military build-up or outright aggression at any sabre-rattling or careless display of force. For an admiral of Nelson's spirit, restraint before an enemy was not a natural response, but he learned to exercise it and prolonged uneasy but convenient stalemates. As Hugh Elliot, who decisively reined Nelson in at one point, observed, 'I do not think that there existed a conjuncture more delicate, or a combination of circumstances more perplexing.'[4]

Apart from pinpoint diplomacy, Nelson had also to address the logistical problems of maintaining a large force far from home in such a way as to prepare it for the ultimate test of battle. And in the end it was that final blood and fire that would make or break his mission. The battle, above all, haunted Nelson's imagination. He could not predict that the war would last another twelve years, fancying rather that it might end quickly, but he saw it as an opportunity, probably a final one, to cap his career with the decisive triumph he had always wanted, one that would secure his future with those he loved and his posterity. This was to be a last 'glorious race' in pursuit of the destiny that had been his lifelong dream. 'We are on the eve of a battle,' he wrote to Emma, 'and I have no doubt but it will be a glorious one.'[5]

2

Ironically his voyage began with a threat to one of the iconic landmarks of this final service, his impressive three-decked flagship, the forty-year-old *Victory*, long the home of famous admirals, of Keppel, Hood and Jervis, but now about to create the most famous partnership between ship and man. Nelson's equipment and provisions had been stowed aboard, but for some time a question lingered over the *Victory*'s part in the unfolding drama.

St Vincent recognised that Cornwallis, who commanded off Brest, held the single most crucial position in Britain's defences, and ordered Nelson to call upon that officer on his outward voyage to offer the *Victory* for service in the Channel. If Cornwallis needed her, Nelson was to continue his journey to the Mediterranean in the *Amphion* frigate, commanded by Captain Hardy, and transfer to a more appropriate ship of the line when he reached his station. A disgruntled admiral endured some dirty weather searching for Cornwallis off Brest, but, unable to find him, Nelson reluctantly transferred to the *Amphion* on 23 May, ordering Sutton to cruise with the *Victory* for another week. The captain carried a letter beseeching Cornwallis to spare the *Victory* for the Mediterranean if he could, but some of Nelson's select possessions went into the frigate in case he lost his flagship. Among essential linen and tableware that crossed to the frigate were the reassuring portraits of Emma and a chubby two-year-old Horatia in shoes, smock and cap. Nelson complained to Addington about the *Victory*. It was his first direct appeal to the Admiralty's masters, but Nelson would send regular reports to the prime minister in the following months until the latter became so overwhelmed with state business that he turned the correspondence over to Lord Hobart, his secretary of war.

One other irritant disturbed the first days of Nelson's new command. A day after leaving Spithead the *Victory* captured a Dutch ship from Surinam with a cargo of cocoa, coffee and sugar. After a prize crew navigated her into Plymouth, Hardy's agent set about piloting the ship through the vice-admiralty court, but Nelson had promised to funnel his prizes through Davison, and Hardy loyally deferred. The issue of prize continued to rankle, however, as Davison, Marsh and Creed, and the admiral's new secretary, John Scott, all wrestled for potentially lucrative shares of the Mediterranean prizes. As for himself, Nelson saw sense in suppressing any get-rich-quick ambitions, and declared that he would be 'perfectly content' to clear his debts, give a reasonable security to Emma and Horatia, and achieve a little independence in 'pecuniary matters' that might make him 'useful' to his friends. To which laudable ends, he resolved to live as frugally as his station would permit.[6]

After parting with the *Victory*, Nelson fought his way southwards through indifferent weather with the *Amphion* and the *Sirius*. On 30 May, when conditions improved, he drafted orders to his captains and commanders, instructing them to seize or destroy all French ships, and to detain Dutch vessels, which would have to wait for the government's decision about their status as prize. He entered the Strait of Gibraltar on the morning of 3 June. A French merchant brig was seized and brought into the bay, providing the hardy occupants of the Rock with their first confirmation that war had been declared.

Gibraltar was a keystone of Britain's control of the Mediterranean. It was not an adequate base, situated as it was so far to the west with neither an abundance of resources nor an adequate harbour or dockyard, but it guarded the entrance to the Mediterranean, protecting the fleet's communication line and the seaway that several thousand British merchant ships used each year. On 4 June Nelson breakfasted at daylight before hurrying ashore to confer with the military governor, Lieutenant General Sir Thomas Trigge, and to inspect the dockyard, where a storekeeper, master shipwright, master attendant and boatswain directed shoals of artificers and labourers. Nelson emphasised the need to manage resources prudently; called for improvements in the number of shipwrights and the complement of a sheer-hulk doubling as a prison ship, and requested the Admiralty to supply additional officers. Security was a major problem at Gibraltar. The through traffic had to run straits haunted by corsairs and anchor in an open bay, and the garrison depended upon food and water imported from Lagos or Tetuan. However stinted Nelson's force, the place would always need the protection of some cruisers, and he immediately detailed two to that service, ordering also that gun- and flatboats be prepared so that privateers could be pursued inshore. In the next couple of months he assigned Gore's *Medusa* and Sutton's *Amphion* to the Strait and its approaches, and on 10 August Richard Strachan's *Donegal*, a ship of the line.

Nelson left Gibraltar the same afternoon. The approach of a strange ship caused a momentary stir when Nelson supposed her to be a French frigate. He ordered the *Amphion* and *Maidstone* to clear for action and weather the newcomer to trap her in the bay, but she proved to be one of his own, and he bore up for Malta. Malta was Britain's other Mediterranean base, and Sir Richard Bickerton, from whom Nelson was to assume command of the station, was said to have gone there. Besides, his old friends Ball, now civil commissioner, and Major General William Anne Villettes, who commanded the garrison, might be able to furnish up-to-date intelligence. A Dutch brig, the *Vrow Agneta*, and a French brig were taken within four hours of each other on the morning of 5 June, and nine days later the *Maidstone*, under Captain Richard Moubray, had the distinction of capturing the first enemy warship of the campaign, the French national brig *Arab* of eight guns and fifty-eight men.[7]

The *Maidstone* was detached to Naples to deliver Elliot and Gaetano Spedillo, as mentioned one of Emma's servants, while the *Amphion* ploughed through waters Nelson well knew, swinging south of Sicily for Malta. On his way Nelson prepared for his return by writing letters to close allies. Reassurances went through William Drummond, Britain's Ambassador Extraordinary and Plenipotentiary in Constantinople, to the Ottoman Porte; to Sardinia through the durable Jackson; and to Corfu, the capital of the new 'Septinsular Republic' of the Ionian Islands, where Britain had a most effective representative in Spiridion Foresti. To all Nelson promised goodwill and all the protection in his power. Most enthusiastically of all, however, he alerted their Sicilian Majesties and Sir John Acton of his return. Addington's last words to him, he told Sir John, were to take care of the king and queen, the 'most faithful allies' of Britain. Nelson's own admiration for them was as strong as ever. He told Elliot that 'the good king of Naples has, under the advice of Sir John Acton, always supported his honour and dignity; and if other powers, more powerful, had done the same, they would not now have become degraded by great sacrifices'. Therein lay Nelson's elemental loyalty to Naples. Europe, through disunity, vacillation and a failure to understand the gravity of their situation, had allowed tyrants to prevail, but Naples had stood tall and created obligations that Britain was bound to honour.[8]

Nelson would have liked to 'fly' to his old comrades, but he realised that Naples and Sicily were very differently placed now than in 1800. Supposedly neutral, the twin kingdoms survived on French sufferance, and had been coerced into paying war reparations and agreeing to maintain any occupation force Napoleon chose to impose. Naples was mortally afraid of provoking additional indignities, and Charles Alquier, the acerbic French minister in Naples, was threatening military occupation if their Majesties did not dismiss Acton, a bulwark of the English party. Nelson knew that his return would encourage Naples, but his power to protect her was limited and he would have to ensure she was not fatally compromised. He would not, therefore, visit their Majesties in person and risk stirring suspicions or jealousies in the French minister. But if it came to the worst and Italy was overrun, Nelson had resolved to preserve Sicily as a refuge for the royal family and their government. This new relationship of outward neutrality and covert fraternity was no easy transition, and involved curbing natural inclinations. In June, for example, Nelson upbraided John Fyffe of the *Cyclops* for infringing the neutrality of Naples by seizing two French ships in the bay. By restoring both vessels to their owners through the Neapolitan authorities, Nelson strengthened their Majesties' status as neutrals and reduced any French impulses to remove them.[9]

Although public affairs predominated, Nelson hoped to receive some personal benefits from Naples, a land that he still regarded as his second home. He anticipated that the queen might assist Emma, unaware that their 'Charlotte' was now far too absorbed with her latest paramour, the Marquis de St Clair, a French émigré barely half her age, to worry about her former confidante. In his letter to the queen, Nelson spoke of Emma's devotion, slipping in that Sir William had left her in poor circumstances, but Her Majesty missed the bait. The admiral was annoyed, but a year later, when he heard that the queen had spoken of writing to the British government in support of Emma's suit for a pension, he would raise the matter again.[10]

Nelson reached Malta on 15 June. Bickerton's squadron had left for Toulon a few weeks before, but over two days the admiral enjoyed an enthusiastic welcome on the island that he had liberated. Valletta was illuminated in his honour, and social niceties were waiting ashore. Nelson sampled Mary, Lady Ball's refreshments amidst stifling heat, and visited Lady Bickerton, one of Fanny's close friends; he dined with General Villettes and took a drive to Floriana to see his 'garden house'; and there was a tour of the Church of St John. But his lordship was brisk for business, and also examined the naval storehouses, received a deputation of islanders, and imbibed the latest on Mediterranean affairs from Ball, now an English baronet as well as a Maltese knight. As civil governor, Ball was making a fair job of reconciling the Maltese to British rule, and had by Nelson's lights adapted so well to politics that he 'appears to forget that he was a seaman'. Nelson gave him official notice of the war, and they got down to basics. Malta, like Gibraltar, would need a constant shield. Garrisoned by fewer than five thousand soldiers, it was the only British base and dockyard east of Gibraltar, and an invaluable strategic possession, guarding the confluence of the eastern and western basins of the Mediterranean and providing a base for watching southern Italy. It was also a crucial staging post for the whole of Britain's maritime traffic with the Adriatic, Levant and Black Sea. In British hands the island was an impregnable bastion, an unmovable thorn in any French plan to dominate the eastern Mediterranean. At the behest of the administration Nelson had disparaged its importance in parliament, but although he recognised its limitations as a base for blockading Toulon, he could not deny its importance for shutting France out of the east. Now he spoke up for the place. 'I consider Malta as an important outwork to India that will ever give us great influence in the Levant and . . . the southern parts of Italy,' he told Addington. 'I hope we shall never give it up.'[11]

However, he saw much further than this, for he knew from his two-year blockade that the island was not self-sufficient in food. It imported some 36,000 salms of grain a year from places as diverse as Corfu, Tunis and the Black Sea, but especially from Sicily. An enemy entrenched in Sicily, with a stranglehold on her food supply, would always be a threat to Malta; and as French armies controlled much of the Italian mainland, Sicily was in deadly danger. Sicily had to be preserved because it was a fall-back position for their Sicilian Majesties and because it fed Malta. It was Nelson's duty to shield both places. Like Gibraltar, Malta would need its quota of ships and a strong military presence, for the war would fill the seas with French corsairs hunting for prey among the trading ships and packets that serviced the island as well as the trade fleets that used Valletta as a rendezvous and staging post in their journeys up and down the Mediterranean. Some of the ships Ball could fit out himself, but four small vessels from Nelson's fleet were detailed to sweep the sea lanes from the toe of Italy, south-west around Sicily and Malta to Tunisia. As for troops, the garrison in Malta was modest but reasonably secure behind the island's towering fortifications. However, Nelson and Villettes agreed that the defence of Sicily was part and parcel of Malta's security, and that the general should prepare a covert detachment of fifteen hundred men to strengthen Messina if the French ever tried to overrun the island. Sicily had about eight thousand indigenous regulars, in addition to militia, but her castle at Messina was so ill prepared that Ball doubted it would withstand an attack of eight days. Fortunately, Nelson's idea had also occurred to Lord Hobart, the secretary of war, and he authorised Villettes to reinforce Sicily with two thousand redcoats if the island was attacked. Encouraged by his own talks, Nelson detailed the *Madras* prison ship, laying at Malta under Captain Charles Schomberg, to contribute to the task force, and undertook to pursue their project with the Neapolitan government.

Nelson's other Maltese dispositions focused upon the eastern Mediterranean. While awaiting an assessment of the area from Foresti in Corfu, the admiral sent Captain William Edward Cracraft with a couple of frigates, *Anson* and *Stately*, to search for privateers as far as Crete. Later they would be reinforced by another frigate, *Juno*. It had taken Nelson just thirty-six hours to do everything practicable at Malta, and he was able to continue his voyage north on 17 June. Navigating the Strait of Messina between Sicily and mainland Italy he was reminded of earlier days when joyful acclamations of 'Viva il Re!' and 'Viva Inglese!' greeted the ships and small boats bumped alongside with offers of fruit. On 25 June the Bay of Naples itself flooded the admiral with memories of dead and absent loved ones and moved him to tears. 'I am looking at *dear* Naples,' he wrote to Elliot, 'if it is what it was.' Its plight tore him 'from the very bottom of my soul'.[12]

Like everyone who returns to cherished places, Nelson risked disillusionment but he had little time to brood. Given the delicacy of the political situation, he declined to go ashore but sent a boat in to communicate with Elliot and John Lewis Falconnet, the Neapolitan banker, and to receive the report of Moubray, whose *Maidstone* was anchored in the bay. A little about the sentiment in Naples also reached Nelson from the repatriated Spedillo, who quickly abandoned his plan of resuming life in his home town and grasped this first opportunity to return to the admiral's service. Apart from intelligence, Nelson wished to inform the British merchants in Naples that a convoy system was being organised for their protection at Malta, and to secure royal approval for his plans to defend Naples and Sicily. Villettes was only prepared to reinforce Messina if his force was allowed to control the citadel free of interference from the Sicilian governor, and terms of an occupation, should it become necessary, had to be negotiated.[13]

The news from all sources was depressing, for the kingdoms were truly in troubled straits. The government was almost bankrupt, its nobility estranged, people discontented and armed services unfit for purpose. To make matters worse, Bonaparte had used Britain's retention of Malta as an excuse to march 13,000 men under General Gouvion St Cyr into the kingdom of Naples, where they established themselves in Pescara on the Adriatic coast, and Brindisi, Otranto and Taranto on the heel of Italy, all dangerously close to Naples, Sicily, and, across the Adriatic, the Greek Morea, a dominion of the Ottoman empire that France particularly coveted. The French clamour for the removal of Acton had also been renewed. Though the recent treaty of Florence had allowed for such a limited occupation, Ferdinand and Maria Carolina were scalded by the humiliation. Naples was being allowed to remain 'neutral' as long as she suffered a French army to occupy key ports and paid for their upkeep from her own purse. Any resistance, or favour shown to Britain, could precipitate the complete conquest of the country. Nelson's return to the Mediterranean was a fillip, but their Majesties could only write forlornly, hoping that like a magician he might save them a second time. 'I pray to God,' wrote Ferdinand, 'that he may hold Admiral Nelson, Duke of Bronte, in his firm and holy safekeeping.'[14]

Confronted with such unpromising circumstances, Nelson had to considerably modify his plan for the defence of Sicily, and its final form owed much to the suggestions of Elliot and Acton. As Nelson knew, Elliot's instructions from home authorised Britain to occupy Messina if the French gained control of Naples, so the minister had no difficulty in agreeing to the basic formula. Equally, their Sicilian Majesties needed no persuading that a Sicily defended by Britain was their best ultimate sanctuary if all else failed, and Villettes' conditions were fully met, 'carried,' said Elliot, 'solely by the respect due to your lordship's name'. Indeed, in covert correspondence it was agreed that Ferdinand would prepare Messina for a British presence by quartering several thousand Neapolitan regulars in Sicily, preparing gunboats to patrol the Strait of Messina, improving batteries and fortifications, and stocking the magazines and larders with the wherewithal to withstand six months' siege. But the matter needed exquisite timing, because their Majesties had no desire to yield their kingdom unnecessarily. If Villettes garrisoned Messina quickly, as Nelson suggested, it could trigger a French attack that would not otherwise have been made; 'any hasty measures,' said Acton, 'would in their Majesties' opinion bring the most horrid and unavoidable evil'. If, on the other hand, Britain dragged her feet, and the French launched their own assault, the redcoats might arrive too late.[15]

It was finally agreed that Britain would only act defensively. Quartered in ports on the east and south-east coasts of Italy, St Cyr's army could only attack Sicily by either marching through Calabria, a mountainous region peopled by bands of armed Italian patriots, or embarking in small coasting vessels. Acton believed that both movements could be detected by a strict vigilance in time for Britain to act. On his recommendation, Nelson also made two improvements to his naval defences. Cracraft's force was increased by the addition of the *Juno* and *Morgiana*, and given the task of patrolling the toe and heel of Italy to prevent St Cyr moving by sea. And to secure Elliot, the royal family and their government a permanent retreat, Nelson promised to keep a warship at Naples. On 30 July the *Monmouth*, one of his less seaworthy ships of the line, was accordingly ordered to Naples.[16]

Nelson had great reservations about the final plan, and would have been happier to see the British moving into Messina immediately. He stressed that its success now depended entirely upon Elliot, Acton and himself keeping 'a good lookout'. He was unsettled by the thought of a sudden rapid French advance catching Naples and the British off guard. He also reminded Naples that although the monarchy appeared to enjoy the support of most of its subjects, there were growing voices for reform. In his view Sicily, where an indifferent aristocracy 'oppressed' the peasantry, was about 'as bad as a civilized country can be'. Nevertheless, the secret agreement to open Messina to the British in an emergency, an agreement which may justly be termed the Nelson–Elliot–Acton accord, helped preserve a stalemate in southern Italy for two whole years. It was one that neither side could comfortably break. France had other fish to fry; Britain could ill spare its regulars, especially when Sardinia as well as Sicily made claims upon them; and Ferdinand lacked the money to make all the military preparations Acton had itemised, even though Elliot and Ball eventually arranged a secret subsidy of £150,000 per annum to be drawn on British Treasury bills. Given this, Lord Harrowby, who succeeded Hawkesbury as Britain's foreign secretary, was probably right when he acknowledged to Elliot that 'the prudence with which you have acted in not pressing any measures which might precipitate the attack of the French has been eminently useful'.

Another reason for military moderation lay in the current state of international negotiations. Russia regarded Bonaparte's occupation of the Neapolitan ports as a breach of the two-year old treaty of Florence between France and Naples, which she had guaranteed, and was demanding the French withdraw. Moreover, she had offered to mediate between France and Britain, creating the possibility of a general peace in which the independence of Naples and Sicily would be an issue. Ferdinand's chief hopes, then, lay not in Britain but in Russia, and he was concerned to avoid any hostilities that might stymie political progress. For him the Nelson plan was not the first line; it was an insurance policy, to be called into being when all else failed. Nor was he entirely deceived, for Napoleon refrained from turning St Cyr's troops upon Naples and even agreed that he, rather than Ferdinand, should pay their wages largely for fear of trampling upon Russian sensibilities.[17]

Whatever the limitations of Russian diplomacy and British naval power, they were reassuring to Ferdinand, who gained the confidence to withstand French demands for the dismissal of Acton and the disarmament of the Calabrians. Indeed, the king used the threat from raiding Barbary corsairs to justify not only the arming of the Calabrians, but also the rehabilitation of a Neapolitan naval squadron, which soon consisted of a ship of the line, six cruisers and forty-two gunboats under the command of Count Thurn. For the time being there was little more that Nelson could do. Considering the small size of his force, the eight ships he had committed to Malta, southern Italy and the east in June and July were a significant gesture.

At Naples Nelson learned that Bickerton had called in on his way to Toulon on 4 June. Heading north-west into the Gulf of Genoa, the new commander-in-chief saw little to encourage him in northern Italy. The French grip was tightening. All but Tuscany and the papacy were client states, harnessed to the imperial progress, and even they were crumbling. Rome was having to pay 720,000 crowns per annum to preserve a shadow of its neutrality, and that did not rid their territory completely of French troops. In March the French also seized Leghorn in Tuscany, packing hundreds of soldiers into the port, crowding some forty ships into its harbour, and extorting 14,000 crowns from the aggrieved government. The British consul was briefly imprisoned and his house plundered of some £1500 worth of property. The Tuscan and Roman ports were so infested with corsairs that most British merchantmen dared not approach without escort. Nelson was not sure what it all meant. His experiences of 1801 had left him suspicious of Bonaparte's plan to invade England, and he continued to believe that the east was the true focus of most of what happened in the Mediterranean. The persistent proliferation of French influence in Italy and Napoleon's drive for bases on the eastern and southern coasts of the peninsula suggested that his old dreams of eastern conquest were still live coals. Once the French had overrun Italy and Sicily it would be a mere hop to the Morea, where the Greeks might be inflamed against their Turkish masters, and the further stops might include Corfu, Crete, Egypt and India. Bonaparte was an extraordinarily difficult man to predict. Little was beyond his ambition and audacity, and he was a master of deception. It was almost impossible to decide which of his many options was the current priority and which the feint. But generally speaking Nelson's money was on the east.[18]

One of the admiral's vexations was the silence from home, and although he exaggerated his isolation, the first dispatches did not reach him until 17 August and the second until 6 October. Nelson developed the habit of scanning foreign newspapers for British as well as international news. Meanwhile, Whitehall was hungrily devouring Nelson's own reports, and finding much to admire and little to object to in their contents. Their man was clearly mastering the politics of the Mediterranean, and he usually anticipated their orders. Hobart, for example, wrote on 23 August that in view of a letter Nelson had written to Addington in June, as well as additional intelligence, the government would declare Genoa and La Spezia under blockade. But Nelson had already acted on his own hook, sending *Niger* to reconnoitre the coasts in the gulf and impose a blockade.

On 8 July Nelson finally found his squadron, nine ships of the line and three cruisers under Bickerton of the *Kent*, riding off the French naval base of Toulon. Here at last was the epicentre of the campaign. From observations made from Gore's frigate, the *Medusa*, it appeared that nine French ships of the line were in the port, seven fully rigged for sea, and eleven or thirteen frigates and corvettes. To cover this force Nelson had barely equal numbers, and one of his capital ships, *Monmouth*, had to station herself at Naples. That meant every ship that left the fleet for repairs, provisions or detached duties increased the numerical odds against Nelson's force. As if that were not enough, the very geography of the region was also against him. Masses of air funnelled through the passes between the Pyrenees, Massif Central and Alps and created dangerous north and north-westerly gales that swept the Gulf of Lions every winter and for much of the year. Gathering speeds of sixty miles an hour or more, these winds, or mistrals, could create huge seas and wild weather that made the area the stormiest in the Mediterranean. Blockading squadrons were regularly driven from their stations, and the hills around Toulon enabled the French to see fairly clearly whether the British were on the coast.[19]

St Vincent, an advocate of the close blockade, knew that squadrons holding the seas off Toulon stood to be torn to pieces, and suggested the British take up a station between Cape Sicié (Toulon) and Hyères and run under the lee of the Île du Levant when the fierce north-westerlies were at their worst. But this was too far eastwards, and Nelson placed his force a little west of Toulon, where he could gain the advantage of the wind if the French put to sea in the prevailing westerlies, and where he could intercept any enemy reinforcements that might be coming from the Strait or Cartagena. This position he named Rendezvous 100. The admiral soon revised his dispositions, however. Unlike St Vincent, Nelson was not enthusiastic about close blockades, which achieved naval supremacy by confining hostile fleets to their ports. He preferred to lure the enemy into a battle. Accordingly, he adopted the practice of leaving a couple of frigates inshore to monitor the movements of the enemy, while retiring his main force out of sight of land to nurture the illusion that the seas might be open. Rendezvous 102, as this offshore station was called, was situated south and some forty miles west of Toulon, and ran along latitude forty-two degrees twenty minutes. Nelson's ships plied back and forth along a forty-mile line, but were warned not to proceed 'to the northward' lest they betray the fleet's presence to the enemy. If a mistral blew from the north-west the most convenient shelter was to be found to the south-west, about ten leagues south of Cape San Sebastian in Spain, which became 'Rendezvous 97'. These positions were strategically well chosen, but they also gave some access to water and fresh provisions. Initially, Nelson had hoped to draw these from Naples, but the Spanish ports of Rosas and Barcelona were more convenient sources, and on 20 July Nelson sent Captain George Elliot of the *Termagant* to open a supply. Elliot found that Rosas not only had many of the fleet's wants in abundance but also an extremely efficient British consul, Edward Gayner, and as long as Spain and Britain remained at peace Rosas remained an invaluable resource.[20]

At this point Nelson had completed a tour of his station, identified the trouble spots, deployed his forces and tackled the problem of supply. His weaknesses were also becoming plain, and he was soon writing to Whitehall about the 'ready money' needed to purchase fresh provisions in areas that refused to accept British Treasury bills, and his want of enough ships and a disposable force of troops. The money came through quickly, but Nelson's request for 10,000 regulars for use in Sicily or Naples made little impression upon Addington's defensively minded administration with greater priorities at home. In the spring of

1804 a detachment of Royal Artillery was sent out, but Nelson's request did not bear tangible fruit for two years.[21]

Looking at the diversity of his tasks, Nelson sometimes wished that he could divide himself into two or more persons. But he was cheered by the speedy arrival of two stalwart ships, the *Victory* on 30 July and the eighty-gun *Canopus* the ensuing month. Rear Admiral George Campbell took *Canopus* for his flagship, while Nelson joyfully reclaimed the *Victory*. 'I can only say to you thanks for not taking the *Victory* from me,' he wrote to Cornwallis. 'It was like yourself.' Sutton had done rather well in her, too, taking three or four prizes since leaving Nelson, the best a French frigate named *Ambuscade*, which Sutton had brought to the Mediterranean under the temporary command of Nelson's protégé, William Layman. As prize master, Layman had also done serious service in her on his way to Gibraltar, capturing one French ship that contained a treasure trove of confidential material, including navigational charts and the current enemy signal books. On 30 July Nelson transferred to the wholly more commodious quarters of the *Victory*, taking with him Hardy, his flag captain, and Murray, the captain of the fleet. The next day the admiral was happily writing to Emma that Hardy was hanging the portraits of her and Horatia in the great cabin, 'and I trust soon to see the other two [portraits] safe arrived from the Exhibition'. Meanwhile, Sutton recovered the *Amphion* and was rewarded with cruises outside the Strait of Gibraltar, where he could combine watching for any enemies who might dare to enter the Mediterranean with prowling a hunting ground notorious for prizes. 'For myself I had rather hear of your destroying two privateers than taking a merchant ship of £20,000 value,' Nelson told the expectant captain. 'I am not a money-getting man, for which I am probably laughed at.' As for the newly refitted *Victory*, she proved one of the fastest capital ships in the fleet and remained the admiral's home for most of his remaining days.[22]

These reinforcements brought Nelson's total of line ships to eleven, but *Monmouth* was locked in Naples and in August Strachan's *Donegal* had to be detailed to command outside the Strait, an area hitherto under the care of a few cruisers. While the frigates, sloops and brigs could handle the privateers stalking those waters, Nelson learned that a French ship of the line, *L'Aigle*, had got into the Spanish port of Cadiz after returning from the West Indies. She, and two consorts, a brig and corvette, were being monitored by James Duff, the British consul in Cadiz, who sent regular reports to the fleet, but they posed a serious threat to Britain's trade passing to and from the Mediterranean. Until the intentions of *L'Aigle* became clearer, Nelson had to deploy a ship of the line such as the *Donegal*. This cut his capital ships off Toulon to nine, and one or two might at any time have to leave for food and water.[23]

Nelson's dispositions of 1803 were clear-sighted and free of the distractions of 1799 and 1800. He had no doubt that control of the Mediterranean meant first and foremost the western Mediterranean, between Gibraltar and Italy, where any threats from the French or the Spanish, whether destined for the east or west, must materialise. Nelson had disparaged the usefulness of Minorca in 1799, but now realised the primary importance of such a base, poised between France and Spain and between the Strait and Toulon. He told Addington that Minorca's 'conveniences are so great that I trust that the moment a Spanish war is certain . . . we shall . . . secure it'. Malta was far too distant, for, with a fleet stationed there, 'the French might do as they pleased between here and Gibraltar'.[24]

At times Nelson came close to acknowledging former errors, though he was never good at it. 'I paid more attention to another sovereign than my own,' he wrote to Abraham Gibbs, but 'I did my duty, to the Sicilifying of my own conscience, and I am easy.' Over and above this, though, he had simply matured. The old Nelson had been a lethal weapon that needed some direction; the new was as keen a sword, but one that thought like the commander-in-chief of a large and important theatre.[25]

3

Nelson's strategy held throughout that first summer, and his ships maintained their stations off Toulon, waiting for their battle. He was unchallenged, and the few ships that ventured out of the port scuttled quickly in again. Towards the end of September Nelson was able to tell St Vincent that he had yet to see 'a French flag at sea'. Occasionally, though, a harbinger of difficulties that lay ahead cast a distant shadow. In the first week of August Nelson took the fleet to Rosas to water and victual, and during his brief absence suffered his first loss. In the small hours of 4 August the *Redbridge* schooner arrived off Toulon searching for the missing fleet with a water ship she had brought from Malta. Lieutenant George Lempriere appears to have also missed Nelson's watch frigates, but a squadron of French cruisers darted out and fired into his vessels, which were soon overpowered and taken. It was a small affair, but one that echoed the wider issues of the safety of his 'open blockade' and efficiency of his communications. On this occasion Nelson got away with no more than a rewriting of lost signal books.[26]

Nelson accepted that his 'open blockade' had inherent risks, especially as the watch frigates and fleet might both be forced from their stations for one reason or another and lose contact with each other. There was always the possibility that the enemy might escape and inflict damage. These were risks that Nelson was prepared to take. His mentor in this, as in so much else, was Lord Hood, his old commander-in-chief. Hood's view was that the annihilation of the enemy in battle, rather than his incarceration in port, was the surest instrument of naval supremacy. 'Therefore,' said he, 'cease blockading the port and tempt it [the hostile fleet] out. I have ever held that opinion, and am persuaded the war has been prolonged by the blockade.' Hood's opinion was particularly relevant in 1803, when the Royal Navy was crippled by St Vincent's reforms. In these circumstances Nelson could expect few reinforcements, and battle looked the best way to establish a working superiority at sea. Nelson never made a secret of the doctrinal core of his strategy, focused as he was on the big battle. 'There seems an idea that I am blocking up the French fleet in Toulon,' he wrote to an acquaintance. 'Nothing can be more untrue . . . My wish . . . is to have them out.' 'I have made up my mind never to go into port till after the battle,' his superiors learned. It would be decisive, 'for I must not have anything like a drawn battle', and if needs be, he would stay out for a year, and asked nothing more than that the government replace such ships as were unequal to the winter gales.[27]

At this stage Nelson envisaged riding off Toulon between Rendezvous 97 and 102, but there were already indications that any kind of blockade would be difficult to maintain. Nelson would learn that gales could strike at any time in the Gulf of Lions. July brought the first, some blowing fiercely for days, and Nelson's diary was soon spotted with such entries as 'all night hard gales and a very heavy sea' and 'all night a dirty Levanter'. The British had learned to handle a degree of rough weather, reefing and unbending sails and striking topmasts and topgallants to ride under bare poles, and Nelson even made preposterous claims not to have lost a single spar to storms. Certainly the *Victory*'s log shows relatively little damage during the command. A jib boom and fore topsail yard were carried away and a topgallant yard and cross-trees damaged, among a much greater problem of split sails, but the flagship had been newly refitted and was unusually advantaged. Many of the other ships suffered more severely. In July the *Triumph*'s bowsprit was sprung in three places, and she retired to Gibraltar, and the *Agincourt* was forced into Malta when a leak spoiled her magazine, while a lower mast and lower yard were sprung in the *Gibraltar*. The following month a foreyard of the *Canopus* was carried away, the mainmast of the *Amazon* frigate damaged, and the *Monmouth* lost her main topmast to a bolt of lightning. Throughout the fleet rotten rigging and worn canvas gave way. Nelson had temporarily lost two ships of the line in a month, and might have paid for it if the French fleet had chosen that moment to offer battle.[28]

Storms and the French fleet or no, Nelson had also to keep an ear towards the political rumblings to starboard and larboard, for at any time they might make his position untenable or transform his priorities. A Spanish war promised rich pickings from ships full of American silver, but Nelson knew that such a conflict would double his adversaries, shut off important sources of provisions and seriously jeopardise his communications with home. Spain, effectively governed by the court favourite, Manuel de Godoy, the 'Prince of Peace', was still the third naval power, and relations with her were deteriorating. At the back of it were the French, who bullied the reluctant Spaniards into a secret agreement of 19 October 1803 by which they would contribute six million livres a month to Napoleon's war chest and repair and rearm French ships in her ports. Although sparing Spain the pain of outright war, it was a breach of neutrality that could not entirely be kept from the watchful Britons. In addition, French pressure gradually compelled the Spaniards to adopt unfriendly policies towards the British. They attempted to restrict the amount of provisions that could be sold to British ships, and refused them entry to ports unless in distress. Both obstacles were given up in the beginning of 1804, but for some months Nelson's ships had to enforce their own codes. When the *Halycon* put in to Alicante on 5 October with damage to her lower rigging and main topmast she was asked to leave after only fourteen hours, although a French privateer had been sitting in the port for weeks. Captain Henry Pearse declined to be so hurried, and lodged a protest. The same month Nelson himself complained to the British vice consul in Barcelona, Jayme Buenaventura Gibert, that French privateers and warships were using Spanish ports as bases to raid British commerce and that their prizes were being sold openly in Barcelona. In March 1804 the Spanish government forbade the sale of captured British ships in their ports, but other difficulties continued. Spain promised but failed to prevent French corsairs from abusing her neutrality, and John Hunter, the consul general in Madrid, finally wrote that 'if the abuse still continues Captain Gore [one of the complainants] will be warranted in taking the remedy into his own hands'.[29]

Such inconveniences routinely disrupted Nelson's attempts to trade with Rosas and Barcelona, but his great concern was that an outbreak of hostilities would catch him unawares. He demanded regular reports from John Hooker Frere, Britain's Envoy Extraordinary and Plenipotentiary in Madrid, suggesting that vital news be sent express to Rosas, where Gayner was on standby to hire a vessel to speed it to the fleet. Apart from Frere and Hunter in Madrid and Gayner in Rosas, the admiral also received reports from Duff in Cadiz, Gibert in Barcelona and Charles Price, the pro-consul in Cartagena. But while he sought a continuation of good relations, he was not prepared to allow Spain to succour the French fleet. In September 1803 Nelson warned Strachan of the *Donegal* that if Spanish warships tried to escort the French *Aigle* out of Cadiz he should deem it a declaration of war and attack 'the whole body'. Anticipating that there might be just such trouble, he reinforced Strachan with the *Agincourt* ship of the line and *Maidstone* frigate. In November the admiral also told Frere that if French corsairs continued to abuse the neutrality of Spanish ports he would attack them wherever they hid. There is evidence that he contemplated using large mortar rafts to bombard ships in Spanish harbours.[30]

Spain was one area that kept Nelson's position in the Mediterranean on a knife edge, and Italy was the other. If reports were true, flotillas of French gunboats and small transports were fitting at Marseilles and Genoa, but no clear indication of their intent was to be had. Nelson knew what an armada of such small boats could do, however, creeping along coasts, exploiting shallows, or making short, opportune dashes across open water in misty weather or at night. Bonaparte had regained Corsica with them in 1796 in the very teeth of the Royal Navy. Nelson's deeper-draught warships could not stem such a tide, he explained to Elliot. 'Nothing but vessels of similar descriptions, and with the same facilities of going into all the little ports in bad weather, can prevent their passage along shore – no, not all the navies of Europe.' Whither these ominous little craft were bound, Nelson knew not but Sicily, Sardinia and the Morea were the likeliest targets.[31]

Italy was a perpetual headache. Despite his contingency plans, Nelson's faith in the ability of Sicily to resist a French attack diminished. He had redcoats ready to rush to its aid, but could not compel the Sicilians to summon them in time. As the summer matured Nelson detected a worrying complacency in Sicily. The governor of Messina, where the dangers were as notorious as noonday, blithely declared that he had no need of the British, and sixteen of his gunboats were beached and rotting. At first even Elliot took their excuses at face value, something Nelson put down to inexperience. Elliot, he told Lord Hawkesbury, 'believes that he is fully acquainted with the whole machinery which governs Naples . . . I doubt that he knows more than they wish him.' The admiral wasted no time in telling Acton that the French were masters of deception and complacency could be fatal. 'I have done my duty representing these matters, and it remains only for me to lament that it is of no avail,' he sighed to Elliot. 'My heart bleeds to hear what I do from Messina, and, as sure as you live, it is lost unless other means are taken to prevent it than are followed at present.'[32]

There was more to the situation in the Two Sicilies than even Nelson knew. Starting at every shadow, the Bourbon regime squirmed to cling to what it had left. At times it played a dangerous double game, here seeking the support of Britain and Russia, and there tittle-tattling to the French about what those powers were doing in a desperate effort to ingratiate itself. Alquier, the French minister in Naples, was actually notified of the secret British plan to garrison Messina. In an obsequious bid for favour, it was represented as a British plot to destroy Neapolitan neutrality, one that the king had uprightly rejected. The playing down of the defences at Messina was part of this attempt to reassure the French and stave off intervention. With Naples twisting all ways, and Russia and Britain incurably suspicious of each other, southern Italy had turned into a diplomatic maelstrom.

But turning that flotilla at Marseilles and Genoa over in his mind, Nelson's worries increasingly centred not on Sicily but on Sardinia, a larger island more fundamentally located between Italy and the French coast. France had already stripped Sardinia of Piedmont on the mainland and Jacobin agitators were busy fanning discontent in the remaining rump of the kingdom, the island itself. The new king, Victor Emanuel, was domiciled in Rome, and it was his brother, Prince Charles Felix Joseph, Duke of Genevois (Savoy), who installed himself in Cagliari to take over the reins of effective government as a viceroy. Like Ferdinand of Naples the King of Sardinia desired nothing more than to rid himself of French interference, and like Ferdinand he saw no clear way to do it. At the beginning of June he was contemplating inviting Britain to occupy the island of San Pietro, off south-western Sardinia, but within days his fears of France had overwhelmed him, and he insisted that on no account would either belligerent be permitted to establish a foothold on his realm. Nevertheless, he flatly told the British that unrestricted numbers of their ships would be welcomed in his ports.[33]

Nelson was beginning to see Sardinia as an answer to his need for a local base, but realised that the island was even more vulnerable to French invasion than Sicily. The Sardinians had only two regular regiments of foot and horse, and an ill-equipped militia of 30,000, and three years of poor harvests had bled its exchequer, which relied upon the duties from grain exports, dry. In the north the island was only separated from French-held Corsica by the narrow Strait of Bonifacio. As early as August, Nelson had written strongly about Sardinia to Addington, suggesting that the British should garrison the island. The people, he reported, were oppressed and ready for change. 'Sardinia will be lost without a struggle,' he said, 'and yet the majority of Sardinians would fly to receive us. But if we will not, then the French [would be chosen] in preference to remaining as they are.'[34]

The conundrum that bedevilled the defence of Sicily repeated itself in Sardinia. On 23 August the *Gibraltar* brought Nelson intelligence that fifteen hundred French – part of the sinister flotilla forming in Marseilles and Genoa – and five thousand Corsicans were ready to invade Sardinia. The Sardinian government, on the other hand, was cautious. It was conceivable that the French merely intended reinforcing Elba, which they had just seized, or suppressing the not inconsiderable internal disaffection inside Corsica. Nor did it see its people as discontented as Nelson maintained. In short, Sardinia was not ready for a strong response to the invasion threat, and like Naples put greater faith in Russian mediation. Without troops or Sardinian cooperation, Nelson had to act within existing means, and on 26 August detailed Donnelly to cruise off Corsica with the *Narcissus* and *Active* to stem any hostile movements.[35]

The Sardinian issue soon worked its way close to the top of Nelson's priorities. As the summer turned into the autumn Nelson's ships maintained their long watch for the French fleet. 'We have nothing in the least new here,' he once said of the unremitting service. 'We cruise, cruise, and one day so like another that they are hardly distinguishable.' The quality of the ships left much to be desired. Many were overdue a refit, and others came from English dockyards denuded of resources and betraying alarming deficiencies. The *Excellent* ship of the line, under Captain Frank Sotheran, which joined in November after bringing the outward British 'trade' to the Mediterranean, had newly fitted rigging that looked incapable of lasting the winter. Nelson reckoned that only the *Victory*, *Belleisle* and *Donegal* were truly seaworthy. Unfortunately, in September they came – the persistent gales that Nelson had dreaded – and with them the first real test of his 'blockade'. On average they lashed the ships for three of every seven days, sometimes whipping up suddenly to attack masts, sails and running rigging at a time when there were few spares to be had. Nelson pleaded his case to the Admiralty while seeking local supplies. Valletta, though nearer than Gibraltar, was also too remote to supply a fleet off Toulon. 'If I had only to look to Malta for supplies,' he said, 'our ships' companies would have been done for long ago.'[36]

But the beatings continued, whether the ships sheltered under Cape San Sebastian, ran southwards, or went under bare poles. 'Such a place for storms and winds I never met with,' Nelson moaned miserably, now almost perpetually seasick as the *Victory* pitched, rolled and shook. 'We now breakfast by candle-light, and all retire at eight o'clock to bed,' he groaned. On 9 October a terrific storm swept from the north-west, driving the squadron before it. It lasted three days, only to be succeeded by a fog as 'thick as buttermilk' that enveloped and infiltrated the ships, penetrating the lungs of the most shrouded sailors, and deadening sound, almost sealing each vessel in a world of its own. In the ghostly murk an easterly picked up, raising fears that the French might use it to bolt for the Strait. Then the *Narcissus* frigate groped her way to the flagship with the alarming news that she had 'spoken' a Spanish craft that claimed to have seen twelve ships of war off Minorca only days before. Nelson was thrown into a fever lest the French had got out, cursing that four of his ships of the line were elsewhere. He had adopted a rota system, in which his ships took turns to leave for supplies, and the *Canopus* was due back from Sardinia on precisely such an errand. The disadvantage of this system was that it left the blockading squadron permanently understrength, as now, but Nelson had to make the best of it. With the residue of his force, 'the finest squadron in the world', he went hunting for the enemy. 'If I should miss these fellows, my heart will break,' he told Clarence. 'God knows, I only serve to fight those scoundrels, and if I cannot do that, I should be better on shore.' But the battle was not to be. On the following day his watch frigate, the *Seahorse*, under his old eleve Courtney Boyle, regained her position off Toulon and put the admiral's mind to rest. The French were still there.[37]

It had been a shock, and an example of how the lack of a base, bad weather and a shortage of ships could threaten the entire naval command of the Mediterranean. Under the rota system Nelson rarely had more than eight line ships with him at any one time, and continued storm damage could erode even that number. Something had to be done to preserve his fleet. The night of 24

October was clear and moonlit, one of several, and Nelson took a necessary risk. Leaving *Narcissus* and *Seahorse* off Toulon, he ordered his entire battle force eastwards to the Maddalena Islands in Sardinia for shelter, water and provisions. He could only hope that the French would not come out in the two weeks he expected to be away.

4

No fleet could operate off Toulon without a convenient base. If another Spanish war broke out Nelson would consider an attack on the Balearic Islands, but as long as the peace with Spain endured Nelson's only viable alternative was neutral Sardinia.

The Maddalenas were an archipelago of small islands scattered off the northern coast of Sardinia, sitting in the eastern entrance of the Strait of Bonifacio, a narrow passage separating Sardinia from Corsica to the north. Maddalena was the largest of the islands, with a town of fifty houses on its southern coast. Directly south of it was a fine and sheltered anchorage, Agincourt Sound, tucked into the northern shore of Sardinia, but covered from Corsica by the archipelago. Sardinia struck some as a desolate, treeless place, where stunted shrubs of wild myrtle and arbutus promised little fuel, but sufficient fruit, fresh beef, grain and water were to be had, and positioned midway between Malta and Toulon, its quiet bays and anchorages were places where victuallers and store ships from Malta could be cleared in all weathers.

The Maddalenas were not well known, but Jackson had sent a map, Troubridge had promised a navigational chart and Ball had recommended Sardinia as the ideal rendezvous for traffic between Malta and the fleet in the Gulf of Lions. Nelson was also encouraged by tentative explorations. Keats had navigated the Strait of Bonifacio both ways and reported a 'good and safe passage' throughout, and Ryves of the *Agincourt* had made a most conscientious survey in the summer, drawing up a chart and sailing directions, and bestowing the name of his ship upon a spacious haven he had found south of Maddalena Island. Scrutinising these admirable materials, Nelson found sound advice about most of the difficulties of what was far from a straightforward journey. 'From Shark's Mouth S.E. by E. per chart near two miles are four or five rocks just above water, a mile from the shore, the outer one near a cable and a half's length from the others, with a passage of ten fathoms between. [It] is not bigger than a barrel. When the water is low there is a second [rock] to be seen, though it is bold close to the rocks. I would not recommend going nearer than 17 fathoms. Between these rocks and Shark's Mouth is a bay in which the *Agincourt* anchored in seventeen fathoms, a fine white clay, good holding ground, and exposed only to a N.E. wind . . .', and so on, all invaluable to the uninitiated mariner. With this in his armoury, Nelson realised that

Sardinia, a mere two hundred miles from Toulon, could be a key to his campaign.[38]

The important voyage of October 1803 was intended to test whether a large force could use the Maddalenas. Squalls and combative winds and currents had the admiral making meteorological entries in his weather journal up to six times a day. Sometimes he lost ground, and one night he was blown two points of the compass off his course and five leagues to leeward. Picking their way through the Bonifacio channel the nine ships, seven of them line of battle ships, tacked skilfully back and forth to avoid the rocks on Ryves's chart and anchored in Agincourt Sound on the evening of 31 October. A delighted Nelson wrote to Ryves that 'we worked the *Victory* every foot of the way from Asinaria [Asinara island] to this anchorage, [the wind] blowing from Lango Sardo [Longon Sardo] under double-reefed topsails. I shall write to the Admiralty [stating] how much they owed to your very great skill and activity in making this survey. This is absolutely one of the finest harbours I have ever seen.' Subsequent soundings confirmed the reliability of the chart, but there were a few unmarked rocks, and the *Excellent* struck one of them while working out of the eastern passage to the Tyrrhenian Sea in May 1804, ripping away her false keel.[39]

If Maddalena was to fulfil its potential, the British had to make themselves welcome. Sardinia had invited Nelson to use her ports but there was no knowing how far the local people or the government would tolerate extensive usage, especially in the face of the expected French resentment. The local military commander, Captain Agostino Millelire, was welcomed aboard the *Victory* with an impressive gun salute, and using the Reverend Scott as his interpreter Nelson explained his need of water, fresh beef, mutton and onions. Provisions were not always available at short notice, but beef, pork, bread, flour, oatmeal and water were taken aboard. Grubby officers were thankful to find a woman ashore happy to receive laundry. The islands had no use for Treasury bills, but with commendable spirit Richard Bromley, the purser of the *Belleisle*, who had offered to act as the fleet's agent victualler, and Captain Hardy dug into their pockets to unearth sufficient hard Spanish dollars.[40]

In the ten days before their departure on 10 November the British successfully courted the community, using Giovanni Brandi, who had helped Ryves, as a consul. Millelire and Lieutenant Pier Francesco Maria Magnon, who commanded the garrison at Longon Sardo, were presented with pressings of Davison's Nile medal by a self-satisfied British admiral, and the enchanted lieutenant reciprocated with gifts of a semi-precious stone and ancient coin and a song he had composed in Nelson's honour. The one durable irritant concerned British deserters, for whom the Sardinians showed inordinate compassion. Nelson asked the people not to inveigle sailors from their duties with drink, and agreed to pay bounties for the apprehension of any who absconded from the shore parties, but the potential for disagreement remained. Magnon declined to arrest deserters unless Nelson promised to exempt them from punishment, but the problem cut both ways, and during a visit in May the British were asked to return two Sardinians who had fled armed service to join a Maltese privateer. It was eventually agreed that the Sardinians would surrender prisoners and Nelson would decline to take their defectors. The most serious incidents occurred in May 1804 when ten sail of the line visited the Maddalenas for a week. One British officer was wounded in the arm while ashore and another seized and robbed, while a few inebriated British tars entered a shepherd's hut and tried to assault a woman. Nevertheless, Nelson preserved a general harmony, and on 18 October presented Santa Maria, the parish church in La Maddalena, with a silver crucifix and two silver candlesticks he had purchased in Barcelona. They are still treasured today.[41]

The value of Sardinia was constantly reinforced. After his first visit Nelson led the fleet back to their rendezvous, taking two prizes on the journey, *Le Titus*, a transport with ninety-six soldiers, and her escort, *Le Renard*, a French national sloop carrying eighteen guns and swivels and eighty men. But the fleet was unable to hold the sea for long, and early in December retired again to Sardinia, this time looking for an anchorage on the south-west coast where they might receive victuallers expected from Malta. San Pietro, which Nelson had used in 1798, was difficult to enter in bad weather so his ships shifted a few miles south-east to an 'excellent and commodious' harbour in the Gulf of Palma, cosily situated between Sardinia and the offshore island of Sant' Antioco. Nelson ordered the master of the *Victory* and Midshipman Charles Royer to make a navigational survey of this fresh discovery, and his letter to the Admiralty rang with praise for the youngster, who had 'no friend to bring him forward' but had proven himself 'a very deserving young man' worthy of promotion.[42]

The processes of exploration and documentation continued throughout the following year. In February Nelson ran his fleet through the eastern part of the Bonifacio passage from the Maddalena to the Tyrrhenian Sea, noting in his diary that it 'looked tremendous by the numbers of rocks and the heavy sea breaking upon them' but was 'perfectly safe when once known' because the pedestal rock on Ryves's chart could 'never be mistaken'. In following months the British found several additional sources of water and provisions at Porto Conte and Porto Torres on the north-west coast of Sardinia, including a site five miles west of the latter settlement, where 'a spring' was discovered 'about 200 yards from the beach . . . where forty casks may be filled at the same time'. On the southern coast, south of Cagliari, Pula sported 'a very fine river of excellent water' that yielded thirteen hundred tons of water in a single visit.[43]

Sardinia was a saviour of Nelson's fleet. By providing shelter and provisions it eased the rigours of sea-keeping and reduced the need to scatter far and wide. The winter gales seldom let up. In December Nelson wrote that 'the whole of this day it blew from the N.N.W. harder than I ever knew it, with constant hail and rain'. The first week in February brought 'one of the heaviest snow storms

I have seen, which continued without intermission all night'. Even with Sardinia relatively close at hand, the wear and tear on the ships accumulated. Two of the frigates lost bowsprits, and in August 1804 the fore- and mainmasts of the *Triumph* had to be secured. The *Kent*'s ordeal was particularly gruelling, for her beams prised open in strong winds, trebling the amount of water breaching her dilapidated hull. Two of Nelson's smaller ships, *Braakel* and *Stately*, were sent home and the *Agincourt*, a capital ship, was slated to follow. So short-handed was the admiral that he temporarily recalled the *Donegal* from Cadiz, leaving *L'Aigle* to be watched by frigates alone. At the end of the year Nelson's fleet was as hard pressed as it had ever been. In Toulon the French had ten ships of the line and twenty cruisers ready for sea or refitting, while Nelson fielded only a dozen capital ships and a score of cruisers to hold down the entire theatre from Cadiz to the Dardanelles. The blockade of Genoa had to be suspended.[44]

Nevertheless, the problems of ships, storms and distant bases had damaged but not destroyed Nelson's campaign. The first crisis of the long watch had passed.

5

If Sardinia was a solution, it was by no means a perfect one. It introduced new problems of its own. It was still two hundred miles from Toulon, and although a couple of cruisers were always left to watch the French, whenever the fleet steered for Sardinia the voyage put two or three days' sailing between Nelson and Toulon even in the finest weather. We have seen that Nelson made no bones about his operation. It was not the 'close' blockade practised by Cornwallis off Brest, as far as was practicable. In its ideal form it was Hood's 'open' blockade, designed to draw the enemy from his fortress. But waiting with the main British force south of Toulon or under Cape San Sebastian was very different from holing up in Sardinia. By taking his ships to Maddalena or Palma, Nelson knew that they risked being away when the French broke out. He understood that his operation was in effect compromised, but simply saw no alternative. 'My plan,' he told Clarence, 'is to spare the ships and men to be ready to follow the enemy if they go to Madras, but never to blockade them, or prevent them putting to sea any day or hour they please.' Unseaworthy ships and sick men, he was saying, would be useless, and something had had to be sacrificed to keep them in respectable shape.[45]

Bad weather, though, could easily disrupt communications between the watch frigates and the fleet in Sardinia, and trips to the Maddalenas could equally be forcibly extended. After his third visit to Sardinia, Nelson attempted to leave the Maddalenas on 15 February, but a fierce wind at WNW prevented his ships from weighing anchor and it was not until the 19th that they cleared the islands and pushed strenuously southwards. Two days later the fleet tried and failed to weather Minorca, and had to shelter under its lee. Nelson regained his rendezvous before the end of the month, having occupied the best part of two weeks achieving what should have been the work of two days in good weather. When such delays were added to the time spent in Sardinia, Nelson's fleet made nine visits between 8 July 1803 and 20 January 1805, and was missing from its cruising ground for some 168 of the 562 days, or for 30 per cent of the time.

For substantial periods, therefore, Nelson's 'open' blockade turned into no blockade, with the watch purely dependent upon the fragile ability of a few frigates to maintain their connections with both the French and British fleets. Some did not approve, and in June 1804 Whitby of the *Belleisle* wrote to his old friend and patron, Cornwallis, that Nelson 'did not cruise upon his rendezvous. I have known him from a week to three weeks, and even a month, unfound by ships sent to reconnoitre. Since I came away the French squadron got out in his absence and cruised off Toulon several days . . . I write this to you in confidence, for I would absolutely not dare to give my opinion on the Mediterranean blockade to any other person.' Some naval historians have compared Nelson's blockade to Bridport's much-derided operations in the English Channel during the previous war, which twice released dangerous enemy squadrons from Brest.[46]

Given Nelson's relative isolation this is an uncharitable view, but Whitby's remark also identifies another serious consequence of Nelson's peregrinations. Every time the fleet left its expected location a ship had to remain behind to redirect couriers, transports, store ships and reinforcements, and when, as sometimes happened, these markers were themselves forced from their stations, communications could collapse. The *Amazon*, which left Spithead to find the fleet in September 1803, wasted 'five weeks' looking for the Mediterranean fleet before locating it at Maddalena on Christmas Eve. Captain Pettet of the *Termagant* did even worse. He left Gibraltar on 23 October 1803 with a store ship and four vessels under convoy and a passenger on board, John Falcon, a diplomat eager to brief the commander-in-chief about Algiers. With orders to join the rendezvous off Toulon 'with all possible despatch', Petêembarked upon a frustrating odyssey, arriving at his destination twice, three times sailing to the Maddalenas, and three times taking directions from British warships along the way. After being 'tossed about during seven weeks in contrary and continual gales of wind' Falcon became so sick that he was invalided ashore without meeting Nelson. Pettet searched on. 'I remained cruising between Cape Sebastian and Toulon in *Termagant* with the transport till the 26th [December],' said the hapless officer, 'when not finding your lordship, and being short of provisions, I was under the necessity of bearing up with the transport for the island of St Peter's [San Pietro, Sardinia], and after having seen her [the transport] safe moored, I mean to proceed to Malta to get my ship victualled . . . I have only to lament that a more favourable opportunity did not present itself to afford my joining your lordship.' Pettet did not find Nelson until 24 January. His experience epitomises the ease with which weather and circumstance could delay ships, drive them away or disrupt schedules. Nelson had asked his watch frigates to look out for the *Termagant* and supplied them with the fleet's intended itinerary, but neither precaution avoided the confusion.[47]

A more obvious consequence of the British reliance upon Sardinia was the island's increased importance. The continued presence of a large fleet, commanded by the undisputed master of naval warfare, unnerved the French. To calm excited Gallic protests his Sardinian Majesty eventually issued an edict restricting the amount of supplies that could be issued to Nelson's fleet at any one time, but the gesture was merely cosmetic, and according to the admiral 'the moment we anchored at Maddalena the 12th [May 1804] 1000 head of fat cattle were brought for sale'. However, the threat of robust French action increased, and the beginning of 1804 found Nelson tormented by a mental picture of the French streaming out of Corsica, Elba or the Riviera in small vessels to overwhelm Sardinia, capitalising upon internal disaffection caused by the king's refusal to countenance urgent constitutional reform. These growing fears were credible, for the French had two good reasons to take over Sardinia: it was a major support of the British fleet, and brought to the borders of Corsica a powerful and daring adversary who had reduced that island before in 1794. The Strait of Bonifacio was a tinderbox frontier separating two sides each afraid of the onslaught from the other.[48]

About the turn of the year the French landed 4500 men in St Florent in the north of Corsica, and several hundred occupied the town of Bonifacio on the southern coast. Some brashly boasted that they were merely waiting for the British fleet to leave to overrun Sardinia. Additional French troops also reached Elba. Nelson, who had captured Elba in 1796, had no worries about the French occupation of that island. When some British politicians at home panicked about it, he reassured Hobart that the island was a 'useless and expensive' acquisition since the harbour of Porto Ferraio was incapable of heaving down ships of the line, and Bonaparte had therefore simply saddled himself with 'a dead load'. The caveat was Elba's position, off the north-west coast of Corsica, where its garrison increased the threat to Sardinia. Then, early in January, Nelson also intercepted some letters that indicated that 30,000 men were embarking at Marseilles for Sardinia. One of the letters was authored by the French minister of war, and Nelson took the intelligence seriously enough to send it to the Sardinian viceroy, the Duke of Genevois, at Cagliari by Major Hudson Lowe. Lowe would earn fame as Napoleon's jailer on St Helena, but here we see him in the role of recruiting agent, charged by the British government with encouraging Sicilians, Sardinians and Corsicans to enlist in the British army. The viceroy told Lowe that he had neither men nor money to defend his island; more, he did not believe the threat to be as great as Nelson said, and was reluctant to antagonise the French. After reading Lowe's report Nelson glumly concluded that if the French invaded Sardinia 'there will be no resistance . . . worth mentioning'. The existing defences were a shambles, and the war chest bare. Meanwhile, in the Strait of Bonifacio tensions were topping new highs. The approach of a British ship was enough to cause a 'tumult' on the French side, sending gunners to their batteries and troops jogging to landing places with their muskets. The Sardinian commander, Magnon, captured the mutual distrust across the frontier in his letters to the British. 'Your fleet, sir,' he told Nelson, 'has thwarted their [the French] plans, because that expedition dare not take to sea because of your presence.' He saw Nelson as Sardinia's 'Guardian Angel' but confessed to Scott, with whom he corresponded, that both sides were motivated by anxieties. 'The fear in Bonifacio [Corsica] . . . is that you will attack them whilst they are under strength.'[49]

In Sardinia, as in Sicily, brinkmanship prevailed. The circumstances were much the same: uncertainty about the French intentions, and about what defences could be raised against a hypothetical invasion without triggering a real one. Elliot, fresh from the Sicilian controversy, pitched in by hinting that he might be able to make £20,000 available to improve fortifications in the Strait of Bonifacio, and suggested a British officer be landed to offer covert advice. The King of Sardinia was interested in the money, but thought the French would soon learn about the officer and accuse Sardinia of breaking her neutrality. Nelson, as in the case of Sicily, favoured a stronger response, and proposed posting five hundred Maltese redcoats in the Maddalenas, not enough to stop a full-blown invasion from Corsica but sufficient to deter opportunist sorties and to hold a large-scale attack until the fleet could come to its relief. Villettes was willing to find the men, but stressed the importance of establishing them behind properly prepared works before a French attack. It was no use Sardinia waiting until the French attacked, and then summoning the redcoats to their aid.[50]

These ideas aroused considerable alarm. In Rome Jackson, Britain's minister to the Sardinian court, wrote that 'authentic accounts' from Corsica indicated that there were no plans to attack Sardinia, and that 'all' the French measures were 'merely defensive'. In London the Sardinian minister was astonished at Nelson's proposals, and declared they would inevitably lay Sardinia open to French retaliation. Whitehall knew about Nelson's ideas. Recently the admiral had written to Hobart that Sardinia was 'the finest island in the Mediterranean' with 'harbours fit for arsenals' as well as the accommodation and supply of the British fleet. He went so far as to recommend the island be purchased; it was 'worth any money to obtain', 'could be maintained for as little as Malta . . . and produce a large revenue', and was absolutely essential to Britain's command of the Mediterranean. At the moment, however, there were no funds for such an imaginative solution, and the government opted to preserve an equitable stalemate. Hawkesbury told the Sardinian minister that he entirely approved of his country's strict neutrality, and promised that orders would be sent to Nelson 'for its most exact and strict observance'. To this mood Jackson must have contributed, because in March he wrote to Hawkesbury reporting that whatever untoward activity had been going on in Marseilles and Toulon had ended, possibly because of the vigilance of Nelson's fleet, and that there was no obvious French interest in Sardinia at the moment. The following month Nelson had to assure the viceroy that no redcoats would be forced upon his island without its consent.[51]

Nelson felt hurt at what he took to be the first rebuttal of his ideas in Whitehall, and penned a mild protest, enclosing letters from Acton, Ferdinand and Maria Carolina to prove the level of satisfaction he was giving. Unrepentant, however, he predicted the loss of Sardinia and added dramatically that 'I do not see that the fleet can then be kept at sea'. Nevertheless, he put in place what he could. He reinforced naval patrols to the east, north and north-west of Sardinia and Corsica, and set up a new 'rendezvous' for British ships twelve miles west of Cape Corse, Corsica, to intercept enemy troops shipping out of the French or Italian mainlands. To counter threats to Maddalena from local Franco-Corsican filibusters, he permanently stationed a cruiser in the Strait of Bonifacio. 'Keep a strict watch during the night, and have your guns loaded with grape,' Nelson warned Pettet, when his *Termagant* was selected for one of the tours of duty at Maddalena. Frigates and bomb vessels took their turns, but perhaps the most eligible appointment was the *Camelion* sloop under Captain Thomas Staines, which possessed auxiliary oars, perfect for inshore work in the Strait of Bonifacio. To assist them Nelson erected at least one wooden observation and signal post in Sardinia, manned by seamen from sunrise to sunset.[52]

Trying another approach, in February Nelson asked the Sardinians to entrust him with three of their galleys so that he could deploy them with his own guard ship for maximum effect. The viceroy jibbed that he might as well declare war on France as put his navy under British command, but agreed that his own sea officer, Baron Giorgio Andrea Des Geneys, would be sent to the Strait of Bonifacio with a galley and a half-galley and secret orders to cooperate with Pettet or whoever was the senior British officer at Maddalena.

None of this was enough as far as Nelson was concerned, and he resurrected the subject whenever new ministers took the reins of power, standing by his story and emphasising the beggarly state of the island's defences. In the summer of 1804 the viceroy squeezed 600,000 livres out of the Sardinian parliament, the *stamenti*, but the money was squandered, and by November even their galleys in the Strait of Bonifacio were laid up. Britain stumped up £12,000 per annum to help the king with his administration, but little of this fed into defence, and at the end of the year Nelson was begging Melville, a new first lord of the Admiralty, to find £30,000 to £40,000 to enable the Sardinians to 'keep up an appearance until something is decided'. Although Nelson always doubted Russia, he thought a Sardinian appeal to the tsar better than doing nothing.[53]

While Nelson's services were universally admired, his strong opinions sometimes invited moderation. The British government thought sleeping dogs were better left undisturbed in Sardinia and had different priorities. In August 1804 Lords Harrowby and Camden, the new secretaries of state for foreign affairs and war, informed their admiral that it was 'absolutely inexpedient' to detach a military force on 'distant expeditions' at the moment, but if more resources could be found in 1805 the matter would be reassessed as a priority. The door was not entirely closed, and Nelson was asked to continue reporting any opportunities to occupy the island that occurred. Harrowby said that a Captain William Leake of the Royal Artillery was going out to assess the military situation in Albania and the Morea; he might usefully drop in on Sardinia, but 'it is particularly important that no premature suspicions should arise of the occupation, in any contingency, of any part of Sardinia by British troops, as such a suspicion would only serve to hasten the attack of the French'. Nelson could scarcely disguise his disappointment. Lowe had already reconnoitred Sardinia. 'We know everything . . . necessary' about Sardinia, he told Harrowby bluntly, 'namely that it has no money, no troops [and] no means of defence, and the people are unhappy . . . in their present state'. He did not even bother to send Leake to the island.[54]

Sardinia shrank from the blatant intervention that Nelson counselled but treated the admiral with great deference. His Sardinian Majesty later paid tribute to the 'efficacious protection' provided by the British admiral, 'by whose attention and delicacy I have not been committed with the enemy, who is constantly on the watch for occasions to injure me'. Sardinia's reservations were not without sense. If the British landed an expeditionary force that was too small and it had to retreat, Sardinia would be left to her enemies; and if Britain took control of the island, might not she hold on to it, as she had Malta, leaving the king without a throne? Weighing all, the king adopted the safer example of Ferdinand, keeping his head down and giving diplomacy room. Russia was still at the table, bracketing demands for the evacuation of Naples with the security of Sardinia and compensation for her loss of Piedmont. Only if that avenue closed, and Russia and France crossed swords, would Sardinia accept a British force, and then only if Britain would pay for it.[55]

Similar objections met an alternative solution to Sardinia's financial problem that Nelson put to Jackson in October, when negotiations between Russia and France began to stumble. Would the king consider selling Sardinia to the British? Jackson dared not even put the idea to the king before he had heard from Whitehall, but warned Nelson that the idea was legless. The king had already lost Piedmont, and Sardinia was his sole remaining possession; it alone 'kept the crown on his head'. Jackson judged that he would only relinquish Sardinia if 'an equivalent territory' on the mainland was offered in lieu, and if the transfer was agreeable to the Sardinian people.[56]

Nelson had no wish to prejudice the king, and was hugely sympathetic to his plight, but his belief that Sardinia was essential to Britain's interests in the Mediterranean would continue to colour his thinking for the remainder of his command. It was, he told Minto, worth 'ten thousand times as much as Malta', for 'if I lose Sardinia, I lose the French fleet'. As for Britain's ministers, they were not 'bold men'.[57]

6

A battle was Nelson's ultimate answer to the problems of the Mediterranean. Not an old victory, but one 'superior to the Nile', big and decisive enough to change the arithmetic of the war. Storms, mountains of paperwork and frustrating choices never drove the thought from his mind. In August 1804 he had to send the *Amazon* to Malta but begged Captain Parker to return as quickly as possible, 'for the day of battle cannot be far off, when I shall want every frigate, for the French have nearly one for every [line of battle] ship, and we may as well have a battle royal, line of battleships opposed to ships of the line, and frigates to frigates'.[58]

Early in the year the men massing between Toulon and Nice, and the news that Latouche Tréville, the admiral who had repulsed the attack on Boulogne, had assumed command of the French Mediterranean fleet, raised expectations. 'We are, my dear friend, on the eve of great events,' Nelson wrote to Ball. The air was indeed thick with talk. The common opinion was that Spain was about to join the war, throwing her squadrons at Ferrol, Cadiz and Cartagena into the reckoning on the side of Napoleon. Others talked about a Franco-Spanish fleet from Brest and Ferrol passing the Strait to join Latouche Tréville in some grand mischief. If such a junction occurred, Nelson's control of the Mediterranean would be lost.[59]

Nelson plumbed for every scrap of intelligence, sending ships to Rosas and Barcelona for newspapers and information, and preparing for a showdown. He ordered Gore's frigates to withdraw from Cadiz if threatened by superior force, falling back towards him, as he would be meeting the new threat head-on. 'Do not let it escape your lips,' he wrote. 'I am determined to have the first blow. Even if they [the Spaniards] come with their whole eighteen, they shall not join the French. If they come up the Mediterranean, and you have a mind for a shooting party, come with your frigates. Every part of your conduct is like yourself – perfect!'[60]

This was bold talk for the commander of such a minimum force. Nelson had received an Admiralty order the previous November warning him that immediate reinforcements were not to be expected, and he would have to replace worn-out ships one by one, as escorts arrived with convoys. In the spring the arrival of the three-decked *Royal Sovereign* under Pulteney Malcolm and the *Leviathan* under Henry William Bayntun made good the loss of the exhausted *Monmouth* and *Agincourt*, which had to be sent home, but the *Gibraltar* had also been recalled by the Admiralty, and the leaking *Kent* was so unequal to the gales off Toulon that she had to be delegated the duty at Naples. As for frigates, sloops and brigs, Nelson reckoned a force of twenty barely enough. Armed with a squadron that was hardly growing with its responsibilities, Nelson knew that his position would truly be lost if he allowed enemy fleets to combine against him.

This febrile climate eased in March. Spain grew more amenable, abandoning an attempt to shut British men-of-war from its ports unless they were in distress, and prohibiting French privateers from selling British prizes on Spanish territory. In May Nelson learned that Spain had emerged from bruising negotiations with France with a tarnished measure of neutrality. It was precarious, but imminent conflict was averted, and Gore was able to return to Cadiz to watch *L'Aigle* and protect Britain's seaway to the Mediterranean with his three cruisers.

The smell of gunpowder had receded, but Nelson continued planning his battle. During his sojourns in Sardinia, Nelson had many opportunities to speak to his officers about the way he hoped to fight, and that perhaps explains why so little written material about the subject survives. What there is emphasises his faith in the close-quarter encounter and the Royal Navy's superior seamanship and gunnery. His stated intention was to attack the French 'in any place where there is a reasonable prospect of getting fairly alongside of them', in or outside of havens, at night or in the day. Thus he asked his captains to familiarise themselves with such likely battle sites as Hyères Bay, Petite Passe, Grande Passe, Gourjean Bay, La Spezia, Ajaccio and Leghorn roads, and supplied each ship with a chart of Gourjean Bay. Among the admiral's notes are fairly detailed sailing directions for attacking an enemy fleet in the southern anchorage of the roads at Leghorn, with attention to shoals and such landmarks as 'a high white building . . . resembling a light house'. A public order, which described how pendants raised over signals 36 and 37 would advise his ships whether to engage an enemy to starboard or larboard, suggests that he had a mind to confuse his opponents by approaching them head-on in a line of battle on the opposite tack, reserving his decision to steer to leeward or windward of the French line until the last moment. A number of measures also tried to reduce the dangers of 'friendly fire' during engagements in darkness or dense smoke. Proud of his fleet, Nelson expressed *esprit de corps* in dramatic 'team colours', garish like those of fish advertising their dangerous toxins. The hulls of his ships were painted in alternating yellow and black bands running fore and aft, a design that the gun ports turned into a chequerboard pattern. The masts were yellow and the inside of the gun ports red. One who saw these ships in 1805 thought them 'very warlike' but they were also eye-catching and easily recognisable. In addition the British went into action under St George's ensign, and carried standing instructions to raise identification lights at night, and, to further distinguish friend from foe, the admiral advised captains to hail a ship before firing if they were in any doubt about its identity. Signalling was another issue. Nelson wanted to minimise signals in a combat situation, where they could easily be mistaken or obscured, but he could never eliminate them entirely. At some stage he adopted Home Popham's improved signal code, which speeded up communications at sea.[61]

Another change was introduced on 13 February 1804, while at the Maddalenas. Nelson divided his fleet into two divisions for the purposes of sailing and fighting. At sea the ships would proceed in two parallel columns, one consisting of *Canopus*, *Donegal*, *Victory*, *Superb* and *Belleisle*, and the other, under Bickerton of the *Kent*, with the *Renown*, *Triumph* and *Excellent*. These dispositions quickly proved their usefulness when the French began to exercise the Toulon ships out of port in March. Latouche Tréville remained unadventurous. His ships slipped out when the sea looked empty and speedily back when threatened, but the skirmishes that developed were a welcome relief from the previous inactivity.[62]

Nelson was returning from the Maddalenas on the morning of 7 April when he first learned of this new French intrepidity. Hoping they might still be at sea he ordered Bickerton's division to haul 'to the southward', furling their topgallants so that they could not been seen from the shore, but keeping just close enough to Nelson's division to see it from the masthead. By keeping part of his force just beyond the enemy's horizon, he hoped to entice them towards the visible – and apparently vulnerable – part of his force before intercepting them or cutting off their retreat with his second division. But by the time he reached Toulon on the 9th the hostile force was already in retreat. A brief scuffle occurred when the *Amazon* pounced upon a French corn brig off Cape Sepet. The enemy batteries at the cape fired, and three French frigates worked out of Toulon on a fair breeze. The wind was poor for Parker, and he got into some difficulty, casting off his prize and using his boats to tow his frigate away from the advancing foes. For a while it looked as if there might be an engagement, as four French ships of the line also emerged to support their frigates, while Nelson signalled *Donegal*, *Excellent* and *Active* to back Parker. But having rescued their brig, the French had no stomach for further hazards and their whole force withdrew.[63]

On board the *Victory* his lordship was exhilarated by even this measure of French resistance, and hoped it augured further and more profitable meetings. The relative strengths of the opposing fleets had not greatly altered. The French had launched a powerful new flagship, the eighty-gun *Bucentaure*, while Nelson acquired the *Leviathan*, a seventy-four, and three bomb vessels on 10 May. Reinforced by the *Excellent*, Nelson's watch force was generally able to stop up the port, driving impudent French gunboats into cover and exchanging a shot or two with the forts, but Nelson advised against any unequal contests. When his main force was off Toulon the admiral resorted to the divisional system, throwing Bickerton's detachment further out, beyond the ken of adversaries, to entice the enemy out. A number of minor fracas took place, but Nelson soon got used to Latouche Tréville's toe-in-the-water tactics, and judged that the French needed to venture as far as Île de Porquerolles, south-east of Toulon, before they justified a reaction.

For Nelson the most aggravating episode occurred on 14 and 15 June, when eight enemy sail of the line and four frigates 'cut a caper off Sepet'. The engagement opened when *Excellent*, *Amazon* and *Phoebe* fired upon three enemy cruisers skulking beneath a fort at Porquerolles, and the entire French squadron in the outer road of Toulon got underway to extricate them. Nelson supposed this was merely another 'gasconade' but recalled *Excellent* to join the *Victory*, *Canopus*, *Donegal* and *Belleisle* in a short line of battle several leagues south-east of Cape Sicié. The next day Nelson twice hove to west of Porquerolles, inviting the superior enemy force to attack him. There was no more to it than that, but Latouche Tréville submitted a dishonest dispatch to his government claiming that the French had driven the British away. The account was published in the French *Moniteur*, and copied into several English newspapers, including the *Morning Chronicle*, and a piqued Nelson swore that if he ever captured his French counterpart he would either refuse to see him or literally force him to eat his words, for which purpose he presumably preserved a copy of an offending news-sheet. Nelson knew that the British public would never believe him capable of such timidity, but he desperately wanted to catch Latouche Tréville and persisted with attempts to lure him out. On 20 August the *Narcissus*, *Fisgard*, *Niger* and *Ambuscade* were ordered to lay off Porquerolles, as if fishing for prizes. Nelson hoped 'to induce the enemy to get to the eastward', while he slipped his larger force westwards into the Gulf of Lions with the intention of picking up a good wind and swinging back towards Toulon in the hope of cutting off any Frenchmen who had ventured out. The ploy failed, but had it succeeded it would not have discomforted Latouche Tréville. The victor of Boulogne had died on 18 August. 'He is gone and all his lies with him,' Nelson grumbled when he heard the news.[64]

Providentially, the death of the French admiral may have denied Nelson a serious crack at the Toulon fleet, for on 2 July Napoleon had ordered him to break out of Toulon with ten or so ships of the line and sixteen hundred soldiers, and sail through the Strait into the Atlantic. He was then to make a junction with the Rochefort fleet and proceed to Cherbourg with the whole force to await further orders. Contrary to Nelson's belief, which viewed Italy or the east as the most likely destination of the Toulon fleet, Bonaparte prioritised his grand design against England.

Of this matter Nelson scarcely knew. After more than a year at his post his knowledge of the French strategies remained opaque. The news from home was thin, and on 8 July he estimated that he had heard nothing from government for three months. What he gleaned on station was buried in contradictory hearsay and speculation. Enemy ships were ready for sea at Brest, Rochefort and Toulon, and the 'capers' outside Toulon implied that the Mediterranean fleet was preparing for something, but what? The Egyptian foray of 1798, Bruix's cruise of 1799, the French presence on the east coast of Italy and interest in the Morea, even experience of the impractical anti-invasion flotilla of 1801, had conditioned Nelson to think in terms of the eastern Mediterranean. 'It is in this country [the Mediterranean] that Buonoparte wishes to make himself great,' he told Acton, 'and therefore this is the country where large armies and fleets should be placed.' He regarded the French plan to invade Britain as impractical, but it was capable of diverting attention, and allowing the enemy to concentrate strength against his undersized squadron in the Mediterranean. Many intelligent observers, equally in the dark, held the same view. Ball argued that France lacked the sea power to support distant colonies, such as those in the West Indies, and would inevitably seek trade, prestige and empire closer to home. He had no doubt that French interest in the eastern Mediterranean would increase. Jackson was inclined to agree, as did Acton, who cited evidence from Constantinople and intercepted enemy correspondence to support a chilling vision of the French horde using Italy as the stepping stone. Another scintilla pointing in that direction came from Captain Pettet. He reported that an American military officer who had just left Marseilles believed that Egypt was the object of the naval preparations then underway in Toulon and Genoa.[65]

Nelson's mind was not fixed. In September 1803 he conceded that the recent growth of Russian naval power in the eastern Mediterranean made the pickings in that quarter much leaner. Perhaps Bonaparte might now be more likely to send his Mediterranean fleet westwards, possibly against the British West Indies or Ireland. If a large French combination got in the West Indies it had a fair chance of capturing St Lucia, Grenada, St Vincent, Antigua, Nevis and St Kitts, and desolating Britain's rich sugar trade.

No one had convincingly penetrated or tracked the volatile ambitions of the new 'emperor' of the French. Nelson, weighing intelligence as diverse as yellow reporting, the statements of spies and diplomats, waterfront gossip and the hunches of the masters of passing ships, remained in darkness. He was drowning in details of all but the pertinent matter. 'A copy of the French admiral's orders, when he is to put to sea, and where he is destined to, is the only useful information I can care about,' he told Ball. On that subject there was nothing but speculation. 'What do you think? Tell me.' That failure of essential intelligence was, through no fault of Nelson's, to bedevil his campaign.[66]

7

On 23 April 1804 there was a general promotion of admirals, and Nelson was raised to his highest ever professional rank, vice admiral of the white. Murray retained his role as captain of the fleet, but got his flag as a rear admiral of the blue, giving the station a total of four flag officers. Sent from the Admiralty on 15 May, the news reached the fleet in August, while Nelson was in Sardinia watering and unloading eight transports, and he changed his flag from blue to white. The colours of the navy's three ancient squadrons retained their relevance only as instruments of promotion. Nelson had risen from the blue to the white squadron, and would need to pass through the red squadron before becoming a full admiral.

Nelson had now been on station for more than a year. There had been no great battles, but numerous anxieties and irresolvable problems, and throughout the relentless battle against the sea. In the *Victory* Murray and Hardy were weary, and Nelson, who had not put a foot on land since visiting Malta in June 1803, was unwell. The winter had damaged him and the early return of protracted gales in July 1804 threatened to wear him out. He coughed, his hernia inflated, and he complained of gout and rheumatism. Sometimes he could hardly see. He dreaded another winter, and by August had decided to return to England and to seek a reappointment in the spring.

Naturally, the idea carried regrets and misgivings. It was possible that he would not be reappointed, and plenty of admirals were waiting in the wings, including Orde, Keith and Bickerton. Furthermore, a Spanish war, with its promise of silver-laden prizes, did not seem far off. And yet, Nelson sighed, 'if I am in my grave, what are the mines of Peru to me?' On 16 August he wrote to William Marsden, the new secretary to the Admiralty, that it was 'absolutely necessary' that he withdrew to spare his health, but that he longed to return when restored. 'No command ever produces so much happiness to a commander-in-chief,' he said, 'whether in the flag-officers, the captains, or the good conduct of the crews', and he had 'constant marks of approbation' from 'every court in the Mediterranean'. He asked Melville, who now ruled at the Admiralty, to permit him to return home in the *Superb*, which needed serious dockyard repairs, and to appoint Bickerton acting commander-in-chief during his absence. The Admiralty would meet all three of his requests in October, but in case his own arguments lacked sufficient weight, Nelson had asked Acton and Elliot if their Sicilian Majesties would lobby for his return through their minister in London. It was an astute move, since Ferdinand and Maria Carolina were deeply conscious of what they owed Nelson. 'It will be impossible for me to find another true friend equal to the brave and steadfast Nelson,' said the king. In fact, he was so alarmed at Nelson's plan that he begged him to stay and offered houses in Naples and Palermo for his recuperation. Nor were their Sicilian Majesties alone concerned. The King of Sardinia, who had retreated to Gaeta in Naples, where Nelson had promised him a ship if he ever needed one, lamented the admiral's proposed sojourn. He 'should consider [it] a very great loss to the inhabitants of the Mediterranean, and particularly to his subjects'.[67]

For despite all, much had been achieved. 'Patience and perseverance', as Nelson used to say, 'will accomplish many things.' Reviewing his work thus far, he could congratulate himself despite the disappointments. With minimal support and guidance he had maintained an effective presence in the Mediterranean, and if enemy privateers continued to be troublesome, particularly in the Strait of Gibraltar and the Adriatic, the seaways had remained open, and in the words of Gore 'there is not such a thing as a French man of war on the ocean'. Due to a lack of ships, the blockade of Genoa had manifestly lacked enough teeth, but the number of ships entering the port fell from 953 in 1802 to 136 in 1804 and its economy was stagnating. The integrity of Sicily and Sardinia had been preserved, despite disagreements about how they might best be defended.[68]

Naples was in a less enviable position. Gallic pressure had grown, and under the threat of invasion Acton was forced to step down as the minister for foreign affairs, retiring to Palermo where he could act more quietly. The king explained to Nelson that he had had no choice. 'To you, my dear Lord Nelson,' he added, 'I recommend myself again whatever may occur in case of the war's renewal.' Acton's replacement was that same Chevalier Antonio Micheroux who had acted the unfortunate go-between in Naples in 1799 and been a negotiator of the treaty of Florence. Without Acton the politics of Naples destabilised. The king resorted to his usual opium – hunting – and the queen, as ever as brave as a lioness, was contemptuous of her leading ministers. Micheroux was stupid and unreliable, and the Prince of Luzzi a shapeless chameleon changing to every circumstance. She became increasingly ungovernable and imprudent. In desperation their Majesties offered France six million livres if she would remove her soldiers from their kingdom, but without success.[69]

Nelson had suffered setbacks here as in Sardinia. Neither power had embraced the internal reforms he thought necessary to counteract the spread of Jacobinism. In fact one of his last letters to Acton warned that the French would benefit from 'the feudal system and oppressive laws of vassalage' in Sicily. 'Turn this over in your enlightened mind,' he said. 'Mankind have more enlarged ideas than in former times . . .. Something must be done, or these countries where the feudal system prevails will be lost.'[70]

In what were perhaps his most questionable ideas, he had also favoured stronger responses to the French threats to the Two Sicilies and Sardinia, at a time when Britain simply lacked the means to contain the likely consequences. Yet the tense brinkmanship prevailed, with each side ready to respond tit for tat to any hostile move. France's occupation of Neapolitan ports on the Adriatic prompted Russia to strengthen the Ionian Islands, which in turn threw Bonaparte into a public rage. Almost foaming at the mouth, he threatened to pack eight thousand more soldiers into Naples and to keep them there until Russia and Britain were out of Corfu and Malta. But in the event only fifteen hundred French soldiers reinforced St Cyr, Britain and Russia remained vigilant without committing the resources to break the stalemate and a simmering peace endured. Britain had lost tens of thousands of redcoats in the West Indies the previous decade, and was still suffering from the mistimed dismemberment of her armed forces during the peace of Amiens. Given her inability to spare substantial forces for the Mediterranean, her ministers endorsed a policy of caution, and if Nelson thought it less than was required it was not entirely barren of results. The admiral eventually conceded that to occupy Messina, as he had formerly advocated, would 'hasten the downfall of the Kingdom of Naples'.[71]

By the end of 1804, however, the great powers were reassessing the situation, and bracing themselves for robust solutions more to Nelson's liking. In the autumn the negotiations between Russia and France had exhausted the patience of both parties. Russia was afraid of French ambitions in the Adriatic and Germany, and in November signed a treaty with Austria that bound the two to support each other if they were attacked by France. Furthermore, Russia and Austria agreed to resist any French expansion into Germany, Italy or the eastern Mediterranean. Encouraged, Maria Carolina began some barely bridled sabre rattling, declaring that she would fall 'gloriously' among 'the long list of those sacrificed to Bonaparte's ambition', and setting Damas the task of reforming her army. Alquier, the French ambassador, spoke of the queen's 'madness' and even Nelson worried whether she was using her head. He knew the value of allies, but was sceptical of their promises, remembering the scorching Austria had given him in 1798.[72]

Britain, too, was finding a new vitality. In May 1804 Addington's lethargic government fell, and Pitt was again summoned to lead a nation at war. His powerful political ally, Henry Dundas, Viscount Melville, formerly a home secretary and conscientious secretary of state for war, accepted the key post of first lord of the Admiralty. Melville and his successors were shocked to see the destruction that St Vincent had left behind him. There were too few seaworthy ships and too few stores to repair them, and relations between the Admiralty and the inferior boards and contractors were at rock bottom. Out on station, Nelson was glad to see the back of the earl and his cronies, whom he blamed for destroying the navy. 'I care nothing about them,' he told Emma, 'and now they can do no harm to any one, I shall not abuse them.' Others were less charitable. Lord Barham, Melville's successor, referred to St Vincent's actions as 'madness and imbecility in the extreme'. Pitt certainly had an enormous task ahead of him. The country's defences, including coastal fortifications, needed renovating; ships had to be built, repaired and manned; and the professional army, which stood at a mere 87,000 men, had to be increased. Britain also wanted a more positive strategy. Addington had fought an unenterprising defensive war. Pitt began the painful job of looking for allies who could help him land a knockout punch.[73]

The only foreseeable spine for a new coalition was the accord that had developed between Britain and Russia. Since 1803 both had collaborated in defending the Morea, as we shall see, and in the summer of 1804 the two began discussing a full-blown alliance. As part of it, Britain resolved to send an expeditionary force of five thousand men to Malta to support Russia in the defence of the Two Sicilies. The combination of Britain, Russia and through the latter Austria was one that Bonaparte genuinely feared. It had temporarily cleared Italy of the French in 1799.[74]

As one buffalo rose to its feet snorting defiantly, its antagonist was advancing with its bossed head down. Bonaparte was refining and invigorating his plan to invade England, although even a member of his own council doubted that the operation was more than an elaborate bluff to distract Britain's attention from other theatres. Napoleon's flotilla of unmanageable shallow-draft vessels needed several tides to cross the Channel, and they were incapable of landing anything like an adequate force in England under the nose of the Royal Navy. To stand a chance the flotilla had to be covered by ships of the line, but the emperor now proposed an imaginative strategy to draw the British fleet from the Channel so that his battleships could slip by and win a temporary command of the narrow seas. As outlined to his minister of marine, Denis Decrès, on 29 September 1804, the plan involved both the Toulon and Rochefort squadrons running their blockades and uniting in the West Indies. Vice Admiral Villeneuve, the veteran of the Nile and Malta, was placed in command of the Toulon fleet and directed to escape in October, dodging Nelson (which Bonaparte thought no difficult task) and passing the Strait to collect *L'Aigle* from Cadiz and make the Atlantic run to join the Rochefort ships under Rear Admiral Edouard Burgues, Comte de Missiessy. All being well the French would eventually be able to count upon fifteen sail of the line, several cruisers and five thousand troops. Their job was to create panic in Britain's overseas colonies by attacks as far apart as the Caribbean, St Helena and West Africa, and while the Royal Navy came out to protect their colonies, Villeneuve would double back to Europe, break the blockade of Ferrol to obtain reinforcements, and join the Brest fleet for an attack on England or Ireland.

It was a grand plan in the Napoleonic style, embracing a destructive feint to divert attention from the real leap for the jugular, and in theory it was plausible. But in detail the strategy was shot through with holes; one wish rested upon another to create a shaky house of cards. It assumed that Missiessy and Villeneuve could both escape, reach the West Indies and return unscathed; that the British fleets could be outwitted and outsailed; and that Britain would endanger her command of the Channel to chase after far-ranging French forces. No less rooted in fantasy was the notion that ill-manned French ships and inexperienced seamen could efficiently execute complicated global movements in real conditions of sea, wind and tide.

With the Anglo-Russian coalition and Bonaparte destined for a major smash-up it was not the most appropriate time for Britain's greatest warrior, the veritable sword of Albion, to talk of quitting the Mediterranean.

XIX

THE EASTERN QUESTION

Nelson, by valour led to deathless fame,
All toils surmounted, and all foes o'ercame,
Braved every danger, calm and undismay'd,
Whilst some new triumph marked each step he
made.

Georgiana, Duchess of Devonshire

I

THEY called it 'the Eastern Question'. An open wound that ran through the politics of nineteenth-century Europe, its heart the chaotic, far-flung, crumbling empire of the Ottoman Porte. Everyone knew that this sprawling brawling archaic structure was slowly collapsing, yet it occupied most of the eastern basin of the Mediterranean, and ran westwards along the shore of North Africa as far as the Strait of Gibraltar, and the fear lay in what might replace it. A weak giant occupying areas of great strategic importance was not, after all, necessarily a threatening one, but if its splintering territories fell into aggressive hands the stability and balance of power in Europe could be threatened. If Nelson was to protect British interests in the Mediterranean and contain the French he had to watch this bubbling cauldron in the east.

Three great powers eyed these wavering regions, France, Russia and Britain. Since Bonaparte's flagrant incursion into the Porte's dominions in 1798, France had been repairing her relations with Turkey, signing a peace treaty in 1802 and re-establishing normal diplomatic relations. French merchantmen again traversed eastern waters, passing the Dardanelles into the Black Sea, but there was little trust, for her ambitions still flickered underneath. Napoleon resented the loss of the Ionian Islands and Egypt, which had promised rich exotic trades and bases for more eastern adventures. In 1801 the French sent Horace Sebastiani to investigate the prospects of exploiting areas within the Turkish empire, including Egypt, and two years later the garrisons that marched into Ancona, Pescara, Brindisi and Otranto on the Adriatic coast of Italy told their own story. They were within striking distance of the Ionian Islands, from which the French had been expelled in 1799, and Albania and the Greek Morea, areas of the Ottoman empire in which Bonaparte also took a special interest. Here, he realised, were possible bridgeheads to new eastern conquests.

In the short run, Britain and Russia saw advantages in maintaining the status quo, propping up the Ottoman empire if only to shut out France. Both committed themselves to defending her if she was attacked. However, if their efforts failed they were equally determined to protect their essential spheres of interest in a general meltdown. Russia would preserve her recently acquired access to the Mediterranean through the Black Sea, and control of the Ionian Islands on the west coast of Greece. Now reincarnated as the Septinsular Republic, with a capital in Corfu, these islands were effectively a client state of Russia, whose government was dominated by the Russian plenipotentiary, Count Giorgio Mocenigo. Russia's other interest was in keeping France out of nearby Albania and the Morea. Ancient attachments, including a commitment to Christianity, had also given Russia a protective interest in Greece, where disaffected populations were vulnerable to interference from any foreign power that promised to reduce the oppression of the Turkish yoke.

For Britain the major interests lay in her extensive eastern commerce and Egypt. British trade in the Levant had declined since its heyday, but some fifty ships still plied those waters with £200,000 worth of exports a year. 'Fish ships' carried Newfoundland fish up the Adriatic to Venice, Trieste and Fiume. English woollen cloth went into the Ionian Sea to Zante, Cephalonia and Patras in the Septinsular Republic, threaded up the Aegean Sea to Constantinople, Smyrna and Salonica, and through the Dardanelles into the Black Sea, or bore towards Cyprus, Syria and Egypt to be exchanged for grain, currants, silk, mohair, alum, cotton, fustick, aloes, honey, olive oil, spices, almonds, drugs and other luxury goods capable of being re-exported from England to the continent for handsome returns. Even the Black Sea, hitherto little known to the British, was attracting interest as a source of grain and naval stores. Nelson had to find the ships to make the sea safe for all this traffic. Egypt, which gave some security to these trades, was also a backdoor to India. After finally overthrowing Bonaparte's expeditionary force in 1801, Britain had no intention of allowing the French back into Egypt, but it remained an area of inherent instability. When Hallowell called at Alexandria in February 1804, he advised the governor and other officers, including the minister of the Porte, to sink ships in the access channels to the harbour and raise other timely defences to frustrate further French attack. Despite current indications that France was preparing another expedition, he could make no headway, and warned Nelson that only British sea power could save Egypt.[1]

Stinted for ships, there was little Nelson could directly do for Egypt except to ensure, as far as he could, that the French did not reach it. In response to

Hallowell's pessimism, Ball took the liberty of sending the *Agincourt* ship of the line to show the flag off Egypt, but Nelson took a dim view of this unauthorised deployment, which doubtfully placed an underpowered force in an isolated place. Action was, rather, needed to protect eastern trade routes from corsairs, and to stop any threatening enemy naval forces nearer home. Eastern merchant convoys left and returned to Malta, where Nelson based a small squadron with orders to protect trade and monitor the French ports. The officer he selected for this difficult work was William Edward Cracraft of the forty-four-gun *Anson*, an experienced and able commander. Mindful of the strain involved, Nelson offered to bring Cracraft back into the main fleet in December 1803, but he stuck grimly to his task and was still at work in 1805.[2]

Malta was a convenient British base, and if this was an area that Nelson entered without active allies, he was not short of sympathy. Again, Bonaparte's compulsive aggression helped, driving the powers towards defensive coalitions. The Porte understood the threat from France, and encouraged by William Drummond, the British minister in Constantinople, Sultan Selim wrote to Nelson to entreat his protecting arm. The admiral's personal standing in the Porte also remained high, and the cabin of Hussein, the *Capitan Pasha*, or grand admiral, was decorated with prints of Nelson's victories. When Hussein died in October 1803, he was succeeded by Nelson's friend Abdul Cadir Bey, who added personal admiration to his partiality for the British. Russia, with the Ionian Islands and the Morea close to her heart, was equally alert. In St Petersburg it was made clear to the British ambassador, Admiral Sir John Borlase Warren, that while Russia preferred the role of neutral mediator, she would set her armies in motion if France struck across the Adriatic. This was an important caveat, because given the immobility of Prussia and Austria the only foreseeable spine to a new anti-French coalition capable of confronting Napoleon was an Anglo-Russian accord. The east, therefore, was not the most salient aspect of Nelson's work, but it was an area where British and Russian interests coalesced, pregnant with diplomatic potential. There were already political meeting points, in Constantinople, where Drummond, Chevalier A. D. Italinsky the Russian minister, and the Porte interfaced, and in Corfu, where Cracraft, Spiridion Foresti the British 'resident', and the Russian plenipotentiary, Count Mocenigo, could also concert policy.[3]

Within months of Nelson's arrival in the Mediterranean, the Morea and Albania threw him into the centre of a new initiative of the first importance. The Morea was the region south of the Gulf of Corinth. It contained some 400,000 people, most of them abused Greeks 'borne down by oppression' and divided among a score of petty semi-autonomous chieftainships, of which Mustapha Pasha of Tripolizza, at Patras, was the ostensible overall governor. Despite Russian and British attempts to encourage the Porte to improve the lot of the Greeks, they were richly discontented, and occupied a ragged terrain of difficult communications, defended by a few ruined, ill-equipped castles. Not surprisingly, Bonaparte saw the Morea as ripe for contamination, and in the spring of 1803 a French naval brig landed powder, lead and arms at Maina and tried to raise a local following among the 15,000 warriors who inhabited the area. Later, captured by Nelson's ships, the commander of the brig admitted that he had been ordered to prepare for a French invasion of the Morea. Overt disaffection was quickly stamped out by the Turks, pro-French chiefs were killed or hounded into the mountains, and their followers 'almost entirely done away'. But a rump remained, seduced by inflammatory messages from French officials in Zante that an army was still coming 'to relieve you from that state of slavery'.[4]

Shortly after Nelson's return to the Mediterranean there was evidence that that larger project was underway. French troops began to crowd into the Italian ports of Ancona, Brindisi, Otranto and Taranto, some only fifty miles across the Strait of Otranto from the Morea, and biscuit was baked for them night and day. Cracraft noted that there were not enough boats in these ports to ship even two hundred men to the Morea or Albania, but that raised the sinister possibility that reinforcements were expected from Toulon, Marseilles, Genoa or Leghorn, where transports were known to be assembling and the Toulon fleet looked ready to sail. As late as June 1804 intelligence milked from a careless French general in Leghorn predicted that an expeditionary force of up to 15,000 men under Jean Louis Reynier, including brigades of Greeks, Copts and Mohammedans, would embark in France and Italy and try to run through Nelson's blockade and establish a foothold in the Morea, where it would rally disaffected Greeks to the north and south. From there it could threaten the Ionian Islands, Belgrade or Constantinople, or simply await a further erosion of the Turkish empire. Whether Napoleon's dreams were flying as high as this is difficult to say. The whole Morea project may have been no more than a blind to divert Nelson's attentions eastwards while his grander design against Britain went forward. Elliot certainly thought so. Nonetheless, Bonaparte was adept at heating several irons in the fire at a time, and watching where opportunities unfolded, so the Morea invasion cannot be ruled out. Nelson, who was not unmindful of Napoleon's penchant for deception, was sure there was something to it. When the French put it about that the transports in Marseilles were bound for the Bay of Biscay, he retorted, 'I do not believe a word of this voyage, but supposing they are fitting out half the g[un] b[oats] reported they can only be for . . . conveying the army which is in the heel of Italy . . . into Sicily and probably to Corfu and the Morea and Adriatic.' British, Russian and Turkish intelligence portrayed a genuine threat to the Morea, and angry French finger-pointing after it was dissipated suggest that at least some were annoyed that the enterprise did not go forward.[5]

This little-known crisis was one of Nelson's most significant contributions in these years. He may have stopped a Morea project in its tracks, and certainly helped draw Britain out of diplomatic isolation. In Constantinople the sultan met the threat by appealing for Nelson's assistance and mobilising his own forces. In St Petersburg Warren had promised that Britain would cooperate with Russia by October 1803, and Foresti, the British 'resident' in Corfu, was given £10,000 to counteract French influence in the Morea. On 11 August, Nelson had already begun increasing Cracraft's squadron to half a dozen cruisers, *Anson*, *Juno*, *Arrow*, *Bittern*, *Morgiana* and *Jalouse*, and extending its operations to cover all the Adriatic ports occupied by the enemy, a serious deployment given his shortage of small ships. Calling at Corfu, Cracraft concerted the defence of the region with Foresti and Mocenigo. Both Turkey and Russia poured resources into the trouble spot. The Porte fielded a regiment of artillery and 11,000 men, about half raised in the Adriatic, repaired castles, stockpiled munitions and supplies, and maintained a significant if intermittent naval presence. Cadir Bey, the *Capitan Pasha*, had sixteen warships in the Adriatic in November 1803, and the following summer Seremet Bey was patrolling with a small detachment of cruisers. In 1803 the crisis had found Russia with only a decommissioned frigate in the Ionian Islands, but by the summer of 1804 that strength had risen to 10,000 troops and six warships, and a year later to 12,000 men and fifteen ships, four of them of the line. The Russo-Turkish forces were a formidable deterrent, but these as yet unaligned powers had to remain scrupulously upon the defensive, and were authorised to engage the enemy only if attacked. It was Nelson's ships, actively blockading Toulon and the Adriatic ports, which really aborted the enemy project.[6]

By the autumn of 1804 the scare had passed. John Philip Morier, a British agent landed in the Morea in April of that year, found little interest in the French. In the autumn the troops in the Italian ports were dispersing, and early in 1805 Nelson's captains reported 'no appearance of any [hostile] preparations whatever' on the coast. But whether a real threat or smoke, the episode had united the eastern powers. The links between the Porte and Russia had become close enough for one to remark that the politics of Constantinople were made in St Petersburg. Nelson held the confidence of all parties. When Turkey's relationship with France withered at the end of 1804, after the sultan refused to recognise Napoleon's claim to be emperor of the French, she renewed her appeals for Nelson's protection. Russia, too, curried his aid, directly from St Petersburg, and through Count Simon Woronzow, the Russian minister in London, and Mocenigo in Corfu. They begged him to cover the Ionian Islands until their reinforcements could get into position, and in the summer of 1804, when Mocenigo drew up a comprehensive plan for the defence of the Septinsular Republic, he submitted it for Nelson's 'superior judgement'. The British admiral advised the Russian Adriatic squadron to remain together so that it could meet emergencies with concentrated force, and found his observations 'highly approved'.[7]

Coalition building was an exasperating road, and Nelson sometimes despaired that it would ever achieve a worthwhile end. Underneath, however, he gauged Bonaparte the common disturber of the human race, and knew that only a coalition would bring him down. 'I cannot help wishing Europe to be the bundle of sticks against France,' he wrote the Queen of Naples. 'If it is good to temporise, let all do it; if to go to war, let all go to war.' Unfortunately the powers allowed 'small states to fall and to serve the enormous power of France, without appearing to reflect that every state which is annexed to France makes their [own] existence as independent state[s] more precarious'.[8]

Not the least consequence of the Morea affair was that it left Britain, Russia and the Porte talking again about common ground and becoming that 'bundle of sticks'.

2

The Morea crisis came, blustered and went, but Nelson's duty to protect British trade in the area was perennial and because of the geography more difficult. The French presence on the east coast of Italy made the Adriatic and Ionian seas a veritable rookery of corsairs, and while French merchantmen were driven off the seas or forced to hide under false flags, privateers thrived on conflict and multiplied. Three British merchant ships were lost in the Adriatic during the summer of 1803. The corsairs in the region operated from the Cisalpine Republic, an Italian client state of France, and ports occupied by the French in Naples or elsewhere, but they also exploited neutral harbours, sensing the reluctance of the non-aligned states to stand up to the colossus of Europe. From the Gulf of Corinth south to Cerigo (Kithira) hostile privateers haunted channels and ports oblivious of sovereignty, pouncing upon unsuspecting merchantmen or virtually blockading them if they took refuge in supposedly safe havens. Further north the Adriatic was controlled by Austria, which had acquired the Venetian territories in the treaty of Campo Formio in 1797, but even her officials seemed unhappy about enforcing the neutrality of their ports. According to accepted practice, hostilities were forbidden within two miles of a neutral territory, but weak local authorities frequently turned a blind eye.

Nelson's means of protecting trade were inadequate. Malta was his base for the outward and inward convoys into the Adriatic, Aegean and Levant, but he often had only one ship to shepherd upwards of a dozen charges instead of the standard two. Some impatient masters chose to 'run' rather than wait for the convoys to form, while others tired of the discipline of sailing in company and abandoned them during the voyage. In May 1804 Nelson was infuriated by the *Betsy*, a fish ship bound for Fiume, which broke with her convoy in spite of the protests of the escorting sloop, *Morgiana*, under Robert Raynsford, and found herself in the hands of a French privateer off the island of Cherso, within a few miles of her destination. Nelson let it be known that such imprudence had to be discouraged, but two ships slipped away from *Morgiana* when she next brought a convoy up the Adriatic in November.[9]

Few powers took a robust stance against abuses of neutrality, but a strong British advocate such as Spiridion Foresti could make a difference. Foresti exposed a French attempt to supply their merchantmen with bogus flags and passes from the Septinsular Republic, and his vociferous complaints about two corsairs that blockaded a Maltese vessel in an Ionian port led to the French minister in Corfu meekly ordering them away. France was wary about offending Russia, but elsewhere it was different and in the summer of 1804 at least fourteen French privateers remained active in the Adriatic.[10]

The first of Nelson's officers to confront the 'neutral' problem in the Adriatic was John Fyffe of the *Cyclops*, who conducted a convoy to Trieste in July 1803. Two of his armed tenders were temporarily detained by the Austrian authorities in Venice after seizing some ships that the British believed to be Cisalpine privateers masquerading under Austrian colours. The issue was whether the legitimacy of the prizes should be decided by due process in the British vice-admiralty courts or by Venetian officials, and it had to be referred to Vienna before Fyffe's case was conceded. Concurrently, Fyffe was embroiled in a second and trickier dispute concerning three British merchant ships taken into Ancona by a Cisalpine corsair. Technically, Ancona was neutral, part of the papal domain, but the French had established a military camp outside the town and pretty much did as they wished. Fyffe complained that the privateer had been illegally manned by Roman subjects, but the town governor said that there was nothing he could do even if that were true. In the brief period of time Fyffe had before leaving for Malta with a return convoy, he managed to retrieve the crews of his tenders, but failed to resolve either dispute. Nelson sympathised, and was so pleased with Fyffe's efforts to defend the British flag that he promised him a more active vessel.[11]

Austria eventually paid reparations, but Ancona remained a thorn in Nelson's side. In February 1804 a prize of HMS *Arrow* sought refuge in the port, and the French attempted to impound her as if the town were her own. 'The neutrality of this port is most shamefully abused,' raged the local British representative, 'the treatment of our poor countrymen in July last throws a slur on Ancona.' Helpless himself, he pleaded for Nelson to flex muscles. 'We have nobody in all this country to attend to our interest, and unless his lordship tells them in some way that they must respect the laws of neutrality, we will every moment become the dupes of French artifices and low intrigues.'[12]

The last straw occurred in June 1804 and the officer at the sharp end was again Raynsford of the *Morgiana*. A convoy he was escorting to Trieste was attacked by two privateers within Austrian territorial waters. *Morgiana* drove the attackers into the neutral port of Umago, south of Trieste, but while thus engaged lost one of her charges, which was pursued by a third corsair into

Trieste itself and seized under the guns of the mole. If Raynsford's account is to be believed both acts were clear infringements of neutrality, and he complained vigorously to the governor of Trieste through the local British consul, the geriatric Edward Stanley. The Austrian authorities were embarrassed but afraid to quarrel with the French, and Stanley was almost as sluggish. As the *Morgiana* made her way back to Malta with the homeward trade, the corsair and her British prize were still being held pending a decision.[13]

In Nelson's opinion, it was time for a strong defence of British rights, and he authorised Cracraft to attack enemy corsairs in any base that allowed them to abuse its neutrality. Moreover, he addressed secret orders to Thomas Staines of the *Camelion* on 1 September 1804, withholding them even from the Admiralty itself. Staines entered the northern Adriatic as if on a routine patrol, but his brief was to hunt down privateers and pirates. If a senior officer tried to redeploy him, he was armed with an exemption signed by the commander-in-chief. Staines was in action in October, and for a couple of months studiously rooted around the many small islands that hid corsairs, but no prizes were taken. He did rescue the British merchant ship the *Morgiana* had left in Trieste, finally relinquished by the Austrians, and was satisfied that he had temporarily driven the raiders into hiding.[14]

The *guerre de course* was never eliminated from the Adriatic, and the lure of plunder constantly attracted new fortune hunters. Off Ragusa Corbet of the *Bittern* came across 'a new species of corsair', one of a number of small, lightly armed boats manned by Cisalpine soldiers and sent out by local military officers without any regular letters of marque whatsoever. Nevertheless, Nelson's system of convoys, patrols and holding neutrals to account reduced serious losses, and a number of privateers met their reckoning. When the British encountered corsairs in neutral waters they became adept at manoeuvring them into firing the first shots, and so justifying retaliation. In January 1804 *Anson* and *Morgiana* cornered a corsair at the island of Milo. When the French landed guns and attempted to deter the British ships with a cross-fire, they unwittingly provided Cracraft with the very pretext he needed to send his boats in to take possession. A creek in the island of Cephalonia saw an exemplary British attack on the morning of 1 May 1804. Lieutenant Robert Corner, commanding two boats of Captain Lewis Shepheard's *Thisbe*, was sent into a craggy opening in the coast to pursue a notorious lateen-rigged corsair, *La Véloce*, which had cocked a snook at neutrality by seizing a British merchantman less than a mile from the neighbouring island of Ithaca. The prize had been recaptured, but her master and a boy were still prisoners on the privateer, which by British lights justified an attack in neutral waters. It was tricky because the hostile vessel disgorged most of her men, who scrambled ashore and squirmed behind rocks to level muskets at the approaching boats. As Corner took the lead boat in he met a sharp volley, including grape from a gun on the prow of the privateer. Two of the lieutenant's men went down, leaving him with only five fit to board, including the ship's clerk. In a moment, Corner decided that rather than stand off to wait for reinforcements from his second boat, he would dash forward before the French could reload. His men stormed impetuously over the side of *La Véloce*, liberating the British prisoners and taking the ship and fourteen or fifteen of her crew. The French protested at Shepheard's breach of neutrality, and Russia complained to London, but Nelson insisted his officers had behaved properly. Neutrals could expect no less, he said, when they habitually allowed French corsairs to abuse their privileges. On this occasion King George himself vindicated the *Thisbe*, but when Corner died in 1820 he was still only a lieutenant.[15]

The protection of trade assumed greater strategic significance in view of Britain's search for cheaper sources of timber, hemp, rope, canvas and tar, the resources that were essential to the country's sea power and security. The crisis in the reserves of English oak was particularly worrying, and before Nelson left England Vansittart had suggested he investigate what was to be had in the Dalmatian forests on the Adriatic. In 1803 the Navy Board commissioned John Leard of Fiume to locate new supplies of timber and other naval stores in the imperial Austrian forests in Hungary, Croatia and Slovenia. The French had imported naval stores from the Adriatic, but Britain's eastern search never quite fulfilled its promise. As Leard described it to Nelson, the pusillanimity of the Austrian emperor was a major stumbling block. Austria prohibited the export of oak to the 'belligerent' powers, and when Leard tried to acquire it covertly through a Hungarian agent, it could not be shipped until a road had been completed in 1805. Albanian oak proved equally difficult to access, hamstrung by inadequate roads and the whim of a local headman, the Bashaw of Scutari. An attempt made by the British government to purchase arms through Trieste also failed, and it wasted the time that two of Nelson's sixty-fours took to visit the port at the end of 1803. Hemp proved an easier commodity to find than timber, and again using the agency of an 'imperial' subject, Leard shipped some through Cherso island, beyond the eyes of French agents. Several shipments of hemp, cordage, tar and associated stores, one alone amounting to fifty-two tons of material, were made at the end of 1803 and beginning of 1804, but the supplies generally proved to be expensive and of uneven quality, and Nelson directed the naval storekeeper at Malta to use Adriatic hemp only when alternative supplies were not available at an affordable rate.[16]

If Leard disappointed, so did the superficially more promising and mesmeric Ali Pasha of Jannina, the Albanian warlord whose writ ran over a wild hinterland that rose grandly from behind a rocky, wave-lashed shoreline. It was the home of numerous fearsome clans dominated by Ali, who manifested only a loose subservience to the Porte while extending his power from northern Albania to the Gulf of Corinth in an astonishing career of conquest, plunder, intrigue, murder and massacre. Russia considered the ambitious chieftain a threat to the

Greeks, especially after his defeat of the Greek Sulliotes in December 1803, and attempted to undermine him, and the British Foreign Office cautioned their diplomats against an involvement in his schemes. But some closer to hand, including Nelson, saw Ali differently. They beheld a powerful, intelligent figure, able to summon 30,000 men to his back, who feared the French and promised an abundance of natural naval resources.

Nelson's attitude to Ali was formed during his previous period in the Mediterranean. The pasha had sent gifts and congratulations, and seemed worth cultivating. Nelson had recommended Britain send a pair of pistols ('a few hundred pounds would have [then] made him ours for ever'), but his recommendations had been passed around several offices until the admiral 'gave it up'. Spiridion Foresti also thought Ali a usable tool. Afraid of both Russia and France, he was keen on a British alliance and ready to offer harbours and raw materials, including timber and fresh beef. Ali's most direct overtures were made through William Hamilton, the secretary of Lord Elgin, former ambassador in Constantinople. In May 1803 Hamilton reported that Ali had offered all Britain desired, including permission to form a permanent settlement at the port of Panormo. True, Ali was cruel, despotic and ill educated, but he had created order in his dominions, was 'one of the most powerful and energetic [pashas] in European Turkey', and 'much attached' to Britain. In September 1803 Lord Hobart, the secretary of war, took the bait and directed Nelson to investigate the uses of Albania.[17]

On 24 November Nelson ordered Cracraft to visit Panormo to ascertain what Ali could supply. The mission was not accomplished without drama, since the *Anson* ran aground off Corfu and had to return to Malta for a refit. With a pilot provided by Foresti, Cracraft persisted and reached his destination, only to find Panormo a depressingly small, steep-sided bay set against bleak, bare marble mountains, and unnavigable to all but boats able to cling close to the shore. After examining several similar bays, Cracraft concluded that 'no establishment' suitable for warships could be made, nor did the population offer any 'considerable' demand for 'our manufactures'. The interior produced only 'precarious' supplies of cattle, and, as for timber, there was none. Morier, who examined the area later, also pointed out that beyond a coastal road the terrain was almost impenetrable, with formidable mountains cut by difficult passes. None of this boded well for the shipment of bulk supplies. Ali was an uncomfortable ally, in constant conflict with neighbouring chiefdoms, but Nelson was loath to give him up and recommended that his request for a cutter and two artillerymen to improve his defences be granted. Even the hitherto suspicious Russians had second thoughts about him after his unblinking promise to furnish thousands of men when the Toulon fleet escaped in February 1805, but hopes that he held the key to safe harbours and naval stores were delusory.[18]

The quest for naval supplies turned over more difficult ground further east, in Russian and Turkish territories about the Black Sea. The British government sent an agent, William Eton, to purchase provisions and stores in the Black Sea in 1803, and the following spring Nelson detailed Lieutenant Frederick Woodman to take two store ships to Odessa to collect the spoils, reconnoitring Russian fortifications at Sebastopol and Cherson and making some appropriate navigational charts while he had the opportunity. Ball also dispatched a representative with 'a large amount' of public money to purchase grain on behalf of Malta, but little but delay and confusion awaited either emissary. Eton was unscrupulous and slippery, and Woodman found nothing more than wheat and forty tons of salted provisions waiting for him, while his naval stores were still making complicated journeys down the Dnieper and elsewhere with delivery dates in September. Woodman was able to make exemplary reports about an area that was still somewhat mysterious to the British, but fluid supplies and stable prices were unrealistic. Moreover, when they filtered through in the autumn they were not always of a satisfactory quality. The pork supplied was unfit to eat, the deal planks too 'sappy' for deck use, and some of the other purchases so unsuitable for naval use that they were sold to the public. By Nelson's lights, the Adriatic and Black Seas were supplementary sources of provisions and stores rather than serious regular alternatives. Apart from issues of price, quantity and quality, their supplies were insecure, depending upon the vagaries of Austrian, Turkish and Russian goodwill.[19]

The eastern Mediterranean remained a potential hot spot, particularly the Adriatic. The French lacked outlets further east, and British ships went relatively unmolested in the Levant and the Aegean and Black Seas. Early in 1805 the build-up of Russian sea power in the Adriatic encouraged Nelson to scale down his commitment, and Cracraft was transferred westwards to the region outside the Strait. The Russian squadron was a deterrent, but Nelson never felt secure about it, and continued to regard a French attempt upon the Morea as a possibility.

However, it was another dominion of the Porte that gave the British admiral the greatest aggravation, one that lay much further west on the coast of North Africa. It was the largest and most formidable of the Barbary states, Algiers.

3

As Nelson expected, the maverick Barbary powers absorbed an unwelcome proportion of time and distracted from greater matters, but they could not be ignored. Under blood-red flags their cruisers stalked the narrow waterways between North Africa and Spain, Sardinia and Sicily, and brazenly hunted prizes and people along the shores of Italy. Some Tunisian raiders landed in Calabria, capturing a four-gun fort and marching a dozen miles inland to round up two hundred prisoners. Although they paid annual tribute to the sultan, these states were largely laws unto themselves, but Nelson felt them worth cultivating. They were sources of fresh provisions, and could, if so minded, offer harbours, trade and false flags and papers to the French, especially as almost all the Barbary ports were influenced by Jewish immigrant communities, some of which had strong mercantile connections to France. In addition, Nelson had the idea that he could increase Britain's influence with Italian states such as Sardinia if he could intercede on their behalf and offer them some protection from the ravages of the feared corsairs of North Africa.[20]

When last on the station, Nelson had found the Barbary powers uncertain about whether Britain or France looked the stronger horse. He had punished, rewarded and exhorted, and established some rapport with Tunis and Tripoli, successfully playing an honest broker in their disputes with Italy and Portugal. Algiers, the most powerful of these powers, had remained its intransigent self, but all were notoriously fickle, and in 1803 Tripoli was in the midst of a naval war with the United States.

Nelson inherited a serious problem with Algiers. John Falcon had taken up the post of British consul general there in 1800, and somehow cajoled its ruler, Mustapha Dey, into recognising his old enemies the Maltese as British subjects under the protection of His Britannic Majesty, a status indeed difficult to deny after Britain's retention of the island. Accordingly, Maltese ships gained immunity to Algerian corsairs by a treaty ratified by the dey on 19 March 1801. But Falcon still ran into great hostility, fanned, he thought, by a group of influential merchants that he called 'the Jew Directory', in imitation of the revolutionary French government. The Jewish community in Algiers amounted to some 10,000 souls, or almost 10 per cent of the total population. Two individuals in particular, Bacri and Busnach, whose wealth was rooted in French trade, had great sway with the dey, providing him with financial services as well as (Falcon reported) bribes to allow them to ship French property under Algerian cover. It was a dangerous arrangement when British cruisers and privateers enjoyed the freedom of the seas, and the dey was still smarting at the seizure of the cargo of *El Veloce*, taken under an Algerian flag, but condemned as French by His Britannic Majesty's vice-admiralty court in Gibraltar. Nor were the howls of protest one way. Falcon himself was complaining that Algerian cruisers had taken Sicilian and Neapolitan ships, despite the fact that they carried safe passes signed by Ball, and even Maltese ships they were sworn to protect.[21]

Nelson did not want 'an Algerine war laid at my charge' and decided to investigate pro and con before charging in like a bull in a china shop. Thinking the problem over in the *Victory*, he discovered that a new chapter had been added to the stormy saga of Anglo-Algerian relations. Back in April two Moorish women had been found in Falcon's house, and the dey was consumed with rage. Falcon insisted that he knew nothing of the women, who had been confidentially admitted by servants, but he had few opportunities to explain. In a dawn raid he and his family were arrested, marched to a ship and expelled from the country. The terrified servants escaped into hiding, but the Moorish women duly received a thousand bastinadoes apiece. When the matter reached Nelson's ears Falcon was at Gibraltar, fuming that apart from anything else his expulsion had been illegal, because the treaty between Algiers and Britain specifically protected the consul general from harassment. Nelson approached the Admiralty for guidance, venturing the opinion that Mustapha Dey was an opportunist who exploited weakness, and 'if we give up one tittle of what we originally demand, we shall always be troubled with his insolence'. A 'sudden blow' against his cruisers was an option. Limply the Admiralty would only suggest that he seek additional information and return Falcon to Algiers to solicit an audience. The admiral was unimpressed. The 'government . . . should decide and not lay an Algerine war at my door,' he grumbled.[22]

While waiting for more details from Falcon, Nelson sent Donnelly of the *Narcissus* to Algiers to test the ground. At the beginning of September, Donnelly confronted the dey in the first of a series of extraordinary interviews endured by different British officers. The captain had a letter from Nelson, but his recitation was continuously interrupted by the excitable potentate, who demanded restitution of *El Veloce* and complained that his letters about the subject had gone unanswered. In a confused and contradictory tirade, Mustapha 'talked of injustices he never received, and grievances which he, on a former occasion, told me were done away'. He would have no more to do with Falcon, but agreed to receive anyone he deemed to be an honest consul. Unable to get further with the dey, Donnelly spoke separately to two of his advisers, his chief minister, or *harnagee*, and Busnach the Jewish merchant, and found both sensible of the folly of antagonising the supreme naval power. They were even inclined to admit a British complaint about the seizure of a ship called the *Ape*, although they hinted that the dey would put them to death if they compromised, and meekly suggested the British look for a way to recover the value of the *Ape* behind Mustapha's back. During his visit Donnelly cast a sharp eye over the city's defences and found many recent improvements towards the sea, where upwards of 350 cannon and a mortar battery were mounted, but the wooden houses heaped on top of each other close to the waterfront were exposed to fire.[23]

For Nelson the Algiers affair was a diversion, and he preferred reconciliation. Not only that, but scrutinising the British complaints about the seizure of Sicilian and Neapolitan ships did not impress him. An island, Malta depended on seaborne trade, but the French occupation had destroyed most of her vessels, and Ball had been granting passes to Sicilian ships bringing in provisions. Such passes were valid for one voyage only, but Nelson suspected that they were being illegally used to cover multiple journeys. Even the discomforted Falcon admitted that the passports of the ships the Algerians had seized were irregular. However, there was one case – that of the *Ape* – and the issue of the expelled consul and its insult to the British flag that could not be ignored. Nelson wanted a peaceful solution, but he was dealing with an irrational, unpredictable and volatile force.[24]

Mustapha was a regal, dignified-looking man in sumptuous clothing, but 'the most ignorant [dey] that can be imagined', peremptory, impatient and forever exploding into uncontrollable frenzies impervious to reason. Probably this impossible personality would contribute to his eventual assassination in August 1805. There was every reason for Algiers to accommodate Britain, for she made her living upon the sea. The country principally relied upon *guerre de course*, seizing ships and cargoes and enslaving their crews. In just forty-five days of 1803 Algerian corsairs took sixteen prizes and 195 prisoners, and twelve hundred Christian slaves were then being held in bondage ashore. The dey ransomed ships and prisoners, granted immunity to the vessels of countries that paid him protection money, and, as we have seen, even charged for the gun salutes that customarily greeted the arrival of foreign warships. Another of Mustapha's tactics was to demand indemnification for a perceived insult. In January last, for example, he had declared war on France, only to settle the dispute the following month on the receipt of presents and the promise of 200,000 Spanish dollars. The Algerians had a considerable treasury, some sixty-five million dollars, and an annual government revenue of about half a million dollars, but its health depended upon the sea and its fourteen cruisers, sixty gunboats and 150 commercial vessels. Algiers could not even send its annual tribute to Constantinople without venturing upon the sea. Any thinking governor would have understood the importance of mollifying Britain, and there was a saying in the country 'that if war should be made with England in the morning, Algiers must hasten to make peace before night'. But this dey not only cast reason to the winds, but half convinced himself that Algiers was impregnable. His only obvious acknowledgement of the British threat to his country was the idleness of his fleet, which had lain low in port ever since Falcon's ignominious departure.

Lord Hobart, the secretary of state for war, produced some bullish orders on 23 August. Nelson should demand the release of any Maltese vessels and crews taken since the treaty of 1801, and adopt 'the most vigorous and effectual measures' to secure compliance; if necessary, he was to seize or destroy the dey's cruisers. Recast by the Admiralty, the orders reached Nelson by the *Childers* on 6 October. He was to proceed cautiously, using an officer who would not risk the capture of his ship if Algiers proved hostile. To be sure of his ground, Nelson wrote to Ball for the essential details of any Maltese vessels taken by Algiers, and chose Captain Keats of the *Superb*, in whom he had unbounded confidence, for the mission. With Keats went the versatile Reverend Scott as secretary and interpreter. Several months later, in January, Hobart retreated from the firm stance he had taken in August, and pointed out that the use of force was inexpedient 'at the present moment', but Nelson had already acted.[25]

Nelson's ships were already overstretched, and if he had to attack the Algerian fleet it had best be done with as few blows as possible, perhaps in a single action at the beginning of April, before the corsairs could get to sea after the winter. First, try negotiations. On 9 January Nelson directed Keats to take Falcon to Algiers with two strongly worded letters from him, one deploring the expulsion of the diplomat as an insult to His Britannic Majesty that needed an apology. Perhaps, Nelson persuaded gently, the dey could acknowledge that his act had occurred in 'an unguarded moment of anger'. The second letter demanded the restitution of Maltese ships 'chartered by the British government'. Neither communication made threats, but they wanted compliance, and expressed a hope that Mustapha would see the propriety and justice of what was required. To help Keats with the practical management of the task, Nelson supplied a detailed memorandum. The captain was to anchor beyond the range of the Algerian batteries. He would not fire the customary salute until relations had been restored, but solicit an audience with the dey. Nelson warned Keats not to be diverted to other matters, nor yield any of the British demands. 'Never appear satisfied with what has been granted, but demand what has not, and leave the question of peace or war entirely open, so that it may hang over his head.' If Mustapha stormed away in one of his passions, Keats should pen a refusal to attend him again until Algiers was ready to meet the British requirements without reservation.[26]

The squadron was under Cape San Sebastian when the *Superb* was detached, but after sending a couple of ships to Rosas for provisions and to assess the status of the Toulon fleet, Nelson ran across to the Barbary coast to lend Keats support. As Nelson's detachment made its way south, Keats arrived at Algiers on 15 January. As ordered, he refused to return a welcoming salute from the Algerian guns, but sent a boat ashore under a lieutenant, who disembarked with a big package. O'Brien, the American consul general, was on hand to conduct the officer to the dey and explain the meaning of Nelson's letters. The audience did not last long. Mustapha got into 'a great squall' and cursed Falcon. He was in an uncommonly bad mood before Keats himself went to see him at noon the next day.[27]

Keats was escorted through long galleries lined with stony-faced axemen before he reached the dey, who received him with initial civility. But the matter of Falcon had barely escaped the captain's mouth before Mustapha stopped him with a 'loud, violent and incoherent' tirade. Keats remained calm, patiently trying to state the British demands for Falcon's reinstatement, the release and compensation of Maltese people and property and a consideration of the claims of Neapolitan ships and crews taken in British service. The interview lasted for one and a half hours, but Keats described it as 'the most strong and violent that could be imagined', while O'Brien, who was present, thought it the most vehement 'ever known or heard in Algiers'. An insult to King George, stormed the dey in 'high latitudes'? Why, the king should have executed Falcon for the offence he had given, adding for good measure that the consul's servant had also ridden over and killed a Moor two years before. Even now the British insulted by declining to return the dey's salute! Keats found it 'impossible to fix' Mustapha's 'attention to any one point for two minutes together'. The dey made one concession, and that with 'violent invectives'. He would accept another consul 'without' the usual dispensation of 'presents', and having so said he marched angrily away.

Back in the *Superb*, Keats wrote to the dey, offering to meet again at any appointed hour in an effort to preserve peace. The evening was tense, especially when Algerian guards posted on mountain heights excitedly reported large ships to the northward. It was Nelson, with seven ships of the line and a frigate. In the morning Keats coolly sent a message to his advancing commander-in-chief, drawing his attention to the crucial state of the proceedings and urging him not to enter the bay. The dey was dangerously emotional, and in no mind to give way; if the British pressed their hand now, they would have to resort to 'extremities'. Consequently, the squadron lay seven leagues to the NNW while pandemonium reigned ashore. The dey himself appeared at the shore batteries, gunboats sped here and there across the harbour like demented water beetles, and soldiers clattered to arms. Everyone thought the city was going to be attacked, and that war between Britain and Algiers was only a gunshot away.

Keats's letter went ashore, and O'Brien took it to the dey, finding him one and a half miles west of the city, perhaps preparing for flight but still boiling with fury. In Algiers, Keats and Scott took the serious risk of being seized as hostages by landing at about one o'clock in the afternoon without an invitation. They were met by the minister of marine, who explained that the dey had left the city. He dismissed the Maltese claims as readily as his master, but offered to set up another interview with the dey and promised to send a boat to the *Superb* in the morning. There was another heavy night, and aboard his ship, three miles from the mole, Keats could see the shore batteries alive with lights and a flurry of movements. The 18th brought an end to the negotiations. The boat promised by the minister of marine did not appear, but O'Brien got word to the British that the dey was as defiant as ever. With some justification Mustapha said that as far as the Neapolitan and Sicilian ships were concerned, he had no treaty with their government and would continue to regard them as his enemies. Keats now saw no further room for talk and withdrew to the fleet.

Nelson could have attacked the city. He had exercised the *Victory*'s guns the day before arriving off Algiers, and the return of Keats and appearance of two more ships gave him a total of nine sail of the line, a frigate and a brig. O'Brien for one thought that he should have done, for although the dey was bloody-minded, the inhabitants of Algiers were terrified. Indeed, said he, 'on the British making themselves respected by these regencies depends their political influence in this sea'. Even after the British left he fully expected them to return for 'a

2d. edition of Copenhagen or a mole hustle'. But in truth Nelson had too few serviceable ships for his main mission, and too few dockyard facilities to put any that were damaged to rights quickly. He could not risk a costly attack on Algiers at that time. He estimated that it would take ten sail of the line and numerous bomb vessels to subdue the city. In 1816 Edward Pellew would do the job with six line of battle ships, nine cruisers and four bomb ketches, but in 1803 Nelson had more important tasks and easier options, and he was wise to withdraw his forces. Reporting to Hobart on the 19th, Nelson praised Keats, who had excelled himself in a very uncomfortable situation, and recommended that no other consul be sent to the dey. Falcon was spirited but unacceptable to the Algerians, and must now return home. It remained to warn British merchantmen to avoid Algiers, and to determine the next step. Given his commitments and resources, it was nigh impossible to mount an efficient blockade of Algiers, but he suggested swooping on the Algerian fleet towards the end of April when it usually put to sea and annihilating it. Whichever, Nelson wanted to reassure Keats, and sent him a personal note, begging 'leave to express my full and entire approbation of the whole of your conduct'.[28]

In the event, Nelson's stroke against Algiers did not fall, and the state of uncertainty continued. The dey built two new batteries, one covering the mole, and kept his vulnerable cruisers in port, forgoing the plunder they would normally have taken. The British government, too, recoiled from a bloody encounter.[29]

Before the end of 1803 the Admiralty had acted to remove one of the difficulties, the confusion about the legality of Ball's passes. New papers would be issued to vessels eligible for British protection, and the Barbary states told they had to be respected. Going further, Hobart's orders of January and March 1804 made it clear that compromise rather than confrontation was now the watchword, and Nelson should act the impartial arbiter between aggrieved parties. The admiral might, for example, claim to have persuaded his government to send a different consul, since the dey objected so much to the old one; as a return favour, he could ask Mustapha to express regret for what had happened and liberate any Maltese ships, crews and cargoes still in his possession. A veil could then be drawn over the unfortunate incident. Nelson had reservations about these orders, but turned again to Keats. On 15 May 1804 the *Superb* was ordered to pick up an interpreter and attendant schooner at Malta and return to Algiers. She carried a letter in which Nelson attributed former difficulties to misunderstandings, and proclaimed himself a 'friend' who had sent Falcon back to England. If the dey delivered the Maltese property and promised never to dismiss a British consul again, Nelson predicted that amity would be restored.[30]

Keats reached Algiers on 10 June and edged patiently towards a solution. Despite the economic difficulties imposed on his country by the inactivity of his cruisers, the dey dug his heels in, barely attending to the reading of Nelson's letter, constantly verging upon an eruption, and at one point becoming so 'unreasonable' that Keats suggested discussions continue through his ministers. For two more days Keats turned the grievances back and forth with the minister of marine, and eventually emerged with a modest advance. Mustapha had expressed regret for the Falcon affair, inviting a new consul to Algiers, and he guaranteed that no further summary dismissals would occur. That for Keats was the end of the Falcon affair, but what of the ships seized in the Maltese trade? Keats had a list of eleven such, but noticed that six were Maltese vessels taken before the treaty of 1801, and all the prisoners from them appeared to have already been released. That left five Neapolitan or Sicilian vessels, taken under British passports in the spring of 1803. The Algerians reasonably contended that as they had no treaty with the Two Sicilies they were entitled to take the ships, and Keats further saw that in four cases the passports Ball had supplied had expired and were being used illegally. Nevertheless, as a gesture, the Algerians now surrendered the masters of all five ships to Keats. Eighty-one crew members remained in captivity, but strictly their situation was one between Algiers and their Sicilian Majesties. According to Keats only one legitimate British complaint remained: the British-owned *Ape*, crewed by Neapolitans, but holding a valid passport from Ball.[31]

Nelson endorsed the whole of Keats's analysis, and told Hawkesbury, the new home secretary, that Mustapha had 'made fully the *amende honorable* for his conduct to Mr Falcon' and extended a finger towards peace. For the sake of agreement some of the old contentious issues should be relinquished, and a new beginning made with the issue of fresh, unequivocal and easily recognisable passports to ships owned by British subjects. There were two sticking points, the *Ape* and a Maltese vessel, the *St Antonio di Padona*, which had been sold in Algiers. Compensation was required for both. Nelson suggested that as Bryan McDonough, the consul for Tripoli, was returning to England, he call at Algiers on his way to Gibraltar to try to settle the two outstanding differences. There was just a chance that Mustapha might accept McDonough as his new consul.[32]

The note of optimism in Nelson's report was soon doused. McDonough, public spirited enough to embrace the unpromising charge, was carried to Algiers by the *Termagant*, Captain Pettet. He delivered a letter from Nelson but could not move the Algerians an inch further than they had gone with Keats. In particular, said the dey, the affair of the *Ape* would only be settled once Britain had compensated Algiers for *El Veloce*. A disappointed Nelson stormily replied that 'not one farthing' of the value of *El Veloce* or its cargo 'belonged either to you or any of your subjects . . . no consul will ever enter into this matter. It is finished . . .' When another overture by Donnelly of the *Narcissus* foundered on the same rock, meeting nothing more than 'the most nonsensical speech I [Donnelly] ever heard', the admiral owned his patience exhausted. 'I have done with him,' he told Lord Camden, the secretary for war and colonies, on 11

October. 'Next spring it will be thought necessary to turn the thoughts of ministers towards Algiers, but the more we appear to give way, the more insolent he is.' This he had known from the beginning.[33]

Looking back, Nelson regretted that the diplomacy had done less than justice to the unfortunate Falcon, who had been offered up as a pawn. In August he wrote to the usurped consul general that 'so far from thinking that you had . . . given me any trouble, I had the greatest pleasure in making your acquaintance, which I hope to renew when I arrive in England'. Falcon's 'whole conduct' at Algiers 'had been most perfectly correct and proper', and Nelson hoped that the end result would be a better appointment elsewhere. The admiral also wished that he had fallen upon the Algerian fleet. 'We never should have given up the cause of Mr Falcon,' he told Ball. 'I do not expect that the Dey will now give up an atom.'[34]

In November 1804, with the dispute eighteen months old, the *Childers* reported a dozen Algerian frigates and corvettes at the mouth of the Adriatic. Nelson asked Ball if any Maltese ships had been taken that year. If one proven case existed he was prepared to stretch his force in a grand sweep across the sea to scoop up the lot. 'I will try and take or destroy his [the dey's] whole fleet,' Nelson told Ball. 'But I will not strike unless I can hit him hard . . . *all* or *none* is my motto.' The Algerian fleet was hunting for Neapolitan prizes around Italy, and Ball advised Nelson to send another ship to Algiers and demand a full compliance with every demand on pain of losing his cruisers. With his fleet out and vulnerable, the dey would probably capitulate, and if he did not there was a perfect justification for the naval action Nelson had mentioned. Neither the demand nor the battle took place. By then a new Spanish war had broken out, and Nelson's hands were full, while the Algerian fleet quickly retired after a skirmish with the escort of a Neapolitan convoy in December.[35]

Fortunately, while Nelson was despairing, his earlier tolerance suddenly paid a dividend. Lagging behind Nelson, the British government did not receive the admiral's reports of Keats's second mission to Algiers until October, when McDonough reached London. Whitehall 'fully adopted' the olive branch Nelson had waved in June, and cheerfully emphasised 'the entire confidence which is placed in your lordship's capacity and judgement'. There could be no question of satisfying the dey about *El Veloce*, which had been caught red-handed shipping French property, and condemned in the vice-admiralty court. An appeal had been heard and the original verdict vouchsafed. Lord Camden set aside the case of the *St Antonio*, but would not give way over the *Ape*, which was a necessary 'preliminary to all accommodation'. With regard to the crews of any Maltese ships in the dey's power, Camden merely suggested that Nelson tell the Algerians that Britain would deem it a favour if the prisoners were liberated.[36]

These letters, with a new consul general for Algiers, Richard Cartwright, reached Nelson on Christmas Day 1804. If the dey agreed to Britain's new conditions, as outlined by Camden, Cartwright could be landed and relations between the two powers normalised. Thus, on 28 December Nelson framed his final orders to the dependable Keats. He would take Cartwright to Algiers, and land him if the outstanding differences were removed. To spare another fractious scene, Nelson suggested Keats first confer with the dey's ministers to ascertain the likelihood of the new terms being accepted, emphasising Britain's importance to Algiers. Indeed, said Nelson, during the peace the British had prevented the French from sending a punitive expedition to Algiers, and in the present dispute had so far exercised great restraint. This time it worked. Keats returned joyously on 15 January 1805, reporting that Cartwright had been landed and relations between Britain and Algiers restored. The dey had grudgingly dropped the *El Veloce* affair, which he nevertheless continued to insist had left him the poorer, ordered the crew of the *Ape* released and agreed that compensation would be paid for the ship and cargo. 'Your Lordship will not fail to observe,' Nelson wrote to Camden, 'that the conduct of Captain Keats merits those encomiums which would fall far short of his merits was I to attempt to express what my feelings are upon this, as upon all other occasions.' He asked Camden to represent the captain's services to the king, and recommended both Scott and the chaplain of the *Superb* for crown livings.[37]

The new British passports did not arrive until 1805, but the crisis subsided. Diplomacy had ultimately triumphed, saving Nelson from what could otherwise have been a drag upon scarce ships. Nelson's plan to destroy the Algerian navy was his only viable alternative, because a blockade was out of the question, but it might not have worked. As it was, the Algerian fleet had confined itself to port for eighteen months, losing considerable amounts of income. In the circumstances Nelson had done reasonably well faced with that exasperating but frequent element of international diplomacy, the obdurate human personality.

Neither Tripoli nor Tunis was as incompetently led as Algiers. Tripoli, although a weaker entity, was illustrating the nuisance value of the Barbary powers in a protracted dispute with the United States. Known as the Tripolitan war, it had begun in 1801, when Yusuf Karamanli, the Bashaw of Tripoli, attempted to extort $225,000 from the newly inaugurated president, Thomas Jefferson. American cruisers had been trying to subjugate Tripoli ever since, with losses accumulating on both sides, but the conflict would last until 1805. Britain had no part in this conflict, although Nelson sympathised with the Americans and declined to supply Tripoli with ammunition, despite the blandishments of the bashaw, who flattered the admiral as 'the redeemer of the Musalman faith'.[38]

Nelson had little to do with Tripoli, and not much more with Tunis. In many respects Tunis had the same difficulties with Britain as Algiers. She enjoyed a healthy trade with France, and given a choice would have favoured her over Britain. It was possible to see thirty merchantmen loading for France in the harbour at a time. British complaints, forwarded by the acting British consul, Henry Clark, included the French use of Tunisian flags to ship their cargoes, and the seizure of ships with British passes by Tunisian cruisers. But Tunis, which seemed to have profited from earlier mistakes, played a far subtler hand than Algiers, contesting the British interpretation of neutral rights with reasoned arguments when necessary but for the most part redressing grievances with apparent open-handedness. When Donnelly of the *Narcissus* met Hamooda Pasha, the Bey of Tunis, on 30 September 1803 he was struck by a man of 'more judgement and good sense than falls to the [common] lot of those barbarians', and one, moreover, very aware of the consequences of alienating British favour. He advised Donnelly that he had no jurisdiction over the Zimbra islands in the Gulf of Tunis, which were 'without cannon shot' of his city, and freed Nelson to act against French corsairs who had recently installed themselves there and taken a British ship. As a result the following May Nelson sent two small brigs, one the *Childers* commanded by his nephew, Billy Bolton, to clean out the nest. And yes, Hamooda agreed, though he had endeavoured to respect British passes, it was possible that mistakes had been made, and he would be grateful to receive a copy of Ball's register of passports so that he could refer to it in every contested case. He would, and did, send a representative to Malta to collect the register and to discuss outstanding cases. Nelson described one Tunisian envoy who visited him as 'a moderate man, and apparently the best disposed of any I ever did business with'.[39]

The Tunisians played both sides, as any small state fighting for survival between bigger predators might do, but with enough skill to encourage Nelson to reciprocate. The admiral passed on the bey's complaints about the excesses of Gibraltar privateers, adding his own jaundiced opinion of that rather lawless breed, who committed abuses 'in these seas every day'. He also helped to secure British safe conduct for a ship carrying Tunisian tribute money that might otherwise have been detained. Britain's relations with Tunis were not straightforward, but both sides compromised enough to avoid serious ruptures.[40]

If nothing else these events remind us of the volatility of the Mediterranean, where numerous competing powers, divided by religion, politics and self-interest abrasively interacted, and storms could rumble out of nowhere hundreds of miles apart. Nelson's naval superiority was paper-thin. A French attack on the Morea, Sicily or Sardinia, or a Spanish or for that matter an Algerian or Tunisian war could have destroyed Nelson's feeble margins overnight. Balancing the sheer diversity and extent of his tasks with the forces at his disposal, Nelson played a shrewd and steady hand in a game of empires that lasted for two years.

For a full assessment of Nelson's relations with the reaches of the Ottoman Porte and dealings in the eastern Mediterranean we would need to know more about the French plans for the Morea. If they were primarily intended to divert or deceive Nelson, as the historian John Holland Rose suggested more than a century ago, they partially succeeded, because when the Toulon fleet did run the blockade in 1805 the British admiral's immediate reactions were to cover Italy, the Morea and Egypt rather than to look westwards. If, on the other hand, the Morea was a credible French strategy awaiting its opportunity, then Nelson must be credited with closing that option down. In either case, he had played safe, containing the French and keeping British trade flowing. His handling of Algiers was hamstrung by the vacillation in London as well as the pressing nature of other matters, but given his mission and resources Nelson had again performed respectably, controlling Tunis by negotiation, and effectively bottling up the Algerian fleet. In these matters he had shown both independence of mind and good judgement. He had, for example, resisted the advice of Ball, whose narrower view had led him to propose a blockade of Algiers, a vigorous defence of the dubious passes and a landing in Egypt, all of which would have dissipated Nelson's strength, threatened his central mission off Toulon, and likely alienated the Porte. Nelson never lost sight of his priorities, and as late as October 1805 was emphasising the need to be 'very friendly' to Algiers, especially as the assassination of the dey that year created an opportunity for a new beginning.[41]

Amidst the ruins of the Ottoman empire he had garnered some achievements, and by cooperating with Turkey and Russia laid a few foundations for a new phase of coalition warfare. It was a creditable record.

XX

IN THE *VICTORY*

I think I have not lost my heart,
Since I, with truth, can swear,
At every moment of my life,
I feel my Nelson there . . .

Then do not rob me of my heart,
Unless you first forsake it;
And then so wretched it would be,
Despair alone will take it.

Emma to Nelson, 1805

I

FOR more than two years Nelson's home was the *Victory*, a huge three-decked floating castle under a magnificent spread of sail, with an extreme width of fifty-two feet and a gun-deck 186 feet long. She was an awesome fighting machine, with a nominal complement of 850 and 104 guns, including two sixty-eight-pound carronades. David Murray managed the fleet from the *Victory* and Captain Hardy the ship, and there were eight lieutenants, including John Quilliam, who had taken over the command of the *Amazon* after Riou's death, Andrew King, wounded in the *Desiree* in the same battle, and John Yule, who had served under Cornwallis and Ball before joining Nelson's entourage in the Mediterranean and Baltic. Yule's brother-in-law, John Carslake, was a midshipman in the *Victory*, rated on 18 April 1803 at the age of eighteen. The senior of three marines officers was the excellent Charles Adair, one of a military line, and among the principal warrant officers was William Rivers the gunner, who had spent more than a dozen years in the *Victory* and now commanded a team of thirty-four men. A professional, Rivers filled notepaper with jottings about such germane matters as ranges, fuses, carriages and rockets. The carpenter, William Bunce, who headed fourteen artificers, had been with Nelson in the *San Josef*, and Thomas Atkinson the master even longer, having been in the old *Theseus* in 1797.[1]

Nelson almost never went on shore, and as the *Victory* was his home he made his quarters as elegant and comfortable as the restrictions allowed. From his cabin came the thousands of commands that moved more than forty ships and six thousand men and boys across a mighty arena, the distillations of hundreds of reports that went to London, and the letters that reached sailors, soldiers, agents, contractors, physicians, diplomats, kings, emperors, beys and bashaws. They covered a formidable range of material, from additions to signal books and the quality of the slop clothing to making the face of Europe.

The heart of the admiral's quarters was an impressive day cabin, situated below the captain's quarters and above the lieutenants' wardroom, and occupying the entire width of the ornamented stern. It drew light from three sides. Sometimes the sunlight hit the water astern of the ship and bounced upwards to throw flickering shadows upon the roof of the cabin, but the woodwork sported whites and gentle hues of buff, pale green, grey and yellow. In the day cabin Nelson could take the air on his stern gallery outside, work at the big table that dominated the interior, or sink into a sofa or one of several armchairs, his favourite being a deep leather but exceedingly plain mahogany seat with pockets on each side for the convenient storage of papers. A foot rest slid from underneath, so he could relax and read, and a small, glass-doored bookcase offered literary excursions into William Stewart Rose's *Naval History of the Late War*, Louis Giradin's *Historical Sketches of Invasions or Descents Upon the British Isles*, *A Few Tracts to Show the Ambitions of France*, five leather-bound volumes of *Asiatic Researches* dealing with the arts, sciences and literature of that continent, collections of the speeches of Sheridan and Lord Moira, and a book of sermons, in which the admiral had marked texts appropriate for reading to sailors. Nelson's 'guardian angels' – Emma's portraits, now reinforced by one of little Horatia – looked down benignly from the walls and were blessed by regular toasts at the behest of the admiral, while usually close at hand were a portable compass, a brass-mounted, velvet-lined grog chest, complete with two glasses, and a much-used medicine chest. The admiral's writing desk, where such essential accompaniments as seals, a watch and quills and ink found a home, was attached to a wall.

Adjoining the day cabin, but extending a little forward along the starboard side of the ship, were two other rooms reserved for Nelson, both small and inconvenienced by the presence of heavy guns, standing ready to be run out of the ports when the ship went into action. Nearest aft was Nelson's dining cabin, where the admiral could seat eight or nine people at a table covered with a linen damask cloth, marked neatly with its owner's initials in minute blue cross stitch. Here guests ate from a Staffordshire blue and white earthenware service decorated with a floral design, using what the admiral called his 'sea list' silver, or sampled choice wines, champagne or claret, poured from ovoid-shouldered carafes or fluted glass decanters, duly inscribed with an 'N', into monogrammed cups or tulip-shaped glasses. The second compartment gave the admiral his retreat, for it contained his cot and a mahogany and boxwood washstand. The last, standing three feet in height, unfolded at the top to place a mirror in front, small trays at the sides and a basin beneath.[2]

Regular staff tripped in and out to spare the admiral daily drudgery. Having disposed of the 'poor foolish' Allen, Nelson felt better served by replacements. Three were rated able seamen on 20 May 1803: Gaetano Spedillo, a valet; Henry Lewis Chevailler, a steward recommended by Davison; and Henry Nicholls. Nelson liked Chevailler, whose pay was back-dated to 1 March, and advised him on the best way to send money to his wife, Elizabeth. Chevailler was 'very much respected' as well as an 'excellent' steward, but there is an indication that he was bullied. In March 1804 he surprised Nelson by confessing that he was 'disagreeably situated in the ship' and wished to return home. 'I never said a harsh thing to him, nor anyone else, I am sure,' the flabbergasted admiral protested. To Davison, Chevailler explained that he had endured 'many disagreeable treatments' from those he could 'never consider . . . as my masters', but 'never once from his lordship'. It sounds as if senior officers were involved, but the matter was obviously resolved, and Chevailler remained in the flagship to find a place beside his dying admiral at Trafalgar. When he left the service he carried a mother-of-pearl box that Nelson had given him. Of the other members of Nelson's retinue, young William Hasleham was from Merton. He drew £18 a year, some of which Nelson had him send home to his parents, and behaved well enough to be promised a rating as able seaman, although he chose not to continue his naval career when the ship was paid off in 1805. Several other servants appear, including the shadowy William Prest, Edward Bartlett, a likeable young doctor marking time for a more suitable posting; and Robert Drummond, an able seaman who joined the ship in July 1803 and ended his days in Greenwich Hospital.[3]

Two other figures in daily attendance were the unrelated Scotts, John the secretary and prize agent, and Alexander John the chaplain, whose working knowledge of French, Italian, Turkish and possibly Spanish eventually got him an Admiralty allowance of £100. Both were bound to their leader in extreme admiration. Alexander, 'the doctor' as Nelson called him, said that he had 'never' before 'met so pure a mind' as the admiral's; 'every thought flowing from . . . selfishness is a stranger to his breast'. Scott spent hours translating, and when the work grew too onerous the overspill went to David Evans of the *Superb*. For the other Scott, a former purser, working for Nelson was a new but entirely 'cheerful and pleasant experience' that brought great 'happiness'. He fussed about his employer, directing Spedillo to keep the admiral's health under close observation, but nursed a complicated ambition of his own. A Scot by nationality as well as name, John was thirty-five, with a wife, Charlotte, and three boys at home, and hoped to supplement his annual salary of £300 by dipping a toe into the prize agency business. An embarrassing rivalry developed. Davison, of course, expected to act for Nelson in matters of prize, but Scott intrigued for that part of the business conducted out on station, using his patron William Marsh, the admiral's banker, to distribute any payments that had to be made in London. Working clandestinely behind Nelson's back, Scott cut in James Cutforth and Patrick Wilkie, the agent victuallers at Gibraltar and Valletta, if they would sign captains to their agency as soon as they arrived on station. Nelson realised that Scott and Davison were squabbling over the business, and was uncomfortable disappointing either. The captains were entitled to nominate whomsoever they wished as their agent, but Nelson suggested that Scott and Davison share the 5 per cent commission in whatever business concerned him. But Davison would have all or nothing. More, in 1805 he made a public appeal to captains to join his agency, using Nelson's name without his permission. Perhaps the presumption annoyed the admiral, because he finally appointed Scott as agent for the flag officers of the fleet. It was the first crack in what had hitherto been an extremely close relationship with Davison. As for Scott, he was not an unprofitable acquisition, for he pressed Nelson's claims to 'good round sums' like a terrier, so much so that the disapproving admiral sometimes had to call him off. 'I have sent to England for the opinion of law,' Scott once bewailed, 'but his lordship, ever anxious to meet equity, has directed me to relinquish the claim.'[4]

Nelson left the routine handling of the ship and its men to Hardy, thus divorcing himself from the darker side of life in the flagship. Hardy's discipline rested in a good measure upon his generous use of the lash. Floggings were a regular feature of life on board. In the year 5 August 1803 to 5 August 1804 the ship saw 204 floggings and a total of 5788 lashes, apart from a few occasions when the *Victory* was required to contribute to the punishment of offenders from other ships during the brutal practice of 'flogging around the fleet'. This works out at an average rate of nearly seventeen strokes a day, but of course the punishments were inflicted in batches. On 14 August 1804 the backs of thirteen men were cut open at the gratings with an accumulative total of 420 strokes. The crew was assembled to witness these grim spectacles, and we can imagine standing to attention under a hot sun during such protracted ordeals was no matter for weak stomachs. Lieutenant Yule, a round-faced, idealistic man with curly hair and long side whiskers, thought the discipline in the *Victory* cruel.[5]

Of course, a degree of punishment was seen as essential by common ratings as well as officers, because thieves, malingerers, brawlers and drunkards all threatened the wellbeing, perhaps even the lives, of the company as a whole. Nelson's distance from Hardy's discipline, as well as his reputation as an admiral with the welfare of his people at heart, helped bind him to his men. He spoke regularly to the ratings, sometimes visiting them between decks and exchanging pleasantries. He kept the ships moving, to alleviate the dreariness of the command, and encouraged the men to produce revues in which plays, music and dancing introduced merriment and light relief, and it was the admiral's custom to attend the performances with his officers. He punctiliously attended the weekly divine services, and when on deck intervened in occasional dramas with good humour as well as decisiveness. There was the evening of 11 September 1804, off the Spanish coast, when a seaman, James Archibald, fell overboard. Master's mate Edward Flynn jumped after him, and kept him afloat until the cutter could be lowered and got alongside, and Nelson was so impressed that he immediately promised to promote Flynn, a reward that gave great satisfaction to the watching company. However, the admiral observed with a knowing eye towards the twenty or so 'young gentlemen' hungry enough to stage a repeat performance, there would be no further promotions for jumping after men overboard. True to his word, Nelson shortly appointed Flynn acting lieutenant of the *Bittern*. A very different incident also stuck in the minds of the ship's company. Once, a fire broke out below decks near the powder magazine, and a flame shot up through the hatchway several feet in height. Terrified seamen leaped into the chains and scrambled up the rigging, or readied themselves to jump overboard, convinced that the magazine would go up and the ship would be blown to pieces. 'At that dreadful moment', said Chevailler, 'where [when] every man thought it his last hour, Lord Nelson was then as cool and as composed as ever I saw him . . . everyone obeyed and in twenty minutes the fire was got under [control].' 'Hardy,' said Nelson calmly, 'go below and see what is the matter.' And soon he had a squad of seamen with wet blankets extinguishing the flames. It was an episode that impressed itself upon the memory of several witnesses.[6]

Even liberated by Hardy from everyday chores, Nelson's day was remarkable for its energy. The admiral rose early, just after daylight, and breakfasted in his cabin at about six. Meal times were useful spaces for meeting his officers and discussing the day's tasks in a convivial way, although they constituted a major expense to the commander-in-chief, who footed the bill. Hardy, Murray, the Scotts, the physician of the fleet and ship's surgeon, and a few commissioned or senior warrant officers generally attended to demolish tea, coffee, hot rolls, toast and cold ham or tongue. Sometimes members of the party then repaired to the deck to watch the sun rising vividly from the sea, bathing the fleet under sail in its golden light. Generally, however, Nelson reserved the hours of seven until two in the afternoon for business, withdrawing to his cabin with his secretaries to read, think and write. Not infrequently he would be seen on deck, pacing the twenty-one feet of space he had on his quarterdeck, occasionally darting to his cabin to write down a precious thought, or applying his telescope to his surviving eye. It was a good eye for weather, and he kept a diary of the movements of the barometer, and reckoned that he could feel a coming cold snap by rheumatic twinges in the stump of his severed arm. Despite his indifferent health, Nelson was notoriously dismissive of bad weather, and resisted its attempts to drive him below. 'The weather has been very stormy,' said Chevailler, who lovingly watched over his master, 'and had it not been for his astonishing care not half the fleet would have a standing start. In all the bad weather, both night and day, that good man was upon deck, maimed as he is, sometimes half naked under such heavy rains as are never seen in England.'[7]

About two or three in the afternoon a drumbeat had the ship's company preparing mess tables and taking their places for dinner, and the food was served to the band's interpretation of 'The Roast Beef of Old England'. To the usual guests at his table, Nelson added juniors from the flagship, and officers from other ships on a rota basis. He was particularly attentive to those who had newly arrived on the station, and even midshipmen proudly wrote home of dining with the commander-in-chief. Seldom less than a dozen graced Nelson's table and Secretary John Scott carved. There were usually three courses and a fruit dessert. Records of purchases suggest a considerable variety of commodities reached Nelson's table, including mutton, pork, beef, poultry, eggs, pears, vegetables and nuts, but the admiral ate sparingly, often applying his combined knife and fork to tackle a few vegetables, cheese, a modest portion of macaroni or the liver and wing of a bird. He used no salt, which he rated a cause of scurvy, but sipped a glass or two of porter, wine or champagne diluted with water, as well as milk and water, which he proclaimed to be good for the gout. Although Nelson's uniform coats were bedecked with the imitations of his knighthoods that he had purchased at four guineas a set in London, he was affable and relaxed at the table, and created an atmosphere of 'urbanity and hospitality'. John Scott testified that his chief had a 'peculiar' ability to make 'everyone happy' and 'the admirals and captains' were 'wonderfully attached to him, and as contented as men can be.' A purser, William Mark, thought dining with Nelson 'the most agreeable thing possible' and noted the admiral's sense of humour. 'One day he sent for his steward and told him to get up an extra plate because he should soon have to entertain the Prefect Maritime of Toulon, Admiral Ganteaume!' Coffee and liqueurs closed the dinners at about 4.30, when the company sometimes adjourned to the deck to enjoy the final performance of the band. At six or seven a tea was served in the admiral's dining cabin, rounded off with a rum punch and cake or biscuit.[8]

Nelson was often in his cot by nine at night, but he slept badly and regularly went up on deck to converse with the officer of the watch beneath a canopy of stars, or pace alone on the deck, supplementing his shirt, flannel waistcoat and coat with a leather waistcoat to give extra protection from cold and damp. It was noticed one rainy night that when the admiral returned to his cabin he kicked off his shoes, and dried his soaking stockings by walking back and forth on his carpet, rather than have his servants disturbed to make a fire.

Not surprisingly, his health deteriorated. Nelson began his tour of duty unusually free of physical discomfort, suffering not so much as a finger ache, a tribute to the care and rest at Merton. A feverish cold that touched him as he entered the Mediterranean soon passed, and it was not until the autumnal gales that his old infirmities returned to the assault. He was regularly seasick ('don't laugh' he wrote to St Vincent), and during the winter suffered from pains in his breast, a bad cough and the pain in his right side that related to a five-year-old hernia. The sudden and alarming heart spasms, which we have noticed before, also struck. They may have indicated angina, but William Beatty, his last surgeon, regarded them as oesophageal and referred to two- or three-day bouts of indigestion. Whichever, Nelson lost so much weight that the rings fell from his fingers, and by the spring reckoned his 'shattered carcase' the 'worst' in the fleet, racked by rheumatic fever, night sweats and flushes, and the hernia. A disturbing new symptom was the sense of blood 'gushing up the left side of my head, and the moment it covers the brain I am fast asleep', possibly something to do with raised blood pressure. He was careless with medicines and found that 'the bark' disagreed with him, but took daily doses of camphor and opium (prescribed by the first of the two surgeons posted to the *Victory*, the excellent George Magrath) and once recommended a 'tooth powder and tincture' that could be purchased from Mary Trotter's establishment, off the Strand.[9]

Beatty tells us that Nelson often spoke of his mortality, remarking that failing a state funeral in St Paul's Cathedral he wanted to be laid with his parents in the little church of Burnham Thorpe, which he had not seen since 1793. He felt age creeping up. 'My wounds have shook me at a time of life when others are in the prime of life,' he told Acton. He most feared living on in darkness, for the 'thick opaque membrane' was again colonising his best eye. 'My eyesight fails me most dreadfully,' he admitted to Davison, and 'firmly' suggested 'that in a very few years I shall be stone blind. It is this only, of all my maladies, that makes me unhappy.' On its own this bilateral pterygium would not have caused blindness, but although Nelson's green shades helped and Baird suggested awnings, Beatty concurred in the admiral's pessimism.

The admiral put much store in fresh food. A merchant of Malta, Alexander Macaulay, supplied special niceties to aid his constitution, including melons and oranges, and forage and animals for the little farmyard that Nelson kept on the ship to furnish his table and provide milk for the sick. He had three goats, some sheep, one of which lambed at sea, and a milk cow that had to be temporarily returned to Macaulay while she was in calf. For all this kindness, Nelson was sure that in the end only Emma's nursing and asses' milk and rest would really restore him to health, and in August 1804 he applied for leave, telling William Marsden, the new principal secretary of the Admiralty, that his 'whole constitution is most severely shocked more than any particular complaint'. His steward, who witnessed his daily struggle, agreed and wrote privately that he was 'afraid' his lordship would 'not mend here'. Yet Nelson would fight on at sea for an entire year beyond that diagnosis.[10]

Professional anxieties and physical infirmities besieged private moments, but this time Nelson had an antidote. Now he had a retreat, a place where cares could melt, wounds heal and needs be fulfilled: Merton, his home, full of his people and happiness and peace. Now, like Collingwood, he had a vision of domestic felicity that waited at the end of the voyage, and helped him endure. He could see beyond his old hunger for action and glory to domestic contentment. 'From my heart I hope that villain Buonaparte will be upset,' he wrote to Cornwallis, 'and that we may have a permanent peace. It is really shocking that *one* animal should disturb the repose of Europe, who I believe wish for peace.' It had been their fate, he commiserated with Waltersdorff, 'to sacrifice our own happiness to the service of our king and country', but of late 'a strong inclination for retirement' had grown upon him.[11]

2

Nothing delighted Nelson more than the letters from England that reunited him with that domestic world. The possibility that his mail might be intercepted caused him to express words of caution, but there was little about home that did not interest him. William was too busy looking for 'a mitre' to write much, and Susannah and Kate relied upon Emma to transmit their news. Davison was the other principal correspondent, filling letters with details of prize court proceedings, naval news and politics. In his own letters Nelson was guarded, and sometimes used the third person, as if he was actually a close associate of the admiral, or employed the old sobriquet of 'Thomson'. The correspondence travelled by many routes, on land and sea, through the Admiralty or hidden in the private letters of well-meaning individuals, and might take a month or more to reach their destinations. The first package from home did not reach the *Victory* until 30 July 1803. But whenever letters arrived, especially those from Merton or Clarges Street, they broke the admiral's isolation, and reconnected him with all he loved.[12]

He missed his little daughter's 'prattle' and dreamed that she called him 'papa'. 'Every scrap' of Emma's letters was 'so interesting that flattering fancy for the moment wafts me home'. More confident of his lover now, Nelson's letters to Emma were fewer, shorter and less passionate than those of 1801. Compared with those written when he was last in the Mediterranean, they were markedly domestic. Emma no longer participated in high politics, and could only play the homebound wife, as Fanny had done, delivering family chit-chat and stories of holidays, relations and the antics of servants. He seemed happy that she remained so, and in another reflection of a growing ability to manage their relationship discouraged her from coming out to the Mediterranean to join him. 'At this moment I can have no home but the *Victory*,' he said firmly, 'and where the French fleet may go, there will the *Victory* be found.' Malta, which she had suggested as a suitable location for her to fix, he dismissed as 'a nasty place with nothing but soldiers and diplomatic nonsense'. Fishing for reassurance, Emma still tried to stir her man's jealousy with stories of such drooling old lechers as Queensberry, but Nelson was secure enough to encourage her to cultivate the duke's interest in case he might bequeath her an allowance. 'We must have confidence in each other,' he told her. 'It is not all the world that could seduce me, in thought, word or deed from all my soul holds most dear. Indeed, if I can help it, I never intend to go out of the ship.' He dismissed her 'nonsensical' letters with the observation that if she believed every malicious report, 'you may always be angry with your Nelson'.[13]

A sense of ease rather than a lack of passion underwrote this comparative serenity, for Nelson still loved Emma intensely. 'I have not a thought except on you and the French fleet,' he wrote. 'All my thoughts, plans and toils tend to those two objects, and I will embrace them both so close when I can lay hold of either one or the other, that the devil himself should not separate us. Don't laugh at my putting you and the French fleet together, but you cannot be separated. I long to see you both in your proper places, the French fleet at sea, you at dear Merton, which in every sense of the word I expect to find a paradise.' Emma was his '*Alpha* and *Omega*', and he thought of her 'all day and all night', for 'my love for you is as unbounded as the ocean', and went 'beyond even this world!' The very thought of the 'inexpressible happiness' of their next meeting at Merton excited him. 'Even the thought of it vibrates through my nerves', and he predicted it would give them 'both real pleasure and exquisite happiness', as well as another child. A stream of gifts made their way to Merton, Spanish honey and Cyprus wine for Queensberry, a box of china, a dozen bottles of tokay, a muff, a comb, Sardinian gloves, material for gowns, a cask of paxoretti, silk shawls, earrings, bracelets, ostrich feathers . . . Many were purchased for him in Naples by the wife of John Lewis Falconnet, a business associate of Gibbs.[14]

Coupled with Emma in his thoughts was Horatia, whose childhood he saw slipping away beyond sight and touch. He was pleased to learn that Emma was making some social headway, and that half a dozen 'ladies of quality' regularly mixed with her, because it boded well for Horatia's ultimate debut in society. Nelson framed his first letter to her on 21 October 1803, when she was in her third year. 'My dear child,' said he, 'Receive this first letter from your most affectionate father. If I live, it will be my pride to see you virtuously brought up, but if it pleases God to call me, I trust to Himself. In that case, I have left dear Lady Hamilton your guardian. I therefore charge you, my child, on the value of a father's blessing, to be obedient and attentive to all her kind admonitions and instructions . . . I shall only say, my dear child, may God Almighty bless you and make you an ornament to your sex, which I am sure you will be . . .' A second letter followed in January. Nelson acknowledged receipt of a lock of her hair, and returned one of his own with a pound to pay for it to be placed inside a locket. Another pound was supplied so that Horatia could buy something for 'Mary and your governess'.[15]

Nelson purchased gifts for Horatia, too. She had wanted a dog and a timepiece, and had given her father a piece of string for his own gold pocket watch. In January 1804 the proud father kissed and sent off a watch that would 'tick for a year instead of a month or two', but he would not stand to the dog. Some months later 'twelve books of Spanish dresses' followed, which 'you will let your Guardian Angel, Lady Hamilton, keep for you when you are tired of looking at them'. In a strongly worded letter to his young niece, Charlotte, whose education Emma had taken in hand, Nelson urged her to befriend 'that dear little orphan, Horatia. Although her parents are lost, yet she is not without a fortune, and I shall cherish her to the last moment of my life, and *curse* them who *curse* her, and Heaven *bless* them who bless her! Dear innocent, she can have injured no one!'[16]

Now that Sir William was out of the way, the admiral was eager to integrate Horatia into the family, and on 6 September 1803 added a new codicil to his will acknowledging 'Miss Horatia Nelson Thomson' as his 'adopted daughter' and leaving her to the guardianship of Emma, 'knowing she will educate my adopted child in the paths of religion and virtue, and give her those accomplishments which so much adorn herself'. He supposed that she would one day become 'a fit wife for my dear nephew, Horatio Nelson'. Thus Nelson had come up with a two-part solution to Horatia's situation. First, she would be brought to Merton as a ward of Lady Hamilton, and second, she would reclaim her station in the Nelson line by marrying her cousin, the heir to the Nelson peerage. On 13 August following Nelson went further down this road by giving Emma a fictitious explanation of the child's history. He had, he said, been asked to care for a child in Italy, and as she had now outgrown a nurse, it was necessary to find her a home. Since Emma had taken a shine to Horatia, 'I am now anxious for the child's being placed under your protecting wing.' Here, therefore, was a document that Emma could produce to ward off sceptical enquiries, but its principal purpose was to clear away obstacles to Horatia's establishment at Merton. 'At Merton she will imbibe nothing but virtue, goodness and elegance of manners, with a good education,' he said hopefully, adding the suggestion that Miss Connor be paid a salary to assist in the moulding.[17]

Largely blind to Emma's faults, Nelson presumed his daughter would flourish under her guidance. True, she was still ostracised by some and refused access to the court, but Emma had been winning a useful degree of social acceptance, and liked children, to whom she was generous to a fault. Nelson naturally wanted to bring his daughter's exile with the Gibsons to an end. He reminded

Emma that the canal at Merton would have to be fenced off to prevent the infant from tumbling in, and expressed his confidence that 'she must turn out an angel if she minds what you say to her'. In fact, Emma did not act on all of Nelson's instructions. She failed to have Horatia inoculated against smallpox, as her father wanted, with the result that the child barely survived a dose of the virus in 1804. And she did not bring her to Merton. As late as March 1805 the admiral was writing to his mistress, 'How is my dear Horatia? I hope you have her under your guardian wing at Merton. May God bless her!'[18]

His one concern was Emma's extravagance, which he attempted to address. In 1804 he gave her an annuity of £500, based on the proceeds from Bronte, and bequeathed her an additional lump sum of £2000. But if Nelson died in service, Horatia would be dependent upon Emma's indifferent housekeeping. 'How I long to settle what [money] I intend upon her [Horatia],' he wrote, 'and not leave her to the mercy of any one, or even to any foolish thing I may do in my old age.' To this end on 6 September 1803 the codicil to his will directed that £4000 be invested and held in trust for 'Horatia Thompson Nelson', his 'adopted daughter', the annual interest to be used by Emma for the girl's upkeep. Perhaps he had reservations, for in May 1805 he announced that he was taking the money out of Emma's hands and placing it with trustees. The child's value may have been raised, if that was possible in such a doting parent, by the fate of another daughter in 1804. For Nelson left Emma pregnant when he returned to the Mediterranean in 1803, and a baby girl was born at the turn of the year. Probably the birth was supervised by Emma's mother at Clarges Street. Named Emma, but possibly not christened, the child died about March 1804, apparently in a convulsive fit. The news reached Nelson at the beginning of April, and he was 'so agitated . . . that I was glad it was night and that I could be by myself'.[19]

Every dainty envelope from Merton induced poignant memories in Nelson. Friends, acquaintances, relatives and children leaped from Emma's lively pages and transported the admiral to that halcyon spot. Charlotte was charming, Horace a model Etonian and the youngest Bolton girls, Ann and Eliza, perpetually feuding, although the former at least had become an articulate teenager capable of turning out a good letter. Some of the news was not so good. Maurice's widow, Sukey, had fallen into debt and Nelson found £90 to spare her selling her plate. Poor Davison had, as we learned earlier, also dug himself into a big hole. An enquiry at the House of Commons revealed that in attempting to get himself elected the member of parliament for Ilchester he had resorted to chicanery that shamed even that sink of corruption, and he was sent down to serve a year's imprisonment in the King's Bench and Marshalsea prisons. Nelson suspected 'those great folks' had it in for him, but cheerfully wrote to the prisoner, 'Do not take it to heart. It will soon pass away, and I shall come and see you in the Christmas holidays, and we shall laugh at the event.'[20]

Still, some matters were not so easily disposed of, and required his lordship's cooperation or supervision, even from so great a distance. Chief among these were the constant demands from family members seeking money or opportunities. The Boltons, still hoping for 'better times', were fingering Emma for money and pressing Nelson for funds to complete Tom's education. A new cause was their son-in-law, Sir William Bolton, who owed his appointment to the *Childers* sloop to Nelson's 'interest'. Nelson had raised young Bolton to the sea, and thought him 'a very attentive, good young man', but had again to protest that his influence was by no means as great as the family supposed. A tall, erect man, with a fair complexion, classic forehead, fine aquiline nose and full blue eyes, Sir William Bolton had the cut of a diplomat, with his mild, extremely likeable disposition, command of French, Italian, German and Spanish, and grounding in literature and the classics. He had served under Nelson in the *Agamemnon*, *Captain*, *Vanguard*, *Foudroyant*, *San Josef* and *St George*, commanded the *Dart* sloop in the Baltic and the Channel, and learned something about leadership. To the end he would be remembered for his cultivation of the 'young gentlemen' and gentle but firm management, and it was his boast that he had never brought anyone to a court martial. A colleague thought him 'truly a man of letters, an excellent scholar, a thorough sailor, and a most amiable and honourable man, kind, humane and feeling in his nature'. Fighting was the side of the business that did not appeal to 'Sir Billy'. Nelson put him in choice positions for taking prizes, but he failed to take a single ship, and the admiral reluctantly concluded him a 'lethargic' captain. As long as Nelson pulled strings Bolton passed up the promotional ladder until he made post-captain in 1805, but he consistently missed opportunities and the admiral felt let down. In private letters he confessed the young man a 'goose'. 'He never will do any good for himself,' he sighed, because 'he has no activity. I move the whole fleet with ten times the rapidity than he does his brig.'[21]

If 'Sir Billy' was a disappointment, Charles Connor, Emma's cousin, was a sad disaster. Nelson placed him among the 'young gentlemen' of the *Phoebe*, but Captain Capel was no hand at shaping adolescents, and Connor was soon frittering his money on boots and shoes and running into debt. In December 1803, when the fleet was watering at Sardinia, Nelson had captain and boy to his table for dinner, and received a fine account of the latter, but he had heard unsettling rumours of his mental condition and was minded of Emma's belief that a streak of insanity ran through the Connor line. 'He had about three months ago something wrong in his head,' Nelson wrote to her. 'The killing [of] a lieutenant and some men belonging to the *Phoebe* made such an impression that he fancied he saw a ghost, &c., but Dr Snipe thinks it is gone off. Was any of his family in that way? He is clever, and I believe Capel has been kind to him.' It was hard to put a finger on the boy's problem. There were 'curious' letters, 'a silly laugh' and 'something very odd about him', and in 1804 he lost the sight of his right eye when some bumptious midshipman flicked an olive stone into it. At times, however, Nelson suppressed his doubts. 'Charles is very much recovered,' he told Emma in June. 'There is no more the matter with his intellects than with mine! Quite the contrary; he is very quick.' Encouraged, Nelson transferred him to James Hillyar's *Niger* to improve his deficient seamanship. 'I am equally obliged to good Hardy about Charles. If Captain Hillyar cannot rate him, Hardy will,' he predicted. And as if those 'excellent' mentors were not enough, the Reverend Scott took Connor 'every day to read and write'. To prime this new beginning, Nelson provided an allowance of £30 a year, 'and that, I am sure, is abundance. The lad is well disposed, and I have no fears about him.' To Connor himself Nelson wrote, 'recollect that you must be a seaman to be an officer, and also that you cannot be a good officer without being a gentleman'. These hopes proved premature. The boy's behaviour in the *Niger* was unsatisfactory, and on 2 March 1805 we find Hillyar writing to Emma 'with extreme sorrow' from Plymouth. 'Within the last two days' Charles had demonstrated such disturbing 'symptoms of derangement' that the surgeon had ordered him bound. He had to be transferred to the hospital, and a 'respectable mercer' of the town appointed to manage his debts.[22]

At times the constant stream of family requests became as inconvenient as they were tedious. 'I am more plagued with other people's business, or rather nonsense, than with my own concerns,' Nelson complained. When his cousin, Robert Rolfe, curried the promotion of Midshipman Thomas Bedingfield, Nelson reminded him 'that we have no deaths in this fine climate, and the French fleet will not give us an opportunity of being killed off'. Less thoughtful still, Lieutenant Colonel Suckling even removed his son from an excellent position in the *Narcissus*, secured through Nelson, to send him to the Mediterranean so that he could continue under the admiral's direct eye. 'I don't blame the child,' groaned Nelson, 'but those who took [him] out of the most desirable situation in the navy. He never will get into such another advantageous ship, but his father is a fool.' It was with difficulty that both boys were served, but Bedingfield got his commission and Suckling switched to the *Ambuscade*.[23]

3

In the cabin of his first-class ship of the line, Nelson quietly worked towards what lay beyond, when his failing eyes and energies would take him away from the sea, and it relieved him to sense that many of the darker clouds over his future were dispersing. Merton – the new seat of his plan – was developing apace. If Emma was the 'Capability Brown' of the project, Davison its banker, Haslewood its solicitor and Cribb the works manager, it was humble Mrs Cadogan who really kept the estate going. 'I was greatly pleased to see that worthy faithful good woman . . . managing your house and lands with as much cleverness as a skilful member of the Agricultural Society,' said one visitor. 'The premises [are] in the highest order, the cattle healthy, the hay well got in and stowed away, and the dairy showing signs of plenty.'[24]

In March 1804 Nelson warned Emma to watch her expenditure, pointing out that the additions to the southern portion of the house, which housed the staff, and the creation of a new entrance to the grounds would be a considerable expense. It was necessary to prioritise. 'The entrance by the corner I would have certainly done,' he told her. 'A common white [painted] gate will do for the present, and one of [the] cottages which is in the barn, can be put up as a temporary lodge. The road [drive] can be made to a temporary bridge [over the 'Nile' stream] for that part of the *Nile* one day, shall be filled up. Downing's canvas awning will do for a passage. For the winter the carriage can be put in the barn, and giving up Mr Bennett's premises will save £50 a year. And another year we can fit up the coach house and stables, which are in the barn. The footpath should be turned. I did show Mr Haslewood the way I wished it done.' Nelson placed great importance on retaining control of the project, and advised Emma against turning it over to a contractor. Rather, Davison's architect, Thomas Chawner, who had drawn up the plans for the improvements, should be retained as an inspector with a fixed budget, and Nelson would assume the responsibility for purchasing materials and hiring 'respectable workmen'. When Emma told him about Spinks, a 'drunken' builder, he ordered his dismissal.[25]

Most of the master's instructions were turned into a reality, in particular the new lodge and driveway, which prospered mightily under Cribb's supervision. There were also the finer touches, such as the orchids Mrs Cadogan planted in the spring of 1805. But costs spiralled. An expensive gardener recommended by the Goldsmids was needed to complete the kitchen garden, and Cribb, who had several children to feed, demanded that his weekly wage be raised to twenty-seven shillings, almost twice the going rate, as well as board. Emma thought the amount 'enormous' and Cribb quit but since he soon returned we must suppose that she met satisfactory terms. Predictably, Davison ran into trouble controlling the expenditure. He wanted to economise by having Chawner design the gardens as well as the house, and successfully resisted Emma's proposal to put a gang of eight labourers at Cribb's command for three months at a cost of £1500. Davison was uncomfortable spending more than £400. However, Nelson was so enchanted with Emma's creative vision that in May 1805 he was insisting that Davison release funds to enable her to add a new kitchen to the south face of the house. The Merton project, like the Scott prize agency, damaged the relationship between Nelson and Davison, but from the pain came a remarkable transformation. As Captain Sutton testified after his return to England, 'I scarcely knew the place again. The alterations and improvements are far beyond anything I could have supposed. When finished it will be a delightful spot.'[26]

Merton grew in Nelson's imagination and sometime in 1804 overthrew his grander design of retiring to Bronte in Sicily. The duchy had much improved under Gibbs's management, and by the end of 1804 was cleared of debts. 'Everything goes on smoothly since we leased the Boschetto, nor shall we have any trouble in recovering the rents as long as General Acton remains in the island,' wrote Gibbs in August. It had been a long haul, which Nelson said had cost him £10,000, but the idea of becoming an improving and benevolent landlord continued to bewitch. He longed to install Emma as the Duchess of Bronte, to see the symbolic eagle of the duchy incorporated into his armorial design, and to fulfil a 'prophecy' that he would make Bronte 'the Happy'. As he said to Marsh in February 1804, 'Every appointment in church and state is mine, and my will pretty near constitutes the law.' The 'happiness or misery of 14,000 poor people' depended upon him, and 'most probably I shall someday reside there'. Yet within months he was also exploring the possibility of surrendering the estate to Ferdinand in return for an annual pension. The political instability of Sicily had knocked the shine from his sanctuary in the sun, and he was disappointed by the difference three years had made to his place in the country. Their Sicilian Majesties showed little interest in Emma. 'As for living in Italy, that is entirely out of the question,' he now told her. 'Nobody cares for us there, and if I had Bronte – which, thank God, I shall not – it would cost me a fortune to go there, and be tormented out of my life. I should never settle my affairs there.' By the summer of 1804 he was viewing Merton, rather than Bronte, as the place where his pilgrimage would end.[27]

So much was clearer, but the stubborn obstacle remained the money he needed to clear his debts, and support two households – his and Fanny's – and his status in society. As a commander-in-chief, Nelson received £1820 per annum in pay, £672 as compensation for sums formerly received for servants and followers, and £365 as 'table money'. By his new deal he would receive £2800 from Bronte, but reckoned that salaries, pensions and feus due each year could whittle his take to only £800. His statutory right to share in the flag eighth of prize money taken on his station was yielding little, as he ruefully concluded from the meticulous notes he kept in his diary. 'There is not one farthing of prize money stirring here,' he complained. 'Except at the first start, I have not got enough to pay my expenses.' More than a year into the job he believed that he was the poorer by upwards of a thousand pounds. Throughout it all, he knew that back home Emma was being her extravagant self. At Christmas 1804 he sent Emma £100 to cover her present, 'a trifle to the servants' and 'something' for 'the poor of Merton' as well as 'Mrs Cadogan, Miss Connor, Charlotte, &c.'. But Emma's outgoings were fluid. She entertained almost daily, and old Queensberry called at least every time she was at home. In April she had had eighty people to her birthday party. Her stream of gifts flowed without remission. 'But indeed,' protested Susannah Bolton, 'I do not like to receive so many presents. Nothing can make me love you better, but so many handsome things as you do for me and mine make me uncomfortable.' As usual, Nelson chided his mistress. 'I am glad that you . . . have made them all happy,' he said, 'and have no doubt but you have made yourself poor.' Yet to waste money to 'please a pack of people' was folly.[28]

Nelson remained conscious of his perilous solvency, especially while Merton continued to consume so much. When the £2100 he owed Greaves was paid in October 1803, he still owed Davison £3800 and George Matcham £4000. George was a sympathetic creditor, but spoke about moving abroad, and it was possible that he would have to call in funds.

He was still chewing on two old bones that promised some relief, government pensions and his prize suit against St Vincent. George Rose, who was proving to be a good friend, prompted Emma to remind Addington about her petition for a public pension, and he might have been inclined to grant her wish had he not a war to fight. Nothing was done before his administration fell in April 1804. Nelson, who was getting the measure of politicians, saw no good in the change. He wrongly expected that the 'hard hearted' Grenville would join the new national government, and predicted that its leader, the sombre Pitt, would be less amenable than Addington had been. 'All their promises are pie-crusts,' he warned Emma, 'made to be broken.' The new first lord of the Admiralty, Henry Dundas, now Viscount Melville, quickly disappointed. Initially Nelson thought Melville might give him 'something for his relatives', and even raised the hoary matter of the Copenhagen medal, but his cynicism was soon vindicated. The first lord, said he, would do nothing for Emma now that he could. Davison begged to differ. He spoke to Melville in 1805, and learned that he had actually approached Pitt about granting Emma £500 a year. Rose also fought gallantly, and secretly drafted a letter for Emma to sign, but Nelson was the truer prophet. 'I do not believe that Pitt will give you a pension any more than Addington, who I supported to the last moment of his ministry,' he told Emma miserably. 'There is no gratitude in any of them.' The same fate overcame his efforts to secure the extra £1000 per annum that would have brought his own pension into line with those of St Vincent and Duncan.[29]

It was all in vain. There was to be neither a state pension for Emma nor an increment to Nelson's, and the struggle merely increased their resentment. Nelson tried a few wild cards. He hoped the Queen of Naples might twist some arms, and she did ask her minister in London to speak in Emma's favour but it was a weak document. 'This is not what you asked for, nor . . . at all adequate to the purpose,' muttered Elliot, who suspected the queen was too wrapped up with her latest lover to attend to much else. Nelson's other recourse was Greville, who might be noble enough to grant his former lover and uncle's widow an allowance from Sir William's estate. Yet Greville merely confirmed his reputation as 'a shabby fellow' and there was nothing in law that could force him to improve Emma's legacy.[30]

15. One of several newly rediscovered watercolours made by Cornelia Knight during Nelson's voyage from Sicily to Malta and back in the spring of 1800. The trip had the character of a working holiday, and in this scene, which occurred at the beginning of May, the Nelson–Hamilton ménage are being rowed into the Anapo River, near Syracuse, presumably to view the Temple of Zeus, which appears on their left. Nelson, in his admiral's hat and uniform coat, sits in the stern, flanked by Emma with a parasol and probably Sir William. The event was sketched from the *Foudroyant* as it happened.

16. Two of Nelson's flagships survived long enough to be photographed, one arguably his favourite, the eighty-gun *Foudroyant*, built to a superior French design and launched in 1798. Carrying Nelson's flag for the year following June 1799, she witnessed the Bourbon restoration and probably the conception of Nelson's daughter, Horatia. During her later career, the ship served as a guard and training ship before being sold to private entrepreneurs. This photograph marks her sad end: shipwrecked on Blackpool Sands on 16 June 1897.

17. Rear Admiral Sir Thomas Graves (1747–1814), second-in-command of Nelson's assault force at Copenhagen, seen sporting the Star of the Order of the Bath awarded for his role in the battle. An engraving of a portrait by James Northcote, published in 1802.

18. Captain Edward Riou (1762–1801), captain of the *Amazon*, whose career had suffered through ill-health and a lack of 'interest'. His heroic death at Copenhagen robbed Nelson of one of his ablest followers.

19. The battle of Copenhagen as reconstructed by Nicholas Pocock (1740–1821), the famous marine artist. Pocock researched his subjects in depth, often interviewing participants before putting brush to canvas. Here, Nelson's ships (*centre*) are seen pummelling the Danish line beyond, with the city in the distance.

20. One of the best of the contemporary engravings of Merton Place, published in 1805 and apparently based on a drawing of the same year. It gives a clear view of the northern facade with its entrance porch, looking towards the bridge over the canal, and the recently improved eastern facade with the 'miradors' towards the lawn.

21., 22. and 23.
Thomas Baxter's sketches of 1803 and 1805 suggest that 'Paradise Merton' abounded in natural verdure and young ladies. Among the latter are Horatia, Nelson's daughter (*left*), Charlotte Nelson (*bottom left*) and one of the admiral's Bolton nieces (*bottom right*).

24., 25. and 26. The protégés of Horatio Nelson met different fortunes: (*top*) James Noble (1774–1851), promoted to commander in 1797 for distinguished service under Nelson, he was never given a ship, and survived decades on 'half pay'. Although he lived long enough to become a vice admiral, his only experience in command of a warship remained two months he had spent in charge of a ketch in 1796. Words he quoted in later years – 'even a flame unfed, or a sword laid by, will eat into itself and rust ingloriously' – reflected the embittered careers of many such officers. (*Top right*) Sir Henry Blackwood (1770–1832), a brilliant frigate captain, contributed greatly to Nelson's success at Trafalgar and rose to command the East Indian and Nore stations. (*Right*) Sir William Parker (1781–1866), one of the great cruiser captains of Nelson's last Mediterranean command, who died as Admiral of the Fleet and counted among his many successes a model operation in command of the China station in 1841–42. This photograph shows him at the time of his last appearance at a royal levee.

27. Rear Admiral George Murray (1759–1819) as he appeared in 1807. Establishing a close relationship with him in the Baltic, Nelson invited him to become his Captain-of-the-Fleet in the Mediterranean in 1803. The two worked in perfect harmony, and when Murray was unable to occupy the same position in the fleet that fought the battle of Trafalgar, Nelson chose to do without a Captain-of-the-Fleet rather than appoint another.

28. Dr William Beatty (1773–1842), a strong-minded and efficient naval surgeon, painted by Arthur W. Devis about 1806. The partnership between Nelson and his medical men created one of the greatest achievements of his command of the Mediterranean in 1803–1805. Beatty succeeded George Magrath as surgeon of the *Victory* in 1804, and four years later contributed to Nelson's immortality by publishing a moving account of his last moments. He became physician to the Duke of Clarence and received a knighthood.

29. Both Murray and Beatty were regular visitors to Nelson's day cabin, shown as it is today in this photograph from the *Victory*.

30. Thomas Masterman Hardy (1769–1839), flag-captain. Noted for his skilful handling of ships and severe discipline, Hardy was a devoted follower of Nelson, to whom he largely owed his prominence. He died a baronet, vice admiral and governor of Greenwich Hospital.

31. John Pollard (1787–1868), the midshipman at Trafalgar who was credited with killing the sniper responsible for Nelson's death. Promoted to lieutenant in 1806, he was retired as a commander in 1864, and appears here in a photograph of about that time.

32. Nelson on the quarterdeck of the *Victory* as she engages the enemy centre: a dramatic reconstruction by William Heysham Overend.

33. William Lionel Wyllie (1851–1931), a marine artist known for his attention to historical detail, exhibited this ambitious interpretation of Trafalgar in 1905. At about 2.30 the *Victory* (*centre*) extricates herself from the tangle composed of the *Fougueux*, *Temeraire* and *Redoutable* to turn some of her larboard guns upon the mutilated *Santissima Trinidad*, just shown at bottom right. Wyllie's enthusiasm extended to a strenuous advocacy of the preservation and restoration of Nelson's famous flagship.

In the end, it was the suit against St Vincent's agent over the right to the flag eighth of the prize money for the capture of the *Santa Brigida* and *Thetis* in 1799 that helped. The action in the Court of Common Pleas in 1802 had been inconclusive. Few commanders-in-chief had left their stations and continued to claim the flag right to prize money, and there were no clear guidelines. Previous practice was trawled with mixed results. Nelson's appeal to a higher court, the King's Bench, was introduced in June 1803. On 14 November, Lord Ellenborough ruled that the moment a superior officer left his station, the right of the remaining flag officers prevailed. It was an important ruling, and a capital victory for Davison, who had masterminded the campaign on the admiral's behalf. When Nelson received the news he declared enthusiastically that 'every person in government or out' would now recognise Davison's talents. A third of the disputed eighth went to Duckworth, but Nelson got the balance, amounting to £6500. It was sufficient, said the admiral, to 'put me out of debt, and, I hope, build my room at Merton, and leave my income, whatever it may be, unclogged'.[31]

There is some doubt about how much Nelson made from his victory. Captain Henry Digby, who had captured the prizes, submitted a counter-claim to the effect that if St Vincent had no claim to the spoils nor did any other admiral. The Marquis of Niza, the Portuguese admiral, also talked about challenging the allocation of Mediterranean prize money, although his ships had never taken any French prizes, and his country had not been at war with Spain. It was apparently not until the spring of 1804 that Nelson's award was confirmed.[32]

At the close of 1804, therefore, Nelson, after many tribulations, began to look financially comfortable for the first time since his break-up with Fanny. Bronte was yielding a modest but sure income, and he had the means of freeing Merton from debt. Furthermore, the war was not yet over, and more prize money could be anticipated. His affairs were wearing a rosier hue, and his course was clear. 'I hope very soon to finish with the French fleet,' he said, 'and return to England and dear Merton, which I think the prettiest place in the world.' The caveat, of course, was that first line. He had to beat the French. 'It will be my last battle,' he told Acton, 'and my whole exertion of knowledge and my life shall be put upon the issue.'[33]

XXI

MASTERING THE MACHINE

Ye mariners of England
That guard our native seas,
Whose flag has braved a thousand years,
The battle and the breeze –
Your glorious standard launch again
To match another foe!
And sweep through the deep
While the stormy winds do blow –
While the battle rages loud and long
And the stormy winds do blow.

Thomas Campbell,
'Ye Mariners of England', *c.*1801

I

In August 1803 Nelson established himself in the Gulf of Lions as the commander-in-chief of a fleet of eleven ships of the line, fifteen frigates and sloops and seven auxiliary vessels. Thirty-three sail to master a sprawling hotbed of conflict and intrigue.

Few reinforcements could be expected. During the peace Britain had decommissioned ships, allowed others to struggle on with insufficient maintenance and built few replacements. Nelson inherited an undersized fleet in poor condition, with some of the ships looking an ill match for the gales they would encounter on constant duty in the Gulf of Lions. Nelson held this important post for the two most difficult years of the war in the Mediterranean, when Britain's naval and military forces were being painfully rebuilt and what extra capacity was being created was being consumed by defences at home. Nelson knew that as long as Napoleon threatened to invade, however chimerically, the Mediterranean theatre would remain a Cinderella. 'I wish the invasion was over,' he wrote, 'for if the enemy do not attempt it we shall always be in hot water.' None of his successors would inherit such dire tools; nor, thanks to Trafalgar, face such a potent naval threat.[1]

He had to keep the seas with ships that should have been docked and repaired, and trickling reinforcements that allowed him to belatedly replace more dilapidated units but not to expand the size of his force. Nine sail of the line joined Nelson in 1803 and 1804, but distressed ships had to be sent home and at the end of the last year the battle fleet only stood at a dozen. However, from first to last Nelson's most strident call was for additional cruisers, but the number of frigates, sloops and brigs stabilised at around twenty-three in the summer of 1804, when he also had three bomb vessels, a schooner and a prison ship. The dockyards at Gibraltar and Malta were small, without a dry dock between them, and could only refit small ships or perform running repairs on the line of battle ships, which had to go home for extensive renovation. In mid-1804 five of Nelson's capital ships were waiting to be ordered home for an overhaul, while another three were obliged to continue service in a condition that placed frustrating limitations upon their use. At a time when the French were strengthening their force in Toulon, and Spain seemed likely to throw in with them, Nelson's fleet barely held its own.[2]

With no slack, every ship in this thin line had to play an important part. 'The going on in the routine of a station, if interrupted, is like the stopping of a watch,' Nelson warned Ball. 'The whole machine gets wrong.' Key detachments secured Gibraltar and Malta, which served as bases and rendezvous for the trade convoys proceeding up or down the Mediterranean, and Toulon was the obvious station for the battle fleet, but ships were more or less permanently stationed off Cadiz, where *L'Aigle* threatened Nelson's communications with England; Naples; the Maddalenas; and in the Adriatic, where Italian ports occupied by the enemy had to be watched. Behind these concentrations, Nelson's smaller ships kept the seas safe for British ships, chaperoned convoys, pursued French privateers, ran provisions, news, dispatches and people here and there, and discharged innumerable mundane tasks. So strapped was Nelson for ships that between 24 November and the end of December 1803 he had not even the means to send a letter.[3]

Whatever depressed Nelson about his fleet, he was enthused by its human resources. A few months after taking over he informed St Vincent that he had never commanded a force so well-mannered and agreeable, and almost a year later it was still a fleet in which 'everyone wishes to please me, and where I am as happy as it is possible for a man to be'. The fleet that won the battle of the Nile – the original band of brothers – may have been more feted, but it was this, the Mediterranean fleet of 1803–5 that made Nelson's ideal team. With such men his expectations transcended all doubts. The result of any meeting with the French, he said, was foregone.[4]

Relatively few of the officers were familiar to Nelson. From his previous

Mediterranean command there came two of the brothers, Hardy and Hallowell, Murray, who had also served in the Baltic, and a goodly number of lesser names, including Thomas Capel of the *Phoebe*, James Hillyar of the *Niger*, and a former lieutenant of the *Foudroyant*, Thomas Staines, now in charge of the *Camelion*. Nelson was particularly pleased with Hillyar, who had been with him in Corsica and done fine boat work in the Mediterranean. To support a needy family he had actually postponed promotion to the rank of commander, preferring regular work as a lieutenant at a time when most commanders were unemployed. Now Nelson got pleasure in increasing the armament of the *Niger* to raise her status and enable Hillyar to command her as a post-captain. 'I shall feel happy if allowed to remain in this country in *any* ship under your command,' the thirty-three-year-old responded. The fleet also included many who had attached themselves to Nelson's star in the Baltic and Channel in 1801. Murray, Gore, Sutton and John Conn, the latter flag captain in the *Canopus*, were notable examples, but some were unlucky. Bedford, commanding the *Thunderer* off Brest, wished himself 'a thousand times' with Nelson, and shared his yearning with young Langford, now recovered from the wounds he had suffered at Boulogne, but tossing about the Channel as commander of the *Lark*.[5]

Among the flag officers and captains Nelson's other old associates were the two admirals Bickerton and Campbell, and the frigate captain Courtenay Boyle of the *Seahorse*, one of the 'young gentlemen' of Nelson's old *Boreas*. Bickerton, 'a very intelligent and correct officer', was a colleague of West Indian days, and had superseded Keith in command of the Mediterranean. Rear Admiral George Campbell had served under Nelson during the blockade of Corsica, but now bonded more strongly. Indeed, when Nelson finally applied for leave to restore his health and predicted the 'pretty general' sorrow it would cause in the fleet, it was Campbell who was particularly downcast. All these standing friends and acquaintances were welcomed with particular accord. 'My dear Boyle,' read the captain of the *Seahorse*, 'I am very happy to have you in so fine a frigate under my command. I am ever, yours most faithfully, Nelson and Bronte.'[6]

But for the most part Nelson found himself in command of 'perfect strangers' who nevertheless revealed themselves to be 'very good men'. Most were experienced officers. Captain Ryves, whose talents as a cartographer have been noticed, was Nelson's age and had been in the navy since 1774. Barlow of the *Triumph* was a year older, and had won a knighthood for a remarkable single-ship action in 1801, in which he had inflicted twenty-six times the number of casualties he had sustained. The captain of the *Narcissus*, Ross Donnelly, had originally been made a commander for taking charge of the *Montagu*, seventy-four, after the death of her captain during 'the Glorious First of June', and had accumulated an excellent service record that recently included the successful evacuation of British shipping from Genoa. Of all the new friends the command brought, Nelson's favourite was Richard Goodwin Keats of the *Superb*, who had distinguished himself under Saumarez in a fight with the Spaniards off Algeciras in 1801. Nelson's new correspondence was peppered with glowing tributes to Keats, whose presence in a battle was 'alone as equal to *one* French 74'. Much like Nelson, prickly, in need of attention and sensitive to others, Keats struck the commander-in-chief as 'one of the most sensible and best officer[s] I almost ever met', willing to dispense clear-cut good sense on matters private and professional. In this 'finest squadron in the world' it was Keats who succeeded to such soulmates as Collingwood, Fremantle, Troubridge and Ball, and became one of the most frequent visitors to the *Victory*.[7]

As always, Nelson had officers to his table, sometimes on a rota basis but often to welcome those newly arrived on the station. He was soon endearing himself as only he knew how. Gore believed the commander-in-chief to be 'the best admiral and kindest friend' the service had 'ever . . . known' and the hero of 'every officer and man'. That was certainly true for some. Malcolm of the *Kent* and Staines of the *Camelion* loved serving under Nelson so much that when their ships were ordered home they asked to exchange their commands with other captains to remain on the station. Strachan of the *Donegal*, who took the admiral as the model for his career, declared that if Nelson retired from the Mediterranean then so would he. It was of such material that Nelson fashioned the 'finest squadron in the world'.[8]

2

Nelson led on the basis of access, example, obligation and reward. He received others with respect and what Gillespie, sometime physician of the fleet, described as a 'noble frankness of manner' and 'freedom from vain formality and pomp'. He created obligations by a sprightly attention to wants and a belief in the power of reward, and inspired by an unremitting dedication to high standards of service. In his diary he wrote the names of promising officers, noting 'a very good young man' or 'a very attentive good man', and expressed joy in assisting them. 'Had the pleasure of rewarding merit in the person of Mr Hindman, gunner's son, of the *Bellerophon* for his conduct', he said, and 'I had the comfort of making an old *Agamemnon* a gunner into the *Camelion*'. No one summarised Nelson's appeal more succinctly than Captain Henry Blackwood, who joined his fleet in 1805. 'He governed those who were under him by the most gratifying acts of kindness, endeavouring to make all sorts of service as pleasant as circumstances would admit. His discernment also made him assign to every officer that service for which his abilities were best calculated, and though he would have duty done, yet he never drew the cord too tight. He carried on the duty of a commander-in-chief, by addressing himself to the feelings of those under him, on which he so well acted, that every officer and man vied who should do his best.'[9]

Unlike many in high positions, Nelson never forgot what he had once been, and understood the insecurities and ambitions of younger or upcoming officers, but he encouraged good teamwork as well as personal initiative, and healed and arbitrated where necessary. 'We must all in our several stations exert ourselves to the utmost,' he encouraged Schomberg of the *Madras*, 'and not be nonsensical in saying I have no order for this, that or the other, if the king's service clearly marks what ought to be done.' On one occasion a difficulty arose between Keats and Murray, the captain of the fleet, whose efficiency was normally relieved by a mild disposition. Nelson assured the petulant Keats that Murray would never withhold supplies from the *Superb*. Rather 'he would stretch the point to comply with your wishes'. Further, 'the situation of first captain is . . . a very unthankful office, for if there is a deficiency of stores he must displease . . . for no ship can have her demands complied with. I wish, my dear Keats, you would turn this in your mind, and relieve Admiral Murray from the uneasiness your conversation has given him, for I will venture to say that if he could . . . show a partiality it would be to the *Superb* because her captain husbands the stores in a most exemplary manner.' He urged Keats to come aboard to 'shake hands' and restore harmony.[10]

The commander-in-chief's interest extended to the youngest in the fleet. He admitted 'young gentlemen' as well as adults to the 'cheerful hours of meals', and in 1803 forsook a meeting with his senior officers to attend a midshipmen's 'party', convened to greet a new arrival. There were boys scarce three feet high in the gathering, but the admiral made an acceptable guest in their world of small troubles. In 1804 twelve Russian cadets temporarily joined the fleet to enlarge their training. Worried that they were 'far removed from . . . country and relations', Nelson beseeched the boys to 'consider' him their 'sincere friend', and wrote to the Russian minister in London to recommend a supplement to their meagre allowance. 'These very fine lads must have hats, shoes and money for their mess,' he said. Lieutenant Charles Tyler of the *Hydra*, the son of one of Nelson's former captains, also benefited from the admiral's paternalism. The foolish young fellow jumped ship to elope with a dancer in Malta, and Nelson wrote to Naples, where he suspected the couple might have fled, offering to pay for the boy's release if he found himself imprisoned. He even begged the frowning Admiralty to consider the 'youthful imprudence' of the 'unfortunate young officer' and to 'allow his name to remain on the list of lieutenants'. The suit was successful, and Tyler died a 'retired' captain in 1846. Such incidents reveal the deep-seated humanity in Nelson. He did not shirk from punishing deserving malcontents, but knew that even the good and the able could find themselves in difficulties, and that mistakes were part of the learning experience.[11]

Demanding professionalism, Nelson's penetrating eye generated letters on almost every conceivable matter. An absent dockyard boatswain, the importance of rolling water casks up beaches at low water to reduce saline contamination, the superiority of Russian 'duck' smocks and trousers, the salvage of a bag of bread that had fallen out of a rowing boat, and the necessity for punctilious accounts, with much else, vied with the terrifying weight of international diplomacy in his ceaseless correspondence. He could be sharp with the slovenly and careless, but hastened to remove crushing clouds from above the heads of luckless officers. After Gore exonerated Henry Whitmarsh Pearse, a newly promoted but disappointing commander of *L'Alcyon* sloop, the admiral admitted that he had been hasty. 'I am satisfied from your account of the state of *L'Alcyon* that blame is not imputable to her commander,' he said, 'and I request you will *tell* him so.' It is not clear whether Gore or Nelson had the truer impression. One who served with Pearse remembered his lethargy and poor discipline, and thought him 'good for nothing'. And yet in September 1809 he took a notorious corsair after a gruelling eight-hour chase.[12]

Despite Nelson's close supervision, he rewarded liberally, remembering the role that praise had played in his own career. Sometimes he bestowed gifts, including pieces of silverware that he had had engraved. We can imagine how the master of the *Victory* treasured the silver boat-shaped coaster that Nelson gave him as a token of his appreciation, and it can still be seen at Lloyd's. Prize money was the most obvious inducement, especially among the lower ranks. Ensconced in the Mediterranean, Nelson continued his fight for the speedy release of prize money. When the *Maria Theresa*, a prize of the *Victory*, was unfairly withheld as a droit of the Admiralty – that is a vessel taken before the formal declaration of war – the admiral urged a speedy resolution. 'When their lordships take into account that the poor sailor . . . has been for these last two years shut up from every comfort of the shore, and [is] in want of his little pittance . . . to procure him some few necessaries of life, I am sure they will agree with me in the propriety of its being immediately paid,' he wrote. No reward compared, in his view, to praise and recognition. The City of London, still dogged by its failure to honour the veterans of Copenhagen, stirred Nelson to new heat when their proposed vote of thanks to the Mediterranean fleet omitted the names of Bickerton and Campbell. 'The constant, zealous and cordial support' of his rear admirals, thundered the commander-in-chief, deserved 'all my thanks and admiration. We have shared together the constant attention of being more than fourteen months at sea, and are ready to share the dangers and glory of a day of battle.' To strengthen his protest he authorised Davison to publish it, and its appearance in the press was said to have 'staggered' the city magnates. Meekly they changed their tribute, but still failed to win Nelson's approval. On his own hook, Nelson never spared due praise, often in brief throwaway lines that revealed how easy it came to him. 'The whole of your conduct is so correct,' he told the harassed naval commissioner at Gibraltar, 'that I can have no doubt but it must always give me satisfaction.'[13]

Encouraging followers and maintaining morale depended much upon a commander-in-chief's ability to promote. All commanders-in-chief were expected to promote eligible candidates to fill vacancies at the levels of lieutenant and commander, but in the Mediterranean, where there was no convenient recourse to the Admiralty, the prerogative was extended to cover the rank of post-captain. Although such appointments were subject to the approval of the Admiralty, they empowered commanders-in-chief by giving them the ability to reward on the spot. It was usual for admirals to gather their favourites in the flagship, where they were at hand for any necessary promotions, but good commanders-in-chief also saw the wisdom of rewarding outstanding merit, however little 'interest' an individual might possess. There were effective limitations to these valuable powers, of course. To promote there had to be vacancies. Existing officers had to die, retire or fall sick, or new posts had to be created, usually by prizes being taken and incorporated into the navy. It was not surprising, therefore, that ambitious aspirants sometimes drank to 'a bloody war', 'a sickly season' or 'sea room'.

Nelson had relatives, friends and followers to serve, but also believed in merit. For him the issue of promotion was a constant headache, swallowing disproportionate amounts of his correspondence and contemplation. He was simply inundated with applicants, and in October 1803 protested to his brother William that he had eighty-six candidates for commissions. Applications on behalf of one person or another poured in from such family members as Emma, Robert Rolfe, William Suckling and Lord Walpole, from friends such as Clarence, Windham, Rose, Spencer, Keith, Kingsmill, Pole and Holloway, and from numerous dignitaries and naval officers with sons or nephews kicking their heels in need of careers, advancement or simply a paternal eye. Some Nelson was able to satisfy. Lord Radstock wrote of his son's ecstatic gratitude for the admiral's 'incessant kindness', while Minto, whose son George and nephew William flourished in the fleet, trilled that Nelson did 'nothing by halves, either to enemies or friends'. The admiral enquired after the nephew of Captain Foley, who was supposed to be in the *Medusa*, and discovered that Gore was so tired of the boy's 'slothful want of care in his person' that he had sent him home. Nelson managed to persuade Captain Durban to bring him out to the Mediterranean again, where the youngster was spurred to reform and given a second chance. Upon reading Nelson's later report, Captain Foley flooded with gratitude for his old chief's protection of 'an outcast without character or a friend' and restoring him to the right road. But others were beyond Nelson's power to help. 'I assure you that I most sincerely wish to promote Brown,' Nelson wrote to his old colleague Pole, but 'alas, nobody [in the fleet] will be so good as to die, nor will the French kill us!' 'I have not the smallest chance of being useful to him,' read Catherine Lutwidge, who had a 'young friend' in the fleet, 'for it is not *two* [captured] French fleets that will clear . . . the Admiralty ordering list.'[14]

The exemplary health of Nelson's fleet, the scarcity of prizes and lack of lethal action all conspired to clog avenues of promotion in the fleet, but the flood of requests from the Admiralty caused the commander-in-chief the greatest grief. Some of the board's relatives were with the fleet, including St Vincent's nephew, William Parker, captain of the *Amazon*, and Troubridge's son and son-in-law, the last the commander of the *Juno*, Henry Richardson. As early as 19 May 1803 the first lord began firing demands for protégés or the relatives of important friends to be fed into whatever positions there were. In thirteen letters the 'Admiralty list' monopolised twenty-one promotions, thirteen lieutenancies, five posts as commander, and three post-captaincies. Little leeway was allowed, and sometimes St Vincent insisted that absolute priority be given his nominees. When Nelson complained the crusty old earl blamed his predecessor, Spencer, who had 'loaded' him with obligations, but cuttingly observed that he himself had gone to the Mediterranean with an even longer list and 'never uttered a murmur' until the pressure began to 'wound my feelings in the extreme'.[15]

Sometimes St Vincent championed the relatives of people his government wished to accommodate, such as Lords Rolle, Camden, Carysfort, Grey and Leven, turning the wheels of political corruption, but Nelson by no means disagreed with all of the Admiralty's sponsorships. Like most admirals, he regarded the children of existing naval officers as wards of the service. Henry Duncan, one Admiralty protégé, was a son of the late victor of Camperdown, while James Hillyar and Peter Parker were on Nelson's private list as well as the Admiralty's. Lieutenant Parker's grandfather, Sir Peter Parker, had nurtured the young Horatio Nelson's career; as the admiral noted in his diary, he 'made me *everything that I am*'. He got Parker to the post of commander before sending him home, where his next step might come easier. Nelson also served Lucius Curtis, the son of Sir Roger Curtis, a notable sea officer, who wrote one of the most moving letters of thanks still in the archives.[16]

But there was no doubt that the Admiralty's list displaced Nelson's own nominees, and reduced his powers to reward the merit around him. By promoting Silas Paddon, an Admiralty eleve, to be a lieutenant in *L'Alcyon* prize, for example, he had to disappoint a more deserving officer at his elbow. Nor was there any relief when Melville succeeded St Vincent as first lord in May 1804. Within six months Melville had submitted a 'long list' of his recommendations, restoring the number of unsatisfied aspirants in the fleet to sixty or seventy. Again Nelson felt impotent to serve his own, and when old colleagues Holloway and Louis asked him to forward their protégés, he had to explain that he could do nothing unless they were on the official Admiralty's list. In letter after letter he reminded anxious patrons that he could not kill people to create vacancies. A cadre of discontented younger officers developed, and some grew so dispirited at prospects in the Mediterranean that they asked permission to return home. Lord Camden's nephew, while admitting his great obligations to Nelson, resolutely declared that 'he never would go to sea again'. Others going home included one Hamilton, tired after a long year as tenth lieutenant of the *Victory*, and even Edmund Palmer, who was a favourite of Clarence and St Vincent. Wherever possible the admiral tried to dissuade the malcontents from making hasty decisions. He transferred a few to other ships in which the prospects for an upward step looked brighter. Admiral Duncan's son shifted between the *Royal Sovereign* and the *Narcissus* before succeeding the ailing Corbet as commander of the *Bittern*.[17]

For most of his command Nelson struggled to reconcile the Admiralty list with his own. On the last were the likes of Midshipman Philip Horn, one of the late Riou's supporters who had been seriously wounded at Copenhagen, and John Woodin, a midshipman at the Nile. Horn became a lieutenant of the *Excellent* and the *Amazon*, while Woodin got his first commission in the *Belleisle*. The ubiquitous but not undeserving Midshipman Faddy, another Nile survivor, whose importuning mother had developed 'the impudence of the devil', shifted his sea chest from the flagship to the *Triumph* with Nelson's commission to act in her as a lieutenant. And the promotion of two Admiralty preferments was delayed so that William Layman, the most brilliant of all Nelson's followers, could command the *Weazle* sloop in 1803. Layman's elevation, said Nelson, demonstrated to all 'the very happy consequence of a fleet looking up to a commander-in-chief for promotion'.[18]

Nelson never got the better of his promotion problem, but while discontent festered it does not seem to have undermined the esteem in which the officers held their chief or their commitment to duty. The admiral's own goodwill was manifest, and everyone knew that under such a commander, with a French fleet ready to sail, the arithmetic could change within hours. Nelson appointed at least 84 commissioned officers in two years, half of them out of the *Victory*. It was a sluggish stream for a large fleet occupying a principal theatre of war, 72 lieutenants (22 of them merely existing lieutenants being elevated within the pecking order), 6 commanders, 4 captains and 2 who took up shore positions. Six moderate prizes taken into the navy and requiring officers had directly or indirectly created twenty-five of these positions, almost as many as the need to replace sick, injured or deceased officers. The capture of a substantial portion of the French battle fleet would hugely accelerate the climb up the promotion ladder.[19]

For many of Nelson's officers the goal of victory promised promotion as well as glory, helping to counter latent disillusionment. It could come that week or the next or the week after. Indeed, as far as battle was concerned, overconfidence rather than disillusion was the greater danger. No one doubted the issue of a contest. The blustering challenges of the seas in the Gulf of Lions continually developed the fleet's seamanship, and on average the ships of the line exercised their guns a little less than once a month. Their French, or potential Spanish, adversaries could offer nothing to match such practical training. Nelson's men had no doubt they could give their foes a sound beating. Gore was ready to tackle a French seventy-four with his frigates, and Capel of the *Phoebe* enjoyed a running discussion with his fellow captain William Parker about whether their two frigates could defeat a ship of the line. Nelson discouraged the experiment, but he saw as gallant a pair of apprentices as graced any fleet and understood their ambitions. 'I dare say,' he said to them concluding one homily, 'that you consider yourself a couple of fine fellows, and when you get away from me, you will do nothing of the sort, but think yourselves wiser than I am!'[20]

3

Lord Nelson's commitment to a new generation of naval talent, irrespective of 'interest', can best be appreciated by looking at individual cases. The greatest of all the little admirals he raised to the sea was William Hoste, the son of a Norfolk parson like himself. Hoste had risen to the rank of post-captain under Nelson's tutelage during the last war, but fell into unemployment during the peace. In 1804 the admiral got a despondent letter from Hoste. 'Fancy the youngster whom you took with you in '93 . . . changed to an old Sea Fencibles captain stationed at Lynn with the very moderate allowance of thirty shillings per diem for literally doing nothing,' William wrote. Nelson did not like the thought, and sent Hoste a powerful testimonial that he could take to Melville, begging the first lord to rescue his favourite protégé. Melville had, in fact, anticipated the request and at the end of the year Captain Hoste returned to the Mediterranean in command of a small frigate, *Eurydice*, and began the second phase of a remarkable naval career.[21]

Exemplifying the young man without interest was Robert Pettet, described by Nelson as 'a very worthy, agreeable companion' who had 'risen from humble origin by his own merits, with a little of my assistance'. Robert had made lieutenant in 1794, when his career faltered until Nelson slotted him into a succession of lieutenancies in the *San Josef*, *St George* and *Victory*. Soon after reaching the Mediterranean the admiral promoted him commander of the *Termagant* sloop, a situation he filled with credit.[22]

Partnering Pettet in the lieutenants' wardrooms of Nelson's ships was one who more than any other typified the sort of officer that Nelson wanted to bring forward. William Layman had many qualities that appealed to the admiral, including loyalty, gratitude, passable manners, an apparent sense of honour and exceptional energy and ability. Indeed, if the navy needed talent, Layman was it. Perhaps he had too much of it, and his irritating tendencies to disregard orders and lecture superiors, as well as his lack of effective 'interest' did not help. Nelson saw it, and, convinced that Layman was a near self-destructing genius, tried to protect him, but the Fates would decree otherwise. Through crisis after crisis, Nelson vociferously supported Layman in the belief that the navy needed him.

Their relationship had begun in 1799, when Nelson was in Sicily and Layman a late entrant to His Majesty's navy, looking for a lieutenancy at the comparatively mature age of thirty-two. A Suffolk man, born on 16 July 1767, Layman was the son of William and Mary Layman of St Clements in Ipswich. His history had been enterprising. He may have joined the navy in the *Portland* in 1782, as he later claimed, but he certainly sailed the English Channel and the North Sea in the *Myrmidon* from 1782 to 1786, quickly rising by dint of labour from ordinary seaman to midshipman and master's mate. By his own account, as a seventeen-year-old officer of the watch he had scuttled the lower deck during a storm and saved the ship. At any rate, he transferred to the *Amphion* frigate, serving in her as master's mate from 1786 to 1788 and attracting the attention of Nelson's friend, Prince William Henry, later the Duke of Clarence. But he went down with fever in Jamaica and was invalided home, just short of the sea time he needed to qualify for a lieutenancy. At this point what slim 'interest' he had failed. Naval appointments were scarce at a time of peace, and Layman joined the East India Company.[23]

There he earned a solid reputation. In 1794, when twenty-six, he was given the formidable charge of taking two or three merchant ships from Bombay to China, New South Wales and the Philippines. A fearful but admiring superior bequeathed him to 'Heaven and your own judgement'. From this and other experiences Layman absorbed much information about the east. Two years later, writing from China as captain of the *Britannia*, he was supplying details of the waters east of Java, information that the commodore of the East India fleet thought deserved 'the thanks of future navigators'. Recognising that Britain's oak forests were being depleted, Layman also surveyed the availability of substitute timber in the east, and in 1797 wrote to the Admiralty with a visionary proposal to build teak ships for the Royal Navy in Bombay. Consumed by the idea, he decided to take a serious gamble with his career. Rather than continue with the Company, he would return to England to seek a shipbuilding contract. His senior in Bombay assured the chairman of the East India Company in London as 'a certainty' that 'he can give you more information respecting matters here in general than any man you can find. Added to a strong head, he constantly lays himself out for information of every kind, and he may be depended on.' These years encapsulated the essence of Layman: a questing mind that produced a ceaseless flow of ideas, and the habit of bombarding government with detailed prospectuses for one scheme or another. When the company chairman commended him to the secretary for war, then Henry Dundas, the latter already knew of the man, having received a memorial from the obscure merchant captain, sent from Manilla.[24]

It was while promoting his plan to build teak ships that Layman approached Nelson in hope of reviving his lapsed naval career. On 12 November 1799 he addressed a letter to the most famous living admiral, who, he had heard, was the decided friend of merit. Because his merchant career did not count, Layman remained four months short of the sea time needed for the king's commission, but expected to pass his examination and needed a ship – and a patron, and he had set his heart on serving with Nelson. His letter mentioned no friends that the admiral knew, but was supported by Fanny, then living near Ipswich, Layman's home town, who wrote to her husband that a certain Mr Reynolds had asked her to recommend the young officer. In April 1800 Reynolds himself tackled Nelson about 'a most superior young man, who wishes for no other happiness but that of being employed as a volunteer or in any way you think him useful'. By now he had served his sea time – finding a temporary post as a midshipman in the *Sulphur* – and passed his examination for lieutenant on 5 June 1800. 'He is uncommonly able as a navigator,' explained Reynolds, 'having commanded a ship in the East Indian country service, and is admirably adapted to fulfil any trying situation where seamanship and spirit might be useful. He is strongly recommended to Sir Thomas Troubridge, but thinks nothing will do but having your sanction to make his appearance.'[25]

Layman had also appealed to St Vincent, then commander-in-chief of the Channel fleet. The craggy earl was interested in the shipbuilding proposal, and would implement a similar, possibly derivative, programme when he became first lord of the Admiralty, and he was impressed with the applicant's 'character . . . and laudable zeal'. In September Layman was rated a lieutenant in the *Formidable*. During the few months he served he claimed to have invented a method of making 'fetid' water 'perfectly sweet and clean', but if so it was not pursued. Instead, an alternative belatedly appeared when Nelson invited him to join his flagship, the *San Josef*, in December. In January 1801 Nelson finally met the 'stout full-faced' young man bubbling with ideas, and took him into the *St George*, bound for the Baltic. He watched with admiration as his new neophyte helped get the *Warrior* off a shoal in the Downs, and put him into a dispatch. In conversation, Layman told Nelson that he did not think 'what I did last night' deserved the commendation. 'But I do,' replied the admiral. 'The loss of one line-of-battle ship might be the loss of a victory.' At Copenhagen the successes continued. Layman distinguished himself in the *Isis*, restoring the larboard lower-deck battery to action after most of the guns had been silenced. A few days afterwards Nelson wrote to Troubridge that the lieutenant was 'really an acquisition when kept within bounds'. The comment is interesting, because it tells us that Nelson was already finding Layman over-enthusiastic.[26]

Unable, for the time being, to return to Nelson's command, Layman promoted himself in his own irrepressible way. During the peace of Amiens he kept his name before government by a flurry of exciting proposals based upon his knowledge of the east and fusing an almost scientific instinct with an eye for the practical and utilitarian. Some had a degree of success. When Britain was troubled with worrying food shortages, Layman pointed out the local sources of supply that enabled ships bound for the East Indies to reduce the quantity of provisions they needed to take with them, suggestions, he said later, that influenced the Admiralty in 1802. More notably, he proposed that the West Indian slave trade be abolished because communities of industrious free Chinese labourers could be imported who would work the fields equally well for a proportion of the profits. Layman flourished a letter of support from Nelson, and for a while the plan was kicked about the Treasury and Colonial Office, but it was not tried until after Layman left for the Mediterranean in 1803 and then badly bungled. It did not resurface until 1810, when a successful plan to introduce Chinese workers to Ceylon got underway. Meanwhile, in April 1802 Layman had resubmitted his plan to build warships in Bombay. It was an opportune moment, since the first lord, St Vincent, was locked in disputes with the British ship-builders and timber suppliers, and ready to grasp any straw that reduced his dependence upon them. St Vincent had already begun building teak ships in Bombay in 1801, possibly inspired by Layman's earlier submissions; now the lieutenant offered to deliver improved teak ships of the line for half the price of comparable vessels built in Britain. With the use of an old sixty-four, a 'decayed' sloop and a handful of experienced dockyard workers, he undertook to furnish a line of battle ship and a frigate every year. St Vincent looked as if he would take the bait, but Layman's bid lapsed when he sailed with Nelson to the Mediterranean in 1803.[27]

Nelson appreciated a mind that explored such inaccessible regions, but he saw the danger of creating enemies, particularly in Troubridge, who had served in the East Indies in his younger days. As the admiral confided to Emma, Layman was a 'very active' and 'good' officer, but had ventured 'to know more about India than Troubridge . . . I often tell him not to let his tongue run so fast, or his pen write so much.' In other words, Layman smacked of the proverbial wise guy who knew too many answers. This judgement was vindicated after the outbreak of war, when Nelson appointed him a lieutenant in the *Victory*. While Nelson proceeded to the Mediterranean in the *Amphion*, Layman followed with Captain Sutton in the flagship, and was soon displaying as much imprudence as activity.[28]

On 28 May the *Victory* took a French frigate, *L'Ambuscade* (thirty-eight), in the Bay of Biscay, and Layman was ordered to take her to Plymouth, wind permitting. The inexperienced officer quickly rewrote his instructions. Deciding that Nelson had need of such vessels as *L'Ambuscade*, and supposing that he might even get the command of her, he headed for Gibraltar instead. On his way south he took two prizes, including a deeply laden French merchantman, the *Maria Theresa*. At Cabrita Point, near Gibraltar, his boats also assisted the

Bittern to take another two vessels on 12 June. Apart from prize goods, Layman captured valuable intelligence, including French signal books, sea charts and a current list of ships' distinguishing pendants. But he quickly annoyed his superior at the Rock. Though a mere lieutenant, he persuaded Governor Trigge to allow him to recruit men from the military garrison to enable him to go in search of a fifty-four-gun French frigate rumoured to be cruising the area. He had the audacity to invite Corbet of the *Bittern* to join him in the campaign, suggesting that as the senior naval officer Corbet should take the *Ambuscade*, a frigate, and allow Layman to command his sloop. Predictably the irascible Corbet had no intention of handing a ship the king had entrusted to his care to a lieutenant, and resented being told his business. He testily ordered Layman to get his prize frigate repaired and await further orders. This was the least of Layman's troubles. The agent victualler at Gibraltar insinuated to Nelson that he had embezzled some of the spoils of the *Maria Theresa* before they had been legally condemned in the prize court. He had certainly been naive, using part of the proceeds to clothe and feed his men and making advance payments on their prize money. He had no business pre-empting the decision of the prize court, exposing himself to charges of corruption. As no request had been made for a court martial, Nelson avoided that ordeal, but he had no alternative but to investigate.[29]

Captains Keats and White got the job of trawling through the evidence, and while they cleared the defendant of embezzlement they concluded that his conduct had been 'indiscreet' and irregular. Nelson breathed a sigh of relief, and hoped his protégé had learned a salutary lesson. But he crushed Layman's hopes of commanding *L'Ambuscade*. Prematurely, Layman was planning to arm the ship with twenty-four-pound carronades and forty-two-pound guns to make her the equal of any single-decked warship, but seemed unaware that even if she had been a weaker vessel, say a lightly armed thirty-two-gun frigate, she would still have been beyond the reach of such a junior officer as himself. Nevertheless, the man was irrepressible and fresh ideas appeared on Nelson's desk, including a detailed plan to cut a French corvette and brig out of Marseilles Bay. 'Should Lord Nelson . . . deem the object worth the risk and give directions for the enterprise, I should beg leave to suggest the following outline for carrying the commodore ship. In a dark night with the wind easterly, all the boats employed should proceed . . .' And so on, in close considered detail, almost as if the admiral had never planned such expeditions himself.[30]

For the moment, Layman had to satisfy himself with being a lieutenant in the *Victory*. He filled his spare time by studying the design of the flagship, and concluding that 'additional riders' fitted during a partial rebuilding of 1800 had added 171 tons to her weight and reduced her draught by seven inches. Of course, he also had improvements to suggest, and according to one account reduced an exasperated Captain Hardy to complaining that either Layman or he would have to leave the ship, for assuredly it was not big enough for both. If so, Hardy was no doubt pleased when Nelson appointed Layman acting commander of the *Weazle* sloop on 6 October 1803, in itself a mark of great confidence considering the Admiralty's insistence that vacancies should be filled with the board's own nominees. Nelson's faith in his industrious subordinate was indeed undiminished. He had 'frequent confidential conversations' with Layman, and found that they shared a concern about the use of unseasoned timber in the building of ships, a practice that caused premature decay. Layman recommended tropical timber, and spoke so convincingly of the resources of the Malabar coast that Nelson advised him to lay his ideas before the Admiralty. Nevertheless, his lordship understood why Layman drove some to distraction. 'I hope Mr Layman will be confirmed,' he wrote to Troubridge. 'He is a very clever fellow, and if he would not prate and write so much he would be better. I tell him it is a pity he ever learned to write.'[31]

Nelson sent the *Weazle* to Gibraltar, where she shipped supplies between Tangier and the garrison, escorted convoys through the Strait, ran errands and harried the numerous small French privateers operating about the Gut. Keeping a station in an eight-mile strait amidst boisterous winds and seas, four strong tides and a current, and chasing privateers in the shallow waters they infested was highly dangerous work, but Layman earned the praise of everyone in Gibraltar. Expecting a war with Spain, he also came up with a plan to seize the Spanish island of Tarifa, then a nest of French corsairs, and turn it into a base for raiding the enemy coasting trade.[32]

On the morning of 29 February 1804 the *Weazle* struck a reef while working into the Bay of Gibraltar in thick fog. Layman had gone below after ordering a subordinate to shorten sail and proceed carefully under partly reefed topsails, keeping a look out and sounding with the lead line. Despite the precautions the ship grounded and all efforts to save her failed, leaving the bedraggled crew no option but to battle through a surging sea to reach the safety of some rocks while the helpless *Weazle* was pounded to pieces. This time a court martial could not be avoided. Layman was acquitted of negligence, but there were no more vacancies on the station and Nelson sent him home with dispatches. In the prevailing circumstances a junior commander could have expected years of under- or unemployment, but Layman had made a lasting impression during his brief period at Gibraltar. A petition of the local merchants adverted to the 'extraordinary and unremitted' campaign he had waged against the privateers. 'No man is more capable of supporting and protecting the trade . . . and convoying the supplies to this place, from his constant study and knowledge of the different bays and inlets, as well on the neighbouring coasts of Spain and Barbary.' Gore and Trigge agreed, and Nelson threw in his demand for Layman's reinstatement in a letter to St Vincent. 'His reappointment to the Gibraltar station would give general satisfaction to the Rock,' he said.[33]

It worked, and early in August the new first lord, Melville, ordered Layman back to the Mediterranean to continue his work as commander of the *Raven* sloop. As soon as the posting was assured, the officer planned a dramatic return, persuading Melville to allow him to experiment with the *Raven* to improve her effectiveness. At Woolwich, Layman excitedly equipped his sloop with eighteen thirty-two-pound carronades and replaced her bow and stern chasers with sixty-eight-pound carronades, one mounted on a revolutionary rotating traverse so that its powerful shot could be hurled over the gunwales in any direction. To enable the ship to work in calm weather or restricted water, he fitted her with sweeps and Chinese sculls. Layman may have unwisely deepened the draught of a vessel intended to confront much shallower water, but he proudly sent a sketch of his improvements to Nelson, who was totally convinced. 'I agree most perfectly in the propriety of having vessels of the aforementioned description stationed in the Straits, and I know of no man so fit to command one of them as Captain Layman,' he wrote to the Admiralty. Sir Sidney Smith, a man interested in innovation, saw the ship at Woolwich and became 'a strong advocate'.[34]

It was with high hopes, therefore, that Captain Layman finally sailed for the Mediterranean on 21 January 1805. His sloop had been turned into a formidable weapon, and his orders, which directed him to resume his work at Gibraltar, were perfect. War had also broken out with Spain, with all that promised in rich prizes, and the full confidence of the Admiralty and commander-in-chief went with him. His troubled struggle for recognition and opportunities seemed to have paid off.

Another eight days found Layman a few leagues off Cadiz, where he was supposed to deposit dispatches with Sir John Orde, who had a squadron blockading the place. He reduced sail and hove to, but the wind being westerly he quit the deck leaving strict orders for soundings to be made every half-hour. At midnight the commander was awoken by his officer of the watch, who told him that the lights of Orde's ships had been seen. But the lights did not belong to the British ships, and almost chillingly, history had begun to repeat itself. The lights were those of Cadiz, and *Raven* was much further inshore than she should have been. She had mistaken her position in the darkness, heavy rain and strengthening wind and current. With mounting dread, Layman's soundings revealed that the ground was shoaling very rapidly beneath them. From eighty fathoms the depth dropped to five. Desperately the captain tried to turn his sloop around, tacking in the blackness one way and then another to avoid foaming rocks and shoals, until he got her to windward of San Sebastian. Then, just as the *Raven* began to look safer, her main yard broke in the slings, and the violent wind and sea drove her towards a looming lee shore. Layman dropped anchors in a risky attempt to hold his position, but they slid helplessly across the rocky bottom, and he had to play his final card and desperately tried to work the unmanageable ship out to sea. The elements were not known for mercy and there came the sickening crash all sailors feared. Layman ordered his dispatches, signals and papers weighted with lead and thrown into the angry sea, and evacuated his doomed ship. All but two men managed to get ashore, where they were surrounded by Spanish soldiers with levelled muskets.[35]

Even in the midst of war, the ultimate and most unpredictable and unforgiving enemy of the sailor was always the sea.

4

Nelson's leadership and commitment to ability and initiative were important props during his difficult years as commander-in-chief of the Mediterranean, but the efficiency of his fleet and its performance on a day of battle ultimately rested upon the general well-being of men and ships. To maintain the terrific exertion of a protracted gun battle, and the constant hauling of ropes and manoeuvring of giant pieces that it entailed, the health as well as morale of the companies had to be maintained. Although hardly as glamorous, the tasks of training and proper maintenance of a fleet, or an army for that matter, were every bit as important to the outcome of a mission as strategy and tactics. Nowhere was the job harder than in a battle fleet far from home, where thousands of men lived in uncomfortably close proximity and endured the privations and rigours of an environment that could be as cruel as it was unpredictable and alien.

This significant but little-told story of Nelson's command was peopled by a different, and almost forgotten, cast of characters, in which some, such as Richard Ford, John Snipe and Edward Gayner deserve to be mentioned in the same breath as Murray, Keats and Gore. It was a strength of Nelson that he recognised the worth of such men and what they contributed to his achievement. The centuries-old battle to keep large forces healthy at sea was at the forefront of his concern, as a memorable letter he penned to his friend Dr Benjamin Moseley on 11 March 1804 testifies:

> The great thing in health, and you will agree with me, that it is easier for an officer to keep men healthy, than for a surgeon to cure them. Situated as this fleet has been, without a real friendly port where we could get all the things so necessary for us, yet I have, by changing the cruising ground, not allowing the sameness of prospect to satiate the *mind*. Sometimes looking at Toulon, Ville Franche, sometimes Barcelona, Rosas, running round Minorca, Majorca, Sardinia and Corsica, and two or three times anchoring for a few days and sending a ship to this place for onions, which I find the best thing which can be given to seamen, having always good mutton for the sick, cattle when we can get it and plenty of fresh water. In the winter giving half the allowance of grog instead of all wine. These things are for the commander-in-chief to look to, and shut very nearly out

from Spain, and only getting refreshments by stealth from other places, my command has been an arduous one. Cornwallis has great merit for his persevering courage, but he has everything sent him. We have nothing.[36]

As a statement of the relationship between provisions and mental and physical health this was as good a statement as Nelson ever made. He believed it implicitly. It was important 'not to be penny wise and pound foolish', he wrote to another medical friend, 'for a small sum well laid out will keep fleets healthy, but it requires large sums to make a sickly fleet healthy'. Whenever he sent captains in search of fresh provisions he reminded them of the supreme value of their pedestrian work, beginning orders with the words, 'Whereas the health of the companies of His Majesty's ships and vessels . . . chiefly depends upon the frequent supplies of fresh beef and other refreshments . . .' No admiral of his time surpassed his understanding of the link between health, service and battle.[37]

Nelson's life of ill health and disability had naturally thrown him into the close company of medical men, and was probably at the back of his appreciation of their worth. From that understanding grew a partnership between an admiral and doctors that produced a remarkable achievement. When the rival fleets of the Mediterranean finally manoeuvred for advantage during the exciting early months of 1805, they carried very different bodies of men. The French and Spanish had spent most of their time in port, where some were stricken by the fierce bouts of the yellow fever that swept Spain's coast in 1800 and 1804, and at sea they miserably succumbed to seasickness, scurvy and typhus. Conversely and somewhat paradoxically, the British fleet emerged from years of punishing active service in the plague-ridden Mediterranean in tip-top physical shape.

Some figures are necessary, but Nelson's own exaggerations need to be dismissed. Just as he claimed that his fleet had survived gales without losing a spar, he was wont to say it had no sick. These embellishments are useful to us as indications of the value he placed upon such achievements, not as statements of fact. Fortunately we have better data, and it reveals an outstanding record. Nelson inherited a fleet with a peacetime sick list that had topped four hundred. However, an analysis of twenty-two sick reports made by John Snipe, the industrious physician of the fleet, between 29 August 1803 and 21 August 1804 records a wartime sick list that fluctuated between 133 and 263. Each return covered only those ships currently accessible to the physician of the fleet, and the variations reflect numbers of ships as well as vibrating levels of sick. However, the average number of sick per ship was only 17.3, and the average number of men actually confined to bed per ship even lower at 1.4. The *Victory* was the largest ship in the fleet, with a complement of some 840, yet during that period her average sick list stood at 26.7 or about a mere 3.2 per cent of the ship's company.

The evidence also shows that there were few hospitalisations and deaths on board. Between 1 August 1803 and 1 March 1804 these totalled sixty-eight, an average of 6.1 for the eleven ships in the return; the *Victory*, given her greater size, reported more but only fourteen. When Leonard Gillespie became physician of the fleet in January 1805 he was astounded to find only one man in the *Victory* confined to bed. The other dozen ships of the line exhibited 'a similar' pattern of 'health, although the most of them had been stationed off Toulon, during which time very few of the men and officers . . . have had a foot on shore'. The great sea diseases failed to get a serious grip of Nelson's fleet. The most persistent ailments, sometimes accounting for a third of the sick list, were sea ulcers. These were the bald facts of an astounding achievement.[38]

Health underpinned all the navy's tasks, and Nelson probably scrutinised the weekly returns of the sick in his fleet as well as those that came once a month from the hospitals at Gibraltar and Malta. He was greatly influenced by medical men, both those with the fleet such as Snipe and Gillespie, the physicians responsible for its overall care, and ship surgeons such as George Magrath and William Beatty of the *Victory*, and correspondents in England, among whom were Andrew Baird, now one of three members of the Sick and Wounded Board, and Moseley. His interest encouraged them, and they saw him almost as one of their own, confiding in him, advising and occasionally experimenting. Towards the end of their association, Snipe wrote that Nelson's 'attention . . . on all occasions' had 'made a deep impression on my heart, and the time I had the honour to serve under your lordship's commands I shall ever consider as the most fortunate period of my life'. The admiral's friendship made Gillespie feel 'one of the family', and, if we may judge from the appearance of the *Victory* in the background of his official portrait, painted in 1837, became the pride of his life, too. Baird, as close to the head of the naval medical service as anybody, still regretted that he was not in the Mediterranean with Nelson, with whom he could only correspond. 'I beg your lordship's pardon for trespassing so much on your time,' wrote Baird, 'but I feel that I am addressing the heart of a noble man whose uniform countenance and goodness to me has been my greatest pride.' The feeling was reciprocal, for to Nelson the physicians and surgeons were unsung heroes of the war. Like the fighting seamen, they were in the front line, salvaging the wreckage of violence and often treating seamen with highly infectious diseases. One of the last acts he ever did in England was to write to the Admiralty in tribute to John Snipe, his former fleet physician, who had died in 1805 of an illness contracted in Messina. Nelson's ability to lead naval officers and men to glory has passed into folklore, but his partnership with the medical men, and the great achievement they shared, has been undervalued.[39]

Of course, Nelson knew that there were rogue surgeons, and he criticised a few in his time, but he remained sensible of the successes the British medical profession had made at sea, and its relatively robust system of training and control. Naval surgeons often held medical degrees, especially those aspiring to become physicians, but whether attached to hospitals or ships, their preparation was largely practical, acquired through seven-year apprenticeships and tested in examinations of the Company of Surgeons in London. This organisation, which recruited and accredited naval surgeons; the Sick and Wounded Board, which examined aspirants in physic as opposed to pure surgery, and held the right to inspect the medical journals of ships; and the supervising physicians of the fleets exercised a degree of control over the profession unknown in the French service.

The British were making landmark strides in improving naval health at this time, and had recently rediscovered something their Tudor ancestors had known, the value of citrus fruits as a cure for scurvy. Though the exact origin of the disease (a deficiency in ascorbic acid, or vitamin C) was not known, it had been associated with a lack of fresh fruit and vegetables. Improved rations, and the growing use of lemon and lime juice to eradicate outbreaks of scurvy, were helping to control the malady in the British navy, although the success of fleets varied according to the dispositions of their physicians and commanders-in-chief. These advances ran hand in hand with better rations of food, which if fully supplied delivered 4500 calories, sufficient to support the energy needed by the average seaman. Contemporaries also acknowledged that the British were particularly aware of the need for shipboard cleanliness and hygiene, essential in such densely populated places, where each man had fourteen inches to sling his hammock and typhus, human lice and rat fleas flourished. In addition, their surgeons were pioneering new techniques, including the use of the trephine rather than the trepan in dealing with head fractures. Nelson strongly believed that the naval surgeons deserved greater rewards than they received. Despite their significance they earned only £5 a month, with an allowance for servants and a contribution towards the costs of instruments and drugs. They were granted neither ward room status nor uniform, and their status and pay lagged considerably behind their army counterparts.[40]

Nelson rebelled against this neglect, and in 1804 led the surgeons' charge for greater recognition and improved conditions by endorsing their petition. The admiral had already told the Sick and Wounded Board that if something was not done the navy would lose its best surgeons to the army. 'I look to you not only to propose it but to enforce it to Lord St Vincent,' he had written to Baird, a shrewd remark addressed to one who not only knew the justice of the surgeons' case but also carried great sway at the Admiralty. Now he urged the new first lord to serve 'so valuable and so respectable a body of men'. The results came the following January, when the pay of naval surgeons rose to up to eighteen shillings a day, half-pay was extended to all unplaced surgeons, and both surgeons and physicians were granted a blue uniform. Gillespie, then the fleet's physician, wrote Nelson a letter of gratitude for his 'very prompt and favourable' support, testifying that he was 'very well satisfied' that the success was due 'in a great measure to your Lordship's efficacious recommendation'. It was co-signed by every surgeon in the fleet. At a stroke Nelson had endeared himself to the entire naval medical service for a lasting and overdue reform that bore directly upon the profession's ability to recruit and retain quality staff. He had never put his influence to better use.[41]

Upon assuming command of the Mediterranean fleet Nelson found that many of his ships had been in service since the last war and were full of scurvy. Though it had not entrenched itself, the disorder had laid a sinister hand on three unfortunate ships. Snipe pronounced 'the whole' crew of the *Triumph* 'more or less afflicted with scurvy'. Scurvy was the most famous of all sea diseases, inflicting symptoms that were fearful to behold, suffer or smell, lethargic debilitated men with jaundiced complexions, swollen limbs, rotten gums, festering ulcers and excruciatingly loose joints. Interruptions to supplies of fresh greens made scurvy difficult to eradicate at sea, and even the Channel fleet, which operated close to home-grown English victuals, ran up substantial sick lists, perhaps because of a misapprehension that beer was an anti-scorbutic. Nelson was not surprised to find it in the Mediterranean, where fresh provisions were more difficult to acquire, and the fleet was flat out of lemon juice. Snipe prescribed a ten-day course of onions as a substitute.[42]

In the longer run, Nelson tackled the problem by monitoring sick lists, procuring as many fresh provisions as possible, and using lemon and lime juice and onions as curatives whenever symptoms of scurvy raised their heads. Not all of his practices were entirely effective. Raw onions were an excellent source of ascorbic acid, but heating or diluting them in water diminished their power, and Nelson may have reduced their potency by recommending they be served with fresh vegetables in a nourishing soup, however much the latter must have enhanced the ships' 'fresh meat days'. Nor is it clear that reducing spirits in favour of what Gillespie later called 'good and wholesome wine' had anything to do with alleviating scurvy. Although the programme in its entirety worked, scurvy in particular remained a lurking menace, ready to appear at every temporary breakdown of fresh provisions, and Snipe and Nelson saw the need to confront outbreaks immediately to prevent them gaining hold. As Strachan reported, the disease made 'a most alarming progress' in the *Donegal* as soon as he exhausted his lime juice. On New Year's Day 1804 there were ten cases of scurvy in Moubray's *Active*, 'the aggregate of whose sick list,' Snipe reported, 'exceeds [that of] any other ship connected with the squadron'. Nelson dispatched her to Spain to purchase as many provisions as were needed to rid the ship of the disease, and to procure curative supplies for the fleet, including onions, vegetables and 30,000 oranges. Despite this in May he was ordering Barlow of the *Triumph* to dose his thirty-seven victims of 'inveterate scurvy' with six additional ounces of lemon juice and two ounces of sugar per day for twelve days, and in July eleven cases of scurvy were shared between the *Canopus*,

Narcissus, *Thunder* and *Donegal*. In a fleet of six or more thousand men these were relatively small outbreaks, but they illustrated the need for constant vigilance.[43]

Scurvy and fevers were underlying nightmares, but the ordinary hazards of the service, the exposure, lifting, hauling, overcrowding and dirt, created ulcers, colds, rheumatism, pulmonary disorders, ruptures, miscellaneous injuries, dysentery, agues and most worryingly typhus, a bacterial infection that could spread quickly and cause coma and death. Maintaining decent hygiene was always difficult. Nelson's officers had to send their linen to Malta, Gibraltar or the Maddalenas for laundering, and some made grubby shirts last longer by wearing them inside out. As far as the men were concerned, the captains adopted the common device of splitting their companies into divisions and assigning each to an officer responsible for upholding satisfactory levels of cleanliness. During her recent refit the *Victory*'s sick-bay had been moved to the starboard upper deck beneath the foc'sle, where it could be heated and ventilated more effectively, and the men easily isolated behind canvas bulkheads. But a solution to one problem often rebounded on another, and we find Nelson reducing the number of times the lower decks were sluiced with water to combat damp.

What most impressed the medics was the admiral's interest in any suggestion for improving the well-being of his men. In September 1803, for example, Snipe complained of inadequate warm and protective clothing and shoes. The tars scampered about barefoot and in short pantaloons, exposing their lower limbs to rheumatic disorders, injury and ulcers. Nelson took the matter up with the Admiralty, submitting samples of Russian 'duck' trousers that Hardy had obtained from the naval storekeeper in Malta. The Navy Board protested that Russian duck had become too expensive because of the heavy demand from the army, but after a tedious delay Nelson's seamen were going about their bad-weather business in the duck trousers, warm Guernsey jackets and cotton smocks that Snipe had recommended. Likewise Snipe and the surgeon of the *Belleisle* drew Nelson's attention to the dangers confronting shore parties sent to cut wood or refill water casks in the low-lying marshy areas of Sardinia, where malarial and other fevers could be contracted and carried back to the ships. The admiral ordered the shore parties to be dosed with a solution of wine or spirits and Peruvian bark, or cinchona, and within a year Gillespie, Snipe's successor, was praising the positive effects. Nelson found Snipe's weekly reports and dinner-table conversation quarries of pertinent observations. The physician thought that the green wood cut for fuel contained contaminants, and recommended that it be smoked before being brought on board, and he had numerous suggestions for preserving the purity of drinking water. Water casks were ordered to be charred once a year to check rot, a portion of lime was introduced to improve the taste of the water and deter infestation, and watering parties were directed to the heads of streams to avoid the pollution that accumulated in lower reaches. Moreover, while the Sick and Wounded Board provided extra necessities for the sick, Snipe recommended additional sources of nutrition. In the spring of 1804 Nelson sent Bolton's *Childers* to Naples to purchase 'the best large pipe macaroni' which, by all accounts, was 'a light, wholesome and nourishing food'. Other treats were milk for patients' tea and a drink made of cocoa and sugar that Snipe considered better than oatmeal or cheese.[44]

Diet, hygiene and clothing could go so far, but cases involving chronic illness or injury and contagious infections required intensive medical care and isolation. There was an eighteenth-century naval hospital at Gibraltar and the *Guerrier* sheer-hulk to handle overspills, but no corresponding provision at Malta, where sick seamen were admitted to the military hospital at Valletta on the sufferance of the army. Relations between the two services were fortunately good, and Nelson ensured they remained so. When the military physician complained that naval patients were being sent to him too late, one arriving 'in the act of death', Nelson issued clear orders that 'the moment any of the people' were 'attacked with an infectious or inflammatory fever' they were to be sent ashore rather than be allowed to remain on board endangering the ship's company. The offending surgeon, James Shaw of the *Madras*, did not have a strong defence, but Nelson plucked the one gem from his otherwise vacuous vindication and ordered that every patient sent ashore must take with him a full statement of his case, stipulating his condition and what treatments he had received. It was essential that receiving doctors had the full picture. But the better solution, as far as Malta was concerned, was the establishment of an independent naval hospital, and Nelson wrote to Baird asking whether one was intended or the fleet was to 'go on the old way'.[45]

Nelson's patronage of the naval hospitals was a lasting legacy of his period as commander-in-chief. The establishment at Gibraltar had emerged from the peace with a reduced and discontented staff simmering under a new presiding physician, William Burd. The key malcontent was the assistant surgeon and dispenser, Pascal Poggioli, whose indiscreet private letters to James Weir, Burd's predecessor and now a member of the Board for Sick and Wounded, inevitably created concern at home. According to Poggioli and some other employees all manner of irregularities and inefficiencies were going on in the hospital. The premises were 'neglected and dirty', and one nurse is said to have complained that 'if it [the dirt] was up to his [Burd's] knees, she believed he would not see it'. To economise medicines were said to have been stinted, and inferior provisions procured. Burd was accused of appropriating hospital medicines for private patients and converting the hospital 'into a bawdy house' by hiring 'women of ill fame' as nurses. There were stories of comings and goings at odd hours, of Burd getting nurses or a maid 'beastly drunk' in his rooms, of 'improper freedoms' being taken, and a lack of order and discipline. According to Hannah

Leard, a former matron and reputed drunkard, the place had gone to the dogs since Weir's departure. 'The day that I left the hospital,' said she, 'Mr [Chaloner] Dent [the victualler] said to me that he supposed that if Dr Weir was now to see the state of the hospital, it would cause him to shed tears.'[46]

Despite the private nature of the initial allegations, on 19 May 1803 the Sick and Wounded Board asked Nelson to investigate. As Gibraltar was Britain's only naval hospital in the Mediterranean, and accommodated up to seventy British seamen and marines, as well as some foreign seamen and prisoners of war, its state was a matter of grave concern and Nelson sent the redoubtable Snipe to get to the bottom of it. Snipe found nothing lacking in the personnel, but highlighted important shortcomings in the physical structures, a leaking roof, the use of uncomfortable wooden 'cradles' rather than iron beds and a serious lack of ventilation in the sheer-hulk. He dismissed the criticisms of Burd as 'frivolous and vexatious', but noted his need of an additional surgeon and a gate porter and more space. A ward that Admiral Keith had surrendered to the military was now sorely needed. A second investigation, in which Snipe probed the charges against Burd more thoroughly, led to Poggioli's dismissal. There was probably more to them than was admitted, but the enquiries forced the hospital to improve its performance. Nelson retrieved the ward from the army, but if Snipe's suggestion that fans and additional portholes be used to improve the quality of the air in the sheer-hulk were adopted, they were insufficient. George Magrath, Nelson's surgeon, later found the ship riddled with typhus fever and its hold 'a perfect compost or dunghill'. The admiral urged the Admiralty to parole prisoners of war rather than allow them to be incarcerated inside.[47]

The need of a naval hospital at Malta could not be ignored. Between 13 May 1802 and 5 December 1803 the military establishment on the island was compelled to admit 744 patients from the ships. Nelson considered using a polacre as a temporary hospital ship, but pushed his plan for a proper establishment with appropriate urgency. The case was undeniable, and John Gray, who had cut his medical teeth in a decade of hospital ships and the hospitals at Lisbon and Gibraltar, was sent from England with a dispenser and agent and orders to place himself under Nelson's orders. By the end of 1803 Nelson was able to send Snipe to Malta to find a suitable 'airy and healthy' site.[48]

When Snipe arrived in Valletta he was 'indefatigable' and conscientiously toured public buildings full of troops or stores in search of an appropriate property. Since sickness could waste a fleet far 'more than the sword of the enemy,' wrote the good doctor, 'there is no part of the service that requires more to be regarded than the choice of a proper situation for an hospital'. Nothing fitted the bill, but Snipe, Ball and Gray decided that the old palace of Bughay, near the waterfront, was the best bet. Though small, it was capable of being extended by the addition of a third storey and two wings, and the grounds were big enough to encompass a kitchen garden and a garden where patients could convalesce. The modifications would cost about £10,000, and Snipe also advocated a high staffing ratio of one nurse to every ten patients. Nelson was enthusiastic, especially about the garden, which he thought indispensable, but it would take years to procure and prepare the site, so a provisional establishment had to be created. He appointed an experienced officer, Lieutenant William Pemberton, to ensure cleanliness and comfort, preserve discipline, prevent desertion and submit monthly returns. Pemberton and his servant were to be accommodated on site, and their names would be carried on the hospital books for board and wages. To oversee the whole operation Nelson also sent Bickerton to Malta on 18 December with orders to inspect whatever premises were utilised and ascertain what medicines were available.[49]

Villettes was kind enough to offer the new establishment a temporary home in two sections of the existing military hospital, and at the end of 1803 an intake of eighty seamen and marines and thirty prisoners of war settled any doubts about need. Care and supplies were put out to tender, using guidelines drawn up by the Sick and Wounded Board. They emphasised 'good wholesome beef', 'the best wheaten bread', 'good sound Madeira', 'good broth', and 'genuine milk', among assorted safeguards of 'quality and strength'. Lime and lemon juice were to be part of the regular diet, but scorbutic patients needed dosing six times daily for twelve days. There was an appropriate emphasis on recruiting 'the most sober, careful and diligent' nurses, and Snipe's staffing ratio was adopted with the addition of a supervisory matron. 'The whole of the hospital is at all times to be kept as sweet and clean as possible.' To ensure quality control the initial contracts were to be negotiated by Snipe, reviewed by Nelson and offered for one year only. Surprisingly adept, Snipe struck a deal to supply and maintain the sick at 1s. 10½d. per man per day, comparable to its counterpart in Gibraltar, but providing for more fruit and vegetables. In 1804 he and Gray went to Messina in search of local commodities needed by the fleet as well as the hospital. John Broadbent, a merchant, stood forward manfully, and on 12 June Snipe agreed the supply of 30,000 gallons of fresh-squeezed lemon juice at a shilling a gallon, some of it destined for use in England. Nelson had no difficulty recommending the Admiralty's acceptance, because even when poor harvests forced Broadbent to increase his price by sixpence a gallon it was still far below that currently being paid for English juice of an inferior quality. In January 1805 Snipe, now with an additional allowance as inspector of hospitals, was back in Messina to clinch a deal for another 30,000 gallons.[50]

Yet for all this the first months of the Maltese naval hospital were full of tribulations. In the spring of 1804 the store ship *Hindustan*, sent from England with the main consignment of medicines and supplies for the new hospital, was lost. They were not replaced until October, and again Villettes had to plug the gap with generous donations from army supplies. Then came tragic losses in personnel. John Gray, who had been a rock in those early days, began complaining of bilious complaints and a pain in his right side. 'I never saw a more correct, zealous, good man,' said Snipe. His whole 'viscera' was found to be diseased, and he was forced to relinquish his place to the surgeon of the *Royal Sovereign* in August. An even greater blow fell early the following year when Snipe himself returned from his second visit to Messina spitting blood from an infection he had picked up. He had signed his last sick return on Christmas Day, and died a few months later; ironically he had already been promoted to a new and safer position in Plymouth. If Nelson had been the umbrella, Snipe had been the cutting edge of medical affairs in the Mediterranean, and he was not easy to replace. Gillespie, who succeeded him, was an accomplished Ulsterman who had studied medicine in Edinburgh, St Andrews and Paris, and was forward-thinking enough to contribute to the literature of tropical diseases, but his weekly reports, compared to Snipe's eager documents, were thin.[51]

The legacy survived, although the Maltese naval hospital was not opened in its own premises at Bughay until 1832. The hospitals gave places to long-term and infectious patients and created space in ship sickbays for short-stay patients. Even so large a battleship as the *Victory* operated with a sickbay of only twenty-two beds. Early in 1805 two hundred patients were being accommodated in the hospitals at Gibraltar and Malta.

The system that Nelson and Snipe had created held for the duration of the admiral's command and helped deflect some serious blows. At the beginning of October 1803 a dreadful pestilence raised its head in Malaga in Spain. It was yellow fever, the infamous 'yellow jack' or 'black vomit' of nautical legend, an acute tropical arbovirus infection capable of devastating human populations. Its ghastly symptoms, most notably the jaundice and gastrointestinal haemorrhages that gave the disease its nicknames, were commonly harbingers of death. We now know that yellow fever is transmitted from animals to humans by the mosquito, but then little about its origin, beyond its association with certain types of environment, was known. What did strike terror was its ability to spread rapidly with lethal effect, and early nineteenth-century medics understood the need for victims to be held in isolation. When the disease struck a pall of fear spread through the Mediterranean. As sailors moved from port to port there was no knowing where the infection had been carried.

Within days of the outbreak at Malaga, Scandinavian merchantmen had taken it to Alicante, Gibraltar and Cadiz, but the onset of cold weather quickly suppressed it and on 20 December a 'Te Deum' was sung at Malaga to give thanks for divine deliverance. But it reappeared in the port in August 1804 and moved rapidly, east to Velez, Cartagena, Alicante, Barcelona and Minorca, and west to Gibraltar and Cadiz. Scattered outbreaks of what may have been the disease occurred in Leghorn and Civita Vecchia on the coast of Italy. The death toll rose hideously. In three non-consecutive days in September 723 died in

Malaga, and at one time 400 were dying a day. One estimate put the total losses in the port as high as a quarter of the population. Four hundred were dead in Alicante by mid-October, and thousands were lost in Cadiz.[52]

Nelson's ships called at Spanish ports but Gibraltar was the biggest threat because almost every British ship going up or down the Mediterranean called there. The pestilence raged through the British outpost, cutting down without distinction. The local newspaper was stopped in its tracks. 'Not a soul' in the settlement 'was out of mourning,' said Captain Parker. Joe King, boatswain of the dockyard, wrote to Nelson that 'my family has all been ill but myself, but thank God they are all recovering. All the officers of the yard [are] ill, excepting the Master Attendant and myself. All the clerks are dead excepting one. If it had not been for the kind attention from the naval officer, Mr Ponnolwell, must have suffered greatly. I am very much fatigue[d] at present with the duty of the yard and removing the sick and burying dead, I scarcely have time to get my meals.' Because they treated the sick the hospital staff were the front line of the defence. On 1 November Burd sent Nelson a chilling letter. Since 12 September about 3400 had died of the fever at Gibraltar, 800 of them members of the garrison, where another 600 were sick. The hospital was on its knees. It had only nineteen patients, but was determined to keep them within its walls, rather than prematurely releasing them to endanger a vulnerable public, rather as Eyam, the seventeenth-century plague village, voluntarily sealed itself off to live or die with its misery alone. Burd himself was weakening, his constitution 'extremely broken down' from fever and the fatigue induced by 'this calamitous visitation'. He warned Nelson to keep clear of the port, but three weeks after writing his letter he, too, was dead. His assistant surgeon, dispenser and victualler perished with him, and an entirely new upper echelon had to be put in place.[53]

Nelson acted decisively. His ships, including convoys, were warned against contacting any suspect ports or vessels, and at Gibraltar they stood well out in the bay. When a boat pulled out to exchange dispatches the packets were twice fumigated, once before they were passed over and again upon receipt. Nelson advised the new governor, Fox, to burn the small houses at the back of the town, which he viewed as a breeding ground of disease. In November he sent George Magrath, his ship's surgeon, to take over Burd's responsibilities. It must have taken courage, but Magrath arrived as the contagion was running itself out and he lived to reach old age and a knighthood. After several weeks of untold worry the fleet survived by isolating itself from everything contaminated, and Nelson wrote in his diary that 'not a man [was] sick in the fleet'. It was a triumph of good management and sheer good luck.[54]

That Nelson's fleet survived this crisis and two years of duty with such minimal damage was remarkable. If the admiral was apt to boast that he had not a sick man in his fleet, the numbers routinely reported by the physician of the fleet tell their own surprising story. Even Nelson, whose record on health had always been good, was taken aback. 'I never experienced anything like the health of this fleet,' he told Elliot. The sick list of the principal battleships peaked at 260 in 1805, but with the arduous nature of the service, the length of its trial and the many difficulties endured, this was a small miracle. It had a decisive bearing upon the effectiveness of the force. As John Snipe so rightly said, sobriety, ventilation, cleanliness, clothing and food were 'absolutely required to keep up that muscular vigour [and] spirit of courage and adventure so necessary in the day of battle'. Nelson knew it too. As early as October 1803 he judged that part of his task convincingly in hand. 'We are healthy beyond example, and in good humour with ourselves, and so sharp-set that I would not be a French admiral in the way of any of our ships,' he wrote. 'I believe we are in the right fighting trim, let them come as soon as they please.' But it would be unjust to suggest that his interest lay solely in maintaining a force fit to fight. It also sprang from a humane belief that the privilege of command carried an obligation to protect those placed in trust. Nelson's old-fashioned paternalism was involved again.[55]

Nelson was not an original thinker as far as health was concerned. His contribution had been to value it, and those who safeguarded it. He created a climate in which the best medical men could do their work secure in the knowledge that they would be supported, protected and praised. Under his leadership they could flourish and make differences. Nelson's role in reforming the standing of the surgeons, establishing the hospital at Malta, encouraging his medical establishment and maintaining the fleet in outstanding health may be regarded as one of his finest achievements. No one put it more succinctly than Snipe himself in May 1804:

> The triumphant state of health which this fleet has enjoyed for nearly twelve months . . . points out in the clearest manner to the most superficial observer the good effects of the wise and salutary measures pursued by our renowned commander-in-chief, under many untoward circumstances which formerly were not experienced in this country. When the thinking mind reflects on the ravages committed in our fleet by diseases in times past and contrasts it with the present we must be strongly impressed with sentiments of admiration and astonishment . . . In the most salubrious situation in Europe containing the same numbers that are in this fleet, I will venture to assert there are more confined in bed by disease.[56]

5

Unlike the Channel fleet, Britain's force in the Mediterranean was fed through a long, exposed communication line from England, some two thousand miles of seaway along which essential goods, personnel and information passed towards and into the Mediterranean. The fleet required enormous quantities of supplies. Not just nourishing food and drinkable water, but also naval stores such as the masts, blocks, timber, canvas, rope, tar and fuel. The job of keeping the supplies flowing was huge and unending. Some sixty transports, store ships and victuallers reached Gibraltar each year, bringing the wherewithal for the fleet, the army and two British bases.[57]

Nelson's fleet of some 8500 souls required prodigious quantities of human fuel. To supply a basic diet capable of maintaining the required energy levels needed an annual intake of 1381 tons of bread; 3,094,000 gallons of beer; 770 tons of beef; 395 tons of pork; 110,500 gallons of peas; 165,750 gallons of oatmeal; 74 tons of butter; 137 tons of cheese and 27,625 gallons of vinegar. More than this had actually to be supplied to cover the considerable wastage, and while the core could be shipped from Deptford by the Victualling Board, additional resources would have to be found on station, particularly fresh meat, fruit, vegetables and water, as well as the special needs of the sick financed by the Sick and Wounded Board. Between October 1804 and January 1805 Nelson's fleet received 659,700 oranges and lemons and more than 15 tons of onions, and consumed 200,000 gallons of wine and 40,000 gallons of brandy. The most continuously pressing need was for fresh water. Ships could carry up to five months of provisions, and the *Victory* alone was able to store 300 tons of water. It was a logistical colossus, involving a large amount of vulnerable shipping. In the two years that followed May 1803 some thirty-three victuallers reached the Mediterranean, travelling for the most part in quarterly convoys and either unloading at the store houses in Gibraltar and Malta or proceeding directly to the fleet. The Victualling Board also used outgoing warships to take supplies to the fleet; the *Excellent* and *Amazon*, for example, went out with enough lime juice and sweetening sugar to last six thousand men for a month. Within the Strait a considerable proportion of the duties undertaken by warships related to the collection and escort of supplies, and victuallers and store ships regularly trundled between the bases and the fleet.[58]

Ships no less than men needed maintainence, and required massive deliveries of bulk stores. A single third-rate ship of the line used more than nine miles of rope and cordage and almost 22,000 square feet of canvas, but a great variety of material was needed and the store ships from Woolwich in England were veritable glory holes of raw materials and individually fashioned items, including rope, twine, cable, canvas, sails, timber, masts, spars, casks, blocks, wedges, rafters, trestle trees, boiler plates, copper, tinplate, iron, turpentine, tar, tallow, paint, beeswax, tools, needles, screws, nails, anchors, artillery, muskets, ammunition, powder, kersey, sailors' slops, cases of shoes, bedding, coal and wooden fuel, among much else. Seventeen such vessels went to the Mediterranean to replenish the fleet and its naval dockyards during Nelson's twenty-two months in the Mediterranean, and just eleven of them sailing in 1803 and 1804 carried

3426 tons of naval stores. Even so, the naval storekeepers at Gibraltar and Malta still had to supplement what was sent from home with materials closer by.[59]

Any failure of supplies would imperil the fleet's ability to perform its duties. A large organisation attempted to coordinate that necessary support, its nucleus in London, where the offices of the Victualling, Navy and Transport boards exercised the overall responsibility for marshalling and shipping Nelson's wants. At Gibraltar and Malta the boards had their local representatives in the agent victuallers, naval storekeepers and agents for transports, whose duties were to manage the resources and supplement them where necessary using bills drawn on London. At any time nearly forty ships could be moving supplies up and down, each hired for about twenty-five shillings per ton a month. Strict monitoring and accounting theoretically oiled this vast machine. In October 1803 the dockyard storekeepers were ordered to make regular returns of their remaining stores so that the commissioners at home would know what to include in their next convoys. 'Surveys of remains', showing how many days of each provision remained in the holds of the individual ships, were also constantly processed by Nelson and Murray. The admiral was thus able to predict upcoming shortages, summon replacements from England, or take what remedial action was required. Everything from the weightiest matters to the sublime and ridiculous found its way into the mountain of paper and statistics. We see Gore complaining that he was reduced to fashioning hammocks from ancient condemned sails, notwithstanding that 'the men nightly fell through them'. The next store ship from Woolwich had 275 beds and 1000 hammocks. And Patrick Wilkie, the agent victualler at Malta, reported to Nelson that the latest bread from England was infested by 'the white worm commonly called bargemen', and asked whether he should use sulphuric or tobacco fumes to drive the invaders out. Nelson did not like the health implications and recommended cutting away the outer layers. It seems that the innards were found to be not 'materially damaged' and suitable for baking into biscuit.[60]

The system worked, but it possessed inherent weaknesses and was always threatened by misadventure. Of the former, perhaps the greatest difficulties arose from the distance between the fleet's usual station and its bases at Malta and Gibraltar, and the inability of either of the latter to conduct major ship repairs. Even a ship with a sound hull but extensive demands for masts, yards and rigging could consume 'the whole strength of the [Gibraltar] yard' for up to eight weeks. Moreover, Nelson began his watch after a period of long Admiralty neglect, and while many of his ships were in disrepair the dockyard store houses were nearly empty. The problem would be slow to mend. Nelson ordered the naval storekeeper at Gibraltar to send the first store ship that arrived from England more or less directly to the fleet, so that his needs could be met without unnecessary delay. Consequently, at the end of August 1803 the *Prevoyante*, under Master William Brown, found Nelson in the Gulf of Lions. 'I have never been better pleased than with the regularity and good order in which the stores . . . have been delivered to the fleet,' Nelson reported. He told the Navy Board that Brown deserved 'every commendation' he was able to bestow.[61]

The other serious problem that faced Nelson upon assuming command concerned victuals and health. As a top priority he had to establish a system for providing fresh food and water, especially as some of the ships were full of scurvy. In peacetime the job was easier. The fleet did not have to remain in any one place, and could go wherever its wants could be supplied, and as there were no major enemies the choice of vendors was considerable. But Nelson had to maintain a station close to Toulon, far away from his bases, and on coasts that were either hostile or afraid to supply him. The Admiralty complacently directed him to Malta, but not only was the nineteen-hundred-mile round trip inconvenient, but Wilkie, the agent victualler, was no William Brown. When Nelson approached him for fresh provisions he imperiously declined to supply the fleet '*anywhere but Malta*'. It was customary for ships to collect victuals from their base, but the imposition was ridiculous given the distance that divided the fleet from Valletta. The admiral concluded that Wilkie was an 'opinionated snuff-taking old gentleman' and even Troubridge, who had recommended his services, owned him 'a poor creature'. Nelson therefore bullied him into creating an efficient system that regularly dispatched victuallers to the fleet based on Nelson's estimates of his requirements. Between June 1803 and March 1805 some twenty-three left Malta to perform this essential duty. At first Nelson sent details of his intended movements so that the carriers knew roughly where to find him, but after October the business was greatly facilitated by the opening of Sardinia, which provided an ideal midway point for the traffic, and havens in which the victuallers could be safely cleared during bad weather.[62]

This innovation was a major step forward, but there was an obvious need to reduce the fleet's over-dependency on any one or two sources of supplies and to increase flexibility. Ships' pursers might be employed to purchase local fresh provisions, but something on a far bigger scale had to be organised. On 12 July Nelson proposed the Admiralty appoint a special agent victualler who would reside with the fleet and have the power to seek and purchase provisions under the direct supervision of the commander-in-chief. Furthermore, a supply of cash was essential because many places refused to take bills drawn on the Victualling Board. Merchants accepting such bills often found that banking houses declined to cash them except at an exorbitant discount, and if they were sent to London, it might take a month or more to get them redeemed. One supplier in Naples protested that he had £15,000 of useless British bills in his hands. Consequently, naval officers wishing to buy emergency local supplies often had to dig cash from their own purses hoping that the government would honour the receipts. Even if he obtained a financial reserve, Nelson felt uncomfortable managing the finances of the procurement system, and appealed for a freedom from smothering red tape. He wanted to be able to entrust captains and pursers with sums without having his accounts held up for years, a captain's receipt being 'a sufficient voucher for the disbursement of such money, and a full discharge from any impress against me'. But the larger purchases would still adhere to the usual forms of procurement, with contractors being invited to tender for the right to supply, and strict systems for assessing the price of local provisions and controlling the quantity and quality of deliveries being put in place. These arrangements would certainly have their inconveniences. Sometimes the ships would become farmyards, collecting sheep, bullocks, pigs and forage wherever they might be had at a satisfactory price, or bringing them from Gibraltar or Malta. But the supply system would at least be lubricated, and the health of the men protected.[63]

The Admiralty quickly responded to Nelson's suggestions, appointing Richard Ford agent victualler to the fleet. Ford had been recommended to the Victualling Board by Lord Hood in 1790, and won sufficient plaudits in the office to be appointed agent victualler at Lisbon. Now he came out with an assistant, John Geohegan, a salary of £500 per annum and a sufficient sum in hard Spanish dollars to facilitate payments. A cash budget was also provided to cover emergencies. James Cutforth, the agent victualler at Gibraltar, was ordered to tide the fleet over with some Spanish dollars, but early the following year the fleet was awarded a float of £3825 as well as £10,000 from the Victualling Board, both supplied in Spanish dollars.[64]

Ford did not reach the fleet until February 1804, and for several months Nelson cast around for supplies. The neutral countries were too afraid to offer anything like enough provisions. Naples and Sicily seemed obvious sources, given their previous relations with the British and the British ship of the line posted in the bay, but Nelson's attempts to secure a regular supply of fresh provisions failed and it was obvious that the government shrank from permitting large-scale exports. What came was little and furtive. A potential saviour appeared in the shape of Archibald McNeil, a merchant who had arrived in Malta after being driven out of Tuscany by the French. Producing various plans to obtain provisions in the Roman territories, Tuscany or Sardinia, and ship them through Neapolitan ports such as Gaeta and Salerno, he wheedled a contract from Nelson before his proposals were revealed to be delusional. After about a year a certain Thomas Warrington took over the defunct contract and managed to supply some oxen through Salerno, but his sources were far too unstable. Nor were naval stores easier to acquire than provisions. After the *Hindustan*, a British store ship, was lost in 1804, Nelson was driven back to Naples and ordered Nathaniel Taylor, the storekeeper at Malta, to visit the city in search of rope, cordage and beds. Taylor arrived in May to a bleak outlook, but working through Captain Malcolm of the *Kent*, then taking her turn in the bay, and the pro-consul, John James, he procured substantial amounts of material, including rope and several hundred beds, much of it sneaked beneath the noses of the authorities. But Nelson did not like James's methods of business, or the quality of all that was provided, and in October admitted himself 'exceedingly angry' about the whole Neapolitan affair. Even Sicily, which furnished valuable citrus fruits, was apt to prohibit the export of food during times of scarcity. Small *speronaras* were able to smuggle out small quantities, but it was thin gruel.[65]

There remained Spain, of course, only a few miles south and west of Toulon. And here Nelson had the good fortune to encounter another who became a significant prop of his command. Edward Gayner was a merchant of Rosas, the deep-water port within a day's sailing of Toulon. A fortyish English Quaker from Bristol, he saw the British fleet as a rare opportunity to combine business with patriotism, and from June 1803 became a conduit for information about Spain, France, and all that appertained to available resources and facilities. He even visited Nelson off Toulon on 2–6 December, attending a religious service in the *Victory*, and returning 'delighted' with the 'regularity' of his countrymen. Spain was uncomfortable about supplying the British in bulk, but despite impediments Gayner arranged for abundant supplies of fresh meat, water, wine and fuel and some fruit, vegetables, corn and fish to be collected at Rosas, devising methods to speed up turnaround and avoid the necessity of British sailors going ashore, where they might attract unwelcome official notice or desert. His boats would pull out to British ships in the bay to collect empty water casks from the fleet, and, when the next ship called, she would find the filled casks on rafts inshore, waiting to be towed away. Gayner also entertained calling naval officers, helped apprehend deserters and used his private family correspondence to Bristol to hide some of the admiral's letters home. Close to the French border, he became an important source of intelligence, and it was he who passed the information that 'a secret expedition' was assembling in Toulon in January 1804, leading to Nelson's attempts to strengthen defences in Sardinia and the Adriatic.[66]

Jayme Buenaventura Gibert, the Spaniard serving as Britain's vice consul in Barcelona, provided similar services, including mail, which he sent out to the fleet by boat. As early as July 1803 the *Cameleon* called at Barcelona for provisions, but while Gibert could send British government bills to be cashed in Madrid, he was frank about his region's difficulties in meeting Nelson's needs. Much of what was available went across the border into France, and the authorities in Barcelona were nervous about supplying the British. Nevertheless, Gibert supplied relatively small amounts in Barcelona, recommended alternative outlets such as Rosas and Alfaques, where there were fewer prying eyes, and sent shiploads of undercover provisions out to the fleet so they did not have to be collected.

Unfortunately, Gibert had not calculated upon the peripatetic nature of Nelson's fleet, which moved sometimes erratically between Spain, France and Sardinia, nor apparently did he forewarn the admiral of his first shipment. In

August, Gibert persuaded some suppliers to contribute to a supply ship, the *Virgin del Carmen*, laden with wine, vegetables, 3000 lemons and 80,000 onions as well as some melons and pears for the admiral's table. She left under the pretence of sailing for Italy, but 'having ran over all the coast of France, and vainly looked for the fleet' she battled bad weather to reach Leghorn, where much of the produce had to be sold at a loss to prevent spoiling. On the return journey the master hoped to deliver the wine at least, but the British were still missing and he had to give a French cruiser the slip and throw letters for Nelson overboard in case of capture. It had been a disaster. Nelson's fleet had been driven off its station by midsummer gales, the first of those that would eventually drive him to the Maddalenas, and inflicted a severe loss on the 'poor people' who had attempted to supply it. Despite all, a second attempt was made in September with no better result. The ship wasted five days cruising off Toulon without sighting a single British ship, but encountered a suspicious French privateer which insisted upon accompanying her into Leghorn. Some of the cargo was sold, including wine at a loss of 50 per cent. The arrival of two ships without specific customers in Leghorn had now attracted dangerous attention in a port occupied by the French, and Gibert's third consignment went to Rosas, where a British ship was supposed to meet her and conduct her to the fleet. But for some reason the cruiser only took the victualler as far as Toulon before leaving her to beat back and forth for three days looking for a fleet that did not appear. She returned to Rosas with a full cargo. 'The misfortunes which have pursued me . . . are perhaps beyond any example,' Gibert complained, 'and after having given . . . the most ardent proofs of my unbounded zeal for the English nation . . . I should have to regret the loss of my funds.' Nelson urged his government to compensate the unfortunate merchants, but Spain's political instability and the loose nature of the blockade had blighted one source of supply.[67]

Spain, particularly Rosas, was a rich source but never a certain one. From 6 September 1803 she made successive attempts to prevent British ships calling at her ports, except in distress, and to restrict the amount or type of provisions they could take. The outbreaks of yellow fever also tightened quarantine regulations, and masters were informed that their ships would be excluded from ports (or, in the parlance, denied 'pratique') until they had been isolated for fifteen days. Though not specifically intended to embarrass the British, it was an impossible requirement of such a busy fleet. Nelson sent Donnelly of the *Narcissus* to Rosas to deliver angry protests for the British minister in Madrid, and to confront the town governor, Manuel Leadan. His unvarnished argument was that Spain's obstructionism amounted to a serious breach of her pretended neutrality. In January 1804 the provincial captain-general agreed to accept a certificate of health signed by Nelson in lieu of formal quarantine restrictions and speeded up the ingress and egress of British warships, but the other problems festered until the spring.[68]

As we have seen, it was Sardinia that eventually unlocked the problem of fresh provisions, offering much that was needed as well as a rendezvous for the Maltese victuallers. Ford's arrival was another plus, for he proved himself an industrious agent victualler. In his first seven and a half months he secured 2571 head of cattle, 379 sheep, 81,685 onions, 21,300 oranges, 913 cabbages, 1000 leeks, 8 loads of vegetables, 3398 lbs of biscuit, and 149,341 gallons of wine and brandy from Spain, Italy, Algiers and the occasional neutral trading ship. Messina in Sicily became his best source of citrus fruits, and yielded about 98,450 oranges and lemons between October 1804 and April 1805, but Ford cast a wide net, travelling as far as Turkey. His efforts were not invariably successful. From Antioch he wrote that 'not a vegetable of any kind is to be met here'. But it was much to his credit that Nelson's fleet survived the outbreak of war with Spain at the end of 1804 so well.[69]

The Spanish war ensured that the search for provisions remained a headache throughout the whole of Nelson's command. The Adriatic should have been a fruitful source, but investigations promised little and those regions controlled by Austria were hampered by an imperial decree of 1803, stipulating that no more than 'daily provisions' could be issued to British ships. Some supplementary outlets were found, including Corfu, Tunis and Tetuan, on the Barbary coast, where fruit-laden donkey trains plodded into small, dusty ports. There were also attempts to tap the Black Sea ports of Odessa and Cherson, and in February 1804 Ball sent a convoy of twenty ships to collect grain that had been purchased at a good price. Unfortunately, the journey to and from Malta was a long one, taking up to five months to complete, and the Black Sea was an unsuitable source for perishable commodities.[70]

While hundreds of detailed accounts testify to Nelson's continual anxiety about water and victuals, the record of the health of his force was the ultimate vindication of his stewardship. The ships, their ageing timbers and rotting ropes and canvas pummelled by seas and winds year on year, fared less well. Nelson assumed command of a fleet in a disturbing state of decay and leaking storehouses denuded of supplies. Some ships had been on the station since the last war, suffering a creeping attrition. Once the severe weather of 1803 set in, the captains' requests for 'surveys' to be made of questionable sails and running rigging multiplied. Nelson admitted his inability to redress; the ships had 'literally nothing on board' and the dockyards were empty. Even at home the supply of hemp needed for making rope was barely sufficient to last two years if eked out by extraordinary economies. The admiral had been saddled with a desperate situation.[71]

He blamed the dead hand of parsimony during the peace, though less St Vincent himself than his misguided advisers, and as that regime was still in place expected little help. 'Was I to begin detailing all the complaints and wants of this fleet,' he wrote to Troubridge, 'it would be exactly the same I dare say as you receive from all other stations, but as it would be attended with no good effect I shall spare myself the trouble of writing and you of reading them.' The replies rang with complacency. Nelson was told to practise a strict economy, which he was doing, and to get cordage at Malta and manufacture rope, caulk and refit as much as possible at sea. However, a system to replace worn-out ships was devised. On 24 September the Admiralty informed Nelson that outgoing convoys would be escorted by ships of the line intended to replace their disabled counterparts in the Mediterranean. Once the exchange had been made, the unseaworthy ships could return home for a refit, bringing a homeward convoy in the process. The turnover was nevertheless sluggish and Nelson was stuck with a semi-decrepit fleet without adequate dockyards or stores to repair the damage. The effects could be seen in the number of ships temporarily put out of action or incapable of holding the seas. By the end of the year the admiral was complaining that his 'crazy fleet' was sliding towards 'a very indifferent state'. If nothing was done 'the finest ships in the service will soon be destroyed'.[72]

The state of Nelson's naval stores reached crisis point early in 1804. Gibraltar, said the new naval commissioner, was 'totally unprovided with stores of every description', lacking even what was 'absolutely *necessary*' to keep a handful of cruisers at sea throughout the winter. Malta was similarly circumstanced, short of most supplies and particularly pitch, tar, resin, paints and oil. One by one the ships were becoming unseaworthy. Nepean learned that 'the upper works of the *Gibraltar* being fir, and her bottom mahogany, the upper works are actually separating from her bottom. The *Kent* is very bad. *Renown*, we have just coiled her with three-inch rope [to hold her timbers together]. She will soon be ruined. *Superb*, we have with large iron bolts and frappings keep her scarf of the stern in its place . . .'[73]

There was reassuring news that some kind of rescue was underway, however. Two store ships, the *Hindustan* and the *Duke of Bronte*, were coming from England with enough supplies to last a year. The *Diana*, under Captain Thomas Maling, which escorted the convoy accompanying the *Duke of Bronte*, also carried twenty-seven tons of stores, including masts, yards and canvas. In January his convoy was scattered by a violent storm off Cape St Vincent, Portugal. Thirty-two ships limped into Gibraltar with the *Sophie* and *Diana*, but five, including the *Duke of Bronte*, were believed to have been taken into Tangier by enemy corsairs. Despite all that Nelson's cruisers had done, the region still bristled with privateers, each typically mounting between six and fourteen guns and carrying sixty to one hundred and twenty men. After a frantic search by the few available British cruisers, the *Duke of Bronte* turned up, but relief turned to disappointment when the stores were unloaded at the dockyard. The sails brought by *Diana* had been left uncovered and been damaged in the storm, and those in the *Duke of Bronte* were purely for the larger ships. To re-equip frigates the storekeeper had to cut down sails intended for sixty-fours.[74]

The *Hindustan*, the principal store ship that followed, carried an immense amount of stores and matériel, enough according to Troubridge to put Nelson's 'whole squadron in a good state'. The cargo amounted to an extraordinary 921 tons of stores, including 110 tons of masts, 181 tons of sails, 213 tons of cable and cordage with machinery for manufacturing the same, 75 tons of slop clothing, winches for winding yarn, a bomb raft, medical supplies for the new hospital at Malta and four 'caldrons' of coal. Compared to the average store ship cargo of 250 tons, this was the Navy Board's attempt to make a decisive difference to Nelson's situation. The *Hindustan*'s master, John Le Gros, got safely to Gibraltar in March, but, in view of the urgent needs of the fleet, Naval Commissioner W. A. Otway took little out of her and sent her forward as quickly as possible. It was a costly decision. Separated from her escort by a severe gale, the *Hindustan* made Rosas Bay, a mere day's sailing from the rendezvous off Toulon. On 2 April her crew were terrified to see thick black smoke billowing from the main hatchway. Fire, one of the most dreaded dangers in wooden sailing ships, had broken out in the fore hold. While some desperately tried to clear the magazine of powder and flammables, others tried to fight their way to the seat of the flames before being driven back by heat and smoke. The blaze became uncontrollable and Le Gros had to evacuate his ship, leaving her to disappear beneath walls of leaping fire and explode at 9.30. Nelson's precious supplies were blown to atoms, thrown across the bay and sent to the bottom. Fortunately, all but three of the crew got ashore. The stalwart Gayner did his best, finding accommodation and sustenance for the shocked survivors, hiring a boat to repatriate them to the fleet, and eventually receiving a silver cup from an appreciative Admiralty. Le Gros, too, emerged with credit. The loss created a sensation throughout the Mediterranean, but Nelson remarked that the preservation of the crew was 'little short of a miracle. I never read such a journal of exertions.' The court martial agreed, the officers of the store ship were acquitted of any negligence, and upon Nelson's recommendation Acting Lieutenant Thomas Banks was awarded a permanent commission. Still, the disaster was a cruel blow to a fleet desperate for supplies. There was talk of using divers to recover some of the items from the seabed, but little seems to have been saved. While Nelson searched frantically for alternatives, the Navy Board grimly bent their hands to rushing out replacements, but it would take another four store ships and several months to make good the loss.[75]

Nor was this quite the end of the catastrophe, which rolled like a set of falling dominoes. The day the *Hindustan* met her appalling destiny in Rosas Bay, the *Swift* cutter under Lieutenant William Leake arrived off Toulon with dispatches from England. The only British ship on the rendezvous, the *Juno*, had been drawn away by the tragedy at Rosas, and the unprotected cutter spent several days searching unsuccessfully for the fleet. On 5 April a hunting French privateer, *L'Esperance*, chased her off Palamos and took her after a short action.

Leake was slain by a musket ball and the entire postbag, with assorted baggage that included three portraits of Emma Hamilton, fell into enemy hands. Nelson hardly dared to think what confidences had been exposed, and consoled himself with the thought that the Admiralty would not have committed premier intelligence to 'a vessel not fit to trust my old shoes in'. In the end the loss of the *Swift* was not as grave as feared, and duplicates of the government's dispatches had been sent by the *Leviathan* ship of the line, but Nelson felt 'uneasy and unwell' for some time. The loss of the *Hindustan* and *Swift* and near loss of the *Duke of Bronte* by a combination of bad weather, accident and enemy action demonstrated just how narrow and precarious were the margins of the fleet's safety and survival.[76]

That spring was the worst moment for Nelson's supply chain, for the next store ships put into Gibraltar safely in July and the following month Nelson was able to report that the replacements and extraordinary efforts in Naples and the Adriatic had left the fleet 'not badly supplied'. Surprisingly the cordage and canvas from Naples was 'excellent' as well as cheap, and Hardy praised its resistance to mildew. The Adriatic hemp had been sent to the fleet from Malta, and was being turned into cordage, and a thirteen-year-old boy was revealing himself to be 'the best rope-maker' in the fleet. For the first time Nelson almost sounded jubilant. It had taken St Vincent's now defunct administration a year to satisfy the fleet's needs.[77]

The lack of ships and repair facilities was never overcome, however. Overstretched and unseaworthy ships kept the seas with little more than emergency maintenance, and by the summer of 1804 eight of the fourteen ships of the line were in need of a total refit in Britain or urgent repairs. At the end of the year the admiral complained bitterly of his lack of small ships, remarking that he had not received a new one in fifteen months. By 'management' he had kept his ships at sea 'but the time must come when we shall break up unless the new Admiralty [under Melville] act very differently from the old, and send out six sail of the line and fifteen frigates and sloops, and I do not believe that the late Admiralty have left them *one* to send'. Of particular shortcomings, he mentioned the need to re-copper his ships to protect their hulls from decay and improve their speed, and in January 1805 confessed his want of 'an entire floating arsenal'.[78]

These remaining weaknesses were beyond Nelson's ability to repair, but what he did as a commander-in-chief was sterling. During a critical period of recovery, when Britain's navy fought to come back from several years of mismanagement and retrenchment, he had maintained a force that exerted its influence across the whole Mediterranean. He had preserved the stream of victuals that helped raise the health of his force to new heights. The ships had been protected as far as means allowed, and while more were needed, they had politically held the line. Not least, the fighting skills of the fleet had been maintained.

Condemned to work with minimal forces in permanent disrepair, the officers and men survived two years as confident of their ability to beat the enemy as ever.

6

If disease had ravaged Nelson's crews, he would have been in hot water because manning was a stubborn problem. In October 1803, when Nelson received the Admiralty's authority to bring his force up to a war establishment, it was nine hundred men short of complement. A survey of forty-three ships over the following year suggests that as a whole they were 1231 men short and 12.8 per cent short of complement. Some men were pressed from British merchantmen, and the Admiralty sent a few hundred men and 'stout boys' but on 29 November admitted that they were unable to supply the men needed and authorised Nelson to recruit foreigners on station, just as long as they were not French. Volunteers would receive the usual bounty, serve for three years, and if they had been taken from the Mediterranean during their term they would be returned upon discharge. The Admiralty pointed Nelson towards Malta. Nelson had tried to recruit men from Malta as early as July and knew that there was little enthusiasm there. Ball, who had difficulty raising a Maltese military regiment, blamed the disruption caused by the long blockade.[79]

As late as Trafalgar fifteen foreigners recruited from Italy, Malta and Portugal were still serving on the *Victory* as seamen or marines. The military side of the business had been entrusted to Captain Charles William Adair, a marine from County Antrim who commanded in the flagship. He marshalled some 250 recruits between February 1804 and January 1805, most Italians of diverse professions, bakers, hairdressers, weavers, labourers, clerks and painters, even the occasional lawyer, writer or surgeon. He was successful enough to send surplus men to England, but in January the Admiralty commissioned Major James Weir to finish the job, relying on his deserved standing with the Maltese.[80]

Desertion weakened the drive to bring the crews up to war-time levels, and became a major concern. As Nelson put it, 'such is the love for roaming of our men that I am sure they would desert from Heaven to Hell merely for the sake of change'. The wood and watering parties that landed in Spain, Sardinia and Malta offered ideal opportunities to the restless or disaffected. On 4 December 1803 a court martial sentenced Robert Dwyer, a marine of the *Belleisle*, to be flogged around the fleet for threatening a superior officer – five hundred lashes across the bare back with a cat-o'-nine-tails. When the first dose of three hundred had been delivered Nelson remitted the remainder of his savage sentence. It was the first such case to be brought before him, the admiral explained in a firm proclamation, but he wished it to be known that sentences for any further instances of mutinous behaviour or 'the shameful and disgraceful crime of desertion', be they flogging around the fleet or death, would be carried out 'without mitigation'. That Nelson bracketed the two offences illustrates how seriously he viewed them. In Spain and Sardinia the local authorities disliked handing over deserters liable to such penalties. The captain-general of Catalonia returned thirteen men found wandering the streets of Barcelona as vagabonds, but only on the condition that they would be pardoned. Still, Nelson paid forty shillings for each runner apprehended, and nine pence per day towards their subsistence while in custody, and a number of deserters were involuntarily repatriated. The recognised price of desertion was not remitted, nor was the problem eradicated. Nelson resorted to arranging for suppliers to deliver provisions to his boats or ships so that his men did not have to be landed.[81]

Difficulties of this kind beset most commands, and there are no grounds for believing that Nelson's crews were any more discontented than most committed to long, difficult and sometimes tedious service. Drink was behind many of the offences. In 1804 a master-at-arms of the *Amphion* was deemed 'a very unsafe person' and dismissed from the service for drunkenness and using a woman to smuggle spirits into the ship. Generally speaking, the officers spoke of amenable ship's companies, and occasioned few complaints themselves. There was a culture of brutality aboard the *Bittern* brig, in which a tyrannical master was charged with beating his quartermaster. Robert Corbet, a ruthlessly efficient cruiser captain, escaped criticism, but he was a gratuitous flogger himself and long after his service with Nelson ended would provoke a serious mutiny. Fortunately, the admiral only had to rebuke one commander, Lieutenant Harding Shaw of the *Spider* brig, who flogged innocent and guilty alike while investigating an offence. His intemperance, said Nelson, was 'foreign to the rules of good discipline and the accustomed practice of His Majesty's navy.'[82]

Despite deserters and martinets most ships in Nelson's fleet were manned by stable, long-standing and well-ordered crews. In this lay their great advantage, for as their days turned into years they improved their trade in real-life situations, chasing sails, exploring unfamiliar anchorages, braving storms and reconnoitring enemy positions. They made the Mediterranean their training ground. In any encounter with enemy ships it was they who were the professionals.

Behind the screen provided by Nelson's line of battle ships the smaller cruisers, his frigates, sloops and brigs, were ceaselessly active, and they, rather than their larger consorts, most often gazed into the face of the enemy. A measure of their success was the relatively small number of French vessels that ventured beyond the creeks, bays, small ports, batteries and shallows of the coast. The French coastal trade proved resilient, and a few of their privateers struck boldly into deeper water, but beyond the shallows the Mediterranean was effectively a British dominion.

These were busy waters, traversed by traders of many nations and criss-crossed by British cruisers on innumerable errands. Historians have devoted most attention to the big units, but the stories of the frigates and 'little ships' also remain in the archives, telling of hazards and frustrations, missions accomplished, the mundane and the spectacular. Some reflect the highest levels of service, and produced noted captains such as Gore, Parker and Cracraft. 'In my last cruise,' wrote the last, 'I looked into all the ports of Puglia [eastern Italy] possessed by the French, made a circuit of the Adriatic and had an interview with Mr Foresti of Corfu . . . The French have no means of embarkation at any of the ports [in which] they hoist Neapolitan colours.' The ships of such men were schools for the service. Robert Heriot Barclay, who would make such a gallant defence of Lake Erie in 1813, had joined the navy under Nelson's fatherly advice and earned his sea time with Cracraft in the Adriatic.[83]

With so few ships, Nelson's cruisers had little time for rest, beginning every new task on the heels of the old. Convoy work was never popular. Merchantmen gathered at the designated collection points for up to two months, often creating unwieldy fleets difficult to discipline or keep in a body. The sixty-one-ship homeward-bound armada that the *Blonde* and *Experiment* took from Gibraltar in September 1803 was by no means unusual. It was regular work, as the trade in perishable goods was impatient of any delay, irrespective of whatever political circumstances demanded the navy's attentions elsewhere. The six homeward-bound convoys that left Malta between July 1803 and September 1804 were not enough for the Smyrna merchants. It was also dangerous, because weakly guarded convoys tempted privateers, some of them fairly well armed. Nelson always tried to post two ships to a convoy, but occasionally had only one, and at Malta, which was the rendezvous for the Italian, Adriatic and Levant trades, the local work had occasionally to be left to underpowered vessels. On 27 April 1804 the tiny *King George* packet, escorting a convoy between Messina and Malta, fought a superior privateer for one and a half hours in an attempt to allow her merchantmen to escape. Eight ships were lost in the attack, and the *King George* suffered severely, losing her commanding officer, who was fatally wounded by a shot that pierced both thighs. It was an act of courage that moved Nelson, who contributed £20 to a fund for his widow.[84]

Isolated tragedies apart, the convoy system worked and losses were exceptional. Going further, Nelson's cruisers prosecuted an active war against corsairs and enemy commerce. In all, the command took or destroyed over a hundred vessels during 1803 and 1804, including seven frigates, two brigs, two schooners and two transports belonging to the French or Spanish navies, some of which Nelson took into his service as needed reinforcements. Because the French shipped property under neutral cover and used false flags, seizures were often tricky. When the boats of the *Niger* investigated a ship under neutral Turkish colours off Genoa on 16 August 1803, they met an unexpected refusal to be allowed alongside. Supposing the ship to be carrying contraband, that is cargoes belonging to the French or their allies, Captain Hillyar sent his boats across, but they were received by a sudden fire from the vessel's stern and quarter guns and musketeers on her deck. In their third bloody attempt to board, the angry tars swarmed over the side of the ship cutting down a dozen defenders and driving the rest below. Yet the ship's papers revealed her to be a legitimate trader, and the hapless crew blamed their intoxicated captain, slain in the fight, for the unnecessary affray. It had cost the British eight casualties, including a lieutenant killed.[85]

Neutrality was a constant irritant. Enemy cargoes used neutral flags, and enemy corsairs abused neutral ports, sometimes darting out to seize approaching merchantmen, even those within the two miles generally accepted as the limits of territoriality. As Gore protested to the British minister in Madrid,

> The whole . . . coast between Cadiz and Alguzeras [Algeciras] affords convenient bays and anchoring places where these [French privateering] vessels take shelter from His Majesty's cruisers, and lay continually at anchor, while part of their crews are looking out upon [from] the adjacent [Spanish] signal towers, from whence they announce the appearance of vessels, and these privateers put to sea after them under Spanish colours. If they discover any British ships of war from the lookout tower, they instantly make the signal to the privateer, and enable her to . . . escape . . . I have seen the crews of the privateers leave their vessels and land and [to] man the guns in the [Spanish] batteries along shore.[86]

Nelson warned his captains against flouting neutrality and restored prizes where clear infringements by his officers were established. Two prizes of the *Cyclops* were restored when Naples complained, and Lieutenant Richard Spencer of the *Renard* schooner was reprimanded for attacking a French privateer in neutral water when it had not fired a shot. But Nelson regularly upbraided Spain, Naples, Austria and Corfu for tolerating French abuses of their neutrality, and went so far as to threaten that any port permitting itself to become an instrument of war would forfeit its neutral status. He ordered his captains to pursue enemy corsairs that had blatantly infringed neutrality wherever it was possible to get at them, whether in neutral havens or not. In reading the reports it is impossible not to suspect that both sides stretched their interpretation of neutrality. Lieutenant Shaw of the *Spider* played a controversial hand, and in August 1803 his superior, George Scott of the *Stately*, forced him to restore the *Intrépide* privateer which had been cut out from beneath a castle at Cape Passero in neutral Sicily. Later the same month the *Spider* was at the Sicilian port of Girgenti, stripping another French privateer of her British prizes. In this case Nelson vindicated Shaw, accepting that the French had forfeited the protection of the port by seizing at least one of their prizes within Sicilian territorial waters. Given claim and counter-claim few of the cases were clear-cut. In an incident that took place in a cove of neutral Fano, one of the Ionian Islands, for example,

La Véloce privateer was taken by the *Arrow*, Captain Richard Budd Vincent. The French technically justified Vincent's action by firing first, but it could be argued that a threatening British approach induced them to do so.[87]

These sorts of difficulties did not deter Nelson's cruisers from showing enterprise and courage. Some used ingenuity, among them Pearse of *L'Alcyon*, who disguised his sloop as a merchantman to incite corsairs to attack him, thus anticipating the tactics of the First World War 'Q' ships. On 21 June 1804 two privateers speeding out of Tarifa near Gibraltar to scoop up what they thought was a defenceless trader found themselves with a tiger by the tail, and one ran ashore while trying to escape.[88]

Nearly a thousand miles to the north-east other officers were taking the war to the enemy's own coast. About midnight of 10 July 1804 the boats of three frigates, *Narcissus*, *Seahorse* and *Maidstone*, swept out of the darkness to attack a French convoy at Le Lavandou in Hyères Bay, near Toulon. A dozen settees lay beneath a shore battery, moored head to stern and attached to each other underneath, but led by Lieutenant John Thomson the British braved a shower of grape and musketry to board and carry most of the vessels in desperate cutlass and pistol work. One of the prizes was cut away and brought out and the rest burned, but the British lost twenty-seven killed and wounded. Lieutenant John Lumley of the *Seahorse* had his right arm pulled out, but made 'a miraculous recovery'. 'Wounds,' Nelson wrote to Donnelly, who had planned the operation, 'must be expected in fighting the enemy. They are marks of honour.'[89]

A little further east on the French Riviera Captain Capel of the *Phoebe* frigate made serious if temporary inroads into the enemy coasting trade using the inshore shallows. His boats were constantly being lowered and raised as he probed, stabbed and landed in amphibious raids reminiscent of those that would later distinguish Lord Cochrane, the most lethal frigate captain of the age. In April two enemy vessels were cut out from beneath batteries, providing intelligence of the French activities in Toulon. Then Capel targeted the coastal batteries and signal stations that sheltered French ships and warned them of British movements. He stormed one battery, driving away its garrison and spiking the guns, and joined the *Childers* in a successful assault on another battery and signal post, making off with enemy signal flags and books. Two more vessels transporting wine and oil were taken at the end of the month. Reporting to Nelson, Capel proudly claimed to have completely disrupted the enemy trade. 'Scarcely anything is moving,' he said.[90]

On 28 August 1804, off Cape Passero, Sicily, close to another thousand miles of sea south and east of where Capel was enjoying himself on the Côte d'Azur, Corbet's sloop, the *Bittern*, performed what was perhaps the most gruelling feat of arms of the year. The captain was a man with a grim mission. He was in pursuit of a notorious ship from Cette that had taken one of the navy's own, for the day before a large French corsair, *L'Hirondelle*, had attacked a British convoy, overwhelming a plucky Maltese brig, the *King George*. Corbet tracked his quarry to Cape Passero, and found her in possession of two captured brigs. The corsair, which was heavily armed with fourteen twelve-pounders and a crew of eighty-one, was in some respects a stiff opponent for a small brig, but the enemy ships scattered. The weather was dead calm, and Corbet dropped all his boats, two to pursue the prizes and the rest to tow his brig after the corsair, and to strengthen the strokes of his oarsmen he fashioned spars into additional oars. Five of his men awaiting trial for desertion were released from their irons to contribute to the remarkable chase that followed, as the British tars heaved at the sweeps for thirty-six windless, punishing hours, snatching brief swallows of water along the way but eschewing meals to crawl over sixty torturous miles, baking in the sun or groping through darkness. As they came up with their prey, the oarsmen came under fire from the French stern guns, while covering shot from their own bow-chasers whined over their heads in reply. But they bagged the corsair, which was taken into the Royal Navy, and recaptured both her prizes. Nelson pardoned the deserters and with good reason. No Trafalgar veteran could have boasted a finer exhibition of duty than the nameless and faceless men who performed this appalling labour with the prospect of a life and death struggle at the end of it.[91]

But perhaps nothing demonstrated the spirit of Nelson's little ships more than a defeat that took place a few leagues north-west of Cape Palos on the eastern coast of Spain. On 4 January 1805 the *Arrow* sloop, armed with twenty-eight thirty-two-pound carronades, and the *Acheron* bomb vessel left Malta with thirty-four merchantmen bound for England. Heading north-west, they ploughed into foul weather and gales, and one ship separated while another rolled on her beam ends and sank with the loss of all hands. In spite of all the convoy was off the Spanish coast on 3 February, steering for the Strait, when two large ships appeared astern. Captain Arthur Farquhar of the *Acheron* dropped behind and signalled the strangers, but receiving no answer warned her consort ahead. Vincent of the *Arrow* was the mild-mannered son of a Berkshire banker and silk merchant, but he had made a respectable reputation for himself in the Adriatic, protecting trade and running down contraband cargoes and corsairs, including a privateer taken at Fano. Now his *Arrow* was in such poor shape that he had been ordered to take a convoy home. About midnight he dropped behind to support the *Acheron*, leaving a merchantman to lead the convoy.[92]

Events then moved quickly. Sure the advancing ships were enemies, Vincent used lights and guns to signal his convoy to scatter. There was an agreed rendezvous at Tetuan, and as the flight got underway and the big French frigates raced forward the lieutenant commanding the *Triad*, a bomb tender, took the crew off a lagging ship and set her on fire. The *Arrow* and *Acheron* were heavily outgunned, but Farquhar came aboard and the two commanders resolved to keep themselves between the convoy and the frigates, creating time for their charges to escape. It was a conscious decision to sacrifice their ships and probably some lives. The 'very unequal contest of considerable length' began in the early hours of the 4th. The *Arrow* took on the *Incorruptible* of forty-two guns and 650 men, one of two 'forty-gun frigates' that had escaped from Toulon. The wind was too variable and light to afford many opportunities to manoeuvre, but Vincent managed to rake his opponent at one point, although at another he had to receive the fire of both enemy frigates and suffered fearful damage. Shot thumped its way through the hull of the little *Arrow*, piercing it above and below the waterline, and dismounted four guns, downed forty men, smashed her lower masts, ripped rigging and sails and disabled her rudder, leaving her an unmanageable 'wreck'. Vincent struck at 7.40 and barely got the men off before his ship settled on her beam ends and went to the bottom, one of the rare instances of a ship being fought until sunk by gunfire. In the meantime the *Acheron* drew the *Hortense* of forty-four guns and six hundred men away from the *Arrow*, but she was knocked to pieces and struck a little after eight o'clock. Farquhar reported that although his crew were largely young and inexperienced they behaved 'with the spirit of veterans', and the vessel was such a ruin that the French removed the prisoners and blew her up. The two ships had been lost, but they had saved most of their convoy, and Vincent told Nelson 'that the officers and crew of the *Arrow* behaved as Englishmen and merit my warmest approbation for their attention and bravery'. The admiral reported a 'most gallant defence' to the Admiralty. Both commanders were cleared of negligence in courts martial and promoted to the rank of post-captain. Deservedly so, because in the depths of the worst disaster that befell Nelson's command at the hands of the enemy the little ships had never acquitted themselves with greater honour.[93]

7

Information was perhaps the hardest commodity to come by, and much of what there was passed along long and insecure channels. That most essential data for seamen, the navigational information that enabled safe travel, was not always available. Local pilots were sometimes unobtainable for areas held by the enemy, and many were unwilling to expose themselves to the risks that naval operations often incurred.

Naval officers could not depend upon having up-to-date charts because the Admiralty's hydrographic service was in its infancy. It was only in 1795 that the board appointed its first hydrographer, Alexander Dalrymple, and his limited powers and tiny staff prevented him satisfying the need, leaving sea officers to arm themselves with additional data when they could. The different captains and masters in a fleet often had varied, even conflicting, navigational information about any particular area. In this respect, Nelson was more fortunate than many in enjoying a far-sighted predecessor and second-in-command, Bickerton. Bickerton had put the peace to good use by ordering his ships' masters, including genuine talents such as Robert Davison and William Kirby, to survey parts of Sardinia, and it was from these explorations that the idea of using Agincourt Sound had grown. Whatever might be said against St Vincent's regime at the Admiralty, it could boast Troubridge's particular interest in charting the Mediterranean. Perhaps he remembered his misfortunes in the *Culloden*, which had twice run ashore. But certainly he more than any other patronised the hydrographic service, studiously transmitting Bickerton's surveys to Dalrymple so that they could be turned into operational charts, which he parcelled up for Nelson in batches of twenty. So in this respect, at least, Nelson was well served by the Admiralty, despite the vast areas of his theatre that remained inadequately explored. It was a beginning, and for the rest the work of lead line and eye and the collection of local information had to go on.[94]

Fresh political information also proved difficult to get, and authentic intelligence of the enemy was more valuable than gold-dust. 'I would give a good deal for a copy of the French admiral's orders,' Nelson once wrote. Important as it was, little that was concrete reached the admiral, who had to guess enemy intentions from a variety of unreliable sources, the gleanings made through spyglasses wielded from the mastheads of watch ships, uncertain statements from ship masters encountered at sea or prisoners, the yellow reporting of newspapers, the movements of troops onshore, and the rumours that filtered through merchants, diplomats and well-wishers. With so little evidence to cross-check information, such fragments were difficult to evaluate, and Nelson often wallowed indecisively amongst the unreliable and contradictory. In moments of crisis the absence of firm intelligence created alarm in all quarters; as Nelson remarked, 'every person thinks they [the French] are destined for his place of residence.' There was little help from home. It took the admiral six or seven weeks to get replies to his letters to government, and sometimes more. 'I have not had a scrap of pen from England ninety days this day,' he complained. Mail was also in danger of being intercepted. Ships of the line or frigates could get through if they were available, and Nelson regularly sent packets to Lisbon for collection, but he also sent much overland through Naples, Vienna and Spain. Sometimes his letters were secreted in the private correspondence of such well-disposed individuals as Falconnet and Gayner.[95]

Britain had a team of diplomats throughout the Mediterranean, all of whom were expected to gather and share intelligence with London, each other and the naval commander-in-chief. There were ministers (ambassadors or envoys) in Madrid, Vienna, St Petersburg, Sardinia, Naples and Constantinople; 'resident' diplomats in Alexandria (Egypt) and the Septinsular Republic; and a number of consuls of different ranks scattered in towns and ports from Cadiz to Smyrna. All strove with the relative isolation, indifferent communications and secrecy of the enemy that vexed Nelson, but a number maintained regular contact with the admiral and transmitted crucial information. Where a consul or agent did not exist, Nelson sometimes appointed a temporary one, such as Nicola Garzia of the Maddalenas. Two individuals were particularly useful informants, James Duff, almost completing forty years of service as British consul in Cadiz, and Spiridion Foresti, the new 'resident' in Corfu.

Duff, who died a baronet in 1815, was particularly well placed to comment upon Spanish or French movements in Cadiz, an important position as far as the security of Nelson's communication line and control of the Mediterranean was concerned. Seventy in 1804, he had first met a fresh-faced Lieutenant Nelson in January 1777, and, growing old in the service, he had become acquainted with most men of consequence in Cadiz, including the Spanish admirals Córdoba and Moreno, defeated at Cape St Vincent. British warships visiting Cadiz habitually anchored close enough to receive boats from Duff, and invariably were given the latest on such matters as the state of Anglo-Spanish relations and the activities of *L'Aigle* and other French ships in the port. Nelson used other consular officials in Spain, such as Gibert and Price, but it was Duff he trusted most.[96]

No diplomat, however, surpassed Foresti in enthusiasm, industry and efficiency. He owed much to Nelson. The two had corresponded since 1798, when Foresti, a merchant of Zante, had served as a British consul in the Ionian Islands. When the French invaded the area they confiscated Foresti's property and confined him for about a year, but Nelson supported his claim to compensation from the British government, and in 1803 he was promoted a 'resident' at the age of fifty-one. 'I can have no claim to your thanks for rendering justice to your unremitting zeal and attention,' Nelson told him. 'It has been your own exertions . . . and . . . you are obliged to no one.' He was unusually active, arguing Britain's corner in the new Septinsular Republic, and conducting 'a daily correspondence with the viziers, pashas and bishops, and most of the leading men in Albania and the Morea'. It was Foresti who came closest to penetrating the plans of the French when he signalled their intention to invade the Morea at the turn of 1803 and sparked the multi-national build-up in the Adriatic that probably contributed to the abandonment of the enemy plan. Moreover, the diplomat offered to tour the threatened regions himself, whipping up anti-French feelings. 'My appearance with the Turks may be very productive of some good consequences,' he ventured.[97]

If Foresti's interpretation of French intentions was correct, his achievement would have been almost unique, since the sum of all Nelson's sources of information fell short of what he really needed – a clear and decisive insight into the minds of his opponents. He could see when the Toulon fleet was ready to sail, but not where it was bound. Bonaparte's orders remained mysterious. This was perhaps the most decisive failure in the Mediterranean. It can hardly be put at Nelson's door, since the admiral did all within his power to relate the scattered facts one to another, but its effect was to divert his attention eastwards at an important moment. Intelligence was the weakest link in his chain mail.

Two years might have been expected to have worn down Nelson's fleet, but at the end of that period it still had the energy of a vital force. It had not yet met its severest test, however. In 1805 that time had finally come.

XXII

THE TEST

Whisper but Nelson in a Frenchman's ear,
And straight from head to foot he quakes with
fear,
Sailors and soldiers all agree together,
To run away, and never mind the weather.

The Barbados Gazette, June 1805

I

On 5 October 1804 four Spanish frigates, returning from South America with a rich haul of wool, fur, Peruvian bark and an eye-watering £170,000 in specie, encountered four British frigates off Cape St Mary near Cadiz. Britain and Spain were at peace but the British were suspicious of naval preparations in the Spanish port of Ferrol, and their detachment was waiting to detain the bullion ships in case of war. Commanded by Graham Moore of the Channel fleet, the British force contained two ships belonging to Nelson's command, Gore's *Medusa* and Sutton's *Amphion*. In the debacle that followed three of the Spanish frigates surrendered and one burst into flames and exploded, killing all but forty-five of her people.

Threatened by Bonaparte, a reluctant Spain had been hectored towards war, but the engagement off Cape St Mary lit the touch paper. Britain restrained herself from formally declaring war, but a Spanish war it was, in all but name. For centuries war with Spain had been synonymous with plunder, and nothing excited British captains more than the thought of heavily laden Spanish treasure ships plodding home across the Atlantic, totally unaware of the outbreak of hostilities in Europe. It was like releasing hares before hounds, and prizes were soon being snapped up. Since the two countries remained officially at peace, the spoils were held as 'droits of the crown' rather than regular prize, but the captors could count upon generous compensation in lieu of prize money. The principals did very well indeed. Gore, who had made a fortune from two Spanish frigates back in 1797, now got a second from the business off Cape St Mary, and became a knight bachelor. Sutton made enough to quit the sea, and even in distant Norfolk petite Susannah Bolton wondered how far the Nelsons would benefit from a toll of 'golden ships'.[1]

Nelson did not believe that Spain wanted war and saw the whole episode as a sordid smash and grab. 'Ah, this love of money!' he sighed. He was astonished at the British action, and realised that it made his position extremely tenuous. The Spanish fleet was not in fighting trim, not least because its ports had been scourged by yellow fever, but if the units at Toulon, Cartagena and Cadiz combined they could field twenty-five ships of the line and greatly outnumber Nelson's fleet. As it was, the Spaniards in Cadiz were well placed to threaten his communication line, and would be supplying no more fresh provisions, intelligence and mail facilities. Nelson's finely balanced command of the Mediterranean was at risk.[2]

In London, Melville, the new first lord of the Admiralty, realised that a stronger force was needed to blockade Cadiz and handle the increased business outside the Strait, and ordered the Channel fleet to detach reinforcements. Had they been incorporated into Nelson's command, which historically covered that area, all might have been well, but Melville carved a new and independent command out of Nelson's jurisdiction, and placed Vice Admiral Sir John Orde in charge of the region outside the Strait of Gibraltar, the very hunting ground in which the current prizes were being taken. Nelson's theatre was now contained within the Mediterranean proper. He had been hurt when Keith superseded him in the Mediterranean in 1799, and resented being elevated to the chief command in the Baltic only after the fighting was over and the main prizes garnered. This was the sequel. Just as the rich pickings of a Spanish war began flooding in, the Admiralty sent another admiral to reap the rewards that had traditionally belonged to the commander-in-chief of the Mediterranean.

Dame Fortune had a strange relationship with Nelson. She granted him great victories, but seldom the financial spoils.

2

Nelson was cruising off Toulon on 12 October when word of the action reached him, and the next day a cutter brought orders from the Admiralty. Pre-dating the battle, they alerted him to the difficulties with Spain and directed him to detain her treasure ships, but to avoid unnecessary acts of hostility unless he had irrefutable evidence of war. Nelson sent Strachan of the *Donegal* to command a few cruisers outside the Strait, but proceeded with caution. A Spanish war would present him with an opportunity to take Minorca, where Port Mahon offered a convenient harbour with dockyard facilities. Intelligence suggested that the people of Minorca were not inimical to British rule, and that the weak garrisons would fall to two thousand men, but for the moment the temptation had to be resisted. Nelson warned his officers to be on their guard when approaching Spanish ports, and sent ships to Rosas and Barcelona to see what could be gained in the way of provisions – perhaps final provisions – and news.[3]

At the time Sardinia was the greater worry, thick with rumours of a French plot to invade from Corsica. Nelson took his main force to Maddalena, where he had arranged for victuallers from Rosas and Malta to rendezvous, and detailed the *Thunder* bomb to remain as a deterrent. In December the Reverend Scott was dispatched to Cagliari but the Prince of Savoy saw no immediate threat. The Sardinians contented themselves with landing a reconnaissance force on Corsica one night to assess the danger and with begging Nelson to keep some 'light ships' off Maddalena.[4]

For several weeks Britain and Spain endured a cold war, and the Admiralty's orders shifted backwards and forwards. In less than good health, Nelson had written for leave in August, and at first the rupture with Spain did not shake his resolve. He would have 'liked an odd hundred thousand pounds' to help family and friends, he told Emma, 'but never mind'. The contents of his wine cellar were already being shifted to the *Superb*, which he had selected to carry him home, as she, like the admiral, was in desperate need of a thorough refit. But when Lambton Este, the son of an old friend, called on Nelson while returning from Egypt on 1 November, he found him wavering. 'Oh my good fellow!' the admiral declared, 'I have abandoned the idea of going to England for the present.' Este was therefore entrusted with papers and dispatches for London, along with some bottles of 'fine Marsala' for luck, and packed off in the *Termagant* sloop five days later.[5]

Back on his cruising ground confronting the Spanish crisis, Nelson felt in serious want of information. Durban of the *Ambuscade* had returned from Barcelona with the news that Spain's declaration of war was daily expected. In his diary of 14 November Nelson wrote, 'At night heard that the Spaniards had declared war.' This intelligence appears to have also come from Durban, who had been sent back to Barcelona. Apparently it consisted of a report that a British merchantman had been fired upon off Minorca, and a letter from Frere, the British minister in Madrid, hinting at imminent hostilities. The report, from whatever source, was wrong but Nelson ordered his captains to seize or destroy Spanish vessels, save for corn ships, in accordance with his original orders from the Admiralty, and spent the latter half of November and part of December off the Spanish coast. In the two months that followed Nelson's receipt of the news about the action off Cape St Mary his forces inflicted considerable damage upon the Spaniards, taking a score of vessels outside and inside the Strait including two frigates, the *Matilda* and *Amphitrite*, a 'national' schooner, the twelve-gun *Ventura* and two transports containing an entire regiment of Spanish regulars. 'I suppose I am the only admiral at war with Spain,' Nelson remarked, satisfied with such activity. The plunder was not inconsiderable, and the captors outside the Strait were said to be expecting £20,000.[6]

Nelson had to return to Sardinia in mid-December. 'Very anxious to get back,' he confided to his diary, 'but fresh provisions is absolutely necessary.' The *Victory* alone was short of twenty-two tons of water and had only ten weeks of provisions left. It was while he was in Pula on 14 December that he received the thunderbolt about Orde. Nelson had already heard of Orde's arrival off Cadiz and thought it 'very extraordinary', but it was not until the *Amazon* brought a letter from Orde dated 17 November, notifying Nelson of his appointment to the new command outside the Strait that the true import struck. Orde had been *persona non grata* while St Vincent was at the Admiralty, and he was not popular in the fleet. Now some of Nelson's captains were 'astonished' at the Admiralty's treatment of their commander-in-chief, and fearful that Orde might succeed to the entire Mediterranean command if he went home. As Parker wrote, Nelson's 'very conciliatory, pleasant manners, and superior abilities have learnt us to respect and feel the value of such a chief'. Campbell raged that Orde was plainly out to 'skim the cream' and damned Melville, 'the Scotch lord at the Admiralty'. Nelson's own feelings spilled out to Marsden:

> We have an odd report that Sir John Orde has been near three weeks off Cadiz. I cannot believe it. It would be so very odd that the last Admiralty should have sent Admiral Campbell to take all my *sugar* from me, which he did completely, and that this Admiralty should send and take all my golden harvest from me. I begin to doubt if I have served well and rendered the state some service. Surely I must have dreamt it, or the Admiralty could not have served me so. As it is, I am, I believe, a poorer man than when I left England . . . But nothing ever shall shake my faithful line of conduct to my king and country. If Sir John does not make haste I shall get hold of the French fleet and then he may hang himself in a golden cord.

Emma also learned that, although Orde 'will get all the money and your poor Nelson all the hard blows', he had decided 'to overwhelm' the intruder 'with respect and attention, and to even make an offer (as Admiral Campbell has gone home) to serve [here] till the Admiralty can send out another flag-officer . . . But I dare say Sir John Orde is too great a man to want my poor services.' No doubt, he grumbled to Sutton, when Orde had 'made money enough he will be removed and the responsibility left where it was before'.[7]

Nelson managed a civil reply to Orde's letter, although he also wrote to Melville, suggesting that his own officer, Strachan, be given the Cadiz command with two sail of the line and eight cruisers. Both admirals were soon quibbling about the demarcation line between their respective jurisdictions. Nelson's suspicions of Orde ran deep. The latter was the senior of the two officers, and Nelson pictured him tapping supplies intended for the Mediterranean, purloining and redeploying ships for his own purposes, and cornering the lion's share of the prize money. Nelson sent the *Anson*, *Niger* and *Childers* to reinforce Strachan outside the Strait in October and November, the last two after learning of Orde's appointment. Partly, he saw it as an opportunity to reward faithful followers by putting them in the way of rich pickings. 'Make your fortune!' he told Strachan. Orde rumbled about the 'intrusion' with a hint of pecuniary interest, and on 27 November ordered Nelson's ships off his station. Nelson responded by telling his captains to avoid Orde; in November he sent Bolton of the *Childers* into the disputed region with 'secret' orders and a command that 'on no account or consideration' was he to allow himself to be redeployed.[8]

After receiving the Admiralty's notification of Orde's command on Christmas Day, Nelson was more circumspect. In the Gulf of Lions he summoned Parker of the *Amazon* to his cabin on 30 December and gave him a package of dispatches to deliver to Lisbon. The admiral warned Parker to pass Cape Spartel, west of the Strait, in the night and to steer south and west to give Orde's ships a wide berth. Nor must Parker have any truck with Orde on the return journey. It was almost as if they were enemy ships. 'Bring to for nothing if you can help it' read Nelson's private letter, but if Parker's later recollections are to be believed, he was more direct in conversation. 'Remember Parker, if you cannot weather that fellow, I shall think you have not a drop of your old uncle's blood in your veins,' he said. There were other reasons why Nelson directed Parker to give the coast of Spain a wide berth. It was rife with yellow fever, and the *Amazon* was far too valuable a ship to get quarantined. Whatever the reason, Parker's cruise was profitable, for apart from delivering the mail to Lisbon he took two prizes containing £71,000 in addition to other goods. His commander-in-chief congratulated the twenty-three-year-old captain, but wished he had earned less, for if he married and left the service the navy would lose a good officer.[9]

When the *Swiftsure* and *Tigre* ships of the line joined Nelson's fleet off Cape San Sebastian on Christmas Day, they brought more than the official announcement about Orde. Nelson's request for temporary leave was also granted. He was still minded to remain with the fleet awhile, and kept the matter to himself to avoid demoralising the men. He was unwell, but the winter had been a mild one, and apart from the Spanish war there were other reasons to stay. Troops were being embarked upon the French ships in Toulon, and Nelson had a hunch that Villeneuve might try to run for it in the short days. Furthermore, his fleet was now a flag officer short. Admiral Campbell had been shipped home on 4 December, sick with fever and a severe disorder of the nervous system, owning that he was 'never . . . more unhinged in my life'. Nelson confided to Emma that 'for several months' he had 'thought that his mind was debilitated, but we tried to laugh him out of it'. It was a dark presentiment of that officer's sad death by his own hand many years later, but in 1805 made another argument for Nelson to postpone his furlough.[10]

It was well that he did.

On 12 December, Spain declared war on Britain. As France and Spain were able to field 102 ships of the line between them, they outnumbered the British at sea. With only 83 capital ships, Albion was now paying a stiff price for St Vincent's imprudent reforms. Had the French and Spanish forces been in better shape, and more geographically concentrated, Britain could have been in serious trouble. On 4 January Spain made a pact with France in Paris, undertaking to provide thirty battleships, most ships of the line, and a substantial army before the end of March. Don Frederico Gravina was appointed commander-in-chief of the Spanish fleet. The French emperor's plan to invade Britain had received a great fillip. Nonetheless, Villeneuve, the admiral at Toulon, had a clear sense of its inadequacies and did not want the commission. At Toulon the dockyard lacked materiel, the men were raw, demoralised and undisciplined, and desertion was rampant. Gravina's fleet was little better placed, plagued by problems of supply and manpower recently aggravated by the pestilence that had worried the Spanish coast. Villeneueve felt that little but confusion and humiliation awaited his fleet at sea, but his coastal lookout towers continued to monitor British movements offshore, and to search for opportunities.

That winter Pitt's strategy of rebuilding a new anti-French coalition, the 'third coalition' as it would be called, was also beginning to flower. In November, Russia had gone so far as to sign a secret treaty with Austria to defend Naples in the event of an attack by France. Austria was notoriously unreliable, and Russia felt the need to encourage her. Britain was asked to commit a significant military force to the Mediterranean, capable of intervening in Italy. In northern Europe Anglo-Russian cooperation foundered on the unmovable rock of Prussia, but in southern Europe the two powers had fashioned a rude accord.

As it happened Britain was already independently organising a military task force to be based in Malta. Relatively small, it consisted of only four thousand men under Sir James Craig, but it was designed to meet Nelson's demand for a mobile amphibious force, capable of being transported to wherever needed in Naples or Sicily. This was far less than Russia wanted, but after Britain had lost the flower of its army in forays into the disease-ridden West Indies it was understandable that Pitt kept his principal remaining forces at home to meet the invasion threat. Anyway, he felt that Craig's expedition was as much as could safely be spared. Size apart, in March 1805 the remit of the task force was widened to include cooperation with the Russians in Italy if circumstances were favourable.

Back in the Mediterranean, Nelson remained unconvinced by Russia, and even less by Austria. Remembering the disaster of 1798, he advised Naples not to antagonise the French on the strength of Russian promises. Nevertheless,

Europe was dividing again into two armed camps, with many small unaligned states struggling to retain their independence. Even Portugal, historically a close ally of Britain, felt pushed towards imposing an embargo on British ships using her ports. As the opposing sides prepared to throw themselves upon each other and forge the great saga of 1805, it was no time for Britain's warrior hero to retire to Merton. He of all the country's admirals was the most capable of winning a major battle and regaining British naval superiority.

3

Nelson left Cape San Sebastian for Agincourt Sound on 2 January 1805 to rendezvous with victuallers from Malta. He was still there at three in the afternoon of the 19th, when the *Active* and *Seahorse*, his watch frigates off Toulon, arrived under full sail. From afar they signalled that the French were at sea!

Eleven sail of the line and nine frigates and brigs, with 6300 soldiers, had left Toulon the day before. Moubray's *Active* and Boyle's *Seahorse* spotted them the same evening, and intermittently kept them in sight until two the following morning, when Villeneuve was some eighty-five miles south of Toulon, steering south or south-west against a powerful north-westerly wind and a large sea, and under a heavy press of sail. Nelson ordered his captains to send their casks and boats ashore to collect what last-minute water and food they could, and hastily weighed the intelligence to hand. He knew absolutely nothing about Villeneuve's intentions, but although the French may have been steering in a southerly direction, the admiral was convinced that 'they could only be bound round the southern end of Sardinia' to threaten Sardinia, Sicily, the Morea or Egypt. It was a logical, even a shrewd, deduction. During the previous fortnight the wind at Toulon had been NE or SE, ideal for a western voyage, yet Villeneuve had only sailed when the breeze swung to NNW. That suggested an easterly destination. But instead of sailing directly eastwards along a friendly Riviera coast, Villeneuve had initially struck south, a course that implied he intended turning east by the south-west coast of Sardinia.[11]

It was the chance Nelson had waited for these last eighteen months, and stores were tumbled aboard his ships before dark. Using a westerly wind the British picked their way out of the Maddalenas eastwards, the *Victory* leading with her stern light pointing the way through the night. By seven the ships had cleared the perilous passage between the Isle of Biche and the coast, barely a quarter of a mile wide, and gained the Tyrrhenian Sea. Nelson then sent *Seahorse* ahead to look for the French on the southern coast of Sardinia, and followed with the *Victory*, *Royal Sovereign*, *Canopus*, *Donegal*, *Superb*, *Spencer*, *Tigre*, *Leviathan*, *Belleisle*, *Conqueror* and *Swiftsure* ships of the line and the *Active* frigate. With Sardinia to starboard they worked south through the remaining stormy hours of darkness, striking topgallants in the high wind and focusing as best they could on Hardy's blue light, blinking in the spray. Nelson threw his fastest ships, *Spencer* and *Leviathan*, on his weather beam, to act promptly against any enemy ships that might appear, and in the morning the ships prepared for battle, forming two close-ordered sailing columns and making what progress they could under storm staysails against strengthening south-westerlies.

Already, the lack of intelligence had played Nelson false: driven to sea by Napoleon, Villeneuve was not heading east but west in pursuit of the emperor's dream of invading England. Missiessy had already got a detachment out of Rochefort, and Villeneuve was supposed to meet him in the West Indies and raid British possessions before doubling back to Europe. Unfortunately, the Toulon fleet performed as Villeneuve knew it would. The storms brought down spars, masts, ropes and sails, and the untrained complements retched as they struggled to cope. On 21 January most of Villeneuve's battered force was back in Toulon. Their admiral composed a damning report of the state of his fleet and tried to resign.

There was little to guide Nelson, who continued to pursue a phantom fleet. On 21 January, when most of Villeneuve's battered ships regained Toulon, the *Seahorse* saw and lost a French frigate off Pula on the southern coast of Sardinia in thick fog and a heavy gale. Nelson believed that the French were struggling to reach Cagliari, a little east of Pula, against the south-westerlies and that he might be able to intercept them. 'I sincerely pray for a favourable wind,' he wrote coming down from the north, 'for we cannot be more than 20 leagues from them, and if Cagliari is their object [and] if the Sardinians wish to defend their capital, we shall be in time to save them. Pray God it may be so.' As Nelson fought to round the south-eastern extremities of Sardinia, his advance frigates returned from Cagliari. No sign of the French. Nelson was nonplussed. 'I have neither eat [sic], drank or slept with any comfort since last Sunday,' he wrote to Acton. 'I would willingly have half of mine [my ships] burnt to effect their destruction. I am in a fever. God send we may find them!'[12]

For some days Nelson beat about the area between Sardinia, Sicily and Italy trying to cover the danger points, while his overstretched small ships sailed, reported and sailed again to close down as many options as possible. In Naples Elliot marvelled at the industry of these ships. 'Having there delivered his dispatches to Captain Sotheran of the *Excellent*, he [Boyle] in a few minutes returned on board [his ship *Seahorse*] . . . and beat out to sea against a gale of wind and heavy sea with a degree of success which created universal admiration, as I believe the attempt would have been deemed impracticable to any other than a British man of war.' The *Morgiana*, *Bittern*, *Seahorse*, *Active*, *Termagant* and *Phoebe*, along with the *Tigre* ship of the line, went to Corsica, Sardinia, Elba and Toulon to the north and north-west, eastwards to Naples, or towards Pantellaria, Tunis and Malta to check the southern passage between the western and eastern basins of the Mediterranean; and as far as the Morea and Crete.

They alerted the endangered, so that defences could be prepared, but found no concrete intelligence. On 19 January the *Phoebe* encountered an eighty-gun French ship of the line, the storm-smashed *Indomptable*, limping towards Ajaccio in Corsica, her topmasts gone. The news got to Nelson a week later, but it was obvious that the Frenchman had run for Corsica after separating from the fleet in bad weather, and the sighting indicated nothing of her original destination. Another report of three French ships making for St Fiorenzo in northern Corsica suggested no more, while the enemy frigate seen by the *Seahorse* off Pula seemed to disappear without trace.[13]

By 28 January, Nelson was suspecting that the enemy might have been scattered and driven back to Toulon, but deemed it his duty to double-check the vulnerable areas to the east before going elsewhere. He struck eastwards across the Tyrrhenian Sea, exchanging communications with Palermo and passing north of the Lipari Islands towards the Strait of Messina. At night the fleet rounded the volcanic island of Stromboli, which blazed fiercely into the black sky, and beat through the Faro – 'a thing unprecedented in nautical history' on account of 'the rapidity of the current' – to reach Messina on the 30th. Amazed observers on distant mountain peaks watched the British ships grimly beating to windward against a violent south-westerly gale. As Naples and Sicily knew no danger, Nelson continued into the blue Ionian Sea battered by squalls. He drew a blank in the Morea, and steered south-east to Egypt, the *Royal Sovereign*, which needed recoppering, straining every sinew to keep company. Making Alexandria on 7 February, he sent Hallowell ashore to confer with the British consul and the governor, but there was no sign of the French, nor any information. This was depressing, since after leaving Italy Nelson had convinced himself without 'a shadow of doubt' that the French were bound for Egypt, largely on account of its weak defences and the hatred the Mamelukes had for the ruling Turks. Back off Crete three days later, Nelson was exhausted. 'I have consulted no man,' he wrote to Melville. 'Therefore the whole blame of ignorance . . . must rest with me. I would allow no man to take from me an atom of my glory had I fallen in with the French fleet, nor do I desire any man to partake of any of the responsibility. All is mine, right or wrong.'[14]

He now rushed back, but declined to linger at Malta on 19 February, 'for I want no intelligence but where to find the French fleet,' he wrote. To access information as quickly as possible, Nelson had named Malta as the place where it should be sent, and also given his captains his intended itinerary in the event of a serious emergency. Both systems were used. In Naples, for example, the 'interval of suspense' during Nelson's absence was 'awful'. On 10 February, Elliot learned that the French had returned to Toulon, and the *Hirondelle* was packed off the following day. But there were fears that Villeneuve would put to sea again before Nelson could return, and on the 14th Corbet of the *Bittern* left to attempt to intercept the admiral 'according to the track described' on his itinerary. As it happened, no one caught Nelson, but the relevant news was sent out to him at Malta. It was a relief, but a sad one, for the French had not retired without drawing blood, and Nelson had suffered the greatest loss of his command. On 4 February two large enemy frigates had attacked the homeward bound convoy from Malta east of the Strait, capturing several vessels and destroying both the escorts, *Arrow* and *Acheron*. Nelson could do little more than dispatch two of his ships to the area to gather the scattered survivors, and press on to Sardinia, where some victuallers and store ships were being assembled for his use.[15]

The news that the French were still in Toulon reached Nelson on the last day of the month, but his visit to Sardinia and appalling weather prevented him from returning to his cruising station until 13 March. Taking stock, he saw a few consolations. The French had fallen to pieces within days, but Nelson's squadron had performed well. Morale was high, and his main force was in 'excellent' health and better physical shape than might have been expected after a voyage of near two thousand miles. Nelson boasted that 'not a yard or mast [was] sprung or crippled, or scarcely a sail split'. He exaggerated. In just two days off Palma one ship had sustained serious damage to her mizzenmast and the *Tigre* lost her fore topmast in furious gales, but overall there were reasons for congratulations. But a convoy had taken a serious hit, an opportunity to destroy the French had been lost, and Nelson's understanding of the French strategy had not improved, for Villeneuve had been forced back to Toulon before he could show his hand. The British admiral remained convinced that his destination had been eastwards, and while he doubled the force of frigates watching Toulon he also posted a sloop ten leagues west of San Pietro in case the French made another attempt to reach Egypt by way of the west coast of Sardinia. Nelson's intelligence remained as flawed after the voyage as before; nothing had occurred that modified his mistaken view that the French were primarily interested in the eastern Mediterranean rather than the English Channel and the Atlantic, and the Admiralty was inclined to agree.[16]

Napoleon was no less trenchant, impervious to the miserable showing of the Toulon fleet, which might at least have raised serious questions about its fitness for the enterprise of England, and the strength of Britain's naval defence. Of three fleets ordered to break the British blockades and unite in the West Indies, only the Rochefort detachment under Missiessy got away with a handful of ships. Hoping to resuscitate his plan, Bonaparte ordered Missiessy to remain in the West Indies until the end of June, and on 2 March framed fresh orders for the other wings of the enterprise. Rear Admiral Honoré Joseph Antoine Ganteaume and Villeneuve were to break out of Brest and Toulon and join Missiessy as before. Villeneuve was ordered to collect the Franco-Spanish forces in Cadiz, reinforce Martinique in the West Indies, and join Ganteaume and Missiessy for the return to Europe. If Ganteaume and Missiessy could not be found, he was to wait up to forty days before doing all possible damage to Britain's Caribbean colonies and returning to Europe on his own. The premier purpose of these complicated manoeuvres was the creation of a huge fleet of forty or more French ships of the line, reinforced by whatever Spanish capital ships could be commandeered in the process. Under the overall command of Ganteaume, it would scare the wits out of Britain's West Indian communities, draw the Royal Navy from its defensive position in the Channel, and then speed back to Europe to gain the temporary mastery of the Channel that was needed to allow Bonaparte to cross from Boulogne. Villeneuve thought the scheme a wild delusion, and saw his future as a humiliated scapegoat, but although Napoleon regarded him as a defeatist who barely knew his business he had few alternative commanders. In fact, in a revised version of the plan dated 13 April, Villeneuve was elevated to the position of supreme commander of the combined fleet. In this version the Toulon fleet would wait in the West Indies up to thirty-five days for Ganteaume, reinforcing the few remaining French islands in the region and seizing the British Windward Islands into the bargain. If the Brest fleet failed to join, he would recross the Atlantic, drive any blockading British ships from Ferrol to release extra capital ships, and storm his way to Boulogne, gathering the Brest fleet along the way. Had Nelson known these plans, he would almost certainly have rewritten history.

As it was, the misconceptions in the minds of Napoleon and Nelson – the commitment of one to a harebrained strategy, and the inability of the other to divine it – contained the seeds of a rerun of the late fiasco. But it would be crowned with an infinitely more dramatic finale.

4

For several weeks Nelson's command settled into its established pattern. The watch on Toulon, the search for provisions and information, the struggle to keep unsound ships at sea and the patrols and convoys continued as a rolling backdrop to occasional crises, inconveniences and adjustments. From what could be seen by his frigates, the French were working hard to restore their ships. With their mission unfulfilled, another breakout looked a strong possibility, and Nelson postponed his sick leave. Nothing mattered more than getting at those ships.

The Spanish 'war' smouldered, as Spain's battle fleet prepared in Cartagena, Cadiz and Ferrol and left the seas to the British. Now that the war was stale news, the chances of the British seizing unwary treasure ships had declined, and a more routine conflict had taken the place of the bullion hunt. On 11 January the Admiralty ordered the seizure or destruction of all Spanish vessels, and some weeks later asked Nelson to send home those Iberian prizes taken before that date so they could be assessed as 'droits' of the crown. Nelson must have shaken his sheep-dog head. He had gathered the prizes at Malta and Gibraltar, but how was he to prepare all of them for a voyage to England? Where were the three hundred men needed to navigate them, or the spare warships to provide escorts? The recent campaign had only underlined his shortage of small ships. 'None are sent me,' he grumbled to Ball, 'and my force decreases every day. Gibraltar is in absolute distress. They have not force sufficient to convoy over their bullock vessels.' Using his trusty initiative, Nelson dispensed with the embarrassing order about the Spanish prizes by ordering ships and cargoes to be sold at public auction in the Mediterranean, and the accruing funds to be held on behalf of the Court of Admiralty.[17]

The frosty relationship with Orde did not thaw, and everyone seemed to trip over the new demarcation line established between the Cadiz and Mediterranean commands. When the lieutenant governor of Gibraltar, General Henry Fox, applied to Nelson for ships to convoy his local supply vessels, the admiral was forced to refer him to Orde. In the end Nelson compelled Orde to retreat, insisting that in order to protect convoys in the Gut, his cruisers needed to operate up to twenty leagues west of the Strait. Orde reluctantly consented to this concession, but he was cut to the quick to learn that the *Amazon* had bypassed him without so much as a courtesy call, and was frustrated at the inadequate force given him by the Admiralty. He flatly asked the Admiralty to place the whole business in 'abler hands'.[18]

The escape of the Toulon fleet had spread fear across the Mediterranean, prompting several governments to put their defences upon alert. They needed to be able to withstand attack long enough for Nelson to arrive and turn the tide. Nelson's awareness of these threats, and the expectations held of him, conditioned his thinking, reinforcing his view that France's greatest ambitions were in Italy or eastwards, and strengthening his sense of responsibility for them. The Morea, now defended by active Russo-Turkish forces, was a harder nut to crack, but Naples and Sardinia worried the British admiral. Both felt a chill wind. Napoleon had threatened war unless their Sicilian Majesties expelled their military adviser, Damas, and the British minister, Elliot, from their kingdom. Maria Carolina resisted as gently as possible. How could she expel Elliot and remain a neutral state, she said, or annoy the supreme naval power? She further denied the emperor's charge that she had encouraged the Russians to strengthen their hold on the Ionian Islands. The queen relented so far as to pack Damas off to Sicily, loaded with gifts, a stipend and a knighthood, but stood firm over Elliot. Slowly France and Naples, led by diametrically opposed but powerful spirits, slipped towards another war, and Elliot grew so despondent that he talked about throwing in his onerous charge and returning to England. Watching this sabre-rattling, Nelson could not afford to weaken his vigilance over the Two Sicilies. As Acton explained, Napoleon had told Ferdinand that he was increasing the French forces occupying the kingdom of Naples to eight thousand men, and by October nearly half that number had arrived. Naples was 'in the worst situation possible' and her hopes 'lay entirely in the English help and protection'.[19]

The other perpetual headache was Sardinia, which gave Nelson the means of watching Toulon. The storm clouds gathering over the island seemed about to break. French *agents provocateurs* were active, fanning discontent at Sardinia's oppressive feudal system, and by April 1805 even the hitherto complacent viceroy, the Prince of Savoy, was beginning to worry. Afraid of being compromised, he would put nothing in writing, but he authorised his minister for war to verbally assure Nelson that he would not resist a British occupation of such key posts as Maddalena or San Pietro. In a personal letter, he asked the admiral to represent the island's plight to His Britannic Majesty. 'I recommend particularly to you the cause of our family,' he added, 'and to the attachment which you have already testified towards us.' Here, as in Naples, Sicily, Tuscany, the Morea and the Septinsular Republic, Nelson was viewed as a saviour and champion, a reputation he took far from lightly. In several letters to Lord Camden, Nelson urged that an armed force be landed to save Sardinia. The blockade of Toulon, even the security of the Levant trade, depended upon it remaining French free. 'The island is all but gone,' he wrote on 10 May, 'and the loss to us will be irreparable.'[20]

A more personal matter caused Nelson much pain: the fate of a favourite, William Layman, whose experimental sloop *Raven* had been shipwrecked off Cadiz and lost. The ship, a highly potent weapon capable of firing through 360 degrees, was a loss in itself, but the officers and men were released by the Spaniards on parole and rejoined the fleet on 7 March. Two days later there was an unavoidable court martial. Hope for Layman was not dead, for the captain-general of Andalusia himself had written that he had 'used all efforts imaginable that depended upon great exertion and good seamanship' to rescue his vessel, 'and manoeuvred with the greatest skill and intelligence'. That was what troubled Nelson. Layman was a brilliant and loyal officer, but this was the second time within a year that he had lost a ship; given that he also had enemies, could his career be saved a second time? Layman blamed his officer of the watch for the disaster. From what could be gathered, 'the lead had not been hove from the time I quitted the deck, and when the lights [of Cadiz] had been seen, the officer of the watch was below, and not then sober'.[21]

At this point Nelson gave some well-intentioned but damaging advice. If Layman threw blame upon the hapless officer of the watch it would destroy his career, and possibly even cost him his life. Moreover, it was the business of a court martial to apportion blame, which would look out of place coming from Layman. 'You will not be censured [in a court martial],' wrote Nelson, 'but it will give an opportunity for ill-natured people to say you had no occasion to make this official statement.' Though publicly Nelson assured Layman that the trial would clear him, privately he worried. 'You must suppose my misery,' he confided in Ball as the enquiry loomed. 'It is at its full and must change.' But he was wrong. Layman emerged from his trial in the *Royal Sovereign* with a severe reprimand. Judged to have shown 'a great want of necessary caution', he was sentenced to have his name placed at the bottom of the list of commanders, and that meant more than a loss of seniority. At a time of great unemployment among commanders, it was tantamount to ending Layman's naval career. Nelson blamed himself, fearing that his sensitivity to the officer of the watch had prevented Layman from making the best of his own case.[22]

'Unhinged' by the sentence, Nelson wrote to Nepean, Melville and even the outgoing first lord, St Vincent, commending Layman to the Admiralty's protection. Layman's efforts to save his ship were 'unequalled by anything they [the Spaniards] ever witnessed,' he wrote. In the meantime the miserable officer returned to England in the *Renown*. He insisted that a forged logbook had been introduced to prejudice the court against him, but the *Renown*'s captain, Strachan, who had been among those sitting in judgement, indicated that one of his fellow members of the court had been 'a bad-hearted man'. Almost lost in the issue of the *Raven* was a report that Layman had made of the defences of Cadiz, based on his observations while a prisoner. Dated 21 February, it was a remarkable document from the hands of a junior commander, no less than an extensive plan for a full-blown amphibious attack on the city, something Nelson himself had once considered. With an attention to diverse detail, the plan identified the relevant strategic targets and their weaknesses, and not only suggested modes of attack but alternatives in case of misadventure. Nelson forwarded it to Melville as the 'useful' study of 'a most intelligent and active mind', worthy of being filed for future consultation.[23]

Nelson's intention was to establish Layman's true value, and it was to that end that he wrote one of his most celebrated letters. It was addressed to Melville:

> And, my dear Lord, give me leave to recommend Captain Layman to your kind protection, for notwithstanding the court-martial has thought him deserving of censure for his running in with the land, yet, my Lord, allow me to say that his misfortune was, perhaps, conceiving that other people's abilities were equal to his own, which indeed, very few people's are. I own myself one of those who do not fear the shore, for hardly any great things are done in a small ship by a man that does. Therefore, I make very great allowances for him. Indeed, his station was intended never to be from the shore in the Straits, and if he did not every day risk his sloop, he would be useless upon that station. Captain Layman has served with me in three ships, and I am well acquainted with his bravery, zeal, judgement and activity. Nor do I regret the loss of the *Raven*, compared to the value of Captain Layman's services, which are a national loss. You must, my dear Lord, forgive the warmth which I express for Captain Layman, but he is in

adversity, and therefore has the more claim to my attention and regard. If I had been censured every time I have run my ship or fleets under my command into great danger, I should long ago have been out of the service, and never in the House of Peers.[24]

Usually the letter has been taken as an example of Nelson's personal sympathy for the afflicted, but the full explanation can only be appreciated in its context. Nelson believed in talent, and the navy's need of it. His fight for Layman reflected sympathy, guilt, and a heartfelt belief that the service was throwing away a fine officer, potentially a great one. Davison received a similar diatribe. 'The testimonies of his exertions to save the sloop are incontrovertible and were never exceeded,' Nelson clamoured, 'I would employ Layman tomorrow if I could.' He begged the agent to renew the fight on his behalf. Sheer bad luck, as Nelson and Hardy thought? Negligence? A noble silence to protect a vulnerable junior? An ill-disposed judge or a false log book? Whatever the root, Layman's career was fatally wounded. He arrived in Portsmouth in May 1805, with letters of introduction that Nelson had given him, and the knowledge that not all voices had abandoned him. The merchants of Gibraltar had again spoken up, remarking that the commander's 'superior knowledge and information with regard to the tides and currents' of the Strait, and his energy in hunting privateers, had given the trade 'a superior satisfaction and security that we had not previously . . . experienced'. In his own cause, Layman threw himself into a campaign for rehabilitation, dredging new ideas from his personal back burner. Among several projects he brought forward at this time was his discovery of a means of improving the strength and durability of timber, and of utilising unseasoned tropical wood for shipbuilding, both highly relevant to Britain's chronic shortage of raw material. Nelson had been impressed by the process, but Melville, who had previously encouraged Layman, had just been driven from office and the new powers were not listening. Worse, they had entered Layman's name in the Admiralty black book, a list of those officers deemed unworthy of appointment or promotion. There the matter stagnated until Nelson himself returned to England later in the year.[25]

There was little time to brood, however. At the end of March Nelson took the fleet to Sardinia to unload the victuallers and store ships sent there from Malta. On the 27th he anchored in the Gulf of Palma, where a frigate brought his new flag officer (Campbell's replacement), his old follower Rear Admiral Thomas Louis, one of the original brothers. Louis was happily installed in Campbell's old *Canopus*, coincidentally a Nile prize, with Francis William Austen, brother of the novelist, as his flag captain. The fleet moved to Pula roads to complete watering, and on 3 April put to sea.

Nelson felt uncomfortable withdrawing from his cruising ground at such a time, and had hit upon an idea to reduce the danger of another French escape.

Before retiring to Sardinia he feinted westwards towards Barcelona, hoping to fool Villeneuve into believing that he had a clear run south. The British fleet had then doubled back towards Sardinia, where it could complete provisioning and put itself in a position to intercept Villeneuve if he took the bait.

On Thursday, 4 April, some leagues west of the island of Toro off south-west Sardinia, where Nelson's fleet lay, a ship materialised through the thin rain and haze. She was the *Phoebe*, one of the watch frigates, coming urgently towards them under a full press of sail with signal flags flying impatiently above her deck.

5

The French were out again. Villeneuve had put to sea with eleven capital ships and seven cruisers on Saturday, 30 March. The wind was light and fair for a westward voyage, but Villeneuve had fallen for Nelson's ruse, and thinking the British off Cape San Sebastian he steered due south with the idea of passing east of the Balearic Islands before turning to starboard and making for the Strait. He was seen by Nelson's watch frigates, *Active* and *Phoebe*, at eight the following morning. For most of the day they shadowed the French, but at eight that night, when the enemy inclined slightly towards the south-west, *Phoebe* left to alert Nelson. She found him almost five days after Villeneuve quit Toulon.

Yet once again the watch frigates lost touch. Within hours of *Phoebe*'s departure, Moubray's *Active* missed the French in the deepening darkness, and also turned towards Sardinia and Nelson. It was decisive. The failure of the frigates to cling to the French long enough to get a fix on their intentions left Nelson 'entirely adrift'. Their ultimate destination might lie to the west or the east.[26]

Certainly Nelson was in a better situation than on the previous occasion. Once his transports had been cleared on 9 April, his ships were provisioned for four months and with wine and spirits for sixty days. Moreover, this time Nelson's fleet was to the west of southern Sardinia, a far more convenient starting point than the Maddalenas. If, as Nelson supposed, the French were ultimately bound eastward, they would have made slow progress in the difficult winds, and the British were ideally positioned to intercept them. As soon as his cruisers and small ships came in, Nelson flung them out, *Seahorse*, *Aetna*, *Hydra* and *Amazon* to his right, covering Naples, Sicily and the south and east coasts of Sardinia, and the *Ambuscade, Active* and *Moucheron* to his left, near the Tunisian coast, while he stationed himself in the relatively narrow channel between Sardinia and Africa. There he could safeguard the Tyrrhenian Sea and the eastern basin of the Mediterranean, including Sardinia, the Two Sicilies and Malta, and intercept any large fleet bound for the east. Had Villeneuve truly been hoping to weather the south-west coast of Sardinia and run eastwards he would have fallen into Nelson's trap.

Villeneuve would not be caught, however. The day after throwing off Nelson's watch frigates he encountered a Ragusan vessel, which informed him that the British fleet was off the southern coast of Sardinia, not Cape San Sebastian. Using an easterly wind, the French therefore deflected westwards, passing north rather than south of the Balearics, and running westwards along the Spanish coast towards the Strait. Thus, they neatly passed beyond the compass of Nelson's fleet, laying in wait to the south-east. Nelson felt 'very uneasy' and 'unlucky' at this second escape of the Toulon fleet, which no doubt some would rate negligence, but he was not psychic and was bereft of good information. Moreover, in view of the recent French threats against Naples and Sicily, and panicky calls for protection from other quarters, he felt obliged to ensure general safety. As he wrote to Ball on 6 April, 'I am, in truth, half dead, but what man can do to find them out shall be done. But I must not make more haste than good speed, and leave Sardinia, Sicily or Naples for them to take, should I go either to the eastward or westward, without knowing something more about them . . . I shall take a position off Ustica [Island, north of Sicily], ready to communicate with the vessels which will join me, and by this position be ready to push for Naples should they be gone there, or to protect Sicily.' Nelson acted reasonably in occupying a strategic area pending the arrival of clearer intelligence.[27]

On 10 April, Hallowell's *Tigre* arrived from Palermo with just such intelligence, courtesy of Acton. Seven Russian ships of the line were reported to be coming to the Mediterranean, and for the first time Nelson heard that Lieutenant General Sir James Craig's task force, the disposable troops he had long since called for, was on its way from England. This introduced the alarming possibility that Villeneuve was actually on his way to intercept and destroy Craig's transports, and that he had a head start on Nelson. 'I may suppose the French fleet are bound to the westward,' he wrote to Ball. 'I must do my best. God bless you. I am very, very miserable.' Leaving the *Aetna* at a new general rendezvous off Sardinia, and five frigates under Captain Capel to handle matters in the Mediterranean, Nelson pressed westwards fighting for every league against westerly and north-westerly winds. On the 16th he met the first clear trace, when a vessel 'spoken' by the *Leviathan* reported that a fleet of sixteen warships had been seen off Cape de Gata, between Cartagena and Gibraltar, nine days before. 'If this account is true, much mischief may be apprehended,' Nelson wrote. 'It kills me, the very thought.' Now bulletins from passing ships tumbled in almost daily, and Nelson learned that the French had passed the Strait on 8 April, their flags flying, and that they had even made a junction with the Spanish ships at Cadiz. If Orde had been driven from Cadiz, and the enemy ships there released, Villeneuve might command a formidable force of some eighteen ships of the line. A nightmarish premonition that Craig's expedition might run into it and be destroyed now gripped the British admiral, as he struggled westwards against a wind 'as foul as it can blow'. A tragedy of those proportions was big enough to sink his reputation into the deepest depths.[28]

As the wake of the French fleet became plainer, Nelson realised that his concern for the east had betrayed him, and that his enemies would circle. Ignorant or contemptuous of his real difficulties, they would castigate him for letting the French escape to reap untold damage – not once, but twice. Perhaps the unhappy fate of the twice-confounded Layman echoed in the back of his mind. Justification crept into his letters to Marsden and Melville on 19 April, and his agitation shouted from every scrap of paper. 'Monday, April 22nd,' he scribbled in his diary. 'Fresh gales N.W.W. and heavy swell. Nothing can be more unfortunate in our winds, but God's will be done. I submit human exertions are absolutely unavailing. What man could do I have done.' To cap all, he still had nothing definite on Villeneuve's ultimate aims and objectives, and on the 18th hurried Parker's *Amazon* forward to Lisbon for intelligence, arranging to rendezvous with him again off Cape St Vincent in Portugal. Two realistic alternatives now confronted Nelson. The French might sail west to threaten Britain's valuable Caribbean colonies; or head north, perhaps to search for Craig's expedition, if they knew about it, or to thrust at Ireland or the Channel. At this stage Nelson favoured the latter hypothesis, apparently believing that the junction of the Toulon and Cadiz contingents portended something grander than a West Indian raid. Although he would evaluate what news he could get from Gibraltar and Lisbon, he wrote to the Admiralty and the commander-in-chief off Ireland that he expected to bring his fleet north, 'as fine ships of war, as ably commanded, and in as perfect order, and in health, as ever went to sea'. The plan was based on nothing more than supposition, but it reflected Nelson's first inkling that the defence of Britain, rather than the Mediterranean, was the core issue of the campaign. And it was sensible in itself, for British admirals had for some time regarded Ushant as the obvious place to rally naval forces defending the homeland.[29]

In this crisis Nelson's exasperation at being 'locked up in the Mediterranean' can readily be imagined. 'I believe easterly winds have left the Mediterranean,' he cursed on 26 April. 'I never have been one week without one until this very important moment. It has half killed me, but fretting is of no use.' In his anguish he turned to wise counsel for support. 'My dear Keats, it is an age since I have had the pleasure of seeing you,' he wrote on 1 May. 'I hope you will come on board after your breakfast that I may have some conversation with you.' Since the wind was so foul, the fleet anchored near Tetuan in Morocco, close to the Strait, and worked feverishly to clear additional Maltese transports of wine and to water the ships for what might become a long voyage. A better breeze helped Nelson get into Rosia Bay at Gibraltar on 6 May, but a welcome easterly sprang up at four in the afternoon and a signal gun recalled all officers and men after only two hours. The remaining transports were cleared and some stores brought from the dockyard. A command structure was put in place for the rump of the fleet that would be left behind, and Bickerton was disembarked with the authority to command more than twenty frigates and small ships. Nelson referred him to Ball if he felt the need for wise counsel. The admiral found time to put his purse at the disposal of his old hand, Joe King, whose increased salary as boatswain of the dockyard had not yet come through. Then the fleet sailed for Cape St Vincent.[30]

Not least, Tetuan and Gibraltar gave Nelson a new perspective to chew over. There the general belief was that Villeneuve was destined for the West Indies, partly because the last news from Lisbon, dated 27 April, had nothing of the enemy to report. It was logical to suppose that if the French had steered north, *something* would have been known at Lisbon. Nelson now had a fine quandary. Could he make a trans-Atlantic voyage on such thin information, taking from England one of its best battle fleets at a time of peril? On the other hand, if Villeneuve was bound to the West Indies with such a large force, could Nelson delay for a moment and risk the loss of Jamaica and other islands of the greatest commercial and strategic importance?[31]

At home the escape of the Toulon fleet had Whitehall at sixes and sevens. The news reached them by the *Fisgard* only days after Craig's expedition had sailed from Spithead in forty-five transports, protected by only two ships of the line, and accompanied by the scores of outward-bound merchantmen. Yet Pitt's first fears were for the West Indies. Nothing had been heard from Nelson, and as Villeneuve's track became clearer it was feared that the hero had been lured to Egypt, and was therefore out of the immediate picture. Rear Admiral Alexander Cochrane had already gone to the West Indies with a small force to deal with Missiessy, who had crossed the Atlantic with five capital ships earlier in the year. Collingwood was now sent to Cadiz with orders to ascertain whether Nelson had gone to the West Indies, and if he had not to sail there himself to support Cochrane. An attempt was made to recall Craig, whose position was now threatened, while the squadrons of Sir Robert Calder and Orde off Ferrol and Cadiz were ordered to fall back to reinforce the Channel fleet's defensive station off Ushant. Thus, without adding Nelson's fleet to the reckoning, the Admiralty had attempted to protect Craig's task force and marshalled the resources to strengthen the West Indies and Britain's key home defence. Napoleon had been completely wrong-footed. He had sought to draw the Royal Navy from its essential positions, and he had signally failed.

Much of the mist cleared around Nelson after he anchored in Lagos Bay, under Cape St Vincent, on 8 May. Some transports left behind by Orde were cleared of usable provisions, extending Nelson's supplies to five months, and the following day two of his frigates came in, *Amazon* and *Amphion*. The information Parker and Sutton brought added up. There was no trace of the enemy fleet to the north, so it must have gone to the West Indies. Nelson immediately decided to pursue. Before he got away, another uncertainty ended. After dinner on the 11th Craig's force came into view, shepherded by the *Queen* and *Dragon* under the command of Rear Admiral John Knight. They had crept gingerly out of the Tagus the day before after hearing of Nelson's presence at Lagos. The admiral sent the Reverend Scott aboard the *Queen*, where he found the leaders of the expedition and some of Nelson's friends, including the elderly but amiable Neapolitan diplomat, the Marchese di Circello, on his way to replace the dying Micheroux as foreign minister at Naples, and one of his entourage, Henry, Abbé Campbell, an Irish priest well known to the Hamiltons. These last hurried over to the *Victory* to impart the latest news from London and Merton. Nelson was eager to be gone, however. With Villeneuve in the west, the way ahead was clear for Craig as far as Cartagena, where six Spanish ships of the line of uncertain capability were still stationed. As a safeguard, Nelson added the hundred-gun *Royal Sovereign* to Knight's escort, and warned Craig against making any premature moves in Italy that would provoke the French to overthrow Naples. The commander-in-chief's mind was thus eased as far as the task force was concerned, but the cost of one of his two largest ships was a high one, leaving him with only ten sail of the line to chase eighteen enemies.[32]

Now Nelson's fleet, many of his ships battered by long service at sea, had to face a greatly superior adversary and an Atlantic voyage, and the feat had to be performed under the gaze of critics primed by his failure to prevent Villeneuve's escape from the Mediterranean. Britain knew that she was endangered, but as yet nothing of the whereabouts of her great champion, and City merchants were complaining about the West Indian islands tottering on the brink of disaster. Nelson was not even sure how much support he commanded in the Admiralty, for by 7 May he had heard that a new first lord was being appointed, Melville having been driven from office by a scandal about the misuse of money in the Navy Office at the time he had been its treasurer. As yet it was unclear who would replace him. Melville had failed to temper Nelson's sense of grievance. The first lord had 'given away a commissionership of both the Navy and Victualling office without considering me – none of them care for me,' the admiral muttered, and yet he could do nothing but cheer Melville's attempt to rebuild the navy after the destructive St Vincent administration, and his successor was an unknown quantity.[33]

Ten capital ships left to cross the Atlantic with Nelson on 12 May, including the dishevelled *Superb*, which Keats was keeping at sea by an enormous effort of will and trouble. The captain pleaded with Nelson to allow him to come. The others were Hardy's *Victory*, Austen's *Canopus*, flying the flag of Louis, Stopford's *Spencer*, Bayntun's *Leviathan*, Hallowell's *Tigre*, Malcolm's *Donegal*, Pellew's *Conqueror*, Hargood's *Belleisle* and Rutherford's *Swiftsure*. Three frigates, *Decade*, *Amphion* and *Amazon*, weighed and put to sea with them on 11 May.

They were a long way behind their quarry. The enemy fleet actually reached

Martinique, the most powerful French stronghold in the New World, on 13 May. But Nelson knew that his own reputation as well as the West Indies depended upon him at that moment. As he told his mistress, 'I suppose if I do not find the French fleet . . . I shall be tried.'[34]

6

This was a complicated game in which admirals in different places, sifting evidence and acting accordingly, were sometimes at cross purposes. The Admiralty, for example, suspecting that Nelson had gone to Egypt, had given Collingwood eleven ships and detached him to the West Indies. Nelson's dispatch of 19 April had made no impression upon this deployment, because it implied that he was coming north to protect the western approaches, and take a station somewhere off the Scilly Islands. But knowing nothing about Collingwood, Nelson changed his plan on 9 May, thinking that the safety of the West Indies rested solely upon him. Even though Collingwood was ordered to cross the Atlantic only if he was sure Nelson had not, two British forces could easily have ended up chasing Villeneuve in the West Indies. Fortunately, Collingwood arrived off Cadiz after Nelson had begun his trans-Atlantic voyage. He therefore stationed himself off the Spanish port, but sent two ships of the line after his old friend as a badly needed reinforcement. Out of confusion had emerged a degree of order.

Thirty-eight leagues from Madeira on 14 May, Nelson penned his latest thoughts for Marsden. If the enemy was not in the West Indies, he would return immediately to Cadiz, hopefully before his absence from the Mediterranean had become fully known. He entreated the Admiralty to leave orders and intelligence for him at Cape St Vincent, which would be his first call when he got back to Europe. As his ships rode the big blue Atlantic rollers the thought of an uneven battle ahead kept bringing loved ones into his mind. Horatia had to be established at Merton, and 'properly educated and brought up' under Emma's tutelage. Mrs Gibson should be pensioned off at £20 a year, and Miss Connor given an allowance to act as a governess. Deep down, he doubted that Emma was carrying out his wishes as far as their little girl was concerned. 'I, again and again, my dearest friend, request your care of my adopted daughter, whom I pray to God to bless.'[35]

The Atlantic voyage, tracing the trade winds, was accomplished with surprising speed, considering the length of time some of Nelson's ships had been in service. On 22 May they crossed the Tropic of Cancer and 'Father Neptune' presided over the usual frivolities, Nelson noting in his diary that for five hundred persons in the *Victory* it was an entirely novel experience. Speed was the essence, and Nelson even refused to shorten sail to gather intelligence, so intent was he on reaching the Caribbean, where a better assessment of the situation could be made. A squad of caulkers was passed around the fleet to seal parting timbers while it remained in motion. The disabled *Superb*, which had been in continuous commission for four years, was the main liability, but Nelson encouraged the anxious Keats. 'I am fearful that you may wish the *Superb* does not go so fast as I could wish,' he wrote on a day that the fleet's progress sank to a mere fifty-nine miles. 'However that may, for if we all went ten knots I should not think it fast enough, yet I would have you assured that I know and feel that the *Superb* does all which is possible for a ship to accomplish, and I desire that you will not fret upon the occasion.' Conditions varied, and towards the end of the month the fleet was making 170 miles a day. Nelson cut ten days off Villeneuve's passage, reaching Barbados in the British Windward Islands after a voyage of 3227 miles from Cape St Vincent lasting twenty-four days.[36]

Nelson still failed to appreciate the wider implications of the crisis, and had apparently concluded that Villeneuve was bent upon no more than a serious onslaught upon the British West Indies. The notion that it was merely a feint, designed to mask a greater objective, was at best secondary. Thus, he regarded Jamaica, the keystone of the British islands, as the most likely French target, although he planned to make his landfall at Barbados, where he hoped Cochrane would be stationed with the latest information and a useful reinforcement. He wanted to surprise the French, and when a mysterious corvette flickered briefly on the horizon some 150 leagues west of Madeira on 16 May, he pictured it as a French corsair racing ahead with tidings that the British were coming. His own courier, the *Martin* sloop, had already been sent ahead to Lord Seaforth, the governor of Barbados, requesting that all ships be prevented from leaving the island to ensure that the imminent arrival of the British fleet was kept inhouse.[37]

If he met the enemy fleet there would be a battle, come what may. 'I am perfectly prepared how to act with either a superior or inferior force,' he said. 'My mind is firm as a rock and my plans for every event fixed in my mind.' Nelson put some of his ideas on paper, and had the *Amazon* distribute copies on 15 May. He had also spoken to some officers personally, seeking opinions about the intentions of the French, and probably introduced the subject of tactics. There was a strong possibility that they would be very different from the ones he had used at the Nile and Copenhagen, where his enemies had been in relatively immobile positions. The infinitely more difficult challenge of securing a decisive victory over a moving target in open water might have to be faced. Nelson's paper of 15 May has not been conclusively identified, but it likely resembled a surviving memorandum that belongs to either 1804 or 1805. The familiar aim of decisiveness was emphasised, along with the tactics he considered essential to achieving it, simplicity, a minimum of time-consuming signalling, an attack beginning from windward and ending from leeward, the use of feints, the concentration of force and sustained close-range fighting. If the enemy ran, Nelson would use only one signal, and direct his ships to chase and engage as they came up. In that case, the first ship to reach their flying opponents would tackle their hindmost ship, and each successive unit would press forward to the next unengaged enemy, making sure that they also fired into those already engaged as they passed. In a way, therefore, a concentration would be achieved, for although every British ship would find an individual opponent, they would weaken other engaged enemy ships as they did so.[38]

Of course, Nelson hoped the French and Spanish would fight rather than run, and create opportunities for a more complete result. In this plan he envisaged the fleets moving towards each other in line of battle on opposite tacks, with the wind to larboard of the British fleet. Nelson planned to keep the enemy guessing as to whether he would steer to leeward or windward of their approaching line as long as possible, but ultimately he would sail to windward to gain the greater agility conferred by the wind. His ships would fire on their opponents in passing, but when the leading British ship was roughly parallel to their sixth ship, Nelson would bear up to cut through and overwhelm the enemy van with superior numbers, engaging it from leeward so that their wounded ships could not fall away with the wind. Effectively he would decapitate the enemy fleet, enfilading and destroying its isolated van. Beyond that the exact nature of the attack would depend upon circumstances, and the memorandum left doubt about finer details. However, in its essence it echoed Howe's famous attack on 'the Glorious First of June' and a celebrated treatise by John Clerk of Elgin. 'The great object,' he said, 'is for us to support each other, and to keep close to the enemy, and to leeward of them.'

Nelson reached Carlisle Bay in Barbados on 4 June. Cochrane, who was there with two useful ships of the line, *Northumberland* and *Spartiate* under Captain Francis Laforey, explained that Missiessy's small detachment from Rochefort had returned to Europe, but Villeneuve was at Martinique, to the north, with large numbers of sick. Nelson was ready to go after him without further ado, but at this critical moment Fate played a fickle hand in the form of a misleading titbit from Brigadier General Robert Brereton, the commandant on St Lucia. It reported that a fleet of twenty-eight sail had passed the island a week before – going south. The only inference was that the combined fleet had left Martinique and was going to attack the British islands of Trinidad or Tobago. Assured that Brereton's information was reliable, Nelson called for urgent action. Within hours Lieutenant General Sir William Myers, the military commander in Barbados, had 2000 infantry and 150 artillerymen marching to Nelson's ships to provide him with a landing force, and the admiral assigned them full victuals, rather than the usual two-thirds rations issued to temporary auxiliaries, so that 'unanimity and a hearty joint cooperation' between the two armed services would be preserved. No less heartening, a skilful black pilot, James Marguette, volunteered to guide the fleet through the islands, and the whole armada began to weigh anchor at 9.30 the following morning.[39]

The ships sailed south, towards the legendary Spanish Main, expecting a battle, but nothing was amiss at Tobago or Trinidad. On the 8th, however, they were overtaken by a dispatch boat from Seaforth at Barbados. Far from abroad, the French were still lingering at Martinique, but they had struck their first blow at a nearby British outpost known as Diamond Rock. Captain James Maurice, who had held the place with a sloop's company and a few eighteen- and twenty-four-pounders, had been attacked by two enemy ships of the line, three cruisers and eleven gunboats, and surrendered after running out of ammunition and water in a three-day siege. Much worse, the combined fleet was now said to have been swollen to thirty-two sail of the line after receiving a reinforcement of French and Spanish ships from Ferrol. If true, Britain's concentration of force in the western approaches had freed another fleet to cross the Atlantic, and Nelson was facing odds of almost three to one!

As it happened, this intelligence too was flawed, for only two ships of the line had joined Villeneuve, giving him a total of twenty. Nelson was fuming at the fool's errand to Trinidad and Tobago. 'Ah, my Emma,' he sighed, 'June 6th would have been a great day, had I not been led astray by false information . . . What a loss! What a relief it would have been for the last two years of cares and troubles.' But even burdened by the fresh fictions about the size of the enemy force he refused to despair. His fleet was 'compact', he said stoically, while 'theirs must be unwieldy, and although a very *pretty* fiddle, I do not believe that either Gravina or Villeneuve know how to play upon it'. Resolutely he steered north to cover Dominica and the British Leeward Islands, and at St George's Bay, Grenada, was found by the *Jason*. The new intelligence, then and after, suggested that the enemy fleet had separated, for sixteen or more of their capital ships had passed Dominica on 6 June heading north. Nelson reasoned that a detachment of the Spanish ships had splintered away towards Havana, the capital of their largest West Indian island, while the rest menaced the British Leeward Islands. Indeed, as Nelson soon learned, on 8 June the French scooped up a convoy of fourteen British sugar ships that had cleared Antigua for England. Therefore, he pressed on 'carrying every rag', keeping the chain of tiny green islands to starboard, until he made St John's, Antigua, on 12 June. Neither Antigua, nor its neighbouring islands of Nevis and St Kitts, had been attacked, and the French were thought to have gone north. Villeneuve's inactivity now demanded an explanation. Although he had taken Diamond Rock and a trade convoy, he had bypassed all of the obvious targets, and there were grounds for believing that his raid, if such it was, had come to an end.[40]

Nelson left Antigua on 13 June without any reliable information about Villeneuve's whereabouts or intentions. '*Very very* low,' he told his diary. 'If I was to ask an opinion of where the enemy's fleet are gone I should have as many opinions as there were persons. Porto Rico, Barbados, Newfoundland, Europe.' Logic told him that the French were running for Europe. Villeneuve had dallied for weeks in the Caribbean, doing no damage to the British colonies, but now his opportunities were fast shrinking. His ships were full of sick, the British islands had been given the time to shine up their defences, the hurricane season was coming and Nelson had appeared. The French were unlikely to embroil themselves in a complicated or difficult operation now, and by some reports had landed many of their soldiers at Guadeloupe. 'My opinion is firm as a rock,' Nelson wrote to Nepean on 16 June, 'that some cause, orders or *inability* to perform any service . . . has made them resolve to proceed direct for Europe, sending the Spanish ships to the Havanna . . . There would have been no occasion for opinions had not General Brereton sent his damned intelligence from St Lucia . . . It has almost broke my heart . . .'[41]

In truth, Villeneuve had reached the West Indies with Napoleon's orders of 2 March in his desk. According to his reading, he was not required to make an ambitious attack upon the British. His job was to wait for Ganteaume to join him from Brest, failing which he was to sail for Europe on about 22 June. That being so, he remained inactive at Martinique until 30 May, when a frigate brought new instructions dated 14 and 29 April. These reiterated his mandate to return to Europe if Ganteaume had not appeared within the allotted period, cautioning him to proceed initially to Ferrol, but also explicitly directed him to attack British possessions in the meantime, mentioning the Windward and Leeward Islands and Trinidad and Tobago. Spurred, Villeneuve and Gravina embarked additional troops at Martinique and Guadeloupe with a view to assaulting Antigua or Barbados, but they had only got as far as taking the British convoy on 8 June before learning from the prisoners the shattering news that Nelson was in the West Indies. The next day Villeneuve declared his intention of returning to Europe. In some ways it was a wise move. Villeneuve's purpose had been to draw the British Channel fleet from its station. With the arrival of Nelson he could do little more to encourage that movement, and arguably his priority was to comply with the balance of his orders and bring his fleet back to Europe in sufficient shape to participate in a campaign against England. If he remained he would simply pile up more sick and run the risk of disabling or losing his fleet in a battle with the British. But it looked bad, particularly as the French commander-in-chief ran for home on 11 June, long before 4 July, the new time allotted for him to wait for Ganteaume. General Jacques Alexandre, Comte Lauriston, who commanded the substantial military force that Villeneuve had brought out with him, boiled that nothing had been done, and accused the admiral of being mortally afraid of Nelson. Although Villeneuve landed some of the local troops he had sequestrated before returning, the governor of Martinique also complained that he had left the French islands in a poorer state of defence that he had found them. Even the prizes taken off Antigua were lost when the officers conducting them to Martinique panicked at the sight of a couple of British warships and burned them.[42]

When Nelson later claimed to have saved the British West Indies, and some two hundred sugar ships plying about them, he had a point. It was not the whole story, but at the beginning of June, with several weeks of its allotted spell in the Caribbean yet to run, the Franco-Spanish fleet had abandoned its campaign in fear of being caught by an aggressive British fleet. Nelson's dash across the Atlantic had done its work.

At Barbuda Nelson disembarked the West Indian troops he had borrowed and left Cochrane to facilitate local business, but temporarily retained the services of his pilot, Marguette, in whom he had discovered 'a very clever, able man', as well as a public-spirited patriot. Then he set out after Villeneuve. He had hounded the French out of the West Indies, but while he remained foggy about where they were going, he could not shake a feeling that the eastern Mediterranean was Napoleon's true goal. Nelson was now seized by the thought that this whole adventure might simply have been a ruse to get him out of the way so that Villeneuve would double back to attack Naples or invade Egypt or the Morea. But with luck he might overtake the combined fleet in the Atlantic or intercept it at the Strait.[43]

Aggravated by every light wind and calm, Nelson sailed eastwards scanning the horizons for his elusive quarry. Yet day succeeded dreary day, revealing nothing but one monotonous mile of rolling grey-blue water after another. On 18 June, the day after Nelson discovered his flagship had only a hundred tons of water left, the *Amazon* reported 'speaking' the *Sally*, a merchant schooner of North Carolina, which had spotted twenty-two sail two days before. It had to be the combined fleet. There was doubt about whether it was steering NNE, as the master insisted, or NNW by the mate's account, but Nelson estimated that he was only eighty leagues away. On the 19th the admiral dispatched the *Martin* to Gibraltar and the *Decade* to Lisbon advertising the approach of the French, and asking for the intelligence to be passed to the senior British officer off Ferrol. At midnight of the next day there was fresh hope, when three planks were spied bobbing in the water, and two days later some debris, a bucket and a topmast. Could they have come from the enemy ships? But the ocean remained empty. When he could, Nelson confided in his captains, and Sutton, Louis, Hargood and Keats, among others, came to dinner, but often the weather was so foul that gigs could not pull across, and the admiral had to satisfy himself with his daily colleagues in the flagship.

Prey and predator were in fact drawing apart during the crossing, Villeneuve steering for Ferrol in north-western Spain and Nelson making for the Strait. The information was brought to England by *Le Curieux*, under Captain George Bettesworth, dispatched from Antigua by Nelson. Arriving at the Admiralty on 9 July her captain breathlessly related how he had sighted Villeneuve some nine hundred miles NNE of Antigua on 19 July, standing northwards. Their lordships, who had been inclined to share Nelson's belief that Villeneuve would return to the Mediterranean, jumped into action. They ordered a squadron watching Rochefort to retreat upon Sir Robert Calder off Ferrol, and the latter to stretch his force towards Cape Finisterre to net the homecoming Franco-Spanish fleet. There were also implications for another military expedition, due to sail for the West Indies.[44]

Nelson had not watered since leaving Gibraltar in May. Richard Ford, who was with him, had purchased forty-one head of cattle from two American ships, but the men had to be put on short rations and salt beef and pork, and it was proposed to anchor in Lagos Bay for urgent provisions. They sighted the cape on 17 July, and Nelson computed that he had made an acceptable thirty-four leagues a day on the return run, travelling 3459 miles out of Barbuda, a little longer than the outward voyage. Intelligence, as well as provisions, was now the great object. Nelson had sent *Amphion* and *Amazon*, the most active ships in his command, to Tangier and Cadiz respectively, with orders to rejoin the fleet at a new rendezvous a few leagues west of Cape Spartel near the Strait. If Villeneuve had not returned, Nelson would wait for him, taking in supplies at Tangier if there was time, but if the French had already gone into the Strait and were close enough to be overtaken, the British would chase. However, when he reached Cape Spartel on 18 July Nelson was disappointed. There was 'no French fleet, or any information about them,' he recorded in his diary. 'How sorrowful this makes me . . .'[45]

Since leaving Sardinia he had chased the French ten thousand miles. He had come close enough to frighten his quarry, but never once had he seen them.

7

Collingwood, he was grateful to learn, had replaced Orde off Cadiz, and the two old comrades exchanged letters. There was no news of Villeneuve, but Nelson learned that Collingwood had sent three ships of the line to Bickerton, still managing matters within the Strait and two after Nelson. Orde had been swallowed by the Channel fleet. As far as the French were concerned, Collingwood's analysis was different from Nelson's. They had both decided that the West Indian ventures were feints, but whereas Nelson supposed Villeneuve's real objectives lay in the Mediterranean, Collingwood predicted that he would return to Ferrol and ultimately participate in an invasion of Ireland. His educated guesses, for they were no more, got close to the French plans.

On 19 July, Nelson's fleet anchored in Rosia Bay, Gibraltar, where Knight, who had brought Craig's expedition to the Mediterranean, was then flying his flag from the *Guerrier* sheer-hulk. The fleet took water and some provisions aboard, and the following day captured a settee, which was burned after the cargo had been removed. That day Nelson also went ashore to visit the governor and naval commissioner, proudly noting in his diary that he had not set foot on land since his visit to Malta on 16 June 1803, nearly two years before. It was about this time that Nelson learned the identity of the new first lord of the Admiralty. Pitt had summoned the octogenarian Sir Charles Middleton from a rural retreat in Kent and turned him into Lord Barham. Nelson had had some dealings with the former comptroller of the Navy Board, but Barham had spent decades ashore and was possibly a mere shade of the man he had once been. His feelings for Nelson were unknown, but he was the man who would ultimately judge the admiral's conduct and was known to speak his mind. Before the end of the day Nelson had addressed his first letter to the new master.

'In forty-eight hours we supplied the ships [of Nelson] abundantly with stores of every description, and having completed the provisions they sailed yesterday morning to Tetuan to water,' the naval storekeeper at Gibraltar informed the Navy Board on 23 July. Nelson thought the supply insufficient. He wanted four months' provisions to support a continuing campaign, and was aware that ugly signs of scurvy were appearing in the fleet. Only twenty-three men were down with the disorder, but scores looked set to join them, and not one ship was unscathed. The *Belleisle* carried 160 cases. So Nelson crossed to Tetuan, just inside the Strait, where some eight miles south-east of a square castle there was a 'very fine and convenient' river 'running for half a mile inside a sandy beach', easily accessible to boats. Many of the ships got two hundred tons of water in one day, and onions and bullocks were also stowed aboard. While thus engaged, the commander-in-chief reviewed the situation in the Mediterranean. If Villeneuve was bound northwards, as Collingwood believed, Nelson would reinforce the Channel fleet and relinquish his command to take advantage of that long postponed leave. But the Mediterranean fleet was still his charge, and he was obliged to leave it in respectable shape. He was alarmed to hear that the Admiralty had ordered three of his frigates in the upper Mediterranean to join Collingwood off Cadiz. Nelson promised Ball that he would get them back, orders or no, and in his first letter to Barham pointed out the many points the commander-in-chief of the Mediterranean had to guard, and of his need for '*many, many* more frigates and sloops' than he had ever been given. And in three letters to the Admiralty from Tetuan, one addressed directly to the first lord, Nelson enlarged on his concerns. The transfer of cruisers from Malta to Cadiz was disastrous, he said. It cut the Mediterranean service to the bone, and left Malta, Sicily and Sardinia dangerously exposed. At least fifteen frigates, ten sloops and brigs and eight smaller vessels were necessary to equip the fleet for its purposes. Speaking straight from the shoulder, Nelson told the new first lord that 'I am taking [back] part of the small craft which were directed to . . . Collingwood, . . . not one of which can with propriety be given up, and I hope the Board will consider it as not wishing to alter any arrangement of theirs, but as a measure absolutely necessary.'[46]

After loading as many stores as possible, Nelson planned to use the first easterly wind to leave the Strait and patrol between Cape St Vincent and Cape Spartel in Tangier, ready to intercept Villeneuve if he tried to run into the Mediterranean. But he was losing hope of that happy meeting, and still brooding over the bad intelligence that had led him to Trinidad and Tobago instead of Martinique. Why, if he could have fought the battle he wanted, he would have become 'the greatest man in his [my] profession that England ever saw'. Still, he wrote to Marsden, he was as ready as ever to go wherever the French led. 'If the case requires', he was prepared to 'go to Madras or round Cape Horn' to find Villeneuve.[47]

On the morning of 25 July, Nelson's fleet was overtaken in the Gut of Gibraltar by the *Termagant* sloop. Captain Pettet had some of Nelson's possessions on board, shipped out of Gibraltar and directed to England, but a packet from Collingwood was more interesting. It contained a Lisbon newspaper that gave Nelson the first definite news of the Toulon fleet. He read of the report that Bettesworth of *Le Curieux* had made to the Admiralty, describing the northerly course Villeneuve had taken across the Atlantic, and realised that he was wasting time screening the Strait. Without further delay, Nelson entrusted his station to Bickerton, Knight and Collingwood, with eight capital ships and every cruiser bar one, and passing Cape Spartel to reach the Atlantic he set a course for home. Letters went forward to Cornwallis off Ushant and Gardner, commanding the Ireland station, advising them of a possible junction, but he refused to own that he had been entirely mistaken about the French. Villeneuve, he decided, had wanted to return to the Mediterranean, but been forced north by his fear of being overtaken by Nelson.[48]

As the *Victory* sailed home the mood in Britain was changing. Some criticism had appeared in the press, especially after the admiral's double failure to intercept the Toulon fleet allowed it to bolt through the Strait and threaten the West Indies. Smelling ruin, many merchants were close to panic, and the mood was only accentuated by the lack of information about the great naval hero. For a short while the question on everyone's lips was, 'Where is Nelson?' But as soon as word reached England that the hunter was indeed on Villeneuve's trail, and speeding across the Atlantic in an epic chase expectations rose to fever pitch. In Brooks's Club in St James's, London, Mr Stepney bet one guinea with Mr Daly and another with Mr Combe 'that an engagement between Ld. Nelson and the French fleet takes place before the latter gets into port'. Whatever the disparity of force, no one doubted the result of an encounter. As the drama unfolded, the vision of that battle dimmed, but in its place stood something no less inspiring: by his prompt action, Nelson had saved the West Indies and with it Britain's economic wellbeing. Once more, he was returning to his country the hero of the hour.[49]

The public acclaim was lifted by a battle that did take place. As a result of the news brought by *Le Curieux*, Vice Admiral Sir Robert Calder was waiting for Villeneuve with fifteen ships of the line off Finisterre. On 22 July the two fleets met in murky weather, and Calder took two Spanish prizes and deflected Villeneuve from his destination of Ferrol to Vigo, further south. The Franco-Spanish fleet soon regrouped in Ferrol, where a depressed Villeneuve reflected on the indiscipline, inexperience and demoralisation in his fleet, and the hundreds of men that were sick. But the British public were disappointed in Calder, who withdrew to join Cornwallis. He had won a victory, but not the sort of victory that Nelson had led the nation to expect. Nelson, like Hawke before him, had raised the bar, transforming the public conception of what actually constituted victory. More focused critics complained that the fault lay in Calder's failure to renew the engagement the next day and to keep the enemy in sight.[50]

All considered, it is difficult to imagine Nelson parting with such a meagre result, but he knew war to be a treacherous and unforgiving business, and sympathised with unfortunate brother officers, even one as self-serving and unlikeable as Calder. When he heard that a court martial was in the wind, he was both surprised and sad. As he wrote to one of his favourite captains, 'Who can, my dear Fremantle, command all the success which our country may wish? We have fought together, and therefore well know what it is. I had had the best disposed fleet of friends, but who can say what will be the event of a battle, and it most sincerely grieves me that in any of the papers it should be insinuated that Lord Nelson could have done better. I should have fought the enemy. So did my friend Calder. But who can say that he will be more successful than another? I only wish to stand upon my own merits, and not by comparison, one way or the other, upon the conduct of a brother officer. You will forgive this dissertation, but I feel upon the occasion.'[51]

On the evening of 15 August, a day after Calder joined the Channel fleet, Nelson reached Cornwallis, who flew his flag from the *Ville de Paris* off Ushant. The admirals exchanged salutes, but Nelson had no opportunity to go aboard his old friend's ship. It was an important moment. Now that the Mediterranean and Channel fleets were united, the senior officer, Cornwallis, took precedence, and Nelson opted to take his leave, bringing his independent command to an end. He asked if he could take the *Victory* and the *Superb*, which carried many of his possessions and needed extensive repairs, to Spithead, and Cornwallis obliged. In bidding farewell to the fleet he had led for more than two years, Nelson addressed his remaining flag officer, Louis. 'I have only a moment,' he said, 'to beg that you will be so good as to express in the manner best calculated to do justice, the high sense I entertain of the merit of the captains, officers and ships' companies lately composing the squadron under my command, and assure their able and zealous commanders that their conduct has met my warmest approbation. I have only to repeat the high opinion I entertain of your [own] distinguished conduct.' Of all his fleets, it had indubitably been the most long-suffering, but also the most pleasurable to command.[52]

Two ships anchored at Spithead on 18 August, saluting the flag of the port admiral, George Montagu, displayed above the *Royal William*. Nelson and Keats were home. The admiral hurried letters to Marsden and the collector of customs, explaining that the two ships' companies only wanted some fresh vegetables and citrus fruits to abolish the remaining scurvy, and that no patients needed to be invalided ashore. The force he had just passed to Cornwallis was in the 'most perfect health'. Hardy, however, was weak, and on a surgeon's certificate got leave ashore. Nelson, who wanted to race to Merton, was placed in quarantine, a novel experience he thought, but hardly surprising considering the disease-ridden hole parts of the Mediterranean had become. He would have to wait.[53]

Nelson's flag flew until the 20th. The extra two days gave him the leisure to wind up essential naval affairs. A list of captured Spanish specie stowed on his ships, including part of the cargoes of seven vessels taken between November and January, totalled £32,300. He was particularly worried about the black pilot, James Marguette, who was 'a perfect stranger in London, and consequently will be apt to be imposed upon. I must beg that he may be taken particular care of, and put in a way for a speedy passage to Barbados.' Nelson had been paying him five shillings a day, but the pilot would need maintenance until he set foot on his native land and compensation for his expenses and inconvenience. Then there were testimonials for other members of his ship's company.[54]

As Nelson enjoyed English air, the French invasion project came apart. In the North Sea Lord Keith's hungry ships were still poised to pounce upon the Boulogne flotilla the moment it ventured out, and the French fleet was no nearer covering it than before. After many manoeuvres that fleet remained divided, with more than thirty capital ships with Villeneuve at Ferrol and twenty-one under Ganteaume at Brest. Situated between them, Cornwallis, now reinforced by some of Nelson's ships, held the seas off Ushant with a force neither felt able to challenge. If by some miracle they had fought their way to Boulogne it would have served little purpose, since the invasion flotilla there was in disarray. No more than two-thirds of the proposed 165,000 men were ready to embark, and those were ill prepared to fight the sea and the British at the same time. Had the French sufficient transports to carry the invasion force, there were not enough gunboats to attend them. Cornwallis felt confident enough to divide his force, and detached Calder to Ferrol with twenty ships to blockade Villeneuve. Before he got there the bird had flown, but not northwards to support the invasion. Villeneuve went south into Cadiz, where Collingwood's detachment obligingly stood off to let him in before immediately reimposing the blockade. Napoleon had been at Boulogne since 3 August, but Talleyrand, the French minister of foreign affairs, besieged him with unwelcome news, including word that Nelson was not only back from the West Indies but sailing north. At the same time as the invasion project floundered, Austria growled threateningly, and on 25 August Napoleon ordered his *Grande Armée* to break its camps at Boulogne in order to address the continental threat. Whatever invasion the emperor had planned was over; the wooden walls of the Royal Navy were simply too strong.

Nelson's command of the Mediterranean was also at an end. Questions were raised about aspects of it, and Barham asked to see the admiral's journal. That Villeneuve escaped from Toulon twice demonstrated the inherent weakness in Nelson's open blockade. His strategy of drawing an enemy out to give battle only made a good argument if it was accompanied by effective arrangements to track and close with the hostile fleet when it emerged. Only the incompetence of the enemy and Nelson's extraordinary energy had averted serious consequences. It was a lesson Nelson learned. But in two respects the admiral had performed with distinction. Beset by serious shortcomings in the penetrative power of the British intelligence system, he had exercised naval power with judgement and finesse, skilfully reassessing the changing strategic configurations, bringing an effective balance of strength and prudence to the diplomacy, and carefully apportioning scarce resources between many and diverse tasks. And if he had wielded the weapon well, he had no less remarkably maintained it in a challenging environment. The test that his fleet had just endured was perhaps its greatest testimonial. Nelson had returned after two years' hard service on a remote station without a convenient base or adequate means of support, and yet in two pursuits of the French fleet towards the end of that labour he had covered some 15,000 miles of sea at a sinew-stretching, ship-straining pace – more than half the distance around the equator. More, he was willing to continue, declaring himself ready to pursue Villeneuve 'round the world' if it became necessary. Of the ten ships of the line he had taken to the West Indies, half had been with him since the summer of 1803, and another two for close on a year. Yet they had still outsailed the Franco-Spanish fleet.[55]

Most of the ships he brought to England were provisioned for three months, and in better shape than might have been expected. The *Superb* needed docking, and particularly wanted a new foremast. The *Victory* and *Spartiate* needed attention, and the *Canopus*, *Belleisle* and *Donegal* would have to be docked before the winter, but the *Spencer*, *Conqueror*, *Tigre*, *Leviathan* and *Swiftsure* were fit for further service. One who saw them wrote that all were 'freshly painted in an uniform manner, in a high state of discipline, and in trim order'. As for the men, all the ships had residual scurvy aboard, but only the *Belleisle* was heavily smitten. Leaving out the *Spartiate*, which had joined in the West Indies, the ten ships had 189 in the sickbays on 4 August, a relatively small proportion of the those manning the fleet. Twenty-three of these were cases of scurvy. In addition, other seamen were being treated as outpatients, many with scorbutic symptoms. Of these the *Conqueror* bore 36, *Spencer* and *Tigre* 40 apiece, and the *Belleisle* 160 cases. Gillespie, the physician of the fleet, admitted that while the refreshments obtained at Gibraltar and Tetuan had reduced the incidence of scurvy, 'a very large proportion of the men' were 'more or less scorbutic'. The outbreak obviously reflected the long chase across the Atlantic, when the supply of fresh provisions and fruits had been dislocated, but when all was considered Nelson had come home with the vast majority of his men able to serve. Even when accidents and enemy action are included in the analysis, Nelson's fleet had only 1–1½ per cent of its men killed or hospitalised. It was an achievement that aroused Gillespie's warmest admiration.[56]

Like Hannibal's crossing of the Alps and Marlborough's march to the Danube, Nelson's great chase across the Atlantic and back revealed decision, energy and tenacity, whether a battle was fought or not. But it gains because it was performed at the end, rather than the beginning, of what should have been an exhausting campaign. People marvelled at the admiral's 'rapid . . . operations'. Camden, writing to Nelson to express his gratitude for the many valuable observations he had sent from the Mediterranean, spoke of the 'admiration I feel in common with the rest of the world of the whole of your conduct after you heard of the enemy having passed the Strait of Gibraltar'. Hugh Elliot, congratulating Nelson from Naples, put it better than any: 'Either the distances between the different quarters of the globe are diminished, or you have extended the powers of human action. After an unremitting cruise of two long years in the stormy Gulf of Lions, to have proceeded without going into port to Alexandria, from Alexandria to the West Indies, from the West Indies back again to Gibraltar; to have kept your ships afloat, your rigging standing, and your crews in health and spirits – is an effort such as never was realized in former times, nor, I doubt, will ever again be repeated by any other admiral. You have protected us for two long years, and you saved the West Indies by only a few days.' It was, he said, 'a perseverance' that outdid all of Nelson's 'former victories'.[57]

It had been the ultimate test of Nelson's fleet, and of the admiral's ability to maintain a first-class fighting force, and he had passed it with his colours flying. In so doing he had placed on record an achievement that may have lacked the drama of the Nile and Trafalgar but surely stood equal to them in substance. Nelson had grown in stature. His politics and strategy were mature and defensible, and he had stabilised emotionally, bringing a steadier hand and clearer head to his business. He had emerged from two years at sea the nearest thing Britain had to a perfect commander-in-chief.

Nelson's mind, however, was now elsewhere. 'I have brought home no honour for my country, only a faithful servant,' he wrote to Emma on 18 August. 'Nor any riches . . . but I have brought home a most faithful and honourable heart.'[58]

XXIII

THE LAST FAREWELL

If from thine Emma's breast her heart
Were stolen, or flown away,
Where, where would she engrave, my Love,
Each tender word you say?

Where, where, would Emma treasure up
Her Nelson's smiles and sighs?
Where mark each joy, each secret look
Of love from Nelson's eyes?

Emma's verses to Nelson, 1805

I

AT 7.45 on the morning of Monday, 19 August, the cheers of a waiting crowd greeted Nelson and Murray as they stepped ashore at Portsmouth. They took tea with Admiral Sir George Montagu, and then Nelson picked up a post chaise at the George. He was so eager to get home that he disappointed milling citizens who wanted to man-haul his carriage, and rumbled northwards towards London, accompanied by the essential accumulated baggage of two years at sea and probably his servants, Chevailler and Spedillo. Many stiff hours on, the admiral peered at the comfortable familiarities of an English countryside nearer home, and early on Tuesday morning the travellers turned right off the turnpike road, passed through iron gates shaded by leafy branches above, and swept down a fine new carriageway to the entrance of Merton Place. Casting his eye around, Nelson saw a revelation. The house had risen above its dubious origins and become the very embodiment of his daydreams.[1]

It was a frantic day for Emma Hamilton and Charlotte Nelson, the one an ageing beauty with a charming countenance but some 'prodigiously large' proportions, and the other an exceedingly slim and pretty eighteen-year-old. The news of Nelson's return had found them at Southend the previous day, sea bathing, and they had raced home. Emma had lived for this. These two years past she had avidly followed Nelson's adventures, upbraiding the Admiralty when their information dried up and rejoicing or scolding at what was delivered. She had wished 'that stumbling block' Orde in Hell, but calmed herself with the thought that her hero was 'thick in great and noble deeds, which t'other poor devil is not, so let dirty wretches get pelf to comfort from. Victory belongs to Nelson!' And throughout she had remained unstoppably in love. 'I am anxious and agitated to see him,' she had written to Davison in 1804. 'I never shall be well till I do see him . . . I love him. I adore him. My mind and soul is now transported with the thoughts of that blessed ecstatic moment when I shall see him again, [and] embrace him. My love is no common love. It may be a sin to love. I say it might have been a sin when I was *another's*, but I had then more merit in trying to suppress it. I am *now free*, and I must sin on and love him more than ever. It is a crime worth going to Hell for . . . I shall be at Merton till I see him as he particularly wishes our first meeting should be there . . . My heart beats every ring of the bell.' On that occasion she had been disappointed. Nelson had not come home, but now he was here.[2]

Emma had excitedly prepared the house and rallied a reception party. Horatia was whisked from Mrs Gibson's, brother William stepped forward smartly, presumably with Sarah and Horace, little Mary Gibbs was probably on hand, and Mrs Cadogan had the staff attending in their finest. 'What a day of rejoicing was yesterday at Merton,' Emma enthused to Kate Matcham, who was in Bath mourning the demise of her last child. 'How happy he is to see us all.'[3]

'The town is wild to see him,' Kate also learned, and indeed Nelson was soon aware that he had again returned a hero. Barham having asked to see his journal, Nelson sent a couple of diaries, both partly written with an eye to informing posterity, and no more was heard. After a few meetings the first lord struck Nelson as 'a wonderful man'. In truth, Nelson had risen above the Admiralty's control. He was effectively the first man in the nation, in direct communication with Pitt and his senior ministers, and could write his own ticket. About this there were no complaints, for Nelson had mastered every detail of the Mediterranean command, and was not only a safe and meticulous manager but also young enough to hunger for victories. If the immediate threat of invasion had eased, it had not disappeared and a new chapter was opening. On 13 August, Villeneuve's Franco-Spanish fleet left Ferrol and sailed for the Mediterranean, but it put into Cadiz for provisions and repairs and was quickly blockaded by Collingwood and Calder. The British view was that such a large force could not subsist in Cadiz indefinitely, and sooner or later would attempt a breakout, and offer a rare opportunity for a serious battle. In and out of government, there was only one opinion about which admiral should be waiting for it.[4]

His adrenalin recharging, Nelson accompanied Emma into London the day he reached Merton. Probably he called upon Barham, who had invited him to Admiralty House, and he renewed his acquaintance with the Bolton nieces, the sparkling teenagers Eliza and Ann, summoned to Clarges Street from their school in Edmonton. On the streets his progress could be traced by the huge crowds and constant huzzas. The admiral shook hands with 'an old friend' and complained of his health but 'appeared perfectly cheerful and in good spirits'. But he may have called at Davison's and been hurt to find his old friend missing, despite a letter the admiral had written from Spithead. Freed from prison in the spring, Davison had gone to Swarland to attend to his Northumberland affairs before making a trip into Scotland. The letter from Nelson had been forwarded, but Davison did not realise how little time the admiral had in England, and saw no need to abort his plans. The two men were not as close as they had been, but Nelson still owed Davison money and now felt uncomfortable about the debt. He told Emma that it 'must not run on', and when Davison wrote putting his purse again at the admiral's service, he declined to indulge. He wished to repay his loans, he replied, 'for long accounts ought to be closed between the dearest friends', even if only to open another one. Before returning to sea Nelson had managed to discharge £3371, which was the greater part of his debt.[5]

The following day Nelson caught up with some letters, one of which went to Lady Collier, assuring her that her son was well and had become a fine officer. But progress was limited as Merton was besieged by Sir Peter Parker 'and God knows who' expecting to see the hero. The stream of visitors rarely abated. Clarence was an early caller, but the curiosity-seeker Andreas Andersen Feldborg, who made the pilgrimage on 26 August, left an account for posterity. A creature of quills, ink bottles and sand, Feldborg had brought a copy of his *Historical Sketch of the Battle of Copenhagen* for the admiral, who leafed through it, pointing out an inaccuracy with the good-natured qualification that 'in the distribution of shadow you would, of course, hold the pencil in a manner different from what an Englishman would have done'. The proud author said he had a new work in preparation, dealing with Scandinavia, and Nelson quickly enquired whether he could use a portrait of the Crown Prince of Denmark. If so, he had one, and so saying the admiral led his guest up a polished oak staircase adorned with a print of the battle of the Baltic to a drawing room, where the prince's likeness had its place upon a wall. Their meeting ended as amicably as it had begun. Remarking that writers, like seamen, did not always receive just rewards, Nelson insisted upon subscribing to the forthcoming work. Feldborg left impressed by the 'most engaging address in air and manners' and noted that his host was a man 'of a middle stature, a thin body and an apparently delicate constitution', but the severity of his countenance was transformed in animation, and his sandy 'luxuriant hair', though streaked with grey, 'flowed in graceful ringlets down his temples'.[6]

Emma had entered a brief period of happiness that lived with her forever, but there were guilty secrets. Nelson had long wanted Horatia to live at Merton, and suspecting procrastination had written to both Emma and Haslewood in May with explicit instructions to pension Mrs Gibson off with £20 a year. It had not yet been done; perhaps because the mail had been slow or Haslewood and Emma too tardy. The child was now four. Charlotte, who spent much time in Emma's company, often wrote of Mary Gibbs, the daughter of Abraham Gibbs, who had arrived in London for her schooling in 1804, but rarely of Horatia. It was Nelson's return that unearthed his little daughter from her hiding place, and she was his constant delight during his last weeks in England. Some portraits show Horatia in the brief sunlight of Merton Place. Here she stands innocently on a chair with her hair clipped short, a shift and long pantellettes, clutching an engraved silver cup her father had brought her from Salter's in the Strand. There she resembles a martinet with a top hat and riding whip, posing impressively beside her rocking horse in the garden beside the east façade. Nelson arranged for her to attend the Reverend Lancaster's Sunday School sessions, where she learned hymns and the catechism, and no doubt expected that Merton would now be her permanent home. Another embarrassment for Emma was the sorry state of her finances. Nelson had considerably enhanced the pension she received from Sir William, and made provision for the household, but she still spent beyond her means and allowed small people to bear the burden. Mrs Gibson's arrears had reached £24 in November 1804, the bills from butchers and bakers topped £100 at one point, and poor Cribb was so 'distressed' for money to meet his everyday expenses that he had gone into his own pockets to pay the mowers. The Tysons had been dunned for £270 and a reluctant Davison had provided more than £730 in 1805. Essential bills had also fallen into arrears. The 1805 accounts of the architect and seven tradesmen employed on the improvements at Merton Place summed £1828, of which £823 was still owed. The admiral took matters in hand, but he understood that Emma was not entirely to blame. Merton could not have been transformed without money, within as well as without. All about were the furnishings she had been compelled to provide, many for a new bedroom that had been built over the dining room at the east end of the servants' block. The account of William Peddieson, the upholsterer of Brewer Street, listed chests of drawers, a feather bed and bolster with 'best goose feathers', a cabriole chair 'with arms stuffed and covered with needlework', ottoman stools, a fire screen, a sofa table, a brass chandelier and a new Kidderminster carpet, as well as sundry cushions and covers. Most of the wooden furniture was in an expensive mahogany. On the whole Nelson liked what he saw, but no doubt he gently rehearsed his regular homily about economy.[7]

Nelson's first few days were much devoted to admiring the progress of Merton Place, which was now the bedrock of the future he planned. Feldborg, who perhaps expected the national hero to inhabit something like Blenheim Palace, thought it small and inelegant, but those who had seen the house before held entirely different opinions. 'Merton Place is astonishingly improved,' naval officer Thomas Bowen had written to Nelson a year before. 'Your lordship will scarcely know it again. Even Capability Brown himself could not have laid it out with more taste than her ladyship has done.' Minto rated the improvements 'excellent' and Nelson's only reservations related to the new bedchamber work above the dining room. There were so many changes, great and small, that Nelson's rambles became something like voyages of discovery, with more surprises still in train, including an African civet cat and an exotic 'crown bird' that would take air on the porch, both on their way from Captain Langford. To accommodate Nelson's predilection for pacing up and down while reflecting or conversing, a habit learned at sea, a 'quarter-deck' walk had been established, located according to tradition on a mound north of the turnpike with views over Wimbledon Hill and rural Wandsworth. The final appearance of the estate, captured in elegant engravings and impromptu drawings, owed much to Emma's vision and energy. It had become an entirely respectable gentleman's residence, sitting in extensive, well-watered pleasure gardens and served by a compact farm. Nelson proclaimed Emma a 'Capability Brown' and even the sceptical Minto capitulated; she was, he confessed, 'a clever being after all'.[8]

Scattered references, deeds, sale descriptions, pictures and plans allow us to see the extent of that work and why it impressed Nelson and featured so vividly in his hopes and aspirations. The house itself was still composed of a northern and southern block, linked by an ante-room on its eastern side. As far as the northern block was concerned, Nelson appears to have done no more than turn the western drawing room into a library. The southern block, originally designed for servants, needed more work. Nelson added the chamber above the dining room on its eastern side, ensuring that its appearance and dimensions matched the upper storey of the northern block, so that the entire eastern side of the house became the symmetrical whole shown in the contemporary engravings. Indeed, this attractive eastern façade, with its ground-floor terrace and 'miradors' towards the garden, was now turned into the principal entrance to the house. Two more improvements to the southern block were planned. An additional cloakroom would buttress up behind the existing ante-room linking the two blocks, and a new kitchen located in a single-floor extension to the rear of the building. A commodious affair, the kitchen would be equipped with a separate scullery and two sets of hotplates on its west wall, the latter probably heated by a flue from the chimney, but it appears not to have been finished until late 1805 or early 1806. These alterations to the southern block allowed a rearrangement of rooms, and increased the number of servants' chambers to eight.[9]

The extent to which the various rooms of the house had been renovated is unclear. In 1801 Nelson purchased a house with only one 'water closet' in the family living quarters, and if the surveyor's report is to be believed even that was not situated on the upper, or 'chamber', floor. But by 1815 a sale notice was able to refer to '5 principal bedchambers (some of which are 24 feet square) with dressing-rooms and water-closet' on the upper floor. The text is ambiguous, but the inference is either that the 'chamber' floor contained a water closet, or that each of the five main bedrooms was so equipped. The latter interpretation has encouraged social historians to cite Merton as a rather advanced villa, with en-suite facilities, possibly employing Joseph Bramah's recently patented ball-cock water closets. It may have been so, but the evidence is being stretched.[10]

The most sweeping improvements were to the grounds. North of the turnpike a kitchen garden had evidently been added, and as a temporary coach house was established in Linton's old barn, Bennett's lease had been relinquished at a saving of £50 a year. South of the turnpike the house now stood in spacious lawns cut by gently curving paths and decorated by choice trees and shrubberies. The 'Nile' canal, once almost circular, had been filled in east and south of the house, and the water quality so improved that it supported fish. The carp and tench had muddied the water, and were regularly consumed by pike, and Nelson had advised that they be removed to the safety of an estate pond. What was left of the 'Nile' still ran beneath the ornamental bridge on the north side of the house, supporting recreational activities with rowing boats and fishing rods, but its reduction had been necessary to provide space for the new carriageway linking the turnpike with the main entrance of the house, which was now in the eastern, rather than the northern, façade. A new estate entrance had been made at the north-eastern corner of the estate, where the turnpike met Abbey Lane. Whether fashionable 'Piccadilly gates' had been installed, or temporary 'common white' substitutes, is not known, but an entrance lodge had been contrived from one of Linton's old outbuildings, and the gravel carriageway swept sedately around the eastern and southern sides of the house to access both the main entrance and the rear, where an extensive orchard stood majestically to the south. Nelson's plan to build a proper coach house and three staff cottages within the eastern limit of the estate, somewhere behind the ruins of Merton Abbey, may have been underway. The pleasure gardens had also been enhanced, unearthing a few Roman artefacts in the process; a small farm fitted out, perhaps south-east of the house near Abbey Lane; and a start made of securing the perimeters of the enlarged estate with palings and trees. Nelson was particularly proud of the improvement to the dramatic subterranean passage that ran beneath the turnpike to link both parts of his estate. It was amplified and brick-lined, and would survive for decades.[11]

Now lost beneath concrete, the Merton of Nelson and Lady Hamilton can only be recovered in fading documents and the drawings and prints of long-dead artists. As the admiral saw it that last time, it was everything he desired, a rural sanctuary where he and his family could live in the honour and affection of the community. As Emma wrote to Davison that September, after 'one fortnight of joy and happiness' at home, 'Nelson is so delighted with Merton, and now he is here 'tis a paradise'.[12]

2

The public appetite for Nelsoniana was unabated. Artists still hectored for sittings, and Robert Bowyer and his niece, the wax sculptress Catherine Andras, sketched him at the same time, an experience which prompted the admiral to remark that it was the first time he had been attacked from both larboard and starboard. The last portrait ever made of him from life was a profile drawn by John Wichelo, who visited Merton impromptu in September. On days when he shopped in London he was attended by enormous crowds, many of whom fell behind him in processions of wonder, thronging the doorways of the stores he entered, parting to let him leave and then continuing in his footsteps.

Friends who accompanied the admiral were astonished at the worship. John Theophilus Lee, a young veteran of the Nile, met Nelson at the Navy Office in Somerset House, and escorted him into the adjacent premises of Thresher and Glenny's and as far as John Salter, the sword cutler, jeweller and silversmith of 35 The Strand, beset by crowds all the way. Minto came across his friend in Piccadilly at the heart of another crowd. Taking his arm to walk with him, he was mobbed, too, for the first and probably the last time in his life. 'It is beyond anything represented in a play or a poem,' he wrote. On a third occasion it was the Reverend Scott who experienced the excitement. An American who witnessed the occasion marked Nelson's sharp-featured profile, sun-burned complexion and 'balancing gait of a sailor'. Nevertheless, he managed to spend a considerable amount of money in these perambulations. Barrett, Corney and Corney of 479 The Strand supplied three additional sets of imitation orders, while several visits to Lock's of St James's Street in August and September netted a hat with a cockade and green shade and a spare shade and cockade for £12. Dolland provided eyeglasses, and James Lavell of St Martin's Lane sent 375 gallons of port worth £308 to Merton early in September. Attempting to raise money, Nelson sold some precious stones to Rundell and Bridge of Ludgate Hill, and on a macabre note visited Peddieson the upholsterer, directing him to prepare the coffin that Hallowell had given him. He might have need of it, he said.[13]

There were surprisingly few private days, and even in London visitors were constantly at his door. Lady Elizabeth Foster, famous for her *ménage à trois* with the Devonshires, and Lady Perceval, called upon their friend Emma Hamilton in Clarges Street. Within they found the William Nelsons ('very strange-looking people') and the bewitching hero, from whom they dragooned kisses before they left. Both women had relatives with the fleet, and doubtless had come with the intention of soliciting patronage. William Perceval Johnson, a godson of the visitor, had joined the *Victory* as a fifteen-year-old midshipman in August 1803 and been transferred to the *Guerrier*. Lady Foster's illegitimate son, Augustus Clifford, another teenage midshipman, was also with the fleet. When he could, Nelson preferred to dine at Merton. Naval colleagues such as Hardy, Jonathan Culverhouse and Thomas Bowen called, and Minto unexpectedly dropped in for the first time on Saturday, 24 August, just as Nelson, William and Sarah, their children and the two Bolton schoolgirls were sitting down at table, with Emma at its head and Mrs Cadogan at the opposite end. The earl received 'a hearty welcome' but noticed that the passion between his host and hostess was 'as hot as ever'. The companies at dinner grew steadily larger, as guests mingled with the final gathering of the Nelson clan.[14]

As they came the family members brought problems as well as pleasures. When the senior Boltons arrived about 28 August, Thomas was not slow to raise his interest in more lucrative employment than farming in Norfolk. Nelson was already subsidising the education of Tom Bolton junior, but the family was growing, and the admiral had acquired his first great-niece, Emma Horatia (the daughter of Sir William and Kitty Bolton), in the spring of 1804. Emma had sent a silver tea service, china and a child's coral to celebrate the occasion. Now Nelson promised to help his brother-in-law towards a commissionership in the Customs, Excise or Navy offices, and wrote to George Rose, the immensely likeable vice president of the Board of Trade and paymaster general, on the 29th. The Matchams arrived from Bath at the beginning of September, looking too thin to feed crows according to Susannah. But George Matcham, Nelson's youngest brother-in-law, was seldom importuning. His family grew and his dream of retiring to the continent loitered, but he showed great forbearance over the £4000 he had loaned the admiral, and seldom wanted much for himself beyond an occasional introduction to this or that person, or written testimonials on behalf of 'poor relatives'. He alone remained uncomfortable with the family's treatment of Fanny. Kate is said to have wished Lady Nelson dead, and Susannah even faulted the way she spread her hands when talking, but in later years George reflected sadly upon the destruction of Nelson's marriage. If the couple had gone abroad, as they had once contemplated, the years 'might have softened mutual seeming asperities' and allowed a peaceful and comfortable association. As for Emma, George disliked the 'Tom Tit' language she deployed against Fanny. Lady Hamilton's 'disposition was satirical, not I believe from malignity of disposition [or] temper, but from an affectation of point and wit,' he said. 'Her letters and even casual notes were never free from this despicable propensity. Lord Nelson, in reply to her, could not but somewhat flatteringly adopt her style.'[15]

Of course, Nelson was his susceptible self. He intervened in sprightly fashion when Sukey, Maurice's wife, ran into more financial difficulties, and stumped up £133 to pay her apothecary, Thomas Bland of Soho Square, for medicines and treatment over a five-year period. He also increased her allowance to £240 per annum. The issue that most concerned him was Emma's pension. When he saw Rose he pressed her claims 'with great earnestness'. Rose, who had once served in the navy, had an unbounded admiration for Nelson, and wanted to help both Emma and Thomas Bolton. He ascertained that the next three vacancies for commissioners of customs were already spoken for, but promised to pursue both causes and to see Nelson in Portsmouth before he sailed.[16]

Friends and acquaintances, and not a few unknowns, some needy and others opportunist, also impinged upon the little time left to the returned hero. George Owen, a seaman of the *Captain*, needed help to get his prize money, Eliza Felton came timorously into his presence at Gordon's Hotel to talk about her son, and naval officers travelled to Merton to pay their respects. Medical men also knew a sympathetic ear. Nelson wrote on behalf of Dr John Gray, pointing out that ten years on station had made him 'the fittest person I know' to become physician of the Mediterranean fleet, and on his very last day at Merton he supported the application John Snipe's widow had made for a pension. 'A better man in private life' than the doctor, 'nor a more able man in his profession I have never met with,' he wrote to Barham.[17]

Disputes over prize money seldom left him alone, and sometimes he was self-serving, but not always; his belief that the system was an essential inducement to service was genuine. When he argued that the *Maria Theresa* had been declared a 'droit' of the crown rather than regular prize because her captor, the *Ambuscade*, was herself a manned prize rather than a formally commissioned naval vessel, he was thinking of the losses the seamen would incur. He ordered Scott, his prize agent, to sort out Murray's entitlements as well as his own. But he had expected to make some money in the Mediterranean, enough to clear his debts and give him security in a future without employment, and all he had had was thin gruel. He defended his corner vigorously, therefore, and smouldered when an Admiralty solicitor ruled out his claim to prizes made by Captain R. H. A. Bennett of the *Tribune*.[18]

One of the saddest supplicants was William Layman, who visited Merton on Thursday, 5 September, fighting for his career. Nelson gave him a letter of introduction to Barham's nephew and private secretary, John D. Thompson, and let in a ray of hope. 'I consider Captain Layman as a most able, active, brave and zealous officer,' he wrote. 'The loss of the services of men of such rare abilities is to be lamented by the country. My wish at present is to place Captain Layman well with Lord Barham, and that his lordship may possess my opinion of him.' Going further, Nelson took Layman to the Admiralty himself, and turned the tide in his favour. The unfortunate officer was not only promised employment, but told that it would be in the Mediterranean, whither Nelson, his favourite patron, was also bound. Alas, tides go out as well as in, and the promises would be forgotten after Trafalgar.[19]

A visitor with a different, and ultimately influential, favour to ask also presented himself. Nelson had known John McArthur as a purser, prize agent and secretary under Hood and St Vincent for most of the previous decade. McArthur had been rated a purser in the *Rattlesnake* cutter in 1779, but his acknowledged skill as a swordsman lent him a rare versatility, and he assisted in the boarding of a superior French vessel. Later, in other ships, his literary competence proved useful, and he helped reform signal books and became a principal mover of the *Naval Chronicle*, which had published Nelson's only connected attempt at autobiography. Through some administrative hiccup McArthur had lost his place as purser of the *Victory* in 1803, and there had been some embittered letters, but he was interested in rebuilding bridges with Nelson now. For 'several years' he had been collecting materials for a life of the admiral. He was living with a wife and daughter in York Place, Portman Square, and perhaps saw some money in his Nelson project. Later he claimed that the admiral endorsed his biography, and 'even direct[ed] me to undertake' the work, 'of which fact I hold ample testimony in his own writing'. He had certainly written to the admiral, stating an intention to visit, and given Nelson's love of self-advertisement and McArthur's entirely sympathetic pen, there are grounds for believing his story. If so, he helped set in motion the most influential book to be published on Nelson in the nineteenth century, and a pillar of his posterity.[20]

Such distractions apart, nowhere that summer could Nelson escape the feeling that he was at the centre of a huge unfolding drama, inexorably gathering pace towards some historic climax. He was the country's champion, arming himself for a decisive contest, and his opinion stood current on everything naval, and much that was not. On Friday, 23 August and the following Monday he was in London, fitting his regular visits to the Navy Office, Marsh and Creed in Norfolk Street and the Admiralty around top level discussions with senior ministers. 'Yesterday,' he wrote to Keats on 24 August, 'the Secretary of State [for war and colonies, Lord Castlereagh], which is a man who has only sat one solitary day in his office and, of course, knows but little of what is passed, and indeed the [Prime] Minister, were all full of the enemy's fleet, and as I am now set up for a *Conjuror* . . . I was asked my opinion, against my inclination, for if I make one wrong guess, the charm will be broken.' Lord Mulgrave, the foreign secretary, was likewise impressed, and Addington (now Lord Sidmouth) was after him, too. The Friday Nelson met Pitt and Castlereagh he ran into the former first minister in Clifford Street, and they talked for an hour, although Addington was weak after being bled by his surgeon and stood in his shirt sleeves. The admiral parted with a promise to visit on Sunday, after attending church. True to it, he arrived at Richmond Park, Addington's residence, and spent another hour in conversation. Addington felt too weak to return the visit, so Nelson made a second trip to Richmond Park on his last Tuesday in England.[21]

At this time Villeneuve's intentions were uncertain, but the City merchants were panicking about the safety of the homeward bound East Indian convoy, while affairs on the continent were beginning to bubble. An Anglo-Russian treaty was in the making, and Austria was expected to take the field as an ally of Russia, although her appointment of the ill-starred Mack as her commander-in-chief would hardly have filled Nelson with confidence. From his first talks with ministers Nelson knew that employment was certain, and before the end of August was speaking of it as foregone. He promised George Elliot a better ship, and tipped off the editor of the *Morning Chronicle*, James Perry, who announced that Nelson would return to the Mediterranean as commander-in-chief in his issue of the 29th. His reservations about resuming the post were cleared away. Cadiz would be restored to the Mediterranean theatre, and there would be no more Ordes. Among other issues aired, probably with Barham, was the insecurity of his communication line. It was decided that a squadron of four cruisers, equipped with the latest Popham signal codes, would protect the line between Finisterre and Gibraltar, but Barham saw problems in Nelson's plans for controlling Spanish threats to Gibraltar. This hoary subject had become critical after the outbreak of the Spanish war, and Nelson authorised Lieutenant General Henry Fox, the military governor of Gibraltar, to tell the Spaniards that if they threatened his outpost the fleet would retaliate against such coastal towns as Cadiz and Malaga.[22]

Nelson felt obliged to raise some of the strategic issues in the Mediterranean. He stood up for Naples, and supported the Neapolitan minister, Castelcicala, in securing a promise that Britain would keep a ship of the line at the capital to give the court a permanent means of escape. Sardinia caused Nelson more concern. As Spain and Britain were at war, the British had the option of seizing Minorca as a base, as they had done in 1799, but Nelson considered Sardinia the better alternative. The thrust of his argument was that Britain would have to invest more in the island's defence. Craig was in the Mediterranean but his force was intended to be a disposable one, capable of being moved about, and the Sardinian strongpoints needed a more permanent reinforcement. Moreover, the island wanted money to make the best of its own resources.[23]

On 28 August Nelson returned to London, booking into Gordon's Hotel in Albermarle Street for the night. By noon callers were flooding into the lobby, including Lords Hood and Braybrooke and a deputation of West India merchants led by Sir Richard Neave, who had passed a powerful vote of thanks to the admiral at a meeting in the London Tavern five days before. He 'breakfasted' with the merchants on 'tea, coffee, chocolate and a dessert of the first quality', and went about some business before dining with Emma at Clarges Street. Minto and Greville, as well as William Nelson and Susannah and Thomas Bolton, were at the table. Sardinia, however, was troubling him, and the admiral was up before six the next morning, writing to Pitt, 'I cannot rest until the importance of Sardinia . . . is taken into consideration', and seeking another audience. Soon after he was knocking at Minto's door, before the diplomat had even risen from his bed. Nelson invited him to dine at Merton the next day, but in the meantime unloaded some papers relating to Sardinia so that Minto could peruse them before they met. He valued the diplomat's counsel, and often flattered his friend by attributing all his 'Mediterranean opinions and politics' to him. The next day at Merton Nelson put copies of his dispatches about Sardinia (his 'great hobby') in front of Minto. Although they discussed the subject, when Minto left, Nelson 'filled' his chaise with books of his correspondence on the matter 'to show how his opinion . . . concurred with mine'. Not only that, but the next day a courier brought Minto 'another load' from the admiral. Nelson got enough satisfaction to write to the Viceroy of Sardinia that he had told Pitt that the island needed 'pecuniary assistance' and believed that 'proper measures' would be 'speedily taken for that essential purpose'.[24]

Listening to Nelson during these talks must have stirred ministers, and Nelson clinched his standing as perhaps the only admiral capable of handling the Mediterranean at such a complicated time and of fighting the battle the country needed. Then, at five in the morning of Monday, 2 September, a mud-flecked chaise and four came with the dawn along the drive of Merton Place, and out of it stepped a stocky but well-made fresh-complexioned naval officer besmirched by a long journey over sea and road. He was Captain Henry Blackwood of the *Euryalus*, one of the first frigate captains of the day, and he had come direct from Collingwood off Cadiz with an urgent packet for the Admiralty. So important, indeed, that he had made this short diversion to the country's premier defender. After weeks of uncertainty, Blackwood confirmed that the enemy's combined fleet of twenty-seven or twenty-eight ships of the line had entered Cadiz on 22 August, where it was being blockaded. As far as Nelson was concerned, this was the starting gun. With such a force Villeneuve would soon exhaust the resources of Cadiz and have to leave, and the British would fight him. If a Franco-Spanish fleet of that magnitude got into the Mediterranean and linked with the Spaniards at Cartagena everything within the Strait – Sardinia, the Sicilies, the Morea, Egypt, Malta and Craig's expeditionary force – would be in deadly danger. But if it could be intercepted and destroyed, Britain would not only have secured the Mediterranean but also regained her general naval superiority, lost the previous year when Spain entered the war. As Blackwood hurtled away to London, an admiral never immune to the exhilaration of battle probably realised that such a chance might never come again. It was his opportunity to change the course of the war, and to annihilate the enemy fleet in the ultimate battle under sail.[25]

Nelson had been priming expectations of what was needed at this great moment. As he told one who met him, 'nothing short of the annihilation of the enemy's fleet will do any good'. And he had been refining the battle tactics he would use. When Keats visited Merton Place Nelson saw the ideal sounding board, and treated the captain to a preview as they paced the 'quarter-deck' on his estate. What Keats heard was the blueprint for Trafalgar. There would be no time-consuming manoeuvres, Nelson said. 'I shall go at them at once' and cut their line 'about one third . . . from their leading ship'. This was a repetition of his standing ideas about dividing an enemy fleet to overwhelm the van or the rear, but now he talked about using two attacking lines with a flying reserve of fast seventy-fours to handle unforeseeable eventualities. 'What do you think of it?' asked the excited admiral, and, before Keats could reply, added, 'I'll tell you what I think of it. I think it will surprise and confound the enemy. They won't know what I am about. It will bring forward a pell-mell battle, and that is what I want.'[26]

Within hours of Blackwood's call Nelson was also travelling into town, where he left Emma and his two sisters at Clarges Street while he made his way to the Admiralty and to Minto. Barham ordered Nelson to proceed immediately to Cadiz to take Collingwood's fleet under his command, and promised a substantial reinforcement. He could take the *Victory* and as many ships as were available out with him, and others would follow. Barham was making a supreme effort, for he had few more than seventy ships of the line fit for sea service anywhere, but he recognised that a national sacrifice was necessary to give Nelson what he needed. He asked the admiral to name his officers. Murray had already written to explain that family reasons precluded him from serving, but Nelson made some suggestions. Berry, injured by the glut of captains and commanders, had appealed to Nelson from Leith, 'wishing to transport myself to your squadron', and fearing that he would otherwise be forced to leave the service to support his family. 'I may wish and hope, write and dance attendance for years without the smallest notice [being] taken of my applications. A man's standing . . . and his reputation . . . all goes for nought,' he moaned. Philip Durham of the *Defiance*, who had fought Villeneuve under Calder, met Nelson at the Admiralty about this time and pledged to have his ship ready for sea if the admiral would take him. Orders to both officers, as well as Blackwood, Keats, Hardy, William Brown of the *Ajax* and William Lechmere of the *Thunderer* were eventually on their way.[27]

As wheels turned to provide Nelson with a great fleet the time he had left in England could be counted in precious days.

3

The weather deteriorated the day after Blackwood's call, and Emma found herself fighting depression, and perhaps what was worse an inner dread. Like Fanny, she knew her man's disposition, even if he kept the details of his plans from her. Nelson certainly did not mislead himself. He needed to meet the combined fleet 'with a force sufficient to do the job well, for half a victory would but half content me', but he knew that the promised reinforcements might not reach him in time, and he could find himself fighting twice his number of capital ships. His plan took that prospect into consideration. He intended to detach, disrupt, enclose and destroy one part of the enemy force before the other could intervene, and would, if necessary, fight two successive battles, first with one part of the enemy fleet, and then with the other, but he knew it was a tall order. 'I will do my best,' he wrote to Davison, 'and I hope God Almighty will be with me.' Some of these apprehensions must have reached Emma, and grown larger in her imagination because of the love she bore him. She had hoped his leave might have given her several months, but now the clock ticked remorselessly and the 'fortnight of joy and happiness' she had enjoyed faded. As she wrote to Lady Kitty Bolton, 'It seems as though I have had a fortnight's dream, and am awoke to all the misery of this cruel separation. But what can I do? His powerful arm is of so much consequence to his country. But I do, nor cannot say more. My heart is broken.' And the clock ticked on.[28]

On Tuesday, 3 September, the day before her candid letter, Emma had presided over a full-scale Nelson family dinner, with the senior Matchams newly arrived and Thomas Bolton due to leave the following day. At least she reigned as Nelson's wife in all but name. Seventeen sat at the table: Emma; Mrs Cadogan; Nelson; William, Sarah, Charlotte and Horace Nelson; Thomas and Susannah Bolton with four of their children, Lady Kitty being detained at Brancaster; William Bolton, Thomas's brother, who appeared that day; George and Kate Matcham; and little Horatia. There were so many that the youngsters had to be given a table to themselves. And another was duly expected, sixteen-year-old George Matcham, Nelson's nephew, who was making his own way from Bath. Cribb was dispatched to meet his coach at the White Horse cellars in Piccadilly, but George did not arrive there till ten at night, and when he got to Merton all but one had retired. Emma welcomed him in her chemise, and directed him to a bedroom he would share with Tom Bolton junior. Most usefully, this worthy young man brought with him a diary that reaches over the centuries to admit us to Nelson's last days at Merton.[29]

Wednesday saw George and his cousin spending a 'tedious' morning hunting in the grounds, but they returned with 'a brace' of birds, apparently brought down by Horace. Nelson was at the Admiralty again but dinner was well attended, and in the games of cards that followed our young diarist lost eleven shillings and sixpence, and only Nelson's gift of a tidy two guineas saved him from ending the day poorer. On Thursday the bulk of Nelson's baggage was loaded on to a cart and directed to Portsmouth, where it would be transferred to the *Victory*. One or both servants, Chevailler and Spedillo, probably went with it.[30]

Nelson may have stayed with Clarence at Bushy House, Teddington, that evening. At least an undated letter from the duke invited him 'next Thursday' and advised him to bring a servant so that he could stay overnight 'that we may talk over the Mediterranean'. The admiral was in town again on Friday, when he saw Pitt in the morning and left a bill at Davison's house. At Merton that day young George fished unsuccessfully in the pond, and 'sauntered' about the grounds. When he came in to dinner he joined another substantial gathering. The admiral introduced his nephews, Tom, Horace and George, as his 'three props' to a portly guest, who obviously thought himself important. Clarence, who had arrived with Lord Errol in tow, 'talked much' but deferred to Nelson's opinions except when the conversation turned to Pitt, against whom His Royal Highness railed most violently. Three other visitors were Lieutenant Colonel William Suckling, his wife Wybrew, and their third son, Nelson, of two years. The Sucklings had delayed christening the boy until the admiral was able to sponsor him in person, and the ceremony was performed in the local church that afternoon. The duke stood in for Prince Adolphus Frederick, who had agreed to be another sponsor, and declared that he would join Nelson as a sponsor of their next child, the imminence of whose birth was plain to see.[31]

Either that day, Friday, 6 September, or the next Nelson received a letter from Marsden, telling him that his orders were ready for collection. On the Saturday, therefore, he was again at the Admiralty, where he spoke to Barham, and wrote a couple of letters. One was for Marsden, complaining about the treatment of the agent victualler at Gibraltar, James Cutforth. Cutforth had faithfully obeyed Nelson's orders and sold the Spanish prizes detained before the official outbreak of war, holding the profits pending the decision of government, but Lord Camden and Lieutenant General Fox had both challenged his proceedings. Nelson asked the Admiralty to support the hapless official. His other letter went to his great friend Collingwood, commanding off Cadiz, telling him that he was on his way.

Nelson had much else to do with ministers, and was in London early on both Sunday and Monday mornings, winding up personal affairs as well as laying foundations for his forthcoming mission. Then and later he was at the Admiralty wanting signalling materials, including fifty copies of Popham's *Telegraphic Signals or Marine Vocabulary* (1803). A faster and more sophisticated communication system that enabled some two thousand words to be spelled out, it had impressed Nelson during his recent pursuit of Villeneuve's fleet. As news of Nelson's appointment spread, the promoters of other naval novelties searched him out. One P. H. Clay arrived at Merton to talk about his newly patented waterproof jackets, which Nelson would endorse after trials, and it was about this time also that the admiral considered whether new weaponry might prise Villeneuve out of Cadiz. Under the alias of 'Robert Francis', the American inventor Robert Fulton had recommended his 'catamarans', which were primitive floating mines equipped with a clockwork firing mechanism. Sent into harbours or closely packed shipping they had the potential to cause panic and damage, but without motive power they had to be towed towards their targets and were of little use in heavily defended anchorages, where batteries, gunboats and harbour booms would be encountered. Fulton had refined the devices since their dismal performance in trials off Boulogne in 1804, and probably explained his proposals to Nelson at the Admiralty. On 12 September the admiral pursued the matter with Sir Sidney Smith, who had experimented with catamarans, but concluded that while the catamaran was another weapon for his armoury it was too limited and unpredictable to depend upon.[32]

At Merton, Sunday, 8 September was relatively quiet. Sir Sidney called, and regaled the company with an account of his defence of Acre, while a letter arrived from Addington begging Nelson to see him before he sailed. The following day George and Horace were packed off to Abraham Goldsmid's 'fine house', Morden Lodge. George thought the property 'gaudy and tasteless' and the kindly bestowed Jewish dinner little more to his liking, while Horace's running wit hardly helped. 'H. cut his jokes on me,' said George, 'Let him go on.' Nelson was in London by 8.30 that morning, and visited Castlereagh at two. On Tuesday Nelson, Emma and the senior Matchams dined with a prominent diplomat, James Crauford, on the condition that 'no person of party' would be present. Harriet, Lady Bessborough was there, however, and the 5th Duke of Devonshire, with his paramour, Lady Elizabeth Foster, who begged Nelson take a letter for her son, Clifford. 'Now kiss it,' the admiral told her, 'and I will carry him the letter and the kiss.' But the company found the admiral unexpectedly modest when the subject of Calder came up: he showed 'great unwillingness' to criticise his brother officer. Perhaps he was reflecting on whether he, like Calder, might disappoint. The same day Nelson made his visit to Addington at Richmond Park, shaking hands with the former premier for the last time.[33]

Letters, like invitations, crowded in fast once the admiral's imminent departure was known. Lord Camden, who vainly called at Gordon's Hotel, was grateful for Nelson's attentions to a nephew who had been promoted lieutenant. Dumouriez was still tantalised by the idea of cooperating with Nelson in some Italian expedition, and hoped the admiral would support a plan he had put to the Austrian emperor. A less distinguished military man, but one also 'set quite aside' by the Establishment, Edward, the Duke of Kent, regretted that he had never served with Nelson, but hoped he would continue to protect his eleve, Midshipman George Raynesford of the *Belleisle*. Richard Bulkeley said his son had insisted he write to thank Nelson for the many favours he had done him.

On Wednesday, Nelson called on William Windham and visited the Navy Office. At home Beckford came to dinner, hoping to gull the admiral to Fonthill again. George's diary pronounced the visitor 'talkative'. He 'praised his own composition. Played extempore on the harpsichord. Sung. I thought it a very horrible noise.' Fortunately, the dependable Horace was there to distract by getting 'into a scrape'.[34]

Thursday the 12th was Nelson's last full day at Merton, and he was again drawn to London for much of the time. The Prince of Wales had asked him to Carlton House to take his leave, but the king, who was at Weymouth, was not to see the nation's champion. Nelson was not surprised, but, according to Gore, His Majesty had softened to the hero over time. Nelson 'never loses time in parley', George had told Gore at a levee in September. 'It is always a word and a blow with him. I glory in him.' But there was much else to do than court royals, and Nelson saw Mulgrave and Castlereagh, with whom he discussed whether troops and catamarans might help dislodge the French from Cadiz. More importantly, Nelson made his last face-to-face appeal for Sardinia. In a written statement he declared that the island 'must have money,' and that he simply could not return to the Mediterranean with a rejection of the viceroy's supplications. If Britain did not aid Sardinia, she would lose it and be faced with more expensive options, such as expelling the French from Sardinian sea ports or capturing Corsica and using it as an alternative base. Castlereagh believed in brinkmanship, and the danger of committing inadequate forces that would merely invite a French attack upon Sardinia, but after conferring with fellow ministers he secured agreement to furnish the island with £40,000 to help it improve defences or raise militia. While waiting for Castlereagh in an ante-room at 12 Downing Street that day, Nelson met a small, hook-nosed army officer in his thirties, just returned from distinguished service in India. Arthur Wellesley, the victor of Assaye and future Duke of Wellington, would be the other great British hero of the war, and this was their only meeting. Nelson began self-importantly, but once he realised the mettle of his decidedly down-to-earth companion he satisfied himself with an informed exchange of views. Nelson wanted Sardinia occupied, but Wellesley did not think himself the man for the job.[35]

Nelson had a meal with Queensberry, Lord William Gordon and a Mr Douglas, members of the Hamilton circle, but returned to Merton for a dinner overshadowed by his imminent departure. Perry and his wife had been invited, and were already *in situ* when the admiral appeared. The editor had been given access to some of his letter-books, and when the admiral drew attention to the importance of Sardinia and his motives for sailing to Alexandria and the West Indies it was obviously with the view that these subjects were meet for a sympathetic airing in the *Morning Chronicle*. Minto, who had dined to excess on a similar diet, arrived unexpectedly to join the table, but the gathering learned that a coach had been ordered to take their host to Portsmouth the following day. Nelson mentioned that the Admiralty hoped to give him forty capital ships, one of the largest fleets in living memory. Emma, usually the soul of any party, cried much of the time, and ate and drank little; sometimes she looked close to fainting. Minto left at about ten in the evening. 'It is a strange picture,' he pondered the next day. 'She tells me nothing can be more pure and ardent than this flame. He is in many points a really great man, in others a baby.' But he admitted, 'His friendship and mine is little short of the other attachment [Emma's], and is quite sincere.' Even so acute a critic as Minto could not help but love the disabled little luminary.[36]

Friday, 13 September 1805, a day of moderate wind and cloud, found the lovers sick inside. Nelson described his departure as being driven from paradise, and Emma was barely able to function. This was the most difficult hour. Recently they had taken 'a private sacrament' together in a church ceremony witnessed by the Dowager Lady Spencer. 'Emma,' Nelson is reported to have said, taking the hand of his mistress, 'I have taken the sacrament with you this day to prove to the world that our friendship is most pure and innocent, and of this I call God to witness.' The Dowager Countess took the profession literally, and thundered to her daughter-in-law, 'Lavinia, I think you will now agree that you have been to blame in your [poor] opinion of Lady Hamilton.' Perhaps she missed the significance of this simple ceremony. The couple could not marry while Fanny lived, but Nelson wanted them to stand united before his God before he put himself in harm's way. It may have been upon this occasion that rings were exchanged. Two such gold betrothal rings, worked into the shape of clasped hands, have recently come to auction. Nelson's was mounted with a large 'H' and had been subsequently engraved with the date 13 September. Emma's bore a miniature of a female eye with a brown iris, a lover's eye painted on ivory after the manner of the time.[37]

Nelson saw the annihilation of the combined fleet as his final mission, and indicated that he would resign his commission if he could secure it. Meanwhile, the Merton project would again fall to Emma and Mrs Cadogan, who would have to complete the kitchen extension and demolish a wall to create additional space. It was principally in connection with Merton that Nelson had to make his last trip into town. An instruction was left at Davison's, ensuring that Emma would continue to receive the £100 a month he had awarded her, and that a bill of Chawner the architect was paid. Marsh and Creed were authorised to settle with one Burlesworth for engraved prints and with Lavell for wine.

Time was racing now. A chaise had been ordered from the King's Head for ten that evening, and Nelson no doubt spent most of the day at home. Sir Sidney Smith, who was about to leave for Boulogne, and the Goldsmids called for dinner. As the light of the summer night faded, Nelson went up to Horatia's bedroom to kneel in prayer beside the sleeping child. He had done all he could to protect her, but for all that felt her fragility in a hostile world, and desperately wanted to see her grow. The chaise arrived at the door, and Nelson's small luggage was loaded. Emma was in tears and would not accompany him outside.

Afterwards she said he came four times back into the house, and on the last occasion knelt to beseech God to bless her. She admitted to William Hayley that she remained haunted by his last words, 'Brave Emma, Heroic Emma, you encourage me to go forth. If there were more Emmas, there would be more Nelsons.' Perhaps, or maybe she was making another claim upon the nation's gratitude. Whatever, finally Nelson stood at the chaise door in the dark with George Matcham, ready to go. The admiral said that he was sorry he had not been able to do all for the family that he had hoped, but maybe this time he would bring back some prize money. George said that he wanted for nothing, and Nelson's safety was all that mattered. Then the door was closed, the last words spoken, and the chaise pulled away into the night.[38]

In his journal Nelson wrote, 'Friday night, at half-past ten drove from dear, dear Merton, where I left all which I hold dear in this world to go to serve my king and country. May the great god whom I adore enable me to fill the expectations of my country, and if it is His good pleasure that I should return, my thanks will never cease being offered up to the throne of His mercy. If it is His good providence to cut short my days upon earth, I bow with the greatest submission, relying that He will protect those so dear to me that I leave behind. His will be done. Amen, amen, amen.'[39]

XXIV

'FOR CHARITY'S SAKE, SEND US LORD NELSON!'

Let's hope this glorious battle will bring a peace,
That our trade in England may prosper and
increase;
And our ships from port to port go free
As before let us with them agree,
May this turn the heart of our enemy.
Huzza, my brave boys!

Nelson's Death and Victory, *c.*1805

I

At six in the morning of Saturday, 14 September, a carriage was pulled into the yard of the George Inn on the High Street, opposite Portsmouth Cathedral, and a tired admiral stepped down. Among those there to meet him was the Reverend Lancaster and his fourteen-year-old son, Henry, who had made a separate journey from Merton. Lancaster tenderly delivered Henry into the admiral's care, ready to begin his training as a 'boy, first class' in the *Victory*. Then the pastor received a note for Emma, notifying her of Nelson's safe arrival, and made his return journey.[1]

Outside the George the ubiquitous crowds hovered. A flag hoisted on one of the churches announced the admiral's presence, and passengers on incoming ships were said to have hastily summoned boats to take them to the hero. After breakfast Nelson made a sortie to the residence of the dockyard commissioner, his old acquaintance Sir Charles Saxton who doubtless apprised him that few of the promised reinforcements had yet arrived. Of thirteen ships that were supposed to be joining Nelson, only the *Victory* and Blackwood's frigate *Euryalus* were here ready to sail. Nelson returned to the George and three guests who had come to see him, George Rose and his wife, who had travelled from their home in Hampshire, and the new treasurer of the navy, George Canning, a rising star in the political firmament. There were also letters, one from Murray, who would have been with Nelson but for the death of his father. A gift of venison accompanied the letter, and Nelson scribbled a brief reply. 'May every success attend you, and health, that greatest of blessings.'[2]

During the day he pressed Rose on behalf of Emma, Bolton and himself, disabusing him of any misconceptions about the size of the Nelson fortune. He had nothing but Merton and £15,000 in government stocks, and debts would wipe out the latter. The conversation must have been encouraging, because Nelson wrote to Emma, asking her to stop Perry from publishing a planned attack on the government, designed to rally public outrage at the inadequacy of the admiral's rewards. Such a notice might crush Rose's suit in the egg. Rose was genuinely moved, and convinced that Pitt would do something. Canning was in awe of the hero, and Nelson thought him 'a very clever deep-headed man' also worthy of confidences. At ten both politicians, with Rear Admiral Sir Isaac Coffin, the port admiral, set off with Nelson for the *Victory*. To avoid the crowds they left by a small livery entrance in Penny Street, and passed along Green Row to Governor's Green, where they took up a path that led through the sally port in the ramparts of the Long Curtain. A footbridge to the Spur Redoubt and another sally port brought the party to the beach by some bathing machines, but hundreds of spectators waited in ambush. As the boat enclosing Nelson, Rose and Canning was pushed off, and the flashing oars found their rhythm, three great cheers rose from the watchers and the man from Burnham Thorpe swept off his hat in farewell. He arrived on board his flagship at about 11.30. Rose and Canning remained some time but when they parted Nelson again 'earnestly entreated' the former 'to use every exertion' and Rose promised to speak to Pitt at 'the earliest opportunity'.[3]

The *Victory* had received some attention during the last few weeks. Guns, sails, masts and yards had been inspected, the ballast and hold purified, the timber scrubbed, caulked and painted and the rigging renewed. Nelson's cabin had been refurbished. Water and provisions were stowed, and most of the old faces were on board, including those of the Scotts. With the combined Franco-Spanish fleet crammed into Cadiz and the British waiting outside, the sense of a coming battle pervaded the fleet as it did the nation. Events seemed to be sweeping towards a grand but uncertain climax. Nelson brought his usual appetite to the command, and told Rose that his new motto was 'touch and take'. It had, of course, always been his policy to close with opponents in order to defeat them, but he seemed to like the alliterative ring of his new coinage, and repeated it, along with the more famous but perhaps derivative 'Nelson touch'. Sending his plan of attack to Ball, Nelson called it 'the Nelson touch, and he hoped it would be touch and take'. On 25 September, Nelson made his first reference to the 'Nelson touch' in a letter to Emma, remarking on his impatience to reach his station before Villeneuve broke out, for 'it would add to my grief if any other man was to give them the Nelson touch, which *we* say is warranted never to fail'.[4]

At eight o'clock the following morning *Victory* and *Euryalus* weighed and sailed with a slight breeze, passing down the Solent and into the Channel. The wind remained poor, as if England was loath to lose sight of her favourite son, and on Tuesday the ships were no further than Portland. When the breeze freshened it was WSW, but Nelson was off Plymouth on the 17th, signalling ships waiting for him there to join. The next day the *Ajax* and *Thunderer* found him in calmer weather off the Lizard, and the three ships of the line and a frigate steered south-west with a human cargo more precious to the fleet than gold. Still believing that his mission would be brief, and that Christmas might see him home, Nelson consoled his loved ones. 'I entreat, dear Emma, that you will cheer up, and we [will] look forward to many, many happy years, and be surrounded by our children's children,' he wrote on the 17th. Then ungenerously, 'God Almighty can, when he pleased, remove the impediment [to marriage, meaning Fanny]. My heart and soul is with you and Horatia.' Still, torn between that old longing for naval glory, and the new domesticity, etched in his mind by those final images of a sleeping Horatia, a tearful Emma and an English paradise fading in the twilight of a late summer, he also found time for local news. 'Thomas seems to do very well, and [is] content,' he informed Emma. 'Tell Mr Lancaster that I have no doubt that his son will do very well.'[5]

Little that was noteworthy happened on the outward trip. A man was lost overboard, and Hardy punished thick and fast, administering floggings in batches of up to eight. Using thirty-six lashes as a standard punishment, he was compelled to answer severer misdemeanours with ferocious penalties, and a private in the marines received seventy-two strokes for theft. Despite a lack of finesse, Hardy was widely acknowledged to be 'very superior in his station', but twenty-seven-year-old Lieutenant Yule, who had served with him in three ships, thought he had 'little consideration' for his men.[6]

On Friday, 20 September, thirty leagues south-west of Scilly, a frigate emerged from a swath of dirty weather. She was the *Decade* from Cadiz, and Nelson's face fell as he contemplated what dispatches she might carry. 'If the battle has been fought I shall be sadly vexed,' he told Emma. In fact, the frigate carried Bickerton, who had resigned his acting command of the Mediterranean after suffering a relapse of health. But he had good news, for the enemy had still been in Cadiz when he left. His major worry alleviated, Nelson's mind focused on other anxieties, including the relatively unknown material among the captains of the fleet. The admiral did not doubt that duty would be done, but wrote to the Admiralty asking whether Lord Henry Paulet and Captain Robert Otway, Baltic veterans who had wanted to serve with him, might be released. He was also worried that news of his approach would reach the enemy and frighten them into abandoning the idea of leaving port. Letters went to the British consul at Lisbon and Captain Sutton, commanding in the Tagus, seeking as many recruits for the fleet as they could muster, and warning them that word of his coming should be kept confidential. The *Euryalus* made her way forward with a dispatch for 'my dear Coll' off Cadiz, directing that no colours should be displayed to herald his arrival, nor salutes fired. Another caution went to Gibraltar, where Fox was asked to keep Nelson's appointment out of the local *Gazette*.[7]

Nelson was hoping for a short campaign, but he could not bank on it, and men and supplies remained crucial. The French and Spanish coasts were hostile, and even England's own ally Portugal was bending to the constant importunities of her powerful neighbours, and citing a 'secret' treaty with Spain to justify withholding provisions from the British in an attempt to expel them from their ports. Nelson confronted the new threat to his communication line by informing Britain's man in Lisbon that his king could have no truck with 'infamous or degrading treaties' but looked for existing obligations to be 'fulfilled in the most liberal manner'. There would be retaliation if British ships were denied water or if they were received by warlike deeds or words. It was not a matter about which he could equivocate. Portugal provided recruits for an undermanned fleet as well as provisions and medicinal supplies, and Cape St Vincent – part of that realm – was the appointed base for the cruisers that Nelson had arranged to protect his communications. All of these services were needed if he was to keep his fleet off Cadiz and protect reinforcements coming from home.[8]

Light airs delayed Nelson awhile off Lisbon, but the news from ashore put the enemy fleet in Cadiz a week before, and he confidently advanced to Cape St Vincent to position the first cruisers in his communication line. John Sykes of the *Nautilus*, who was intercepted carrying Collingwood's dispatches home, was reassigned to cruise off the Cape to collect intelligence, safeguard the rear and usher forward any reinforcements. Another vessel, the *Juno*, would be posted off Cape Spartel by early October. So situated, these ships were singularly well placed to forewarn Nelson of the approach of any enemy forces, either from the north or the south.

Noon of 28 September brought Nelson in sight of the first of Collingwood's ships, and he joined the fleet about six the same evening. Collingwood had half a dozen capital ships inshore watching Cadiz, and twenty out at sea, blockading a superior Franco-Spanish fleet of thirty-seven ships of the line, massed in the inner harbours that hid snugly behind an arm of the isle of Cadiz as it swept in a circuitous fashion across the southern half of the bay. If they chose to remain, it would be hard to shift them, as Nelson knew from his unsuccessful bombardments of 1797, and perhaps Layman's plan for an attack on Cadiz came to mind. Irrespective, the sight of the combined fleet securely behind the steeples of Cadiz was as good a birthday gift as the admiral could have imagined.

The following day was Sunday, 29 September, and Nelson had reached the age of forty-seven. He had only another twenty-two days to live.

2

Nelson's greatest problem was to prise Villeneuve out, but unknown to the British it had already been solved – by Napoleon.

The combined fleet had been in Cadiz since 22 August. Villeneuve had returned to Europe burdened with sick, and even after discharging numerous invalids in Vigo he had to establish two field hospitals in Cadiz. At the end of September some seventeen hundred men aboard the French and Spanish ships were still sick, and in the following month the French ships were short of 2207 hands, despite the use of raw recruits, black prisoners from the West Indies and several thousand troops, who, if useless as seamen, could at least man fighting tops and guns and form boarding parties. In some ships 50 per cent of the crew were infantrymen. Villeneuve had a sound but insufficient core, some sharpened up in gunnery exercises by Latouche Tréville, but neither time nor opportunity to weave a satisfactory fabric of the whole. He shook his head at the sight of fine ships manned by 'herdsmen and beggars'. As for the Spanish fleet, its men had been scratched together from fever-ridden ports and wasted on the Atlantic voyage, but the admiral, Don Frederico Gravina, fielded a select fifteen adequately manned vessels. His main shortages were in trained gunners and hands experienced in war, for relatively few of his men had seen serious naval action. Provisions and naval stores were also scarce in Cadiz. Winter was coming, Spain was in financial crisis and the merchants were refusing the dubious drafts and paper money tendered by the French. It took the arrival of a newly appointed agent victualler from Paris, ambassadorial pressure in Madrid, government loans, several orders from Godoy and a transfusion of cash to lubricate what meagre supplies could be found. Nor were relations between the allied fleets satisfactory. In addition to the practical difficulties of coordinating forces divided by language, tradition and practice, there was a feeling amongst the Spaniards that Villeneuve had failed to support them during the action with Calder, which cost them the only two ships lost in the fighting. Some Spaniards also realised that the war was none of their making, and they were oxen being led to slaughter by an admiral they did not respect and for a cause in which they had no interest. Villeneuve's stock was even falling in his own force, and the military in particular shared Napoleon's view that he was a coward. Not least, both French and Spanish admirals knew that unless they were greatly favoured by numbers they could not win a battle with the British. Gravina had long since acknowledged the superior gunnery of the Royal Navy, which he attributed to their better carriages and replacement of the slow match with the firing lock. He had once even visited England and inspected Portsmouth dockyard.[9]

Reservations aside, on 14 September Napoleon issued new orders to his diffident admiral. The cooperation between Britain and Russia in the Mediterranean, the Russian military and naval build-up in the Adriatic and Craig's expedition to Italy were all beginning to worry the emperor. He now insisted that the combined fleet leave Cadiz and sail through the Strait to support the French army under St Cyr, which looked dangerously isolated in Italy. Villeneuve received his fresh orders on the 27th, two days before Nelson's arrival. The port was enlivened and troops began embarking, but with little enthusiasm. Then October brought two new pieces of intelligence. Despite Nelson's precautions, the arrival of his three ships of the line had been spotted from the enemy's signal stations, and on 2 October word from Lisbon revealed the identity of their commander. To add to Villeneuve's innumerable perplexities, he now knew that Nelson was out there, waiting to destroy him. In the ensuing days it also became clear that Napoleon had lost all faith in him, and sent Admiral François-Etienne Rosily-Mesros, an uninspiring elderly hydrographer, to Cadiz to succeed him and inflict a humiliating dismissal.

On 8 October the leaders of the combined fleet held a tempestuous council of war in Villeneuve's flagship, the *Bucentaure*, and decided to postpone sailing. Gales were predicted, and, clutching at straws, the allied commanders hoped that the British might be driven from their station or at least weakened, and present an opportunity to escape. If the predicted storms did not scatter the British, maybe shortages of food and water would compel them to relax their blockade in order to forage. Moreover, if the combined fleet put to sea in the teeth of the impending storms, the badly handled and hurriedly prepared ships would be thrown into chaos. It made sense to bide time, putting the ships in order and waiting for a better opportunity. Sometimes those opportunities rode on the tail end of a gale, in the brief space between the weather clearing up and the blockading ships regrouping. Ideally, Villeneuve needed an easterly wind to get his ships out of Cadiz, and then a westerly to make the Strait. But however the cards were cut, with Napoleon pushing from behind and Nelson waiting ahead, the French admiral held a singularly dismal hand.

Out at sea his British counterpart found much more to his satisfaction. True, he had fewer ships, but they were of an altogether different stamp from those of the combined fleet. Seven had been part of the Mediterranean fleet, *Victory*, *Canopus*, *Tigre*, *Conqueror*, *Leviathan*, *Donegal* and *Spencer*, still displaying their characteristic black and yellow chequerboard paintwork, and Nelson could speak for them, albeit that the last was now riddled with scurvy. The *Spartiate* had crossed the Atlantic with Nelson, and in command of three of the remaining ships were two tested and trusty colleagues with whom Nelson had forged particularly close bonds, Collingwood, whose flag flew in the *Dreadnought*, and Fremantle of the *Neptune*. Other old shipmates were scattered throughout the fleet, some who had grown much in the years since he had last seen them. A twenty-six-year-old lieutenant of the *Defence* had been one of Nelson's 'young gentlemen' in the *Captain* and *Theseus*, George Kippen. Others were less familiar. There were four flag officers: Collingwood and another vice admiral, the unfortunate Calder, in the *Prince of Wales*, and two rear admirals, Thomas Louis, one of the brothers, whose flag still few above the *Canopus*, and William Carnegie,

Earl of Northesk, of the *Britannia*, one of four patricians in the higher command. All the admirals were inferior to Nelson in naval rank, but older in years. Calder had been born in 1745, Collingwood in 1748, Northesk in 1756 and Louis in 1758. Most of the captains in the fleet were in their forties, and in some respects might be held to have lacked experience. Of the twenty-seven who would take ships of the line into the melee off Trafalgar, only five had captained a capital ship prior to their present command, and only five had held their present commands since 1803. Few had been in a significant action, but all had been schooled in serious seafaring in the Channel or Mediterranean fleets.[10]

Nelson took command of twenty-nine ships of the line, which Collingwood had divided into two detachments, the smaller an inshore squadron under Louis that beat back and forth off Cadiz, and the other about fifteen miles offshore. These were the dispositions of the close blockade, designed to keep opponents in port, but inimical to Nelson's intentions of drawing them out and into battle. Immediately upon taking command on 29 September, Nelson redeployed his force so that it created uncertainty in the minds of his enemies and encouraged them to attempt an escape. Louis's detachment was withdrawn into the fleet, and the whole stood much further out, some fifty nautical miles to the west, well beyond the reach of the snooping signal towers. Nelson hoped to prevent Villeneuve from seeing the arrival of expected reinforcements, or indeed whether the British ships were in the offing or no, in order to draw him out. By taking a position further out to sea, he also minimised the danger of being swept towards the Strait by powerful westerly winds, a fate that had once overcome Keith's ships off Cadiz, and placed himself to intercept any French reinforcements from the northward. Thus far, then, it was the open blockade Nelson had employed off Toulon, but now he improved it in accordance with the hard lessons learned in the spring. A first-class officer was needed to lead a detachment of cruisers tasked with watching Cadiz and maintaining a chain of communication to the main fleet. Blackwood was the ideal captain, enterprising, diligent and sensible, and one, moreover, thoroughly acquainted with Nelson's plans. On the voyage out he had been on board the *Victory* at least four times. At first Nelson could give Blackwood only two frigates, *Euryalus* and *Hydra*, and they adopted an inshore cruising position about five or six miles from the enemy fleet and its surrounding flotilla of gunboats. But other ships were necessary, and Nelson did something he had deplored in the spring; he wrote to Admiral Knight, stationed at Gibraltar, asking him to part with the *Phoebe*.

Having made his initial dispositions, Nelson got down to winning over his principal officers and explaining his ideas, now for the last time. Fremantle saw the fleet reverberate with a new 'energy and activity'. On the whole it rejoiced at Nelson's arrival, eager to become part of his story. Collingwood was the perfect partner. A sensitive, introspective man, he was middle-aged but spare, with steady blue eyes that illuminated a round, homely and disarming countenance. In his articulate letters he revealed humanity and his ability to balance a love of his profession with the leavening influence of home. If Nelson's heart was in Merton, Collingwood's had long been in Morpeth, Northumberland, where his wife Sarah and two daughters passed beneath oaks and poplars that he had planted with his own hands, and the common sounds were those of garden songbirds and the creaking of wagons rattling by at dawn. A piece of that home was with him in the cabin of his flagship, his faithful dog, Bounce. Collingwood lacked Nelson's fire, decision and amiability, weaknesses that detracted from his abilities as a fighting admiral, but his measured judgement made him an extremely effective diplomat, administrator and commander-in-chief. Reserved and aloof, he had relatively few friends. Edward Codrington of the *Orion*, one of the captains off Cadiz, called him 'another stay-on-board admiral who never communicates with anybody but upon service', and whose refusal to allow boats to put out not only flattened inter-ship visiting but also blighted private attempts to purchase fresh fruit from local traffickers. 'For charity's sake, send us Lord Nelson, ye men of power!' Codrington cried in a letter to his wife. The hero did not disappoint. One of the first acts of the new commander-in-chief was an order that boats might be lowered to allow officers to replenish their tables. The 'whole system' was 'completely changed', wrote Codrington, as 'a general joy' spread through the fleet. He rejoiced that he had lived to meet 'a commander-in-chief' who endeavoured 'to make a hard and disagreeable service as palatable . . . as circumstances will admit'. Inasmuch as Nelson was concerned, this was far from an unrepresentative view, and the admiral described his reception as 'the sweetest sensation of my life'.[11]

The day Nelson took over the fleet he began inviting his captains to dine with him in batches, introducing himself in an informal way and drawing them into his plans for the great task that lay ahead. The first consignment of captains arrived on 29 September, when several old acquaintances embraced the admiral in a flood of emotion. Fremantle, who called with the junior captains the following afternoon, recalled that he had 'never spent a pleasanter day'. Nelson brought him the news of the birth of a child. Would Fremantle prefer a boy or a girl, teased the commander-in-chief? Fremantle wanted a girl, as Nelson knew, and was happily informed that his wish had been granted. Nelson also promised that Fremantle would have his 'old place in the line of battle, which is second', and 'desired me to come to him whenever I choose, and to dine with him so often as I could make it'. Captain George Duff, a voluminous, fair-haired Scot from Banff who commanded the *Mars*, wrote home after the 'very merry dinner' on 30 September to speak of a chief he little knew. 'He is so good and pleasant a man that we all wish to do what he likes, without any kind of orders. I have been myself very lucky with most of my admirals, but I really think the present the pleasantest I have met with.' The night after the second dinner Nelson woke at four in the morning with one of his 'dreadful spasms'. It may have been indigestion, but Nelson blamed the seven hours of writing that had engaged him the previous day, and was sure that the disorder would one day be his death. Feeling 'weak', he dined quietly that afternoon with Collingwood and Louis, but two days later was inviting Captain Eliab Harvey of the *Temeraire* to the flagship, desiring 'an opportunity of cultivating your acquaintance'.[12]

The one personnel problem concerned Sir Robert Calder, the oldest flag officer in the fleet. The letters Nelson brought had alerted Calder to the hammering he was taking back home for his scrappy battle with Villeneuve. He immediately demanded a court martial. It was not unexpected, but in 'a very distressing' interview, Nelson advised Calder to withdraw his request, knowing the ordeal that awaited him, and suspecting that he would not emerge from it unscathed. 'He is in adversity, and if he ever has been my enemy, he now feels the pang of it, and finds me one of his best friends.' But the older man would not relent. Although Calder and Collingwood had received their flags on the same day in 1799, it was the younger admiral who had been entrusted with the supreme command off Cadiz, and the arrival of Nelson, whom Calder had long thought an upstart, rubbed salt in the wound by pushing him further down the pecking order. He insisted on returning to England, and with a surprising insensitivity asked if he might depart in his flagship, the ninety-gun *Prince of Wales*. He was 'cut . . . to the soul' at the thought of being 'turned out' of his ship, but to expect a commander-in-chief to surrender one of his few big three-deckers in the shadow of a crucial battle with a superior fleet was downright irresponsible. Barham expected him to use a frigate, but Nelson granted the boon. Fearing the Admiralty would censure him for disobeying their orders, he explained that 'I trust that I shall be considered to have done right as a man, and to a brother officer in affliction. My heart could not stand it, and so the thing must rest.' Unfortunately, the matter did not stop there. Calder asked some of the captains to return with him to bear witness to his conduct, and Nelson had to appoint acting officers to the *Ajax* and *Thunderer*. Durham of the *Defiance*, who arrived from England to join Nelson, was also named a witness but flatly refused to accompany Calder. Calder urged Nelson to order Durham home, but the commander-in-chief declined to do so. He saw that the request was, apart from anything else, counter-productive. Durham had fought for the opportunity to join the fleet, and would only have painted an unfavourable picture of Calder if he had been forced to forgo it.[13]

Within a few days Nelson had taken a vital step in preparing his fleet for a battle in which they would be outnumbered and outgunned. In this, his reputation had been a great help. His name was synonymous with victory, as if he could ordain it by some baffling act of prestidigitation. Midshipman Henry Walker told his mother that Nelson filled men with so much 'additional confidence' that 'everyone felt himself more than a match for any enemy'. Thomas Atkinson, master of the *Victory*, newly qualified to handle a first-rate ship, fully expected that 'we shall at least take half the combined fleet'. To advertise the fleet's new identity, the admiral had the ships painted in his regimental black and yellow, 'à la Nelson' as Duff put it, creating a visual symbol of unity and purpose. It was practical, too, helping ships to distinguish friend from foe in a smoke-filled conflict. The lower masts of the British ships were painted yellow, including the hoops, which the French daubed in black. Most significant of all, Nelson used those introductory dinners to impart the basic elements of his plan of battle, gathering his captains behind their common objective and enabling them to predict what his intentions would be on the day.[14]

Two accounts have come to us, both through Nelson, and therefore almost certainly exaggerated. Yet their gist is consistent with other evidence. In one the admiral flattered himself that his plan had been 'clearly perceived and understood' as well as 'generally approved'. The more famous narrative was penned in a letter to Emma on 1 October: 'I believe my arrival was most welcome, not only to the commander of the fleet [Collingwood], but also to every individual in it, and when I came to explain to them the Nelson touch, it was like an electric shock. Some shed tears, all approved. "It was new, it was singular, it was simple!" And from the admirals downwards, it was repeated, "It must succeed, if ever they will allow us to get at them. You are, my Lord, surrounded by friends who you inspire with confidence."'[15]

This unanimity and spirit was essential because Nelson was committed to fighting an extraordinary battle. The expected reinforcements would give him the most powerful fleet he had ever wielded, and it would take on the combined strength of the second and third navies of the world. What was coming was more than a battle. It was a matter of national survival. Like every informed observer, Nelson discounted the idea of defeat, but had Britain suffered such a heavy blow, the safety of the realm would have been in the balance, for at this point Napoleon had postponed rather than abandoned his plans to invade. Nelson for one was sure that unless Napoleon received a severe check he would try to invade Britain 'some day or other'. Nor was a mediocre British victory acceptable. If the enemy fought their way into the Mediterranean, mauled or not, they could still seriously threaten weaker domains, such as Sardinia, Naples, Sicily and the Morea, or Craig's task force. All of Nelson's pertinent remarks in these tense weeks testify to his understanding that something overwhelmingly decisive was required, something capable of changing the war. A great victory could protect Britain from further threats of invasion; while it would not ensure that the British would ultimately win the war, it could almost guarantee that she would not lose it. Nelson was looking for an unparalleled success that would secure his country and succour Europe.[16]

He did not say, but implicitly understood, that there was even more at stake. For this was not so much a battle of three European nations, but of three worldwide empires. It was a struggle for the command of the sea, and all that it entailed. The ripples of the victory Nelson wanted would wash far beyond the petty confines of the European continent, or indeed the chronological limits of the present war.

He knew what the seas meant to Britain, but even he could not have guessed how crucially he was to bear upon the nineteenth century. For this, more than any other battle of the war, by land or sea, was the crucial contest for global domination.

Seldom had a British commander left his country with such a burden on his shoulders. He was intelligent enough to see some of those vast implications, and what failure might cost, and he knew it was going to be bloody. As he wrote to Davison, 'Day by day, my dear friend, I am expecting the [combined] fleet to put to sea – every day, hour and moment, and you may rely that, if it is within the power of man to get at them, that it shall be done, and I am sure that all my brethren look to that day as the finish of our laborious cruise. The event no man can say exactly, but I must think, or render great injustice to those under me, that, let the battle be when it may, it will never have been surpassed . . . If I fall on such a glorious occasion, it shall be my pride to take care that my friends shall not blush for me. These things are in the hands of a wise and just Providence, and His will be done . . . Do not think I am low-spirited on this account, or fancy anything is to happen to me. Quite the contrary, my mind is calm, and I have only to think of destroying our inveterate foe.'[17]

3

Letters were written to allies and colleagues in the Mediterranean, assuring them that Nelson would not neglect them, and that Britain would cooperate with the Austrian and Russian forces squaring up to the French. His first concern, however, was to keep his fleet in position and full fettle. The old problem of provisions had to be confronted again. Nelson got some supplies locally, sending a ship to Lagos for cattle and benefiting from the grapes and other commodities Portuguese traders brought to the fleet, and a few prizes yielded extras. The *Pickle*, a ten-gun schooner that arrived from England in October, took a ship trying to get into Cadiz with a cargo of Tetuan bullocks, and a week later *Phoebe* seized a Spanish schooner. 'All kinds of necessaries', including laundry services, were also sought from Gibraltar. Unfortunately, although at least three victuallers soon reached the fleet from Gibraltar, there were difficulties about a long-term large-scale supply. The community at the Rock drew many of its supplies from Morocco, but Admiral Knight, the local naval commander, had upset the Moorish merchants at Tetuan. Moreover, the King of Morocco had begun restricting beef exports and, given the limited supplies he allowed, the needs of Nelson's ships now clashed with those of the garrison at Gibraltar. It was essential that these obstacles were removed, but the British representative at Tangier, James Matra, was elderly, ill and inefficient.[18]

Early in October a number of victuallers from England arrived in the fleet, and the slow business of clearing them of four months' provisions began. Unfortunately, they had no fresh water, and by the middle of the month Nelson's ships were running low. Fresh provisions were also needed, especially as the *Spencer* and *Zealous* had dozens of cases of scurvy and fever. Remembering the near-disastrous escapes of the Toulon fleet, Nelson decided that his fleet would not retire to Gibraltar and Tetuan en masse, as it had to the Maddalenas. Rather detachments would leave on a rota basis, and Louis was directed to lead out the first, consisting of the *Canopus*, *Tigre*, *Queen*, *Spencer*, *Zealous* and *Endymion*. The latter was a frigate in desperate need of repairs to her mainmast and bowsprit, but the danger of this decision was that it weakened Nelson's presence off Cadiz semi-permanently. One wonders whether he needed to detach so large a force. Louis's detachment included a three-decker and two eighties. Yet the need itself was undeniable. With Louis went Richard Ford, the agent-victualler of the fleet. While Nelson would order Knight to welcome Moorish ships at Gibraltar, he relied upon Ford to restore those 'gentry' to 'good humour' and open supplies, and entrusted him with a royal letter and presents for the King of Morocco. Ford did not fail. He restored relations with Morocco, engaged a Moorish detachment to guard a watering place at Tetuan to ensure that Nelson's ships had permanent access, and concluded a contract to acquire cattle. As a result Louis's detachment was liberally supplied and the *Amphion* frigate also collected immediate provisions for the fleet, including onions and citrus fruits for the sick.[19]

Not all were pleased, however. Louis was miserable, especially as Nelson's order of battle had chosen his ship, the *Canopus*, to follow the *Victory* into battle. He and his flag captain, Francis Austen, dined with Nelson the day before their departure for Gibraltar and observed sadly that they might miss the battle. Nelson could say little in extenuation, but trusted that Louis would get his job done and return before the French made their move. The downcast rear admiral did as he was bidden on 3 October, but with a lifelong regret. His departure cut Nelson's capital force to only twenty-three sail.[20]

While Nelson awaited his reinforcements and a movement from the combined fleet, he completed his preparations. Copies of Popham's improved signal book were distributed to all captains, and a complicated table of recognition signals, based upon the positions ten different pendants could occupy in the rigging, was composed to help identify the large number of ships. An alternative system was created for use in battle, when visibility and the destruction of spars and cordage increased communication problems, and the fleet was briefed on the use of low-visibility signals such as blue lights and false fires.[21]

One worrying possibility was that Villeneuve would not leave Cadiz, but attempt to sit out the winter. The British gave thought to ways of encouraging them, especially as Blackwood was reporting that a dozen of their capital ships were anchored in a vulnerable position. Nelson considered bombarding them with Congreve rockets, or dislodging them with explosion vessels and fireships or the diabolical catamarans of 'Mr Francis'. His captains were inundated with volunteers willing to serve in the small boats needed for such dangerous work, and two bomb vessels, three fireships and two detachments of Royal Marine artillery were placed on stand-by. But in the end neither 'Francis' nor Congreve were sent to the fleet, largely because Nelson wrote to Castlereagh that he had 'little faith' in their inventions. Instead, he hoped to starve the combined fleet out. This was less than easy, since Villeneuve was still managing to import some commodities by sea despite Blackwood's inshore squadron. Cargoes from Nantes and Bordeaux were being loaded on to Danish neutrals and carried to local Spanish ports between Cape St Mary and the Strait, where they were transferred to shallow-draught coasters able to slip through shallows and offshore reefs to reach Cadiz. Nelson wrote home recommending that an order Collingwood had given to detain these neutrals be endorsed. Castlereagh did not like it, but agreed to the declaration of a formal blockade of the Spanish ports involved in the contraband trade, although by then Nelson had initiated the action on his own authority.[22]

Another anxiety, if a distant one, was that the Spanish squadron in Cartagena might emerge from the Strait and intervene. By 9 October, Blackwood's inshore squadron was up to strength with five frigates, a sloop and a schooner. 'I see you feel how my heart is set on getting at these fellows, whom I have hunted so long,' Nelson wrote to him, asserting his utmost confidence that they would not be allowed to 'slip through our fingers'. Blackwood adopted the practice of keeping the lighthouse at Cadiz under surveillance, since intelligence indicated that it would be lit if the Spaniards from Cartagena were expected to make a night-time dash through the blockade. Blackwood's service in the *Brilliant* and *Penelope* had been distinguished, but here in the *Euryalus* he had found his finest hour as the indispensable link between Nelson and the enemy fleet. Most appropriately, he as much as any officer was tuned to the same drum as his commander-in-chief, sharing his ambition 'to make the most decisive battle . . . that ever was'.[23]

On his part, Nelson established the chain of communication between Blackwood's cruisers and the fleet. Some fifty sea miles divided the two, and the admiral detached an intermediate squadron of capital ships to fill the void, choosing as its commander Captain Duff of the *Mars*. Duff was over forty, with unspectacular but solid experience in British and West Indian waters, but he was to perform more than adequately. The *Mars*, *Defence* and *Colossus* took a station twelve miles east of the fleet, closer to Cadiz, ready to fall back upon Nelson or advance towards Blackwood as necessary. One of Duff's ships would be thrown in advance, towards the most westerly of Blackwood's frigates. If the enemy came out, Blackwood's alert would pass along the line to the most westerly of Duff's ships, which would rush it to the fleet, firing signal guns by day or night to give the earliest possible alarm. On 14 October, Nelson reinforced Duff with the newly arrived *Agamemnon*, commanded by the erratic Berry, and Duff divided his squadron into two. The *Defence* and *Agamemnon* stood nearest to Blackwood, while a little further west the *Mars* and *Colossus* occupied a position fifteen miles from the fleet. Berry, who owed his appointment to Nelson, had an ambiguous reputation. He lacked initiative as an officer, but was courageous in arms and had the reputation of being a lucky captain, having been at Cape St Vincent, the Nile and the taking of the *Généreux* and *Guillaume Tell*. In times of uncertainty, as Blackwood remarked, 'such [a] bird of good fortune' seemed a good omen.[24]

Louis's departure left Nelson at his weakest, and desperate for the promised reinforcements. On about 5 October intelligence gathered by the inshore squadron indicated that the combined fleet was ready to sail. The French and Spanish ships had begun embarking troops, and it was said that they only wanted a good easterly wind to attempt a breakout. Alarmingly, that wind arrived on the 5th, creating a tense period of disturbing possibilities. The easterly gave Villeneuve an opportunity to leave Cadiz, and furthermore, if the Spanish squadron at Cartagena really did have a mind to reinforce him, it would have found the same wind useful for pushing towards the Strait. Nelson fired letters to Barham, Marsden, Castlereagh and Rose with not inconsiderable urgency, telling them that if they wanted the victory he had promised he needed their reinforcements, ships both large and small. As he told Rose, 'it is, as Mr Pitt knows, *annihilation* that the country wants, and not merely a splendid victory of twenty-three to thirty-six, honourable to the parties concerned but absolutely useless in the extended scale to bring Bonaparte to his marrow bones. *Numbers* can only annihilate.'[25]

Nelson's luck held, however. Easterly or not, neither Villeneuve nor the Cartagena squadron moved, and during the second week of October some of the British reinforcements trickled in, the *Defiance*, *Royal Sovereign*, *Belleisle*, *Agamemnon* and *Africa* from home and the *Leviathan* from Gibraltar. Of the *Superb* and *Barfleur*, which were also expected, there was no sign, and when the *Prince of Wales* left for England with the forlorn Calder on 14 October, and the *Donegal* sailed for Gibraltar to collect a ground-tier of casks and undergo speedy repairs three days later, the twenty-seven ships of the line that remained were those that Nelson would take into the battle of Trafalgar. Barham's order to Vice Admiral Duckworth to join Nelson with the *Superb*, *Powerful* and *Acasta* ('if ready') was not written until 28 October, a week after the battle had been fought. Against Nelson's twenty-seven capital ships, the French and Spaniards in Cadiz had – if Blackwood's reconnaissance of 8 October could be replied upon – thirty-four ships of the line, including three three-deckers and nine cruisers.[26]

The *Royal Sovereign*, which arrived on 8 October and became Collingwood's new flagship, brought Nelson a cash reserve for the use of his fleet and secret orders dated 21 September. They reminded him of what he already knew, that his remit included the protection of Craig's force, with which he was to maintain communication. In replying on 10 October Nelson pointedly observed that communication depended upon cruisers, of which he also had far too few. Those he had were constantly being lost to duty. One went home with Calder and another to Algiers. Two of his frigates were used to take a convoy and part of the fleet's money to Gibraltar and Malta; on 15 October Nelson had to send an additional order after Louis, asking him to extend his mission to ensure that the convoy got safely past Cartagena.[27]

Considering the constant need for small ships in the Mediterranean, Nelson had understandably used his enhanced status in London to stipulate what he would need in the way of cruisers. A figure of thirty-two frigates, sloops and brigs had been agreed with Barham, of which only twenty-two were currently available. Weighing it up, Nelson now decided that he had understated his requirements, and added nine more cruisers to the list. In all, he wanted forty-one. His purpose, he said, was not to demand the 'impossible', but to offer an honest assessment of need, leaving their lordships at the Admiralty to provide what they could in the knowledge that 'whatever force' could be 'spared' he would 'do all in my power to make the most of them'. However, he did inform Castlereagh that 'the last fleet was lost to me for want of frigates. God forbid this should!'[28]

The secret orders brought by the *Royal Sovereign* added at least one crucial piece of intelligence: although Craig was based at Malta, his troops might operate on the Italian mainland. This strengthened Nelson's conviction that the combined fleet would be ordered to the Mediterranean. He warned Blackwood that Villeneuve would probably use an easterly to clear Cadiz and run south, and then try to catch a westerly at the mouth of the Strait to take him through. However, said he, 'watch all points, and all winds and weathers'.[29]

The showdown seemed close now, and on 10 October Nelson almost convinced himself that the enemy would run that night. Their fleet had gathered towards the mouth of the harbour, and showed every indication of sailing. A spate of orders went out to the British captains to prepare them for imminent chase and battle. Any damage to their ships at this moment could be costly, and Nelson cautioned his officers to shorten sail and take down topgallant yards and masts at night so they would not be caught out by sudden gales. The admiral also reminded the captains to keep accurate records of the families of dead and wounded seamen, so that they could be contacted by the Patriotic Fund for the injured and bereaved. The same day Nelson dined with Collingwood, reviewing the battle plan one more time, but the night that followed was tense. The British were not entirely mistaken, because Villeneuve had ordered his fleet to prepare to sail, but the weather began to deteriorate, with strong westerlies whipping up, and he changed his mind. For seven days the westerlies blew and the combined fleet remained in port, while Blackwood's hungry watch prowled offshore.[30]

4

On Wednesday, 9 October, Nelson dispatched a document to Collingwood. 'I send you my plan of attack,' he wrote to his second-in-command. 'It is to place you perfectly at ease respecting my intentions, and to give full scope to your judgement for carrying them into effect. We can, my dear Coll, have no little jealousies. We can have only one great object in view, that of annihilating our enemies and getting a glorious peace for our country. No man has more confidence in another than I have in you, and no man will render your services more justice than your very old friend, Nelson and Bronte.' Nelson had consulted Collingwood in finalising his plan, and sent a copy of the written version, a paper commonly known as 'the Nelson memorandum'. To further demonstrate his confidence in Collingwood, Nelson sent a trunk of papers relating to their task. Collingwood at least assimilated the memorandum, and distributed copies to his captains in a meeting held to 'converse on the general plan to be executed'.[31]

It was a remarkable document. Other admirals, including Hood and Collingwood, had avowed the complete destruction of the enemy fleet as their objective, but it was unusual to plan an encounter in such detail, and even more unusual to frame it in a written memorandum. Apart from St Vincent, who provided sketches of potential battle tactics, Nelson's attempt to prepare his captains has few precedents. It was, however, a defining characteristic of a man who placed so much emphasis upon communication. He would never have understood those commanders, even great ones such as Napoleon, who were happy to go into battle with their plans locked in their heads.

At this stage Nelson assumed that his battle force might rise to forty or so ships, and that the combined fleet might field as many as forty-six, but in most respects the memorandum reflected verbal and written statements he had been making since 1803. It was not a precise blueprint, but an ideal, suggesting how his basic principles would apply in suitable circumstances. The attack assumed that the British fleet would have the advantage of the wind, and the enemy force would be to leeward, travelling in the same direction in a line-ahead formation. Nelson planned to strike quickly, confusing the enemy about his intentions to paralyse him if he could, but intent upon breaking through the hostile line at several points to create a series of close-quarter duels in which the British could engage from leeward and prevent their injured adversaries from retreating before the wind. No formalised exchange this, but a semi-chaotic melee in which the superior gunnery, seamanship and sense of direction and purpose of the British could count. Initially, Nelson hoped to mass force upon the enemy centre and rear, defeating it before the van could turn and support, but order would soon break down, and it was essential that the British captains possessed prior knowledge of the plan so that they could modify it to achieve the wanted result as circumstances demanded. If Nelson's plan succeeded, the combined fleet would be disadvantaged in every way. They would be outnumbered at the decisive point, outgunned and outmanoeuvred, and their command and control system entirely disrupted.[32]

Darkness was falling about six each evening, so Nelson preferred a morning attack, and to avoid squandering time and opportunities forming into battle he declared that the order of sailing would double as the order for battle. He intended to attack at speed, under full sail. The fleet would be divided into two lines of sixteen or so ships, one commanded by himself and the other by Collingwood, and if he had enough ships he would form a small reserve to use wherever circumstances dictated. Once the engagement commenced, Collingwood would have 'the entire direction of his line'.

Nelson assumed that the Franco-Spanish fleet would have an extended line of about forty-six capital ships. The British would approach from the rear in their two lines, possibly parallel to or forming an acute angle with the enemy line, with Collingwood's line furthest to leeward and nearer the enemy ships, and Nelson's abreast of it to windward. Divided, the British lines would be far shorter than Villeneuve's, but Nelson intended advancing until they covered the enemy centre and rear at extreme gun range before signalling Collingwood to bear up towards the combined fleet and make a direct attack upon the last twelve of the enemy ships under every stitch of canvas. It seems that Collingwood's ships were to perform this manoeuvre simultaneously, deploying first into a line abreast formation, and then bearing down upon the allied line, each ship steering to breach it behind the stern of her opposite number and then engaging from leeward. Probably some of the British ships would not be able to cut through, but 'they will always be at hand to assist their friends', and effectively put the enemy ships in a crossfire. This action would form the first focus of the battle, in which Collingwood's sixteen ships would overwhelm an inferior allied rear in a bruising point-blank encounter.

As Collingwood made his attack, Nelson would lead his line through the Franco-Spanish centre, while the flying reserve would strike the enemy even further forward with the primary intention of securing the French commander-in-chief. Together they would destroy the enemy centre and prevent it from intervening in Collingwood's battle, and, because the Franco-Spanish van could turn only slowly, Nelson hoped to master some twenty-six enemy ships with his forty and screen the prizes before a credible rescue could be mounted. If, however, the decapitated enemy van did make a late attack, Nelson would effectively fight a second battle, and had 'no fears as to the result'.

The attack was designed to confuse the enemy, committing Collingwood's lee line to action, while leaving the intentions of Nelson's windward line and the flying column momentarily unclear. When Nelson introduced a new flag, 'yellow with blue fly', as the signal for Collingwood to deploy, he explained that he would 'probably advance his fleet to the van of theirs before he makes the signal, in order to deceive the enemy by inducing them to suppose it is his intention to attack their van'. But confusion could never be entirely eliminated from either side once the fleets had collided and intermingled in a sprawling, bloody, smoke-shrouded engagement. Inevitably, it would become an affair of numerous small but desperate encounters between ship and ship, or between one ship and two or three opponents. Once that point of the battle had been reached, signals and orders almost became redundant, and Nelson's advice for his captains was simple: 'no captain can do very wrong if he places his ship alongside that of an enemy.'[33]

The memorandum said little about the dangers of such an attack, which every officer must have appreciated. In particular, the final leg of the British attack, when the ships bore up to fall upon the enemy line, meant exposing their vulnerable bows, defended largely by bow and quarter guns, to the full broadside batteries of the enemy. That was the reason why Nelson stressed that this crucial move had to be performed under 'all sails, even steering sails . . . to get as quickly as possible to the enemy's line'. Anticipating also that his own, and possibly even Collingwood's line, might have to attack in a follow-my-leader style, with the ships hitting the enemy line one by one, Nelson placed some of his most heavily armed ships at the front, where they could absorb the greatest punishment and create shock impact.

The Nelson memorandum has rightly been regarded as the blueprint for Trafalgar, but the battle would be fought rather differently. It is the memorandum, however, that has often been acclaimed the finer conception. Its ideas were not new, and almost all the tactical elements had appeared before, in print as well as in action. The use of divisions harked back to the seventeenth century, when fleets were divided into squadrons, each under a flag officer, and they also marked the recent engagements of Duncan and Calder. The father of Collingwood's attack on the rear was surely Howe's plan of 1794, and the notion of attacking centre and rear had lately misfired under Calder. Nelson's idea of weighting the front of his lines with larger ships for shock impact could be found in Bigot de Morogues's *Tactique Navale*, published in 1763. These are just some possible prototypes. What Nelson had done was to distil from experience and theory usable principles and to tailor them into a meaningful whole. His judgement lay in the selection and arrangement of the materials. If there was originality in Nelson's attack, it lay perhaps in the freedom of action he conferred upon Collingwood once he had begun his final advance. But the whole reflected a salient feature of Nelson's management. Unlike most admirals who tried to control their battles with signals, Nelson had prepared his fleet to anticipate his intentions as far as possible, a process in which the memorandum played a pivotal role. It did not entirely work. One captain, Robert Moorsom, seemed unclear about what he was to do beyond the idea of breaking to leeward, and there would be more signals than Collingwood wanted or needed. But overall it must be accounted one of the finest elucidations a master warrior ever made of his trade.

The day after Nelson wrote his 'memorandum' he issued his orders of battle and sailing. This told each ship to which division, Nelson's or Collingwood's, she belonged, and what position she should ideally take in the line. Forming it, Nelson kept most of his old Mediterranean ships in his own line, but also took into account such slow-sailing giants as the *Prince*, *Britannia* and *Dreadnought*. The careful positioning of heavy ships was also plain. Nelson's 'van or starboard divison' was headed by the *Temeraire* (98), *Victory* (100) and *Neptune* (98), and Collingwood's 'rear or larboard division' by the *Prince* (98), *Mars* (74), *Royal Sovereign* (100) and *Tonnant* (80). There were later alterations to this order. The lumbering hundred-gun *Britannia* was removed from Collingwood's line to the rear of Nelson's, and the *Prince* joined the *Dreadnought*, both labouring ninety-eights, at the end of Collingwood's. There they would not slow down an attack, but might enliven a flagging action or defend the rear if the enemy van swung around more quickly than expected. Blackwood's *Euryalus* was given the job of repeating the flagship's signals, and handed authority over the other frigates. The captain later wrote that Nelson 'also gave me a latitude, seldom or ever given, that of . . . ordering any of the stern-most line of battle ships to do what struck me as best'. If true, Nelson authorised Blackwood to resuscitate the idea of a flying column by redeploying the lagging ships according to the progress of the action.[34]

5

Under the darkening sky the routine business of the fleet continued. On each ship discipline and day-to-day maintenance were conscientiously maintained. The commander-in-chief addressed the issue of his fleet's health, reiterating the measures that had been successful in the Mediterranean. Captains were authorised to purchase beef, lemons, onions and other fresh supplies providing they furnished the commander-in-chief with the standard vouchers. Pursers were warned that onions specifically supplied for medical purposes were not to be used in the regular vegetable soup and could only be accessed through the admiral's specific order, and masters that deliveries made to ships had to be authenticated against contractors' bills of lading or the advice notes of agent victuallers. Surgeons were ordered to send a full report with every patient invalided ashore. In those final days off Cadiz the transports were also cleared, leaving the fleet short only of water.

Nelson promoted efficiency and duty, but never drudgery. At no time, perhaps, was occasional relief from the thought of what lay ahead more welcome. 'I dined again with Lord Nelson a few days ago,' Fremantle wrote to his wife on 6 October, 'and sat with him until 8 o'clock, when he detained me to see a play that was performed by the seamen on board the *Victory*. I assure you, it was very well conducted, and the voice of the seaman who was dressed in great form and performed the female part was entertaining to a degree. We poor sloops have not ingenuity to attempt anything of the sort.'[35]

Nelson was also glad to see some reassuring old faces, and *Agamemnons* to boot. Berry arrived with the old ship herself, as well as his reputation for sniffing out action. 'Here comes Berry,' Nelson is reputed to have said. 'Now we shall have a battle!' Another reunion was with William Hoste, now commanding the *Eurydice* frigate. The young man soon made his presence felt, seizing several vessels, including a Spanish privateer, and when Sutton withdrew to England to recover his health Nelson rewarded him with the larger *Amphion*. Hoste thought the admiral 'as good a man as ever lived', but was disappointed at his first assignment at the helm of the *Amphion*. Nelson selected him to take some of the cash reserve to Gibraltar, and then to pay Algiers a goodwill visit. Just when a battle was expected! While Hoste sadly steered for the Strait, Nelson was able to pass the *Eurydice* to another old *Agamemnon*, William's former messmate Sir Billy Bolton. The appointment rescued Sir Billy from a depressing post in the *Guerrier* sheer-hulk at Gibraltar, and pleased the Bolton clan at home. Among other eleventh-hour boons to protégés, Nelson slotted two junior officers of the *Victory* into acting lieutenancies, sending Midshipman William Foster, a nephew of Lady Berry, to the *Colossus*, and Master's Mate Henry Jones to the *Eurydice*. Jones, Nelson told Marsden at the Admiralty, was 'a very valuable officer of great abilities and merit'.[36]

The oppressive workload left Nelson little time for quiet reflection, but he wrote his last-known love poem, which he entitled 'Henry (off Cadiz) to Emma'. Was there a sense that paradise had no sooner been found than it began disappearing in the world?

> No calm at sea this heart shall know,
> While far from thee, midst lengthening hours of absence and of woe,
> I gaze – in sorrow – o'er the boundless deep,
> With eyes which, were they not ashamed, would weep.

He meant it too, for he had little stomach for service beyond the battle. 'Poor man,' recalled a midshipman when it was all done. 'How he wished so much to see England again.'[37]

Among concerns that dragged his mind away from these sad reflections was the news on 14 October that half a dozen French ships of the line and half as many cruisers had escaped from Rochefort, commanded by Rear Admiral Zacharie Allemand, perhaps France's finest flag officer. Under normal circumstances Nelson would have delighted at the possibility of having a crack at another French detachment, but now it was merely an unwelcome complication in a much bigger game. At the very least Allemand could fall upon Nelson's communications. On 14 October, Nelson invited Collingwood to the *Victory* promising to enlighten him with 'all I know, and my intentions', and they doubtless agreed contingency plans.[38]

Then, at about midnight on Friday, 18 October, the wind at Cadiz shifted to the eastward, and the following morning Villeneuve ordered his fleet to sail. He had heard that Rosily had reached Madrid, apparently on his way to take over the fleet, and was determined to avoid a humiliating scene. But it was hot news from his telegraph that gave him a glimmer of hope. A British detachment (actually Louis's) had reached Gibraltar. That meant that Nelson's fleet, wherever it was stationed, was weakened. A thin rope had been thrown to the drowning Villeneuve and he seized it. At dawn on Saturday, 19 October the combined fleet began using a light north-easterly breeze to work out of harbour. It was a slow process, and the wind soon fell, leaving much of the fleet becalmed in the bay, but the following day a south-westerly enabled it to steer north-west to clear the coast before wearing and proceeding south-west.

Villeneuve's first movements on the 19th were seen by the *Sirius*, the British frigate closest inshore, and telegraphed to the *Euryalus*. By seven in the morning Blackwood had satisfied himself that the enemy was coming out, and excitedly signalled the *Naiad* further west, using three flags, a yellow diagonal cross on a blue ground, a flag of white and blue vertical stripes, and one of white and blue. It was signal 370, proclaiming that the enemy ships were leaving port or getting under sail, and the game was afoot! From *Naiad* it went to Capel's *Phoebe*, and then to the first ship of the line, the *Defence*, whose guns instantly tolled across the deep below her flying signals. By 9.30, little more than two hours after the combined fleet had begun to make sail, the news had reached Nelson, almost fifty miles WSW of Cadiz. This time his watch system had worked immaculately.

Neglecting nothing, Blackwood dispatched the *Weazle* brig to Gibraltar to find Louis, and the *Pickle* to Cape Spartel in search of the ship standing guard in that quarter. Either might otherwise have run into the combined fleet unawares. After alerting all relevant parties, Blackwood's job was to track the enemy force and use blue lights, signal guns and rockets to keep Nelson informed. At his service was Home Popham's improved telegraph system, and he managed to report hourly.[39]

The first news caught Nelson summoning some of his captains to the *Victory*, but he instantly signalled a 'general chase' to the south-east, supposing that the enemy would run for the Strait. Despite a feeble westerly wind, the fleet bustled as captains braced themselves to compete one against the other in a final race for glory. Nelson soon superseded the 'general chase' signal with an order to form order of sailing, and therefore of battle. In the first departure from his instructions, he allowed the formation to develop at the convenience of the captains. In other words, the ships were not to delay for the sake of creating the precise order planned, and the sluggish need not impede their consorts.

About noon Nelson sat quietly in his cabin, writing two letters. The first was to 'my dearest, beloved Emma, the dear friend of my bosom'. He scratched the bare details, that the enemy was coming out but the wind was so light that he did not expect to fight until tomorrow. 'May the God of Battles crown my endeavours with success,' he continued. 'At all events, I will take care that my name shall ever be most dear to you and Horatia, both of whom I love as much as my own life, and as my last writing before the battle will be to you, so I hope in God that I shall live to finish my letter after the battle.'[40]

He left the document open so that he could 'finish' it, and began another to his child. 'My dearest Angel, I was made happy by the pleasure of receiving your letter of September 19th, and I rejoice to hear that you are so very good a girl, and love my dear Lady Hamilton, who most dearly loves you. Give her a kiss for me. The combined fleet of the enemy are now reported to be coming out of Cadiz, and therefore I answer your letter, my dearest Horatia, to mark to you that you are ever uppermost in my thoughts. I shall be sure of your prayers for my safety, conquest and speedy return to dear Merton, and our dearest good Lady Hamilton. Be a good girl. Mind what Miss Connor says to you. Receive, my dearest Horatia, the affectionate, parental blessing of your father, Nelson & Bronte.' In this, which he knew might be his last, he unequivocally told Horatia that she was his daughter.[41]

Duff's squadron came in during the day, and that evening Nelson placed *Mars* at the head of a flying column consisting also of the *Orion*, *Belleisle*, *Leviathan*, *Bellerophon* and *Polyphemus* with orders to go ahead towards the Strait, carrying a light to guide those following. It was a tribute to the confidence Nelson had in so recent an acquaintance.

The dark morning of Sunday, 20 October found Nelson in the proximity of the Strait amidst mist, wind-driven rain and poor visibility. Yet there was no sign of the combined fleet, nor for that matter of Louis, who was then actually two hundred miles to the east, guiding the money consignment past Cartagena. The admiral was on tenterhooks, afraid that the enemy had retreated back into port, as he had done so often in the past. Not everyone was of a like mind; the master of the *Prince* found the idea rather comforting, given the greatly superior force of the combined fleet. For some time the British rode impatiently under close-reefed topsails, but there was a danger that westerlies might push the larger ships into the Strait, and Nelson wore his fleet and began retracing his steps towards the north-west in search of his enemy.[42]

Blackwood's frigates were still clinging like limpets to the skirts of the enemy armada, and at about seven in the morning the *Phoebe* arrived in Nelson's fleet signalling that the combined fleet was to the north. Relieved, Nelson realised that he now had to draw the enemy further out, away from the Cadiz bolthole, and to avoid playing his hand too soon. That morning Collingwood was rowed to the *Victory* for what would be his final meeting with his friend, and suggested that they proceed immediately to attack. But Nelson demurred. He saw the danger in starting an engagement late in the afternoon, when the days were so short, and more importantly of confronting the combined fleet while it was too close to Cadiz. A battle he would have, however. That same morning he telegraphed the *Africa* and *Belleisle*, ordering the hoops around their masts to be painted yellow so that they were uniform with the rest of the fleet.[43]

The looming encounter was going to be a huge smash-up. The Franco-Spanish fleet consisted of forty sail, thirty-three of them ships of the line. Villeneuve's flag flew from the *Bucentaure*, one of four eighty-gun ships in a force of fourteen French capital ships. The Spanish admiral, Gravina, was in the *Principe de Asturias* of 112 guns, and his force contained the world's largest warship, Nelson's old adversary, the four-decked *Santissima Trinidad* of between 130 and 140 guns, as well as another ship of 112 guns, one of 100 guns, and two of 80 guns. Against these Nelson could deploy twenty-seven ships of the line, half a dozen less than the enemy, four frigates, a schooner and a cutter. He had three three-deckers, the *Victory*, *Royal Sovereign* and *Britannia*, all rated at 100 guns. The *Temeraire*, *Neptune*, *Prince* and *Dreadnought* had nominal armaments of 98 guns, and the *Tonnant* was an 80. At the other end of the scale, though, Nelson fielded three underpowered sixty-fours to the enemy's one, and they had twenty-four- rather than thirty-two-pounders on their lower decks.

The details of men and armaments are imprecise, however. It seems clear that France and Spain had learned much from their previous defeats, and worked hard to increase the punching power of their ships by adding many mortars and carronades to their decks. The *Principe de Asturias* and *Santa Ana*, for instance, though rated at 112 guns each, may have carried 120. And the British had done likewise. Some of their seventy-fours, such as *Belleisle*, *Revenge*, *Achille* and *Colossus*, had been reinforced with enough carronades to give them a chance against three-deckers. The differences between the British and continental pounds in weight have also sometimes been overlooked in comparisons of armaments. Two things are certain. Both sides were unusually heavily armed, and the advantage lay with Villeneuve.

Nelson had 17,000 men and boys, about 2000 short of a full complement, whereas the enemy possessed 30,000. The Spaniards had manned all but two of their ships fully, and accounted for 11,847 of the total personnel of the combined fleet. According to a recent historian, Nelson's fleet carried some 2370 guns of all kinds to the combined fleet's 3237. Restricting the analysis to ships of the line gave Villeneuve a 33 per cent advantage in firepower.

In terms of the early nineteenth century the strength of both fleets was awesome. In one discharge Nelson's fleet could hurl some 23.2 tons of lethal metal with terrific force. A single broadside from the *Victory* alone, amounting to some 1148 lbs of shot, was equivalent to 67 per cent of Wellington's entire firepower at Waterloo. If the *Victory* double-shotted her guns, as she commonly did at close quarters, this one ship could massively outgun the duke's army. Indeed, the total firepower of both armies at Waterloo amounted to a mere 7.3 per cent of the firepower at Trafalgar.[44]

The greatest clash of armour in the twenty-two-year struggle against revolutionary and Napoleonic France was about to begin.

XXV

'IRRESISTIBLE LINES OF SHIPS'

But hark! I hear,
The signal gun!
Farewell! My dear!
The *Victory* leads on!
The fight's begun!

'Henry (off Cadiz) to Emma', 1805

I

CAUTIOUSLY the British sailed towards their foe, sweeping wide WNW to avoid a premature head-on encounter. At all events, Nelson could not afford to frighten the combined fleet back into Cadiz, and he needed to position himself to attack its flank. Lacking enough ships to form a reserve, the admiral had decided to use just the two divisions under Collingwood and himself. To maintain contact with his quarry, he briefed the captains of the *Mars*, *Colossus* and *Defence* and returned them to their task of standing between Blackwood and the fleet.[1]

By noon Nelson was twenty-five miles south-west of Cadiz, heading roughly north-west. Villeneuve's day had been fraught. After extricating his fleet from Cadiz, he had tried to gain 'sea room' by sailing westwards, fighting the south-westerly that had taken Nelson's fleet to the Strait, but dark, stormy weather and tossing seas wearied his inexperienced crews and when the wind veered to WNW it took the ships aback and deflected them to the SSW. In a gloomy evening the distant flash of rockets, flares and guns revealed the proximity of British ships, and Villeneuve tried to form a single line of battle, but darkness fell upon an untidy mass of ships, some in line ahead and others abreast, and squadron mixed with squadron. Ironically, the previous December the French admiral had predicted that Nelson would try to cut his line and envelop his rear, creating close-quarter slugging bouts between individual ships and groups of ships. It was uncannily accurate, and Villeneuve hoped to frustrate the British tactics by deploying a tight line of battle bristling with broadside firepower and a reserve of twelve capital ships. If the British got amongst him, he would close and use his superiority in manpower and soldiers to board. But when the 20th closed that stout, organised defence was still far away.[2]

The wind that threw Villeneuve aback in the afternoon also checked the British fleet, coming north-west from the Strait, and, like his French counterpart, Nelson was forced on to a south-westerly course. It was not until about four that he managed to wear his ships and, getting up topgallants, continue northwards with the wind to larboard. He knew from Blackwood that Villeneuve was in the NNE, sailing in a westerly direction on a course that would take him across Nelson's path. In fact, at about 7.30 that evening two sails of the combined fleet were briefly seen from the starboard bow of the *Victory*. After five the British admiral telegraphed Blackwood again, imploring him not to lose sight of the enemy during the night. All being well, daylight would bring the giant combatants together.

Nelson was not sure who commanded the combined fleet, as rumour had it that Villeneuve had been replaced by Decrès. Whoever he was, he remained uncomfortably close to Cadiz. Nelson therefore kept clear by wearing seawards, continuing gently south-west under top- and foresails, away from the Franco-Spanish ships. All saw and obeyed Nelson's new signal except the sixty-four-gun *Africa* under Henry Digby, which maintained her northerly course too long and could easily have missed the battle. That night Nelson had little rest. He was racked by the thought that the French might once again slip through his fingers. Throughout the hours of darkness the guns and blue lights of his scouts reported every hour, and at about four or five in the morning of 21 October 1805 the admiral judged it was time to close in. With the wind at WNW he ordered the fleet to wear again, this time to race through what was left of the night north by east directly towards the combined fleet.

Heralding a new day, the sun lifted its head from behind the combined fleet to reveal a mass of French and Spanish ships standing east by south on the starboard tack towards the Strait. The British saw their masts rising above the haze eleven miles away, and knew that another ten or more miles beyond lay the cape and treacherous shoals of Trafalgar on the coast of Spain. The combined fleet, consisting of forty war machines, including thirty-three of the line, was an astonishing spectacle. Captain Codrington of the *Orion* had never seen such a sight, while to an able seaman of the *Victory* it looked like 'a great wood on our lee bow'. Another witness wrote that 'the human mind cannot form a grander or more awesome sight'.[3]

Two thoughts predominated throughout the British fleet. In the full knowledge that Nelson would take them into the bloody heart of that mighty force, the vision of a sure and glorious victory, of a day that would live in history, was coupled with apprehensions about the cost. The talking about a battle-to-be was over; every person in the fleet would be put in harm's way, and most had to control fear. First Lieutenant William Cumby of the *Bellerophon* swung out of his cot that morning to make 'a short but fervent prayer' for a victory and his own salvation. After breakfast his captain, John Cooke, called him into his cabin. Cooke bade him read Nelson's memorandum in case he was 'bowl'd out' and the lieutenant would have to take command. In the *Victory* a nineteen-year-old midshipman, Robert Smith, scribbled hurriedly to his 'dear and honour'd parents', assuring them that if he fell it would be with 'a clear conscience, pure heart and in peace with all men'. Among 'few requests' was a wish that the 'dearest of mothers' would 'not give way' to 'low spirits' and remember that her 'affectionate son' could not have died 'in a more glorious cause'. Similar thoughts were running through every ship. The 'dear' parents of Midshipman Thomas Aikenhead of the *Royal Sovereign*, which would lead the lee line into battle, read that their son felt 'not the least dread' at falling 'in defence of my king'. To his sister the young man admitted that this might be 'the last time' she received her 'brother's love', but 'every British heart pants for glory. Our old admiral [Collingwood] . . . is quite young with the thought of it.' Older men thought of wives and children. 'Adieu, my dearest wife,' wrote Blackwood, who had done so much to create the day. 'Your Henry will not disgrace his name, and if he dies, his last breath will be devoted to the dearest of dear wives. Take care of my boy. Make him a better man than his father.' Captain Duff thought of Sophie, the girl he had known since childhood and married, and wished he had spent more time with her in that little home in Castle Street in Edinburgh. Their thirteen-year-old son, Norwich, was with him in the *Mars*, fresh to the navy. The boy had taken a fast frigate from Portsmouth to reach the ship, where he had joined his cousin, Thomas, fourteen years old, two boys together in a great adventure.[4]

Collingwood's servant found the admiral up before light, shaving at his mirror with little apparent concern. In the *Victory*, which carried the burden of leading the weather line, many of the officers 'were very pensive and thoughtful'. Nelson was on deck early, looking as if no more than the business of an ordinary day stared him in the face. He was attired in cotton stockings and woollen breeches, a non-regulation waistcoat and an undress uniform coat of dark blue wool, with thirty-six gilt buttons and two gold epaulettes, each adorned with twin silver-spangled stars. As usual the empty right sleeve was looped over one of the buttons on his breast. Beneath, the admiral's shirt had a shortened right sleeve, the end of which had been drawn together over the stump of the severed arm by means of a string. The admiral's hat was equipped with the green silk shade to protect his eyes, and a stock of black silk covered the throat. He carried a long green stocking purse of woven silk containing some gold and silver coins, and an expensive pocket watch made by Josiah Emery of London, but it was noticed that the last time he appeared on deck he neglected to bring his sword. The imitation stars of knighthood sewn on to the left breast of the admiral's coat made a target for enemy snipers, but he declined to change his coat. On the whole the commander-in-chief seemed in high spirits. This was 21 October, he said, a lucky date in his family. On that day in 1757 his uncle, Captain Maurice Suckling of the *Dreadnought*, had fought a gallant action against the French in the West Indies. And the date was also significant for Nelson's home village, Burnham Thorpe, for it was the day of the annual fair. He had not seen his birthplace, where his parents lay buried, for twelve years but it passed through his mind that day.[5]

Nelson studied the weather, and consulted Atkinson the master. The blustery conditions of the night had eased and the day showed promise. The water was smooth but rolling heavily as a light wind at WNW blew directly towards the enemy. Like many a good 'weather man', Nelson saw a storm coming. The wind favoured his attack, but its lightness would make the advance painfully slow, and he had no time to waste. The October days were short, and if the combined fleet panicked it might yet turn back for Cadiz, only twenty-five miles northward. Nelson decided to attack in the most direct way, eschewing any complicated manoeuvring, and throwing his two columns upon the enemy in a line-ahead charge. It would be dangerous because the first ships in the British lines would suffer the raking broadsides of several opponents long before they could reply, but Nelson had weighted the front of his columns with heavy ships capable of absorbing punishment and delivering a shock impact, and once at close quarters he was sure that the sheer efficiency of the British would prevail.

Everywhere his ships sprang to life. In the *Victory* a breakfast was served at about eight, and then 822 men and boys made their final preparations. Not all were natives of the British Isles. About 8 per cent of the flagship's crew were foreigners, including twenty-six from North and South America, five from the West Indies, ten from Italy and six from Malta. Two hailed from India. Three were from France and four from Holland, countries that were at war with Britain. There were twenty-eight boys aged between thirteen and eighteen, of whom Cornelius Carroll, a 'boy, 2nd class', from Plymouth, who was training to become a commissioned officer, and Samuel Robbins, a 'boy, 3rd class', from London, earning £7 a year for his service, may have been the youngest. At least one woman was on board, the wife of a Maltese seaman, serving as a powder monkey carrying powder and cartridges from the magazines to the guns. According to the ship's medical journal, not a soul began the day sick.[6]

Dawn had found the British fleet in an irregular order, and after six the *Victory* hoisted signals 72 and 76, directing the ships to form their two divisions and sail large towards the ENE in order to get to windward of the enemy. To prevent his three cumbersome, badly coppered three-deckers, *Britannia*, *Prince* and *Dreadnought*, from holding up matters, Nelson signalled them to join their lines as convenient, excusing them from taking up their prescribed positions. As it happened all three did rather better than expected, and the *Britannia* worked her way forward to a respectable sixth position in the admiral's 'weather' line.

Slowly order emerged from what had looked like a chaotic collection of ships, as the *Victory*, her steering sails and royals set to catch the most wind, and the *Royal Sovereign* led off, and their followers bore up behind, transmuting first into two divisions and some two hours later into two misshapen columns. In accordance with Nelson's most recent orders, Collingwood had fifteen ships in his 'lee' line, and one of those, the *Africa*, was still struggling to rejoin the fleet. With fourteen sail of the line at his disposal, Collingwood steered a little more easterly than Nelson to open water between the two lines, making for the twelve enemy ships to the right. Nelson's memorandum had assumed that it would have been the rear of the Franco-Spanish fleet, but, as it now stood, Collingwood would be attacking the van, nearest the Strait. Whichever, his job was to overwhelm that force, leaving Nelson's twelve ships to shield him with an attack further along the enemy line.[7]

In the hurried advance most of the British ships made the best speeds they could, some such as the *Victory* and the newly coppered *Royal Sovereign* achieving up to three knots and others managing only one or two. Given the speed of the operation, this variability was unavoidable. Eighteen of the twenty-seven capital ships had had their copper sheathing repaired or replaced within the last two years, enabling them to slip more easily through the water; some ships simply handled better than others. Moreover, each ship had to extricate herself from the pack as circumstances allowed, and started from a unique position. The *Defence*, which had been one of Duff's scouts, began her day far from her allotted position, and had to pass through Nelson's line to reach her place with Collingwood, and the undersized *Africa* never got that far. Her headlong dash to get into the battle was to be one of the dramatic events of the day, but she was too late to join Collingwood's line, and threw herself into Nelson's fracas instead. To some extent these disparities weakened the attack, opening gaps between faster and slower ships and leaving some better supported than others. Fortunately, the heavy-hitters in Nelson's line fared well. Three three-deckers with a hundred or so guns each, *Victory*, *Temeraire* and *Neptune*, led the line, and another, the *Britannia*, struggled up among the seventy-fours that followed in relatively close order behind. Collingwood's *Royal Sovereign* led the 'lee' line, but his other three-deckers, *Prince* and *Dreadnought*, trailed so far behind that one unkind witness said they 'might as well have been in Spithead'. He would have to rely on the eighty-gun *Tonnant* and his seventy-fours to follow him into the melee. Outside the lines, the four British frigates, *Euryalus*, *Naiad*, *Phoebe* and *Sirius*, were thrown on Nelson's larboard flank, where the little *Pickle* and *Entreprenante* cutter also found a place. They could not engage the enemy ships of the line, but Villeneuve had five frigates, four of them big forty-gunners, as well as two brigs that might need to be dealt with, and, if the battle developed as Nelson planned, the smaller ships would be needed to repeat signals, tow damaged ships, board prizes and ferry passengers and messages.[8]

Nelson's fear that the combined fleet might abandon its mission and recoil towards Cadiz soon looked justified. After seven Villeneuve ordered his ships to wear together and form a tight line of battle on the larboard tack with Cadiz on its lee bow to the north-east. It was not a manoeuvre they had practised, and the light wind and large swell offered little help, but using studding-sails to corner every breath, the ships clumsily turned their heads from the British to come round on the opposite tack to face Cadiz. In so doing the order of the combined fleet was reversed. The old rear under Admiral Pierre Dumanoir of the *Formidable* now became the van; while the old van, under Admiral Ignatio María de Alava of the *Santa Ana* (112), was the new rear.

It took the French and Spanish two hours to complete the manoeuvre, and they failed to accomplish it properly. Rather than a single compact line of battle, able to maximise its broadside fire, the result assumed a ragged crescent shape, sagging leewards in the centre while leaving both extremities closer to the British. French and Spanish ships were mixed promiscuously, some close together, others spaced out, some in line, some to leeward and some even line abreast. The new allied rear was particularly ungainly, incorporating a 'corps de reserve' under Gravina in the *Principe de Asturias* (118), which was supposed to be available for action wherever most needed. When Villeneuve signalled Gravina to keep to windward and shield his centre from Nelson's attack at about 11.30, he was unable to respond. Whatever happened that day, Villeneuve was going to lose ships, but this muddled performance with a perilous shore to leeward risked disaster.

Nelson had been on deck when Villeneuve began his manoeuvre, but after satisfying himself that he could still catch them, he withdrew to his cabin to find a silent space. It had probably already been stripped of most furniture to allow its twelve-pounders to be manned, and the portraits of Emma and Horatia and other precious possessions had been found a safe refuge. The dining-room chairs were folded flat and stowed. However, left was 'a little table fixed to the side of the ship' where Nelson was accustomed to write with a portable compass at his elbow. The entry he now made in his diary was a prayer. It is a remarkable document, made by a man on the brink of a terrible battle, and, ever mindful of posterity, Nelson ensured its survival by making a second copy:

> At seven the enemy wearing in succession. May the Great God whom I worship grant to my country, and for the benefit of Europe in general, a great and glorious victory. And may no misconduct in anyone tarnish it, and may humanity after victory be the predominant feature in the British fleet. For myself individually, I commit my life to Him who made me, and may His blessing light upon my endeavours for serving my country faithfully. To Him I resign myself, and the just cause which is entrusted to me to defend. Amen, Amen, Amen.[9]

About this time the admiral invited his four frigate captains aboard the *Victory* for a final briefing. Blackwood found the admiral on the poop, and, with Hardy, accompanied him into the grand cabin, where Nelson wanted them to witness a codicil he had just made to his will. There could be little doubt that if he died the state would provide for his family, but those closest to his heart were tainted by illegitimacy. In snatched silences he thought of them, probably as he had last seen them at Merton, Emma flush with tears and little Horatia sleeping so peacefully and safely with the world outside on fire. Now Nelson made his last appeal for his loved ones, an appeal only hours ahead of a fury no living man had seen at sea, and surely one of the most moving ever bequeathed to the British nation. 'October the twenty-first, one thousand eight hundred and five,' he began, 'then is [in] sight of the combined fleets of France and Spain, distant about ten miles.' He reviewed the services and supposed services that Emma had performed for her country, how she had warned Britain of Spain's intention to declare war in 1796 and facilitated the watering of the Nile fleet in 1798, and then he went on:

> Could I have rewarded *these* services, I would not now call upon my country, but as that has not been in my power, I leave Emma, Lady Hamilton, therefore, a legacy to my King and Country, that they will give her an ample provision to maintain her rank in life. I also leave to the beneficence of my country my adopted daughter, Horatia Nelson Thompson, and I desire she will use in future the name Nelson only. These are the only favours I ask of my King and Country at this moment, when I am going to fight their battle.[10]

2

At about ten, as the British attack got underway, signal 13 flew above the *Victory*. It ordered the ships to prepare for battle. The final adjustments were made, mess tables hitched up, remaining bulkheads and partitions removed, furniture and hammocks stowed away, galley fires doused and the lower yards slung and topsail sheets 'stoppered' to enable the men to concentrate on the guns. Drums and whistles summoned men to their quarters. In the *Victory* the gun crews, up to seven to a piece, gathered around the lower-deck thirty-two-pounders, the twenty-four-pounders above, and the 'twelves' on the upper deck. Two massive sixty-eight-pound carronades added colossal close-up punching power on the forecastle. Some of the gunners wore checked shirts, but most stripped to the waist, binding handkerchiefs around their heads and ears or pulling on woollen caps to keep sweat and noise at bay. They wore canvas or duck trousers, flapping loosely above the ankles, and many went barefoot. In those final hours some hastily bequeathed their possessions, assigning pitiful keepsakes to their comrades in brief but grave conversations. Lieutenants Edward Williams, Andrew King, John Yule and George Browne, with a few midshipmen, were also about the batteries to supervise, clear wreckage and dead or wounded men and restore guns to action. A thousand shot had been placed on each deck but more would be needed, and men and boys moved back and forward between the batteries and the magazines, some ready to form a human chain. William Rivers, the gunner, and his mates distributed powder, shot, wooden boxes filled with cartridges and small arms, or prepared further supplies. Captain Charles William Adair, the twenty-nine-year-old marines officer, one of a military family, inspected his corps of 145 redcoats, and posted them in strategic positions, ready to deal with enemy snipers, defend magazines, hatchways and principal cabins, and help with the guns. The carpenter, William Bunce, a man of twenty-five, prepared his team to repair damage, clear debris and support the sailing and steering functions of the ship, and down in the dark bowels of the cockpit, below the lower deck, William Beatty and two surgical assistants laid out a grim array of instruments and 150 drugs and preparations, ready to receive the mass casualties of round, bar, chain and grape shot, small arms fire, and flying wood and metal. Based on the quarterdeck, where he could command the ship, stood the burly Hardy, assisted by First Lieutenant John Quilliam, a native of the Isle of Man; the ship's master, Thomas Atkinson; and such junior lieutenants as Alexander Hills, George Miller Bligh and William Ram. Nelson stood with Hardy, but John Scott the secretary served him as aide, and the signal lieutenant, John Pasco (actually the oldest of the nine lieutenants on board) was close by with Popham's telegraph system to hand.

As the spiritless breeze took the British languidly forward, the individual enemy ships became distinguishable from the forest of masts. Some, like the British, were painted with double yellow lines punctuated by the open gun ports, while others displayed a broad single red or yellow line, or simply a ubiquitous and ominous black. The great *Santissima Trinidad*, the only four-decker afloat, which ultimately ran up the flag of a Spanish rear admiral, was a particularly terrific sight, her sides painted in alternate lines of red and white, and her majestic white figurehead representing the three members of the Holy Trinity. But intimidating as the Franco-Spanish display was, a steely purpose characterised the determined advance of the British columns, the ships beneath bellying white canvas, their studding sails set to harness every inch of wind. Some jettisoned casks, stores and livestock to lighten their weight and gain speed, but, while gaps opened in Collingwood's line, Nelson's ships sometimes 'pressed so much upon each other as to be obliged to go bow and quarter instead of ahead'. Their progress became almost surreal when their bands struck up tunes, gliding serenely forward to 'Hearts of Oak', 'God Save the King', 'The Downfall of Paris' 'Rule, Britannia' and 'Britons Strike Home'. Men, 'as if in mere bravado', danced the hornpipe to relieve the tension. On the guns of the

Bellerophon, the old 'Billy Ruffian' as her people affectionately called her, someone had chalked the words 'Victory or Death'. The spirit was as evident in the small as well as the large ships, and not a few were amused to see the tiny *Pickle* schooner slipping perkily along to larboard of Nelson's line as if she was the most fearsome vessel afloat, her half a dozen little carronades run out, her deck cleared for action and her boarding nets raised.[11]

At eleven raw pork and half a pint of wine were served the men of the *Victory*, and at about the same time Nelson toured the decks, speaking familiarly with different hands. He promised a more glorious day than the Nile, and they cheered. As usual, the admiral's eye did not miss the minutiae, and on top he ordered the stowed hammocks to be saturated with water to resist fire. Out on the quarterdeck the admiral's bedecked uniform aroused concern among his closest followers. The enemy fighting tops were crowded with French and Spanish marksmen, probably soldiers who knew how to handle muskets, and they would be looking for the best targets. Nelson refused to change his coat for something plainer; the men were used to seeing him accoutred in his stars, and to shed them now would set a bad example.[12]

There was a similar reaction to Blackwood's suggestion that he conduct the battle from the *Euryalus* frigate, and to pleas that at least he allow Eliab Harvey's *Temeraire* or Fremantle's *Neptune* to lead the weather line and take the position of greatest danger. Pressed on all sides, the admiral seemed to prevaricate, and agreed that Harvey should go ahead. He hailed the *Temeraire* to concede her the honour of leading the fleet, but she was out of earshot and Blackwood left to deliver the message by boat. It was no use. Nelson simply could not do it, and, instead of giving way, drove the *Victory* forward with all sail.[13]

In fact, both British admirals almost resembled rival greyhounds plunging for a hare. According to Nelson's written plan, Collingwood's line was to have been led by the *Mars*, but looking across to starboard he could see the *Royal Sovereign* bravely forging ahead, her newly coppered hull cutting fiercely through the water. Afraid that his friend might outrun his support, Nelson twice signalled *Mars* to take her assigned lead, but Collingwood afforded Duff no opportunity and advanced with undiminished urgency. Nelson was lost in admiration. 'See how that noble fellow Collingwood carries his ship into action,' he said. With such an example, he could do no less himself. About noon Nelson sealed his decision by specifically signalling the *Temeraire* to remain astern of the *Victory*, directly countermanding the previous order sent by Blackwood. He had often told Emma that whatever happened he would be first, and now he made that good.

Nelson's line bore down on the combined fleet at almost a right angle, the ships adopting a ragged follow-my-leader or line-ahead formation that likened it to a charging column of infantry. As we have seen, the admiral's memorandum had assigned the lee line under Collingwood a distinct form of attack, in which the ships formed line-abreast almost parallel to the enemy line, and advanced simultaneously to break it in several places, much as Duncan had broken the Dutch fleet at the battle of Camperdown. But Collingwood quickly concluded that the formation of such a 'line of bearing' would be too time-consuming, and discounted the idea. Instead, his lee line proceeded in a ragged 'bow-and-quarter' line, in which the bows of the following ship closed upon the starboard quarter of the ship ahead. Both the British lines, therefore, assumed the character of shock columns. Rather than cutting the Franco-Spanish line at many points, the ships would reach the enemy one by one, punching their way through in a smaller number of places.

Despite the inherent risk, Nelson's concern was not whether he would win his battle, but whether the scale of his triumph would suffice. As the distance between the belligerent fleets closed, it became obvious that the combined fleet was going to make a fight of it. Encouraged, Nelson remarked that they were putting on a brave face, but 'I'll give them such a dressing as they never had before'. Blackwood said that if fourteen ships of the line were taken it would be a great victory, but Nelson disagreed. 'I shall not, Blackwood, be satisfied with anything short of twenty,' he said. He had promised Pitt and his ministers a battle of annihilation, and he intended to live up to it.[14]

Nelson's first intended target was the enemy centre, but when near enough to make out most of the enemy ships the *Victory* hauled to port to steer towards the van under Dumanoir. This movement is still mysterious. It has generally been taken to be a feint, designed to fill the enemy with doubt and indecision, and if the intention was truly to divert it succeeded if the amount of reportage in the French accounts is any guide. The log of the *Orion*, the only British ship to refer to the movement other than the *Victory*, clearly regarded it as a feint. But it is arguable that this swing to port betokened a significant, if temporary, change in Nelson's plan. The *Euryalus*, which repeated the admiral's signals, logged one that suggests that Nelson had switched his attack from the centre to the van. 'I intend to push or go through the end of the enemy's line to prevent them getting into Cadiz,' the signal ran. We do not know when it was made, because of the varying times kept by the different ships. The master of the *Euryalus* put it at 11.40, but his timings were some seventeen minutes fast, which would put the correct time about 11.23. A lieutenant's log of the same frigate timed it even earlier, at 11.00, but he had the famous 'England Expects' signal at 11.30, about fifteen minutes too early. The evidence of the *Euryalus*, therefore, suggests that between 11.15 and 11.30 Nelson signalled his intention to cut through the enemy van to seal off its retreat to Cadiz.[15]

Nelson did not pursue this plan, however. Shortly he swung again to starboard to resume his attack on the enemy centre. We can only speculate about what may have changed his mind. Possibly he thought that an attack on the van could not have prevented the centre from interfering in Collingwood's difficult battle further south, or perhaps he was influenced by the identification flags hoisted by the combined fleet about 11.45, just before firing began. An eyewitness in the *Victory* remembered that Nelson was particularly anxious to secure the enemy commander-in-chief, and Blackwood had certainly encouraged him to do so. He had always understood the importance of trying to destroy or capture the command centre of an enemy force. The identification flags would have revealed some of these targets to the British, if they had not guessed them already. In the centre of the enemy line were two impressive enemy flagships, the giant *Santissima Trinidad*, which carried the flag of a Spanish rear admiral, Baltasar Hidalgo de Cisneros, and just astern Villeneuve's *Bucentaure* bearing the flag of the commander-in-chief. And when the *Victory* abandoned her course towards the hostile van, and steered to starboard, these were the targets she reached. As the log of the *Spartiate* recorded, the *Victory* bore 'down on a Spanish four-decker (*Santissima Trinidad*) and a French two-decker with an Admiral's flag at the fore'. The evidence is too thin to speak with certainty, but Nelson may well have seen the perfect opportunity to combine a crushing attack on the centre with the demolition of the enemy commander-in-chief.[16]

As usual Nelson read the battle carefully, adjusting his ideas as he did so, but Villeneuve reacted slowly to events. It was not until about 11.30 that he futilely signalled Gravina to keep to windward and support his centre. Nor when Nelson turned towards his centre did he summon the ships in his van to come to his assistance. Although he tried to form a more tightly packed, impenetrable formation, and ordered his ships to conserve their ammunition until at closer range, he seemed transfixed by the thundering, hell-bent attack. As he later admitted to Blackwood, 'he never saw anything like the irresistible line of our ships'.[17]

Nelson's last signals were made just before firing with the combined fleet dead ahead. Most of them urged ships forward with every sail consistent with the safety of the masts, sometimes singling out the *Africa*, which had been mislaid the previous night but now suddenly appeared in the north-west, flying to join the attack. One signal directed the fleet to anchor at the close of the day. Nelson may have been thinking of the coming storm, or the dangerous sandbanks, shoals and reefs of San Pedro and Trafalgar that lay to leeward of the combined fleet. A damaged ship, unable to work out to sea, might easily be driven by wind and tide upon those banks and wrecked. In either case, this precautionary signal had a tragically prophetic dimension.[18]

Blackwood and the other frigate captains were still in the *Victory* at about 11.45, when Nelson remarked that he would 'amuse' the fleet. Perhaps he was remembering his *Henry V*, and looking for some rousing appeal that would encourage his men as his hero was said to have done before Agincourt. Turning to Pasco, the signal lieutenant on the poop, he said, 'I wish to say to the fleet, "England confides that every man will do his duty",' adding, 'You must be quick, for I have one more [signal] to make, which is for close action.' Pasco leafed through his signal book and then suggested substituting the word 'expects' for 'confides' as the former was already listed, and the latter would have to be spelled letter by letter. 'That will do, Pasco,' said Nelson without hesitation, 'Make it directly.' The famous signal, 'England Expects That Every Man Will Do His Duty', required thirty-one flags, and duly climbed the mizzen topgallant masthead in twelve hoists. A twenty-three-year-old landsman from Battersea, John Rome, later claimed to have done the hauling. Legend says that Collingwood expressed annoyance at what he took to be a superfluous signal, and not every ship acknowledged it in the log, but bursts of cheering broke out from many British ships. Hardy thought 'its effects were felt throughout the fleet', and Blackwood remembered 'the shout' it aroused as 'truly sublime'. A witness on one of the frigates recalled that after receiving the signal the men on the ship went down to their guns 'without confusion, and a cool, deliberate courage . . . seemed to rest on the countenance of every man I saw'. 'It was received,' said another, 'with a burst of applause and every individual seemed animated with a determination to conquer.'[19]

Shortly before firing, the frigate captains left the *Victory* to carry final messages to the captains of the capital ships, reminding them that Nelson relied upon their exertions and adding, in an echo of the memorandum, that in cases of difficulty each should use his own judgement 'provided it led them quickly and closely alongside the enemy'. For Harvey and Fremantle, whose ships immediately followed the *Victory*, there was a further notice, recorded in the *Neptune*'s log: 'At 11.50 Captn. Blackwood of the *Euryalus* came alongside and acquainted us it was Lord Nelson's intention to cut through the enemy's line about the 13th or 14th ship [and] then to make sail on the larboard tack for their van.' Again, the admiral was revising his plan according to circumstance, and now hoped to break the centre, raking the ships on either side as he cut through, and then turning to port, engaging the enemy van from leeward as he progressed up their line.[20]

Blackwood's accounts of his last words with Nelson are well known, and have inspired pages of misguided ink about premonitions and suicide. According to the better-known version, which was recalled some years afterwards, the two men shook hands. Preparing to leave, Blackwood said, 'I trust, my lord, that on my return to the *Victory*, which will be as soon as possible, I shall find your Lordship in possession of twenty prizes.' 'God bless you, Blackwood,' Nelson replied. 'I shall never speak to you again.' Reminiscences set down long after the events they describe are almost always unreliable, but Blackwood also said as much the day after the battle. Writing to his wife, the captain mentioned that Nelson 'told me, at parting, we should meet no more', a remark that made him come away 'with a heart very sad'. Was this so odd, however? Most men go into battle with anxieties about life and death, and Nelson was fully conscious of the extreme danger he risked. To function in an engagement it is necessary to suppress such misgivings, but on this occasion the emotional commander-in-chief allowed them to surface. Nor was his the only poignant farewell as the frigate captains quit the *Victory*. Captain William Prowse of the *Sirius* frigate exchanged his last words with his nephew, Captain Adair of the flagship's marines. Adair, like Nelson, had only hours to live.[21]

But the *Victory* did not have the honour of opening the greatest naval battle of the nineteenth century. Close to noon a dull roar and spurts of flame and smoke came from the larboard batteries of the French seventy-four, *Fougueux*, and perhaps the huge 120-gun, black-painted *Santa Ana*, bearing the flag of Alava, a Spanish vice admiral, ahead. These first range-finding shots were hurled at the oncoming *Royal Sovereign*, as she outstripped the *Belleisle* and *Mars* to reach a distance of one thousand yards. Soon the firing intensified, and others joined in, including the *San Justo* and *San Leandro* ahead, and the *Monarca*, *Pluton* and *Algésiras* astern, the last commanded by Rear Admiral Charles Magon, the most truculent of the French flag officers. Much of the fire was too high, and one observer thought it 'confused and random-like', but some of it went home. On the British ships the identification flags and remaining colours unfurled to cheers in the fleet, Nelson's white ensign advertising his standing as a vice admiral of the white. The ships sailed boldly on under the white and red flag of St George and occasional Union Jacks. The trial of fire promised by Nelson's head-on tactics had begun.[22]

However carefully a commander might prepare and attempt to control events, something unforeseen can always intervene. The results of an encounter do not always reflect the worth of the plan, for a good one can fail and a bad succeed. The role of the commander is to stack the odds as far as he is able. Fate was already dealing one blow to Nelson's calculations that 21 October 1805. He had wanted to mass superior force against a part of the enemy line, and to crush it before it could be reinforced. But the wind was so light that his ships were dripping torturously slowly into the battle. Inadequately supported by consorts struggling up behind, they battered their way into a tight-packed enemy formation, sometimes two or three ships deep, and took on superior numbers of the enemy ships. The pell-mell battle that Nelson wanted occurred, but not quite the concentration of force intended. In the first and decisive stage of the fighting, it was the British, not the French and Spanish, ships that were outnumbered. Nelson's ships not only had to advance under a heavy fire they could barely return, but finally entered a fray in which they were surrounded by foes.

3

Collingwood's leading ships were converging with the enemy line at an angle of seventy to eighty degrees, rather than perpendicularly, but they were still disadvantaged. Relatively few of their guns could reply to the broadsides from the enemy ships ahead, and the ordeal was prolonged by the wind, which began to lose what little power it had to push them forward. For several minutes a number of opponents tried to find their range, most directing bar and chain as well as round shot high at the British masts, rigging and sails in the continental manner. Their gunners, relatively few of whom had much experience in open water, were lifted and pitched by the powerful swell, making it difficult for them to fix a target, but the *Royal Sovereign* took some direct hits. Despite the occasional thumps of pierced sails, the crunch of fractured timber and shrieks of stricken men, Collingwood could do little more with his forward guns than create a thin masking smoke.

How Nelson envied Collingwood at that moment, and William Hargood's seventy-four-gun *Belleisle* which gamely moved forward into second place, behind the *Royal Sovereign*. As his ship overtook the larger *Tonnant*, Hargood called a greeting to her captain. 'A glorious day for Old England!' Charles Tyler cheeringly replied, trusting that both would make a prize. *Belleisle* edged forward towards the *Royal Sovereign*'s starboard quarter and a marines officer was able to count seven or eight ships firing upon the flagship. Standing on a quarterdeck carronade to get a better view, Hargood ordered his men to lie down at their quarters to escape the inevitable shot and flying splinters. His ship observed an 'almost awful' silence as it sailed into danger, broken only on the upper deck by the orders that passed from captain to master and master to the quartermaster at the helm. Then the seventy-four was also receiving fire and suffering casualties. Hargood declined to reply, saving his shot for close range, and when his first lieutenant suggested that they fire to make smoke, he would admit of no such nonsense. His ship was 'ordered to go through the line', he replied firmly, 'and go through she shall, By God!'[23]

But ahead Collingwood had made a potentially damaging mistake. He was supposed to cut the enemy line at the twelfth ship, concentrating his fifteen upon a manageable rear, but with all sails set he steered slightly to port to strike the combined fleet further up, between the stern of the Spanish three-decker, *Santa Ana*, and the French *Fougueux*, a seventy-four. Perhaps he was attracted by Alava's distinguishing flag, or maybe the double banking of ships in the enemy rear made accurate counting difficult, but the move pitted him against sixteen of the enemy ships rather than twelve, and threw away one of the advantages Nelson had tried to garner. On top of that, a considerable gap had opened in his lee line between the first eight ships and the remaining seven. The slow progress made by the rear of Collingwood's force meant that he would have to win his battle with only eight ships. Nelson's plan to mass force on the rear had dramatically failed.

Captain Louis-Alexis Beaudouin of the *Fougueux* saw that Collingwood intended breaking the line ahead and tried to close on the towering black stern of the *Santa Ana* to shut the British ship out. Unabashed, the *Royal Sovereign* bore unflinchingly forward, and Beaudoin had to back his main topsail and check his ship to avoid a collision. A few minutes after noon Collingwood slashed away his studding sails to prevent them getting in the way, and barged under the *Santa Ana*'s stern, her weakest part, delivering the first British broadside of the battle, a terrific double- or triple-shotted volley that blazed its destructive course along the full length of the Spanish ship. Some of the Spaniard's men, seeing what was coming, had already scrambled over her far bulwark, clinging to her offside to hide, but the great vessel was shaken from stern to stem. A starboard broadside from the *Royal Sovereign* slammed almost simultaneously into the side of the *Fougueux*, hitting her so hard that she rocked crazily to starboard. Then, putting his helm to starboard and hauling on the braces to trim sails, Collingwood swung his ship to port to engage the wounded *Santa Ana* side by side from leeward.

An awful scene ensued, as for several minutes Collingwood's massive three-decker fought surrounded and alone. She was lashed by fire from the *Santa Ana* alongside, the French eighty-gun *Indomptable* to leeward, the *Fougueux* astern, and two Spanish seventy-fours ahead, the *San Leandro* and *San Justo*. 'I looked once out of our stern ports,' wrote Midshipman George Castle, 'but saw nothing but French and Spaniards round, firing at us in all directions. It was shocking to see the many brave mangled seamen so, some with their heads half shot away, others with their entrails mashed, lying panting on the deck.' Collingwood himself had several narrow escapes, one when the master was almost cut in two at his side, and fell upon the admiral dying, with his head on his shoulder. Yet in those terrible fifteen or so minutes the fury of the *Royal Sovereign* was irresistible, and she inflicted more casualties upon the *Santa Ana* alone than she received from all five of her enemies combined. In the battle the Spanish flagship lost 241 casualties and the *Royal Sovereign* 141. As other British ships entered the maelstrom, diverting the enemy ships, Collingwood's ship was left locked in a deadly duel with the *Santa Ana*, dealing fearful damage. In less than two hours the Spanish ship was forced to strike her colours and dismasted, but the *Royal Sovereign* had been turned into an exhausted, unmanageable wreck with only a splintered foremast standing. Blackwood's *Euryalus* had to fight her way through the floating wreckage and embattled ships to take her in tow.[24]

Following *Royal Sovereign*, Hargood's *Belleisle*, her sails and rigging already mutilated, pushed through the enemy line astern of the *Fougueux*, her guns thundering in succession as they found their targets in the Frenchman's stern and quarter. But then she found herself sandwiched between the *Fougueux* behind and the *Indomptable* directly ahead, both raking her with severe fire. In the hideous combat that followed *Belleisle* also engaged *Achille*, *Aigle*, *Neptune* and probably others. Her gun decks became demonic, as sweat-soaked men slaved at the ordnance in an atmosphere drained of oxygen by the explosions. Powder monkeys scampered with ammunition amidst darting flame, and huge guns bucked at their tackle in deafening noise, blinding and choking smoke, and sudden and grotesque injury and death. 'At every moment the smoke accumulated more and more thickly,' said a survivor, 'stagnating on board between decks at times so densely as to blur over the nearest objects, and often blot out the men at the guns from those close at hand on each side. The guns had to be trained . . . mechanically by means of orders passed down from above, and on objects that the men fighting the guns hardly ever got a glimpse of . . . In fact, the men were as much in the dark as . . . if they had been blindfolded, and the only comfort . . . was that every man was so isolated from his neighbour that he was not put in mind of his danger by seeing his messmates go down all round. All that he knew was that he heard the crash of the shot smashing through the rending timbers, and then followed at once the hoarse bellowing of the captains of the guns, as men were missed at their posts, calling out to the survivors, "Close up there! Close up!"' The only British ship to be entirely dismasted and her remaining guns encumbered with wreckage, the *Belleisle* fought on until relieved by *Defiance*, *Polyphemus* and *Swiftsure*, three of the ships towards the end of Collingwood's line. The *Swiftsure*, under Captain William Rutherford, engaged the wounded *Aigle* and *Achille*, forcing the first to strike in half an hour and setting the last on fire. Hargood still managed to take possession of another beaten prize, the Spanish *Argonauta*, before the *Naiad* frigate got her in tow. Said one who saw the price she had paid, 'So many bodies in such a confined place . . . would affect the most obdurate heart.' As the broken hulk was towed from the fray the men of the *Swiftsure* turned up to cheer.[25]

Duff in the *Mars*, another seventy-four, was the third British ship to engage, shearing away the Spanish *Monarca* with a starboard broadside before attempting to penetrate the hostile line ahead of the oncoming *Pluton*. The *Mars* was soon boxed in and taking savage hits from three or more enemy ships too close to miss, losing her running rigging, braces and sails, and sustaining so much damage to masts and rudder that she became unmanageable. The powder smoke hung about her so thickly that the adversaries were almost invisible to each other, even at point-blank range. Peering into the murk over the side of his quarterdeck to assess the situation, Captain Duff was decapitated by a shot, and two seamen were struck dead at his side. The first lieutenant assumed command of the ship amongst mounting casualties. The master's log recorded that the 'the poop and quarter deck [were] almost left destitute, the carnage was so great'. Duff's nephew, Acting Lieutenant Alexander Duff, was also killed in the battle, leaving the captain's thirteen-year-old-son to write to his mother about her husband's death. 'He died like a hero', and by 'the will of Heaven,' said Midshipman Norwich Duff, 'ever . . . dear to his king and his country and his friends.' The boy would die a vice admiral in 1862.[26]

Across to larboard Nelson saw the leading ships of the lee line disappearing in furious discharges of artillery, smoke, flame and flying debris. In minutes only the tops of their highest royals could be seen above the dense smoke, and the flashes of their guns from within. Standing next to Lieutenant Quilliam and Midshipman George Westphal, a twenty-year-old protégé of the Duke of Kent, Nelson strained to make their movements out. 'Nobly done, Hargood!' he exclaimed as the *Belleisle* sliced her way into the enemy ships with swingeing blows.[27]

Now it was the turn of the *Victory* and her weather line.

The first ranging shots were fired at Nelson's oncoming flagship soon after noon at a range of perhaps a thousand yards. Hurtling from the *Formidable* and *Scipion* in the enemy van, they fell short, and hissed angrily into the deep, expelling fountains of foam and water. Then a round shot sliced through the *Victory*'s main topgallant, and the bombardment intensified. After Nelson turned his ship to starboard to make for the enemy centre, he exposed her larboard side to the enemy van and her bows to the ships ahead, and was soon being cut up by eight to ten adversaries, including the *Héros*, the four-decked *Santissima Trinidad* of more than 130 guns, the *Bucentaure* of 80 guns, and the *Redoutable* of 74. About 12.24, Nelson fired some long shots at the van to larboard, an expression of defiance that provoked cheers from ships in both British lines.[28]

The wind had almost dropped, and the *Victory*'s lower sails had been furled to free her crews to fight. Closing the remaining distance so slowly, the ship was a sitting target for hundreds of guns, and within point-blank range – about 630 yards – they told formidably. Shot whined overhead, plunged alongside, thumped holes through sails, ripped away rigging and smashed through timber. The foresail of the *Victory*, still preserved at Portsmouth, bears testimony to the onslaught. Measuring 3618 square feet, it is severely torn in the centre and perforated by twenty round shot and some sixty musket balls. The ship's fore topsail yard, fore topmast and main topgallant crashed down, and her mizzen and mizzen topmast were damaged and her wheel smashed, sending the master scuttling below to arrange for her to be steered from the gunroom by means of tackle and the tiller. On the open decks men were quickly scythed down. One of the first to die was Nelson's secretary, John Scott, who was almost torn in half by a round shot while talking to an officer on the quarterdeck. 'Was that Scott?' asked Nelson, as he saw a body being lifted from the blood-drenched deck and thrown overboard. When a midshipman confirmed his fear the admiral said, 'Poor fellow.' Plymouth-born Thomas Whipple, a captain's clerk of twenty years, soon followed, fatally slashed open by a splinter while in conversation with Midshipman Westphal. A shot flew between Nelson and Hardy as they stood on the quarterdeck, hitting the fore-brace bits and flinging a splinter that struck the buckle from one of the captain's shoes. The two officers stopped to see if the other was hurt, and then the admiral smiled. 'This is too warm work, Hardy, to last long,' he remarked. When a last attempt was made to persuade him to remove his coat he merely said that it was too late. Forty grim-faced marines stationed with Captain Adair on the poop were particularly vulnerable, and it is surprising that Nelson and Hardy neglected to tell them to lie down. A single doubled-headed shot intended to slash away rigging butchered eight of them at a stroke. It was but the beginning of a systematic attrition, and there was a tinge of bitterness in Second Lieutenant Lewis Rotely's recollection that 'no men went down until knocked down' and 'the poop became a slaughter-house'.[29]

Despite the attrition on the upper decks, the gunners had been ordered to lie down until it was time to fire, but for agonising minutes only the larboard and forward guns had the opportunity to reply. As the *Victory* closed on the enemy line, the *Bucentaure*, Villeneuve's flagship, hauled to the wind to close an opening behind the *Santissima Trinidad* and frustrate Nelson's obvious intention to run under her stern. Putting his helm to port to turn the prow of the *Victory* to starboard, Nelson then made for the gap between the *Bucentaure* and the *Redoutable* coming up astern, braving full broadsides and a storm of musket balls fired 'at short musket range' from the French flagship in the process. The combatants were blanketed in a thick, almost impenetrable, smoke. Although Captain Jean Lucas of the *Redoutable* tried to close the gap, Nelson put up his helm and jammed his ship so close under *Bucentaure*'s vulnerable stern that his larboard yardarms passed over the classical carved figures of the Frenchman's poop. Now, for the first time, the British ship could repay her tormentors in full. A heavy sixty-eight-pound carronade, located on the forecastle and loaded with a round shot and a canister containing four hundred and seventy-seven musket balls, began the destruction of the French flagship, exploding her stern galleries into fragments of flying glass and timber, and then a full larboard broadside, fifty-one double-shotted twelves, twenty-fours and thirty-twos, visited death and destruction along the entire length of the enemy gun decks. Perhaps a quarter of the French guns were smashed or disabled in the onslaught, and scores of men flung off their feet, dead, wounded or traumatised, some dreadfully mangled. The French flagship may have carried as many as eighty-six guns, but for a short while only a few muskets and after guns could reply. She rallied, but never recovered from that one cataclysmic blizzard. It was at about this point that Villeneuve signalled his van to come to his support, but if Dumanoir saw it through the smoke he did not respond.[30]

Instead of the clear water that Nelson hoped would greet him to leeward of the Franco-Spanish line he found the eighty-gun French *Neptune*, which probably put some dangerous raking shots into the emerging battle-scarred prow of the British flagship. To larboard the *Victory* continued to pound *Bucentaure*, and more desultorily fired upon the *Santissima Trinidad* beyond, but to starboard she collided heavily with the *Redoutable*, grinding alongside her and pushing both ships to leeward in a tangled whole, the British starboard fore topmast studding sail boom locked into the Frenchman's fore topsail. Although the

Redoutable had eighty-four or more guns she would have been no match for the *Victory* in normal circumstances, and was held in a death hug. At times the ships were so close that some of the *Victory*'s guns could not be run out properly, and the British seamen were reduced to hurling bucketfuls of water into the French ports in case fires there endangered both vessels.

The ordeal of the *Redoutable* was brutal. At thirty yards most of the *Victory*'s guns could smash their way through more than four feet of solid, seasoned oak. This close, the double or treble-shotted starboard discharges punched their way through the French ship relatively cleanly, without scattering as many murderous splinters as they would otherwise have done, but the fusillade was heavier, faster and more relentless than the French had ever seen. The standard British gun was designed on the Blomefield pattern, built to withstand great internal power and capable of extreme velocity. They may have been ignited by a lanyard and flintlock mechanism rather than a slow match, but more probably a 'quick match' of worsted and cotton, and they were certainly served by professional gunners able to work with purposed precision in appalling conditions. The *Victory*'s guns had last been exercised only five days before, and the forty step process ran like clockwork. The gun was stabilised after recoiling into its breechings, the bore sponged and wormed to remove debris and a cartridge rammed home, followed by up to three wadded shot. The cartridge was pierced for ignition through an aperture in the gun breech, and prepared for firing. Primed, the weapon was hauled to its open port and under the supervision of the gun captain adjusted with tackle, handspikes and wedges, aimed and fired according to the roll of the ship. A good British crew could fire a round in about three minutes for a short time, although the rhythm would have been unsustainable in a protracted contest, when men tired and guns overheated. Nevertheless, the gunner of the *Victory* recorded that in little more than four hours she used six to seven tons of powder to fire 4243 round shot and 371 double-headed, grape and case shot, and threw four thousand musket balls. An officer of marines on one of the gun decks of the *Victory* 'fancied' himself 'in the infernal regions, where every man appeared a devil. Lips might move, but orders and hearing were out of the question. Everything was done by signs.' Yet not a single accident was recorded, so smooth and disciplined were the crews. This awesome power was now unleashed upon the *Redoutable*. At first the French tried to kill the British gunners by discharging muskets and pistols through the ports, but their own artillery was soon silenced as fiery discharges slammed into the hull of the doomed ship, smashing its physical and human insides to pieces.[31]

The innards of the *Redoutable* were being pulped, but Captain Lucas was one of the most tenacious and enterprising officers in the French service. He had disciplined and drilled his men, instilling an outstanding *esprit de corps* that kept them fighting. Lucas, like most of the continental officers, still believed in old-fashioned battles, in which boarding would play a key role and had made it his speciality. The crew were trained in the use of the grapnels that held ships together, and in boarding weaponry of all kinds, including short carbines fitted with bayonets, and grenades, for which the captain had devised belts that enabled chosen men to carry two at a time. Thus equipped, the French could project a veritable shower of missiles on to an enemy deck to clear it before boarding. Totally incapable of withstanding the terrific beating the British guns were administering below, Lucas played this one crucial card. The marksmen bristling in his fighting tops were already spattering the upper decks of the *Victory* with a lethal fire, and now trumpets summoned reinforcements from the gun decks. The lower gun ports were closed as seamen and soldiers responded, spilling on to the upper deck and into the shrouds and netting of the *Redoutable*, brandishing swords, pistols, muskets and pikes. To pave the way, scores of grenades, perhaps two hundred or more in all, were hurled into the British ship.[32]

Minutes after forcing the enemy line, Nelson's attack had been only partly successful. The line had been fractured, but, instead of passing to leeward and turning to port towards Villeneuve's van, the *Victory* had been unable to break through and was embedded in the hostile defences like a flattened bullet. And while the French ship was being pulverised to fragments below, her musketry and grenades were clearing the *Victory*'s poop, quarterdeck and waist, and exposing them to a threatening counterattack. It was just as this crisis was maturing that the British suffered a devastating blow. One of the snipers in the fighting top of the *Redoutable*'s mizzen mast was scanning the quarterdeck of the enemy ship, looking for targets amidst gaps in the swinging sails, masts, rigging and drifting smoke. His light *Ancien Régime* musket was charged with an '18-to-the-pound' lead ball measuring 0.69 inches in diameter and weighing 0.71 ounces. Seeing an opportunity, the marksman focused on two officers some fifty-five feet away. On a high moving platform, it was a quick and difficult shot, and the larger man would have made the easier target. But the marksman recognised his small but distinguished companion, and, squinting along his sight, saw the admiral turn briefly towards the *Redoutable*. He took his chance and squeezed the trigger.[33]

About fifteen minutes after one o'clock, perhaps fifty minutes into the *Victory*'s battle, Nelson and Hardy were still pacing up and down the quarterdeck between the steering wheel beneath the poop and the hatchway that led to the lower decks. Nelson saw Walter Burke the purser on deck, and sent him down to the cockpit to help the surgeon. As the two commanders approached their turning point near the hatchway, with Nelson on the port side, the admiral complimented one of his ships and turned left, momentarily facing the French ship on their starboard side. In the din of conflict no one heard the crack of the musket. The ball struck Nelson high in the front of his left shoulder, piercing the epaulette and dragging pieces of gold lace, silk pad and bullion with it as it drove deep into his small body. After slightly fracturing the left shoulder bone, it coursed straight and obliquely down into the thorax (chest), breaking the left second and third ribs and cutting the associated intercostal blood vessels. Then it tore through the left lung, fracturing the sixth and seventh thoracic vertebrae and penetrating the left side of the spine. In so doing it severed one of several large branches of the left pulmonary artery at the root of the lung in the vicinity of the sixth vertebra. The ball, flattened against bone during its destructive course, finally exited the right side of the spine and embedded itself in the trapezius muscle of the back, about two inches below the point of the right shoulder blade. Nelson felt the bullet smack into his backbone, and fell on his knees, trying to support himself with his one hand before crumpling forward upon his left side.[34]

Two or three men immediately ran to his assistance, including Sergeant James Secker of the Royal Marines, a Norfolk man. As the admiral was partially lifted a shocked Hardy knelt beside him. The admiral's uniform was covered with the blood of an earlier casualty on the deck. 'Hardy, I believe they have done it at last,' said Nelson, managing the faintest of smiles. Hardy said he hoped the wound would not be mortal, but the admiral replied, 'My backbone is shot through.' He had to be got to the surgeon. Four men managed to get him down the three ladders that led into the surgeon's cockpit in the belly of the ship, an agonising and dangerous journey for a man with a serious spinal injury. Reputedly, Nelson pulled a handkerchief over his face and breast to avoid dispiriting the men. Down in the gloomy cockpit, amidst the groans and stink of blood, Beatty and his assistants were working at full stretch, with forty casualties arriving about the same time as Nelson. Indeed, the Reverend Scott, who had been helping the surgeons, had been so distressed by the grisly scene that he fled up top for a respite, despite the enemy fire. Beatty had just pronounced death over the bodies of the captain's clerk, Whipple, and Lieutenant William Alexander Ram, who had suffered multiple injuries when a round shot smashed upwards through the quarterdeck, scattering broken splinters everywhere. Only twenty-one and recently promoted, Ram was in extreme pain, and bled to death after tearing away a tourniquet the surgeon had applied. Beatty's distress was interrupted by an urgent voice. 'Mr Beatty, Lord Nelson is here,' it called. 'Mr Beatty, the admiral is wounded!'[35]

4

Above decks the crisis in the *Victory* peaked after the admiral had been brought down. An early casualty was the marksman who had fired the most famous shot in the battle. Using the poop and quarterdeck, two British midshipmen, nineteen-year-old John Pollard from Cawsand in Cornwall, and twenty-year-old Edward Francis Collingwood from Milford in Wales, directed a steady fire at the mizzen top of the *Redoutable*, supported by a man named King, who reloaded muskets. The number of snipers cut down depends upon the version one accepts, but one of the Frenchmen was hit as he tried to escape down the rigging. However, Pollard's lethal role was acknowledged at the time, and if his story is to believed Hardy called him into the wardroom after the action and personally thanked him for avenging the admiral's death.[36]

Lucas made his bid to board the *Victory*. It was probably a forlorn venture, given his markedly inferior manpower, and the greater height of the British ship and rolling of the swell made her hard to enter from the *Redoutable*, even though the French took their main yard down to throw across as a bridge. The crisis was serious but short-lived. French claims that they virtually commanded the upper decks of the *Victory* were exaggerated, but they certainly inflicted severe casualties in the open upper decks. When most of the marines on the poop and quarterdeck were down, Adair sent Rotely for reinforcements below, where some of his corps had stripped off their red coats to help man guns. Supported by seamen armed with tomahawks, cutlasses and pikes, they stormed up top and threw themselves into the fray. By then Adair had only ten men left, and the din was so deafening that he had to bellow into the ears of subordinates to be heard. He was an inspiration, continuing to load and fire his musket after being wounded in the forehead by a splinter, but a ball ploughed into the back of his head and killed him instantly. Marines Lieutenant Rotely took command, and ordered the men to clear the enemy tops of snipers, especially the mizzen that hid Nelson's killer, claiming that 'in five minutes not a man was left alive in it'. In the action the *Victory*'s marines suffered forty-three killed and wounded, almost a third of the total force, the dead including James Berry, a twenty-one-year-old drummer from Norwich. But their loss was not entirely in vain, because they helped keep Lucas's boarders at bay. James Robertson Walker, a twenty-two-year-old midshipman in the forecastle, remembered that the marines and seamen about him 'fell like corn before the sickle' but with the help of a sixty-eight-pound carronade, which recoiled quickly on a sliding platform and hurled frightening discharges of round and grape shot at a fast pace, they prevented the French from boarding. Signal Lieutenant John Pasco agreed that 'not a single man from *Redoutable* ever set foot on the *Victory*'s deck'. Perhaps memory was skewing the facts to some extent, but Lucas's attempt to board was thwarted and the French captain, who later fell into British hands, would acknowledge the devastation the *Victory*'s carronade caused among his massed boarders.[37]

This failure destroyed Lucas's thin chance to avoid defeat by about twenty minutes past one o'clock, but the *coup de grâce* was delivered by Eliab Harvey's *Temeraire*, the second ship in Nelson's line, which fouled with the *Redoutable* at about that time. Immortalised in Turner's great canvas, the 'fighting *Temeraire*' of ninety-eight guns had suffered substantial damage during her approach, delivering only a few blows in return, and she buried herself in the combined fleet almost unmanageable, with her bowsprit and all three masts wounded.

Nevertheless, she raked the *Redoutable* with a mighty broadside that slaughtered some two hundred men, and ran upon her starboard side, sandwiching the luckless French seventy-four between herself and the *Victory*, two of the heaviest ships in the British fleet. Thus trapped, Lucas abandoned all further thought of boarding the British flagship, and struggled to work guns and muskets on both sides. To starboard Harvey lashed the French ship to the *Temeraire* in a fatal embrace, while to larboard the *Victory*'s gunners were said to have begun to depress their pieces for fear that their shot would pass right through the *Redoutable* and into the *Temeraire*. In this corner of the battle, at least, Nelson's plan to mass strength worked, and *Redoutable* made a brief, futile resistance. The sight that greeted the prize crew that went aboard the *Redoutable* was almost beyond belief. Most of the French guns had been catapulted over or smashed. The hull was shot through with holes, her ports stoved in, her poop and stern almost unrecognisable, and her decks 'torn up'. Four of her six pumps had been destroyed and the tiller, helm and rudder shot away, while her masts lay in a 'mass of wreckage', with the main strewn across the poop of the *Temeraire*. So many fires were breaking out that the men of the *Victory* were trying to pole their ship away to avert danger. As Lucas remarked, 'He who has not seen the *Redoutable* in this state can never have any concept of her destruction. I do not know of anything on board which was not cut up by shot.' The ship was filled with shattered bodies. By Lucas's reports 522 of 643 men were dead or wounded, including nearly all the officers, and the official return put the butcher's bill even higher at 571. The *Redoutable* had fought until 80 per cent or more of her complement had fallen. Few more gallant defences have been recorded, but she gained no reward. The ship sank the following day, and the British were only able to save 169 of her crew.[38]

With the *Redoutable* conquered, *Temeraire* was free to deal with other opponents, several of whom had been firing into her. The *Fougueux* came along her starboard side, so that all four vessels – *Victory*, *Redoutable*, *Temeraire* and *Fougueux* – lay together, bows forward, as if snug in a harbour. Harvey transferred gunners to his starboard guns to open a savage fire into the *Fougueux*, and then sent boarders leaping into her rigging and through her gun ports. The French captain was found mortally wounded on his quarterdeck, among 546 casualties, comparable to those suffered by the *Redoutable*. Between the two French prizes, the exhausted *Temeraire* lay covered by a layer of debris, with 123 of her men killed and wounded. She had never seen a finer hour. As for the crippled *Victory*, she fired some of her larboard batteries at the *Santissima Trinidad* and such other adversaries as she could reach, and extricating herself from the rubble, struggled northwards while her men fought to clear wreckage and restore capability.[39]

The third and fourth ships of Nelson's line, Fremantle's three-decked *Neptune* and two seventy-fours, Bayntun's *Leviathan* and Israel Pellew's *Conqueror*, all got into action astern of the *Bucentaure*, where some water had opened after the

Victory and *Redoutable* fell to leeward. At a signal Fremantle's men, crouching low to avoid shot, sprang to their guns and sent a multi-shotted broadside into the French flagship, stripping her upper deck of its remaining guns and able-bodied men. Breaking through the line, Fremantle luffed up to larboard to attack *Bucentaure* from leeward, simultaneously opening a systematic fire into the stern of the *Santissima Trinidad*. He was reinforced by *Leviathan* and *Conqueror*, which fired into the dying French flagship, intensified the attack upon the gargantuan *Santissima Trinidad*, positioning themselves to do maximum damage while keeping away from her fearful broadsides, and extended the battle to the *San Augustín*, which was smashed into defeat in thirty minutes.

Less than two hours after the *Victory* opened fire, the battle in the centre was drawing to a close. The *Bucentaure* was a helpless wreck, her masts broken stumps, her rigging, sails and spars spattered in all directions and trailing over shot-ridden sides, and 282 of her men killed and wounded, some of the former decapitated by shot as they stooped at their guns. Latterly, her colours had only been kept flying by a plucky midshipman, who had wrapped them around his body and stood on the upper deck. At one point Villeneuve considered transferring to another ship, but all his boats were smashed. He struck at about two o'clock, and one of Nelson's objectives, the destruction of the enemy command centre, had been achieved. Northwards the same fate was overtaking the *Santissima Trinidad*, now also beset by the sixty-four-gun *Africa*. Exemplifying the best of the Royal Navy, the *Africa* had regained the fleet after a frantic voyage from the north, jettisoning valuable provisions to increase her pace. Too late to take her allotted place in Collingwood's line, but remembering Nelson's orders to seek out the enemy if all else failed, Digby went straight into the nearest storm, exchanging fire with the entire Franco-Spanish van as he passed each of its ships in turn, and finally bearing up to rake the *Santissima Trinidad* fore to aft. The contest progressed to its inexorable end. The mizzen and mainmasts of the Spanish colossus went down simultaneously, plunging over the side in one of the 'most magnificent sights' one officer of *Conqueror* had 'ever beheld'. Fifteen minutes later the *Santissima Trinidad*'s foremast fell backwards on to her stern. Taking life-threatening hits between wind and water as she helplessly heeled one way or another in the swell, she was a fallen giant, littered with shattered wood, canvas, cordage, broken guns, flesh, bone and blood. Some of the 332 casualties lay helplessly on the blood-patterned decks without arms or legs. About 2.15 a Union Jack was hung over the starboard quarter of the largest warship in the world to advertise her surrender.[40]

All ten of the ships that had defended the allied centre had given way. Four were prizes, and the rest bloodily dispersed, two bearing away to the north-east and four becoming embroiled in the battle to the rear. The failure of those six ships to engage more seriously had yielded a fortunate advantage to the British, enabling four ships of the line to overwhelm the *Santissima Trinidad*. This part of the battle had not gone entirely to Nelson's plan, however. He had not prevented fragments of the disintegrating centre from falling back to increase the pressure upon Collingwood as intended, nor been able to advance northwards with his ships to attack the Franco-Spanish van. But two flagships, one the command centre, had been taken, and the entire Franco-Spanish fleet hewn in two like a broken bough, with an extensive battle in progress to the south and a relatively unengaged van to the north.

Collingwood's lee column had more on its hands than either Nelson or he had intended. In the fierce cannonade the hot air rose, leaving the ships to struggle to manoeuvre or extricate themselves from difficulty with barely a wind. The *Royal Sovereign*, *Belleisle* and *Mars* had borne the brunt of the initial fire and crunched their way through the enemy ships, but the *Tonnant*, *Bellerophon* and *Colossus* came behind to turn the tide of the battle, though at a heavy cost. All three ships saw their captains cut down, and two returned the highest casualties in the British fleet.

Charles Tyler's eighty-gun *Tonnant* pierced the line astern of the Spanish *Monarca*, disposing of her with two raking broadsides before engaging the *Algésiras*, the flagship of the French rear admiral, Charles-René Magon. 'The Spaniard I hauled up for was very soon silenced,' Tyler reported, 'but his second astern, Admiral Magon in the *Algizeras*, a new ship of 80 guns, made sail to prevent my cutting through, but I owed him one, and prevented his assistance for some time. He again made sail and was going to rake us. Our sails etc. all gone, [but] I put the helm hard a-port and caught his jib boom in our mizzen rigging, and in a very little time not a man was to be seen on his decks. They had 300 men ready to board us, but the fire from our quarter-deck and all the guns that could bear soon altered their plans. We set her on fire by our [blazing] wads [from the guns] in her bow, but put it out with our engine. The Admiral Magon was killed and his captain wounded, and near 300 men, as they say. My officers and men behaved with the utmost coolness and bravery.' In the course of the fight, however, a musket ball ripped through Tyler's right thigh, and he had to quit the deck, leaving his first lieutenant to finish the battle. When he forced the Spanish *Monarca* to surrender he did not have a boat left to go over to take possession.[41]

John Cooke, the captain of the *Bellerophon*, was less fortunate than Tyler. Pushing into the combined fleet between the Spanish *Bahama* and *Montanes*, he put two broadsides and three blasts from a carronade into the first before colliding with the French *Aigle* ahead, striking her on the larboard quarter with his starboard bow and pushing his foreyard into the enemy mainsail. The French ship was the larger, more heavily armed and generously manned, and she had assistance from three or more consorts, which tried to position themselves to fire into the *Bellerophon*. A desperate fight ensued with the muzzles of the guns of the principal opponents almost touching, and the crews close enough to look each other in the eye, snatch at each other's ramrods or fire pistols through the open ports. Using their superiority in troops, the French twice attempted to board, tossing fizzing grenades on to the British upper deck or through ports and hatchways. Some of the murderous projectiles exploded, throwing iron fragments and musket balls in every direction, killing and maiming men and kindling the timber beams. A single blast downed twenty-five of the *Bellerophon*'s men. Captain Cooke was reloading his pistols on the quarterdeck when one or two musket balls slammed into his chest and killed him. His sailing master went down with a mangled leg and the captain of marines was carried below with eight balls in his body and his right arm severed. First Lieutenant William Pryce Cumby ordered all men off the poop. Yet throughout the torment those British guns continued to pound away relentlessly. 'Our fire was so hot that we soon drove them from the lower deck,' a witness said, 'after which our people took the quoins out and elevated their guns so as to tear her [upper] decks and sides to pieces.' The *Aigle* lost two-thirds of her company, and one side of the ship 'was entirely beaten in'. Seeking an escape, the dismasted Frenchman raised a sail on an improvised jib to crawl away to leeward, where she eventually struck to the *Defiance*. The exhausted *Bellerophon*, her main and mizzen topmasts hanging over the starboard side, her jib boom, spanker boom and gaff shot away, and not a brace or bowline 'serviceable', had become 'totally unmanageable' and suffered 150 casualties.[42]

No British ship suffered the casualties endured by the *Colossus*. She got into action before one o'clock, mauled the French *Swiftsure* to larboard and then locked yardarms with another Frenchman, the *Argonaute*, which suddenly materialised ghostlike out of the smoke to starboard. For half an hour or so *Colossus* engaged both ships, trading blistering volleys until the *Argonaute* fell to leeward, a wreck with more than two hundred dead and wounded on her decks. But the *Colossus* herself had a singularly hard battle. According to a marine of the *Sirius* frigate, she was almost carried by boarders, who gained possession of her forecastle and main hatchway, but was rescued by heroic lower-deck tars who climbed out of their ports, scaled the outside of the ship to reach the quarter-deck, and turned some of her guns forward to expel the attackers. Drama was also heightened by Captain James Nichol Morris, who was hit in the thigh, but continued to direct the fight with a tourniquet tied above his wound in the manner of the legendary Admiral John Benbow. The battle with the *Swiftsure* lasted longer, and left the Frenchman a helpless hulk, tossing in the waves with two masts down, the wheel shattered and the hull leaking like a sieve, but the British ship had enough fight along the way to also force the Spanish *Bahama* to surrender after a heroic resistance. The process cost *Colossus* two hundred men dead and injured. As her quartermaster wrote, 'although we had a great many killed and wounded, and our decks afloated with blood, two more [ships] came bearing down upon us. We were much disabled, it had fallen little wind, so that some heavy ships of ours could not get to our assistance, but no matter, we were Englishmen. "Sink or Conquer" was the word, three cheers, and to it . . .' After a 'continued blaze' of several hours the *Colossus* was relieved by the arrival of the *Orion*, which finished off the *Swiftsure*; in her protracted trial she had inflicted more than twice her own casualties upon three adversaries.[43]

Two more ships of Collingwood's line got in action within thirty minutes of the *Royal Sovereign*. Richard King's *Achille* cut a remarkable swath through the Franco-Spanish rear, raking the *Montanes* and luffing up to leeward to knock her out of the fight. Then, swinging north-east, she destroyed resistance in the Spanish *Argonauta*, leaving her with an English ensign slung over her larboard quarter in a token of surrender, and went on to hammer the *Berwick*, turning her decks and cockpit into a shambles, killing her captain and inflicting 250 other casualties. One British ship had defeated three enemies and inflicted hundreds of casualties for a loss of seventy-two of her own men.

Robert Moorsom's *Revenge*, a new and powerfully armed seventy-four bearing one of the most distinguished names in naval history, had a reputation for gunnery among British colleagues who were themselves professionals. Her fight developed into a battle with the two seventy-fours, *San Ildefonso* and the French *Achille*, and the 112-gun *Principe de Asturias*, the flagship of Gravina, the senior Spanish admiral. One opponent ran her bowsprit over the poop of the *Revenge* and provided an ideal opportunity to board, but as the enemy soldiers and sailors attempted to swarm across the rudimentary bridge they were knocked off like flies by canister shot from Moorsom's poop carronades and small arms fire. It was many galling minutes before the next British ship arrived. Philip Durham's *Defiance* eventually spared the *Revenge* by falling upon the *Principe de Asturias*. Gravina's shot flew 'so high that they shot away our main-topgallant truck,' wrote a midshipman, but 'every one of our shot told upon her and made the splinters fly'. When the Spanish flagship limped away to leeward, *Defiance* turned upon the ragged *Aigle*. In desperation the French resorted to a primitive chemical weapon, jars of sulphur and combustibles thrown into the British ports as an incendiary and gas shell, emitting noxious fumes. Durham replied by recalling his boarders, standing off and resuming a more distant but ferocious bombardment, 'every shot . . . going through and through'.[44]

A lieutenant of the *Conqueror*, Humphrey Senhouse, later an admiral, put his finger on a flaw in the British tactics. 'Instead of doubling on the enemy, the British were on that day themselves doubled and trebled on,' he said. The first seven ships 'were placed in such situations . . . that nothing but the most heroic gallantry and practical skill at their guns could have extricated them'. Although not strictly true – Nelson did not literally plan to 'double' his opponents – there was much in this. The battle of Trafalgar was essentially won by fourteen ships, which together suffered 85 per cent of the fleet's casualties. In Nelson's battle five ships, *Victory*, *Temeraire*, *Neptune*, *Leviathan* and *Africa* engaged at least seven opponents, and were spared greater odds because others fled the centre. The last prize taken in that contest was the *San Augustín*, boarded in twenty minutes by the men of the *Leviathan*. The first nine ships in Collingwood's line engaged twenty opponents. For over an hour Nelson's intended British concentration backfired, undermined principally by the light wind. It was the enemy, not the British, who had the advantage of numbers and firepower. The balance of the engagement, and its character, tilted as the afternoon matured, and Nelson's later arrivals made relatively short work of the remaining opposition.[45]

As these reinforcements sailed into action the begrimed companies 'crowded upon the beams, poops and quarters and every part of the[ir] ships to cheer us'. The *Royal Sovereign*, *Belleisle*, *Bellerophon* and *Colossus*, which headed Collingwood's line, each reported casualties of between 126 and 200 killed and wounded, whereas those in the rear, *Prince*, *Polyphemus*, *Swiftsure*, *Dreadnought*, *Defence* and *Thunderer*, suffered between none and thirty-six casualties respectively, and together summed only 108. The British *Swiftsure* helped *Defiance* destroy the resistance of the *Aigle*, 'fast' firing into her as the men of the *Defiance* boarded, 'driving the Frenchmen overboard in all directions', and *Dreadnought*, *Thunderer*, *Defence* and *Prince* also reinvigorated a flagging attack, completing the defeat of the *San Ildefonso*, *San Juan de Nepomuceno* and the French *Achille*. Three crushing broadsides from the lumbering three-decked *Prince* dismasted the *Achille* and left her enveloped in flames, providing the final spectacle of the battle. The French ship had survived encounters with several British ships, but now rushed towards her end with horrible urgency, and the *Prince* stood off, expecting a violent explosion. 'We could plainly see the blood running out of the *Achille*'s scuppers,' recorded a log of the British *Swiftsure*. Terrified figures, silhouetted black against the licking flames, were seen hurling debris into the sea to serve as crude rafts and leaping overboard. Despite the danger, British boats from the *Prince*, *Pickle*, *Naiad* and *Entreprenante* circled, snatching what survivors they could from the sea. The most famous was Jeanne Caunant, a twenty-five-year-old woman who was found clinging stark-naked to some wreckage. Hastily wrapped in clothes donated by the oarsmen of the *Pickle*'s boat, she had injuries and burns but survived to tell her remarkable story. The wife of a maintopman, she had served in *Achille* as a powder monkey until the ship took fire, when she was trapped below. Eventually she escaped through a gunroom port, climbed down the chains to the rudder, and although she could not swim leaped into the sea and thrashed her way to some life-saving wreckage. Hers was a happy end, since she was reunited with her husband, who also survived, but nothing could spare the *Achille* herself. The ship disintegrated in a large explosion at about 5.30, commemorating both the sunset and the end of the battle with a wrathful red fountain that shot into the air and briefly illuminated the scene of carnage on the darkening waters below.[46]

5

An important contribution to the result off Cape Trafalgar was made by Dumanoir of the *Formidable*, who commanded the allied van. For two hours the battle raged without his division making any serious attempt to intervene. Even when it fired upon the *Africa* as she passed to support Nelson, it remained stubbornly unstirred by her example. Dumanoir's inaction was akin to the failure of the French rear to react at the Nile, but on that occasion the defaulting rear admiral was no less a person than Villeneuve himself. Now the boot was upon the other foot. Nelson had supposed the enemy van would not be able to react quickly enough to save the centre and rear, but was blessed on the day by an inertia even he could not have predicted. Reinforced by refugees from the centre, Dumanoir eventually had ten ships to dispose, enough to have influenced the conflict if they had been committed at a decisive stage.

About the time Nelson's column hit his centre, Villeneuve summoned his unengaged ships to his aid, but probably that and a second signal to the same effect were lost in the thick powder smoke. Apparently acting upon his own hook, Dumanoir eventually ordered the van to tack with the intention of threatening the rear of Nelson's line as it progressed slowly towards the fight. The wind was so light that small boats had to be used to tow the heads of some of Dumanoir's ships round, and it was almost three o'clock before they got underway. Only three ships followed Dumanoir's *Formidable* as she made her way south to windward. Four others wore to leeward instead, where they hoped to link with the remains of Gravina's division, then making its last stand against Collingwood's ships, and the remaining two pursued truly heroic courses of their own. The French *Intrépide*, under Captain Louis-Antoine-Cyprien Infernet, came to windward and headed straight into the heart of the embattled centre, now in British hands, determined to vindicate national honour by cutting her way through the mass of enemy ships to rescue the commander-in-chief. Not dissimilarly, Captain Cayetano Valdes of the Spanish *Neptuno* felt obliged to support the *Santissima Trinidad* and trailed after Dumanoir's detachment nursing a wholly different agenda.

None of these manoeuvres, diffident, hopeful or magnificently foolish, was successful. Seeing Dumanoir coming round with three seventy-fours and two eighties, Hardy signalled the British ships of the weather column to come to the wind on the larboard tack and shield their damaged consorts and prizes. Several managed to respond, including *Leviathan*, *Africa*, *Neptune*, *Agamemnon* and *Conqueror*, while the last two of Nelson's original attack line, *Spartiate* and *Minotaur*, temporarily hauled up across Dumanoir's path to fire raking broadsides into the oncoming foe before joining the defensive formation. It was enough for Dumanoir, who saw that Villeneuve had surrendered and was beyond help, and after a brief exchange of shots made off to windward. He worked southwards, but Collingwood, like Hardy, had extricated some of his torn belligerents to resist, and Dumanoir recoiled and steered for the Strait. The battle was then in its final moments, and Gravina, who had suffered a mortal wound when his left arm was smashed by grape, was rallying what remained of his force to run for Cadiz. In the meantime, the brave *Intrépide* made her astonishing effort to reach the dismasted *Bucentaure*. She had no chance, and was soon entangled in a battle for survival. Codrington's *Orion* decisively quit an attack on the *San Augustín* to leeward to compel *Intrépide* to strike at about five o'clock. Her mizzen and main topmasts had gone by the board, and half her men were down. On her part the *Neptuno* surrendered to the *Spartiate* and *Minotaur* after suffering seventy-three casualties, one her captain, who was injured by the falling mizzen.

The battle saw many acts of heroism on both sides. Thomas Robinson, boatswain of the *Bellerophon*, went down to the cockpit, dressed both his badly injured hands with the aid of a purser's steward to spare the surgeon, and returned to his fighting deck, entreating an officer to use him in whatever capacity he might be useful. He died of his wounds in Gibraltar two weeks later. Nineteen-year-old Midshipman William Rivers of the *Victory*, his left foot hanging by a thread of skin, pluckily descended to the cockpit unaided to spare another for further duty. 'Nothing is the matter with me,' he told his father, the gunner. 'Only lost my leg, and that in a good cause!' James Spratt, a flammable Irishman of the *Defiance*, famously swam to the French *Aigle*, boarded her single-handed, and tried to raise British colours. Though badly injured, he held his ground until reinforced, keeping the thrusting bayonets of three French soldiers at bay with his swinging cutlass and tomahawk. It got down to a struggle with bare hands, but Spratt survived to become a commander and father an admiral.[47]

If the French van performed less than satisfactorily, by no means all the British lived up to Nelson's expectations. One witness opined that some 'in enviable situations . . . did not . . . do quite as much as they might have done'. Collingwood's flag captain fingered Richard Grindall of the *Prince* and Rear Admiral the Earl of Northesk of the *Britannia*, while Codrington of the *Orion*, who contributed to the taking of the French *Swiftsure* and *L'Intrépide*, saw Berry as a weak link. According to Codrington, Berry's *Agamemnon* was 'far astern of us' during the approach, and while *Orion* prudently reserved her fire until it could be used with effect, Berry was 'blazing away and wasting her ammunition'. Collingwood declined to sully the victory by making an issue of such shortcomings, but was disappointed that some of his ships failed to get up in time to play a full part. He asked to see the *Dreadnought*'s log, but knew that the three-decker sailed badly, and concluded that Captain Conn had done well to get into the action in time to make a notable contribution. The wind was exceptionally light, of course, but some ships reputed for their sailing qualities made poor progress, including the *Polyphemous*, *Swiftsure* and *Defence*. The *Defence*, like the *Africa*, had been disadvantaged by her starting point far to the northwest. But some captains probably took a narrow view of their duty, and instead of hurrying forward as fast as possible became absorbed with finding and keeping their designated place in the official sailing order. Yet Nelson had not demanded a slavish adherence to the prescribed order. He had emphasised the importance of speed and close-quarter firing, and ultimately released his captains to act according to circumstances. In the words of his memorandum, 'no captain can do very wrong if he places his ship alongside that of an enemy'.[48]

British casualties, as initially reported to Collingwood, amounted to 1663 killed and wounded. Submissions to the Patriotic Fund, established by Lloyd's in 1803 to provide relief for the veterans and their families, produced a higher figure, 1734, but this was still modest for such a closely fought encounter. By Collingwood's figures, only six ships sustained more than one hundred casualties. One was the *Victory*. After the battle her losses were given as 132, but Beatty later claimed that twenty-seven men were treated for injuries after the returns had been made out, which increased the total to 159. The Patriotic Fund gave the flagship's loss as 136, with relatively light injuries probably accounting for the disparity. The ship itself had also suffered grievously. Her mizzen topmast and yards had been shot away, and her fore- and mainmasts, main topmast, fore and maintops, jib boom and bowsprit seriously damaged. Her sails and rigging were cut to shreds, two of her anchors disabled, and 134 shot holes had been battered through the hull. Her human loss was greater than that of any ship in the weather line. Indeed, laying aside the *Temeraire*, the *Victory* sustained more casualties than the next six ships of her line combined. Nelson had always led from the front, but never more dramatically than in this conflict 'so grand, so awful, and so tremendous'.[49]

The battle had been the greatest test of naval power in living memory. In numbers of ships, guns and men, and to some extent in tactical position, Villeneuve had a clear advantage, and a competent fleet would have repulsed Nelson's attack. Yet while eighteen French and Spanish ships had been taken or destroyed, not a single British ship had surrendered and only one had been totally dismasted. Of the surviving ships of the defeated fleet, eleven got to Cadiz with Gravina, many badly damaged, and four fled with Dumanoir. Five of the seven French and Spanish flag officers who gave battle that day were captured or killed. The disparity in human losses was no less stark. Although heavily outnumbered in the decisive phase of the battle, the British lost about 1700 killed and wounded, but they killed, wounded or captured about 14,000 of their enemies. A recent estimate put the Spanish loss, including those killed and wounded on the ships that escaped, at 7495, or about 63 per cent of their total manpower. There had been no more graphic demonstration of the potency of the British war machine.[50]

If the Nile and Copenhagen had been smaller victories they had been more complete, but they were fought in enclosed spaces from which the enemy had no ready escape. That so decisive a victory as Trafalgar could have been won in open water was almost incredible. It ultimately rested upon the investment Britain had put into its navy, and upon the superior training, discipline, experience and health of her crews. The British possibly had a technical advantage in their greater use of heavy carronades, but the superiority of their seamanship and gunnery had told formidably. The French and Spanish knew it, and had tried to avoid the battle. 'It is only possible to be better served by the [Spanish] gunnery,' said one of their officers, 'when their assembly and tools are of the level of perfection of the enemy's.' And the British banked on it. 'Our men,' observed a lieutenant of the *Conqueror*, 'who from constant practice had gained great quickness in the use of their guns, aimed with deliberate precision, as if they had only been firing at a mark, and tore their opponent to pieces.'[51]

But the victory belonged firmly to Nelson. The circumstances were not ideal. He had far fewer ships than envisaged, his opponents were more heavily armed than experience predicted and the light air seriously exposed the British attack. Nor had all of Nelson's tactics been successful. The enemy control centre was destroyed, but once the battle had begun Villeneuve's signals had hardly been effective anyway, and while the van of the combined fleet had been kept out of the decisive phase of the battle, as Nelson had intended, it was as much a result of its own inertia as the British admiral's feint. The concentration that Nelson had wanted had also been elusive. The feeble breeze and slow advance; the failure to implement the line of bearing that might have brought Collingwood's line into action more or less simultaneously; and the pattern of the conflict had all militated against the British plan to mass strength. But Nelson had recognised the overwhelming superiority of the weapon in his hand and measured the risks that had to be taken to unleash its full power. He had seized his moment and taken enough ships directly into the heart of the enemy fleet, where they were needed, creating that close-range pell-mell encounter in which his forces excelled. And in that blinding smoke-wreathed chaos and carnage he had, through his previous written and verbal communications, given his captains purpose and direction, whilst many of their opponents fought isolated and alone. Digby of the *Africa*, for example, could throw away the plan and use his initiative to make a difference because he knew what Nelson expected. If the ultimate unpredictability of war had frustrated key elements of Nelson's plan, its fundamentals – the health, experience, seamanship, gunnery and focus of the British fleet – were sound. Indeed, the admiral had exceeded his expectations. He had said that only numbers could annihilate, but he was wrong. He had annihilated without numbers.

6

They laid him on a makeshift bed against the larboard side of the cockpit, normally a midshipmen's berth, its huge oak ribs still shuddering to the discharge of great guns on the main deck above. The purser, Walter Burke, at sixty-five the oldest man in the ship, had helped to receive the admiral from the men who had brought him down the ladder, and temporarily supported his chief's head on his lap. Nelson had fractured ribs, a perforated lung, a spinal injury and ruptured arteries, but apparently made little complaint. He seems, indeed, to have been barely conscious, and asked who had carried him. 'Burke, my back is broke,' said the injured man.[52]

Beatty received the same dire prognosis. 'Ah, Mr Beatty,' Nelson said, 'you can do nothing for me. I have but a short time to live. My back is shot through.' He wanted the surgeon to attend to his other patients. Beatty saw blood, much of it in fact picked up from the stained deck rather than Nelson's own. The surgeon had formed a great attachment to Nelson since arriving in the *Victory* as a replacement for George Magrath. He remarked that he hoped the wound would not be a bad one, and quickly got to work, cutting the injured man's clothes away to avoid increasing his pain and covering his pale fragile body with a sheet. The Reverend Scott was also soon on the spot, wringing his hands in distraction. Nelson was made as comfortable as possible, and his coat was given to young Midshipman Westphal, who lay nearby with a head wound and needed a pillow. And there, in the gloom of that awful place, where a surgeon, assistant, surgeon's mate and a few helpers performed operations on a table beneath the light of half a dozen lanterns, and men lay everywhere groaning in pain and blood, with the timber pitching and rolling or shaking to the guns, the life of Horatio Nelson began to ebb away.[53]

Scott looked at Beatty, waiting desperately for his judgement, and Nelson saw his agonised face. 'Doctor, I told you so,' he said. 'Doctor, I am gone.' His mind wandered to the refuge still waiting for him back home, and in an agitated whisper he said, 'Remember me to Lady Hamilton. Remember me to Horatia. Remember me to all my friends.' Convinced he had little time, he tried to include everything. 'Doctor, remember me to Mr Rose. Tell him I have made a will, and left Lady Hamilton and Horatia to my country.' These words, or others like them, were repeated several times. Beatty remembered him saying, 'I have to leave Lady Hamilton and my adopted daughter, Horatia, as a legacy to my country.' Those matters dealt with, he grew more relaxed, but returned to them several times.[54]

Beatty gently examined the injuries, passing his left arm around the admiral's body to raise it while he felt for wounds in the thin back with the forefinger of his right hand. There was no exit wound, and Beatty told the patient that he suspected the ball was in his spine. He did not say, but knew that any attempt to probe the spine would be highly dangerous and painful and would probably hasten the end. The admiral's breath was short and laboured now, and his pulse weak and irregular. What did he feel, the surgeon asked? Nelson reported 'a gush of blood every minute within his breast', but there was no feeling in the lower part of his body. When he inhaled there was a terrific pain in the lower part of his spine. 'I felt it break my back,' he said.

His hopes fading, Beatty checked the admiral's pulse. He spoke discreetly, but eventually shared his fears with his assistants and Scott, Burke and Hardy. The exact nature of Nelson's injuries was not discovered until Beatty performed a post-mortem, and they have inspired disagreement since. In particular, historians have tried to find out what it was that actually killed Nelson. The damage to the spinal column deprived him of feeling in the lower body and by itself would have left the admiral a paraplegic, but it would not have caused death within hours. The left lung was also perforated, allowing air to escape and accumulate outside the lung, building pressure upon it and threatening a collapse. This 'pneumothorax' caused pain in the admiral's left side and increasing shortness of breath. In addition Nelson was bleeding internally, and 'a large branch of the pulmonary artery' had been divided, but there has been disagreement about how much blood was lost. Beatty concluded that the loss of blood was not 'very great.' Part of the answer to this apparent paradox – the rupture of an arterial vessel and restricted loss of blood – may have been low blood pressure. The pressure of the pulmonary vessels is low compared to that of the main artery, and there is also a tendency for a traumatically damaged artery not to bleed, because the muscle in the wall curls up and blocks the end of the vessel. Beatty's view was that, as the ruptured vessel was near the heart, what blood was lost was removed from the circulatory system early and 'produced death sooner than would have been effected by a larger quantity of blood lost from an artery in a more remote part of the body.' However, more recent medical analyses have emphasized that a steady loss of blood from the pulmonary vessels, as well as bleeding from the intercostals and lung tissue, would have combined with a profound fall in blood pressure caused by the damage to the spine. Low blood volume and low blood pressure stifled the supply of oxygen to Nelson's organs, hastening his end. He might have survived his spinal injury or the damage to his lungs and arteries, but not both.[55]

Nelson's vital organs were failing, and in the heat of the cockpit, where burning candles and lamps exhausted the air and dozens of human bodies were packed, he felt intolerably hot and thirsty, and tried to push the sheet that covered him away. 'Fan, fan,' he would gasp, and 'drink, drink'. Lemonade, water and some wine were given for the remaining moments of his life. Beatty may also have administered laudanum, but the pain and slow respiration made it hard for the wounded admiral to speak in sentences.

He 'repeatedly' asked for Hardy, desperate to know whether he had, after all, secured the victory he had promised the British people. Sudden bursts of cheering from the decks above stirred his curiosity, and Lieutenant Pasco, lying nearby with serious grape shot wounds to his right arm and side, suggested that prizes were being taken. As the minutes dragged, Nelson began to fear for Hardy's safety. The enemy was being decisively defeated, Burke reassured without the slightest knowledge of the fact, adding that Nelson would live to carry the news to England, but Nelson was not deceived. 'It is nonsense, Mr Burke, to suppose I can live,' he said. 'My sufferings are great, but they will soon be over.' The miserable Scott, who refused to leave his side, tried to object, but Nelson whispered, 'Ah, Doctor, it is all over. It is all over.'

Still, he called for his captain. 'Will no one bring Hardy to me?' he cried, 'He must be killed; he is surely destroyed.' In response, Hardy's aide, Midshipman Bulkeley, who owed his place in the ship to Nelson, came below to report that the captain was well and would come as soon as he could leave the deck. Nelson heard the voice and asked whose it was. 'It is Mr Bulkeley, my Lord,' said Burke. Nelson asked the boy to remember him to his father. It was probably a little after 2.30 that Hardy came at last, bending low to fit his large body between the decks. Nelson seemed relieved, and the two men shook hands affectionately. 'Well, Hardy,' asked the admiral, 'how goes the battle? How goes the day with us?'

'Very well, my Lord,' said the captain. 'We have got twelve or fourteen of the enemy's ships in our possession, but five of their van have tacked and show an intention of bearing down upon the *Victory*. I have therefore called two or three of our fresh ships round us, and have no doubt of giving them a drubbing.'

'I hope none of our ships have struck, Hardy?'

'No, my Lord. There is no fear of that.'[56]

'I am a dead man, Hardy. I am going fast. It will be all over with me soon. Come nearer to me. Pray let my dear Lady Hamilton have my hair, and all other things belonging to me.' Such personal matters led Burke to attempt a tactful withdrawal, but Nelson asked him to stay.

Hardy could not accept his friend's bleak prediction. Nelson had plucked him from obscurity, given him one opportunity after another, and placed him on the page of history. Hardy had cut the admiral's meat, and spared him the daily chore of managing his ships. Never a strategist, tactician or diplomat, Hardy knew a ship as few others, but stood in distant amazement of his friend's wider abilities. Now it was all fading fast. He hoped, he said, that Beatty might still save his life. 'Oh no,' Nelson answered firmly. 'It is impossible. My back is shot through. Beatty will tell you so.'

Dumanoir's threat to the fleet demanded Hardy's presence, and he had to go. The two friends shook hands again, and the captain climbed out of that dark wretched hole into the light, no doubt glad of the pressing business to hand. The flagship was soon emptying its larboard guns at Dumanoir's ships passing to windward, and Nelson, lying directly below the discharges, is alleged to have said, 'Oh *Victory*, *Victory*, how you distract my poor brain.'

Beatty had never been under more pressure; his battle was a grim litany of triumphs and tragedies, of lives saved and lost in wretched conditions. William Browne, an able seaman in his forties, mangled by grape shot, died of a huge haemorrhage in the left cavity of the chest. Richard Jewell of twenty-five years, severely wounded near the top of a femur by 'great violence', had an entire leg amputated, but perished from the amount of blood lost before reaching the cockpit. And an eighteen-year-old Scot from Paisley, Colin Turner, his stomach punctured by a musket ball, survived the initial treatment only to die of gangrene. But of the eleven amputations that Beatty performed in the action and its immediate aftermath, all but two survived, including Daniel McPherson, a twenty-two-year-old from Dumbarton, who had a femur smashed by a cannon shot and 'several pieces of bone' carried away. After amputating a foot of young Midshipman Rivers, Beatty returned to the admiral, leaving his assistants to treat two marines, Lieutenants James Peake and Lewis Reeves, both of whom would survive. 'You can do nothing for me,' Nelson said, begging the surgeon to resume his other duties. The protesting medic withdrew, but Scott soon summoned him back. 'Ah, Mr Beatty,' breathed the admiral when he appeared. 'I have sent for you to say what I forgot to tell you before, that all power of motion and feeling below my breast are gone, and *you* very well *know* I can live but a short time.' He was remembering the recent case of James Bush, who had died in the *Victory* in July after thirteen days of suffering with a spinal injury. The symptoms had not been dissimilar.

Beatty reminded Nelson that he had mentioned the loss of feeling before, but now pressed his limbs. The admiral said that Scott and Burke, who were alternately supporting the bed beneath his shoulders to give him relief, had both tried it already. '*You know* I am gone,' he emphasised. It was as if he needed to know the truth, however grave. Thus prompted, Beatty's eyes began to fill with tears as he pronounced the faltering words he hardly dared to say. 'My Lord, unhappily for our country, nothing can be done for you.' He turned his head and stepped back to hide his emotions.[57]

'I know it,' Nelson went on. He placed his hand to his left side. 'I feel something rising in my breast which tells me I am gone.' He referred to what he thought was a regular rush of blood, but which might have been a movement of blood and other fluids within the left thorax. Composing himself, Beatty recommended Scott and Burke to supply drink whenever it was requested, and they fanned him almost mechanically with paper. The three bent over the fallen man for some time. He murmured, and occasionally they picked out the words, 'God be praised, I have done my duty.'

About an hour after the admiral's arrival his pulse began to fail, but his mind seemed clear. Beatty asked if the pain was still great, and Nelson admitted that it was so severe that he wished he was dead. 'Yet,' he added in a whisper, 'one would like to live a little longer too.' He did not speak again for several minutes, and when it came his voice was low and difficult, and the attendants had difficulty hearing against the background noise. 'What would become of poor Lady Hamilton, if she knew my situation?' he said.

Up above Captain Hardy could wait no longer, and at about four in the afternoon a boat left the *Victory* to thread its way southwards, through water filled with wreckage and tired ships drawing upon their last reserves of strength and courage. It carried Lieutenant Alexander Hills on a serious errand. He reached the ruins of the *Royal Sovereign*, only one of her masts still standing, and climbed aboard. Collingwood was nursing a badly injured leg, but remained very much in command of his ship, which was a relief to Hills, for he had been charged to tell the second-in-command that their chief was badly wounded. Collingwood must have known that the boat would never have come on a trivial errand, and as he listened gravely he realised that Hardy was warning him to prepare to take command of the fleet. 'I asked the officer if his [Nelson's] wound was dangerous,' wrote Collingwood. 'He hesitated, [and] then said he hoped it was not. But I saw the fate of my friend in his eye, for his look told what his tongue could not utter.'[58]

After sending Hills, Hardy made his way back down into the cockpit for a final meeting. He knelt beside the dying admiral, and shook his hand, holding on to it as he spoke. Hardy was not an emotional man, but the grief oozes from the brief details of that last meeting. He congratulated Nelson on a brilliant victory. It 'was complete' and 'though he did not know how many of the enemy were captured, as it was impossible to perceive every ship distinctly, he was certain . . . of fourteen or fifteen having surrendered'.

'That is well, but I bargained for twenty,' Nelson whispered, a perfectionist to the last sand of the glass. Then, as strongly as he could, he said, '*Anchor*, Hardy, *anchor*!' He knew the damaged ships were on a dangerous lee shore, and that a storm was brewing, and foresaw that the end of the battle would bring no relief from travail.

'I suppose, my Lord, Admiral Collingwood will now take upon himself the direction of affairs,' suggested Hardy, knowing that Hills was on his way to the *Royal Sovereign*.

'Not while I live, I hope, Hardy,' Nelson gasped, trying to raise himself to emphasise the importance of his final command. 'No, do *you* anchor, Hardy.' And when the captain asked if he should make the signal, he went on, 'Yes, for if I live, I'll anchor.' In fact, Collingwood did not carry out Nelson's last order, and consequences followed that might have been anticipated. But Nelson was satisfied that his task was done.[59]

Hardy wanted to know if the other's pain was great. Nelson predicted he had only a few more minutes, and begged Hardy not to throw his body overboard. 'Oh no, certainly not,' managed the captain.

'Then you know what to do, and take care of my dear Lady Hamilton, Hardy. Take care of poor Lady Hamilton.' He knew Hardy would do his best, and that the void now lay before him, a void few wanted to face alone. His last order came immediately and softly. 'Kiss me, Hardy,' he said.[60]

The captain leaned forward and kissed the admiral's cheek. 'Now I am satisfied,' Nelson whispered. 'Thank God, I have done my duty.' Hardy rose and for one or two minutes stood in silence, their life together running out before his eyes. Then, unbidden, the big man knelt again. The admiral's eyes were closed, and Hardy kissed his forehead.

'Who is that?' Nelson asked.

'It is Hardy,' replied the grief-stricken comrade.

'God bless you, Hardy,' Nelson replied. And then the captain was gone, overcome with the tragedy.[61]

Nelson now wanted Chevailler to turn him on his right side, an understandable request, given that his left lung may have been collapsing. When it had been done, he expressed a wish that he had never left the deck, as he would soon be gone. Somewhere, deep in the recesses of his mind, he had the idea that an admiral should die at his post. But the change in his position hardly helped. The admiral's breath became dreadfully difficult and shallow, his voice began to fail, and his mind rambled. Several times he repeated the order to anchor, and returned to his loved ones. 'Doctor,' he said to Scott, 'I have not been a *great* sinner.' Pausing, he added, '*Remember* that I leave Lady Hamilton and my daughter, Horatia, as a legacy to my country . . . never forget Horatia.' Indeed, his final lucid moments focused on those at Merton, and the hopes he had of Rose. 'Doctor, I was right, I told you so,' he gasped, as if to advertise the approach of death. 'George Rose has not yet got my letter. Tell him . . .' The pain interrupted, and then he said, 'Mr Rose will remember. Don't forget, doctor, mind what I say.'[62]

He asked Scott to pray for him, and they said a prayer together. His requests for a drink and fan continued, but with such diminished strength that they were almost inaudible, and he bade Scott rub his chest, which seemed to give relief. On occasions he summoned the last of his strength to repeat, 'Thank God, I have done my duty.' Scott remembered his last words as 'God and my country.'[63]

Some time after Hardy's departure, about fifteen minutes according to Beatty, Nelson lost the power of speech. After five minutes of silence Chevailler went to find Beatty, and said he feared the admiral was at the end. Immediately the surgeon was beside his chief, feeling his hand. It was cold and there was no pulse. Beatty put a hand to the admiral's forehead and extremities, and found that they too were cold, but Nelson's eyes fluttered open. He looked up and closed them again without trying to speak. An emergency then drew Beatty away, leaving Burke, Scott and Chevailler with the dying man breathing shallow and silently. Chevailler soon found Beatty again, and said he thought the admiral had gone.

Beatty checked and nodded. He had slipped away without a sound, with Burke still supporting the admiral's head and shoulders and Scott mechanically rubbing his chest as if in a trance. It was 4.30, and the guns were falling silent. Those still firing were distant and few.

No announcement was made to the fleet, but as night fell sharp observers saw that the *Euryalus*, to which Collingwood had temporarily shifted his flag, carried the lights of the commander-in-chief. But from the *Victory* no such lights shone. There was only darkness.[64]

7

Two battles were fought off Cape Trafalgar on that memorable occasion, one on 21 October between the rival fleets, and the other, beginning that night and sprawling over two more terrible days, between the survivors, both victors and vanquished, and the violent storm that Nelson had foreseen. So many damaged ships and men tossed towards lee shores created new dramas, and fresh spine-tingling stories of heroism and cowardice. Instead of anchoring, as Nelson had wished, Collingwood tried to work his crippled force out to sea. Some prisoners were released, and others saved from their foundering ships, but Collingwood had to destroy most of the prizes. Only four of the captured ships were brought into Gibraltar.

There was the added complication of an enemy counterattack. As the storm abated, Captain Julien Marie Cosmao-Kerjulien of the *Pluton* led five of the sail of the line that had escaped the battle from Cadiz, confronting heavy seas in a daring effort to recapture some of the British prizes. They did rescue two, but in the process lost another four, three going ashore and one first taken by the British and then also shipwrecked. There would be no more sorties, for Collingwood reunited his force and restored his blockade of Cadiz. Even this was not the end, however. Dumanoir's detachment, which had also fled Trafalgar, was driven from the Strait by a southerly gale and tried to run north to Rochefort. But on 4 November it encountered a British squadron under Strachan, that diehard Nelson apostle, and all four ships were taken. Napoleon's great combined fleet was gone. In all, twenty-four had been lost at Trafalgar or in the engagements off Cadiz and Rochefort, and the total loss of manpower – some 17,000 killed, wounded, captured and lost in the sea – equalled the entire force Nelson had brought to the battle on 21 October. Only two of the nine surviving ships in Cadiz were seaworthy.

It was the greatest naval triumph since the defeat of the Spanish Armada in 1588, but the prevailing feeling in the victorious fleet was one of sadness. 'I never set eyes on him,' wrote a seaman in the *Royal Sovereign*, 'for which I am both sorry and glad, for . . . the men in our ship who have seen him are such soft toads, they have done nothing but blast their eyes and cry ever since he was killed. God bless you, chaps that fought like the devil sit down and cry like a wench!' Another survivor agreed that 'every hero in the fleet shed a tear on hearing the news of his death'.[65]

For Nelson, the soul of the fleet, the man with whom everyone wanted to share the jubilation, had suddenly been snatched away. 'I could forever tell you the qualities of this beloved man,' the Reverend Scott wrote to a friend. 'I have not shed a tear for years before the 21st of October, and since, whenever alone, I am quite a child.' Hardy, stern and manly Hardy, thought he would mourn forever, and Berry, who rushed to the *Victory* to congratulate the commander-in-chief, was thunderstruck to hear of the death of 'the best friend I ever had'. So, too, thought Collingwood. 'I cannot tell you how deeply I am effected,' he wrote home. 'My friendship for him was unlike anything that I have left in the navy, a brotherhood of more than thirty years.' Codrington, who had known Nelson for so very short a time, lamented that 'the navy lost not only their best, their dearest, but their only friend'. Nelson 'never met with a distressed sailor without assisting him with his purse, or attention, or advice; nor did he ever neglect to encourage merit. He was easy of access, and his manner was particularly agreeable and kind. No man was ever afraid of displeasing him, but everybody was afraid of not pleasing him.'[66]

No one spoke of that combination of personal and professional inspiration more effectively than Blackwood. In a long letter to his wife the day after the battle he wrote,

> My heart . . . is sad and penetrated with the deepest anguish. A victory – such a one as has never been achieved – yesterday took place in the course of five hours, but at such an expense in the loss of the most gallant of men and best of friends as renders it to me a victory I never wished to have witnessed . . . In my life I never was so shocked or so completely upset as, upon flying to the *Victory* even before the action was over, to find Lord Nelson was then at the gasp of death . . . Such an admiral has the country lost, and every officer and man so kind, so good, so obliging a friend as never was . . . I hope it is not [an] injustice to the second-in-command, who is now on board the *Euryalus*, and who fought like a hero, to say that the fleet under any other never would have performed what they did under Lord Nelson.[67]

XXVI

'ALL TOILS SURMOUNTED . . .'

This noble martyr in the glorious cause,
Of British liberty and British laws,
Has taught us how to fight and (ah too high
A price for knowledge), taught us how to die.

Anonymous, 1805

I

WEDNESDAY, 6 November 1805. The autumn was beautiful at Merton, even in November, when fine early morning mist obscured the brilliant golds and yellows of the trees. Emma felt unwell, but Susannah Bolton was staying, sitting by the bedside exchanging morning pleasantries, when their reveries were disturbed by a distant thunder. It was the guns of the Tower of London pealing some auspicious event. Susannah was momentarily excited, imagining that it betokened news from the fleet, but Emma said there had not been enough time, and it was probably related to some victory in Germany. Several minutes later a carriage stopped at the door, and a servant announced the arrival of an officer. It was Captain Whitby with a letter from Hamond, the comptroller of the Navy Board, but his complexion was pale and his voice faint and unsteady. 'We have gained a great victory,' he began, but was soon 'unable to speak' and it was the 'tears in his eyes, and a deathly paleness over his face' that imparted the news the two women feared. According to Emma, 'for ten hours after I could neither speak nor shed a tear'.[1]

The *Pickle* had brought the news home, reaching England on 4 November. Two days later, a little after midnight on the 6th, her travel-worn commander, John Richards Lapenotiere, alighted from his coach at a fog-bound Admiralty and alerted the night porter that he had come from the fleet. A stunned Marsden roused Barham from his cot by candlelight, and clerks were soon at work copying Collingwood's dispatch. A messenger rushed it to Pitt in little more than an hour. Pitt had served the king as principal minister for twenty-four years, and was accustomed to receiving momentous news at the dead of night, but this was the first and only time that he was unable to regain his sleep. He rose again at three in the morning. The king received the news at Windsor at 6.30 and sat in complete silence for five minutes, unable to compose a word.

When the nation awoke it was hit by a sledgehammer. Never had Britain won such a triumph at sea. Although the blockade and Barham's dispositions had defeated Napoleon's plan to invade England in the summer, Trafalgar put its resuscitation out of the question and returned to Albion a naval superiority over France and Spain that she enjoyed for the rest of the war. Britain was safe, but the atmosphere was one of shock and deep sadness. When a large crowd gathered at the Admiralty for news Marsden looked wretched and the people stood in an uncanny silence. No one could remember suffering such a loss before, nor would Britain experience it again until, perhaps, Sir Winston Churchill was laid to rest in 1965. But even Churchill's end, which came after an extensive and steady decline in the fullness of years, and long after his war had been won, did not hit the public so dramatically. Nelson's body was returned to England preserved in a cask of spirits, laid in state in the magnificent Painted Hall in Greenwich, and on 9 January 1806 conveyed to St Paul's Cathedral for the most elaborate state funeral ever known. Encased in two coffins, one the memento of the battle of the Nile supplied by Hallowell, the body was finally put to rest beneath a huge sarcophagus originally intended for Cardinal Wolsey almost three centuries before, while the whole capital yielded to grim pageantry.

Among officers of the Royal Navy the news of Trafalgar created mixed emotions of envy, exhilaration and sorrow. Louis's detachment, which had missed the battle, was particularly chagrined. Recalling Nelson's 'happy talent' for 'conciliating . . . all ranks', one of its captains testified that 'exertions till that moment unknown' had been made to rejoin the fleet, but in vain. So too thought Hoste. 'Not to have been in it is enough to make one mad', he wrote, 'but to have lost such a friend besides is really sufficient to overwhelm me.' Hallowell likewise could not 'bear up against the disappointment of being out of the action and the loss of the commander whom he had so long loved'. For Codrington, still off Cadiz, life was empty. 'As there is now no longer a Lord Nelson . . . I should wish to get home as soon as possible,' he said. '*Never* whilst I live shall I cease to regret his loss.'[2]

Emma took to her bed in Clarges Street in a state of protracted misery. As she later wrote to Davison, 'I have been very ill all day, my heart broken and my head consequently weak from the agitation I suffer. I tell you truly I am gone, nor do I wish to live. He that I loved more than life, he is gone. Why, then, should I live or wish to live? I lived but for him . . . All is now a dreary prospect before me . . . Nothing gives me a gleam of comfort but the hope that I shall soon follow . . .' On the 13th she was still in bed with the admiral's letters strewn about her. Fanny, who received the news in Bath, fared better. Unlike Emma, she had a personal note from Barham, and it was she with whom the organisers of the funeral communicated. 'Everybody loves my lady,' wrote her maid on 24 November, 'and she looks so well in her widow's weeds, and we are all in black. All the great folks come after her.' Fanny's carriage was in the cortege of 9 January, while Emma spent the day at Clarges Street.[3]

Within weeks the artistic, literary and stone monuments were in full flood. On the Sunday after the news reached the county of Cork in Ireland a captain of the Royal Navy and nearly a thousand volunteers threw up 'a lofty and solid arch' of granite on the top of 'the highest hill' they could find near Castle Townsend. In certain overseas territories the response was also immediate. The news interrupted a society ball in Montreal, and a public subscription was immediately launched to finance a memorial. A cross-section of the British and French-Canadian inhabitants contributed, including the Seminary of St Sulpice, and in 1808 a huge column and statue was raised in the Place Jacques Cartier, where it was considered 'a very great improvement to the city of Montreal'. These were among the first in a series of studies in stone that has continued until the present time, bequeathing the modest and the massive, the indifferent and magnificent, the hated and the beloved, in different parts of the world.[4]

Implicit was the belief that something of supreme importance had occurred, and yet notwithstanding Nelson's hopes for peace the immediate strategic influence of Trafalgar was limited. Napoleon had already abandoned his plan to invade England, and easily crushed the Austrians and Russians at Ulm and Austerlitz, destroying the third coalition and re-establishing military supremacy in continental Europe. He was thus able to dismiss the expensive, ill-conceived enterprise of England and his useless sacrifice of the combined fleet, and to pile the blame upon scapegoats, especially Villeneuve. The French admiral was released by the British in 1806 and returned to France, where he died in a mysterious stabbing that has been regarded as both suicide and assassination. Although the Mediterranean fleet had been destroyed, the collapse of the coalition led to a resurgence of French power in southern Europe and to a rerun of history. The kingdom of Naples was overrun in 1806, and their Sicilian Majesties driven into exile in Sicily, which became a British protectorate. The invaders proclaimed Joseph Bonaparte, Napoleon's brother, the new king. Reflecting on the loss of her old guardian, Maria Carolina admitted that 'I shall regret him all my life. Twenty vessels [at Trafalgar] may increase his glory, but nothing can console for his loss. So much courage, virtue and modesty, all united in one individual, is not to be found again. For him it is happiness, for us a heavy misfortune.' Shrunken and worn out, the once formidable Queen of Naples died of a stroke in Vienna in September 1814, only months before Britain and her victorious allies finally overthrew Napoleon at Waterloo. She never saw Ferdinand restored to his throne.[5]

Trafalgar did not, therefore, liberate Europe. The war went on for another ten years, and France had even rebuilt a powerful battle fleet by 1813. But the character of the conflict had changed in 1805. Trafalgar had demonstrated Britain's invincibility at sea, and there were no more significant attempts to challenge her command of the ocean. The war turned into a struggle of attrition between a supreme land and a supreme naval power, neither able to directly overthrow the other, but both attempting to floor their opponent with slow and inefficient economic strangleholds. Napoleon tried to ruin Britain by a 'continental system' that locked her trade out of Europe, and the Royal Navy replied with a rigorous blockade of the enemy coasts. In the end the invidious influence of sea power began to prevail. It enabled Britain to diversify her overseas trade, compensating for difficulties in Europe; to strip enemies of territorial possessions and their blue-water commerce; and to create the resources to subsidise allied armies in Europe. Britain supplied £20 million to the final campaign of 1814–15 alone. Naval power also sustained the British army that drove the French out of Portugal and Spain after 1808, and, more significantly, by compelling Napoleon to rely upon his 'continental system' British sea power led him into decisive conflict with other European powers. It was Bonaparte's attempt to bully Russia into closing her ports to Britain that led to the disastrous campaign of 1812, a debacle that cost him half a million men and signalled the decline of his power. As the noted military historian J. F. C. Fuller observed long ago, there was a distinct chain of causality between Trafalgar and the collapse of Napoleon's empire. What was even more important, when the war ended in 1815 it left Britain the greatest naval power on earth with the world at her fingertips.[6]

Not all who had shared Nelson's dream of peace lived to see it. On 15 January 1815, just five months before the battle of Waterloo, Emma Hamilton died. After Nelson's death George Rose and Hardy tried hard to secure the favours he had asked of his country, and both Pitt and the Prince of Wales seemed disposed to comply. But Pitt's sudden death in January 1806 damaged hopes that the 'legacy' Nelson had left to his country, his mistress and his daughter, would be honoured. The new premier was Lord Grenville, whom the Hamiltons had long numbered an enemy, and excuses were found to do nothing.[7]

The illegitimacy of Emma and Horatia, as well as a lingering dislike of the former in some quarters, also played relevant parts. Nelson left relatively little money. Apart from Merton, which passed with seventy-two choice acres of its land to Emma, and £6302 worth of investments in government consols mortgaged to provide Fanny her annuity of £1000, his estate, as registered at the Stamp Office on 16 November 1810, amounted to only £12,163, and that was burdened with considerable debts as well as annuities to Sukey, John Tyson, Mrs Graefer and Mrs Gibson. True, the admiral's share of the money the government stumped up to compensate captors for the destruction of the Trafalgar prizes added an impressive £18,518, but these resources passed by due process into the hands of Nelson's regular family.[8]

By comparison with Emma, the Nelsons benefited from considerable government largesse. Nelson's sisters were awarded £10,000 each, something that must have compensated Susannah for her husband's disappointment over the place he had coveted on one of the public boards. William Nelson did best. He got an earldom, as well as his brother's other titles, with a net annuity of £5,000, and a grant of £90,000 to purchase and furnish a suitable residence. In 1814 he acquired an estate in Wiltshire which he renamed Trafalgar House. Nonetheless, all did not go well for William, for his only male heir, Horace, died of typhus fever in January 1808, and after his death in 1835 the title passed to his nephew, Tom Bolton. By then the 2nd earl's parents were dead, Susannah in 1813 and Thomas in 1834, and Tom himself enjoyed only months of ennoblement before suffering a premature death. His heir, another Horatio, then held the title for seventy-eight years until he died on the eve of the Great War of 1914. A reforming Labour government of 1947 finally abolished the pension, and death duties and other financial misfortunes compelled the 6th earl to sell Trafalgar House in the fifties.[9]

Considering the generous grants made to the Nelsons, Emma could justly claim to have been unfortunate. She inherited Merton, but it proved impossible to maintain or sell, and while she had £800 a year from her husband, the annuity of £500 that Nelson had left her on the Bronte estate went unpaid for a considerable time. That left her Nelson's bequest of £2000 and the interest from £4000 held in trust for Horatia. Despite all, she continued to live extravagantly, shunned by those who had put up with her for Nelson's sake, and deserted by such fair-weather friends as the newly elevated William Nelsons. Despite hawking off some of the admiral's heirlooms, Emma ran up debts of £18,000 within three years. In 1808 she sold the house in Clarges Street and the next year Asher Goldsmid, brother of Abraham and Benjamin, bought Merton. Further appeals for a public grant, based on the strength of her services in the Mediterranean and the appeal Nelson had made on the eve of Trafalgar, failed to save Emma and Horatia from being committed for debt in 1813 and condemned to living in 'a sponging house' within the rules of the King's Bench prison. Her dependants fell away. Poor Fatima is said to have ended her days in the asylum for the insane at St Luke's Hospital.[10]

Not in his wildest dream could Nelson have envisaged that the very dearest of his people, including a child of thirteen with whooping cough, the legacies he had entrusted to the care of his country within hours of fighting the battle of Trafalgar, would have been allowed to sink so low. But thus did the astonishing life of Emma Hamilton, from blacksmith's daughter to artist's model, acclaimed artiste, ambassadress, confidante of a queen and mistress of the first man in England, come full circle and beyond. Satisfying her most urgent creditors, she was discharged from the King's Bench in 1814 and fled to France to escape the remaining pursuers. The memories of those last days were burned into Horatia's mind forever. Emma was probably dying of cirrhosis of the liver, and lay for most of the time on a pallet in a dingy alcove of miserable lodgings in the rue Française in Calais, embittered, frustrated, abusive in her cups to the child she was sworn to protect, a child who for the most part was her only attendant. She was barely sensible at the end, and died at one in the afternoon, beneath the portraits of the two men who had shared her paradise on earth, Sir William Hamilton and Nelson. She was a few months short of her fiftieth birthday. Horatia remembered that she had some fine qualities, but in the long years that followed refused to accept that Lady Hamilton was her mother as if the very idea was repugnant. By then what was left of Emma's public reputation was being shredded by anonymous publications, *Letters of Lord Nelson to Lady Hamilton*, probably contributed by her own hired hack, James Harrison, and *The Memoirs of Lady Hamilton*, which relied for much of its vindictive copy upon a former servant, Francis Oliver.

Happily, Horatia fared much better. After Emma's death she was adopted and restored to health by Catherine Matcham, Nelson's surviving sister. In the care of the Matchams at their home at Ashfold Lodge, Horsham, and later with the remains of the Bolton family, then living at Burnham Market in Norfolk, Horatia bloomed into an eligible young lady, filling notebooks with private thoughts that blended piety, good intentions and a lively mind. In 1822 she married Philip Ward, a young clergyman, at the church in Burnham Westgate. They lived gentle country lives at Stanhoe and Bircham Newton in Norfolk and Tenterden in Kent until Philip's sudden death in 1859. He left behind eight children, of whom one, Nelson, survived until 1917. Nelson's little Horatia died at Pinner on Sunday, 6 March 1881, at the venerable age of eighty-one.

Try as she did, she never learned the truth about her parentage, although she knew that Nelson was her father. The few who could have told her remained silent or evasive. However, Horatia did live to see an unexpected righting of one injustice. A belated appeal on her behalf led the government to grant Horatia's daughters an annuity of £100 each in 1854, and an additional lump sum of £1428 was raised by a public subscription in 1855. There was also a small legacy from a well-wisher and sponsorships for the other children. And so, modestly but usefully, did good people of the nation attempt to fulfil Nelson's plea.[11]

Fanny, Viscountess Nelson was less tempestuous and vibrant than her overpowering rival, but in many respects made of sterner stuff. The many vicissitudes of life did not destroy her. In addition to the £1000 a year Nelson had left her, she received an annuity of £2000 from the government, and cut a respected figure in Bath, Brighton, London or Exmouth, where she eventually retired to an agreeable cliff-side residence. Though freed to remarry, she chose a single life, and remained on good terms with some of Nelson's old circle, including Elizabeth Locker; even the William Nelsons attempted a kind of reconciliation. Fanny was happy to renew her acquaintance with Charlotte, who married into the Hood family, but knew William and Sarah too well to entangle herself in their company. In 1830, however, she had the pleasure of entertaining William IV, formerly the Duke of Clarence, at her lodgings in Brighton. The king remembered giving her away to Nelson at that marriage in Nevis so long before. Nelson remained the love of Fanny's life to the last. She never remarried, nor is there evidence of any lasting relationships with men, but she enjoyed a dignified retirement that latterly included extensive travels on the continent.

To this degree of contentment the wayward Josiah finally contributed. After returning from the Mediterranean at the age of twenty in 1800 he never got another ship. In 1825 seniority brought him within hailing distance of the summit of the post-captains' list, but he was denied a flag and shunted straight into the ranks of superannuated captains. Mother and son seemed a strange pair. One who saw them in 1808 marked the contrast between a 'very amiable good woman' and 'the greatest oddity I ever beheld'. For long Josiah's means were modest, amounting to little more than his naval half-pay and a small legacy from his mother's uncle, but, wonder of wonders, fortune eventually smiled in the form of successful investments in the French funds. In the 1820s Captain Nisbet acquired a house on quai Voltaire in Paris. He married one of Fanny's godchildren, Frances Herbert Evans, and gave his mother pleasure in several grandchildren. Josiah died of pleurisy in Paris in 1830, at the age of fifty, but three daughters survived him, two of whom lived into the twentieth century. Fanny herself died in London on 6 May 1831 and was buried next to Josiah in Littleham, near Exmouth.[12]

Alexander Davison struck hard times. In 1809 he was convicted of fraud and the abuse of public funds and began two years in Newgate prison. His bank failed in 1816, and he sold his mansion in St James's Square, although he did manage to hold on to his estate at Swarland, Northumberland, where he planted oak trees to represent the positions of the ships at the battle of the Nile. Davison died in 1829, Swarland Hall was demolished in 1947, and an axe taken to all but four of the Nile oaks, but his other monument to Nelson, a forty-foot obelisk, was recently restored and can still be seen standing a lonely sentinel on a windy hill top near the Felton by-pass. Perhaps the civilian most affected by Nelson's death was his chaplain, Scott, who reverently attended the admiral's body on its long journey from Trafalgar to St Paul's Cathedral, as if afraid to relinquish it to the guardianship of any other. 'When I think . . . what an affectionate, fascinating little fellow he was,' he famously wrote, 'how dignified and pure his mind, how kind and condescending his manners, I become stupid with grief for what I have lost.' Nelson had promised to help Scott to a prebendary stall, but those ambitions had to be shelved, and the chaplain satisfied himself with more pedestrian appointments in Southminster and Catterick. He died in 1840 at the age of seventy-two, revering his hero to the end.[13]

Nelson's naval colleagues passed from the scene with various degrees of distinction, but those who had been closest did well enough. Many died in harness. In 1807 Troubridge was drowned when his ship was sucked into the Indian Ocean by a cyclone as he made his way from the East Indies to the Cape of Good Hope, where he had been named commander-in-chief. Ball got his flag in 1805, but remained civil commissioner in Malta, confounding critics of his administration by leaving a name venerated throughout the island. In 1809 he died in Malta, where his tomb can still be seen. After Trafalgar Collingwood became a distinguished commander-in-chief of the Mediterranean, but he never went home to his beloved Northumberland, and died worn out in the service in 1810. Fremantle was decorated by Austria, Malta, Spain and Britain, and died a vice admiral and commander-in-chief of the Mediterranean at Naples in 1819. Keats missed Trafalgar, but distinguished himself in Duckworth's victory off San Domingo the following year, hanging a portrait of Nelson in his rigging to inspire his men. Although ill health dogged his later years, he commanded in the Baltic, served briefly as second-in-command in the Mediterranean, and ended his days a full admiral and governor of Greenwich Hospital in 1834. Blackwood's golden days ended with Trafalgar, but he commanded in the East Indies and at the Nore, and was knighted and made a baronet. He died of a fever in Ballyleidy, County Down, in 1832, and lies in Killyleagh churchyard. And Hardy? Despite his limitations, he prospered. Raised to a baronetcy for Trafalgar, he was made a KCB and knight bachelor in 1815, and in 1819 raised his pendant in command of a squadron operating off South America. He became a vice admiral, a transient member of the board of Admiralty and governor of Greenwich Hospital, where he died in 1839.

Nelson had befriended merit, and those who missed him most were the younger protégés with careers still to make. Some had alternative patrons, but without Nelson even the most able could find that merit alone was not enough. Sir William Bolton, the amiable but complacent officer who had married Nelson's niece, had often disappointed the admiral, and blew another chance in 1805. Nelson had arranged for him to bring out the *Melpomene* frigate, but he missed Trafalgar. 'Billy, Billy, out of luck!' the admiral is said to have sighed. A scholarly, humane officer, who boasted that he had never court-martialled a man, Sir William possessed a natural modesty that prevented him from pushing himself forward. He enjoyed a few more commands, but made relatively little of his opportunities, and died much loved on 16 December 1830, leaving three daughters. John Yule, a lieutenant of the *Victory*, was also perhaps too gentle for his profession. 'The action,' he said of Trafalgar, 'will be, by the nation, conceived a glorious one, but when the devastation is considered, how can we glory in it? How many orphans and fatherless has it made?' More, without Nelson's guiding hand the future was bleak, and Yule foresaw the end of his 'golden dreams'. He was right. Although promoted a commander in December 1805 he spent most of the following years unemployed, despite a useless appeal to the new Earl Nelson, and died in 1841.[14]

The fortunes of Nelson's other protégés varied because the navy was neither a career open to talent nor a mere theatre for 'interest'. William Hoste, rescued by Nelson from the trough of the Sea Fencibles, did not look back. When he destroyed an enemy squadron at Lissa in the Adriatic in 1811 he roused his men with the signal 'Remember Nelson'. But perhaps he mirrored his mentor most of all when he took three powerful fortresses in Dalmatia and Albania in operations that few naval commanders would have attempted. Nelson had taught Hoste that with well-managed and disciplined forces the navy could challenge its barriers and transcend traditional roles. Hoste did not live long enough to reach flag rank. He died of consumption at the age of forty-eight in 1828, but he had been made a baronet and was honoured with a statue in St Paul's Cathedral. William Parker of the *Amazon* did even better. He commanded the Mediterranean and Channel fleets, and in the Chinese opium war of 1841–42 conducted a campaign that one historian has described as 'an unprecedented feat of amphibious warfare'. Towards the end he reached the very pinnacle of the service by becoming Admiral of the Fleet.[15]

By contrast, James Noble, Hoste's messmate in the *Agamemnon*, did badly, despite comparable courage and enterprise. Nelson got him to the rank of commander in 1797, when Noble was twenty-three, but there were no ships for new arrivals, and reaching 'post' as part of a general promotion in 1802 did not help. He spent decade after futile decade trying to support a growing family on naval half-pay and applying to one first lord of the Admiralty after another. During those empty, dreary years he steadily climbed the captains' and flag lists to become a vice admiral, albeit one who had only commanded a ketch for seventy-five days in 1796 as a lieutenant. In disappointed old age Noble wished he had been more assertive, and that he had made more use of Nelson, his 'trump card'. After Trafalgar it was too late, although Hardy admitted that the admiral 'frequently spoke of you, and regretted very much that it had been out of his power to get you afloat'; 'had he . . . survived . . . you may rely on it you would not have been forgotten'. As it was, an eager officer languished on the beach for half a century, dying in 1851 with a total estate worth less than £200. 'Circumstances has [have] taught me experience,' he remarked wistfully, 'and in me is exemplified that merit without a quid pro quo or influential connection may rot!'[16]

For the brilliant William Layman, whose career Nelson had tried to save on several occasions, there was no happy ending. Before leaving England in September 1805, Nelson had obtained a promise from the Admiralty that Layman would be given a ship and returned to the Mediterranean, but after Trafalgar it was forgotten. Without his sole powerful supporter, Layman fought back the only way he knew, digging into his fertile mind for more projects that might pluck him from obscurity and disgrace. He reappraised his plan to increase the lifespan and strength of ship timber, and offered to build an experimental frigate according to its principles, but while he intrigued a few scientific and political brains, he was shunned by the Admiralty and Navy Board. The influential *Naval Chronicle*, edited by Nelson's biographers, became a strong advocate, and published a two-part biography in 1817, an honour normally reserved for distinguished flag officers and captains. To these editors, as to Nelson, Layman was a 'disappointed genius' and his story an epitome of the 'discouraging instances of merit struggling with misfortune' and the 'skill, courage and activity fruitlessly exerted'. The Admiralty's neglect was nothing less than 'disgraceful'. Some others agreed, characterising the stubborn refusal to examine Layman's schemes and promote him to the rank of post captain a 'narrow-minded and illiberal jealousy'. Momentarily encouraged, the commander continued his long and lonely battle, authoring pamphlets and a full maritime history, but the years of hostility and neglect knocked the heart out of him and his courage failed. Latterly he was said to suffer from delusions. One bleak spring day in 1826 his life ended in a public wash-house in Cheltenham, where he cut his own throat with a razor at the age of fifty-eight.[17]

Nelson died, and as time rolled on those who had been part of his world moved along their individual paths towards a myriad of different destinies. One by one they disappeared. The last of the Nelsons of Burnham Thorpe was Catherine Matcham, the admiral's youngest sibling, who died in 1842, and the last niece or nephew to remember the admiral, her son George, died in 1877, outliving Charlotte by four years. Ann Melton of Docking, who died in 1879, was believed to be the last person in Norfolk to have known Nelson, but in January 1889 a ninety-five-year-old man, James Hudson, the son-in-law of old Cribb, died after spending nearly all of his life in one of the cottages the admiral had built at Merton. He always claimed to have been present when Nelson left his paradise for the last time in 1805. The period of high Victorianism saw the remnants of Nelson's old crews gathered to their fathers. James Chapman, a landsman who said he had been the stroke oar of Nelson's cutter, passed away quietly in Dundee in 1876. Perhaps the last officer of the victorious fleet at Trafalgar was Lieutenant-Colonel James Fynmore, a midshipman of the *Africa* on that historic day, who died in April 1887.[18]

Places often live much longer than people. The first Elizabethans were so stunned by the exploits of Drake that they tried to preserve the *Golden Hind* in a specially constructed dock at Deptford. The vessel rotted in Stuart times, but Drake's home at Buckland Abbey in Devon did survive, and there something of his restless spirit can still be recaptured by the introspective visitor. Two centuries later Nelson suffered equally mixed fortunes. The parsonage at Burnham Thorpe, where he had been born, was demolished in 1803, and two years later the diarist Farington recorded that 'not a stone' of it could be found, 'but [Daniel] Everitt [the current rector] showed us a tree which touched the kitchen chimney'. Paradise Merton, where Nelson found peace, was treated in a like manner in 1823, when the remains of the grounds were sold. After Emma's friends purchased it in 1808 no buyer would take it off their hands, and it lay empty, decaying and ghostly for years. The site disappeared under rows of Victorian dwellings, and today one has to walk along Nelson Grove Road to pass over what had once been such a venerated spot. Ironically Roundwood, which Nelson only saw twice and never slept in, survived until 1961. Ironic, too, that now the only one of the admiral's houses still standing is Maniace, at Bronte, which he never saw at all. It passed through Charlotte, Nelson's niece, to the Hood-Bridport family, from whom it was purchased by the Sicilian government in 1980. Castello Nelson is open to the public, a reminder of that other retreat that figured so much in his later dreams.[19]

But in Britain we have one iconic residence. Nelson spent much of his life in ships, rather than houses, and maybe it is they which evoke his memory most poignantly. The eighteenth-century ship of the line, as beautiful to behold as it was fearful to fight, passed into history with the thousands of largely forgotten men who had sailed her. Of Nelson's favourites, the *Agamemnon* was shipwrecked in Maldonado Bay on the coast of South America in 1809, and the *Foudroyant* on the sands of Blackpool as late as 1897. But at Portsmouth the most famous of them all, the *Victory*, can still be seen, heroically preserved much as she was, to remind us not only of Nelson but the remarkable weapon that had made his and her country mistress of the seas.

2

In time none could seriously deny that British sea power was one of the great shaping influences of world history. Empires fell and rose upon the back of it. As we have seen, it destabilised the French and Napoleonic empires, both within Europe and without. When Napoleon sold Louisiana Territory to the United States in 1803, doubling the extent of that infant republic and setting her on the road to a new continental empire, he did so knowing that the impending renewal of his war with Britain and the power of the Royal Navy effectively debarred him from exploiting his greatest overseas possession. Indeed, it could only be lost. The eclipse of the French and the rise of the American empire were not untouched by Britain's naval greatness.

While Trafalgar was only the most dramatic expression of British naval superiority, it created psychological as well as physical barriers towards resuming a contest so one-sided. Ships might be built, but to what effect in the face of such overwhelming power? The consequences for Spain's overseas empire were considerable. After the defeat of the Spanish Armada in 1588, Spain quickly cobbled up a second and a third armada, although none reached English shores. But after Trafalgar there was no comparable renaissance in the Spanish navy. Between 1808 and 1830 therefore, when the Latin American republics won their independence in armed struggles with Spain and Portugal, neither power had the naval resources to restore their colonies to obedience, especially in the face of British disapproval. President James Monroe's doctrine of 1823, declaring that hands should be kept off America, had standing only inasmuch as it was backed by British ships of the line.

While the Spanish, French and Portuguese empires crumbled, one strode mightily forward, turning the nineteenth century into its own. Classically trained minds in Britain saw themselves as the new Romans. The relative peace the British claimed to have imposed on the world throughout the nineteenth century, in which wars remained local rather than global, they termed the 'Pax Britannica' in memory of the 'Pax Romana'. And when, in 1843, a huge column and statue was raised in Trafalgar Square, proclaiming the debt the country owed to its greatest admiral, the design by William Railton was a conscious copy of Rome's Temple of Mars Ultor, honouring Julius Caesar. It did more than identify the man and means by which Britain had risen to the height of greatness. It declared that Britain was the new global superpower. So potent a symbol of the nation's greatness did the column become that Hitler planned to dismantle it and remove it to Berlin if he ever managed to conquer Britain.

And in some ways Britain's evocation of the Roman empire barely did justice to the scale of what was now being created. The far mightier Mongol empire would have made a fairer comparison, but even that paled before Britannia's achievement. For this was a sea-borne empire with few limits on earth. Protected by the navy, the maritime highways gave Britain safe access to the world's resources and markets, allowing her commerce to outpace rivals and create unprecedented prosperity and confidence at home. It pushed Britain through the first industrial revolution and made her 'the workshop of the world', and where economics and trade led, colonisation and annexation often reluctantly followed, dragging English culture, language, law and institutions in their wake. At its peak the empire was colossal, containing a quarter of the world's population and more than a fifth of its land surface, scattered in big and small parcels across the planet and glued together by naval, maritime and economic power. There was good and bad in that empire. It both suppressed the sea-going slave trade, and dispossessed or disempowered indigenous peoples, but it was a unique and astonishing artefact, the more remarkable for being the creation of a small offshore island in northern Europe.

Trafalgar, therefore, cannot be seen as simply another great battle in a brief but troubled period of European history. It ushered in Britain's century. By the end of the Victorian period Britain was visibly flagging, as Germany, the United States and Japan, among others, industrialised and built rival battle fleets, but the Royal Navy was still able to play a crucial role in the country's survival during the great wars of the twentieth century.

More than any other British hero, Nelson was identified with that undeniable success. If sea power was essential to national security and worldwide expansion, influence and prosperity, Nelson was seen as its high priest. As early as 1811 the publisher John Murray looked firmly to the future when he commissioned Robert Southey to write a life of Nelson that could 'become the heroic text of every midshipman in the navy'. At the end of the same century the first serious interpretative biography of the admiral was fittingly penned by A. T. Mahan, the American author of the classic studies of the influence of sea power. Soon after, Britain's greatest naval theorist and historian, Sir Julian Corbett, produced one of the two first scholarly studies of Trafalgar. And by and large Nelson has retained this status. Wellington was a comparable military figure, but his aloof, aristocratic caste as well as a questionable political career damaged him as a popular hero, and the armies of the world, barring the British, never adopted him as a crucial role model. There were many alternatives. But wherever the role of the admiral is studied, Nelson is acknowledged the exemplar. A bicentennial commemoration of Trafalgar in the Solent in 2005 was attended by ships from thirty-two countries, representing all six of the inhabited continents. Rightly or wrongly, his standing in the profession of arms at sea remains unique.[20]

3

The British naval victory in the French wars rested on the shoulders of many men and women. They were taxpayers and wives, naval architects and shipwrights, artisans of many hues, men who led short lives in the fierce heat of foundries, victuallers and store keepers, administrators and informers, surgeons and many others, apart from the thousands of seamen who manned the ships. We sometimes do an injustice to corporate sacrifices when we remember the few names that have come down to posterity, some entirely fortuitously. Nelson had many flaws. His petulance, cloying hunt for love and attention, constant self-promotion, brooding sensitivity to slights and occasional ruthlessness tire, and his life was not always above reproach. His deep need for recognition also made him vulnerable to flattering influences, and his relationships with Prince William Henry, the Hamiltons and the Bourbons of Naples all damaged his private and public reputation. The period between the summer of 1799 and end of 1801 was particularly rocky, when his domestic affairs were turned upside down and his professional judgement most compromised. But for all this Nelson deserves his reputation as one of the country's greatest public servants, and his achievements need no exaggeration.

Trafalgar, great victory though it was, created obvious problems as a tactical model. Nelson's attack was of its time, when the qualitative difference between the belligerent fleets justified the risks that Nelson took to create his close-quarter 'pell mell' battle. It had been exquisitely tailored to its historical circumstances.

To have applied such tactics in another time or situation could have courted disaster. He was not, therefore, a simple template.

Not a few dodged the subject by simply labelling the admiral a 'genius' and therefore, in effect, above the comprehension of mortal men. For them he stands on a pedestal, as in Trafalgar Square, beyond comparison, understanding and therefore emulation. Collingwood would not quite have agreed. Nelson, he said, 'possessed the zeal of an enthusiast, directed by talents which Nature had very bountifully bestowed upon him, and everything seemed as if by enchantment to prosper under his direction. But it was the effect of *system and nice combination, not of chance*.' In other words, his success did not belong to the unfathomable realms of the supernatural, but to the adoption of sound principles that were capable of yielding lessons.[21]

But what were these potent qualities and principles, and how original or unusual were they? Nelson was a strikingly successful admiral, and tactics naturally jump to mind, but we now know that far from being original these were a common property of his peers in the British fleet. Such ideas as attacking from windward, cutting the enemy line, sealing off the retreat to leeward, massing strength upon a part of the opposing force, and using Britain's advantage in close-range gunnery were well known to several officers who had noted the combat superiority of their fleet. The battles of 'the Glorious First of June', Cape St Vincent and Camperdown, and the naval treatise of John Clerk of Eldin, which Hardy tells us Nelson had read, all reflect this trend. Indeed, Duncan's attack at Camperdown in 1797 was not only similar to Nelson's at Trafalgar, but achieved comparable results, knocking out nine of the fifteen Dutch ships of the line. Had the numbers been greater, the ships larger and the enemy the French or the Spanish, we would have heard much more of a battle that has almost been forgotten. Nelson's tactics were the product of unusual and clear forethought, but they were not strokes of inspiration from a clear blue sky, nor, for that matter, were they entirely successful. We can never quarrel with the overall results of his most remarkable encounters, or deprecate the heroism and careful planning that went into them, but, as we have seen, turning theory into practice is not always easy. The concentration of force that Nelson valued did not tell at the Nile until some two hours into the battle, was almost lost through the early British losses at Copenhagen and was questionable throughout most of Trafalgar.

Nelson's conscientious study of tactics was important, but modern historians have cited his management style as a more unique contribution, and here, certainly, the admiral outshone his contemporaries. He stands in a different kingdom from such formidable or self-contained figures as Howe, Hood, St Vincent, Keith, Cornwallis, Collingwood and Duckworth. There can be no doubt that his sympathetic and accessible regime was endearing, helping bond the admiral to his followers and providing one solution to the growing communication problem bedevilling the exercise of command. The increasingly large forces deployed in modern warfare made it difficult for generals and admirals to exercise close supervision or control. Communications could easily break down on fast-moving or wide fronts or in sprawling, complicated encounters wreathed in smoke. Nelson never dispensed with signals, and embraced Popham's improved telegraph, but he did reduce his dependence upon them by briefing his senior officers beforehand in written and verbal communications. His purpose was to draw them into the spirit and detail of the enterprise, and to harness them to his expectations and standards of performance, so that they might use their judgement more effectively. Again, he was not always successful. Sometimes events rushed forward too quickly, or officers simply misunderstood. But he had a practice with the potential to solve problems and inspire a degree of imitation.

But to emphasise tactical innovations or management style is to compartmentalise Nelson in an unsatisfactory way, for he impresses not for this or that attribute so much as the whole package, a package that he constantly refined and developed. Nelson was a perfectionist with a clear idea of what the navy should be doing. As far as battle was concerned, for example, he aimed for complete and decisive results. He wanted knockouts, not unconvincing decisions that solved little. This principle was not universal, but to adopt it calls for a complete reappraisal of ways and means. It demands different tactics and practices than more modest objectives. To this and other ends Nelson distilled worthwhile insights, ideas and procedures from life's journey – among them the tactics we have mentioned – and synthesised them into a remarkable and unique whole.

Although opinionated and strong-minded, Nelson was an educable man, who constantly refined his experiences for what was valuable. In his earlier career, he took much inspiration from Hood, whose commitment to decisive victory was so great that he condemned the close blockades that got in the way. Nelson never lost sight of those lessons, which fitted his self-image, personality and ambition. Throughout life he was driven by an unquenchable thirst for glory and distinction, and it was that which gave him the intense energy, focus and aggression that made him such a force to be reckoned with. But to that star he added the detailed planning that was needed to produce the desired result; the tireless activity that developed first-rate crews; outstanding leadership; moral as well as immense physical courage and a willingness to act according to his own judgement, even at the expense of orders; and what he called 'spur of the moment thinking', a rare ability to remain composed under fire and take decisive action. It was never more evident than at Cape St Vincent, when he wore out of line to pursue an independent course, and at Copenhagen, where he constantly revised his plan to meet developing crises. All of these components turned him into a first-class fighting admiral.

Nelson also learned that the work of an admiral began long before the enemy was sighted. The infrastructure for victory had to be assembled and maintained. Only well-fed and healthy crews had the stamina to endure long campaigns and intense battles with either the enemy or the sea; only well-trained and disciplined crews could deliver a fire as devastating as the one the *Victory* poured into the *Bucentaure* and *Redoutable*; and men needed to be motivated and inspired to confront the dangerous and difficult. Nelson had learned much from such early influences as Maurice Suckling, William Locker and Lord St Vincent, but even in his final years he was listening to and benefiting from new mentors such as Baird, Snipe and Gillespie. His later work in the Mediterranean reveals him as a master of fleet management.

During that same command he also proved himself an outstanding commander-in-chief. The wherewithal needed for this was perhaps less instinctive in one so strong-willed and potentially impatient. Yet Nelson's maturation was never more evident than in his growing appreciation of the strategic and diplomatic aspects of command. As a young man he had shown extraordinary political courage in supporting the navigation laws in the West Indies, at the risk of his career, and this steel core persisted. To the end he stood ready to back his own judgement. Such self-confidence, while potentially subversive, was essential to the commander-in-chief of a distant station, where close oversight was impossible, but it was useless – nay, potentially disastrous – if it was not informed by political and strategic insight.

In this Nelson visibly grew in stature. Always a good inter-service man, he gained from relationships with the military and diplomatic arms of His Majesty's service. As a commodore operating off the Italian coast in 1795–97 he had benefited from the guidance of the career diplomats, Sir Gilbert Elliot (later Lord Minto), Francis Drake and John Trevor, and it was his consequent understanding of the Mediterranean that led the government to send him back there in 1798. However, his grasp of the theatre as a whole was then unsteady; he thought regionally, allowed himself to be sucked into doubtful activities in Italy to the detriment of wider concerns. With fewer distractions, understanding grew in the following years. His Baltic campaign was arguably his most flawless, politically as well as militarily, and his two years in the Mediterranean saw a fine blend of naval, political and administrative insight. He was not only a far more energetic commander-in-chief than Hood, Hotham and St Vincent had been, but partly as a result of it more informed. The interest, sometimes deference, with which the politicos in the Mediterranean and their masters in London greeted Nelson's pronouncements about the station testify to the respect he had won in the field. At the comparatively young age of forty-five Nelson had become a consummate all-rounder with a thorough command of almost every relevant facet of his complex business.

This successful career development is one of the most marked features of

Nelson. To isolate, say, his management style or his strategy or his tactics, is to miss the comprehensive nature of his strengths. He could create and maintain a top-rate fighting force, even in difficult circumstances. He had the aggression, skill, daring and leadership to take it into battle and win naval superiority, as he had done in the Baltic and the Mediterranean. And he developed the strategic and political wisdom to *exercise* naval command across a large theatre, to identify priorities and deploy forces to support them; and in effect, to become much more than a mere admiral. The attention he gave to the situations and needs of diverse communities, the links he saw between internal governance and political security in an age of revolution, the attempts he made to broker truces between allies and potential allies, his calls for unity against a great peril and the measurement of where and when scant resources could best be deployed all betokened the elements of statesmanship. While some of his contemporaries distinguished themselves as fighting admirals, fleet managers, and – in the case of Collingwood – commanders-in-chief, Nelson's grasp of all three has no parallel.

There was something else. Nelson, more than any admiral of his time, *inspired*. 'We shall want more victories yet,' Minto wrote after Nelson's death, but 'to whom can we look for them? The navy is certainly full of the bravest men, but . . . there was a sort of heroic cast about Nelson that I never saw in any other man, and which seems wanting to the achievement of impossible things which became easy to him, and on which the maintenance of our superiority at sea seems to depend.'[22]

Nelson was a patriot, who completed years of dedicated service to his country, but it was the scale of his ambitions, the heroism, come danger, injury or death, with which he pursued them, and his successes that transformed him into a national hero. His dream was no common thing. He aimed to do more than any sea officer had done before, and perhaps to achieve perfection. He never put it better than in a letter of 1795, describing his disappointment with a minor British victory won off Genoa: 'had we taken ten sail, and allowed the eleventh to have escaped, if possible to have been got at, I could never call it well done'. Of course, Nelson did not fool himself into believing that perfection could always be achieved, but the idea of the overwhelming victory never left him. 'I have had a good race of glory,' he acknowledged in 1804, but 'never' felt 'satisfied'.[23]

As he chased the naval holy grail, mastering victories and reverses along the way, he consciously presented himself as the champion of his people, a new Henry V, the famous medieval warrior-king who had authored England's greatest triumph over the French at Agincourt. He put laudatory accounts of his exploits in the press and appeared before his public in 'walkabouts', and as his status increased so he swept ever more people into his march through history. Lady Foster said she remembered no one with Nelson's ability to stir the enthusiasm of the British people. At a time when the realm was confronting the frightening military power of Napoleon, Nelson was a reassuring presence, and his credibility increased with every triumph.

Perhaps his greatest contribution to the navy was to lift its standing to unprecedented heights. Nelson knew that he had a fine weapon, but it had to be tested to reach its true potential. That, in effect, meant stretching the navy, sometimes beyond what we would now call its 'comfort zone'. He was by no means the only admiral to attack the boundaries. The close blockades of St Vincent and Cornwallis wore down ships and men, but they took seamanship to new levels. More spectacularly, Nelson took the navy where few admirals would have dared to go. As a young officer he led naval forces into engagements ashore that even some members of the the military did not think were winnable. The other two flag officers of the Baltic fleet would not have attacked the Danish position at Copenhagen, and there is no evidence that Collingwood had a clear tactical plan to cope with Villeneuve. On all of these occasions Nelson placed men and ships where they had to fight for their survival, but in the doing they won victories that raised the morale and reputation of the service and reached new horizons.

It was a risky course, and Nelson overreached himself at Tenerife and Boulogne. His sorties into amphibious warfare were not always nicely calculated, but experience had given him the measure of his opponents at sea and his meticulous planning was usually vindicated. Nelson's ambition led him to his greatest triumph at Trafalgar. He fulfilled the promises he had made to those who had sent him, and the expectations of his people. And then he was gone. The navy had to continue under his shadow, and there was a sense of anti-climax in the long years of warfare that followed. When Keats hoisted Nelson's portrait on his rigging to inspire his men at San Domingo in 1806 and Hoste urged his squadron to 'Remember Nelson' off Lissa in 1811 they were both trying to reclaim Nelson's spirit. But the idea that the service as a whole was enthused by 'the Nelson touch' is far from correct, as the lethargic attack upon the French fleet in the Basque roads in 1809 demonstrated. Lord Cochrane, the hero of the debacle, was disgusted that more enemy ships were not destroyed by a fleet that played it safe. At stake, he believed, was that vital potency that Nelson had bequeathed. 'If,' he wrote after a court martial had acquitted his commander-in-chief, 'the anticipation of possible danger is to awe a British fleet, when the enemy is within its reach, and by an effort of no uncommon enterprise might be destroyed, we must take our farewell of those gallant exploits . . . that have thrown a lustre over the annals of our country.'[24]

Even before the battle of the Basque roads there was some public disquiet. The Lakes poet William Worsdworth lamented how 'deplorable' it was 'to think what fools' occupied 'the highest stations' in the navy. Anxiety intensified in the two years that followed the outbreak of the War of 1812, in which the navy was defeated by American forces in a run of small, mainly single-ship, actions. The 'Nelson touch' appeared to have emigrated. Honour was belatedly retrieved by the striking victory that Philip Broke's *Shannon* scored over the American *Chesapeake* in 1813 and the near destruction of the United States economy in 1814, and two years later Admiral Edward Pellew's thundering subjugation of Algiers reaffirmed that Britannia was still very much the unrivalled mistress of the oceans. Yet some of the glitter of Trafalgar had already been knocked away.[25]

But Nelson, 'the immortal memory' as the service chose to remember him, was always going to be a difficult act to follow. It is as true today as it was then. The age of sail and Britain's command of the sea is passed, and no one now needs to know how to win a battle with wooden ships and iron men, but Horatio Nelson is still an inspiration. He remains a symbol of service, endeavour and spirit. His quest to succeed by exceeding, to lift the bar of human achievement in a respectable cause, whatever the frailties of the body or the difficulties of the task, still contains a powerful challenge. His dream was to become not just an admiral, but a great admiral, perhaps the greatest admiral of all. It is a terrifying glove to throw down, and few would care to take it up today, whatever our walk of life. To consciously set out to become, say, not just a good poet, parent, surgeon, dancer, teacher, entrepreneur, technologist, scientist, friend or sportsman, but a *great* one, we must first define what constitutes that excellence, and then modify our behaviour to reach out to it, making what sacrifices are necessary. It requires us to sharpen our thinking, reshape our attitudes and reorient our practices. Few of us would care to take up such a forbidding challenge. But that need to achieve, perfect and strive, is perhaps the nearest we can now get to 'the Nelson touch'. When that combination of missionary zeal and exceptional ability succeeds it can make a true difference. It drove Brunel to become our greatest engineer, and Cook our greatest explorer. It turned a discontented middle-class Victorian lady, Florence Nightingale, into our greatest Englishwoman, who left us a legacy that still serves us today at the point of our greatest need.

It made Nelson, lifting him from the common run of efficient admirals. No one put it better than the Polish-born novelist Joseph Conrad in a much-quoted but superbly relevant passage of autobiography, *The Mirror of the Sea*. 'In a few short years he [Nelson] revolutionised not the strategy or tactics of sea warfare, but the very conception of victory itself. He brought heroism into the line of duty. Verily he is a terrible ancestor.'[26]

ACKNOWLEDGEMENTS

THE idea of writing this book was born in Kingston-upon-Hull in the East Riding of Yorkshire, some miles north on the same coast as Nelson's Norfolk. It was a time very different from the present one, and I was of a community of folk that hewed hard livings in local factories, dock-related industries and ships that plied cold northern seas. Hull was then one of the greatest shipping ports in the world, and I suppose most of our personal histories were crossed in some way by ships and sailors. My father's people had lived, worked and sometimes been born on boats that carried freight along the coast and up and down the Humber and the Ouse. My mother's father and grandfather had been blue water seamen. For a boy fascinated by the great stories of history, perhaps searching for an escape from the workaday world outside, the sea had an obvious attraction. By the time I was eighteen or nineteen, I had conceived the unlikely notion that one day I would write a life of Nelson. Today, of course, I look at the subject differently, but still feel an affinity with the earlier writers who helped inspire this quest.

Oliver Warner and Carola Oman, with whom I had corresponded in the sixties, had died long before I rehabilitated this project two decades later. But I owe Sir Ludovic Kennedy a double debt, first for his *Nelson and His Captains*, which reawakened my interest at the beginning of the eighties, and secondly for his valuable assistance. Although I was hitherto unknown to him, Sir Ludovic read the full manuscript of my first volume, and became an enthusiastic supporter. I greatly regret that I was unable to finish before his death in 2009. Another for whom this book came too late was Surgeon Vice-Admiral Sir James Watt, with whom I became acquainted as long ago as 1981. His unfailing encouragement and advice, in which he gave freely of his immense knowledge of the medical aspects of naval history, has been an important standby. He had written only a short time before his death in 2010, although typically making no reference to his own serious health problems. I miss both men greatly, and hope that this book does some justice to their faith.

The publication of my earlier volume introduced me to a number of other scholars, whose help and inspiration have maintained morale during a long campaign. Roger Knight, then winding up his magnificent *Pursuit of Victory*, was among the first to write, in exactly the same spirit as one captain might cheer another, whose ship disappears into the enemy smoke ahead. I met Andrew Lambert, the distinguished author of *Nelson: Britannia's God of War* and numerous other naval titles, at a book event about the same time. I am grateful for the encouragement of both. Among other able scholars I am particularly indebted to Guy St Denis and Brian Vale. Guy, who focuses on the War of 1812 period, epitomises the intrepid researcher, turning every available stone in his quests for information and accuracy; and Brian stands out among new naval historians for his readiness to challenge conventional perspectives and to worry boundaries. I also benefited from the aid or encouragement given by Anthony Cross, Martyn Downer, Judith Goodman, Peter Hopkin, Charles Lewis, Huw-Lewis Jones, Janet MacDonald, Peter Padfield and Richard Venn. As usual I have resorted to the expert translating skills of two of my most valued friends, Professor Roberta Ferrari of the University of Pisa, and Dr Harold Smyth.

Serious study of Nelson depends primarily upon four huge collections of original material of almost unfathomable depths; indeed, it is fair to state that no one has ever plumbed them. The best organised and richest is the British Library, St Pancras, which contains 129 volumes of relevant Nelson and Hamilton papers as well as several significant related collections, and I am indebted to the staff of the Department of Manuscripts for their unfailing patience and assistance over a dozen years of study, particularly David Hunt and Brenda Hockley who kept bringing an efficient supply of bulky tomes to my desk, and to Joanne Cox of the Customer Services section at Wetherby, Yorkshire. The National Archives, formerly the Public Record Office, at Kew houses the extensive files of the relevant government departments, and here I have had to concentrate primarily upon the Admiralty, Foreign and Colonial departments, knowing that more yet exists within and beyond their boundaries in such other classifications as the War Office. The National Archives is, in my experience, a heavily bureaucratised organisation, but there are staff at different levels who struggle to make it work. Among such heroes and heroines I simply have to mention Julie Ash, whose incredible industry and efficiency have solved many problems in the production of manuscripts over the years. I once tried to thank her, but she was far too brisk for business for such nonsense, and left me with only this means to express what I and no doubt many other customers owe to such rare individuals. The Nelson materials at the National Maritime Museum, Greenwich, grow steadily. The key holdings were described by K. F. Lindsay-MacDougall in 1955, and the largest collection, the Croker papers, which I examined paper by paper, has recently been expertly calendared by Jane Knight. I was extremely fortunate in doing the bulk of my work in the old Caird Library, which had a judicious flexibility essential to extended research as well as an architectural charm of its own. Library staff have come and gone over the years, but they set standards of courtesy hard to find in these pressured times. I must apologise to those whose names I never knew, but who were appreciated along the way, but Gareth Bellis, Michael Bevan, Eleanor Gawne, Kiri Ross-Jones, Graham Thompson and Brian Thynne all made important contributions. Special thanks are due to Sonia Bacca, Andrew Davies, Daphne Knott and Martin Salmon, who on different occasions went beyond the call of duty to get me out of dangerous shoal water. In Monmouth the Nelson Museum has a deceptively large quarry of manuscripts and memorabilia based on the collection of Lady Llangattock, who gathered into her custody much that had earlier belonged to such nineteenth-century forerunners as Matthew Barker, Thomas Pettigrew and Alfred Morrison, and more besides. The manuscripts are itemised under 993 'E' designations, and contain the most valuable run of the letters that Nelson wrote to his wife, and six little-used letterbooks that extensively cover the period 1796–1804. My thanks go to all the staff, but especially the senior curator, Andrew Helme, whose unparalleled knowledge of the collection was always at my service, and who even arranged for me to work additional out-of-public-hours to get me through my brief. I am much in his debt.

Among other people and institutions furnishing timely assistance and access to materials I must mention Anne Buchanan, Local Studies Librarian at Bath Central Library; Rachel Clare, Library and Archives Assistant at the Birmingham Central Library; Andrew Currie and the other staff at Bonham's auctioneers, London; Tony Sharkey, Local History Librarian, the Blackpool Central Library, Blackpool, Lancashire; John C. Dann, Barbara De Wolfe, and the ever gracious staff of the William L. Clements Library at the University of Michigan, Ann Arbor, USA, with very special thanks to Janet P. Bloom, a wonderful lady who kindly offered to surrender her breaks to give me more time with the manuscripts; archivists Jennie Hancock, Alison Spence and Katrina Griffiths who were most helpful at the Cornwall Record Office, Truro; Nils G. Bartholdy, State Archives of Denmark, Copenhagen; Katherine Collett and Randall L. Ericson, Couper Librarian at the Burke Library, Hamilton College, Clinton, New York; Jennie Rathbun, Micah Hoggatt and Emilie L. Hardman of the Houghton Library, Harvard University, Cambridge, Massachusetts; Marianne Percival, Hereford Reference Library; the Brymnor Jones Library in the University of Hull and the Central Reference Libary, Hull; Melissa Lindberg, the Huntington Library, San Marino, California; Dr Patricia McGuire, archivist at King's College, Cambridge; the library of the University of Lancaster; the London Library, St James's Square; Amy Proctor, Senior Information Officer at the London Metropolitan Archives; Sarah Gould, Heritage Officer at the Merton Local Studies Centre, Morden; the National Archives, formerly the Scottish Record Office, in Edinburgh; the National Library of Scotland, Edinburgh; Faith Carpenter, then curator of the Nelson Museum of Great Yarmouth, a relatively new but happily thriving resource for all things Nelsonian; Patricia Belier at the University of New Brunswick archives, Fredericton, Canada; Elaine Archbold, Special Collections, Robinson Library, Newcastle University; the Newspaper Library, Colindale, London, where it is still possible to browse the full files of rare and valuable periodicals; Ian Palfrey, Senior Archivist, Norfolk Record Office, Norwich; Professor Bernard de Neumann, Royal Hospital School, Holbrook, Suffolk; Margaret Newman in the Library of the Royal Naval Museum, Portsmouth, a particularly pleasant workplace; Arianna Cona, secretary at the Fondazione Salvare Palermo Onlus, Palermo, Sicily; Tessa Milne and Gabriel Heaton of Sotheby's Auctioneers, who afforded me access to important manuscript lots; Andrea Cameron, Honorary Librarian at Stationers' Hall, London; Rhona Elstone and the staff of the Surrey History Centre, Woking; James W. Cheevers, Associate Director and Senior Curator, and his staff at the United States Naval Academy Museum at Annapolis, Maryland, to whom I owe another special vote of thanks for their splendid support; and the staff of the Wellcome Institute Library in London.

R. T. T. Bramley, Ron Cansdale, Richard S. J. Clarke (of Royal Victoria Hospital, Belfast), Michael Crumplin, Linda Ebrey, Ron Fiske, Dr Simon Harris, Barry E. Kelly, Gary Kent, April Place, Stephen Locker-Lampson, Randy Mafit (editor of *The Kedge Anchor*), Michael Nash (whose valuable study of the funeral of Nelson's father appeared as this book was going to press), Robert Le Noble Noble, Malcolm Paton, Alex Revell, Ian Sayer, Pamela Webb, Peter D. Winterbottom and Jim Woolward contributed pieces of information or timely shoulders to the wheel. At the Bodley Head, sister publishers to Jonathan Cape, I was fortunate indeed to recover many of the 'old team' that had so signally served my previous volume. Jörg Hensgen has again been outstanding. One of the finest editors in the business, he is also a delight to work with, and his understanding and enthusiasm have been nothing less than inspirational. His support, especially during those last long miles, was decisive. I am also much indebted to Chloe Johnson-Hill and Ruth Waldram, who ushered me through the post-publication processes with unfailing good humour; Richard Collins, who carefully scrutinised my embryonic texts; and to Katherine Ailes and Kay Peddle. The project also received a great boon from the appointment of the able Stuart Williams, who takes the helm at Bodley Head this year. In New York I am again indebted to Jack Macrae at Henry Holt. Among old and new friends I would particularly like to salute Bruce Crowther, an East Riding original now ensconced in Spain; Mavis Richards, who we have now sadly lost; Art and Shirley Wolfe of Ann Arbor in Michigan; and Jackie Stevenson of Crediton in Devon for their encouragement, hospitality and persevering interest. Not least, anyone embarking on a long voyage to windward needs a social network to intervene during absences and keep the home fires in good shape. I am especially grateful to Anita and Brian Randall, the Hawcroft family and Mu and Bob Potter, who stepped in to help while I was away on long spells of 'service'.

Emma Lefley, Tracey Walker, Stephen Courtney, Chris Turner and Emma Butterfield were instrumental in gathering illustrations, and the maps were drawn by Martin Lubikowski.

My thanks go to all of these people, but the opinions expressed in this book are mine, as are its faults. The extent of the material available on Nelson, both in manuscript and print, surprised even me, and although I have spent fourteen years exploring regions accessible and not so accessible, the landscape still contains unreached peaks and hidden valleys. It did not sit well, but I find solace in the wise words of my late friend, Helen Hornbeck Tanner, during my forays into a very different intellectual wilderness. 'Never be afraid,' she said, 'of leaving something for the next scholar.' It was good advice. Whether anyone will tackle Nelson in depth again I cannot say. Many manuscripts are more thoroughly catalogued and reachable than they were years ago, but a bland homogeneity and rigid and sometimes stifling bureaucracy is invading a growing number of our archives and libraries, and despite the internet and digitalisation, the job of serious grass-root research is not for the faint-hearted. Taking this banner from the three Nelson writers who inspired me as a youth has led me as close to my physical limits as any project I have undertaken, but we need to encourage new enquirers. No two pairs of eyes see things in exactly the same way, and nothing attracts new discoverers more than the prospect of 'treasure yet to be lifted', as Stevenson would say. It is pleasing to envisage a new and vigorous generation of Nelson interpreters stepping forward to take the flag from the old.

Lastly, this book is dedicated to the three people who were always at its heart. My brother Philip has been my university department throughout life, sharing enthusiasms, tossing thoughts back and forth, and lending a hand when necessary. My partner, Terri, has had to live with Nelson far longer than she would have wished, and I could never have reached this point without her constant forbearance, support and sacrifice. And Will Sulkin has taken me through Pimlico, Jonathan Cape and the Bodley Head. He is a great editor, a master of the frontier between publishers and writers, and a staunch friend. It was Will's enthusiasm, vision, advocacy and support that brought this project to life and saw it through, whatever the obstacles. My debt to him is incalculable, and in many ways the best of this book is Will's as well as mine.

John Sugden,
Cumbria, 2012

NOTES

Introduction

1. James, Earl of Malmesbury, *Diaries*, 4, pp. 341–42. • **2**. Egerton MS 2240, f. 143; Emma to Nelson, 2/4/1802, Egerton MS 1623. • **3**. Clarke to Hamilton, 2/2/1806, Hilda Gamlin, *Nelson's Friendships*, 2, p. 77; McArthur to Nelson, 19/5/1803, NMM: CRK/8. • **4**. Among the best monographs are Tim Clayton and Peter Craig's *Trafalgar*; Brian Lavery's *Nelson's Fleet at Trafalgar*; Rina Prentice's *Authentic Nelson*; Peter Goodwin's encyclopaedic *Nelson's Ships* and *Ships of Trafalgar*; Colin White's selection of largely unpublished *New Letters*; Richard Walker's *Nelson's Portraits*; Martyn Downer's life of Alexander Davison; and Lawrence Brockliss, John Cardwell and Michael Moss's *Nelson's Surgeon*. The Society for Nautical Research samples the scholarship in a special issue of *The Mariner's Mirror* (vol. 91, no. 2, 2005); Anthony Cross and Huw Lewis-Jones have turned *The Trafalgar Chronicle* into an essential annual fest of valuable papers; while the Nelson Society's *Nelson Dispatch* offers a valuable running commentary. • **5**. Nelson to Emma, 3/5/1804, Egerton MS 1614. • **6**. Nelson to Emma, 25/4/1801, Egerton MS 1614. In an aside to the shortcomings of Europe's rulers, Nelson once described his aspirations as 'happiness, doing good to the poor, and setting an example of virtue and godliness worthy of imitation even to kings and princes': Nelson to Emma, 10/3/1801, *HANP*, 2, p. 127. • **7**. Nelson to Acton, 2/6/1800, Zabriskie Collection, US Naval Academy, Annapolis. But it should be said that Nelson's empathies were less engaged when it came to slavery in the West Indies. He once described the arguments of William Wilberforce as a 'damnable and cruel doctrine' that destabilised the West Indian islands and incited rebellion: Nelson to Taylor, 11/6/1805, Add. MS 34959. Nelson had probably been influenced by the friendships and connexions he had made among the West Indian planters, but how far this letter represented his real views is uncertain. It was written at a time he was being accused of risking the safety of the British West Indies, and when he needed to emphasise the importance he attached to their protection. As we shall see, Nelson fought hard for the rights of individual black men who gave him good service. • **8**. Churchill, *Marlborough: His Life and Times* (reprinted, Chicago, 2002), 1, p. 19.

I Recovering

1. *London Chronicle*, 5/9/1797; Nepean to Nelson, 2/9/1797, Add. MS 34933; Spencer to Nelson, 3/9/1797, Add. MS 34906; *Seahorse* log, ADM 51/1190. • **2**. *Bath Journal*, 11/9/1797; Louis Hodgkin, *Nelson and Bath*, pp. 3, 9. Useful biographies of Fanny have been published by Edith M. Keate and Frances Hardy. • **3**. Nelson to William Nelson, 7/9/1797, and Kate Matcham to Nelson, 6/10/1798, Add. MSS, 34988; *Bath Journal*, 11/9/1797. The little evidence about Nelson's voice converges. A midshipman of 1801 described it as 'a squeaking little voice' with a 'true Norfolk drawl,' while at the same time a soldier spoke of it as 'thin [and] rather feeble': Jean Pond, 'Nelson's Voice', *ND*, 7 (2000), p. 130; Mary Agnes FitzGibbon, *Veteran of 1812*, p. 39. • **4**. Fanny Nelson to Suckling, 6/9/97, *D&L*, 2, p. 440; Nelson's expenses, 1797, *NLTHW*, p. 378; Nelson to William, 6/9/1797, Add. MS 34988. • **5**. MS 'Auto-biography of James Noble', written in 1826 and revised in 1846. Nelson probably paid for the lodgings in Porto Ferraio, cf. Pollard to Nelson, 7/1/1797, NMM: CRK/10, which includes an entry, 'Cash pd. Adelaide as per order, £20'. On this subject, John Sugden, 'New Light', revises earlier accounts. • **6**. Josiah Nisbet's 'passing certificate', 7/4/1797, ADM 6/95, stated that he appeared to be twenty years old. He was, in fact, born in 1780, possibly on 7 July (Sotheby's, *Davison*, p. 200). The certificate also claimed that he had served for more than two years as a captain's servant in the *Champion* and *Unicorn* between 1 February 1784 and 5 July 1786, when he was actually between four and six years old. In 1817 Josiah had forgotten Nelson's contrivance of 1797, and offered a different, but equally bogus, version of his sea time in his 'Return of Services' to the Admiralty, 25 August 1817, ADM 9/2. He now asserted that he had served two years on his stepfather's frigate, *Boreas*, between 1785 and 1787. See also *Dolphin* muster, ADM 36/12339. Josiah's career is described and documented in John Sugden, 'Fine Colt'. • **7**. Man to Nelson, and Man to Thompson, Nelson and Calder, 22/9/1797, Add. MS 34906. • **8**. *London Chronicle*, 13/9/1797; account with Marsh and Creed, *HANP*, 2, pp. 384–9; statement of Marsh, Sibbald and Strachey, 28/9/1797, Add. MS 34906; account of Maurice Nelson and Davison, NMM: CRK/3/168. • **9**. *The Times*, 4/9/1797; *True Briton*, 4, 5 and 6/9/1797; *Sun*, 10/11/1797. Whig attacks on the expedition in *Morning Chronicle*, 4 and 7/9/1797, omitted criticism of Nelson. • **10**. Clarence to Nelson, 7/9/1797, Coke to Nelson, 19/9/1797 and Worrell to Nelson, 20/9/1797, Add. MS 34906; William Nelson to Nelson, 7/10/1797, Monmouth MS E653; Nelson to St Vincent, 6/10/1797, *D&L*, 2, p. 448; Gillian Ford, 'Nelson References'; *True Briton*, 24/1/1798. • **11**. Man to Nelson, 22/9/1797, Add. MS 34906. The house was situated between Bruton and Grosvenor Streets, the sixth property from the former, with Little Bruton Street to its rear. It was renumbered 147 the following century, and thus depicted in Peter Jackson, *Tallis's . . . Views*, pp. 58–9. For the original numbers and positions see Paul Laxton and Joseph Wisdom, *A to Z*, map 12. Valuable studies of Nelson's family have been been written by 'Thomas Foley' (actually Florence Horatia Suckling), Mary Eyre Matcham and Thomas Nelson. • **12**. Elliot to his wife, 5/10/1797, NLS MS. 11051; Anne Fremantle, *Wynne Diaries*, 2, p. 195; Bulkeley to Nelson, 12/3/1800, Thomas J. Pettigrew, *Memoirs*, 2, p. 276. • **13**. Fanny to Nelson, 7/6/1799, Add. MS 34988; Thomas to Nelson, 21/9/1797, Hamond (Westacre) Papers, Norwich Record Office, HMN 4/3900; Davison to Nelson, 3/5/1801, NMM: CRK/3; William to Nelson, 7/10/1797, 11 and 30/11/1797, Monmouth MSS E653, 655, 656; James Harrison, *Life*, 1, p. 226; *The Times*, 28/9/1797, 2 and 3/10/1797. Maurice referred to Sukey (Mrs Susannah Ford) as 'Mrs Nelson' although no formal marriage was admitted. In 1801 Davison said that the couple had lived together for 'upwards of twenty years'. The date is supported by James Preston, who recalled that as a naval lieutenant he used to spend Sundays with Maurice, who had a 'little country abode for the health of his lady at Roehampton near Putney Common'. Maurice introduced Preston to Nelson after the latter returned from the West Indies, which would have been in 1781. Sukey may have been older than Maurice. Her health steadily deteriorated, especially after 1789, when regular medication became necessary, and she eventually lost her sight. However, she wrote a respectable hand as her only surviving letter attests. In his will in 1797 Maurice referred to her as 'Mrs Susannah Ford,' which implies she had been a widow, and there is evidence of two children from an earlier union. Nevertheless, an administration of her effects in 1811 named James Price, a coloured servant, as her only beneficiary. See Preston to Nelson, 19/5/1801, NMM: CRK/10; Bland to Nelson, 3/9/1805, Add. MS 34988; Sukey to Nelson, 11/9/1801, NMM: CRK/20; and Diana N. Jarvis, 'Maurice Nelson', pp. 609–10. • **14**. Elliot to his wife, 5/10/1797, NLS MS 11051. • **15**. Richard Edgcumbe, *Diary*, 1, p. 77; Spencers to Nelson, 19/9/1797, 8 [December?] 1797, Add. MS 34906; *The Times*, 20/9/1797. • **16**. Poyntz's letters to his sister, the Dowager Countess, are in Add. MS 75574. • **17**. *The Times*, 28 and 29/9/1797; *True Briton*, 29/9/1797; *London Chronicle*, 28 and 29/9/1797; *London Gazette*, 30/9/1797; Townsend to Nelson, 22/9/1797, Add. MS 34906; Horace Twiss, *Eldon*, 1, p. 208. The 'Biographical Memoir' of Nelson published in *NC*, 3 (1800), p. 180, which *may* have reflected a witness statement, reported that the king expressed a hope that Nelson's injury would not deprive his country of further service, to which the admiral replied that 'so long as I have a foot to stand on, I will combat for my king and country!'. Much later, Lady Louise Berry said that her husband, Captain Edward Berry, accompanied Nelson to the levee. When the king commiserated with Nelson over the loss of his arm, the admiral cheerfully introduced Berry as his 'right hand' (*D&L*, 2, p. 448). The press reports contain no reference to Berry's presence, but he may have been there; Fremantle was present, despite the failure of the newspapers to notice him (Fremantle, *Wynne Diaries*, 2, p. 203). • **18**. *True Briton*, 26/10/1797, 9 and 23/11/1797, 7 and 21/12/1797; *The Times*, 5/10/1797. Trevor, Drake and Elliot had all supported Nelson's application for a crown pension. • **19**. *The Times*, 16/11/1797; *Bath Journal*, 4/12/1797; Mrs Henry Baring, *Windham*, p. 382; Nelson to Wilkes, 22/11/1797, *D&L*, 2, p. 452, where the speeches at the Guildhall are reprinted under an incorrect date that places the event after Wilkes's death. • **20**. Nelson's expenses, *NLTHW*, p. 378; William Nelson to Nelson, 7/10/1797, Monmouth MS E653; Elliot to his wife, 5/10/1797, NLS MS 11051; *True Briton*, 20/9/1797. • **21**. Nelson to Robinson, 5/10/1797, H. T. A. Bosanquet, 'Lord Nelson', plate facing p. 194; John Drinkwater Bethune, *Narrative*, p. 97. • **22**. *True Briton*, 14 and 17/10/1797; *The Times*, 14 and 16/10/1797; *London Gazette*, 17 and 18/10/1797; *Courier*, 17/10/1797, 8/11/1797. • **23**. Clarke and McArthur, *Life and Services*, 2, p. 67. The circumstances and some little known details in this account, such as the name of Nelson's landlord, are verifiable. Clarke and McArthur got the story from Lady Nelson, who saw the proofs of the book, so it was probably substantially correct. • **24**. *The Times*, 17 and 21/10/1797; *True Briton*, 18/10/1797; *Sun*, 7/11/1797. • **25**. Mary Eyre Matcham, *Nelsons*, p. 149; 'Admiral Horatio Nelson's Combined Knife and Fork'; *Morning Chronicle*, 4/2/1801. • **26**. Nelson to Bertie, 11/12/1797, *D&L*, 2, p. 458; Foley, *Nelson Centenary*, p. 39. • **27**. *True Briton*, 20/12/1797; *The Times*, 20/12/1797; *London Chronicle*, 19 and 20/12/1797; *Oracle*, 25/12/1797; *Morning Chronicle*, 20/12/1797; *D&L*, 2, p. 458; Marsden to Nelson, 12/12/1797, Add. MS 34933; Add. MS 34906, f. 298. The omission of Nelson's name in lists of officers accompanying the procession implies he made his own way. • **28**. David White, 'Heralds', and Ron C. Fiske, 'Nelson's Arms', are informed accounts. For the figurehead of the *Captain* see Miller's account, Add. MS 34906, f. 321. • **29**. Fanny to Nelson, 6/5/1798, *NLTHW*, p. 428. Richard Walker, *Nelson Portraits*, with its supplementary papers, is the standard work. The portrait by Daniel Orme was probably based upon a sketch made for a tableau painting showing Nelson at Cape St Vincent. Orme may have sketched several of the other figures in the scene from life. At least six of the seven companions shown beside Nelson in the finished canvas had returned to England, and were theoretically available for sittings. Orme also based his painting of the Spanish sword being surrendered to Nelson on a sketch made of the original trophy. For this line of thought, see Francis William Blagdon, [Edward] *Orme's Graphic History*, which prints the sketches. Edward Orme, the Bond Street engraver, was the brother of Daniel the artist. Concerning Gahagan's sculpture, Walker's statement (*Nelson's Portraits*, p. 209) that the artist arranged the hair on his first bust 'to conceal the Nile scar' is erroneous, as that work was being exhibited as early as May 1798, two months before the injury was sustained. • **30**. Fanny to Nelson, 23/7/1798, *NLTHW*, p. 441. John McArthur considered his portrait too flattering, and claimed William Nelson agreed. He asked Nelson to sit again, although it is not clear that he did so: McArthur to Nelson, 1/12/1800, NMM: CRK/8. • **31**. On the issue of the *Jane and Elizabeth*, which was referred to the Treasury, see Sugden, *Nelson*, ch. xiv, and pp. 396–7; Heseltine to Nelson and Hume to Heseltine, both 11/1/1798, Add. MS 34906. • **32**. *Ipswich Journal*, 9, 16 and 23/9/1797; 'Particulars and Conditions of Sale', Add. MS 30170; Esther Hallam Moorhouse, *Nelson in England*, pp. 111–12. • **33**. *Ipswich Journal*, 4/11/1797; Edmund Nelson to Catherine Matcham, 30/10/1797, in Matcham, *Nelsons*, p. 146; articles of agreement, 13/11/1797, Add. MS 30170, f. 23. • **34**. Matcham, *Nelsons*, p. 154–5; Marsh, Sibbald and Stracey to Nelson, 2/1/1798, Add. MS 34906; Nelson to Fanny, 7/4/1798, *NLTHW*, p. 392; Jim Saunders, 'Roundwood'. Fanny and Edmund surrendered their rented properties in Bath to occupy Roundwood, but by mid-September 1798 were asking Kate Matcham, Nelson's youngest sister, to find them a short-term winter let in Bath. • **35**. Cockburn to Nelson, 1/6/1798, Add. MS 34907; Marsh, Sibbald and Stracey to Nelson, 28/9/1797, and Parker to Thompson, 22/10/1797, Add. MS 34906. • **36**. Thompson to Nelson, 6 and 11/12/1797, Add. MS 34906; agreement of Thompson, et al., Add. MS 34906, f. 268; *D&L*, 2, p. 459. • **37**. Nelson to Spencer, 27/9/1797, enclosing the certificates of 1794 and 1797, Add. MS 75813. • **38**. Nelson to naval commissioners, 1/10/1797, 6/10/1797, NMM: MON 1/8, and *D&L*, 7, p. cxlviii; Nelson to Sick & Hurt Board, 29/3/1798, Wellcome MS 3677; Nelson to St Vincent, 6/10/1797, *D&L*, 2, p. 448; Bosanquet, 'Lord Nelson', p. 13; accounts with Marsh, Sibbald and Stracey, *HANP*, 2, p. 389; Harrison, *Life*, 1, pp. 226, 229–30, which contains material from Thomas Bolton. • **39**. Surgeons' Company to Sick & Hurt Board, 1/3/1798, the Board to Nepean, 26/3/1798, and Nelson to the Board, 21/3/1798, *NLTHW*, 377, 378; Bosanquet, 'Lord Nelson', 13; Add. MS 34933, ff. 78, 82; Nelson to Nepean, 28/11/1797, *D&L*, 2, p. 454. • **40**. Nelson to Loughborough, 12/10/1797, Loughborough to Nelson, 15/10/1797, Nelson to Halkett, 23/10/1797, and Edmund Nelson to Halkett, 25/12/1797, Add. MS 34906; Matcham, *Nelsons*, p. 146. • **41**. Nelson to William, 29/11/1797, NMM: BRP/6; William to Nelson, 7/10/1797, 30/11/1797, Monmouth MSS E653, 656; Nelson to Loughborough, 2/12/1797, Add. MS 34906; *The Times*, 3/10/1797. • **42**. Nelson to Miller, 11/12/1797, *D&L*, 2, p. 456; Miller to Nelson, 17/10/1797, Add. MS 34906; Taylor to Nelson, 11/3/1799, Add. MS 34909. • **43**. Lucas to Nelson, 13/9/1797, Coulson to Nelson, 5/3/1798, King to Nelson, 28/1/1798, Fellows to Nelson, 3/3/1798, Add. MS 34906; Nelson to Fellows, 2/10/1797, Huntington, HM 34017. • **44**. St Vincent to Keith, 4/9/1801, David Bonner-Smith, *St Vincent*, 1, p. 22; N. A. M. Rodger, *Command of the Ocean*, p. 518. • **45**. St Vincent to Spencer, 24/9/1797, enclosing Spencer to St Vincent, 20/8/1797, Add. MS 75813; St Vincent to Jackson, 9/8/1778, Jedediah S. Tucker, *St Vincent*, 1, p. 85; Ms 'Auto-Biography of James William Noble'. This subject, with fresh data on Nelson's early Mediterranean service, is fully treated in John Sugden, 'Rusting Ingloriously'. • **46**. Nelson to Berry, 8/12/1797, *D&L*, 2, p. 456. • **47**. Galwey 'passing certificate', 7/2/1793, ADM 6/92; return of service, 1817, ADM 9/2; Galwey to Nelson, 27/9/1797, 22/11/1797, Add. MS 34906; Nelson to Nepean, 14/12/1797, *D&L*, 2, p. 460; Marsden to Nelson, 15/12/1797, Add. MS 34933; *Vanguard* muster, ADM 36/15356; John Marshall, *Royal Navy Biography*, 2, pp. 653–4. Galwey, however, suffered from the blight that destroyed the careers of Spicer and Noble. Becoming a commander on 8

October 1798, he returned to England, where he was stymied by the shortage of ships. As Nelson had promised him a letter of introduction to Lady Spencer, he applied for help to Nelson (Galwey to Nelson, 17/9/1799, Add. MS 34913). Made post-captain in the general promotion of 1802, he died a rear admiral of the red on 9 August 1844. For brief details of naval officers' careers see NA: G. C. Pitcairn-Jones, 'Sea Officers List', and David Syrett and R. L. DiNardo, *Commissioned Sea Officers*. • **48**. Master's log, *Vanguard*, ADM 52/3516; Berry to Nelson, 25/2/1798, Add. MS 34906; *Bath Journal*, 25/12/1797; *True Briton*, 27/12/1797; Nelson to Suckling, 3/1/1797, *D&L*, 3, p. 1. • **49**. *St James's Chronicle*, 20/2/1798, 14/3/1798; Nelson to St Vincent, 6/10/1797, *NLTHW*, p. 380; Nelson to St Vincent,10/1/1798, *D&L*, 3, p. 3; Lady St Vincent to Nelson, 29/12/1797, Add. MS 34906. • **50**. Matcham, *Nelsons*, pp. 148, 151; Carola Oman, *Nelson*, p. 688, n. 31; Edgar Vincent, *Nelson*, p. 351; Thomas Taylor to Nelson, 30/12/1797, Add. MS 34906; *Vanguard* muster, ADM 36/15356. • **51**. Nelson to Lloyd, 29/1/1798, John Rylands Library. This letter survives in multiple copies. The probable explanation is that an original was used as a model for forgeries. See for example, *Notes & Queries*, 9th series, 10 (1902), p. 425; *Toronto Daily News*, 15/1/1919, and three letters of 1935–6 in the Archives of Ontario, Toronto, Canada, Box MU 7838. • **52**. Edgcumbe, *Diary*, 1, pp. 77–8. • **53**. Harrison, *Life*, 1, pp. 230–31; Nelson to Edmund, 14/3/1798, Monmouth MS E600; Nelson to William, 31/3/1798, Add. MS 34988; William to Sarah Nelson, 27/2/1798, NMM: BRP/1/2; Matcham, *Nelsons*, p. 151–2. No. 96 Bond Street, between Blenheim and Brook Streets, was renumbered 103 and is now distinguished by a blue plaque. • **54**. Nelson to Suckling, 9/4/1798, *D&L*, 3, p. 9; Nelson to Mary Nelson, 2/3/1798, Add. MS 34988; Fanny to Nelson, 7/4/1798, Add. MS 34988; will, 21/3/1798, *NLTHW*, p. 405; *London Chronicle*, 2/3/1798. • **55**. Waldegrave to Nelson, 17/3/1798, Add. MS 34906; *The Times*, 2 and 15/3/1798; *True Briton*, 15/3/1798; Baring, *Windham*, p. 389; Berry to Nelson, 8/3/1798, Add. MS 34906. • **56**. Nepean to Nelson, 16, 17, 20 and 27/3/1798, Add. MSS 34933 and 34906. • **57**. Berry to Nelson, 8 and 12/3/1798, Add. MS 34906. • **58**. Campbell to Nelson, 16/3/1798, Parker to Nelson, 13/3/1798, and Pinney to Nelson, 11/3/1798, Add. MS 34906; Nelson to Campbell, 16/3/1798, Morgan Library, New York. • **59**. Nelson to Collier, 14/3/1798, 8/4/1798, *D&L*, 3, pp. 5, 7; Collier to Nelson, 27/3/1798, March 1798, April 1798, Add. MS 34906; Berry to Nelson, 30/12/1798, Add. MS 34909; *Vanguard* muster, ADM 36/15356; William O'Byrne, *Biographical Dictionary*, pp. 215–16. • **60**. *Vanguard* log, ADM 52/3516; Parker to Nepean, 15/3/1798, ADM 1/1028; Nelson to Nepean, 29/3/1798, *D&L*, 3, p. 7; Nepean to Nelson, 30/3/1798, Add. MS 34906. • **61**. Lloyd to Nelson, 9/3/1798, *HANP*, 2, p. 5. • **62**. Fanny to Nelson, 7/4/1798, Add. MS 34988. • **63**. Fanny to Nelson, 30/3/1798, 4 and 7/4/1798, Add. MS 34988. • **64**. *D&L*, 2, p. 457, and 3, pp. 3, 8; Smith to Nelson, 12/3/1798, Ives to Nelson, 14/3/1798, Rumsey to Nelson, 9/4/1798, Add. MS 34906; Nelson to Gaskin, 26/1/1798, NMM: AGC/17/3. • **65**. The admiral's personal retinue included John Campbell, secretary; Anthony Leary, an Irish cook from County Cork, later rated a landsman; and two unsatisfactory servants, Thomas Spencer, a twenty-seven-year-old man from Gotham, Nottinghamshire, and the vastly overhallowed Tom Allen. Allen was from Sculthorpe, about ten miles from Burnham Thorpe, and had been baptised in the parish on 23 December 1771 (Graham Dean, 'The Nile Musters', p. 12). For the complement of the *Vanguard* see her muster, ADM 36/15356, and Eric Tushingham, *HMS Vanguard*. • **66**. *Vanguard* muster, ADM 36/15356. • **67**. Carysfort to Nelson, 30/3/1798, Add. MS 34906; O'Byrne, *Biographical Dictionary*, p. 934; Antram to Nelson, 26/3/1798, Add. MS 34906. Both men became commissioned officers. • **68**. Nelson to Fanny, 29 and 31/3/1798, 7/4/1798, *NLTHW*, pp. 388, 389, 392; Fanny to Nelson, 4 and 23/4/1798, 28/5/1798, Add. MS 34988; William Cooper, *A Sketch of the Life of the Late Henry Cooper* (c. 1856), written by his brother,

p. 7. • **69**. Nelson to Bertie, 4/1/1798, *D&L*, 3, p. 1. • **70**. Spencer to Nelson, 31/3/1798, Add. MS 34906; Parker to Nepean, 1 and 9/4/1798, 15/3/1798, ADM 1/1028. • **71**. Nelson to Fanny, 3/4/1798, *NLTHW*, p. 390; Fanny to Nelson, 5 and 15/4/1798, NLTHW, p. 423, and Add. MS 34988.

II The Band of Brothers

1. Nelson to Miller, 31/3/1798, Add. MSS 36608. The logs of the *Vanguard*, ADM 51/1288 and ADM 52/3516, are a basis for some of the following. For the ship's sailing qualities see ADM 95/39/2. On the *Vanguard* and other Nelson's ships see Peter Goodwin, *Nelson's Ships*, a work of great industry. Nelson's activities in the Mediterranean between 1798 and 1800 are principally documented in his letterbooks (Add. MS 34963 and Monmouth MSS E 989 and 991), order books (Add. MSS 30260, 36608–36609) and incoming correspondence (Add. MSS 34907–17); ADM 1/397–401; NMM: JER/3–6;and the Hamilton papers in the Egerton and Add. MSS, the NMM (HML) and FO 70. • **2**. Nelson to Fanny, 24/4/1798, Monmouth MS E 940; *Dolphin* log, ADM 51/1277; John Marshall, *Royal Naval Biography*, 3, p. 187; St Vincent to Nelson, 23/10/1797, Add. MS 34949. For Josiah see John Sugden, 'Fine Colt'. • **3**. St Vincent to Spencer, 1/5/1798, Julian S. Corbett, *Spencer*, 2, p. 441; Ludovic Kennedy, *Nelson and His Captains*, p. 108. • **4**. Acton to Hamilton, 3/4/1798, Egerton MS 2640. • **5**. Eden to Grenville, 23 and 28/3/1798, 14 and 16/4/1798, FO 7/51. My impressions of Austria depend upon British Foreign Office records, but I have also used Karl A. Roider, *Thugut*, with some reservations, and Gunther E. Rothenberg, *Napoleon's Great Adversaries*, which reviews the military dimension in Austrian resistance. • **6**. Acton to Hamilton, 9/4/1798, Egerton MS 2640. • **7**. Day, 31/3/1798, and Jackson to St Vincent, 31/3/1798, NMM: CRK/18. • **8**. J. C. Herold, David Chandler and Charles Esdaile have written of Napoleon's expedition, but the indispensable secondary accounts of Nelson's campaign are those by Brian Lavery and Michele Battesti. • **9**. Minto to Nelson, 25/4/1798, Jedediah S. Tucker, *St Vincent*,1, p. 348; Minto to Spencer, 24/4/1798, Add. MS 75820. • **10**. Duke of Buckingham, *Courts and Cabinets*, 2, p. 405. • **11**. Spencer to St Vincent, 29/4/1798, Corbett, *Spencer*, 2, p. 437. • **12**. Nepean to St Vincent, 2/5/1798, Add. MS 34933. • **13**. Jackson to Grenville, 7 and 28/4/1798, 5, 12 and 19/5/1798, FO 67/26; Eden to Grenville, 21 and 28/4/1798, FO 7/51; Day to St Vincent, 31/3/1798, 13/4/1798, ADM 1/397; intelligence from Lisbon, 17 and 20/5/1798, NMM: CRK/18. • **14**. St Vincent's instructions, 2/5/1798, ADM 1/397. • **15**. Nelson to Fanny, 1/5/1798, Monmouth MS E941; St Vincent to Nelson, 17/7/1798, Augustus Phillimore, *Last*, 1, p. 25; Richard D. Barnett, 'Barnett', p. 192. Orde's grudge against St Vincent ran deeper than Nelson: see Tucker, *St Vincent*, 1, pp. 351–5, and Edward Pelham Brenton, *St Vincent*, 1, chaps xiv–xv. For Parker's long-standing differences with Nelson see John Sugden, *Nelson*, pp. 365–6, 712, 873–4, n. 52. • **16**. Order book, Add. MS 30260. • **17**. Saumarez and Ball have received useful monographs, but deserve serious modern biographies. John Ross, *Saumarez*, prints relevant papers, some of which have recently come to auction. Ball's letters to Nelson survive in discrete collections, including ADM 7/55, NMM: CRK/1, and Add. MS 37268. For some of Nelson's captains see the works by W. H. Fitchett, Ludovic Kennedy and Nicholas Tracy, and the anthology edited by Peter Le Fevre and Richard Harding. • **18**. Nelson to St Vincent, 8 and 17/5/1798, Colin White, *New Letters*, p. 210, and ADM 1/397; *Terpsichore* log, ADM 51/4507. I have also drawn upon the logs of the *Orion, Alexander, Emerald* and *La Bonne Citoyenne* (ADM 51/1253, 1260, 1268, 1247). For an incomplete list of prizes and stoppages with a summary of intelligence gained, see 'Report of Vessels Spoke', Add. MS 34907, ff.111–16. • **19**. Thomas Spencer to his parents, 3/8/1798, Stephen

Howarth, 'Nelson's Steward'. • **20**. The accounts Ball later gave his secretary, Samuel Taylor Coleridge (Barbara E. Rooke, *Friend*, 2, p. 293), and Francis Laing (*D&L*, 3, p. 21) fit the gratitude Nelson expressed after the storm, but Berry wrote to his father-in-law on 29 May (*D&L*, 3, p. 17) 'that we had determined to order the *Alexander* to cast off the hawser and desire her to shift for herself', but stops short of saying that it happened. The log of the *Alexander* modestly states that after seven in the morning of 22 May the ship 'spoke' the admiral, and at three in the afternoon took *Vanguard* in tow. • **21**. Nelson to St Vincent, 24/5/1798, Add. MS 34963; Nelson to Fanny, 24/5/1798, Monmouth MS E960. • **22**. Ross, *Saumarez*, 1, p. 196; Lavery, *Nelson and the Nile*, p. 110. • **23**. Quotations and details from Sardinian sources are given by John R. Gwyther, 'Nelson in Carloforte', which draws upon the researches of local historians. • **24**. Day to St Vincent, 13/4/1797, ADM 1/397; Desmond Gregory, *Napoleon's Italy*, p. 30. • **25**. Gregory, *Napoleon's Italy*, p. 37; Jackson to Grenville, 7 and 28/4/1798, 16 and 23/6/1798, FO 67/26. A useful, if opaque, study is Michael Broers, *Napoleonic Empire in Italy*. • **26**. Nepean to St Vincent, 2/5/1798, Add. MS 34933; Jackson to Grenville, 26/5/1798, 16/6/1798, FO 67/26. • **27**. Details of purchases, Add. MS 34906, f. 425; Jackson to Nelson, 18/7/1798, Add. MS 34907; Ross, *Saumarez*, 1, p. 196. Jackson received Nelson's complaint about his reception at San Pietro, but consoled himself in a belief that 'the day after the date of the letter an order came from the Viceroy of Sardinia to furnish' Nelson with 'whatever he might want'. This does not appear to be true; in fact, on 8 June the viceroy informed the court at Turin that he disapproved of De Nobili's firing a salute and supplying the British: Jackson to Grenville, 7 and 21/7/1798, FO 67/27; Gwyther, 'Nelson in Carloforte', p. 26. • **28**. Nelson to St Vincent, 31/5/1798, NMM: JER/3–4; *Mutine* log, ADM 51/1244. The *Orion* and *Alexander* rejoined Nelson on 8 and 9 June, both with prizes. • **29**. Intelligence of Hope, 28/5/1798, 2/6/1798, NMM: CRK/14/42; Edward Berry, *Narrative*, p. 3; St Vincent to Hamilton, 22/5/1798, FO 7/52. • **30**. There is much to be said about Troubridge, but we have fine introductions by Kennedy, *Nelson and his Captains*, and Pat Crimmin, in Le Fevre and Harding, *British Admirals*, pp. 294–321, 392–4. • **31**. Collingwood to Edward Collingwood, 14/12/1798, in C.H.H. Owen, 'Letters', 166; Rooke, *Friend*, 2, p. 293; St Vincent to Nepean, 23/4/1798, 1/7/1798, ADM 1/397. • **32**. St Vincent to Emma Hamilton, 27/2/1799, NMM: CRK/20; Nelson to Emma, 23/4/1804, NMM: CRK/19. • **33**. Nelson first applied the phrase to his squadron on 25 September. • **34**. St Vincent to Nepean, 5/6/1798, ADM 1/397; Nelson to his captains, 11 and 18/6/1798, Add. MS 30260; Berry, *Narrative*, p. 9; R. Gamble, *Letters*, p. 10; Sugden, *Nelson*, p. 645. For a defence of Hope and the voyages of the missing cruisers see M.K. Barritt, 'Nelson's Frigates'. • **35**. Nelson to Hamilton, 17/6/1798, Add. MS 34963; Berry, *Narrative*, p. 12; orders, 11 and 18/6/1798, Add. MS 30260. • **36**. St Vincent to Nelson, 21/5/1798, and St Vincent to Emma, 22/5/1798, Tucker, *St Vincent*, 1, pp. 442, 443; 'Report of Vessels Spoke', Add. MS 34907; Thompson to St Vincent, 8/6/1798, ADM 1/397; Ross, *Saumarez*, 1, pp. 200–201; Ball to Ross, 28/9/1798, ADM 7/55. One of the prizes, *Il Carriere de Cadiz*, a 200-ton polacre with 80 men and 8 guns, yielded the information. The other was the five-gun *Acquilon* brig. Berry painted his countrymen in glowing colours, saying that the vessel was released because it contained up to 90 priests driven from Rome by French cruelties (*Narrative*, p. 4), but in fact only 42 priests were on board, and the ship was actually ransomed for $10,000 Spanish dollars. The practice of ransoming prizes to evade the protracted and expensive proceedings in the admiralty courts had been outlawed by the prize acts but was still commonly practised. • **37**. Pitt to Grenville, 1–10/6/1798, HMC, *Dropmore*, 4, p. 229. • **38**. Edmund to Nelson, 2/7/1798, and Fanny to Nelson, 23/4/1798, Add. MS 34988. • **39**. Edmund to Nelson, 4/7/1798, and Fanny to Nelson, 28/5/1798, 11/6/1798, 23/7/1798, Add.

MS 34988. • **40**. Fanny to Nelson, 9, 16 and 23/7/1798, Add. MS 34988; Phyl and Stanley Excell, 'Lord Nelson's Home in Ipswich'. • **41**. William to Nelson, 7/6/1798, Add. MS 34988. • **42**. Nelson to St Vincent, 11/6/1798, NMM: JER/3–4. • **43**. Cooper Willyams, *Voyage*, p. 8. • **44**. Udny to Nelson, 20/4/1798, 28/5/1798, Add. MS 34906. That Nelson had received letters from Udny is shown by Jackson to Nelson, 18/7/1798, Add. MS 34907. • **45**. Hamilton to Grenville, 15 and 29/5/1798, 5/6/1798, and Hamilton to St Vincent, 15/4/1798, FO 70/11; Acton to Hamilton, 3/4/1798, Egerton MS 2640. John A. Davis, *Hamilton Letters*, and Hilda Gamlin, *Nelson's Friendships*, 2, Appendix, reprint some of the diplomat's reports. • **46**. Hamilton to Jervis, April 1798, enclosing letters of Acton, Add. MS 34906; Acton to Hamilton, 22/5/1798, FO 70/11. The Austro-Neapolitan treaty had been signed in Vienna on 20 May, but ratification was delayed on several counts, one of which was Naples's need for a guarantee of support in the event of France attacking her for supplying and succouring the British fleet. For some of this see Morton Eden to Grenville, 7/5/1798, 4 and 14/7/1798, FO 7/51, FO 7/52. On Naples see the studies by Harold Acton and John A. Davis. • **47**. Grenville to Hamilton, 20/4/1798, 5/6/1798, FO 70/11; Grenville to Eden, 28/4/1798, 29/5/1798, FO 7/51; Eden to Grenville, 26/5/1798, 19/6/1798, FO 7/52; Hamilton to Grenville, 5 and 18/6/1798, FO 70/11; Gallo, 12/6/1798 [my italics], ADM 1/397; Queen of Naples to Emma, 11/6/1798, HMC, *Dropmore*, 4, p. 237. Davis makes considerable play of British pressure upon Naples, but while that kingdom was certainly in an unenviable position, it needs to be emphasised that Nelson's force had been solicited by Austria and Naples, and could only be sustained with logistical support. Austria vacillated, but eventually acknowledged that the appearance of the fleet placed her under an obligation, and duly modified the defensive treaty with Naples to meet it. Nor did Naples deny that these events originated in their own appeals. As Acton wrote, 'we have requested by two successive couriers the court of England to come to the assistance of the Two Sicilies with a fleet . . . we have begged of you to help us' (Acton to Hamilton, 22/5/1798, FO 70/11). It is unfair, therefore, to charge Britain with requiring the support that the solicited action entailed. • **48**. Nelson to Hamilton, 22 and 23/7/1798, ADM 1/397 and ADM 1/398; Nelson to St Vincent, 22/6/1798, *D&L*, 7, p. cliii; Hamilton to St Vincent, 16–17/6/1798, ADM 1/397; Hamilton to Nelson, 17/6/1798, Add. MS 34907; Acton to Hamilton, 18/6/1798, 1/8/1798, Egerton MS 2640, and Add. MS 34907; Eden to Grenville, 14/7/1798, FO 7/52; Acton to the governors of Messina, Syracuse and Trapani, 17/6/1798, Add. MS 34941, f. 235. The italics are mine. • **49**. Nelson to Hamilton, 18/6/1798, *HANP*, 2, p. 11. St Vincent was even more dogmatic about the will to defend Naples. He asked Emma to give the queen his 'most inviolable assurance that I will spill every drop of my blood in the defence of her sacred person': St Vincent to Emma, 15/7/1798, Add. MS 31161. • **50**. Eden to Grenville, 14/7/1798, FO 7/52; Acton to Hamilton, 25/6/1798, Egerton MS 2640; Willyams, *Voyage*, pp. 11–18. • **51**. Nelson to Hamilton, 20/7/1798, *HANP*, 2, p. 12; Ball to Nelson, 21/6/1798, and the 'Report of Vessels Spoke', Add. MSS 34907. Nelson's reference was to Acton's letter to Hamilton of 3 April, which included the words, 'Will England see all Italy and even the Two Sicilies in the French hands with indifference?'. • **52**. Hamilton to Nelson, 9, 10 and 16/6/1798, Add. MS 34907. • **53**. Hamilton to Grenville, 3/4/1798, 18 and 20/6/1798, FO 70/11; Acton to Hamilton, 18/6/1798, Egerton MS 2640; Hamilton to Nelson, 26/6/1798, Add. MS 34907. • **54**. Hamilton to Grenville, 8/8/1798, FO 70/11; Hamilton to St Vincent, 12/8/1798, ADM 1/398. • **55**. Hamilton to Acton, 27/8/1798, Egerton MS 2640. This is the original wording in draft, later modified. • **56**. Eden to Grenville, 23/5/1798, 18/8/1798, FO 7/52; Eden to Hamilton, 11/7/1798, Egerton MS 2640; Hamilton to Eden, 28/9/1798, Egerton MS 2638. • **57**. Eden to Grenville, 7, 9, and 29/5/1798, 10/7/1798, 18/8/1798, FO 7/51 and 7/52; Hamilton to Acton,

27/8/1798, Egerton MS 2640. • **58**. Emma to Nelson, 17/6/1798, and undated (f. 3), Add. MS 34989; Nelson to Emma, 17/6/1798, Egerton MS 1614. The queen's letter Emma referred to is almost certainly that filed in Egerton MS 1618, f. 8. Captain Thomas Bowen of the *Transfer* brig had arrived at Naples on 10 June with letters from St Vincent, giving news of Nelson's approach. Years later Emma claimed that it was she who got permission for the British ships to provision and water, through her influence with the queen. Doubtless Emma supported her husband's attempts to secure Nelson's fleet full access to Sicilian ports, but as the queen's letter of 11 June and Gallo's of 12 June made clear, Naples stopped short of breaking her treaty with France. Troubridge got more on 17 June, using Hamilton and Acton. Emma's claim was at least misleading. • **59**. Emma to Nelson, 30 June 1798, NMM: CRK/20. • **60**. Corbett, *Spencer*, 2, pp. 448, 449. • **61**. Conference, 22/6/1798, NMM: CRK/14. • **62**. Despite the Egyptian protestations, Alexandria was being strengthened as a result of intelligence from Leghorn that Bonaparte was bound for Malta and Egypt: Ball to Nelson, 1/7/1798, Add. MS 34912. • **63**. Berry, *Narrative*, p. 7. • **64**. Nelson to St Vincent, 29/6/1798, Add. MS 34963; Ball to Nelson, 1/7/1798, Add. MS 34912. • **65**. Nelson to Hamilton, 20/7/1798, ADM 1/398; Berry, *Narrative*, p. 7; 'Report of Vessels Spoke', Add. MS 34907. • **66**. Hamilton to Nelson, 26/6/1798, Add. MS 34907; Nelson to Hamilton, 22/7/1798, ADM 1/398; *Orion* log, ADM 51/1253. The usual confusion about this episode is dispelled by Torre's report to Acton, 22/7/1798, enclosed in Hamilton to Grenville, 4/8/1798, FO 70/11. • **67**. Peyton to Nelson, 3/7/1798, Add. MS 34907; medical journal of the *Swiftsure*, ADM 101/121/3. • **68**. Medical journals of the *Vanguard*, *Swiftsure* and *Theseus* (respectively filed in ADM 101/124/1, 101/121/3 and 101/123/2) are the only ones that survive for Nelson's squadron. It is difficult to assess the health of the squadron. The admiral's extraordinary claim (Nelson to St Vincent, 22/7/1798, *NLTHW*, p. 412) that he had not a sick man in the force was patently dishonest. Even the minimalist sick reports in the weekly musters of his ships of the line gives a total of forty-two sick at that time, which, if true, would still have suggested a very good level of health in a squadron of some 8600 souls. According to these musters (ADM 36/11860, 12174–75, 12318, 12458, 12508, 12546, 12649, 13733, 13756, 14334, 14345–46, 14416, 145356) the levels of sick were low and did not significantly change in the ships under Nelson during June and July. Comparing the numbers of sick reported at the beginning and end of that service, and ignoring minor fluctuations between, we find almost identical figures. The numbers reported for Nelson's initial command (*Orion*, *Vanguard* and *Alexander*) fell from 8 to 4, and those on the ships of line reinforcing him in June increased from 38 to 39. But while the musters indicate that some ships carried more sick than others, they are poor indicators of the true sick lists in the squadron. The *Vanguard*, *Swiftsure* and *Theseus* musters, for example, record no sick for the period during which those ships were involved in the campaign, but their medical journals tell a different story. In the *Theseus* twenty-four men went on the sick list between 9 June and 26 July. The three surviving medical journals suggest that while the health of the squadron was generally good, the sick lists were higher than these other records indicate, and that surgeons were concerned about the persistence of intermittent fevers, sea ulcers and scurvy. For health in the navy see the studies by Christopher Lloyd and J. L. S. Coulter, James Watt and Brian Vale and Griffith Edwards. • **69**. Nelson to Hamilton, 23/7/1798, ADM 1/398; order book, Add. MSS, 30260; Grant's diary, NMM: GRT/6. • **70**. Acton to Hamilton, 1 and 15/8/1798, FO 70/11, and Egerton MS 2640; Hamilton to Nelson, 1/8/1798, Add. MS 34907; Hamilton to Grenville, 4/8/1798, FO 70/11; Hamilton to St Vincent, 12/8/1798, ADM 1/398; Le Cheze to Gallo, 1798, Add. MS 34942, f. 130; Eden to Grenville, 14, 18 and 21/7/1798, FO 7/52; Eden to Hamilton, 16/7/1798, Egerton MS 2638. • **71**. Medical journal of *Swiftsure*, ADM 101/121/3; Berry, *Narrative*, p. 8;

Gamble, *Letters*, p. 12; Ball to Nelson, 21/6/1798, Add. MS 34907; Nelson to Fanny, 15/6/1798, Monmouth MS 944; Nelson to Hamilton, 23/7/1798, *HANP*, 2, p. 14; Willyams, *Voyage*, pp. 23–8. • **72**. Add. MS 34907, f. 75 following. • **73**. St Vincent issued a version of Howe's signal book of 1790, if we can judge from Berry's personal copy, sold at Bonham's in 2005. • **74**. Berry, *Narrative*, pp. 10–11. Berry repeated this assertion several times, insisting that Nelson had formed his plan two months before the battle of the Nile, and that his orders were 'minutely and precisely executed' (pp. 13, 15, 28). His wholly partisan view of Nelson should be noted. • **75**. Russell F. Weigley, *Age of Battles*. • **76**. Orders, 8 and 18/6/1798, Add. MS 30260; Berry, *Narrative*, pp. 9, 12. • **77**. Grant's diary, NMM: GRT/6; Ross, *Saumarez*, 1, pp. 198, 202, 208, 209, 210. Sir John Ross, who worked from family papers, has several allusions to the discussion of battle tactics. He noted a disagreement between Nelson and Saumarez as to the propriety of doubling an enemy line and attacking both sides simultaneously. Sir James 'had seen the evil consequences of doubling on the enemy, especially in a night action', and maintained that 'it never required two English ships to capture one French'. The last words are quoted as reported speech, and perhaps came from Saumarez's diary (pp. 228–9). Given the one-for-one superiority of the British ships, Saumarez is represented as having suggested that two be concentrated on the enemy three-decker and the rest take an individual opponent. • **78**. Samuel Grant's diary, NMM: GRT/6. • **79**. Ross, *Saumarez*, 1, p. 215. • **80**. T. Sturges-Jackson, *Logs*, 2, pp. 12, 30; *Memoir of . . . Sir George Elliot*, pp. 9–10. There were thirteen sail of the line, but the man at the masthead of the *Zealous* mistakenly included three frigates in his count. About fifteen minutes later *Zealous* signalled a reliable count of 17 sail of the line, 4 frigates and 2 brigs. • **81**. Ross, *Saumarez*, 1, p. 215.

III 'Victory is . . . Not a Name Strong Enough for Such a Scene'

1. Nelson to Howe, 8/1/1799, Add. MS 34963. • **2**. T. Sturges-Jackson, *Logs*, 2, pp. 56–59. Anchoring by the stern, however, did increase the risk of running out too much cable, as George Elliot, a midshipman of the *Goliath*, later explained (Charles Ekins, *Naval Battles*, pp. 259–62). It may have been responsible for the *Goliath* being brought up against *Le Conquérant* rather than *Le Guerrier*, and more seriously for *Bellerophon* finding herself pitted against the huge *L'Orient*. Berry*'s Narrative* was written with the aid, and possibly at the behest, of the editor of the *True Briton*. The pamphlet sold well, with proceeds going to those wounded in the battle (Berry to Nelson, 30/12/1799, Add. MS 34909). See also Oliver Davis's diary, NMM: WAL/21/b; R. Gamble's *Letters* and Cooper Willyams's *Voyage*. Willyams, chaplain of the *Swiftsure*, drew some material from earlier published sources, and was in turn plumbed heavily by John Theophilus Lee, *Memoirs*, pp. 73–115. French sources published in *D&L*, 3, include an account by Blanquet, the original of which is filed in Add. MS 37076. Among other French material see *Copies of Original Letters*, which includes accounts of Brueys and Ganteaume; and especially Clément de La Jonquière, *Expedition d'Egypte*, 2, pp. 389–432, which prints testimony from many of the French ships. William James, *Naval History*, 2, pp. 158–86, pioneered secondary accounts. • **3**. Troubridge to St Vincent, 16/8/1798, Julian S. Corbett, *Spencer*, 2, p. 478; *Memoir of . . . George Elliot*, p. 17; Hood to Viscount Hood, 10/8/1798, Sturges-Jackson, *Logs*, 2, p. 14; Willyams, *Voyage*, p. 44. An early plan of the battle, based on a sketch by a French officer, was published in *NC*, 1 (1799), p. 521. Other early plans include one Captain William Gage of the *Terpsichore* (which missed the battle) sent to Captain Thomas B. Capel, Add. MS 37076, f. 32; the 'Nelson for Ever' chart 'copied from one of Capt. Host[e]', which has a more accurate listing of the French line, Add. MS 37076, f. 33; a plan in the

William Windham papers, Add. MS 37878, f. 26; and a crude pen and ink said to have been done by Nelson himself on 18 February 1803 at 23 Piccadilly, Add. MS 18676. More useful is the plan based on the work of Captain Miller of the *Theseus*, published by Clarke and McArthur in 1809, but the course of the *Audacious* and the order of the rearmost French ships are in error. Four plans of the battle by Captain Ball, sold by Sotheby's in 2005, are in several respects the most authentic representations, but are less sure in depicting the attacks of the first British ships: Sotheby's, *Trafalgar*, pp. 122–3. • **4** So sure was Brueys that his rear would come under attack first that he gave it no instructions to support the van and centre, whereas he provided for the van and centre to assist the rear. See Villeneuve to Blanquet, 12/11/1800, Sturges-Jackson, *Logs*, 2, p. 77. • **5**. The evidence about the armaments of the fleets is contradictory. Battesti arms *L'Aquilon* with 74 long guns and 4 carronades, but a British seaman in the battle recorded her total armament as 68 cannons, 14 carronades and 6 swivels: Scott to his father, 1798, *Gentleman's Magazine*, 68 (1798), pt. ii, p. 1139. Some of the French guns were not mounted, and there are particular difficulties in assessing the numbers of carronades deployed. Battesti's figure of 116 carronades for Nelson's fleet is merely an educated guess. The *Vanguard* had ten 24-pound carronades, while the *Goliath* had 24-pounders and some large 68-pound Spanish guns on her poop, captured the year before. Battesti, *Bataille d'Aboukir*, pp. 16–18, 217–18, and Lavery, *Nelson and the Nile*, pp. 173–5, 193, make spirited attacks upon the problem. For gun drills on the *Vanguard* and *Goliath* see ADM 52/3516 and ADM 51/1261. See also *NC*, 4 (1800), pp. 143–8, 222–26, for sample contemporary comment. • **6**. Eric Tushingham, *HMS Vanguard*, p. 15; *D&L*, 3, p. 67. • **7**. Jaubert to his brother, 8/7/1798, and Brueys to Bruix, 12/7/1798, *Copies of Original Letters*, 1, pp. 18, 40; Villeneuve to Bruix, 6/9/1798, MS, A. M. Broadley, 'Nelsoniana', BL, 4, f.p. 82. • **8**. Berry, *Narrative*, p. 14. Hardy's *Mutine* did, however, snap up 'a country boat' from Alexandria. • **9**. William Henry Webley, 21/5/1810, Sturges-Jackson, *Logs*, 2, p. 26; *Vanguard* log, ADM 52/3516. • **10**. Berry, *Narrative*, pp. 15–16. • **11**. Foley's manoeuvre has consumed much ink. The motive is the common but questionable belief that the initiative was the decisive act of the battle. Thus, for example, Laura Foreman and Ellen Blue Phillips, *Napoleon's Lost Fleet*, p. 123, claim that it conferred 'an extraordinary advantage' upon the attackers. Nelson's most voluble admirers have resented suggestions that such a key move did not originate with the admiral, and found support in Berry, who not only asserted that his chief's orders were 'minutely and precisely executed' but also that Nelson himself observed Foley's opportunity with the remark that 'where there was room for an enemy's ship to swing, there was room for one of our own to anchor' (Berry, *Narrative*, pp. 13, 15). Foley's manoeuvre does not seem to have been part of a generally pre-concerted plan, however. He claimed it as his independent idea (John Marshall, *Royal Naval Biography*, 1, pp. 364–5; Browne to Nicolas, 27/4/1845, *D&L*, 3, p. 474), and Hood of the *Zealous* admitted his astonishment at Foley's manoeuvre, while Miller of the *Theseus*, the fifth British attacker, doubted its utility. Of course, Nelson may have discussed the possibility with Foley in the preceding weeks. Foley dined with Nelson on 7 July, and possibly again on 31 July, and there must have been other opportunities for the two to discuss tactics. There is also evidence that Nelson spoke of passing along both sides of the French line to Saumarez (Ross, *Saumarez*, 1, pp. 227–9), though a claim that Foley, Hood and Troubridge had thrashed the idea out the day before the battle (Marshall, *Royal Naval Biography*, 1, pp. 364–5 n.) must be doubted in the light of Hood's contemporary remark. There were precedents for Foley's attack, but even if the captain was not an historian he had been flag captain in Hood's fleet when an identical assault upon the French fleet in Golfe Jouan near Nice was considered in June 1794 (John Sugden, *Nelson*, p. 499). Furthermore, an experienced commander, Foley would have known that there were two ways of fulfilling Nelson's order of 1 August to concentrate force on the French van and centre. The British could either turn the enemy's left flank, as he did, and engage the enemy from both sides, or group a superior number of British ships on their starboard side only. Having said all this, it is reasonable to ask whether Foley's bold move had any material effect on the outcome of the battle. Even successfully performed, the manoeuvre was not without risk, since British vessels subjecting the French to a crossfire also exposed themselves to the danger of 'friendly fire' from their consorts on the other side of the French line. Was it therefore necessary? Given the extended spaces between the French ships, there was ample room to build a concentration upon the enemy's line using only its starboard side, placing British ships on the bow and quarter of each Frenchman. In some places British ships could even have stationed themselves between two enemy vessels, raking sterns and bows simultaneously. This attack would have reduced the perils of the shoals and 'friendly fire'. Saumarez seems to have been willing to dispense with the principle of concentration entirely, except in dealing with the bigger French vessels, and to have relied upon Britain's ship-for-ship combat superiority. He appears to have favoured attacking from the French rear, each British ship taking an opposite number as far as possible, trapping it against the lee shore. Providing the enemy van did not attempt flight, this tactic would have engaged more of the French capital ships, and might have yielded a more complete result. Certain phrases in Hood to Lord Hood, 10/8/1798, Sturges-Jackson, *Logs*, 2, p. 14, suggest that he would also have preferred to have engaged the enemy entirely from one side. Foley's initiative surprised the French, but it cannot be regarded as decisive. Given the enemy's vulnerable and inflexible position and the efficiency of the British there were viable alternatives. • **12**. John Nicol, *Life*, pp. 174–75; muster of the *Goliath*, ADM 36/14817; Grant diary, NMM: GRT/6; petition of Christian White, c. 1801, Wellcome MS 3676. The gunner of the *Goliath*, mentioned by Nichol, was George Neal, but I found no reference to his wife in the muster. One wonders if the children of the *Goliath* survived. In the year 2000 excavations on Aboukir or Bequier Island (now Nelson's Island) began to uncover graves from the period of British occupation between 1798 and 1801. The remains of three infants were found. One, believed to date from 1798 and wrapped in a shroud once held by a small bronze pin, may have been one of the children born in the *Goliath*. Adjacent to the child was another coffin marked 'G' which contained the remains of a woman, who appeared to have been buried in a dress with her face covered by a handkerchief. Perhaps the 'G' signified a personal name, or perhaps *Goliath*; if the latter, we must conclude she was probably Mrs Holcombe, who was buried on the island according to Nicol. See three reports by Nick Slope, 'Developments on Nelson's Island', 'Photographs from the Excavations' and 'Nelson's Island Update'. • **13**. Ekins, *Naval Battles*, p. 260. *Le Peuple Souverain* was the next oldest ship of the line, launched in 1757, but *Le Spartiate* and *Franklin* were both new ships, finished only a year earlier. • **14**. Grant's diary, NMM: GRT/6; Ross, *Saumarez*, 1, p. 217; Sturges-Jackson, *Logs*, 2, pp. 10, 32, 37; John Tancock's account, Add. MS 37076, f. 60; Miller in *D&L*, 7, p. clv; Ekins, *Naval Battles*, p. 262; report from *La Serieuse*, La Jonquiere, *Expedition d'Egypte*, 2, p. 417; Battesti, *Bataille d'Aboukir*, p. 99. • **15**. Gould to Nelson, 1/8/1798, Add. MS 34907; Gould to his uncle, 2/12/1798, Sturges-Jackson, *Logs*, 2, p. 29; Berry, *Narrative*, p. 17; Miller in *D&L*, 7, p. clvi. Some accounts have the *Audacious* breaking through the enemy line between the *Guerrier* and *Conquérant*, but her log states that she fired on the former with her *larboard* guns, reasonably establishing that she followed *Goliath*'s path: Sturges-Jackson, *Logs*, 2, p. 28. • **16**. Nicol, *Life*, p. 176. • **17**. Berry, *Narrative*, p. 15. • **18**. Miller in *D&L*, 7, pp. clv, clvi; Emeriau's report, 2/8/1798, La Jonquiere, *Expedition d' Egypte*, 2, p. 409; John Hill's account, Bonham's auction lot, 2005. • **19**. Lady

Berry, *D&L*, 3, p. 55; Nelson to St Vincent, 3/8/1798, Add. MS 34263; medical journal of the *Vanguard*, ADM 101/124/1. • **20**. *Vanguard* medical journal, ADM 101/124/1; *Vanguard* muster, ADM 36/15356; Graham Dean and Keith Evans, *Nelson's Heroes*, pp. 23–5. • **21**. E. H. Fairbrother, 'Nelsoniana', pp. 321–4; Berry to Miller, 2/8/1798, Tushingham, *HMS Vanguard*, p. 43. The course of the scar destroys the story of the flap of skin falling across Nelson's good eye and temporarily blinding him, as given by early biographers. About the severity of the wound opinions have differed. T. C. Barras, 'Nelson's Head Injury', p. 217, contends that it was 'a simple minor injury'. The skin of the forehead splits easily under impact, and can bleed copiously without indicating severe head damage. It is true that most blows to the head do not cause brain injuries, and that Nelson was not knocked unconscious, but he referred to headaches and confusion in ensuing weeks, which indicate post-traumatic syndrome. • **22**. Hill's account, Bonham's lot, 2005; *NC*, 1 (1799), p. 287, and 3 (1800), pp. 182–3. Although Hill's statement may have been based on a private log, the ship's logs (ADM 51/1271 and 52/3229) do not mention the incident. • **23**. Nelson to Berry, 10/12/1798, Add. MS 34908; Berry, *Narrative*, p. 17; Gamble, *Letters*, p. 17; *Vanguard* log, ADM 52/3516; report from *L'Aquilon*, 2/8/1798, La Jonquière, *Expedition d'Egypte*, 2, p. 409. • **24**. Troubridge to St Vincent, 16/8/1798, Corbett, *Spencer*, 2, p. 478; Sturges-Jackson, *Logs*, 2, pp. 72–3. • **25**. Gamble, *Letters*, p. 18. The failure of the British *Culloden* and the French *Généreux, Guillaume Tell, Diane* and *Justice* to participate reduced the French superiority in the nominal number of guns from 170 to 10. • **26**. Gamble, *Letters*, p. 18; Blanquet, *D&L*, 3, p. 69; Berry, *Narrative*, p. 16; Willyams, *Voyage*, p. 51 n. • **27**. Report from *L'Orient*, Battesti, *Bataille d'Aboukir*, pp. 107–8; Gamble, *Letters*, p. 24. • **28**. Blanquet, *D&L*, 3, pp. 68–9; Ganteaume to Bruix, 23/8/1798, and his abstract, 5/8/1798, *Copies of Original Letters*, 1, pp. 219, 230; Poussielque's account, based on the statements of French officers who escaped to Alexandria in a boat, Add. MS 34907, f. 186 following. The wounds of Brueys and Dupetit-Thouars are described differently in these accounts. Ganteaume, for example, states that Brueys was hit in the body and hand, but then descended from the poop to be slain on his quarterdeck. • **29**. Blanquet and Miller link the fire to the poop, and Gamble, *Letters*, p. 19, who was on the adjacent *Swiftsure*, mentions the main chains. An incendiary may have been involved. The French as well as Ball made use of them. Hallowell later discovered that unorthodox weapons carried by *Le Spartiate* included a smoke ball that emitted a black pitch-like substance, and a ball that exploded on ignition. The French also sent a fire raft, a more common recourse, towards the British ships during the battle. A party from the *Orion* was organised to push it away, but it drifted clear of the ship's larboard bow by about twenty-five yards: Sturges-Jackson, *Logs*, 2, p. 32; Willyams, *Voyage*, pp. 144–5; Thomas J. Pettigrew, *Memoirs*, 1, pp. 130–32; and Lee, *Memoirs*, pp. 90–91, 134–5. • **30**. Scott to his father, 1798, *Gentleman's Magazine*, 68 (1798), pt. ii, p. 1139; Berry, *Narrative*, p. 18; Lady Berry, *D&L*, 3, p. 56; Blanquet, *D&L*, 3, pp. 69–70. • **31**. Gamble, *Letters*, p. 19; Blanquet, *D&L*, 3, p. 69; Ross, *Saumarez*, 1, p. 220. • **32**. John Jupp to his parents, 26/11/1798, in John B. Hattendorf, *Naval Documents*, 421; Miller, *D&L*, 7, p. clvi; Grant's diary, NMM: GRT/6; Kleber's journal, La Jonquière, *Expedition d'Egypte*, 2, pp. 420–21. Underwater archaeological work in the bay has recently improved our knowledge of the explosion. • **33**. *D&L*, 3, p. 70; Berry, *Narrative*, p. 18; Willyams, *Voyage*, p. 55; Gamble, *Letters*, pp. 19–20; *Alexander* log, ADM 51/1260; Sturges-Jackson, *Logs*, 2, p. 67; Barbara E. Rooke, *Friend*, 2, p. 294. As Sturges-Jackson observed, the times given by the different British logs vary. The destruction of *L'Orient* was put at ten o'clock in the *Vanguard*, *Alexander*, *Bellerophon* and *Goliath*, but others timed it between 9.37 (*Swiftsure*) and 11.30 (*Orion*). • **34**. Gamble, *Letters*, pp. 25–26; Ross, *Saumarez*, 1, p. 221; Sturges-Jackson, *Logs*, 2, p. 68; Jupp to his parents, 26/11/1798, Hattendorf, *Naval Documents*, p. 421. However, Miller, *D&L*, 7, p.

clvi, speaks of a disconnected firing during the pause. • **35**. Berry, *Narrative*, pp. 18–19; Sturges-Jackson, *Logs*, 2, p. 54; *D&L*, 3, pp. 69–70. • **36**. Foley to Nelson, 2/8/1798, Add. MS 34907; Ball's 'Second Position' plan of the battle, Sotheby's lot, 2005. • **37**. Villeneuve to Blanquet, 12/11/1800, in Sturges-Jackson, *Logs*, 2, p. 77; Lejoille to the Minister of Marine, 8/9/1798, Edward P. Brenton, *Naval History*, 1, p. 412 • **38**. Gamble, *Letters*, p. 21. The surrender of the frigate is variously timed, but many logs put it before the arrival of *Goliath*. • **39**. Report from *Le Timoleon*, La Jonquière, *Expedition d'Egypte*,2, p. 417. • **40**. Hood to Viscount Hood, 10/8/1798, Sturges-Jackson, *Logs*, 2, p. 14 • **41**. Casualty returns of the British ships, Add. MS 34907; Nelson to Fanny, 11/8/1798, *NLTHW*, p. 399; Troubridge, 26/10/1798, Add. MS 34908; Ganteaume to Bruix, 23/8/1798, *Copies of Original Letters*, 1, p. 219; Martyn Downer, *Nelson's Purse*, pp. 133–34. Saumarez's estimate, made to claim 'head money', contrasts sharply with the 218 fatalities suffered throughout the British squadron. For another recent attempt to compute the French casualties, see Battesti, *Bataille d'Aboukir*, 97, pp. 117–18. • **42**. Nelson to the fleet, 2/8/1798, Ross, *Saumarez*, 1, p. 224; Berry, *Narrative*, pp. 24–25; Nelson to his father, 25/9/1798, Add. MS 34988. • **43**. Berry to Miller, 3/8/1798, *D&L*, 3, p. 66; Miller, *D&L*, 7, pp. clviii, clix. • **44**. Nelson order book, Add. MS 30260; negotiations between Troubridge and the commandant at Aboukir, 16/8/1798, Add. MS 34907, f. 171; Berry, *Narrative*, pp. 22–3, 26; Ross, *Saumarez*, 1, p. 225; Troubridge to St Vincent, 16/8/1798, Corbett, *Spencer*, 2, p. 478. • **45**. Nelson to Spencer, 19/9/1798, Add. MS 34963; Saumarez to his wife, 2/8/1798, Ross, *Saumarez*, 1, p. 232. Spencer agreed to serve Faddy, and sums from the Admiralty and the Lloyd's Committee for assisting the families of casualties raised the net annual income of Martha Faddy and her children to £90. However, the kindness somewhat backfired. Mrs Faddy began 'plaguing' the Lloyd's Committee to increase her entitlement, claiming that her son was wounded in the battle. 'She is a very troublesome woman,' said Berry, 'and ought to be ashamed of herself.' Despite all, young Faddy stuck to the sea, served under Nelson in the *Victory* and died on active service in 1811: Add. MS 34907, f. 130; Faddy to Nelson, 25/10/1798, 19/6/1799, 30/8/1799, Add. MS 34908, 34912–13; Berry to Nelson, 1/3/1802, NMM: CRK/2. • **46**. *Vanguard* log, ADM 51/1288; Sturges-Jackson, *Logs*, 2, p. 67; Troubridge to St Vincent, 16/8/1798, Corbett, *Spencer*, 2, p. 478; Nelson to Spencer, 9/8/1798, Add. MS 34963. • **47**. Nelson to St Vincent, 14/8/1798, 1/9/1798, *D&L*, 7, p. clxii; Nelson to Wyndham, 21/8/1798, Add. MS 34963. • **48**. Nelson to St Vincent, 3/8/1798, Add. MS 34963; Nelson to Berry, 20/12/1798, Add. MS 34908; St Vincent to Nepean, 6 and 25/8/1798, ADM 1/398. • **49**. Nelson to Minto, 29/8/1798, *D&L*, 3, p. 100. • **50**. Saumarez to Nelson, 3/8/1798, Add. MS 34907; Nelson to captains, 3/8/1798 [my italics], Sotheby's lot, 2005; Ross, *Saumarez*, 1, pp. 227–8, 231, which gives, but does not source the conversations of 2 and 3 August. They probably come from retrospective accounts of Saumarez, preserved in his family papers. But see James Davey, 'Nelson's Second,' for a different view of the relationship between Nelson and Saumarez. The commemorative sword, commissioned from Rundell and Bridge of Ludgate Hill, London, was gold, with its hilt tooled to represent a Nile crocodile and a guard engraved with the names of the 'band of brothers'. The item was stolen from Greenwich in 1900, but similar pieces made for other members of the Egyptian Club have recently come to auction. • **51**. Nelson to St Vincent, 19/10/1798, Jedediah S. Tucker, *St Vincent*, 1, p. 455. Nelson's cover note to St Vincent was lost in the capture of the *Leander*. • **52**. Thompson's orders, 2/8/1798, Add. MS 46119; Thompson to Nelson, 13/10/1798, Add. MS 34907. • **53**. Nelson to Nepean, 7/8/1798, Add. MS 34963; Nelson to Emma, 11/8/1798, Pettigrew, *Memoirs*, 1, p. 140; Capel to Nelson, 4/9/1798, Add. MS 34907. According to Francis Seymour, Hardy's nephew by marriage, who based an account on Hardy's recollections in 1838, the captain 'found Lord Nelson's ship in extremely bad order, for . . . he was no seaman'. The men were unable to 'take in a reef in the main topsail', and Nelson 'defied' Hardy 'to get it done'. Hardy's success in putting the ship to rights cemented their relationship: John Gore, *Nelson's Hardy*, pp. 16–17. Seymour exaggerated, but Nelson certainly had no reputation among his peers as a seaman. Harriet Hoste and Tom Pocock have produced handy biographies of Hoste, but a more scholarly account is needed. • **54**. For India and Duval's mission see Nelson to the governor of Bombay, 9/8/1798, Add. MS 37878; Duval to Nelson, 17/8/1798, Add. MS 34907; James, *Naval History*, 2, p. 388; *D&L*, 3, pp. 97, 98, 99; and Ross, *Saumarez*,1, p. 247. • **55**. Nelson to Spencer, 7/9/1798, and Nelson to Nepean, 18/8/1798, ADM 1/398; Cathcart to his parents, 20/8/1798, John Knox Laughton, *Naval Miscellany*, 1, p. 272. Downer, *Nelson's Purse*, chs. 5 and 6, is a succinct account of Davison, based upon records that were auctioned and dispersed in 2005. Though the adjutant general of *L'Orient* declared that the flagship carried £600,000 in ingots of gold and diamonds (Nelson to Wyndham, 21/8/1798, Add. MS 34963) and reports of the ship's wealth circulated in the British squadron the story had little foundation: Brian Tarpey, 'Malta Treasure'. • **56**. Tushingham, *HMS Vanguard*, p. 137; Perkins Magra to Portland, 31/7/1798, FO 77/4. St Vincent's sudden return to his former pessimism about Josiah was probably fed by John Obra, one of the admiral's lower-deck followers, who had been promoted to the position of carpenter in the *Dolphin* on 6 March 1797. Obra did not enjoy serving under Nisbet, and remarkably resigned his warrant to return to St Vincent's flagship, *Ville de Paris*, on 23 December. Probably Obra explained his resignation by referring to Nisbet's conduct in the *Dolphin*. See Obra to Nisbet, 22/12/1797, Hilda Gamlin, *Nelson's Friendships*, 1, p. 15; *Dolphin* muster, ADM 36/12340. It should be noted that St Vincent's contempt for privileged protégés did not extend to his own favourites, although he remained genuinely alert to the importance of merit. • **57**. Troubridge to Nelson, 1798, Add. MS 34907, f. 218; Nelson to Fanny, 28/2/1794, 9/1/1800, Monmouth MSS E809, E972; John Sugden, 'Fine Colt', pp. 36 7. • **58**. St Vincent to Nelson, 27/9/1798, Tucker, *St Vincent*, 1, p. 452; Saumarez's orders of 12 August and 1 September were sold at Sotheby's in 2005. Ross, *Saumarez*, reprints his journal covering the period. • **59**. Albert Nute, translator, 'Charles Norry's Narrative'. • **60**. Grenville to Spencer, 18/9/1798, Corbett, *Spencer*, 2, p. 463. • **61**. Nelson to Hamilton, 8/8/1798, 7/9/1798, *Letters*, 2, p. 240, and FO 70/11; Hamilton to Acton, 25/8/1798, Add. MS 34907; Acton to Hamilton, 24 and 28/9/1798, Egerton MS 2640; Hamilton to St Vincent, 12/8/1798, ADM 1/398. • **62**. Le Roy to Thevenard, 4/9/1798, and Avrieury to Descorches, 29/8/1798, *Copies of Original Letters*, 2, pp. 180, 202; Nelson to St Vincent, 9/8/1798, ADM 1/398; the logs of the *Zealous*, *Swiftsure* and *Goliath* (ADM 51/1283, 1247 and 1261) ; Ball to Vaubois, 9/11/1798, ADM 7/55; Richard D. Barnett, 'Barnett', p. 194; Willyams, *Voyage*, pp. 75–7; Hood to Nelson, 19/9/1798, FO 70/11, and several papers in Add. MS 34907, especially account by Hallowell, 10/8/1798, Hope to Hood, 22/8/1798, Foley to Hood, 25/8/1798, Hood to Nelson, September 1798, and Hood to Nelson, 26/8/1798. The *Swiftsure* was particularly active in this work, taking, in addition to the above, four supply vessels between 19 August and 17 September. • **63**. Nelson to the tsar, 1798, NMM: CRK/14/31; Grenville to Spencer, 18/9/1798, Corbett, *Spencer*, 2, p. 463; Stanford J. Shaw, *Between Old and New*, chs 16–17. • **64**. Nelson to Jackson, 27/8/1798, Add. MS 34963; Add. MS 34942, ff. 137, 162, 172; Smith to Nelson, 22 and 29/8/1798, Add. MS 34942; Grenville to Smith, 23/10/1798, Add. MS 34933; Warren R. Dawson, *Nelson Collection*, pp. 496–7; Shaw, *Between Old and New*, p. 158. John Spencer Smith, Britain's new minister plenipotentiary in Constantinople, gained George III's permission for Nelson to accept and wear the chelengk (Smith to the Porte, 28/11/1798, Add. MS 34908). This famous piece was stolen from the National Maritime Museum at Greenwich in 1951, and broken up for sale on the jewellery market. • **65**. Whitworth to Grenville, 19/10/1798, FO 65/41; Hamilton to Grenville, 7/3/1799, FO 70/12; Ushakov to Nelson, September 1798, Add. MS 34907. For Russian policy, see Norman E. Saul, *Russia*, and Hugh Ragsdale, *Paul I*. • **66**. Nelson to Minto, 29/8/1798, *D&L*, 3, p. 110; Nelson to Hamilton, 8/8/1798, and Nelson to Wyndham, 21/8/1798, Add. MS 34963; Nelson to St Vincent, 1/9/1798, NMM: JER/3–4. • **67**. The Portuguese detachment consisted of the *Principe Real*, Niza's flagship, a first-rate, two seventy-fours, *Rheine de Portugal*, Captain Thomas Stone, and *Alfonso d'Albuquerque*, Donald Campbell, and a sixty-four, *St Sebastian*, Sampson Mitchell. • **68**. Jackson to Grenville, 19/10/1798, FO 65/41. • **69**. Fanny to Nelson, 11/9/1798, 1/10/1798, Add. MS 34988; Edmund to Nelson, undated, Add. MS 34988, f. 290; Lavinia to the Dowager Countess Spencer, 5 and 28/7/1798, Add. MS 75599. • **70**. *Ipswich Journal*, 6/10/1798; Mary Eyre Matcham, *Nelsons*, p. 159. • **71**. Nelson to Saumarez, 24/3/1798, Huntington, HM 23680; Ross, *Saumarez*, 1, pp. 245–47; Saumarez's letters to Nelson in Add. MS 34907. • **72**. Barnett, 'Barnett', p. 194; Nisbet to Nepean, 14/7/1803, ADM 1/2229. Nisbet commanded *La Bonne Citoyenne* from 13 September 1798 to 2 April 1799. • **73**. Nelson to Hamilton, 13/9/1798, FO 70/11; Hood to Nelson, 26/8/1798 (two letters), Add. MS 34907; Willyams, *Voyage*, p. 92. • **74**. Add. MS 34907, f. 408; Hamilton to Nelson, 10/9/1798, Add. MS 34907; Acton to Hamilton, 11 and 12/9/1798, Egerton MS 2640; Nelson to Hamilton, 13/9/1798, FO 70/11; Saumarez to Nelson, 26/9/1798, Add. MS 34907; Saumarez to St Vincent, 10/10/1798, with enclosures, ADM 1/398; Willyams, *Voyage*, p. 92. Wiliam Hardman, *Malta*, is an indispensable documentary history of the campaign, but see also Desmond Gregory, *Malta*. • **75**. Nelson to Spencer, 16/9/1798, Add. MS 34963. • **76**. This mainly follows the logs of *Vanguard* and *Thalia*, ADM 51/1288 and 4507. • **77**. Nelson to St Vincent, 1 and 20/9/1798, NMM: JER/3–4, and *D&L*, 3, p. 128; Nelson to his captains, 7/9/1798, Add. MS 34963; medical journals of the *Swiftsure* and *Vanguard*, ADM 101/121/3 and 101/123/2; musters of *Culloden*, *Alexander* and *Vanguard*, ADM 36/12175, 14354 and 15356. • **78**. Hamilton to Grenville, 25/9/1798, Add. MS 37077.

IV 'Nostro Liberatore!'

1. Johann Wolfgang von Goethe, *Italian Journey*, p. 211; James Lowry, *Fiddlers and Whores*, p. 124; Troubridge to Nelson, 19/8/1799, Add. MS 34913. • **2**. Capel to Nelson, 4/9/1798, Add. MS 34907; Hoste to his mother, September 1798, Harriet Hoste, *Hoste*, 1, p. 104. • **3**. Hamilton to Nelson, 8 and 10/9/1798, Add. MS 34907; queen to Emma, 2/9/1798, Thomas J. Pettigrew, *Memoirs*, 1, p. 140; Emma to Nelson, 8/9/1798, Add. MS 34989; *NC*, 3 (1800), p. 292. Hamilton's importance to diplomacy, arts and sciences demands a versatility rare in scholars, but the studies by Brian Fothergill, David Constantine and I. Jenkins and K. Sloan complement each other. Published primary sources are *HANP*, Vittorio Accardi's *Hamilton Papers* and John A. Davis's *Hamilton Letters*. • **4**. Nelson to Fanny, 25/9/1798, Monmouth MS E947; Hamilton to Grenville, 25/9/1798, FO 70/11; Cornelia Knight, *Autobiography*, 1, pp. 115–18, and 2, pp. 258–9; James Harrison, *Life*, 1, pp. 320–21; Vanguard logs, ADM 51/1288 and ADM 52/3516. With regard to the differences between Nelson and Caracciolo, the above revises John Sugden, *Nelson*, p. 853, n. 70. Though the disagreement concerned Admiral William Hotham's fleet action with the French in March 1795, its exact nature is unclear. Knight thought that Caracciolo resented Nelson for overtaking him in going into action on that occasion, but Hotham's nephew (who was no more present than Knight, and who also wrote long afterwards) stated that it was Nelson who took umbrage, complaining that the Italian had got in his way. There is no good reason to suppose that this encounter affected the future relationship of the two men, which foundered upon very different rocks. • **5**. *D&L*, 3, pp. 474–5; Nelson to Spencer, 25/9/1798, Add. MS 34963; Nelson to Fanny, 25/9/1798, Monmouth MS E147; Hamilton to Grenville, 25/9/1798, FO 70/11. A typical panegyric was D. Giuseppe Gargamo, *Il Felice Arrivo Nella Citta Di Napoli del Gran Ammiraglio di S. M. Brittannica Orazio Nelson . . . Cantata, Avoce sola con cori Musica* (Naples, 1798). • **6**. Nelson to Spencer, 29/9/1798, Add. MS 34963, borrowing from a letter Emma had written him; Nelson to Hamilton, 27/10/1798, WLC; Nelson to Fanny, 28/9, 1/10/1798, Monmouth MSS E948, 949; order book, 25/9/1798, 3/10/1798, Add. MS 30260; Ball to Saumarez, 11/10/1798, Ross, *Saumarez*, 1, p. 275; Hamilton to Grenville, 9/10/1798, FO 70/11; Hamilton to Acton, 24 and 25/9/1798, NMM: HML/21; Hamilton to Nelson, 22/11/1798, Add. MS 34908; Acton to Hamilton, 24, 25, 26 and 28/9/1798, Egerton MS 2640; Knight, *Autobiography*, 1, pp. 116–17. Miss Knight's addition to the national anthem should not be confused with her *The Battle of the Nile . . . A Pindarick Ode*, dedicated to Hamilton on 16 September and also sent to the printers. For a copy see FO 70/11. The story about Josiah (Harrison, *Life*, 1, pp. 328–9) probably came from Emma, the author's chief informant. By then she hated Josiah, but the story is consistent with other reports of his conduct at this time. • **7**. Nelson to Edmund, 25/9/1798 [italics mine], Add. MS 34988; Nelson to St Vincent, 27/9/1798, *D&L*, 3, p. 133; Nelson to Hamilton, 7/9/1798, FO 70/11. • **8**. Hamilton to Eden, 6/11/1798, Add. MS 37077; Nelson to Fanny, 25/9/1798, Monmouth MS E947; Emma to Fanny, 2/12/1798, Add. MS 34989. • **9**. Nelson to Fanny, 28/9/1798, 1/10/1798, 11/12/1798, Monmouth MSS E948, 949, 954. That Fanny resented Emma's supposed mastery of Josiah seems evident by her later endorsement on the letter of 11 December, asserting that her son had never liked the Hamiltons, who had tried to make him dance against his inclinations. • **10**. Lori Ann Touchette, 'Pantomime Mistress', pp. 123, 126. Though rich in biographers, Emma Hamilton has no satisfactory biography, conjuring for the most part destructive prejudices for or against. The anonymously published *Memoirs* (1815) buried little known truths in a vindictive presentation. Among nineteenth-century accounts John Cordy Jeaffreson got the better of Hilda Gamlin, although both works retain interest. Walter Sichel's *Lady Hamilton* superseded previous work, but is deeply flawed by the author's extreme partiality for his subject. Few would justify his portrait of Emma the 'stateswoman'. Admirers and detractors produced biographies in roughly equal measure thereafter, but nothing approaching Sichel's industry or scholarship has appeared. Among recent biographies, that by Kate Williams contains important revisions, but the safest account was written by Flora Fraser, while Julia Peakman offers a level-headed introduction. Studies by Patricia Jaffe, K. G. Holmstrom and Touchette are essential to an understanding of Emma's art, while Jack Russell and Winifred Gérin offer hard-nosed perspectives based on extensive research. • **11**. Touchette, 'Pantomime Mistress', pp. 129, 141, 143. • **12**. Countess Elgin to her mother, 4/10/1799, Nisbet Hamilton Grant, *Letters*, p. 21; Pryse Lockhart Gordon, *Memoirs*, 2, pp. 384–85. • **13**. Mackinnon to Grenville, 30/11/1798, FO 70/11. • **14**. Lavinia to Dowager Countess Spencer, 8 and 20/10/1798, Add. MS 75599; Lavinia to Nelson, 1/10/1798, Add. MS 34907; Lady Parker to Nelson, 29/10/1798, Add. MS 34908. • **15**. *Ipswich Journal*, 20/10/1798. Hughes had called at Roundwood to pay his respects early in October, and was invited to join Fanny, Edmund, William Nelson and Berry's sister at dinner, a pleasing sequel to the sometimes strained relationships Hughes and Nelson had endured in the West Indies: Hughes to Nelson, 9/10/1798, Add. MS 34907. • **16**. Fanny to Hood, 18/10/1798, *NLTHW*, 458; Matthew Sheldon, 'Nelson's Appearance'; Marianne Czisnik, 'Nelson and the Nile'; John May, 'Nelson Commemorated'; Lily McCarthy, *Nelson Remembered*; *The Times*, 19/1/1999. Eleven political cartoons featured the admiral immediately after the Nile, the most famous James Gillray's depiction of the hero, a hook for a right hand, wading into the river and clubbing and subduing its crocodiles, held to represent the French ships. • **17**. Fanny to Nelson, 1/10/1798, 7/6/1799, Add. MS 34988; Fanny to Hood, 18/10/1798, *NLTHW*, p.458; Nelson to Fanny, 25/9/1798, Monmouth MS E947; Kate to Nelson, 6/10/1798, Add. MS 34988; *The Times*, 23/11/1798; Berry to Nelson, 26/11/1798, Add. MS 34908. William Suckling, a major influence upon the young Nelson, was then sixty-eight. Sensing the end, he visited his birthplace at Barsham in Suffolk, calling at Roundwood on both the outward and return journeys. Back home he declined rapidly, and Maurice Nelson took his leave in October. 'I went to Kentish Town this morning and saw him very feeble indeed, and I think in exactly the same way as the late Comptroller [Captain Maurice Suckling, William's brother] was. He seems perfectly easy and sleeps a great deal (by far too much) . . . He has certainly a confirmed dropsy' (Maurice to Fanny, 19/10/1798, *NLTHW*, p. 454). There may have been an hereditary problem, because none of the Sucklings lived long. Catherine (Nelson's mother) died at forty-two, her brother Maurice at fifty-two, and William at sixty-eight. William died on 15 December 1798, survived by his second wife, three sons and a daughter. The eldest boy, William, was an army colonel in the 3rd Dragoon Guards, and the daughter married a captain in the same regiment. Suckling's widow, Mary, lost her father two weeks later. She sold her husband's house in Kentish Town in the spring of 1799 at a price inflated by its connections with Nelson, but there was also property in Norfolk and Suffolk. Nelson and a Mr Hume of the Board of Customs were joint executors of the will, for which service the admiral was bequeathed £100: Maurice to Nelson, 21/12/1798, Add. MS 34988; Mary Suckling to Nelson, 14/11/1799, Add. MS 34914. • **18**. Nelson to Fanny, 16/9/1798, Monmouth MS E947. • **19**. Hood to Nelson, 15 and 29/10/1798, Add. MSS 34907 and 34908; Goodall to Nelson, 3/10/1798, Add. MS 34907; Maurice Nelson to Fanny, 5/10/1798, and to Nelson, 25/11/1798, Add. MS 34988; Davison to Nelson, 6/4/1799, 7/5/1799, Add. MSS 34910 and 34911; Lord Rosebery, *Windham Papers*, 2, p. 78; Spencer to Nelson, 7/10/1798, Add. MS 34907. • **20**. Denis Driscoll, 'Lord Nelson'. Nelson's new title required augmentations to the coat of arms granted in 1797. The top of the shield appropriated a design incorporating a palm tree, a disabled ship and the castle at Aboukir; a new crest included the chelengk; a baronial coronet was displayed above the arms; and there was a fresh motto, '*Palmam Qui Meruit Ferat*', said to have been suggested by Lord Grenville. See Ron C. Fiske, 'Nelson's Arms', p. 550, and David White, 'Heralds', p. 63. • **21**. Galwey to Nelson, 25/4/1799, Add. MS 34910; Davison to Marsh and Creed, 13/11/1799, Hilda Gamlin, *Nelson's Friendships*, 1, p. 159; Sotheby's, *Davison*, pp. 62–9, and *Trafalgar*, pp. 126–33; John Braun, 'Lord Nelson'; Edmund to Susannah Bolton, 1799, NMM: GIR/1. • **22**. Marsh to Nelson, 14/11/1799, Add. MS 34914. • **23**. Nelson's information about French naval power: Add. MS 34908, f. 16. • **24**. Nelson to St Vincent, 27/9/1798, *D&L*, 3, p. 133; Nelson to Spencer, 25/9/1798, Add. MS 34963; Ball to Nelson, 22/9/1798, 1 and 4/10/1798, ADM 7/55; Add. MS 34907, f. 433; order, 13/10/1798, ADM 30260; *Vanguard* log, ADM 51/1288. • **25**. Nelson to Spencer, 9/10/1798, Add. MS 34963; medical journal of the *Vanguard*, ADM 101/124/1. There are some discrepancies between the patient-by-patient reports and the general medical summary. • **26**. Grenville to Spencer, 9/9/1798, and Spencer to St Vincent, 16/9/1798, Corbett, *Spencer*, 2, pp. 458, 459; Spencer to St Vincent, 3/10/1798, Add. MS 34933. • **27**. Letters of Grenville and Spencer in Corbett, *Spencer*, 2, pp. 463, 470, 491. • **28**. Grenville to Jackson, 14/9/1798, and Jackson to Grenville, 6/10/1798, 3/11/1798, FO 67/27. • **29**. Letter to Wyndham, 17/10/1798, FO 165/167; Wyndham to Grenville, 15/9/1798, FO 79/16; Jackson to Nelson, and Wyndham to Nelson, both 24/10/1798, Add. MS 34908; Jackson to Wyndham, 31/10/1798, and Wyndham to Hamilton, 20/11/1798, Add. MS 39793. • **30**. Hamilton to Nelson, 8/9/1798, Add. MS 34907; Acton to Nelson, 8/9/1798,

Add. MS 34907; queen to Circello, Add. MS 34907, f. 144. • **31**. Eden to Grenville, 7/5/1798, 22/8/1798, FO 7/51 and FO 7/52; Piers Mackesy, *Statesmen at War*, pp. 54–6. • **32**. Hamilton to Nelson, 26/10/1798, WLC; Grenville to Hamilton, 6/11/1798, FO 70/11; Nelson to St Vincent, 27/9/1798, Add. MS 34963. • **33**. Acton to Hamilton, 20/9/1798, Egerton MS 2640; Jackson to Grenville, 29/9/1798, 3 and 7/11/1798, FO 67/27; Jackson to Nelson, 26/9/1798, Add. MS 34907; Wyndham to Hamilton, 7, 11 and 14/11/1798, Add. MS 39793; Graham to Hamilton, 17/10/1798, Egerton MS 2638; Hamilton to Nelson, 26/10/1798, Add. MS 34908; Hamilton to Grenville, 9 and 16/10/1798, FO 70/11; Nelson to Emma, 3/10/1798 [italics mine], Add. MS 34989; Roger de Damas, *Memoirs*, p. 249. Among abler critics are Davis, *Napoleon and Naples*, p. 78, and H. C. Gutteridge, *NATNJ*, pp. xxiv–xxv, who asserts that Nelson mistook the pacific intentions of the French Directory for weakness and made himself the main instrument of a precipitate campaign. Nelson did not view the French as weak; the reverse. He believed that the French threat to Naples was potentially overwhelming, and that the best prospect of defeating it lay in a pre-emptive attack that would both disrupt the enemy's preparations and draw Austria into the war. As he told St Vincent on 6 December, 'It was not a case of choice, but necessity, which forced the King of Naples to march . . .' (Add. MS 34963). Events proved his course to be disastrous because it misjudged the disposition of Austria, but the intelligence at his disposal lent it credibility. • **34**. Grenville to Hamilton, 3/10/1798, 23/11/1798, FO 70/11; Grenville to Whitworth, 16/11/1798, FO 65/41; HMC, *Dropmore*, 4, pp. 332, 419; Minto to his wife, 9/1/1799, Countess of Minto, *Elliot*, 3, p. 44. • **35**. Nelson to St Vincent, 28/9/1798, *D&L*, 3, p. 133; Hamilton to Grenville, 28/9/1798, 16/10/1798, FO 70/11; Acton to Hamilton, 1/10/1798, Egerton MS 2640. • **36**. Acton to Hamilton, 25/11/1798, Add. MS 34943; Eden to Grenville, 14/7/1798, FO 7/52; Young to Nelson, June 1799, Add. MS 34912; Nelson to Duckworth, 6/12/1798, Add. MS 34963; Nelson to Spencer, 9/10/1798, Dawson, *Nelson Collection*, p. 115. • **37**. Nelson to St Vincent, 13/10/1798, Add. MS 34963; Nelson to Fanny, 11/12/1798, Monmouth MS E954; Harold Acton, *Bourbons*, p. 289. The Queen of Naples, Maria Carolina, became a hate figure for her contemporary opponents, and afterwards among those who traced modern Italian democracy to her Jacobin foes. Freihers von Helfert and John Cordy Jeaffreson mounted a serious defence, but she remains irretrievably controversial. See the detailed biography by Egon Caesar Conte Corti. • **38**. Eden to Grenville, 3/10/1798, FO 7/53; Nelson to St Vincent, 4 and 13/10/1798, NMM: JER/3–4. For the scolding itself, which closes with the foolish maxim that 'the boldest measures are the safest', see Nelson to the queen, 3/10/1798, Add. MS 34989. • **39**. Eden to Grenville, 10/10/1798, FO 7/53; Acton to Hamilton, 13 and 26/10/1798, Add. MSS 34907 and 34908; Nelson to St Vincent, 13/10/1798, Add. MS 34963; Hamilton to Grenville, 16/10/1798, FO 70/11; Hamilton to Nelson, 26/10/1798, Add. MS 34908. • **40**. St Vincent to Hamilton, 7/12/1798, *NLTHW*, p. 497; St Vincent to Nelson, 28/10/1798, *D&L*, 3, p. 145; Spencer to Nelson, 30/9/1798, 25/12/1798, Add. MSS 34907 and 34908; Nelson to St Vincent, 13/10/1798, Add. MS 34963. • **41**. Ushakov to Nelson, September 1798, Add. MS 34933. Ushakov distrusted the British and believed them capable of seizing the Ionian Islands. He concentrated upon securing the islands even after the tsar had ordered him to send a detachment to support Nelson. • **42**. Nelson to Emma, 25/4/1801, Egerton MS 1614; Hood to Nelson, 19/9/1798, FO 70/11; Hood to Nelson, 25/10/1798, 26/11/1798, and Hood to Smith, 28/12/1798, Add. MS 34908; Add. MS 34908, ff. 182, 183; Hallowell to Hood, 24 and 30/10/1798, Add. MS 34908; Willyams, *Voyage*, pp. 119–28; Nelson to St Vincent, 30/9/1798, *D&L*, 3, p. 138; Acton to Hamilton, 1/10/1798, Egerton MS 2640. • **43**. Grenville to Hamilton, 3/10/1798, FO 70/11; Nelson to Hamilton, 9/10/1798, *HANP*, 2, p. 22; Nelson to St Vincent, 22/10/1798, Add. MS 34963; Emma to Nelson,

20/10/1798, Add. MS 34989; Hamilton to Acton, 15/10/1798, NMM: HML/21. • **44**. Ball, 'State of . . . Malta and Gozo', 12/10/1798, NMM: HML/2. • **45**. Ball to Saumarez, 11/10/1798, John Ross, *Saumarez*, 1, p. 275; Ball to Nelson, 8/11/1798, ADM 7/55; Add. MS 34907 f. 408. • **46**. Ball to Nelson, 30/11/1798, 27/12/1798, 29/1/1799, ADM 7/55; Michael Nash, 'A Letter'; Nelson to Hamilton, 24 and 27/10/1798, *Letters*, 2, pp. 245, 247. • **47**. Order, 30/10/1798, Add. MS 30260; St Vincent to Nelson, 27/2/1799, Add. MS 34940; Nelson to Campbell, 3/7/1799, Add. MS 34963; Cornelia Knight, *Autobiography*, 1, pp. 127–8; Ball to Nelson, 10/12/1798, ADM 7/55. • **48**. Vaubois to the Directory, 27/11/1789, William Hardman, *Malta*, p. 149; Ball to Nelson, 30/11/1798, 10/12/1798, 29/1/1799, ADM 7/55; Wyndham to Grenville, 18/11/1798, FO 79/16. • **49**. Ball to Nelson, 30/10/1798, 1/10/1798, ADM 7/55; Nelson to St Vincent, 1/11/1798, ADM 1/398; Knight notes, *D&L*, 3, p. 475. • **50**. Acton to Hamilton, 15/11/1798, Egerton MSS 2640; Hamilton to Grenville, 19/11/1798, FO 70/11; Hamilton to Acton, 5/11/1798, NMM: HML/21. For Josiah Nisbet see the master's log of *La Bonne Citoyenne*, ADM 52/2777, and Add. MS 34908, ff. 93, 122. • **51**. Queen to Gallo, November 1798, Maurice Weil, *Correspondance Inédite*, 1, p. 530.

V Nelson's Great Gamble

1. Queen to Emma, September 1798, Thomas J. Pettigrew, *Memoirs*, 1, p. 149; Hamilton to Nelson, 20/10/1798, Add. MS 34908. • **2**. Emma to Nelson, 20, 26 and 27/10/1798, Add. MS 34989. Effendi, by all accounts an amiable fellow, is said to have attired himself in ceremonial robes to present Nelson with the chelengk on a cushion: *NC*, 1 (1799), p. 340. • **3**. Nelson to Emma, 16/10/1798, Egerton MS 1614; Nelson to St Vincent, 4/10/1798, NMM: JER/3–4. • **4**. Nelson to Emma, 24/10/1798, NMM: CRK/19; Nelson to Hamilton, 27/10/1798, *Letters*, 2, p. 247. • **5**. Letters of Troubridge, October and November 1798, Egerton MS 2638. • **6**. Emma to Fanny, 2/12/1798, Add. MS 34989; Davison to Nelson, 26/11/1798, 7/12/1798, Add. MS 34908; Cornelia Knight, *Autobiography*, 1, p. 139. • **7**. St Vincent to Emma, 28/10/1798, Monmouth MS E415. • **8**. Hamilton to Eden, 27/10/1798, Add. MS 37077. • **9**. Nelson to Fanny, 11/12/1798, Monmouth MS E954; Nelson to St Vincent, 3 and 9/11/1798, NMM: JER/3–4. • **10**. Emma to Nelson, 24 and 25/11/1798, Add. MS 34989. • **11**. Nelson to Emma, 19/5/1799, NMM: CRK/19. Emma was thirty-four years Sir William's junior. In 1784 Nelson had been attracted to thirty-two-year-old Mary Moutray, who was six years his senior and some thirty years younger than her husband, John Moutray, a naval commissioner. He had written about Mary in the same fulsome way he wrote about Emma. In John Sugden, *Nelson*, pp. 260, 822 n., Mary's age may have been misstated. Her obituary in the *Northern Whig* (Belfast), 1/6/1841, indicates a birth year of 1750 or 1751; however, J. D. Davies, *ODNB*, 39 (2004), pp. 568–9, has discovered her baptism, which occurred on 15 October 1752 in Charles Parish, York, Virginia, where her father then served in the *Triton*. It is possible that Mary's baptism was simply delayed, but the probability is that she was born in 1752. It is worth noting that Davies gives the date of Mary's death incorrectly. • **12**. Grenville to Whitworth, 23/11/1798, FO 65/41; Eden to Grenville, 13 and 20/10/1798, 8 and 10/11/1798, 8/12/1798, and Grenville to Eden, 23/11/1798, FO 7/53; Eden to Hamilton, 15/11/1798, Add. MS 2638. • **13**. Emma to Nelson, 24/10/1798, Add. MS 34989. Reporting Thugut's contrariness in matters relating to conflict with France, Eden remarked that the Austrian foreign minister could respond to one official in his 'same dilatory uncertain nature', and to another 'with . . . much seeming approbation' of strong action, and that in the latter mood he suggested the pope repair to Rome and declare 'a war of religion' (Eden to Grenville, 15/12/1798, FO 7/53). • **14**. Wyndham to Grenville, 15/9/1798, 18 and 24/11/1798, 4/12/1798, FO 79/16; Wyndham to Hamilton, 7 and 14/11/1798, Add. MS 39793; Hamilton to Grenville, 19/11/1798, FO 70/11. • **15**. Hamilton to Grenville, 19/11/1798, FO 70/11; Roger de Damas, *Memoirs*, p. 255. • **16**. Nelson to Spencer, 13/11/1798, Add. MS 34963; Hamilton to Grenville, 19/11/1798, FO 70/11; St Vincent to Nelson, 31/12/1798, 1/1/1799, Add. MSS 31161 and 34940. • **17**. Nelson to Duckworth, 6/12/1798, Add. MS 34963; queen to Gallo, November 1798, Maurice Weil, *Correspondance Inédite*, 1, p. 540. • **18**. Hamilton to Grenville, 2/12/1798, FO 165/167. • **19**. Hamilton to Nelson, 25/11/1798, Add. MS 34908; Jacques Macdonald, *Recollections*, 1, p. 192; Damas, *Memoirs*, chs. 12 and 13. • **20**. Nelson to Hamilton, 16/11/1798, Huntington Library, HM 34027; Wyndham to Grenville, 24/11/1798, 4/12/1798, FO 79/16; Acton to Hamilton, 15 and 17/11/1798, Egerton MS 2640; Hamilton to Grenville, 19 and 28/11/1798, FO 70/11. • **21**. Wyndham to Grenville, 26/12/1798, FO 79/16; Hamilton to Grenville, 28/11/1798, FO 70/11; Emma to Nelson, 2/12/1798, Add. MS 34989; Nelson to St Vincent, 28/11/1798, ADM 1/399; order, 22/11/1798, Add. MS 30260; Nelson to Wyndham, 10/12/1798, Add. MS 34963. • **22**. Wyndham to Grenville, 24/11/1798, 4 and 23/12/1798, FO 79/16. In addition to the logs of the *Vanguard*, I have referred to those of the *Culloden*, *Minotaur*, *La Bonne Citoyenne* and *Alliance* in ADM 51/1294, 1271, 1278, and ADM 52/2777. • **23**. The Leghorn expedition has been little understood. The most telling accounts are Wyndham to Nelson, 29/11/1798, Add. MS, 34908; Wyndham to Grenville, 4/12/1798, with its enclosures, FO 79/16; and Nelson's private memorandum of 2/12/1798, *HANP*, 2, p. 27. See also Wyndham to Nelson, 28 and 30/11/1798, Add. MS 34908; Nelson to St Vincent, 28/11/1798, ADM 1/398; Nelson to Spencer, 29/11/1798, Add. MS 34963; and Hamilton to Grenville, 11/12/1798, FO 70/12. • **24**. Wyndham to Grenville, 4 and 11/12/1798, FO 79/16; Wyndham to Nelson, 20/11/1798, Add. MS 34908; Watson to Hamilton, 13/10/1798, FO 165/167; Nelson to St Vincent, 29/11/1798, ADM 1/399; Nelson to Hamilton, 29/11/1798, *HANP*, 2, p. 27. • **25**. Wyndham to Nelson, 29/11/1798, Add. MS 34908; Wyndham to Hamilton, 30/11/1798, Add. MS 37077. See also Wyndham to Hamilton, 3/12/1798, Add. MS 39793, which questions the right of Naselli to assume control of the Tuscan troops as well as his own. Though unhappy with the treatment of Tuscany, Wyndham accepts that the occupation force could save the kingdom 'from the deadly blow the French intended'. • **26**. Nelson to Hamilton, 3/12/1798, Huntington Library, HM 34029; Order, 29/11/1798, Add. MS 30260. • **27**. Nelson to Wyndham, 30/11/1798, Add. MS 34963. • **28**. Nelson to Hamilton, 3/12/1798, Huntington Library, HM 34029. • **29**. Nelson to Wyndham, 30/11/1798, 10/12/1798, and Nelson to Troubridge, 9/12/1798, Add. MS 34963; Troubridge to Nelson, 4 and 6/12/1798, Add. MS 34908; Acton to Hamilton, 8/12/1798, Egerton MS 2640. • **30**. Nelson to St Vincent, 6/12/1798, and Nelson to Spencer, 7/12/1798, Add. MS 34963. Spencer's solution was to exclude Troubridge's first lieutenant from the general Nile promotion, but to slate him for the first vacancy that occurred thereafter: Add. MS 34907, f. 402. • **31**. Nelson to Spencer, 18/12/1798, Add. MS 34963. • **32**. Nelson to Ushakov, 12/12/1798, Add. MS 34908; Hamilton to Grenville, 23/10/1798, FO 70/11. For the scurvy, Add. MS 34908, f. 242. • **33**. Acton to Hamilton, 28/11/1798, Egerton MS 2640. • **34**. Nelson to St Vincent, and Nelson to Stuart, both 6/12/1798, Add. MS 34963; *The Times*, 22/11/1798, 1/1/1799; Whitworth to Paget, 28/12/1798, Augustus B. Paget, *Paget Papers*, 1, p. 144; Eden to Grenville, 12/9/1798, FO 7/53. • **35**. Hamilton to Grenville, 6/1/1799, *HANP*, 2, p. 33; Nelson to Spencer, 11/12/1798, Add. MS 34963. For views of the campaign from the opposing sides see Macdonald's *Recollections* and Damas's frank *Memoirs*. Pietro Colletta, *History of the Kingdom of Naples*, 1, pp. 248–51, who served in Ferdinand's army as a youth, remembers the confusion. • **36**. Nelson to Eden, 10/12/1798, Add. MS 34963. • **37**. Wyndham to Grenville, 23/12/1798, FO 79/16; Jackson to Canning,

4/12/1798, FO 67/27; Eden to Grenville, 8, 19 and 22/12/1798, FO 7/53; Eden to Hamilton, 5/3/1799, Egerton MS 2638; Whitworth to Grenville, 20/11/1798, 25 and 29/1/1799, 12/2/1799, FO 65/41 and FO 65/42; Grenville to Whitworth, 25/1/1799, FO 65/42. The Austrian emperor had ordered Archduke Charles, his premier general, to prepare his army for combat at the beginning of February 1798 (Gunther E. Rothenberg, *Napoleon's Great Adversary*, p. 66). • **38**. Queen to Emma, 17 (endorsement) and 21/12/1798, John C. Jeaffreson, *Queen of Naples*, 2, pp. 32, 37; Acton to Nelson, 20/12/1798, Egerton MS 1623. • **39**. Acton to Hamilton, 19, 20 and 21/12/1798, Egerton MS 2640; queen to Emma, 17, 18 and 19/12/1798, Egerton MS 1615; Nelson to St Vincent, 28/12/1798, ADM 1/399; Hamilton to Greville, 6/1/1799, *HANP*, 2, p. 33; Hamilton to Grenville, 28/12/1798, FO 70/11; Patricia Jaffe, *Catalogue*, 54; logs of the *Alcmene* (ADM 51/4408) and *Vanguard*. The account by an officer of the *Vanguard*, 2/1/1799 (*The Times*, 15/2/1799) states that between six and seven hundred casks of silver, and some containing gold, were transferred. If not an exaggeration, this presumably refers to the valuables brought to both ships. • **40**. Acton to Nelson, 20/12/1798, Pettigrew, *Memoirs*, 1, p. 181; queen to Gallo, 27/12/1798, Weil, *Correspondance Inédite*, 2, p. 1; Guglielmo Pepe, *Memoirs*, p. 52; Knight, *Autobiography*, 1, p. 125. • **41**. Queen to Gallo, 27/12/1798, Weil, *Correspondance Inédite*, 2, p. 4; Acton to Hamilton, 21/12/1798, Egerton MS 2640; Hamilton to Grenville, 28/12/1798, FO 70/11. • **42**. Acton to Nelson, 21/12/1798, Egerton MS 1623; Emma's endorsement on queen to Emma, 21/12/1798, Egerton MS, 1615; queen to Gallo, 21/12/1798, Weil, *Correspondance Inédite*, 1, p. 54. • **43**. In addition to sources listed above, see Nelson to St Vincent, 28/12/1798, ADM 1/399; evacuation plan, 20/12/1798, *D&L*, 3, p. 206; queen's account in Walter Sichel, *Lady Hamilton*, 252; queen to Gallo, 27/12/1798 (second letter), Weil, *Correspondance Inédite*, 2, p. 4; Emma to Grenville, 7/1/1799, *HANP*, 2, p. 35; embarkation lists, Pettigrew, *Memoirs*, 1, pp. 183–5; passenger list, 23/12/1798, Wellcome MS 3676; Acton to Hamilton, 21, 28 and 31/12/1798, Egerton MS 2640; Pryse Lockhart Gordon, *Memoirs*, 1, pp. 205–06; Nelson to Acton, 20 and 21/12/1798, Zabriskie Collection, US Naval Academy, Annapolis; account from the *Sannita* in B. Maresca, 'Caracciolo', pp. 76–79; and James Harrison, *Life*, 1, p. 383. Antonius, Count de Thurn (1723–1806), succeeded Caracciolo as the principal Neapolitan naval commander, and with Acton produced *Istruzioni Peril Servizio de Bastimenti Della Real Marina di Guerra* (Naples, 1800) to regulate the service. • **44**. Nelson to Lady Knight, 20/12/1798, *HANP*, 2, p. 31; Knight, *Autobiography*, 1, pp. 124–9; *Alliance* log, ADM 51/1278. After dark the next day Nelson ordered the boats of his ships to the *molesiglio* to pick up more persons and baggage (order, 22/12/1798, Add. MS 30260). However, the evacuation failed to take off Mesdames Adelaide and Victoire, the elderly daughters of Louis XV of France, who had fled Paris in 1791 and were now at Caserta with a retinue of some eighty persons. A courier was sent to Caserta, but they missed the embarkation and travelled overland to Trieste. • **45**. Queen to Gallo, 27/12/1798, Weil, *Correspondance Inédite*, 2, p. 1; Harold Acton, *Bourbons*, p. 321. • **46**. Nelson to St Vincent, 28/12/1798, Add. MS 34963; queen to Gallo, 27/12/1798, Weil, *Correspondance Inédite*, 2, p. 4; Nelson to Acton, 'Wednesday', Zabriskie collection, US Naval Academy. • **47**. Acton to Hamilton, 15 and 29/1/1799, Egerton MS 2640. • **48**. Queen to Gallo, 27/12/1798, Weil, *Correspondance Inédite*, 2, p. 1. • **49**. Knight, *Autobiography*, 1, pp. 134–5; queen to Emma, c. 1799, Egerton MS 1620, f. 145; Hamilton to Grenville, 8/4/1799, *HANP*, 2, p. 40. • **50**. Wyndham to Hamilton, 13/12/1798, Add. MS 39793. • **51**. Dixon to Hood, 29/12/1798, Add. MS 34908. • **52**. William and Anne Compton to Nelson, 9/12/1799, Add. MS 34915; Spencer to Nelson, 24 and 25/12/1798, Add. MS 34908; Nelson to Spencer, 6/4/1799, Add. MS 75832; Nelson to Berry, 10/4/1799, Add. MS 34910. Nelson was dissatisfied with the compensation for the Nile prizes that he had burned, claiming that they had been undervalued. • **53**. Denis Orde, *In The Shadow of Nelson*, p. 226. • **54**. Spencer to Grenville, 3/10/1798, HMC, *Dropmore*, 4, p. 332; Whitworth to Grenville, 22/10/1798, FO 65/41; St Vincent to Nelson, 28/4/1799, Add. MS 34940; John Barrow, *Smith*, vol. 1, prints several relevant documents. • **55**. Smith's letters, 11/12/1798, to Hamilton (*HANP*, 2, p. 29), Nelson and St Vincent (Add. MS 34908); St Vincent to Smith, 26/11/1798, Add. MS 34908; Spencer to St Vincent, 9/10/1798, Add. MS 34907. • **56**. Nelson to St Vincent, 30 and 31/12/1798, and Nelson to Spencer, 1–2/1/1799, Add. MS 34963. • **57**. St Vincent to Nelson, 17/1/1799, *D&L*, 3, p. 215; St Vincent to Nepean, 16/1/1799, Warren R. Dawson, *Nelson Collection*, p. 117. • **58**. Nelson to Cornwallis, 31/1/1799, HMC, *Various Collections*, 6, p. 392; Nelson to Fanny, 2/1/1799, Monmouth MS E955.

VI 'The Mainspring'

1. Nelson to Goodall, 31/1/1799, *D&L*, 3, p. 246; Nelson to St Vincent, 25/1/1799 to 1/2/1799, Add. MS 34963; queen to Emma, Egerton MS 1620, f. 147; Nelson to Berry, 10/4/1799, Add. MS 34910; Roger de Damas, *Memoirs*, p. 277. Regarding St Vincent's imperfect grasp of Nelson's situation, in February he believed that the problems of Malta and Egypt were on the point of being 'decided', when they survived until 1800 and 1801 respectively: St Vincent to Nelson, 25/2/1799, Add. MS 31162. • **2**. Nelson to St Vincent, 9/5/1799, 5/6/1799, Add. MS 34963; Nelson to Acton, 9/5/1799, *NANJ*, p. 17; Hood to Nelson, 26/1/1799, and Louis to Nelson, 7/6/1799, Add. MS 34909; Ball to Nelson, 31/3/1799, Add. MS 34910; order book, 26 and 27/3/1799, Add. MS 30260; Acton to Hamilton, 1/1/1799, Egerton MS 2640. The medical journal of the *Vanguard* (ADM 101/124/1) records 9 new fever and ulcer cases between 1 September and 10 December 1798, but the report for 24 December to 8 June 1799 claimed 20 fever patients, 29 ulcer cases and 30 venereal patients. Most were returned to duty, but a few fatalities occurred, and a general survey of the health of the squadron was ordered on 1 June in order that serious cases could be transferred to Minorca (orders of 18/5/1799, 1 and 5/6/1799, Add. MS 36608). • **3**. Nelson to Magra, 15/3/1799, Add. MS 34963; Nelson to Davison, 21/4/1799, Egerton MS 2240. • **4**. Countess Elgin to her mother, 28/9/1799, in Nisbet Hamilton Grant, *Letters*, p. 17; Emma to Greville, 5/8/1799, *HANP*, 2, p. 61; Nelson to Ball, 21/1/1799, *D&L*, 3, p. 236; Nelson to Cadogan, 17/7/1799, *HANP*, 2, p. 55; Nelson to Emma, May 1799, NMM: CRK/19; Ball to Tyson, 26/4/1799, Add. MS 34910; Monmouth MS E69. • **5**. Nelson to Smith, 12/3/1799, Add. MS 34909; Nelson to Emma, 19/5/1799, NMM: CRK/19; queen to Emma, 19–20/5/1799, Thomas J. Pettigrew, *Memoirs*, 1, p. 223; Keith to his sister, 10 and 19/4/1799, 13/7/1799, NMM: KEI/46; Duchess of Sermoneta, *Locks*, p. 164; Damas, *Memoirs*, p. 278; Edward J. Foote, *Vindication*, pp. 17, 66; *Alcmene* log, ADM 51/4408. • **6**. Master's log, *La Bonne Citoyenne*, ADM 52/2777. • **7**. Add. MS 34908, ff. 269, 276, 277; Wyndham to Nelson, 25/1/1799, Add. MS 34912; Acton to Nelson, 8/3/1799, Add. MS 34909. • **8**. Nelson to Fanny, 17/1/1799, 2/2/1799, Monmouth MS E 956, and *NLTHW*, p. 481. • **9**. Fanny's maid to her brother, 25/11/1806, Hamilton College Library, Clinton, NY. • **10**. Nelson to Fanny, 4 March 1801, Add. MS 28333. • **11**. Ball to Nelson, 31/3/1799, Add. MS 34910; musters of *La Bonne Citoyenne* and *Thalia*, ADM 36/14514 and 14652; Nisbet to Nepean, 14/7/1803, ADM 1/2229; St Vincent to Nelson, 25 and 27/2/1799, Add. MS 34940. • **12**. Ball to Nelson, 26/4/1799, Add. MS 34910; Nisbet to Nelson, 4/5/1799, NMM: NWD/6; Nelson to Ball, 21/4/1799, *D&L*, 3, p. 332. Nisbet was still neglecting to write his mother: Berry to Nelson, 4/6/1799, Add. MS 34911. • **13**. For contemporary accounts of the fall of Naples see the diary, 15–24/1/1799, in FO 79/17, and Mario Battaglini, *Monitore Napoletano*. • **14**. Nelson's orders to Niza, 3/1//1799, and Campbell to Nelson, 13/1/1799, Add. MS 34909; Acton to Nelson, 14/1/1799, Add. MS 75832; Hamilton to Grenville, 3 and 14/1/1799, FO 70/12. In the circumstances, the eventual destruction of most of the Neapolitan ships was probably unavoidable, but the timing of the act, when the king's colours still flew over the city castles and resistance to the French was continuing, was demoralising. Subsequently, the lack of reliable Neapolitan ships increased the burdens on Nelson's squadron. Acton, for example, had to ask British ships to collect 20,000 muskets from Trieste: Acton to Nelson, 30/1/1799, Add. MS 34909. • **15**. Grenville to Hamilton, 25/3/1799, FO 165/168; Nelson to Stuart, 7/1/1799, Nelson to Spencer, 7/1/1799, and Nelson to St Vincent, 17/4/1799, Add. MS 34963. • **16**. Freihers von Helfert, *Ruffo*, pp. 528, 537; Harold Acton, *Bourbons*, p. 276; queen to Emma, 19/1/1799, Pettigrew, *Memoirs*, 1, p. 201. • **17**. Queen to Emma, 13/5/1799, Egerton MS 1620, f. 69; Acton to Nelson, 10/1/1799, and Nelson to Spencer, 24/1/1799, Add. MS 75832; St Vincent to Nelson, 17/1/1799, Add. MS 34909; Nelson to Emma, 25/1/1799, Egon Caesar Conte Corti, *Marie Karoline*, f.p. 488. • **18**. Hamilton to Grenville, 6 and 7/3/1799, enclosing the *Raccolta di Notizie* [*Palermo Gazette*], 5/3/1799, containing an account of the installation, FO 70/12; Sotheby's, *Trafalgar*, p. 34–5. • **19**. Nelson to St Vincent, 25/1/1799 to 1/2/1799, Add. MS 34963. • **20**. Acton to Hamilton, 10/2/1799, Egerton MS 2640; Jacques MacDonald, *Recollections*, 1, pp. 217, 219; queen to Emma, undated, Pettigrew, *Memoirs*, 1, p. 213. • **21**. Sermoneta, *Locks*, p. 123; Hamilton to Nelson, 28/12/1798, Add. MS 34908; Acton to Hamilton, 28 and 31/12/1798, Egerton MS 2640; Acton to Nelson, 6/1/1799, 8 and 10/3/1799, Add. MS 34909; papers in Add. MS 34909, ff. 374, 385; Hamilton to Grenville, 17 and 19/1/1799, FO 70/12; Nelson to Acton, 8 and 10/3/1799, *NANJ*, p. 7. • **22**. Hamilton to Grenville, 16/1/1799, 7 and 13/2/1799, FO 70/12; Nelson to Minto, 19/1/1799, *D&L*, 3, p. 235; Nelson to Wyndham, 28/1/1799, and Nelson to Spencer, 6/3/1799, Add. MS 34963. For Nelson's politics, see John Sugden, *Nelson*, pp. 401–11. • **23**. Acton, *Bourbons*, pp. 337–9; Nelson to Wyndham, 28/1/1799, and Nelson to Louis, 28/1/1799, Add. MS 34963; Ball to Magra, 25/1/1799, ADM 7/55. Nelson put the French killed at 87 and Ball 102. • **24**. Nelson's comment on p. 317 of Helen Maria Williams, *Sketches*, NMM: PHB/P/19; O'Hara to Nelson, 31/12/1798, Add. MS 34908; St Vincent to Nelson, 1/1/1799, Add. MS 34940; Darby to Nelson, 17/4/1799, Add. MS 34910. • **25**. Pryse Lockhart Gordon, *Memoirs*, 1, pp. 201–2. • **26**. Gordon, *Memoirs*, 1, pp. 208–11, 228–9; Sermoneta, *Locks*, pp. 177, 178, 193. I surmised that the dinner took place on 6 March from Nelson to St Vincent, 6/3/1799, Add. MS 34963. Conceivably the Turkish sword survives at Eglinton Castle, Lord Montgomerie being the son of the Earl of Eglinton. • **27**. The counter-revolutionary movements are discussed by Owen Chadwick, *Popes*, and Michael Broers, *Napoleonic Empire*. • **28**. Hamilton to Grenville, 13 and 17/2/1799, 6/3/1799, FO 70/12; Whitworth to Grenville, 2 and 25/1/1799, 12/2/1799, FO 65/42; Acton to Nelson, 9, 15 and 16/2/1799, 18/3/1799, Add. MSS 34909 and 34910; Wyndham to Nelson, 9/2/1799, Add. MS 34909. • **29**. Nelson to Stuart, 16/2/1799, and Stuart to Duckworth, 28/2/1799, ADM 1/399; Stuart to Dundas, 27/3/1799, 13/4/1799, WO 1/297. • **30**. Stuart to Dundas, 13/4/1799, and Stuart to Hamilton, 28/3/1799, WO 1/297; Stuart to Nelson, 3/4/1799, Add. MS 34910; Hamilton to Grenville, 22/3/1799, 8/4/1799, FO 70/12; Acton to Hamilton, 28/3/1799, Egerton MS 2640. • **31**. Wyndham to Nelson, 28/12/1798, 6/2/1799, Add. MSS 34908 and 34909; Nelson to Wyndham, 28/1/1799, Add. MS 34963. • **32**. Wyndham to Grenville, 6 and 8/1/1799, 2/2/1799, 27/4/1799, and Gage to Wyndham, 7/1/1799, FO 79/17; Wyndham to Nelson, 16/3/1799, Add. MS 34909; Hamilton to Grenville, 26/1/1799, 29/4/1799, FO 70/12; Jackson to Grenville, 8 and 16/12/1798, FO 67/27; Nelson to Acton, 9/5/1799, *NANJ*, p. 17. • **33**. Nelson to St Vincent, 8/3/1799, Add. MS 34963; Spencer to Nelson, 12/3/1799, and Smith to Troubridge, 3 and 3/3/1799 (two letters), Add. MS 34909; John Barrow, *Smith*, 1, pp. 251,

255; Nelson to Berry, 10/4/1799, Add. MS 34910. • **34**. Nelson to Smith, 8/3/1799, Add. MS 34963. • **35**. Nelson to Spencer, 24/1/1799, Add. MS 75832; Nelson to Acton, 26/2/1799, *NANJ*, p. 49; Troubridge to Nelson, 6/2/1799, March 1799, Add. MSS 34909 and 34910; Hallowell to Nelson, 11/3/1799, Add. MS 34909. • **36**. Nelson to Smith, 18/3/1799, and Nelson to Wyndham, 22/3/1799, Add. MS 34963; Hamilton to Grenville, 8/4/1799, FO 70/12; order book, 29/4/1799, Add. MS 30260. Smith put a different interpretation on the loan of the *Lion* in his letter to Nepean, 7/3/1799, ADM 1/399. • **37**. Burton to Nelson, 17/3/1799, Add. MS 34909; Smith to Grenville, 6/3/1799, Pettigrew, *Memoirs*, 1, p. 195; Dixon to Nelson, 6/5/1799, Add. MS 34911. Smith replied to the rebukes of superiors in letters to Nelson, 31/5/1799, and St Vincent, 2/6/1799, Add. MS 34911. • **38**. Nelson to Ball, 9/2/1799, *HANP*, 2, p. 38; Nelson to St Vincent, 17/4/1799, Add. MS 34963; Nelson to Spencer, 7 and 17/2/1799, Add. MS 75832; Ball to Nelson, 4, 5 and 23/2/1799, 26/4/1799, Add. MSS 34909 and 34910; Foley to the governor of Messina, 21/4/1799, Add. MSS 34910. • **39**. Ball to Nelson, 25 and 27/12/1798, 6/1/1799, ADM 7/55; Menard to the Minister of Marine, 17/1/1799, William Hardman, *Malta*, p. 165. • **40**. Ball to Hamilton, 7/12/1798, NMM: HML/2; Ball to St Vincent, 27/12/1799, ADM 1/399; Ball to Nelson, 6/1/1799, 4 and 5/2/1799, Add. MS 34909, and 29/1/1799, ADM 7/55; Nelson to St Vincent, 3/2/1799, Add. MS 34963; Acton to Hamilton, 19/5/1799, Egerton MS 2640; Menard to Minister of Marine, 17/1/1799, Hardman, *Malta*, p. 165. • **41**. Hardman, *Malta*, pp. 169, 171; Ball to Nelson, 9 and 10/2/1799, Add. MS 34909, and 3 and 15/3/1799, ADM 7/55; Ball to Hamilton, 9/2/1799, *NLTHW*, p. 498; Acton to Nelson, 3 and 20/2/1799, Add. MS 34909; Acton to deputies, 19/2/1799, Add. MS 34943; Hamilton to Grenville, 6/3/1799, FO 70/12; Acton to Hamilton, 21/4/1799, Egerton MS 2640; order, 28/2/1799, Add. MS 36608. Ferdinand officially approved of Ball's appointment as governor in August: Acton to Nelson, 25/8/1799, NMM: CRK/1. • **42**. Ball to Hamilton, 19/10/1798, 9/2/1799, NMM: HML/2; Ball to Tyson, 26/4/1799, Add. MS 34910; Ball to Nelson, 7/5/1799, Add. MS 34911. • **43**. Nelson to St Vincent, 17/4/1799, Add. MS 34963; Ball to Nelson, 26/4/1799, Add. MS 34910; Ball to Hamilton, 26/4/1799, NMM: HML/2. • **44**. Nelson to Nepean, 21/9/1799, ADM 1/400. • **45**. Ball to Nelson, 12/4/1799, Add. MS 34910; Acton to Nelson, 18/11/1799, Add. MS 34915. • **46**. Magra to Nelson, 10/1/1799, 20 and 23/3/1799, Add. MSS 34909 and 34910; 'Case of the Polacre . . .' 1/2/1799, ADM 7/55. • **47**. Magra to Nelson, 27/11/1798, 7/12/1798, 17/1/1799, Add. MSS 34908 and 34909. • **48**. Nelson's letters to the bey, 15/3/1799, St Vincent, 2/2/1799, and Niza, 9/1/1799, Add. MS 34963. • **49**. Magra to Stuart, 5/5/1799, Add. MS 34911; Magra's letters to Nelson, 6 and 8/3/1799 (Add. MS 34909), 16 and 24/3/1799, 19/4/1799 (Add. MS 34910) and 16/12/1799 (Add. MS 34932). • **50**. Bey to Nelson, 25/3/1799, 27/6/1799, Add. MS 34910 and *HANP*, 2, p. 51; Acton to Nelson, 5/4/1799, 30/6/1799, Add. MS 34910 and NMM: CRK/17; Nelson to Acton, 10/5/1799, 23/9/1799, *NANJ*, 2, p. 18, and Zabriskie Collection, US Naval Academy; Nelson to Magra, 20/6/1799, 10/8/1799, and Nelson to the bey, 16/8/1799, Add. MS 34963; Magra to Nelson, 21/5/1799, 13 and 29/6/1799, Add. MSS 34911 and 34912. • **51**. Magra to Portland, 15/2/1800, FO 77/4. • **52**. Magra to Nelson, February 1799, and Lucas to Ball, 3 and 5/3/1799, Add. MS 34909; Lucas to Nelson, 5 and 28/3/1799, Add. MS 34910; Hamilton to Grenville, 8/4/1799, FO 70/12. • **53**. McDonough to Portland, 15/5/1801, FO 76/5; Ball to Tyson, 26/4/1799, Add. MS 34909; St Vincent to Nelson, 30/4/1799, Add. MS 34940; Nelson to the bashaw, 28/4/1799, Add. MS 34910; Nelson to St Vincent, 5/6/1799, Add. MS 34963. • **54**. McDonough to Nelson, 11/5/1799, Campbell to Nelson, 17/5/1799, 1/6/1799, and Lucas to Nelson, 2/6/1799, Add. MS 34911. • **55**. Lucas to Nelson, 14/10/1799, Add. MS 34914. • **56**. Wyndham to Nelson, 21/11/1799, Add. MS 34915; Nelson to Wyndham, 2/12/1799, and Nelson to Hoste, 3/12/1799, FO 79/17; Bensamon to Erskine, 27/11/1799, and O'Brien to commanding officer at Minorca, 8/11/1799, FO 3/8. • **57**. O'Brien to commanding officer at Minorca, 8/11/1799, and Falcon to Elgin, 7/1/1800, FO 3/8; O'Brien, 'Remarks & Abuses', Add. MS 34932, f. 214; Hope, 20/2/1799, ADM 1/399. These paragraphs principally depend upon several documents in FO 3/8, Add. MSS 34915 and 34916, and ADM 1/401. • **58**. Bensamon to Nelson, 5/1/1800, Falcon to Portland, 2/6/1800, and Falcon to Keith, 2/6/1800, FO 3/8. • **59**. Note on Anglo-Algerian agreement, 7/12/1800, Add. MS 34918.

VII Coming Back

1. Acton to Nelson, 18/3/1799, Add. MS 34910. • **2**. John A. Davis, *Naples*, p. 116; Guglielmo Pepe, *Memoirs*, 1, p. 65. • **3**. Nelson to St Vincent, 2/3/1799, Add. MS 34963; Nelson to Spencer, 6/3/1799, 6/4/1799, Add. MS 75832; Add. MS 34910, f. 42; Hamilton to Grenville, 22/3/1799, FO 70/12. • **4**. Acton to Nelson, 19 and 20/3/1799, Add. MS 34910. • **5**. Nelson to Berry, 10/4/1799, Add. MS 34910; Cooper Willyams, *Voyage*, pp. 176–78. • **6**. Nelson to Troubridge, 28 and 30/3/1799, Add. MSS 30260 and 34963; king's instructions, 30/3/1799, *NANJ*, p. 28. • **7**. Acton to Nelson, 11/2/1799, Add. MS 34909; order book, 5/3/1799, 29/4/1799, Add. MS 30260; Nelson to Acton, 18/3/1799, Add. MS 34963; Nelson to Wherry, 1/4/1799, *D&L*, 3, p. 311. • **8**. Troubridge to Nelson, 3, 4, 7, 9, 13 and 18/4/1799, 7/5/1799, Add. MSS 34910 and 34911; R. Gamble, *Letters*, p. 58; Willyams, *Voyage*, pp. 181–2. The trials conducted by the new justice, Vincenzo Speciale, sent from Palermo, proved controversial. Perhaps a score of defendants were executed on Procida. • **9**. Troubridge to Nelson, 4, 13, 16, 18 and 20/4/1799, 7, 9 and 11/5/1799, Add. MSS 34910 and 34911; his undated note on Add. MSS 34911, f. 148; Nelson to Acton, 14/4/1799, 13/5/1799, *NANJ*, p. 11, and Add. MS 34911; Acton to Nelson, 2/5/1799, NMM: CRK/17; order book, 6/5/1799, Add. MS 36608. For letters of Trabia see Add. MSS 34943 and 34944. • **10**. Troubridge to Nelson, 4, 18, 21, 25 and 27–29/4/1799, 1/5/1799, Add. MSS 34910 and 34911; Nelson to Clarence, 11/4/1799, Add. MS 46356; Acton to Hood, 8/5/1799, Add. MS 34911; Hood to Troubridge, 28/4/1799, and Darley to Hood, 26/4/1799, Add. MS 34910; 'Tableau', 22/4/1799 to 1/5/1799, Maurice Weil, *Correspondance Inédite*, 2, p. 69; order book, 8/5/1799, Add. MS 36608; Add. MS 34944, f. 77; logbooks of the *Culloden*, *Minotaur*, *Swiftsure*, *Zealous* and *Seahorse* in ADM 51/1294, 1300, 1274 and 1270. Caracciolo contributed to defending Castellammare with his gunboats, but the truth about his defection only dawned on Troubridge gradually. Early in April he reported a rumour that Caracciolo had been drummed into the enemy forces and obliged to perform common guard duty at the Caserta Palace, which the French had made their headquarters, but a few days later he intercepted one of the seaman's letters, establishing that he was now the head of the Jacobin marine. Even so, Troubridge hoped that time would show that he had been 'forced' into the position and that alleged signatures on revolutionary documents were forgeries or had been made under duress (Troubridge to Nelson, 9, 13, 18 and 21/4/1799, and Harriman to Nelson, 20/4/1799, Add. MS 34910). Not until May did Troubridge accept that Caracciolo seemed to have become a Jacobin, but even then he prayed that he was innocent (Troubridge to Nelson, 1 and 5/5/1799, Add. MS 34911). Nelson was inclined to agree, believing that Caracciolo 'was fool enough to quit his master when he thought his case desperate', but was no Jacobin (Nelson to Spencer, 29/4/1799, Add. MS 34963). Finding Caracciolo's name on proclamations denigrating the monarchy, the queen was less patient, and pronounced him to be a scoundrel. It was put beyond doubt on 17 May, when the Neapolitan commander led an attack on the king's ships at Procida. See Francesco Lemmi, *Nelson e Caracciolo*, pp. 50–56. • **11**. Troubridge to Nelson, 26 and 27/4/1799, Add. MS 34910; his undated letter, Add. MS 24911, f. 297; Hood to Troubridge, 1799, Add. MS 34932, f. 15. Three Tschudys were in Neapolitan service at this time, Joseph Anton Xavier, Ludwig Sebastian and Joseph Anton, and more work is needed to differentiate them. • **12**. Nelson to Troubridge, 25/4/1799, Add. MS 34963; Troubridge to Nelson, 11/5/1779, Add. MS 34911; Acton to Nelson, 30/4/1799, Add. MS 34910. • **13**. King to Ruffo, 1/5/1799, *NANJ*, p. 45. • **14**. Acton to Ruffo, 4/4/1799, *NANJ*, p. 34; king to Ruffo, 11/4/1799, 1/5/1799, *NANJ*, pp. 38, 45; queen to Ruffo, 5/4/1799, 14/6/1799, *NANJ*, pp. 36, 82. • **15**. Queen to Ruffo, 5/4/1799, *NANJ*, p. 36; queen to Gallo, 17/5/1799, Weil, *Correspondance Inédite*, 2, p. 92. The royals reserved the right of judgement to themselves and their intended commission, but they were not entirely consistent. Thus, on 10 June Ferdinand stated that summary exile – rather than trial by courts – might be extended to 'several rebels, even to the leaders, according to circumstances, if the general good, the promptitude of the operation and reasons of weight make it advisable'. Moreover, the king wanted the enemy forts in Naples to be 'speedily evacuated . . . at any cost, and, should it be necessary, to employ any other means besides force': king to Prince Royal, 10/6/1799, *NANJ*, p. 67. • **16**. Nelson to Clarence, 10/5/1799, Add. MS 46356; Nelson to Spencer, 1/5/1799, *D&L*, 3, p. 340; Nelson to Acton, 8/5/1799, *NANJ*, p. 14. • **17**. Oswald to Troubridge, undated, Add. MS 34911, f. 152; Troubridge to Oswald, 12/5/1799, and Troubridge to Nelson, 4 and 6/5/1799, Add. MS 34911; Nelson to Acton, 8/5/1799 [my italics], *NANJ*, p. 16; Nelson to Hamilton, 26/5/1799, *HANP*, 2, p. 48. Yauch was court-martialled, but the French retreated from Longone in May. • **18**. Nelson to Troubridge, 7/4/1799, Add. MS 34963. The supposed Jacobin was D. Charles Granozio di Giffoni: James Stanier Clarke and John McArthur, *Life and Services*, 2, p. 236 n. But a widow of a man of that name, D. Carlo Granozio, was later compensated in April 1800 for the loss of her husband, who had perished in the royalist cause: Alfonso Sansone, *Avvenimenti*, p. 433. • **19**. Nelson to Spencer, 17/4/1799, Add. MS 75832; Spencer to Nelson, 12/3/1799, *D&L*, 3, p. 335. • **20**. For the Bruix affair see *NC*, vol 1 and 2; Christopher Lloyd, *Keith Papers*, 2, pp. 30–60; St Vincent's dispatches and letters in ADM 1/399 and Add. MS 34940; Corbett, *Spencer*, 3, pp. 43–103; William James, *Naval History*, 2, pp. 284–302; John Sugden, 'Lord Cochrane', pp. 48–50; and G. Douin, *Campagne de Bruix*. • **21**. Nelson to Ball, 12/5/1799, Add. MS 34963; Troubridge to Nelson, 14/5/1799, Add. MS 34911. • **22**. Nelson to St Vincent, 12/5/1799, Add. MS 34963; Graham to Hamilton, 9/5/1799, Egerton MS 2638; queen to Gallo, 14, 17 and 18/5/1799, Weil, *Correspondance Inédite*, 2, pp. 89, 92, 95. Dissatisfied with Danero, the king replaced him with Prince Cuto, who, with Graham and the Prince di Scaletta, were responsible for military defence: Acton to Hamilton, 24/5/1799, Egerton MS 2640. • **23**. Nelson to St Vincent, 13/5/1799, *D&L*, 3, p. 355. • **24**. Nelson to St Vincent, 23/5/1799, ADM 1/399. • **25**. Nelson to St Vincent, 14/5/1799, and Nelson to his captains, 21/5/1799, Add. MS 34963; order book, 16/5/1799, Add. MS 36608; note in Add. MS 34911, f. 246; sailing order, 14/6/1799, Add. MS 36609. Ball's detachment consisted of *Alexander*, *Audacious* and *Goliath*. The *Principe Real* had ninety-two guns; all of the other capital ships were seventy-fours, except for Dixon's *Lion* and the *St Sebastian*, which were sixty-fours. Nelson could make twelve ships of the line by including George Burlton's armed transport, *Haerlem*, which was being rearmed to pass for another sixty-four. His 'cruisers' were the frigates *Minerve*, *Thalia* and *Pallas*, the *San Leon* brig, *Incendiary* fireship and *L'Entreprenant* cutter. • **26**. Nelson to Emma, 21 and 22/5/1799, *D&L*, 7, pp. clxxxii, clxxxiii; Nelson to Hamilton, 23/5/1799, Huntington Library, HM 34032. • **27**. Nelson to Emma, 21/5/1799, *D&L*, 7, p. clxxxii; Hamilton to Nelson, 21/5/1799, Add. MS 34911; St Vincent to Nelson, 21, 22 and 31/5/1799, Add. MS 34940. • **28**. Intelligence, 22/5/1799, and Hallowell to Nelson, 23/5/1799, Add. MS 34911. • **29**. Nelson to Hamilton, 23 and 25/5/1799, Huntington Library, HM 34032, 34033. • **30**. The line consisted of *Vanguard*,

Culloden, Zealous, Alexander, Swiftsure, Alfonso d'Albuquerque, Principe Real, St Sebastian, Goliath, Lion, Audacious and *Minotaur*: order book, 28/5/1799, Add. MS 36608. The *Lion* was eventually sent to Malta to reimpose the lapsed blockade. • **31**. Hood to Foote, 7/5/1799, Foote to Nelson, 22/5/1799, and Oswald to Nelson, 17, 21 and 22/5/1799, Add. MS 34911. • **32**. Vivion to Hamilton, 31/5/1799, Add. MS 37077. • **33**. Nelson to Dixon, 20/6/1799, Add. MS 36609; Vivion to Nelson, 31/5/1799, 19 and 25/6/1799, and Vivion to Ball, 1/7/1799, Add. MS 34940. But see Ball to Duckworth, 3/8/1799, ADM 7/55, who claimed the French had imported not 'the smallest supply' in the last four months. • **34**. Keith to Nelson, 3, 6 and 17/6/1799, Add. MS 34911. • **35**. Hamilton to Grenville, 5/6/1799, FO 70/12; St Vincent to Nelson, 27 and 31/5/1799, Add. MS 34940; *Foudroyant* log, ADM 51/1279; Peter Goodwin, *Nelson's Ships*, pp. 179–95. The other two ships reinforcing Nelson were the *Northumberland* and *Majestic*. The followers who accompanied Nelson to his new flagship included Lieutenants William Standway Parkinson, William Bolton, Henry Compton, Edward Thornbrough Parker and John Lackey; 'young gentlemen' rated either as midshipmen or master's mates, Richard Walsh, George Antrim, Clement Ives, Atkin Hayman, Francis Collier, the Hon. Granville Proby West and John Woodin; and several seamen: John Marsh, Richard Searle, James McLaughlin, Spry Roberts, John Hextram, William Randall, Walter Grosse, William Clothier, Robert Tripp, William Pedwin, James Johnson, Christian Coleman, John Budd, George Shirley and Forbes Clark (orders of 7/6/1799, Add. MS 36608). Lieutenant Parkinson had been with Nelson in the *Boreas* in 1784. Bolton and Compton were old *Agamemnons*, and seventeen of the lower-deck ratings had been at the Nile. Most of the latter were able seamen in their twenties. The oldest may have been John Hextram, a Swede some thirty-nine years old. • **36**. Nelson to St Vincent, 10 and 12/6/1799, *D&L*, 3, pp. 377, 379. • **37**. The king's instructions, 10/6/1799, *NANJ*, pp. 62, 67; Acton to Nelson, 8 and 10/6/1799, NMM: CRK/1. • **38**. St Vincent to Nelson, 31/5/1799, Add. MS 34940; queen to Ruffo, 14/6/1799, queen to Nelson, 11/6/1799, and Emma to Nelson, 12/6/1799, in *NANJ*, pp. 82, 72, 74. This volume, edited by H. C. Gutteridge, collects most of the pertinent documents about this episode. Nelson had already stipulated the need for Sir William's presence as an interpreter: Acton to Hamilton, 11/6/1799, Egerton MS 2640. • **39**. Nelson to St Vincent, 12/6/1799, NMM: JER/5; Acton to Nelson, 11 and 12/6/1799, Add. MS 34911; Hamilton to Grenville, 16/6/1799, FO 70/12. • **40**. Acton to Hamilton, 15 and 19/6/1799, Add. MSS 34911 and 34912. Keith's best course might have been to send the two ships of the line to cover Minorca, and to have pressed on to engage the French fleet. • **41**. Order of battle and sailing, 14/6/1799, Add. MS 36609; Nelson to Keith, 16/6/1799, Add. MS 34963; Nelson to Emma, 18/6/1799, Egerton MS 1614; Nelson to Hamilton, 16/6/1799, *HANP*, 2, p. 51. • **42**. Hamilton to Nelson, 18/6/1799, Add. MS 34912. • **43**. Nelson to Emma, 18 and 19/6/1799, Egerton MS 1614; Foley to Nelson, 20/6/1799, and Acton to Hamilton, 20/6/1799, Add. MS 34912; Nelson to Hamilton, 20/6/1799, *D&L*, 7, p. clxxxv; Nelson to Magra, 20/6/1799, Add. MS 34963. • **44**. Keith to Nelson, 17/6/1799, Add. MS 34912. • **45**. Hamilton to Nelson, 20/6/1799, and Acton to Hamilton, 20/6/1799, Add. MS 34912. • **46**. *D&L*, 3, p. 491; endorsement on queen to Emma, 2/7/1799, Egerton MS 1616; Nelson to Keith, 27/6/1799, ADM 1/400. • **47**. Foote to Nelson, 11, 13, 15 and 26/6/1799, Add. MSS 34911 and 34912. • **48**. Foote to Ruffo, 20/6/1799, and Foote to Nelson, 18–20/6/1799, Add. MS 36873; Micheroux to Ruffo, 19/6/1799, *NANJ*, p. 124. • **49**. Micheroux, *NANJ*, p. 106; Foote to Ruffo, 20/6/1799, and Foote to Nelson, 23/6/1799, Add. MS 36873; Ruffo to Acton, 21/6/1799, *NANJ*, p. 149. • **50**. Capitulation, 23/6/1799, *NANJ*, p. 155. • **51**. *NANJ*, p. 159; queen to Ruffo, 14/6/1799, *NANJ*, p. 82. On 19 June, however, the queen obscured the picture by informing Ruffo that it was necessary to 're-establish good order and quiet, and to cleanse society by removing the perturbers of the public peace', and that Caracciolo was 'the only one among the guilty scoundrels' she did 'not wish to go to France' (*NANJ*, p. 133). Presumably, she was giving a private opinion, not intended to subvert the judicial process that Ferdinand intended to establish. • **52**. Hamilton to Nelson, 17/6/1799, Add. MS 34912; king to Ruffo, 20/6/1799, *NANJ*, p. 139. • **53**. Queen to Ruffo, 21/6/1799, *NANJ*, p. 165; king to Ruffo, 25/6/1799, John A. Davis, *Hamilton Letters*, p. 231; Acton to Hamilton, 23/6/1799, Egerton MS 2640; Hamilton to Grenville, 14/7/1799, FO 70/12. • **54**. Hamilton to Nelson, 17/6/1799, Add. MS 34912; Nelson to Foote, 6/6/1799, Add. MS 36873; king to Ruffo, 25/6/1799, Davis, *Hamilton Letters*, p. 231; Nelson letter of August 1799, NMM: CRK/14. • **55**. Hamilton to Acton, 22/6/1799, *NANJ*, p. 177.

VIII The Bourbon Restoration

1. Cooper Willyams, *Voyage*, p. 203. • **2**. Nelson's 'observations', 24/6/1799, *NANJ*, p. 197. • **3**. Nelson to Drummond, 25/6/1799, Add. MS 36608; *Majestic* log, ADM 51/1260; Hamilton to Acton, 25/6/1799, NMM: HML/21. • **4**. Foote to Nelson, 24/6/1799, and his statement of 26/6/1799, Add. MS 36873; Hamilton to Grenville, 14/7/1799, FO 70/12. Foote spoke well of Nelson's treatment of him at the time. It was only after the admiral's death that he felt impelled to justify his conduct, and attacked Nelson's handling of the rebels. • **5**. Nelson to Duckworth, 25/6/1799, *D&L*, 3, p. 387, and Nelson to Keith, 27/6/1799, ADM 1/400. • **6**. Hamilton to Grenville, 14/7/1799, FO 70/12; Nelson to Méjean, 25/6/1799, Add. MS 36609. A note of 25 June (NMM: CRK/17) records that the Duke of Salandra sent a boat to the *Foudroyant* with a complaint that Ruffo had 'taken too cold a part and given the rascals time to invent more mischief, and that the people . . . were burning with impatience to fall upon the French and Jacobins without loss of time'. • **7**. Nelson to Keith, 27/6/1799, ADM 1/400; Hamilton to Grenville, 14/7/1799, FO 70/12; Nelson's opinion, 25/6/1799, *NANJ*, p. 217. • **8**. Domenico Sacchinelli, *Ruffo*, pp. 252–3, is the source for the statement that the Jacobins were encouraged to slip into the city. Sacchinelli was Ruffo's secretary and apologist, and is by no means trustworthy, but this seems confirmed by Carlo de Nicola, *Diario*, pp. 259–60, and *NANJ*, p. 330. Likewise, the 'protest' comes from Sacchinelli, p. 251, and may be one of his paraphrases of documents or just possibly an invention. • **9**. Pryse Lockhart Gordon, *Memoirs*, 1, pp. 217–18; Guglielmo Pepe, *Memoirs*, p. 106; 'Fiat Justitia', 'The Nelson Dispatches', part 3, pp. 452–5. • **10**. Hamilton to Ruffo, 26 and 27/6/1799 [my italics], *NANJ*, pp. 231, 252; Nelson to Ruffo, 26/6/1799, Add. MS 34963. • **11**. Hamilton to Acton, 27/6/1799, *NANJ*, p. 249; Hamilton to Greville, 4/8/1799, FO 70/12; and two retrospective accounts of Rushout, Add. MS 30999, ff. 75 and 82, which are unreliable in detail, but contain some genuine impressions. • **12**. Hamilton to Acton, 27/6/1799, NMM: HML/21. Notable protagonists in the debate over this affair include Edward James Foote, Robert Southey, Domenico Sacchinelli, Francis. P. Badham (Foote's grandson), Constance Giglioli and Terry Coleman, who write critically of Nelson; and Jeaffreson Miles, Nicholas Harris Nicolas, Benedetto Maresca, Hermann Hueffer, John Knox Laughton, A. T. Mahan, H. C. Gutteridge, Marianne Csisnik and Andrew Lambert, who articulate a robust defence. The determination to vindicate or accuse is often apparent. Blame has also been freely lodged with Ruffo, Micheroux, the royals and both Hamiltons. • **13**. Nelson to Acton, 26/6/1799, *NANJ*, p. 271; Hamilton to Acton, 28/6/1799, *NANJ*, p. 267; Hamilton to Acton, 27/6/1799, NMM: HML/21. In all cases the italics are mine. • **14**. Hamilton to Grenville, 14/7/1799, FO 70/12. That Nelson expected an evacuation to follow his assurances of 26 June, and allowed it to proceed according to the 'treaty' rather than his summons, strongly indicates that he had accepted the capitulation, and was not merely reviving a defunct armistice. The rebels were not incarcerated as prisoners until 28 June, when Nelson's policy again altered, as discussed below. • **15**. *NANJ*, p. 217. The note delivered by the British captains, reproduced as a facsimile at the end of Sacchinelli, *Ruffo*, is written in Italian. It suggests Hamilton's hand, containing some of his flourishes and letter formations. • **16**. *Culloden* log, ADM 52/2902; Troubridge to Nelson, 13/7/1799, Add. MS 34912; Nelson to Spencer, 15/7/1799, Add. MS 75832; Nelson to Niza, 27/6/1799, Add. MS 34963; *Foudroyant* log, ADM 51/1279. • **17**. Micheroux, *NANJ*, p. 106; Smith to Nelson, undated, NMM: CRK/12/63; R. Gamble, *Letters*, pp. 64–5; Emma to Greville, 19/7/1799, *HANP*, 2, p. 56; Sacchinelli, *Ruffo*, p. 254; Harold Acton, *Bourbons*, p. 395; Wade to Nelson, June 1799, Add. MS 34912. • **18**. Ruffo to Nelson, 26/7/1799, Add. MS 34944. • **19**. Queen to Emma, 24 and 26/6/1799, *NANJ*, pp. 195, 210; king to Ruffo, 25/6/1799, Davis, *Hamilton Letters*, p. 291; king to Nelson, 27/6/1799, NMM: CRK/17. Acton's letters (Egerton MSS 2640) are printed in *NANJ*, pp. 224, 225, 227. I am assuming that the queen's letter of the 24th arrived at the same time, or just before, those of the 25th. • **20**. Hamilton to Acton, 28/6/1799, quoting his letter to Ruffo, NMM: HML/21. • **21**. Gordon, *Memoirs*, 1, pp. 215–16; Lock to his father, July 1799, 9/8/1799, Duchess of Sermoneta, *Locks*, pp. 170, 178; Lock to Graham, 19/7/1799, 22/8/1799, National Library of Scotland, NLS 3598. Both of these reporters are suspect. Lock resented the Hamiltons, and from 23 July blamed Nelson for blocking his attempt to be named an agent victualler to the fleet. Lock apparently influenced Gordon, whose memoirs recapitulate several of Lock's charges. • **22**. Nelson to Spencer, 13/7/1799, Add. MS 75832; Hamilton to Grenville, 14/7/1799, FO 70/12; Nelson to Davison, 9/5/1800, Egerton MS 2240. Hamilton spoke more openly to his friend Acton. On 28 June he wrote that 'Lord Nelson, *finding* that His Sicilian Majesty totally disapproved . . . and those rebels being *still* on board . . . [the] polacres . . . thought himself sufficiently authorised to seize all these polacres . . .' [italics mine]. This admits the change of direction that resulted in the final seizure of the vessels, and the role of the king's responses in bringing it about: Hamilton to Acton, 28/6/1799, NMM: HML/21. • **23**. Nelson to Sargent, 28/6/1799, Add. MS 36609; *NANJ*, p. 320. See also the logs of *Foudroyant*, *Culloden*, *Seahorse*, *Zealous*, *Leviathan*, *Majestic* and *Swiftsure*, ADM 51/1279, 1294, 1270, 1300, 1282 and 1274, and ADM 52/2902. • **24**. Nelson to Acton, 28 and 30/6/1799, *NANJ*, p. 271, and NMM: CRK/1. • **25**. Acton to Hamilton, 26/6/1799, Egerton MS 2640; Acton to Nelson, 30/6/1799, 1/8/1799, NMM: CRK/17 and CRK/1; king to Ruffo, 27/6/1799, *NANJ*, p. 276; Hamilton to Acton, 30/6/1799, NMM: HML/21. • **26**. Troubridge to Nelson, 2 and 7/7/1799, Add. MS 34912; Nelson's proclamation to the rebels, 29/6/1799, Add. MS 36609; Hamilton to Nelson, 30/6/1799, NMM: HML/2 [copy erroneously dated 3 June]. • **27**. A list of the prisoners held on board the ships of the British fleet, made after the departure of the *Alexander* and *Alfonso d'Albuquerque* on 2 July, shows fifty-one names distributed between sixteen ships. On 5 July eighty-one prisoners were being held at the Castel Nuovo, and possibly nineteen at Castel dell'Uovo: see lists in NMM: GIR/3a. It is not clear whether those at Castel dell'Uovo had been paroled. • **28**. Hamilton to Acton, 20/6/1799, *NANJ*, p. 276; Nelson to Thurn, 29/6/1799, Add. MS 34912. • **29**. George S. Parsons, *Reminiscences*, p. 1; report of Thurn, 29/6/1799, Sacchinelli, *Ruffo*, p. 265; Hamilton to Acton, 29/6/1799, *NANJ*, p. 276, Parsons could not understand Italian, and it is difficult to see how he divined the conversation he reported years later. No transcript of the court martial has been found. • **30**. James Stanier Clarke and John McArthur, *Life and Services*, 2, p. 273. According to John Rushout, later Lord Northwick, Add. MS 30999, f. 75, Caracciolo came up from below after his trial and almost went on his knees in supplication to the British officers on deck. But Rushout was remembering an incident of nearly half a century before and shows confusion. Among other unverified stories about the incident was one that may have come from the Locks (Gordon, *Memoirs*, 1, p. 219). The day Caracciolo died Emma started at dinner when a roasted pig was beheaded, and said that it reminded her of the unfortunate Caracciolo. Rushout, another of the diners, maintained that Emma said 'Thank God' when she heard the cannon shot marking the execution, and rose to propose a toast. Yet another present, Francis Augustus Collier, recalled that Emma only said, 'Thank God, we are rid of a traitor!' and made no toast. The generally reliable Matthew H. Barker knew Emma in her last days in 1815. 'I saw her a short time previously to her death at a rustic fete, about four miles from Calais,' he wrote. 'There were still remains of beauty, but it was tempered by advancing age, and saddened by sorrow. I was near her when she died. She loudly exclaimed against the ingratitude of her country, but her last hours were passed in wild ravings, in which the name Caracciolo was frequently distinguished' (Barker, *Life of Nelson*, p. 485). However, Nicolas, the editor of the admiral's letters, found another witness to Emma's passing (possibly Horatia Nelson) who refuted the report (*D&L*, 3, pp. 521–2). • **31**. Acton to Nelson, 2/7/1799, NMM: CRK/1. Nelson anticipated the wishes of the Sicilian government. On 30 June, Acton wrote to Hamilton from Palermo, 'I flatter myself that the scoundrel Caracciolo and his adherents will have received a proper reward before His Majesty's arrival, and that we shall have in the king's forces all those who triumphantly are still walking the streets and may do further mischief.' His view was that the sailor's execution would have 'a proper and useful effect on the people' (Acton to Hamilton, 30/6/1799, 2/7/1799, *NANJ*, pp. 289, 290) and contribute towards creating an environment in which the king could return. Nelson had anticipated Acton's suggestion the day before the letter was written, but it is conceivable that Acton's opinion had already reached him through other channels. • **32**. For the siege of St Elmo see documents in *D&L*, 3, pp. 390–405; Troubridge to Nelson, 5, 7 and 13/7/1799, Add. MS 34912; Nelson to Keith, 13/7/1799, ADM 1/400; papers in Add. MS 34911, ff. 295, 298, and Add. MS 34912, ff. 177, 181, 250; return of ordnance captured, 13/7/1799, Add. MS 34963; Acton to Harrison, 17/6/1799, Egerton MS 2640; Ball to Pigot, 1/9/1799, Thomas Joseph Pettigrew, *Memoirs*, 1, p. 393; Willyams, *Voyage*, pp. 205–6. • **33**. Nelson to Keith, 13/7/1799, ADM 1/400. Nelson's suggestion that the Admiralty 'bestow some mark of . . . royal favour' on Troubridge was deleted from the version of the dispatch released to the press, but succeeded nonetheless. Troubridge became a baronet on 20 November: George III to Spencer, 3/9/1799, Add. MS 75829. • **34**. Nelson to Keith, 13/7/1799, ADM 1/400; Troubridge to Nelson, 2 and 7/7/1799, Add. MS 34912; Compton to Emma, 3/7/1799, Pettigrew, *Memoirs*, 1, p. 276; Wade to Nelson, June 1799, Add. MS 34912. Nelson's concern that the British set a good example in the Sicilies is evident in several letters and orders. For instance, he censured the commander of the *Alceste* for raising 'a great outcry' by impressing Sicilian subjects, including some regimental musicians, without the king's permission, and prejudicing goodwill to 'other British ships' (Nelson to Bailey, 7/9/1799, Add. MS 34963). British patrols in the city of Naples continued throughout the summer, and successfully restored order, and the opportunities to misbehave ashore produced relatively few serious misdemeanours. Two seamen of the *Vanguard* were flogged for looting the quarters of a Calabrian officer in the Nuovo, 'to the great disgrace of British seamen' (Nelson to Duckworth, 8/7/1799, and Nelson to Hood, Add. MS 36609; court martial, 9/7/1799, ADM 1/5350) but the most contentious case involved John Jolly, a marine of the *Alexander* doing duty below St Elmo. Becoming intoxicated, he threatened to shoot a lieutenant of his corps and began to 'curse and bugger every man's eyes that came near him'. Jolly was tried on the *Leviathan* on 6 July and sentenced to be executed in the marine encampment ashore. Imprisoned in the *Foudroyant* in the meantime, Jolly wrote two letters to Emma Hamilton, pleading for his life, and Nelson suspended the sentence at the final moment pending the pleasure of his sovereign. In 1800 Jolly was pardoned and returned to his ship with 'such admonitions for his future conduct' as his captain judged 'necessary and proper'. Responsible for the delicate state of public order ashore, Troubridge immediately reproached Nelson for his lenience. 'I wish the mercy shown may have the desired . . . effect; for my own part, I cannot think [so]. Six since my report to your lordship yesterday have got drunk and committed irregularities . . . I fear Ball neglected to give you Jolly's character. He told me so great a villain did not exist in the fleet, [and] that he had long deserved hanging.' Pointedly, he asked how he was to deal with such serious offenders since 'legally we cannot flog them here?' Nelson responded on 9 July with an open declaration that no clemency would be given for further such offences, but Troubridge refused to be palliated. The escape of 'so great a miscreant' had caused 'more discontent among the captains than your lordship can conceive', he said. Going further he warned of 'the known interference of Lady Hamilton, and her talking of it. These things get home and are talked of . . .' For Troubridge, the Jolly case demonstrated Emma's malign influence upon the admiral. See the court martial, 6/7/1799, ADM 1/5350; Nelson to Keith, 14/7/1799, ADM 1/400; Nelson to Troubridge, 6 and 9//7/1799, Add. MSS 36609 and 34963; Nelson to Ormsby, 22/5/1800, ADM 7/55; Troubridge to Nelson, 7/7/1799, 28/12/1799, Add. MSS 34912 and 34915; Jolly to Emma, 6/7/1799, NMM: CRK 22. • **35**. Emma to Greville, 19/7/1799, *HANP*, 2, p. 56; *NC*, 2 (1799), p. 547; Parsons, *Reminiscences*, p. 3. • **36**. Clarke and McArthur, *Life and Services*, 2, pp. 277–8 (Hardy's account); Foote, *Vindication*, p. 44; Parsons, *Reminiscences*, pp. 3–4, which was influenced by Gordon, *Memoirs*, 1, pp. 220–21; Rushout's account, Add. MS 30999, f. 83, perhaps the most embellished; and James Lowry, *Fiddlers and Whores*, p. 45. • **37**. Nelson to Troubridge, 17/7/1799, Add. MS 34963; Hamilton to Smith, 25/7/1799, Add. MS 34912. • **38**. Keith to Nelson, 21–27 and 27/6/1799, Add. MS 34912. • **39**. Nelson to Keith, 13/7/1799, Add. MS 34963; Keith to Nelson, 9/7/1799, with 'intelligence received at Mahon', Add. MS 34912. • **40**. Keith to Nelson, 28/6/1799, ADM 1/400; Nelson to Keith, 19/7/1799, Add. MS 34963; Nelson to Spencer, 19/7/1799, Add. MS 75832. This last letter is misdated in the letterbook, Add. MS 34963. • **41**. Nelson to Nepean, 19/7/1799, ADM 1/400. • **42**. Acton to Nelson, 19/7/1799, NMM: CRK/17; Nelson to Smith, 20/7/1799, Add. MS 34963; Keith to Nelson, 13, 14, 15 and 17/7/1799, ADM 1/400, and 16/7/1799, Add. MS 34912. • **43**. Nelson to Spencer, 23/7/1799, 1–4/8/1799, Add. MSS 75832 and 34963; Keith to St Vincent, 17/7/1799, ADM 1/400. • **44**. Duckworth to Nelson, 27/7/1799, NMM: CRK/4/157. • **45**. Troubridge to Nelson, 22, 25, 26, 27 and 29/7/1799, Add. MS 34912, with an undated letter and a journal of the siege at ff. 386, 466; Nelson to Duckworth, 1/8/1799, and Nelson to Spencer, 6/11/1799, Add. MS 34963; Willyams, *Voyage*, pp. 206–8; 'articles' of surrender, 30/7/1799, ADM 1/400. • **46**. Nelson to Hoste, 25/6/1799, Add. MS 36609; Hoste to Nelson, 8/7/1799, Add. MS 34912; Nelson to Louis, 30/7/1799, 4/8/1799, Add. MS 36609, and Add. MS 34963; Louis to Nelson, 2, 4 and 5/8/1799, 10/11/1799, Add. MSS 34913 and 34914; Hamilton to Grenville, 5/8/1799, FO 70/12; 'return' of ordnance and garrisons, ADM 1/400. • **47**. Petitions of Harriet Parente, Add. MS 34932, ff. 42–4; Troubridge to Nelson, 20/8/1799, 16/9/1799, Add. MS 34913. Different figures have been given. Harold Acton, *Bourbons*, p. 409, states that of 8000 tried in Naples, 544 were sentenced to further imprisonment, 355 exiled and 99 executed. Davis, *Naples*, pp. 93, 121, has two contradictory sets of figures. A pardon of 1803 allowed the banished to return. • **48**. Queen to Emma, undated and 28/7/1799, Pettigrew, *Memoirs*, 1, pp. 267, 272; Maria to Gallo, 17/5/1799, Maurice Weil, *Correspondance Inédite*, 2, p. 92. John Cordy Jeaffreson, *Queen of Naples*, 2, pp. 14, 293–4, argued that the queen was severer in letters likely to be seen by the king, and more merciful in confidential letters to Emma. She implored Emma to assist Count

Belmonte, a minor offender, on account of his brother, Prince Belmonte, a staunch royalist. Nelson accordingly had the count removed to the *Culloden*, perhaps to shield him, and the queen sent her thanks under cover of a letter to Mrs Cadogan. 'You have rescued him [Prince Belmonte] from the tomb,' she wrote. He had wept with gratitude upon reading Nelson's 'compassionate' note. Many petitions to Nelson and Emma are filed in Egerton MSS 1622 and 1623. • **49**. Queen to Emma, 2 and 7/7/1799, Pettigrew, *Memoirs*, 1, pp. 260, 261; Add. MSS 34912, f. 34; Parsons, *Reminiscences*, p. 5. Among others, the Duchess of Sorrentino was said to have benefited from Emma's intercession (Raffaele Palumbo, *Maria Carolina*, pp. lxxxviii, 213). • **50**. Nelson to Cadogan, 17/7/1799, Monmouth MS E448. • **51**. 'List of Jacobins', NMM:GIR/3a; Cirillo to Emma, 3/7/1799, *HANP*, 2, p. 56; Cirillo to Nelson, 14 and 18/7/1799, Add. MS 34912; statement of Nelson, NMM: PHB/P/19; Pietro Colletta, *History*, 1, pp. 383–4. Nor were any representations Nelson might have made in response to the other petition from the *Leviathan* successful, for the father and grown son of that family were also among the executed. • **52**. Nelson to Nepean, 1/8/1799, Add. MS 34963; petition for 'bat and forage money', 24/2/1801, NA: T1/856. Nelson's order book (Add. MS 36609) contains details of appointments. His recognition of those whose duties were essential but mundane rather than eye-catching, or who acted beyond a strict naval remit, was a trait. He strongly recommended Philip Lamb, the agent for transports responsible for the movement of victuals and naval stores, to the Transport Board. 'A more able, sober and zealous officer does not exist in any service,' he wrote. Magra and Spiridion Foresti, Britain's representatives in Tunis and Corfu respectively, were praised as 'the only ones [in the consular service] I have found who really and truly do their duty and merit every encouragement and protection' (Nelson to the Transport Board, 17/10/1799, and Nelson to Nepean, 28/11/1799, ADM 1/400). • **53**. Order of 1/8/1799, Darby's pocket book, Bonham's auction lot, 2005. • **54**. Wyndham to Grenville, 4 and 18/7/1799, FO 79/17; Cockburn to Nelson, 2/8/1799, Add. MS 34913. • **55**. Emma to Greville, 19/7/1799, *HANP*, 2, p. 56; Hamilton to Greville, 4/8/1799, FO 70/12; Thomas A. Hardy, 'Matthew Boulton's Neapolitan Medal'. • **56**. Nepean to Nelson, 20/8/1799, Add. MS 34933; Spencer to Nelson, 4 and 19/8/1799, 7/10/1799, Add. MS 75832; Nelson to Nepean, 20/9/1799, ADM 1/400; Young to Nelson, 17/11/1799, Add. MS 34915. • **57**. Cyrus Redding, *Recollections*, 3, p. 252; Spencer to Nelson, 18/8/1799, NMM:CRK/11. • **58**. Nelson to his captains, 10/3/1799, Add. MS 36609. • **59**. Nelson to his captains, 24/7/1799, Add. MS 34912; John Tyson's notes, 23/7/1799, Add. MS 34912, f. 373; numerous letters of the Locks published in Sermoneta, *Locks*, p. 137 following. • **60**. Pursers to Lock, 29/7/1799, Add. MS 34912. Lock did admit that he wrote 'too warmly' from a sense of disappointment. The captains vindicated their pursers, denying extravagance, and reporting that the receipts indicated that reasonable rates had been paid for provisions, despite the inflation created by the distressed state of the country. For captains' reports, including those of Troubridge and Louis on 27 and 28 July, see Add. MS 34912. On the matter of Ruffo's treaty Lock seems to have been genuinely shocked, but balked at pressing it further. He burned his account of it, but some of his details found their way into the letter he wrote to Thomas Graham, cited above in n. 21. • **61**. Victualling Board to Nelson, 2/9/1799, Add. MS 34933. • **62**. Nelson to Davison, 9/5/1800, Egerton MS 2240; Nelson's critique of Williams, NMM: PHB/P/19, and Add. MS 34991. • **63**. Foote, *Vindication*, pp. 17, 31, 39, 66. Marianne Czisnik, 'Nelson at Naples: The Development of a Story', is an excellent review of the controversy. • **64**. Nelson to Clarence, 10/5/1801, Add. MS 46356. • **65**. Acton, *Bourbons*, p. 431.

IX Duke of Bronte

1. Lady Minto to Malmesbury, 6/7/1800, Countess of Minto, *Elliot*, 3, p. 138; Hamilton to Grenville, 17/8/1799, Add. MS 37077; Nelson's letters to Keith and Nepean, 5/8/1799, ADM 1/400. • **2**. Troubridge to Nelson, 16/9/1799, Add. MS 34913; Hamilton to Acton, 1/11/1799, NMM: HML/21; Add. MS 37077, f. 134; Hamilton to Grenville, 19/12/1799, FO 70/12; Paget to Grenville, 13/5/1800, Augustus B. Paget, *Paget Papers*, 1, p. 207. • **3**. Cornelia Knight, *Autobiography*, 2, p. 288; Hamilton to Grenville, 17/8/1799, and Hamilton to Greville, 22/9/1799, FO/12; Nelson to Nepean, 24/9/1799, with enclosure, ADM 1/400; Nelson to Duckworth, 16/8/1799, Add. MS 34963; 'The Lost Sword', *ND*, 3 (1990), pp. 214–15. • **4**. Nelson to Luzzi, 15/8/1799, ADM 1/400. For this subject see Jane Knight, 'Nelson and the Bronte Estate', and Michael Pratt, *Nelson's Duchy*. • **5**. Castelcicala to Grenville, 30/12/1800, FO 70/14; Nelson to Edmund, 15/8/1799, Sotheby's lot, 2005; Edmund to Susannah, 29/10/1799, and Nelson to William, 21/8/1799, Add. MS 34988. • **6**. Nelson to Davison, 15/8/1799, Egerton MS 2240; Nelson to Fanny, 15/12/1799, Monmouth MS E971. • **7**. Graefer to Nelson, 21/11/1799, 4, 11 and 12/12/1799, NMM: CRK/17. • **8**. Davison to Nelson, 6/4/1799, Add. MS 34910; Nelson to Davison, 15/8/1799, Egerton MS 2240. Davison supplied silver medals to all participating lieutenants, and copper gilt and copper bronze medals to lower ranks and ratings. The medals described Nelson as 'Europe's Hope and Britain's Glory', and displayed his portrait, supported by a bare-breasted Britannia representing Hope. These were the first officially endorsed service medals to be struck by a private individual. They were much prized by recipients, who sometimes had their medals engraved with their names and those of the ships in which they had served. Davison also sent medals to Ferdinand of Naples, Paul of Russia and the Grand Vizier: Grenville to Whitworth, 27/8/1799, FO 65/44. • **9**. Hamilton to Grenville, 8/11/1799, FO 70/12; Nelson to Nepean, 28 November 1799, ADM 1/400; Ali Pasha to Nelson, January 1800, Add. MS 34916; Smith to Nelson, 8 and 9/9/1799, Add. MS 34913. In March 1800 Nelson was introducing himself as 'Horatio, Lord Nelson of the Nile, K.B., Duke of Bronte in Sicily, First Knight of the Imperial Order of the Crescent . . .' (order, 21/3/1800, Add. MS 36609). • **10**. Emma to Minto, 3/3/1800, *NLTHW*, p. 522; George S. Parsons, *Reminiscences*, pp. 9, 128; Pryse Lockhart Gordon, *Memoirs*, 1, p. 223, and 2, p. 388; Hamilton to Trabia, 28/9/1799, Warren R. Dawson, *Nelson Collection*, p. 151. • **11**. Gordon, *Memoirs*, 1, p. 223; Add. MS 34907, f. 225; Maurice Nelson to Nelson, 10/11/1799, Add. MS 34988; Lock to his father, 9/8/1799, Duchess of Sermoneta, *Locks*, p. 178; Roger de Damas, *Memoirs*, p. 278; Knight, *Autobiography*, 2, p. 290; and Parsons, *Reminiscences*, pp. 9–13, who misdates the event. Regarding the Russo-Turkish squadron, thirteen Russian and nine Turkish ships arrived at Messina on 14 August: *Raccolti di Notizie* (Palermo), 25/8/1799, FO 70/12. • **12**. Richard Walker, *Nelson Portraits*, ch. 4; James to Nelson, 29/9/1799, Add. MS 34914. • **13**. Keith to Nelson, 24/7/1799, ADM 1/400. Officially, Keith remained acting commander-in-chief of the Mediterranean after he left the Mediterranean. On 15 November he was appointed commander-in-chief, and returning to Gibraltar on 6 December effectively ended Nelson's unofficial role as acting commander of the theatre. • **14**. Nepean to Nelson, 20/8/1799, Add. MSS 34933. • **15**. Nelson to Duckworth, 20/8/1799 (two letters), ADM 1/400, and Add. MS 36609; Duckworth to Nelson, 1/9/1799, Add. MS 34913; Nelson to Foley, 4/9/1799, Add. MS 36609; Nelson to Nepean, 17/8/1799, with enclosure, Add. MS 34963; Wyndham to Grenville, 9/8/1799, FO 79/17. • **16**. Hamilton to Grenville, 7/9/1799, and Hamilton to Greville, 22/9/1799, FO 70/12. • **17**. Duckworth to Nelson, 30/8/1799, Martin to Nelson, 31/8/1799, and Nelson to Smith, 10/9/1799, Add. MS 34913; Smith to Nelson, 20/10/1799, Add. MS 34914; Sermoneta, *Locks*, p. 178; Hamilton to

Grenville, 22/9/1799, with enclosures, FO 70/12. • **18**. Nelson to Spencer, 6/9/1799, and Nelson to Drummond, 19 and 29/8/1799, Add. MSS 34913; Nelson to Elgin, Thomas J. Pettigrew, *Memoirs*, 1, p. 362; Nelson to Italinsky, 28/8/1799, Add. MS 34963; Norman Saul, *Russia*, pp. 115–25. The *Leander* was finally handed over to the British *Chichester* at Corfu in December 1799. • **19**. Minto, *Elliot*, 3, pp. 93–6; Wyndham to Grenville, 3, 8 and 27/9/1799, 12/10/1799, FO 79/17; Hamilton to Erskine, 29/2/1799, Add. MS 37077; Paget, *Paget Papers*, 1, p. 207. • **20**. Acton to Nelson, 19/7/1799, 21/8/1799 [my italics], NMM: CRK/1 and 17. • **21**. Hamilton to Grenville, 7/9/1799, FO 70/12. • **22**. Correspondence between Hallowell and Belair, 24 and 25/8/1799, Add. MS 34945; Hallowell to Nelson, 24–25/8/1799, and Erskine to Nelson, 5/9/1799, Add. MS 34913; Troubridge to Nelson, 26/8/1799, 12 and 22/9/1799, Add. MSS 34913 and 34914. • **23**. Troubridge to Nelson, 28/8/1799, 11/9/1799, Add. MS 34913; Hamilton to Grenville, 24/8/1799, 7/9/1799, FO 70/12; Acton to Nelson, 25/8/1799, NMM: CRK/1; Nelson to Troubridge, 7/9/1799, Add. MS 34963. • **24**. Louis to Troubridge, 17/9/1799, Add. MS 34913; Troubridge to Nelson, 27 and 29/9/1799, and Acton to Nelson, 6/10/1799, Add. MS 34914; Wyndham to Grenville, 12/10/1799, FO 79/17; Harriet Hoste, *Hoste*, 1, p. 114; *London Gazette*, 16/11/1799; *D&L*, 4, p. 259; Add. MS 34990, f. 70; *Culloden* log, ADM 51/1294. • **25**. Hamilton to Grenville, 14/10/1799, FO 70/12; Troubridge to Nelson, 30/9/1799, 8/10/1799, and Acton to Nelson, 1/10/1799, Add. MS 34914; Acton to Hamilton, 15/10/1799, Egerton MS 2640; Nelson to Bayley, 2/10/1799, Add. MS 36609; Nelson to Troubridge, 1/10/1799, Add. MS 34963; Minto, *Elliot*, 3, p. 101. • **26**. *NC*, 3 (1800), p. 145; Sagar to Nelson, NMM: CRK 22/63; Troubridge to Nelson, 20/12/1799, Add. MSS 34915; Hamilton to Nelson, 16/10/1799, Add. MS 34913; Acton to Nelson, 16/11/1799, 7/6/1800, Add. MS 34915 and NMM: CRK/1; Nelson to Acton, 26/11/1799, Add. MS 34963. • **27**. Wyndham to Grenville, 9/8/1799, FO 79/17; Duckworth to Nelson, 30/8/1799, and Martin to Nelson, 31/8/1799, Add. MSS 34913. • **28**. Among many documents see Ball to Hamilton, 22/3/1800, NMM: HML/2; Ball to Nelson, 17/7/1799, 28/8/1799, 15/9/1799, 2 and 23/10/1799 and 7 and 11/11/1799, Add. MSS 34912, 34913 and 34914; Nelson to Nepean, 3/11/1799, ADM 1/400; Nelson to Hamilton, 14/1/1800, Monmouth MS E87; Acton to Hamilton, 1/9/1799, 21/1/1800, Egerton MSS 2640; Acton to Nelson, 27/11/1799, Add. MSS 34915; Hamilton to Acton, 30/1/1800, NMM: HML/21; Hamilton to Grenville, 6/12/1799, 17/1/1800, FO 70/12, FO 70/13. • **29**. Nelson to Smith, 20/8/1799, Add. MS 34913. The explosion on the *Theseus* also wounded Lieutenant James Summers and killed Major Thomas Oldfield of the Royal Marines, both former officers of Nelson: casualty list enclosed by Smith, 30/5/1799, ADM 1/399. Nelson felt for Miller. While Berry thought 'a plain monument' acceptable, Nelson wanted a more extended subscription to raise £500 to place a sculpture by John Flaxman in St Paul's Cathedral: Nelson to Saumarez, c. January 1801, Sotheby's lot, 2005. • **30**. Louis to Nelson, 16/12/1799, Add. MS 34915. • **31**. Nelson to Spencer, 21 September 1799, Pettigrew, *Memoirs*, 1, p. 281; Nelson to Davison, September 1799, Egerton MS 2240. • **32**. Jackson to Grenville, 28/9/1799, FO 67/68; Nelson to Long, 17/10/1799, and Nelson to Blackwood, 9/11/1799, Add. MS 36609; Nelson to Niza, 3/10/1799, 24/11/1799, Nelson to Troubridge, 1/10/1799, and Nelson to Acton, 2/10/1799, Add. MS 34963; Ball to Nelson, 7/11/1799, 10 and 11/12/1799, Add. MS 34914 and 34915; St Vincent to Souza Continho, 5/3/1799, ADM 1/399. • **33**. Ball to Nelson, 17/7/1799, 20/8/1799, 3/9/1799, Add. MSS 34912 and 34913; Graham to Nelson, 3/9/1799, Add. MS 34913; Hamilton to Grenville, 14/10/1799, FO 70/12. • **34**. Nelson to Erskine, 17/9/1799, 11/10/1799, Nelson to Troubridge, 16/9/1799, and Nelson to Graham, 3/10/1799, Add. MS 34963; Erskine to Nelson, 31/10/1799, Add. MS 34914; Dundas to Fox, 17/9/1799, Warren R. Dawson, *Nelson Collection*, p. 149. • **35**. Nelson to Troubridge, 1/10/1799, Add. MS 34963; Nelson to Nepean, 15/10/1799, ADM 1/400. • **36**.

Countess Elgin to her mother, 4 and 5/10/1799, Nisbet Hamilton Grant, *Letters*, pp. 21, 23. • **37**. Nelson to Spencer,15/10/1799, Add. MS 34963; Troubridge to Nelson, 30/9/1800, Add. MS 34917. Parsons, *Reminiscences*, pp. 15–16, 23, spoke of the indiscipline on board the *Foudroyant* under Berry's custody, and of his indecision in action. As for shipboard discipline, the logs of the *Vanguard* and *Foudroyant*, ADM 51/1288 and 1279, show that Hardy ordered about 129 floggings between 1 January and 12 October 1799. The common sentences were for 24 or 36 lashes, although twice thieves were compelled to run the gauntlet, a more unorthodox punishment. This was almost four times the rate of punishment under Berry between 12 October 1799 and 29 June 1800 (*Foudroyant* log, ADM 51/1330). Both captains inflicted mass punishments. On 9 October 1799 Hardy administered a total of 288 strokes to ten men, and on 22 March 1800 Berry punished eight men with a total of 252 strokes. Neglect of duty, disobedience, absenteeism, sleeping on duty, fighting, drunkenness and theft were the usual offences. The different levels of punishment could suggest that Berry had better discipline than Hardy and needed to administer fewer punishments; but contemporaries gave Hardy a reputation for severity – Lieutenant John Yule thought him cruel – and credited him with producing a more orderly ship. • **38**. Nelson to *Duckworth*, 14/10/1799, Add. MS 34963. • **39**. Nelson to Nepean, 10/11/1799, ADM 1/400; Nelson to Hamilton, 13/10/1799, WLC; Hamilton to Grenville, 12/11/1799, FO 70/12. • **40**. Nelson to Hamilton, 13/10/1799, WLC; Erskine to Nelson, 11/11/1799, and Erskine to Dundas, 16/10/1799, Add. MS 34914. With regard to the withdrawal of forces from Minorca, Nepean had directed Nelson to facilitate the return of the 28th Regiment on 10 October but the letter had not yet reached him: Nepean to Nelson, 10/10/1799, Add. MS 34933. • **41**. Ball to Nelson, 20/8/1799, Add. MS 34913; Nelson to Berry, 28/10/1799, Add. MS 36609. • **42**. Blackwood to Nelson, 17/11/1799, Add. MS 34915; Duckworth to Nelson, 4/12/1799, NMM: CRK/4; and several documents in ADM 1/400: Cockburn to Keith, 2/3/1800, Blackwood to Duckworth, 21/10/1799, Nelson to Nepean, 7/12/1799, and the list of prizes filed with Duckworth to Nepean, 6/12/1799. • **43**. Nelson to Nepean, 9/11/1799, ADM 1/400; Hamilton to Minto, 22/9/1799, *NLTHW*, p. 514; Nelson to Minto, 24/10/1799, Add. MS 34963. • **44**. Countess Elgin to her mother, 4–6/10/1799, Grant, *Letters*, p. 21; Hamilton to Minto, 3/3/1800, *NLTHW*, p. 521; Hamilton to Greville, 4/8/1799, FO 70/12. • **45**. *The Times*, 14 and 28/11/1799; *Morning Chronicle*, 7/12/1799; Kennett to Hamond, 22/11/1799, Hamond (Westgate) Papers, Norwich Record Office; Brian Connell, *Whig Peer*, p. 417; Grant, *Letters*, pp. 21, 25–6. • **46**. Harold Acton, *Bourbons*, pp. 184–5; James Lowry, *Fiddlers and Whores*, pp. 118–19, 124, 126. • **47**. Troubridge to Nelson, 22/12/1799, Add. MS 34963; Hamilton to Grenville, 4/7/1800, Add. MS 37077. • **48**. John Sugden, *Nelson*, p. 848, prematurely dismissed the *Times* testimony. • **49**. Nelson codicil, 6/3/1801, *HANP*, 2, p. 125; Hamilton to Grenville, 4/1/1800, FO 70/13; Troubridge to McDonald, 17/4/1799, Add. MS 34910; Sermoneta, *Locks*, p. 191; Minto, *Elliot*, 3, p. 138. • **50**. Hamilton to Greville, 4/8/1799, FO 70/12; Nelson to Berry, 7/2/1800, Add. MS 34916. • **51**. Countess de Boigne, *Memoirs*, p. 101. • **52**. Duckworth to Nelson, 17/6/1800, Pettigrew, *Memoirs*, 1, p. 367; Paget to Grenville, 13/5/1800, Paget, *Paget Papers*, 1, p. 217; Minto to Malmesbury, 6/7/1800, Minto, *Elliott*, 3, p. 138; Prince Augustus Frederich, Duke of Sussex, to his equerry, 24/12/1799, *ND*, 6 (1997), p. 40. • **53**. Iain Gordon Brown, 'Henry Aston Barker', pp. 707–8. • **54**. Troubridge to Nelson, 15 and 28/12/1799, Add. MS 34915; Troubridge to Emma, 14/1/1800, Pettigrew, *Memoirs*, 1, p. 339. • **55**. Nelson to Paul I, 31/10/1799, and Nelson to Italinsky, 24/10/1799, Add. MS 34963; Hamilton to Grenville, 25/10/1799, FO 70/12; Ushakov to Nelson, 4/11/1799, Add. MS 34946. • **56**. Nelson to Erskine, 26/10/1799, 12/11/1799, ADM 1/400; Nelson to Clarence, 9/11/1799, Add. MS 46356; Nelson to Spencer, 6/11/1799, Add. MS 34963. • **57**. O'Hara to Nelson, 3/11/1799, Fox to Nelson,

12/11/1799 and Stewart to Graham, 12/11/1799, Add. MS 34914; Fox to Dundas, 12/11/1799, and Graham to Fox, 4 and 10/12/1799, WO 1/291; Duckworth to Nelson, 12/11/1799, NMM: CRK/4; Nelson to Nepean, 14/12/1799, ADM 1/400. • **58**. Nelson to Troubridge, 25/11/1799, and Nelson to Weir, 6/12/1799, Add. MS 36609; Nelson to Troubridge, 28/11/1799, Add. MS 34963; Nelson to Fox, 25/11/1799, WO 1/291. With his usual scepticism, Troubridge dissented from Nelson's view of Italinsky, describing him as 'an artful, cunning designing fellow' (Troubridge to Nelson, undated, c. 1800, Add. MS 34917). • **59**. Nelson to Spencer, 28/11/1799, Add. MS 34963; Nelson to Nepean, 2/12/1800, ADM 1/400. Nelson took a pessimistic view of Fox's orders, which actually referred to extraordinary rather than conventional expenses. Fox had decreed that the army was responsible for 'such [expenses] as shall be in your judgement necessary for the subsistence, comfort and health of your troops'. Nelson must provide 'stores and supplies . . . their subsistence excepted': Fox to Graham, 12/11/1799, and Fox to Nelson, 12/11/1799, WO 1/291. • **60**. Graham to Fox, 10 and 28/12/1799, Lindenthal to Fox, 10, 28 and 31/12/1799, and Fox to Nelson, 28/12/1799, WO 1/291. • **61**. Ball to Nelson, 10/12/1799, Troubridge to Nelson, 4 and 9/12/1799, and Martin to Nelson, 20/12/1799, Add. MS 34915; Nelson to Fox, 14/12/1799, WO 1/291. • **62**. Wyndham to Nelson, 30/11/1799, WO 1/291; Nelson to Wyndham, 13/12/1799, and Wyndham to Grenville, 10/1/1800, FO 79/18. The Austrians generals involved in the overtures to Nelson were Johann von Klenau, Leopold Comte Palfy and Peter Carl Ott.

X 'Come Back to Your Family Here'

1. Troubridge to Hamilton, 7/2/1800, Egerton MS 2638. • **2**. Troubridge to Nelson, 15/12/1799, Add. MS 34915; Nelson to Nepean, 23/12/1799, ADM 1/400; Mike K. Barritt, 'Hydrographic Surveying and Charting'. • **3**. Nelson to Troubridge, 29/12/1799, Add. MS 34963; Ball to Nelson, 18/11/1799, Add. MS 34915; Troubridge to Nelson, 14/1/1800, 10 and 13/4/1800, Add. MSS 34916 and 34917; Ball to Emma, 17/10/1799, NMM: CRK/20. • **4**. Troubridge to Hamilton, 11/3/1800, Egerton MS 2638; Troubridge to Nelson, 22 and 28/12/1799, 31/12/1799-1/1/1800, 7/1/1800, Add. MSS 34915 and 34916. • **5**. 'Nelson's Second Visit to Naples', *United Services Magazine*, 1845, part 2, p. 328; Troubridge to Nelson, 23/12/1799, Add. MS 34915. • **6**. Troubridge to Nelson, 23/12/1799, 2 and 5/1/1800, Add. MSS 34915 and 34916; Troubridge to Hamilton, 6/2/1800, Egerton MS 2638; Ball to Nelson, 21/12/1799, Add. MS 34915; Graham to Fox, 4/12/1799, WO 1/291. • **7**. Troubridge to Nelson, 5, 6, 7 and 8/1/1800, Add. MS 34916. • **8**. Nelson to Troubridge, 7, 8 and 14/1/1800, 28/3/1800, *D&L*, 4, pp. 168, 172, 176, 211; Nelson to Hamilton, 10/1/1800, *Letters*, 2, p. 254; Graham to Fox, 12/1/1800, WO 1/291. • **9**. Hamilton to Grenville, 17/1/1800, Add. MS 37077; Graham to Keith, 12–25/1/1800, WO 1/291. • **10**. Troubridge to Emma, 14/1/1800, Thomas J. Pettigrew, *Memoirs*, 1, p. 339; Troubridge to Nelson, 9/1/1800, Add. MS 34916; Nelson to Acton, 21/4/1800, Zabriskie Collection, US Naval Academy. • **11**. Ball to Macauley, 22/3/1800, Pettigrew, *Memoirs*, 1, p. 341; Ball to Nelson, 25/3/1800, James Stanier Clarke and John McArthur, *Life and Services*, 2, p. 328. • **12**. Nelson to Nepean, 16/1/1800, and Graham to Hamilton, 22/1/1800, ADM 1/401; Hamilton to Grenville, 16/1/1800, FO 70/13; Graham to Keith, 12–25/1/1800, WO 1/291. • **13**. Nelson to Fox, 7/1/1800, Add. MS 34963; Villettes to Nelson, 27/11/1799, 16/4/1800, Add. MSS 34915 and 34917; Smith to Nelson, 8/9/1799, Add. MS 34913; Villettes to Erskine, 17/12/1799, WO 1/298; Ball to Fox, 15/12/1799, WO 1/291. • **14**. Nelson to Spencer, 23/1/1800, WLC; Nelson to Keith, 7/1/1800, Add. MS 34963. • **15**. Nepean to Nelson, 11 and 16/10/1799, 13/12/1799, Add. MS 34933; Nelson to Long, 8/1/1800, Add. MS 36609; Nelson to Spencer, 21/1/1800, Add. MS 34963. • **16**. Nelson to Fanny, 7/11/1799, Monmouth MS E970; Nelson to Minto, 6/4/1800, *D&L*, 4, p. 221; Nelson to Davison, 15/8/1799, 12/3/1800, Egerton MS 2240. • **17**. Brown to Nelson, 2/2/1803, NMM: CRK/2; Brown's register, Add. MS 36613. • **18**. Suvorov to Nelson, 12/1/1800 [my italics], *Athenaeum*, 1 (1876), p. 396; Goodall to Nelson, 15/11/1799, Add. MS 34914; Martyn Downer, *Nelson's Purse*, p. 145. Goodall referred to the story of the knight, Rinaldo, who was lured into a magic garden by a Saracen princess. • **19**. Nelson to Victualling Board, 14/11/1799, Add. MS 34914. • **20**. Lock to Nelson, 30/11/1799, and Lock to Tyson, 2/12/1799, Add. MS 34915; Duchess of Sermoneta, *Locks*, pp. 188–90; *D&L*, 4, pp. 127–8; Hamilton to Nelson, 26/2/1799, Add. MS 34916. • **21**. Victualling Board to Nelson, 20/12/1799, Add. MS 34933; Hardy to Nelson, 12/1/1800, Add. MS 34916. Hardy called on the Victualling Board in London, and found them astonished at suggestions that they would have corresponded with Lock. • **22**. Lock to Nelson, 3/12/1799, Add. MS 34933; Nelson to Lock, 4 December 1799, Add. MS 34963. • **23**. Nelson to Victualling Board, 5/12/1799, Add. MS 34963. • **24**. Victualling Board to Nelson, 13/2/1800, Add. MS 34934; Sermoneta, *Locks*, 198. • **25**. Louis to Nelson, 29/12/1799, Add. MS 34915. • **26**. Keith to Nelson, 14/12/1799, 7/1/1800, Add. MSS 34915 and 34916; Keith to Spencer, 25/1/1800, Add. MS 75840. • **27**. Hoste to his parents, 7/3/1800, 21/5/1802, Harriet Hoste, *Hoste*, 1, pp. 136, 169. • **28**. Nelson to Emma, 29/1–2/2/1800, *ND*, 3 (1989) p. 133. • **29**. Nelson to Emma, 3/2/1800, NMM: CRK/19. • **30**. Grenville to Spencer, 24/12/1799, Add. MS 75829; Hamilton to Nelson, 7/2/1800, Add. MS 34916. • **31**. Jack Russell, *Nelson and the Hamiltons*, p. 110; Acton to Hamilton, 4 and 13/2/1800, Egerton MS 2640; Acton to Grenville, 11/2/1800, Add. MS 37077. • **32**. Thomas Cochrane and George Butler Earp, *Autobiography*, 1, pp. 88–9. • **33**. Keith to Nepean, 6 and 9/2/1800, and Keith to Ponda de Lina, 6/2/1800, ADM 1/401; Keith to Dundas, 9/2/1800, WO 1/291; Hamilton to Grenville, 11/2/1800, Add. MS 37077. • **34**. Nelson to Emma, 17/2/1801, *HANP*, 2, p. 115; Pettigrew, *Memoirs*, 1, p. 305; Nelson to Emma, 13/2/1800, Pettigrew, *Memoirs*, 1, p. 299. • **35**. Diary extract, Egerton MS 1614. • **36**. Blackwood to Nelson, December 1799, Add. MS 34915; Keith to Nepean, 20 and 21/2/1800, ADM 1/401. • **37**. Keith to Nepean, 15 and 20/2/1800, and Ball to Dixon, 14/2/1800, ADM 1/401; account of Andrew Thompson of the *Foudroyant*, 27/2/1800, FO 70/13. • **38**. Keith to Spencer, 22/2/1800, Add. MS 75840; *Alexander* log, ADM 51/1362; Mark West, 'Capture of the Généreux.' • **39**. George S. Parsons, *Reminiscences*, pp. 7–9. • **40**. Nelson's diary, Egerton MSS 1614. • **41**. Keith to Spencer, 6/3/1800, Add. MS 75840; Keith to Dundas, 19/2/1800, WO 1/291; Tyson to Hamilton, 22/2/1800, Add. MS 42069; losses enclosed with Keith to Nepean, 21/2/1800, ADM 1/401. Ball claimed that the two prizes carried fifteen hundred French troops, which would have made the total haul of prisoners even higher: Ball to Lucas, 4/2/1800, Bonham's lot, 2005. • **42**. Nelson to Keith, 18/2/1800, ADM 1/401; Nelson to Minto, 26/2/1800, *D&L*, 4, p. 193; Keith to Nelson, undated, Add. MS 34932. • **43**. Nelson to Martin, 7/3/1800, Add. MS, 36609; Troubridge to Nelson, 16/3/1800, Add. MS 34916; Nelson Journal, 19–20/2/1800, NMM: CRK/14; Nelson to Emma, 20/2/1800, NMM: CRK/19; Keith to Spencer, 20/2/1800, Add. MS 75840; Martin to Nelson, 5/3/1800, Wellcome Library, MS 3680. Troubridge was not impressed with Cochrane. 'Lord Keith passed the Faro in the night with a hard southerly gale,' he wrote. 'I feel for [damaged] *Genereux*. The Honble. Cockrane [sic] seemed a thick-headed fellow. If she has not a short passage, I begin to think they will contrive to lose her' (Troubridge to Nelson, 18/3/1800, Add. MS 34916). The voyage of *Généreux* did indeed suffer 'a very stormy passage' and 'the most severe gale' that John Tyson, who accompanied her as Nelson's local prize agent, remembered: Tyson to Nelson, 21/3/1800, Add. MS 34917. For a fuller account see John Sugden, 'Lord Cochrane', pp. 50–51. • **44**. Ball to Emma, 27/2/1800, 10/3/1800, Pettigrew, *Memoirs*, 1, pp. 330, 338. • **45**. Keith to Nepean,

20/2/1800, *D&L*, 4, p. 187; Nelson to Maurice, February 1800, *D&L*, 4, p. 101. • **46**. Keith to Spencer, 20/2/1800, Add. MS 78540; Keith to Fox, 5 and 20/2/1800, WO 1/291; Fox to Keith, 17 and 19/3/1800, WO 1/291; Graham to Hamilton, 19/5/1800, William Hardman, *Malta*, p. 295. • **47**. Nelson to Keith, 24/2/1800, Add. MS 34963; Keith to Nelson, 24/2/1800, 20/3/1800, Add. MS 34916. • **48**. Ball to Emma, 27/2/1800, Pettigrew, *Memoirs*, 1, p. 330; Hamilton to Nelson, 7/2/1800, Add. MS 34916. Nelson bestowed Ball's decoration, a large Maltese cross, during a dinner on the *Foudroyant*. Emma proudly wore her smaller cross, and was later granted a coat of arms by the College of Arms in London on 19 November 1806: *ND*, 7 (2002), pp. 660–61. • **49**. Nelson to Keith, 28/2/1800, 20/3/1800, Add. MS 34963; Nelson to Foresti, 28/3/1800, *D&L*, 4, p. 213. • **50**. Troubridge to Nelson, 24/2/1800, 8/8/1800, *D&L*, 4, p. 195, and Add. MS 34917. • **51**. Nelson's journal, 26/2/1800–8/3/1800, NMM: KEI/18/4; Ball to Macauley, 22/3/1800, Pettigrew, *Memoirs*, 1, p. 341; Ball to Nelson, 22/3/1800, Add. MS 34917; Graham to Keith, 24/5/1800, Christopher Lloyd, *Keith Papers*, 2, p. 171; Graham to Nelson, 3/3/1800, Add. MS 34916; Tyson to Hamilton, 22/2/1800, Add. MS 42069. • **52**. Ball to Nelson, 27/2/1800, 5/3/1800, Add. MS 34916; Nelson to Keith, 10/3/1800, NMM: KEI/18/4. • **53**. Nelson to Troubridge, 10 and 20/3/1800, Add. MSS 36609 and 34963; Troubridge to Hamilton, 31/3/1800, Egerton MS 2638; Troubridge to Nelson, 21 and 22/2/1800, 21/3/1800, Add. MSS 34916 and 34917; Nelson to Emma, 4/3/1800, Egerton MS 1614; Nelson to Hamilton, 8/3/1800, NMM: CRK/14; Keith to Nepean, 24/3/1800, ADM 1/401; *Foudroyant* log, ADM 51/1330. • **54**. Hamilton to Nelson, 26 and 27/2/1800, Add. MS 34916. • **55**. Nelson to Spencer, 29/11/1799, Add. MS 34963. • **56**. Troubridge to Nelson, 29/3/1800, 7/4/1800, Add. MS 34917, and 1/4/1800, ADM 1/401; Blackwood to Nelson, 31/3/1800, Add. MS 34917; Dixon to Troubridge, 31/3/1800, 7/4/1800, Add. MS 34917; log of *Foudroyant*, ADM 51/1330; Berry to Hamilton, 31/3/1800, Warren R. Dawson, *Nelson Collection*, p. 156; Berry to Nelson, 30/3/1800, ADM 1/400; Nelson to Spencer, 8/4/1800, Add. MS 34963; Nelson to Berry, 5/4/1800, Add. MS 34917; Nelson to Keith, 8/4/1800, ADM 1/401; Ball to Troubridge, 16/3/1800, Add. MS 34916; Wyndham to Grenville, 24/4/1800, FO 79/18; *NC*, 4 (1801), p. 253. • **57**. Nelson to Blackwood, 5/4/1800, NMM: CRK/7; Blackwood to Nelson, 4/1/[1799]1800, *HANP*, 2, p. 33. See Leslie H. Bennett, *Nelson's Eyes*, for a sound biography of Blackwood. • **58**. Parsons, *Reminiscences*, pp. 26–7. • **59**. Nelson to Nepean, 4/4/1800, ADM 1/401. On 24 August the remaining Nile frigates tried to escape from Valletta, and the *Diane* was captured. The *Justice* alone reached Toulon. • **60**. Minto to his wife, 28/3/1800, Countess of Minto, *Elliot*, 3, p. 113. • **61**. Spencer to Nelson, 30/3/1800, 25/4/1800, Add. MS 34917. • **62**. Nelson to Keith, 3/4/1800, NMM: KEI/18/4. • **63**. Spencer to Keith, 9/5/1800, Add. MS 75840; Spencer to Nelson, 9/5/1800, Add. MS 34917; Nelson to Spencer, 20/6/1800, Add. MS 75841. • **64**. Paget to Grenville, 13/5/1800, 4/7/1800, Augustus B. Paget, *Paget Papers*, 1, pp. 217, 246; Keith to Spencer, 6/5/1800, Add. MS 75840; Keith to Nelson, 27/2/1800, Add. MS 34916; Sermoneta, *Locks*, p. 198; Hamilton to Acton, 15 and 16/4/1800, Egerton MS 2640; queen to Emma, undated, transcript in Egerton MS 1620, f. 169. • **65**. Nelson to Berry, 21/3/1800, Add. MS 36609; Acton to Hamilton, 4/5/1800, Egerton MS 2640; Cornelia Knight, *Autobiography*, 1, p. 146. At one time Nelson fretted that Berry would not get to Palermo to collect him. Troubridge assured him that Berry would not be allowed to malinger: 'do not listen to the damned crying of the thing [Berry]. I will get her [the *Foudroyant*] up for you . . .': Troubridge to Nelson, 13/4/1800, Add. MS 34917. • **66**. Nelson to Emma, 26/1/1801, *HANP*, 2, p. 109; Knight sketchbook, Bonham's lot, 2010. • **67**. Ball to Emma, 19/5/1800, Pettigrew, *Memoirs*, 1, p. 372; Ball to Nelson, 22/3/1800 and March 1800, and Troubridge to Nelson, 1 and 7/4/1800, Add. MS 34917. • **68**. Nelson to Keith, 23/4/1800, 10 and 19/5/1800, NMM: KEI/18/4; Villeneuve to Minister of Marine and Colonies,

14/6/1800, William Hardman, *Malta*, p. 301; Keith to Nepean, 7/5/1800, ADM 1/402; Keith to Paget, 16/7/1800, Paget, *Paget Papers*, 1, p. 252; Nelson to Paul I, 4/9/1800, NMM: CRK/14. • **69**. Keith to Nelson, 6/5/1800, 3, 5 and 6/6/1800, Add. MS 34917; Keith to Spencer, 5/6/1800, 13/7/1800, Add. MS 75840; Nelson to Acton, 9/5/1800, Zabriskie Collection, US Naval Academy. • **70**. Nelson to Acton, 2/6/1800, Add. MS 34963. • **71**. Nelson to Keith, 6/6/1800, Add. MS 34963; queen to Emma, undated, transcript, Egerton MS 1620, f. 171; Nelson to Spencer, 20/6/1800, Add. MS 75841. • **72**. Queen to Emma, undated, and Troubridge to Emma, 30/3/1800, Pettigrew, *Memoirs*, 1, pp. 343, 374; Acton to Nelson, 7 and 8/6/1800, NMM: CRK/1, and Add. MS 34917. • **73**. Acton to Nelson, 4/7/1800, NMM: CRK/1. • **74**. Blackwood to Nelson, 15/4/1800, Foresti to Nelson, 16/4/1800, Hoste to Nelson, 26/4/1800, Troubridge to Nelson, 8/8/1800, and Tough to Nelson, 9/6/1800, Add. MS 34917; Nelson to Foresti, 29/10/1799, and Nelson to Keith, 3/6/1800, Add. MS 34963; Collier to Nelson, 28/10/1800, NMM: CRK/3; the Comptons to Nelson, 9/12/1799, Add. MSS 34915. • **75**. Nelson to Keith, 10/8/1799, Add. MS 34963; Nelson to Berry, 8/4/1800, Add. MS 34917; barge crew to Nelson, 26/6/1800, Add. MS 34917. • **76**. Hamilton to Grenville, 4/7/1800, Add. MS 37077.

XI 'A Weak Man in Bad Hands'

1. *Foudroyant* and *Alexander* logs, respectively filed in ADM 51/1330 and 1362; queen to Gallo, 15/6/1800, Maurice Weil, *Correspondance Inédite*, 2, p. 159. • **2**. Suzanne d'Huart, *Journal de Marie-Amelie*, pp. 28–9; Nelson to Spencer, 17/6/1800, Add. MS 34963; Hamilton to Keith, 16/6/1800, NMM: KEI/18/4; Parsons, *Reminiscences*, p. 30; Wyndham to Grenville, 21/6/1800, FO 79/18. The first chapter of Cornelia Knight's *Autobiography* and volume two of James Harrison's *Life*, which cross-checks reasonably well with the other sources on this subject, are useful for the present chapter throughout. The letter that Maria Carolina and her four children sent to Nelson can be seen in NMM: CRK/3. The children, aged between twenty-one and ten, were Christina (known as Mimi), Amelie, Antoinette and Leopold. • **3**. D'Huart, *Journal*, pp. 29–30. • **4**. *ND*, 4 (1994), p. 21; D'Huart, *Journal*, p. 30. The sword, a present of the 'Egyptian Club' founded to commemorate the Nile, had been shipped to the Mediterranean by the manufacturers, Rundell and Bridge of London. According to Princess Amelie the captains had 'contributed 80 guineas apiece, two thirds of which was for widows and children of the dead, and the remainder for this sword'. It was engraved on the guard with the names of the Aboukir brotherhood, but was stolen from Greenwich in 1900 and never recovered. A sword and a dirk, commemorative pieces made for other members of the Egyptian Club, have recently come to the auction market, often distinguished by the crocodile motif. Some examples are in the National Maritime Museum, but see also Sotheby's, *Davison*, pp. 46–53. • **5**. Keith to Nelson, 15/6/1800, Add. MS 75840; Hamilton to Keith, 16/6/1800, Lloyd, *Keith Papers*, 2, p. 116. • **6**. Keith to Nelson, 17/6/1799, Add. MS 34917; D'Huart, *Journal*, p. 30; Nelson to Downman, 19/6/1800, Add. MS 36609. • **7**. Keith to Nelson, 19/6/1799 (several letters), Add. MS 34917; Keith to Spencer, 18/6/1800, Add. MS 75840. • **8**. Keith to Paget, 20/6/1800, Augustus B. Paget, *Paget Papers*, 1, pp. 232, 252; queen to Gallo, 29/6/1800, 2, 6 and 11/7/1800, Weil, *Correspondance Inédite*, 2, pp. 161, 163, 166, 167; Keith to Nelson, 21/6/1800, Add. MS 34917. • **9**. Queen to Gallo, 2/7/1800, Weil, *Correspondance Inédite*, 2, p. 163; Nelson to Berry, 9/7/1800, Add. MS 34917; J. F. Maurice, *Moore*, 1, p. 367; Keith to Nelson, 27/6/1800, Add. MS 34917; Keith to Nepean, 22/6/1800, ADM 1/402; Jackson to Grenville, 2/7/1800, FO 67/29. Thirty-one packages of Nelson's baggage consisted of thirty packages of paintings, prints, plate, glass, furniture, clothing, swords, wine, sugar, rum, coffee, the Hallowell coffin and 'certain minerals': Sotheby's, *Davison*, p. 31. They went home in the *Serapsis*, but several additional boxes of papers made the journey in the *Hindustan* store ship. Berry and Tyson searched for the missing letters at Port Mahon without success: Tyson to Nelson, 26/7/1800, Add. MS 34917. • **10**. Nelson to Keith, 1/7/1800, NMM: KEI/18/4, Keith to Nelson, 9/7/1800, Add. MS 34917; Keith to Nepean, 22/6/1800, ADM 1/402; Jackson to Grenville, 3–4/7/1800, FO 67/29. • **11**. Nelson to Berry, 9/7/1800, *D&L*, 4, p. 262; Jackson to Grenville, 10/7/1800, FO 67/29; Penrose to Frere, 10/7/1800, FO 79/18; D'Huart, *Journal*, p. 31; Knight, *Autobiography*, pp. 149–50; James Harrison, *Life*, 2, pp. 247–9. • **12**. Jackson to Grenville, 2 and 11/7/1800, FO 67/29; Wyndham to Grenville, 21 and 24/6/1800, FO 79/18; Nelson to Keith, 11/7/1800, NMM: KEI/18/4; Keith to Spencer, 13/7/1800, Add. MS 75840; Knight to Berry, 2 and 16/7/1800, *D&L*, 4, p. 263; Berry to Nelson, 24/6/1800, Add. MS 34917. When he returned to London Nelson joined Castelcicala, the Neapolitan minister, in recommending Ormsby for a permanent appointment, and he received the command of the *Scout*. • **13**. Lady Minto to Malmesbury, 10/7/1800, Countess of Minto, *Elliot*, 3, p. 139. • **14**. A fugitive document records 950 ducats' worth of boatswain's and carpenter's stores being issued to four ships from Palermo arsenal in 1799: see Sotheby's, *Trafalgar*, p. 156. • **15**. Acton to Nelson, 15/8/1800, Egerton MS 1623; Knight to Berry, 2 and 24/7/1800, 9/8/1800, *D&L*, 4, pp. 263–5; Penrose to Frere, 24/7/1800, FO 79/18. • **16**. Comelate to Nelson, 1/8/1801, 3/1/1804, *HANP*, 2, p. 159, and Add. MSS 34922; Messer to Nelson, 9/11/1800 and undated, NMM: CRK/9/37, 38; D'Huart, *Journal*, pp. 31–32. • **17**. D'Huart, *Journal*, p. 32; Knight to Berry, 9/8/1800, *D&L*, 4, p. 265; Graefer to Nelson, 10/12/1800, NMM: CRK/17. • **18**. Thomas Blumel, 'Nelson's Overland Journey'. This and Otto Erich Deutsch, *Admiral Nelson and Joseph Haydn*, based on disparate continental sources, are the standard accounts. • **19**. Deutsch, *Nelson and Haydn*, p. 71; Nathanial Wraxall, *Memoirs*, 1, pp. 164–65; Winifred Gérin, *Horatia Nelson*, p. 49; Marianne Czisnik, 'Unique Account', p. 119. • **20**. *Notes and Queries*, 12a, series IV, p. 129. • **21**. Deutsch, *Nelson and Haydn*, p. 75; Harrison, *Life*, 2, p. 251. • **22**. Deutsch, *Nelson and Haydn*, p. 58; Tom Malcolmson, 'Vienna's Reaction to Nelson's Victory', p. 95; Richard Walker, *Nelson Portraits*, pp. 107–12; *ND*, 8 (2003) p. 18; Von Herz to Nelson, 19/11/1800, 6/6/1801, NMM: CRK/6; Thaller and Ranson to Nelson, 6/12/1801, NMM: CRK/13. A circular needlework showing Nelson and Emma walking at Merton with her dog depicts one of the admiral's black suits. It is reputed, on no good evidence, to have been made by Emma Hamilton: Richard Walker, 'Nelson Portraits,' *TC*, 15 (2005), pp. 264–65. • **23**. Minto, *Elliot*, 2, p. 364. • **24**. Lady Minto to Lady Malmesbury, 1800, Minto, *Elliot*, 3, p. 146; Nelson to Minto, 19/9/1800, *D&L*, 4, p. 266. • **25**. Deutsch, *Nelson and Haydn*, pp. 81–2. • **26**. Deutsch, *Nelson and Haydn*, pp. 98–9; Lord Malmesbury, *Series of Letters*, 2, p. 23. • **27**. Deutsch, *Nelson and Haydn*, pp. 99, 101. • **28**. Malmesbury, *Series of Letters*, 2, pp. 22–3; *HANP*, 2, pp. 404–5; Deutsch, *Nelson and Haydn*, pp. 97–8. It is sometimes said that the fine mass in D minor, widely known in Germany after 1805 as *The Nelson Mass*, was written by Haydn to celebrate the battle of the Nile. The evidence does not convince. Haydn seems to have written the mass in July and August 1798, before news of the battle reached Vienna early in September, and Haydn later called the work *A Mass for Times of Distress*. That said, the mass was not performed until 23 September 1798, and it is possible that the joyful trumpets and drums in the chorus at the end of the 'Benedictes' were inspired by news of Nelson's victory. Some connection is indicated by the use of the name *Nelson Mass* before the composer's death, but it is possible that it merely acquired this appellation because Haydn performed the work for Nelson in 1800: Deutsch, pp. 60–62, 141–2; H. C. Robbins-Landon, *Haydn*, pp. 327–8, 433, 557–65. • **29**. Harrison, *Life*, 2, p. 252; Deutsch, *Nelson and Haydn*, pp. 87–90. • **30**. Egerton MS 1616, f. 121. • **31**. Noble to Nelson, 9/9/1800,

Add. MS 34917; Desmond Gregory, *Malta*, pp. 74, 89, 301. The journal of Vaubois, published in French in William Hardman, *Malta*, pp. 556–642, clearly demonstrates the progressive deterioration of the enemy garrison's ability to sustain itself. • **32**. Deutsch, *Nelson and Haydn*, p. 130. • **33**. Von Herz to Nelson, 19/11/1800, NMM: CRK/6. • **34**. Knight, *Autobiography*, 1, p. 154; Dean of Westminster, *Remains*, pp. 105–6. Mrs St George's reference to Emma as 'exceedingly embonpoint' partly reflects the latter's pregnancy. • **35**. Westminster, *Remains*, p. 105; Elliot to Grenville, 12/10/1800, FO 68/14; Blumel, 'Nelson's Overland Journey', p. 166. Nelson's reduced physical stature may not have been exaggerated. An examination of a surviving uniform coat of 1801 suggests a chest size of 35 inches, and incredibly thin arms. Subsequent uniforms from his final years imply additional weight, for he required a chest size of 37½ inches and a waist of 33 inches: Keith Levett, 'A Tailor's Nelson', studies the admiral's surviving uniforms. • **36**. Elliot to Grenville, 12/10/1800, FO 68/14. • **37**. Westminster, *Remains*, pp. 110–12. Mrs St George is often seen as a hostile commentator, but her recall of detail was close and accurate, and she was not invariably critical. In 1814 she defended Nelson as 'liberal, charitable, affectionate, indifferent to the common objects of pursuit [wealth], and clear-sighted' (*Remains*, p. 293). • **38**. Blumel, 'Nelson's Overland Journey', p. 171. • **39**. Glennie to Hammond, 4/11/1800, FO 33/20. • **40**. Knight, *Autobiography*, 1, p. 156; Harrison, *Life*, 2, pp. 264–5; *The Times*, 11/12/1800; Dumouriez to Nelson, 1800, 13/1/1801, 30/4/1804, NMM: CRK/4; A. M. Broadley, *Dumouriez*, pp. 208, 327–28; Nelson to Emma, 26/8/1803, Thomas J. Pettigrew, *Memoirs*, 2, p. 337; Brumel, 'Nelson's Overland Journey', p. 178. • **41**. Brian Gould to the *ND*, 7 (2001), p. 347; Knight, *Autobiography*, 1, p. 157; Harrison, *Life*, 2, p. 262. • **42**. Harrison, *Life*, 2, pp. 265–6; Brumel, 'Nelson's Overland Journey', p. 180; Czisnik, 'Unique Account', p. 111. For James George ('Major') Semple (b. 1759), see *The Life of Major J. G. Semple Lisle* (1800); *Memoirs of the Northern Imposter, or Prince of Swindlers . . .* (1786) and *ODNB*, 49 (2004), p. 748. Semple, who operated under various aliases, was born in Ayrshire in 1759, the son of an exciseman. In an erratic career, he regularly resorted to confidence trickery, and in 1786 was convicted of obtaining goods under false pretences and sentenced to transportation for a period of seven years. Through agreement, he undertook to exile himself on the continent for the stipulated period, and subsequently returned to England, but in 1795 he was again convicted, this time for cheating tradesmen. Surviving Newgate prison and a couple of attempts at suicide, he was shipped as a convict to Australia in the *Lady Jane Shore* in 1797. Providentially, there was a mutiny on board, and Semple, who had tried to warn the captain, was placed with the officers and loyal seamen in an open boat. Semple surrendered to the British authorities in Tangier, returned to England, and was committed to Tothill Fields house of correction, where he was domiciled when his *Autobiography* appeared in 1799. The brush with Nelson suggests that he again accepted exile in lieu of transportation, a not unusual practice of the time, and that his representation of himself as a penniless outcast was accurate. • **43**. Nelson to Coleman, 23/10/1800, Bonham's lot, 2005. • **44**. *Ipswich Journal*, 6/11/1800. • **45**. Spencer to Keith, 18/8/1800, *NLTHW*, p. 526. • **46**. Nelson to William, 10/4/1799, Add. MS 34988. • **47**. St Vincent to Nepean, 9/11/1800, NMM: AGC/J/6/1. St Vincent was not the only colleague who thought Nelson's discipline was not as strong as it should have been: *NC*, 36 (1816), pp. 468–9. • **48**. St Vincent to Nelson, 20/11/1800, NMM: CRK/11. • **49**. Brown's register of prizes, Add. MS 36613; Brown to Nelson, 2/2/1803, NMM: CRK/2. Using papers dispersed after auction, Martyn Downer, *Nelson's Purse*, pp. 150–52, assessed Nelson's prize and head money for the Nile at £1366, equal to the payments made to five non-participating flag officers, and inferior to the £2186 awarded each captain and St Vincent's share of £8198. The commander-in-chief had chosen the officers and men who fought the battle, and thus had some moral claim to a reward. The sale of captured stores and ordnance raised Nelson's share to about £2300. A common seaman's share amounted to barely £15. Another summing of the Nile plunder, including prize and head money, compensation for the prizes that had to be destroyed, and the sale of stores, which put the total at £195,938, would also have given Nelson about £2000 (NMM: Dav/3/8, 9). However, in another estimate Davison concluded that Nelson made £2146 and £2358 from the battles of Cape St Vincent and the Nile respectively, compared with the £10,730 and £14,150 the earl received for the same engagements (note reproduced in Sotheby's, *Davison*, p. 86, and *Trafalgar*, pp. 226–7). Nelson does not seem to have complained unduly about his lot, which arose from the practices of the service. His suit of 1800, however, was not clear cut, and divided legal and naval opinion. • **50**. Leveson V. Harcourt, *Rose*, 1, p. 342. • **51**. Suckling to Nelson, 17/11/1800, NMM: CRK/12; McArthur to Nelson, 15/7/1795, Wellcome MS 3676. • **52**. Davison to Nelson, 4/4/1801, 3/5/1801, NMM: CRK/3; Diana N. Jarvis, 'Maurice Nelson'. • **53**. Nelson to Emma, 16/10/1801, NMM: CRK/19; William to Nelson, 8/11/1799, Add. MS 34988. • **54**. Thomas Foley, *Nelson Centenary*, p. 43; Fanny to Nelson, 10/12/1799, *NLTHW*, p. 541; William to Nelson, 8/11/1799, 18/1/1800, Add. MS 34906; William to Emma, 19/3/1801, Pettigrew, *Memoirs*, 1, p. 446. • **55**. Edmund to Nelson, 21/2/1800, Add. MS 34988; Mary E. Matcham, *Nelsons*, p. 174. Nelson's promise to provide his father with another daughter in 1783 referred to a plan to marry Elizabeth Andrews, a clergyman's daughter he had met in St Omer, but she refused him. See John Sugden, 'Looking For Bess', which identified the Andrews family and recovered details of Elizabeth's life. • **56**. Maurice to Nelson, 26/1/1800, and Fanny to Nelson, 11 and 23/2/1800, Add. MSS 34988; Fanny to Davison, 18/7/1799, NMM: Dav/2; Charlotte to Sarah Nelson, 22/1/1800, NMM: BRP/1. • **57**. Fanny to Davison, 28/4/1801, NMM: Dav/2; Fanny to Nelson, 14/10/1799, 26/12/1799, 15/4/1800, Add MS 34988, and 26/12/1799, *HANP*, 2, p. 78. • **58**. Nelson to Davison, 20/9/1800, *D&L*, 7, p. cxcviii. • **59**. Fanny to Nelson, 25/11/1799, Add. MS 34988. • **60**. Fanny to Davison, 2/3/1801, NMM: Dav/2; St Vincent to Nelson, 15/12/1799, Add. MS 34940; Fanny to Nelson, 14/10/1799, Add. MS 34988. • **61**. Fanny to Nelson, 21/10/1799, Add. MS 34988. • **62**. St Vincent to Nelson, 25 and 27/2/1799, Add. MS 34940. These paragraphs revise the fuller reconstruction of Nisbet's career in John Sugden, 'Fine Colt'. • **63**. Captain's log, ADM 51/1333 and 4507; lieutenant's log, ADM 51/4507; Nisbet to commandant of Civita Vecchia, 23/7/1799, Nisbet to Nelson, 27/7/1799, and Foote to Nelson, 19 and 23/7/1799, Add. MS 34912; Nelson to Nisbet, 3/8/1799, Add. MS 34963. The episode at Civita Vecchia took place two months before Troubridge captured the town in September. • **64**. Darby to Nelson, 26/9/1799, Add. MS 34914. • **65**. Troubridge to Nelson, 29/8/1799, and Martin to Nelson, 13 and 31/8/1799, 5/9/1799, Add. MS 34913; Louisa to Edward Berry, 21/10/1799, Add. MS 34914; Nelson to Austen, 22/8/1799, Add. MS 36609; Nelson to Duckworth, 16/10/1799, NMM: PST/39. • **66**. Briarly to Tyson, 19/2/1800, Add. MS 34916; Fanny to Josiah, 15/4/1800, Add. MS 34988. • **67**. Nelson to Duckworth, 14/10/1799, Add. MS 34963; Nelson to Duckworth, 14/10/1799, Add. MS 36609; Duckworth to Nelson, 12/11/1799, NMM: CRK/4. • **68**. Louis to Nelson, 29/12/1799, Add. MS 34915; minutes of the Bulkely court martial, 28/12/1799, ADM 1/ 5492. The minutes of the court martial are filed (perhaps misfiled) with the courts martial of marines officers ashore, although the incident occurred on board the *Thalia*. • **69**. Duckworth to Nelson, 4/12/1799, NMM: CRK/4; Louis to Nelson, 28/12/1799, Add. MS 34915; Nelson to Fanny, 20/1/1800, Monmouth MS E973; Troubridge to Nelson, 14/1/1800, Add. MS 34916. • **70**. Keith to Nelson, 15/1/1800, Briarly to Nisbet, 10/2/1800, and Briarly to Tyson, 19/2/1800, Add. MS 34916. • **71**. Briarly to the Navy Board, 10/2/1800, and Briarly to Tyson, 19/2/1800, Add. MS 34916; Duckworth to Nelson, 17/6/1800, Pettigrew, *Memoirs*, 1, p. 367; *Thalia* muster book,

ADM 36/14652. • **72**. Murdoch to Keith, 24/5/1800, *NLTHW*, p. 524; Nisbet to Nepean, 6 and 20/10/1800, 8 and 17/11/1800, 8 and 9/12/1800, ADM 1/2227.

XII Domestic Strife

1. *Morning Post*, 10/11/1800; *Morning Chronicle*, 21/11/1800; *NC*, 4, p. 429; Cornelia Knight, *Autobiography*, 1, p. 158; Nelson to Nepean, 6/11/1800, ADM 1/579. • **2**. *Ipswich Journal*, 15/11/1800; Fanny to Davison, 20/10/1800, NMM: Dav/2. • **3**. Troubridge to Nelson, 30/9/1800, and Nelson to Berry, 5/12/1800, Add. MS 34917; Hardy to Manfield, 8/11/1800, A. M. Broadley, *Nelson's Hardy*, p. 53. • **4**. James Harrison, *Life*, 2, p. 270; Davison to Nelson, 26 and 29/1/1801, NMM: CRK/3. I have principally drawn my account of Nelson in London from the *Morning Post*, *Morning Herald*, *The Times*, *Porcupine*, *Morning Chronicle* and *Ipswich Journal*. A close reading of the numerous reports therein accounts for Nelson's activities on thirty of the sixty-six days between 9 November and 13 January, when he left to command the *San Josef*. • **5**. Edmund to Kate Matcham, 15/11/1800, M. E. Matcham, *Nelsons*, 181; Nelson to Richards, 1/12/1800, *ND*, 1 (1984), p. 197; Hardy to Manfield, 10/11/1800; Broadley, *Nelson's Hardy*, p. 54; Young to Keith, 10/11/1800, C. C. Lloyd, *Keith Papers*, 2, p. 146; Harrison, *Life*, 2, pp. 271–2; K. S. Cliff, *Lock*, p. 7. • **6**. *Morning Herald*, 13 and 14/11/1800; Nelson to Heard, 20/9/1800, Monmouth MS E79; Troubridge to Nepean, 8/10/1800, Warren R. Dawson, *Nelson Collection*, p. 158. • **7**. *ND*, 1 (1984), p. 197; accounts with Davison, NMM: CRK/3/168; Matcham, *Nelsons*, p. 180; David Constantine, *Fields of Fire*, p. 257; Emma to Fanny, November 1800, Walter Sichel, *Lady Hamilton*, p. 511; Nelson to Emma, November 1800, Egerton MS 1614. • **8**. Richard Edgcumbe, *Diary*, 1, pp. 77–9; Cornelia Knight, *Autobiography*, 1, pp. 161–2; Nelson to Emma, 15/10/1801, NMM: CRK/19. • **9**. Elizabeth and Florence Anson, *Mary Hamilton*, pp. 326, 328; Castelcicala to Nelson, 15/12/1800, NMM: CRK/3. • **10**. This may have been the last time that Fanny accompanied her husband to the theatre. Nelson invited Davison to join a party for dinner on 26 November, from which they were to proceed to a box at the Royalty Theatre, but the members of the gathering are not named: Nelson to Davison, 26/11/1800, Egerton MS 2240. He did not always venture into society in female company. About 19 November Nelson and Sir William Hamilton visited 'the paintings at the Panorama' with an unnamed group of friends: *Morning Chronicle*, 20/11/1800. • **11**. James Grieg, *Farington Diary*, 3, p. 131. Farington recorded Hamond's story twice, the last time on 13 June 1805, which at least suggests consistency. The uglier version in the *Memoirs of Lady Hamilton*, pp. 222–3, contains the key elements, but Emma's dinner-table pique is occasioned by another guest, rather than Fanny, although Lady Nelson failed to condemn the offender. In this story Emma's illness is genuine stomach sickness (she was, in fact, in an advanced pregnancy), and she withdraws with Fatima. Nelson insists his wife also attends the distressed woman, accusing her of causing it, and Fanny finds herself holding a basin to catch Emma's vomit. In both versions the incident is presented as a significant step in the disintegration of the Nelsons' marriage. Considering Hamond's account of the argument that occurred between Nelson and his wife the following morning, one wonders whether it relates to a more graphic story that Emma later gave James Harrison, *Life*, 2, pp. 278–9, in which Nelson abandons his wife's bed after a domestic broil one night and quits the house to wander the empty streets until arriving at the Hamiltons' house in Grosvenor Square at about four in the morning. • **12**. *Journals of the House of Lords*, 42, p. 661. • **13**. Mrs Henry Baring, *Windham*, p. 434. • **14**. Matcham, *Nelsons*, p. 180; documents in NMM: MAM/6, 35; William Nelson to George Matcham, 29/11/1800, Sotheby's lot, 2005; Matcham to Nelson, 15/7/1802, NMM: CRK/20. • **15**. Nelson to Horace Nelson, 1800, Add.

MS 34988; Brown to Nelson, 19/11/1800, Barrons to Nelson, 8/12/1800, and Barry to Nelson, 21/11/1800, NMM: CRK/2; Atkinson to Nelson, 21/11/1800, NMM: CRK/1; Doreen Scragg, 'Thomas Atkinson'; Graham to Nelson, 19/11/1800, NMM: CRK/6/77; Ron C. Fiske, 'Nelson and the Gregorians'. Nelson did serve some of the supplicants. Atkinson was appointed to the *San Josef*, and Nelson attempted to find another correspondent a place in Greenwich Hospital: Nepean to Nelson, 2/12/1800, Add. MS 34934. • **16**. Inventory of a service, Add. MS 34990, f. 7; John May, 'The Nelson Silver'; Cliff, *Lock*, pp. 7–8. Forty-five pieces of the service survive in the National Maritime Museum and Lloyd's. • **17**. Keith Levett, 'Tailor's Nelson'; Brian Connell, *Whig Peer*, p. 440. • **18**. D. M. Stuart, *Dearest Bess*, p. 133; Richard Walker, *Nelson Portraits*, is supplemented by his 'The Nelson Portraits: Addendum, 2005', p. 268; Hayley to Flaxman, 17/11/1805, Monmouth MS E495. • **19**. Walker, *Nelson Portraits*, believes the bust by Damer was based on sittings in Naples in 1798. While the Common Council of London commissioned Damer to produce a bust of Nelson in 1799, I do not think that any significant sittings occurred in Naples. One version of the Damer bust was dated 1801, and the commission for the City fathers was not fulfilled until 1804. It showed the Sicilian order that Nelson received in 1800. Further evidence that the busts had their origin in England in 1800 rather than in Naples at an earlier time comes in an 1806 engraving that bears the rubric that the original was executed upon Nelson's return to England in '1801'. Most tellingly, in a reference missed by Walker, *The Times* for 29 November 1800 records that Nelson had been sitting to Mrs Damer an hour a day for several days. • **20**. Beckford to the Hamiltons, 24/11/1800, Lewis Melville, *Life and Letters*, p. 232. In support of Hamilton's claim, Nelson claimed that the diplomat had spent more than £13,000 maintaining his establishment in Palermo during his last year of occupancy: Nelson statement: Egerton MS 1614, f. 11. • **21**. *Ipswich Journal*, 27/12/1800; *The Times*, 24/12/1800. • **22**. George S. Hilliard, *Ticknor*, 1, p. 63. The best known account of Nelson's visit, published in the *Gentleman's Magazine* of 1801 and reprinted by Tom Malcolmson, 'Visit to Fonthill', has been credited to Henry Tresham, but it was actually adapted from a letter Miss Mary and Susan Beckford wrote Lady Anne Hamilton on 29/12/1800, an abridgment of which can be found in Hilda Gamlin, *Nelson's Friendships*, 1, p. 169. See also Marjorie Bowen, *Patriotic Lady*, pp. 279–82; Cyrus Redding, *Reminiscences*, 3, pp. 111–28; and 'William Beckford in Farington's Diary', p. 66. Secondary accounts in Nelson biographies are confused, but Jim Millington's 'Where Nelson Went in Fonthill Abbey' provides the essential guide. • **23**. Redding, *Recollections*, 3, pp. 127–8. The estate eventually had two carriageways, one the 'Nine Miles Walk' and another a winding four-mile stretch which skirted the southern part of the grounds from east of the abbey to 'the great Western Avenue': Robert J. Gemmett, *Beckford's Fonthill*, p. 99. • **24**. Beckford to Emma, 30/8/1805, 'A Letter to Emma Hamilton from Beckford'; Nelson to Emma, 29/12/1800, Thomas J. Pettigrew, *Memoirs*, 1, p. 392; Edward Hawke Locker, *Memoirs*, ch. 16; Locker to Nelson, 28/2/1804, NMM: CRK/8. • **25**. Bourne to Smith, 3/1/1801, Monmouth MS E89; Collingwood to Blackett, 25/1/1801, *D&L*, 4, p. 278; Grenville to the Admiralty, 3/1/1801, ADM 1/4186; Jim Saunders, 'Roundwood', p. 348; Nelson to Fanny, 9/1/1801, Add. MS 34902; Nelson to Foresti, 29/12/1800, Cornwall Record Office, J3/35/36. • **26**. *The Times*, 13/1/1801; financial statement, 1801, Add. MS 28333; Nelson to Fanny, 13/1/1801, *NLTHW*, p. 618. • **27**. Nelson to Emma, 14/1/1801, Pettigrew, *Memoirs*, 1, p. 409; Hardy to Manfield, 16/1/1801, Broadley and Bartelot, *Nelson's Hardy*, p. 60. • **28**. *Morning Chronicle*, 20/1/1801; Yolanda C. Stanton, 'Nelson Sword'. • **29**. Nelson to Fanny, 16/1/1801, *NLTHW*, p. 618; Nelson to Davison, 2/2/1801, Egerton MS 2240; Nelson to Spencer, 17/1/1801, Add. MS 34940; Nelson to Emma, 17 /1/1801, 16/3/1801, Pettigrew, *Memoirs*, 1, p. 410, and *HANP*, 2, p. 126; St Vincent to Nepean, 17/1/1801, NMM: AGC/J/6/2.

• **30**. *NC*, 5, p. 94; Navy Board to Nelson, 1/12/1800, Add. MS 34934; *ND*, 7 (2001), p. 567; Nelson to Spencer, 17 and 22/1/1801, Add. MSS 34940 and 75849; Nelson to Spencer, 31/1/1801, NMM: CRK/11; Nelson to Addington, 2/2/1801, *D&L*, 4, p. 282; Nelson to St Vincent, 28/1/1801, *D&L*, 7, p. ccxxviii*. The 'guardian angels' are more often mentioned than identified. One was the well-known portrait Schmidt had painted in Dresden, but the other was apparently sketched by Cornelia Knight and showed Emma crowning a rostral column. In April Emma sent a third, Romney's portrait of her in the guise of St Cecilia: Nelson to Emma, 26/3/1801, 5/4/1801, Egerton MS 1614; Stewart to Emma, 23/4/1801, *HANP*, 2, p. 141. • **31**. St Vincent to Nelson, 3/2/1801, Add. MS 31164; Nelson to Emma, 29/1/1801, 1/2/1801, Pettigrew, *Memoirs*, 1, p. 419, and *HANP*, 2, p. 110; Nelson to Davison, 4/2/1801, Egerton MS 2240; Nelson to Spencer, 26/1/1801, and Spencer to Nelson, 29/1/1801, Add. MS 75849; Warren R. Dawson, *Nelson Collection*, p. 163. Nelson's followers included Hardy and Parker; 9 lieutenants (including Philip Lyne, a Troubridge eleve, Robert Pettet, John Yule, William Bolton, Frederick Langford, George Elliot and William Layman); Thomas Atkinson, master; Stephen Comyn, chaplain; 13 midshipmen (including Michael L. Raven, one of the Ravens of Burnham Thorpe); 2 clerks (one Thomas Wallis), 2 supernumeraries (one Richard Bulkeley), 4 servants (one Tom Allen); and 15 men and boys, including young William Faddy. Readers will recognise relatives, long standing followers and the protégés of friends in this collection. Nelson felt obliged to Faddy, whose father had died at the Nile, even though Hardy thought him an officer with little potential. The actual transfers (muster of the *St. George*, ADM 36/14293) slightly exceeded a list Nelson furnished the Admiralty (Nelson to Nepean, 16/2/1801, ADM 1/118), although some names on the latter did not, in fact, follow the admiral. • **32**. Nelson to Emma, 17/1/1801, Pettigrew, *Memoirs*, 1, p. 410; Mark Philp, 'I'll Sing of Fame'd Trafalgar'. • **33**. Nelson to Emma, 28/1/1801, Monmouth MS E91; Trotter to Millar, 3/2/1806, Add. MS 34990. • **34**. Nelson to Emma, 11 and 22/2/1801, 6/3/1801, *HANP*, 2, pp. 113, 120, 126; Nelson to Emma, 24/1/1801, 12/2/1801, MS in A. M. Broadley's 'Nelsoniana', BL, f.p. 5, 256, and Pettigrew, *Memoirs*, 1, p. 424; *NC*, 5 (1801), pp. 94, 180. Nelson visited Captain Robert Kingsmill in March 1781, and may have met the unidentified woman there, but the allusion to seventeen years suggests that he last saw her in 1784, when he was ordered to the West Indies in the *Boreas*. Troubridge kept his house at Plymouth for the use of his 'girls' (Troubridge to Nelson, 31/7/1800, Add. MS 34917). • **35**. Nelson to Emma, 14/2/1801, *HANP*, 2, p. 114; John Gore, *Nelson's Hardy*, p. 18. • **36**. Mary Simpson had since come to England, and in 1801 took up an apartment in the Royal Hospital, Chelsea, where her husband, Lieutenant Colonel Robert Mathews, was appointed a major: see John Sugden, 'Mary Simpson'. • **37**. Nelson to Emma, 25/1/1801, 14/2/1801, *HANP*, 2, pp. 108, 114; Nelson to Emma, 15/2/1801, Pettigrew, *Memoirs*, 1, p. 425. The portrait was possibly that now owned by the Frick Foundation, New York, showing Emma with a dog, which just might be Mira, a pet of the Hamiltons in Palermo. • **38**. Nelson to Emma, 21/1/1801, 11/2/1801, Egerton MS 1614, and Sichel, *Lady Hamilton*, p. 520; Nelson to Fanny, 20 and 21/1/1801, 3/2/1801 [my italics], *NLTHW*, pp. 618, 619; Davison to Nelson, 20/2/1801, NMM: CRK/3. • **39**. Nelson to Emma, 25/1/1801, *HANP*, 2, p. 108. • **40**. Fanny to Davison, 20 and 24/2/1801, NMM: Dav/2; Fanny to Sarah Nelson, 22/1/1801, Add. MS 34988. • **41**. Nelson to Emma, February 1801, Egerton MS 1614; Fanny to Davison, 24/2/1801, NMM: Dav/2; account with Davison, NMM: CRK/3/168. • **42**. Nelson to Emma, 17/2/1801, *HANP*, 2, p. 115; Nelson to Davison, 17/2/1801, Egerton MS 2240. • **43**. Dundas to the Duke of York, 23/2/1801, ADM 1/4186. • **44**. The child was called 'Horatia' in Emma's first surviving note to Mrs Gibson dated 7/2/1801: *D&L*, 7, p. 372, but not until a note of 15 March was she referred to as 'Miss Thomson'. Sometimes the name was rendered 'Thompson'.

The Memoirs of Lady Hamilton, which states that she was born at 23 Piccadilly and carried to Little Titchfield Street in a large muff, adds that Francis Oliver accompanied Emma on the occasion. This is the strongest indication that the 'inside' information in this account came from Oliver. Understanding Emma's need for secrecy, Nelson recommended that Mrs Gibson be occasionally given 'an additional guinea' and that 'a small pension' be offered to preserve her silence: Nelson to Emma, 6/2/1801, Houghton, MS Eng. 196.5. For Emma's dealings with Gibson see NMM: NWD and Winifred Gérin's splendid biography of Horatia. • **45**. Nelson to Emma (undated but written on 23/2/1801), WLC, refers to twins. It is reasonable to suppose that if both survived and one was a boy, he would have been the preferred child, given the practice of primogeniture. Searches of the parish baptismal and burial records of St James's have not thrown any light on the missing twin. The possibility that Emma might have felt inadequate to raising two secret children and placed a girl in an institution has directed attention to Coram's Foundling Hospital in London, but the admissions (London Metropolitan Archives, A/FH/A/09/001–198) show only one child who *might* be a candidate. On 19 April 1801 five new foundlings were baptised with names associated with Nelson, two of them girls. Emma patronised the hospital, and may have sponsored these children. Of the girls, 'Emma Hamilton' (no. 18643) was later adopted by one Sarah Snelling, who reported her progress to Emma, but the records reveal her to have been born on 2 March 1801, the daughter of William and Mary James. The other girl, baptised 'Mary Thompson' (no. 18641), had also been admitted on 18 April, when she was thought to be three months old. This age, and the use of the same surname applied to Horatia, makes Mary a possible candidate for the missing sibling. However, the hospital records suggest she was the daughter of a 'Dinah Minis'. Mary Thompson was apprenticed on 12 January 1816: General Register, X41/4, and baptisms, A/FH/A14/004/001, London Metropolitan Archives. The possibility of a fostering elsewhere also remains, but the greater likelihood is that the other twin died at or shortly after birth. • **46**. Nelson to Emma, 21 and 24/1/1801, Egerton MS 1614 and MS inserted into Broadley's 'Nelsoniana', BL, 5, f.p. 256; Nelson to Emma, 25/1/1801, *HANP*, 2, p. 108; Nelson to Emma, March 1801, NMM: CRK/19. • **47**. Nelson to Emma, 1 and 3/2/1801, *HANP*, 2, p. 110. • **48**. Marsh to Nelson, 25 and 26/11/1800, NMM: CRK/8; Nepean to Nelson, 23/1/1801, Add. MS 34934. • **49**. Drafts codicil, 5/2/1801, Egerton MS 1614. See also *NLTHW*, p. 580; *HANP*, 2, pp. 130, 131; Nelson to Emma, 6/3/1801, *HANP*, 2, p. 125; Add. MS 28333, f. 5; *Daily Telegraph*, 22/6/2007. • **50**. Nelson to Emma, 5 and 22/2/1801, 10/3/1801, *HANP*, 2, pp. 111, 120, 127, and 16/2/1801, NMM: CRK/19. • **51**. Flora Fraser, 'Cartoonists' Dream', and Matthew Sheldon, 'Nelson's Appearance in Caricature', are valuable on this. • **52**. Nelson to Emma, 26/1/1801, 4, 17 and 19/2/1801, 10 and 11/3/1801, *HANP*, 2, pp. 109, 111, 116, 118, 127, 128; *Morning Herald*, 2/2/1801. • **53**. Nelson to Emma, 6 and 17/2/1801, 6/3/1801, Houghton, MS Eng. 196.5, and *HANP*, 2, p. 116. • **54**. Nelson to Emma, 18 and 19/2/1801, *HANP*, 2, pp. 117, 118. • **55**. Hamilton to Nelson, 19/2/1801, NMM: CRK/7; Nelson to Emma, undated, and 19/2/1801, *HANP*, 2, pp. 113, 118; Hamilton to Nelson, 19/2/1801, *NLTHW*, p. 576. • **56**. Nelson to Emma, 20–21 and 22/2/1801, *HANP*, 2, p. 120. • **57**. William to Emma, 19/2/1801, Pettigrew, *Memoirs*, 1, p. 429. • **58**. Emma to Sarah Nelson, 20/2/1801, 4/3/1801, Add. MS 34989; Nelson to Emma, 10/3/1801, *HANP*, 2, p. 127. • **59**. Nelson to Emma, 23/2/1801, WLC; Emma to Sarah, 24/2/1801, 2/3/1801, Add. MS 34989. It appears from an entry in Nelson's accounts (*HANP*, 2, p. 392), that Edward Parker, his current protégé, was his aide in London. Parker probably travelled from Portsmouth with Nelson, but was appointed to command the *Trimmer* at the end the month and sent to Sheerness. • **60**. Nepean to Nelson, 26/2/1801, Add. MS 34934; Nelson to Spencer, 26/2/1801, Add. MS 75849; Emma to Sarah,

26/2/1801, Add. MS 34989; Nelson to Emma, 27/2/1801, *HANP*, 2, p. 121; Spencer to Nelson, 2/3/1801, NMM: CRK/11. • **61**. Nelson to Troubridge, 7 and 11/3/1801, 27/4/1801, Huntington, HM 34208, 34210, 34222. • **62**. Nelson to Fanny, 4/3/1801, *HANP*, 2, p. 125; Troubridge to Nelson, 10/9/1801, NMM: CRK/13. • **63**. Nelson to Emma, 1/3/1801, Houghton, MS Lowell, 10. • **64**. Nelson to Emma, 6/2/1801, Houghton, MS Eng. 196.5. • **65**. Nelson to Fanny, 4/3/1801, *HANP*, 2, p. 125 [part in Add. MS 28333]. • **66**. Fanny to Davison, 20/2/1801, 2/3/1801, 28/4/1801, NMM: Dav/2; Edmund to Fanny, 14/3/1801 and Susannah to Fanny, 8/3/1801, Monmouth MS E669. • **67**. Fanny to Davison, 1/3/1801, NMM: Dav/2. • **68**. Nelson to Emma, 6 and 11/3/1801, *HANP*, 2, pp. 126, 128; Nelson to Emma, undated, but evidently 9/3/1801, University of New Brunswick, Canada, Beaverbrook collection; Nelson to Emma, 17/3/1801, NMM: Mon/1/18. Rolfe, however, got a chaplaincy out of his intervention. • **69**. Fremantle to his brother, 27/2/1801, Ann Parry, *Fremantle*, p. 52; list of 28/2/1801, ADM 1/4; Nepean to Nelson, 5/3/1801, Add. MS 34934; Nelson to Troubridge, 4/3/1801, Huntington, HM 34209; Nelson to Emma, 13/3/1801, Egerton MS 1614. Stewart's contemporary journal was published in *The Cumloden Papers*, and a narrative he wrote for Clarke and McArthur, quoted above, in *D&L*, 4, pp. 299–313. • **70**. Fremantle to his brother, 11/3/1801, Parry, *Fremantle*, p. 53. • **71**. Nelson to Davison, 11/3/1801, Egerton MS 2240; Nelson to St Vincent, 1/3/1801, *D&L*, 4, p. 290; Nelson to Troubridge, 7 and 10/3/1801, Huntington, HM 34208, 34210. • **72**. St Vincent to Parker, 11/3/1801, 5/4/1801, Add. MS 31169; Parker to Nepean, 12/3/1801, ADM 1/ 4. • **73**. Nelson to Troubridge, 13/3/1801, Huntington, HM 34212; sailing orders, 10/3/1801, Add. MS 34918; Nelson to Emma, 26/5/1801, *HANP*, 2, p. 149. • **74**. Nelson to Emma, 13/3/1801, Egerton MS 1614; Nelson to Berry, 9/3/1801, Add. MS 34918; Nelson to St Vincent, 1/3/1801, *D&L*, 4, p. 290. • **75**. Nelson to Emma, 8/2/1801, *Letters*, 1, p. 23. • **76**. Nelson to Emma, 16/2/1801, NMM: CRK/19; *HANP*, 2, p. 143.

XIII 'Champion of the North'

1. Ole Feldbaek, *Denmark and the Armed Neutrality*, is the best study of the politics of the Baltic. • **2**. St Vincent to Cornwallis, 9/3/1801, Add. MS 31169. • **3**. Tomlinson's narrative, dated June 1801, is published in J. G. Bullocke, *Tomlinson Papers*, pp. 305–12. The first book-length study of the Baltic campaign appeared in Olav Bergersen's *Noytralited og Krig*, a detailed account of the Danish–Norwegian navy. For long the only extended account in English was that by William James, but two thoughtful studies, Dudley Pope's *Great Gamble* and Ole Feldbaek's *Battle of Copenhagen*, supersede previous writing. Stephen Howarth, *Battle of Copenhagen*, assembles useful papers. For Nelson, see the dispatches and associated miscellania in ADM 1/ 4; letterbooks (Monmouth MSS E990, 991); order book (sampled by Colin White, *New Letters*, from a microfilm in the National Archives of Denmark, D/173) and journal, 12 March to 13 May 1801 (NMM: CRK/14). The Stewart narratives are in the *Cumloden Papers* and *D&L*, 4, pp. 299–304. The original of the first part of the last narrative, covering events up to 26 March, is in Add. MS 34918, ff. 315–18, but Nicolas had to reprint the last section from James Stanier Clarke and John McArthur's biography. These sources are worth comparing with Parker's journal in ADM 50/65. The logs of the fleet are cited as necessary, but those of the *St George* are filed in ADM 51/1371 and 52/2968. T. Sturges-Jackson, *Logs*, vol. 2, contains extracts covering the actual battle. • **4**. Nelson to Emma, 16/3/1801, 12/5/1801, Egerton MS 1614, and Thomas J. Pettigrew, *Memoirs*,2, p. 61. • **5**. Nelson to Troubridge, 7, 8, 11 and 13/3/1801, 7/5/1801, Huntington, HM 34208, 34210, 34212, 34225. • **6**. St Vincent to Nelson, 8/3/1801, Add. MS 31168. • **7**. W. H. Fitchett and Ludovic Kennedy have written of Riou, but see also

Kennedy's edition of the 'Log of the *Guardian*'. • **8**. Nelson's journal, NMM: CRK/14; Parker's journal, ADM 50/65. Nelson's seamanship may not have impressed colleagues, but he was a careful recorder of navigational information. 'I would always recommend,' ran one of several observations in his Baltic journal, 'unless the wind is at E.S.E. and you have the Swedish shore close abreast, to always make Anholt. If the wind blows strong westerly you may always anchor under the lee of it in very smooth water . . .' • **9**. Nelson to Troubridge, 16 and 23/3/1801, Huntington, HM 34212, 34220. The turbot anecdote (*NC*, 37 [1817], p. 446) originated in Layman, but see also Nelson's journal and Parker to Nelson, 14/3/1801, NMM: CRK/9/168. • **10**. Nelson to Troubridge, 20/3/1801, Huntington, HM 34213; Nelson to Davison, 20/3/1801, Egerton MS 2240. • **11**. Vansittart to Parker, 21/3/1801, ADM 1/4. • **12**. Parker to Nepean, 23/3/1801, Add. MS 23207; Domett to Nelson, March 1801, NMM: CRK/4. • **13**. Nelson to Troubridge, 23/3/1801, Huntington, HM 34214. • **14**. Feldbaek, *Battle of Copenhagen*, is the most reliable account. • **15**. Layman's account, *NC*, 37 (1817), p. 46; Domett to Bridport, 4/5/1801, Add. MS 35201; Nelson to Vansittart, 12/5/1801, *D&L*, 4, p. 368. • **16**. George Pellew, *Sidmouth*, 1, p. 368; Scott to Lavington, 23/3/1801, Monmouth MS E473. • **17**. Nelson to Troubridge, 29/3/1801, Huntington, HM 34215; Nelson to Parker, 24/3/1801, ADM 1/4; Parker to Nepean, 23/3/1801 (second letter), Add. MS 23207. • **18**. The deployment of the experienced seamen at Copenhagen illustrates the concentration of strength in the northern part of the Danish line of battle. The eight southern units in the line contained a greater proportion of untrained volunteers and pressed men: Feldbaek, *Battle of Copenhagen*, p. 97. • **19**. Vansittart to Nelson, 8/4/1801, WLC. • **20**. Parker to Nelson, 24/3/1801, NMM: CRK/9; Parker to his wife, 6/4/1801, Peter Le Fevre, 'Little Merit', 21; Domett to Bridport, 4/5/1801, Add. MS 35201; Nelson to Troubridge, 29/3/1801, Huntington, HM 34215; Nelson to Parker, 24/3/1801, ADM 1/ 4. • **21**. St Vincent to Parker, 15/3/1801, Add. MS 34934. • **22**. *Cumloden Papers*, p. 11; Parker to Nepean, 6/4/1801, ADM 1/4; Nelson journal, NMM: CRK/14. • **23**. Feldbaek, *Battle of Copenhagen*, p. 86; *NC*, 6 (1801), pp. 117–20; *Cumloden Papers*, p. 11. • **24**. Parker to Nepean, 6/4/1801, ADM 1/4; Parker to his wife, 27/3/1801, Le Fevre, 'Little Merit', p. 18; Domett to Nelson, 26/3/1801, NMM: CRK/4. • **25**. Muster of the *Elephant*, ADM 36/15342; John Finlayson, 'Signal Midshipman', p. 87; Nelson to Emma, 26/5/1801, Egerton MS 1614. Finlayson was rated as an eighteen-year-old in the muster of the *St George* (ADM 36/14293), but he may have exaggerated his age to enhance his chances of promotion. His account was written long afterwards, and draws upon published sources as well as memory. Some of the small personal episodes are convincing, but when Finlayson supports earlier printed accounts on the larger details his narrative should be regarded as a plagiarism rather than an independent source. • **26**. Musters of the *Agamemnon* and *Ganges*, ADM 36/14590 and 15393. A late reminiscent account by Major John B. Glegg, who sailed in the *Monarch*, suggests the role of the military in the battle: F. Loraine Petre, *Royal Berkshire Regiment*, 1, pp. 77–9. • **27**. Fremantle to Betsy Fremantle, 29/3/1801, and Fremantle to Buckingham, 29/3/1801, Anne Fremantle, *Wynne Diaries*, 3, pp. 37, 38; Nelson's journal, NMM: CRK/14. • **28**. *Cumloden Papers*, p. 12. • **29**. John Hopper to Nelson, 1801, NMM: CRK/7; *NC*, 5 (1801), pp. 308–11, and 6 (1801), p. 118. • **30**. Nelson to Troubridge, 30/3/1801, John Knox Laughton, *Naval Miscellany*, 1, p. 425. • **31**. *Events of the War Between Denmark and England*, p. 10; Nelson to Emma, 30/3/1801, *HANP*, 2, p. 132; Mosse to his wife, 23, 29 and 30/3/1801, NMM: Mss/78/145. • **32**. Feldbaek, *Battle of Copenhagen*, p. 107. It should be noted that a Danish 36-pound shot weighed nearly 40 English pounds, and their 24-pound shot weighed almost 26½ English pounds. • **33**. Pope, *Great Gamble*, p. 450. • **34**. Parker journal, ADM 50/65; Nelson to Emma, 30/3/1801, *HANP*, 2, p. 132. • **35**. Stewart's narrative, *D&L*, 4, p. 303; Mosse to his wife, 1/4/1801, NMM: Mss/78/145. According to Stewart, Nelson was thinking about how to meet the Russians and Swedes at sea, and spoke of 'attacking the head of their line, and confusing their movements as much as possible'. If true, these were ideas that would reappear at Trafalgar. • **36**. Frederick M. Millard, 'Battle of Copenhagen', p. 84. • **37**. *Cumloden Papers*, p. 16; Danish account, 3/4/1801, enclosed with Caulfield to Hawkesbury, 7/4/1801, FO 33/21. • **38**. Stewart, *D&L*, 4, p. 304; Nelson to Emma, 5/4/1801, Egerton MS 1614. I deduce that Stewart and the army lieutenant colonels were present from an allusion that Lieutenant Colonel William Hutchinson of the 49th, berthed in the *Monarch*, attended (Millard, 'Battle of Copenhagen', p. 84), although that irascible officer did not mention it in his own account. • **39**. Fremantle to Buckingham, 4/4/1801, Fremantle, *Wynne Diaries*, 3, p. 42; Graham Dean, 'Nelson's Heroes', *ND*, 7 (2001), p. 479. • **40**. Parker to Nelson, 26/3/1801, NMM: CRK/9. The *Defence*, *Ramillies* and *Veteran* never got within gunshot of the battle. Parker's other capital ships, *London*, *St George*, *Warrior*, *Saturn* and *Raisonnable*, made no contribution, although boats from Parker's division did join the *Elephant* while the action was in progress. The non-participation of part of the British fleet later complicated the issue of rewards and prize money. • **41**. Nelson's instructions, 1/4/1801, ADM 1/4. • **42**. Nelson to St Vincent, September 1801, *D&L*, 4, p. 499. • **43**. Sturges-Jackson, *Logs*, 2, p. 113. • **44**. Millard, 'Battle of Copenhagen', p. 86. • **45**. *Cumloden Papers*, p. 21. • **46**. Charlton to Nelson, 20/6/1801, NMM: CRK/3. • **47**. Lieutenant Thomas Southey of the *Bellona*, brother of the poet, throws a critical light upon Thompson (Oliver Warner, 'Lieut. Tom Southey', pp. 58–9), but for another account from the same ship see Midshipman William Anderson's letter to his parents, with 'minutes' of the action, Add. MS 40730. • **48**. The logs of the *Polyphemus* (ADM 51/1371; ADM 52/3299; Sturges-Jackson, *Logs*, 2, pp. 95–8) provide a record of signals that reflect Nelson's close monitoring of the battle. • **49**. Stewart to Clinton, 6/4/1801, NMM: AGC/14/27. • **50**. Feldbaek, *Battle of Copenhagen*, p. 142; Fremantle to Buckingham, 4/4/1801, Fremantle, *Wynne Diaries*, 3, p. 42; account of signal midshipman of the *Ganges*: *Canadian Courant* (Montreal), 26/5/1819. • **51**. *Cumloden Papers*, p. 22. Two contemporary British sketches preserve remarkable views of the battle, one by Robinson Kittoe, Graves's secretary (Pope, *Great Gamble*, plate 9) and the other probably the work of Captain Peter Fyers of the Royal Artillery (Thomas A. Hardy, 'Battle Plans', p. 88). For the versatility of carronades see Mark Lardas, 'Carronades'. • **52**. Danish account, Caulfield to Hawkesbury, 7/4/1801, FO 33/21; logs of the *Elephant*, ADM 51/1356, and 52/2968; Thomas A. Hardy, 'Peter Willemoes'; *NC*, 14 (1805), p. 398; J. A. Andersen, *A Dane's Excursion*, p. 15. • **53**. Nelson to Angerstein, 17/1/1802, Add. MS 34918. • **54**. Millard, 'Battle of Copenhagen', pp. 87–89; Green to Nelson, 14/9/1801, NMM: CRK/6. • **55**. Feldbaek, *Battle of Copenhagen*, p. 171. • **56**. For different views of Parker's signal see Sturges Jackson, *Logs*, 2, pp. 83–5, Oliver Warner, *Nelson's Battles*, pp. 121–2, and especially Pope, *Great Gamble*, pp. 514–21. • **57**. Nelson to Emma, 2/4/1801, Egerton MS 1614. • **58**. Graves to Graves, 3/4/1801, Sturges Jackson, *Logs*, 2, p. 101. According to James, *Naval History*, 3, p. 73, who had access to witnesses, Graves repeated Parker's signal in the *Defiance*, but on the lee main topsail yardarm, where it could not easily be seen, leaving Nelson's signal for close action prominently displayed at the main topgallant masthead. • **59**. Stewart to Clinton, 6/4/1801, NMM: AGC/14/27; *Cumloden Papers*, p. 24; Countess of Minto, *Elliot*, 3, pp. 215, 218. • **60**. *Elephant* muster, ADM 36/15342; James Harrison, *Life*, 2, p. 295. An extensive quotation from an account by a 'Mr Ferguson' also appears in James Stanier Clarke and John McArthur, *Life and Services*, 2, pp. 420–22. • **61**. *D&L*, 4, pp. 308–9. • **62**. For other references to Nelson's habit of 'working' his stump when agitated, see George Magrath's testimony in Cyrus Redding, *Recollections*, 3, p. 252, and George S. Parsons, *Reminiscences*, p. 8. • **63**. *NC*, 37 (1817), p. 450. Rather than remain inactive in the *St George*, Layman volunteered to serve in Nelson's attack force, finding a place on the lower deck of the *Isis*, 'when, from five guns only working . . . [he] by great exertions, manned and replaced the whole of the larboard battery': Layman to Nelson, 12/3/1801, *NC*, 37 (1817), p. 451; Stewart to Layman, 26/5/1802, *NC*, 37 (1817), p. 452. • **64**. Stewart to Clinton, 6/4/1801, NMM: AGC/14/27. • **65**. Nelson to Addington, 8/5/1801, *D&L*, 4, p. 360; Nelson to the Danes, 2/4/1801, ADM 1/4; Fremantle to his wife, 4/4/1801, Fremantle, *Wynne Diaries*, 3, p. 41; Pope, *Great Gamble*, pp. 418, 566. • **66**. Caulfield to Hawkesbury, 7/4/1801, FO 33/21. • **67**. *D&L*, 4, p. 310; Horace G. Hutchinson, 'Nelson at Copenhagen', pp. 326–7. Five of Nelson's seven bomb vessels were being prepared to bombard, *Terror*, *Explosion*, *Volcano*, *Discovery* and *Zebra*. Each was equipped with sixty-eight-pound carronades capable of firing carcasses, and thirteen-inch mortars, capable of projecting shells at a high angle to create a long-range but imprecise bombardment. • **68**. Nelson to Emma, 8/5/1801, Egerton MS 1614; *D&L*, 4, p. 312. • **69**. Hardy to Manfield, 5/4/1801, A. M. Broadley, *Nelson's Hardy*, p. 63; Stewart to Clinton, 6/4/1801, NMM: AGC/14/27; Fremantle, *Wynne Diaries*, 3, pp. 41, 43. Susan Harmon, 'The Serpent and the Dove', is a thoughtful weighing of Nelson's motives. • **70**. Account of the *Edgar*, NMM: CRK/14/169. • **71**. Nelson to Danes, 2/4/1801, ADM 1/4; Nelson to his captains, 2/4/1801, White, *New Letters*, 259. The logs of the bomb vessels refer to the bombardment, for example that of the *Volcano*, ADM 51/1358, which times its commencement at 2.10. • **72**. Pope, *Great Gamble*, p. 424. The number of prisoners has been differently stated, but I have used the figure certified by the Danes on 7/5/1801, Baltic collection, WLC. • **73**. Caulfield to Hawkesbury, 7/4/1801, FO 33/21; Graves to Graves, 3/4/1801, Sturges Jackson, *Logs*, 2, p. 101. • **74**. Nelson's journal, 2/4/1801, NMM. CRK/14. • **75**. Nelson to Emma, 2/4/1801, Egerton MS 1614; Pettigrew, *Memoirs*, 2, p. 17. The reference in the poem to 'Henry's anchor fixed in [the] heart' may have been inspired by a poem by Lord William Gordon: Nelson to Emma, 21/1/1801, Egerton MS 1614.

XIV Controlling the Baltic

1. Nelson to Parker, 3/4/1801, *D&L*, 4, p. 331: Domett to Nelson, 3/4/1801, NMM: CRK/4. • **2**. *D&L*, 4, p. 325. Nelson and Lindholm's exchange of letters about Fischer, dated 22 April and 2 May, are in Add. MS 34918. • **3**. Nelson to Parker, 3/4/1801, ADM 1/4; Fancourt to Nelson, 9/4/1801, NMM: CRK/5/57. • **4**. Parker to Nepean, 6/4/1801, ADM 1/4; Nelson to Troubridge, 3, 9 and 28/4/1801, Huntington, HM 34216, 34217 and 34223. A few months later, however, Nelson was less complimentary about Thesiger, and complained that the Admiralty had promoted him 'in preference to merit': Troubridge to Nelson, 14/8/1801, NMM: CRK/13. • **5**. Parker to Nepean, 30/4/1801, ADM 1/ 4; Nelson to Davison, 22/4/1801, July 1801, Egerton MS 2240; Nelson to St Vincent, April 1801, *D&L*, 4, p. 336; St Vincent to Parker, 10/3/1801, Add. MS 31169; Dickson to Nelson, 31/3/1802, *HANP*, 2, p. 186. • **6**. Hardy to Manfield, 5/4/1801, A. M. Broadley, *Nelson's Hardy*, p. 63; Nelson to Addington, 4/4/1801, *D&L*, 4, p. 322; *NC*, 14 (1805), pp. 397–9. Stewart's oft-repeated assertion that Nelson's aide, Edward T. Parker, was present on the occasion is incorrect. Far from accompanying Nelson to the Baltic, Parker was in England preparing the *Trimmer* for sea until 24 April (ADM 35/1935; ADM 52/3503), and came out with Rear Admiral Totty, joining Nelson off Bornholm in the Baltic on 24 May, where he delivered a packet from Davison. • **7**. Vansittart to Nelson, 8/4/1801, and 'minute of a conversation with His Royal Highness, Prince Royal of Denmark', 3/4/1801, WLC. • **8**. Nelson to Addington, 9/4/1801, *D&L*, 4, p. 339. • **9**. Lindholm to Nelson, 2/5/1801, Add. MS 34918. • **10**. Nelson to Clarence, 10/5/1801, Add. MS 46356; Nelson to Addington, 4/4/1801,

D&L, 4, p. 332. • **11**. Nelson to Thompson, 12/4/1801, Add. MS 46119. • **12**. Parker to the Danes, 6/4/1800, ADM 1/4. • **13**. Nelson to Troubridge, 9/4/1801, Huntington, HM 34217. • **14**. Nelson to Addington, 9/4/1801, *D&L*, 4, p. 339. • **15**. Stewart, *D&L*, 4, p. 326. • **16**. Nelson to Addington, 9/4/1801, *D&L*, 4, p. 339. • **17**. Fremantle to his wife, 1/5/1801, Anne Fremantle, *Wynne Diaries*, 3, p. 53. • **18**. Nelson to Troubridge, 9/4/1801, Huntington, HM 34217; Nelson to Lindholm, 12/4/1801, *HANP*, 2, p. 137. • **19**. Nelson to Emma, 9/4/1801, *HANP*, 2, p. 136; Waltersdorff to Nelson, 16/6/1801, Lindholm to Nelson, 15/1/1801, and Nelson to Lindholm, 15/4/1801, WLC; Thomas A. Hardy, 'Boulton's Neapolitan Medal', p. 198. • **20**. Nelson to St Vincent, 9/4/1801, *D&L*, 4, p. 341. • **21**. Clarence to Nelson, 20/4/1801, Egerton MS 1623; Huskisson to Admiralty, 21/4/1801, FO 22/41; Addington to Nelson, 20/4/1801, NMM: CRK/1; Nepean to Nelson, 22/4/1801, Add. MS 34934; Nelson to Addington, 5 and 8/5/1801, *D&L*, 4, pp. 355, 360. • **22**. Nelson to Emma, 9 and 27/4/1801, *HANP*, 2, pp. 136, 142, and 11/5/1801, Thomas J. Pettigrew, *Memoirs*, 2, p. 60. • **23**. Nelson's journal, NMM: CRK/14; Nelson to Troubridge, 12/4/1801, Huntington, HM 34218. • **24**. Domett to Bridport, 26/4/1801, Add. MS 35201; Parker to Nepean, 25/4/1801, ADM 1/4; Nepean to Parker, 4/5/1801, Add. MS 34934. • **25**. Briarly's account, 19/4/1801, *NC*, 5 (1801), p. 452; Nelson's journal, NMM: CRK/14; Nelson to Troubridge, 20/4/1801, Huntington, HM 34219; Nelson to Emma, 8/6/1801, Egerton MS 1614; Mary Agnes FitzGibbon, *Veteran of 1812*, p. 39. • **26**. St Vincent to Parker, 17/4/1801, Add. MS 31169; Nathaniel Wraxall, *Historical Memoirs*, 1, pp. 164–6; G. S. Street, *Ghosts of Piccadilly*, pp. 184–5; Hamilton to Nelson, 16/4/1801, NMM: CRK/7. • **27**. Fanny to Nelson, April 1801, *NLTHW*, p. 585; Nelson to Davison, 23/4/1801, Egerton MS 2240; Edmund to Nelson, April 1801, *NLTHW*, p. 586. • **28**. St Vincent to Parker, 17/4/1801, Add. MS 34934. • **29**. Leveson V. Harcourt, *Rose*, 1, p. 347; Davison to Rundell and Bridge, 22/8/1801, NMM: CRK/3; Rundell and Bridge to Davison, 6/9/1801, Sotheby's, *Davison*, p. 121; Addington to Nelson, 9/7/1801, NMM: CRK/1. The new peerage entitled Nelson to add a viscount's coronet to his coat of arms. Lloyd's made two awards of £500 to Nelson at this time, one belated compensation for the injury he had received in the battle of Cape St Vincent, and the other for Copenhagen: Angerstein to Nelson, 3/6/1801, 30/7/1801, NMM: CRK/1, and *HANP*, 2, p. 159. • **30**. Nelson's journal, NMM: CRK/14; J. G. Bullocke, *Tomlinson Papers*, pp. 310–11; Domett to Bridport, 26/4/1801, Add. MS 35201; Crauford to Hawkesbury, 22/4/1801, FO 33/21; Parker to Nelson, 21 and 22/4/1801, NMM: CRK/9. • **31**. Nepean to Parker, 6/5/1801, Add. MS 34934. • **32**. Parker to Pahlen, 26/4/1801, Add. MS 34918; Nelson to Tyler, 24/4/1801, W. H. Wyndham-Quin, *Tyler*, p. 115; Nelson to Fremantle, 24/4/1801, Fremantle, *Wynne Diaries*, 3, p. 52; A. and M. Gatty, *Recollections*, p. 76. Graves's medal, made of bronzed copper, is illustrated in Sotheby's, *Trafalgar*, pp. 128–9. • **33**. Nelson to Clarence, 4/4/1801, Add. MS 46356; Nelson to Emma, 8/6/1801, Egerton MS 1614; Nelson to Ball, 4/6/1801, Warren R. Dawson, *Nelson Collection*, p. 165; Nelson to Dickson, 23/5/1801, Nelson to Troubridge, 2 and 7/5/1801, and Nelson to Nepean, 25/4/1801, Huntington, HM 34047, 34224–34225, 34221. • **34**. Nelson to Emma, 23 and 27/4/1801 (*HANP*, 2, p. 142), 28/4/1801 (Zabriskie Collection, US Naval Academy) and 12/5/1801 (Pettigrew, *Memoirs*, 2, p. 61); Nelson to Hamilton, 27/4/1801, *HANP*, 2, p. 143; Ferdinand to Nelson, April 1801, Egerton MS 1623; Tyson to Nelson, 8/4/1801, Add. MS 34918; Nelson to Lindholm, 12/4/1801, WLC. • **35**. Parker's journal, 5/5/1801, ADM 50/65; Sturges Jackson, *Logs*, 2, p. 92; Peter Le Fevre, 'Little Merit', p. 21; Ann Parry, *Fremantle*, p. 57; Troubridge to Nelson, 25/4/1801, Bonham's lot, 2005; Nelson to Nepean, 5/5/1801, ADM 1/4. • **36**. Nelson to Clarence, 10/5/1801, Add. MS 46356. • **37**. A list of Baltic ships in the Huntington, HM 34231, gives the sail of the line as *St George*, *Warrior*, *Raisonable*, *Polyphemus*, *Glatton*, *Invincible*, *Edgar*, *Zealous*, *Saturn*, *London*, *Ganges*, *Ardent*, *Defence*, *Bellona*, *Elephant*, *Ramillies*, *Veteran*,

Russell, Agamemnon, Defiance and *Powerful. Monarch* and *Isis*, which had suffered the greatest damage in the battle, had been sent home. • **38**. Nelson to Nepean, 5, 7, 17 and 22/5/1801, ADM 1/4. • **39**. Nelson to Emma, 25/4/1801, Egerton MS 1614. • **40**. *D&L*, 4, p. 386; Nelson to Emma, 8/5/1801, Pettigrew, *Memoirs*, 2, p. 54; Nelson to Clarence, 10/5/1801, Add. MS 46356. • **41**. Nelson to Nepean, 5/5/1801, ADM 1/4; • **42**. Nelson to St Vincent, 22/5/1801, *Cumloden Papers*; Nelson to Emma, 5/6/1801, Pettigrew, *Memoirs*, 2, p. 84; Clarke and McArthur, *Life and Services*, 2, p. 421; *D&L*, 4, p. 386. • **43**. Nelson to the Swedish admiral, 8/5/1801, FO 73/29. • **44**. Nelson to Carysfort, 8/5/1801, WLC; Nelson to Pahlen, 9/5/1801, ADM 1/4. • **45**. Garlike to Nelson, 18/5/1801, FO 65/48. • **46**. Nelson to Emma, 15/5/1801, Egerton MS 1614; Balascheff to Nelson, 12/5/1801, WLC; Domett to Bridport, 17/5/1801, Add. MS 35201. • **47**. Nelson to Pahlen, 16/5/1801, and Nelson to Nepean, 17/5/1801, ADM 1/4. • **48**. Fremantle concluded that all the Russian ships were unseaworthy and the dockyard denuded of stores, but the shore defences were in reasonable order. The harbour fielded 160 guns and mortars, and there was a citadel and a forty-eight-gun fort on the south-west side of the port. Fremantle also noted that two hundred British merchantmen were detained at St Petersburg and Riga: Fremantle to Nelson, 23/5/1801, NMM: CRK/5; Fremantle, *Wynne Diaries*, 3, p. 59. • **49**. Nelson to Carysfort, 19/5/1801, *D&L*, 4, p. 375; Nelson to Nepean, 24/5/1801, ADM 1/4; Nelson to Panin, 20/5/1801, and Nelson's declaration, 20/5/1801, FO 73/29; Tchitchagoff's declaration, 20/5/1801, NMM: CRK/13. • **50**. St Helens to Hawkesbury, 21/5/1801, FO 65/48. • **51**. Davison to Nelson, 22 and 24/4/1801, WLC, and NMM: CRK/3; *Gentleman's Magazine*, 71, pt. 1 (1801), p. 381; *NC*, 5 (1801), p. 376; Nelson to St Vincent, 22/5/1801, *D&L*, 4, p. 379; Martyn Downer, *Nelson's Purse*, pp. 185–7. • **52**. Sotheby's, *Davison*, p. 82; Mary E. Matcham, *Nelsons*, p. 187; Nelson to Maurice, 15/4/1801, Huntington, HM 34046; St Vincent to Nelson, 25/4/1801, Add. MS 31169. • **53**. Davison to Nelson, 3/5/1801, NMM: CRK/3; Nelson to Davison, 22 and 25/5/1801, *D&L*, 4, pp. 378, 391; Nelson to Sukey, 2/7/1801, *HANP*, 2, p. 156; Nelson to Emma, 26/5/1801, and Susannah to Emma, 1/3/1811, *HANP*, 2, pp. 139, 348; Diana N. Jarvis, 'Maurice Nelson, 1753–1801', pp. 609–11. • **54**. Nelson to Nepean, 22/5/1801, and Nelson to Booth, 28/5/1801, ADM 1/4; Balfour to Nelson, 17/4/1801, NMM: CRK/2; Victualling Office to Nelson, 8/10/1801, and Nepean to Nelson, 2/6/1801, Add. MS 34934; Nelson to Murray, 19/5/1801, Colin White, *New Letters*, p. 266; Cockburn to Hawkesbury, 11/4/1801, FO 33/21. • **55**. Nelson to Emma, 1/6/1801, *HANP*, 2, p. 150; Cockburn to Nelson, 29/5/1801, NMM: CRK/3; Tyckson to Nelson, 5/6/1801, Egerton MS 2240; Thomas Blumel, 'Nelson in Warnemuende Roads', pp. 765, 766, 769. This article, based on local sources, fleshes out Nelson's visit. • **56**. Totty to Nelson, 2/6/1801, NMM: CRK/12. • **57**. Nelson to Cronstedt, 23/5/1801, and the proclamation of King Gustav Adelph, 19/5/1801, FO 73/29; Totty to Nelson, 25/5/1801, NMM: CRK/12; Crauford to Hawkesbury, 2/6/1801, FO 33/21. • **58**. Nelson to Troubridge, 27/5/1801, Huntington, HM 34228; Pahlen to Nelson, May 1801, ADM 1/4; St Helens to Nelson, 5/6/1801, NMM: CRK/14; Domett to Bridport, 27/5/1801, Add. MS 35201. • **59**. Stewart, *D&L*, 4, p. 393. • **60**. St Vincent to the Lord Mayor of London, 3/6/1801, Add. MS 31169; Garlike to Hawkesbury, 24/5/1801, FO 65/48. • **61**. St Helens to Hawkesbury, 31/5/1801, and Garlike to Hawkesbury, 24/5/1801, FO 65/48; Thesiger to Nelson, 5/7/1801, NMM: CRK/13. • **62**. Royal decree of 4/6/1801, FO 65/48. • **63**. Nelson to Lindholm, 6/5/1801, 5, 7, 12 and 16/6/1801, WLC. • **64**. Nelson to St Vincent, 12–14/6/1801, *D&L*, 4, p. 412; Nelson to Nepean, 12/6/1801, ADM 1/4; Lindholm to Nelson, 10/6/1801, WLC; Bernstorff to Nelson, 8/5/1801, Egerton MS 1623. • **65**. Nelson to Berry, 11/6/1801, Add. MS 34918; Stewart to Nelson, 8/6/1801, and Lindholm to Nelson, 10/6/1801, WLC; Charles Fenwick, 21/5/1801, FO 22/41; Waltersdorff to Nelson, 15/6/1801, NMM: CRK/14. • **66**. Nelson to Davison, 15/5/1801, *D&L*,

4, p. 416. • **67**. Nelson to Nepean, 12/6/1801, ADM 1/4; Nepean to Nelson, 26/6/1801, Add. MS 34934; *St George* log, ADM 51/1371; Andrew Lambert, *Nelson*, p. 213. • **68**. Nelson to Emma, 20/4/1801, 17/5/1801, 8/6/1801, *HANP*, 2, p. 139, and Pettigrew, *Memoirs*, 2, pp. 68, 86. • **69**. St Vincent to Nelson, 31/5/1801, Add. MS 31169. • **70**. Clarke and McArthur, *Life and Services*, 2, p. 422; Nelson's memorandum, 18/6/1801, *D&L*, 4, p. 420; Nelson to Clarence, 15/6/1801, Add. MS 46356. Lieutenant William Davies of the *Tigress* was removed from his command for persistent drunkenness, while the case of Lieutenant Henry of the *Terror*, charged with ill-treating a boy and 'uncleanliness', went forward to Pole's jurisdiction (Pole to Graves, 20/6/1801, Add. MS 40668). Two other lieutenants, David Dickson and Robert Crosby of the *Zealous* and *Vengeance*, who had been officers of the watch when their ships collided in the night of 15 May, were sent to England: Nelson to Nepean, 13 and 14/6/1801, ADM 1/4; Nepean to Nelson, 24/6/1801, Add. MS 34934. • **71**. Fremantle to his wife, 4/4/1801, Fremantle, *Wynne Diaries*, 3, p. 41; Brisbane to Nelson, 16/6/1801, NMM: CRK/2; Totty to Nelson, 22/6/1801, NMM: CRK/14. • **72**. Log of *St George*, ADM 51/1371; Nelson to Emma, 14/6/1801, Pettigrew, *Memoirs*, 2, p. 101. • **73**. Graves to Nelson, June 1801 and 8/8/1801, NMM: CRK/6. • **74**. *D&L*, 4, p. 413; Fremantle to his brother, 3/7/1801, Parry, *Fremantle*, p. 60.

XV The Guardian

1. *The Times*, 1/7/1801; *Morning Chronicle*, 1/7/1801; *Trewman's Exeter Flying Post*, 1/7/1801; *Ipswich Journal*, 4/7/1801. The account of the visit to the hospital was given to Sir Walter Scott by a witness, and published in 1828: Esther H. Moorhouse, *Nelson in England*, pp. 160–61. • **2**. Nelson to Stewart, 3/7/1801, *Cumloden Papers*; *Morning Chronicle*, 3/7/1801; Nelson to Parker, 8/7/1801, NMM: CRK/14. • **3**. St Vincent to Nelson, 12/9/1801, Add. MS 31169; Nelson to Yorke, 23/7/1801, privately owned; Nelson to Suckling, 21/11/1801, Add. MS 21506; Suckling to Nelson, 1/11/1803, NMM: CRK/12; Teissier to Nelson, 8/7/1801, NMM: CRK/13. • **4**. Nelson to St Vincent, 23/9/1801, *D&L*, 7, p. ccxxix; Addington to Nelson, 11 and 13/7/1801, NMM: CRK/1. • **5**. Lord to Lady Cathcart, 8/7/1801, John Knox Laughton, *Naval Miscellany*, 1, p. 290; Nelson to Sukey, 2/7/1801, Huntington, HM 34049; Sukey to Emma, 11/9/1801, NMM: CRK/20; Nelson to Davison, 9/7/1801, Egerton MS 2240; *The Times*, 16/7/1801; Emma's note and Gordon's poem, Egerton MS 1623; Nelson to Emma, 26/9/1801, *NLTHW*, p. 590; James Harrison, *Life*, 2, p. 348; *ND*, 8 (2003), pp. 16–17. One deduces that Quasheebaw was Fatima's original name. • **6**. Mary Ann Parker (1786– 1829), who shared her brother's good nature, married Daniel Shewen, a naval lieutenant, in 1805. Their son, Edward Thornbrough Parker, died a colonel in the Royal Marines in 1864. My discussion of Parker depends heavily upon the assiduous research of Richard Venn, who approached me for assistance with his project and exceeded all expectations. • **7**. Nelson to Baird, 20/9/1801, *D&L*, 4, p. 491; Nelson to St Vincent, 27/9/1801, *D&L*, 4, p. 497. • **8**. Admiralty to St Vincent, 26/12/1798, ADM 2/292; Hardy to Manfield, 20/8/1801, A. M. Broadley, *Nelson's Hardy*, p. 71; 'Account of the removes of Commissioned Officers', 1798, ADM 6/64. • **9**. Parker to Nelson, 26/9/1799, 9/12/1799, Add. MS 34914; Count de Front to Grenville, 24/10/1799, and Nepean to Frere, 29/10/1799, FO 67/28; Nelson to Troubridge, 1/10/1799, Add. MS 34963; Hilda Gamlin, *Nelson's Friendships*, 1, pp. 382–83; Fanny to Nelson, 21/10/1799, Add. MS 34988. • **10**. Gamlin, *Nelson's Friendships*, 1, p. 249, and 2, pp. 251– 2; *HANP*, 2, p. 392; Sarah to William Nelson, Sept, 1801, NMM: BRP/4. • **11**. Nepean to Nelson, 26/7/1801, NMM: CRK/9; Richard Saxby, 'Blockade of Brest'. • **12**. Nelson to Stewart, 23/9/1801, *Cumloden Papers*. • **13**. List, 2/8/1801, order book, Royal Naval Museum, MS. 200; Add. MS 34918, ff. 90–95; Add. MS 34934, f. 136; and 'A List of His Majesty's

Ships and Vessels . . . Under the Command of Lord Viscount Nelson', Add. MS 34918. The 'line' ships eventually coming within his jurisdiction were the *Ardent* (William Nowell), *Leyden* (William Bedford), *York* (John Ferrier), *Ruby* (Edward Berry), *Glatton* (John Devonshire), *Isis* (Thomas Masterman Hardy) and *Berschermer* (Alexander Fraser), although the floating battery, *Batavier* (William R. Broughton), was a fifty. The *Alliance* store ship and *Serapsis* block mounted forty-four guns apiece. At the other end of the scale, some of Nelson's units were single-gun affairs, such as row galleys armed with a 68-pound carronade, or flats carrying a 12-pounder: list of needs at Sheerness Yard, 28/7/1801, NMM: CRK/14. • **14**. St Vincent to Nelson, 8, 11 and 14/8/1801, Add. MS 31169; Nelson's memorandum, 25/7/1801, ADM 1/531. Parker's personal service to Nelson is illustrated by his early request that Emma send them cream cheese, one of the admiral's favourites, so that he could cut it up for him: Parker to Emma, 30/7/1801, Houghton, MS Eng. 196.5. Nelson's official correspondence for this command is filed with the papers of the North Sea squadron in ADM 1/531–532, and the letters sent him by the Admiralty can be found in NMM: CRK/15 and 16. See also Monmouth MSS E990 and 991 (Nelson letter books) and Royal Naval Museum MS 200 (order book). • **15**. The principal locations for Nelson's defensive inshore ring ran from Yarmouth to Rye Bay, and excluding major naval bases were Orfordness; Hollesley Bay; the Woodbridge river; the Wallet (Felixstowe); Harwich; the Colne, Blackwater and Maldon rivers; the Swin; the East Swale; Whitstable flats; Herne Bay; Pan Sand; Margate; a station under Dungeness; and Rye and Winchelsea: Nelson to Nepean, 28/7/1801, ADM 1/531; Add. MS 34918, ff. 90–95; Graeme's 'Disposition of Vessels Under Nelson', 11/8/1801, NMM: CRK/6/60; and the list of stations for gun barges, NMM: CRK/6/65. • **16**. Nelson to Emma, 31/7/1801, 21/9/1801, NMM: CRK/19. • **17**. Fanny to Davison, 26/6/1801, NMM: DAV/2. • **18**. Fanny to Davison, 27/5/1801, NMM: Dav/2; Fanny to Nelson, 1801, Monmouth MS E981. • **19**. Fanny to Davison, 24 and 27/5/1801, 15/6/1801, NMM: Dav/2. • **20**. Susannah to Fanny, 14/5/1801, Monmouth MS E670. • **21**. Fanny to Davison, 26/4/1801, 7/5/1801, NMM: Dav/2; Edmund to Nelson, 3, 9 and 16/7/1801, 1/8/1801, NMM: CRK/9. • **22**. Edmund to Emma, August 1801, Warren R. Dawson, *Nelson Collection*, p. 172; Edmund to Fanny, 21/8/1801, Monmouth MS E649; Fanny to Edmund, September and October 1801, Monmouth MSS E688, 689; *Ipswich Gazette*, 12/9/1801. • **23**. Edmund to Fanny, 17/10/1801, Monmouth MS E650. • **24**. Matcham, *Nelsons*, p. 191. • **25**. Log of *Unite*, ADM 51/1384; Parker to Emma, 30/7/1801, Houghton, MS Eng. 196.5. • **26**. Nelson to St Vincent, 30/7/1801, *D&L*, 4, p. 432; Nelson to captains, 10/8/1801, order book, Royal Naval Museum, MS 200; *Leyden* log, ADM 51/1358. • **27**. List of ships, ADM 1/531, f. 704. • **28**. Somerville to Lutwidge, 28/7/1801, ADM 1/670; Richardson to Lutwidge, 2/8/1801, Philips to Philips, 5/8/1801, Philips to Nelson, 9/8/1801, and Russel to Nelson, 17 and 18/8/1801, NMM: CRK/10; St Vincent to Nelson, 29 and 31/7/1801, Add. MS 31169; *Medusa* log, ADM 51/1437. Thomas Wallis, secretary, Lieutenant Frederick Langford and Commander Edward Parker, accompanied Nelson to the *Medusa* (*Medusa* muster, ADM 36/15155). • **29**. Somerville to Lutwidge, 1/8/1801, ADM 1/670; Parker to Davison, 3/8/1801, Sotheby's lot, 2002; Rémi Monaque, 'Latouche-Tréville', which gives the French perspective. • **30**. Nelson to Nepean, 3/8/1801, ADM 1/531; Nelson to St Vincent, 13/8/1801, *D&L*, 4, p. 456. • **31**. Vansittart to Nelson, 30/7/1801, NMM: CRK/13. • **32**. This account of the attacks on Boulogne draws upon Nelson's letters to St Vincent and Addington, 4/8/1801, *D&L*, 4, p. 438; Nelson to Nepean, 4/8/1801, ADM 1/531; Nelson to Stewart, 4/8/1801, *Cumloden Papers*; Nelson to Clarence, 5/8/1801, Add. MS 46356; Nelson to Emma, 4/8/1801, Egerton MS 1614; Cathcart to Cathcart, 7/8/1801, Laughton, *Naval Miscellany*, 1, p. 292; Nowell to Nelson, 7/8/1801, ADM 1/670; various ships' logs, especially *Medusa*, *Discovery* and *Gannet*, ADM 51/1437, 1352 and

1463; eyewitness accounts in the *Morning Chronicle*, 6 and 8/8/1801, and *Hampshire Telegraph*, 10/8/1801; John Charnock, *Biographical Memoirs*, p. 334; Sotheby's, *Davison*, p. 122; Monaque, 'Latouche-Tréville', pp. 276–8. • **33**. Nelson to Nepean, 6/8/1801, ADM 1/531; Owen to Bedford, 14/8/1801, Add. MS 34918; Brodie to Owen, 19/8/1801, NMM: CRK/9. • **34**. Owen to Nelson, 9, 12, 13, 14 and 22/8/1801, Add. MS 34918; Nepean to Nelson, 1/10/1801, NMM: CRK/16. • **35**. St Vincent to Nelson, 7, 14, 17 and 26/8/1801, Add. MS 31169; Brodie to Owen, 19/8/1801, and Owen to Nelson, 21/8/1801, NMM: CRK/9. • **36**. Victualling Board to Nelson, 26/8/1801, and Sick and Wounded Office to Nelson, 2/9/1801, Add. MS 34934; Graeme to Nelson, 7, 11, 28 and 30/8/1801, NMM: CRK/6; Coffin to Nelson, 25/9/1801, NMM: CRK/3; Office of Ordnance to Baseley, 6/8/1801, and letters of Mathews, Geast and Marshall to Nelson, 8–10 and 14/8/1801, with related documents, Add. MS 34934. • **37**. Graeme to Nelson, 18, 28 and 30/8/1801, NMM: CRK/6; Graeme to Nepean, 7, 8 and 19/8/1801, ADM 1/734; Gore to Nelson, 21/9/1801, and a list of ships at the Nore and Sheerness, 1801, NMM: CRK/6; Bedford to Nelson, 1, 2, 3 and 31/8/1801, with enclosed list, NMM: CRK/2; Harvey to Bedford, 6/8/1801, NMM: CRK/6; Dorvey and Atkins, 13/9/1801, NMM: CRK/15; Lutwidge to Nepean, 3 and 23/8/1801, ADM 1/670; Nelson to Nepean, 22/8/1801, ADM 1/531; Spence to Nelson, 11/8/1801, NMM: CRK/12. Disaffection was more feared than real. Nelson ordered an enquiry into a crew accused of plotting to seize control of their gun vessel and taking her into Calais. The story proved to be the fabrication of a cabin boy: Nelson to Nepean, 23/8/1801, and Bedford and Gore to Nelson, 21/8/1801, ADM 1/531. • **38**. Nelson to captains, 6/8/1801, and Nelson to Nepean, 10/8/1801, ADM 1/531; letters to Nelson in Add. MS 34918, especially those by Berry, 13/8/1801, Shield, 7/8/1801, Edge, 9, 13, 19 and 28/8/1801, Schomberg, 13/8/1801, Becker, 9 and 27/8/1801, and Hamilton, 8/8/1801; Melhuish to Nelson, 16/8/1801, 16/9/1801, NMM: CRK/9; Troubridge to Nelson, 16/8/1801, NMM: CRK/13. The Sea Fencibles were placed under regular naval officers, many of whom had been unable to secure appointments in Her Majesty's ships. Some old *Agamemnons* with the Fencibles hoped to use Nelson's offices to find a way back into regular employment. One of Shield's assistants was James Noble, a commander. Noble offered to command any boat under Nelson, but Shield kept him on shore. Further afield, Lieutenant Maurice William Suckling, the admiral's cousin, commanded the *Furnace* gunboat stationed at Blakeney in Norfolk. Suckling asked Nelson to help him achieve promotion, but seemed unsure as to whether to remain at sea or focus on managing an inherited estate in Suffolk. At Blakeney he was accused of hiring out the Fencibles placed under his command to local farmers and shipowners, and of absenting himself from his post to visit his estate: Suckling to Nelson, 10, 8/1801, and Skene to Nelson, 29/8/1801, NMM: CRK/12. In Tiverton, Devon, another *Agamemnon*, Captain George Andrews, who was unemployed, would even have taken a blockship to return to Nelson's command: Andrews to Nelson, 13/9/1801, NMM: CRK/1. • **39**. Nelson to St Vincent, 7/8/1801, *D&L*, 4, p. 446. • **40**. *Medusa* log (captain), ADM 51/1437; *Medusa* log (master), ADM 52/3208; Spence to Nelson, 11/8/1801, NMM: CRK/12; Nelson to Nepean, 10/8/1801, ADM 1/531; *NC*, 6 (1801), p. 161; 'The Medusa Channel', *ND*, 4 (1991), pp. 4–6; 'Surveys of Graeme Spence'. • **41**. Ferrier to Nelson, 12/8/1801, ADM 1/531. • **42**. Nelson's orders, 15/8/1801, Add. MS 34918; *Morning Herald*, 19/8/1801. Cotgrave of the *Gannet* was one of Nelson's earliest naval acquaintances, having been with him and Charles Boyles in Captain Suckling's *Triumph* at Blackstakes: Cotgrave to Nelson, 2/6/1801, NMM: CRK/3. • **43**. Graham Smith, 'Nelson's Revenue Cutters'. • **44**. *Morning Chronicle*, 10, 15 and 28/8/1801; Latouche Tréville to the Minister of Marine, 16/8/1801, in Charnock, *Biographical Memoirs*, 335; logs of the *York* and *Leyden*, ADM 51/1330 and 1358. The timings given in the logs are suspect. The *York*, which records hoisting her boats out at 7.00, has the action commencing at 12.30; but the *Medusa* (ADM 51/1437) logged hoisting out her boats at 8.10 and the action as beginning at 1.30. This suggests a discrepancy in timekeeping of an hour. • **45**. Nelson to Emma, 15/8/1801, Pettigrew, *Memoirs*, 2, p. 154; Nelson to Stewart, 26/8/1801, *Cumloden Papers*. • **46**. This description of the engagement is based upon the logs of the attacking ships; Nelson's dispatches to St Vincent and Nepean, 16/8/1801, ADM 1/531; reports of the five divisional commanders dated 16/8/1801, Add. MS 34918; Nowell to Nelson, 7/8/1801, NMM: CRK/9; Nelson to Stewart, 26/8/1801, *Cumloden Papers*; Lord to Lady Cathcart, 29/8/1801, 1/9/1801, and Gore to Cathcart, 28/8/1801, Laughton, *Naval Miscellany*, 1, pp. 296, 298, 300; Hardy to Manfield, 20 and 26/8/1801, Broadley, *Nelson's Hardy*, pp. 71, 73. Copies of official French documents can be found in NMM: MRF/181. • **47**. List of casualties, 1/9/1801, ADM 1/532; Ferrier to Nelson, 19 and 22/8/1801, 17–30/9/1801, NMM: CRK/5; Somerville to Nelson, 26/9/1801, 2/10/1801, NMM: CRK/11. • **48**. Hood to Cornwallis, 31/8/1801, HMC, *Various Collections*, 6, p. 395. • **49**. Baird to Nelson, 1/8/1801, NMM: CRK/1; Nelson to Emma, 18/8/1801, NMM: CRK/19; *Morning Chronicle*, 19/8/1801; *NC*, 6 (1801), p. 172. • **50**. Nelson to St Vincent, 17– 19/8/1801, *D&L*, 4, p. 470; Troubridge to Nelson, 19/8/1801, NMM: CRK/13; St Vincent to Nelson, 28/8/1801, and St Vincent to Milbanke, 20/3/1801, Add. MS 31169. • **51**. Nelson to Hill, 6/9/1801, *D&L*, 4, p. 485; 'Remarks by a Seaman', Nelson to Nepean, 6/9/1801, and Hill to Nelson, 28/8/1801, NMM: CRK/14; Nepean to Nelson, 8 and 11/9/1801, Add. MS 34918; *Morning Chronicle*, 28/9/1801; St Vincent to Nelson, 9/9/1801, Add. MS 31169; Anthony Cross, 'School of Fear', which makes an informed analysis of Hill's charges. • **52**. Nelson to the fleet, 19/8/1801, order book, Royal Naval Museum, MS 200; Nelson to St Vincent, 17–19/8/1801, *D&L*, 4, p. 470; Nepean to Nelson, 11, 12, 20, 28 and 29/8/1801, Add. MS 34918; Emma to William, 4/9/1801, NMM: BRP/4. • **53**. Russel to Nelson, 19/8/1801, NMM: CRK/10; Nelson to Nepean, 25/8/1801, ADM 1/531; Owen to Nelson, 22 and 29/8/1801, 8/9/1801, Add. MS 34918; Owen to Nelson, 21/8/1801, with sketch, NMM: CRK/9; annotations on George Thompson's map of 1794, made during the reconnaissance, NMM: CRK/16/47. • **54**. Rose to Nelson and Sarradine to Nelson, 21/8/1801, ADM 1/531; Cotgrave to Nelson, 22/8/1801, NMM: CRK/3; *Gannet* log, ADM 51/1463; Philips to Nelson, 8/9/1801, NMM: CRK/10; Gore to Nelson, 7/9/1801, NMM: CRK/6. • **55**. Helvoet plan, ADM 1/531, f. 697; St Vincent to Nelson, 31/9/1801, Add. MS 31169; Gore to Nelson, 18/9/1801, NMM: CRK/6; Owen to Nelson, 26/9/1801, NMM: CRK/9; Nelson to Rose and Somerville, 1/10/1801, Add. MS 34918; Nelson to Nepean, 21/9/1801, NMM: CRK/15. According to the muster of the *Amazon* (ADM 36/14681) Nelson transferred on 28 August with Thomas Wallis and five servants, Joshua Webb, James Bell, Tom Allen, Benjamin Cook and Samuel Parton. • **56**. Nelson to Nepean, September 1801, NMM: CRK/15. Nelson's complaints were not entirely mistaken. Success *always* breeds professional jealousy, and the repulse at Boulogne had attracted criticism, but he exaggerated. Typical of many letters from those eager to serve under him was that of John Lackey of the *Earl of St Vincent* cutter, who begged to be included in Nelson's next foray, when he would 'show you what the cutter is able to perform': Lackey to Nelson, 1/9/1801, NMM: CRK/8. • **57**. Ferrier to Gore, 21/8/1801, NMM: CRK/5/86; Troubridge to Nelson, 2/9/1801, NMM: CRK/13; Davison to Nelson, 4/9/1801, NMM: CRK/3; Parker to Emma, 18/8/1801, Sotheby's lot, 2005; Nepean to Nelson, 26/7/1801, Add. MS 34934. • **58**. Parker to Emma, 21/8/1801, Monmouth MS E544. • **59**. Nelson to Emma, 19/8/1801, Pettigrew, *Memoirs*, 2, p. 161. • **60**. Nelson to Emma, 19/8/1801, 16/10/1801, Huntington, HM 34052, and NMM: CRK/19; *Morning Chronicle*, 24/9/1801; Sarah Nelson's letters to her husband, 27/8/1801 to 16/9/1801, NMM: BRP/3. H. Clay, who then owned a Japan factory in Birmingham and was an associate of Hamilton, claims the ménage stayed at the Ship Inn in Deal, kept by a Mr Michener. He was introduced to Nelson in their upstairs room overlooking the sea, and the admiral recollected seeing some of Clay's work in King Street, Covent Garden, about 1798, including a print of his former captain, George Farmer. Clay subsequently sent Nelson a copy, which the recipient pronounced a 'wonderful' likeness: *Memoirs of the Rt. Hon. Lord Viscount Nelson*, pp. 56–57. Contemporary letters clearly identify the Three Kings, however (NMM: CRK/22 and BRP/3), and Nelson was accustomed to taking meals there when ashore. Probably in reflection Clay confused the two inns. The Ship Inn, which was situated further south on Beach Street, closed in 1857, but the Three Kings is now the Royal Hotel. • **61**. Nepean to Nelson, 28/8/1801, Add. MS 34918. • **62**. Nelson to Emma, 20/9/1801, Pettigrew, *Memoirs*, 2, p. 181; Nelson to Stewart, 23/9/1801, *Cumloden Papers*; Nelson to Baird, 20 and 21/9/1801, *D&L*, 4, pp. 491, 492; Nelson to St Vincent, 20/9/1801, *D&L*, 4, p. 491; Nelson to Miss Parker, 24/9/1801, *D&L*, 4, p. 494. • **63**. Nelson to Emma, 24 and 27/9/1801, Pettigrew, *Memoirs*, 2, pp. 187, 190; *Amazon* log, ADM 51/4409. • **64**. Nelson to Emma, 29/9/1801, *HANP*, 2, p. 168; Nelson to Nepean, 28/9/1801, ADM 1/532. • **65**. *The Times*, 30/9/1801; *NC*, 6 (1801), pp. 318, 540–41; *Kentish Chronicle*, 27/9/1801; Nelson to Emma, 28/9/1801, *HANP*, 2, p. 168. The tomb which Nelson established may be seen today: Jim Jeffreys, 'In Passing', *ND*, 7 (2000), pp. 62–4. • **66**. Enery to Nelson, 3/9/1801, NMM: CRK/5/7; Gore to Nelson, 30/8/1801, NMM: CRK/6/15; Nelson to Baird, 6/10/1801, *D&L*, 4, p. 505; Nelson to Emma, 8/10/1801, NMM: CRK/19; Nelson to Stewart, 10/10/1801, *Cumloden Papers*. Thomas Parker died in Gloucester, where he was buried on 21 July 1803. • **67**. Berry to Nelson, 20/7/1801, NMM: CRK/2; Emma to Bedford, 13/2/1802, Add. MS 30182. Charles Connor, one of the Connor tribe related to Emma, was only twelve years old. Stanislaw Banti, an Italian of fourteen years, was the son of Emma's friend, Brigida Banti, the opera singer then resident in Knightsbridge. Both were rated first-class boy volunteers, which put them firmly on the commissioned officer ladder, but in Nelson's opinion Banti had imbibed too many of the vices of London to succeed and in 1802 he gave up the sea to return to Italy: *Amazon* muster, ADM 36/14681. • **68**. *Amazon* log, ADM 51/4409; St Vincent to Nelson, 5/9/1801, Add. MS 31169; Nelson to Nepean, 2, 4 and 7/9/1801, ADM 1/532. • **69**. Nelson to Nepean, 7 and 24/9/1801, ADM 1/532; Sherlock to Cathcart, 7/9/1801, NMM: CRK/12; Nelson to Emma, 20/10/1801, NMM: CRK/19. • **70**. Addington to Nelson, 8/10/1801, Add. MS 34918; Nelson to Emma, 15/10/1801, NMM: CRK/19.

XVI Looking for Paradise

1. Nelson to Emma, 12/10/1801, NMM: CRK/19. • **2**. Nelson to Emma, September 1801, *HANP*, 2, p. 165. • **3**. Nelson to Emma, 31/7/1801, 11 and 21/8/1801, NMM: CRK/19. • **4**. Nelson to Emma, 21/8/1801, NMM: CRK/19; St Vincent to his sister, 3/1/1806, Add. MS 29915; A. Aspinall, *Later Correspondence*, 3, p. 542; Parker to Davison, 9/8/1801, Sotheby's, *Davison*, pp. 122–3. • **5**. David Constantine, *Fields of Fire*, pp. 261–4. • **6**. Emma to Bedford, 13/2/1802, Add. MS 30182; Emma to Sarah, September 1801, and Sarah to William, 2/9/1801, NMM: BRP/3; William to Emma, 13/6/1801 [italics mine], 23/8/1801, Thomas J. Pettigrew, *Memoirs*, 2, p. 152, and NMM: CRK/20; William to Nelson, 18/1/1800, Add. MS 34988; Sarah to Emma, 1803, Monmouth MS E538. • **7**. Nelson to Emma, 5/8/1801, Egerton MS 1614; Troubridge to Nelson, 14/8/1801, NMM: CRK/13. The differences over promotions can be traced in Add. MSS 31168 and 31169 and St Vincent's letters in NMM: CRK/11. • **8**. St Vincent to Nelson, 8/8/1801, Add. MS 31169; Nelson to Emma, 11/8/1801, NMM: CRK/19; Troubridge to Nelson, 14 and 17/8/1801, NMM: CRK/13. • **9**. Nelson to William, 10/4/1802, Add. MS 34988; Nelson to Emma, 12, 16 and 20/10/1801, NMM: CRK/19; Ludovic Kennedy, *Nelson and his Captains*, p. 265; Troubridge to Nelson, 20/9/1801, NMM: CRK/13. • **10**. Nelson to Davison, 13/8/1801, Egerton MS 2240; Nelson to Boothby, 1/1/1802, Add. MS 34918; Nelson to Emma, 22/8/1801, Pettigrew, *Memoirs*, 2, p. 169. • **11**. Nelson to Emma, 9/4/1801, Egerton MS 1614; Nelson to Scott, 31/7/1801, Robinson Library, Newcastle; Marianne Czisnik, 'Unique Account', p. 111. • **12**. Throughout this book I have converted money values from Sicilian 'ounces' to English pounds at the contemporary equivalent of one ounce to ten shillings. • **13**. Graefer to Nelson, 26/9/1801, *HANP*, 2, p. 166; Tyson to Nelson, 21/10/1801, Pettigrew, *Memoirs*, 2, p. 240; Nelson to Sutton, 16/2/1802, WLC; Graefer to Nelson, 10/12/1800, and Leckie to Nelson, 8/10/1800, NMM: CRK/17. • **14**. Nelson to Emma, 23/9/1801, Monmouth MS E107; Hardy to Manfield, 7/11/1801, A. M. Broadley, *Nelson's Hardy*, p. 77. • **15**. Nelson to Marsh and Creed, 15/9/1801, 29/12/1801, *HANP*, 2, p. 165, and Egerton MSS 1614; Nelson to Emma, 2/10/1801, *HANP*, 2, p. 170. • **16**. Nelson to Emma, 13/8/1801, Sotheby's lot, 2005; sale particulars, 1801, Surrey History Service, Woking, G85/2/1/1/42; Peter Hopkins, *History*, pp. 6, 31, 33. 'Paradise Merton', as Nelson called it, has been obliterated. The house was demolished in 1823, and the grounds disappeared under Victorian tenements. As a result, many erroneous statements have been made about its nature, extent and location. Percy Mundy, J. K. Laughton, Esther H. Moorhouse, James E. Jagger, Carola Oman, Philip Rathbone and Peter Warwick made brave attempts to clarify. However, until the deeds (now in the Surrey History Service) came to light in 1975, and the careful research of John Wallace, Peter Hopkins and Judith Goodman, the subject remained mysterious. Goodman's '200 Years Ago' supplements Hopkins's *History*, which is the standard work. I have reviewed the evidence, but remain greatly indebted to both these informed members of the Merton Historical Society for putting me on the right track. Key primary accounts, other than the deeds, include the sale advertisement of 1801, cited above; Cockerell to Haslewood, 31/8/1801, Add. MS 34918; sale description, 1808, *HANP*, 2, p. 308; sale particulars, 1815, Surrey History Service, G85/2/1/1/103; Hopkins, *History*, p. 26; *The Times*, 22/3/1815; and sale particulars, 1823, Goodman, '200 Years Ago', pp. 8–9. Surviving plans include the Rocque map, 1746, Warwick, 'Here Was Paradise', p. 41; *Thomas Milne's Land Use Map of London & Environs in 1800*; Thomas Chawner's plan of the ground floor, January 1805, Local Studies Library, Morden; C. T. Crackow's map of the seventy-two acres retained by Emma in 1806, Surrey History Service, 7883/3, which is superimposed on tithe maps for greater effect in Hopkins, *History*, p. 23; and a plan made in 1823 after the house itself was demolished, reproduced in Goodman, '200 Years Ago', p. 9. • **17**. Haslewood to Nelson, 25 and 31/8/1801, Add. MS 34918. • **18**. Cockerell's report, 31/8/1801, and Haslewood to Nelson, 2 and 9/9/1801, Add. MS 34918; Nelson to Haslewood, 27/8/1801, 4/9/1801, Monmouth MS E96, 100. • **19**. *HANP*, 2, pp. 165, 394–95; Marsh, Page and Creed to Nelson, 10/9/1801, Add. MS 34918; Emma, October 1801, Add. MS 34989; Fanny to Davison, 3/9/1801, NMM: Dav/2. Nelson's diamonds, including the chelengk, Ferdinand's sword and portrait and the Russian, Turkish and Sardinian snuff boxes, were held in a mahogany box by Davison. The market value of diamonds was low in 1801, and Nelson prevaricated about selling, but a few may have been traded at Rundell and Bridge: Nelson to Davison, 8/1/1801, October 1801, Add. MS 34988 and Egerton MS 2240; *NC*, 14 (1805), pp. 174–5. With regard to the possessions at Dods's, a 'list of Sundries' dated 5 March 1801 (Add. MS 34990) contains a poignant list of the remnants of the old triumvirate, including Edmund's bookcase and desk; Fanny's trunk, dressing screen and glassware; and a broken spinning wheel, bronzes and chimney ornaments. The extensive wine cellar included 51 hampers, 9 casks, a pipe and 27 bottles of ale, cider, red and white wine, sherry, port and brandy. Much of the table and hardware, from a coffee roaster to a copper boiler and ironing board, and the larger objects such as a mahogany wardrobe, bedstead and dining tables, a black writing desk, and a Kidderminster carpet probably went to Merton. Nelson also owned large numbers of books and prints, and his professional aids and trophies included a compass, printing machine, and relics of *L'Orient*, among them a piece of the mast and Captain Hallowell's coffin. • **20**. Nelson to Davison, December 1801, *D&L*, 4, p. 536; Nelson to Emma, 26/9/1801, 19/10/1801, NMM: CRK/19; Nelson to Emma, 9/10/1801, Egerton MS 1614. • **21**. Emma to Sarah, October 1801, Add. MS 34989. • **22**. Deeds, 23–24/10/1801, Surrey History Service, 7883/1–2; declaration of trust, 19/5/1807, Surrey History Service, 7883/6; Matcham to Nelson, 1801, NMM: CRK/9; Booth and Haslewood to Nelson, 21/11/1802, 22/9/1803, NMM: CRK/2 and 6; Nelson to Haslewood, 27/9/1801, Monmouth MS E109. • **23**. Emma to Sarah, November 1801, Add. MS 34989. • **24**. Walterstorff to Nelson, 4/12/1801, Add. MS 34918. • **25**. Emma to Sarah Nelson, October 1801, NMM: BRP/4. The accusation that Fanny had abandoned Josiah may have originated in Nelson's last meeting with his stepson at Deal on 6 September. The admiral did not invite the visitor to stay to dinner, but spoke to him. Josiah may have tried to ingratiate himself by denigrating his mother. If so, Nelson should have known Fanny better than to have believed it. Sarah to William, 9/9/1801, NMM/BRP/3. • **26**. Edmund to Nelson, 23/9/1801, 8/10/1801, NMM: BRP/5, and *HANP*, 2, p. 173; Nelson to Emma, 26/9/1801, 13/10/1801, NMM: CRK/19 and Monmouth MS E112. • **27**. St Vincent to Nelson, 1/5/1801, Add. MS 31169; Crew to Nelson, 22/9/1801, Add. MS 34934. • **28**. Nelson to Eamer, 20/11/1801, 22/6/1802, Egerton MS 1614; *Ipswich Gazette*, 14/11/1801. • **29**. St Vincent to Nelson, 21/11/1801, Add. MS 34918; St Vincent to Addington, 3/1/1802, D. Bonner-Smith, *St Vincent*, 1, p. 105. • **30**. Nelson to St Vincent, 22/11/1801, *D&L*, 4, p. 528; St Vincent to Nelson, 23/11/1801, Add. MS 34918. • **31**. Nelson to Davison, 28/11/1801, Egerton MS 2240; Nelson to Sutton, 16/2/1802, WLC; *Ipswich Gazette*, 12 and 26/12/1801; St Vincent to Nelson, 3/6/1802, Add. MS 31169. • **32**. Addington to Nelson, 26/10/1801, Add. MS 34918; *Morning Chronicle*, 14/11/1801; Nelson to Addington, 2/12/1801, *D&L*, 4, p. 534; Nelson to Emma, 19/10/1801, NMM: CRK/19. Nelson had written to Pitt as early as 1787, when he was unravelling corrupt practices in the Antigua dockyard: Nelson to Pitt, 4/5/1787, NA: PRO 30/8/187. • **33**. Nelson to Keith, 14/9/1801, NMM: KEI/18/4. • **34**. Nelson to Stewart, 10/10/1801, *Cumloden Papers*. • **35**. Nelson to Boothby, 1/5/1802, Add. MS 34918; Nelson to Emma, 9/10/1801, Egerton MS 1614. • **36**. J. Steven Watson, *Reign of George III*, p. 409; Nelson to Pelham, 17/10/1801, Add. MS 33108; Nelson to Emma, 5 and 18/10/1801, *HANP*, 2, p. 171, and Egerton MS 1614; John Sugden, *Nelson*, pp. 241–3. • **37**. Nelson to Emma, 20/10/1801, NMM: CRK/19. • **38**. Johnson to Jowett, 1/3/1982, Nelson file, Local Studies Library, Morden; *Morning Chronicle*, 31/10/1801, 13 and 14/11/1801; Nelson to Sutton, 31/10/1801, WLC; *Parliamentary Debates*, 36, columns 185–6. • **39**. Jack Russell, *Nelson and the Hamiltons*, p. 249; Maria Carolina's letters, Pettigrew, *Memoirs*, 2, pp. 238, 243; memorandum on Malta, Houghton, MS Eng. 196.5. • **40**. Addington to Nelson, 26/12/1801, NMM: CRK/1. • **41**. *Ipswich Journal*, 26/12/1801. • **42**. Horace to Sarah Nelson, December 1801, NMM: BRP/4; Nelson to Sutton, 6 and 21/1/1802, Monmouth MS E116 and WLC. • **43**. Fanny to Nelson, 18/12/1801, Monmouth MS E979. • **44**. Mark Girouard and Christopher Christie explore these trends. • **45**. The exact nature of the canal is mysterious. A Rocque plan of 1746 (Warwick, 'Here Was Paradise', p. 41) shows a pool to the north of the house, fed by a circuitous canal that struck south-west and then east to meet the Wandle, which flowed through the adjacent estate of Merton Abbey. The grounds, as depicted in the map, were changed by 1801. Nelson appears to have extended the canal on the north side of the house, but eliminated the southern arm that joined the Wandle. Wells on either side of the western arm of the canal in 1823 suggest an underground source for the reduced canal, once the link with the river had been broken. See the plan of 1823 in Goodman, '200 Years Ago'. • **46**. William A. Bartlett, *History and Antiquities*, pp. 170–71. Saker would have been about twenty-one years old in 1801. • **47**. Hamilton to Nelson, 16/10/1801, *HANP*, 2, p. 175; Nelson to Davison, 4/10/1803, *D&L*, 5, p. 219. • **48**. Nelson to Emma, 1803, *HANP*, 2, p. 219; Mundy, 'Nelson . . . at Merton', p. 209; receipts from Bennett, 1803–1805, Monmouth MS E401. • **49**. 'Specification of the Several Artificers', 5/4/1801, Houghton, MS. Eng. 196.5; James Harrison, *Life*, 2, pp. 373, 375, 377. • **50**. Matcham to Nelson, 28/10/1802, NMM: NWD/7; Haslewood to Nelson, 18/11/1801, *HANP*, 2, pp. 200, 201; Mary Eyre Matcham, *Nelsons*, pp. 200, 203; deed of selection, 4/3/1802, Surrey History Service, 7883/3; Shadwell's opinion, 11 /11/1802, Add. MS 34990; Nelson to Haslewood, 22/12/1803, Add. MS 34954; letters in NMM: MAM, especially nos. 19, 21–23, 27, 47. • **51**. John May, 'Nelson Silver', pp. 148–9; Rita Prentice, *Authentic Nelson*, pp. 120, 125, 143; Sotheby's, *Trafalgar*, pp. 48–61; Rosemary Jewers, 'Nelson's Staircase'. • **52**. Nelson to Bolton, 10/6/1802, NMM: GIR/1; Emma to Bedford, 13/2/1802, Add. MS 30182; Nelson to Emma, Autumn 1804, NMM: NWD/4; Patterson to Nelson, 13/4/1803, NMM: CRK/10; Nelson to Patterson, Huntington, HM34198. • **53**. Matcham to Nelson, 28/10/1802, *HANP*, 2, p. 200; *ND*, 9 (2007), p. 377. Hopkins, *History*, p. 41, usefully superimposes the estate upon a modern map, and provides an indispensable guide to any current adventurer seeking the site of Paradise Merton. In brief the Wimbledon holdings were confined within modern South Park Road (north), Merton High Street (south), Haydons Road (east) and Merton Road (west). The area south of the turnpike (Merton High Street) is bordered by Abbey and Deer Park roads in the east and south, and Brisbane Avenue in the west. Merton Place itself stood between present-day Nelson Grove Road and Merton High Street, roughly where a small block of flats, also named Merton Place, now stands. A good starting point for the walker is the Nelson Arms public house on Merton High Street, which approximates the site of the lodge at Nelson's new entrance, and is straight across the High Street from what was once the plot leased from Bennett. • **54**. E. A. Kempson, *Bygone Merton*, p. 240; 'Some Recollections of Nelson', p. 183; J. F. Allan, 'Was Nelson a Fly Fisher?' *MM*, 77 (91), p. 184. • **55**. Matcham, *Nelsons*, p. 285; Nelson to Banks, undated, Monmouth MS. E 199/200; Harrison, *Life*, 2, p. 404; Nelson to Bentham, 10/11/1802, Houghton, MS Eng. 196.5; *HANP*, 2, pp. 396, 398, 406–17; Add. MS 34989, ff. 53–4; *Daily Telegraph*, 19/5/2009. • **56**. Emma to Nelson, 8/10/1805, *HANP*, 2, p. 268; James E. Jagger, *Parish Church*, p. 5; T. G. Jackson, 'Eagle House', in Henry Copeland, *The Wimbledon and Merton Annual* (1903), p. 21; Emma and Horace Nelson to Sarah, November 1802, NMM: BRP/4; *D&L*, 7, p. ccxviii; Evelyn M. Jowett, *Illustrated History*, p. 104; Lancaster's verses, NMM: CRK/16/93; J. C. Beaglehole, *The Life of Captain James Cook* (1974), p. 693. Elizabeth Cook, widow of the explorer, briefly resided at Merton Abbey after the death of her cousin in 1827, but never saw Nelson, as some biographers have stated. • **57**. Among many sources, Cadogan to Emma, 3/8/1804, 21/9/1804, NMM: CRK/20; Tyson to Nelson, 14/3/1803, Add. MS 34919; Nelson to Emma, 11/3/1801, 12/8/1801, Egerton MS 1614; Hamilton to Emma, 16/7/1802, NMM: WAL/16A; Adrian Bridge, 'Tom Allen's Job Reference'. • **58**. Emma to Nelson, 8/10/1805, *HANP*, 2, p. 268; James Grieg, *Farington Diary*, 3, pp. 134–5; Nelson to Emma, 10/9/1803, NMM: CRK/19; Nelson to Elliot, 8/9/1803, *D&L*, 5, p. 198; W. H. Chamberlain, *Reminiscences*, p. 27. • **59**. Tyson to Emma, 28/12/1802, *HANP*, 2, p. 203. • **60**. Alfred T. Mahan, *Nelson*, p. 537; John Horsely, *Recollections*, pp. 7–8; Nelson to Emma, 19/10/1801, NMM: CRK/19; Grieg, *Farington Diary*, 1, p. 348; Richard Walker, *Nelson Portraits*, pp. 144–9, 257–9. • **61**. Nelson probably met Robert and Mary Mathews of Quebec fame when he visited Moseley, because Robert had been appointed major of the hospital in 1801. • **62**. K. S. Cliff,

Lock, pp. 7–13. • **63**. *Memoirs of Lady Hamilton*, pp. 271–2, 275–7. Jacqui Livesey, 'Literary Assassin', identifies the author as John Watkins, a noted polemicist, who had tried to gain access to Sir William's papers after his death for the purposes of writing a memoir. Oliver was apparently his informant. • **64**. Nelson to Murray, 10/11/1802, *D&L*, 5, p. 34; Bulkeley to Nelson, 12/3/1800, Pettigrew, *Memoirs*, 2, p. 277; *NC*, 37 (1817), p. 445; Emma and Horace to Sarah Nelson, undated, NMM: BRP/4. • **65**. 'Auto-Biography of James William Noble', MS in private hands; Noble to Nelson, undated, NMM: CRK/9. • **66**. Minto, 22/3/1802, 18/4/1803, Countess of Minto, *Elliot*, 3, pp. 242, 283; Emma to Sarah, March 1802, NMM: BRP/4. • **67**. Elizabeth and Florence Anson, *Mary Hamilton*, p. 328; A. T. Mahan, *Life of Nelson*, p. 537; Nelson to Nepean, 21/11/1802, Warren R. Dawson, *Nelson Collection*, p. 180; Nelson to Berry, 29/5/1802, NMM: BER/6. • **68**. Emma to Kate, 23/12/1802, Sotheby's lot, 2005; Charlotte to Emma, undated, and Horace to Nelson, 21/5/1804, NMM: CRK/20. Kate's children were George, Catherine, Elizabeth, Frank, Harriett, Horatia, Susannah and Horatio. She would have three more between 1805 and 1811, the last Nelson. • **69**. Matcham, *Nelsons*, pp. 203, 205; 'Favourite Sultana', Monmouth MS E206; Horace to his mother, 1802, NMM: BRP/4. • **70**. Will of Emma Hamilton, 16/10/1808, *HANP*, 2, p. 320; Tyson to Emma, 28/12/1802, *HANP*, 2, p. 203. A 'Miss Connor' appears in several letters as a governess, but Thomas Baxter, who visited Merton several times, specifically stated that two of the Connor girls served in that capacity. • **71**. Fanny to Nelson, 1800, Add. MS 34988, f. 376; William to Nelson, 8/5/1802, Hilda Gamlin, *Nelson's Friendships*, 1, p. 301; accounts, 21/9/1802, Huntington Library, HM 34060; Nelson to Matthew Nelson, 7/3/1803, Thomas Nelson, *Genealogical History*, p. 24; Nelson to Emma, 26/8/1803, Pettigrew, *Memoirs*, 2, p. 337; Hamilton to Greville, 23/12/1802, *HANP*, 2, p. 202; Walter Sichel, *Emma, Lady Hamilton*, p. 512. • **72**. Accounts, *HANP*, 2, Appendix D; Emma to Kate Matcham, 23/12/1802, Sotheby's lot, 2005. The drawings are now in NMM: WAL/49. The card players cannot be positively identified, but probably included Charlotte.

XVII No Common Love

1. Emma to Davison, 24/7/1804, Add. MS 40739. • **2**. Susannah to Nelson, 1799, Add. MS 34988, f. 329; Susannah to Emma, 27/4/1803, and Bolton to Emma, 16/10/1803, NMM: CRK/22. • **3**. Edmund to Nelson, 26/2/1802, 23/3/1802, NMM: CRK/9; Edmund to Fanny, 20/4/1802, Monmouth MS E651. • **4**. Matcham to Nelson, 14/2/1802, 24/4/1802, NMM: NWD/7; Nelson to Matcham, 26/4/1802, Sotheby's lot, 2005; Nelson to Davison, 27/4/1802, Sotheby's, *Davison*, p. 129; W. H. Chamberlain, *Reminiscences*, p. 27. Edmund's will (NMM: CRK/9/87), witnessed by Abraham Cook, had been dated 12 January 1801. Fatima was probably named for a friend of Emma's, who had an inn on the Windsor Road: see her entertaining letters in NMM: CRK/22. • **5**. William to Nelson, 8 and 12/5/1802, Hilda Gamlin, *Nelson's Friendships*, 1, pp. 299, 302; William to Nelson, 4, 14 and 16/5/1802, NMM: NWD/7; Nelson's letters to George Matcham in NMM: MAM. Edmund was survived by two sisters, Thomasine Goulty and Alice Rolfe. Mrs Goulty had lost her husband days before. Alice, the last of the generation, died on 24 July 1823, at the age of ninety-three. • **6**. Nelson to Davison, 3/5/1802 and May 1802, Egerton MS 2240. Regarding the legacies paid Nelson, £300 was found to reimburse him for expenses incurred as executor of Maurice's will, £227 came as his portion of a sum Edmund had inherited from his wife, and it was believed that £400 would accrue from his sister Ann's will, which had finally passed through probate. • **7**. Susannah to Fanny, 13/5/1802, Monmouth MS E671; Nelson to Bolton, 10/6/1802, NMM: GIR/1; Kate Williams, *England's Mistress*, p. 287; Hardy to Manfield, 24/6/1802, A. M. Broadley, *Nelson's Hardy*, p. 94; HMC in *Various*

Collections, p. 406. • **8**. Matcham to Nelson, 9/1/1803, NMM: CRK/9; Nelson and Emma to Matcham, 11/1/1803, Sotheby's lot, 2005. The position of the Matchams is unclear. In late 1801 Kate wrote to Fanny that she longed for a '*chit chat* letter' from her. According to Lady Nelson's partly substantiated story the Matchams also upbraided William Nelson for discourteous remarks he made about Fanny during a visit to Bath. Emma's frustration with Kate's reluctance to endorse the new regime also speaks for itself. She told Sarah that Nelson loved her more than either of his sisters, and that she and her husband were the 'only people worthy to be by him beloved'. Susannah was characterised as 'close fisted and jealous'. However, after Edmund's death Kate attempted to avoid Fanny, and is even said to have wished her 'in Heaven'. Long afterwards she excused her brother's conduct on the ground that Fanny was 'so very cold': Kate to Fanny, 1801, Monmouth MS E673; Mary E. Matcham, *Nelsons*, p. 183; Fanny to Davison, April 1801, NMM: Dav/2; Emma to Sarah, October 1801, and Emma to Sarah and William, 8/9/1801, NMM: BRP/4; Kate to Emma, 1/12/1804, 20/1/1805, and Bolton to Emma, 7/7/1805, NMM: NWD/8, 9. • **9**. Nelson to Gibson, 19/11/1802, NMM: NWD/16. • **10**. Hamilton to Emma, 16/7/1802, NMM: WAL/16A. • **11**. Hamilton to Greville, 24/1/1802, *HANP*, 2, p. 182. • **12**. Hamilton to Greville, 5/12/1801, and to the Marquis of Douglas, 2/7/1802, *HANP*, 2, pp. 177, 195; Walter Sichel, *Emma, Lady Hamilton*, p. 389. • **13**. Hamilton to Emma, 16/7/1802, NMM: WAL/16A. • **14**. Nelson to Stewart, 28/8/1802, *Cumloden Papers*. • **15**. Harrison, *Life*, 2, p. 404; Nelson to Davison, 19/7/1802, 11/9/1802, and Emma to Davison, 20/9/1802, Egerton MS 2240; *Ipswich Journal*, 29/5/1802. • **16**. Nelson to Melville, 22/6/1804, 10/10/1804, Add. MSS 34956 and 34957; Nelson to Addington, 15/7/1802, Huntington, HM 34056; James Harrison, *Life*, 2, pp. 468–9. • **17**. For Nelson and naval charities see William to Nelson, 26/5/1803, NMM: CRK/9; John Sugden, 'Forgotten *Agamemnons*'; accounts with Marsh and Creed, 1803, NMM: CRK/8; Aubrey to Nelson, 29/1/1800, NMM: CRK/1; Nelson to Newby, 3/3/1802, Warren R. Dawson, *Nelson Collection*, p. 175; *HANP*, 2, p. 388; *A Brief Account of the Naval Asylum at Paddington-Green*, pp. 10, 14; *NC*, 7 (1802), pp. 516–18; minutes of the Naval Asylum, 7 and 19/2/1802, 19/3/1802, 11 and 25/2/1803, ADM 67/253; Edward Locker to Nelson, 22/2/1799, Wellcome MS 3676. • **18**. Glasse to Nelson, 2/6/1804, NMM: CRK/6; Davison to Nelson, 7/5/1799, Add. MS 34911; accounts, NMM: CRK/3/168; *The Times*, 29/11/1800; Dod to Nelson, 21/11/1800, NMM: CRK/4; *Morning Post*, 11/12/1800; *Abstract from the Account of the Asylum, or House of Refuge*; John Callcott Horsley, *Recollections*, pp. 7–8; Charlotte Nelson to her mother, 21/4/1800, NMM: BRP/1. • **19**. Nelson to Keighley, 31/8/1805, Add. MS 34992; Reed to Nelson, 25/1/1803, NMM: CRK/10; Harris to Nelson, 20/10/1804, Wellcome MS 3676; Brent to Nelson, 27/11/1800, 10/5/1803, NMM: CRK/2; Addington to Nelson, 4/10/1802, Thomas J. Pettigrew, *Memoirs*, 2, p. 266; Johnston petition, 11/9/1802, Monmouth MS E122. • **20**. Beach to Nelson, 16/11/1802, NMM: CRK/2. A Samuel Beach from Norwick, Cheshire, was a twenty-three-year-old ordinary seaman in the *St George* (ADM 36/14293), but this might not be the same man. • **21**. *The Whole Proceedings on the King's Commission of the Peace, Oyer and Terminer, and Gaol Delivery for the City of London . . .* (1802), pp. 427–32, and (1803), pp. 500–01. I suspect Beach was reprieved, and that Nelson may, after all, have saved his life. In 1802, when his case first came up, the country was at peace. On that occasion Nelson's intervention probably produced the diminution of sentence. But in 1803, when Beach was convicted the second time, Britain was at war and in desperate need of men. It was common in such times for minor malefactors to be offered a reprieve if they would enlist in the armed forces. Given Beach's profession, and his trial defence, which stressed his readiness to rejoin the navy, he probably escaped execution. • **22**. Joseph and William Brodie Gurney, *Trial*, p. 174; *Gentleman's Magazine*, 73 (1803), pt 1, pp. 173–7; studies of Despard by M. Elliott and Mike Jay. • **23**. Bulkeley to Nelson, 17/2/1803, 9/3/1803, *HANP*, 2, pp. 207, 208; James Grieg, *Farington Diary*, 2, p. 83; Despard to Nelson, 15/2/1803, and Catherine Despard to Nelson, NMM: CRK/4; Petition of Despard, HO 42/70; Palmer to Nelson, undated, NMM: CRK/10; Earl of Malmesbury, *Diaries*, 4, p. 214; Countess of Minto, *Elliot*, 3, pp. 273, 274. • **24**. *The Whole Proceedings on the King's Commission of the Peace, Oyer and Terminer, and Gaol Delivery for the City of London* (1803), pp. 233–42; *NC*, 9 (1803), pp. 317–26; Macnamara to Nelson, 9/4/1803, NMM: CRK/8; Nelson to Emma, 27/8/1804, Houghton, MS. Eng. 196.5. • **25**. Eric Tushingham, *HMS Vanguard*, p. 133; Nelson to Davison, 27/4/1802, Sotheby's, *Davison*, p. 129; Nelson to the Lord Chancellor, 24/6/1802, Bonham's lot, 2005. For a particularly moving supplication see Mrs A. Burke to Nelson, undated, NMM: CRK/2. • **26**. Nelson to Sutton, March and 10/4/1802, *D&L*, 5, pp. 8, 10. • **27**. Nelson to William, 10/4/1802, Add. MS 34988. • **28**. William to Emma, undated, Pettigrew, *Memoirs*, 2, p. 252; Nelson to Addington, 17/7/1802, *D&L*, 7, p. ccxii. • **29**. Hamilton to Emma, 16/7/1802, HMM/WAL/49. • **30**. Nelson to Davison, 30/3/1802, Egerton MS 2240; Emma to Matcham, 23/12/1802, Sotheby's lot, 2005. • **31**. Addington to Nelson, 30/5/1802, NMM: CRK/1; William to Nelson, 25/3/1803, NMM: CRK/9. • **32**. Emma to Matcham, 23/12/1802, Sotheby's lot, 2005. • **33**. *Parliamentary Debates*, 36, columns 936–38; Minto, *Elliot*, 3, pp. 258, 273; *Ipswich Gazette*, 19/2/1803. • **34**. Nelson to Addington, 8/3/1803, Add. MS 34988; *Daily Mail*, 22/6/2007. • **35**. Nelson to Parker, 4/2/1803, NMM: CRK/14; Davison to Nelson, 17/3/1804, 7/1/1805, NMM: CRK/3; document on Nelson's claims to proceeds of *Thetis* and *Santa Brigida* in February 1802, and Nelson to Berry, 27/11/1802, Add. MS 34918; letter to Bridport, 23/6/1801, Add. MS 35201. • **36**. Nelson to Addington, 29/12/1802, Colin White, *New Letters*, p. 18. • **37**. Nelson to William, 18/10/1803, *D&L*, 5, p. 252; Nelson to Davison, 12/12/1803, 13/1/1804, Egerton Mss. 2240; Nelson to Emma, 22/8/1804, 2/10/1804, Pettigrew, *Memoirs*, 2, p. 419, and *HANP*, 2, p. 240. • **38**. Roger Morriss, 'St Vincent and Reform', is a careful appraisal. On the duration of the peace see Nelson to Bedford, 13/2/1802, Add. MS 30182. • **39**. *Parliamentary Debates*, 36, columns 1144–45. • **40**. Prize court charges, NMM: CRK/16/30. • **41**. Nelson's 'examination', 1/4/1803, Add. MS 46356; Nelson proposal, NMM: JER/9. The greater delays were caused, of course, by litigation. It could take years to determine whether a prize was lawful, and who was entitled to share in the proceeds. In 1802 Nelson had to visit the lodgings of Captain Cockburn in Conduit Street, London, to untangle the complicated cases of two prize corn ships captured in 1795. The proceeds amounted to £3000, but, while three captains had an agreement to pool their takings, irrespective of who was the actual captor, their crews had not. The distributing agent, John McArthur, had therefore to be clear about which ships were present upon each occasion: Nelson to Marsh, Page and Creed, 23/4/1802, Huntington, HM 34055, and documents in *HANP*, 2, p. 186, and *D&L*, 5, pp. 11, 13, 15. For prize, see the study by J. Richard Hill. • **42**. Nelson to Nepean, 28/2/1803, Dawson, *Nelson Collection*, p. 181. • **43**. *D&L*, 5, p. 44. • **44**. St Vincent to Nelson, 1/3/1803, Add. MS 31168. • **45**. Nelson to Mobbs, 28/9/1802, letter in private hands. • **46**. Hamilton to Greville, 24/1/1802, *HANP*, 2, p. 182. • **47**. *HANP*, 2, pp. 401–4. This tour, with an improved chronology, has been reconstructed from *Jackson's Oxford Journal*, 24/7/1802, 18/6/2008; *Gloucester Journal*, 26/7/1802, 2, 23 and 30/8/1802, 6/9/1802; *Berrow's Worcester Journal*, 29/7/1802, 26/8/1802 and 2/9/1802; *The Times*, 31/7/1802, 7, 12, 13 and 20/8/1802, 2 and 7/9/1802; *Hereford Journal*, 25/8/1802; *Aris's Birmingham Gazette*, 30/8/1802, 6/9/1802; *Coventry Mercury*, 30/8/1802, 6/9/1802; *Ipswich Journal*, 21/8/1802, 28/8/1802, 4/9/1802; *Derby Mercury*, 2/9/1802; *Memoirs of the Rt. Honourable Lord Viscount Nelson*, 58; and Harrison, *Life*, 2, pp. 379–404. Additional sources are cited as appropriate. Edward Gill, *Tour*, is valuable, although my sources are divergent on some points.

• **48**. Nelson to George, 16/7/1802, NMM: MAM/20; *Oxford Journal*, 18/6/2008. • **49**. Nelson's memorandum, *D&L*, 5, pp. 24–8; Roger Knight, 'Nelson and the Forest of Dean'. • **50**. Monmouth Corporation to Nelson, 14/2/1802, NMM: CRK/9/50; Charles Heath, *Kymin Pavilion*. • **51**. Nelson to Churchney, 3/8/1802, *TC*, 12 (2002), p. 5. When the report in the *Gloucester Journal* went to press the fate of the boy was not known. • **52**. Nelson to St Vincent, 22/5/1803, NMM: JER/9; St Vincent to Greville, 21/10/1802, Hilda Gamlin, *Nelson's Friendships*, 1, p. 307. • **53**. Nelson to Westfaling, 9/8/1802, and Nelson to Foley, 1/10/1802, Houghton, MS Eng. 196.5; Esther Hallam Moorhouse, *Nelson in England*, pp. 209–10. • **54**. Banks to Greville, 30/9/1802, *HANP*, 2, p. 197; Gill, *Tour*, p. 40. • **55**. Nelson's message of thanks, printed 17/8/1802, NMM: CRK/16/74. • **56**. In several articles Mike Baker argues that Nelson detoured to Chepstow, rather than taking the more direct route to Monmouth from Newport, to tackle a damaging deadlock that had developed between the Admiralty and a timber cartel represented by John Bowsher, a resident of Chepstow. Catalyst for the dispute was St Vincent, who attributed the growing costs of shipbuilding and repair to corruption and the development of monopolistic cartels of merchants, who undermined the competitive basis of the contract system. There were, in fact, several causes for the inflation, including shortages of indigenous timber, but St Vincent further aggravated timber suppliers by appointing inspectors, whose function was to assess the quality of incoming deliveries. Merchants began to complain about their deliveries being cut up and despoiled by zealous 'timber masters'. The dispute damaged the maintenance of the fleet at a time of unstable foreign relations, and only when the Admiralty relented and allowed the contractors an increase of 25 per cent was normality resumed. For intelligent comment see the studies by Robert G. Albion, Bernard Pool and Roger Morriss. Baker cites evidence that Bowsher met Nelson at the Three Cranes (Baker, 'Lord Nelson, Timber Merchants', p. 24), which he links with the subsequent departure from Chepstow, on 22 August, of timber-laden river trows destined for the royal dockyards. This, and his belief that Nelson helped persuade the Admiralty to allow an increase in prices, enables Baker to credit Nelson with a key role in breaking the impasse. The theory is plausible, but rests upon circumstantial evidence. Nelson bemoaned his inability to influence the Admiralty at this period, and, while Baker identifies Bowsher as one of five timber merchants who acted in informal concert in 1802, the authoritative Roger Knight, 'Nelson and the Forest of Dean', questions whether a timber cartel existed. • **57**. *NC*, 20 (1808), pp. 110–11; Heath, *Kymin Pavilion* (final two pages). Nelson's concern for national unity appears in his correspondence at this time. 'God grant that we may be true to ourselves,' he wrote to Stewart on 24 August 1803 (*Cumloden Papers*). His references echo *King John*, which read 'Come the three corners of the world in arms/And we shall shock them;/Nought shall make us rue/If England to herself do rest but true'. It is one of several of Shakespeare's patriotic allusions that Nelson remembered. • **58**. Rina Prentice, *Authentic Nelson*, pp. 140–41, 146–7, 181, reproduces the entry in Chamberlain's order book, curiously dated 26 August. The *Worcester Journal* clearly shows that the visit occurred on 30 August. See also John May, 'The "Emma" Cup and Saucer', which describes two of the pieces, painted by Thomas Baxter. Baxter, a painter on porcelain, may have met Nelson at the factory. He visited Merton several times, once at Christmas 1802. Nelson never saw the finished sets. Part of the breakfast service was completed in 1805 for a price of £120 10s. 6d., but after Nelson's death the balance of the order was cancelled: *ND*, 8 (2004), p. 514. • **59**. Frederick Pollock, *Macready's Reminiscences*, 1, pp. 5–7. See also Mark Barrett's informative articles, 'Nelson and the Theatre' and 'Nelson in Birmingham'. • **60**. The snuff box was auctioned in 1900: *Weekly Argus News* [Crawfordsville, Indiana], 3 February 1900. The box was inscribed with the date 4 September 1802, which indicates that it must have been sent to Nelson three days after he left Birmingham. • **61**. Banks to Greville, 30/9/1802, *HANP*, 2, p. 197. • **62**. Nelson to Davison, 11/9/1802, and Emma to Davison, 20/9/1802, Egerton MS 2240. • **63**. Notes between the Hamiltons, September 1802, *HANP*, 2, pp. 195–6; Houghton, MS Eng. 196.5 (64). • **64**. Newspaper clipping, 1/10/1802, Monmouth MS E8; Hamilton to Emma, 1802, *HANP*, 2, p. 197; David Constantine, *Fields of Fire*, p. 134. • **65**. Hamilton's will, 31/3/1803, Add. MS 34990. • **66**. Nelson to Murray, 2/4/1803, *D&L*, 5, p. 55; Oliver to Matcham, 2/4/1803, NMM: MAM/43. • **67**. Nelson to Davison, 6/4/1803, Egerton MS 2240; Nelson to Perry, 6/4/1803, *Notes & Queries*, 4th series, 5, p. 293; Nelson to Clarence, 6/4/1803, Add. MS 46356; Pettigrew, *Memoirs*, 2, p. 295. • **68**. Expenses, 7–18/4/1803, MS, A. M. Broadley, 'Nelsoniana', BL, 6, p. 312. • **69**. Nelson to Davison, 17/5/1803, Egerton MS 2240; NMM: CRK/22/72. • **70**. Jack Russell, *Nelson and the Hamiltons*, p. 337. • **71**. Grieg, *Farington Diary*, 3, p. 135. • **72**. Acton to Nelson, 2/3/1803, Egerton MS 1623; Nelson to Addington, 4/12/1802, *D&L*, 5, p. 36. • **73**. Gibbs to Nelson, 5 and 30/7/1803, NMM: CRK/17; Michael Pratt, *Nelson's Duchy*, pp. 88–9; Nelson to Emma, 18/10/1803, *D&L*, 5, p. 253; Ball to Nelson, 8/11/1802, NMM: CRK/1; Nelson to Gibbs, 11, 12 and 13/8/1803,16/9/1803, *D&L*, 5, pp. 159, 164, 167, and Add. MS 34953. The standard work on Bronte is the fine résumé by Jane Knight. • **74**. Graefer to Nelson, 10/12/1800, and Gibbs to Nelson, 12/9/1803, 27/11/1803, NMM: CRK/17; Nelson to Acton, 2/6/1800, Zabriskie collection, US Naval Academy; Pratt, *Nelson's Duchy*, pp. 89–90, 109. • **75**. Gibbs to Nelson, 5/11/1803, 24/12/1803, 9/8/1804, NMM: CRK/17; note of lease, NMM: CRK/17/40. • **76**. Nelson to Addington, 9/3/1803, George Pellew, *Sidmouth*, 3, p. 170. • **77**. Nelson to Sutton, 16 and 28/4/1803, WLC; Emma to Bedford, 13/2/1802, Add. MS 30182; Nelson to Bedford, 21/4/1803, Huntington, HM 34060; Nelson to Murray, 22/3/1803, 13/4/1803, *D&L*, 5, pp. 50, 58. For Nelson's visits to the Admiralty, see *The Times*, 14/3/1803, 8–17/5/1803; *Ipswich Gazette*, 12/3/1803, 21/5/1803; and Nelson to Clarence, 8/5/1803, Add. MS 46356. • **78**. Scott to Nelson, 4/9/1801, NMM: CRK/11. Writing to Charles Hamilton, 10/4/1803, NLS 1030, f. 36, Nelson listed eight lieutenants whose abilities he had judged in earlier commands, five from the *St George* and the rest from the *Amazon*, *Desiree* and *Medusa*. Most of these were posted to the *Victory*. Having suffered from experience, Nelson advised captains taking unknown 'young gentlemen' into their ships to seek a bond from the parents to cover maintenance: Nelson to Benjamin Page, 2/12/1802, 4/3/1803, 'Some Recollections of Nelson'. • **79**. Salter's list 'for sea service', 7/5/1803, Add. MS 34990; *Daily Mail*, 22/6/2007; Nelson to Emma, 19/5/1803, NMM: MAM/26. • **80**. Will, NA: PROB 1/22; T. E. Christopher, 'Lord Nelson's Wife', p. 62. • **81**. Nelson to Emma, 14/3/1804, *D&L*, 5, p. 439. • **82**. Thomas Foley, *Nelson Centenary*, p. 63; Nelson to Davison, 11 and 12/5/1803, and Pelham to Nelson, May 1803, Egerton MS 2240. • **83**. Nelson to Emma, 18 and 20/5/1803, Houghton, MS Eng. 196.5, and *HANP*, 2, p. 210. • **84**. *NC*, 9 (1803), p. 420.

XVIII 'By Patience and Perseverance'

1. Charles Esdaile, *Napoleon's Wars*, is a recent reappraisal. Piers Mackesy, *War in the Mediterranean*, remains a classic account of that phase. • **2**. Key sources for Nelson's command of 1803–1805 are his order books, Add. MSS 34970, 36610; letterbooks, Add. MSS 34953–60, 34964–65, 40094–95, and Monmouth MSS E991–92; correspondence, Add. MSS 34919–33, 34935–36, and NMM: CRK passim, ELL/301–308 and JER/9–10; diaries, Add. MSS 34966–68, 35191; and the official correspondence in ADM 1/407–11. See also the logbooks of *Amphion* (ADM 51/1446 and 52/3562) and *Victory* (ADM 51/1498 and 4514 and 52/3711). • **3**. Nelson's diary, 16/6/1803, Add. MS 35191. • **4**. Elliot to Nelson, 22/6/1803, FO 70/21. • **5**. Nelson to

Emma, 10/2/1804, Egerton MS 1614. • **6**. Nelson to Davison, 24/8/1803, Egerton MS 2240; Davison to Nelson, 7/6/1803, NMM: CRK/3; Nelson to Emma, 22/5/1803, 1/8/1803, NMM: CRK/19/28, 30. • **7**. A. and M. Gatty, *Recollections*, p. 102; Moubray to Nelson, 14/6/1803, ADM 1/407. • **8**. Nelson to Elliot, 26/12/1803, *D&L*, 5, p. 335. • **9**. Nelson to Acton, 10/6/1803, 19/6/1803, Add. MS 34965. • **10**. Nelson to Emma, July 1803, NMM: CRK/19/29; Nelson to Maria Carolina, 10/7/1804, *D&L*, 6, p. 105. • **11**. Gatty, *Recollections*, pp. 104–106; Nelson to Emma, 21/8/1803, Thomas J. Pettigrew, *Memoirs*, 2, p. 331; Nelson to Addington, 28/6/1803, CO 173/1; Desmond Gregory, *Malta*, ch. 10. • **12**. Nelson to Elliot, 25/6/1803, Add. MS 34965. • **13**. Nelson to merchants, 19/6/1803, ADM 1/407; Nelson to Villettes, 5/8/1803, Monmouth MS E189. • **14**. Ferdinand to Nelson, June 1803, NMM: CRK/5. • **15**. Elliot to Nelson, 22/6/1803, Acton to Nelson, 5/7/1803, Elliot's instructions, 18/5/1803, and Elliot to Hawkesbury, 19/7/1803, FO 70/21. • **16**. Nelson to Richardson, 26/6/1803, and Nelson to Hart, 30/7/1803, Add. MS 36610; Elliot to Hawkesbury, 10/1/1804, FO 70/22. • **17**. Nelson to Addington, 28/6/1803, CO 173/1; Nelson to Acton, 2/12/1803, Add. MS 34953; Harrowby to Elliot, 3 and 6/7/1804, FO 70/22; Elliot to Hawkesbury, 24/7/1803, 21/8/1803, 3/9/1803, 31/1/1804, FO 70/21 and FO 70/22. • **18**. Wyndham to Hawkesbury, 16/4/1803, FO 79/20; Nelson to Nepean, 2/9/1803, ADM 1/407. • **19**. James Beresford, 'Roar of the Lion'. • **20**. Nelson to St Vincent, 12/12/1803, Add. MS 34954; Nelson to Elliot, 20/7/1803, 13/6/1804, Nelson to Boyle, 11/10/1803, Nelson to Moubray, 22/3/1804 and Nelson to Staines, 6/6/1804, Add. MS 36610. • **21**. Nelson to Hobart, 18/7/1803, Colin White, *New Letters*, p. 318; Nelson to Nepean, 30/7/1803, ADM 1/497; St Vincent to Nelson, 24/9/1803, Add. MS 31169. • **22**. Nelson to Cornwallis, July 1803, HMC, *Various Collections*, 6, p. 399; Layman to Nelson, 27/6/1803, Add. MS 34919; Nelson to Emma, 1/8/1803, NMM: CRK/19; Nelson to Sutton, 15/8/1803, WLC. • **23**. Nelson to Elliot, 30/7/1803, Add. MS 34965; Duff to Campbell, 14/7/1803, Add. MS 34919. By the end of August line ships were *Victory* (104); two eighties, *Canopus*, Captain John Conn, Rear Admiral George Campbell, and *Gibraltar*, George Frederick Ryves; the seventy-fours, *Kent*, John Stuart, Rear Admiral Richard Bickerton; *Renown*, John Chambers White; *Belleisle*, John Whitby; *Superb*, Richard Goodwin Keats; *Triumph*, Robert Barlow; and *Donegal*, Richard John Strachan; and two sixty-fours, *Agincourt*, Thomas Briggs; and *Monmouth*, George Hart. • **24**. Nelson to Addington, 27/9/1803, Add. MS 34965. • **25**. Nelson to Gibbs, 11/8/1803, *D&L*, 5, p. 159. • **26**. Nelson to St Vincent, 27/9/1803, NMM: JER/9; Nelson to Nepean, 9/8/1803, ADM 1/407. • **27**. Hood's comment in HMC, *Various Collections*, 6, p. 395; Nelson to Axe, 31/5/1804, Monmouth MS E289; Nelson to Addington, 24/8/1803, Add. MS 34965. • **28**. Nelson to Melville, 22/2/1805, Melville papers, SNA, GD51/2/1082; Barlow to Nelson, 8/7/1803 and Nelson to Nepean, 19/7/1803, ADM 1/407; Nelson to Troubridge, 21/10/1803, Add. MS 34954; Nelson's diaries, 14 and 15/7/1803, 8 and 14/10/1803, Add. MSS 35191 and 34966; report of Davison, Foxton and Trench, 2/12/1802, Wellcome MS 3670. • **29**. Nelson to Gibert, 13/9/1803, Add. MS 34965; Pearse to Strachan, 12/10/1803, Add. MS 34921; Hunter to Gibert, 23/3/1804, NMM: CRK/7/97; Hawkesbury to Frere, 21/1/1804, Frere to Hawkesbury, 10/4/1804 and Frere to Harrowby, 22/7/1804, FO 72/52; Hunter to Harrowby, 25/9/1804, FO 72/53. • **30**. Nelson to Frere, 13/9/1803, 25/11/1803, WLC; Nelson to Hunter, 24/9/1803, and Nelson to Duff, 4/10/1803, Add. MS 34953; Nelson to Strachan, 26/9/1803, *D&L*, 5, p. 211; Nelson to Addington, 27/9/1803, Add. MS 34965. • **31**. Nelson to Elliot, 30/7/1803, Add. MS 34365. • **32**. Nelson to Hawkesbury, 16/10/1803, Add. MS 34964; Nelson to Elliot, 2/9/1803, *D&L*, 5, p. 192. • **33**. Jackson to Hawkesbury, 4, 18 and 25/6/1803, FO 67/32. • **34**. Nelson to Addington, 24/8/1803, Add. MS 34965. • **35**. Nelson diary, 24 and 26/8/1803, Add. MS 34967; Nelson to Jackson, 6/9/1803, Add. MS 34953; Jackson to Nelson, 21/6/1803, 16/8/1803, 4/10/1803, Add. MSS 34919 and

34920; Nelson to Donnelly, 26/8/1803, Add. MS 36610; Jackson to Hawkesbury, 24/9/1803, 15 and 22/10/1803, 5/11/1803, FO 67/32. • **36**. Nelson to Emma, 26/9/1803, 30/5/1804, NMM: CRK/19 and Egerton MS 1614. • **37**. Nelson to Davison, 21/10/1803, Egerton MS 2240; Nelson to Emma, 18/10/1803, NMM: CRK/19; Nelson to Clarence, 15/10/1803, *D&L*, 5, p. 247. • **38**. Keats, 1/8/1803, Add. MS 34919; Ryves, sailing directions, Add. MS 34932; Troubridge to Nelson, 16/6/1803, 26/8/1803, NMM: CRK/13; Ball, 'Malta', Add. MS 34932, f. 181; David Hilton, 'La Maddalena', pp. 224–5. • **39**. Nelson to Ryves, 1/11/1803, and Nelson to Jackson, 1/11/1803, Add. MS 34954. • **40**. For Nelson's connections with Sardinia see four valuable papers by John R. Gwyther. • **41**. Scott to Nelson, 19/10/1804, NMM: CRK/11; William S. Lovell, *Personal Narrative*, pp. 32–3; Nelson to Villettes, 3/8/1804, Nelson to Gibert, 25/9/1804 and Nelson to the Church of Santa Maria, 18/10/1804, Add. MS 34957. • **42**. Nelson to Nepean, 19 and 26/12/1803, ADM 1/407. • **43**. Nelson's diary, 8/8/1804, 6/9/1804, Add. MS 34967. • **44**. Nelson's diary, 9/12/1803, 7/2/1804, Add. MS 34966; Malcolm to Nelson, 22/4/1804, enclosing report, 25/4/1804, ADM 1/408. • **45**. Nelson to Clarence, 24/5/1804, 12/10/1804, Add. MSS 46356 and 34957. • **46**. Russell Grenfell, *Nelson the Sailor*, p. 166. • **47**. Parker, 25/12/1803, Augustus Phillimore, *Parker*, 1, p. 225; Nelson to Pettet, 6/10/1803, Add. MS 36610; Falcon to Yorke, 9/12/1803, and Pettet to Nelson, 30/12/1803, Add. MS 34921; Nelson to Boyle, 27/11/1803, Bonham's lot, 2010; Nelson to his captains, 4/12/1803, and Nelson to Moubray, 5/12/1803, Add. MS 36610. • **48**. Nelson to St Vincent, 25/5/1804, Add. MS 34955. • **49**. Jackson to Hawkesbury, 18/2/1804, FO 67/33; Lowe to Nelson, 5/2/1804, and Lowe to Elliot, 12/2/1804, NMM: CRK/17; Nelson to Elliot, 23/2/1804, *D&L*, 5, p. 472; Gwyther, 'Nelson in Turin', p. 57, and Magnon's letters in his 'Tower at Longon Sardo', pp. 143, 148, 150; intelligence from Donnelly, 16/3/1804, Add. MS 34922. • **50**. Jackson to Hawkesbury, 11, 18 and 25/2/1804, 10/3/1804, FO 67/33; Nelson to Jackson, 10/2/1804, Add. MS 34955; Villettes to Nelson, 22/1/1804, 28/2/1804, Add. MS 34922. • **51**. Nelson to Hobart, 22/12/1803, CO 173/1; Jackson to Hawkesbury, 17 and 24/3/1804 [nos 18, 20], FO 67/33; Jackson to Nelson, 3/4/1804, Add. MS 34923. • **52**. Nelson to Hawkesbury, 22/6/1804, FO 70/22; Nelson to Jackson, 26/4/1804, Add. MS 34955; Nelson to Bickerton, 13/2/1804, *Daily Telegraph*, 25/11/2008; Nelson's orders to Staines, 26/1/1804, Donnelly, 30/1/1804 and Pettet, 31/1/1804, Add. MS 36610; court martial of Brown, Collins and Marshall, 17/2/1804, Add. MS 34922. • **53**. Nelson to Hobart, 31/5/1804, and Nelson to Camden, 3/11/1804, CO 173/1; Nelson to Melville, 29/12/1804, Add. MS 34958. • **54**. Camden to Nelson, 29/8/1804, Add. MS 34956; Harrowby to Nelson, 29/8/1804, FO 70/23; Nelson to Harrowby, 11/10/1804, Add. MS 34957. • **55**. Jackson to Harrowby, 11/8/1804, FO 67/33. • **56**. Nelson to Jackson, 7/10/1804, Add. MS 34957; Jackson to Harrowby, 16/6/1804, 20 and 27/10/1804, 17/11/1804, FO 67/34. • **57**. Nelson to Minto, 11/1/1804, Add. MS 34954; Nelson to Ball, 3/8/1804, Add. MS 34956. • **58**. Nelson to Parker, 28/8/1804, Add. MS 34957; Nelson to Elliot, 3/1/1805, Add MS 34958. • **59**. Nelson to Ball, 11/2/1804, Add. MS 34955. • **60**. Nelson to Gore, 17/2/1804, *D&L*, 5, p. 422. • **61**. Nelson to his captains, 28/4/1804, *D&L*, 5, p. 519; Nelson letter of 1804, Huntington, HM 34071; Lady Bourchier, *Codrington*, 1, p. 52; Frederick Hoffman, *Sailor of King George*, p. 133. • **62**. Order of sailing, 1804, Monmouth MS E371; intelligence sent by Moubray, April 1804, Add. MSS 34923, f. 158. • **63**. Nelson to Bickerton, 7/4/1804, Add. MS 34955. • **64**. Nelson to Donnelly, 20/8/1804, Add. MS 36610; Nelson to Ball, 4/10/1804, Add. MS 34957. • **65**. Nelson to Acton, 12/7/1804, Add. MS 34956; Ball to Nelson, 20/11/1803, and his observations of 7/7/1804, NMM: CRK/1; Acton to Nelson, 12/2/1804, 2/4/1804, NMM: CRK/1; Pettet to Nelson, 20/1/1804, Add. MS 34922. • **66**. Nelson to Ball, 6/9/1804, *D&L*, 6, p. 191. • **67**. Nelson to Emma, 23/11/1804, NMM: CRK/19; Nelson to Marsden, 16/8/1804, ADM 1/408; Nelson to Acton, 29/8/1804, Add. MS 34957; Ferdinand to

Nelson, 19/1/1805, WO 1/282; Jackson to Harrowby, 4/8/1804, FO 67/33. • **68**. Nelson to Strachan, 4/10/1803, Add. MS 34953; Gore to Nelson, 21/6/1804, NMM: CRK/6. • **69**. Ferdinand to Nelson, 22/5/1804, Egerton MS 1623. • **70**. Nelson to Acton, 28/3/1805, Zabriskie Collection, US Naval Academy. • **71**. Elliot to Harrowby, 2, 9 and 16/10/1804, FO 70/23; Warren to Harrowby, 23/9/1804, FO 65/56; Nelson to Camden, 14/5/1805, WO 1/282. • **72**. Acton, *Bourbons*, pp. 495, 498; Warren to Harrowby, 30/8/1804, FO 65/55. • **73**. Nelson to Emma, 22/9/1804, Pettigrew, *Memoirs*, 2, p. 423; Middleton to Melville, 17/3/1805, John Knox Laughton, *Barham*, 3, p. 66. • **74**. These negotiations can be followed in FO 65/54–55.

XIX The Eastern Question

1. Hallowell to Nelson, 16/3/1805, Add. MS 34923. Jane Knight's informed paper, 'Nelson and the Eastern Mediterranean', offers an alternative interpretation of this subject. • **2**. Ball to Nelson, 31/3/1804, 16/5/1804, 7/7/1804, NMM: CRK/1. • **3**. Drummond to Nelson, 12/9/1803, NMM: CRK/4; Drummond to Hawkesbury, 4/7/1803, 9/9/1803, FO 78/40; Warren to Hawkesbury, 10/8/1803, FO 65/53. A professional seaman with a 'fair character', Abdul Cadir Bey was perhaps too old for his post. He was deposed at the end of 1804 and confined on charges of embezzling funds at Acre: Stratton to Hawkesbury, 10/10/1803, FO 78/41; Stratton to Harrowby, 9/12/1804, FO 78/43. • **4**. Foresti to Hawkesbury, 22/2/1804, 27/4/1804, 22/6/1804, and Foresti to Harrowby, 6/10/1804, FO 42/5; Morier to Hawkesbury, 24/4/1804, FO 78/44; Morier to Nelson, 26/5/1804, NMM: CRK/9; Elliot to Hawkesbury, 24/7/1803, FO 70/21. • **5**. Nelson diary, July 1803, Add. MS 34966; Elliot to Hawkesbury, 5/2/1804, FO 70/23. The subject runs through many dispatches in FO 65, FO 78 and FO 42. See, for example, Foresti to Hawkesbury, 1/2/1804, 20/6/1804, FO 42/5. In France some blamed Italinsky, the Russian minister in Constantinople, for thwarting the project, whereas residual French agitators in the Morea explained that it had been postponed for 'internal concerns' in France: Warren to Harrowby, 24/8/1804, FO 65/55; Foresti to Harrowby, 28/1/1805, FO 42/7. • **6**. Warren to Hawkesbury, 9, 16 and 30/12/1803, FO 65/53; Foresti to Hawkesbury, 21/11/1803, 10/12/1803, FO 42/5; Foresti to Harrowby, 28/1/1805, and Foresti to Mulgrave, 16/4/1805, FO 42/7; return of 6/8/1805, ADM 1/411; Nelson's orders to Richardson and Raynsford, 11/8/1803, Add. MS 36610; and the series of letters from Foresti to Nelson between 23/8/1803 and 3/8/1804, NMM: CRK/5. • **7**. Morier to Hawkesbury, 30/6/1804, 31/7/1804, FO 78/44; Pisani to Stratton, 30/10/1804, FO 78/43; Foresti to Hawkesbury, 27/3/1804, 28/6/1804, FO 42/5; Foresti to Harrowby, 28/1/1805, 19/2/1805, FO 42/7; Foresti to Nelson, 28/6/1804, 7/8/1804, NMM: CRK/5; Warren to Nelson, April 1804, NMM: CRK/13. • **8**. Nelson to Maria Carolina, 10/7/1804, 19/12/1804, Add. MSS 34956 and 34965. • **9**. Letters of Nicholas Strane between 5/10/1803 and 11/2/1804 in NMM: CRK/12; Kensington to Marsden, 5/5/1804, Add. MS 34936. • **10**. Foresti to Nelson, 8/10/1803, 31/1/1804, NMM: CRK/5; Foresti to Hawkesbury, 22/2/1804, FO 42/5. • **11**. Fyffe's tribulations are fully detailed in Add. MSS 34919 and 34920, but see also Stuart to Nelson, 1/9/1803, NMM: CRK/12. • **12**. MacGill to Vincent, 26/2/1804, Add. MS 34922; Jackson to Hawkesbury, 20/8/1803, FO 67/32. • **13**. Raynsford to Nelson, 30/7/1804, with enclosure, Add. MS 34924; Nelson to Raynsford, 2/9/1804, *D&L*, 6, p. 185; Cracraft to Nelson, 24/10/1804, ADM 1/408; Nelson to Cracraft, 5/10/1804, Add. MS 34957. • **14**. Nelson to Staines, 1/9/1804, Add. MS 36610; Staines to Nelson, 5/12/1804, 4/1/1805, *HANP*, 2, p. 249, and NMM: CRK/11; Nelson to Foresti, 18/4/1804, 3/8/1804, Cornwall Record office, J3/35/36. • **15**. Corbet to Cracraft, 17/11/1804, Cracraft to Nelson, 23/1/1804, and Nelson to Marsden, 8/6/1804, ADM 1/408; Corner to Shepheard, 1/5/1804, Shepheard to Nelson, 1 and 6/5/1804, and Foresti to Shepheard, 6/5/1804, Add. MS 34923; Nelson to Corner, 3/8/1804, Add. MS 34956. • **16**. Leard to Nelson, 30/11/1803, 17/12/1803, 20/3/1804, Add. MSS 34921 and 34923; Stuart to Leard, 24/9/1803, and paper by Leard, 17/12/1803, Add. MS 34920; Taylor to Nelson, 23/1/1804, and Henry to Leard, 3/3/1804, Add. MS 34922; letters of Leard in ADM 106/1559 and FO 78/43. • **17**. Nelson to Addington, 24/8/1803, Add. MS 34965; Foresti to Nelson, 31/1/1804, 3/8/1804, NMM: CRK/5; Hamilton to Paget, 26/5/1803, and Hamilton to Hawkesbury, 6/5/1803, Add. MS 34919. • **18**. Cracraft to Nelson, 13/1/1804, Add. MS 34922; Foresti to Nelson, 31/1/1804, NMM: CRK/5; Morier to Harrowby, 31/7/1804, Add. MS 34924; Nelson to Hobart, 17/3/1804, 16/4/1804, CO 173/1. • **19**. Woodman, 23/5/1804, FO 78/43; Chapman to Warren, 1/6/1804, FO 65/55; Park, Sotheran and Ros report, 8/12/1804, and Wilkie to Nelson, 18/2/1805, Wellcome MS 3678; Taylor and Lawson to Otway, 10/12/1804, Wellcome MS 3679. • **20**. Nelson to Jackson, 6/9/1803, Add. MS 34953. • **21**. O'Brien to the British commandant at Minorca, 8/11/1799, FO 3/8; document dated 19/3/1801, Add. MS 34918; Falcon to Nelson, 4/6/1803, Add. MS 34919. Two papers are useful on this subject, Falcon's 'Reflection Upon Algiers', 1803, Add. MS 34921, and 'Remarks &c. On the Insults and Abuses which Great Britain received from Algiers', unsigned but apparently the work of Richard O'Brien, the US consul general at Algiers, Add. MS 34932. • **22**. Nelson to Nepean, 22/6/1803, ADM 1/407; Nelson to Villettes, 29/8/1803, *D&L*, 5, p. 189; Falcon to Pelham, 22/4/1803, Add. MS 34919. • **23**. Donnelly to Nelson, 3/9/1803, Add. MS 34920. • **24**. Ball to Nelson, 7/8/1803, 29/10/1803, NMM: CRK/1, and Add. MS 34921; Falcon to Ball, 23/6/1803, Add. MS 34919; Falcon to Nelson, 15/8/1803, Add. MS 34920. • **25**. Hobart to Nelson, 23/8/1803, 7/1/1804, *D&L*, 5, p. 220 and WLC; Nepean to Nelson, 26/8/1803, *D&L*, 5, p. 232; Nelson to Hobart, 16/10/1803, WLC. • **26**. Nelson to Keats, 9/1/1804, *D&L*, 5, p. 345; Nelson to the dey, 9/1/1804, and memorandum, CO 173/1. • **27**. The visit is documented in Add. MS 34922, in which see especially O'Brien to Clark, 29/1/1804; six letters of Keats to Nelson, 17 and 18/1/1804; O'Brien to Keats, 18/1/1804; and Falcon to Yorke, 18/1/1804. • **28**. O'Brien to a merchant of Alicante, 18/2/1804, and O'Brien to Clark, 29/1/1804, Add. MS 34922; Nelson to Hobart, 19 and 20/1/1804, CO 173/1; Nelson to Keats, 19/1/1804, *D&L*, 5, p. 380. • **29**. Keats to Nelson, 24/6/1804, Add. MS 34924; Nelson to Ball, 25/11/1804, Add. MS 34958. • **30**. Hobart to Nelson, 9/1/1804, WLC; Hobart to Nelson, 8/3/1804, Nelson to the dey, 14/5/1804, and Nelson to Keats, 15/5/1804, CO 173/1; Keats to Nelson, 20/6/1804, Add. MS 34924. • **31**. Keats to Nelson, 20 and 24/6/1804, and Keats to Ball, 18/6/1804, Add. MS 34924; 'List of Sicilians and Neapolitans . . . having English passports', 17/6/1804, NMM: CRK/8; O'Brien to British consul, 3/6/1803, Add. MS 34919; dey to Nelson, 15/6/1804, CO 173/1. The *Ape*, a xebec also known as the *Bee*, was owned by the English merchant Thomas Pollard, and manned by Pietro Gonzi and fourteen men. Her passport, issued on 30 April 1803, licensed her to carry wine from Malta to Messina, but she was taken by a corsair on 16 May. One of her crew had died in Algiers, her master was handed over to Keats but twelve remained in captivity. The ship and cargo were valued at £1394: Falcon to Ball, 23/6/1803, Add. MS 34919; petition of Fuevaino, 14/10/1803, Add. MS 34921; valuation, NMM: CRK/16/39. • **32**. Nelson to Hawkesbury, 29/6/1804, CO 173/1. It appears that the issue of the *St Antonio* was, in fact, already settled. She had been taken in November 1803, but some documents imply her crew were surrendered into the custody of O'Brien, and the restitution of the ship and compensation promised. According to Ball to Keats, 29/5/1804, Add. MS 34924, the compensation was short by six hundred dollars. • **33**. Nelson to the dey, 1/7/1804, 26/8/1804, Nelson to Camden, 11/10/1804, and Donnelly to Nelson, 3/9/1804, CO 173/1; Dey to Nelson, 6/7/1804, NMM: CRK/17; McDonough to Nelson, 26/7/1804, Add. MS 34924. McDonough, a surgeon, was the adopted son and secretary of Simon Lucas, the British consul in Tripoli, who had died in 1801. McDonough stood in until an official replacement, William Lanford, was announced in 1804. • **34**. Nelson to Falcon, 8/8/1804, Huntington, HM 34069; Nelson to Ball, 1/1/1805, *D&L*, 6, p. 310. • **35**. Nelson to Ball, 25/11/1804, Add. MS 34958; Ball to Nelson, 30/11/1804, NMM: CRK/1. • **36**. Camden to Nelson, 29/10/1804, Add. MS 34936. • **37**. Nelson to Camden, 16/1/1805, Add. MS 34958; Nelson to Ball, 16/1/1805, Add. MS 34958; documents respecting the mission filed in WO 1/282. • **38**. McDonough to Nelson, 4/8/1803, CO 173/1. • **39**. Nelson to Emma, 18/10/1803, NMM: CRK/19; Durban to Nelson, 20/8/1803, and several letters of Clark to Nelson between 27/7/1803 and 20/6/1804, NMM: CRK/17; Nelson to Clark, 2/3/1804, Clark to Nelson, 20/8/1803, 2/10/1803, and Hamooda Pasha to Nelson, 18/8/1803, CO 173/1; Nelson to Clark, 23/9/1803, Add. MS 34953. • **40**. Nelson to Hobart, 8/6/1804, CO 173/1; Nelson to Tough, 6/6/1804, Add. MS 34956, Nelson to Magnon, c. July 1804, Add. MS 34956. • **41**. Nelson to Cartwright, 8/10/1805, Add. MS 34960; Nelson to Castlereagh, 23/9/1805, WO 1/282. For an appreciation of Nelson's differences with Ball, see Donald Sultana, *Coleridge in Malta*.

XX In the Victory

1. The other lieutenants were William Layman, Robert Pettet, John Lackey, George Miller Bligh and John Pasco: *Victory* musters, ADM 36/15895–15900. • **2**. Kenneth Fenwick and Arthur Bugler have written of HMS *Victory*. Well-illustrated works by Lily Lambert McCarthy, Pieter van der Merwe and Margaret Lincoln depict much surviving memorabilia, but see especially Rina Prentice, *Authentic Nelson*. • **3**. Nelson to Emma, July 1803, 26/8/1803, NMM: CRK/19; Nelson to Davison, 28/3/1804, Egerton MS 2240; *ND*, 4 (1991), p. 76; Chevailler to Davison, 16/3/1804, 14/3/1805, RNM: 2002/76; Hardy to Manfield, 5/9/1803, A. M. Broadley, *Nelson's Hardy*, p. 110; Hasleham to Nelson, 27/8/1805, 3/9/1805, Wellcome MS 3676. • **4**. Scott to Lavington, 25/8/1809, Monmouth MS E468; John Scott to Emma, 18/7/1803, *HANP*, 2, p. 214; Nelson to Davison, 12/12/1803, Egerton MS 2240; Nelson to Marsh, 27/2/1804, Hilda Gamlin, *Nelson's Friendships*, 1, p. 352; Scott to Evans, 16/3/1804, and Scott to Marsh and Creed, 16/3/1804, 5/10/1805, RNM: 1996/1. As a prize agent John Scott operated on the principle of 'where there is the least doubt of right, lay claim'. Interestingly, when Nelson left the Mediterranean to pursue the French to the West Indies in 1805, leaving Bickerton in acting command of the station, Scott continued to claim Nelson's half of the flag eighth for prizes taken during his absence. This put Nelson dangerously close to St Vincent's position, when he was challenged over his right to prizes taken by his ships after he left the Mediterranean station in 1799: Scott to Cutforth, 16/3/1805, 20/9/1805, RNM: 1996/1. William Marsh (1755–1846) was the son of George Marsh, a former naval commissioner, and he was an admirer of both Lord and Lady Nelson. By his second wife, Frances Graham, he had his ninth child, Georgiana Nelson Marsh, on 7 January 1801, apparently naming her for Lady Nelson, her godmother. Marsh's bank failed in 1824. • **5**. Nelson does not seem to have involved himself in this matter. In September 1803 he told one correspondent that only two men had been punished in the ship for upwards of two months, 'we are so orderly and quiet'. In fact at least six had been lashed during that period: Nelson to Gaskin, 9/9/1803, Add. MS 34953. • **6**. Chevailler to Davison, 14/3/1805, RNM: 2002/76; Cyrus Redding, *Recollections*, 3, p. 253 (recollection by George Magrath, the ship's surgeon); Gillespie, 14/8/1805, J. Holland Rose, 'Nelson's Fleet', 77. • **7**. Chevailler to Davison, 14/3/1805, Royal Naval Museum, 2002/76. Nelson's interesting weather diary for October 1803 to August 1804 is in the Karpeles Library,

Santa Barbara. For Nelson's day see Gillespie to his sister, 12/1/1805, John Gillespie Deacon, 'Gillespie', 341; William Beatty's *Authentic Narrative*; and Scott to his wife, 12/11/1803, *The Times*, 29/9/1923. • **8**. William Mark, *At Sea With Nelson*, pp. 179, 183. • **9**. For this and the following paragraph, Nelson to St Vincent, 5/10/1803, *D&L*, 5, p. 223; Nelson to Baird, 30/5/1804, Monmouth MS E152; Nelson to Emma, March 1804, 23/11/1804, *HANP*, 2, p. 226, and NMM: CRK/19; Nelson to Davison, 12/12/1803, 23/11/1804, Egerton MS 2240; statement of Este, *D&L*, 6, p. 256; Nelson to Acton, 1/8/1804, Add. MS 34956; Trotter to Nelson, 29/8/1805, Wellcome MS 3676. • **10**. Macaulay to Nelson, 18/9/1803, 22/1/1804, NMM: CRK/8; Nelson to Marsden, 16/8/1804, ADM 1/408. • **11**. Nelson to Cornwallis, 19/3/1804, HMC, *Various Collections*, p. 402; Waltersdorff to Nelson, 9/5/1804, Add. MSS 34923. • **12**. Davison to Nelson, 3/12/1803, NMM: CRK/3. Between July 1804 and 5 March 1805 Nelson wrote to Emma twenty-five times: Add. MS 34967. Emma's letters to Davison during this period are in Add. MS 40739. • **13**. Nelson to Emma, 7–21/12/1803, 13/1/1804, March 1804, Sotheby's lot, 2005, NMM: CRK/19 and *HANP*, 2, p. 225; Nelson to Emma, 5/10/1803, Egerton MS 1614; Nelson to Emma, 27/8/1804, Thomas J. Pettigrew, *Memoirs*, 2, p. 420; *Memoirs of Lady Hamilton*, pp. 267–68. • **14**. Nelson to Emma, 21 and 26/8/1803, Pettigrew, *Memoirs*, 2, p. 331, and NMM: CRK/19; Nelson to Emma, 16/3/1805, NMM: TRA/13. • **15**. Nelson to Horatia, 21/10/1803, 14/1/1804, Winifred Gérin, *Horatia Nelson*, pp. 68–69. The references are probably to one of the Connor girls and young Mary Gibbs. Mary Gibbs, the daughter of Abraham Gibbs, the former British consul at Palermo who was administering Bronte, went to England by the *Cyclops*, Captain Fyffe ('a good commander who is fond of children'), and arrived in Merton in January 1804. Under Nelson's patronage she was put in Mrs Cleveland's school in Cumberland Street, London, 'the first school in England': Gibbs to Nelson, 12/9/1803, NMM: CRK/17; Nelson to Gibbs, 15/4/1804, Add. MS 34955. • **16**. Nelson to Emma, 20/1/1804, *HANP*, 2, p. 222; Nelson to Horatia, 20/1/1804, 13/4/1804, Monmouth MS E161 and NMM: CRK/15; Nelson to Charlotte, 19/4/1804, NMM: CRK/15. • **17**. Codicil, 6/9/1803, NA: PROB 1/22; Nelson to Emma, 13/8/1804, *HANP*, 2, p. 239. • **18**. Nelson to Emma, 10/4/1804, 9/3/1805, NMM: CRK/19, and *Letters*, 2, p. 87. In 1796 Edward Jenner had shown that a vaccine based on cowpox could protect against smallpox. • **19**. Codicil, 6/9/1803, NA: PROB 1/22; Nelson to Emma, 2/4/1804, 4/4/1805, NMM: CRK/19, and *HANP*, 2, p. 256; *Memoirs of Lady Hamilton*, p. 260. This Emma should not be confused with her godchild, Emma Horatia Bolton, born in March 1804. • **20**. Nelson to Davison, 9/8/1804, 16/9/1805, Egerton MS 2240 and Add. MS 34960; Nelson to Emma, 27/6/1804, *HANP*, 2, p. 232. • **21**. Bolton to Emma, 16/4/1805, NMM: NWD/9; Nelson to Emma, 23/11/1804, 9–31/3/1805, 4/4/1805, NMM: CRK/19, *Letters*, 2, p. 87, and Monmouth MS E445. For Bolton's career see John Marshall, *Royal Navy Biography*, vol. 2, part 2, p. 936, and the 'Biographical Memoir'. • **22**. Nelson to Emma, 26/12/1803, 21/4/1804 (Pettigrew, *Memoirs*, 2, pp. 359, 384), 27/5/1804, 6/6/1804 (NMM: CRK/19), 13/8/1804 (*HANP*, 2, p. 238), and 9–31/3/1805 (*Letters*, 2, p. 87); Hillyar to Emma, 2/3/1805, NMM: NWD/9; Nelson to Connor, 20/8/1804, Add. MS 34956. • **23**. Nelson to Emma, 9–31/3/1805, *Letters*, 2, p. 87; Nelson to Rolfe, 7/4/1804, *D&L*, 5, p. 488. • **24**. Unwin to Nelson, 28/1/1804, NMM: CRK/13. • **25**. Nelson to Emma, 13/1/1804 (part in NMM: CRK/19, and balance in *HANP*, 2, p. 219), 14/3/1804 (NMM: CRK/19) and 9/9/1804 (Pettigrew, *Memoirs*, 2, p. 423). • **26**. Davison to Emma, 17/6/1804, Add. MSS 34989; Nelson to Davison, 7/5/1805, Egerton MS 2240; Cadogan to Emma, 21/9/1804, 2/10/1804, NMM: CRK/20; Emma to Davison, 17/10/1804, Add. MS 40739; Sutton to Nelson, 6/2/1805, NMM: CRK/12. • **27**. Nelson to Emma, 18/10/1803, 27/8/1804, NMM: CRK/19, and Houghton, MS Eng. 196.5; Nelson to Marsh, 27/2/1804, Hilda Gamlin, *Nelson's Friendships*, 1, p. 352; Nelson to Graefer, 10/9/1803, Add. MS 34953; Nelson to Gibbs, 11 and 12/2/1804, 1, 26 and 29/8/1804, Add. MSS 34955–57. • **28**. Nelson to Davison, 18/3/1804, Egerton MS 2240; Susannah to Emma, 31/10/1804, NMM: NWD/8; Nelson to Emma, 26/8/1803, 10/9/1803 (NMM: CRK/19), and November 1804 (WLC). Using a conversion rate of one Spanish dollar to 51 pence, I estimate Nelson's share of seven prizes given in one list to be about £2983: ADM 298/12. • **29**. Nelson to Emma, 27/6/1804, November 1804, *HANP*, 2, p. 232, and WLC; Nelson to Davison, 29/12/1804, Add. MS 34958; Davison to Nelson, 7/1/1805, NMM: CRK/3; Rose to Emma, 9/3/1804, NMM: NWD/8; Rose, *Diaries*, p. 239. Rose did help Nelson to obtain a revision of the patent of his barony to extend the attached pension to the next two heirs male of his father, if he had no male issue himself. In effect, the barony, restyled 'of the Nile and Hilborough', would pass to William Nelson: Rose to Nelson, 15/9/1803, NMM: CRK/10. • **30**. Elliot to Nelson, 27/7/1804, NMM: ELL/307; Nelson to Emma, 31/8/1804, NMM: CRK/19; *Memoirs of Lady Hamilton*, p. 269. • **31**. Minutes of proceedings in Court of Common Pleas, 17/5/1802, Monmouth MS E735; Nelson to Davison, 13/1/1804, *D&L*, 5, p. 370; Davison to Nelson, 15/11/1803, NMM: CRK/3; *NC*, 10 (1804), p. 432. • **32**. Marsh to Nelson, 23/11/1803, 7/12/1803, 31/3/1804, NMM: CRK/8; Haslewood to Nelson, 9/4/1804, NMM: CRK/6; Nelson to Haslewood, 19/3/1804, 24/5/1804, Add. MS 34955. • **33**. Nelson to Haslewood, 24/5/1804, Add. MS 34955; Nelson to Acton, 18/3/1804, Zabriskie Collection, US Naval Academy.

XXI Mastering the Machine

1. Nelson to Otway, 5/4/1804, Add. MS 34955. • **2**. The capital ships that reinforced Nelson in 1803 and 1804 were the *Victory*, *Canopus* and *Excellent* in 1803; and the *Royal Sovereign*, *Leviathan*, *Spencer*, *Conqueror*, *Tigre* and *Swiftsure* the following year. • **3**. Nelson to Ball, 7/6/1804, *D&L*, 6, p. 51. • **4**. Nelson to St Vincent, 17/10/1803, *D&L*, 7, p. ccxxxi*; Nelson to Nepean, 4/8/1804, *D&L*, 6, p. 54. • **5**. Hillyar to Nelson, 7/8/1803, Add. MS 34919; Bedford to Nelson, 5/9/1803, NMM: CRK/2; Langford to Nelson, 20/5/1804, NMM: CRK/8. • **6**. Nelson to Villettes, 9/7/1803, *D&L*, 5, p. 126; Nelson to Emma, 29/9/1804, NMM: CRK/19; *NC*, 30 (1813), p. 34. Campbell was ill at the end of 1804, and had to quit the fleet. 'I never was more unhinged in my life,' he wrote, a sad portent of his eventual suicide: Campbell to Nelson, November 1804, NMM: CRK/3/15. • **7**. Nelson to Davison, 13/1/1804, Egerton MS 2240; *D&L*, 5, p. 370; Nelson to Elliot, 11/7/1803, *D&L*, 5, p. 130; Nelson to Nepean, 20/1/1804, Warren R. Dawson, *Nelson Collection*, p. 187. • **8**. Gore to Nelson, 26/8/1804, NMM: CRK/6; Nelson to Durban, 27/8/1803, Norfolk Record office, MC646/1. • **9**. John Gillespie Deacon, 'Gillespie', p. 340; Nelson's diary, 1/8/1803, 7/11/1803, Add. MS 34966; James Stanier Clarke and John McArthur, *Life and Services*, 3, pp. 208–9. Midshipman John Hindman of the *Victory* was promoted acting lieutenant of the *Phoebe* in 1803. • **10**. Nelson to Schomberg, 7/10/1803, Add. MS 34953; Nelson to Keats, 30/3/1805 (two letters), *D&L*, 6, p. 386, and Add. MS 34959. • **11**. Nelson to Emma, 7–21/12/1803, Sotheby's lot, 2005; Nelson to Russians, 16/3/1804, *D&L*, 5, p. 448; Nelson to Woronzow, 31/5/1804, Add. MS 34956; Nelson to Marsden, 11/4/1805, ADM 1/410. • **12**. Gore to Nelson, 1/7/1804, Add. MS 34924; Nelson to Gore, 6/8/1804, *D&L*, 6, p. 137; William Mark, *At Sea With Nelson*, p. 186. • **13**. Nelson to Marsden, 1/8/1805, ADM 1/411; Nelson to Lord Mayor of London, 1/8/1804, and Davison to Emma, 22/10/1804, Thomas J. Pettigrew, *Memoirs*, 2, pp. 413, 430; Perrington to Nelson, 25/10/1804, NMM: CRK/10; Nelson to Otway, 14/8/1804, Add. MS 34956. • **14**. Nelson to William, 18/10/1803, Add. MS 34988; Radstock to Nelson, 18/1/1805, NMM: CRK/10; Minto to Nelson, 2/9/1803, NMM: CRK/9; Foley to Nelson, 25/8/1803, 21/5/1804, 7/10/1804, NMM: CRK/5; Nelson to Pole, 25/5/1804, and Nelson to Lutwidge, 24/5/1804, Add. MS 34955. In fact, Nelson was able to assist Mrs Lutwidge's eleve. 'I really cannot inform [you] how truly happy your kindness towards him has made his family and friends,' she replied. 'They are . . . one of the most delighted circles in England': Lutwidge to Nelson, 8/3/1804, NMM: CRK/8. • **15**. Nelson to Ball, 5/8/1804, *D&L*, 6, p. 135; St Vincent to Nelson, 7/3/1804, Add. MS 31169. • **16**. Nelson's diary, Add. MS 34966. • **17**. Nelson to Melville, 10/10/1804, Nelson to Holloway, 10/10/1804, Nelson to Louis, 12/10/1804 and Nelson to Duncan, 4/10/1804, Add. MS 34957; Nelson to Hamilton, 3/8/1804, and Nelson to Melville, 4 and 24/8/1804, Add. MS 34956. Paddon may not have distinguished himself. Despite his 'interest' and capture of a gun brig in 1800 he remained a lieutenant for twenty-two years. • **18**. Nelson to Berry, 8/8/1804, Add. MS 34956; Nelson to Nepean, 7/10/1803, ADM 1/407. • **19**. Six returns of commissioned officers are haphazardly filed in ADM 6/64. • **20**. Augustus Phillimore, *Parker*, 1, pp. 255, 308. Apart from gunnery skills, Nelson's fleet made some improvements to technical firepower. Logs occasionally refer to ships receiving heavier guns or carronades, although the flintlock firing mechanism, often described as a British advantage, does not appear to have been general. On 26 June 1804 the Admiralty recommended the use of 'a new description of slow match': Nelson to Marsden, 10/10/1804, ADM 1/408. • **21**. Hoste to Nelson, 7/1/1804, 27/5/1804, NMM: CRK/6; Nelson to Melville, 12/10/1804, Add. MS 34957. • **22**. Este statement, 4/11/1804, *D&L*, 6, p. 256; Pettet to Nelson, 18/3/1803, NMM: CRK/10. • **23**. Layman's passing certificate, 5/6/1800, ADM 6/98, and return of service, 1817, ADM 9/4. • **24**. Tate to Layman, 28/7/1794, Rees to Layman, 27/10/1796, Tate to Scott, 3/5/1798, and Scott to Layman, 6/5/1799, all in Add. MS 34914. • **25**. Layman to Nelson, 12/11/1799, Add. MS 34914; Fanny to Nelson, 13/11/1799, *NLTHW*, p. 537; Reynolds to Nelson, 14/4/1800, Add. MS 34917; Troubridge to Nelson, 26/11/1800, NMM: CRK/13. There are three sketches, 'Biographical Memoir', *NC*, 37 (1817); John Marshall, *Royal Navy Biography*, 3, ii, pp. 323–44; and John Sugden, 'William Layman'. • **26**. 'Biographical Memoir', pp. 177, 444–53; Hardy to Manfield, 11/3/1805, Broadley, *Nelson's Hardy*, p. 125; Nelson to Troubridge, Huntington, HM 34217. • **27**. 'Biographical Memoir', pp. 177, 457; William Layman, *Plan for . . . the British West Indies*; Pettigrew, *Memoirs*, 2, p. 667. • **28**. Nelson to Emma, 2/4/1804, NMM: CRK/19/40. • **29**. The affair runs through numerous documents in Add. MSS 34919, but see especially Layman to Nelson, 27/6/1803, 10 and 23/7/1803, and also Cutforth to Nelson, 30/7/1803, NMM: CRK/3. • **30**. Report of Keats and White, 24/8/1803, Layman's remarks on the *Ambuscade*, 12/8/1803, and his report of 18/9/1803, Add. MS 34920. • **31**. Layman's memorandum on the *Victory*, Add. MS 34920; John Gore, *Nelson's Hardy*, p. 18; Layman to Melville, 9/4/1812, Marshall, *Royal Navy Biography*, p. 336; Nelson to Troubridge, 20/10/1803, Add. MS 34954. • **32**. Strachan to Nelson, 3/11/1803, Layman to Nelson, 2/11/1803, and Gore to Nelson, 14/1/1804, Add. MS 34922; Layman to Nelson, 6/2/1804, NMM: CRK/8. • **33**. Layman to Nelson, 20/3/1804, ADM 1/408; Nelson to St Vincent, 6/4/1804, Add. MS 34955; Gore to Nelson, 19/3/1804, and court martial, 2/4/1804, Add. MS 34923; Otway to Nelson, 18/2/1804, and address of the merchants, 6/3/1804, Add. MS 34922; Trigge to Nelson, 12/3/1804, NMM: CRK/12. • **34**. Layman to Nelson, 13/4/1804, memorial, endorsed with Nelson to Marsden, 14/4/1804, Add. MS 34923; Layman to Emma Hamilton, 21/9/1804, NMM: CRK/22; Layman to Nelson, 30/1/1805, ADM 1/410. • **35**. Layman to Nelson, 30/1/1805, 8/3/1805, ADM 1/410 and NMM: CRK/8. • **36**. Nelson to Moseley, 11/3/1804, Add. MS 37076. • **37**. Nelson to Baird, 19/3/1804, Wellcome MS 7362/2; Nelson to Keats, 27/8/1803, Add. MS 36610. • **38**. Sick reports, 1803–4, Wellcome MS 3680; John Gillespie Deacon, 'Gillespie', p. 340. • **39**. Snipe to Nelson, 16/3/1805, NMM: CRK/12; Baird to Nelson, 27/1/1803, 10/6/1804, NMM: CRK/1 and Add. MS 34924. Baird and a rival physician, Thomas

Trotter, disagreed about the efficacy of lemon juice in the treatment of scurvy, and Baird asked Nelson for his observations. As a surgeon Snipe had inspected recruits in receiving ships at Sheerness before serving as physician of Nelson's fleet. • **40**. C. C. Lloyd and J. L. S. Coulter, Jane Bowden-Dan, James Watt, Laurence Brockliss, et al., Janet Macdonald, Brian Vale and David McLean have written authoritatively on aspects of these subjects. • **41**. Nelson to Baird, 30/5/1804, Add. MS 34956; Nelson to Melville, 12/10/1804, ADM 1/408; Nelson to surgeons, 12/10/1804, Add. MS 34957; Sick and Wounded Board circular, 28/1/1805, Wellcome MS 3677; Gillespie to Nelson, 15/4/1805, Add. MS 34929. • **42**. Nelson to Baird, August 1803, *D&L*, 7, p. ccxiv; Nelson to Nepean, 27/7/1803, ADM 1/407; Snipe to Barlow, 24/7/1803, Add. MS 34919. • **43**. Memorandum, 30/12/1803, *D&L*, 7, p. ccxvii; Strachan to Nelson, 19/2/1804, NMM: CRK/11; sick lists, 1/1/1804, 8/7/1804, Add. MS 34922 and 34924; Nelson to Moubray, 8/3/1804, Add. MS 36610; Nelson to Barlow, 15/5/1804, *D&L*, 6, p. 19. It should be noted that supplies of citrus fruits, like those of fresh greens and onions, fluctuated. Few lemons or oranges could be procured in Rosas except through Majorca, and this source was threatened by the Spanish War of 1804. Even Sicily, which afforded a more ample and secure supply, could disappoint, as in 1804, when the lemon crop failed: Ford to Nelson, 22/3/1804, Wellcome MS 3677; Snipe to Nelson, 20/1/1805, ADM 1/410. • **44**. Nelson to Marsden, 12/8/1804, ADM 1/408; Snipe's observations, 7/11/1803, 23/11/1803, Wellcome MS 3680; Felix to Whitby, 16/12/1803, Add. MS 34921; Snipe to Nelson, 21/12/1803, 30/3/1804, Add. MSS 34921 and 34923; Nelson to captains, 21/12/1803, Add. MS 36610; *D&L*, 5, p. 318; Nelson to Bolton, 30/3/1804, *D&L*, 5, p. 479; Navy Board to Marsden, 27/8/1804, Add. MS 34936. • **45**. Franklin to Villettes, 28/7/1803, and Shaw to Franklin, 24/7/1803, Add. MS 34919; *D&L*, 7, p. ccxvi; Nelson to Baird, August 1803, *D&L*, 7, p. ccxiv. • **46**. Among many documents, see Poggioli to Weir, 30/3/1803, Add. MS 34919; Leard to Long, 27/8/1803, and the statement of Burd, transmitted by Poggioli, 22/9/1803, Add. MS 34920. • **47**. Snipe to Nelson, 26 and 30/6/1803, 22/8/1803, Add. MSS 34919 and 34920; Snipe to Sick and Wounded Board, 29/6/1803, Burd, 13/6/1803, and Burd to Nelson, 14/6/1803, Add. MS 34919; minutes of an enquiry, 22/12/1803, Add. MS 34921; Snipe's report, 16/1/1804, and Snipe and others to Nelson, 18/1/1804, Add. MS 34922; Trigge to Nelson, 15/9/1803, Add. MS 34920; Magrath to Nelson, 28/2/1805, ADM 1/410. • **48**. Dickson to Snipe, 5/12/1803, and Gray to Nelson, 19/11/1803, Add. MS 34921; Nelson to Snipe, 25/11/1803, *D&L*, 5, p. 294. • **49**. Snipe to Nelson, 7 and 9/12/1803, 4/7/1804, Add. MSS 34921 and 34924; Ball to Nelson, 5/12/1803, NMM: CRK/1; Nelson to Marsden, 10/5/1804, ADM 1/408. • **50**. Sick and Wounded Board notes, Add. MS 34920; contract between Snipe and Higgins, 21/12/1803, and Sick and Wounded Board to Nelson, 29/5/1805, Wellcome MS 3681; Snipe to Nelson, 7/12/1803, 20/1/1805, ADM 1/407 and ADM 1/410; Ball to Nelson, 9/7/1804, NMM: CRK/1; Nelson to Marsden, 7/8/1804, 4/2/1805, ADM 1/408, ADM 1/410; contract between Snipe and Broadbent, 12/6/1804, ADM 1/408. • **51**. Snipe to Nelson, 29/5/1804, Add. MS 33924. • **52**. Regular reports reached Nelson from Hunter in Madrid: see Hunter to Nelson, 4/1/1804, 29/8/1804, 22/9/1804, and reports in NMM: CRK/7; Duff to Nelson, 22/10/1803, 24/11/1804, NMM: CRK/4. • **53**. Parker to his mother, 25/1/1805, Phillimore, *Parker*, 1, p. 269; King to Nelson, 22/10/1804, NMM: CRK/8; Burd to Nelson, 1/11/1804, NMM: CRK/2. Between 1 September and 8 December 1804 the military garrison suffered 894 men dead: return, Wellcome MS 3681. • **54**. Nelson's diary, 27/10/1804, Add. MS 34967. • **55**. Snipe's observations, 19/9/1803, Wellcome MS 3680; Nelson to Davison, 4/10/1803, Egerton MS 2240. • **56**. Snipe report, 7/5/1804, Wellcome MS 3680. • **57**. Eleven returns of transports, 9/2/1804–4/2/1805, Wellcome MS 3680; Victualling Office reports, Wellcome MS 3678. For a full consideration of victualling see the excellent studies by Roger Knight and Janet Macdonald.

• **58**. Estimates based on Instructions to Richard Ford, 13/12/1803, Wellcome MS 3678; Troubridge to Nelson, 22/9/1803, NMM: CRK/13; returns of the Victualling Office and agent victuallers in Wellcome MSS 3677 and 3678. • **59**. Estimates based upon the returns and correspondence regarding Navy Board storeships, Wellcome MS 3679; stores aboard the *Duke of Bronte*, Add. MS 34921. • **60**. Serle to Nelson, 25/6/1803, Add. MSS 34919; Gore to Nelson, 4/12/1803, ADM 1/408; Wilkie to Nelson, 15/12/1804, 8/2/1805, Wellcome MS 3678. • **61**. Otway to Ryves, 13/6/1804, Add. MS 34924; Nelson to Navy Board, 21/9/1803, *D&L*, 5, p. 207. • **62**. Nelson to St Vincent, 12/7/1803, Add. MS 34965; Nelson to Troubridge, 21/10/1803, Add. MS 34954; Troubridge to Nelson, 28/12/1803, NMM: CRK/13; Nelson to Wilkie, 8/8/1803, 6/7/1804, 7/9/1804, 5/10/1804, 26/2/1805, Wellcome MS 3678. • **63** Nelson to Nepean, 12/7/1803, ADM 1/408; Briggs to Bickerton, 15/6/1803, Brigham to Villettes, 16/6/1803, and Noble to Nelson, 26/7/1803, Add. MS 34919. • **64**. Marsh to Nelson, 23/11/1803, NMM: CRK/8; Hood to Nelson, 21/11/1803, NMM: CRK/6; St Vincent to Nelson, 24/9/1803, 20/11/1803, Add. MS 31169 and NMM: CRK/11; White to Nelson, 26/7/1803, Add. MSS, 34919. • **65**. Scott to Nelson, 28/7/1803, and Keats to Nelson, 2/8/1803, Add. MS 34919; Falconnet to Nelson, 13/2/1804, NMM: CRK/5; McNeil to Nelson, 4 to 26/11/1803, and Macaulay to Nelson, 13/9/1803, NMM: CRK/8; Taylor to Nelson, 3/6/1804, and Malcolm to Nelson, 3/6/1804, Add. MS 34924; Malcolm to Nelson, 28/6/1804, 26/7/1804, 16/10/1804, NMM: CRK/8; Warrington to Nelson, 26/7/1804, NMM: CRK/13; Nelson to Taylor, 21/10/1803, Add. MS 34954. • **66**. Nelson to Emma, 7/12/1803, Sotheby's lot, 2005; note from Gayner, 13/1/1804, *HANP*, 2, p. 222; Ford to Nelson, 22/3/1804, 28/6/1804, 3/7/1804, Wellcome MS 3677. Gayner, who died in Minorca in 1846, is treated by Ben Burgess, David Donaldson and Justin Reay. • **67**. Gibert to Nelson, 30/7/1803, 13 and 30/8/1803, 7, 12 and 26/9/1803, 7/10/1803, 1 and 26/12/1803, Add. MSS 34919, 34920 and 34921; Felix Gibert to Nelson, 16/8/1803, Add. MS 34920; Nelson to Gibert, 13/9/1803, Add. MS 34953. • **68**. Gibert to Nelson, 12/9/1803, Add. MS 34920; Keats to Frere, 14/12/1803, Add. MS 34921; Gayner to Nelson, 16/1/1804, Leadan to Donnelly, 12/1/1804, 14/1/1804, and Moubray to Nelson, 25/1/1804, Add. MS 34922. • **69**. Ford to Nelson, 14/12/1804, and his accounts, 13/2/1803 to 9/4/1804, Wellcome MS 3677; letterbook, ADM 114/55. • **70**. Comelate to Nelson, 3/1/1804, Add. MS 34922; Baird to Nelson, 30/10/1803, NMM: CRK/1; Foresti to Nelson, 8/10/1803, NMM: CRK/5; Gough to Donnelly, October 1803, Add. MS 34920; Ball to Nelson, 15/12/1803, 18/9/1804, NMM: CRK/1. • **71**. Nelson to St Vincent, 17/10/1803, *D&L*, 7, p. ccxxxi; Taylor to Nelson, 25/9/1803, Add. MS 34920. • **72**. Nelson to Davison, 12/12/1803, Egerton MS 2240; St Vincent to Nelson, 24/9/1803, Add. MS 31169. • **73**. Otway to Nelson, 2/11/1803, Add. MS 34921; Taylor to Nelson, 10/2/1804, Add. MS 34922; Nelson to Nepean, 14/1/1804, Warren R. Dawson, *Nelson Collection*, p. 499. • **74**. Otway to Nelson, 31/1/1804, Maling to senior officer, 23/1/1804, and Strachan to Nelson, 2/2/1804, Add. MS 34922; Maling to Nelson, 2/2/1804, NMM: CRK/8. • **75**. Taylor to Nelson, 1/4/1804, Le Gros's letters to Marsden and Nelson, 3/4/1804, and the court martial, 19/4/1804, Add. MS 34923; Otway to Nelson, 18/2/1804, Add. MSS 34922; Nelson to St Vincent, 19/4/1804, Add. MS 34955; Nelson to Marsden, 19 and 22/4/1804, ADM 1/408; Troubridge to Nelson, 28/12/1803, NMM: CRK/13; Wellcome MS 3679. • **76**. Watson to Nelson, April 1804, and Gibert to Nelson, 7/4/1804, Add. MS 34923; Nelson to Emma, 28/4/1804, *HANP*, 2, p. 229. The *Espérance* was herself captured by the British *L'Alcyon* on 20 September 1804. • **77**. Nelson to Taylor, 5/11/1803, *D&L*, 5, p. 279; Nelson to Otway, 14/8/1804, Add. MS 34956; Elliott to Harrowby, 24/7/1804, FO 70/22. • **78**. Nelson to Elliot, 7/7/1804, Add. MS 34956; Nelson to Otway, 18/1/1805, Add MS 34958. • **79**. Troubridge to Nelson, 20 and 21/9/1803, NMM: CRK/13; Ball to Nelson, 27/8/1801, NMM: CRK/1; musters, December 1803–December 1804,

Wellcome MS 3681. • **80**. List of recruits, 1804–1805, Wellcome MS 3676; Pietro Veivas, 19/4/1804, Huntington, HM 1857; Adair to Nelson, 20/1/1803, 20/3/1805, ADM 1/410. • **81**. Nelson to Villettes, 6/9/1804, Add. MS 34957; Nelson to officers, 10/11/1803, and Nelson to Kerr, 9/9/1804, Add. MS 36610; Gibert to Nelson, 30/8/1803, Add. MS 34920. • **82**. Nelson to Sutton, 2/8/1804, Add. MS 36610; Nelson to Shaw, 4/10/1804, Monmouth MS E991. • **83**. Cracraft to Nelson, 13/5/1804, Add. MS 34924; Barclay to Nelson, 5/9/1804, NMM: CRK/2. • **84**. Wherry to Nelson, 24/8/1804, NMM: CRK/13; Nelson to Wherry, 22/10/1804, Add. MS 34957; Scott to Wilkie, 1/8/1804, Scott letterbook, RNM: 1996/1. • **85**. Hillyar to Nelson, 20/8/1803, Add. MS 34920. • **86**. Gore to Frere, 24/6/1804, 10/9/1804, NMM: CRK/6. • **87**. Scott to Nelson, 13/8/1803, Shaw to Nelson, 30/8/1803, 14/2/1804, and Schomberg to Nelson, 7/4/1804, Add. MS 34923. Vincent's dispatch (3/6/1804, Add. MS 34924) justified the British advance by alluding to the hostile 'disposition' of the French, who hauled their ship close to the beach and assumed a defensive posture. This 'induced me to attempt cutting her out, conceiving the offensive arrangements made in shore by the enemy to be a sufficient indication that they meant not to claim the neutrality of the island, but had by their operations grossly violated it'. • **88**. Pearse to Gore, 22/6/1804, Add. MS 34924. • **89**. Donnelly to Nelson, 11/7/1804, and Thomson to Donnelly, 11/7/1804, Add. MS 34924; Nelson to Donnelly, 12/7/1804, Add. MS 36610. • **90**. Capel to Nelson, 24/4/1804, 1/5/1804, Add. MS 34923. • **91**. Corbet to Schomberg, 3/5/1804, Add. MS 34923. • **92**. Vincent's report, 10/3/1804, Add. MS 34918. • **93**. Farquhar's letters to Nelson and Strachan, 11/2/1805, Coggan to Schomberg, 13/2/1805 and Nelson to Marsden, 29/3/1805, ADM 1/410; Vincent to Nelson, 14/2/1805, ADM 1/411. • **94**. I am indebted to M. K. Barritt, who is preparing a conscientious study of the hydrographic service. • **95**. Nelson to Ball, 6/10/1803, Add. MS 34953; Nelson to Emma, 19/12/1804, *HANP*, 2, p. 251; Nelson to Foresti, 1/1/1805, Cornwall Record Office, J3/35/36. • **96**. Duff to Nelson, 28/10/1803, Add. MS 34921. • **97**. Foresti to Nelson, 9/2/1805, NMM: CRK/5; Foresti to Hawkesbury, 27/4/1804, FO 42/5; Nelson to Foresti, 4/11/1803, Cornwall Record Office, J3/35/36.

XXII The Test

1. Julian de Zuleta, 'Battle'; Susannah to Emma, 25/10/1804, *HANP*, 2, p. 243. • **2**. Nelson to Ball, 12/10/1804, and Nelson to Gore, 13/10/1804, Add. MS 34957. • **3**. Nelson to Strachan, 13/10/1804, ADM 1/409; Nelson to Villettes, 28/11/1804, and Nelson to Melville, 23/11/1804, Add. MS 34958. • **4**. Brandi to Nelson, 28/12//1804, NMM: CRK/18; Savoy to Nelson, 15/12/1804, Thomas J. Pettigrew, *Memoirs*, 2, p. 441. • **5**. Marsden to Nelson, 15/11/1804, Add. MS 34936; Nelson to Emma, 13/10/1804, NMM: CRK/19; *D&L*, 6, p. 256. • **6**. Nelson's diary, 14/11/1804, Add. MS 34967; Nelson to Otway, 1/12/1804, and Nelson to Capel, 9/12/1804, Add. MS 34958; Hillyar to Nelson, 26/11/1804, NMM: CRK/6; *Victory* log, ADM 51/4514. The incident at Minorca was exaggerated, the Spaniards having fired to keep a ship away that it was feared might bring the yellow fever. • **7**. Diary, 2 and 19/12/1804, Add. MS 34967; Augustus Phillimore, *Parker*, 1, p. 269; Campbell to Nelson, 15/12/1804, NMM: CRK/3; Nelson to Marsden, 4/12/1804, Add. MS 34958; Nelson to Emma, 4 and 19/12/1804, Egerton MS 1614 and Monmouth MS E159; Nelson to Sutton, 14/3/1805, WLC. • **8**. Orde to Marsden, 28/11/1804, Orde to Nelson's ships, 27/11/1804, and Nelson to Bolton, 23/11/1804, ADM 1/409; Nelson to Strachan, 15/11/1804, Add. MS 34958. • **9**. Nelson to Parker, 30/12/1804, *D&L*, 6, p. 309; Phillimore, *Parker*, 1, pp. 259, 266–68. On the issue of prize money, John Scott, Nelson's agent, ordered Cutforth, his co-agent, to scrupulously lay claim to any prize taken by Orde's ships in the *sight* of any of Nelson's ships: Scott to Cutforth, 10/1/1805, Scott letterbook, RNM, 1996/1. • **10**. Nelson to Emma, 4/12/1804, Pettigrew, *Memoirs*, 2, p. 438; Campbell to Nelson, 1804, NMM: CRK/3. • **11**. Nelson's diary, 19/1/1805, Add. MS 34967; Nelson to Ball, 1/1/1805, Add. MS 34958. • **12**. Nelson's diary, 22/1/1805, Add. MS 34967; Nelson to Acton, 25/1/1805, Warren R. Dawson, *Nelson Collection*, p. 195. • **13**. Elliot to Harrowby, 29/1/1805, FO 70/24. • **14**. Nelson to Marsden, 12/2/1805, ADM 1/410; Nelson to Ball, 11/2/1805, Add. MS 34958; Nelson to Melville, 14/2/1805, *D&L*, 6, p. 342. • **15**. Nelson's diary, 19/2/1805, Add. MS 34967; Elliot to Harrowby, 12, 16 and 17/2/1805, FO 70/24. • **16**. Nelson to Marsden, 22/2/1805, ADM 1/410; Marsden to Nelson, 17/4/1805, NMM: CRK/9. • **17**. Nelson to Ball, 29/3/1805, *D&L*, 6, p. 382. • **18**. Orde to Melville, 27/3/1805, *D&L*, 6, p. 383. • **19**. Acton to Nelson, 21/10/1804, CO 173/1. • **20**. Nelson to Camden, 10/3/1805, 10/5/1805, with enclosures, CO 537/151. • **21**. Solana to Duff, 13/2/1805, and Layman to Nelson, 30/1/1805, ADM 1/410. • **22**. *NC*, 38, p. 4; John Marshall, *Royal Navy Biography*, p. 330; Nelson to Ball, 8/3/1805, Add. MS 34959. • **23**. Nelson to Marsden, 10/3/1804, and enclosures, ADM 1/410; Nelson to Emma, 9–10/3/1805, *Letters*, p. 102; Nelson to Melville, 10/3/1805, Add. MS 34959. • **24**. Nelson to Melville, 10/3/1805, Add. MS 34959. It was reading this paragraph, accurately published in *NC*, that gave Nicolas the idea of editing Nelson's letters. • **25**. Nelson to Davison, 11/3/1805, Add. MS 34959; Marshall, *Royal Navy Biography*, pp. 334, 336. • **26**. Nelson to Sotheran, 7/4/1805, *D&L*, 6, p. 402. • **27**. Nelson's diary, 16/4/1805, Add. MS 34968; Nelson to Ball, 6/4/1805, *D&L*, 6, p. 399; Foresti to Nelson, 9/2/1805, NMM: CRK/5; Acton to Nelson, 8/4/1805, NMM: CRK/1; Ball to Nelson, 20 and 21/2/1805, 1/4/1805, NMM: CRK/1. • **28**. Nelson to Ball, 10/4/1805, Add. MS 34959; Nelson to Elliot, 16/4/1805, *D&L*, 6, p. 405; Nelson's diary, 18/4/1805, Add. MS 34968. The Admiralty notification of the sailing of Craig's expedition did not reach Nelson until 1 May. • **29**. Nelson's diary, 22/4/1805, Add. MS 34968; Nelson to Marsden, 19/4/1805, ADM 1/410; Nelson to Melville, 19/4/1805, SNA, GD 51/2/1082. The station of Ushant, identified by Drake in 1587 and developed by Anson in the mid-eighteenth century, had become the central plank in Britain's defences. • **30**. Nelson's diary, 30/4/1805, Add. MS 34968; Nelson to Otway, 26/4/1805, *D&L*, 6, p. 415; Nelson to Keats, 1/5/1805, *D&L*, 6, p. 419; Nelson to Bickerton, 11/5/1805, Add. MS 34959. • **31**. Nelson to Emma, 4/5/1805, Monmouth MS E169. • **32**. WO 1/280 for Craig's dispatches. • **33**. Nelson to Emma, 9/5/1805, Pettigrew, *Memoirs*, 2, p. 471. • **34**. Nelson to Emma, 13/5/1805, Pettigrew, *Memoirs*, 2, p. 471. • **35**. Nelson to Emma, 16/5/1805, *D&L*, 6, p. 441. • **36**. Nelson's diary, 22/5/1805, Add. MS 34968; Nelson to Keats, 19/5/1805, *D&L*, 6, p. 442. I was criticised for referring to the Neptune ceremony at the crossing of the Tropic of Cancer by the *Boreas* in 1784 (*Nelson*, p. 251), a reference which came from the reminiscences of a lieutenant of that ship. The reviewer presumed these ceremonies to be uniquely a feature of the crossing of the Equator. In fact, the earliest allusion to them in respect of the Tropic of Cancer that I know is in Henri Joutel's journal of La Salle's voyage of 1684, and the practice was still alive among the British in 1816: John Richardson, 'Recollections of the West Indies', *The New Era or Canadian Chronicle* (Brockville, Canada), 2/3/1842. • **37**. Nelson to Keats, 19/5/1805, *D&L*, 6, p. 442; A. and M. Gatty, *Recollections*, p. 173. • **38**. Nelson to Emma, 14/7/1804, Egerton MS 1614; Nelson to Keats, 27/5/1805, *D&L*, 6, p. 443; Phillimore, *Parker*, 1, pp. 287–9. The memorandum shows evidence of having been hastily written, and at one point assumes the enemy fleet to have ten or a dozen ships of the line and at another only eight or nine. Since Villeneuve crossed the Atlantic with eighteen capital ships, naval historians have rightly speculated that the document was written in 1803 or 1804. • **39**. Nelson to Marsden, 26/6/1805, ADM 1/411. • **40**. Nelson to Seaforth, 8/6/1805, SNA, GD 46/17/16; Nelson to Emma, 10 and 16/6/1805, Pettigrew, *Memoirs*,

2, p. 478, and Monmouth MS E416. • **41**. Nelson's diary, 13/6/1805, Add. MS 34968; Nelson to Nepean, 16/6/1805, Add. MS 34959. • **42**. Edouard Desbriere's study is essential for this campaign. • **43**. Nelson to Marsden, 10/7/1805, ADM 1/411; Phillimore, *Parker*, 1, p. 295. • **44**. Intelligence from the *Sally*, 18/6/1805, ADM 1/411; Camden to Coote, 4/7/1805, and July 1805, Coote Papers, WLC. • **45**. Nelson's diary, 18/7/1805, Add. MS 34968. • **46**. Report to the Navy Board, 23/7/1805, ADM 106/2022; Nelson's diary, 22/7/1805, Add. MS 34968; Nelson to Bayntun, 19/6/1805, *ND*, 7 (2000), p. 116; Brian Lavery, *Nelson's Fleet*, pp. 85–6; Nelson to Barham, 23/7/1805, Add. MS 34958. • **47**. Nelson to Davison, 24/7/1805, Add. MS 34958; Nelson to Marsden, 23/7/1805, ADM 1/411. • **48**. Nelson to Keats, 17/8/1805, *D&L*, 7, p. 7. The *Amazon* frigate was ordered to accompany the fleet home. 'Make haste and join me,' wrote Nelson, 'if all plans fail you will find me at Spithead.' Nelson may have wanted to bring the *Amazon* home for recoppering and repairs, but Parker was delighted to remain under Nelson's direct orders. 'I have no wish to remain on this station after the departure of our chief,' he told his mother: Phillimore, *Parker*, 1, p. 298. He followed Nelson, but did not catch him, reaching England at the end of August. • **49**. Betting book, 1805–6, Brooks's Club, p. 196. • **50**. Nicholas Tracy, 'Sir Robert Calder's Action'. • **51**. Nelson to Fremantle, 16/8/1805, Add. MS 34958. • **52**. Nelson to Louis, 15/8/1805, *D&L*, 7, p. 4. • **53**. Nelson to the collector of customs, 18/8/1805, ADM 1/411. • **54**. Nelson to Marsden, 18/8/1805, ADM 1/411; Nelson to Scott, 17/8/1805, Warren R. Dawson, *Nelson Collection*, p. 356. Nelson furnished Marguette with a letter of introduction 'that due attention may be paid this valuable man, who very cheerfully offered his services'. In response, the Board paid Marguette six shillings per diem from 18 August, when he was discharged from the *Victory*, and gave him six weeks' allowance in advance. He was borne on the books of the *Royal William* until a passage home could be arranged: Nelson to Marsden, 18/8/1805, ADM 1/411. • **55**. Nelson to Curtis, 19/8/1805, Huntington, HM 34075. • **56**. Nelson's report, 15/8/1805, HMC, *Various Collections*, 6 (1909), p. 412; Joseph Allen, *Hargood*, p. 137; J. Holland Rose, 'State of Nelson's Fleet', p. 77. • **57**. Vera Foster, *Two Duchesses*, p. 235; Camden to Nelson, 7/9/1805, Add. MS 34936; Elliot to Nelson, 18/8/1805, NMM: ELL/308. • **58**. Nelson to Emma, 18/8/1805, Pettigrew, *Memoirs*, 2, p. 486.

XXIII The Last Farewell

1. *Morning Chronicle*, 22/8/1805. • **2**. James Grieg, *Farington Diary*, 2, pp. 274–5; Emma to Davison, 30/10/1804, Add. MS 40739. Emma was plagiarising a letter Richard Bulkeley had written to her. • **3**. Mary Eyre Matcham, *Nelsons*, p. 226. Lady Nelson, who may not have been fully informed, listed the admiral's personal staff at Merton in 1805 as Chevailler, Spedillo, Cribb, a gardener and 'under gardener', a 'second man', two footmen and a coachman postillion: undated fragment, c. 1805, Bonham's lot, 2005. • **4**. Nelson to Bickerton, 20/9/1805, Monmouth MS E187. • **5**. NMM: CRK/9/17; *Ipswich Gazette*, 24/8/1805; Nelson to Emma, 13/5/1805, Thomas J. Pettigrew, *Memoirs*, 2, p. 474; Nelson to Davison, 31/8/1805, Egerton MS 2240; Add. MS 34992, f. 77. • **6**. J. A. Andersen, *Dane's Excursion*, 1, pp. 15–23. • **7**. Nelson to Emma, 16/5/1805, NMM: TRA/14; Cadogan to Emma, 18/7/1805, *HANP*, 2, p. 259; Emma to Tyson, 8/5/1805, Walter Sichel, *Lady Hamilton*, p. 512; Add. MS 34988, f. 404; Peddieson and Thomas Molyneux accounts, Monmouth MSS E400 and E397. The bill for the architect and tradesmen (Merton Place file, Morden Public Library) included £24 for 'house and chaise hire' and identifies the local tradesmen as Spinks, bricklayer; Betley, plasterer; Molyneux, plumber, painter and glazier; Messenger, mason; Williams, slater; Smith, facer; and Bowyer, joiner and carpenter. James Bowyer's bill was the largest, at £646. • **8**. Bowen to Nelson,

24/9/1804, NMM: CRK/2; Countess of Minto, *Elliot*, 3, p. 362; Langford to Emma, 14/8/1805, *HANP*, 2, p. 260. • **9**. Nelson to Emma, 26/8/1803, 9/5/1805, Pettigrew, *Memoirs*, 2, pp. 337, 471; Nelson to Emma, 12/8/1804, NMM: CRK/19; Nelson to Davison, 16/9/1805, Egerton MS 2240. In the new layout, shown in Chawner's January 1805 plan of the ground floor (Peter Hopkins, *Merton Place*, p. 39), a housekeeper's room created at the western end of the southern block may have been occupied by Mrs Cadogan. There is doubt about when various changes were made. Chawner's plan creates confusion by describing some of the pre-Nelson changes to the property (the addition of a dining room to the east end of the southern block and the ante-room linking the blocks) as 'lately built'. Some have taken this to mean that they were built by Nelson between 1801 and 1805. However, that they pre-dated Nelson, and were part of the property as purchased by him, is evident from the sale particulars of 1801. The reference in the latter to the two blocks being 'attached' seems conclusive, since they were only linked by the ante-room and dining room marked by Chawner as 'lately built'. It seems clear, therefore, that these features pre-dated Nelson's occupancy. I deduced that Nelson's new kitchen was built in late 1805 or early 1806 from comparing Nelson's letter to Davison, cited above, with Gyford's drawing of Merton, published on 1 March 1806. Thomas Baxter's sketches of Merton (NMM: WAL/49), made in 1803 and 1805, give views of the western, eastern and north-eastern façades of the house, as well as of such specific items as the garden, greenhouse, entrance gates and bridge over the canal. Particularly useful is his view of the grounds to the east of the house, which shows the new entrance lodge and carriageway. Of the engravings of the house the best are one showing the northern façade done by Edward Hawke Locker in 1804, and two depicting the northern and eastern façades, one based on the aforementioned drawing by Gyford. For two others, showing the eastern and northern façades, see Hopkins, *Merton Place*, p. 27, and Edward Gill, *Nelson and the Hamiltons on Tour*, p. 3. • **10**. For example, 'In Nelson's house . . . each of the five bedrooms had a WC fitted in the adjoining dressing-room, together with a washstand and bowl, lead tank and tap, and a bath filled by servants': Roy Porter, *English Society*, p. 273. • **11**. An account of James Hudson, Cribb's son-in-law, who spent most of his life in the estate cottages, says that two existed at the bottom of the lane linking the new lodge with the back of Merton Abbey. This must have been adjacent to Abbey Lane (clippings in Monmouth MS E8). The tunnel, like the rest of Merton Place, disappeared in the nineteenth century, but it was rediscovered in 1889, when excavations were made for a sewer. An item of that year recorded that it was 'situated as near as possible between the shops now occupied by Mr Smith, oilman, and Mr Corke, butcher, and passed beneath the road in a slanting fashion towards Haydons Lane into The Shrubbery'. See Hopkins, *Merton Place*, p. 32. H. P. Smith's establishment was situated about 250 feet west of the present Nelson Arms and Joseph Corke was further west but adjacent to him at 61 High Street. Corke was later interviewed by John Knox Laughton, and said that when he came to Merton in 1845 the subway was still open. Nelson's well was situated in his yard (Laughton, 'Nelson at Merton', pp. 34–5). The terminus of the tunnel near the house is uncertain. Nelson to Emma, 9/9/1804, Egerton MS 1614, wanted it to stop short of the kitchen which was at the rear of the southern block. • **12**. Emma to Davison, 6/9/1805, in Sotheby's, *Davison*, p. 155. • **13**. Lee, *Memoirs*, pp. 175–6; Minto, *Elliot*, 3, p. 362; Alison Lockwood, 'Nelson', pp. 33–5; Kenneth S. Cliff, *Lock*, pp. 10–11; Nelson to Dolland, 11/9/1805, Monmouth MS E179; receipt from Barrett, Corney and Corney, Monmouth MS E178; *Daily Telegraph*, 22/9/1997; Anne Fremantle, *Wynne Diaries*, 3, p. 221. • **14**. Dorothy M. Stuart, *Dearest Bess*, pp. 123–4; Minto, *Sir Gilbert Elliot*, 3, p. 362. Lady Perceval was probably Isabella, wife of the 3rd Earl of Egmont. • **15**. Matcham to Nelson, August 1805, and Susannah to Emma,

18/10/1805, NMM: NWD/9; Matcham, *Nelsons*, p. 287; James Harrison, *Life*, 2, p. 466. • **16**. Bland to Nelson, 3/9/1805, Add. MS 34988; Nelson to Davison, 16/9/1805, Egerton MS 2240; Nelson to Rose, 29/8/1805, NMM: GIR/1; Rose to Nelson, 1 and 11/9/1805, Add. MS 34931; Rose to Abercorn, 9/4/1808, Leveson V. Harcourt, *Rose*, 1, p. 254. • **17**. Owen to Nelson, 3/9/1805, Eliza Felton to Nelson, 5/9/1805, Add. MS 34931; Nelson to Barham, 8/9/1805, ADM 1/411; Nelson to Barham, 13/9/1805, Bonham's lot, 2005. • **18**. Bicknell to Marsden, 24/8/1805, ADM 1/411; Scott to Cutforth, 18/3/1805, Scott letterbook, RNM, 1996/1. • **19**. Layman's memorandum of services, 29/8/1817, John Marshall, *Royal Navy Biography*, 3, ii, p. 335. • **20**. McArthur to Nelson, 16/7/1799, 9 and 11/4/1803, 2 and 11/5/1803, 6/9/1805, Add. MSS 34912, 34919, 34931; McArthur to William Nelson, 10/12/1806, Add. MS 34992. McArthur (1755–1840) generated extensive papers, a small number of which survive in the British and Rosenbach Libraries. • **21**. Nelson to Keats, 24/8/1805, *D&L*, 7, p. 15; Nelson to Ball, 11/10/1805, *D&L*, 7, p. 112; George Pellew, *Sidmouth*, 2, pp. 380–82; Sidmouth to Nelson, 8/9/1805, Add. MS 34931; *The Times*, 24, 26 and 27/8/1805. • **22**. Hood to Nelson, 26/8/1805, Add. MS 34930; Minto, *Elliot*, 3, p. 367; Nelson to Fox, 27/9/1805, Warren R. Dawson, *Nelson Collection*, p. 215; Julian Corbett, *Trafalgar*, p. 181. • **23**. Barham to Nelson, 12/9/1805, Add. MS 34931. • **24**. *Ipswich Journal*, 31/8/1805; Nelson to Pitt, 29/8/1805, NMM: GIR/2; Minto, *Elliot*, 3, pp. 366–7; Nelson to the Viceroy, 27/9/1805, John Gwyther, 'Nelson in Turin', p. 69. • **25**. Blackwood's reports of 18/8/1805, 2/9/1805, ADM 1/1534; Matcham, *Nelsons*, pp. 234–5; Harrison, *Life*, 2, p. 457; James S. Clarke and John McArthur, *Life and Services*, 3, p. 119. • **26**. Countess Granville, *Gower*, 2, p. 113; *D&L*, 7, p. 241; Nelson to Beckford, 31/8/1805, *D&L*, 7, p. 22. • **27**. Minto, *Elliot*, 3, p. 368; Harrison, *Life*, 2, pp. 458–9; Berry to Nelson, 23/8/1805, *D&L*, 7, p. 23. • **28**. Nelson to Davison, 6/9/1805, Egerton MS 2240; Emma to Bolton, 4/9/1805, *D&L*, 7, p. 28. • **29**. Matcham, *Nelsons*, pp. 228–31, has George's diary; Harrison, *Life*, 2, p. 460. • **30**. *The Times*, 5/9/1805. Tom Allen was no longer with Nelson. He always claimed that the *Victory* sailed before he could reach it in 1803, and inadvertently left him behind. In fact, Nelson had dismissed the fellow. When he applied for employment with the Rev. J. Glasse of Burnham Thorpe, the admiral declined to give him a 'character'. Allen, he said, 'did not make a very grateful return to my kindness to him' and had never been his steward, as he professed. 'Nor,' he added, 'do I think him able to perform such a service well.' Nelson usually had compassion for old shipmates, and his words suggest genuine anger against Allen: Adrian Bridge, 'Tom Allen's Job Reference'; 'Nelson, His Valet, and His Native Coast'; *Notes & Queries*, 2nd series, 2 (1856), p. 385. • **31**. Clarence to Nelson, Add. MS 34932, f. 1; Joseph Allen, *Hargood*, p. 114; J. E. Jagger, *Lord Nelson's Home Life*, p. 12; Thomas Foley, *Nelson Centenary*, pp. 66–67. Nelson Suckling had been born on 31 December 1803. The next child, named William Nelson Suckling for both Clarence and the admiral, was born in February 1806. • **32**. *The Times*, 10 and 14/9/1805; Nelson to Marsden, 6/9/1805, ADM 1/411; John Barrow, *Autobiography*, pp. 280–81; Hardy to Rose, 9/12/1805, Bonham's lot, 2005; Clay to Nelson, 9/9/1805, Add. MS 34931; Francis to Nelson, 4/9/1805, Add. MS 34931. • **33**. Sidmouth to Nelson, 8/9/1805, Add. MS 34931; Granville, *Gower*, 2, pp. 111–13; Matcham, *Nelsons*, p. 235; Stuart, *Dearest Bess*, pp. 123, 125. Nelson kept his word to Lady Foster, inviting Clifford to dine in the *Victory* and delivering the packet entrusted to him: Nelson to Emma, October 1805, Monmouth MS E438. Paul Emden, 'Brothers Goldsmid', p. 236, records a story told by Lionel Goldsmid, one of Benjamin Goldsmid's sons, to the effect that Nelson spent his last night in England at his father's villa at Roehampton. Insofar as the date is concerned this is an error, but some of Lionel's memories of the admiral ring true, and the incident probably occurred at another time. He remembered Nelson's careless appearance, and the rapport he developed with Lionel and his younger sister. 'He was kind in the extreme, and we all loved him,' remembered Lionel. • **34**. Mrs Henry Baring, *Windham*, p. 452. • **35**. *The Times*, 14/9/1805; Gore to Nelson, 1/2/1805, NMM: CRK/6; John Sugden, *Nelson*, pp. 11, 796; *Edinburgh Review* (1838), pp. 321–2; Nelson's opinion, WO 1/282, f. 113; Nelson to Castlereagh, 13/10/1805, Add. MS. 34960; Nelson to Craig, 15/10/1805, Add MS 34960; Castlereagh to Nelson, 24/9/1805, 27/10/1805, WO 1/282. • **36**. Minto, *Elliot*, 3, p. 370. • **37**. Richard Edgcumbe, *Diary*, 1, p. 79; Stuart, *Dearest Bess*, pp. 127–9. The rings were sold at Bonham's in 2005. The one Emma gave Nelson appears to have been brought back to Merton by Chevailler after Trafalgar. According to a third-hand story, Nelson was wearing it on his last day, and as he lay dying told Chevailler to return it to Emma. • **38**. *The Times*, 13/9/1805; Emma to Hayley, 29/1/1806, Colin White, 'Further Unpublished Letters', p. 68; Harrison, *Life*, 2, pp. 472–4; *Memoirs of Lady Hamilton*, p. 322. • **39**. Oliver Warner, *Last Diary*, pp. 34–5.

XXIV 'For Charity's Sake, Send us Lord Nelson!'

1. Muster of the *Victory*, ADM 36/15900. • **2**. Allison Lockwood, 'Nelson as Seen by an American', pp. 33–4; Nelson to Murray, 14/9/1805, Warren R. Dawson, *Nelson Collection*, p. 215; David Shannon, 'Utmost Expression of Nautical Affection', pp. 136–7. • **3**. Nelson to Emma, 15/9/1805, Bonham's lot, 2005; Leveson V. Harcourt, *Rose*, 1, pp. 264–5; Rose's statement, 10/2/1806, NMM: GIR/5; Oliver Warner, *Last Diary*, p. 36; James Harrison, *Life*, 2, p. 475. Nelson's route from the George to the beach is reconstructed in Tertius, 'You Who Tread his Footsteps', pp. 236–8, and Colin White, 'Nelson's Last Walk', pp. 382–5. • **4**. Nelson to Rose, 17/9/1805, and Nelson to Ball, 11/10/1805, Add. MS 34960; Nelson to Emma, 25/9/1805, Monmouth MS E183. The 'we' could either refer to Nelson and his officers or to conversations that had occurred between Nelson and Emma at Merton. • **5**. Log of the *Victory*, ADM 51/4514; Nelson to Emma, 17–18/9/1805, NMM: CRK/19. 'Thomas' may have been Thomas Dear, an able seaman who had joined Nelson's personal retinue. • **6**. Lady Bourchier, *Codrington*, 1, p. 68; Peter Yule Booth, 'John Yule', pp. 396–400. • **7**. Nelson to Emma, 20/9/1805, *HANP*, 2, p. 266. • **8**. Nelson to Strangford, 3/10/1805, *D&L*, 7, p. 67. • **9**. Edouard Desbriere, *Trafalgar*, 2, p. 96. • **10**. Jocelyn Godley, 'A Captain's Career'; A. H. Taylor, 'Battle of Trafalgar', p. 283. For the ships and personnel of the fleet at Trafalgar, see Peter Goodwin, *Ships of Trafalgar*; Brian Lavery, *Nelson's Fleet*; A. M. Broadley, *Three Dorset Captains*; Robert Holden Mackenzie, *Trafalgar Roll*; Hilary L. Rubinstein, *Trafalgar Captain*; Leslie H. Bennett, *Nelson's Eyes*; John D. Clarke, *Men of H.M.S. Victory*; and Colin White, *Trafalgar Captains*. • **11**. *MM*, 16 (1930), p. 409; Bourchier, *Codrington*, 1, pp. 46–51; *NC*, 15, p. 37. A comprehensive biography of Collingwood is needed, but see those by George Newnham Collingwood, Geoffrey Murray and Oliver Warner. • **12**. Anne Fremantle, *Wynne Diaries*, 3, p. 210; *MM*, 16 (1930), pp. 409–10; Duff to his wife, 1 and 10/10/1805, *D&L*, 7, pp. 70, 71; Nelson to Emma, 1/10/1805, Egerton MS 1614; Nelson to Collingwood, 30/9/1805, Add. MS 34960; Nelson to Harvey, 3/10/1805, Sam Willis, *Fighting 'Temeraire'*, p. 161. • **13**. Nelson to Emma, *HANP*, 2, p. 267; Calder to Nelson, 12/10/1805, Add. MS 34931; Nelson to Barham, 30/9/1805, 13/10/1805, and Nelson to Gambier, 2/10/1805, Add. MS 34960. Calder left the fleet on 14 October. He was found guilty of failing to do his best to defeat the enemy and never employed at sea again, although he did become commander-in-chief at Plymouth. • **14**. T. Sturges-Jackson, *Logs*, 2, p. 322; Atkinson to Paul, 3/10/1805, Doreen Scragg, 'Thomas Atkinson', p. 90; William Beatty, *Authentic Narrative*, p. 8; Duff to his wife, 10/10/1805, *D&L*, 7, p. 71; Fremantle, *Wynne Diaries*, 3, p. 210. • **15**. *NC*, 15 (1806), p. 37; Nelson to Emma, 1/10/1805, Egerton MS 1614. • **16**. Nelson to

Stewart, 8/10/1805, *Cumloden Papers*. • **17**. Nelson to Davison, *NC*, 14 (1805), p. 475. • **18**. Ram to his sister, 1/10/1805, Charley Ram, 'Letters', p. 185. • **19**. Nelson to Middleton, 2/10/1805, Sotheby's lot, 2005; Castlereagh to Nelson and Matra, 4/9/1805, Add. MS 34931; Nelson to Knight, 17/10/1805, *Daily Mail*, 16/7/2010; Nelson to Ford, 2/10/1805, Add. MS 34960; Ford to Collingwood, 2/1/1805, ADM 114/55. Janet Macdonald has justly remarked that Nelson might have organised a victualling service between Gibraltar-Tetuan and the fleet, as he had established one from Malta in 1803, and obviated the need to deplete his main force. There was, of course, the problem of unloading victuallers at sea during the autumn and winter weather, but conceivably Nelson felt that time was against him. Water and fresh provisions were needed urgently, and it was probably quicker to collect them, loading directly, rather than to send a courier with orders to prepare transports. • **20**. Recollections of Austen, *D&L*, 7, p. 63; Warner, *Last Diary*, p. 53; Louis to Emma, 9/11/1805, Thomas J. Pettigrew, *Memoirs*, 2, p. 543. Although not one of Nelson's closest confidants, Louis adored his chief as few others. After the admiral's death he wrote to Emma to ask for a keepsake. 'I never made such a request before, nor ever shall again,' he said, 'for no man can ever have the warmth of my heart and soul so strong and sincere.' • **21**. Add. MS 21506, f. 155; *ND*, 5 (1995), p. 158. • **22**. Blackwood to Nelson, 10/10/1805, Add. MS 34931; Castlereagh to Nelson, 24/9/1805, 27/10/1805 and October 1805, WO 1/282; Nelson to Castlereagh, 2/10/1805, Add. MS. 34960. • **23**. Nelson to Blackwood, 4 and 8/10/1805, NMM: CRK/7; Blackwood to his wife, 19/10/1805, *D&L*, 7, p. 73. • **24**. Nelson to Blackwood, 4/10/1805, Add. MS 37076; Blackwood to Nelson, 15/10/1805, Add. MS 34931; Nelson to Duff, 4/10/1805, Houghton, MS Eng. 196.5; Warner, *Last Diary*, p. 53. • **25**. Nelson to Rose, 6/10/1805, *D&L*, 7, p. 80 [my italics]; Nelson to Barham, 1/10/1805, 5/10/1805, Bonham's lot, 2005, and Add. MS 34960; Collingwood to Nelson, 6/10/1805, Add. MS 34931; Nelson to Gambier, 6/10/1805, Add. MS 34960. • **26**. Barham to Duckworth, 28/10/1805, Bonham's lot, 2005; Blackwood to Nelson, 8/10/1805, Add. MS 34931. • **27**. Warner, *Last Diary*, p. 52; Nelson to Knight, 8/10/1805, Add. MS 34960. • **28**. Nelson to Marsden, 7 and 10/10/1805, ADM 1/411; Nelson to Castlereagh, 5/10/1805, Add. MS. 34960. • **29**. Nelson to Blackwood, 9/10/1805, NMM: CRK/7. • **30**. Nelson to Collingwood, 10/10/1805, MS in A. M. Broadley, 'Nelsoniana', BL, 6, f.p. 440. • **31**. Nelson to Collingwood, 9/10/1805, Add. MS 34960; Warner, *Last Diary*, p. 20. The memorandum (NMM: GIR/3) is printed in *D&L*, 7, p. 89. In 2002 Colin White drew attention to an informal ink sketch which, he hypothesised, may have been an earlier representation of the plan, done in the summer of 1805. The sketch has been much reproduced since, and the supposition that it relates to Trafalgar, while inconclusive, is plausible: *Observer*, 20/5/2002. • **32**. Nelson's prevailing principles, distilled from various statements, may be summarised as follows: (1) the objective was the destruction, rather than the mere defeat, of the enemy force; (2) it was imperative to fight at close range so that the advantages of British gunnery could be maximised; (3) complicated and time-consuming sailing manoeuvres were to be avoided, and the enemy engaged as quickly as possible, using a combined sailing and battle order; (4) it was important to induct captains and flag officers into the battle plan to reduce a dependence upon signalling and maximise command and control; (5) the attack should be made from windward, but by cutting through the enemy line it would be possible to disrupt his formation and by engaging from leeward seal off his retreat; (6) wherever possible the enemy was to be kept in doubt about the nature of the attack, perhaps by the use of a feint; (7) force was to be massed against part of the enemy line; (8) a flying column could act as a reserve, ready to intervene as necessary; (9) the command centre of the enemy fleet, commonly the flagship, was a desirable target; and (10) a simple and flexible plan was preferable, capable of being modified according to the actual circumstances of battle. • **33**. For the signal flag, see Tim Clayton, 'Difficulty', p. 18. • **34**. *D&L*, 7, p. 226. Several copies of the order of sailing that I have seen show that Nelson continued to refine it until the day of battle; two different listings were made on the same day. • **35**. Fremantle, *Wynne Diaries*, 3, p. 211. • **36**. *D&L*, 7, pp. 98, 117; Nelson to Marsden, 12/10/1805, ADM 1/411. • **37**. Pettigrew, *Memoirs*, 2, p. 654; A. M. Broadley, *Nelson's Hardy*, p. 260. • **38**. Nelson to Blackwood, 14/10/1805, NMM: CRK/7; Nelson to Collingwood, 14/10/1805, *D&L*, 7, p. 121. • **39**. Hardy to Rose, 9/12/1805, Bonham's lot, 2005. • **40**. Warner, *Last Diary*, p. 73. • **41**. *D&L*, 7, p. 132. • **42**. Anderson's account of Trafalgar, NMM: MSS/80/201.2. • **43**. Roberts's account, in Broadley, *Nelson's Hardy*, pp. 139–46. • **44**. Clayton, 'Difficulty', p. 22; Peter Goodwin, *Ships of Trafalgar*, pp. 9–11, 163–4, 208–9, 240–42.

XXV 'Irresistible Lines of Ships'

1. Apart from the dependable William James, *Naval History*, the British produced little on Trafalgar during the nineteenth century. After the centennial three monumental studies became the basis of subsequent scholarship: the histories by Edouard Desbriere (1907, translation 1933) and Julian Corbett (1910) and the *Report of a Committee of the Admiralty* (1913). In the thirties the research of A. H. Taylor, summarised in a paper of 1950, became the basis of a new round of popular studies, of which the best were those by Oliver Warner and Dudley Pope, published in 1959. Alan Schom's *Trafalgar* (1990) set the battle in the context of the French invasion project of 1803–5. The bicentennial inspired several studies, of which those by Tim Clayton and Peter Craig (2004) and Brian Lavery (2005) are outstanding. Among several short analyses see especially those by Marianne Czisnik, Michael Duffy, Roger Knight and Tony Beales. Edward Fraser, *Sailors*, and Peter Warwick, among others, reprint several first-hand narratives; Peter Goodwin deals with the *Ships of Trafalgar*, and Mark Adkin pulls together much introductory matter. Fraser, *Enemy*, was the only British historian to write extensively of the Spanish and French side of the story, but the tradition of scholarship in Spain extends as far back as the mid-nineteenth century, prompted much by indignation at the aspersions of the French historian Thiers. Of the older works Pelayo Alcala Galiano, *Combate de Trafalgar*, repays scrutiny, but for modern appraisals see the papers by Julian de Zulueta, John Habron's *Trafalgar and the Spanish Navy*, and José Cayuela Fernandez and Angel Pozuelo Reina's *Trafalgar*. Jean-Pierre Jurien de la Graviere, *Sketches*, offered authoritative post-Napoleonic war French comment, but Desbriere has now been supplemented by two fine modern works by French historians Michele Battesti and Rémi Monaque. • **2**. Villeneuve's instructions, 21/12/1804, Edouard Desbriere, *Trafalgar Campaign*, 2, p. 129. • **3**. Edward Fraser, *Enemy*, pp. 60–61; Pope, *England Expects*, p. 201; Hewson to Strange, 2/11/1805, Houghton, MS Eng. 196.5. • **4**. Ernest Waring, 'Cumby Letter'; David Shannon, 'In Case I should Fall'; John Webb, 'Midshipman at Trafalgar'; Blackwood to his wife, 21/10/1805, *D&L*, 7, p. 138; A. N. and H. Tayler, *Book of the Duffs*, 1, p. 264. • **5**. Lesley Edwards, 'Recreation'; Ron Fiske, 'Visit'; Alfred Gatty in *Notes & Queries*, series 1, vol. 3 (1851), p. 517. The uniform, stained with the blood of another casualty, perhaps John Scott, can be seen at the National Maritime Museum. • **6**. Medical journal, ADM 101/125; *Victory* muster, ADM 36/15900, but see Edward Fraser, *Sailors*, pp. 242–3, and interpretations by Charles P. Addis, *Men Who Fought . . . in HMS Victory*, and John Clarke, *Men of H.M.S. Victory*. • **7**. Michael Duffy, 'All Was Hushed Up', pp. 220–4, contains a convincing analysis of the changing order of sailing. • **8**. Thomas Huskisson, *Eyewitness*, p. 70; 'The Naval Officer', *United Service Journal*, p. 362. • **9**. Pasco to Huggins, 25/5/1835, Monmouth MS E360; Fiske, 'Visit', p. 19; William Beatty, *Authentic Narrative*, p. 14;

Oliver Warner, *Last Diary*, pp. 58–60. • **10**. Warner, *Last Diary*, pp. 61–7. • **11**. Lady Bourchier, *Codrington*, 1, p. 63; Lady Ellis, *Memoirs*, p. 4; Hercules Robinson, *Sea Drift*, p. 206. For an excellent account of the schooner and her commander see the paper by Peter Hore. • **12**. E. H. Fairbrother, 'Nelsoniana', p. 322; James Greig, *Farington Diary*, 3, p. 138. • **13**. William James, who interviewed Hardy and other survivors, stated that when Lieutenant Yule attempted to adjust an inadequately set studding sail on the forecastle, Nelson feared he was shortening sail and ran impatiently forward to upbraid him: *Naval History*, 4, p. 46. • **14**. Blackwood's account in *D&L*, 7, p. 146. But William Wilkinson of the frigate *Sirius*, who had the story from his captain, also an eyewitness, reported Nelson's words as 'I must have twenty, but ten will do': Keith Pybus, 'Stinkpots and Villains', p. 303. • **15**. *Report of a Committee*, pp. 24, 26, 37, 63; *The Times*, 2/1/1806 (Dumanoir's account); *D&L*, 7, p. 154; Peter Hicks, 'Harsh, but Necessary, Apprenticeship', p. 42. The manuscript plan of the battle by Jean-Jacques Magendie, captain of the *Bucentaure*, in the National Maritime Museum, clearly delineates Nelson's deviation. • **16**. Joseph Allen, *Hargood*, p. 140 (Owen's account); A. M. Broadley, *Nelson's Hardy*, p. 264 (Roberts's account); *Report of a Committee*, p. 53; Blackwood to Nelson, 10/10/1805, Add. MS 34931. For the enemy flags, see for example the reports of Berenger, Lucas and Bazin in Desbriere, *Trafalgar Campaign*, 2, pp. 165, 211, 220. Apart from flags identifying the admirals, the combined fleet's national colours were the French tricolour and the Banner of Castile. • **17**. Blackwood to his wife, 23/10/1805, *D&L*, 7, p. 226. • **18**. NMM: Wellcome MS 30 (William Rivers). Nelson made twenty-three signals in the hours before the battle commenced, and only one thereafter. • **19**. Pasco to Cole, 29/10/1840, Bourchier, *Codrington*, 1, p. 60; *D&L*, 7, pp. 149, 150; undated holograph by Pasco, Bonham's lot, 2005; Hardy to Rose, 9/12/1805, Bonham's lot, 2005; *United Services Magazine*, 1829, pt 1, p. 362; Hewson to Strange, 2/11/1805, Houghton, MS Eng. 196.5; *Niagara Chronicle* (Canada), 12/2/1852. The word 'duty' had to be spelled, and needed four flags. The other words used three numerical flags each. • **20**. *Report of a Committee*, p. 36. For fuller reproductions of the logs, see T. Sturges Jackson, *Logs*, vol. 2. • **21**. *D&L*, 7, pp. 150, 224. • **22**. Bazin to Rosily, 12/11/1805, and Villemadrin to Rosily, 1805, Desbriere, *Trafalgar Campaign*, 2, pp. 229, 267; Allen, *Hargood*, p. 138. • **23**. Allen, *Hargood*, pp. 139, 142 (Owen's account); Fraser, *Sailors*, p. 220 (Nicholas's account). • **24**. Castle to his sister, 3/11/1805, *ND*, 6 (1998), 346; Edward Fraser, *Enemy*, p. 258. It is not known how long Collingwood was unsupported. The *Belleisle*, which followed, said she cut the line at 12.13, only five minutes after the *Royal Sovereign*; the log of the flagship, however, records that she opened fire at 11.50, at noon 'no other ship [was] in action', and that the *Santa Ana* surrendered at 12.40, 'at this [which] the *Belleisle* came up' (*Report of a Committee*, pp. 9, 49). • **25**. Fraser, *Sailors*, pp. 271, 274. Taylor reasoned that *Pluton* rather than *Achille* was *Belleisle*'s opponent, but Allen, Hargood's biographer, who spoke to witnesses, and an account from the British *Swiftsure*, were sure it was *Achille*: Allen, *Hargood*, pp. 127–8; Barker to his uncle, 22/10/1805, in Dean Appleton, 'Letters from Trafalgar'. • **26**. *Report of a Committee*, p. 29; *NC*, 15 (1806), p. 371; Tayler, *Book of the Duffs*, including Robinson to his mother, 29/1/1805, 1, pp. 263, 265. • **27**. Westphal's account, Allen, *Hargood*, 123; *ND*, 1 (1984), pp. 13–35; Roberts's account, Broadley, *Nelson's Hardy*, p. 264; Clement to his father, 30/11/1805, Appleton, 'Letters from Trafalgar', p. 539. • **28**. 'Louis Rotely Recalls Trafalgar', pp. 383–5; John to his parents, 3/12/1805, *ND*, 7 (2000), p. 269; Michael Applebe, 'Personal Account', p. 37; David Shannon, 'The Engagement Began Very Hot', pp. 238–9; Barton to his parents, 27/10/1805, Graham Dean, *Nelson's Heroes*, p. 26. • **29**. Lavery, *Nelson's Fleet at Trafalgar*, pp. 163, 166; *Morning Chronicle*, 28/12/1805; 'Louis Rotely Recalls Trafalgar', pp. 384–5. On Nelson's uniform, as early as December 1805 Pasco, who was present, attributed an unreasonably pompous speech to the admiral: 'No, whatever may be the consequence, the insignia of the honours I now wear, I gained by the exertions of British seamen under my command in various parts of the world, and in the hour of danger I am proud to show them and the enemies of Old England I will never part from them. If it pleases God I am to fall, I will expire with these trophies entwined round my heart' (*Morning Chronicle*, 9/12/1805). He may have said something to that effect, but would hardly have employed such melodramatic language, and a more succinct version later appeared. However, W. H. Smyth, 'Nelson Vindicated', pp. 390–91, who spoke to Hardy, Quilliam and other officers of the *Victory*, flatly denied the story, and said that Nelson merely professed it was too late to be changing a coat. Beatty, *Authentic Narrative*, and A. and M. Gatty, *Recollections*, are the principal sources for Nelson's final hours. • **30**. Magendie to Decrès, 1805, and Villeneuve to Decrès, 14/11/1805, Desbriere, *Trafalgar Campaign*, 2, pp. 137, 191. • **31**. 'Louis Rotely Recalls Trafalgar', p. 384; Roberts's account, Broadley, *Nelson's Hardy*, p. 258; Rivers gunnery book, Royal Naval Museum, 1998/41/1. • **32**. Lucas report, 2/1/1806, Desbriere, *Trafalgar Campaign*, 2, p. 211. • **33**. Line soldiers were accustomed to volley fire, discharging muskets at massed ranks it was difficult to miss, but marksmen sought individual targets. In the circumstances, when smoke, sails and shrouds intermittently obscured the British upper deck, firing blind made little sense. Rivers, the gunner of the *Victory*, also testified that the sniper 'was seen to take deliberate aim by Mr [Francis] Collingwood and [David] Oglevee [Ogilvee] on the quarter-deck or poop': Rivers notes, NMM: Wellcome/30. • **34**. Two accounts of Nelson's injuries have been found. The autopsy report of 15/12/1805 (Special Collections, Wellcome MS 5141) was presumably the letter that Dr Gillespie read to the Medical Society of London on 23 December (minutes of the Medical Society of London, 23/12/1805, Wellcome Library). Beatty developed his account for the *Authentic Narrative*. See also Ron Fiske, 'Visit', p. 18; 'Tertius', 'The Bullet That Killed Nelson'. In two conscientious enquiries D. Wang, 'Admiral Lord Nelson's Death', and Michael Crumplin and Anthony Harrison, 'A Fatal Shot', drew attention to the uncertain trajectory of the ball, which I have supposed might have been deflected from its straight course as it passed through Nelson's body. Crumplin and Harrison argue that it pursued a straight course, and would have missed the left pulmonary artery, which Beatty insisted had been damaged; moreover, a division of the artery would also have caused a large blood loss, something Beatty's autopsy had failed to find. The points are well considered and may be right, but I am inclined to stick with Beatty. He was a fine surgeon – the mortality rates of his patients were low – and an astute and conscientious enquirer, and was unlikely to have been mistaken about something of such public importance. The course of the ball carries relatively little weight. A low velocity ball, especially one dragging threads of clothing with it, can easily pursue an erratic or complex course in collision with bone and human tissue, as many military surgeons have attested. Nor would a division of a branch of the major pulmonary artery necessarily create high blood loss. • **35**. Collingwood to Clarence, 12/12/1805, *D&L*, 7, p. 240; Greig, *Farington Diary*, 3, p. 138; James S. Clarke and John McArthur, *Life and Services*, 3, p. 155; James, *Naval History*, 4, pp. 43, 80, 103; Roberts's account, Broadley, *Nelson's Hardy*, p. 264; Lady Foster's account, Dorothy M. Stuart, *Dearest Bess*, p. 131; Burke's account, *Morning Chronicle*, 10/12/1805; William Turner's account, Dean, *Nelson's Heroes*, p. 140. The first six accounts derive ultimately from Hardy. The statements of any single witness will vary in detail over time. It is the general thrust of them that matters. According to Bess Foster, for example, Hardy said that Nelson's first words after being hit were 'Hardy, they have winged me at last', which roughly squares with his more famous account. • **36**. Varying statements were made about the identities of both the killer and avenger of Nelson. Rotely of the *Victory*'s marines said his men cleared the French fighting tops ('Louis Rotely Recalls Trafalgar', pp. 384–5), but a week after the battle an officer of the *Sirius* frigate, which towed the damaged *Temeraire* out of action, claimed that the marines of *that* ship shot all those left in the tops of the *Redoutable* (Wilkinson to his uncle, 30/10/1805, Pybus, 'Stinkpots and Villains', p. 303). Pollard was clearly regarded by the British as Nelson's avenger at the time: Senhouse to his mother, 27/10/1805, *Macmillan's Magazine*, 81 (1900), p. 415; *Gibraltar Gazette*, 2/11/1805; Hewson to Strange, 2/11/1805, MS Eng. 196.5, Houghton Library; and John to his parents, 3/12/1805, *ND*, 7 (2000), p. 269. His claim was endorsed by James Harrison, *Life*, 2, p. 501, and William Beatty's *Authentic Narrative*, and as late as 13 May 1865 by Thomas Goble, 'one of the surviving officers of the quarter-deck' of the *Victory*, actually a master's mate (Malcolm Paton, 'Thomas Goble at Trafalgar', Ms). Pollard, who died a retired commander in 1868, was a modest man, but he gave his own account in 1863. During the battle he was hit by a splinter in the right arm, and his spyglass and pocket watch were smashed by bullets. See Fraser, *Sailors*, pp. 329–36; David Shannon, 'John Pollard'; and Jack Spence's *Nelson's Avenger*. The 'King' mentioned by Pollard was either John King, the quartermaster, or Thomas King, the quartermaster's mate. • **37**. In the mid-nineteenth century veterans of the battle agreed that the French failed to board. Pasco, *The Times*, 2/5/1853, said that he manned the poop and quarterdecks throughout the engagement, and no boarders got on the *Victory*. Two midshipmen of 1805 also addressed *The Times* to similar import. On 5 May John Carslake owned that one Frenchman boarded, but he was knocked over the side. Five days later Walker stressed the role of the sixty-eight-pound carronade in repulsing the invasion: see Charles Addis, 'Fog of War', pp. 253–4, and Rivers notebook, Royal Naval Museum, 1998/41/1. • **38**. Lucas's report, 2/1/1806, Desbriere, *Trafalgar Campaign*, 2, p. 211. Beatty mentions the depression of the *Victory*'s starboard guns, although James, *Naval History*, 4, p. 57, who interviewed several witnesses, denied it. • **39**. Hope to his brother, 4/11/1805, NMM. Sam Willis has given a revealing account of the *Temeraire* and her captain. • **40**. Fraser, *Enemy*, p. 270; Richards to Parrish, 21/10/1805, Royal Naval Museum, MS 414/92(1). • **41**. Tyler to Collingwood, 2/11/1805, Bonham's lot, 2005; Tyler to his wife, 29/10/1805, 3/11/1805, W. H. Wyndham-Quin, *Tyler*, p. 147. • **42**. *D&L*, 7, p. 170; Waring, 'Cumby Letter'; Fraser, *Sailors*, pp. 289–90. David Cordingly, *Billy Ruffian*, tells the story of this ship. • **43**. Hull to his mother, 11/11/1805, Douglas W. Smith, 'Now Safe Returned', p. 534; 'Isaac May, Marine', pp. 209–10. • **44**. Campbell's account, Hilary L. Rubinstein, *Trafalgar Captain*, pp. 183, 186. • **45**. Senhouse's account, *Macmillan's Magazine*, 81 (1900), p. 420. • **46**. Hilton to his brother, 3/11/1805, Dean, *Nelson's Heroes*, p. 95; Reid to his sister, 28/10/1805, *Notes & Queries*, series 1, vol. 9 (1854), pp. 297–8; *Swiftsure* log, Sotheby's, 2005. The 'Jeannette' episode, which inspired a dramatic painting by L. A. Wilcox and a passage in Thomas Hardy's *The Dynasts*, has been told by Edward Fraser and others, but see the very pertinent remarks of Peter Hore, 'John Richards Lapenotiere', pp. 803–4. • **47**. William Rivers gunner notebook, Royal Naval Musuem, MS 1998/41/1. • **48**. Warren R. Dawson, *Nelson Collection*, pp. 429, 439, 454; 'The Naval Officer', p. 362; Rotherham letterbook, NMM: LBK/38; Codrington to his wife, 30/10/1805, Bourchier, *Codrington*, 1, p. 63; Collingwood to Conn, 8/3/1806, Monmouth MS E224; Michael Duffy, 'All Was Hushed Up', and Tony Beales are essential reading on these points. • **49**. Dawson, *Nelson Collection*, pp. 347–89; Roberts's account, Broadley, *Nelson's Hardy*, p. 261; Codrington to his wife, 15/11/1805, Bourchier, *Codrington*, 1, p. 71; John D. Clarke, *Men of H.M.S. Victory*, pp. 53–9; Rivers notes, NMM: Wellcome/30. • **50**. J. de Zulueta, 'Trafalgar', p. 307; James Watt, 'Surgery at Trafalgar', pp. 84–5; Desbriere, *Trafalgar Campaign*, 1, pp. 296–7, 300–301. • **51**. Augustin Guimera, 'Trafalgar', p. 52; Fraser, *Sailors*, pp. 299–300. • **52**. Fiske, 'Visit', 18; *Morning Chronicle*, 10/12/1805. The exact place has been the subject of controversy. Some have cited the contemporary sketches of Arthur William Devis and Benjamin West. Devis visited the *Victory* in Spithead in December 1805 and made a pen and ink drawing of the spot where Nelson died. Unfortunately, Devis was willing to use artists' licence (for example, expanding the space in the cockpit) and the several renovations of that part of the ship during the nineteenth and twentieth century make it difficult to compare his work with the ship that survives today. Peter Goodwin, 'Where Nelson Died', and Charles Addis, 'Where Nelson Died', both informed authorities, argue that the traditional identification of the spot is incorrect, and that Nelson was laid some twenty-five feet further forward, nearer the cable tier. Heinrich Siemers, 'Where Nelson Really Died', disagrees, and believes that the position was 'passed on to us correctly', and that Nelson was propped against a standing knee on the larboard side of the cockpit (p. 87). That continuing traditions of the places where Nelson fell and died existed seems clear (T. H. McGuffie, *Peninsular Cavalry General*, p. 51; Egerton Ryerson, 30/4/1833, in the [Canadian] *Christian Advocate*, 12/7/1833). See also 'Tertius', 'Where Did Nelson Die?' • **53**. Westphal to Nicolas, 20/11/1844, *D&L*, 7, p. 249. William Westerburgh was assistant surgeon and Neil Smith the surgeon's mate. • **54**. The medical journal of the *Victory*, ADM 101/125/1, is the basic source for events in the cockpit. Gatty, *Recollections*, pp. 187, 188, contains Scott to Rose, 22/12/1805, one of the primary documents for Nelson's death. 'The Last Moments of Lord Nelson' (*Morning Chronicle*, 9/10/1805) preserves early views of Lieutenant Pasco, who was present both on the quarterdeck and in the cockpit. 'Lord Nelson' (*Morning Chronicle*, 10/12/1805) drew on the observations of Burke, while 'Lord Nelson' (*Morning Chronicle*, 28/12/1805) appears to be the work of Burke, Beatty and perhaps Hardy. Beatty's *Authentic Narrative* was a more considered reflection, based also, no doubt, upon published sources and conversations with other witnesses, and it deserves its status as the best single account. It can only have been an approximation of the reality. Nelson's words were not taken down verbatim, and different witnesses remembered the gist of his remarks and some vivid phrases. But Beatty's account is roughly convergent with the previous sources, and faithfully reflects the admiral's professional and personal concerns. There are, however, a small number of discrepancies in the evidence which I have noticed as appropriate. William James, *Naval History*, 4, pp. 81–2, contains detail obtained from discussions with Hardy, and perhaps others. See also Broadley, *Nelson's Hardy*, pp. 258, 264, for the account of Roberts, who was also in the cockpit at the time, and Warner, *Last Diary*, p. 30. • **55**. Beatty, autopsy report, 15/12/1805, Wellcome MS 5141; Beatty, *Authentic Narrative*, final page. After the capture of the *Guillaume Tell* in March 1800 Nathan Wilson, surgeon of the *Penelope*, visited the decks of the defeated ship and found seriously injured men who had lain for many hours without attention, some without arms or legs, yet 'without a haemorrhage of the least consequence taking place, two of whom I have two days afterwards doing well' (Medical journal of the *Penelope*, ADM 101/112/6). I am greatly indebted to Sir James Watt, Michael Crumplin and Simon Harris for their detailed medical observations. • **56**. A supplement to the *Gibraltar Chronicle*, 2/11/1805, drawing on witness statements, said that Nelson responded, 'What, only twelve. There should have been fifteen or sixteen by my calculation.' But after a pause he added that 'twelve are pretty well'. • **57**. Burke recalled that Nelson was afraid that 'the lower part of me is dead' and asked Burke to lift one of his legs. The purser raised both legs high, one after the other, but Nelson was unable to feel either movement (*Morning Chronicle*, 10/12/1805). • **58**. Collingwood to Clarence, 12/12/1805, *D&L*, 7, p. 240. • **59**. The accuracy of some of the remembered remarks is suggested here by the use of old Norfolk dialect. The phrase, 'Do you . . . ,' as an instruction, was once common to the different parts of Norfolk, though it has since largely disappeared: R. T. T. Bramley of Gillingham, Beccles, Suffolk, to Sugden,

8/7/2009. It also appears in letters of Nelson and members of his family. • **60**. Hardy's remark to Scott that Nelson's last words to him were 'Do be kind to poor Lady Hamilton' (Hardy to Scott, 10/3/1807, Gatty, *Recollections*, p. 212), probably reflects this final conversation. • **61**. According to the Burke–Beatty account of 1805, Nelson said, 'You have all done your duty, God bless you.' • **62**. This follows Scott's principal account, but Lady Foster got a similar story from him, including the words, 'I have not been a great sinner, have I?' In this version Scott did not answer but kissed Nelson's forehead: Stuart, *Dearest Bess*, p. 132. • **63**. This is the most authoritative version of Nelson's final words, but there are alternatives, some quite fanciful. Many consoled themselves with the thought that Nelson had died knowing that he had triumphed. Pasco (*Morning Chronicle*, 9/12/1805) said that Nelson's last word was 'Victory!' but that in 'attempting to repeat it he convulsively grasped the hand of one of his friends near him, the blood rushed from the lungs into the throat, and he expired calmly and without a groan'. Unlike Pasco, Robert Hilton, a surgeon's mate of the *Swiftsure*, was not present, but heard that upon being told of his success the admiral died with the words, 'I have lived then long enough' (Hilton to his brother, 3/11/1805, Dean, *Nelson's Heroes*, p. 95; Duff to his mother, 21/10/1805, Tayler, *Duffs*, 1, p. 265; *Gibraltar Gazette*, 24/10/1805). James Bayley wrote to his sister from the fleet that Nelson's last words to Hardy were 'that it was his [Nelson's] lot . . . to go, but I am going to Heaven, but never haul down your colours to France, for your men will stick to you' (Shannon, 'The Engagement Began Very Hot', p. 238). Something like this might have gone round for Senhouse of the *Conqueror* sent a similar story home on 27 October, combining it with Nelson's order to anchor (*Macmillan's Magazine*, p. 415). By far the most authoritative statement in this train is the Burke–Beatty account of 1805, which also states that Nelson died while Hardy was present. Hearing the good news, Nelson remarked, 'I could have wished to have lived to enjoy this, but God's will be done.' 'My lord, you die in the midst of triumph,' said Hardy. 'Do I, Hardy?' Nelson replied with a faint smile. 'God be praised.' Then he expired (*Morning Chronicle*, 28/12/1805). Captain Fremantle, who must have spoken to Hardy, wrote to his wife that Nelson learned of his victory and 'expressed a wish that he might have lived to see the end of the victory' but 'thanked God for the success he had granted to the King's arms, and expired sending a farewell to all his brother seamen' (Fremantle to his wife, 28/10/1805, Anne Fremantle, *Wynne Diaries*, 3, p. 221). The other thrust of the 'last words' reports, popularised by Scott and Beatty, had Nelson giving thanks to God and speaking of duty. Burke's account of the following December reported 'his last words' as 'I have done my duty, I praise God for it', after which a few moments passed before 'he expired without a groan' (*Morning Chronicle*, 10/12/1805). The gunner of the *Victory*, William Rivers, whose son was in the cockpit at the time, reported Nelson's final words as 'I have done my duty. I praise God for it', but has them directed to Hardy (Rivers notebook, Royal Naval Museum, MS 1998/41/1). • **64**. Waring, 'Cumby Letter', p. 244. • **65**. Fraser, *Sailors*, p. 258; John to his parents, 3/12/1805, *ND*, 7 (2000), p. 269. • **66**. Scott to Lavington, 10/12/1805, Monmouth MS E470; 'Memoir of the Late . . . Berry', p. 510; Collingwood to Blackett, 2/11/1805, *D&L*, 7, p. 234; Bourchier, *Codrington*, 1, pp. 121, 124–5. • **67**. *D&L*, 7, p. 224.

XXVI 'All Toils Surmounted . . .'

1. D. M. Stuart, *Dearest Bess*, pp. 127–8. • **2**. Hoste to his father, 9/11/1805, Harriet Hoste, *Hoste*, 1, p. 251; Austen account, NMH; AUS/2; Lady Bourchier, *Codrington*, 1, pp. 71, 95. • **3**. Flora Fraser, *Beloved Emma*, p. 326; Sotheby's, *Davison Collection*, p. 175; maid to her brother, 24/11/1805, Hamilton College Library. • **4**. *The Quebec Mercury*, 12/5/1806; Johnson to Rylands,

29/10/1807, 23/11/1807, 14, 21 and 28/12/1807, Civil and Provincial Secretary, Library and Archives, Canada, Ottawa, Record Group 4, A1, vols. 96–7. The Montreal monument had a chequered history. In 1893 French-Canadian radicals waged a campaign against it in *Le National*, but there was almost unanimous condemnation of three youths who were apprehended in the act of dynamiting the monument that November. The monument survives to the present day, and has recently been carefully restored, a happy outcome that reflects not only the widespread cross-cultural support for the original project, but also the fact that the memorial is the oldest neo-classical survivor in the city: *Toronto Globe*, 9, 11, 21, 23 and 29/11/1893. The Dublin statue, another impressive early nineteenth-century work, was not so fortunate, and was felled by Irish republicans in 1966. • **5**. Harold Acton, *Bourbons*, p. 516. • **6**. For the naval war after Trafalgar see Richard Glover, 'The French Fleet', and N. A. M. Roger, *Command of the Ocean*. • **7**. Rose's statement, 15/2/1806, NMM: GIR/5; *Notes & Queries*, 153 (1927), p. 295. • **8**. Haslewood to Thomas Bolton, 17/11/1810, NMM: GIR/5; ADM 238/12. • **9**. Michael Nash, 'Earl Nelson', summarises this story. • **10**. The tradition that Fatima died in St Luke's Hospital is not borne out by their register of 'incurables' in the London Metropolitan Archives. • **11**. Winifred Gérin, *Horatia Nelson*, is an indispensable work of family history. • **12**. Bridges to her son, 3/6/1808, *ND*, 7 (2000), p. 263; *United Services Magazine*, 1831, pt 2, p. 287. E. M. Keate, Sheila Hardy and John Sugden ('Fine Colt') give a reasonable picture of Fanny and her son. • **13**. Martyn Downer, *Nelson's Purse*; Scott to Emma, January 1806, *HANP*, 2, p. 274. • **14**. 'Biographical Memoir of . . . Sir William Bolton', p. 86; Peter Yule Booth, 'John Yule', p. 398. • **15**. Andrew Lambert, *Admirals*, p. 231. • **16**. 'Auto-Biography of James William Noble', MS. For this officer see John Sugden, 'Rusting Ingloriously'. • **17**. 'Biographical Memoir,' p. 441; *NC*, 37 (1817), p. 469; *The Times*, 27/5/1826; Will, 24/4/1817, NA: PROB 11/1713; John Sugden, 'William Layman'. • **18**. David Shannon, 'Trafalgar's Last Survivors'; Huw Lewis-Jones, 'Trafalgar Old Boys'. • **19**. James Greig, *Farington Diary*, 3, p. 124. • **20**. Robert Southey, *Life of Nelson*, unsigned note to undated Hutchinson edition edited by A. D. Power, p. 355. • **21**. Collingwood to Pasley, 16/12/1805, *D&L*, 7, p. 241 [my italics]. • **22**. Countess of Minto, *Elliot*, 3, p. 373 • **23**. Nelson to Fanny, 1/4/1795, Monmouth MSS E855; Nelson to Villettes, 6/9/1804, *D&L*, 6, p. 189. • **24**. Thomas Cochrane, *Notes on a Court Martial* pp. 20–21. • **25**. Wordsworth to Stuart, 26/3/1809, E. de Selincourt, *Letters*, 2, p. 295. • **26**. Joseph Conrad, *Mirror of the Sea*, ch. 47.

ABBREVIATIONS

PUBLISHED sources use short titles keyed to the bibliography. The following abbreviations were used in citing manuscripts:

Add. MSS	Additional Manuscripts in the British Library
ADM	Admiralty papers, National Archives
BL	British Library, St Pancras, London
CO	Colonial Office papers, National Archives
D&L	Nicolas, *Dispatches and Letters*
Egerton MSS	Egerton Manuscripts in the British Library
FO	Foreign Office papers, National Archives
HANP	Morrison, *Hamilton and Nelson Papers*
HMC	Historical Manuscripts Commission
Houghton	Houghton Library, Harvard University, Cambridge, Mass.
Huntington	Huntington Library, San Marino, California
MM	*Mariner's Mirror* (Journal of the Society of Nautical Research)
Monmouth MSS	Manuscripts at the Nelson Museum, Monmouth
NA	National Archives, Kew (former PRO)
NC	*Naval Chronicle*
ND	*Nelson Dispatch* (Journal of the Nelson Society)
NLS	National Library of Scotland, Edinburgh
NLTHW	Naish, *Nelson's Letters to his Wife*
NMM	National Maritime Museum, Greenwich
ODNB	*Oxford Dictionary of National Biography*
RNM	Royal Naval Museum, Portsmouth
SNA	Scottish National Archives (former Scottish Record Office)
TC	*Trafalgar Chronicle* (Yearbook of the 1805 Club)
WLC	William L. Clements Library, Ann Arbor, Michigan
WO	War Office papers, National Archives

SELECT BIBLIOGRAPHY

Manuscripts

British Library, London

Additional Mss., Dept. of Mss., vols 14273, 14275, 40096–97, 52780, 81595 (Collingwood papers)

18204, 21506, 24813, 30170, 30999, 34274, 38737, 41567, 42071, 42773 (miscellaneous)

18676 (plan of battle of the Nile)

20107, 20162, 20177, 20189, 29543, 56088, 80775 (Lowe)

23207 (victory despatches)

28333, 30260, 34902–92, 35191, 36604–13, 40094–95, 46356 (Nelson)

29914–15, 31158–64, 31168–69 (St Vincent)

30114 (Wilson)

30182 (Bedford)

30927 (Southey)

33107–08 (Pelham)

35201–02 (Bridport)

36873 (Foote)

37076–77, 39793, 39793, 40739, 41200, 42069 (Hamilton)

37268 (Ball)

37875–82 (Windham)

40667–68 (Graves)

40730 (Anderson)

42773–74 (Rose)

46119 (Thompson)

75812–13, 75819, 75824–25, 75829, 75832, 75840–41, 75847–49, 75574, 75599 (Spencer)

Egerton Mss., Dept. of Mss., vols 1614–23, 2638–40 (Hamilton)

2240–41 (Nelson)

A. M. Broadley, 'Nelsoniana' (1902, 8 vols of printed pages with interleafed mss.), Department of Rare Books.

Log of the *Britannia*, 10R/L/MAR/B/285VV, Asian and African Reading Room.

National Archives, Great Britain, Kew (formerly Public Record Office)

Adm 1/ 4 (Baltic)
Adm 1/118–20 (Channel)
Adm 1/396–411 (Mediterranean)
Adm 1/530–32 (North Sea)
Adm 1/579 (admirals' letters)
Adm 1/670 (Downs)
Adm 1/734 (Nore)
Adm 1/1026 (Portsmouth)
Adm 1/1534, 2073–74, 2079–80, 2083, 2226–27, 2229, 2332–33 (captains' letters)
Adm 1/2809–11 (lieutenants' letters)
Adm 1/3974–75, 3985–86, 6034–35, 6038 (intelligence)
Adm 1/4015 (ordnance)
Adm 1/4186 (Secretary of State)
Adm 1/4551 (miscellaneous)
Adm 1/5346, 5347–55, 5363–70, 5492 (courts-martial)
Adm 2/135–50 (instructions)
Adm 2/285–308 (Admiralty out-letters)
Adm 6/64 (commissions)
Adm 6/86, 92, 94–5, 98 (passing certificates)
Adm 7/55 (Ball letterbook)
Adm 8/86–90 (disposition of ships)
Adm 9/2 (returns of service)
Adm 12 (digests of correspondence)
Adm 35/1935 (pay books)
Adm 36/11860, 12174–75, 12318, 12339–40, 12458, 12508, 12546, 12649, 13733, 13756, 14012, 14293, 14334, 14345–46, 14381–82, 14416, 14514, 14652, 14681–82, 14817, 14946, 15125, 15155, 15303, 15342, 15356–58, 15392–93, 15895–900, 16116, 16390, 16645 (ships' musters)
Adm 50/65 (admirals' journals)
Adm 51/1168, 1190, 1204, 1228, 1241, 1244, 1247–49, 1253, 1255, 1260–63, 1266, 1268, 1270–71, 1273–74, 1277, 1279, 1282–83, 1288, 1293–94, 1300, 1307, 1313–15, 1317, 1321, 1324, 1330–31, 1333, 1339, 1346, 1349–54, 1356–58, 1360–61, 1363–64, 1366, 1368, 1371–72, 1375, 1377, 1384, 1388–90, 1399, 1421, 1437, 1441, 1443, 1446, 1448, 1450–51, 1453–54, 1456, 1458, 1463, 1468–69, 1471, 1473–74, 1476–84, 1486, 1488–89, 1492–94, 1497–99, 1503–04, 1506, 1508–13, 1515–16, 1519, 1529, 1531, 1533, 1539, 1545–46, 1550, 1558, 1562, 1595, 1640, 4408–09, 4412, 4417, 4444, 4461, 4473, 4507, 4514–15 (captains' logs)
Adm 52/2653–54, 2777, 2902, 2962, 2968, 3229, 3299, 3175, 3208, 3399, 3489, 3464, 3503, 3516, 3711, 3564, 4018 (masters' logs)
Adm 101/112/6, 121/3, 123/2, 124/1, 125/1 (medical journals)
Adm 102/231, 236–37 (Gibraltar hospital)
Adm 106/2021–22 (Gibraltar dockyard)
Adm 107/4, 15, 24 (passing certificates)

Adm 114/55 (Ford letterbook)
Adm 196/5 (service records)
Adm 238/12 (prize lists)
CO 91/40–45 (Gibraltar)
CO 158/7–10, 15 (Malta)
CO 159/1–2 (Malta)
CO 173/1 (Nelson)
CO 537/151 (Nelson)
FO 3/8 (Algiers)
FO 7/51–53, 59–60, 67–76 (Austria)
FO 22/40–41 (Denmark)
FO 24/2 (Egypt)
FO 28/18 (Genoa)
FO 33/20–21 (Hamburg)
FO 37/59–60 (intelligence)
FO 42/3–7 (Ionian Islands)
FO 43/3 (Italy)
FO 52/12 (Morocco)
FO 65/40–46, 52–59 (Russia)
FO 67/26–29, 32–34 (Sardinia)
FO 68/14 (Saxony)
FO 70/11–14, 21–4 (Naples and Sicily)
FO 72/51–53 (Spain)
FO 73/29 (Sweden)
FO 76/5–6 (Tripoli)
FO 77/3–5 (Tunis)
FO 78/20–29, 40–45 (Turkey)
FO 79/16–18, 20 (Tuscany)
FO 120/1 (Austria)
FO 121/4 (Austria)
FO 165/167–70 (Naples and Sicily)
HCA 49/100 (Maltese prize court)
HO 32/7 (Home/Foreign Office correspondence)
HO 42/70 (Despard)
PRO 30/8/163, 187 (Pitt papers)
PROB 1/22 (Nelson wills and codicils), 11/1713, 1775
T 1/856 (Treasury)
WO 1/280 (Craig's expedition)
WO 1/282 (Nelson's correspondence with Camden and Castlereagh)
WO 1/291–93 (Malta)
WO 1/297–98 (Minorca)
WO 6/55 (Minorca)

Caird Library, National Maritime Museum, Greenwich
Admiralty lieutenants' logs (ADM/L)
Anderson diary, 1805 (Mss/80/201.2)
Autograph Collections (AGC)
Autograph Collections, Nelson (AGL/N)
Barham papers (BAR)
Baxter, Thomas, drawings (WAL/49)
Bayntun papers (BNY)
Berry papers (BER)
Bridport papers (BRP)
Cockburn papers (COC)
Codrington papers (COD)
Collingwood papers (COL)
Cornwallis papers (COR)
Croker-Phillipps papers (CRK and PHB)
Davison papers (DAV)
De Coppet collection (COP)
Duckworth papers (DUC)
Elliot papers (ELL)
French Boulogne dispatches (MRF/181 microfilm)
Girdlestone papers (GIR)
Grant diary (GRT)
Hamilton papers (HML)
Hamilton and Rose letterbook (LBK/50)
Haslewood papers (HAS)
Hood papers (HOO)
Hope letter
Hoste papers (HOS)
Jervis papers (JER)
Keats papers (KEA)
Keith papers (KEI)
Kingsmill papers (KIN)
Louis papers (LOU)
Matcham papers (MAM)
Melville papers (MEL)
Monserrat papers (MON)
Mosse papers (Mss/78/145)
Nelson papers (BGY/5D and K2)
Nelson photocopies (PST/39)
Nelson's book annotations (PHB/P/19)
Nelson–Ward papers (NWD)
Nepean papers (NEP)

Nile miscellania (Mss/88/054.5)
Pitcairn-Jones, C. G. 'Sea Officers' List'
Rivers notes (Wellcome/30)
Rotherham letterbook (LBK/38)
Stewart papers (STW)
Sutcliffe-Smith papers (SUT)
Trafalgar House papers (TRA)
Walter papers (WAL)
Western papers (WES)
Xerox autographs (XAGC)

Nelson Museum, Monmouth, Wales

Nelson manuscripts, E1–E993 (especially letter-books, 1796–1804, E987–E992), and memorabilia

Wellcome Institute Library, London

Western Ms. 7362
Western Mss. 3667–81 (Nelson papers)
Special Collections, volume 5141 (Medical Society of London)

Royal Naval Museum, Portsmouth

John Scott Letters, 1990/167
John Scott Letterbook, 1996/1
Chevailler papers
William Rivers gunnery papers
Nelson order-book, 1801 (Ms. 200)
Samuel Richards letter, Ms. 414/92(1)

Nelson Museum, Great Yarmouth, Norfolk

Miscellaneous Nelson manuscripts and memorabilia

Bodleian Library, Oxford

Beckford papers, c. 1, 16, 31 and 33

Centre for Buckinghamshire Studies, Aylesbury

Fremantle papers

Cornwall Record Office, Truro

Foresti papers, J3/35/36 (two small letterbooks and letters of Foresti to Hawkins)

National Archives, Edinburgh, Scotland (Scottish Record Office)

Seaforth papers (GD 46)
Melville papers (GD 51)
Dundonald papers (GD 233)

National Library of Scotland, Edinburgh

Minto papers
Lynedoch papers
Malcolm of Burfoot (Pulteney Malcolm) papers
Barker journals
Cochrane papers

London Metropolitan Archives, London

Foundling Hospital admissions (A/FH/A/09/001–198)
Foundling Hospital baptisms (A/FH/A/14/004/001)
Foundling Hospital general register (X41/4)
Admissions at St Luke's Hospital

Local Studies Collection, Morden

Merton Place and Nelson files
Local maps, especially O.S., 1871, 1898

Norfolk Record Officc, Norwich

Hamond (Westacre) Papers
MC 154/1, 646/1, 834/110, 2577/7/21/1–9 and PT 16/1 (letters and a facsimile)

Surrey History Service, Woking

Merton, Wimbledon and Mitcham deeds, 1801–1808, 7883/1–3, 5, 6
Merton Place (engravings), 4348/1/62/6–7
Sales particulars, 1801, 1815 , G85/2/1/1/42 and 103

Miscellaneous British and European Items

Nelson letter and annotated typescript of Oman's *Nelson* (Bath Central Library)
Bonham's auction lots, 2005
Betting book (Brooks's Club, St James's, London)
Hotham papers (Brymnor Jones Library, Hull University)
Nelson letter, NM/Nelson/1 (King's College, Cambridge)
Noble papers (Robert Le Noble)
Nelson letter, 1801, Ms. album (Robinson Library, Newcastle University)
Nelson letter (John Rylands Library, Manchester)

Sotheby's auction lot, 2005
Nelson letter and memorabilia (Nelson and Victory Hotels, Stockholm, Sweden)

Burke Library, Hamilton College, Clinton, New York
Beinecke Lesser Antilles Collection

William L. Clements Library, University of Michigan, Ann Arbor, USA
Hubert S. Smith papers (Nelson letters)
Baltic campaign collection
Fenno–Hoffman papers (Sutton papers)
Eyre Coote papers
Croker papers
Melville papers

Houghton Library, Harvard University, Cambridge, Mass.
Ms.Eng.196.5 (Joseph Husband collection of Nelson papers)
Ms. Lowell 10, 17 (Amy Lowell collection)
Autograph file

Huntington Library, San Marino, California
Nelson papers

Karpeles Library, Santa Barbara, California
Miscellaneous Nelson papers

Morgan Library, New York City
Miscellaneous Nelson papers

Rosenbach Museum and Library, Philadelphia
John McArthur papers (1073/12)
Nelson letter (E Ms. 491/11)

United States Naval Academy, Annapolis, Maryland
William F. Kurfess collection
Christian A. Zabriskie collection

University of New Brunswick, Fredericton, Canada
Beaverbrook ms. collection, C-MS 154 (Nelson letter)

Printed Sources

(Works are published in London unless otherwise stated)

A Brief Account of the Naval Asylum at Paddington-Green (1802)
Accardi, Vittorio, ed., *The Hamilton Papers* (Napoli, 1999)
Acton, Harold, *The Bourbons of Naples* (1956)
Addis, Charles P., ed., *The Men Who Fought with Nelson in HMS Victory at Trafalgar* (Nelson Society, 1988)
—— 'The Fog of War', *ND*, 7 (2000): 252–57
—— 'Where Nelson Died', *TC*, 11 (2001): 52–54
Adkin, Mark, *The Trafalgar Companion* (2005)
'Admiral Horatio Nelson's Combined Knife and Fork', *Bulletin of the New York Academy of Medicine*, 47 (1971): 1025–27
Albion, Robert G., *Forests and Sea Power* (Cambridge, Mass., 1926)
Alcala Galiano, Pelayo, *El Combate de Trafalgar* (Madrid, 1909–30, 2 vols)
Allan, J. F., 'Was Nelson a Fly-Fisher?' *MM*, 77 (1991): 184
Allen, Derek, and Hore, Peter, *News of Nelson: John Lapenotiere's Race from Trafalgar to London* (Greenwich, 2005)
Allen, Joseph, *Life of Lord Viscount Nelson, K.B., Duke of Bronte* (1853)
Allen, Joseph, and Hargood, Maria, Lady, *Memoir of the Life and Services of Admiral Sir William Hargood* (1841)
An Abstract from the Account of the Asylum or House of Refuge . . . for . . . Friendless and Deserted Orphan Girls (1794)
An Account of the Institution and Regulations of the Guardians of the Asylum, or House of Refuge (1793)
Andersen, J. A., *A Dane's Excursions in Britain* (1809)
Anson, Elizabeth and Florence, ed., *Mary Hamilton* (1925)
Applebe, Michael M., 'Personal Account of Trafalgar Vice Admiral William Stanhope Lovell', *ND*, 9 (2006): 34–41
Appleton, Dean, 'Letters from Trafalgar', *ND*, 7 (2001): 538–42
Aris's Birmingham Gazette
Aspinall, A., ed., *The Later Correspondence of George III* (Cambridge, 1962–70, 5 vols)
Aspinall-Oglander, Cecil, ed., *Freshly Remembered* (1956)
Avery, William P., 'An Imposing Array: Fact or Fiction', *MM*, 70 (1984): 31–44
Badham, Francis Pritchett, 'Nelson and the Neapolitan Republicans', *English Historical Review*, 13 (1898): 261–82
—— *Nelson at Naples* (1900)
—— *Nelson and Ruffo* (1905)
Baggally, John W. *Ali Pasha and Great Britain* (Oxford, 1938)
Baker, Mike, 'The English Timber Cartel in the Napoleonic Wars', *MM*, 86 (2000): 79–81
—— 'Lord Nelson and the English Timber Cartel', *ND*, 8 (2005): 823–32

—— 'Lord Nelson, Timber Merchants and the "Great Attraction of History"', *ND*, 10 (2009), 22–26

Baring, Mrs Henry, ed., *The Diary of the Rt. Hon. William Windham* (1866)

Barker, Alison and Mark, et al., '"Not a Brace or Bowline Left": Midshipman Babcock's Trafalgar Log', *ND*, 7 (2001): 526–30

Barker, Matthew H. ('The Old Sailor'), *The Life of Nelson* (1836)

Barnett, Richard D., ed., 'Richard Barnett: An Anglo-Jewish Sailor at the Battle of the Nile', *MM*, 71 (1985): 185–200

Barras, T. C., 'Nelson's Head Injury at the Battle of the Nile', *ND*, 2 (1987): 217

Barrett, Mark, 'Nelson and the Theatre', *ND*, 7 (2000): 151–60

—— 'Nelson in Birmingham, August 1802', *ND*, 7 (2002): 750–58

Barritt, Michael K. 'Nelson's Frigates, May to August 1798', *MM*, 58 (1972): 281–95

—— 'The Evolution of Hydrographic Surveying and Charting in Support of Naval Operations, 1793–1815' (ms.)

Bartlett, William A., *The History and Antiquities of Wimbledon, Surrey* (1865)

Barrow, John, *An Auto-Biographical Memoir of Sir John Barrow* (1847)

—— *The Life and Correspondence of Admiral Sir William Sidney Smith* (1848, 2 vols)

The Bath Journal

Battaglini, Mario, ed., *Il Monitore Napoletano 1799* (Naples, 1999)

Battesti, Michele, *La Bataille d'Aboukir, 1798* (Paris, 1998)

—— *Trafalgar* (Saint-Cloud, 2004)

'Battle of Trafalgar and Death of Nelson', *Notes & Queries*, 1st series, 9 (1854): 297–98

Baugh, Daniel A., *British Naval Administration in the Age of Walpole* (Princeton, N.J., 1965)

Beales, Tony, '"Great Expectations": The Approach of British Ships at the Battle of Trafalgar', *MM*, 96 (2010): 455–67

Beatty, William, *Authentic Narrative of the Death of Lord Nelson* (1807; second ed., 1808)

Bennett, Leslie H., *Nelson's Eyes: The Life and Correspondence of Vice-Admiral Sir Henry Blackwood* (Brussels, 2005)

Bergersen, Olav, *Noytralited og Krig* (Oslo, 1966, 2 vols)

Berrow's Worcester Journal

Berry, Edward, *An Authentic Narrative of the Proceedings of His Majesty's Squadron, under the Command of Rear-Admiral Sir Horatio Nelson* (Dublin, 1799)

'Biographical Memoir of Captain William Layman of the Royal Navy', *NC*, 37 (1817): 441–58, and 39 (1818): 177–85

'Biographical Memoir of the Honourable Captain Courtney Boyle', *NC*, 30 (1813): 1–41

'Biographical Memoir of the Late Captain Sir William Bolton, Knt., R.N', *United Services Magazine*, 1832, part 1, 84–88

'Biographical Memoir of the Right Honourable Lord Nelson of the Nile, K.B', *NC*, 3 (1800): 157–91, and 14 (1805): 397–99

Blagdon, Francis William, *Orme's Graphic History of the Life, Exploits and Death of Horatio Nelson* (1806)

Blumel, Thomas, 'Nelson's Overland Journey, 1800', *ND*, 7 (2000): 82–96, 162–86

—— 'Nelson in Warnemuende Roads, 1801', *ND*, 7 (2002): 762–72, 849

Boigne, Louisa, Countess de, *Memoirs* (New York, 1907)

Bonner-Smith, David, ed., *Letters of Admiral of the Fleet the Earl of St Vincent* (Navy Records Society, 1922–27, 2 vols)

Booth, Peter Yule, 'Lt. John Yule, R.N., and John Carslake, Midshipman, in "Victory" at Trafalgar', *ND*, 5 (1996): 396–400

Bosanquet, H. T. A., 'Lord Nelson and the Loss of His Arm', *MM*, 38 (1952): 184–94

Bourchier, Lady, *Memoir of Sir Edward Codrington* (1873, 2 vols)

Bowden-Dan, Jane, 'Diet, Dirt and Discipline: Medical Developments in Nelson's Navy. Dr John Snipe's Contribution', *MM*, 90 (2004), 260–72

Bowen, Marjorie, *Patriotic Lady* (1935)

Braun, John, 'Lord Nelson and the Livery Companies', *TC*, 2 (1992): 53–57

Brenton, Edward P., *The Naval History of Great Britain* (1823–25; revised ed., 1837, 2 vols)

Brenton, Edward Pelham, *Life and Correspondence of John, Earl of St Vincent* (1838, 2 vols)

Brett-James, Anthony, *General Graham, Lord Lynedoch* (1959)

Bridge, Adrian, 'Tom Allen's Job Reference from Nelson', *ND*, 5 (1996), 295–97

Bridport, Viscount, Duke of Bronte, and Morris, Sue, 'The Duchy of Bronte', *ND*, 7 (2000): 20–26

Broadley, A. M., and Bartelot, R. G., *Three Dorset Captains at Trafalgar* (1906)

—— *Nelson's Hardy* (1909)

— and J. Holland Rose, *Dumouriez and the Defence of England against Napoleon* (1909)

Brockliss, Laurence, Cardwell, John, and Moss, Michael, *Nelson's Surgeon William Beatty, Naval Medicine and the Battle of Trafalgar* (Oxford, 2005)

Broers, Michael, *The Napoleonic Empire in Italy, 1796–1814* (2005)

Brown, Iain Gordon, ed., 'Henry Aston Barker and Lord Nelson's "Sicilification"', *ND*, 8 (2005): 702–709

Browne, George Lathom, *Nelson* (1890)

Buckingham, Duke of, ed., *Memoirs of the Courts and Cabinets of George III* (1853, 2 vols)

Bullocke, J. G., ed., *The Tomlinson Papers* (NRS, 1935)

Burgess, Ben, 'Edward Gayner – Spy for England', *ND*, 4 (1991): 65–68

Cannadine, John, ed., *Admiral Lord Nelson: Context and Legacy* (Basingstoke, 2005)

—— ed., *Trafalgar in History* (Basingstoke, 2006)

Cardwell, M. John, 'The Royal Navy and Malaria, 1756–1815', *TC*, 17 (2007): 84–97

Chadwick, Owen, *The Popes and the European Revolution* (Oxford, 1981)
Chamberlain, W. H., *Reminiscences of Old Merton* (1925)
Charnock, John, *Biographical Memoirs of Lord Viscount Nelson* (1806)
Christie, Christopher, *The British Country House in the Eighteenth Century* (Manchester, 2000)
Christopher, T. E., 'Lord Nelson's Wife and the Distribution of Certain Items of His Estate', *ND*, 6 (1997), 61–63
Clark, S. G., 'The Lad Who Caught Nelson's Eye', *MM*, 64 (1978): 347–48
Clarke, James Stanier, and McArthur, John, eds, *The Naval Chronicle* (1799–1819, 40 vols)
—— *The Life of Admiral Lord Nelson, K.B., From His Lordship's Manuscripts* (1809, 2 vols)
—— *The Life and Services of Horatio, Viscount Nelson, Duke of Bronte, Vice-Admiral of the White, K.B.* (1840, 3 vols)
Clarke, John D., ed., *The Men of HMS Victory at Trafalgar* (Vintage Naval Library, 1999)
Clarke, R. S. J., 'Ulster Connections with Nelson and Trafalgar', *Ulster Medical Journal*, 75 (2006): 81–84
Clayton, Tim, and Craig, Peter, *Trafalgar: The Men, the Battle, the Storm* (2004)
—— 'The Difficulty of Reconstructing the Battle of Trafalgar', *TC*, 15 (2005): 14–25
Cliff, Kenneth S., 'Mr Lock and Lord Nelson's Eye', *ND*, 6 (1999): 486–90
—— 'Mr Lock, Hatter to Lord Nelson's Navy', *TC*, 9 (1999): 22–28
—— *Mr Lock the Hatter Went to Sea* (Alresford, 2005)
Clowes, William Laird, et al., *The Royal Navy: A History* (1897–1903, 7 vols)
Coleman, Terry, *Nelson: The Man and the Legend* (2001; revised ed., 2002)
—— 'Nelson, the King, and His Ministers', *TC*, 13 (2003): 6–12
Colletta, Pietro, *History of the Kingdom of Naples, 1734–1825* (Edinburgh, 1858, 2 vols)
Collinge, J. M., *Navy Board Officials, 1660–1832* (1978)
Connell, Brian, *Portrait of a Whig Peer* (1957)
Constantine, David, *Fields of Fire: A Life of Sir William Hamilton* (2001)
Copeland, Henry, ed., *The Wimbledon and Merton Annual* (1903)
Copies of Original Letters from the Army of General Bonaparte in Egypt, Intercepted by the Fleet under the Command of Admiral Lord Nelson (1798–99, 2 vols)
Corbett, Julian S., *The Campaign of Trafalgar* (1910)
Corbett, Julian S., and Richmond, H. W., eds, *Private Papers of George, Second Earl Spencer* (1913–24, 4 vols)
Cordingly, David, *Billy Ruffian* (2003)
Cornwallis-West, G., *The Life and Letters of Admiral Cornwallis* (1927)
Correspondance de Napoléon I (Paris, 1858–69, 32 vols)
Corti, Egon Caesar Conte, *Ich, eine Tochter Maria Theresias: Ein Lebensbild der Königin Marie Karoline von Neapel* (Munich, 1950)
—— *Nelsons Kampf um Lady Hamilton* (Munich, 1983)

The [London] *Courier*

The Coventry Mercury

Creasy, Richard, 'I Have Then Lived Long Enough', *Mail on Sunday*, 4 March 2007

Creswell, John, *British Admirals of the Eighteenth Century: Tactics in Battle* (1972)

Crimmin, P. K., 'The Royal Navy and the Levant Trade, *c.* 1795–*c.* 1805,' in Jeremy Black and Philip Woodvine, eds., *The British Navy and the Use of Naval Power in the 18th Century* (Leicester, 1988), 219–36

—— 'John Jervis, Earl of St Vincent', in Le Fevre, P., and Harding, R., ed., *Precursors of Nelson* (2000), 324–50, 418–20

Cross, Anthony, 'The School of Fear. The Case of Lord Nelson Blackmailed', *TC*, 10 (2000): 57–67

—— 'Primary Sources. Notice of the Execution of William White', *TC*, 16 (2006): 76–77

Crumplin, Michael K. H., 'The Most Triumphant Death. The Passing of Vice-Admiral Lord Horatio Nelson, 21st October 1805', *Journal of the Royal Naval Medical Service*, 91 (2005): 92–95

—— and Harrison, Anthony, 'A Fatal Shot. The Death of Admiral Horatio, Viscount Lord Nelson', *ND*, 9 (2006): 156–62

The Cumloden Papers (Edinburgh: 1871)

Czisnik, Marianne, 'Nelson and the Nile: The Creation of Admiral Nelson's Public Image', *MM*, 88 (2002): 41–60

—— 'Nelson at Naples', *TC*, 12 (2002): 84–121

—— 'Nelson at Naples: The Development of a Story', *TC*, 13 (2003): 35–55

—— 'Admiral Nelson's Tactics at the Battle of Trafalgar', *History*, 89 (2004): 549–59

—— *Horatio Nelson: A Controversial Hero* (2005)

—— 'A Unique Account of Lady Hamilton's Attitudes in Hamburg, 1800', *TC*, 20 (2010): 108–20

Damas, Roger de, *Memoirs of the Comte Roger de Damas* (1913)

D'Auvergne, Edmund B., *The Dear Emma* (1936)

Davenport, R. A., *Life of Ali Pasha* (1861)

Davey, James, 'Nelson's Second', *TC*, 20 (2010): 92–107

Davies, David, *A Brief History of Fighting Ships* (1996; reprinted, 2002)

Davis, John A., *Naples and Napoleon: Southern Italy and the European Revolutions, 1780–1860* (Oxford, 2006)

—— and Capuano, Giovanni, eds., *The Hamilton Letters: The Naples Despatches of William Hamilton* (2008)

Dawson, Warren R., ed., *The Nelson Collection at Lloyds* (1932)

Deacon, John Gillespie, 'Dr Leonard Gillespie, MD, EN, 1758–1842', *ND*, 5 (1996): 340–41

Dean, Graham, 'The Nile Musters', *ND*, 5 (1994): 11–12

Dean, Graham, and Evans, Keith, *Nelson's Heroes* (Norwich, 1994)
The Derby Mercury
Desbriere, Edouard, *The Naval Campaign of 1805. Trafalgar* (1907; translated and edited by Constance Eastwick, Oxford, 1933, 2 vols.)
Deutsch, Otto Erich, *Admiral Nelson and Joseph Haydn* (Slinfold, West Sussex, 2000)
D'Huart, Suzanne, ed., *Journal de Marie-Amélie, reine des Français* (Paris, 1981)
The Dictionary of National Biography (1885–90; reprinted, 1908–1909, 22 vols)
'Different Letters from the Past', *Annals of the Royal College of Surgeons*, 62 (1980): 388–89
Donaldson, David, 'Edward Gayner and the Nelson Legend in Minorca', *ND*, 5 (1996): 430–35
Donatone, Guido, ed., *William Hamilton. Diario Segreto Napoletano, 1764–1789* (Naples, 2000)
Douin, G. *La Campagne de Bruix en Méditerranée* (Paris, 1923)
Downer, Martyn, *Nelson's Purse* (2004)
—— 'Brother Nelson', *TC*, 14 (2004): 39–46
Drinkwater-Bethune, John, *A Narrative of the Battle of St Vincent* (1840)
Driscoll, Denis, 'Lord Nelson – the "Nile" Annuity', *ND*, 5 (1996): 302
Duffy, Michael, ed., *The Naval Miscellany* (Aldershot, 2003)
—— '"All Hushed Up": The Hidden Trafalgar', *MM*, 91 (2005): 216–40
—— 'Trafalgar: Myth and Reality', in Richard Harding, ed., *A Great and Glorious Victory* (2008), 58–69, 118–19
Dull, Jonathan R. *The Age of the Ship of the Line* (Barnsley, 2009)
Dumas, Alessandro, *I Borboni di Napoli* (Naples, 1862–63, 10 vols)
Edgcumbe, Richard, ed., *The Diary of Frances, Lady Shelley, 1787–1817* (1912)
The Edinburgh Review, July 1838, p. 322
Edwards, Lesley, 'Horatio Nelson and Lady Hamilton's Twins', *MM*, 86 (2000): 313–15
—— 'The Recreation of Nelson's Trafalgar Uniform', *ND*, 7 (2001): 333–35
Ekins, Charles, *The Naval Battles of Great Britain* (1828)
Elliott, M. 'The "Despard Conspiracy" Reconsidered', *Past & Present*, 75 (1977): 46–61
Ellis, Lady, ed., *Memoirs and Services of the Late Lieutenant-General Sir S. B. Ellis* (1866)
Emden, Paul, 'The Brothers Goldsmid and the Financing of the Napoleonic Wars', *Transactions* [of] *the Jewish Historical Society of England*, 114 (1940): 225–46
Esdaile, Charles, *Napoleon's Wars* (2007)
Evans, Carol, 'The Illegitimate Children of Emma, Lady Hamilton', *TC*, 5 (1995): 96–103
Evans, Thomas A., *A Statement of the Means by which the Nelson Coat . . . Was Obtained . . .* (1846)
Events of the War between Denmark and England from the 30th of March 1801 till the Cessation of Hostilities on the 2nd April, from Official Reports and Ocular Witnesses (Copenhagen, 1801)

Excell, Phyl and Stanley, 'Lord Nelson's Home in Ipswich', *Suffolk Roots*, 6 (1980): 69–71

Fairbrother, E. H., 'Nelsoniana', *Notes & Queries*, 11 (1922): 321–24

Faure, Maurice, *Souvenirs du Général Championnet* (Paris, 1905)

Feldbaek, Ole, *Denmark and the Armed Neutrality* (Copenhagen, 1980)

—— *The Battle of Copenhagen, 1801: Nelson and the Danes* (2002)

Feldborg, Andreas Anderson, *A Tour in Zealand in the Year 1802, with an Historical Sketch of the Battle of Copenhagen, By a Native of Denmark* (1804)

Fenwick, Kenneth, *HMS Victory* (1962)

Fernandez, Jose Cayuela, and Reina, Angel Pozuelo, *Trafalgar, Hombres y Naves Entre Dos Epocas* (Barcelona, 2004)

'Fiat Justicia', 'The Nelson Dispatches', *United Services Magazine*, pt. 3 (1845): 452–55, 588–91

Finlayson, John, 'A Signal Midshipman at Copenhagen', *TC*, 11 (2001): 80–97

Fiske, Ron C., *Notices of Nelson Extracted from 'Norfolk and Norwich Notes and Queries'* (Nelson Society, 1989)

—— 'A Visit to HMS *Victory*, 7 January 1806', *ND*, 4 (1991): 16–19

—— 'Nelson's Arms and Hatchments', *ND*, 6 (1999): 549–54

—— 'Nelson, Levett Hanson and the Order of St Joachim', *ND*, 7 (2002): 649–58

—— 'Nelson and the Gregorians', *ND*, 7 (2001): 472–74

Fitchett, W. H., *Nelson and His Captains* (1902)

FitzGibbon, Mary Agnes, *A Veteran of 1812: The Life of James FitzGibbon* (Toronto, 1894)

Foley, Thomas (Florence Horatia Suckling), *The Nelson Centenary* (Norwich, 1905)

Foote, Edward J., *Vindication of his Conduct . . . in the Bay of Naples* (1807; second ed., 1810)

Ford, Gillian, 'Nelson References in Holkham Game Books', *ND*, 1 (1982): 51–52

Foreman, Laura, and Phillips, Ellen Blue, *Napoleon's Lost Fleet: Bonaparte, Nelson, and the Battle of the Nile* (1999)

Foster, Vere, ed., *The Two Duchesses* (1898)

Fothergill, Brian, *Sir William Hamilton, Envoy Extraordinary* (1969)

Fournier, August, *Life of Napoleon I* (1911, 2 vols)

Fraser, Edward, *The Enemy at Trafalgar* (1906)

—— *The Sailors Whom Nelson Led* (1913)

—— 'HMS *Victory*', *MM*, 8 (1922): 258–64

Fraser, Flora, 'A Cartoonist's Dream', *ND*, 2 (1986): 143–44

—— *Beloved Emma* (1986)

Fremantle, Anne, ed., *The Wynne Diaries* (1935–40, 3 vols)

—— *The Wynne Diaries* (1952)

Gagniere, Albert, *La Reine Marie-Caroline de Naples, Lady Hamilton et Nelson* (Paris, 1886)

Gamble, R., *Letters from the Mediterranean in 1798 and 1799* (Bungay, *c.* 1799)

Gamlin, Hilda, *Emma, Lady Hamilton* (Liverpool, 1891)
—— *Nelson's Friendships* (1899, 2 vols)
Gatty, Alfred and Margaret, *Recollections of the Life of the Reverend A. J. Scott, D.D., Lord Nelson's Chaplain* (1842)
Gemmett, Robert J., *Beckford's Fonthill* (Norwich, 2003)
The Gentleman's Magazine
Gérin, Winifred, *Horatia Nelson* (1970)
Gibbons, Leslie A., 'Was Lord Nelson a Freeman?' *ND*, 5 (1996): 450–52
The Gibraltar Chronicle Supplement, 2 November 1805
Giglioli, Constance, *Naples in 1799* (1903)
Gill, Edward, *Nelson and the Hamiltons on Tour* (Gloucester, 1987)
Girouard, Mark, *Life in the English Country House* (1978)
The Gloucester Journal
Goddard, John, '1805: Captain Conn's Year', *TC*, 13 (2003): 68–78
Godley, Jocelyn, 'A Captain's Career in Nelson's Navy', *Family Tree Magazine* (August 2004): 67–70
Goethe, Johann Wolfgang von, *Italian Journey* (1970)
Gonzalez-Aller Hierro, J. L., ed., *La Campana de Trafalgar (1804–1805): Corpus Documental, Conservado en los Archives Españoles* (Madrid, 2004, 2 vols)
Goodden, Angelica, *Miss Angel: The Art and World of Angelica Kauffman* (2005)
Goodman, Judith, 'More Information on Merton Place', *ND*, 9 (2006): 182–83
—— '200 Years Ago – Merton Place After Nelson', *Merton Historical Society Bulletin*, 157 (2006): 8–10
Goodwin, Peter, 'Where Nelson Died', *MM*, 85 (1999): 272–87
—— *Nelson's Ships* (2002)
—— *The Ships of Trafalgar* (2005)
Gordon, Pryse Lockhart, *Personal Memoirs* (1830, 2 vols)
Gore, John, *Nelson's Hardy and His Wife* (1935)
Goulty, George A., 'Nelson Memorial Rings', *ND*, 3 (1990): 225–31
Grab, Alexander, 'Popular Uprisings in Napoleonic Italy', *Consortium on Revolutionary Europe Proceedings* (1989), 112–19
—— 'State, Power, Brigandage and Rural Resistance in Napoleonic Italy', *European History Quarterly*, 25 (1995): 39– 70
Grant, Nisbet Hamilton, ed., *The Letters of Mary Nisbet of Dirleton, Countess of Elgin* (1926)
Granville, Castalia, Countess, ed., *Lord Granville Leveson Gower, First Lord Granville* (1916, 2 vols)
Green, Peter, 'Alexander John Ball', *ND*, 9 (2007): 411–20
Gregory, Desmond, *Malta, Britain and the European Powers, 1793–1815* (1996)
—— *Minorca, the Illusory Prize* (1990)
—— *Napoleon's Jailer: Lt. Gen. Sir Hudson Lowe, a Life* (1996)
—— *Sicily: The Insecure Base* (1988)
—— *Napoleon's Italy* (2001)

Greig, James, ed., *The Farington Diary* (1922–28, 8 vols)
Grenfell, Russell, *Horatio Nelson* (1949; reprinted, 1968)
Guidotto, Gaetano, *Il Castello Nelson* (Bronte, n.d.)
Guimera, Agustin, 'Trafalgar: Myth and History', in Richard Harding, *Great and Glorious Victory* (2008): 40–57, 116–18
Gurney, Joseph, and William Brodie, *Trial of Edward Marcus Despard* (1803)
Gutteridge, H. C., ed., *Nelson and the Neapolitan Jacobins* (1903)
Gwilliam, H. W., *Old Worcester People and Places* (1975)
Gwyther, John R., 'Nelson's Gifts to La Maddalena', *TC*, 10 (2000): 47–56
—— '"In Order to Thank Your Excellency"', *TC*, 11 (2001): 35–37
—— 'Nelson in Turin', *TC*, 12 (2002): 47–71
—— 'Nelson in Carloforte', *TC*, 13 (2003): 13–33
—— 'Nelson and Francesco Carboni', *TC*, 14 (2004): 23–38
—— 'Nelson and Agostino Millelire', *TC*, 15 (2005): 145–55
—— 'From the Tower at Longon Sardo: Correspondence between Lieutenant Magnon, Dr Alexander Scott and Lord Nelson', *TC*, 16 (2006): 141–58, and 17 (2007): 268–63
Hales, E. E. Y., *Revolution and the Papacy, 1769–1846* (1960)
The Hampshire Telegraph (Portsmouth)
Hanioglu, M. Sukru, *A Brief History of the Late Ottoman Empire* (Princeton and Oxford, 2008)
Harbron, John D., *Trafalgar and the Spanish Navy* (1988)
Harcourt, Leveson Vernon, ed., *The Diaries and Correspondence of the Rt. Hon. George Rose* (1860, 2 vols)
Harding, Richard, ed., *A Great and Glorious Victory: New Perspectives on the Battle of Trafalgar* (2008)
Hardman, William, and Holland-Rose, J., *A History of Malta during the Period of the French and British Occupation, 1798–1815* (1909)
Hardwick, Mollie, *Emma, Lady Hamilton* (1969)
Hardy, Sheila, *Frances, Lady Nelson* (Staplehurst, 2005)
Hardy, Thomas A., 'Battle Plans of Copenhagen and Notes on the Bomb Vessels Employed', *ND*, 1 (1983): 88–92
—— 'Nelson's Turkish Scimitar', *ND*, 1 (1983): 108–109
—— 'Matthew Boulton's Neapolitan Medal', *ND*, 1 (1984): 194–201
—— 'After the Nile', *ND*, 2 (1985): 14–15
—— 'Peter Willemoes: Admiral Nelson's Opponent at Copenhagen', *ND*, 2 (1985): 22–25
—— *'Remember Nelson': Campaign and Commemorative Medals, Portrait Medallions and Associated Insignia, 1797–2005* (Nelson Society, 2005)
Harmon, Susan, 'The Serpent and the Dove: Studying Nelson's Character', *MM*, 75 (1989): 43–51
Harrison, James, *Life of the Rt. Honourable Horatio, Lord Viscount Nelson* (1806, 2 vols)

Harrison, Jon, 'From Armchair to Archive: Intercepted Foreign Letters from 1804', *TC*, 18 (2008): 72–79
Hattendorf, John B., et al., *British Naval Documents, 1204–1960* (Aldershot, 1998)
Heales, Alfred, *The Records of Merton Abbey* (1898)
Heath, Charles, *Historical and Descriptive Accounts of . . . Monmouth* (Monmouth, 1804)
—— *Descriptive Account of the Kymin Pavilion and Beaulieu Grove* (Monmouth, 1807)
Helfert, Joseph Alexander, Freiherr von, *Königin Karolina von Neapel und Sicilien in Kampfe gegen die Französische Weltherrschaft, 1790–1814* (Vienna, 1878)
—— *Fabrizio Ruffo* (Vienna, 1882)
—— *Maria Karolina von Oesterreich, Königin von Neapel und Sicilien* (Vienna, 1884)
The Hereford News and Journal
Herold, J. C., *Bonaparte in Egypt* (1963)
Hewitt, James, ed., *Eye-Witnesses to Nelson's Battles* (1972)
Hicks, Peter '"A Harsh, but Necessary, Apprenticeship": New French Accounts and a Previously Unknown Sketch of the Battle of Trafalgar', *TC*, 17 (2007): 42–52
Hill, J. Richard, *Prizes of War* (Stroud, 1998)
Hilliard, George S., ed., *Life, Letters and Journals of George Ticknor* (Boston, 1876)
Hills, Ann Mary, 'His Eye in Corsica', *ND*, 6 (1998): 294–99
—— 'Nelson: War Pensioner', *ND*, 6 (1999): 427–31
—— 'Nelson's Wounds: The Evidence of the Artists', *ND*, 7 (2000): 107–15
—— 'Nelson and Preventative Medicine', *ND*, 8 (2005): 833–36
—— *Nelson: A Medical Casebook* (Stroud, 2006)
—— 'The Nelson Touch, A New Interpretation', *ND*, 9 (2007): 349–50
Hilton, David, 'La Maddalena,' *ND*, 9 (2006): 222–29
Historical Manuscripts Commission, *Report on Manuscripts in Various Collections* (1909)
—— *Report on the Manuscripts of J. B. Fortescue . . . at Dropmore* (1905)
Hodgkin, Louis, *A Brief Guide to Nelson and Bath* (Corsham, 1991)
Hoffman, Frederick, *A Sailor of King George* (2003)
Holmes, Richard, *Coleridge: Darker Reflections* (1998)
Holmström, Kirsten Gram, *Monodrama, Attitudes, Tableaux Vivants: Studies on Some Trends of Theatrical Fashion, 1770–1815* (Stockholm, 1967)
Hopkins, Peter, *A History of Lord Nelson's Merton Place* (1998)
Hore, Peter, 'John Richards Lapenotiere and HM Schooner *Pickle*', *ND*, 7 (2002): 799–815
—— ed., *The Habit of Victory: The Story of the Royal Navy, 1545–1945* (2005)
Horsley, John Calcott, ed., *Recollections of a Royal Academician* (1903)
Hoste, Harriet, ed., *Memoirs and Letters of Captain Sir William Hoste* (1833, 2 vols)
Houston, Matilda C., *A Woman's Memories of World Known Men* (1883, 2 vols)

Howarth, Stephen, 'Nelson and the Magdalen', *TC*, 1 (1991): 18–25
—— 'Nelson's Steward at the Nile', *TC*, 8 (1998): 100–107
—— ed., *Battle of Copenhagen 1801: 200 Years* (The 1805 Club, 2003)
Hueffer, Hermann, 'Die Neapolitanische Republik des Jahres 1799', in Wilhelm Maurenbrecher, ed., *Historisches Taschenbuch* (Leipzig, 1884): 279–388
—— 'La Fin de la République Napolitaine', *La Revue Historique* [Paris], 83 (1903): 243–76, and (1904): 33–50
Hughes, Edward, ed., *The Private Correspondence of Admiral Lord Collingwood* (1957)
Hunt, Graham, 'Lieutenant John Neale, RN, of HMS Dreadnought at Trafalgar', *ND*, 2 (1986): 129–33
Huskisson, Thomas, *Eyewitness to Trafalgar* (1985)
Hutchinson, Horace G., 'Nelson at Copenhagen', *Blackwood's Magazine*, 166 (1899): 323–32
'Isaac May, Marine, A Relic of Trafalgar', *United Service Magazine*, part 2 (1869): 206–16
The Illustrated London News
Imbruglio, Girolamo, ed., *Naples in the Eighteenth Century* (Cambridge, 2000)
Inglis, John A., *The Nisbets of Carfin* (1916)
The Ipswich Journal
Jackson, Peter, *John Tallis's London Street Views* (1969)
Jackson's Oxford Journal
Jaffe, Patricia, *Lady Hamilton in Relation to the Art of Her Time* (1972)
Jagger, J. E., *Lord Nelson's Home and Life at Merton* (1926)
—— *Parish Church of St Mary the Virgin, Merton. Historical Notes* (n.d.)
James, William, *Naval History of Great Britain* (1822–24; reprinted 1837, 6 vols)
Jarvis, Diana N., 'Maurice Nelson, 1753–1801', *ND*, 7 (2002): 609–11
Jay, Mike, *The Unfortunate Colonel Despard* (2004)
Jeaffreson, John Cordy, *Lady Hamilton and Lord Nelson* (1888, 2 vols)
—— *The Queen of Naples and Lord Nelson* (1889, 2 vols)
Jenkins, Ian, and Sloan, Kim, eds, *Vases and Volcanoes: Sir William Hamilton and His Collection* (1996)
Jennings, Louis J., ed., *Correspondence and Diaries of John Wilson Croker* (1884, 3 vols)
Jewers, Rosemary, 'Searching for Nelson's Staircase', *ND*, 10 (2009): 99–105
Journals of the House of Lords
Jowett, Evelyn M., *An Illustrated History of Merton and Morden* (1951)
Jupp, Peter, *Lord Grenville, 1759–1834* (Oxford, 1985)
Jurien de la Gravière, Jean-Pierre, *Sketches of the Last Naval War* (1848)
Keate, Edith M., *Nelson's Wife* (1939)
Keevil, J. J., 'Leonard Gillespie, M.D., 1758–1842', *Bulletin of the History of Medicine*, 28 (1954): 301–32

Keigwin, R. P., 'Admiral Nelson's Journey Through Germany', *MM*, 21 (1939): 153–57

Kemble, James, *Idols and Invalids* (1933)

Kempson, E. A., *Bygone Merton* (1895)

Kennedy, Ludovic, *Nelson and His Captains* (1951; revised ed., 1975)

—— 'The Log of the *Guardian*, 1789–1799', in C. Lloyd, ed., *Naval Miscellany* (Navy Records Society, 1952)

The Kentish Chronicle

Knight, Carlo, 'The British at Naples in 1799', *TC*, 11 (2001): 15–34

Knight, Cornelia, *Autobiography of Miss Cornelia Knight* (1861, 2 vols)

Knight, Jane, 'Nelson and the Bronte Estate', *TC*, 15 (2005): 133–44

—— 'Nelson and the Eastern Mediterranean, 1803–1805', *MM*, 91 (2005): 195–215

Knight, Roger, 'Nelson and the Forest of Dean', *MM*, 87 (2001): 88–92

—— *The Pursuit of Victory: The Life and Achievement of Horatio Nelson* (2005)

—— 'The Fleet at Trafalgar', in Cannadine, *Trafalgar in History*, 61–71

—— 'Politics and Trust in Victualling the Navy, 1793–1815', *MM*, 94 (2008): 133–49

—— 'Captivity, Marriage and Influence', *TC*, 20 (2010): 49–57

—— and Wilcox, Martin, *Sustaining the Fleet, 1793–1815* (Woodbridge, 2010)

Kossman, Robby, *Lord Nelson und der Herzog Franz Caracciolo* (Berlin, 1895)

La Jonquière, Clément de, *L'Expédition d'Egypte, 1798–1801* (Paris, 1900, 5 vols)

Lambert, Andrew, 'Sir William Cornwallis, 1744–1819', in Le Fevre and Harding, eds, *Precursors of Nelson*, 351–75, 420–21

—— *Nelson: Britannia's God of War* (2004)

—— 'Nelson's Search for the Sublime' (Burnham address, October 2005)

—— 'Making a Victorian Nelson: Albert, Nicholas and the Arts', *TC*, 15 (2005): 192–216

—— *The Immortal and the Hero: Nelson and Wellington* (Southampton, 2005)

—— 'Patriotism and Popular Identities: Nelson Revived, 1885–1914', *TC*, 17 (2007): 212–30

Lardas, Mark N., 'Carronades: Myths and Realities of the Guns that Changed Naval Battle', *Artilleryman*, 25 (2005), no. 2

Laughton, John Knox, ed., *Letters and Despatches of Horatio, Viscount Nelson, K.B.* (1886)

—— *The Nelson Memorial: Nelson and His Companions-at-Arms* (1896)

—— 'Nelson at Naples', *Athenaeum*, 26 August 1899

—— ed., *The Naval Miscellany* (Navy Records Society, 1902–12, 2 vols)

—— 'Nelson's Home at Merton', *Wimbledon and Merton Annual* (1903): 32–44

—— ed., *Letters and Papers of Charles, Lord Barham* (Navy Records Society, 1906–10, 3 vols)

—— ed., *The Barker Collection* (1913)

Lavery, Brian, *Nelson's Navy* (1989)

—— ed., *Shipboard Life and Organisation, 1731–1815* (1998)

—— *Nelson and the Nile* (1998)
—— 'George Keith Elphinstone, Lord Keith', in Le Fevre and Harding, *Precursors of Nelson*, 377–99, 421
—— *Nelson's Fleet at Trafalgar* (2005)
Lawrence, Christine, *The History of the Old Naval Hospital, Gibraltar* (Lymington, 1994)
Laxton, Paul, and Wisdom, Joseph, *The A-Z of Regency London* (1985)
Le Brun, Elisabeth Vigée, *Souvenirs* (Paris, 1984, 2 vols)
'Lector', 'Original Anecdotes of Nelson,' *United Services Magazine*, Part 3 (1847): 433–34
Lee, John Theophilus, *Memoirs of the Life and Services of Sir J. Theophilus Lee, of the Elms, Hampshire* (1836)
Le Fevre, Peter, and Harding, Richard, eds, *Precursors of Nelson* (2000)
—— 'Little Merit Will be Given to Me', in Howarth, *Battle of Copenhagen*, 1–29
—— and Harding, Richard, eds, *British Admirals of the Napoleonic Wars* (2005)
Legg, Stuart, ed., *Trafalgar: An Eye-Witness Account of a Great Battle* (1966)
Lemmi, Francesco, *Nelson e Caracciolo e la Repubblica Napoletana, 1799* (Florence, 1898)
Le Quesne, Leslie, 'Did One Bad Move by the Ship's Steward Lead to Nelson's Death?' *TC*, 7 (1997): 77–78
—— 'Nelson and his Surgeons', *Journal of the Royal Naval Medical Service*, 86 (2000): 85–88
'A Letter from Edward Nosworthy – a Sailor in Nelson's Fleet', *ND*, 2 (1985): 78–80
'A Letter to Emma Hamilton from Beckford in 1805', *The Beckford Journal*, 1 (1995): 17–22
Letters of Lord Nelson to Lady Hamilton (1814, 2 vols)
Levett, Keith, 'A Tailor's Nelson', *TC*, 10 (2000): 68–85
Lewis, Charles, *'I Am Myself a Norfolk Man': Nelson, the Norfolk Hero* (Cromer, 2005)
Lewis, Michael, *A Social History of the Navy, 1793–1815* (1960)
Lewis-Jones, Huw, 'Trafalgar Old Boys: A Graphic Portrait', *TC*, 17 (2007): 182–92
Leyland, John, ed., *The Blockade of Brest, 1803–1805* (1898–1901, 2 vols)
'The Life of Stephen Humphries, Royal Marine, Written by Himself, 1853', *TC*, 2 (1992): 59–61
Lincoln, Margaret, ed., *Nelson and Napoleon* (2005)
Lindsay-MacDougall, K. F., 'Nelson Manuscripts at the National Maritime Museum', *MM*, 41 (1955): 227–32
Livesy, Jacqui, 'The Literary Assassin', *ND*, 10 (2011): 623–34
Lloyd, Christopher C., ed., *The Keith Papers* (1927–55, 3 vols)
—— *St Vincent and Camperdown* (1963)
—— *Mr Barrow of the Admiralty* (1970)
—— and Coulter, J. L. S., *Medicine and the Navy, 1714–1815* (1961)

Locker, Edward Hawke, *Memoirs of Celebrated Naval Commanders* (1832)
Lockwood, Allison, 'Nelson as Seen by an American Just Before Trafalgar', *ND*, 2 (1985): 33–35
The London Chronicle
The London Evening Mail
The London Gazette
'The Lost Sword', *ND*, 3 (1990): 214–15
Lovell, W. S., *Personal Narrative of Events from 1799 to 1815* (1879)
Lowry, James, *Fiddlers and Whores: The Candid Memoirs of a Surgeon in Nelson's Fleet* (2006)
Luttrell, Barbara, *The Prim Romantic: A Biography of Ellis Cornelia Knight* (1965)
McCarthy, Lily, and Lea, John, *Nelson Remembered* (Portsmouth, 1995)
Macdonald, Jacques, *Recollections* (1892, 2 vols)
Macdonald, Janet, *Feeding Nelson's Navy* (2004)
—— 'Two Years off Provence', *MM*, 92 (2006): 443–54
—— *The British Navy's Victualling Board, 1793–1815* (Woodbridge, 2010)
—— 'A Giant in Promises, a Pigmy in Performance,' *TC*, 20 (2010): 58–65
McGuffie, T. H., ed., *Peninsular Cavalry General* (1951)
Mackenzie, Robert Holden, *The Trafalgar Roll* (1913)
Mackesy, Piers, *The War in the Mediterranean, 1803–1810* (1964)
—— *Statesmen at War: The Strategy of Overthrow, 1798–1799* (1974)
McLean, David, *Surgeons of the Fleet* (2010)
McLynn, Frank, 'Brief Encounters: Wellington and Nelson', *BBC History* (March 2005): 8
Maffeo, Steven E., *Most Secret and Confidential: Intelligence in the Age of Nelson* (2000)
Mahan, A. T., *The Influence of Sea Power upon the French Revolution and Empire, 1793–1815* (1892, 2 vols)
—— *The Life of Nelson* (1898, 2 vols; revised ed., 1899)
—— 'The Neapolitan Republicans and Nelson's Accusers', *English Historical Review*, 14 (1899): 471–501
—— 'Nelson at Naples', *English Historical Review*, 15 (1900): 699–727
Malcolmson, Tom, 'Vienna's Reaction to Nelson's Victory at the Battle of the Nile', *ND*, 6 (1997): 95
—— ed., 'The Visit to Fonthill', *ND*, 7 (2000): 223–37
Malmesbury, James Harris, Earl of, ed., *Diaries and Correspondence of James Harris, First Earl of Malmesbury* (1844, 4 vols)
—— *A Series of Letters of the First Earl of Malmesbury* (1870, 2 vols)
Manners, Victoria, and Williamson, G. C., *Angelica Kauffman* (1924)
Marcus, Geoffrey J., *The Age of Nelson* (1971)
Maresca, Benedetto, ed., 'Dell'Ammiraglio Francesco Caracciolo', *Archivo Storico per le Province Napoletane*, 10 (1885): 48–84

—— 'Memoria Sugli Avvenimenti di Napoli Nell'Anno 1799', *Archivo Storico per le Province Napoletane*, 13 (1888): 36–94
The Mariner's Mirror (Journal of the Society for Nautical Research)
Marione, Patrick, 'A Great Coxcomb', *TC*, 12 (2002): 8–44
Marks, Richard, *Nautical Essays* (1818)
Mark-Wardlaw, William Penrose, *At Sea with Nelson, Being the Life of William Mark, a Purser . . .* (1929)
Marriott, Leo, *What's Left of Nelson* (Littlehampton, 1995)
Marsh, Lieutenant, 'Spanish and French Accounts of the Battle of Trafalgar, with Notes', *Royal United Services Magazine*, part 3 (1851): 337–52
Marshall, John, *Royal Navy Biography* (1823–35, 8 vols)
Marshall, K. N., 'The Tattered Flag', *ND*, 2 (1986): 103–107
Matcham, Mary Eyre, *The Nelsons of Burnham Thorpe* (1911)
Matheson, C., *The Life of Henry Dundas, First Viscount Melville, 1742–1811* (1933)
Maurice, J. F., ed., *The Diary of Sir John Moore* (1904, 2 vols)
May, John, 'The Nelson Silver', *ND*, 2 (1986): 147–55
—— 'Nelson Commemorated', in Colin White, ed., *Nelson Companion* (Stroud, 2005)
—— 'The "Emma" Cup and Saucer', *TC*, 11 (2001): 7–14
'The Medusa Channel', *ND*, 4 (1991): 4–6
Melville, Lewis, ed., *Life and Letters of William Bedford of Fonthill* (1910)
Memoir of Admiral the Hon. Sir George Elliot (1863)
'Memoir of the Late Rear-Admiral Sir Edward Berry, Bart., K.C.B', *Royal United Services Magazine*, part 1 (1831): 508–11
'Memoir of the Public Services of the Late Sir Thomas Troubridge, Bart., Rear-Admiral of the White Squadron', *NC*, 23 (1810): 1–29
Memoirs of Emma, Lady Hamilton (1815; ed. W. H. Long, 1891)
Memoirs of the Right Honourable Lord Viscount Nelson, Duke of Bronte, &c. (Birmingham, 1805)
Middleton, Judy, 'Admiral Sir George Augustus Westphal', *ND*, 1 (1984): 132–35
Miles, Jeaffreson, *Vindication of Admiral Lord Nelson's Proceedings in the Bay of Naples* (1843)
Millard, Frederick M., 'Battle of Copenhagen', *Macmillan's Magazine*, 72 (1895): 81–93
Millington, Jon, 'Where Nelson Went in Fonthill Abbey', *The Beckford Journal*, 8 (2002): 43–49
Minto, Countess of, ed., *A Memoir of the Rt. Hon. Hugh Elliot* (1868)
—— *Life and Letters of Sir Gilbert Elliot, First Earl of Minto* (1874, 3 vols)
Monaque, Rémi, 'Latouche-Tréville: The Admiral Who Defied Nelson', *MM*, 86 (2000): 272–84
—— *Latouche-Tréville, 1745–1804* (Paris, 2000)
—— *Trafalgar* (Paris, 2005)

Moorhouse, Esther Hallam, *Nelson in England* (1913)
The Morning Chronicle
The Morning Herald
The Morning Post
Morris, Roland, *HMS Colossus: The Story of the Salvage of the Hamilton Treasure* (1979)
Morrison, Alfred, *The Hamilton and Nelson Papers* (1893–94, 2 vols)
Morriss, Roger, 'St Vincent and Reform, 1801–1804', *MM* 69 (1983): 269–90
—— *The Royal Dockyards during the Revolutionary and Napoleonic Wars* (Leicester, 1983)
—— *Cockburn and the British Navy in Transition* (Exeter, 1997)
—— and Lavery, Brian, Deucher, Stephen, and Van der Merwe, Pieter, *Nelson: An Illustrated History* (1995)
Mowl, Timothy, *William Beckford* (1998)
Mundy, Percy, 'Nelson and Lady Hamilton at Merton', *Home Counties Magazine*, 3 (1901): 205–11
Murray, Geoffrey, *The Life of Admiral Collingwood* (1936)
Naish, George P. B., and Lindsay-MacDougall, K. F., eds, *Nelson's Letters to His Wife and Other Documents, 1785–1831* (1958)
Nance, E. M., *Pottery and Porcelain of Swansea and Nantgarw* (1942)
Napoleon, Nelson and Their Time: The Calvin Bullock Collection (1985)
Nash, Michael, 'Earl Nelson and the Line of Succession', *ND*, 1 (1984): 191–93
—— *From Bladud's Fountains to Burnham Thorpe: The Death and Funeral of the Reverend Edmund Nelson* (Hoylake & Tattenhall, 2011)
Naval Anecdotes, Illustrating the Character of British Seamen . . . (1806)
The Naval Chronicle
'The Naval Officer', *The United Service Journal and Naval and Military Magazine*, part 1 (1829): 361–65
The Navy List
Nelson, Thomas, *Genealogical History of the Nelson Family* (King's Lynn, 1908)
The Nelson Dispatch (Nelson Society, 1982–2012, 11 vols)
'Nelson and the Duke of Bronte', *United Services Magazine*, pt. 2 (1835): 516–19
'Nelson: Unpublished Letters', *Notes & Queries*, 11th series, 10 (1914): 305–10
'Nelson, His Valet, and His Native Coast', *United Services Magazine* (1836): 201–208
Newbolt, Henry, *The Year of Trafalgar* (1905)
The Niagara Chronicle (Canada), 12 February 1852
Nicol, John, *The Life and Adventures of John Nicol, Mariner* (1822; reprinted, Edinburgh, 1997)
Nicola, Carlo de, *Diario Napoletano, 1798–1800* (Milan, 1963)
Nicolas, Nicholas Harris, ed., *The Dispatches and Letters of Vice-Admiral Lord Viscount Nelson* (1844–46, 7 vols)
Noble, James, *Auto-Biography of James William Noble* (n. p., *c.* 1850)
Norie, J. W., *Sailing Directions for the River Thames to the Nore and Sheerness* (1847)

Notes & Queries
Nuñez, José Maria Blanco, et al., *XXXI Congreso Internacional de Historia Militar* (Madrid, 2006)
Nute, Albert, 'Charles Norry's Narrative of the Egyptian Exhibition', *ND*, 2 (1985): 69–73
O'Byrne, William, *A Naval Biographical Dictionary* (1849)
Oman, Carola, *Nelson* (1946)
—— *Sir John Moore* (1953)
The [London] *Oracle*
Owen, C. H. H., ed., 'Letters from Vice-Admiral Lord Collingwood, 1794–1809', in Michael Duffy, ed., *The Naval Miscellany* (Aldershot, 2003), 149–220
The Oxford Dictionary of National Biography (2004)
Padfield, Peter, *Guns at Sea* (1973)
—— *Maritime Power and the Struggle for Freedom* (2003)
Paget, Augustus B., ed., *The Paget Papers* (1896, 2 vols)
Paget, John, *Paradoxes and Puzzles* (1874)
Palmer, Peggy, 'Nelson's Norfolk', *Norfolk Fair*, June 1977, 48–49
Palumbo, Raffaele, *Carteggio di Maria Carolina, Regina delle due Sicilie, con Lady Hamilton. Documenti Inedite* (Naples, 1877)
Parliamentary Debates
Parry, Ann, *The Admirals Fremantle* (1971)
Parsons, George S., *Nelsonian Reminiscences: Leaves from Memory's Log* (1843; reprinted, 1998)
Peakman, Julia, *Emma Hamilton* (2005)
Pellew, George, ed., *The Life and Correspondence of the Rt. Hon. Henry Addington, First Viscount Sidmouth* (1847, 3 vols)
Pepe, Guglielmo, *Memoirs of General Pepe* (1846, 3 vols)
Perrin, W. G., 'Letters of Lord Nelson, 1804–1805', *The Naval Miscellany*, 3 (1901), 173–90
Petrie, F. Loraine, *The Royal Berkshire Regiment* (Reading, 1925, 2 vols)
Pettigrew, Thomas Joseph, *Memoirs of the Life of Vice-Admiral Lord Viscount Nelson* (1849, 2 vols)
Phillimore, Augustus, *The Life of Admiral of the Fleet, Sir William Parker* (1876–80, 3 vols)
Phillips, I. Lloyd, 'Lord Barham at the Admiralty, 1805–1806', *MM*, 64 (1978): 217–33
Philp, Mark, '"I'll Sing of Fam'd Trafalgar if You'll Listen unto me": Nelson in Popular Song', *TC*, 15 (2005): 65–81
Plomer, William, *Ali the Lion* (1936)
Pocock, Tom, *Remember Nelson: The Life of Captain Sir William Hoste* (1977)
—— *Horatio Nelson* (1987)
Pollock, Frederick, ed., *Macready's Reminiscences and Selections from his Diaries and Letters* (1875, 2 vols)

Pool, Bernard, *Navy Board Contracts, 1660–1832* (1966)
Pope, Dudley, *England Expects* (1959)
—— *The Great Gamble: Nelson at Copenhagen* (1972)
Porter, Robert Ker, *Travelling Sketches in Russia and Sweden* (1809, 2 vols)
Pratt, Michael, *Nelson's Duchy: a Sicilian Anomaly* (Staplehurst, 2005)
Prentice, Rina, *The Authentic Nelson* (2005)
Price, C., *English Theatre in Wales* (1948)
Pugh, P. D. Gordon, *Nelson and his Surgeons* (1968)
Pybus, Keith, 'Stinkpots and Villains: William Wilkinson's Life, Career and Trafalgar Letter', *ND*, 7 (2001): 302–306.
Ragsdale, Hugh, ed., *Paul I* (Pittsburgh, 1979)
Ralfe, James, *The Naval Biography of Great Britain* (1828, 4 vols)
Ram, Charley, 'Letters of Lt. William Andrew Ram, Killed at Trafalgar', *ND*, 6 (1998): 184–87
Rao, Anna Maria, ed., *Napoli, 1799* (Naples, 2002)
Rathbone, Philip, *Paradise Merton: The Story of Nelson and the Hamiltons at Merton Place* (1973)
Reay, Justin, 'In the Footsteps of the Hero: Nelson at the Admiralty in London', *TC*, 16 (2006): 24–43
—— 'In Search of Nelson's Spy', *TC*, 19 (2009): 1–15
Redding, Cyrus, *Fifty Years' Recollections* (1858, 3 vols)
Report of a Committee Appointed by the Admiralty to Examine and Consider the Evidence Relating to the Tactics Employed by Nelson at the Battle of Trafalgar (1913)
Robbins-Landon, H. C. *Haydn: The Years of 'The Creation', 1796–1800* (1977)
Robinson, Hercules, *Sea Drift* (1858)
Robinson, William ('Jack Nasty-Face'), *Nautical Economy, or Forecastle Recollections* (1836; reprinted, 2005)
Rodger, Alexander Bankier, *The War of the Second Coalition, 1794 to 1801* (Oxford, 1964)
Rodger, Nicholas, *The Wooden World. An Anatomy of the Georgian Navy* (1986; reprinted, 1988)
—— *The Command of the Ocean* (2004)
—— 'Nelson and the British Navy: Seamanship, Leadership, Originality', in David Cannadine, *Admiral Lord Nelson*, 7–29
Rodriguez Gonzalez, A. R., *Trafalgar y el Conflicto Anglo-Español del Siglo XVIII* (Madrid, 2005)
Roider, Karl A., *Baron Thugut and Austria's Response to the French Revolution* (Princeton, 1987)
Rooke, Barbara E., ed., *The Friend* (1969, 2 vols)
Rose, J. Holland, 'The State of Nelson's Fleet Before Trafalgar', *MM*, 8 (1922): 75–81
Rosebery, Lord, ed., *The Windham Papers* (1913, 2 vols)
Ross, John, *Memoirs and Correspondence of Admiral Lord de Saumarez* (1838, 2 vols)
Rossen, S. F., and Caroselli, S. L., eds., *The Golden Age of Naples: Art and*

Civilisation under the Bourbons, 1734–1805 (Detroit, 1981, 2 vols)
Rothenberg, Gunther E., *Napoleon's Great Adversaries: The Archduke Charles and The Austrian Army, 1792–1814* (Bloomington, Indiana, 1982)
Rubinstein, Hilary L., *Trafalgar Captain* (Stroud, 2005)
Russell, Jack, *Nelson and the Hamiltons* (New York, 1969)
Sacchinelli, Domenico, *Memorie Storiche Sulla Vita del Cardinale Fabrizio Ruffo* (Naples, 1836)
The St James's Chronicle
Sainty, J. C., *Admiralty Officials, 1660–1870* (1974)
Sansone, Alfonso, *Gli avvenimenti del 1799 nelle Due Sicilie* (Palermo, 1901)
Saul, Norman E., *Russia and the Mediterranean, 1797–1807* (Chicago and London, 1972)
Saunders, Jim, 'The Roundwood, Nelson's Home at Ipswich, 1797–1801', *ND*, 5 (1996): 345–48
—— 'Alexander Davison and Horatio Nelson', *ND*, 8 (2003): 81–105
Saxby, Richard, 'The Blockade of Brest in the French Revolutionary War', *MM*, 78 (1992): 25–35
Schom, Alan, *Trafalgar: Countdown to Battle, 1803–1805* (1990)
Scragg, Doreen, 'The Career of Thomas Atkinson, Master of the *Victory* at Trafalgar, and First Master Attendant, Portsmouth Yard', *TC*, 8 (1998): 80–99
Sermoneta, Vittoria Caetani, Duchess of, *The Locks of Norbury* (1940)
Shannon, David, 'The Nelson Effigy at Westminster Abbey', *ND*, 4 (1991): 26–30
—— 'Trafalgar's Last Survivors', *ND*, 5 (1995): 116–27
—— 'In Case I Should Fall in the Noble Cause', *ND*, 6 (1998): 188–90
—— 'Three Pipes of Port by Desire of My Lord', *ND*, 6 (1998): 191–93
—— 'The Engagement Began Very Hot', *ND*, 7 (2000): 238–39
—— 'John Pollard, Nelson's Avenger', *ND*, 8 (2005): 615–20
Sharman, Victor T., *Nelson's Hero* (Barnsley, Yorkshire, 2005)
Shaw, Stanford J., trans., *Ottoman Egypt in the Age of the French Revolution* (Cambridge, Mass., 1964)
—— *Between Old and New: The Ottoman Empire under Sultan Selim III, 1789–1807* (Cambridge, Mass., 1971)
Sheldon, Matthew, 'A Survey of Nelson's Appearance in Caricature', *TC*, 14 (2004): 1–10
'Ship *Bellerophon*, Mediterranean, September 14, 1798', *TC*, 4 (1994): 77–78
Sichel, Walter, *Emma, Lady Hamilton* (1905; revised ed., 1907)
Siemers, Heinrich, 'Where Nelson Really Died', *TC*, 10 (2000): 86–98
'Sketch of the Life of Admiral Lord Nelson of the Nile', *Lady's Magazine*, 29 (1798): 483–5
Smith, Douglas Whiteley, 'Now Safe Returned from Dangers Past', *ND*, 6 (1999): 532–37
Smith, Graham, 'Nelson's Revenue Cutters at Boulogne', *ND*, 7 (2001): 462–63
Smith, Jane, *The Story of Nelson's Portsmouth* (Tiverton, 2005)

Smyth, W. H., 'Nelson Vindicated from Vanity in his Last Moments', *United Services Magazine*, 1842, part 2, 390–91
'Some Recollections of Nelson', *United Services Magazine*, 1839, part 3, 180–86
Sotheby's, *Nelson: The Alexander Davison Collection* (2002)
—— *Trafalgar, Nelson and the Napoleonic Wars* (2005)
Southey, Robert, *The Life of Nelson* (1813; reprinted, 1903)
Southwick, Leslie, 'Historic Tokens: The Nelson Collection at Lloyds of London', *TC*, 6 (1996): 71–86
Spence, Jack, *Nelson's Avenger* (Cawsand, Cornwall, 2005)
Stanton, Yolanda C., '"Nelson" Tokens of the Napoleonic Period', *ND*, 1 (1984): 136–40
—— 'The Exeter Nelson Sword', *ND*, 2 (1986): 110–11
Steer, Michael, 'The Blockade of Brest and the Victualling of the Western Squadron, 1793–1805', *MM*, 76 (1990): 307–16
Street, G. S., *The Ghosts of Piccadilly* (1914)
Stromeyer, C. E., 'Trafalgar and the Nelson Touch', *The Times*, 21 October 1905
Stuart, Dorothy M., *Dearest Bess* (1955)
Sturges-Jackson, T., ed., *Logs of Great Sea Fights, 1794–1805* (Navy Record Society, 1899–1900, 2 vols)
Sugden, John, *Lord Cochrane: Naval Commander, Radical and Inventor, 1775–1860* (Ph.D., Sheffield University, 1981)
—— 'Looking for Bess', *ND*, 5 (1995–6), 219–22, 260–64, 387–89
—— 'Forgotten *Agamemnons*: Nelson's Marine Society Boys', *ND*, 8 (2004): 485–88, 549–54
—— *Nelson: A Dream of Glory* (2004; revised ed., 2005)
—— 'Mary Simpson: A New Look at Nelson's First Love', *TC*, 15 (2005): 120–32
—— 'Rusting Ingloriously: James Noble and Peter Spicer, Nelson's "St Vincent" Heroes', *TC*, 16 (2006): 5–23
—— 'New Light on Adelaide Correglia', *MM*, 93 (2007): 91–94
—— '"Fine Colt", "Cub" or "Vile Spue"? Recovering Captain Josiah Nisbet', *TC*, 17 (2007): 31–41, and 18 (2008): 80–99
—— 'Vive L'Amiral', in J. D. Markham and Mike Resnick, ed., *History Revisited* (Dallas, Texas, 2008), 291–304
—— 'The Stormy Life and Strange Death of Captain William Layman', *TC*, 22 (2012): 68–100
—— 'The Unhappy Admiral', *BBC History* (November 2012): 26–30
Sultana, Donald, ed., *Samuel Taylor Coleridge in Malta and Italy* (1969)
The Sun
'The Surveys of Graeme Spence', *The Nautical Magazine and Naval Chronicle*, (1842): 313–19
'Swiftsure, Gibraltar, Nov. 3rd, 1805', *TC*, 2 (1992): 18–20

Syrett, David, and DiNardo, R. L., *Commissioned Sea Officers of the Royal Navy, 1660–1815* (Aldershot, 1994)

Talbott, John E., *The Pen and Ink Sailor* (1998)

Tarpey, Brian, 'Nelson's Blockade of Malta', *ND*, 2 (1986): 136–38

—— *Nelson's Marines at Malta* (Milton Keynes, 1995)

—— 'Nelson at Malta', *ND*, 6 (1999): 498–501

Tayler, Alistair and Henrietta, *The Book of the Duffs* (Edinburgh, 1914)

Taylor, A. H., 'The Battle of Trafalgar', *MM*, 36 (1950): 281–321

Terraine, John, *Trafalgar* (1976)

'Tertius', 'Where Did Nelson Die?' *ND*, 2 (1987): 169–72

—— 'You Who Tread In His Footsteps Remember His Glory', *ND*, 2 (1987): 236–38

—— 'The Bullet That Killed Nelson', *ND*, 2 (1987): 204–208

The Times

Touchette, Lori-Ann, 'Sir William Hamilton's "Pantomime Mistress": Emma Hamilton and her Attitudes', in C. Hornsby, ed., *The Impact of Italy* (2000), 123–46

Tracy, Nicholas, 'Sir Robert Calder's Action', *MM*, 77 (1991): 259–70

—— *Nelson's Battles* (1996)

—— *The Battle of Copenhagen* (2003)

—— *Who's Who in Nelson's Navy* (2005)

The Trafalgar Chronicle (The 1805 Club, 1991–2012, 22 vols)

Trewman's Exeter Flying Post

Trotter, Thomas, *Medicina Nautica* (1803, 3 vols)

The True Briton

Tucker, Jedediah Stephens, ed., *Memoirs of Admiral the Rt. Hon. The Earl of St Vincent, G.C.B.* (1844, 2 vols)

Tunstall, Brian, and Tracy, Nicholas, *Naval Warfare in the Age of Sail* (1990)

Turquan, Joseph, and D'Auriac, Jules, *A Great Adventuress: Lady Hamilton and the Revolution, 1753–1815* (1914)

Tushingham, Eric, Morewood, John, and Hayes, Derek, *HMS Vanguard at the Nile* (Nelson Society, 1998)

—— and Mansfield, Clifford, *Nelson's Flagship at Copenhagen: HMS Elephant. The Men, the Ship, the Battle* (Nelson Society, 2001)

Twiss, Horace, *The Public and Private Life of Lord Chancellor Eldon* (1844; reprinted, 1846, 2 vols)

United Services Magazine

Vale, Brian, 'The Conquest of Scurvy in the Royal Navy, 1793– 1800: A Challenge to Current Orthodoxy', *MM*, 94 (2008): 160–75

—— and Edwards, Griffith, *Physician to the Fleet: The Life and Times of Thomas Trotter 1760–1832* (Woodbridge, 2011)

Van Der Merwe, Peter, 'Nelson's Last Provision for Lady Hamilton, 1805', *MM*, 68 (1982): 42

Vane, Charles, Marquess of Londonderry, ed., *Memoirs and Correspondence of Castlereagh* (1848–53, 12 vols)
Vendôme, Duchesse de, ed., *La Jeunesse de Marie Amélie, reine des Français, d'après son Journal* (Paris, 1935, 2 vols)
Vigo, Pietro, *Nelson e Livorno* (Siena, Italy, 1903)
Vincent, Edgar, *Nelson, Love and Fame* (New Haven, Conn., 2003)
Voigt, Christian, 'Admiral Nelsons Deutschlandreise', *Marine-Offiziers Verband*, 11 (1934): 157–60, and 12 (1934): 173–75
Volke, Finn, *The Battle of Copenhagen* (Shelton, Notts., 2003)
Vulpius, Christian A., *Die Russen und Engländer in Neapel* (Leipzig, 1800)
Walker, Richard, *The Nelson Portraits* (Portsmouth, 1998)
—— 'The Nelson Portraits: Addendum 2005', *TC*, 15 (2005): 257–68
—— 'The Nelson Portraits: Addendum II, 2006', *TC*, 16 (2006): 182–85
Wang, D, et al., 'Admiral Lord Nelson's Death: Known and Unknown – A Historical Review of the Anatomy', *Spinal Cord*, 43 (2005): 573–76
Ward, Robert, 'Robert Mylne, Matthew Boulton, and the Treasure in Nelson's Tomb', *TC*, 17 (2007): 53–61
Waring, Ernest, ed., 'The Cumby Letter', *ND*, 6 (1998): 233–46
Warner, Oliver, *Lord Nelson: A Guide to Reading* (1955)
—— *A Portrait of Lord Nelson* (1958)
—— *Emma Hamilton and Sir William* (1960)
—— 'Lieut. Tom Southey, R.N., and His Brother's *Life of Nelson*', *MM*, 50 (1964): 57–59
—— *Nelson's Battles* (1965)
—— *The Life and Letters of Vice-Admiral Lord Collingwood* (1968)
—— *Nelson* (1975)
—— ed., *Nelson's Last Diary* (1971)
Warwick, Peter, 'Here Was Paradise – A Description of Merton Place', *TC*, 4 (1994): 36–47
—— *Voices from Trafalgar* (2005)
Watson, J. Steven, *The Age of George III, 1760–1815* (Oxford, 1960)
Watt, James, 'The Injuries of Four Centuries of Naval Warfare', *Annals of the Royal College of Surgeons of England*, 57 (1975): 3–24
—— 'Surgery at Trafalgar', *Journal of the Royal Naval Medical Service*, 91 (2005): 83–91
—— 'Naval and Civilian Influences on Eighteenth- and Nineteenth-Century Medical Practice,' *MM*, 97 (2011): 148–66
Webb, David, 'A Midshipman at Trafalgar', *MM*, 69 (1983): 164
Weigley, Russell F., *The Age of Battles* (1991)
Weil, Maurice H., and Circelo, Carlo, Marquis C. di Somma, eds, *Correspondance inédite de Marie-Caroline . . . avec le Marquis de Gallo* (Paris, 1911, 2 vols)
West, Mark, 'The Capture of the *Généreux* and the *Guillaume Tell*: A Study in Prize Litigation', *TC*, 20 (2010): 66– 91

Westminster, Dean of, ed., *The Remains of the Late Mrs Richard Trench* (1862)
Wheatley, H. B., *A Short History of Bond Street, Old and New* (1911)
Wheeler, Dennis, 'Looking at Logbooks: Science and the Nelsonian Legacy', *TC*, 16 (2006): 130–40
'Where Nelson Died: An Historical Riddle Resolved', *MM*, 85 (1999): 272–87
White, Colin, 'Nelson's Last Walk', *ND*, 5 (1996): 382–85
—— ed., *Nelson: New Letters* (2005)
—— *Nelson the Admiral* (2005)
—— 'Further Unpublished Letters by Nelson and Emma Hamilton', *TC*, 18 (2008): 66–71
—— and the 1805 Club, *The Trafalgar Captains* (2005)
White, David, 'Heralds and their Clients: The Arms of Nelson', *TC*, 8 (1998): 56–73
White, Joshua, *Supplement to the Life of the Late Horatio, Lord Viscount Nelson . . . with a Circumstantial Narrative of the . . . Funeral* (1806)
'William Beckford in Farington's Diary', *The Beckford Journal*, 11 (2005): 50–74
Williams, David, 'Nelson Commemorated', *TC*, 14 (2004): 88–99
Williams, Helen Maria, *Sketches of the State of Manners and Opinions in the French Republic* (1801, 2 vols)
Williams, Kate, *England's Mistress* (2006)
Willis, Sam, *Fighting at Sea in the Eighteenth Century* (Woodbridge, 2008)
Willyams, Cooper, *A Voyage up the Mediterranean in His Majesty's Ship the Swiftsure, One of the Squadron under the Command of Rear-Admiral Sir Horatio Nelson, K.B.* (1802)
Wilmot, Catherine, ed., *An Irish Peer on the Continent* (1920)
Woolf, Stuart, 'The Mediterranean Economy during the Napoleonic Wars', in Erik Aerts and F. Crouzet, eds, *Economic Effects of the French Revolutionary and Napoleonic Wars* (Leuven, 1990)
Wraxall, Nathaniel William, *Historical and Posthumous Memoirs of Sir Nathaniel William Wraxall* (1884, 5 vols)
Wybourn, T. Marmaduke, *Sea Soldier: The Letters and Journals of Major T. Marmaduke Wybourn, R.M., 1797–1813* (Tunbridge Wells, 2001)
Wyndham-Quin, W. H., *Sir Charles Tyler, G.C.B., Admiral of the White* (1912)
Zorlu, Tuncay, *Innovation and Empire in Turkey* (2008)
Zulueta, J. de, 'Trafalgar – the Spanish View', *MM*, 66 (1980): 293–318
—— 'Health in the Royal Navy during the Age of Nelson – Health in the Spanish Navy during the Age of Nelson', *Journal of the Royal Naval Medical Service*, 86 (2000): 89–92
—— 'The Final Sacrifice off Cape Trafalgar', *MM*, 91 (2005): 251–65
—— 'The Battle of Cape Santa Maria, 5 October 1804', *MM*, 96 (2010): 197–202

GLOSSARY

ABLE-SEAMAN An experienced seaman, senior to an 'ordinary seaman' and a 'landman', the latter a beginner

ABOUT, GO To change tacks

ADMIRAL An officer eligible to command a fleet and fly a distinguishing flag. In descending order of seniority the three grades were admiral, vice admiral and rear admiral

ADMIRALTY The senior naval board, whose first lord was a cabinet minister

AFT Towards the rear or stern of a ship

ARTICLES-OF-WAR A statutory disciplinary code, regularly read to the ship's company

BACK To brace a sail so that the wind blows directly onto the front of it and retards the ship's progress

BEAM The width of a boat or ship, or a frame supporting the decks

BENDING SAILS Attaching sails to yards, gaffs or stays

BITTS A frame to which mooring cables are attached

BLOCKSHIP A decommissioned hulk often used to guard entrances

BLUE, THE The junior of three groups (red, white and blue) across which flag ranks were distributed. In former times a battle fleet would be divided into three squadrons commanded by admirals, designated by the three colours

BOATSWAIN A warrant officer responsible for the ship's boats, rigging, sails, cables and routine discipline aboard the ship

BOMB VESSEL A vessel reinforced to carry heavy mortars to fire explosive shells

BOOM A spar that extends the foot of a sail

BOW-CHASERS Guns mounted in the bows of a ship

BOWER An anchor on the bow of a ship

BOWSPRIT A spar extending forward from the bows of a ship

BRIG A merchant ship with two masts; also a type of rig in which the mainsail was 'fore and aft' rigged, often used on small cruisers

BULKHEAD An internal partition in a ship

BUMPKIN A short boom used to extend the lower edges of the principal sails on the masts

CABLE'S LENGTH 200 yards
CANISTER/CASE SHOT Cased shot designed to scatter among opponents
CAPITAL SHIP A ship of the line
CAPSTAN A man-powered winch to work anchors, weights or heavy sails
CAPTAIN OF THE FLEET Appointed to the flagship, responsible to the admiral for the administration of the fleet as well as the running of the flagship
CARCASS An incendiary shell filled with combustible material
CARRONADE A heavy short gun used for close-quarter action
CATHEAD Timber projection near the bows of a ship to hold an anchor ready for dropping
CHAINS Platforms on the outside of a ship from which the shrouds and ratlines lead to the masts
CHAIN SHOT Shot linked by a bar or chain, used to clear decks of men or bring down sails, spars and rigging
CHASE A ship being pursued
CLERK OF THE CHEQUE A dockyard official responsible for accounts
CLEW UP To draw up the lower edges of a square sail for furling, using the clew and clew-lines
COCKPIT Place below the lower gundeck, near the aft hatchway, used by surgeons as an operating theatre in a battle
COMMANDER A 'rank' between lieutenant and post-captain, entitling its holder to command a ship no larger than a sixth-rate
COMMISSIONED OFFICER An officer of the rank of lieutenant or above, holding the king's commission from the Admiralty
COMMODORE A temporary post held by a senior captain, usually one given the command of a squadron; entitled to fly a broad pendant
COMPTROLLER The head of the Navy Board
CONTRABAND Goods prohibited from entering the ports of an enemy by a declaration of blockade
CORVETTE A French sloop
COURSE Sail set upon the lower yards
COXSWAIN Helmsman and commander of a ship's boat
CROSS JACKYARD The lower yard of the mizzen mast
CROW A crowbar used in handling guns
CRUISER Originally a ship deployed to reconnoitre or search for hostile ships, but loosely used to indicate naval frigates, sloops and brigs
CUTTER A small single-masted vessel
DOCKYARD COMMISSIONER A commissioned officer in charge of a dockyard, responsible to the Navy Board
DOG WATCH Two two-hour watches between four and eight p.m.
DOUBLE/TRIPLE SHOTTING The loading of two or three shot within a single charge to increase short-range velocity

DRIVER Additional sail for the mizzen

DROITS OF THE CROWN Prize money accruing to the crown from the seizure of ships suspected of contraband

FATHOM Six feet

FELUCCA A small oared vessel, sometimes equipped with a lateen sail

FIFTY A 'ship of the line' of fifty long guns, but almost obsolete by the end of the eighteenth century

FIGHTING INSTRUCTIONS Code for tactical signals and movements, frequently elaborated by individual admirals

FISH To strengthen or splint a broken spar

FLAG RANK Loosely, an admiral with the right to fly his flag at the masthead

FORECASTLE An area beneath the short raised forward deck of a ship; loosely, the living quarters of a crew, distinguished from those of the officers aft

FOREMAST The mast nearest the bow of a ship, extended upwards by the fore topmast and carrying the foresail, fore topsail and fore topgallant sail

FREIGHT MONEY Payment received by captains or admirals for shipping freight or specie

FRIGATE A three-masted square-rigged warship mounting between twenty-four and forty-four guns; light and fast, frigates cruised against enemy merchantmen and small warships and gathered intelligence, but were too weak to stand in the line of battle

GAFF The spar on the after side of a mast, used to suspend a supplementary sail

GALLERY Stern or quarter walkway

GALLEY An oared fighting ship, or a rowing boat, usually with one or two masts

GALLIOT A small single-masted galley

GIG A narrow, light, fast ship's boat

GRAPE Anti-personnel shot that scatters

GUARDA COSTA A Spanish guard boat

GUARDSHIP A warship stationed to protect a harbour or port

GUNBOAT A small, lightly armed boat

GUNWALE Timbers covering the upper edge of a ship's side

HALF PAY Reduced salary payable to unemployed commissioned officers

HALYARDS Tackle for raising sails, spars or yards

HAUL UP To turn closer to the direction from which the wind is blowing

HAWSE The space between a ship's bow and the ground in which her anchor is fastened

HEAD MONEY Money paid to the captors of warships, based on the sizes of their crews

HEAVE DOWN To turn (a ship) on her side for careening

HELM Originally the steering tiller but latterly the wheel

HOWITZER A short heavy siege gun
IMPRESS SERVICE The service for raising men for the navy, under the command of a regulating captain
INDIAMAN A merchantman trading with the East or West Indies
INTEREST Influence with people able to advance one's cause
JIB An extension of the bowsprit
JOLLY BOAT A small, general-purpose boat
JURY MAST A temporary mast
KEDGE ANCHOR A small anchor used to haul grounded ships towards deeper water or to move ships when they are becalmed in shallows
KEELSON An internal keel to strengthen a frame
KETCH A vessel with main- and mizzen masts
LARBOARD The left-hand side of a ship, looking forward to the bow
LARBOARD TACK To sail with the wind coming over the larboard side of a ship
LATEEN A triangular sail suspended on a yard at an angle of some forty-five degrees to the mast
LEE An area sheltered or further from the wind
LEEWARD The direction to which the wind is blowing. A vessel to leeward is on the sheltered side of a ship. A lee shore faces an onshore wind. A ship adopting the leeward position in battle places the enemy between herself and the wind. If crippled, such a ship can escape by running to leeward before the wind
LEVANTER A strong easterly or northeasterly Mediterranean wind
LIEUTENANT A commissioned officer, eligible to command unrated ships but usually supporting a commander or post-captain
LINE OF BATTLE The regular battle formation of fleets was line ahead, so that each ship presented a broadside towards the enemy
LOWER DECK Deck of a ship above the orlop
LUFF To change course into the wind
MAINMAST The middle mast of a three-masted ship, extended upwards by the main topmast and carrying the mainsail, main topsail and main topgallant
MASTER Warrant officer in charge of navigation and handling of the ship
MASTER AND COMMANDER In some small cruisers the commander also acted as master
MASTER-AT-ARMS Warrant officer responsible for discipline
MASTER'S MATE Technically an assistant to the sailing master, but often a trainee commissioned officer analogous to a midshipman
MERCHANTMAN A merchant ship
MIDSHIPMAN A petty officer, generally a boy or youth training to become a lieutenant
MIZZEN MAST In a three-masted ship the rearmost mast, extended by the mizzen topmast

NAVY AGENT An official who receives and distributes pay

NAVY BOARD A board accountable to the Admiralty Board, consisting of commissioned officers and civilians responsible for administrating the dockyards

ORDNANCE BOARD A board reporting to the Master-General of the Ordnance, a cabinet minister, responsible for supplying cannon, shot, gunpowder and small arms to the armed services

ORLOP The lowest deck of a ship, above the hold

PASSING CERTIFICATE A certificate attesting to a candidate's success in an examination for lieutenant

PINNACE Oared ship's boat, sometimes able to raise a temporary mast

PISTOL SHOT A range of about 25 yards

POINT BLANK The range at which shot can reach its target in a straight line, without falling, about 600 yards

POLACRE A three-masted Mediterranean vessel, generally possessing square sails on the mainmast and lateen sails on the fore- and mizzen masts

POOP DECK A short high deck at the rear of a ship

POST-CAPTAIN An officer eligible to command any size of warship, and entered on an official list according to the date of his first captain's commission

POWDER MONKEY A person, normally a boy, employed to carry powder from the magazine to the gundeck

PRIVATEER A private man-of-war authorised to attack enemy commerce during wartime

PRIZE AGENT A civilian appointed by a ship's captain or a group of such officers, who saw prize cases through the Vice-Admiralty courts and distributed the proceeds

PRIZE CREW A skeleton crew put on a prize to conduct her to port

PROCTOR An official of the Vice-Admiralty courts, responsible for preparing cases for the advocates

QUARTER After parts of a ship on either side of the stern; the direction from which the wind blows

QUARTER-DECK A raised part of the upper deck to the rear of the mainmast, reserved for the use of officers

QUARTERMASTER A petty officer who assisted the sailing master

RATE Six categories of warship, based on the number of guns, excluding carronades. First rates (one hundred guns or more), second rates (eighty-four or more) and third rates (seventy or more) were the principal ships of the line

RIGGING Network of ropes supporting a ship's masts. Standing rigging refers to fixed ropes, and running rigging to ropes managing sails

ROYAL Auxilliary sail raised above the topgallant

SAIL LARGE To sail before the wind, with the wind coming from behind

SCHOONER A two- or three-masted vessel rigged fore and aft
SEA FENCIBLES A maritime militia raised after 1798 to defend Britain from invasion
SEA-TIME The six years of sea-going experience necessary to become a lieutenant
SETTEE A French Mediterranean vessel with two or three masts and lateen (triangular) sails
SEVENTY-FOUR The most numerous ship of the line, with seventy-four guns
SHALLOP A large heavy boat with fore and aft sails or lug sails, or a shallow-draught boat using oars or a sail
SHEET Rope manipulating a sail
SHEET ANCHOR An anchor supporting the bower
SHEER-HULK A decommissioned ship equipped with sheers to lift heavy weights. Ships needing masts lifting in or out were brought alongside a sheer-hulk
SHIP OF THE LINE A capital ship, usually of sixty-four or more long guns, strong enough to stand in the line of battle
SHIPS IN ORDINARY Laid up or decommissioned ships
SHROUDS Standing rigging from masts to the ship sides
SICK AND HURT BOARD A subsidiary board of the Admiralty, responsible for ships' surgeons and hospitals, abolished in 1806
SLING The middle part of a yard, encircled by a sling hoop from which it is suspended from the mast and hoisted or lowered
SLOOP Loosely used in the navy to describe a warship smaller than a frigate, possibly a two-masted brig or a three-master
SLOPS Clothing supplied by the Navy Board, obtained through a ship's purser, who deducted the cost from due wages. A slop ship was used to store such clothing
SNOW A two-masted merchantman
SPANKER A supplementary sail raised on a boom attached to the mizzen
SPAR A generic term for a mast, yard, boom or gaff
SPOKE The word used to report an interchange of information between two vessels, either by hailing or by a boat from one going alongside the other
SPRINGS Supplementary ropes attached to an anchor cable at an angle to pull the ship's head or stern round
SPRITSAIL A small sail suspended from the bowsprit
SQUADRON A number of warships too small to constitute a fleet
SQUARE-RIG Four-sided sails placed across the yards
STARBOARD Right-hand side of a ship, looking forward to the bows
STARBOARD TACK To sail with the wind coming from starboard
STAY Fore and aft rope supporting masts
STAYSAIL Triangular sail suspended from a stay

STERN CHASERS Guns mounted on the stern

STUDDING SAIL Sail set out upon a boom from a square sail in good weather

SUPERNUMERARY A passenger carried on the books for victuals, but not a member of the regular ship's company

SWIVEL A light anti-personnel gun that turned on a pivot

TACK To turn a ship by putting her head against the direction of the wind

TARTAN A Mediterranean vessel, generally with one mast, a large lateen sail and a foresail

THREE/TWO DECKER Terms referring to the number of gundecks on a warship

TOPGALLANT Sail above the topsail on the mast of a square rigger

TOPMAST Extension to a fore-, main- or mizzen mast

TOPSAIL The sail above the principal sail on a mast of a square-rigger

VAN The front of a fleet

VICE-ADMIRALTY COURT An overseas branch of the High Court of Admiralty

VICTUALLING BOARD A subsidiary board of the Admiralty responsible for supplying processed provisions and fresh meat and vegetables at home and abroad

WAD A bundle of rags rammed down the muzzle of a cannon to prevent shot rolling out

WARD ROOM A mess for commissioned officers

WARRANT OFFICER An officer appointed by a warrant of the Navy Board, such as a master, surgeon or purser

WATCH A period of duty on a ship, usually four hours long; one of two contingents into which the crew is divided, so that some seamen rest while others handle the ship

WEAR To turn a ship by putting the bow away from the wind

WEATHER GAUGE A ship in the windward position was said to have the weather gauge. Thus situated, it had advantages over an opponent to leeward. Ships with the weather gauge could manoeuvre more easily than those to leeward, which attacked against the wind

WINDWARD Anything to windward of a ship is between that ship and the wind. In a naval action a ship with her enemy to leeward is said to have the windward position or the weather gauge and the advantage of the wind

XEBEC A small three-masted vessel with both square and lateen sails

YARD A spar across a mast, supporting a sail

YAWL A yacht or small sailing boat

YEOMAN OF THE POWDER ROOM A petty officer with responsibility for the magazine

INDEX

THE HISTORY OF THE BODLEY HEAD

The Bodley Head was founded in 1887 by John Lane and Elkin Matthews. Initially trading in antiquarian books in London, in 1894 Lane and Matthews began to publish works of 'stylish decadence', including the notorious literary periodical *The Yellow Book*. The Bodley Head became a private company in 1921 and in the 1970s formed a publishing group with Jonathan Cape and Chatto & Windus. It was bought by Random House in 1987 and ceased trading as an adult imprint in 1990.

2008 saw the launch of an exciting and entirely new imprint within Random House's VINTAGE division with the revival of the distinguished Bodley Head name. In its new incarnation The Bodley Head is devoted to excellence in non-fiction in all fields. Its two principal strands are books of impeccable scholarship in the humanities and sciences, and books which directly address the intellectual and cultural issues of our times.